WORLD CIVILIZATIONS

THE GLOBAL EXPERIENCE

AP* EDITION   DBQ UPDATE
FOURTH EDITION

PETER N. STEARNS
George Mason University

MICHAEL ADAS
Rutgers University

STUART B. SCHWARTZ
Yale University

MARC J. GILBERT
North Georgia College & State University

PEARSON
Longman

New York San Francisco Boston
London Toronto Sydney Tokyo Singapore Madrid
Mexico City Munich Paris Cape Town Hong Kong Montreal

Acquisitions Editor: Janet Lamphier
Development Editor: Barbara Conover
Supplements Editor: Kristi Olson
Media Editor: Patrick McCarthy
Executive Marketing Manager: Sue Westmoreland
Production Manager: Eric Jorgensen
Project Coordination, Text Design, and Electronic Page Makeup: Electronic Publishing Services Inc., NYC
Cover Designer/Manager: Wendy Ann Fredericks
Cover Art: The Art Archive/Coptic Museum Cairo/Dagli Orti, Picture Desk, Inc./Kobal Collection
Photo Researcher: Jullie Chung, Photosearch, Inc.
Senior Maufacturing Buyer: Dennis J. Para
Printer and Binder: Von Hoffmann Corporation
Cover Printer: Coral Graphic Services, Inc.

Library of Congress Cataloging-in-Publication Data
World civilizations : the global experience / Peter N. Stearns ... [et al.].--Advanced
    Placement ed.
        p. cm.
    Includes bibliographical references and index.
    ISBN 0-321-19447-0
    1. Civilization--History. 2. Civilization--History--Sources. I. Stearns, Peter N.

CB69.W666b 2003
909--dc22   2003058063

Please visit us at http://www.ablongman.com

ISBN
AP Edition DBQ Update 0-13-193927-0
SVE 0-321-16425-3 (©2004)

    4 5 6 7 8 9 10—VH—08 07 06

BRIEF CONTENTS

Detailed Contents   v

List of Maps   xv

Preface   xvii

Supplements   xxv

About the Authors   xxvii

Prologue   xxix

PART I

THE RISE OF AGRICULTURE AND AGRICULTURAL CIVILIZATIONS   2

1 From Human Prehistory
to the Early Civilizations   6

PART II

THE CLASSICAL PERIOD, 1000 B.C.E.–500 C.E.   30

Document-Based Questions   32

2 Classical Civilization: China   34

3 Classical Civilization: India   50

4 Classical Civilization
in the Mediterranean: Greece and Rome   68

5 The Classical Period: Directions, Diversities,
and Declines by 500 B.C.E.   90

PART III

THE POSTCLASSICAL ERA   112

Document-Based Questions   118

6 The First Global Civilization:
The Rise and Spread of Islam   120

7 Abbasid Decline and the Spread
of Islamic Civilization
to South and Southeast Asia   146

8 African Civilizations
and the Spread of Islam   170

9 Civilization in Eastern Europe:
Byzantium and Orthodox Europe   192

10 A New Civilization Emerges
in Western Europe   213

11 The Americas on the Eve of Invasion   238

12 Reunification and Renaissance
in Chinese Civilization: The Era
of the Tang and Song Dynasties   262

13 The Spread of Chinese Civilization:
Japan, Korea, and Vietnam   286

14 The Last Great Nomadic Challenges:
From Chinggis Khan to Timur   312

15 The West and the Changing
World Balance   334

iii

PART IV

THE WORLD SHRINKS, 1450–1750   350

Document-Based Questions   356

16   The World Economy   358

17   The Transformation of the West, 1450–1750   380

18   The Rise of Russia   402

19   Early Latin America   418

20   Africa and the Africans in the Age of the Atlantic Slave Trade   446

21   The Muslim Empires   472

22   Asian Transitions in an Age of Global Change   498

PART V

INDUSTRIALIZATION AND WESTERN GLOBAL HEGEMONY, 1750–1914   524

Document-Based Questions   532

23   The Emergence of Industrial Society in the West, 1750–1914   534

24   Industrialization and Imperialism: The Making of the European Global Order   562

25   The Consolidation of Latin America, 1830–1920   588

26   Civilizations in Crisis: The Ottoman Empire, the Islamic Heartlands, and Qing China   616

27   Russia and Japan: Industrialization Outside the West   640

PART VI

THE 20TH CENTURY IN WORLD HISTORY   662

Document-Based Questions   668

28   Descent into the Abyss: World War I and the Crisis of the European Global Order   670

29   The World in the 1920s: Challenges to European Dominance   700

30   The Great Depression and the Authoritarian Response   726

31   A Second Global Conflict and the End of the European World Order   750

32   Western Society and Eastern Europe in the Decades of the Cold War   778

33   Latin America: Revolution and Reaction into the 21st Century   812

34   Africa, the Middle East, and Asia in the Era of Independence   834

35   Rebirth and Revolution: Nation-building in East Asia and the Pacific Rim   862

36   Globalization and Resistance: World History 1990–2003   892

Glossary   G-1

Credits   C-1

Index   I-1

DETAILED CONTENTS

List of Maps   xv

Preface   xvii

Supplements   xxv

About the Authors   xxvii

Prologue   xxix

PART I

The Rise of Agriculture and Agricultural Civilizations   2

Chapter 1   From Human Prehistory to the Early Civilizations   6

The Neolithic Revolution   11

Civilization   13

VISUALIZING THE PAST: Mesopotamia in Maps   17

DOCUMENT: Hammurabi's Law Code   19

IN DEPTH: The Idea of Civilization in World Historical Perspective   23

The Heritage of the River Valley Civilizations   24

IN DEPTH: The Legacy of Asia's First Civilizations   26

The First Civilizations   28

GLOBAL CONNECTIONS: The Early Civilizations and the World   29

Further Readings   29

On the Web   29

PART II

The Classical Period, 1000 B.C.E.–500 C.E.   30
Document-Based Questions   32

Chapter 2   Classical Civilization: China   34

Patterns in Classical China   35

Political Institutions   38

Religion and Culture   40

DOCUMENT: Teachings of the Rival Chinese Schools   42

Economy and Society   44

IN DEPTH: Women in Patriarchal Societies   45

How Chinese Civilization Fits Together   47

GLOBAL CONNECTIONS: Classical China and the World   48

Further Readings   49

On the Web   49

Chapter 3   Classical Civilization: India   50

The Framework for Indian History: Geography and a Formative Period   51

Patterns in Classical India   53

v

Political Institutions   55

Religion and Culture   57

Economy and Society   61

IN DEPTH: Inequality as the Social Norm   62

VISUALIZING THE PAST: The Pattern of Trade
in the Ancient Eurasian World   64

Indian Influence   65

China and India   66

GLOBAL CONNECTIONS: India
and the Wider World   66

Further Readings   67

On the Web   67

Decline in China and India   98

Decline and Fall in Rome   99

The New Religious Map   103

DOCUMENT: The Popularization of Buddhism   104

VISUALIZING THE PAST: Religious Geography   109

GLOBAL CONNECTIONS: The Late Classical
Period and the World   110

Further Readings   110

On the Web   111

PART III

The Postclassical Era   112
Document-Based Questions   118

**Chapter 4   Classical Civilization
in the Mediterranean:
Greece and Rome   68**

The Persian Tradition   70

Patterns of Greek and Roman History   71

Greek and Roman Political Institutions   74

IN DEPTH: The Classical Mediterranean
in Comparative Perspective   77

Religion and Culture   79

Economy and Society
in the Mediterranean   83

VISUALIZING THE PAST: Commerce and Society   84

DOCUMENT: Rome and a Values Crisis   86

Toward the Fall of Rome   87

GLOBAL CONNECTIONS: Greece, Rome,
and the World   88

Further Readings   88

On the Web   89

**Chapter 5   The Classical Period:
Directions, Diversities,
and Declines by 500 C.E.   90**

Expansion and Integration   91

Beyond the Classical Civilizations   92

IN DEPTH: Nomads and Cross-Civilization Contacts
and Exchanges   94

**Chapter 6   The First Global
Civilization: The Rise
and Spread of Islam   120**

Desert and Town: The Arabian World
and the Birth of Islam   122

The Life of Muhammad
and the Genesis of Islam   127

The Arab Empire of the Umayyads   130

IN DEPTH: Civilization and Gender Relationships   136

From Arab to Islamic Empire:
The Early Abbasid Era   138

DOCUMENT: *The Thousand and One Nights* as a Mirror
of Elite Society in the Abbasid Era   141

GLOBAL CONNECTIONS: Early Islam
and the World   142

VISUALIZING THE PAST: The Mosque as a Symbol
of Islamic Civilization   143

Further Readings   145

On the Web   145

**Chapter 7   Abbasid Decline
and the Spread of Islamic Civilization
to South and Southeast Asia   146**

The Islamic Heartlands in the Middle
and Late Abbasid Eras   147

DOCUMENT: Ibn Khaldun on the Rise and Decline
of Empires   152

An Age of Learning
and Artistic Refinements   153

VISUALIZING THE PAST: The Patterns
of Islam's Global Expansion   157

The Coming of Islam to South Asia   158

The Spread of Islam to Southeast Asia   165

IN DEPTH: Conversion and Accommodation
in the Spread of World Religions   166

GLOBAL CONNECTIONS: Islam:
A Bridge Between Worlds   168

Further Readings   168

On the Web   169

Chapter 8   African Civilizations and the Spread of Islam   170

African Societies: Diversity and Similarities   172

Kingdoms of the Grasslands   176

DOCUMENT: The Great Oral Tradition and the Epic
of Sundiata   178

The Swahili Coast of East Africa   182

IN DEPTH: Two Transitions in the History
of World Population   184

Peoples of the Forest and Plains   185

GLOBAL CONNECTIONS: Internal Development
and Global Contacts   189

Further Readings   190

On the Web   191

Chapter 9   Civilization in Eastern Europe: Byzantium and Orthodox Europe   192

The Byzantine Empire   195

VISUALIZING THE PAST: Women and Power
in Byzantium   198

The Spread of Civilization
in Eastern Europe   203

DOCUMENT: Russia Turns to Christianity   207

IN DEPTH: Eastern and Western Europe: The Problem
of Boundaries   209

GLOBAL CONNECTIONS: Eastern Europe
and the World   210

Further Readings   210

On the Web   210

Chapter 10   A New Civilization Emerges in Western Europe   212

Stages of Postclassical Development   214

IN DEPTH: Western Civilization   223

Western Culture in the Postclassical Era   224

Changing Economic and Social Forms
in the Postclassical Centuries   227

VISUALIZING THE PAST: Peasant Labor   228

DOCUMENT: Changing Roles for Women   231

The Decline of the Medieval Synthesis   232

GLOBAL CONNECTIONS: Medieval Europe
and the World   236

Further Readings   236

On the Web   236

Chapter 11   The Americas on the Eve of Invasion   238

Postclassic Mesoamerica, 1000–1500 C.E.   240

Aztec Society in Transition   246

DOCUMENT: Aztec Women and Men   248

IN DEPTH: The "Troubling" Civilizations
of the Americas   250

Twantinsuyu: World of the Incas   251

VISUALIZING THE PAST: Archeological Evidence
of Political Practice   253

The Other Indians   257

GLOBAL CONNECTIONS: The Americas
and the World   260

Further Readings   260

On the Web   261

Chapter 12 Reunification and Renaissance in Chinese Civilization: The Era of the Tang and Song Dynasties 262

Rebuilding the Imperial Edifice in the Sui-Tang Era 264

DOCUMENT: Ties That Bind: Paths to Power 268

Tang Decline and the Rise of the Song 271

Tang and Song Prosperity: The Basis of a Golden Age 275

IN DEPTH: Artistic Expression and Social Values 281

GLOBAL CONNECTIONS: China's World Role 284

Further Readings 284

On the Web 285

Chapter 13 The Spread of Chinese Civilization: Japan, Korea, and Vietnam 286

Japan: The Imperial Age 287

The Era of Warrior Dominance 293

IN DEPTH: Comparing Feudalisms 295

Korea: Between China and Japan 299

Between China and Southeast Asia: The Making of Vietnam 302

VISUALIZING THE PAST: What Their Portraits Tell Us: Gatekeeper Elites and the Persistence of Civilizations 304

DOCUMENT: Literature as a Mirror of the Exchanges Between Civilized Centers 308

GLOBAL CONNECTIONS: In the Orbit of China: The East Asian Corner of the Global System 309

Further Readings 310

On the Web 310

Chapter 14 The Last Great Nomadic Challenges: From Chinggis Khan to Timur 312

The Mongol Empire of Chinggis Khan 314

DOCUMENT: A European Assessment of the Virtues and Vices of the Mongols 317

The Mongol Drive to the West 320

VISUALIZING THE PAST: The Mongol Empire as a Bridge Between Civilizations 321

The Mongol Interlude in Chinese History 325

IN DEPTH: The Eclipse of the Nomadic War Machine 330

GLOBAL CONNECTIONS: The Mongol Linkages 332

Further Readings 333

On the Web 333

Chapter 15 The West and the Changing World Balance 334

The Decline of the Old Order 335

The Rise of the West 338

VISUALIZING THE PAST: Population Trends 339

DOCUMENT: Italian Renaissance Culture 342

Western Expansion: The Experimental Phase 343

Outside the World Network 344

IN DEPTH: The Problem of Ethnocentrism 346

GLOBAL CONNECTIONS: 1450 and the World 348

Further Readings 348

On the Web 348

PART IV
The World Shrinks, 1450–1750 350
Document-Based Questions 356

Chapter 16 The World Economy 358

The West's First Outreach: Maritime Power 360

IN DEPTH: Causation and the West's Expansion 365

Toward a World Economy 366

VISUALIZING THE PAST: West Indian Slaveholding   368

Colonial Expansion   370

DOCUMENT: Western Conquerors: Tactics and Motives   373

GLOBAL CONNECTIONS: The World Economy—And the World   378

Further Readings   378

On the Web   379

Chapter 17   The Transformation of the West, 1450–1750   380

The First Big Changes: Culture and Commerce   382

Science and Politics: The Next Phase of Change   388

VISUALIZING THE PAST: Versailles   391

IN DEPTH: Elites and Masses   393

The West by 1750   394

DOCUMENT: Controversies About Women   396

GLOBAL CONNECTIONS: Europe and the World   399

Further Readings   400

On the Web   400

Chapter 18   The Rise of Russia   402

Russia's Expansionist Politics Under the Tsars   403

Russia's First Westernization, 1690–1790   406

DOCUMENT: The Nature of Westernization   411

Themes in Early Modern Russian History   412

VISUALIZING THE PAST: Oppressed Peasants   414

IN DEPTH: Multinational Empires   416

GLOBAL CONNECTIONS: Russia and the World   416

Further Readings   416

On the Web   417

Chapter 19 Early Latin America   418

Spaniards and Portuguese: From Reconquest to Conquest   421

DOCUMENT: A Vision from the Vanquished   425

The Destruction and Transformation of American Indian Societies   428

IN DEPTH: The Great Exchange   430

Colonial Economies and Governments   432

Brazil: The First Plantation Colony   435

Multiracial Societies   437

VISUALIZING THE PAST: Race or Culture? A Changing Society   439

The 18th-Century Reforms   440

GLOBAL CONNECTIONS: Latin American Civilization and the World Context   444

Further Readings   445

On the Web   445

Chapter 20   Africa and the Africans in the Age of the Atlantic Slave Trade   446

The Atlantic Slave Trade   449

African Societies, Slavery, and the Slave Trade   454

VISUALIZING THE PAST: Symbols of African Kingship   458

White Settlers and Africans in Southern Africa   461

IN DEPTH: Slavery and Human Society   463

The African Diaspora   464

DOCUMENT: An African's Description of the Middle Passage   465

GLOBAL CONNECTIONS: Africa and the African Diaspora in World Context   470

Further Readings   470

On the Web   471

Chapter 21
The Muslim Empires   472

The Ottomans: From Frontier Warriors
to Empire Builders   473

DOCUMENT: An Islamic Traveler Laments the Muslims'
Indifference to Europe   481

The Shi'a Challenge of the Safavids   482

IN DEPTH: The Gunpowder Empires and the Shifting
Balance of Global Power   484

The Mughals and the Apex of Muslim
Civilization in India   489

VISUALIZING THE PAST: The Basis of Imperial Power
in the Rival Muslim Empires   491

GLOBAL CONNECTIONS: Gunpowder Empires
and the Restoration of the Islamic Bridge
Between Civilizations   496

Further Readings   496

On the Web   497

Chapter 22   Asian Transitions
in an Age of Global Change   498

The Asian Trading World and the Coming
of the Europeans   500

VISUALIZING THE PAST: Intruders: The Pattern
of Early European Expansion into Asia   506

Ming China: A Global Mission Refused   508

DOCUMENT: Exam Questions as a Mirror
of Chinese Values   509

IN DEPTH: Means and Motives
for Overseas Expansion: Europe
and China Compared   515

Fending Off the West: Japan's Reunification
and the First Challenge   517

GLOBAL CONNECTIONS: An Age
of Eurasian Closure   521

Further Readings   522

On the Web   522

PART V
Industrialization
and Western Global
Hegemony, 1750–1914   524
Document-Based Questions   532

Chapter 23   The Emergence
of Industrial Society in the West,
1750–1914   534

The Age of Revolution   536

VISUALIZING THE PAST: The French Revolution
in Cartoons   539

The Consolidation of the Industrial Order,
1850–1914   543

DOCUMENT: Women in the Industrial Revolution   545

Cultural Transformations   550

Western Settler Societies   552

IN DEPTH: The United States in World History   556

Diplomatic Tensions and World War I   558

GLOBAL CONNECTIONS: Industrial Europe
and the World   559

Further Readings   560

On the Web   560

Chapter 24   Industrialization
and Imperialism: The Making
of the European Global Order   562

The Shift to Land Empires in Asia   564

IN DEPTH: Western Education and the Rise
of an African and Asian Middle Class   571

Industrial Rivalries and the Partition
of the World, 1870–1914   573

Patterns of Dominance:
Continuity and Change   576

VISUALIZING THE PAST: Capitalism and Colonialism 577

DOCUMENT: Contrary Images: The Colonizer Versus the Colonized on the "Civilizing Mission" 581

GLOBAL CONNECTIONS: A European-Dominated World Order 586

Further Readings 587

On the Web 587

Chapter 25 The Consolidation of Latin America, 1830–1920 588

From Colonies to Nations 590

New Nations Confront Old and New Problems 593

DOCUMENT: Confronting the Hispanic Heritage: From Independence to Consolidation 596

Latin American Economies and World Markets, 1820–1870 598

Societies in Search of Themselves 606

IN DEPTH: Explaining Underdevelopment 609

The Great Boom, 1880–1920 610

GLOBAL CONNECTIONS: New Latin American Nations and the World 614

Further Readings 614

On the Web 615

Chapter 26 Civilizations in Crisis: The Ottoman Empire, the Islamic Heartlands, and Qing China 616

From Empire to Nation: Ottoman Retreat and the Birth of Turkey 619

IN DEPTH: Western Dominance and the Decline of Civilizations 620

Western Intrusions and the Crisis in the Arab Islamic Heartlands 624

The Last Dynasty: The Rise and Fall of the Qing Empire in China 629

DOCUMENT: Building a New China 636

GLOBAL CONNECTIONS: Muslim and Chinese Decline and a Shifting Global Balance 637

Further Readings 638

On the Web 638

Chapter 27 Russia and Japan: Industrialization Outside the West 640

Russia's Reforms and Industrial Advance 642

DOCUMENT: Conditions for Factory Workers in Russia's Industrialization 647

Protest and Revolution in Russia 649

Japan: Transformation Without Revolution 652

IN DEPTH: The Separate Paths of Japan and China 654

VISUALIZING THE PAST: Two Faces of Western Influence 657

GLOBAL CONNECTIONS: Russia and Japan in the World 660

Further Readings 661

On the Web 661

PART VI
The 20th Century in World History 662
Document-Based Questions 668

Chapter 28 Descent into the Abyss: World War I and the Crisis of the European Global Order 670

The Coming of the Great War 671

A World at War 675

VISUALIZING THE PAST: Trench Warfare 676

Failed Peace   682

World War I and the Nationalist Assault
on the European Colonial Order   684

DOCUMENT: Lessons for the Colonized
from the Slaughter in the Trenches   685

IN DEPTH: Women in Asian and African Nationalist
Movements   694

GLOBAL CONNECTIONS: World War
and Global Upheavals   696

Further Readings   697

On the Web   698

Chapter 29   The World in the 1920s: Challenges to European Dominance   700

The Disarray of Western Europe,
1918–1929   702

Industrial Societies Outside Europe   706

Revolution: The First Waves   710

IN DEPTH: A Century of Revolutions   718

GLOBAL CONNECTIONS: The 1920s
and the World   724

Further Readings   724

On the Web   725

Chapter 30   The Great Depression and the Authoritarian Response   726

The Global Great Depression   727

IN DEPTH: The Decline of the West?   733

Economic and Political Changes
in Latin America   736

The Militarization of Japan   740

Stalinism in the Soviet Union   742

DOCUMENT: Socialist Realism   745

VISUALIZING THE PAST: Socialist Realism   746

New Political and Economic Realities   747

GLOBAL CONNECTIONS: Depression
and Retreat   747

Further Readings   748

On the Web   748

Chapter 31   A Second Global Conflict and the End of the European World Order   750

Old and New Causes
of a Second World War   752

Unchecked Aggression and the Coming
of War in Europe and the Pacific   753

IN DEPTH: Total War   754

The Conduct of a Second Global War   757

DOCUMENT: Japan and the Loss in World War II   763

War's End and the Emergence
of the Superpower Standoff   764

Nationalism and Decolonization   766

VISUALIZING THE PAST: On Nationalist Leadership   770

GLOBAL CONNECTIONS: Persisting Trends
in a World Transformed by War   775

Further Readings   775

On the Web   776

Chapter 32   Western Society and Eastern Europe in the Decades of the Cold War   778

After World War II: International Setting
for the West   779

The Resurgence of Western Europe   783

Political Stability and the Question Marks   785

IN DEPTH: The United States and Western Europe:
Convergence and Complexity   790

Cold War Allies: The United States, Canada,
Australia, and New Zealand   790

Culture and Society in the West   793

VISUALIZING THE PAST: Women at Work in France
and the United States   795

Eastern Europe After World War II:
A Soviet Empire   799

Soviet Culture: Promoting New Beliefs
and Institutions   802

DOCUMENT: 1986: A New Wave
of Soviet Reform   808

GLOBAL CONNECTIONS: The Cold War
and the World 809

Further Readings 810

On the Web 810

Chapter 33 Latin America: Revolution and Reaction into the 21st Century 812

Latin America After World War II 815

Radical Options in the 1950s 816

VISUALIZING THE PAST: Murals and Posters:
Art and Revolution 818

The Search for Reform
and the Military Option 821

DOCUMENT: The People Speak 822

IN DEPTH: Human Rights in the 20th Century 827

Societies in Search of Change 829

GLOBAL CONNECTIONS: Struggling Toward
the Future in the Global Era 832

Further Readings 833

On the Web 833

Chapter 34 Africa, the Middle East, and Asia in the Era of Independence 834

The Challenges of Independence 836

IN DEPTH: Artificial Nations and the Rising Tide
of Communal Strife 842

DOCUMENT: Cultural Creativity in the Emerging Nations:
Some Literary Samples 847

Paths to Economic Growth
and Social Justice 848

VISUALIZING THE PAST: Globalization and Postcolonial
Societies 857

GLOBAL CONNECTIONS: Postcolonial Nations in
the Cold War World Order 860

Further Readings 860

On the Web 861

Chapter 35 Rebirth and Revolution: Nation-building in East Asia and the Pacific Rim 862

East Asia in the Postwar Settlements 864

Japan, Incorporated 868

The Pacific Rim: New Japans? 871

VISUALIZING THE PAST: Pacific Rim Growth 873

IN DEPTH: The Pacific Rim as a U.S. Policy Issue 875

Mao's China and Beyond 876

DOCUMENT: Women in the Revolutionary
Struggle 881

Colonialism and Revolution in Vietnam 883

GLOBAL CONNECTIONS: East Asia
and the Pacific Rim
in the Contemporary World 889

Further Readings 890

On the Web 890

Chapter 36 Globalization and Resistance: World History 1990–2003 892

The End of the Cold War 895

The Great Powers and New Disputes 902

IN DEPTH: How Much Historical Change? 904

Globalization 908

DOCUMENT: Protests Against Globalization 914

A World of Religious and Ethnic Conflict 916

Global Warming and Other Perils 918

Toward the Future 920

GLOBAL CONNECTIONS: Civilizations
and Global Forces 922

Further Readings 922

On the Web 924

Glossary G-1

Credits C-1

Index I-1

LIST OF MAPS

Page

10 The Spread of Human Populations, c. 10,000 B.C.E.
12 The Spread of Agriculture
21 Egypt, Kush, and Axum, Successive Dynasties
36 China from the Later Zhou Era to the Han Era
54 India at the Time of Ashoka
55 The Gupta Empire
72 Greece and Greek Colonies of the World, c. 431 B.C.E.
73 Alexander's Empire, c. 323 B.C.E., and the Hellenistic World
74 The Roman Empire from Augustus to 180 C.E.
97 Civilizations of Central and South America
101 Germanic Kingdoms After the Invasions
102 The Mediterranean, Middle East, Europe, and North Africa, c. 500 C.E.
114 The Postclassical World Takes Shape
115 The Postclassical World in Transition, c. 1400 C.E.
123 The Expansion of Islam in the 7th and 8th Centuries
125 Arabia and Surrounding Areas Before and During the Time of Muhammad
148 The Abbasid Empire at Its Peak
159 The Spread of Islam, 10th–16th Centuries
177 Empires of the Western Sudan
182 The Swahili Coast; African Monsoon Routes and Major Trade Routes
197 The Byzantine Empire Under Justinian
203 The Byzantine Empire, 1000–1100
205 East European Kingdoms and Slavic Expansion by c. 1000
218 Charlemagne's Empire and Successor States
233 Western Europe Toward the End of the Middle Ages, c. 1360 C.E.
241 Central Mexico and Lake Texcoco
252 Inca Expansion

Page

254 The Ancient Cities of Peru
265 China During the Era of Division, the Sui Dynasty, and the Tang Dynasty
273 China in the Song and Southern Song Dynastic Periods
289 Japan in the Imperial and Warlord Periods
299 The Korean Peninsula During the Three Kingdoms Era
303 South China and Vietnam on the Eve of the Han Conquest
314 The Mongol Empire of Chinggis Khan
322 The Four Khanates of the Divided Mongol Empire
347 Polynesian Expansion
353 World Boundaries, c. 1453
353 World Boundaries, c. 1700
362 Spain and Portugal: Explorations and Colonies, c. 1600
364 French, British, and Dutch Holdings, c. 1700
387 Western Europe During the Renaissance and Reformation
392 Europe Under Absolute Monarchy, 1715
405 Russian Expansion Under the Early Tsars, 1462–1598
407 Russia Under Peter the Great
412 Russia's Holdings by 1800
422 Spanish and Portuguese Explorations, 1400–1600
450 Portuguese Expansion and Major African Kingdoms
475 The Ottoman, Safavid, and Mughal Empires
476 The Expansion of the Ottoman Empire
483 The Safavid Empire
490 The Growth of the Mughal Empire, from Akbar to Aurangzeb
502 Routes and Major Products Exchanged in the Asian Trading Network, c. 1500

Page

514 Ming China and the Zhenghe Expeditions, 1405–1423

518 Japan During the Rise of the Tokugawa Shogunate

525 Industrial Development in Key Regional Centers, c. 1900

525 Main Colonial Holdings, c. 1914

540 Napoleon's Empire in 1812

543 Industrialization in Europe, c. 1850

547 The Unification of Italy

547 The Unification of Germany, 1815–1871

555 19th-Century Settlement and Consolidation in the United States, Canada, Australia, and New Zealand

559 The Balkan Wars, 1912–1913

566 European Colonial Territories, Before and After 1800

567 The Stages of Dutch Expansion in Java

568 The Growth of the British Empire in India, from the 1750s to 1858

575 The Partition of Africa Between c. 1870 and 1914

576 The Partition of Southeast Asia and the Pacific Islands to 1914

594 Independent States of Latin America

619 The Ottoman Empire in the Late 18th Century

629 China During the Qing Era

644 Russian Expansion, 1815–1914

659 Japanese Colonial Expansion to 1914

664 World Distribution of Manufacturing, 1930

Page

666 The World in 1995

673 World War I Fronts in Europe and the Middle East

689 The Middle East After World War I

706 Eastern Europe and the Soviet Union, 1919–1939

707 From Dominions to Nationhood: Formation of Canada, Australia, and New Zealand

721 China in the Era of Revolution and Civil War

741 The Spread of Japan to the Outbreak of World War II

759 The Main Theaters of World War II

774 The Partition of Palestine after World War II

781 Soviet and Eastern European Boundaries by 1948

782 Germany After World War II

787 The European Union in the Europe of 2003

826 U.S. Intervention in Central America and the Caribbean, 1898–1981

838 The Colonial Division of Africa and the Emergence of New Nations

839 The Partition of South Asia: The Formation of India, Pakistan, Bangladesh, and Sri Lanka

849 The New West African Nations

852 The Middle East in the Cold War Era

865 The Pacific Rim Area by 1960

876 China in the Years at the End of World War II, the Final Phase of the Civil War

884 Vietnam: Divisions in the Nguyen and French Periods

899 Post–Soviet Union Russia, Eastern Europe, and Central Asia

905 The Implosion of Yugoslavia, 1991–1999

PREFACE TO THE AP* EDITION, DBQ UPDATE

When we first began to work on *World Civilizations: The Global Experience*, we did so out of the conviction that it was time for a world history textbook that is truly global in its approach and coverage and yet manageable and accessible for today's students. Our commitment to that goal continues with this DBQ Update of the AP* Edition of the text. Here we present a truly global history—one that discusses the evolution and development of the world's leading civilizations—and balances that coverage with examination of the major stages in the nature and degree of interactions among different peoples and societies around the globe. We view world history not as a parade of facts to be memorized or a collection of the individual histories of various societies, but rather as the study of historical events in a global context. The study of world history combines meaningful synthesis of independent development within societies with comparative analysis of the results of interaction between societies.

Several decades of scholarship in world history and in area studies by historians and other social scientists have yielded a wealth of information. The challenge is to create a coherent and comprehensible framework for organizing all this information. Our commitment to world history stems from our conviction that students will understand and appreciate the present world by studying the myriad forces that have shaped that world and created our place within it. Furthermore, study of the past in order to make sense of the present will help them prepare to meet the challenges of the future.

Approach

This AP* Edition of *World Civilizations: The Global Experience* has been especially adapted for the AP* World History course and test. Rather than including the numerous, longer chapters that earlier editions and most other texts otherwise devote to world history developments before 500 C.E., this text substitutes a single chapter on prehistory and early civilizations and a single part, composed of four chapters, covering the classical civilizations of China, India, Greece, and Rome and the crucial developments toward the end of the classical period. These five chapters survey major patterns up to the postclassical era, at which point the more detailed treatment of the postclassical period can come into play. The goal is to provide students with a manageable presentation that can then be supplemented by more detailed library reading or handouts on particular issues (including additional map exercises) on the early period of world history. The chapters highlight characteristics in the major civilizations, patterns of trade and exchange within and among major societies, and of course basic features of agricultural economies. Thus, both comparative work and a focus on global processes can be applied to this introductory segment.

The two principal distinguishing characteristics of this book are its global orientation and its analytical emphasis. This is a true *world* history textbook. *World Civilizations: The Global Experience*, AP* Edition, examines the histories of all areas of the world and all peoples according to their growing or waning importance. It also considers what happened across regions by examining cross-civilizational developments such as migration, trade, the spread of religion, disease, plant exchange, and cultural interchange. Civilizations or societies sometimes slighted in world history textbooks—such as the nomadic societies of Asia, Latin American societies, the nations of the Pacific Rim, and the societies of nonurban sedentary peoples—receive attention here.

Many world history textbooks function as factual compendia, leaving analytical challenge to the classroom. Our goal throughout this book has been to relate fact to interpretation while still allowing ample opportunity for classroom exploration. Our analytical emphasis focuses on how key aspects of the past and present have been shaped by global forces such as the exchange of technology and ideas. By encouraging students to learn how to assess continuity and change, the text helps them relate the past to the present. Through analysis and interpretation students become active, engaged learners, rather than passive readers of the facts of historical events.

Periodization

This text pays a great deal of attention to periodization, an essential requirement for coherent presentation. *World Civilizations: The Global Experience*, AP* Edition, identifies six periods in world history, each period determined by three basic criteria: a geographical rebalancing among major civilizational areas, an increase in the intensity and extent of interaction across civilizations (or, in the case of the earliest period, cross-regional interaction), and the emergence of new and roughly parallel developments in most, if not all, of these major civilizations. The book is divided into six parts corresponding to these six major periods of world history. In each part, basic developments of each period are referred to in chapters that discuss the major civilizations in the Middle East, Africa, Asia, Europe, and the Americas, and in several cross-cutting chapters that address larger world trends. Part introductions identify the fundamental new characteristics of parallel or comparable developments and regional or international exchange that define each period.

After sketching the hunting-and-gathering phase of human existence, the single chapter of Part 1, The Rise of Agriculture and Agricultural Civilizations, provides an overview of the rise of agriculture and the emergence of civilizations in parts of Africa, the Middle East, parts of Asia, and southern Europe—the sequence of developments that set world history in motion from the origin of the human species until about 3000 years ago.

Part 2, The Classical Period, deals with the growing complexity of major civilizations in several areas of the world. During the classical period, civilizations developed a new capacity to integrate large regions and diverse groups of people through overarching cultural and political systems. Yet many regions and societies remained unconnected to the increasingly complex centers of civilization. Coverage of the classical period of world history, then, must consider both types of societies.

The Postclassical Era, the period covered in Part 3, saw the emergence of new commercial and cultural linkages that brought most civilizations into contact with one another and with nomadic groups. The decline of the great classical empires, the rise of new civilizational centers, and the emergence of a network of world contacts, including the spread of major religions, are characteristics of the postclassical era.

Developments in world history over the three centuries from 1450 to 1750 mark a fourth period in world history—the period covered in Part 4, The World Shrinks. The rise of the West, the intensification of global contacts, the growth of trade, and the formation of new empires define this period and separate it from the preceding postclassical period.

Part 5, Industrialization and Western Global Hegemony, 1750–1914, covers the period of world history dominated by the advent of industrialization in western Europe and growing European imperialism. The increase and intensification of commercial interchange, technological innovations, and cultural contacts all reflected the growth of Western power and the spread of Western influence.

The 20th Century in World History, the focus of Part 6, defines the characteristics of this period as the retreat of Western imperialism, the rise of new political systems such as communism, the surge of the United States and the Soviet Union, and a variety of economic innovations, including the achievements of Japan, Korea, and the Pacific Rim. Part 6 deals with this most recent period of world history into the 21st century and with some of its portents for the future.

Themes

We make world history accessible to today's students by using several themes as filters for the vast body of information that constitutes the subject. These themes provide a perspective and a framework for understanding where we have come from, where we are now, and where we might be headed.

Commonalities Among Societies

World Civilizations: The Global Experience, AP* Edition, traces several key features of all societies. We look at the technologies people have developed—for humans were toolmaking animals from an early date—and at the impact of technological change on the physical environment. We examine social structure, including the inequalities between the two genders and among different social classes. We detail the intellectual and cultural developments occurring within various societies. We also discuss the role of human agency: how individuals have shaped historical forces. These four areas—technology and the environment, inequalities and reactions to inequalities, intellectual and cultural development, and human agency—are four filters through which to examine any human society.

Contacts Among Civilizations

Large regional units that defined aspects of economic exchange, political institutions, and cultural values began to spring up more than 5000 years ago. These civilizations—that is, societies that generate and use an economic surplus beyond basic survival needs—created a general framework for the lives of most people ever since. But different regions had a variety of interactions, involving migration, trade, religious missionaries, exchanges of diseases and plants, and wars. Diplomatic relations between societies—what we now call international relations—also were organized. Many aspects of world history can be viewed in terms of whether societies had regular connections, haphazard interchange, or some mix of the two.

Features

The features in *World Civilizations: The Global Experience*, AP* Edition, have been carefully constructed and honed over the course of its earlier editions. Our aim has been to analyze change and continuity.

DBQs

This edition contains a number of AP*-like and AP*-level Document Based Questions (DBQs), which can train students in the experience of document analysis as well as providing models for teachers. Each of the major time periods is covered by two questions, which also involve different types of documents and a variety of topics. Here is a chance to integrate serious, realistic DBQ work with the rest of the AP* world history course.

Full-Color Design

The AP* Edition of *World Civilizations: The Global Experience* is published in full color and in a large format. Full-color maps, specially developed to provide a global orientation, aid students to easily recognize and distinguish geographical features and areas. Full-color photos, with their thought-provoking captions, help bring history to life.

Part Introductions

Part introductions define the characteristics of the period of world history covered in that part, examine parallel or comparable developments that occurred

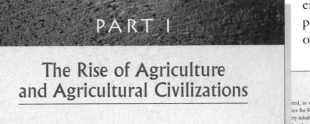

PART I

The Rise of Agriculture and Agricultural Civilizations

CHAPTER
1 From Human Prehistory to the Early Civilizations

Introduction

The idea that the world is becoming smaller is, like much folk wisdom, only partly true. For several hundred years, but particularly during the past century, worldwide transportation and communication facilities have become steadily more elaborate and rapid. It was less than 500 years ago that a ship first sailed around the entire world, a dangerous and uncertain journey that took many months. Now, political leaders, business people, and even wealthy tourists can routinely travel across half the world in less than a day. Telephone and radio communications have for several decades provided worldwide linkages, and, thanks to satellites, even global television hookups have become routine. As a result, for the first time in world history, events of widespread interest can be simultaneously experienced by hundreds of millions of people in all parts of the globe. World Cup soccer finals and recent Olympic games have drawn audiences of over a billion people.

The smallness of our world involves more than speedy international contact; it also involves the nature and extent of that contact. The 20th century was the first to experience world wars, as well as the fear of surprise attacks by enemies 6000 miles away. International negotiations and diplomatic contacts are not so novel, but the impact of events in distant parts of the globe has obviously increased. As an example, we can consider the conflicts between Christians and Muslims in unfamiliar parts of the Balkans that prompted several interventions by American troops in the late 1990s. In 2001, terrorist attacks on the United States brought home tensions that combined Middle Eastern problems, American policy, and contemporary technology. Worldwide economic contacts have increased at least as fast as those in the

among different societies as well as the new kinds of global interactions that arose, and identify the key themes to be explored in the chapters that follow. Part introductions give students a context for analyzing the content of each chapter as well as a framework for seeing how the chapters within a part relate to one another. Part timelines summarize the events of the chronological period covered.

Chapter Introductions

Introductions to each chapter identify the key themes and analytical issues that will be explained in the chapter. Chapter 3, for example, on the classical civilization of India, emphasizes India's distinctive and enduring characteristics. Whereas the focus in classical China was on politics and related philosophical values, the empha-

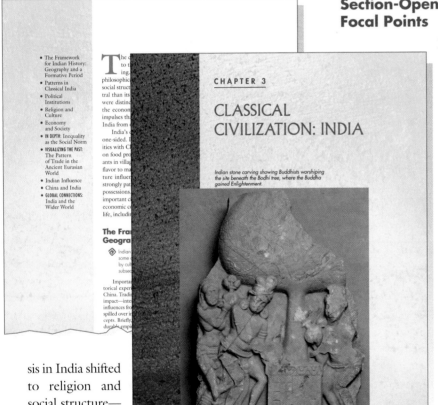

CHAPTER 3

CLASSICAL CIVILIZATION: INDIA

Indian stone carving showing Buddhists worshiping the site beneath the Bodhi tree, where the Buddha gained Enlightenment.

- The Framework for Indian History: Geography and a Formative Period
- Patterns in Classical India
- Political Institutions
- Religion and Culture
- Economy and Society
- IN DEPTH: Inequality as the Social Norm
- VISUALIZING THE PAST: The Pattern of Trade in the Ancient Eurasian World
- Indian Influence
- China and India
- GLOBAL CONNECTIONS: India and the Wider World

sis in India shifted to religion and social structure—characteristics still apparent today. The introduction gives the reader a context for understanding the similarities and differences between the classical civilization of India and the classical civilization of China in particular.

Timelines

Each part introduction begins with an extensive timeline that outlines the period under consideration. The timeline includes major events in all the societies dis-

2.5 MILLION B.C.E.	30,000 B.C.E.	10,000 B.C.E.	6000 B.C.E.	4000 B.C.E.	3000 B.C.E.	2000 B.C.E.
2.5 million B.C.E. Emergence of more humanlike species, initially in eastern Africa **750,000** Further development of species into *Homo erectus,* an upright, tool-using human **600,000** Wide spread of species across Asia, Europe, Africa; development of fire use **40,000–140,000** Completion to date of basic human evolution; emergence of *Homo sapiens sapiens* in Africa; *Homo sapiens sapiens* replaces other	**30,000–8000** Passage of people from Siberia to tip of South America **14,000** End of great ice age	**9000** Domestication of sheep, pigs, goats, cattle **8500–3500** Development of farming in Middle East	**6000** First potter's wheel **5000** Domestication of maize (corn) in Mesoamerica **5000–2000** Huanghe culture develops in China	**4000–3000** Age of innovation in Middle East: writing, bronze metalworking, wheel, plow **3500–1800** Sumerian civilization, with some disruptions through conquest **3100** Rise of Egyptian civilization	**2500–1500** Indus civilization in south Asia **2050–1750** Babylonian Empire in Middle East	**1500** Shang kingdom in China; writing develops **1122** Western Zhou kings in China

cussed in the part. Each chapter begins with a timeline that orients the student to the period, countries, and key events of the chapter.

Section-Opening Focal Points

Focal point sections after each main chapter head give students a focus with which to understand the topic. In Chapter 24, on industrialization and imperialism, the first section of the chapter discusses how imperialism in Asia drew in the European powers of the time. The focal point in that section introduces the contrasts between colonizers who were willing to adopt the lifestyles of the people they sought to rule, such as the

The Shift to Land Empires in Asia

From the mid-18th century onward, the European powers began to build true empires in Asia similar to those they had established in the Americas beginning in the 16th century. Using divide-and-conquer tactics, first the Dutch on Java and then the British in India began the process of carving up Asia, Africa, and Oceania into colonial possessions. In this first phase of the colonization process, Europeans overseas were willing to adapt their lifestyles to the climates and cultures of the peoples they had gone out to rule.

Although we usually use the term *partition* to refer to the European division of Africa at the end of the 19th century, the Western powers had actually been carving up the globe into colonial enclaves for centuries (see Map 24.1). At first, this process was haphazard and often quite contrary to the interests and designs of those in charge of European enter-

Dutch in Java, and those who imposed Westernization from early on, such as the British in India. This focus gives the reader a point of view with which to evaluate colonization during a particular era, not just a set of places, dates, and events to memorize.

Visualizing the Past

In most chapters, a *Visualizing the Past* feature asks students to analyze pictorial evidence, maps, or tables to interpret historical patterns. Text accom-

Visualizing the Past

The Mosque as a Symbol of the Islamic Civilization

From one end of the Islamic world to the other, Muslim towns and cities can be readily identified by the domes and minarets of the mosques where the faithful are called to prayer five times daily. The following illustrations trace the development of the mosque and the refinement of mosque architecture, the crowning glory of Islamic material culture, during the early centuries of Muslim expansion. As you look at these pictures and follow the development of the mosque, consider what the functions of the mosque and the evolving style of mosque architecture can tell us about Muslim beliefs and values and the impact of earlier religions, such as Judaism and Christianity, on Islam.

Given the low level of material culture in pre-Islamic Arabia, it is not surprising that the earliest prayer houses were simple in design and construction. In fact, these first mosques were laid out along the lines suggested by Muhammad's own house. They were square enclosures with a shaded porch on one side, a columned shelter on the other, and an open courtyard in between. The outer perimeter of the earliest mosques was made of reed mats,

but soon more permanent stone walls surrounded the courtyard and prayer areas. After Mecca was taken and the Ka'ba became the central shrine of the new faith, each mosque was oriented to the qibla, or Mecca wall, which always faced in the direction of the holy city.

In the last years of the prophet, his chair was located so that the faithful could see and hear him during prayer sessions. During the time of the first caliphs, the raised area became the place from which sermons were delivered. From the mid-8th century, this space evolved into a genuine pulpit. Somewhat earlier, the practice of build-
(continued)

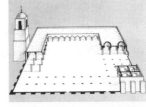

Dome and Minaret, Iranian Mosque

panying the illustrations provides a level of analysis, and a series of questions draws the students into providing their own analyses. In Chapter 6, for example, this feature illustrates, in both its text and its visuals, the importance of the mosque as a symbol of Islamic civilization.

Documents

Excerpts from original documents are included in *Document* boxes to give the reader contact with diverse

Document

A Vision from the Vanquished

History usually is written by the victors, so it is rare to find a detailed statement from the vanquished. In the 17th century, Guaman Poma de Ayala, an acculturated Peruvian Indian who claimed to trace his lineage to the provincial nobility of Inca times, composed a memorial outlining the history of Peru under the Incas and reporting on the current conditions under Spanish rule. Guaman Poma was a Christian and a loyal subject. He hoped that his report would reach King Philip III of Spain, who might then order an end to the worst abuses, among which were the Spanish failure to recognize the rank and status of Indian nobles. His book was not published in his lifetime and was not recovered until the 20th century.

Guaman Poma was an educated, bilingual Indian who spoke Quechua as well as Spanish and who had a profound understanding of Andean culture. His book is remarkable for its revelations of Indian life, for its detailed criticism of the abuses suffered by the Indians, and especially because Guaman Poma illustrated his memorial with a series of drawings that give his words a visual effect. The illustrations also reveal the worldview of this interesting man. The drawings and text offer a critical inside view not of the laws, but of the workings of Spain's empire in America from an Indian point of view.

Miners

At the mercury mines of Huancavelica the Indian workers are punished and ill-treated to such an extent that they die like flies and our whole race is threatened with extermination. Even the chiefs are tortured by being suspended by their feet. Conditions in the silver-mines of Potosí and Chocllococha, or at the gold-mines of Carabaya are little better. The managers and supervisors, who are Spaniards or mestizos, have virtually absolute power. There is no reason for them to fear justice, since they are never brought before the courts.

Beatings are incessant. The victims are mounted for this purpose on a llama's back, tied naked to a round pillar or put in stocks. Their hair is cut off and they are deprived of food and water during detention.

Any shortage in the labor gangs is made an excuse for punishing the chiefs as if they were common thieves or traitors instead of the nobility of the county. The wor

Proprietors

Your Majesty has granted large estates, including the right to employ Indian labor, to a number of individuals of whom some are good Christians and the remainder are very bad ones. These encomenderos, as they are termed, may boast about their high position, but in reality they are harmful both to the labor force and to the surviving Indian nobility. I therefore propose to set down the details of their life and conduct.

They exude an air of success as they go from their card games to their dinners in fine silk clothes. Their money is squandered on these luxuries, as well it may, since it costs them no work or sweat whatever. Although the Indians ultimately pay the bill, no concern is ever felt for them or even for Your Majesty or God himself.

Official posts like those of royal administrator and judge ought not to be given to big employers or mine-owners or to their obnoxious sons, because these peoples
(continued)

CAPI:TVLODELOSPASAGEROS
ESPAñOLESDELa
bo ycriollos mestizos ymula
tos ycriollas mestizas yespa
ñoles cristianos
decastilla

voices of the past. We share a firm commitment to include social history involving women, the nonelite, and experiences and events outside the spheres of politics and high culture. Each document is preceded by a brief, scene-setting narration and followed by probing questions to guide the reader through an analysis of the document. In Chapter 19 on early Latin America, for example, the *Document* box presents a detailed statement not by the victor but by the vanquished: an educated bilingual Peruvian Indian who composed a memorial outlining the history of Peru under the Incas and reporting on later conditions under Spanish rule. The text and the drawings that accompany it offer a critical inside view of the workings of Spain's empire in America from a Native American point of view.

In Depth Sections

Each chapter contains an analytical essay on a topic of broad application. The essay is followed by questions intended to probe student appreciation of the topic

In Depth

Eastern and Western Europe: The Problem of Boundaries

Deciding where one civilization ends and another begins is not always easy, particularly when many political units and some internal cultural differences are involved. Defining the territory of the two related civilizations that developed in Europe is particularly difficult. A number of states sat, and still sit, on the borders of the two civilizations, sharing some characteristics of each. Furthermore, political disputes and nationalist attachments, fierce in this border territory of east central Europe during the past two centuries, make territorial definitions an emotional issue. So the question of defining Europe's civilizations is a particularly thorny case of a larger problem.

If a civilization is defined simply by its mainstream culture, then east and west Europe in the postclassical period divide logically according to Orthodox and Catholic territories (and use of the Cyrillic and Greek or of the Latin alphabets). By this reckoning, Poland, the Czech areas, and the Baltic states (these latter did not convert to Catholicism until the 14th century) are western, and Hungary is largely so. South Slavs are mainly but not entirely Orthodox, a regional division that can provoke recurrent violence. Russia and Ukraine are decidedly Orthodox in tradition. Religion matters. Poland and other Catholic regions have long maintained much more active ties with western Europe than Russia has. At the end of the postclassical period, a Czech religious dissenter, named Hus, even foreshadowed the later Protestant Reformation in his attacks on the Catholic church.

Politically, the case is more complicated. Poland, Hungary, and Lithuania formed large regional kingdoms at various times during and after the postclassical period. But these kingdoms were very loosely organized, much more so than the feu-

dal monarchies that were developing in western Europe. Exceptionally large aristocracies in Poland and Hungary (by western or by Russian standards) helped limit these states.

Trade patterns also did not closely unite Poland or Hungary with western Europe until much later, when the two regions were clearly different in economic structure. Also, Polish and Hungarian societies often shared more features with Russia than with western Europe.

Russian expansion later pulled parts of eastern Europe, including Poland, into its orbit, although it never eliminated strong cultural identities. It is also important to remember that borders can change. The Mongol invasions that swept through Russia also conquered Poland and Hungary, but the armies did not stay there. Part of the Ukraine was also free from direct Mongol control, which helped differentiate it from Russia proper. For two centuries, at the end of the postclassical period, the divisions within eastern Europe intensified. Since 1989, many east European countries have again achieved full independence from Russia, and they want to claim their distinctive pasts. Not an easy border area to characterize in terms of a single civilization, east central Europe has also been a victim of many conquests interspersed with periods of proud independence.

Questions: What were the main characteristics of Russian civilization as it first emerged in the postclassical period? In what ways did Poland, Hungary, and the Czech lands differ from these characteristics? Are there other civilization border areas, in the postclassical period or later, that are similarly difficult to define because of their position between two other areas?

and suggest questions or interpretive issues for further thought. For example, the *In Depth* section in Chapter 9, which covers the Byzantine Empire, steps aside slightly from the discussion of Byzantium and Orthodox Europe to look at the question of where one civilization ends and another begins—a question still relevant today. How do we define states that sit between clearly defined civilizations and share some characteristics of each culture? The analytical argument in this section encompasses contested borders, mainstream culture, religion, language, and patterns of trade and looks more specifically at Poland, Hungary, and Lithuania, with elements of both western and eastern Europe and Russia in their cultures. The questions after the analysis prompt the reader to think about these difficult-to-define civilization border areas.

NEW Global Connections

Each chapter ends with a new section—Global Connections—which reiterates the key themes and issues raised in the chapter and makes clear their importance not only to the areas of civilization discussed in the chapter but also to the world as a whole. For example, in Chapter 13, this new summary section emphasizes that the spread of ideas, organizational models, and material culture from a common Chinese center spawned the rise of three distinct patterns of civilized development in Japan, Korea, and Vietnam. However, direct influences from other parts of the world were

ttled on
clashed
into the
the Viet-
s proved
rces and
French
ate 18th
h of the
territory

but from a distant land and religion about which the Vietnamese knew and cared nothing—France and the conversion-minded Roman Catholic church.

GLOBAL CONNECTIONS: In the Orbit of China: The East Asian Corner of the Global System

The first millennium C.E. was a pivotal epoch in the history of the peoples of east Asia. The spread of ideas, organizational models, and material culture from a common Chinese center spawned the rise of three distinct patterns of civilized development in Japan, Korea, and Vietnam. In contrast to the lands of the nomadic peoples who had long been in contact with China from the north and west, each of these regions contained fertile and well-watered lowland areas that were suited to sedentary cultivation, which was essential to the spread of the Chinese pattern of civilized development. In fact, each provided an ideal environment for the cultivation of wet rice, which was increasingly replacing millet and other grains as the staple of China.

Common elements of Chinese culture, from modes of writing and bureaucratic organization to religious teachings and art, were transmitted to each of these three areas. In all three cases, Chinese imports, with the important exception of popular Buddhism, were all but monopolized by court and provincial elite groups, the former prominent in Japan and Korea, the latter in Vietnam. In all three cases, Chinese thought patterns and modes of social organization were actively and willingly cultivated by these local elites, who knew that they were the key to a higher lev

s moved
noi, the
difficult
ting and
rs inter-
ns of the
and atti-
herners.
selves as
ir coun-
he Viet-
as less
t. As the
outhern
manders
e north
ickering
he 16th
to chal-
nily that

ne were
the two

slight, because there was no sense that any other place had examples worth emulating. The intensity of interactions within the east Asian region generated a degree of isolation from the world beyond.

Further Readings

Each chapter includes several annotated paragraphs of suggested readings. Students receive reliable guidance on a variety of books: source materials, standards in the field, encyclopedic coverage, more readable general-interest titles, and the like.

On the Web

Each chapter ends with a list of annotated Web sites. Every effort has been made to find stable sites that are likely to endure. However, the annotations also give students the key words necessary to search for similar sites.

Glossary

The comprehensive page-referenced glossary is another feature that sets this book apart. It includes

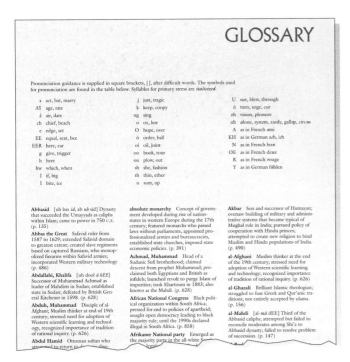

conceptual terms, frequently used foreign terms, and names of important geographical regions and key characters on the world stage. Much of world history will be new to most students, and this glossary will help them develop a global vocabulary.

Organizational Changes to This Edition

In order to give the student a clearer chronological view of major world events, we have made a number of changes to both chapter order and topical organization within chapters.

Chapter 16 now emphasizes the world economy, rather than specifically stressing the importance of the West in the world.

For reasons of connection among regions, the chapter on Africa and Africans in the age of the Atlantic slave trade, now Chapter 20, precedes the chapter on the Muslim empires, now Chapter 21. This facilitates connections with Chapter 19 on the Americas.

The text of a number of chapters within Part 6, The 20th Century in World History, has been heavily reorganized to give the student a clearer view of major events that affected the entire world: Chapter 28 now details World War I and the crisis of the European world order; Chapter 29, the world in the 1920s; Chapter 30, the decade of the Great Depression and the growth of authoritarian politics; and Chapter 31, World War II and the end of the European world order.

Chapter 35, Rebirth and Revolution, combining two chapters of the previous edition, relates post–World War II events in China, Japan, Korea, and other countries of the Pacific Rim.

Chapter 36 has been extensively revamped to deal with globalization and its challenges as the leading themes of the 21st century.

Acknowledgments

Grateful acknowledgment is made to the following reviewers, who made many useful suggestions during the development of this AP* Edition.

Sharlene Sayegh, California State University, Long Beach

J. Michael Allen, Brigham Young University, Hawaii Campus

David R. Smith, California State Polytechnic, Pomona

PETER N. STEARNS
MICHAEL ADAS
STUART B. SCHWARTZ
MARC JASON GILBERT

SUPPLEMENTS

For Qualified Adopters

Companion Web site (www.ablongman.com/stearns 4eAP).* Teachers can take advantage of the online course companion that supports this text. The instructor section of the Web site includes the instructor's manual, a list of instructor links, and downloadable images from the text.

Instructor's Resources. This helpful manual to *World Civilizations: The Global Experience*, AP* Edition, written by Jay Harmon, now contains DBQ rubrics, as a guide for teachers. Additionally, there are lesson and discussion suggestions and activities for the high school world history AP* classroom, along with chapter summaries, vocabulary, and various types of review and skills activities and reproducible worksheets. The manual also contains pacing and assignment guides as well as review questions to promote the needed history and world history skills.

*AP*Test Bank.* Compiled and edited by Jay Harmon specifically for the AP* Edition of *World Civilizations: The Global Experience*, this supplement contains AP-style multiple-choice and essay questions.

AP TestGen Computerized Testing System.* This easy-to-customize test generation software package presents a wealth of multiple-choice and essay questions and allows users to add, delete, and print test items.

For the Student

Companion Web site (www.ablongman.com/stearns 4eAP).* The online course companion provides a wealth of resources for students using *World Civilizations*. Students can access chapter summaries, practice test questions, dozens of Web activities, and hundreds of annotated Web links.

AP Student Review Manual.* This text-specific student supplement written by Jay Harmon aims to help students achieve success on the AP* exam. Like the Instructor's Resources, this supplement contains chapter summaries, key terms, AP-style multiple-choice and essay questions, and map exercises. It also includes a photo exercise, two full-length practice multiple-choice exams, four original DBQs, and a chapter providing tips and strategies for success on the World History test.

ABOUT THE AUTHORS

Peter N. Stearns

Peter N. Stearns is Provost and Professor of History at George Mason University. He received his Ph.D. from Harvard University, and, before moving to George Mason University, he taught at Rutgers University, the University of Chicago, and Carnegie Mellon, where he won the Robert Doherty Educational Leadership Award and the Elliott Dunlap Smith Teaching Award. He teaches world history and has for the past fifteen years. He currently serves as chair of the Advanced Placement World History Committee and also founded and is the editor of the *Journal of Social History*. In addition to textbooks and readers, he has written studies of gender and consumerism in a world history context. Other books address modern social and cultural history and include studies on gender, old age, work, dieting, and emotion. His most recent book in this area is *Anxious Parents: A History of Modern Childrearing in the United States.*

Michael Adas

Michael Adas is the Abraham Voorhees Professor of History and a Board of Governor's Chair at Rutgers University in New Brunswick, New Jersey. Over the past couple of decades his teaching has been focused on patterns and processes of global and comparative history. His courses on race and empire in the early modern and industrial eras and on world history in the 20th century have earned him a number of teaching prizes. In addition to texts on world history, Adas' writings have been devoted mainly to the comparative history of colonialism and its impact on the peoples and societies of Asia and Africa. Recent books include *Machines as the Measure of Men: Science, Technology and Ideologies of Western Dominance,* which won the Dexter Prize, and his forthcoming study of *Dominance by Design: Technological Imperatives and America's Civilizing Mission.* He is also currently writing a global history of the First World War.

Stuart B. Schwartz

Stuart B. Schwartz was born and educated in Springfield, Massachusetts, and then attended Middlebury College and the Universidad Autonoma de Mexico. He has an M.A. and Ph.D. from Columbia University in Latin American history. He taught for many years at the University of Minnesota and joined the faculty at Yale University in 1996. He has also taught in Brazil, Puerto Rico, Spain, France, and Portugal. He is a specialist on the history of colonial Latin America, especially Brazil, and is the author of numerous books, notably *Sugar Plantations in the Formation of Brazilian Society* (1985), which won the Bolton Prize for the best book in Latin American History. He is also the author of *Slaves, Peasants and Rebels* (1992), *Early Latin America* (1983), and *Victors and Vanquished* (1999). He has held fellowships from the Guggenheim Foundation and the Institute for Advanced Study (Princeton). For his work on Brazil he was recently decorated by the Brazilian government. He continues to read widely in the history and anthropology of Latin America, Africa, and early modern Europe.

Marc Jason Gilbert

Marc Jason Gilbert is a Professor of History at North Georgia College & State University. He is also a University System of Georgia Board of Regents Distinguished Professor of Teaching and Learning and codirector of that system's programs in India and southeast Asia.

He received his Ph.D. in history from UCLA in 1978, where he built his own program in world history out of a mixture of more traditional fields. He was a founding member of the World History Association and one of its initial officers. More than a decade ago, he founded the Southeastern World History Association, a regional affiliate of the World History Association, of which he continues to serve as Executive Director. He has codirected two Summer Institutes for Teaching AP World History. He has attempted to bring global dimension to south and southeast Asian history in numerous articles and books, such as *How the North Won the Vietnam War*.

PROLOGUE

The study of history is the study of the past. Knowledge of the past gives us perspective on our societies today. It shows different ways in which people have identified problems and tried to resolve them, as well as important common impulses in the human experience. History can inform through its variety, remind us of some human constants, and provide a common vocabulary and examples that aid in mutual communication.

The study of history is also the study of change. Historians analyze major changes in the human experience over time and examine the ways in which those changes connect the past to the present. They try to distinguish between superficial and fundamental change, as well as between sudden and gradual change. They explain why change occurs and what impact it has. Finally, they pinpoint continuities from the past along with innovations. History, in other words, is a study of human society in motion.

World history is not simply a collection of the histories of various societies but a subject in its own right. World history is the study of historical events in a global context. It does not attempt to sum up everything that has happened in the past. It focuses on two principal subjects: the evolution of leading societies and the interaction among different peoples around the globe.

The Emergence of World History

Serious attempts to deal with world history are relatively recent. Many historians have attempted to locate the evolution of their own societies in the context of developments in a larger "known world": Herodotus, though particularly interested in the origins of Greek culture, wrote also of developments around the Mediterranean; Ibn Khaldun wrote of what he knew about developments in Africa and Europe as well as in the Muslim world. But not until the 20th century, with an increase in international contacts and a vastly expanded knowledge of the historical patterns of major societies, did a full world history become possible. In the West, world history depended on a growing realization that the world could not be understood simply as a mirror reflecting the West's greater glory or as a stage for Western-dominated power politics. This hard-won realization continues to meet some resistance. Nevertheless, historians in several societies have attempted to develop an international approach to the subject that includes, but goes beyond, merely establishing a context for the emergence of their own civilizations.

Our understanding of world history has been increasingly shaped by two processes that define historical inquiry: debate and detective work. Historians are steadily uncovering new data not just about particular societies but about lesser-known contacts. Looking at a variety of records and artifacts, for example, they learn how an 8th-century battle between Arab and Chinese forces in central Asia brought Chinese prisoners who knew how to make paper to the Middle East, where their talents were quickly put to work. And they argue about world history frameworks: how central European actions should be in the world history of the past 500 years, and whether a standard process of modernization is useful or distorting in measuring developments in modern Turkey or China. Through debate

xxix

comes advances in how world history is understood and conceptualized, just as the detective work advances the factual base.

What Civilization Means

Humans have always shown a tendency to operate in groups that provide a framework for economic activities, governance, and cultural forms—beliefs and artistic styles. These groups, or societies, may be quite small—hunting-and-gathering bands often numbering no more than 60 people. World history usually focuses on somewhat larger societies, with more extensive economic relationships (at least for trade) and cultures.

One vital kind of grouping is called civilization. The idea of civilization as a type of human society is central to most world history, though it also generates debate and though historians are now agreed that it is not the only kind of grouping that warrants attention. Civilizations, unlike some other societies, generate surpluses beyond basic survival needs. This in turn promotes a variety of specialized occupations and heightened social differentiation, as well as regional and long-distance trading networks. Surplus production also spurs the growth of cities and the develop-

ment of formal states, with some bureaucracy, in contrast to more informal methods of governing. Most civilizations have also developed systems of writing.

Civilizations are not necessarily better than other kinds of societies. Nomadic groups have often demonstrated great creativity in technology and social relationships, as well as promoting global contacts more vigorously than settled civilizations sometimes did. And there is disagreement about exactly what defines a civilization—for example, what about cases like the Incas where there was no writing?

Used carefully, however, the idea of civilization as a form of human social organization, and an unusually extensive one, has merit. Along with agriculture (which developed earlier), civilizations have given human groups the capacity to fundamentally reshape their environments and to dominate most other living creatures. The history of civilizations embraces most of the people who have ever lived; their literature, formal scientific discoveries, art, music, architecture, and inventions; their most elaborate social, political, and economic systems; their brutality and destruction caused by conflicts; their exploitation of other species; and their degradation of the environment—a result of changes in technology and the organization of work.

WORLD CIVILIZATIONS

PART I

The Rise of Agriculture and Agricultural Civilizations

CHAPTER

1 From Human Prehistory to the Early Civilizations

Introduction

The idea that the world is becoming smaller is, like much folk wisdom, only partly true. For several hundred years, but particularly during the past century, worldwide transportation and communication facilities have become steadily more elaborate and rapid. It was less than 500 years ago that a ship first sailed around the entire world, a dangerous and uncertain journey that took many months. Now, political leaders, business people, and even wealthy tourists can routinely travel across half the world in less than a day. Telephone and radio communications have for several decades provided worldwide linkages, and, thanks to satellites, even global television hookups have become routine. As a result, for the first time in world history, events of widespread interest can be simultaneously experienced by hundreds of millions of people in all parts of the globe. World Cup soccer finals and recent Olympic games have drawn audiences of over a billion people.

The smallness of our world involves more than speedy international contact; it also involves the nature and extent of that contact. The 20th century was the first to experience world wars, as well as the fear of surprise attacks by enemies 6000 miles away. International negotiations and diplomatic contacts are not so novel, but the impact of events in distant parts of the globe has obviously increased. As an example, we can consider the conflicts between Christians and Muslims in unfamiliar parts of the Balkans that prompted several interventions by American troops in the late 1990s. In 2001, terrorist attacks on the United States brought home tensions that combined Middle Eastern problems, American policy, and contemporary technology. Worldwide economic contacts have increased at least as fast as those in the military and diplomatic fields. Production surges in China or Mexico vitally affect Americans as consumers and workers; shifts in the oil prices levied by Middle Eastern nations influence the driving habits of Americans and Europeans. Cultural linkages have also proliferated, as witness the existence of international sporting events and the widespread audience for French films or American television. In the 21st century, a traveler to cities on every inhabited continent can find buildings that look just like those at home. Indeed, U.S. hotel and restaurant chains now literally span the earth.

To some observers, our smaller world is also an increasingly homogeneous world. Certain people lament the widespread adoption of various customs that seem to reduce valuable and interesting human diversity. Thus, purists in France deplore the practice of modern French supermarkets in imitating American packaging of cheese, just as many in Japan or Egypt deplore the decline of traditional costumes in favor of more Western-style dress. Probably more people, or at least more Americans, rejoice that our lifestyle has been adopted by other societies. Many Americans, comfortable in their own ways, are pleased to see familiar products and styles in other countries. Others, firm believers in the importance of international harmony, are eager to minimize the strangeness of foreign lands.

Despite new and important international linkages, our world is also marked by fundamental, often agonizing, divisions and diversities. Japan, in 1984, ordered a government inquiry into the use of chopsticks among schoolchildren. Their use had been declining because of a growing eagerness to eat quickly. Surely, to many American eyes, this might seem to represent a quaint, if harmless, concern for distinctive traditions. But such concerns are not altogether different from those of Muslim leaders, many of whom from the late 1970s to the present have thundered against Western influences, ranging from styles of women's dress to the idea that economic development rather than religion should be society's foremost priority. Varied reactions to Western influence reflect serious global divisions. And there are the direct conflicts over identity that rage in various parts of the world.

Correspondingly, certain systematic separations shape our world as much as linkages. As Russia experiments with democracy, China resolutely combines political authoritarianism with economic innovations. Stark divisions separate societies that have industrialized, and in which a minority of people are directly engaged in food production, from the larger number of nations in which full industrialization remains a distant dream. Cultural divisions also remain strong. India is the leading producer of films in the contemporary world, but these films, steeped in traditional Indian themes and values, rarely find non-Indian audiences. The United States, although able to export some films and television shows widely, also enjoys certain sports, notably football, that have only modest appeal to other cultures. Japan, in copying televised American quiz shows, imposes shame on losing contestants in a fashion that would seem bizarre to the West. Changes in the role of women in the workplace and their growing assertiveness and independence, commonplace factors in Western societies, find incomplete echoes in the Muslim world or even in Japan.

The point is clear: The smallness of the world, as represented by the new and sometimes beneficial exchanges among diverse peoples, exists alongside deep divisions. International contacts do not necessarily bring harmony or friendship. Any interpretation of the contemporary world must take into account this complex tension, involving the undeniable existence of certain patterns that have worldwide influence but the equally undeniable existence of divergencies and conflicts that stubbornly persist. Policymakers face

2.5 MILLION B.C.E.	30,000 B.C.E.	10,000 B.C.E.	6000 B.C.E.	4000 B.C.E.	3000 B.C.E.	2000 B.C.E.
2.5 million *B.C.E.* Emergence of more humanlike species, initially in eastern Africa **750,000** Further development of species into *Homo erectus*, an upright, tool-using human **600,000** Wide spread of species across Asia, Europe, Africa; development of fire use **40,000–140,000** Completion to date of basic human evolution; ermergence of *Homo sapiens sapiens* in Africa; *Homo sapiens sapiens* replaces other human species	**30,000–8000** Passage of people from Siberia to tip of South America **14,000** End of great ice age	**9000** Domestication of sheep, pigs, goats, cattle **8500–3500** Development of farming in Middle East	**6000** First potter's wheel **5000** Domestication of maize (corn) in Mesoamerica **5000–2000** Huanghe culture develops in China	**4000–3000** Age of innovation in Middle East: writing, bronze metalworking, wheel, plow **3500–1800** Sumerian civilization, with some disruptions through conquest **3100** Rise of Egyptian civilization	**2500–1500** Indus civilization in south Asia **2050–1750** Babylonian Empire in Middle East	**1500** Shang kingdom in China; writing develops **1122** Western Zhou kings in China

this conflict in applying their beliefs to the wider world: Should U.S. policy be based on assumptions that most of the world will become increasingly like us, or should it build on assumptions of permanent political and cultural differences? U.S. policy in recent decades has, in fact, oscillated between both approaches, in part because each approach—the vision of expanding contact and imitation, and the vision of deep-seated, possibly growing differentiation—has much to commend it.

The same tension must inform any study of how the world became what it is today—that is, any effort to convey the basic dynamics of world history. Both international influences and major diversities are rooted in the past. Humankind has always been united in some respects. The human species displays certain common responses, and as a result, all human societies share certain basic features. Moreover, there have always been some links among different human societies in various parts of the world, although admittedly such linkages have only recently become complex and rapid. Cultural diffusion—the process by which an idea or technique devised in one society spreads to another—describes the way plowing equipment first invented in China ultimately was adopted in Europe, or the way a numbering system conceived in India reached the Middle East and then Europe many centuries ago. The same basic process of cultural diffusion, now speeded up, indicates how the Japanese copied and then improved upon American assembly-line production during the 1970s and 1980s. There have always been, in other words, some common themes in world history, affecting many peoples and establishing a common dynamic for developments in many parts of the world in a given set of centuries. However, there also have always been important differences among the world's peoples, as even prehistoric

4

societies differed markedly in how they viewed death, how they treated the elderly and children, or the kind of government they established.

There are two ways to make the study of these complexities relatively manageable. The evolution of worldwide processes—that is, developments that ultimately shaped much of the world's population—can be understood by dividing the past into coherent periods of world history, from the prehistoric age to the development of agriculture to the spread of the great religions and on to more recent stages. The leading diversities of human society for at least the past 3000 years can be conveyed by concentrating on the development of particularly extensive and durable civilizations, whose impact runs from their own origins to the present time. These civilizations, while not embracing the entire human species even today, have come to include most people, and they are, fortunately, not infinite in number. Five early traditions—in the Middle East (Mesopotamia and Persia), the Mediterranean (the Middle Eastern coast, north Africa, and southern Europe), India, China, and Central America—ultimately were replaced by seven major patterns of government, society, and culture. Exploring the nature of these patterns in the world's seven regions—east Asia; India and southeast Asia; the Middle East; eastern Europe; sub-Saharan Africa; western Europe and North America; and Latin America—and then assessing their interaction with the larger processes of world history provide the key to understanding the essential features of human society past and present.

Think of a pattern as follows: Each civilization deals with some common issues, such as how to organize a state, how to define a family, how to integrate technology and whether or not to encourage technological change, how to explain and present the natural universe, and how to define social inequality. The distinctive ways that each civilization handles these issues follow from geographical differences plus early cultural and historical experience. The goal in comparing the major civilizations involves understanding these different approaches to common social issues. But civilizations were never entirely isolated, and ultimately they all had to decide what to do about growing international trade, migrations, spreading diseases, and missionary religions. They also had to decide how to respond to examples and influences from other societies. Responses to these common forces sometimes drew civilizations together, but they also often reflected very diverse adjustments. The puzzle of world history—its pieces composed of distinct civilizations, contacts, and ongoing change—is not hard to outline but it is undeniably challenging.

Not long ago, many Americans believed that world history consisted of the rise of their own Western civilization and its interaction with the rest of the globe. Not long ago, many Chinese believed that world history involved little more than the fascinating story of the evolution of the only civilization that mattered—their own. These were attractive visions, adequate for many purposes; they certainly offered simpler explanations than a focus on the interaction and differentiation of several vibrant civilizations. But just as many people today see that the world is growing "smaller," in the same way, many also observe that it is growing more complex. A study of world history can and should respond to this complexity.

CHAPTER 1

FROM HUMAN PREHISTORY TO THE EARLY CIVILIZATIONS

Cave paintings discovered in Lascaux, France, in 1940—an example of which is shown here—probably served a ritualistic purpose for the Paleolithic artists who created them.

- The Neolithic Revolution
- Civilization
- VISUALIZING THE PAST: Mesopotamia in Maps
- DOCUMENT: Hammurabi's Law Code
- IN DEPTH: The Idea of Civilization in World Historical Perspective
- The Heritage of the River Valley Civilizations
- IN DEPTH: The Legacy of Asia's First Civilizations
- The First Civilizations
- GLOBAL CONNECTIONS: The Early Civilizations and the World

The human species has accomplished a great deal in a relatively short period of time. There are significant disagreements over how long an essentially human species, as distinct from other primates, has existed. However, a figure of 2 or 2.5 million years seems acceptable. This is approximately $1/4000$ of the time the earth has existed. That is, if one thinks of the whole history of the earth to date as a 24-hour day, the human species began at about 5 minutes before midnight. Human beings have existed for less than 5 percent of the time mammals of any sort have lived. Yet in this brief span of time—by earth-history standards—humankind has spread to every landmass (with the exception of the polar regions) and, for better or worse, has taken control of the destinies of countless other species.

To be sure, human beings have some drawbacks as a species, compared to other existing models. They are unusually aggressive against their own kind: While some of the great apes, notably chimpanzees, engage in periodic wars, these conflicts can hardly rival human violence. Human babies are dependant for a long period, which requires some special family or child-care arrangements and often has limited the activities of many adult women. Certain ailments, such as back problems resulting from an upright stature, also burden the species. And, insofar as we know, the human species is alone in its awareness of the inevitability of death—a knowledge that imparts some unique fears and tensions.

Distinctive features of the human species account for considerable achievement as well. Like other primates, but unlike most other mammals, people can manipulate objects fairly readily because of the grip provided by an opposable thumb on each hand. Compared to other primates, human beings have a relatively high and regular sexual drive, which aids reproduction; being omnivores, they are not dependant exclusively on plants or animals for food, which helps explain why they can live in so many different climates and settings; the unusual variety of their facial expressions aids communication and enhances social life. The distinctive human brain and a facility for elaborate speech are even more important: Much of human history depends on the knowledge, inventions, and social contracts that resulted from these assets. Features of this sort explain why many human cultures, including the Western culture that many Americans share, promote a firm separation between human and animal, seeing in our own species a power and rationality, and possibly a spark of the divine, that "lower" creatures lack.

Although the rise of humankind has been impressively rapid, its early stages can also be viewed as painfully long and slow. Most of the 2 million plus years during which our species has existed are described by the term **Paleolithic (Old Stone) Age.** Throughout this long time span, which

7

		TRANSITION PHASE		NEOLITHIC AGE		METAL AGE	
2.5 MILLION B.C.E.	*30,000 B.C.E.*	*10,000 B.C.E.*	*6000 B.C.E.*	*4000 B.C.E.*	*3000 B.C.E.*	*2000 B.C.E.*
2.5 million Emergence of more humanlike species, initially in eastern Africa **750,000** Further development of species into *Homo erectus* **600,000** Wide spread of species across Asia, Europe, Africa; development of fire use **120,000** Completion to date of basic human evolution; *Homo sapiens sapiens* displaces other human species	**25,000** Passage of people from Siberia to tip of South America **14,000** End of great ice age **12,000** Fashioning of stone tools; end of Paleolithic, or Old Stone, Age	**10,000–8000** Development of farming in the Middle East **9000** Domestication of sheep, pigs, goats, cattle **8000** Transition of agriculture; introduction of silk weaving in China	**6000** First potter's wheel **5500** Çatal Hüyük at its peak **5000** Domestication of maize (corn) in Mesoamerica	**4000** Yangshao culture in China **4000–3000** Age of innovation in the Middle East: introduction of writing, bronze metalwork, wheel, plow **3500–1800** Civilization of Sumer; cuneiform alphabet	**3100** Rise of Egyptian civilization **2500** Emergence of Harappan (Indus) civilization	**2000** Kotosh culture in Peru **2000** Conversion to agriculture in northern Europe, southern Africa **1500** Emergence of Shang kingdom in China; writing develops **1500** First ironwork in the Middle East **1200** Jews settle near the Mediterranean; first monotheistic religion **1122** Western Zhou kings

runs until about 14,000 years ago, human beings learned only simple tool use, mainly through employing suitably shaped rocks and sticks for hunting and warfare. Fire was tamed about 750,000 years ago. The nature of the species also gradually changed during the Paleolithic, with emphasis on more erect stature and growing brain capacity. Archeological evidence also indicates some increases in average size. A less apelike species, whose larger brain and erect stance allowed better tool use, emerged between 500,000 and 750,000 years ago; it is called, appropriately enough, *Homo erectus.* Several species of *Homo erectus* developed and spread in Africa, to Asia and Europe, reaching a population size of perhaps 1.5 million 100,000 years ago.

Late Paleolithic Developments

Considerable evidence suggests that more advanced types of humans killed off or displaced many competitors over time, which explains why there is only one basic human type throughout the world today, rather than a number of rather similar human species, as among monkeys and apes. The newest human breed, ***Homo sapiens sapiens,*** of which all humans in the world today are descendants, originated about 120,000 years ago, also in Africa. The success of this subspecies means that there have been no major changes in the basic human physique or brain size since its advent.

Even after the appearance of *Homo sapiens sapiens,* human life faced important constraints. People who hunted food and gathered nuts and berries could not support large numbers or elaborate societies. Most hunting groups were small, and they had to roam widely for food. Two people required at least one square mile for survival. Population growth was slow, partly because women breast-fed infants for several years to limit their own fertility. On the other hand, people did not have to work very hard—hunting took about seven hours every three days on average. Women, who gathered fruits and vegetables, worked harder but there was significant equality between the sexes based on common economic contributions.

Paleolithic people gradually improved their tool use, beginning with the crude shaping of stone and wooden implements. Speech developed with *Homo erectus* 100,000 years ago, allowing more group cooperation and the transmission of technical knowledge. By the later Paleolithic period, people had developed rituals to lessen the fear of death and created cave paintings to express a sense of nature's beauty and power. Goddesses often played a prominent role in the religious pantheon. Thus, the human species came to develop cultures—that is, systems of belief that helped explain the environment and set up rules for various kinds of social behavior. The development of speech provided rich language and symbols for the transmission of culture and its growing sophistication. At the same time, different groups of humans, in different locations, developed quite varied belief systems and corresponding languages.

The greatest achievement of Paleolithic people was the sheer spread of the human species over much of the earth's surface. The species originated in eastern Africa; most of the earliest types of human remains come from this region, in the present-day countries of Tanzania, Kenya, and Uganda. But gradual migration, doubtless caused by the need to find scarce food, steadily pushed the human reach to other areas. Key discoveries, notably fire and the use of animal skins for clothing—both of which enabled people to live in colder climates—facilitated the spread of Paleolithic groups. The first people moved out of Africa about 750,000 years ago. Human remains (Peking man, Java man) have been found in China and southeast Asia dating from 600,000 and 350,000 years ago, respectively. Humans inhabited Britain 250,000 years ago. They first crossed to Australia 60,000 years ago, followed by another group 20,000 years later; these combined to form the continent's aboriginal population. Dates of the migration from Asia to the Americas are under debate. Most scholars now believe that humans crossed what was then a land bridge from Siberia to Alaska about 30,000 years ago, with several subsequent migration waves until warmer climates and rising ocean levels eliminated the land bridge by 8000 B.C.E.* Many of the new arrivals quickly spread out, reaching the tip of the South American continent possibly within a mere

---

*In Christian societies, historical dating divides between years "before the birth of Christ" (B.C.) and after (A.D., *anno Domini,* or "year of our Lord"). This system came into wide acceptance in Europe in the 18th century, as formal historical consciousness increased (although ironically, 1 A.D. is a few years late for Jesus' actual birth). China, Islam, Judaism, and many other societies use different dating systems, referring to their own history. This text, like many recent world history materials, uses the Christian chronology (one has to choose some system) but changes the terms to B.C.E. ("before the common era") and C.E. ("of the common era") as a gesture to less Christian-centric labeling.

thousand years. Settlers from China reached Taiwan, the Philippines, and Indonesia 4500 to 3500 years ago.

In addition, soon after this time—roughly 14,000 years ago—the last great ice age ended, which did wonders for living conditions over much of the Northern Hemisphere. Human development began to accelerate. In the Mesolithic (Middle Stone) Age, a span of several thousand years, from about 12,000 to 8000 B.C.E., human ability to fashion stone tools and other implements improved greatly. People learned to sharpen and shape stone, to make better weapons and cutting edges. Animal bones were used to make needles and other precise tools. From the Mesolithic also date the increased numbers of log rafts and dugouts, which improved fishing, and the manufacture of pots and baskets for food storage. Mesolithic people domesticated more animals, such as cows, which again improved food supply. Population growth accelerated, which also resulted in more conflicts and wars. Skeletons from this period show frequent bone breaks and skull fractures caused by weapons.

In time, better tool use, somewhat more elaborate social organization, and still more population pressure led people in many parts of the world to the final Stone Age—the **Neolithic (New Stone) Age** (see Map 1.1). From Neolithic people, in turn, came several more dramatic developments that changed the nature of human existence—the invention of agriculture, the creation of cities, and other foreshadowings of civilization, which ended the Stone Age altogether throughout much of the world.

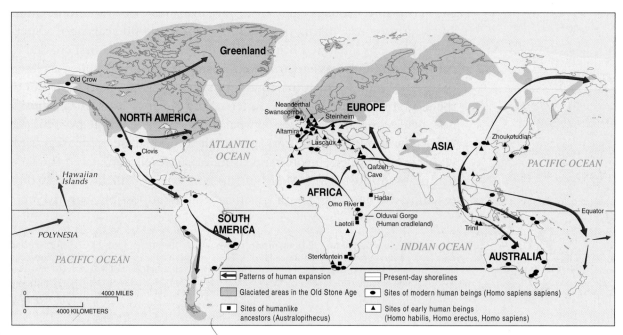

Map 1.1   *The Spread of Human Populations, c. 10,000 B.C.E.*

The Neolithic Revolution

 The Neolithic revolution involved the development of agriculture. This occurred in different times in different places. Agriculture created important changes from humankind's hunting-and-gathering past, going well beyond food supply.

Human achievements during the various ages of stone are both fascinating and fundamental, and some points are hotly debated. Our knowledge of Stone Age society is of course limited, although archeologists have been creative in their interpretations of tool remains and other evidence, such as cave paintings and burial sites, that Stone Age people produced in various parts of the world. What people accomplished during this long period of prehistory remains essential to human life today; our ability to make and manipulate tools thus depends directly on what our Stone Age ancestors learned about physical matter.

However, it was the invention of agriculture that most clearly moved the human species toward more elaborate social and cultural patterns of the sort that people today would find recognizable. With agriculture, human beings were able to settle in one spot and focus on particular economic, political, and religious goals and activities. Agriculture also spawned a great increase in the sheer number of people in the world—from about 6 to 8 million across the earth's surface during early Neolithic times, to about 100 million some 3000 years later.

The initial development of agriculture—that is, the deliberate planting of grains for later harvest—was probably triggered by two results of the ice age's end. First, population increases, stemming from improved climate, prompted people to search for new and more reliable sources of food. Second, the end of the ice age saw the retreat of certain big game animals, such as mastodons. Human hunters had to turn to smaller game, such as deer and wild boar, in many forested areas. Hunting's overall yield declined. Here was the basis for new interest in other sources of food. There is evidence that by 9000 B.C.E., in certain parts of the world, people were becoming increasingly dependant on regular harvests of wild grains, berries, and nuts. This undoubtedly set the stage for the deliberate planting of seeds (probably accidental to begin with) and the improvement of key grains through the selection of seeds from the best plants.

As farming evolved, new animals were also domesticated. Particularly in the Middle East and parts of Asia, by 9000 B.C.E. pigs, sheep, goats, and cattle were being raised. Farmers used these animals for meat and skins and soon discovered dairying as well. These results not only contributed to the development of agriculture but also served as the basis for nomadic herding societies.

Farming was initially developed in the Middle East, in an arc of territory running from present-day Turkey to Iraq and Israel. This was a very fertile area, more fertile in those days than at present. Grains such as barley and wild wheat were abundant. At the same time, this area was not heavily forested, and animals were in short supply, presenting a challenge to hunters. In the Middle East, the development of agriculture may have begun as early as 10,000 B.C.E., and it gained ground rapidly after 8000 B.C.E. Gradually during the Neolithic centuries, knowledge of agriculture spread to other centers, including parts of India, north Africa, and Europe. Agriculture, including rice cultivation, soon developed independently in China. Thus, within a few thousand years agriculture had spread to the parts of the world that would produce the first human civilizations (Map 1.2). We will see that agriculture spread later to much of Africa south of the Mediterranean coast, reaching west Africa by 2000 B.C.E., although here too there were additional developments with an emphasis on local grains and also root crops such as yams. Agriculture had to be invented separately in the Americas, based on corn cultivation, where it was also a slightly later development (about 5000 B.C.E.).

Many scholars have termed the development of agriculture a **Neolithic revolution.** The term is obviously misleading in one sense: Agriculture was no sudden transformation, even in the Middle East where the new system had its roots. Learning the new agricultural methods was difficult, and many peoples long combined a bit of agriculture with considerable reliance on the older systems of **hunting and gathering.** A "revolution" that took over a thousand years, and then several thousand more to spread to key population centers in Asia, Europe, and Africa, is hardly dramatic by modern standards.

The concept of revolution is, however, appropriate in demonstrating the magnitude of change involved. Early agriculture could support far more people per square mile than hunting ever could; it also allowed people to settle more permanently in one area. The system was nonetheless not easy. Agriculture required more regular work, at least of men, than hunting did. Hunting groups today, such as the pygmies of the Kalahari desert in southwest Africa, work an average of 2.5 hours a day, alternating long, intense hunts

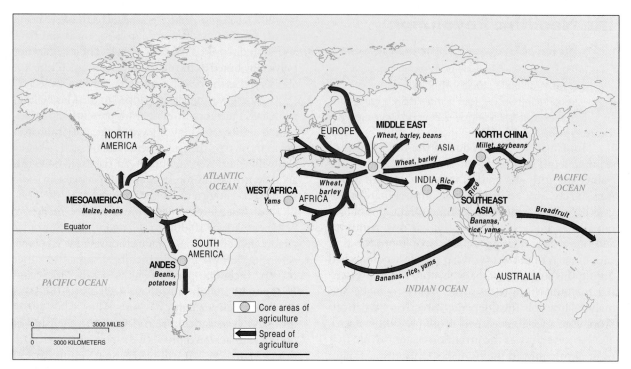

Map 1.2   *The Spread of Agriculture*

with periods of idleness. As much as agriculture was demanding, it was also rewarding: Agriculture supported larger populations, and with better food supplies and a more settled existence, agricultural peoples could afford to build houses and villages. Animals provided not only hides but also wool for more varied clothing.

We know next to nothing of the debates that must have raged when people were first confronted with agriculture, but it is not hard to imagine that many would have found the new life too complicated, too difficult, or too unexciting. Most evidence suggests that gathering-and-hunting peoples resisted agriculture as long as they could. Gradually, of course, agriculture did gain ground. Its success was hard to deny. And as farmers cleared new land from forests, they automatically drove out or converted many hunters. Disease played a role: Settled agricultural societies suffered from more contagious diseases because of denser population concentrations. Hunting-and-gathering peoples lacked resistance and often died when agriculturists who had developed immunity to these diseases carried them into their areas.

Not all the peoples of the world came to embrace the slowly spreading wave of agriculture, at least not until very recently. Important small societies in southern Africa, Australia, the islands of southeast Asia, and

even northern Japan were isolated for so long that news of this economic system simply did not reach them. The white-skinned hunting tribes of northern Japan disappeared only about a hundred years ago. Northern Europeans and southern Africans converted to agriculture earlier, about 2000 years ago, but well after the Neolithic revolution had transformed other parts of their continents. Agriculture was initiated in the Americas as early as 5000 B.C.E. and developed vigorously in Central America and the northern part of South America. However, most Indian tribes in North America continued a hunting-and-gathering existence, sometimes combined with limited agriculture, until recent centuries. Finally, the peoples of the vast plains of central Asia long resisted a complete conversion to agriculture, in part because of a harsh climate; herding, rather than grain-growing, became the basic socioeconomic system of this part of the world. From this area would come waves of tough, nomadic invaders whose role in linking major civilizations was a vital force in world history until a few centuries ago.

Development possibilities among people who became agriculturists were more obvious than those among smaller populations who resisted or simply did not know of the system: Agriculture set the basis for more rapid change in human societies. Greater wealth and larger populations freed some people for other specializations, from which new ideas or techniques might spring. Agriculture itself depended on control over nature that could be facilitated by newly developed techniques and objects. For example, during the Neolithic period itself, the needs of farming people for storage facilities, for grains and seeds, promoted the development of basket-making and pottery. The first potter's wheel came into existence around 6000 B.C.E., and this, in turn, encouraged faster and higher-quality pottery production. Agricultural needs also encouraged certain kinds of science, supporting the human inclination to learn more about weather or flooding.

Much of what we think of as human history involves the doings of agricultural societies—societies, that is, in which most people are farmers and in which the production of food is the central economic activity. Nonagricultural groups, like the nomadic herders in central Asia, made their own mark, but their greatest influence usually occurred in interactions with agricultural peoples. Many societies remain largely agricultural today. The huge time span we have thus far considered, including the Neolithic revolution itself, is all technically "prehistorical"—involved with human patterns before the invention of writing allowed the kinds of recordkeeping historians prefer. In fact, since we now know how to use surviving tools and burial sites as records, the prehistoric–historic distinction means less than it once did. The preagricultural–agricultural distinction is more central. Fairly soon after the development of agriculture—although not, admittedly, right away—significant human change began to occur in decades and centuries, rather than in the sizeable blocks of time, several thousand years or more, that describe preagricultural peoples.

Indeed, one basic change took place fairly soon after the introduction of agriculture, and, again, societies in the Middle East served as its birthplace. The discovery of metal tools dates back to about 4000 B.C.E. Copper was the first metal with which people learned how to work, although the more resilient metal, bronze, soon entered the picture. In fact, the next basic age of human existence was the **Bronze Age.** By about 3000 B.C.E., metalworking had become so commonplace in the Middle East that the use of stone tools dissipated, and the long stone ages were over at last—although, of course, an essentially Neolithic technology persisted in many parts of the world, even among some agricultural peoples.

Metalworking was extremely useful to agricultural or herding societies. Metal hoes and other tools allowed farmers to work the ground more efficiently. Metal weapons were obviously superior to those made from stone and wood. Agricultural peoples had the resources to free up a small number of individuals as toolmakers, who would specialize in this activity and exchange their products with farmers for food. Specialization of this sort did not, however, guarantee rapid rates of invention; indeed, many specialized artisans seemed very conservative, eager to preserve methods that had been inherited. But specialization did improve the conditions or climate for discovery, and the invention of metalworking was a key result. Like agriculture, knowledge of metals gradually fanned out to other parts of Asia and to Africa and Europe.

Gradually, the knowledge of metal tools created further change, for not only farmers but also manufacturing artisans benefited from better tools. Woodworking, for example, became steadily more elaborate as metal replaced stone, bone, and fire in the cutting and connecting of wood. We are still living in the metal ages today, although we rely primarily on iron—whose working was introduced around 1500 B.C.E. by herding peoples who invaded the Middle East—rather than copper and bronze.

Civilization

 The emergence of civilization occurred in many though not all agricultural societies. It often built on additional changes in technology including the introduction of metal tools. Most civilizations had common features including cities, writing, and formal states. Early civilizations formed in Mesopotamia, Egypt, the Indus River basin, and China. These can be compared to determine other commonalities plus early differences.

Agriculture encouraged the formation of larger as well as more stable human communities than had existed before Neolithic times. A few Mesolithic groups had formed villages, particularly where opportunities for fishing were good, as around some of the lakes in Switzerland. However, most hunting peoples moved in relatively small groups, or tribes, each containing anywhere from 40 to 60 individuals, and they could not settle in a single spot without the game running out. With agriculture, these constraints changed. To be sure, some agricultural peoples did move around. A system called **slash and burn agriculture** existed in a few parts of the world, including portions of the American South, until about 150 years ago.

Here, people would burn off trees in an area, farm intensively for a few years until the soil was depleted, and then move on. Herding peoples also moved in tribal **bands,** with strong kinship ties. But most agricultural peoples did not have new lands close by to which they could move after a short time. Also, there were advantages to staying put: Houses could be built to last, wells built to bring up water, and other "expensive" improvements afforded because they would serve many generations. In the Middle East, China, and parts of Africa and India, a key incentive to stability was the need for irrigation devices to channel river water to the fields. This same need helps explain why agriculture generated communities and not a series of isolated farms. Small groups simply could not regulate a river's flow or build and maintain irrigation ditches and sluices. Irrigation and defense encouraged villages—groupings of several hundred people—as the characteristic pattern of residence in almost all agricultural societies from Neolithic days until our own century. Neolithic settlements spread widely in agricultural societies. New ones continued to be founded as agriculture spread to regions such as northern Europe, as late as 1500 B.C.E. (Figure 1.1).

One Neolithic village, **Çatal Hüyük** in southern Turkey, has been elaborately studied by archeologists. It was founded about 7000 B.C.E. and was unusually large, covering about 32 acres. Houses were made of mud bricks set in timber frameworks, crowded together, with few windows. People seem to have spent a good bit of time on their rooftops in order to experience daylight and make social contacts—many broken bones attest to frequent falls. Some houses were lavishly decorated, mainly with hunting scenes. Religious images, both of powerful male hunters and "mother goddesses" devoted to agricultural fertility, were common, and some people in the village seem to have had special religious responsibilities. The village produced almost all the goods it consumed. Some trade was conducted with hunting peoples who lived in the hills surrounding the village, but apparently, it was initiated more to keep the peace than to produce economic gain. By 5500 B.C.E., important production activities developed in the village, including those of skilled toolmakers and jewelers. With time also came links with other communities. Large villages like Çatal Hüyük ruled over smaller communities. This meant that some families began to specialize in politics, and military forces were organized. Some villages became small cities, ruled by kings who were typically given divine status.

By 3000 B.C.E., Çatal Hüyük had become part of a civilization. Although many of the characteristics of

Figure 1.1 *Skara Brae in the Orkney Islands off the Scottish coast is an excellent example of a late Neolithic settlement that dates from 1500 B.C.E.*

civilization had existed by 6000 or 5000 B.C.E. in this Middle Eastern region, the origins of civilization, strictly speaking, approximately date to only 3500 B.C.E. The first civilization arose in the Middle East along the banks of the Tigris and Euphrates rivers. Another center of civilization started soon thereafter in northeast Africa (Egypt), and a third by around 2500 B.C.E. along the banks of the Indus River in northwestern India. These three early centers of civilization had some interaction. The fourth and fifth early civilization centers, a bit later and considerably more separate, arose in China and Central America.

Unlike an agricultural society, which can be rather precisely defined, **civilization** is a more subjective construct. Some scholars prefer to define civilizations only as societies with enough economic surplus to form divisions of labor and a social hierarchy involving significant inequalities. This is a very inclusive definition, and under it most agricultural societies and even some groups like North American Indians who combined farming with hunting would be drawn in. Others, however, press the concepts of civilization further, arguing, for example, that a chief difference between civilizations and other societies (whether hunting or agricultural) involves the emergence of formal political organizations, or states, as opposed to dependence on family or tribal ties. Most civilizations produce political units capable of ruling large regions, and some characteristically produce huge kingdoms or empires.

The word *civilization* itself comes from the Latin term for *city*, and in truth most civilizations do depend on the existence of significant cities. In agricultural civilizations, most people do not live in cities. But cities are crucial because they amass wealth and power, they allow the rapid exchange of ideas among relatively large numbers of people, thereby encouraging intellectual thought and artistic expression, and they promote specialization in manufacturing and trade.

Most civilizations developed writing, starting with the emergence of **cuneiform** (writing based on wedge-like characters) in the Middle East around 3500 B.C.E. Societies that employ writing can organize more elaborate political structures because of their ability to send messages and keep records. They can tax more efficiently and make contracts and treaties. Societies with writing also generate a more explicit intellectual climate because of their ability to record data and build on past, written wisdom. (One of the early written records from the Middle East is a recipe for making beer—a science of a sort.) Some experts argue that the very fact of becoming literate changes the way people think, encouraging them to consider the world as a place that can be understood by organized human inquiry, or "rationally," and less by a host of spiritual beliefs. In all agricultural civilizations—that is, in all human history until less than 200 years ago—only a minority of people were literate, and usually that was a small minority. Nonetheless, the existence of writing did make a difference in such societies.

Since civilizations employ writing and are by definition unusually well organized, it is not surprising that almost all recorded history is about what has happened to civilized societies. We simply know the most about such societies, and we often are particularly impressed by what they produce in the way of great art or powerful rulers. It is also true that civilizations tend to be far more populous than noncivilized societies. Therefore, the history of civilization generally covers the history of most people.

But the history of civilization does not include everybody. No hunting or nomadic peoples could generate a civilization—they lacked the stability and resources, and, with the exception of a limited number of signs and symbols, they never developed writing, unless it came from the outside. Furthermore, some agricultural peoples did not develop a full civilization, *if* our definition of civilization goes beyond the simple acquisition of economic surplus to formal states, cities, and writing. Portions of west Africa, fully agricultural and capable of impressive art, have long lacked writing, major cities, or more than loose regional government.

People in civilizations, particularly during the long centuries when they were surrounded by noncivilized peoples, characteristically looked down on any society lacking in civilization. The ancient Greeks coined the word *barbarian* to describe such cases— indeed, they were prone to regard all non-Greeks as barbarians. As a result of labels like this, it is easy to think of much human history as divided between civilizations and primitive **nomads.**

Such a distinction is incorrect, however, and it does not follow from the real historical meaning of civilization. In the first place, like agriculture, civilization brings losses as well as gains. As Çatal Hüyük moved toward civilization, distinctions based on social class and wealth increased. Civilizations often have firmer class or caste divisions, including slavery, than do "simpler" societies. They also often promote greater separation between the rulers and ruled, monarchs and subjects. Frequently, they are quite warlike, and there is greater inequality between men and women than in "noncivilized" societies. With civilization, more fully patriarchal structures emerged. In cities, male superiority was even clearer than in agriculture, as men did most of the manufacturing and assumed political and religious leadership, thus relegating women to subordinate roles. "Civilization," then, is not a synonym for "good."

By the same token, noncivilized societies may be exceptionally well regulated and have interesting, important cultures. Many noncivilized societies, in fact, have more regulations—in part, because they depend on rules transmitted by word of mouth—than civilized societies. Some of the societies most eager to repress anger and aggression in human dealings, such as Zuni Indians in the American Southwest, are noncivilized. Although some noncivilized societies treat old people cruelly, others display more respect and veneration toward elders than most civilizations do. In other words, noncivilized societies are not all alike. They are not characteristically populated with cannibals and warmongers, but rather are often shocked by the doings of civilized peoples. For example, American Indians were appalled at the insistence of European settlers on spanking their children, a behavior they regarded as vicious and unnecessary. A fascinating, although probably unanswerable, question involves determining whether or not the civilization form has left more or less good in its wake.

It is also important to note that many nomadic peoples contributed greatly to world history. While many remaining hunting-and-gathering peoples became increasingly isolated, except in parts of the Americas, nomadic herding economies continued to flourish in many places. They depended on the domestication of animals and on key technological improvements, for example in riding equipment and weaponry. Precisely because they traveled widely, nomadic peoples could play vital roles in world trade and in developing contacts among more settled areas. Nomadic groups in central Asia would play a particularly great role in world history, but groups in the Middle East and Africa were significant as well.

Despite the importance of alternatives, it remains true that the development of civilization most obviously continued the process of technological change and political organization. Civilizations also generated the largest populations and the most elaborate artistic and intellectual forms. It is in this context that the term has real meaning and in which it legitimately commands the attention of most historians.

Civilizations also increased human impact on the environment. For example, the first center of copper production in Europe, along the Danube valley, led to such deforestation that the fuel supply was destroyed, and the industry collapsed after about 3000 B.C.E. The extensive agriculture needed to support Indus River cities opened the land to erosion and flooding because of overuse of the soil and removal of trees.

Having started in 3500 B.C.E., civilization developed in its four initial centers—the Middle East, Egypt, northwestern India, and northern China—over the following 2500 years. These areas covered only a tiny portion of the inhabited parts of the world, although they were the most densely populated. Such early civilizations, all clustered in key river valleys, were in a way pilot tests of the new form of social organization. Only after about 1000 B.C.E. did a more consistent process of development and spread of civilization begin—and with it came the main threads of world history. However, the great civilizations unquestionably built on the achievements of the river valley pioneers, and so some understanding of this contribution to the list of early human accomplishments is essential.

Tigris-Euphrates Civilization

The most noteworthy achievements of the earliest civilizations were early versions of organizational and cultural forms that most of us now take for granted—writing itself, formal codes of law, city planning and architecture, and institutions for trade, including the use of money. Once developed, most of these building blocks of human organization did not have to be reinvented, although in some cases they spread only slowly to other parts of the world.

It is not surprising then, given its lead in agriculture, metalworking, and village structure, that the Middle East generated the first example of human civilization. Indeed, the first civilization, founded in the valley of the Tigris and Euphrates rivers in a part of the Middle East long called **Mesopotamia,** forms one of only a few cases of a civilization developed absolutely from scratch—and with no examples from any place else to imitate. (Chinese civilization and civilization in Central America also developed independently.) By 4000 B.C.E., the farmers of Mesopotamia were familiar with bronze and copper and had already invented the wheel for transportation. They had a well-established pottery industry and interesting artistic forms. Farming in this area, because of the need for irrigation, required considerable coordina-

Visualizing the Past

Mesopotamia in Maps

The Mesopotamian civilizations steadily expanded from their roots in the fertile valley between the Tigris and Euphrates rivers throughout their centuries of existence. Reading the maps can help explain the nature of the civilizations in the region.

What do these maps suggest about the relationship between Mesopotamian civilizations and the topography of the Middle East? Does geography suggest reasons for invasion and political instability in this civilization center? Did later empires in the region have the same relationship to river valleys as did the earlier states? What might have caused the change? Why did even the larger empires not spread through the Arabian peninsula? What were the potential contacts between Mesopotamia and other river valley civilization centers? Why has the Middle East been so significant in European, African, and Asian history?

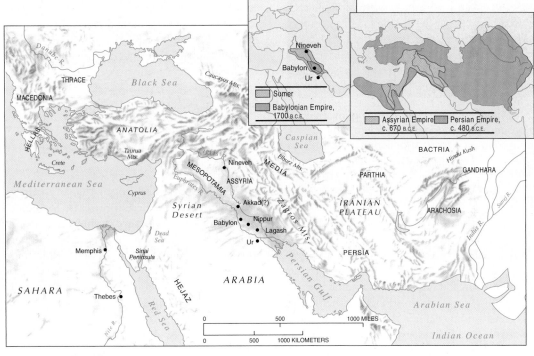

Mesopotamia and the Middle East

tion among communities, and this in turn served as the basis for complex political structures.

By about 3500 B.C.E., a people who had recently invaded this region, the **Sumerians,** developed a cuneiform alphabet, the first known case of human writing. Their alphabet at first used different pictures to represent various objects but soon shifted to the use of geometric shapes to symbolize spoken sounds. The early Sumerian alphabet may have had as many as 2000 such symbols, but this number was later reduced to about 300. Even so, writing and reading remained complex skills, which only a few had time to master. Scribes wrote on clay tablets, using styluses shaped quite like the modern ballpoint pen (see Figures 1.2 and 1.3).

Sumerian art developed steadily, as statues and painted frescoes were used to adorn the temples of the gods. Statues of the gods also decorated individual

Figure 1.2 *One of the early uses of writing involved marking property boundaries. This picture shows cuneiform writing on a Mesopotamian map from about 1300 B.C.E. The map focuses on defining the king's estate, with sections for priests and for key gods such as Marduk. In what ways did writing improve property maps?*

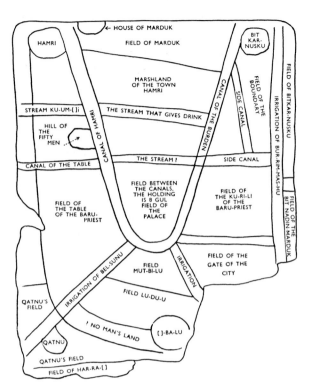

Figure 1.3 *Translation of the cuneiform writing in Figure 1.2.*

homes. Sumerian science aided a complex agricultural society, as people sought to learn more about the movement of the sun and stars—thus founding the science of astronomy—and improved their mathematical knowledge. (Astronomy defined the calendar and provided the astrological forecasts widely used in politics and religion.) The Sumerians employed a system of numbers based on units of 10, 60, and 360 that we still use in calculating circles and hours. In other words, Sumerians and their successors in Mesopotamia created patterns of observation and abstract thought about nature that a number of civilizations, including our own, still rely on, and they also introduced specific systems, such as charts of major constellations, that have been current at least among educated people for 5000 years, not only in the Middle East, but by later imitation in India and Europe as well.

Sumerians developed complex religious rituals. Each city had a patron god and erected impressive shrines to please and honor this and other deities. Massive towers, called **ziggurats,** formed the first monumental architecture in this civilization. Professional priests operated these temples and conducted the rituals within. Sumerians believed in many powerful gods, for the nature on which their agriculture depended often seemed swift and unpredictable. Prayers and offerings to prevent floods as well as to protect good health were a vital part of Sumerian life. Sumerian ideas about the divine force in natural objects—in rivers, trees, and mountains—were common among early agricultural peoples; a religion of this sort, which sees gods in many aspects of nature, is known as polytheism. More specifically, Sumerian religious notions, notably their ideas about the gods' creation of the earth from water and about the divine punishment of humans through floods, later influenced the writers of the Old Testament and thus continue to play a role in Jewish, Christian, and Muslim cultures. Sumerian religious ideas, which had a decidedly gloomy cast, also included a belief in an afterlife of punishment—an original version of the concept of hell.

Sumerian political structures stressed tightly organized **city-states,** ruled by a king who claimed divine authority. The Sumerian state had carefully defined boundaries, unlike the less formal territories of precivilized villages in the region. Here is a key early example of how civilization and a more formal political structure came together. The government helped regulate religion and enforce its duties; it also provided a court system in the interests of justice. Kings were originally military leaders during times of war, and the function of defense and war, including leadership of a trained army, remained vital in Sumerian politics. Kings and the noble class, along with the priesthood, controlled considerable land, which was worked by slaves. Thus began a tradition of slavery that would long mark Middle Eastern societies. Warfare remained vital to ensure supplies of slaves taken as prisoners during combat. At the same time, slavery was a variable state of existence, and many slaves were able to earn money and even buy their freedom.

The Sumerians added to their region's agricultural prosperity not only by using wheeled carts but also by learning about fertilizers and by adopting silver as a means of exchange for buying and selling—an early form of money. However, the region was also hard to defend and proved a constant temptation to outside invaders from Sumerian times to the present. The Sumerians themselves fell to a people called the Akkadians, who continued much of Sumerian culture. Another period of decline was followed by conquest by the **Babylonians,** who extended their own empire and thus helped bring civilization to other parts of the Middle East. It was under Babylonian rule that the king **Hammurabi** introduced the most famous early code of law, boasting of his purpose:

> to promote the welfare of the people, I, Hammurabi, the devout, god-fearing prince, cause justice to prevail in the land by destroying the wicked and the evil, that the strong might not oppress the weak.

Hammurabi's code established rules of procedure for courts of law and regulated property rights and the duties of family members, setting harsh punishments for crimes.

Document

Hammurabi's Law Code

Hammurabi, as king of Babylon, united Mesopotamia under his rule from about 1800 to 1750 B.C.E. His law code, the earliest such compilation still in existence, was discovered on a stone slab in Iran in 1901 C.E. Not a systematic presentation, it was a collection of exemplary cases designed to set general standards of justice. The code provides vital insights into the nature of social relations and family structure in this ancient civilization. Examples of the Hammurabic code follow:

When Marduk commanded me to give justice to the people of the land and to let [them] have [good] governance, I set forth truth and justice throughout the land [and] prospered the people.

At that time:

If a man has accused a man and has charged him with manslaughter and then has not proved [it against] him, his accuser shall be put to death.

If a man has charged a man with sorcery and then has not proved [it against] him, he who is charged with the sorcery shall go to the holy river; he shall leap into the holy river and, if the holy river overwhelms him, his accuser shall take and keep his house; if the holy river proves that man clear [of the offense] and he comes back safe, he who has charged him with sorcery shall be put to death; he who leapt into the holy river shall take and keep the house of his accuser.

If a man has come forward in a case to bear witness to a felony and then has not proved the statement that he has made, if that case [is] a capital one, that man shall be put to death.

If he has come forward to bear witness to [a claim for] corn or money, he shall remain liable for the penalty for that suit.

If a judge has tried a suit, given a decision, caused a sealed tablet to be executed, [and] thereafter varies his judgment, they shall convict that judge of varying [his] judgment and he shall pay twelvefold the claim in that suit; then they shall remove him from his place on the bench of judges in the assembly, and he shall not [again] sit in judgment with the judges.

(continued)

If a free person helps a slave to escape, the free person will be put to death.

If a man has committed robbery and is caught, that man shall be put to death.

If the robber is not caught, the man who has been robbed shall formally declare whatever he has lost before a god, and the city and the mayor in whose territory or district the robbery has been committed shall replace whatever he has lost for him.

If [it is] the life [of the owner that is lost], the city or the mayor shall pay one maneh of silver to his kinsfolk.

If a person owes money and Adad [the river god] has flooded the person's field, the person will not give any grain [tax] or pay any interest in that year.

If a person is too lazy to make the dike of his field strong and there is a break in the dike and water destroys his own farmland, that person will make good the grain [tax] that is destroyed.

If a merchant increases interest beyond that set by the king and collects it, that merchant will lose what was lent.

If a trader borrows money from a merchant and then denies the fact, that merchant in the presence of god and witnesses will prove the trader borrowed the money and the trader will pay the merchant three times the amount borrowed.

If the husband of a married lady has accused her but she is not caught lying with another man, she shall take an oath by the life of a god and return to her house.

If a man takes himself off and there is not the [necessary] maintenance in his house, his wife [so long as] her [husband is delayed], shall keep [herself chaste; she shall not] enter [another man's house].

If that woman has not kept herself chaste but enters another man's house, they shall convict that woman and cast her into the water.

If a son strikes his father, they shall cut off his forehand.

If a man has put out the eye of a free man, they shall put out his eye.

If he breaks the bone of a [free] man, they shall break his bone.

If he puts out the eye of a villain or breaks the bone of a villain, he shall pay one maneh of silver.

If he puts out the eye of a [free] man's slave or breaks the bone of a [free] man's slave, he shall pay half his price.

If a man knocks out the tooth of a [free] man equal [in rank] to him[self], they shall knock out his tooth.

If he knocks out the tooth of a villain, he shall pay one-third maneh of silver.

If a man strikes the cheek of a [free] man who is superior [in rank] to him[self], he shall be beaten with 60 stripes with a whip of ox-hide in the assembly.

If the man strikes the cheek of a free man equal to him[self in rank], he shall pay one maneh of silver.

If a villain strikes the cheek of a villain, he shall pay ten shekels of silver.

If the slave of a [free] man strikes the cheek of a free man, they shall cut off his ear.

Questions: What can you tell from the Hammurabic code about the social and family structure of Mesopotamia? What is the relationship between law and trade? Why did agricultural civilizations such as Babylon insist on harsh punishments for crimes? What religious and magical beliefs does the document suggest? Using specific examples, show how interpreting this document for significant historical meaning differs from simply reading it.

For many centuries during and after the heyday of Babylon, peace and civilization in the Middle East were troubled by the invasions of hunting and herding groups. Indo-European peoples pressed in from the north, starting about 2100 B.C.E. In the Middle East itself, invasions by Semitic peoples from the south were more important, and Semitic peoples and languages increasingly dominated the region. The new arrivals adopted the culture of the conquered peoples as their own, so the key features of the civilization persisted. But large political units declined in favor of smaller city-states or regional kingdoms, particularly during the centuries of greatest turmoil, between 1200 and 900 B.C.E. Thereafter, new invaders, first the Assyrians and then the Persians, created large new empires in the Middle East.

Egyptian Civilization

A second center of civilization sprang up in northern Africa, along the Nile River. Egyptian civilization, formed by 3000 B.C.E., benefited from the trade and technological influence of Mesopotamia, but it produced a quite different society and culture. Less open to invasion, Egypt retained a unified state throughout most of its history. The king, or **pharaoh,** possessed immense power. The Egyptian economy was more fully government-directed than its Mesopotamian counterpart, which had a more independent business class. Government control may have been necessary because of the complexity of coordinating irrigation along the Nile. It nonetheless resulted in godlike status for the pharaohs, who built splendid tombs for themselves—the **pyramids**—from 2700 B.C.E. onward.

During periods of weak rule and occasional invasions, Egyptian society suffered a decline, but revivals kept the framework of Egyptian civilization intact until after 1000 B.C.E. (Map 1.3). At key points, Egyptian influence spread up the Nile to the area now known as the Sudan, with an impact on the later development of African culture. The kingdom of **Kush** interacted with Egypt and invaded it at some point.

Neither Egyptian science nor the Egyptian alphabet was as elaborate as its Mesopotamian equal, although mathematics was more advanced in this civilization. Egyptian art was exceptionally lively; cheerful and colorful pictures decorated not only the tombs—where the belief in an afterlife made people want to be surrounded by objects of beauty—but also palaces and furnishings. Egyptian architectural forms were also quite influential, not only in Egypt but in other parts of the Mediterranean as well. Egyptian mathematics produced the idea of a day divided into 24 hours, and here too Egypt influenced the development of later Mediterranean cultures.

Indian and Chinese River Valley Civilizations

River valley civilizations developed in two other centers. A prosperous urban civilization emerged along the **Indus River** by 2500 B.C.E., supporting several large cities, including **Harappa** and **Mohenjo Daro,** whose houses even had running water (Figure 1.4). Indus River peoples had trading contacts with Mesopotamia, but they developed their own distinctive alphabet and artistic forms. Infiltrations by Indo-Europeans, however, plus natural calamities, resulted in such destruction that it makes it hard to speak with confidence about either the nature of this culture or its subsequent influence on India. Harappan writing, for example, has yet to be deciphered. It remains true that civilization never had to be fully reinvented in India. The Indo-European migrants combined their religious and political ideas with those that had taken root in the early cities. In recent times, Indians' pride in their early civilized history has become an important part of their national identity.

Civilization along the **Huanghe (Yellow River)** in China developed in considerable isolation, although some overland trading contact with India and the Middle East did develop. Huanghe civilization was the subject of much later Chinese legend, which praised the godlike kings of early civilization, starting with the mythic ancestor of the Chinese, P'an Ku. The Chinese had an unusually elaborate concept of their remote ori-

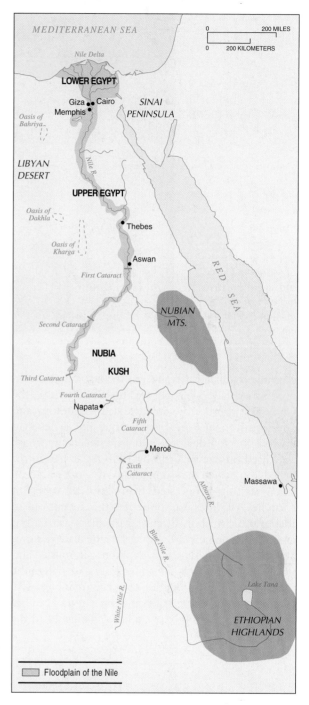

Map 1.3 *Egypt, Kush, and Axum, Successive Dynasties. As Egypt weakened, kingdoms farther up the Nile and deeper into Africa rose in importance.*

gins, and they began early to record a part-fact, part-fiction history of their early kings. What is clear is the following: First, the existence of an organized state that

Figure 1.4 *The ruins at Mohenjo Daro are still impressive more than four millennia after the city was established.*

carefully regulated irrigation in the fertile but flood-prone river valley. Second, by about 2000 B.C.E. the Chinese had produced an advanced technology and developed an elaborate intellectual life. They had learned how to ride horses and were skilled in pottery; they used bronze well and by 1000 B.C.E. had introduced iron, which they soon learned to work with coal. Their writing progressed from knotted ropes to scratches of lines on bone to the invention of **ideographic** symbols. Science, particularly astronomy, arose early. Chinese art emphasized delicate designs, and the Chinese claim an early interest in music (Figure 1.5). Because of limits on building materials in the region, the Chinese did not construct many massive monuments, choosing to live in simple houses built of mud. By about 1500 B.C.E., a line of kings called the

Figure 1.5 *This elaborately decorated bronze incense vessel from the Shang era, with its whimsical horse and catlike figure, shows the high level of artistic expression achieved very early in Chinese history. It also demonstrates a high level of metalworking ability, which carried over into Shang weapons and tools. Although the design of these ritual vessels often was abstract, mythical creatures such as dragons and sacred birds were deftly cast in bronzes that remain some of the great treasures of Chinese art.*

In Depth

The Idea of Civilization in World Historical Perspective

The belief that there are fundamental differences between civilized and "barbaric" or "savage" peoples is very ancient and widespread. For thousands of years the Chinese set themselves off from cattle- and sheep-herding peoples of the vast plains to the north and west of China proper, whom they saw as barbarians. To the Chinese, being civilized was cultural, not biological or racial. If barbarians learned the Chinese language and adopted Chinese ways—from the clothes they wore to the food they ate—they were regarded as civilized.

A similar pattern of demarcation and cultural absorption was found among the American Indian peoples of present-day Mexico. Those who settled in the valleys of the mountainous interior, where they built great civilizations, lived in fear of invasions by peoples they regarded as barbarous and called **Chichimecs,** meaning "sons of the dog." The latter were nomadic hunters and gatherers who periodically moved down from the desert regions of north Mexico into the fertile central valleys in search of game and settlements to pillage. The Aztecs were simply the last, and perhaps the most fierce, of a long line of Chichimec peoples who entered the valleys and conquered the urban-based empires that had developed there. But after the conquerors settled down, they adopted many of the religious beliefs and institutional patterns and much of the material culture of defeated peoples.

The word *civilization* is derived from the Latin word *civilis,* meaning "of the citizens." The term was coined by the Romans. They used it to distinguish between themselves as citizens of a cosmopolitan, urban-based civilization and the "inferior" peoples who lived in the forests and deserts on the fringes of their Mediterranean empire. Centuries earlier, the Greeks, who had contributed much to the rise of Roman civilization, made a similar distinction between themselves and outsiders. Because the languages of the non-Greek peoples to the north of the Greek heartlands sounded like senseless babble to the Greeks, they lumped all the outsiders together as *barbarians,* which meant "those who cannot speak Greek." As in the case of the Chinese and Aztecs, the boundaries between civilized and barbarian for the Greeks and Romans were cultural, not biological.

Until the 17th and 18th centuries C.E., the priority given to cultural attributes (e.g., language, dress, manners) as the means by which civilized peoples set themselves off from barbaric ones was rarely challenged. But in those centuries, a major change occurred among thinkers in western Europe. Efforts were made not only to define the differences between civilized and barbarian but to identify a series of stages in human development that ranged from the lowest savagery to the highest civilization. Depending on the writer in question, candidates for civilization ranged from Greece and Rome to (not surprisingly) Europe of the 17th and 18th centuries. Most of the other peoples of the globe, whose "discovery" since the 15th century had prompted the efforts to classify them in the first place, were ranked in increasingly complex hierarchies. Nomadic, cattle- and sheep-herding peoples, such as the Mongols of central Asia, usually were classified as barbarians. Then in the 19th century racial differences were added to the hierarchy, with white people seen as having evolved the most advanced civilizations.

The second major shift in Western ideas about civilization began at the end of the 18th century but did not really take hold until a century later. In keeping with a growing emphasis in European thinking and social interaction on racial or biological differences, modes of human social organization and cultural expression were increasingly linked to what were alleged to be the innate capacities of each human race. Although no one could agree on what a race was or how many races there were, most European writers argued that some races were more inventive, moral, courageous, and artistic—thus more capable of building civilizations—than others. Of course, white (or Caucasian) Europeans were considered by white European authors to be the most capable of all. The hierarchy from savage to civilized took on a color dimension, with white at the top, where the civilized peoples clustered, to yellow, red, brown, and black in descending order.

Some authors sought to reserve all the attainments of civilization for whites, or peoples of European stock. As the evolutionary theories of thinkers such as Charles Darwin came into vogue in the late 1800s, race and level of cultural development were seen in the perspective of thousands of years of human change and adaptation rather than as being fixed in time. Nevertheless, this new perspective had little effect on the rankings of different human groups. Civilized whites were simply seen as having evolved much further than backward and barbaric peoples.

(continued)

The perceived correspondence between race and level of development and the hardening of the boundaries between civilized and "inferior" peoples affected much more than intellectual discourse about the nature and history of human society. These beliefs were used to justify European imperialist expansion, which was seen as a "civilizing mission" aimed at uplifting barbaric and savage peoples across the globe. In the last half of the 19th century virtually all non-Western peoples came to be dominated by the Europeans, who were confident that they, as representatives of the highest civilization ever created, were best equipped to govern lesser breeds of humans.

In the 20th century much of the intellectual baggage that once gave credibility to the racially embedded hierarchies of civilized and savage peoples was discarded. Racist thinking was discredited by 20th-century developments, including the revolt of the colonized peoples and the crimes committed by the Nazis before and during World War II in the name of racial purification. In addition, these ideas have failed because racial supremacists cannot provide convincing proof of innate differences in mental and physical aptitude between various human groups. These trends, as well as research that has resulted in a much more sophisticated understanding of evolution, have led to the abandonment of rigid and self-serving 19th-century ideas about civilization. Yet even though non-European peoples such as the Indians and Chinese are increasingly given credit for their civilized attainments, much ethnocentrism remains in the ways social theorists determine who is civilized and who is not.

Perhaps the best way to avoid the tendency to define the term with reference to one's own society is to view civilization as one of several human approaches to social organization rather than attempting to identify specific kinds of cultural achievement (e.g., writing, cities, monumental architecture). All peoples, from small bands of hunters and gatherers to farmers and factory workers, live in societies. All societies produce cultures: combinations of the ideas, objects, and patterns of behavior that result from human social interaction. But not all societies and cultures generate the surplus production that permits the levels of specialization, scale, and complexity that distinguish civilizations from other modes of social organization. All peoples are intrinsically capable of building civilizations, but many have lacked the resource base, historical circumstances, or desire to do so.

Questions: Identify a society you consider to be civilized. What criteria did you use to determine that it was civilized? Can you apply those criteria to other societies? Can you think of societies that might not fit your criteria and yet be civilizations? Do the standards that you and others use reflect your own society's norms and achievements rather than neutral, more universal criteria?

Shang ruled over the Huanghe valley, and these rulers did construct some impressive tombs and palaces. Invasions disrupted the Shang dynasty and caused a temporary decline in civilization. However, there was less of a break between the river valley society and the later, fuller development of civilization in China than occurred in other centers.

The Heritage of the River Valley Civilizations

River valley civilizations left a number of durable achievements. But most river valley civilizations declined after about 1200 B.C.E. A number of small centers emerged in the Middle East; these introduced further innovations including the religion of Judaism.

Many accomplishments of the river valley civilizations had a lasting impact. Monuments such as the Egyptian pyramids have long been regarded as one of the wonders of the world. Other achievements, although more prosaic, are fundamental to world history even today: the invention of the wheel, the taming of the horse, the creation of usable alphabets and writing implements, the production of key mathematical concepts such as square roots, the development of well-organized monarchies and bureaucracies, and the invention of functional calendars and other divisions of time. These basic achievements, along with the awe that the early civilizations continue to inspire, are vital legacies to the whole of human history. Almost all the major alphabets in the world today are derived from the writing forms pioneered in the river valleys, apart from the even more durable concept of writing itself. Almost all later civilizations, then, built on the massive foundations first constructed in the river valleys.

Despite these accomplishments, most of the river valley civilizations were in decline by 1000 B.C.E. The civilizations had flourished for as many as 2500 years, although of course with periodic disruptions and revivals. But, particularly in India, the new waves of invasion did produce something of a break in the history of civilization, a dividing line between the river valley pioneers and later cultures.

This break raises one final question: Besides the vital achievements—the fascinating monuments and the indispensable advances in technology, science, and art—what legacies did the river valley civilizations impart for later ages? The question is particularly important for the Middle East and Egypt. In India, we must frankly admit much ignorance about possible links between Indus River accomplishments and what came later; in China, there is a definite connection between the first civilization and subsequent forms. Indeed, the new dynasty in China, the Zhou, took over from the Shang about 1000 B.C.E., ruling a loose coalition of regional lords; recorded Chinese history flowed smoothly at this point. But what was the legacy of Mesopotamia and Egypt for later civilizations in or near their centers?

Europeans, even North Americans, are sometimes prone to claim these cultures as the "origins" of the Western civilization in which we live. These claims should not be taken too literally. It is not altogether clear that either Egypt or Mesopotamia contributed much to later political traditions, although the Roman Empire emulated the concept of a godlike king, as evidenced in the trappings of the office, and the existence of strong city-state governments in the Middle East itself continued to be significant. Ideas about slavery may also have been passed on from these early civilizations. Specific scientific achievements are vital, as the Greeks, for example, carefully studied Egyptian mathematics. Scholars argue, however, over how much of a connection exists between Mesopotamian and Egyptian science and later Greek thinking, aside from certain techniques of measuring time or charting the stars.

Some historians of philosophy have asserted a basic division between a Mesopotamian and Chinese understanding of nature, which they claim affected later civilizations around the Mediterranean in contrast to China. Mesopotamians were prone to stress a gap between humankind and nature, whereas Chinese thinking developed along ideas of basic harmony. It is possible, then, that some fundamental thinking helped shape later outlooks, but the continuities here are not easy to assess. Mesopotamian art and Egyptian architecture had a more measurable influence on Greek styles, and through these, in turn, later European and Muslim cultures. The Greeks thus learned much about temple building from the Egyptians, whose culture had influenced island civilizations, such as Crete, which then affected later Greek styles.

There was a final connection between early and later civilizations in the form of regional cultures that sprang up under the influence of Mesopotamia and Egypt, along the eastern shores of the Mediterranean mainly after 1200 B.C.E. Although the great empires from Sumer through Babylon were disrupted and the Egyptian state finally declined, civilization in the Middle East had spread widely enough to encourage a set of smaller cultures capable of surviving and even flourishing after the great empires became weak. These cultures produced important innovations that would affect later civilizations in the Middle East and throughout the Mediterranean. They also created a diverse array of regional identities that would continue to mark the Middle East even as other forces, like the Roman Empire or the later religion of Islam, took center stage. Several of these small cultures proved immensely durable, and in their complexity and capacity to survive, they would influence other parts of the world as well.

A people called the **Phoenicians,** for example, devised a greatly simplified alphabet with 22 letters around 1300 B.C.E.; this alphabet, in turn, became the predecessor of Greek and Latin alphabets. The Phoenicians also improved the Egyptian numbering system and, as great traders, set up colony cities in north Africa and on the coasts of Europe. Another regional group, the Lydians, first introduced coined money.

The most influential of the smaller Middle Eastern groups, however, were the Jews, who gave the world the first clearly developed monotheistic religion. We have seen that early religions, both before and after the beginnings of civilization, were polytheistic, claiming that many gods and goddesses worked to control nature and human destiny. The Jews, a Semitic people influenced by Babylonian civilization, settled near the Mediterranean around 1200 B.C.E. The Jewish state was small and relatively weak,

In Depth

The Legacy of Asia's First Civilizations

In their size, complexity, and longevity, the first civilizations to develop in south Asia and China match, and in some respects surpass, the earliest civilizations that arose in Mesopotamia and Egypt. But the long-term impact of the **Harappan civilization** in the Indus basin was strikingly different from that of the Shang and Zhou civilization in north China. The **loess** zone and north China plain where the Shang and Zhou empires took hold became the center of a continuous civilization that was to last into the 20th century C.E. and, some historians would argue, to the present day. Although regions farther south, such as the Yangtze basin, would in some time periods enjoy political, economic, and cultural predominance within China, the capital and center of Chinese civilization repeatedly returned to the Yellow River area and the north China plain. By contrast, the Indus valley proved capable of nurturing a civilization that endured for more than a thousand years. But when Harappa collapsed, the plains of the Indus were bypassed in favor of the far more lush and extensive lands in the basin of the Ganges River network to the east. Although the Indus would later serve, for much shorter time spans, as the seat of empires, the core areas of successive Indian civilizations were far to the east and south.

The contrast between the fates of the original geographic centers of Indian and Chinese civilizations is paralleled by the legacies of the civilizations themselves. Harappa was destroyed, and it disappeared from history for thousands of years. Although the peoples who built the Indus complex left their mark on subsequent Indian culture, they did not pass on the fundamental patterns of civilized life that they had evolved. Their mother-goddess, yoga positions, and the dancing god of fertility endured. Some of their symbols, such as the swastika and the *lingam* (a phallic image, usually made of stone), were prominent in later artistic and religious traditions. The Harappans' tanks, or public bathing ponds, remain a central feature of Indian cities, particularly in the south. Their techniques of growing rice and cotton were preserved by cultivating peoples fleeing nomadic incursions and were later taken up by the newly arrived Indo-Aryan tribes.

Nearly everything else was lost. In contrast to the civilizations of Mesopotamia, which fell but were replaced by new civilizations that preserved and built on the achievements of their predecessors, much of what the Harappan peoples had accomplished had to be redone by later civilized peoples. The cities of the Indus civilization were destroyed, and comparable urban centers did not reappear in south Asia for more than a thousand years. The Harappans' remarkably advanced standards for measuring distance and weight ceased to be used. Their system of writing was forgotten, and when rediscovered it was celebrated as an intriguing but very dead language from the past. Harappan skills in community planning, sewage control, and engineering were meaningless to the nomadic peoples who took control of their homelands. The Harappan penchant for standardization, discipline, and state control was profoundly challenged by the brawling, independent-minded warriors who supplanted them as masters of the Indian subcontinent.

In contrast to the civilization of the Indus valley, the original civilization of China has survived nomadic incursions and natural catastrophes and has profoundly influenced the course of Chinese history. Shang irrigation and dike systems and millet and wheat cultivation provided the basis for the innovations and expansion of subsequent dynasties. Shang and Zhou fortified towns and villages surrounded with stamped earth walls have persisted as the predominant patterns of settlement throughout Chinese history. The founders of the Shang and Zhou dynasties have been revered by scholars and peasants alike as philosopher-kings who ought to be emulated by leaders at all levels. The Shang and Zhou worship of heaven and their veneration of ancestors have remained central to Chinese religious belief and practice for thousands of years. The concept of the **Mandate of Heaven** has been pivotal in Chinese political thinking and organization.

Above all, the system of writing that was originally formulated for Shang oracles developed into the key means of communication between the elites of the many peoples who lived in the core regions of Chinese civilization. The scholar-bureaucrats, who developed this written language and also profited the most from it, soon emerged as the dominant force in Chinese culture and society. Chinese characters provided the basis for the educational system and bureaucracy that were to hold Chinese civilization together through thousands of years of invasions and political crises. Many of the key ingredients of China's early civilizations have remained central throughout Chinese history. This persistence has made for a continuity of identity that is unique to the Chinese people.

It has also meant that China, like the early civilizations of Mesopotamia, was one of the great sources of civilizing influences in human history as a whole. The area affected by ideas developed in China was less extensive than that to which the peoples of Mesopotamia gave writing, law, and their other great achievements. But contacts with China provided critical impetus for the development of civilization in Japan, Korea, and Vietnam. Writing and political organization were two areas in which the earliest formulations of Chinese civilization vitally affected other peoples. In later periods, Chinese thought and other modes of cultural expression such as art, architecture, and etiquette also strongly influenced the growth of civilized life throughout east Asia.

China's technological innovation was to have an impact on global civilization comparable to that of early Mesopotamia. Beginning with increasingly sophisticated irrigation systems, the Chinese have devised a remarkable share of humankind's basic machines and engineering principles. In the Shang and Zhou eras they also pioneered key processes such as silk manufacturing.

The reasons for the differing legacies of Harappan and early Chinese civilizations are numerous and complex. But critical to the disappearance of the first and the resilience of the second were different patterns of interaction between the sedentary peoples who built early civilizations and the nomadic herders who challenged them. In India, the nomadic threat was remote—perhaps nonexistent—for centuries. The Harappan peoples were deficient in military technology and organization. When combined with natural calamities, the waves of warlike nomads migrating into the Indus region proved too much for the Harappan peoples to resist or absorb. The gap between the nomads' herding culture and the urban, agriculture-based Harappan civilization was too great

to be bridged. Conflict between them may well have proved fatal to a civilization long in decline.

By contrast, the loess regions of northern China were open to invasions or migrations on the part of the nomadic herding peoples who lived to the north and west. Peoples from these areas moved almost continuously into the core zones of Chinese civilization. The constant threat posed by the nomads forced the peoples of the north China plain to develop the defenses and military technology needed to defend against nomadic raids or bids for lasting conquest. Contrasting cultures and ways of life strengthened the sense of identity of the cultivating peoples. The obvious nomadic presence prodded these same peoples to unite under strong rulers against the outsiders who did not share Chinese culture. Constant interaction with the nomads led the Shang peoples to develop a culture that was receptive to outside influences, social structures, and political systems. Nomadic energies reinvigorated and enriched the kingdoms of the Shang and the Zhou, in contrast to India, where they proved catastrophic for the isolated and far less adaptable peoples of the Indus valley civilization.

Questions: Compare the early civilizations of India and China with those of Sumer and Egypt. Which are more similar in terms of longevity? Which factors were critical in the failure of the Indus civilization to persist? Which best explain Chinese longevity? Are these the same as those that account for the long life of Egyptian civilization? Why did the Indus civilization have such a limited impact on subsequent civilizations in India, in contrast to Sumer and the other civilizations of Mesopotamia? What is the chief legacy of each of these early civilizations to subsequent human history?

retaining independence only when other parts of the Middle East were in political turmoil. What was distinctive about this culture was its firm belief that a single God, Jehovah, guided the destinies of the Jewish people. Priests and prophets defined and emphasized this belief, and their history of God's guidance of the Jews formed the basis for the Hebrew Bible. The Jewish religion and moral code persisted even as the Jewish state suffered domination by a series of foreign rulers, from 772 B.C.E. until the Romans seized the state outright in 63 B.C.E. Jewish **monotheism** has sustained a distinctive Jewish culture to our own day; it would also serve as a key basis for the development of both Christianity and Islam as major world religions.

Because Judaism stressed God's special compact with the chosen Jewish people, there was no premium placed on converting non-Jews. This belief helps explain the durability of the Jewish faith itself; it also kept the Jewish people in a minority position in the Middle East as a whole. However, the elaboration of monotheism had a wide, if not immediate, significance. In Jewish hands, the concept of God became less humanlike, more abstract. This represented a basic change in not only religion but also humankind's overall outlook. Jehovah had not only a power but also a rationality far different from what the traditional gods of the Middle East or Egypt possessed. These gods were whimsical and capricious; Jehovah was orderly and just, and individuals would know what to expect if they obeyed God's rules. God was also linked to ethical conduct, to proper moral behavior. Religion for the Jews was a way of life, not merely a set of rituals and ceremonies. The full impact of this religious transformation on Middle Eastern civilization would be realized only later, when Jewish beliefs were embraced by other, proselytizing faiths. However, the basic concept of monotheistic religion was one of the legacies of the end of the first great civilization period to the new cultures that would soon arise.

The First Civilizations

 The first civilization developed in the Middle East, in the valleys of the Tigris and Euphrates rivers. Mesopotamian civilization featured distinctive culture and political institutions, along with basic tools of civilization including writing and formal government.

Overall, the river valley civilizations, flourishing for many centuries, created a basic set of tools, intellectual concepts such as writing and mathematics, and political forms that would persist and spread to other parts of Europe, Asia, and Africa. Invasion and natural calamities in India, and invasion and political decline in Egypt, marked a fairly firm break between the institutions of these river valley civilizations and those that would later develop. Huanghe civilization, in contrast, flowed more fully into the more extensive Chinese civilization that would follow. The Middle East, where civilization had first been born, provided the most complex heritage of all. Here too there was a break between the initial series of riverine empires and the civilizations of Greece and Persia that would later dominate the region. However, the development of smaller cultures, such as that of the Jews, provided a bridge between the river valley period and later Middle Eastern society, producing vital new inventions and ideas. The smaller cultures also generated a deeply entrenched network of regional or minority values and institutions that

would continue to make the Middle East a complex, vibrant, and sometimes troubled part of the world.

One final result of the first, long period of human civilization is certainly clear: a pattern of division among the world's peoples. The diffusion of *Homo sapiens sapiens* set the initial stage. Small groups of people spread to almost every corner of the world but maintained little contact with each other thereafter. Separate languages and cultures developed widely. The rise of agriculture stimulated new links, and the spread of farming and new technologies began to cut into local isolation. Trade soon entered the picture: Although most commerce centered within a region, linking a city to its hinterland, a few routes traveled greater distances. By 1000 B.C.E., Phoenicians traded with Britain for metals (they bought lead to make bronze), while Chinese silk was reaching Egypt. Here we have one of the basic themes of world history: steadily proliferating contacts against a background of often fierce local identity.

The rise of civilization further reduced local autonomy, as kings and priests tried to spread trade contacts and cultural forms and warred to gain new territory. Civilization itself was an integrating force at a larger regional level, although, as we have seen in the Middle East, smaller identities persisted. However, individual civilizations had only sporadic contacts with each other. They, and their leading institutions and cultural forms, developed separately. Thus, four distinct centers of civilization developed (five, if the emerging Olmec culture in Mexico is included), each with widely varied patterns, from style of writing to beliefs about nature.

The early civilizations shared important features, including cities, trade, and writing, that helped them meet the common basic definition of civilization in the first place. They also frequently developed some mutual relationships, although the Huanghe culture in China is one example of a civilization that flourished in relative isolation. Egypt and Mesopotamia, in particular, had recurrent contacts through trade and war. But the values or belief systems of each civilization, and their manifestation in political and business styles, were not so easily disseminated. Even relatively close neighbors, such as Egypt and Mesopotamia, developed radically different political attitudes, beliefs about death, and artistic styles. Civilization and considerable diversity thus coexisted hand in hand.

GLOBAL CONNECTIONS: The Early Civilizations and the World

Mesopotamia and Egypt presented two different approaches to relationships outside the home region. Mesopotamia was flat, with few natural barriers to recurrent invasion from the north. Perhaps for this reason, Mesopotamian leaders thought in terms of expansion. Many conquering emperors expanded their territory, though within the Middle East. Many traders pushed outward, dealing either with merchants to the east or sending expeditions into the Mediterranean and beyond, and also to India. The Middle East's role as active agent in wider contact was clearly being established.

Egypt, though not isolated, was more self-contained. There was important trade and interaction along the Nile to the south, which brought mutual influences with the peoples of Kush and Ethiopia. Trade and influence also linked Egypt to Mediterranean islands like Crete, south of Greece. A few interactions, finally, occurred with Mesopotamia. But most Egyptians, including the leaders, thought of Egypt as its own world. There was less need or desire to learn of wider horizons. Correspondingly, ancient Egypt played less of a role as intermediary among regions than did Mesopotamia.

Further Readings

Two collections of sources offer some materials on early China and India: W. T. De Bary Jr. et al., eds., *Sources of Chinese Tradition* (1960), and W. T. De Bary Jr. et al., eds., *Sources of Indian Tradition* (1958). On prehistory, see Robert J. Wenke, *Patterns in Prehistory* (1984); Brian Fagan, *The Journey from Eden: The Peopling of Our World* (1990); Richard Adams, *Prehistoric Mesoamerica* (1991); and Chris Scarre, ed., *Smithsonian Timelines of the Ancient World* (1994). On early civilizations, see C. L. Redman, *The Rise of Civilization: From Early Farmers to Urban Society in the Ancient Near East* (1988); H. Crawford, *Sumer and the Sumerians* (1991); J. Bright, *A History of Israel* (1981); and A. Nibbi, *Ancient Egypt and Some Eastern Neighbors* (1981). On India and China, see G. O. Possehl, ed., *Harappan Civilization: A Contemporary Perspective* (1982); V. & R. Allchin, *The Rise of Civilization in India and Pakistan* (1982); Ping-ti Ho, *Cradle of the East: An Inquiry into the Indigenous Origins of Techniques and Ideas of Neolithic and Early History in China* (1975); Wolfram Eberhard, *History of China* (1977 ed.); and K. C. Wu, *The Chinese Heritage* (1982). On the crucial issue of gender, see M. Ehrenberg, *Women in Prehistory* (1989), and G. Robins, *Women in Ancient Egypt* (1993). On other key topics, refer to Richard Gabriel, *The Culture of War: Invention and Early Development* (1991), and Paul Bairach, *Cities and Economic Development: From the Dawn of History to the Present* (1988). For a challenging statement on the legacy of African and Middle Eastern societies to later Greece, read Martin Bernal, *Black Athena*: *The Africanistic Roots of Classical Civilization* (1987). On the environment, see I. G. Simmons, *Environmental History* (1993). On patterns of contact, see Luce Boulnois, *The Silk Road* (1966); Philip D. Curtin, *Cross-Cultural Trade in World History* (1984); Xinru Liu, *Ancient India and Ancient China: Trade and Religious Exchanges* (1988); and Shereen Ratnagar, *Encounter: The Westerly Trade of the Harappan Civilization* (1981). The science and technology of the ancient world are discussed in Richard Bulliet, *The Camel and the Wheel* (1975); George Ifrah, *From One to Zero: A Universal History of Numbers* (1985); and Edgardo Marcorini, ed., *The History of Science and Technology: A Narrative Chronology* (1988).

On the Web

On early human life forms, up to *Homo sapiens sapiens*, see http://www.iinet.net.au/~chawkins/heaven.htm and http://pecosrio.com; for a virtual tour of Egyptian cities, see http://www.ancientegypt.co.uk/menu.html; on the Gilgamesh epic, see http://www.wsu.edu/~dee/meso/gilg.htm; on the evolution of Hindu epics and beliefs, see http://campus.northpark.edu/history/WebChron/India/India.html. Chinese ethical systems are explored at http://www.san.beck.org/EC13–Chou.html.

PART II

The Classical Period, 1000 B.C.E.–500 C.E.

CHAPTERS

2 Classical Civilization: China

3 Classical Civilization: India

4 Classical Civilization in the Mediterranean: Greece and Rome

5 The Classical Period: Directions, Diversities, and Declines by 500 C.E.

Introduction

Having quickly reviewed the hundreds of thousands of years of human prehistory and the 3000 years of developments in the river valley civilizations, we now slow down our discussion considerably. In the remainder of this book, we deal with the most recent 3000 years of human experience, from roughly 1000 years before the common era (B.C.E.) until the present. There are several reasons for this radical change of pace. Available knowledge is one. Civilizations over the past 3000 years have produced far more records than their predecessors. We not only know more about events such as wars and rebellions, but we also have a fuller sense of how ordinary people in these societies thought about daily issues such as health and family. More important is the fact that civilizations created after 1000 B.C.E. have direct links to civilizations that exist today. Chinese civilization, indeed, flows quite coherently from the middle of the Zhou dynasty (500 B.C.E.) to the present, with surges and declines and significant changes but with equally important connections to preceding events. Even in Western society, where there have been far more shattering disruptions than in China, we can look back to Greek and Roman civilizations and find philosophies and political institutions directly related to contemporary ideas and forms.

The period in the history of civilization after the decline of the river valley cultures is known as *classical*; it runs from about 1000 B.C.E. until the 5th century C.E. In three parts of the world—China, India, and the Mediterranean area (which extends from the Middle East to southern Europe and north Africa)—new or renewed civilizations arose that proved very durable. These civilizations did not touch all the world's peoples, although they spread well beyond the boundaries of the river valleys. It is important to remember that the history of classical civilization does not reflect the whole of world history during this period, because it does not include northern Europeans, central Asians, most Africans below the Sahara, and of course all American Indians. Historical developments in these regions beyond the classical civilizations were significant, but they followed patterns different from those in the classical world.

Also during the classical period, new empires arose around the Tigris-Euphrates valley, resuming the developments of those started by the Sumerians and Babylonians. First the Assyrians and then the Persians established large empires that at times extended throughout the Middle East and even into Europe and India. These empires boasted not only great power but also important new religious ideas and artistic styles that influenced both Greek and Indian cultures later on.

The three classical civilizations of China, India, and the Mediterranean left the most substantial legacies, however, and they also included the largest population concentrations in the world at that time. Moreover, all three classical civilizations set in motion institutions and values that would continue to shape these key parts of the world long after the classical period was over. Some of the continuing diversity of our world is the result of distinctions created during the classical period. Examples include the intense political centralization of the Chinese in contrast to the greater regionalism of Indian political life, or the emotional restraint the Chinese and Japanese were taught to exhibit compared with the greater display of feeling allowed many Mediterranean peoples.

All three classical civilizations built on the achievements of the river valley societies. In the Mediterranean, Greeks benefited from the influence of the earlier Minoan civilization, which had been centered on the Greek islands and partially derived from the greater Egyptian culture. Here, and still more obviously in India and China, classical peoples relied on the technologies developed in the river valley societies; they also utilized earlier artistic styles and possibly some more abstract ideas. And, of course, they adapted earlier writing systems and mathematical concepts.

However, the classical civilizations were not, in the final analysis, simple continuations of the earlier societies from which they derived. Use of iron weapons, first by invading peoples, gave governments a new military edge. Classical civilizations also created larger political structures, capable of controlling more territory. They shifted their geographical base: The center of Indian development moved from the Indus to the Ganges River; China expanded to include the rice-growing Yangtze River (Chiang Jiang) as well as the Huanghe, or Yellow River. All the classical civilizations improved on earlier technologies for agriculture, manufacturing, and urban life. They established more elaborate philosophical and religious systems and expanded scientific and mathematical knowledge. The sophistication of these achievements helps account for the enduring influence of classical civilizations today, not only in the regions where they flourished but also in other areas of the world to which their heritage ultimately spread.

Expansion and integration dominated the outcomes of classical civilizations, even though each created a distinctive, specific culture. Each classical civilization spread beyond a regional center to embrace a growing diversity of people and a growing amount of territory. This, in turn, created the challenge of building institutions and beliefs that could integrate these peoples, without necessarily homogenizing them. Integration

2000 B.C.E.	1000 B.C.E.	500 B.C.E.	250 B.C.E.	1 C.E.	250 C.E.	500 C.E.
1700 Indo-European invasions in Mediterranean **1500–1000** Vedic Age in India, formative period **1400** Kingdom of Mycenae **1029–258** Zhou dynasty	**c. 1000** Polynesians reach Fiji, Samoa **1000–600** Epic Age in India, beginnings of early Hinduism **800** Rise of Greek city-states; Homeric epics, beginnings of Rome **800–400** Spread of Olmec civilization: cultivation of maize (corn), potatoes, domestication of turkeys, dogs **700** Zhou decline **563–483** Gautama Buddha **551–478** Confucius **509–450** Beginnings of Roman republic; Twelve Tables of Law	**c. 500** Laozi and Daoism **500–449** Greek defeat of Persia; spread of Athenian Empire **470–430** Athens at height: Pericles, Phidias, Sophocles, Socrates **431–404** Peloponnesian Wars **402–201** Warring States period in China **338–323** Macedonian Empire, Alexander the Great **330–100** Hellenistic period **264–146** Rome's Punic Wars **322–184** Mauryan dynasty in India	**221–202** Qin dynasty; Great Wall **202** B.C.E.**–220** C.E. Han dynasty **140–87** Rule of Wu Ti **133** Decline of Roman republic **30** B.C.E.**–220** C.E. Kushan rule in India, Hindu beliefs develop **27** Augustus Caesar, rise of Roman Empire	**23–220** Later Han dynasty; invention of paper, compass **30** Crucifixion of Jesus **c. 100** Root crops introduced to southern Africa through trade **180** Death of Marcus Aurelius; beginning of decline of Roman Empire **2nd century** Development of porcelain in China **220–589** Nomadic invasions, disorder, considerable spread of Buddhism in China **231** Initial Germanic invasion effort	**312–337** Constantine; division of Roman Empire administration; toleration of Christianity **319–540** Gupta Empire **450** Beginning of Hun invasions in India **476** Last Roman emperor deposed, fall of Rome	**527–565** Justinian, Eastern emperor **589–618** Sui dynasty in China **600** Harsha's Empire **618** Tang dynasty

included politics, so it was no accident that massive empires grew, at least toward the end of the classical era, around each center. Integration also included growing internal trade as well as cultural systems deliberately designed to draw people together in common beliefs. The problem of integrating new territories, and the processes that resulted, led to the fundamental characteristics of the classical period.

Expansion resulted from massive population growth and encouraged the further development of the classical civilizations. In the final centuries before the common era, China's population tripled, to 60 million. At 14 B.C.E., the Roman Empire had a population of about 54 million people and India about 50 million. Expansion included the migration of farming populations from the regional center to escape crowding, and deliberate commercial efforts to seek new sources of food supply—the factor behind Greek colonies scattered around the Mediterranean. It also included explicit military expansion, particularly by the great empires of China, India, Greece, and Rome, which often resulted in significant resettlement efforts. Military conquest by these three civilizations was backed by well-organized political units and often the advantage in weaponry that iron-based technology provided.

In the Mediterranean, expansion was actually aided by the various diseases settlers brought to the new lands: It reduced local populations and hence the pressure or need to deal with local diversities. Expansion in China and India meant embracing large local populations, already resistant to the contagions of agricultural society. This resulted in greater attention to social, cultural, and political institutions. Both China and India, though in very different ways, worked harder on the process of integration than Greece and Rome.

Everywhere, however, the need to innovate in response to expansion, to draw peoples and territories into manageable interaction, determined many of the key characteristics of this period of world history.

Each classical civilization operated separately for the most part. Trade brought silk from China to the Middle East and the Roman Empire, but while such luxuries were welcomed, no economy was deeply affected by international commerce. There was important cultural exchange between Greece and India, but India's adaptation of Greek artistic style and the Mediterranean's adoption of Indian religious concepts were unusual occurrences. For the most part, developments within each expanding civilization, more than contacts between them, marked this phase of world history.

CHAPTER 2

CLASSICAL CIVILIZATION: CHINA

This bronze miniature of a horse and carriage demonstrates the high level of both artistic and technological proficiency that the Chinese had attained by the last centuries B.C.E. The elaborate harness and finely crafted wheels and axle were as refined as those of any world culture at that time.

- Patterns in Classical China
- Political Institutions
- Religion and Culture
- **DOCUMENT**: Teachings of the Rival Chinese Schools
- Economy and Society
- **IN DEPTH**: Women in Patriarchal Societies
- How Chinese Civilization Fits Together
- **GLOBAL CONNECTIONS**: Classical China and the World

China generated the first of the great classical societies. The region remained rather isolated. This limited its ability to learn from other cultures but also spared it frequent invasion and encouraged an intense, and distinctive, Chinese identity. The decline of the Shang dynasty did not result in as much internal chaos as did invasions of parts of the Middle East and particularly India. Hence, the Chinese could build more strongly on Huanghe precedents. Particularly important was a general, if somewhat vague, worldview developed by Huanghe thinkers and accepted as a standard approach in later Chinese thinking. This intellectual heritage stressed the basic harmony of nature: Every feature is balanced by an opposite, every *yin* by a *yang*. Thus for hot there is cold, for male, female. According to this philosophy, an individual should seek a way, called **Dao,** to relate to this harmony, avoiding excess and appreciating the balance of opposites. Individuals and human institutions existed within this world of balanced nature, not, as in later Mediterranean philosophy, on the outside. Chinese traditions about balance, Dao, and yin/yang were intrinsic to diverse philosophies and religions established in the classical period itself, and they provided some unity among various schools of thought in China.

Despite important cultural continuity, classical China did not simply maintain earlier traditions. The formative centuries of classical Chinese history were witness to a great many changes, as the religious and particularly the political habits of the Shang kingdom were substantially modified as part of building the world's largest classical empire. As a result of these new centuries of development, resulting in much diversity but often painful conflict, the Chinese emerged with an unusually well-integrated system in which government, philosophy, economic incentives, the family, and the individual were intended to blend into a harmonious whole.

Patterns in Classical China

 China developed in many ways from its river valley period. The Zhou dynasty featured centralized politics but important cultural innovation. Later dynasties emphasized order and centralization.

Of all the societies in the world today, it is China that has maintained the clearest links to its classical past—a past that has been a source of pride but also the cause of some problems of adaptation. Already in the period of classical Chinese history, a pattern was set in motion that lasted until the early part of the 20th century. A family of kings, called a *dynasty*, would start its rule of China with great vigor, developing strong political institutions and encouraging an active economy. Subsequently, the dynasty grew weaker and tax revenues declined, while social divisions increased in the larger society. Internal rebellions and sometimes invasions from the

1200 B.C.E.	500 B.C.E.	250 B.C.E.
1029–258 Zhou dynasty; introduction of standard spoken language **551–478** Confucius	**c. 500** Laozi and Daoism **c. 500** Editing of the Five Classics **c. 450** Development of calendar **402–201** Era of the Warring States	**221–202** Qin dynasty: the First Emperor, the Great Wall begun, single basic language **202 B.C.E.–220 C.E.** Han dynasty **c. 200** Introduction of ox-drawn plow, horse collar, water mill **141–87** Reign of Han Wu Ti, increased bureaucracy; examinations, spread of Confucianism

outside hastened the dynasty's decline. As the ruling dynasty declined, another dynasty emerged, usually from the family of a successful general, invader, or peasant rebel, and the pattern would start anew. Small wonder that many Chinese conceive of history in terms of cycles, in contrast to the Western tendency to think of steady progress from past to present.

Three dynastic cycles cover the many centuries of classical China: the Zhou, the Qin, and the Han (Map 2.1). The **Zhou** dynasty lasted from 1029 to 258 B.C.E. Although lengthy, this dynasty flourished,

in fact, only until about 700 B.C.E.; it was then beset by a decline in the political infrastructure and frequent invasions by nomadic peoples from border regions. Even during its strong centuries, the Zhou did not establish a powerful government, ruling instead through alliances with regional princes and noble families. The dynasty initially came into China from the north, displacing its predecessor, the Shang rulers. The alliance systems the Zhou used as the basis for their rule were standard in agricultural kingdoms. (We will see similar forms later emerge in Japan,

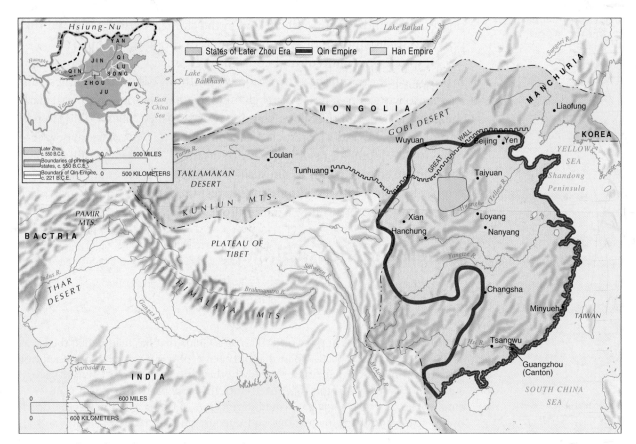

Map 2.1 *China from the Later Zhou Era to the Han Era*

India, Europe, and Africa.) Rulers lacked the means to control their territories directly and so gave large regional estates to members of their families and other supporters, hoping that their loyalties would remain intact. The supporters, in exchange for land, were supposed to provide the central government with troops and tax revenues. This was China's feudal period, with rulers depending on a network of loyalties and obligations to and from their landlord-vassals. Such a system was, of course, vulnerable to regional disloyalties, and the ultimate decline of the Zhou dynasty occurred when regional land-owning aristocrats solidified their own power base and disregarded the central government.

The Zhou did, however, contribute in several ways to the development of Chinese politics and culture in their active early centuries. First, they extended the territory of China by taking over the Yangtze River valley. This stretch of territory, from the Huanghe to the Yangtze, became China's core—often called the "Middle Kingdom." It provided rich agricultural lands plus the benefits of two different agricultures—wheat-growing in the north, rice-growing in the south—a diversity that encouraged population growth. The territorial expansion obviously complicated the problems of central rule, for communication and transport from the capital to the outlying regions were difficult. This is why the Zhou relied so heavily on the loyalty of regional supporters.

Despite these circumstances, the Zhou did actually heighten the focus on the central government itself. Zhou rulers claimed direct links to the Shang rulers. They also asserted that heaven had transferred its mandate to rule China to the Zhou emperors. This political concept of a Mandate of Heaven remained a key justification for Chinese imperial rule from the Zhou onward. Known as Sons of Heaven, the emperors lived in a world of awe-inspiring pomp and ceremony.

The Zhou worked to provide greater cultural unity in their empire. They discouraged some of the primitive religious practices of the Huanghe civilization, banning human sacrifice and urging more restrained ceremonies to worship the gods. They also promoted linguistic unity, beginning the process by which a standard spoken language, ultimately called Mandarin Chinese, would prevail over the entire Middle Kingdom. This resulted in the largest single group of people speaking the same language in the world at this time. Regional dialects and languages remained, but educated officials began to rely on the single Mandarin form. Oral epics and stories in Chinese, many gradually recorded in written form, aided in the development of a common cultural currency.

Increasing cultural unity helps explain why, when the Zhou empire began to fail, scholars were able to use philosophical ideas to lessen the impact of growing political confusion. Indeed, the political crisis spurred efforts to define and articulate Chinese culture. During the late 6th and early 5th centuries B.C.E., the philosopher known in the West as **Confucius** wrote an elaborate statement on political ethics, providing the core of China's distinctive philosophical heritage. Other writers and religious leaders participated in this great period of cultural creativity, which later reemerged as a set of central beliefs throughout the Middle Kingdom.

Cultural innovation did not, however, reverse the prolonged and painful Zhou downfall. Regional rulers formed independent armies, ultimately reducing the emperors to little more than figureheads. Between 402 and 201 B.C.E., a period known aptly enough as the Era of the Warring States, the Zhou system disintegrated.

At this point, China might have gone the way of civilizations such as India, where centralized government was more the exception than the rule. But a new dynasty arose to reverse the process of political decay. One regional ruler deposed the last Zhou emperor and within 35 years made himself sole ruler of China. He took the title Qin Shi Huangdi, or First Emperor. The dynastic name, **Qin,** conferred on the whole country its name of China. **Shi Huangdi** was a brutal ruler, but effective given the circumstances of internal disorder. He understood that China's problem lay in the regional power of the aristocrats, and like many later centralizers in world history, he worked vigorously to undo this force. He ordered nobles to leave their regions and appear at his court, assuming control of their feudal estates. China was organized into large provinces ruled by bureaucrats appointed by the emperor. Shi Huangdi was careful to select his officials from nonaristocratic groups, so that they would owe their power to him and not dare to develop their own independent bases. Under Shi Huangdi's rule, powerful armies crushed regional resistance.

The First Emperor followed up on centralization by extending Chinese territory to the south, reaching present-day Hong Kong on the South China Sea and even influencing northern Vietnam. In the north, to guard against barbarian invasions, Shi Huangdi built a **Great Wall,** extending over 3000 miles, wide enough for chariots to move along its crest. This wall, probably the largest construction project in human history, was built by forced labor, conscripted by the central bureaucracy from among the peasantry.

The Qin dynasty was responsible for a number of innovations in Chinese politics and culture. To determine the empire's resources, Shi Huangdi ordered a national census, which provided data for the calculation of tax revenues and labor service. The government standardized coinage, weights, and measures through the entire realm. Even the length of axles on carts was regulated to promote coherent road planning. The government also made Chinese written script uniform, completing the process of creating a single basic language in which all educated Chinese could communicate. The government furthered agriculture, sponsoring new irrigation projects, and promoted manufacturing, particularly that of silk cloth. The activist government also attacked formal culture, burning many books. Thinking, according to Shi Huangdi, was likely to be subversive to his autocratic rule.

Although it created many durable features of Chinese government, the Qin dynasty was short-lived. Shi Huangdi's attacks on intellectuals, and particularly the high taxes needed to support military expansion and the construction of the Great Wall, made him fiercely unpopular. One opponent described the First Emperor as a monster who "had the heart of a tiger and a wolf. He killed men as though he thought he could never finish, he punished men as though he were afraid he would never get around to them all." On the emperor's death, in 210 B.C.E., massive revolts organized by aggrieved peasants broke out. One peasant leader defeated other opponents and in 202 B.C.E. established the third dynasty of classical China, the **Han.**

The Han dynasty, which lasted over 400 years, to 220 C.E., rounded out China's basic political and intellectual structure. Han rulers retained the centralized administration of the Qin but sought to reduce the brutal repression of that period. Like many dynasties during the first flush of power, early Han rulers expanded Chinese territory, pushing into Korea, Indochina, and central Asia. This expansion gave rise to direct contact with India and also allowed the Chinese to develop contact with the Parthian Empire in the Middle East, through which trade with the Roman Empire around the Mediterranean was conducted. The most famous Han ruler, Wu Ti (140–87 B.C.E.), enforced peace throughout much of the continent of Asia, rather like the peace the Roman Empire would bring to the Mediterranean region a hundred years later, but embracing even more territory and a far larger population. Peace brought great prosperity to China itself. A Han historian conveys the self-satisfied, confident tone of the dynasty:

> The nation had met with no major disturbances so that, except in times of flood or drought, every person was well supplied and every family had enough to get along on. The granaries in the cities and the countryside were full and the government treasures were running over with wealth. In the capital the strings of cash had stacked up by the hundreds of millions until ... they could no longer be counted. In the central granary of the government, new grain was heaped on top of the old until the building was full and the grain overflowed and piled up outside, where it spoiled and became unfit to eat.... Even the keepers of the community gates ate fine grain and meat.

Under the Han dynasty, the workings of the state bureaucracy also improved and the government was linked to formal training that emphasized the values of Confucian philosophy. Reversing the Qin dynasty's policies, Wu Ti urged support for Confucianism, seeing it as a vital supplement to formal measures on the government's part. Shrines were established to promote the worship of the ancient philosopher as a god.

The quality of Han rule declined after about two centuries. Central control weakened, and invasions from central Asia, spearheaded by a nomadic people called the Huns, who had long threatened China's northern borders, overturned the dynasty entirely. Between 220 and 589 C.E., China was in a state of chaos. Order and stability were finally restored, but by then the classical or formative period of Chinese civilization had ended. Well before the Han collapse, however, China had established distinctive political structures and cultural values of unusual clarity, capable, as it turned out, of surviving even three centuries of renewed confusion.

Political Institutions

 Political institutions became one of classical China's hallmarks. The power of the emperor, the development of a bureaucracy, and the expansion of state functions combined together.

The Qin and Han dynasties of classical China established a distinctive, and remarkably successful, kind of government. The Qin stressed central authority, whereas the Han expanded the powers of the bureaucracy. More than any other factor, it was the structure of this government that explained how such a vast territory could be effectively ruled—for the Chinese empire was indeed the largest political system in the classical world. This structure would change after the classical period, particularly in terms of streamlining and expanding bureaucratic systems and procedures, but it never required fundamental overhaul.

The political framework that emerged as a result of the long centuries of China's classical period had several key elements. Strong local units never disappeared. Like most successful agricultural societies, China relied heavily on tightly knit patriarchal families. Individual families were linked to other relatives in extended family networks that included brothers, uncles, and any living grandparents. Among the wealthy land-owning groups, family authority was enhanced by the practice of ancestor worship, which joined family members through rituals devoted to important forebears who had passed into the spirit world. For ordinary people, among whom ancestor worship was less common, village authority surmounted family rule. Village leaders helped farming families regulate property and coordinate planting and harvest work. During the Zhou dynasty, and also in later periods when dynasties weakened, the regional power of great landlords also played an important role at the village level. Landed nobles provided courts of justice and organized military troops.

Strong local rule was not the most significant or distinctive feature of Chinese government under the Qin and Han dynasties, however. Shi Huangdi not only attacked local rulers but also provided a single law code for the whole empire and established a uniform tax system. He appointed governors to each district of his domain, who exercised military and legal powers in the name of the emperor. They, in turn, named officials responsible for smaller regions. Here indeed was a classic model of centralized government that other societies would replicate in later times: the establishment of centralized codes and appointment of officials directly by a central authority, rather than reliance on arrangements with numerous existing local governments. The effectiveness of a central government was further enhanced by the delegation of special areas and decisions to the emperor's ministers.

Some dealt with matters of finance, others with justice, others with military affairs, and so on.

Able rulers of the Han dynasty resumed the attack on local warrior-landlords. In addition, they realized the importance of creating a large, highly skilled bureaucracy, one capable of carrying out the duties of a complex state. By the end of the Han period, China had about 130,000 bureaucrats, representing 0.2 percent of the population. The emperor Wu Ti established examinations for his bureaucrats—the first example of civil service tests of the sort that many governments have instituted in modern times. These examinations covered classics of Chinese literature as well as law, suggesting a model of the scholar-bureaucrat that would later become an important element of China's political tradition. Wu Ti also established a school to train men of exceptional talent and ability for the national examinations. Although most bureaucrats were drawn from the landed upper classes, who alone had the time to learn the complex system of Chinese characters, individuals from lower ranks of society were occasionally recruited under this system. China's bureaucracy thus provided a slight check on complete upper-class rule. It also tended to limit the exercise of arbitrary power by the emperor himself. Trained and experienced bureaucrats, confident in their own traditions, could often control the whims of a single ruler, even one who, in the Chinese tradition, regarded himself as divinely appointed—the "Son of Heaven." It was no accident then that the Chinese bureaucracy lasted from the Han period until the 20th century, outliving the empire itself.

Small wonder that from the classical period at least until modern times, and possibly still today, the Chinese were the most tightly governed people in any large society in the world. When it worked well—and it is important to recall that the system periodically broke down—Chinese politics represented a remarkable integration of all levels of authority. The edicts of an all-powerful emperor were administered by trained scholar-bureaucrats, widely respected for their learning and, often, their noble birth. Individual families also emphasized this strong principle of authority, with the father in charge, presumably carrying on the wishes of a long line of ancestors to which the family paid reverence. The Chinese were capable of periodic rebellions, and gangs of criminals regularly came to disrupt the social scene—indeed, frequently harsh punishments reflected the need of the government to eradicate such deviant forces. Nevertheless, whether within the family or the central state, most Chinese in ordinary times believed in the importance of respect for those in power.

Government traditions established during the classical period included an impressive list of state functions. Like all organized states, the Chinese government operated military and judicial systems. Military activity fluctuated, as China did not depend on steady expansion. Although classical China produced some enduring examples of the art of war, the state was not highly militaristic by the Han period. Judicial matters—crime and legal disputes—commanded more attention by local government authorities.

The government also sponsored much intellectual life, organizing research in astronomy and the maintenance of historical records. Under the Han rulers, the government played a major role in promoting Confucian philosophy as an official statement of Chinese values and in encouraging the worship of Confucius himself. The government developed a durable sense of mission as the primary keeper of Chinese beliefs.

The imperial government was also active in the economy. It directly organized the production of iron and salt. Its standardization of currency, weights, and measures facilitated trade throughout the vast empire. The government additionally sponsored public works, including complex irrigation and canal systems. Han rulers even tried to regulate agricultural supplies by storing grain and rice in good times to control price increases—and potential popular unrest—when harvests were bad.

China's ambitious rulers in no sense directed the daily lives of their subjects; the technology of an agricultural society did not permit this. Even under the Han, it took over a month for a directive from the capital city to reach the outlying districts of the empire—an obvious limit on imperial authority. A revealing Chinese proverb held that "heaven is high, and the emperor is far away." However, the power of the Chinese state did extend considerably. Its system of courts was backed by a strict code of law; torture and execution were widely employed to supplement the preaching of obedience and civic virtue. The central government taxed its subjects and also required some annual labor on the part of every male peasant—this was the source of the incredible physical work involved in building canals, roads, and palaces. No other government had the organization and staff to reach ordinary people so directly until virtually modern times, except in much smaller political units such as city-states. The power of the government and

the authority it commanded in the eyes of most ordinary Chinese people help explain why its structure survived decline, invasion, and even rebellion for so many centuries. Invaders like the Huns might topple a dynasty, but they could not devise a better system to run the country, and so the system and its bureaucratic administrators normally endured.

Religion and Culture

 Chinese culture featured the development of the Confucian system. Daoism, a distinctive science, and artistic traditions complemented this emphasis.

The Chinese way of viewing the world, as this belief system developed during the classical period, was closely linked to a distinct political structure. Upper-class cultural values emphasized a good life on earth and the virtues of obedience to the state, more than speculations about God and the mysteries of heaven. At the same time, the Chinese tolerated and often combined various specific beliefs, so long as they did not contradict basic political loyalties.

Rulers in the Zhou dynasty maintained belief in a god or gods, but little attention was given to the nature of a deity. Rather, Chinese leaders stressed the importance of a harmonious earthly life, which would maintain proper balance between earth and heaven. Harmony included carefully constructed rituals to unify society and prevent individual excess. Among the upper classes, people were trained in elaborate exercises and military skills such as archery. Commonly, ceremonies venerating ancestors and even marking special meals were conducted. The use of chopsticks began at the end of the Zhou dynasty; it encouraged a code of politeness at meals. Soon after this, tea was introduced, although the most elaborate tea-drinking rituals developed later on.

Even before these specific ceremonies arose, however, the basic definition of a carefully ordered existence was given more formal philosophical backing. Amid the long collapse of the Zhou dynasty, many thinkers and religious prophets began to challenge Chinese traditions. From this ferment came a restatement of the traditions that ultimately reduced intellectual conflict and established a long-lasting tone for Chinese cultural and social life.

Confucius, or Kung Fuzi (which means Kung the philosopher), lived from roughly 551 to 478 B.C.E. His life was devoted to teaching, and he traveled through many parts of China preaching his ideas of political virtue and good government. Confucius was not a religious leader; he believed in a divine order but refused to speculate about it. Chinese civilization was unusual, in the classical period and well beyond, in that its dominant values were secular rather than religious.

Confucius saw himself as a spokesman for Chinese tradition and for what he believed were the great days of the Chinese state before the Zhou declined. He maintained that if people could be taught to emphasize personal virtue, which included a reverence for tradition, a solid political life would naturally result. The Confucian list of virtues stressed respect for one's social superiors—including fathers and husbands as leaders of the family. However, this emphasis on a proper hierarchy was balanced by an insistence that society's leaders behave modestly and without excess, shunning abusive power and treating courteously those people who were in their charge. According to Confucius, moderation in behavior, veneration of custom and ritual, and a love of wisdom should characterize the leaders of society at all levels. With virtuous leaders, a sound political life would inevitably follow: "In an age of good government, men in high stations give preference to men of ability and give opportunity to those who are below them, and lesser people labor vigorously at their husbandry to serve their superiors."

Confucianism was primarily a system of ethics—do unto others as your status and theirs dictate—and a plea for loyalty to the community. It confirmed the distaste that many educated Chinese had developed for religious mysteries, as well as their delight in learning and good manners. Confucian doctrine, carefully recorded in a book called the *Analects*, was revived under the Han emperors, who saw the usefulness of Confucian emphasis on political virtue and social order. Confucian learning was also incorporated, along with traditional literary works, into the training of aspiring bureaucrats.

The problems Confucius set out to rectify, notably political disorder, were approached through an emphasis on individual virtuous behavior, both by the ruler and the ruled. "When the ruler does right, all men will imitate his self-control. What the ruler does, the people will follow." According to Confucius, only a man who demonstrated proper family virtues, including respect for parents and compassion for children and other inferiors, should be considered for political service. "When the ruler excels as a father, a son, and a brother, then the people imitate him." Confucius thus built into his own system the links among many levels of authority that came to

characterize larger Chinese politics at its best. His system also emphasized personal restraint and the careful socialization of children.

For subordinates, Confucius largely recommended obedience and respect; people should know their place, even under bad rulers. However, he urged a political system that would not base rank simply on birth but would make education accessible to all talented and intelligent members of society. The primary emphasis still rested nonetheless on the obligations and desirable characteristics of the ruling class. According to Confucius, force alone cannot permanently conquer unrest, but kindness toward the people and protection of their vital interests will. Rulers should also be humble and sincere, for people will grow rebellious under hypocrisy or arrogance. Nor should rulers be greedy; Confucius warned against a profit motive in leadership, stressing that true happiness rested in doing good for all, not individual gain. Confucius projected the ideal of a gentleman, best described by his benevolence and self-control, a man always courteous and eager for service and anxious to learn.

During the Qin and early Han periods, an alternate system of political thought, called "Legalism," sprang up in China. Legalist writers prided themselves on their pragmatism. They disdained Confucian virtues in favor of an authoritarian state that ruled by force. Human nature for the Legalists was evil and required restraint and discipline. In a proper state, the army would control and the people would labor; the idea of pleasures in educated discourse or courtesy was dismissed as frivolity. Although Legalism never captured the widespread approval that Confucianism did, it too entered the political traditions of China, where a Confucian veneer was often combined with strong-arm tactics.

Confucianists did not explicitly seek popular loyalty. Like many early civilizations, China did not produce a single system of beliefs, as different groups embraced different values, with the same individual even turning to contrasting systems depending on his or her mood. Confucianism had some obvious limits in its appeal to the masses and indeed to many educated Chinese. Its reluctance to explore the mysteries of life or nature deprived it of a spiritual side. The creed was most easily accepted by the upper classes, who had the time and resources to pursue an education and participate in ceremony. However, elements of Confucianism, including a taste for ritual, self-control, and polite manners, did spread beyond the upper classes. But

Document

Teachings of the Rival Chinese Schools

The brief passages quoted here are taken from the writings of Confucius, Mencius, Xunzi, and Laozi. Identify whether each passage is Confucian or Daoist and explain why you made each choice.

> I take no action and the people are reformed.
> I enjoy peace and people become honest.
> I do nothing and people become rich.
> I have no desires and people return to the good and simple life.

> The gentleman cherishes virtue; the inferior man cherishes possessions.
> The gentleman thinks of sanctions; the inferior man thinks of personal favors.

> The nature of man is evil; his goodness is acquired.
> His nature being what it is, man is born, first, with a desire for gain.
> If this desire is followed, strife will result and courtesy will disappear.

> Keep your mouth closed.
> Guard your senses.
> Temper your sharpness.
> Simplify your problems.
> Mask your brightness.
> Be at one with the dust of the earth.
> This is primal union.

> Personal cultivation begins with poetry, is made firm with rules of decorum, and is perfected by music.

> When it is left to follow its natural feelings, human nature will do good. That's why I say it is good. If it becomes evil, it is not the fault of man's original capability.

Questions: Which of these ideas are most compatible? Which of them could best be called religious? Which are most secular? Which philosophers propose ideas that are best suited to people who want to build a strong and unified political order?

most peasants needed more than civic virtue to understand and survive their harsh life, where in constant toil they eked out only a precarious and meager existence. During most of the classical period, polytheistic beliefs, focusing on the spirits of nature, persisted among much of the peasant class. Many peasants strove to attract the blessing of conciliatory spirits by creating statues, emblems, and household decorations honoring the spirits, and by holding parades and family ceremonies for the same purpose. A belief in the symbolic power of dragons stemmed from one such popular religion, which combined fear of these creatures with a more playful sense of their activities in its courtship of the divine forces of nature. Gradually, ongoing rites among the ordinary masses integrated the Confucian values urged by the upper classes.

Classical China also produced a more religious philosophy—Daoism—which arose at roughly the same time as Confucianism, during the waning centuries of the Zhou dynasty. Daoism first appealed to many in the upper classes, who had an interest in a more elaborate spirituality. Daoism embraced traditional Chinese beliefs in nature's harmony and added a sense of nature's mystery. As a spiritual alternative to Confucianism, Daoism produced a durable division in China's religious and philosophical culture. This new religion, vital for Chinese civilization although never widely exported, was furthered by Laozi, who probably lived during the 5th century B.C.E. Laozi (often called Lao-tsu in popular Daoist texts) stressed that nature contains a divine impulse that directs all life. True human understanding comes in withdrawing from the world and contemplating this life force. Dao, which means "the way of nature," refers to this same basic, indescribable force:

> There is a thing confusedly formed,
>
> Born before heaven and earth.
>
> Silent and void
>
> It stands alone and does not change,
>
> Goes round and does not weary.
>
> It is capable of being the mother of the world.
>
> I know not its name,
>
> So I style it "the way."

Along with secret rituals, Daoism promoted its own set of ethics. Daoist harmony with nature best resulted through humility and frugal living. According to this movement, political activity and learning were irrelevant to a good life, and general conditions in the world were of little importance.

Daoism, which would join with a strong Buddhist influence from India during the chaos that followed the collapse of the Han dynasty, guaranteed that China's people would not be united by a single religious or philosophical system. Individuals did come to embrace some elements from both Daoism and Confucianism, and indeed many emperors favored Daoism. They accepted its spread with little anxiety, partly because some of them found solace in Daoist belief but also because the religion, with its otherworldly emphasis, posed no real political threat. Confucian scholars disagreed vigorously with Daoist thinking, particularly its emphasis on mysteries and magic, but they saw little reason to challenge its influence. As Daoism became an increasingly formal religion, from the later Han dynasty onward, it provided many Chinese with a host of ceremonies designed to promote harmony with the mysterious life force. Finally, the Chinese government from the Han dynasty onward was able to persuade Daoist priests to include expressions of loyalty to the emperor in their temple services. This heightened Daoism's political compatibility with Confucianism.

Confucianism and Daoism were not the only intellectual products of China's classical period, but they were the most important. Confucianism blended easily with the high value of literature and art among the upper classes. In literature, a set of Five Classics, written during the early part of the Zhou dynasty and then edited during the time of Confucius, provided an important tradition. They were used, among other things, as a basis for civil service examinations. The works provided in the Five Classics included some historical treatises, speeches, and other political materials; a discussion of etiquette and ceremonies; and in the Classic of Songs, over 300 poems dealing with love, joy, politics, and family life appeared. The Chinese literary tradition developed on the basis of mastering these early works, plus Confucian writing; each generation of writers found new meanings in the classical literature, which allowed them to express new ideas within a familiar framework. Several thinkers during the Han dynasty elaborated Confucian philosophy. In literature, poetry commanded particular attention because the Chinese language featured melodic speech and variant pronunciations of the same basic sound, a characteristic that promoted an outpouring of poetry. From the classical period onward, the ability to learn and recite poetry became the mark of an educated Chinese. Finally, the literary tradition established in classical China reinforced the Confucian emphasis on human life, although the subjects included romance and sorrow as well as political values.

Chinese art during the classical period was largely decorative, stressing careful detail and craftsmanship (Figure 2.1). Artistic styles often reflected the precision and geometric qualities of the many symbols of Chinese writing. Calligraphy itself became an important art form. In addition, Chinese artists painted, worked in bronze and pottery, carved jade and ivory, and wove silk screens. Classical China did not produce monumental buildings, aside from the awe-inspiring Great Wall and some imperial palaces and tombs, in part because of the absence of a single religion; indeed, the entire tone of upper-class Confucianism was such that it discouraged the notion of temples soaring to the heavens.

In science, important practical work was encouraged, rather than imaginative theorizing. Chinese astronomers had developed an accurate calendar by 444 B.C.E., based on a year of 365.5 days. Later astronomers calculated the movement of the planets Saturn and Jupiter and observed sunspots—more than 1500 years before comparable knowledge developed in Europe. The purpose of Chinese astronomy was to make celestial phenomena predictable, as part of the wider interest in ensuring harmony between heaven and earth. Chinese scientists steadily improved their instrumentation, inventing a kind of seismograph to register earthquakes during the Han dynasty. The Chinese were also active in medical research, developing precise anatomical knowledge and studying principles of hygiene that could promote longer life.

Chinese mathematics also stressed the practical. Daoism encouraged some exploration of the orderly processes of nature, but far more research focused on how things actually worked. For example, Chinese scholars studied the mathematics of music in ways that led to advances in acoustics. This focus for science and mathematics contrasted notably with the more abstract definition of science developed in classical Greece.

Figure 2.1 *A Han relief on a funeral tile found in the Chengdu region in Sichuan (eastern Han dynasty, 25 B.C.E.–221 C.E.). The hunting scene in a luxuriant landscape in the upper panel is linked with a scene (lower panel) of peasants working in the fields. Such illustrations enable historians to track the development of toolmaking and weaponmaking in ancient civilizations such as China. They also make it possible to study patterns of organization in agrarian and artisan production (for which direct evidence is sparse) as well as the leisure activities of officials and the landed elites.*

Economy and Society

 China's economy featured extensive internal trade but some ambivalence about merchants. Important technological innovations occurred. Social inequality included some respect for the peasant masses. China's family system stressed a rigid patriarchy.

Although the most distinctive features of classical China centered on politics and culture, developments in the economy, social structure, and family life also shaped Chinese civilization and continued to have an impact on the empire's history for a significant period of time.

As in many agricultural societies, considerable gaps developed between China's upper class, which controlled large landed estates, and the masses, farmer-peasants who produced little more than what was needed for their own subsistence. The difficulty of becoming literate symbolized these gaps, for landlords enjoyed not only wealth but also a culture denied to most common people. Prior to the Zhou

dynasty, slaveholding may have been common in China, but by the time of the Zhou the main social division existed between the land-owning gentry—about 2 percent of the total population—and peasants, who provided dues and service to these lords while also controlling some of their own land. The Chinese peasantry depended on intensive cooperation, particularly in the southern rice region; in this group, property was characteristically owned and regulated by the village or the extended family, rather than by individuals. Beneath the peasantry, Chinese social structure included a group of "mean" people who performed rough transport and other unskilled jobs and suffered from the lowest possible status. In general, social status was passed from one generation to the next through inheritance, although unusually talented individuals from a peasant background might be given access to an education and rise within the bureaucracy.

Officially then and to a large extent in fact, classical China consisted of three main social groups. The landowning aristocracy plus the educated bureaucrats, or Mandarins, formed the top group. Next came the laboring masses, peasants and also urban

In Depth

Women in Patriarchal Societies

Most agricultural civilizations, including China, downgraded the status and potential of women, at least according to modern Western standards and to the implicit standards of hunting and gathering societies. Agricultural civilizations were characteristically patriarchal; that is, they were run by men and based on the assumption that men directed political, economic, and cultural life. Furthermore, as agricultural civilizations developed over time and became more prosperous and more elaborately organized, the status of women deteriorated from its initial level. Individual families were normally set up on a patriarchal basis. The husband and father determined fundamental conditions and made the key decisions, and the woman gave humble obedience to this male authority at least in principle. Patriarchal family structure rested on men's control of most or all property, starting with land itself. Marriage was based on property relationships, and it was assumed that marriage, and therefore subordination to men, was the normal condition for the vast majority of women. A revealing symptom of patriarchy in family life was the fact that after marrying, a woman usually moved to the orbit (and often the residence) of her husband's family.

Characteristic patriarchal conditions had developed in Mesopotamian civilization. Marriages were arranged for women by their parents, and a formal contract was drawn up. The husband served as authority over his wife and children just as he did over his slaves. Early Sumerians may have given women greater latitude than they enjoyed later on. Their religion attributed considerable power to female sexuality, and their law gave women important rights, so that they could not be treated as outright property. Still, even in Sumerian law, the adultery of a wife was punishable by death, while a husband's adultery was treated far more lightly—a double standard characteristic of patriarchalism. Mesopotamian societies after Sumerian times began to emphasize the importance of a woman's virginity at marriage and to impose the veil on respectable women when they were in public to emphasize their modesty. These changes showed a progressive cramping of women's social position and daily freedom. At all points a good portion of Mesopotamian law (such as the Hammurabic code) was given over to prescriptions for women, assuring certain basic protections but clearly emphasizing limits and inferiority.

Specific patriarchal conditions varied from one agricultural civilization to another. This means that comparisons are important, and sometimes subtle. Egyptian civilization gave upper-class women more credit than Mesopotamia did, and there were several powerful queens. Jewish law traced descendance from mothers rather than fathers, though it held women to be separate and inferior even in worship. Confucianism, in China, had important implications for women, involving recommendations of good treatment but amid demonstrations of deference and subservience to men. Variety, in other words, operated within a clearly patriarchal framework.

Why was patriarchalism so pervasive? As agriculture improved with the use of better techniques, women's labor, though still absolutely vital, became less important than it had been in hunting-and-gathering societies. This was particularly true in the upper classes and in cities, where men frequently took over the most productive work—craft production, for example—and political leadership. The inferior position of women was less marked in peasant families, where their work was essential. More generally, agricultural societies were based on concepts of property. It seemed essential for men to know who their heirs were, in order to pass along land; and this meant attention to regulating women's sexuality, to try to assure faithfulness. All this helps explain why women became seen as both inferior and ornamental, really as part of men's property. Patriarchalism, in sum, responded to economic and legal conditions in agricultural civilizations and often deepened over time.

Patriarchalism raises important questions about women themselves. Many women internalized patriarchal culture, believing that they should obey and please men and agreeing that they were inferior. But patriarchalism did not preclude some important options for women. In many societies a minority of women could gain some relief through religious functions, which could provide them a chance to operate independent of family structures. Patriarchal laws defined some rights for women even within marriage, protecting them at least in theory from the worst abuses. Confucian theorists argued that women must obey men but urged men to treat them decently in return. Women could also wield informal power in patriarchal societies by their emotional hold over husbands or sons. Such power was indirect, behind the scenes, but a forceful woman might use these means to figure prominently in a society's history. Women could also form networks, within a large household. Older women, who commanded the obedience of many daughters-in-law as well as unmarried daugh-

(continued)

ters and servant women, could powerfully shape the activities of a family.

The fact remains that patriarchalism was a commanding theme in most agricultural civilizations. Enforcement of patriarchalism, through law and culture, provided one means by which these societies regulated their members and tried to achieve order. While women were not reduced to literal servitude by most patriarchal systems, they might have come close. Their options were severely constrained. Girls were reared to accept patriarchal conditions, and boys were fully conscious of their own superiority. In many agricultural civilizations, patriarchalism dictated that boys, because of their importance in carrying on the

family name and chief economic activities, were more likely to survive. When population excess threatened a family's well-being, patriarchal assumptions often determined that female infants be killed as a means of population control.

Questions: How do you think most women reared in a patriarchal society would react to their conditions? What might cause differences in women's conditions in patriarchal societies, or from one society to another? Why were upper-class women often considered more inferior to men than lower-class women were?

artisans who manufactured goods. These people, far poorer than the top group and also condemned to a life of hard manual labor, sometimes worked directly on large estates but in other cases had some economic independence. Finally, came the mean people, the general category we already identified as applying to those without meaningful skills. Interestingly, performing artists were ranked in this group, despite the fact that the upper classes enjoyed plays and other entertainments provided by this group. Mean people were punished for crime more harshly than other groups and were required to wear identifying green scarves. Household slaves also existed within this class structure, but their number was relatively few and China did not depend on slaves for actual production.

Trade became increasingly important during the Zhou and particularly the Han dynasties. Much trade focused on luxury items for the upper class, produced by skilled artisans in the cities—silks, jewelry, leather goods, and furniture. There was also food exchange between the wheat- and rice-growing regions. Copper coins began to circulate, which facilitated trade, with merchants even sponsoring commercial visits to India. Although significant, trade and its attendant merchant class did not become the focal points of Chinese society, and the Confucian emphasis on learning and political service led to considerable scorn for lives devoted to moneymaking. The gap between the real importance and wealth of merchants and their officially low prestige was an enduring legacy in Confucian China.

If trade fit somewhat uncomfortably into the dominant view of society, there was no question about the importance of technological advance; here, the

Chinese excelled. Agricultural implements improved steadily. Ox-drawn plows were introduced around 300 B.C.E., which greatly increased productivity. Under the Han, a new collar was invented for draft animals, allowing them to pull plows or wagons without choking—this was a major improvement that became available to other parts of the world only many centuries later. Chinese iron mining was also well advanced, as pulleys and winding gear were devised to bring material to the surface. Iron tools and other implements such as lamps were widely used. Production methods in textiles and pottery were also highly developed by world standards. Under the Han, the first water-powered mills were introduced, allowing further gains in manufacturing. Finally, during the Han, paper was invented, which was a major boon to a system of government that emphasized the bureaucracy. In sum, classical China reached far higher levels of technical expertise than Europe or western Asia in the same period, a lead that it would long maintain.

The relatively advanced technology of classical China did not, however, steer Chinese society away from its primary reliance on agriculture. Farming technology itself helped increase the size of the population in the countryside; with better tools and seeds, smaller amounts of land could support more families. But China's solid agricultural base, backed by some trade in foodstuffs among key regions, did permit the expansion of cities and of manufacturing. Nonagricultural goods were mainly produced by artisans, working in small shops or in their homes. Even though only a minority of the workforce was involved in such tasks that used manual methods for the most part, the output of tools, porcelain, and textiles increased considerably, aided in this case as well by the interest in improving techniques.

In all major social groups, tight family organization helped solidify economic and social views as well as political life. The structure of the Chinese family resembled that of families in other agricultural civilizations in emphasizing the importance of unity and the power of husbands and fathers. Within this context, however, the Chinese stressed authority to unusual extremes. Confucius said, "There are no wrongdoing parents"—and in practice, parents could punish disobedient children freely. Law courts did not prosecute parents who injured or even killed a disobedient son, but they would severely punish a child who scolded or attacked a parent. In most families, the emphasis on obedience to parents, and a corresponding emphasis on wives' obedience to husbands, did not produce great friction. Chinese popular culture stressed strict control of one's emotions, and the family was seen as the center of such an orderly, serene hierarchy. Indeed, the family served as a great training ground for the principles of authority and restraint that applied to the larger social and political world. Women, although subordinate, had their own clearly defined roles and could sometimes gain power through their sons and as mothers-in-law of younger women brought into the household. The mother of a famous Confucian philosopher, Mencius, continually claimed how humble she was, but during the course of his life she managed to exert considerable influence over him. There was even a clear hierarchical order for children, with boys superior to girls and the oldest son having the most enviable position of all. Chinese rules of inheritance, from the humblest peasant to the emperor himself, followed strict primogeniture, which meant that the oldest male child would inherit property and position alike.

How Chinese Civilization Fits Together

 Chinese civilization featured well-defined parts, like the imperial systems and Confucianism. These also fit together, which is a key reason emperors ultimately encouraged Confucianism. Even family structures related to larger institutions and values.

China's politics and culture meshed readily, especially around the emergence of a Confucian bureaucracy. Economic innovation did not disrupt the emphasis on order and stability, and family structures were closely linked to political and cultural goals.

Classical Chinese technology, religion, philosophy, and political structure evolved with very little outside contact. Although important trade routes did lead to India and the Middle East, most Chinese saw the world in terms of a large island of civilization surrounded by barbarian peoples with nothing to offer save the periodic threat of invasion. Proud of their culture and of its durability, the Chinese had neither the need nor the desire to learn from other societies. Nor, except to protect their central territory by exercising some control over the mountainous or desert regions that surrounded the Middle Kingdom, did Chinese leaders have any particular desire to teach the rest of the world. A missionary spirit was foreign to Chinese culture and politics. China displayed some patterns that were similar to those of the other agricultural civilizations, and it occasionally embraced the concepts of these cultures. Indeed, the spread of Buddhism from India, during and after the Han decline, was a notable instance of a cultural diffusion that altered China's religious map and also its artistic styles. Nevertheless, the theme of unusual isolation, developed during the formative period of Chinese civilization, was to prove persistent in later world history—in fact, it has not entirely disappeared to this day.

Chinese civilization was also noteworthy for the relative harmony among its various major features. We have, in this chapter, examined the pattern of leading historical events in classical China and then the systems of government, belief, economy, and social structure. All these facets were closely meshed. Although the centralized government, with its elaborate functions and far-reaching bureaucracy, gave the clearest unity and focus to Chinese society, it did not do so alone. Confucianism provided a vital supplement, making the bureaucracy more than a collection of people with similar political objectives, but rather a trained corps with some common ideals. An appreciation of distinctive artistic styles, poetry, and the literary tradition added to this common culture. Cohesive government and related beliefs about human ideals and aesthetics were linked, in turn, to the economy. Political stability over a large and fertile land aided economic growth, and the government took a direct role in encouraging both agriculture and industry. A strong economy, in turn, provided the government with vital tax revenues. Economic interests were also related to the pragmatic Chinese view of science, whose aim was to determine how nature worked. Finally, social relationships reinforced all these systems. The vision of a stable hierarchy and tight family structures meshed with the strong impulse toward orderly politics and helped instill the virtues of obedience and respect that were important to the larger political system.

Not surprisingly, given the close links among the various facets of their civilization, the Chinese tended to think of their society as a whole. They did not distinguish clearly between private and public sectors of activity. They did not see government and society as two separate entities. In other words, these Western concepts that we have used to define classical China and to facilitate comparisons with other societies do not really fit the Chinese view of their own world. Confucius himself, in seeing government as basically a vast extension of family relationships, similarly suggested that the pieces of the Chinese puzzle were intimately joined.

A grasp of Chinese civilization as a whole, however, should not distract us from recognizing some endemic tensions and disparities. The division in belief systems, between Confucianism and Daoism, modifies the perception of an ultimately tidy classical China. Confucianists and Daoists tolerated each other. Sometimes, their beliefs coincided in such a way that a single individual who behaved politically as a Confucianist might explore deeper mysteries through Daoist rituals. However, between both groups there was considerable hostility and mutual disdain, as many Confucianists found Daoists superstitious and overexcited. Daoism did not inherently disrupt the political unity of Chinese culture, but at times the religion inspired attacks on established politics in the name of a mysterious divine will.

Tension in Chinese society showed in the way Confucian beliefs were combined with strict policing. Chinese officials did believe in fundamental human goodness and the importance of ceremony and mutual respect. However, they also believed in stern punishment, not only against criminals but also as warnings to the larger, potentially restless population. People arrested were presumed guilty and often subjected to torture before trial. The Chinese, in fact, early discovered the usefulness of alternating torture with benevolence, to make accused individuals confess. In the late Han period, a thief who refused to confess even under severe torture was then freed from chains, bathed, and fed, "so as to bring him in a happy mood"—whereupon he usually confessed and

named his whole gang. In sum, both Confucianism and the Chinese penal system supported tight control, and the combination of the two was typically effective; however, they involved quite different approaches and quite different moral assumptions.

All of this suggests that classical China, like any vigorous, successful society, embraced a diversity of features that could not be fully united by any single formula. Elites and masses were divided by both economic interests and culture. Some shared the same values, particularly as Confucianism spread, and upper-class concern for careful etiquette and the general welfare of the population mitigated the tension. But such calm was a precarious balance, and when overpopulation or some other factor tipped the scale, recurrent and often violent protest could be the result.

Despite any divisions, the symbiosis among the various institutions and activities of many people in classical China does deserve strong emphasis. It helps account for the durability of Chinese values. Even in times of political turmoil, families would transfer beliefs and political ideals by the ways in which they instructed their children. The overall wholeness of Chinese society also helps account for its relative immunity to outside influence and for its creativity despite considerable isolation.

Chinese wholeness, finally, provides an interesting contrast to the other great Asian civilization that developed in the classical period. India, as fully dynamic as China in many ways, produced different emphases, but also a more disparate society in which links among politics and beliefs and economic life were less well defined. Many would argue that this contrast between the two Asian giants persists to our own time.

GLOBAL CONNECTIONS: Classical China and the World

The short-lived Qin dynasty and four centuries of Han rule established the basic components of a civilization that would last for thousands of years, making it the longest-lived in world history. As the achievements of the classical age demonstrate, China had also become one of the most creative and influential civilizations of all human history. The strength of its agrarian base has allowed China to carry about one-fifth of the total human population from the last centuries B.C.E. to the present day. The productivity of its peasants has made it possible for some of the world's largest cities to flourish in China, and nurtured one of history's largest and most creative elites. In China's classical age, the world's largest and for much of history its best-run bureaucracy was established, and civil service exams were invented. The Chinese also pioneered in the development of a whole range of basic technologies that were later disseminated over much of Eurasia and northern Africa. These ranged from paper and compasses, which created new possibilities for human communication and cross-cultural interaction, and water mills, which provided new sources of power and food processing, to porcelain, which elevated dining to unparalleled levels of elegance and opened up exciting possibilities for artistic expression. Over the centuries, beginning in this classical period itself, Chinese merchants and central Asian nomads disseminated these inventions over much of the globe, and have consequently contributed to technological transformations in societies as diverse as those found in Japan, Rome, the Middle East, and England.

Chinese influence was directly involved in the patterns of world trade that began to emerge during the classical centuries. China's production of silk was unusually high quality, and the product began to be valued elsewhere, in India, the Middle East, and even the distant Mediterranean during the Roman Empire. Trade in silk and other luxury products generated a network of roads through central Asia known collectively as the **Silk Roads.** Under the Han, the Chinese government actively encouraged this trade with regions to the west. Improved roads, both in China and in the Middle East, encouraged trade as well. One Chinese emissary, Zhang Qian, actually traveled to western India. Most trade along the Silk Roads was carried by nomadic merchants, and until well after the classical period no one seems to have traveled all the way from China to the Mediterranean or vice versa. But the trade was lively, spurring attention also to sea routes in the Indian Ocean. While we do not know the volume of goods involved, Silk Road trade was important enough to win considerable attention in upper-class and government circles, and it provided an initial framework on which global trading patterns would later elaborate. China's role was

greater still in the huge swath of territory from central Asia to the Pacific.

Over much of central and east Asia, Chinese influence in political thought and organization, approaches to warfare, art and architecture, religion, and social norms was pervasive. For nearly two thousand years, China would serve as the "Middle Kingdom" for the diverse peoples of this vast area—the focus of their trade and the model for their often successful efforts to fashion their own variants of empire, prosperity, and sophisticated lifestyles.

Further Readings

Several sources offer original materials on classical Chinese thought and politics: John Fairbank, ed., *Chinese Thought and Institutions* (1973); Wing-stit Chan, *A Source Book in Chinese Philosophy* (1963); and P. Ebrey, *Chinese Civilization and Society: A Sourcebook* (1981). Two excellent general surveys for this period and later ones are John Fairbank and Albert Craig, *East Asia: Tradition and Transformation* (1993); E. O. Reischauer and John Fairbank, *A History of East Asian Civilization, Vol. I: East Asia, The Great Tradition* (1961); see also Arthur Cotterell, *The First Emperor of China* (1981). Briefer but useful are M. J. Coye and J. Livingston, eds., *China, Yesterday and Today* (1975); Wolfram Eberhard, *A History of China* (1977); and X. Z. Liu, *Ancient India and Ancient China* (1988). See also D. Twitchett and M. Loewe, eds., *The Cambridge History of China*, Vol. 1 (1986). On more specialized topics, see E. Balazs, *Chinese Civilization and Bureaucracy* (1964); J. Needham, *Science and Civilization in China*, 4 vols. (1970); Richard J. Smith, *Traditional Chinese Culture: An Interpretive Introduction* (1978); Benjamin Schwartz, *The World of Thought in Ancient China* (1983); Michael Loewe, *Everyday Life in Early Imperial China* (1968); Cho-yun Hsu and K. M. Linduff, *Western Chou Civilization* (1988); Michele Pirazzoli-t'Sersteven, *The Han Civilization of China* (1982); R. Wilke and M. Wolf, *Women in Chinese Society* (1975); and Bella Vivante, ed., *Women's Roles in Ancient Civilizations: A Reference Guide* (1999).

On the Web

On Daoism, see http://www.his.com/~merkin/DaoBrief.html. For a virtual tour of the Great Wall, see http://www.chinavista.com/travel/greatwall/greatwall.html.

CHAPTER 3

CLASSICAL CIVILIZATION: INDIA

Indian stone carving showing Buddhists worshiping the site beneath the Bodhi tree, where the Buddha gained Enlightenment.

- The Framework for Indian History: Geography and a Formative Period
- Patterns in Classical India
- Political Institutions
- Religion and Culture
- Economy and Society
- IN DEPTH: Inequality as the Social Norm
- VISUALIZING THE PAST: The Pattern of Trade in the Ancient Eurasian World
- Indian Influence
- China and India
- GLOBAL CONNECTIONS: India and the Wider World

The classical period of Indian history includes a number of contrasts to that of China—and many of these contrasts have proved enduring. Whereas the focus in classical China was on politics and related philosophical values, the emphasis in classical India shifted to religion and social structure; a political culture existed, but it was less cohesive and central than its Chinese counterpart. Less familiar but scarcely less important were distinctions that arose in India's scientific tradition and the tenor of the economy and family life. Here, too, the classical period generated impulses that are still felt in India today—and that continue to distinguish India from other major civilizations in the world.

India's distinctiveness was considerable, but a comparison must not be one-sided. India was an agricultural society, and this dictated many similarities with China. Most people were peasant farmers, with their major focus on food production for their own family's survival. The clustering of peasants in villages, to provide mutual aid and protection, gave a strong localist flavor to many aspects of life in China and India alike. In addition, agriculture influenced family life, with male ownership of property creating a strongly patriarchal flavor, and women held as inferiors and often treated as possessions. As agricultural civilizations, both China and India produced important cities and engendered significant trade, which added to social and economic complexity and also created the basis for most formal intellectual life, including schools and academies.

The Framework for Indian History: Geography and a Formative Period

 Indian civilization was shaped by geography and climate, which help explain some differences from China. Classical Indian civilization was further prepared by cultural and social developments during the centuries of Aryan invasion and subsequent consolidation.

Important reasons for India's distinctive paths lie in geography and early historical experience. India was much closer to the orbit of other civilizations than China. Trading contacts with China, developed late in the classical period, had little impact—interestingly, China was more affected. But India was frequently open to influences from the Middle East and even the Mediterranean world. Persian empires spilled over into India at several points, bringing new artistic styles and political concepts. Briefly, **Alexander the Great** invaded India, and while he did not establish a durable empire, he did allow important Indian contacts with Hellenistic culture. Periodic influences from the Middle East continued after the classical age, forcing India to react and adapt in ways that China largely avoided because it was more isolated.

In addition to links with other cultures, India's topography shaped a number of vital features of its civilization. The vast Indian subcontinent is partially separated

51

1600 B.C.E.	**1200** B.C.E.	**750** B.C.E.	**500** B.C.E.	**250** B.C.E.	**1** C.E.
1600–1000 Period of Aryan invasions **1500–1000** Vedic Age	**1200–700** Sacred Vedas composed **1000–600** Epic Age: *Mahabharata, Ramayana, Upanishads* composed	**700–c. 550** Era of unrivaled brahman dominance **563–483** Life of the Buddha	**327–325** Alexander the Great's invasion **322–298** Chandragupta Maurya rules **269–232** Reign of Ashoka	**200** B.C.E.–**200** C.E. Period of greatest Buddhist influence	**319** Beginning of the Gupta Empire; one of the world's first universities established **535** Gupta Empire overturned by the Huns

from the rest of Asia, and particularly from east Asia, by northern mountain ranges, notably the **Himalayas.** Important passes through the mountains, especially in the northwest, linked India to other civilizations in the Middle East; although it lacked the isolation of China's Middle Kingdom, the subcontinent was somewhat set apart within Asia. At the same time, divisions within the subcontinent made full political unity difficult: India was thus marked by greater diversity than China's Middle Kingdom. The most important agricultural regions are those along the two great rivers, the Indus and the Ganges. However, India also has mountainous northern regions, where a herding economy took root, and a southern coastal rim, separated by mountains and the Deccan plateau, where an active trading and seafaring economy arose. India's separate regions help explain not only economic diversity but also the racial and language differences that, from early times, have marked the subcontinent's populations.

Much of India is semitropical in climate. In the river valley plains, heat can rise to 120°F during the early summer. Summer also brings torrential **monsoon** rains, crucial for farming. But the monsoons vary from year to year, sometimes bringing too little rain or coming too late and causing famine-producing drought, or sometimes bringing catastrophic floods. Certain features of Indian civilization may have resulted from a need to come to terms with a climate that could produce abundance one year and grim starvation the next. In a year with favorable monsoons, Indian farmers were able to plant and harvest two crops and could thus support a sizeable population.

Indian civilization was shaped not only by its physical environment but also by a formative period, lasting several centuries, between the destruction of the Indus River civilization and the revival of full civilization elsewhere on the subcontinent. During this formative period, called the Vedic and Epic ages, the **Aryan** (Indo-European) migrants—hunting and herding peoples originally from central Asia—gradu-

ally came to terms with agriculture but had their own impact on the culture and social structure of their new home. Also during the Vedic Age, from about 1500 to 1000 B.C.E., Indian agriculture extended from the Indus River valley to the more fertile Ganges valley, as the Aryans used iron tools to clear away the dense vegetation.

Most of what we know about this preclassical period in Indian history comes from literary epics developed by the Aryans, initially passed on orally. They were later written down in **Sanskrit,** which became the first literary language of the new culture. These sacred books were called the **Vedas.** The initial part of this formative period, the Vedic Age, takes its name from the Sanskrit word *Veda,* or "knowledge." The first epic, the *Rig-Veda,* consists of 1028 hymns dedicated to the Aryan gods and composed by various priests. New stories, developed during the Epic Age between 1000 and 600 B.C.E., include the *Mahabharata,* India's greatest epic poem, and the *Ramayana,* both of which deal with real and mythical battles; these epics reflect a more settled agricultural society and better-organized political units than the *Rig-Veda.* The Epic Age also saw the creation of the *Upanishads,* epic poems with a more mystical religious flavor.

Aryan ideas and social and family forms also became increasingly influential. As the Aryans settled down to agriculture, they encouraged tight levels of village organization that came to be characteristic of Indian society and politics. Village chiefs, initially drawn from the leadership of one of the Aryan tribes, helped organize village defenses and regulate property relationships among families. Family structure emphasized patriarchal controls, and extended family relationships among grandparents, parents, and children were close.

The characteristic Indian caste system also began to take shape during the Vedic and Epic ages, perhaps initially as a means of establishing relationships between the Aryan conquerors and the indigenous people, whom the Aryans regarded as inferior. Aryan social classes (**varnas**) partly enforced divisions familiar in agricultural societies. Thus, a warrior or governing class, the Kshatriyas, and the priestly class, or brahmans, stood at the top of the social pyramid, followed by Vaisyas, the traders and farmers, and Sudras, or common laborers. Many of the Sudras worked on the estates of large landowners. A fifth group gradually evolved, later called the **untouchables,** who were confined to a few jobs, such as transporting the bodies of the dead or hauling refuse. It was widely believed that touching these people would defile anyone from a superior class. Initially, the warrior group ranked highest, but during the Epic Age the brahmans replaced them, signaling the importance of religious links in Indian life. Thus, a law book stated, "When a brahman springs to light he is born above the world, the chief of all creatures, assigned to guard the treasury of duties, religious and civil." Gradually, the five social groups became hereditary, with marriage between castes forbidden and punishable by death; the basic castes divided into smaller subgroups, called *jati*, each with distinctive occupations and each tied to its social station by birth.

The *Rig-Veda*, the first Aryan epic, attributed the rise of the caste system to the gods:

> When they divided the original Man
> into how many parts did they divide him?
> What was his mouth, what were his arms,
> what were his thighs and his feet called?
> The brahman was his mouth, of his
> arms was made the warrior.
> His thighs became the vaisya, of
> his feet the sudra was born.

The Aryans brought to India a religion of many gods and goddesses, who regulated natural forces and possessed human qualities. Thus, **Indra,** the god of thunder, was also the god of strength. Gods presided over fire, the sun, death, and so on. This system bore some resemblances to the gods and goddesses of Greek myth or Scandinavian mythology, for the very good reason that they were derived from a common Indo-European oral heritage. However, India was to give this common tradition an important twist, ultimately constructing a vigorous, complex religion that, apart from the Indo-European polytheistic faiths, endures to this day.

During the epic periods, the Aryans offered hymns and sacrifices to the gods. Certain animals were regarded as particularly sacred, embodying the divine spirit. Gradually, this religion became more elaborate. The epic poems reflect an idea of life after death and a religious approach to the world of nature. Nature was seen as informed not only by specific gods but also by a more basic divine force. These ideas, expressed in the mystical *Upanishads*, added greatly to the spiritual power of this early religion and served as the basis for later Hindu beliefs. By the end of the Epic Age, the dominant Indian belief system included a variety of convictions. Many people continued to emphasize rituals and sacrifices to the gods of nature; specific beliefs, as in the sacredness of monkeys and cattle, illustrated this ritualistic approach. The brahman priestly class specified and enforced prayers, ceremonies, and rituals. However, the religion also produced a more mystical strand through its belief in a unifying divine force and the desirability of seeking union with this force. Toward the end of the Epic period one religious leader, Gautama Buddha, built on this mysticism to create what became Buddhism, another major world religion.

Patterns in Classical India

 Two major empires formed at crucial periods in classical Indian history, the Mauryan and, later, the Gupta.

By 600 B.C.E., India had passed through its formative phase. Regional political units grew in size, cities and trade expanded, and the development of the Sanskrit language, although dominated by the priestly brahman class, furthered an elaborate literary culture. A full, classical civilization could now build on the social and cultural themes first launched during the Vedic and Epic ages.

Indian development during the classical era and beyond did not take on the convenient structure of rising and falling dynasties characteristic of Chinese history. Political eras were even less clear than in classical Greece. The rhythm of Indian history was irregular and often consisted of landmark invasions that poured in through the mountain passes of the subcontinent's northwestern border.

Toward the end of the Epic Age and until the 4th century B.C.E., the Indian plains were divided among powerful regional states. Sixteen major states existed by 600 B.C.E. in the plains of northern India, some of them monarchies, others republics dominated by assemblies of priests and warriors. Warfare was not uncommon. One regional state, Magadha, established dominance over a considerable empire. In 327 B.C.E., Alexander the Great, having conquered Greece and much of the Middle East, pushed into northwestern India, establishing a small border state called Bactria.

Political reactions to this incursion produced the next major step in Indian political history, in 322 B.C.E., when a young soldier named **Chandragupta Maurya** seized power along the Ganges River. He became the first of the **Mauryan** dynasty of Indian rulers, who in turn were the first rulers to unify much of the entire subcontinent. While it is difficult to know what, if anything, the Mauryan dynasty borrowed directly from Persian political models or the example of Alexander the Great, Chandragupta and his successors maintained large armies, with thousands of chariots and elephant-borne troops. The Mauryan rulers also developed a substantial bureaucracy, even sponsoring a postal service.

Chandragupta's style of government was highly autocratic, relying on the ruler's personal and military power. This style would surface periodically in Indian history, just as it did in the Middle East, a region with which India had important contacts. A Greek ambassador from one of the Hellenistic kingdoms described Chandragupta's life:

> Attendance on the king's person is the duty of women, who indeed are bought from their fathers. Outside the gates [of the palace] stand the bodyguards and the rest of the soldiers…. Nor does the king sleep during the day, and at night he is forced at various hours to change his bed because of those plotting against him. Of his non-military departures [from the palace] one is to the courts, in which he passed the day hearing cases to the end … [When he leaves to hunt,] he is thickly surrounded by a circle of women, and on the outside by spear-carrying bodyguards. The road is fenced off with ropes, and to anyone who passes within the ropes as far as the women, death is the penalty.

Such drastic precautions paid off. Chandragupta finally designated his rule to a son and became a religious ascetic, dying peacefully at an advanced age.

Chandragupta's grandson, **Ashoka** (269–232 B.C.E.), was an even greater figure in India's history. First serving as a governor of two provinces, Ashoka enjoyed a lavish lifestyle, with frequent horseback riding and feasting. However, he also engaged in a study of nature and was strongly influenced by the intense spiritualism not only of the Brahman religion but also of Buddhism. Ashoka extended Mauryan conquests, gaining control of all but the southern tip of India through fierce fighting (Map 3.1). His methods were bloodthirsty; in taking over one coastal area, Ashoka himself admitted that "one hundred and fifty thousand were killed (or maimed) and many times that number later died." But, Ashoka could also be compassionate. He ultimately converted to Buddhism, seeing in the belief in **dharma,** or the law of moral consequences, a kind of ethical guide that might unite and discipline the diverse people under his rule. Ashoka vigorously propagated Buddhism throughout India, while also honoring Hinduism, sponsoring shrines for its worshippers. Ashoka even sent Buddhist missionaries to the Hellenistic kingdoms in the Middle East, and also to Sri Lanka to the south. The "new" Ashoka urged humane behavior on the part of

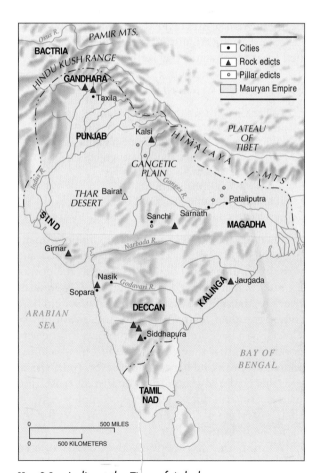

Map 3.1 *India at the Time of Ashoka*

his officials and insisted that they oversee the moral welfare of his empire. Like Chandragupta, Ashoka also worked to improve trade and communication, sponsoring an extensive road network dotted with wells and rest stops for travelers. Stability and the sheer expansion of the empire's territory encouraged growing commerce.

The Mauryan dynasty did not, however, succeed in establishing durable roots, and Ashoka's particular style of government did not have much later impact, although a strong Buddhist current persisted in India for some time. After Ashoka, the empire began to fall apart, and regional kingdoms surfaced once again. New invaders, the **Kushans,** pushed into central India from the northwest. The greatest Kushan king, Kanishka, converted to Buddhism but actually hurt this religion's popularity in India by associating it with foreign rule.

The collapse of the Kushan state, by 220 C.E., ushered in another hundred years of political instability. Then a new line of kings, the **Guptas,** established a large empire, beginning in 320 C.E. (Map 3.2). The Guptas produced no individual rulers as influential as the two great Mauryan rulers, but they had perhaps greater impact. One Gupta emperor proclaimed his virtues in an inscription on a ceremonial stone pillar:

> His far-reaching fame, deep-rooted in peace, emanated from the restoration of the sovereignty of many fallen royal families.... He, who had no equal in power in the world, eclipsed the fame of the other kings by the radiance of his versatile virtues, adorned by innumerable good actions.

Bombast aside, Gupta rulers often preferred to negotiate with local princes and intermarry with their families, which expanded influence without constant fighting. Two centuries of Gupta rule gave classical India its greatest period of political stability, although the Guptas did not administer as large a territory as the Mauryan kings had. The Gupta empire was overturned in 535 C.E. by a new invasion of nomadic warriors, the Huns.

Classical India thus alternated between widespread empires and a network of smaller kingdoms. Periods of regional rule did not necessarily suggest great instability, and both economic and cultural life advanced in these periods as well as under the Mauryas and Guptas.

Political Institutions

 India did not place as much emphasis on politics as China did, in part because of the structures implanted in the caste system. Regional political units were often highlighted.

Classical India did not develop the solid political traditions and institutions of Chinese civilization, or the high level of political interest that would characterize classical Greece and Rome. The most persistent political features of India, in the classical period and beyond, involved regionalism, plus considerable diversity in political forms. Autocratic kings and emperors dotted the history of classical India, but there were also aristocratic assemblies in some regional states with the power to consult and decide on major issues.

As a result of India's diversity and regionalism, even some of the great empires had a rather shaky base. Early Mauryan rulers depended heavily on the power of their large armies, and, as we have seen, often feared betrayal and attack. Early rulers in the Gupta dynasty used various devices to consolidate

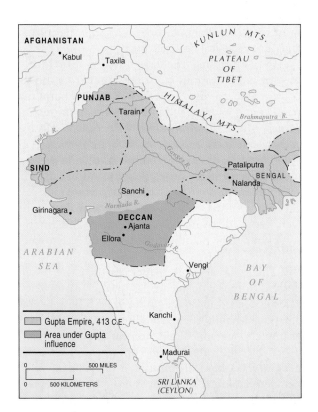

Map 3.2 *The Gupta Empire*

support. They claimed that they had been appointed by the gods to rule, and they favored the Hindu religion over Buddhism because the Hindus believed in such gods. The Guptas managed to create a demanding taxation system, seeking up to a sixth of all agricultural produce. However, they did not create an extensive bureaucracy, rather allowing local rulers whom they had defeated to maintain regional control so long as they deferred to Gupta dominance. The Guptas stationed a personal representative at each ruler's court to ensure loyalty. A final sign of the great empire's loose structure was the fact that no single language was imposed. The Guptas promoted Sanskrit, which became the language of educated people, but this made no dent in the diversity of popular, regional languages.

The Guptas did spread uniform law codes. Like the Mauryan rulers, they sponsored some general services, such as road building. They also served as patrons of much cultural activity, including university life as well as art and literature. These achievements were more than enough to qualify the Gupta period as a golden age in Indian history.

The fact remains, however, that the political culture of India was not very elaborate. There was little formal political theory and few institutions or values other than regionalism that carried through from one period to the next. Chandragupta's chief minister, **Kautilya,** wrote an important treatise on politics, but it was devoted to telling rulers what methods would work to maintain power—somewhat like the Legalists in China. Thinking of this sort encouraged efficient authority, but it did not spread political values or a sense of the importance of political service very widely, in contrast to Confucianism in China and also to the intense interest in political ethics in Greece and Rome. Ashoka saw in Buddhism a kind of ethic for good behavior, as well as a spiritual beacon, but Buddhist leaders in the long run were not greatly interested in affairs of state. Indeed, Indian religion generally did not stress the importance of politics, even for religious purposes, but rather the preeminence of priests as sources of authority.

The limitations on the political traditions developed during this period of Indian history can be explained partly by the importance of local units of government—the tightly organized villages—and particularly by the essentially political qualities of social relationships under the caste system. Caste rules, interpreted by priests, regulated many social relationships and work roles. To a great extent, the caste system and religious encouragement in the faithful performance of caste duties did for Indian life what more conventional government structures did in many other cultures, in promoting public order.

India's caste system became steadily more complex after the Epic Age, as the five initial classes subdivided into ultimately almost 300 jati (or livings), which became further divided into a multitude of subcastes—the true basis of the caste system—which defined the groups that a person could eat with or marry within. Hereditary principles grew ever stronger, so that it became virtually impossible to rise above the caste in which a person was born or to marry someone from a higher caste. It was possible to fall to a lower caste by marrying outside one's caste or by taking on work deemed inappropriate for one's caste. Upward mobility could occur within castes, as individuals might gain greater wealth through success in the economic activities appropriate to the caste. Rulers, like the Mauryans, might spring from the merchant castes, although most princes were warrior-born. It is important not to characterize the caste system in an oversimplified way, for it did offer some flexibilities. Nevertheless, the system gave India the most rigid overall framework for a social structure of any of the classical civilizations.

In its origins, the caste system provided a way for India's various races, the conquerors and the conquered, to live together without perpetual conflict and without full integration of cultures and values. Quite different kinds of people could live side by side in village or city, separated by caste. In an odd way, castes promoted tolerance, and this was useful, given India's varied peoples and beliefs. The caste system also meant that extensive outright slavery was avoided. The lowest, untouchable castes were scorned, confined to poverty and degrading work, but their members were not directly owned by others.

The political consequences of the caste system derived from the detailed rules for each caste. These rules governed marriages and permissible jobs, but also social habits such as eating and drinking. For example, a person could not eat or drink with a lower-caste individual or perform any service for that person. This kind of regulation of behavior made detailed political administration less necessary. Indeed, no state could command full loyalty from subjects, for their first loyalty was to caste.

More of the qualities of Indian civilization rested on widely shared cultural values than was the case in China. Religion, and particularly the evolving Hindu religion as it gained ground on Buddhism under the Guptas, was the clearest cultural cement of this society, cutting across political and language barriers and across the castes. Hinduism itself embraced considerable variety, and it gave rise to important religious dissent. Nor did it ever displace important minority religions. However, Hinduism has shown a remarkable capacity to survive and is the major system of belief in India even today. It also promotes other features in Indian culture. Thus, contemporary Indian children are encouraged to indulge their imaginations longer than Western children, and are confronted less sharply with outside reality. Some observers argue that even Indian adults, on average, and are less interested in general, agreed upon truths than in individually satisfying versions. A mindset of this sort goes back to the religious patterns created over 2000 years ago in classical India, where Hinduism encouraged imaginative links with a higher, divine reality. It is this kind of tradition that illustrates how classical India, although not the source of enduring political institutions beyond the local level, produced a civilization that would retain clear continuity and cultural cohesiveness from this point onward—even though the subcontinent was rarely politically united, at least under indigenous rulers.

Religion and Culture

 Two major religions, Hinduism and Buddhism, marked classical India. Artistic patterns were linked to religion. A significant scientific tradition developed as well.

Hinduism, the religion of India's majority, developed gradually over a period of many centuries. Its origins lie in the Vedic and Epic ages, as the Aryan religion gained greater sophistication, with concerns about an overarching divinity supplementing the rituals and polytheistic beliefs supervised by the brahman caste of priests. The *Rig-Veda* expressed the growing interest in a higher divine principle in its Creation Hymn:

> Then even nothingness was not, nor existence.
> There was no air then, nor the heavens beyond it.
> Who covered it? Where was it? In whose keeping...? The gods themselves are later than creation, so who knows truly whence it has arisen?

Unlike all the other world religions, Hinduism had no single founder, no central holy figure from whom the basic religious beliefs stemmed. This fact helps explain why the religion unfolded so gradually, sometimes in reaction to competing religions such as Buddhism or Islam. Moreover, Hinduism pursued a number of religious approaches, from the strictly ritualistic and ceremonial approach many brahmans preferred, to the high-soaring mysticism that sought to unite individual humans with an all-embracing divine principle. Unlike Western religions or Daoism (which it resembled in part), Hinduism could also encourage political and economic goals (called artha) and worldly pleasures (called karma)—and important textbooks of the time spelled out these pursuits. Part of Hinduism's success, indeed, was the result of its fluidity, its ability to adapt to the different needs of various groups and to change with circumstance. With a belief that there are many suitable paths of worship, Hinduism was also characteristically tolerant, coexisting with several offshoot religions that garnered minority acceptance in India.

Under brahman leadership, Indian ideas about the gods gradually became more elaborate (scholars call early Hinduism *brahmanism* for this reason, though Hindus always called their religion *dharma*, or moral path). Original gods of nature were altered to represent more abstract concepts. Thus, Varuna changed from a god of the sky to the guardian of ideas of right and wrong. The great poems of the Epic Age increasingly emphasized the importance of gentle and generous behavior, and the validity of a life devoted to concentration on the Supreme Spirit. The *Upanishads,* particularly, stressed the shallowness of worldly concerns—riches and even health were not the main point of human existence—in favor of contemplation of the divine spirit. It was in the *Upanishads* that the Hindu idea of a divine force informing the whole universe, of which each individual creature's soul is thought to be part, first surfaced clearly, in passages such as the following:

> "Fetch me a fruit of the banyan tree."
> "Here is one, sir."
> "Break it."
> "I have broken it, sir."
> "What do you see?"
> "Very tiny seeds, sir."
> "Break one."
> "I have broken it, sir."
> "What do you see now?"

"Nothing, sir."

"My son, … what you do not perceive is the essence, and in that essence the mighty banyan tree exists. Believe me, my son, in that essence is the self of all that is. That is the True, that is the Self."

However, the *Upanishads* did more than advance the idea of a mystical contact with a divine essence. They also attacked the conventional brahman view of what religion should be, a set of proper ceremonies that would lead to good things in this life or rewards after death. From the Epic Age onward, Hinduism embraced this clear tension between a religion of rituals, with fixed ceremonies and rules of conduct, and the religion of mystical holy men, seeking communion with the divine soul.

The mystics, often called **gurus** as they gathered disciples around them, and the brahman priests agreed on certain doctrines, as Hinduism became an increasingly formal religion by the first centuries of the common era. The basic holy essence, called *brahma,* formed part of everything in this world. Every living creature participates in this divine principle. The divine aspects of brahma are manifested in the forms of several gods, including **Vishnu,** the preserver, and **Shiva,** the destroyer, who could be worshipped or placated as expressions of the holy essence. The world of our senses is far less important than the world of the divine soul, and a proper life is one devoted to seeking union with this soul. However, this quest may take many lifetimes, and Hindus stressed the principle of **reincarnation,** in which souls do not die when bodies do but pass into other beings, either human or animal. Where the soul goes, whether it rises to a higher-caste person or falls perhaps to an animal, depends on how good a life the person has led. Ultimately, after many good lives, the soul reaches full union with the soul of brahma, and worldly suffering ceases.

Hinduism provided several channels for the good life. For people who renounced this world in search of salvation, there was the meditation and self-discipline of *yoga,* which means "union," allowing the mind to be freed to concentrate on the divine spirit. For others, there were the rituals and rules of the brahmans. These included proper ceremonies in the cremation of bodies at death, appropriate prayers, and obedience to injunctions such as treating cows as sacred animals and refraining from the consumption of beef. Many Hindus also continued the idea of lesser gods represented in the spirits of nature, or purely local divinities, which could be seen as expressions of Shiva or Vishnu (Figure 3.1). Personal devo-

Figure 3.1 *Perhaps the most frequently depicted Indian religious image is of god in the form of Shiva as the celestial dancer, here portrayed in a south Indian bronze. His dance represents the patterns of creation and destruction that are inescapable elements of the cosmos. The drum in his far left hand keeps the time between cycles of birth and death. The left hand below the drum is open as a gesture of reassurance to the righteous of their ultimate salvation. His foot crushes the demon of ignorance, shown as small compared with divine truth and welcoming of its own inevitable conquest by divine knowledge.*

tion to these divinities through prayer could aid the process of reincarnation to a higher state. Thus, many ordinary Hindus placed a lot of importance on prayers. Symbolic sacrifices or gifts to the gods might also bring them salvation or entry, through reincarnation, into a higher caste.

Hinduism also provided a basic, if complex, ethic that helped supply some unity amid the various forms of worship. The epic poems, richly symbolic, formed the key texts. They illustrated a central emphasis on the moral law of dharma as a guide to living in this world and simultaneously pursuing higher, spiritual goals. The concept of dharma directed attention to the moral consequences of action and at the same time the need to act. Each person must meet the obligations of life, serving the family, producing a livelihood and even earning money, and serving in the army when the need arises. These actions cannot damage, certainly cannot destroy, the eternal divine essence that underlies all creation. In the *Bhagavad Gita*, a classic sacred hymn, a warrior is sent to do battle against his own relatives. Fearful of killing them, he is advised by an incarnation of Brahma (Krishna) that he must carry out his duties. He will not really be killing his victims because their divine spirit will live on. This ethic urged that honorable behavior, even pleasure seeking, is compatible with spirituality and can lead to a final release from the life cycle and to unity with the divine essence. The Hindu ethic explains how devout Hindus could also be aggressive merchants or eager warriors. In encouraging honorable action, it could legitimize government and the caste system as providing the frameworks in which the duties of the world might be carried out, without distracting from the ultimate spiritual goals common to all people.

The ethical concept of dharma was far less detailed and prescriptive than the ethical codes associated with most other world religions, including Christianity and Islam. Dharma stresses inner study and meditation, building from the divine essence within each creature, rather than adherence to a fixed set of moral rules.

The spread of Hinduism through India and, at least briefly, to some other parts of Asia had many sources. The religion accommodated extreme spirituality. It also provided satisfying rules of conduct for ordinary life, including rituals and a firm emphasis on the distinction between good and evil behavior. The religion allowed many people to retain older beliefs and ceremonies, which they may have derived from a more purely polytheistic religion. It reinforced the caste system, giving people in lower castes hope for a better time in lives to come and giving upper-caste people, including the brahmans, the satisfaction that if they behaved well, they might be rewarded by communion with the divine soul. Even though Hindu beliefs took shape only gradually and contained many ambiguities, the religion was sustained by a strong cadre of priests and through the efforts of individual gurus and mystics.

At times, however, the tensions within Hinduism broke down for some individuals, producing rebellions against the dominant religion. One such rebellion, which occurred right after the Epic Age, led to a new religion closely related to Hinduism. Around 563 B.C.E., an Indian prince, Siddhartha Gautama, was born who came to question the fairness of earthly life in which so much poverty and misery abounded. Gautama, later called **Buddha** or "enlightened one," lived as a Hindu mystic, fasting and torturing his body. After six years, he felt that he had found truth, then spent his life traveling and gathering disciples to spread his ideas. Buddha accepted the spiritual truth behind many Hindu beliefs, such as reincarnation, but he denied the validity of others, such as caste. He held the material world to be a snare that warped human relations and caused pain via the frustrations inherent in it: All worldly things decay, but men and women suffer and harm others as they struggle to hold onto youth, health, and life itself, though all are destined to pass away. Buddha did not reject the possibility of rewards after life, but he saw salvation as arising from the destruction of the self, whose annihilation opens the door to a realm where suffering and decay are no more, literally a world beyond existence itself: **nirvana.** Individuals could regulate their lives and aspirations toward this goal, without elaborate ceremonies. Great stress was placed on self-control: "Let a man overcome anger by love, let him overcome evil by good, let him overcome the greedy by liberalness, the liar with the truth." By arguing that a holy life could be achieved through individual effort by people at every level of society, Buddhism denied the spiritual value not only of caste and the performance of rituals, but also of priests. This was another sign of the complexity of Indian social life in practice.

Buddhism spread and retained coherence through the example and teachings of groups of monks, organized in monasteries but preaching throughout the world (Figure 3.2). Buddhism attracted many followers in India itself, and its growth was greatly spurred by the conversion of the Mauryan emperor Ashoka. Increasingly, Buddha himself was seen as divine. Prayer and contemplation at Buddhist holy places and works of charity and piety gave substance to the idea of a holy life on earth. Ironically, however, Buddhism did not witness a permanent following in India. Brahman opposition was strong, and it was ultimately aided by the influence of the Gupta emperors. Furthermore, Hinduism showed its adaptability by emphasizing its mystical side, thus retaining the loyalties of many Indians. Buddhism's greatest successes, aided by the missionary encouragement of Ashoka and later the Kushan emperors, came in other parts of southeast Asia, including the island of Sri Lanka, off the south coast of India, and in China, Korea, and Japan. Still, pockets of Buddhists remained in India, particularly in the northeast. They were joined by other dissident groups who rejected aspects of Hinduism. Thus,

Figure 3.2 *This beautifully detailed sandstone statue of the Buddha meditating in a standing position was carved in the 5th century C.E. Note the nimbus, or halo, which was common in later Buddhist iconography. The calm radiated by the Buddha's facial expression suggests that he has already achieved Enlightenment. As Buddhism spread throughout India and overseas, a wide variety of artistic styles developed to depict the Buddha himself and key incidents of his legendary life. The realism and stylized robes of the sculpture shown here indicate that it was carved by artists following the conventions of the Indo-Greek school of northwestern India.*

Hinduism, although dominant, had to come to terms with the existence of other religions early on.

If Hinduism, along with the caste system, formed the most distinctive and durable products of the classical period of Indian history, they were certainly not the only ones. Even aside from dissident religions, Indian culture during this period was vibrant and diverse, and religion encompassed only part of its interests. Hinduism itself encouraged many wider pursuits.

Indian thinkers wrote actively about various aspects of human life. Although political theory was sparse, a great deal of legal writing occurred. The theme of love was important also. A manual of the "laws of love," the **Kamasutra,** written in the 4th century C.E., discusses relationships between men and women.

Indian literature, taking many themes from the great epic poems and their tales of military adventure, stressed lively story lines. The epics themselves were recorded in final written form during the Gupta period, and other story collections, like the *Panchatantra*, which includes Sinbad the Sailor, Jack the Giant Killer, and the Seven League Boots, produced adventurous yarns now known all over the world. Classical stories were often secular, but they sometimes included the gods and also shared with Hinduism an emphasis on imagination and excitement. Indian drama flourished also, again particularly under the Guptas, and stressed themes of romantic adventure in which lovers separated and then reunited after many perils. This literary tradition created a cultural framework that still survives in India. Even contemporary Indian movies reflect the tradition of swashbuckling romance and heroic action.

Classical India also produced important work in science and mathematics. The Guptas supported a vast university center—one of the world's first—in the town of Nalanda that attracted students from other parts of Asia as well as Indian brahmans. Nalanda had over a hundred lecture halls, three large libraries, an astronomical observatory, and even a model dairy. Its curriculum included religion, philosophy, medicine, architecture, and agriculture.

At the research level, Indian scientists, borrowing a bit from Greek learning after the conquests of Alexander the Great, made important strides in astronomy and medicine. The great astronomer Aryabhatta calculated the length of the solar year and improved mathematical measurements. Indian astronomers understood and calculated the daily rotation of the earth on its axis, predicted and explained eclipses, and developed a theory of gravity, and through telescopic observation they identified seven planets. Medical research was hampered by religious prohibitions on dissection, but Indian surgeons nevertheless made advances in bone setting and plastic surgery. Inoculation against smallpox was introduced, using cowpox serum. Indian hospitals stressed cleanliness, including sterilization of wounds, while leading doctors promoted high ethical standards. As was the case with Indian discoveries in astronomy, many medical findings reached the Western world only in modern times.

Indian mathematics produced still more important discoveries. The Indian numbering system is the one we use today, although we call it Arabic because Europeans imported it secondhand from the Arabs. Indians invented the concept of zero, and through it they were able to develop the decimal system. Indian advances in numbering rank with writing itself as key human inventions. Indian mathematicians also developed the concept of negative numbers, calculated square roots and a table of sines, and computed the value of pi more accurately than the Greeks did.

Finally, classical India produced lively art, although much of it perished under later invasions. Ashoka sponsored many spherical shrines to Buddha, called **stupas,** and statues honoring Buddha were also common. Under the Guptas, sculpture and painting moved away from realistic portrayals of the human form toward more stylized representation. Indian painters, working on the walls of buildings and caves, filled their work with forms of people and animals, captured in lively color. Indian art showed a keen appreciation of nature. It could pay homage to religious values, particularly during the period in which Buddhism briefly spread, but could also celebrate the joys of life.

There was, clearly, no full unity to this cultural outpouring. Religion, legalism, abstract mathematics, and art and literature coexisted. The result, however, was a somewhat distinctive overall tone, different from the more rational approaches of the West or the Chinese concentration on political ethics. In various cultural expressions, Indians developed an interest in spontaneity and imagination, whether in fleshly pleasures or a mystical union with the divine essence.

Economy and Society

 India developed extensive internal and maritime trade. Family life combined patriarchy with an emphasis on affection.

The caste system described many key features of Indian social and economic life, as it assigned people to occupations and regulated marriages. Low-caste individuals had few legal rights, and servants were often abused by their masters, who were restrained only by the ethical promptings of religion toward kindly treatment. A brahman who killed a servant for misbehavior faced a penalty no more severe than if he had killed an animal. This extreme level of abuse was uncommon, but the caste system did unquestionably make its mark on daily life as well as on the formal structure of society. The majority of Indians living in peasant villages had less frequent contact with people of higher social castes, and village leaders were charged with trying to protect peasants from too much interference by landlords and rulers.

Family life also emphasized the theme of hierarchy and tight organization, as it evolved from the Vedic and Epic ages. The dominance of husbands and fathers remained strong. One Indian code of law recommended that a wife worship her husband as a god. Indeed, the rights of women became increasingly limited as Indian civilization took clearer shape. Although the great epics stressed the control of husband and father, they also recognized women's independent contributions. As agriculture became better organized and improved technology reduced (without eliminating) women's economic contributions, the stress on male authority expanded. This is a common pattern in agricultural societies, as a sphere of action women enjoyed in hunting cultures was gradually circumscribed. Hindu thinkers debated whether a woman could advance spiritually without first being reincarnated as a man, and there was no consensus. The limits imposed on women were reflected in laws and literary references. A system of arranged marriage evolved in which parents contracted unions for children, particularly daughters, at quite early ages, to spouses they had never even met. The goal of these arrangements was to ensure solid economic links, with child brides contributing dowries of land or domestic animals to the ultimate family estates, but the result of such arrangements was that young people, especially girls, were drawn into a new family structure in which they had no voice.

However, the rigidities of family life and male dominance over women were often greater in theory than they usually turned out to be in practice. The emphasis on loving relations and sexual pleasure in Indian culture modified family life, since husband and wife were supposed to provide mutual emotional

In Depth

Inequality as the Social Norm

The Indian caste system is perhaps the most extreme expression of a type of social organization that violates the most revered principles on which modern Western societies are based. Like the Egyptian division between a noble and a commoner and the Greek division between a freeperson and a slave, the caste system rests on the assumption that humans are inherently unequal and that their lot in life is determined by the families and social strata into which they are born. The caste system, like the social systems of all other classical civilizations, presumed that social divisions were fixed and stable and that people ought to be content with the station they had been allotted at birth.

Furthermore, all classical social systems (with the partial exception of the Greeks, at least in Athens) played down the importance of the individual and stressed collective obligations and loyalties that were centered in the family, extended kin groups, or broader occupational or social groups. Family or caste affiliation, not individual ambition, determined a person's career goals and activities.

All of these assumptions directly contradict some of the West's most cherished current beliefs. They run counter to one of the most basic organizing principles of modern Western culture, rooted in a commitment to equality of opportunity. This principle is enshrined in European and American constitutions and legal systems, taught in Western schools and churches, and proclaimed in Western media. The belief in human equality, or at least equality of opportunity, is one of the most important ideas that modern Western civilization has exported to the peoples of Africa, Asia, and Latin America.

The modern concept of equality rests on two assumptions. The first is that a person's place in society should be determined not by the class or family into which he or she is born but by personal actions and qualities. The second is that the opportunity to rise—or fall—in social status should be open to everyone and protected by law. Some of our most cherished myths reflect these assumptions: that anyone can aspire to be president of the United States, for example, or that an ordinary person has the right to challenge the actions of the politically and economically powerful.

Of course, equality is a social ideal rather than something any human society has achieved. No one pretends that all humans are equal in intelligence or talent, and there are important barriers to equality of opportunity. But the belief persists that all humans should have an equal chance to better themselves by using the brains and skills they have. In the real world, race, class, and gender differences often favor some individuals over others, and laws and government agencies often do not correct these inequities. But the citizens of modern Western societies, and increasingly the rest of the world, champion the principles of equality of opportunity and the potential for social mobility as the just and natural bases for social organization and interaction.

However, what is just and natural for modern societies would have been incomprehensible in the classical age. In fact, most human societies through most of human history have been organized on assumptions that are much closer to those underlying the Indian caste system than to those underlying modern Western norms. Ancient Egyptians or Greeks, or for that matter medieval Europeans or early modern Chinese, believed that career possibilities, political power, and social privileges should be set by law according to the position of one's family in the social hierarchy. The Indian caste structure was the most rigid and complex of the systems by which occupations, resources, and status were allotted. But all classical civilizations had similar social mechanisms that determined the obligations and privileges of members of each social stratum.

In some ways, classical Chinese and Greek societies provided exceptions to these general patterns. In China, people from lowly social origins could rise to positions of great status and power, and well-placed families could fall on hard times and lose their gentry status. But "rags to riches" success stories were the exception rather than the rule, and mobility between social strata was limited. In fact, Chinese thinkers made much of the distinctions between the **scholar-gentry** elite and the common people.

Although some of the Greeks, particularly the Athenians, developed the idea of equality for all citizens in a particular city-state, most of the people of these societies were not citizens, and many were slaves. By virtue of their birth the latter were assigned lives of servitude and often drudgery. Democratic participation and the chance to make full use of their talents were limited to the free males of the city-states.

In nearly all societies, these fixed social hierarchies were upheld by creation myths and religious beliefs that proclaimed their divine origins and the danger of punishment if they were challenged. Elite thinkers stressed the importance of the established social order to human peace and well-being; rulers were duty bound to defend it. Few challenged the naturalness of the hierarchy itself; fewer still proposed alternatives to it. Each person was expected to accept his or her place and to concentrate on the duties and obligations of that place rather than worry about rights or personal desires. Males and females alike were required to subordinate their individual yearnings and talents to the needs of their families, clans, communities, or social superiors. In return for a person's acceptance of his or her allotted place in the hierarchy, he or she received material sustenance and a social slot. Of course, these benefits were denied to people who fought the system. They might be outcast or exiled, physically punished, or even killed.

Questions: What arguments did the thinkers of the classical civilizations of Greece, China, and India use to explain and justify the great differences in social status and material wealth? How did those who belonged to elite groups justify their much greater status, wealth, and power compared to the peasants, artisans, and servants who made up most of the population? Why did people belonging to these subordinate social strata, including oppressed groups such as slaves and untouchables, accept these divisions? Comparing these modes of social organization with the ideals of your own society, what do you see as the advantages and drawbacks of each?

support as a marriage developed. The Mahabharata epic called a man's wife his truest friend: "Even a man in the grip of rage will not be harsh to a woman, remembering that on her depend the joys of love, happiness, and virtue." Small children were often pampered. "With their teeth half shown in causeless laughter, their efforts at talking so sweetly uncertain, when children ask to sit on his lap, a man is blessed." Families thus served an important and explicit emotional function as well as a role in supporting the structure of society and its institutions. They also, as in all agricultural societies, formed economic units. Children, after early years of indulgence, were expected to work hard. Adults were obligated to assist older relatives. The purpose of arranged marriages was to promote a family's economic well-being, and almost everyone lived in a family setting.

The Indian version of the patriarchal family was thus subtly different from that in China, although women were officially just as subordinate and later trends—as in many patriarchal societies over time— would bring new burdens. But Indian culture often featured clever and strong-willed women and goddesses, and this contributed to women's status as wives and mothers. Stories also celebrated women's emotions and beauty.

The economy of India in the classical period became extremely vigorous, certainly rivaling China in technological sophistication and probably briefly surpassing China in the prosperity of its upper classes. In manufacturing, Indians invented new uses for chemistry, and their steel was the best in the world. Indian capacity in ironmaking outdistanced European levels until a few centuries ago. Indian techniques in textiles were also advanced, as the subcontinent became the first to manufacture cotton cloth, calico, and cashmere. Most manufacturing was done by artisans who formed guilds and sold their goods from shops.

Indian emphasis on trade and merchant activity was far greater than in China, and indeed greater than that of the classical Mediterranean world. Indian merchants enjoyed relatively high caste status and the flexibility of the Hindu ethic. They also traveled widely, not only over the subcontinent but by sea to the Middle East and east Asia. The seafaring peoples along the southern coast, usually outside the large empires of northern India, were particularly active. These southern Indians, the Tamils, traded cotton and silks, dyes, drugs, gold, and ivory, often earning great fortunes. From the Middle East and the Roman Empire, they brought back pottery, wine, metals, some slaves, and above all gold. Their trade with southeast Asia was even more active, as Indian merchants transported not only sophisticated manufactured goods but also the trappings of India's active culture to places like Malaysia and the larger islands of Indonesia. In addition, caravan trade developed with China.

Visualizing the Past

The Pattern of Trade in the Ancient Eurasian World

The period of Maurya rule in India coincided with a great expansion in trade between the main centers of civilization in Eurasia and Africa. In the centuries that followed, a permanent system of exchange developed that extended from Rome and the Mediterranean Sea to China and Japan. The trading networks that made up this system included both those established between ports connected by ships and sea routes and those consisting of overland exchanges transmitted along the chain of trading centers that crossed central Asia and the Sudanic region of Africa. By the last centuries B.C.E., this far-flung trading system included much of the world as it was known to the peoples of the Eastern Hemisphere.

Some products produced at one end of the system, such as Chinese silks and porcelains, were carried the entire length of the network to be sold in markets at the other edge, in Rome, for example. As a general rule, products carried over these great distances tended to be high-priced luxury goods such as spices and precious jewels. But most of the exchanges, particularly in bulk goods such as metal ores or foodstuffs, were between adjoining regions. The ports of western India, for example, carried on a brisk trade with those in the Red Sea and Persian Gulf, while trading centers in southeast Asia supplied China with forest products and other raw materials in exchange for the many items manufactured by China's highly skilled artisans. Although

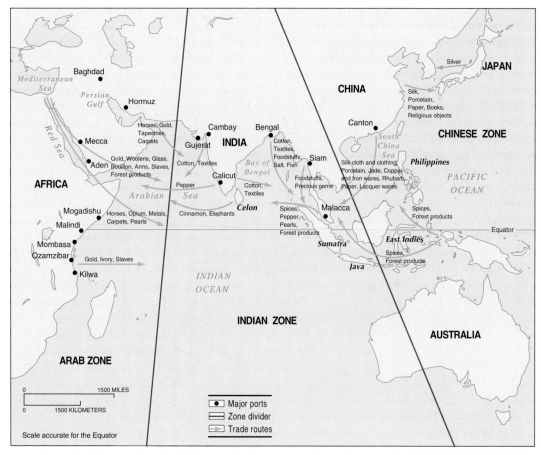

Eurasian and African Trading Goods Routes, c. 300 B.C.E. to 300 C.E.

some merchants and seamen, particularly the Chinese and Arabs, could be found in ports far from their homelands, most confined their activities within regional orbits, such as the Arabian Sea, the Persian Gulf, or the South China Sea.

This map provides an overview of this great trading network in the age of the classical civilizations, roughly the 3rd century B.C.E. to the 3rd century C.E. It shows the main centers of production, the goods exported overland and overseas, and the main directions of trade in these products. In each of the main sectors participating in the system, key ports, inland trading centers, and the products produced in different regions are shown.

Questions: Which civilizations or areas in the global trading network were the main centers for the production of finished products, such as cloth and pottery? What major centers supplied raw materials, such as forest products or foods? Which areas and port centers strike you as key points of convergence for the various types of trade? What advantages would these areas enjoy? Why were luxury goods likely to be transported the greatest distances? Why were bulk goods, especially foods, usually shipped only short distances, if at all? What were the advantages and disadvantages of sea and land transport? Besides trade goods, what other things might be transmitted through the trading networks? How great a role do you think the trading system played in the development of global civilization?

The Indian economy remained firmly agricultural at its base. The wealth of the upper classes and the splendor of cities like Nalanda were confined to a small group, as most people lived near the margins of subsistence. But India was justly known by the time of the Guptas for its wealth as well as for its religion and intellectual life—always understanding that wealth was relative in the classical world and very unevenly divided. A Chinese Buddhist on a pilgrimage to India wrote:

> The people are many and happy. They do not have to register their households with the police. There is no death penalty. Religious sects have houses of charity where rooms, couches, beds, food, and drink are supplied to travelers.

Indian Influence

 Because of extensive trade, Indian artistic and cultural influence spread widely, particularly in southeast Asia. Buddhism was a leading cultural export.

Classical India, from the Mauryan period onward, had a considerable influence on other parts of the world. In many ways, the Indian Ocean, dominated at this point by Indian merchants and missionaries, was the most active linkage point among cultures, although admittedly, the Mediterranean, which channeled contact from the Middle East to north Africa and Europe, was a close second. Indian dominance of the waters of southern Asia, and the impressive creativity of Indian civilization itself, carried goods and influence well beyond the subcontinent's borders. No previous civilization had developed in southeast Asia to compete with Indian influence. And while India did not attempt political domination, dealing instead with the regional kingdoms of Burma, Thailand, parts of Indonesia, and Vietnam, Indian travelers or settlers did bring to these locales a persuasive way of life. Many Indian merchants married into local royal families. Indian-style temples were constructed and other forms of Indian art traveled widely. Buddhism spread from India to many parts of southeast Asia, and Hinduism converted many upper-class people, particularly in several of the Indonesian kingdoms. India thus serves as an early example of a major civilization expanding its influence well beyond its own regions.

Indian influence had affected China, through Buddhism and art, by the end of the classical period. Earlier, Buddhist emissaries to the Middle East stimulated new ethical thinking that informed Greek and Roman groups like the Stoics and through them aspects of Christianity later on.

Within India itself, the classical period, starting a bit late after the Aryan invasions, lasted somewhat longer than that of China or Rome. Even when the period ended with the fall of the Guptas, an identifiable civilization remained in India, building on several key factors first established in the classical period: the religion, to be sure, but also the artistic and literary tradition and the complex social and family network. The ability of this civilization to survive, even under long periods of foreign domination, was testimony to the meaning and variety it offered to many Indians themselves.

China and India

 China and India offer important contrasts in political emphases, social systems, and cultures. They also resembled each other in seeking to build stable structures over large areas and in using culture to justify social inequality.

The thrusts of classical civilization in China and India reveal the diversity generated during the classical age. The restraint of Chinese art and poetry contrasted with the more dynamic sensual styles of India. India ultimately settled on a primary religion, though with important minority expressions, that embodied diverse impulses within it. China opted for separate religious and philosophical systems that would serve different needs. China's political structures and values found little echo in India, whereas the Indian caste system involved a social rigidity considerably greater than that of China. India's cultural emphasis was, on balance, considerably more other-worldly than that of China, despite the impact of Daoism. Quite obviously, classical India and classical China created vastly different cultures. Even in science, where there was similar interest in pragmatic discoveries about how the world works, the Chinese placed greater stress on purely practical findings, whereas the Indians ventured further into the mathematical arena.

Beyond the realm of formal culture and the institutions of government, India and China may seem more similar. As agricultural societies, both civilizations relied on a large peasant class, organized in close-knit villages with much mutual cooperation. Cities and merchant activity, although vital, played a secondary role. Political power rested primarily with those who controlled the land, through ownership of large estates and the ability to tax the peasant class. On a more personal level, the power of husbands and fathers in the family—the basic fact of patriarchy—encompassed Indian and Chinese families alike.

However, Indian and Chinese societies differed in more than their religion, philosophy, art, and politics. Ordinary people had cultures along with elites.

Hindu peasants saw their world differently from their Chinese counterparts. They placed less emphasis on personal emotional restraint and detailed etiquette; they expected different emotional interactions with family members. Indian peasants were less constrained than were the Chinese by recurrent efforts by large landlords to gain control of their land. Although there were wealthy landlords in India, the system of village control of most land was more firmly entrenched than in China. Indian merchants played a greater role than their Chinese counterparts. There was more sea trade, more commercial vitality. Revealingly, India's expanding cultural influence was due to merchant activity above all else, whereas Chinese expansion involved government initiatives in gaining new territory and sending proud emissaries to satellite states. These differences were less dramatic, certainly less easy to document, than those generated by elite thinkers and politicians, but they contributed to the shape of a civilization and to its particular vitality, its areas of stability and instability.

Because each classical civilization developed its own unique style, in social relationships as well as in formal politics and intellectual life, exchanges between two societies like China and India involved specific borrowings, not wholesale imitation. India and China, the two giants of classical Asia, remain subjects of comparison to our own time, because they have continued to build distinctively on their particular traditions, established before 500 C.E. These characteristics, in turn, differed from those of yet another center of civilization, the societies that sprang up on the shores of the Mediterranean during this same classical age.

GLOBAL CONNECTIONS: India and the Wider World

No classical civilization was more open to outside influences than those of the Indian subcontinent. None were more central to cross-cultural exchanges in the centuries that ushered what we have come to label the common era (C.E.) of world history. The brahman-dominated, caste-ordered civilization, which flourished at the end of the Vedic era and later under the Guptas, produced some of humanity's most sublime art and philosophy; important breakthroughs in mathematics, the sciences, and technology; prosperous urban centers; and a population that has been second only to that of China through much of human history.

The period dominated by the Mauryas in between saw the rise of Buddhism, one of a handful of truly world religions. In this era and the age of the Guptas that followed, Buddhism was but one of numerous components of Indian civilization that were exported to China and east Asia, across the steppes of central Asia, throughout most of southeast Asia, and as far west as the Mediterranean.

In mainland and island southeast Asia, the impact of Indian civilization was especially critical. Indian merchants played a key role in trade with these regions, and other influences followed. Indian religions and epics, art and architecture, and concepts of kingship sparked the rise of centralized states and complex societies that culminated in great civilizations, such as those centered at Angkor Wat in Cambodia and the kingdom of Majapahit in central Java. In the Mediterranean, Indian influences were felt in areas as diverse as artistic techniques, philosophies such as Stoicism, and religious ideas that significantly affected Christianity. Central to all of these developments was the fact that in the centuries that witnessed the flowering of Indian civilization under the Mauryas and Guptas, the coastal areas of the Indian subcontinent became, and would remain for millennia, one of the core areas of an ever expanding trading network that would eventually encompass most of the Eastern Hemisphere. Indian manufactured goods, such as cotton textiles and bronze statuary, soon became some of the most coveted commodities in this system of exchange. Indian merchants and sailors would carry them throughout the Indian Ocean and to the emporiums of the Silk Roads that dominated overland trade beyond the Himalaya Mountains. Indian religions, artwork, scientific discoveries, and epic literature came to enrich, and at times spur major transformations in, civilizations over much of the known world.

Further Readings

Two useful sources for Indian religion and philosophy are Franklin Edgerton, trans. and ed., *The Bhagavad Gita, Translated and Interpreted* (1944), and S. Radhakrishnan and Charles Moore, eds., *A Source Book in Indian Philosophy* (1957). Among the most accessible surveys of early Indian history are Romila Thaper, *A History of India,* Vol. 1 (1966); P. Spear, *India* (1981); Stanley Wolpert, *A New History of India* (1994); and D. D. Kosambi, *Ancient India, A History of Its Culture and Civilization* (1965). On more specialized topics, see J. W. Sedlar, *India and the Greek World* (1952); H. Scharff, *That State in Indian Tradition* (1988); Jeannine Auboyer, *Daily Life in Ancient India* (1961); A. L. Basham, *A Cultural History of India* (1975); and Trevor Ling, *The Buddha* (1973).

On the Web

For an overview of early Indian history and culture, see http://www.historyofindia.com/ancfrm.html.

Alexander the Great's invasion of India is the subject of a mock ancient newspaper article and of a critical review entitled "Alexander the Ordinary" at http://www.itihaas.com/ancient/alex.html and http://www.itihaas.com/ancient/1.html. The Emperor Ashoka is "interviewed" at http://www.itihaas.com/ancient/ashoka.html. His edicts are illuminated at http://www.cs.colostate.edu/~malaiya/ashoka.html. The beauty and global reach of the Mahabharata and Ramayana are examined at http://web.utk.edu/~jftzgrld/MBh1Home.html, http://www.maxwell.syr.edu/maxpages/special/Ramayana, and at http://www.askasia.org/frclasrm/lessplan/1000054.htm.

CHAPTER 4

CLASSICAL CIVILIZATION IN THE MEDITERRANEAN: GREECE AND ROME

Vase art played a prominent role in Greece, with more vivid action and emotion than in earlier Egyptian styles. Here, Hercules brings a boar to Eurystheus, who is so frightened he has hidden in a wine jar.

- The Persian Tradition
- Patterns of Greek and Roman History
- Greek and Roman Political Institutions
- IN DEPTH: The Classical Mediterranean in Comparative Perspective
- Religion and Culture
- Economy and Society in the Mediterranean
- VISUALIZING THE PAST: Commerce and Society
- DOCUMENT: Rome and a Values Crisis
- Toward the Fall of Rome
- GLOBAL CONNECTIONS: Greece, Rome, and the World

The classical civilizations that sprang up on the shores of the Mediterranean Sea from about 800 B.C.E. until the fall of the Roman Empire in 476 C.E. rivaled their counterparts in India and China in richness and impact. Centered first in the peninsula of Greece, then in Rome's burgeoning provinces, the new Mediterranean culture did not embrace all of the civilized lands of the ancient Middle East. Greece rebuffed the advance of the mighty Persian Empire and established some colonies on the eastern shore of the Mediterranean, in what is now Turkey, but it only briefly conquered more than a fraction of the civilized Middle East. Rome came closer to conquering surrounding peoples, but even its empire had to contend with strong kingdoms to the east. Nevertheless, Greece and Rome do not merely constitute a westward push of civilization from its earlier bases in the Middle East and along the Nile—although this is a part of their story. They also represent the formation of new institutions and values that would reverberate in the later history of the Middle East and Europe alike.

For most Americans, and not only those who are descendants of European immigrants, classical Mediterranean culture constitutes "our own" classical past, or at least a goodly part of it. The framers of the U.S. Constitution were extremely conscious of Greek and Roman precedents. Designers of public buildings in the United States, from the early days of the American republic to the present, have dutifully copied Greek and Roman models, as in the Lincoln Memorial and most state capitols. Plato and Aristotle continue to be thought of as the founders of our philosophical tradition, and skillful teachers still rely on some imitation of the Socratic method. Our sense of debt to Greece and Rome may inspire us to find in their history special meaning or links to our own world; the Western educational experience has long included elaborate explorations of the Greco-Roman past as part of the standard academic education. But from the standpoint of world history, greater balance is obviously necessary. Greco-Roman history is one of the three major classical civilizations, more dynamic than its Chinese and Indian counterparts in some respects but noticeably less successful in others. The challenge is to discern the leading features of Greek and Roman civilization and to next compare them with those of their counterparts elsewhere. We can then clearly recognize the connections and our own debt without adhering to the notion that the Mediterranean world somehow dominated the classical period.

2000 B.C.E.	1000 B.C.E.	500 B.C.E.	250 B.C.E.	1 C.E.	250 C.E.
1700 Indo-European invasions of Greek peninsula **1400** Kingdom of Mycenae; Trojan War	**800–600** Rise of Greek city-states; Athens and Sparta become dominant **c. 700** Homerian epics *Iliad, Odyssey;* flowering of Greek architecture **550** Cyrus the Great forms Persian Empire **509** Beginnings of Roman republic	**470–430** Athens at its height: Pericles, Phidias, Sophocles, Socrates **450** Twelve Tables of Law **431–404** Peloponnesian Wars **359–336** Philip II of Macedonia **338–323** Macedonian Empire, Alexander the Great **300–100** Hellenistic period **264–146** Rome's Punic Wars	**49** Julius Caesar becomes dictator; assassinated in 44 **27** Augustus Caesar seizes power; rise of Roman Empire **c. 4** Birth of Jesus	**c. 30** Crucifixion of Jesus **63** Forced dissolution of independent Jewish state by Romans **101–106** Greatest spread of Roman territory **180** Death of Marcus Aurelius; beginning of decline of Roman Empire	**313** Constantine adopts Christianity **476** Fall of Rome

Classical Mediterranean civilization is complicated by the fact that it passed through two centers during its centuries of vigor, as Greek political institutions rose and then declined and the legions of Rome assumed leadership. Roman interests were not identical to those of Greece, although the Romans carefully preserved most Greek achievements. Rome mastered engineering; Greece specialized in scientific thought. Rome created a mighty empire, whereas the Greek city-states proved rather inept in forming an empire. It is possible, certainly, to see more than a change in emphases from Greece to Rome, and to talk about separate civilizations instead of a single basic pattern. And it is true that Greek influence was always stronger than Roman in the eastern Mediterranean, whereas western Europe would encounter a fuller Greco-Roman mixture, with Roman influence predominating in language and law. However, Greek and Roman societies shared many political ideas; they had a common religion and artistic styles; they developed similar economic structures. Certainly, their classical heritage would be used by successive civilizations without fine distinctions drawn between what was Greek and what was Roman.

The Persian Tradition

 The development of classical Mediterranean civilization includes the rise of city-states in Greece. This was followed by the expansion of the Hellenistic period. Rome emerged as a separate republic but strongly influenced by Greece. Roman expansion led to a decline of republican forms and the rise of a great empire.

As a vibrant classical civilization developed in the Mediterranean, a second center flourished in the Middle East, inheriting many of the achievements of the earlier Mesopotamian society. By 550 B.C.E., **Cyrus the Great** established a massive Persian Empire across the northern Middle East and into northwestern India. Although tolerant of local customs, the Persians advanced iron technology, developed a new religion—**Zoroastrianism**—and a lively artistic style. While the Persians had only limited influence on the Mediterranean coast and were ultimately toppled by the Greek-educated conqueror Alexander the Great, Persian language and culture survived in the northeastern portion of the Middle East, periodically affecting developments elsewhere in the region even into the 20th century. A separate empire in the area, the Sassanid, emerged again during Rome's imperial centuries.

Patterns of Greek and Roman History

 The rise of the dynamic city-states of classical Greece began around 800 B.C.E., reaching a high point in the 5th century. Then decline set in, but a new pattern of expansion occurred under Alexander the Great. Greek values spread widely in the ensuing Hellenistic period. By the time Hellenism declined, Rome was emerging as an expanionist republic, later becoming the Roman Empire. So the pattern was: Greek rise and decline, Hellenism, Roman republic, Roman Empire.

Greece

Even as Persia developed, a new civilization took shape to the west, building on a number of earlier precedents. The river valley civilizations of the Middle East and Africa had spread to some of the islands near the Greek peninsula, although less to the peninsula itself. The island of Crete, in particular, showed the results of Egyptian influence by 2000 B.C.E., and from this the Greeks were later able to develop a taste for monumental architecture. The Greeks themselves were an Indo-European people, like the Aryan conquerors of India, who took over the peninsula by 1700 B.C.E. An early kingdom in southern Greece, strongly influenced by Crete, developed by 1400 B.C.E. around the city of Mycenae. This was the kingdom later memorialized in Homer's epics about the Trojan War. Mycenae was then toppled by a subsequent wave of Indo-European invaders, whose incursions destroyed civilization on the peninsula until about 800 B.C.E.

The rapid rise of civilization in Greece between 800 and 600 B.C.E. was based on the creation of strong city-states, rather than a single political unit. Each city-state had its own government, typically either a tyranny of one ruler or an aristocratic council. The city-state served Greece well, for the peninsula was so divided by mountains that a unified government would have been difficult to establish. Trade developed rapidly under city-state sponsorship, and common cultural forms, including a rich written language with letters derived from the Phoenician alphabet, spread throughout the peninsula. The Greek city-states also joined in regular celebrations such as the athletic competitions of the **Olympic games.** Sparta and Athens came to be the two leading city-states: The first represented a strong military aristocracy dominating a slave population; the other was a more diverse commercial state, also including the extensive use of slaves, justly proud of its artistic and intellectual leadership. Between 500 and 449 B.C.E., the two states cooperated, along with smaller states, to defeat a huge Persian invasion. It was during and immediately after this period that Greek and particularly Athenian culture reached its highest point. Also during this period several city-states, and again particularly Athens, developed more colonies in the eastern Mediterranean and southern Italy, as Greek culture fanned out to create a larger zone of civilization (Map 4.1).

It was during the 5th century B.C.E. that the most famous Greek political figure, **Pericles,** dominated Athenian politics. Pericles was an aristocrat, but he was part of a democratic political structure in which each citizen could participate in city-state assemblies to select officials and pass laws. Pericles ruled not through official position but by wise influence and negotiation. He helped restrain some of the more aggressive views of the Athenian democrats, who urged even further expansion of the empire to garner more wealth and build the economy. Ultimately, however, Pericles' guidance could not prevent the tragic war between Athens and Sparta, which would deplete both sides.

Political decline soon set in, as Athens and Sparta vied for control of Greece during the bitter **Peloponnesian Wars** (431–404 B.C.E.). Ambitious kings from Macedonia, in the northern part of the peninsula, soon conquered the cities. **Philip II of Macedon** won the crucial battle in 338 B.C.E., and then his son Alexander extended the Macedonian Empire through the Middle East, across Persia

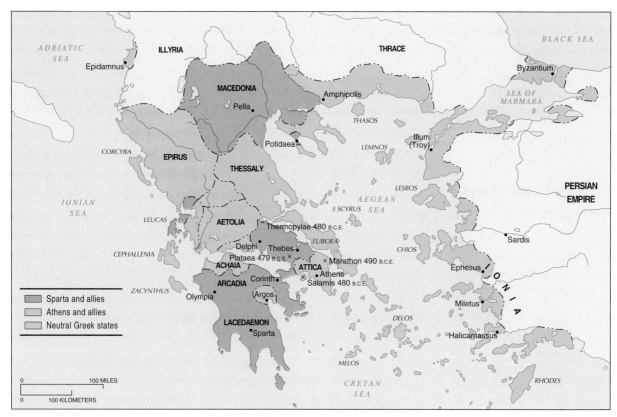

Map 4.1 *Greece and Greek Colonies of the World, c. 431 B.C.E. On the eve of the Peloponnesian War, Greek civilization had succeeded in spreading to key points around the Mediterranean world.*

to the border of India, and southward through Egypt (Map 4.2). Alexander the Great's empire was short-lived, for its creator died at the age of 33 after a mere 13 years of breathtaking conquests. However, successor regional kingdoms continued to rule much of the eastern Mediterranean for several centuries. Under their aegis, Greek art and culture merged with other Middle Eastern forms during the **Hellenistic period,** the name derived because of the influence of the Hellenes, as the Greeks were known. Although there was little political activity under the autocratic Hellenistic kings, trade flourished and important scientific centers were established in such cities as **Alexandria** in Egypt. In sum, the Hellenistic period saw the consolidation of Greek civilization even after the political decline of the peninsula itself, as well as some important new cultural developments.

Rome

The rise of Rome formed the final phase of classical Mediterranean civilization, for by the first century B.C.E. Rome had subjugated Greece and the Hellenistic kingdoms alike. The Roman state began humbly enough, as a local monarchy in central Italy around 800 B.C.E. Roman aristocrats succeeded in driving out the monarchy around 509 B.C.E. and established more elaborate political institutions for their city-state. The new **Roman republic** gradually extended its influence over the rest of the Italian peninsula, among other things conquering the Greek colonies in the south. Thus, the Romans early acquired a strong military orientation, although initially they may have been driven simply by a desire to protect their own territory from possible rivals. Roman conquest spread more widely during the three **Punic Wars,** from 264 to 146 B.C.E., during

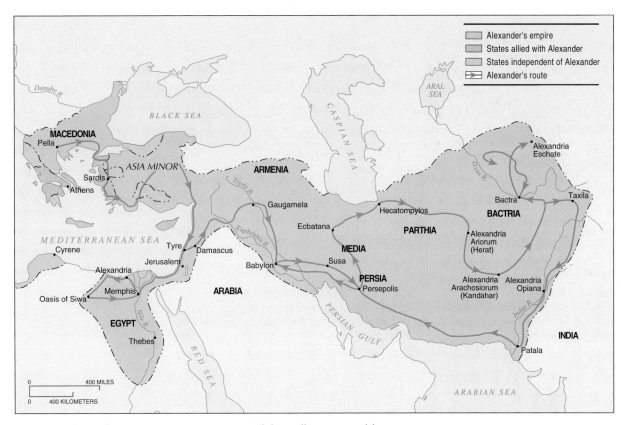

Map 4.2   *Alexander's Empire, c. 323 B.C.E., and the Hellenistic World*

which Rome fought the armies of the Phoenician city of **Carthage,** situated on the northern coast of Africa. These wars included a bloody defeat of the invading forces of the brilliant Carthaginian general **Hannibal,** whose troops were accompanied by pack-laden elephants. The war was so bitter that the Romans in a final act of destruction spread salt around Carthage to prevent agriculture from surviving there. Following the final destruction of Carthage, the Romans proceeded to seize the entire western Mediterranean along with Greece and Egypt.

The politics of the Roman republic grew increasingly unstable, however, as victorious generals sought even greater power while the poor of the city rebelled. Civil wars between two generals led to a victory by **Julius Caesar,** in 45 B.C.E., and the effective end of the traditional institutions of the Roman state. Caesar's grandnephew, ultimately called **Augustus Caesar,** seized power in 27 B.C.E., following another period of rivalry after Julius Caesar's assassination,

and established the basic structures of the Roman Empire. For 200 years, through the reign of the emperor Marcus Aurelius in 180 C.E., the empire maintained great vigor, bringing peace and prosperity to virtually the entire Mediterranean world, from Spain and north Africa in the west to the eastern shores of the great sea. The emperors also moved northward, conquering France and southern Britain and pushing into Germany. Here was a major, if somewhat tenuous, extension of the sway of Mediterranean civilization to western Europe (Map 4.3).

Then the empire suffered a slow but decisive fall, which lasted over 250 years, until invading peoples from the north finally overturned the government in Rome in 476 C.E. The decline manifested itself in terms of both economic deterioration and population loss: Trade levels and the birth rate both fell. Government also became generally less effective, although some strong later emperors, particularly **Diocletian** and **Constantine,** attempted to reverse the tide. It was

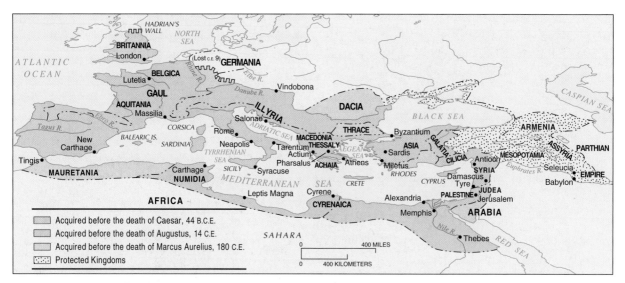

Map 4.3   *The Roman Empire from Augustus to 180 C.E. The empire expanded greatly in its first centuries, but such far-flung colonies proved impossible to maintain, both militarily and economically. How do the size and location of the empire compare with the earlier expansion of the republic?*

the emperor Constantine who, in 313, adopted the then somewhat obscure religion called Christianity in an attempt to unite the empire in new ways. However, particularly in the western half of the empire, most effective government became local, as the imperial administration could no longer guarantee order or even provide a system of justice. The Roman armies depended increasingly on non-Roman recruits, whose loyalty was suspect. Then, in this deepening mire, the invasion of nomadic peoples from the north marked the end of the classical period of Mediterranean civilization—a civilization that, like its counterparts in Gupta India and Han China during the same approximate period, could no longer defend itself.

To conclude: The new Mediterranean civilization built on earlier cultures along the eastern Mediterranean and within the Greek islands, taking firm shape with the rise of the Greek city-states after 800 B.C.E. These states began as monarchies but then evolved into more complex and diverse political forms. They also developed a more varied commercial economy, moving away from a purely grain-growing agriculture; this spurred the formation of a number of colonial outposts around the eastern Mediterranean and in Italy. The decline of the city-states ushered in the Macedonian conquest and the

formation of a wider Hellenistic culture that established deep roots in the Middle East and Egypt. Then Rome, initially a minor regional state distinguished by political virtue and stability, embarked on its great conquests, which would bring it control of the Mediterranean with important extensions into western and southeastern Europe plus the whole of north Africa. Rome's expansion ultimately overwhelmed its own republic, but the successor empire developed important political institutions of its own and resulted in two centuries of peace and glory.

Greek and Roman Political Institutions

 Greece and Rome featured an important variety of political forms. Both tended to emphasize aristocratic rule. But there were significant democratic elements in some cases, as well as examples of autocracy. Later Rome added emphasis on law and the institutions of a great, though somewhat decentralized, empire.

Politics were very important in classical Mediterranean civilization, from the Greek city-states through the early part of the Roman Empire. Indeed, our word *politics* comes from the Greek word for city-state, **polis,** which correctly suggests that intense political interests were part of life in a city-state in both Greece and Rome. The "good life" for an upper-class Athenian or Roman included active participation in politics and frequent discussions about the affairs of state. The local character of Mediterranean politics, whereby the typical city-state governed a surrounding territory of several hundred square miles, contributed to this intense preoccupation with politics. Citizens felt that the state was theirs, that they had certain rights and obligations without which their government could not survive. In the Greek city-states and also under the Roman republic, citizens actively participated in the military, which further contributed to this sense of political interest and responsibility. Under the Roman Empire, of course, political concerns were restricted by the sheer power of the emperor and his officers. Even then, however, local city-states retained considerable autonomy in Italy, Greece, and the eastern Mediterranean—the empire did not try to administer most local regions in great detail. The minority of people throughout the empire who were Roman citizens were intensely proud of this privilege.

Strong political ideals and interests created some similarities between Greco-Roman society and the Confucian values of classical China, although the concept of active citizenship was distinctive in the Mediterranean cultures. However, Greece and Rome did not develop a single or cohesive set of political institutions to rival China's divinely sanctioned emperor or its elaborate bureaucracy. So in addition to political intensity and localism as characteristics of Mediterranean civilization, we must note great diversity in political forms. Here the comparison extends to India, where various political forms—including participation in governing councils—ran strong. Later societies, in reflecting on classical Mediterranean civilization, selected from a number of political precedents. Monarchy was not a preferred form; the Roman republic and most Greek city-states had abolished early monarchies as part of their prehistory. Rule by individual strongmen was more common, and our word *tyranny* comes from this experience in classical Greece. Many tyrants were effective rulers, particularly in promoting public works and protecting the common people against the abuses of the aristocracy. Some of the Roman generals who seized power in the later days of the republic had similar

characteristics, as did the Hellenistic kings who succeeded Alexander in ruling regions of his empire.

Greece

Democracy (the word is derived from the Greek *demos,* "the people") was another important political alternative in classical Mediterranean society. The Athenian city-state traveled furthest in this direction, before and during the Peloponnesian Wars, after earlier experiences with aristocratic rule and with several tyrants. In 5th-century Athens, the major decisions of state were made by general assemblies in which all citizens could participate—although usually only a minority attended. This was **direct democracy,** not rule through elected representatives. The assembly met every 10 days. Executive officers, including judges, were chosen for brief terms to control their power, and they were subject to review by the assembly. Furthermore, they were chosen by lot, not elected—on the principle that any citizen could and should be able to serve. To be sure, only a minority of the Athenian population were active citizens. Women had no rights of political participation. And half of all adult males were not citizens at all, being slaves or foreigners. This, then, was not exactly the kind of democracy we envision today. But it did elicit widespread popular participation and devotion, and certainly embodied principles that we would recognize as truly democratic. Pericles, who led Athens during its decades of greatest glory between the final defeat of the Persians and the agony of war with Sparta, described the system this way:

> The administration is in the hands of the many and not of the few. But while the law secures equal justice to all alike in their private disputes, the claim of excellence is also recognized; and when a citizen is in any way distinguished he is preferred to the public service, not as a matter of privilege but as the reward of merit. Neither is poverty a bar, but a man may benefit his country whatever be the obscurity of his condition.

During the Peloponnesian Wars, Athens even demonstrated some of the potential drawbacks of democracy. Lower-class citizens, eager for government jobs and the spoils of war, often encouraged reckless military actions that weakened the state in its central dispute with Sparta.

Neither tyranny nor democracy, however, was the most characteristic political form in the classical

Mediterranean world. The most widely preferred political framework centered on the existence of aristocratic assemblies, whose deliberations established guidelines for state policy and served as a check on executive power. Thus, Sparta was governed by a singularly militaristic aristocracy, intent on retaining power over a large slave population. Other Greek city-states, although less bent on disciplining their elites for rigorous military service, also featured aristocratic assemblies. Even Athens during much of its democratic phase found leadership in many aristocrats, including Pericles himself. The word *aristocracy*, which comes from Greek terms meaning "rule of the best," suggests where many Greeks—particularly, of course, aristocrats themselves—thought real political virtue lay.

Rome

The constitution of the Roman republic, until the final decades of dissension in the 1st century B.C.E., which led to the establishment of the empire, tried to reconcile the various elements suggested by the Greek political experience, with primary reliance on the principle of aristocracy. All Roman citizens in the republic could gather in periodic assemblies, the function of which was not to pass basic laws but rather to elect various magistrates, some of whom were specifically entrusted with the task of representing the interests of the common people. The most important legislative body was the **Senate,** composed mainly of aristocrats, whose members held virtually all executive offices in the Roman state. Two **consuls** shared primary executive power, but in times of crisis the Senate could choose a dictator to hold emergency authority until the crisis had passed. In the Roman Senate, as in the aristocratic assemblies of the Greek city-states, the ideal of public service, featuring eloquent public speaking and arguments that sought to identify the general good, came closest to realization.

The diversity of Greek and Roman political forms, as well as the importance ascribed to political participation, helped generate a significant body of political theory in classical Mediterranean civilization. True to the aristocratic tradition, much of this theory dealt with appropriate political ethics, the duties of citizens, the importance of incorruptible service, and key political skills such as oratory. Roman writers like **Cicero,** himself an active senator, expounded eloquently on these subjects. Some of this political writing resembled Confucianism, although there was less emphasis on hierarchy and obedience or bureaucratic

virtues, and more on participation in deliberative bodies that would make laws and judge the actions of executive officers. Classical Mediterranean writers also paid great attention to the structure of the state itself, debating the virtues and vices of the various political forms. This kind of theory both expressed the political interests and diversity of the Mediterranean world and served as a key heritage to later societies.

The Roman Empire was a different sort of political system from the earlier city-states, although it preserved some older institutions, such as the Senate, which became a rather meaningless forum for debates. Of necessity, the empire developed organizational capacities on a far larger scale than the city-states; it is important to remember, however, that considerable local autonomy prevailed in many regions. Only in rare cases, such as the forced dissolution of the independent Jewish state in 63 C.E. after a major local rebellion, did the Romans take over distant areas completely. Careful organization was particularly evident in the vast hierarchy of the Roman army, whose officers wielded great political power even over the emperors themselves.

In addition to considerable tolerance for local customs and religions, plus strong military organization, the Romans emphasized carefully crafted laws as the one factor that would hold their vast territories together. Greek and Roman republican leaders had already developed an understanding of the importance of codified, equitable law. Aristocratic leaders in 8th-century Athens, for example, sponsored clear legal codes designed to balance the defense of private property with the protection of poor citizens, including access to courts of law administered by fellow citizens. The early Roman republic introduced its first code of law, the Twelve Tables, by 450 B.C.E. These early Roman laws were intended, among other things, to restrain the upper classes from arbitrary action and to subject them, as well as ordinary people, to some common legal principles. The Roman Empire carried these legal interests still further, in the belief that law should evolve to meet changing conditions without, however, fluctuating wildly.

The idea of Roman law was that rules, objectively judged, rather than personal whim should govern social relationships; thus, the law steadily took over matters of judgment earlier reserved for fathers of families or for landlords. Roman law also promoted the importance of common-sense fairness. In one case cited in the law texts of the empire, a slave was being shaved by a barber in a public square; two men were

In Depth

The Classical Mediterranean in Comparative Perspective

The three great classical civilizations lend themselves to a variety of comparisons. The general tone of each differed from the others, ranging from India's otherworldly strain to China's emphasis on government centralization, although it is important to note the varieties of activities and interests and the changes that occurred in each of the three societies. Basic comparisons include several striking similarities. Each classical society developed empires. Each relied primarily on an agricultural economy. Greco-Roman interest in secular culture bears some resemblance to Confucian emphasis in China, although in each case religious currents remained as well. But Greco-Roman political values and institutions differed from the Confucian emphasis on deference and bureaucratic training. Greek definitions of science contrasted with those of India and China, particularly in the emphasis on theory. Several focal points can be used for comparison.

Each classical civilization emphasized a clear social hierarchy, with substantial distance between elites and the majority of people who did the manual and menial work. This vital similarity between the civilizations reflected common tensions between complex leadership demands and lifestyles and the limited economic resources of the agricultural economy. Groups at the top of the social hierarchy judged that they had to control lower groups carefully to ensure their own prosperity. Each classical society generated ideologies that explained and justified the great social divisions. Philosophers and religious leaders devoted great attention to this subject.

Within this common framework, however, there were obvious differences. Groups at the top of the social pyramid reflected different value systems. The priests in India, the bureaucrats in China, and the aristocrats in Greece and the Roman republic predominated. The status of merchants varied despite the vital role commerce played in all three civilizations.

Opportunities for mobility varied also. India's caste system allowed movement within castes, if wealth was acquired, but little overall mobility. This was the most rigid classical social structure because it tied people to their basic social and occupational position by birth. China's bureaucratic system allowed a very small number of talented people from below to rise on the basis of education, but most bureaucrats continued to come from the landed aristocracy. Mediterranean society, with its aristocratic emphasis, limited opportunities to rise to the top, but the importance of acquired wealth (particularly in Rome) gave some nonaristocrats important economic and political opportunities. Cicero, for example, came from a merchant family. Various classes also shared some political power in city-state assemblies; the idea of citizens holding basic political rights across class lines was unusual in classical civilizations.

Each classical civilization distinctively defined the position of the lowest orders. India's untouchables performed duties culturally evaluated as demeaning but often vital. So did China's "mean people," who included actors. As Greece and then Rome expanded, they relied heavily on the legal and physical compulsions of slavery to provide menial service and demanding labor. Greece and Rome gave unusual voice to farmers when they maintained their own property but tended to scorn manual labor itself, a view that helped justify and was perpetuated by slavery. Confucianism urged deference but offered praise for peasant work.

Finally, each classical civilization developed a different cultural glue to help hold its social hierarchy together. Greece and Rome left much of the task of managing the social hierarchy to local authorities; community bonds, as in the city-states, were meant to pull different groups into a sense of common purpose. They also relied on military force and clear legal statements that defined rights according to station. Force and legal inequalities played important roles in China and India as well, but there were additional inducements. India's Hinduism helped justify and sustain the hierarchy by promising rewards through reincarnation for those who submitted to their place in any given existence. Chinese Confucianism urged general cultural values of obedience and self-restraint, creating some agreement—despite varied religions and philosophies—on the legitimacy of social ranks by defining how gentlemen and commoners should behave.

In no case did the social cement work perfectly; social unrest surfaced in all the classical civilizations, as in major slave rebellions in the Roman countryside or peasant uprisings in China. At the same time, the rigidity of classical social structures gave many common people some leeway. Elites viewed the masses as being so different from themselves that they did not try to revamp all their beliefs or community institutions.

(continued)

Differences in approach to social inequality nevertheless had important results. China and particularly India generated value systems that might convince people in the lower classes and the upper ranks that there was some legitimacy in the social hierarchy. Greece and Rome attempted a more difficult task in emphasizing the importance of aristocracy while offering some other elements a share in the political system. This combination could work well, although some groups, including slaves and women, were always excluded. It tended to deteriorate, however, when poorer citizens lost property. Yet no sweeping new social theory emerged to offer a different kind of solace to the masses until Christianity began to spread. It is no accident, then, that Indian and Chinese social structures survived better than Mediterranean structures did, lasting well beyond the classical period into the 20th century.

Questions: Why did the classical civilizations seem to need radical social inequalities? What was the relationship between wealth and social position in each classical civilization? If India used religion to compensate for social inequalities, what did China and the Mediterranean use?

playing ball nearby, and one accidentally hit the barber with the ball, causing him to cut the slave's throat. Who was responsible for the tragedy: the barber, catcher, or pitcher? According to Roman law, the slave—for anyone so foolish as to be shaved in a public place was asking for trouble and bore the responsibility himself.

Roman law codes spread widely through the empire, and with them came the notion of law as the regulator of social life. Many non-Romans were given the right of citizenship—although most ordinary people outside Rome preferred to maintain their local allegiances. With citizenship, however, came full access to Rome-appointed judges and uniform laws. Imperial law codes also regulated property rights and commerce, thus creating some economic unity in the vast empire. The idea of fair and reasoned law, to which officers of the state should themselves be subject, was a key political achievement of the Roman Empire, comparable in importance, although quite different in nature, to the Chinese elaboration of a complex bureaucratic structure.

The Greeks and Romans were less innovative in the functions they ascribed to government than in the political forms and theories they developed. Most governments concentrated on maintaining systems of law courts and military forces. Athens and, more durably and successfully, Rome placed great premium on the importance of military conquest. Mediterranean governments regulated some branches of commerce, particularly in the interest of securing vital supplies of grain. Rome, indeed, undertook vast public works in the form of roads and harbors to facilitate military transport as well as commerce. And the Roman state, especially under the empire, built countless stadiums and public baths to entertain and distract its subjects. The city of Rome itself, which at its peak contained over a million inhabitants, provided cheap food as well as gladiator contests and other entertainment for the masses—the famous "bread and circuses" that were designed to prevent popular disorder. Colonies of Romans elsewhere were also given theaters and stadiums. This provided solace in otherwise strange lands like England or Palestine.

Governments also supported an official religion, sponsoring public ceremonies to honor the gods and goddesses; civic religious festivals were important events that both expressed and encouraged widespread loyalty to the state. However, there was little attempt to impose this religion on everyone, and other religious practices were tolerated so long as they did not conflict with loyalty to the state. Even the later Roman emperors, who advanced the idea that the emperor was a god as a means of strengthening authority, were normally tolerant of other religions. They only attacked Christianity, and then irregularly, because of the Christians' refusal to place the state first in their devotion.

Localism and fervent political interests, including a sense of intense loyalty to the state; a diversity of political systems together with the preference for aristocratic rule; the importance of law and the development of an unusually elaborate and uniform set of legal principles—these were the chief political legacies of the classical Mediterranean world. The sheer accomplishment of the Roman Empire, which united a region never before or since brought together, still stands as one of the great political monuments of world history. This was a distinctive political mix. Although there was attention to careful legal procedures, no clear definition of individuals' rights existed. Indeed, the emphasis on duties to the state could lead, as in Sparta, to an essentially totalitarian framework in which the state controlled even the raising of children. Nor, until the peaceful centuries of the early Roman Empire, was it an entirely successful political structure, as wars and instability were common. Nonetheless, there can be no question of the richness of this political culture or of its central importance to the Greeks and Romans themselves.

Religion and Culture

 Greek and Roman culture did not directly generate a major religion, though Christianity arose in the classical Mediterranean context. Emphasis on philosophy and science and a strong artistic tradition described classical Mediterranean culture.

The Greeks and Romans did not create a significant, world-class religion; in this they differed from India and to some extent from China. Christianity, which was to become one of the major world religions, did of course arise during the Roman Empire. It owed some of its rapid geographical spread to the ease of movement within the huge Roman Empire. However, Christianity was not really a product of Greek or Roman culture, although it would ultimately be influenced by this culture. It took on serious historical importance only as the Roman Empire began its decline. The characteristic Greco-Roman religion was a much more primitive affair, derived from a belief in the spirits of nature elevated into a complex set of gods and goddesses who were seen as regulating human life. Greeks and Romans had different names for their pantheon, but the objects of worship were essentially the same: A creator or father god, Zeus or Jupiter, presided over an unruly assemblage of gods and goddesses whose functions ranged from regulating the daily passage of the sun (Apollo) or the oceans (Neptune) to inspiring war (Mars) or human love and beauty (Venus). Specific gods were the patrons of other human activities such as metalworking, the hunt, even literature and history. Regular ceremonies to the gods had real politi-

cal importance, and many individuals sought the gods' aid in foretelling the future or in ensuring a good harvest or good health.

In addition to its political functions, Greco-Roman religion had certain other features. It tended to be rather human, of-this-world in its approach. The doings of the gods made for good storytelling; they read like soap operas on a superhuman scale. Thus, the classical Mediterranean religion early engendered an important literary tradition, as was also the case in India. (Indeed, Greco-Roman and Indian religious lore reflected the common heritage of Indo-European invaders.) The gods were often used to illustrate human passions and foibles, thus serving as symbols of a serious inquiry into human nature. Unlike the Indians, however, the Greeks and Romans became interested in their gods more in terms of what they could do for and reveal about humankind on this earth than the principles that could elevate people toward higher planes of spirituality.

This dominant religion also had a number of limitations. Its lack of spiritual passion failed to satisfy many ordinary workers and peasants, particularly in times of political chaos or economic distress. "Mystery" religions, often imported from the Middle East, periodically swept through Greece and Rome, providing secret rituals and fellowship and a greater sense of contact with unfathomable divine powers. Even more than in China, a considerable division arose between upper-class and popular belief.

The gods and goddesses of Greco-Roman religion left many upper-class people dissatisfied also. They provided stories about how the world came to be, but little basis for a systematic inquiry into nature or human society. And while the dominant religion promoted political loyalty, it did not provide a basis for ethical thought. Hence, many thinkers, both in Greece and Rome, sought a separate model for ethical behavior. Greek and Roman moral philosophy, as issued by philosophers like **Aristotle** and Cicero, typically stressed the importance of moderation and balance in human behavior as opposed to the instability of much political life and the excesses of the gods themselves. Other ethical systems were devised, particularly during the Hellenistic period. Thus, **Stoics** emphasized an inner moral independence, to be cultivated by strict discipline of the body and by personal bravery. These ethical systems, established largely apart from religious considerations, were major contributions in their own right; they would also be blended with later religious thought, under Christianity.

The idea of a philosophy separate from the official religion, although not necessarily hostile to it, informed classical Mediterranean political theory, which made little reference to religious principles. It also considerably emphasized the powers of human thought. In Athens, **Socrates** (born in 469 B.C.E.) encouraged his pupils to question conventional wisdom, on the grounds that the chief human duty was "the improvement of the soul." Socrates himself ran afoul of the Athenian government, which thought that he was undermining political loyalty; given the choice of suicide or exile, Socrates chose the former. However, the Socratic principle of rational inquiry by means of skeptical questioning became a recurrent strand in classical Greek thinking and in its heritage to later societies. Socrates' great pupil **Plato** accentuated the positive somewhat more strongly by suggesting that human reason could approach an understanding of the three perfect forms—the absolutely True, Good, and Beautiful—which he believed characterized nature. Thus, a philosophical tradition arose in Greece, although in very diverse individual expressions, which tended to deemphasize the importance of human spirituality in favor of a celebration of the human ability to think. The result bore some similarities to Chinese Confucianism, although with greater emphasis on skeptical questioning and abstract speculations about the basic nature of humanity and the universe.

Greek interest in rationality carried over to an inquiry into the underlying order of physical nature. The Greeks were not outstanding empirical scientists. Relatively few new scientific findings emanated from Athens, or later from Rome, although philosophers like Aristotle did collect large amounts of biological data. The Greek interest lay in speculations about nature's order, and many non-Westerners believe that this tradition continues to inform what they see as an excessive Western passion for seeking basic rationality in the universe. In practice, the Greek concern translated into a host of theories, some of which were wrong, about the motions of the planets and the organization of the elemental principles of earth, fire, air, and water, and into a considerable interest in mathematics as a means of rendering nature's patterns comprehensible. Greek and later Hellenistic work in geometry was particularly impressive, featur-ing among other achievements the basic theorems of Pythagoras. Scientists during the Hellenistic period made some important empirical contributions, especially in studies of anatomy; medical treatises by Galen were not improved on, in the Western world, for many centuries. The mathematician Euclid produced what was long the world's most widely used compendium of geometry. Less fortunately, the Hellenistic astronomer Ptolemy produced an elaborate theory of the sun's motion around a stationary earth. This new Hellenistic theory contradicted much earlier Middle Eastern astronomy, which had recognized the earth's rotation; nonetheless, it was Ptolemy's theory that was long taken as fixed wisdom in Western thought.

Roman intellectuals, actively examining ethical and political theory, had nothing to add to Greek and Hellenistic science. They did help to preserve this tradition in the form of textbooks that were administered to upper-class schoolchildren. The Roman genius was more practical than the Greek and included engineering achievements such as the great roads and aqueducts that carried water to cities large and small. Roman ability to construct elaborate arches so that buildings could carry great structural weight was unsurpassed anywhere in the world. These feats, too, would leave their mark, as Rome's huge edifices long served as a reminder of ancient glories. But ultimately, it was the Greek and Hellenistic impulse to extend human reason to nature's principles that would result in the most impressive legacy.

In classical Mediterranean civilization, however, science and mathematics loomed far less large than art and literature in conveying key cultural values. The official religion inspired themes for artistic expression and the justification for temples, statues, and plays devoted to the glories of the gods. Nonetheless, the human-centered qualities of the Greeks and Romans also registered, as artists emphasized the beauty of realistic portrayals of the human form and poets and playwrights used the gods as foils for inquiries into the human condition. Early Greek poets included a woman author, Sappho (around 600 B.C.E.) (Figure 4.1).

All the arts received some attention in classical Mediterranean civilization. Performances of music and dance were vital parts of religious festivals, but their precise styles have unfortunately not been preserved. Far more durable was the Greek interest in

Figure 4.1 *This Roman painting features a young woman in an unusual role, as a student of the early Greek poet Sappho.*

drama, for plays, more than poetry, took a central role in this culture. Greek dramatists produced both comedy and tragedy, indeed making a formal division between the two approaches that is still part of the Western tradition, as in the labeling of current television shows as either form. On the whole, in contrast to Indian writers, the Greeks placed the greatest emphasis on tragedy. Their belief in human reason and balance also involved a sense that these virtues were precarious, so a person could easily become ensnared in situations of powerful emotion and uncontrollable consequences. The Athenian dramatist **Sophocles,** for example, so insightfully portrayed the psychological flaws of his hero Oedipus that modern psychology long used the term *Oedipus complex* to refer to a potentially unhealthy relationship between a man and his mother.

Greek literature contained a strong epic tradition as well, starting with the beautifully crafted tales of the *Iliad* and *Odyssey,* attributed to the poet Homer, who lived in the eighth century B.C.E. Roman authors, particularly the poet Vergil, also worked in the epic form, seeking to link Roman history and mythology with the Greek forerunner. Roman writers made significant contributions to poetry and to definitions of the poetic form that would long be used in Western literature. The overall Roman literary contribution was less impressive than the Greek, but it was substantial enough both to provide important examples of how poetry should be written and to furnish abundant illustrations of the literary richness of the Latin language.

In the visual arts, the emphasis of classical Mediterranean civilization was sculpture and architecture.

Figure 4.2   *The square simplicity of Doric style is reflected in these columns at the Parthenon. Varied column designs marked the progression of Greek architecture from Doric simplicity through Ionic (the outer columns in image at right) to the more ornate Corinthian (center column in image at right).*

Greek artists also excelled in ceramic work, whereas Roman painters produced realistic (and sometimes pornographic) decorations for the homes of the wealthy. In Athens's brilliant 5th century—the age of Pericles, Socrates, Sophocles, and so many other intensely creative figures—sculptors like Phidias developed unprecedented skill rendering simultaneously realistic yet beautiful images of the human form, from lovely goddesses to muscled warriors and athletes. Roman sculptors, less innovative, continued this heroic-realistic tradition. They molded scenes of Roman conquests on triumphal columns and captured the power but also the human qualities of Augustus Caesar and his successors on busts and full-figure statues alike.

Greek architecture, from the 8th century B.C.E. onward, emphasized monumental construction, square or rectangular in shape, with columned porticoes (Figure 4.2). The Greeks devised three embellishments for the tops of columns supporting their massive buildings, each more ornate than the next: the **Doric,** the **Ionic,** and the **Corinthian.** The Greeks, in short, invented what Westerners and others in the world today still regard as "classical" architecture, although the Greeks themselves were influenced by Egyptian models in their preferences. Greece, and later Italy, provided abundant stone for

ambitious temples, markets, and other public buildings. Many of these same structures were filled with products of the sculptors' workshops. They were brightly painted, although over the centuries the paint would fade so that later imitators came to think of the classical style as involving unadorned (some might say drab) stone.

Roman architects adopted the Greek themes quite readily. Their engineering skill allowed them to construct buildings of even greater size, as well as new forms such as the free-standing stadium. Under the empire, the Romans learned how to add domes to rectangular buildings, which resulted in some welcome architectural diversity. At the same time, the empire's taste for massive, heavily adorned monuments and public buildings, while a clear demonstration of Rome's sense of power and achievement, moved increasingly away from the simple lines of the early Greek temples.

Classical Mediterranean art and architecture were intimately linked with the society that produced them. There is a temptation, because of the formal role of classical styles in later societies, including our own, to attribute a stiffness to Greek and Roman art that was not present in the original. Greek and Roman structures were built to be used. Temples and

Figure 4.3 *This sarcophagus, or tomb, from the 4th century shows Christ and the apostles in typical Roman dress, a glimpse at how Roman men looked in public.*

marketplaces and the public baths that so delighted the Roman upper classes were part of daily urban life. Classical art was also flexible, according to need. Villas or small palaces—built for the Roman upper classes and typically constructed around an open courtyard—had a light, even simple quality rather different from that of temple architecture. Classical dramas were not merely examples of high art, performed in front of a cultural elite. Indeed, Athens lives in the memory of many humanists today as much because of the large audiences that trooped to performances of plays by authors like Sophocles as for the creativity of the writers and philosophers themselves. Literally thousands of people gathered in the large hillside theaters of Athens and other cities for the performance of new plays and for associated music and poetry competitions. Popular taste in Rome, to be sure, seemed less elevated. Republican Rome was not an important cultural center, and many Roman leaders indeed feared the more emotional qualities of

Greek art. The Roman Empire is known more for monumental athletic performances—chariot races and gladiators—than for high-quality popular theater. However, the fact remains that, even in Rome, elements of classical art—the great monuments if nothing more—were part of daily urban life and the pursuit of pleasure. Roman styles were also blended with Christianity during the later empire (Figure 4.3) providing another lasting expression.

Economy and Society in the Mediterranean

Greek and Roman economies featured commercial agriculture, trade, and slavery. Patriarchal family structure was characteristic.

Politics and formal culture in Greece and Rome were mainly affairs of the cities—which means

Visualizing the Past

Commerce and Society

Greek commerce expanded along with the colonies. In this painting on the interior of the Arkesilas Cup, dating from 560 B.C.E., the king of Cyrene, a Greek colony in northern Africa, is shown supervising the preparation of hemp or flax for export. What does the picture suggest about the nature and extent of social hierarchy? How can costumes be used in this kind of assessment? What is the king most concerned with? What kinds of technology are suggested? Can you think of other types of evidence to use in analyzing this kind of colonial commercial economy?

that they were of intense concern only to a minority of the population. Most Greeks and Romans were farmers, tied to the soil and often to local rituals and festivals that were rather different from urban forms. Many Greek farmers, for example, annually gathered for a spring passion play to celebrate the recovery of the goddess of fertility from the lower world, an event that was seen as a vital preparation for planting and that also suggested the possibility of an afterlife—a prospect important to many people who endured a life of hard labor and poverty. A substantial population of free farmers, who owned their own land, flourished in the early days of the Greek city-states and later around Rome. However, there was a constant tendency, most pronounced in Rome, for large landlords to squeeze these farmers, forcing them to become tenants or laborers or to join the swelling crowds of the urban lower class. Tensions between tyrants and aristocrats or democrats and aristocrats in Athens often revolved around free farmers' attempts to preserve their independence and shake off the heavy debts they had incurred. The Roman republic declined in part because too many farmers became dependant on the protection of large landlords, even when they did not work their estates outright, and so no longer could vote freely.

Farming in Greece and in much of Italy was complicated by the fact that soil conditions were not ideal for grain growing, and yet grain was the staple of life. First in Greece, then in central Italy, farmers were increasingly tempted to shift to the production of olives and grapes, which were used primarily for cooking and winemaking. These products were well suited to the soil conditions, but they required an unusually extensive conversion of agriculture to a market basis. That is, farmers who produced grapes and olives had to buy some of the food they needed, and they had to sell most of their own product in order to do this. Furthermore, planting olive trees or grape vines required substantial capital, for they would not bear fruit for at least five years after planting. This was one reason so many farmers went into debt. It was also one of the reasons that large landlords gained increasing advantage over independent farmers, for they could enter into market production on a much larger scale if only because of their greater access to capital.

The rise of commercial agriculture in Greece and then around Rome was one of the prime forces leading to efforts to establish an empire. Greek city-states, with Athens usually in the lead, developed colonies in the Middle East and then in Sicily mainly to gain access to grain production; for this, they traded not only olive oil and wine but also manufactured products and silver. Rome pushed south, in part, to acquire the Sicilian grain fields and later used much of north Africa as its granary. Indeed, the Romans encouraged such heavy cultivation in north Africa that they promoted a soil depletion that helps account for the region's reduced agricultural fertility in later centuries.

The importance of commercial farming obviously dictated extensive concern with trade. Private merchants operated most of the ships that carried agricultural products and other goods. Greek city-states and ultimately the Roman state supervised the grain trade, promoting public works and storage facilities and carefully regulating the vital supplies. Other kinds of trade were vital also. Luxury products from the shops of urban artists or craftsworkers played a major role in the lifestyle of the upper classes. There was some trade also beyond the borders of Mediterranean civilization itself, for goods from India and China. In this trade, interestingly, the Mediterranean peoples found themselves at some disadvantage, for their manufactured products were less sophisticated than those of eastern Asia; thus, they typically exported animal skins, precious metals, and even exotic African animals for Asian zoos in return for the spices and artistic products of the east.

For all the importance of trade, merchants enjoyed a somewhat ambiguous status in classical Mediterranean civilization. Leading Athenian merchants were usually foreigners, mostly from the trading peoples of the Middle East—the descendants of Lydians and Phoenicians. Merchants had a somewhat higher status in Rome, clearly forming the second most prestigious social class under the landed patricians, but here, too, the aristocracy frequently disputed the merchants' rights. Overall, merchants fared better in the Mediterranean than in China, in terms of official recognition, but worse than in India; classical Mediterranean society certainly did not set in motion a culture that distinctly valued capitalist moneymaking.

Slavery was another key ingredient of the classical economy. Philosophers such as Aristotle produced elaborate justifications for the necessity of slavery in a proper society. Athenians used slaves as household servants and also as workers in their vital silver mines, which provided the manpower for Athens' empire and commercial operations alike. Sparta used slaves extensively for agricultural work. Slavery spread steadily in Rome from the final centuries of the republic. Since most slaves came from conquered territories, the need for slaves was another key element in military expansion. Here was a theme visible in earlier civilizations in the eastern Mediterranean, and within later societies in this region as well, that helps explain the greater importance of military forces and expansion in these areas than in India or China. Roman slaves performed household tasks—including the tutoring of upper-class children, for which cultured Greek slaves were highly valued. They also worked the mines, for precious metals and for iron; as in Greece, slave labor in the mines was particularly brutal, and few slaves survived more than a few years of such an existence. Roman estate owners used large numbers of slaves for agricultural work, along with paid laborers and tenant farmers. This practice was another source of the steady pressure placed upon free farmers who could not easily compete with unpaid forced labor.

Partly because of slavery, partly because of the overall orientation of upper-class culture, neither Greece nor Rome was especially interested in technological innovations applicable to agriculture or manufacturing. The Greeks made important advances in shipbuilding and navigation, which were vital for their trading economy. Romans, less adept on the water, developed their skill in engineering to provide greater urban amenities and good roads for the swift and easy movement of troops. But a technology designed to improve the production of food or manufactured goods did not figure largely in this civilization, which mainly relied on the earlier achievements of previous Mediterranean societies. Abundant slave labor probably discouraged concern for more efficient production methods. So did a sense that the true goals of humankind were artistic and political. One Hellenistic scholar, for example, refused to write a handbook on engineering because "the work of an engineer and everything that ministers to the needs of life is ignoble and vulgar." As a consequence of this

Document

Rome and a Values Crisis

Rome's increasing contact with the eastern Mediterranean, particularly Greece, brought important debates about culture. Many conservatives deplored Greek learning and argued that it would corrupt Roman virtue. Cicero, a leading politician in the Senate and a major Latin writer, here defends Greek literature, using Hellenistic justifications of beauty and utility. Cicero played a major role in popularizing Greek culture during the 1st century B.C.E. His comments also reflect the concerns that Greek culture inspired a source of change.

Do you think that I could find inspiration for my daily speeches on so manifold a variety of topics, did I not cultivate my mind with study, or that my mind could endure so great a strain, did not study provide it with relaxation? I am a votary of literature, and make the confession unashamed; shame belongs rather to the bookish recluse, who knows not how to apply his reading to the good of his fellows, or to manifest its fruits to the eyes of all. But what shame should be mine, gentlemen, who have made it a rule of my life for all these years never to allow the sweets of a cloistered ease or the seductions of pleasure or the enticements of repose to prevent me from aiding any man in the hour of his need? How then can I justly be blamed or censured, if it shall be found that I have devoted to literature a portion of my leisure hours no longer than others without blame devote to the pursuit of material gain, to the celebration of festivals or games, to pleasure and the repose of mind and body, to protracted banqueting, or perhaps to the gaming-board or to ballplaying? I have the better right to indulgence herein, because my devotion to letters strengthens my oratorical powers, and these, such as they are, have never failed my friends in their hour of peril. Yet insignificant though these powers may seem to be, I fully realize from what source I draw all that is highest in them. Had I not persuaded myself from my youth up, thanks to the moral lessons derived from a wide reading, that nothing is to be greatly sought after in this life save glory and honour, and that in their quest all bodily pains and all dangers of death or exile should be lightly accounted, I should never have borne for the safety of you all the brunt of many a bitter encounter, or bared my breast to the daily onsets of abandoned persons. All literature, all philosophy, all history, abounds with incentives to noble action, incentives which would be buried in black darkness were the light of the written word not flashed upon them. How many pictures of high endeavor the great authors of Greece and Rome have drawn for our use, and bequeathed to us, not only for our contemplation, but for our emulation! These I have held ever before my vision throughout my public career, and have guided the workings of my brain and my soul by meditating upon patterns of excellence.

But let us for the moment waive these solid advantages; let us assume that entertainment is the sole end of reading; even so, I think you would hold that no mental employment is so broadening to the sympathies or so enlightening to the understanding. Other pursuits belong not to all times, all ages, all conditions; but this gives stimulus to our youth and diversion to our old age; this adds a charm to success, and offers a haven of consolation to failure. In the home it delights, in the world it hampers not. Through the night watches, on all our journeying, and in our hours of country ease, it is an unfailing companion.

If anyone thinks that the glory won by the writing of Greek verse is naturally less than that accorded to the poet who writes in Latin, he is entirely in the wrong. Greek literature is read in nearly every nation under heaven, while the vogue of Latin is confined to its own boundaries, and they are, we must grant, narrow. Seeing, therefore, that the activities of our race know no barrier save the limits of the round earth, we ought to be ambitious that whithersoever our arms have penetrated there also our fame and glory should extend; for the reason that literature exalts the nation whose high deeds it sings, and at the same time there can be no doubt that those who stake their lives to fight in honour's cause find therein a lofty incentive to peril and endeavor. We read that Alexander the Great carried in his train numbers of epic poets and historians. And yet, standing before the tomb of Achilles at Sigeum, he exclaimed, "Fortunate youth, to have found in Homer an herald of thy valor!" Well might he so exclaim, for had the *Iliad* never existed, the same mound which covered Achilles' bones would also have overwhelmed his memory.

Questions: What kind of objections to Greek learning is Cicero arguing against? Which of his arguments had the most lasting appeal to those who were reshaping Roman culture? Can you think of similar debates about foreign culture in other times and places in history? How would you use this document to reconstruct the debate Cicero was participating in and why it seemed important?

Source: Cicero, *Pro Archia Poeta*. Translated by N. H. Watts. Loeb Classical Library. Cicero, Pro Archia (Harvard University Press, 1965), 12–14, 16, 23–24.

outlook, Mediterranean society lagged behind both India and China in production technology, which was one reason for its resulting unfavorable balance of trade with eastern Asia.

Both Greek and Roman society emphasized the importance of a tight family structure, with a husband and father firmly in control. Women had vital economic functions, particularly in farming and artisan families. In the upper classes, especially in Rome, women often commanded great influence and power within a household. But in law and culture, women were held inferior. Families burdened with too many children sometimes put female infants to death because of their low status and their potential drain on the family economy. Pericles stated common beliefs about women when he noted, "For a woman not to show more weakness than is natural to her sex is a great glory, and not to be talked about for good or for evil among men." Early Roman law stipulated that "the husband is the judge of his wife. If she commits a fault, he punishes her; if she has drunk wine, he condemns her; if she has been guilty of adultery, he kills her." (Later, however, such customs were held in check by family courts composed of members of both families.) Here was a case where Roman legal ideas modified traditional family controls. If divorced because of adultery, a Roman woman lost a third of her property and had to wear a special garment that set her apart like a prostitute. On the other hand, the oppression of women was probably less severe in this civilization than in China. Many Greek and Roman women were active in business and controlled a portion, even if only the minority, of all urban property.

Because of the divisions within classical Mediterranean society, no easy generalizations about culture or achievement can be made. An 18th-century English historian called the high point of the Roman Empire, before 180 C.E., the period in human history "during which the condition of the human race was most happy or prosperous." This is doubtful, given the technological accomplishments of China and India. And certainly, many slaves, women, and ordinary farmers in the Mediterranean world itself might have disagreed with this viewpoint. Few farmers, for example, actively participated in the political structures or cultural opportunities that were the most obvious mark of this civilization. Many continued to work largely as their ancestors had done, with quite similar tools and in very similar poverty, untouched by the doings of the great or the bustle of the cities except when wars engulfed their lands.

We are tempted, of course, exclusively to remember the urban achievements, for they exerted the greatest influence on later ages that recalled the glories of Greece and Rome. The distinctive features of classical Mediterranean social and family structures had a less enduring impact, although ideas about slavery or women were revived in subsequent periods. However, the relatively unchanging face of ordinary life had an important influence as well, as many farmers and artisans long maintained the habits and outlook they developed during the great days of the Greek and Roman empires, and because their separation from much of the official culture posed both a challenge and opportunity for new cultural movements such as Christianity.

Toward the Fall of Rome

 Rome began to decline after about 180 C.E. Symptoms were gradual, including loss of territory and economic reversals. Ultimately, Rome was periodically invaded and the empire finally collapsed.

Classical Mediterranean society had one final impact on world history through its rather fragmentary collapse. Unlike China, classical civilization in the Mediterranean region was not simply disrupted only to revive. Unlike India, there was no central religion, derived from the civilization itself, to serve as link between the classical period and what followed. Furthermore, the fall of Rome was not uniform; in essence, Rome fell more in some parts of the Mediterranean than it did in others. The result, among other things, was that no single civilization ultimately rose to claim the mantle of Greece and Rome. At the same time, there was no across-the-board maintenance of the classical Mediterranean institutions and values in any of the civilizations that later claimed a relationship to the Greek and Roman past. Greece and Rome would live on, in more than idle memory, but their heritage was unquestionably more complex and more selective than proved to be the case for India or China.

GLOBAL CONNECTIONS: Greece, Rome, and the World

Like other classical civilizations, and notably China, classical Greeks had a definite sense of the inferiority of the non-Greek world, which they indiscriminately called barbarian. Some Greek city-states, like Sparta, were quite closed to outside influences. But overall, the Greeks were also a trading and expansionist people. They set up Greek colonies in various parts of the Mediterranean. They traded even more widely, and relied heavily on foreigners for part of this trade. Some Greeks were immensely curious about other peoples and their habits. The historian and traveler Herodotus (484–425 B.C.E.) talked enthusiastically about customs very different from his own, though he was also capable of believing wild exaggerations about how some people lived.

Greek outreach was obviously extended by Alexander the Great, who did not have such a keen belief in Greek superiority. Alexander forged important new contacts between the eastern Mediterranean, the rest of the Middle East, and western India. He even hoped to extend his system into China, but obviously this did not occur. The system did not last, but the interest in setting up stronger links with Asia remained an important concern. The Greek world, in other words, was a Mediterranean world, looking eastward primarily, though also to northeastern Africa.

During the early centuries of Rome's development, its leaders were quite conscious of a wider Mediterranean world. Rome's expansion reflected this awareness of powerful competitors. The wars with Carthage brought Rome into contact, and ultimate victory, with a powerful state in north Africa. Roman leaders were also alert to the influence of Greek culture in the eastern Mediterranean. Some feared elaborate Greek art and lifestyles as a distraction from pure Roman virtue, but even more were drawn to the benefit of further incorporating Greek culture. The movement toward the east drew Rome into interaction with many Middle Eastern peoples, as far as Persia.

At the height of the empire, Rome seemed to have created its own world. There was trade on the fringes of the empire. On the northern border in Europe, Germanic tribes learned about the empire through trade and occasional fighting. This helped some decide, ultimately, that they wanted to move into the empire directly. Trade also occurred with other parts of Africa, particularly in the northeast. Wealthy Romans were also quite aware of luxury goods from Asia, particularly Chinese silks, though they knew almost nothing of China itself. The goods were brought to the Mediterranean by nomadic merchants. But the big focus in Rome was internal development in a territory that clearly surpassed any empire ever established in the area. Tolerant of local diversities, Romans also built the same kinds of monuments and amenities in Asia, Africa, and Europe—a testimony to their confidence in the validity of their own styles and to their sense that there was little to learn beyond their borders.

Further Readings

There are a number of excellent sources on classical Greece and Rome, even aside from translations of the leading thinkers and writers. See M. Crawford, ed., *Sources for Ancient History* (1983); C. Fornara, *Translated Documents of Greece and Rome* (1977); N. Lewis, *Greek Historical Documents: The Fifth Century B.C.* (1971); M. Crawford, *The Roman Republic* (1982); P. Green, *Alexander to Actium: The Historical Evolution of the Hellenistic Ages* (1990); and M. M. Austin, *The Hellenistic World from Alexander to the Roman Conquest* (1981). Useful surveys on ancient Greece include K. Dover, *The Greeks* (1981), and F. J. Frost, *Greek Society* (1980). Important specialized works include M. Crawford and D. Whitehead, *Archaic and Classical Greece* (1983); Cyril Robinson, *Everyday Life in Ancient Greece* (1987); W. Burkert, *Greek Religions* (1985); G. E.R. Lloyd, *The Revolutions of Wisdom: Studies in the Claims and Practices of Ancient Greek Science* (1987); Sarah Pomeroy, *Goddesses, Whores, Wives, and Slaves: Women in Classical Antiquity* (1975); A. R. Burn, *Persia and the Greeks* (1962); and Moses Finley, *Slavery in the Ancient World* (1972). On Rome, K. Christ, *The Romans: An Introduction to Their History and Civilization* (1984), is eminently readable and provocative. See also M. Crawford, *The Roman Republic* (1978); L. P. Wilkinson, *The Roman Experience* (1974); B. Cunliffe, *Rome and the Empire* (1978); Cyril Robinson, *Everyday Life in Ancient Rome* (1987); J. Boardman et al., *Oxford History of the Classical World* (1986); and R. Saller, *The Roman Empire* (1987).

On early history, see H. H. Scullard, *A History of the Roman World, 753–146 B.C.* (1961). For social aspects, good sources include R. MacMuleen, *Roman Social Relations, 50* B.C.–A.D. *284* (1981); P. Garnsey and R. Saller, *The Roman Empire: Economy, Society and Culture* (1987); K. Hopkins, *Conquerors and Slaves, Slaves and Masters in the Roman Empire* (1987); K. R. Bradley and W. Philips Jr., *Slavery from Roman Times to the Early Transatlantic Trade* (1985); Peter Gamsey and R. Saller, *The Roman Empire: Economy, Society, and Culture* (1987); and Y. Garlan, *War in the Ancient World* (1975).

A useful reference on women's history in the classical period is R. Bridenthal and C. Koonz, eds., *Becoming Visible: Women in European History* (1977); see also M. Lefkowitz and M. Faut, *Women and Life in Greece and Rome* (1992). The rise and spread of Christianity are treated in two outstanding studies, R. MacMullen, *Christianizing the Roman Empire* (1984), and Peter Brown, *The World of Late Antiquity, A.D. 150–750* (1971).

On the Web

For Web sites on Alexander, see http://www.mediatime.net/alex; on Greek religion, see http://www.greekcivpdx.edu/religion/relig.htm; for a virtual tour of ancient Athens and Rome, see http://www.in-athens.com/archeological/acropolis.htm and http://library.thinkquest.org/11402/homeforum.html; on Roman women, see http://library.thinkquest.org/11402/womeninrome.html.

CHAPTER 5

THE CLASSICAL PERIOD: DIRECTIONS, DIVERSITIES, AND DECLINES BY 500 C.E.

The conversion of kings, such as Clovis, king of the Franks, helped inspire wider conversions and gave the clergy some symbolic power over the state. This relief shows Clovis being converted to Christianity.

- Expansion and Integration
- Beyond the Classical Civilizations
- **IN DEPTH:** Nomads and Cross-Civilization Contacts and Exchanges
- Decline in China and India
- Decline and Fall in Rome
- The New Religious Map
- **DOCUMENT:** The Popularization of Buddhism
- **VISUALIZING THE PAST:** Religious Geography
- **GLOBAL CONNECTIONS:** The Late Classical Period and the World

The basic themes of the three great classical civilizations involved expansion and integration. From localized beginnings in northern China, the Ganges region, or the Aegean Sea, commercial, political, and cultural outreach pushed civilization through the Middle Kingdom and beyond, through the Indian subcontinent, and into the western Mediterranean. The growth set in motion deliberate but also implicit attempts to pull the new civilizations together in more than name. Correspondingly, the most telling comparisons among the three classical civilizations—identifying similarities as well as differences—involve this same process of integration and some of the problems it encountered.

Throughout the classical world, integration and expansion faltered between 200 and 500 C.E. Decline, even collapse, began to afflict civilization first in China, then in the Mediterranean, and finally in India. These developments signaled the end of the classical era and ushered in important new themes in world history that would define the next major period. The response of major religions to political decline formed a leading direction for world history to come.

Classical civilizations (including Persia) had never embraced the bulk of the territory around the globe, although they did include the majority of the world's population. Developments outside the classical orbit had rhythms of their own during the classical period, and they would gain new prominence as the great civilizations themselves faltered. This describes the third historical theme—along with basic comparisons and the process of decline and attendant religious responses—that must be addressed in moving from the classical period to world history's next phase.

Expansion and Integration

 Common themes for the classical civilizations involve territorial expansion and related efforts to integrate the new territories. Integration included a mixture of central political values and institutions, common cultures and social values, and commercial links.

The heritage of the classical civilizations involves a host of new ideas, styles, technologies, and institutions. Many of these arose as part of the broad process of adjusting to the expansion of civilization. Thus, it was not entirely accidental that in scarcely more than a century, between about 550 and 400 B.C.E., seminal thinkers arose in all three civilizations—Confucius and Laozi, Buddha, and Socrates. The thinkers had no contact with each other, and their specific ideas varied widely. However, all three were inspired by the common need to articulate central values in their respective societies, as part of a larger process of generating a shared culture on the basis of which their expanding societies might operate.

1000 B.C.E.	1 C.E.	250 C.E.	500 C.E.
c. 1000 Polynesians reach Fiji, Samoa **1000** Independent kingdom of Kush **800–400** Spread of Olmec civilization: cultivation of maize (corn), potatoes; domestication of turkeys, dogs **c. 300** Rise of Axum	**c. 30** Crucifixion of Jesus **c. 100** Root crops introduced to southern Africa through trade **100** Beginning of decline of Han dynasty **180** Rome begins to decay **c. 200** Extensive agriculture in Japan **227** Beginning of Sassanid Empire in Persia	**284–305** Reign of Diocletian **c. 300** Ethiopia adopts Christianity **c. 312–337** Reign of Constantine **370–480** Nomadic invasions of western Europe **c. 400** Growth of Mayan civilization **c. 400** Polynesians reach Hawaii **450** Huns begin to invade India **476** Collapse of Rome	**c. 500** Buddhism takes root in east and southeast Asia **c. 500** Formation of Ghana **c. 600** Beginning of Islam **618** Tang dynasty in China: glorious cultural period **700** Shintoism unified into single national religion in Japan

China, India, and the Mediterranean set about the tasks of uniting their expanding civilizations in different ways. China emphasized greater centralization, particularly in politics, generating a political culture to match. India and the Mediterranean remained more localized and diverse. India, however, used key religious values, and particularly the spread of Hinduism, to cement its civilization even across political boundaries. Mediterranean cultural achievements spread widely also, but involved less of the population—one reason the region proved more vulnerable to fragmentation after its political unity collapsed under Rome.

Integration involved two basic issues, the most obvious of which was territorial. China had to reign in its new southern regions, and the government devoted considerable attention to settling some northerners in the south, promoting a common language for the elite, and other techniques. The southward spread of the caste system and ultimately Hinduism in India addressed territorial issues. Rome combined considerable local autonomy and tolerance with common laws, the expansion of citizenship to elites across the empire, and a tight commercial network that created interdependencies between grain-growing regions and the olive and grape regions.

The second challenge to integration was social. All three classical civilizations fostered great inequalities between men and women and between upper and lower classes. The nature of the inequalities varied, from Mediterranean slavery to the Indian caste system to the Confucian sense of hierarchy; these differences were significant. Nevertheless, the assumption of inequality as normal was common to all three societies. Most leading thinkers—Buddha was an exception—did not oppose inequalities, writing openly of the need for deference and even (in the case of the Mediterranean) for slavery.

All the classical civilizations made some efforts to maintain a basic social cohesion while acknowledging inequality. None took the modern, Western-inspired route of arguing for opportunities of upward mobility. Confucianism stressed mutual respect between upper and lower classes, along with special deference on the part of the lower social orders. Shared values about family and self-restraint provided some further links across the social hierarchy. Mediterranean aristocrats treated some locals as clients, offering them protection; they also supported civic rituals intended to foster loyalty. India offered a religion that was shared by all social classes and gave the hope of future incarnation to the lower castes. None of these approaches consistently united the society. Lower-class risings, even slave rebellions, were part of the classical experience as well. On balance, however, some techniques may have worked better than others. Again, as the Roman Empire fell, many elements of the lower classes quickly turned their attention to other interests. This suggests that here, too, the integration of Mediterranean society was slightly more tenuous than that of the classical civilizations of Asia.

Beyond the Classical Civilizations

 Outside the classical civilizations important development occurred in other parts of the world. Significant civilizations operated in the Americas and also in Africa outside the immediate classical orbit. Agriculture and other developments occurred in northern Europe and northern Asia. Nomadic societies played a vital role, particularly in central Asia, in linking and occasionally disrupting classical civilizations.

Although the development of the three great civilizations is the central thread in world history during the classical period, significant changes also occurred in other parts of the world. On the borders of the major civilizations, as in northeastern Africa, Japan, and northern Europe, these changes bore some relationship to the classical world, although they were partly autonomous. Elsewhere, most notably in the Americas, new cultures evolved in an entirely independent way. In all cases, changes during the classical period set the stage for more important links in world history later on. Southeast Asia gained access to civilization during the classical period mainly through its contacts with India. Regional kingdoms had already been established, and agricultural economies were familiar on the principal islands of Indonesia as well as on the mainland. Participation in wider trade patterns developed through the efforts of Indian merchants. Hindu and particularly Buddhist religion and art also spread from India. Here was a case of the outright expansion of civilization without the creation of a fully distinctive or unified culture.

A similar case of expansion from an established civilization affected parts of sub-Saharan Africa; indeed, in this case the interaction had begun well before the rise of Greece and Rome. By the year 1000 B.C.E., the independent kingdom of Kush was flourishing along the upper Nile. It possessed a form of writing derived from Egyptian hieroglyphics (and which has not yet been fully deciphered) and mastered the use of iron. Briefly, around 750 B.C.E., armies from Kush conquered Egypt (Figure 5.1). Major cities were built. The Kushites seem to have established a strong monarchy, with elaborate ceremonies illustrating a belief that the king was divine. The kingdom of Kush was defeated by a rival kingdom called **Axum** by about 300 B.C.E.; Axum ultimately fell to another regional kingdom, **Ethiopia.** Axum and Ethiopia had active contacts with the eastern Mediterranean world until after the fall of Rome. They traded with this region for several centuries. The activities of Jewish merchants brought some conversions to Judaism, and a small minority of Ethiopians have remained Jewish to the present day. Greek-speaking merchants also had considerable influence, and it was through them that Christianity was brought to Ethiopia by the fourth century C.E. The Ethiopian Christian church, however, was cut off from mainstream Christianity thereafter, flourishing in isolation to modern times. And Ethiopia could boast, into the late 20th century when it was abolished, of having the oldest continuous monarchy anywhere in the world.

Figure 5.1 *This tomb painting from about 1300 B.C.E. highlights black-skinned people from the rising kingdom of Kush, who interacted increasingly with Egyptian society and at one point controlled Egypt directly.*

In Depth

Nomads and Cross-Civilization Contacts and Exchanges

Through much of recorded human history, nomadic peoples have been key agents of contact between sedentary, farming peoples and town dwellers in centers of civilization across the globe. Nomadic peoples pioneered all the great overland routes that linked the civilized cores of Eurasia in ancient times and the Middle Ages. The most famous were the fabled **Silk Roads** that ran from western China across the mountains and steppes of central Asia to the civilized centers of Mesopotamia in the last millennium B.C.E. and to Rome, the Islamic heartlands, and western Europe in the first millennium and a half C.E.

Chinese rulers at one end of these trading networks, and Roman emperors and later Islamic sultans at the other end, often had to send their armies to do battle with hostile nomads, whose raids threatened to cut off the flow of trade. But perhaps more often, pastoral peoples played critical roles in establishing and expanding trading links. For periodic payments by

merchants and imperial bureaucrats, they provided protection from bandits and raiding parties for caravans passing through their grazing lands. For further payments, nomadic peoples supplied animals to transport both the merchants' goods and the food and drink needed by those in the caravan parties. At times, pastoralists themselves took charge of transport and trading, but it was more common for the trading operations to be controlled by specialized merchants. These merchants were based either in the urban centers of the civilized cores or in the trading towns that grew up along the silk road in central Asia, the oases of Arabia, and the savanna zones that bordered on the north and south the vast Sahara desert in Africa.

Until they were supplanted by the railroads and steamships of the Industrial Revolution, the overland trading routes of Eurasia and the Americas, along with comparable networks established for sailing vessels, were the most important channels for contacts

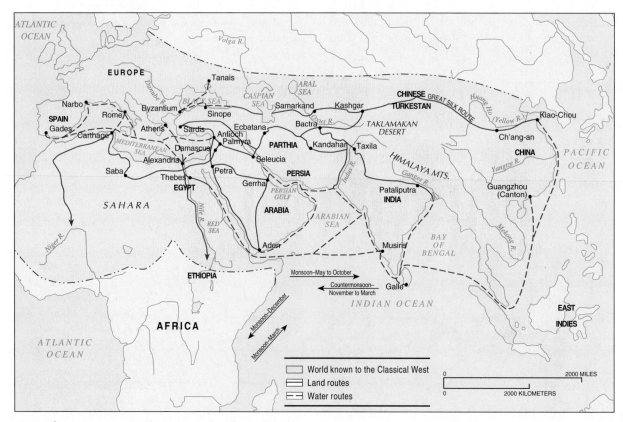

Main African–Eurasian Trade Routes in the Classical Age

between civilizations. Religions such as Buddhism and Islam spread peacefully along the trading routes throughout central Asia, Persia, and Africa. Artistic motifs and styles, such as those developed in the cosmopolitan Hellenistic world created by Alexander the Great's conquests, were spread by trading contacts in northern Africa, northern India, and western China.

Inventions that were vital to the continued growth and expansion of the civilized cores were carried in war and peace by traders or nomadic peoples from one center to another. For example, central Asian steppe nomads who had been converted to Islam clashed with the armies of the Chinese Empire in the 8th century C.E. The victorious Muslims found craftspeople among their prisoners who knew the secrets of making paper, which had been invented many centuries earlier by the Chinese. The combination of nomadic mobility and established trading links resulted in the rapid diffusion of papermaking techniques to Mesopotamia and Egypt in the 8th and 9th centuries and across northern Africa to Europe in the centuries that followed.

Nomadic warriors also contributed to the spread of new military technologies and modes of warfare, particularly across the great Eurasian land mass. Sedentary peoples often adopted the nomads' reliance on heavy cavalry and hit-and-run tactics. Saddles, bits, and bow and arrow designs developed by nomadic herders were avidly imitated by farming societies. And defense against nomadic assaults inspired some of the great engineering feats of the preindustrial world, most notably the Great Wall of China (discussed in Chapter 2). It also spurred the development of gunpowder and cannons in China, where the threat of nomadic incursions persisted well into the 19th century.

In addition, nomadic peoples have served as agents for the transfer of food crops between distant civilized cores, even if they did not usually themselves cultivate the plants being exchanged. In a less constructive vein, nomadic warriors have played a key role in transmitting diseases. In the best-documented instance of this pattern, Mongol cavalrymen carried the bacterium that causes the strain of the plague that came to be known as the Black Death from central Asia to China in the 14th century. They may also have transmitted it to the West, where it devastated the port cities of the Black Sea region and was later carried by merchant ships to the Middle East and southern Europe.

Questions: What other groups played roles as intermediaries between civilizations in early global history? What features of the nomads' culture and society rendered them ideal agents for transmitting technology, trade goods, crops, and diseases between different cultural zones? Why have the avenues of exchange they provided been open only for limited time spans and then blocked for years or decades at a time? What agents of transmission have taken the place of nomadic peoples in recent centuries?

It is not clear how much influence, if any, the kingdoms of the upper Nile had on the later history of sub-Saharan Africa. Knowledge of ironworking certainly spread, facilitating the expansion of agriculture in other parts of the continent. Patterns of strong, ceremonial kingship—sometimes called divine kingship—would surface in other parts of Africa later, but whether this occurred through some contact with the Kushite tradition or independently is not known. Knowledge of Kushite writing did not spread, which suggests that the impact of this first case of civilization below the Sahara was somewhat limited.

For most of Africa below the Sahara, but north of the great tropical jungles, the major development up to 500 C.E. was the further extension of agriculture. Well-organized villages arose, often very similar in form and structure to those that still exist. Farming took earliest root on the southern fringes of the **Sahara,** which was less arid than it is today. Toward the end of the classical era, important regional kingdoms were forming in western Africa, leading to the first great state in the region—Ghana. Because of the barriers of dense vegetation and the impact of African diseases on domesticated animals, agriculture spread only slowly southward. However, the creation of a strong agricultural economy did prepare the way for the next, more long-lasting and influential wave of African kingdoms, far to the west of the Nile. New crops, including root crops and plantains introduced through trade with southeast Asia about 100 C.E., helped African farmers push into new areas.

Advances in agriculture and manufacturing also occurred in other parts of the world besides sub-Saharan Africa. In northern Europe and Japan, there was no question, as yet, of elaborate contacts with the great civilizations, no counterpart to the influences that affected parts of southeast Asia and the upper Nile valley. Japan, by the year 200 C.E., had established extensive agriculture. The population of the islands had been formed mainly by migrations from the peninsula of Korea, over a 200,000-year span. These migrations had ceased by the year 200. In Japan, a regional political organization based on tribal chiefs evolved; each tribal group had its own god, thought of as an ancestor. A Chinese visitor in 297 described the Japanese as law-abiding, fond of drink, expert at agriculture and fishing; they observed strict social differences, indicated by tattoos or other body markings. Japan had also developed considerable ironworking; interestingly, the Japanese seem to have skipped the stage of using bronze and copper tools, moving directly from stone tools to iron. Finally, regional states in Japan became increasingly sophisticated, each controlling somewhat larger territories. In 400 C.E., one such state brought in scribes from Korea to keep records—this represented the introduction of writing in the islands.

Japan's religion, **Shintoism,** provided for the worship of political rulers and the spirits of nature, including the all-important god of rice. Many local shrines and rituals revolved around Shinto beliefs, which became unified into a single national religion by 700 C.E. However, this was a simple religion, rather different in ritual and doctrine from the great world religions and philosophies developing in the classical civilizations. Something like national politics arose only around 400 C.E., when one regional ruler began to win the loyalty and trust of other local leaders; this was the basis for Japan's imperial house, with the emperor worshipped as a religious figure. Such growing political sophistication and national cultural unity were just emerging by 600 C.E., however. It was at this point that Japan was ready for more elaborate contacts with China—a process that would move Japan squarely into the orbit of major civilizations.

Much of northern Europe lagged behind Japan's pace. Teutonic or Celtic peoples in what is today Germany, England, and Scandinavia, and Slavic peoples in much of eastern Europe, were loosely organized into regional kingdoms. Some, in Germany and England, had succumbed to the advances of the distant Roman Empire, but after Rome's decline the patterns of regional politics resumed. There was no written language, except in cases where Latin had been imported. Agriculture, often still combined with hunting, was rather primitive. Scandinavians were developing increasing skill as sailors, which would lead them into wider trade and pillage in the centuries after 600 C.E. Religious beliefs featured a host of gods and rituals designed to placate the forces of nature. This region would change, particularly through the spread of the religious and intellectual influences of Christianity. However, these shifts still lay in the future, and even conversions to Christianity did not bring northern and eastern Europe into the orbit of a single civilization. Until about 1000 C.E., northern Europe remained one of the most backward areas in the world.

Yet another portion of the world was developing civilization by 600 C.E.—indeed, its progress was greater than that of much of Europe and Africa. In Central America, an Indian group called the Olmecs developed and spread an early form of civilization from about 800 until 400 B.C.E. The Olmecs seem to have lacked writing, but they produced massive, pyramid-shaped religious monuments.

The first American civilization was based on many centuries of advancing agriculture, expanding from the early cultivation of corn. Initially, in the wild state, corn ears were scarcely larger than strawberries, but patient breeding gradually converted this grain into a staple food crop. In the Andes areas of South America, root crops were also grown, particularly the potato. The development of American agriculture was limited by the few domesticated animals available—turkeys, dogs, and guinea pigs in Central America. Nevertheless, **Olmec culture** displayed many impressive achievements. It explored artistic forms in precious stones such as jade. Religious statues and icons blended human images with those of animals. Scientific research produced accurate and impressive calendars. Olmec culture, in its religious and artistic emphases, powerfully influenced later Indian civilizations in Central America. The Olmecs themselves disappeared without a clear trace around 400 B.C.E., but their successors soon developed a hieroglyphic alphabet and built the first great city—**Teotihuacan**—in the Americas, as a center for trade and worship. This culture, in turn, suffered setbacks from migrations and regional wars but from its base developed a still fuller American civilization, starting with the **Maya,** from about 400 C.E. onward.

In essence, the Olmecs and their successors had provided for the Central American region the equivalent of the river valley civilizations in Asia and the Middle East, although many centuries later (Map 5.1). A similar early civilization arose in the Andes region in present-day Peru and Bolivia, where careful agriculture allowed the construction of elaborate cities and religious monuments. This culture would lead, later, to the civilization of the **Inca.** The two centers of early civilization in the Americas developed

Map 5.1 *Civilizations of Central and South America*

in total isolation from developments elsewhere in the world. As a result, they lacked certain advantages that come from the ability to copy and react to other societies, including such basic technologies as the wheel or the capacity to work iron. However, the early American Indian cultures were considerably ahead of most of those in Europe during the same period. And they demonstrate the common, although not invariable, tendency of humans to move from the establishment of agriculture to the creation of the more elaborate trappings of a civilized society.

Another case of isolated development featured the migration of agricultural peoples to new island territories in the Pacific. **Polynesian** peoples had reached islands such as Fiji and Samoa by 1000 B.C.E. Further explorations in giant outrigger canoes led to the first settlement of island complexes such as Hawaii by 400 C.E., where the new settlers adapted local plants, brought in new animals (notably pigs), and imported a highly stratified caste system under powerful local kings.

Agriculture, in sum, expanded into new areas during the classical period; early civilizations, or early contacts, were also forming. These developments were not central to world history during the classical period itself, but they folded into the larger human experience thereafter.

The herding peoples of central Asia also contributed to world history, particularly toward the end of the classical period. Some nomadic groups gained new contacts with established civilizations, like China, which brought changes in political organization as well as some new goals for conquest. Central Asian herders played a vital role in trade routes between east Asia and the Middle East, transporting goods like silk across long distances. Other herding groups produced important technological innovations, such as the stirrup, which allowed mounted horsemen to aim weapons better. The herding groups thus enjoyed an important history of their own and also provided important contacts among the civilizations that they bordered. Finally, perhaps because of internal population pressure as well as new appetites and opportunities, herding groups invaded the major civilizations directly, helping to bring the classical period as a whole to an end.

Decline in China and India

 A combination of internal weakness and invasion led to important changes, first in China, then in India.

Between 200 and 600 C.E., all three classical civilizations collapsed entirely or in part. During this four-century span, all suffered from outside invasions, the result of growing incursions by groups from central Asia. This renewed wave of nomadic expansion was not as sweeping as the earlier Indo-European growth, which had spread over India and much of the Mediterranean region many centuries before, but it severely tested the civilized regimes. Rome, of course, fell directly to Germanic invaders, who fought on partly because they were, in turn, harassed by the fierce Asiatic Huns. The Huns themselves swept once across Italy, invading the city of Rome amid great destruction. Another Hun group from central Asia overthrew the Guptas in India, and similar nomadic tribes had earlier toppled the Chinese Han dynasty. The central Asian nomads were certainly encouraged by a growing realization of the weakness of the classical regimes. For Han China as well as the later Roman Empire suffered from serious internal problems long before the invaders dealt the final blows. And the Guptas in India

had not permanently resolved that area's tendency to dissolve into political fragmentation.

By about 100 C.E., the Han dynasty in China began to enter a serious decline. Confucian intellectual activity gradually became less creative. Politically, the central government's control diminished, bureaucrats became more corrupt, and local landlords took up much of the slack, ruling their neighborhoods according to their own wishes. The free peasants, long heavily taxed, were burdened with new taxes and demands of service by these same landlords. Many lost their farms and became day laborers on the large estates. Some had to sell their children into service. Social unrest increased, producing a great revolutionary effort led by Daoists in 184 C.E. Daoism now gained new appeal, shifting toward a popular religion and adding healing practices and magic to earlier philosophical beliefs. The Daoist leaders, called the **Yellow Turbans,** promised a golden age that was to be brought about by divine magic. The Yellow Turbans attacked the weakness of the emperor but also the self-indulgence of the current bureaucracy. As many as 30,000 students demonstrated against the decline of government morality. However, their protests failed, and Chinese population growth and prosperity both spiraled further downward. The imperial court was mired in intrigue and civil war.

This dramatic decline paralleled the slightly later collapse of Rome, as we shall see. It obviously explained China's inability to push back invasions from borderland nomads, who finally overthrew the Han dynasty outright. As in Rome, growing political ineffectiveness formed part of the decline. Another important factor was the spread of devastating new epidemics, which may have killed up to half of the population. These combined blows not only toppled the Han, but led to almost three centuries of chaos—an unusually long span of unrest in Chinese history. Regional rulers and weak dynasties rose and fell during this period. Even China's cultural unity was threatened as the wave of Buddhism spread—one of the only cases in which China imported a major idea from outside its borders until the 20th century. Northern China, particularly, seemed near collapse.

Nonetheless, China did revive itself near the end of the 6th century. Strong native rulers in the north drove out the nomadic invaders. The **Sui** dynasty briefly ruled, and then in 618 C.E. it was followed by the **Tang,** who sponsored one of the most glorious periods in Chinese history. Confucianism and the bureaucratic system were revived, and indeed the bureaucratic tradition became more elaborate. The period of chaos left its mark somewhat in the continued presence of a Buddhist minority and new styles in art and literature. But, unlike the case of Rome, there was no permanent disruption.

The structures of classical China were simply too strong to be overturned. The bureaucracy declined in scope and quality, but it did not disappear during the troubled centuries. Confucian values and styles of life remained current among the upper class. Many of the nomadic invaders, seeing that they had nothing better to offer by way of government or culture, simply tried to assimilate the Chinese traditions. China thus had to recover from a serious setback, but it did not have to reinvent its civilization.

The decline of classical civilization in India was less drastic than the collapse of Han China. The ability of the Gupta emperors to control local princes was declining by the 5th century. Invasions by nomadic peoples, probably Hun tribes similar to those who were pressing into Europe, affected some northern portions of India as early as 500 C.E. During the next century, the invaders penetrated much deeper, destroying the Gupta empire in central India. Many of the invaders were integrated into the warrior caste of India, forming a new ruling group of regional princes. For several centuries, no native ruler attempted to build a large Indian state. The regional princes, collectively called **Rajput,** controlled the small states and emphasized military prowess. Few political events of more than local significance occurred.

Within this framework, Indian culture continued to evolve. Buddhism declined further in India proper. Hindu beliefs gained ground, among other things converting the Hun princes, who had originally worshipped gods of battle and had no sympathy for the Buddhist principles of calm and contemplation. Within Hinduism, the worship of a mother goddess, **Devi,** spread widely, encouraging a new popular emotionalism in religious ritual. Indian economic prosperity also continued at high levels.

Although Indian civilization substantially maintained its position, another threat was to come, after 600 C.E., from the new Middle Eastern religion of **Islam.** Arab armies, fighting under the banners of **Allah,** reached India's porous northwestern frontier during the 7th century, and while there was initially little outright conquest on the subcontinent, Islam did win some converts in the northwest. Hindu leaders reacted to the arrival of this new faith by strengthening their emphasis on religious devotion, at the expense of some other intellectual interests. Hinduism also underwent further popularization; Hindu texts were written in vernacular languages such as Hindi, and use of the old classical language, Sanskrit, declined. These reactions were largely successful in preventing more than a minority of Indians from abandoning Hinduism, but they distracted from further achievements in science and mathematics. Islam also hit hard at India's international economic position and affected its larger impact throughout Asia. Arab traders soon wrested control of the Indian Ocean from Tamil merchants, and India, though still prosperous and productive, saw its commercial dynamism reduced. In politics, regionalism continued to prevail. Clearly, the glory days of the Guptas were long past, although classical traditions survived particularly in Hinduism and the caste system.

Decline and Fall in Rome

 Decline in Rome was particularly complex. Its causes have been much debated. Developments varied between the eastern and western portions of the empire as the Mediterranean region pulled apart.

The Roman Empire exhibited a great many symptoms of decay after about 180 C.E. There was statistical evidence in the declining population in addition to growing difficulties in recruiting effective armies. There were also political manifestations in the greater brutality and arbitrariness of many Roman emperors—victims, according to one commentator at the time, of "lustful and cruel habits." Tax collection became increasingly difficult, as residents of the empire fell on hard times. The governor of Egypt complained that "the once numerous inhabitants of the aforesaid villages have now been reduced to a few, because some have fled in poverty and others have died … and for this reason we are in danger owing to impoverishment of having to abandon the tax-collectorship."

Above all, there were human symptoms. Inscriptions on Roman tombstones increasingly ended with the slogan, "I was not, I was, I am not, I have no more desires," suggesting a pervasive despondency over the futility of this life and despair at the absence of an afterlife.

The decline of Rome was more disruptive than the collapse of the classical dynasties in Asia. For this reason, and because memories of the collapse of this great empire became part of the Western tradition, the process of deterioration deserves particular attention. Every so often, Americans or western Europeans concerned about changes in their own society wonder if there might be lessons in Rome's fall that apply to the uncertain future of Western civilization today.

We have seen that the quality of political and economic life in the Roman Empire began to shift after about 180 C.E. Political confusion produced a series of weak emperors and many disputes over succession to the throne. Intervention by the army in the selection of emperors complicated political life and contributed to the deterioration of rule from the top. More important in initiating the process of decline was a series of plagues that swept over the empire. As in China, the plagues' source was growing international trade, which brought diseases endemic in southern Asia to new areas like the Mediterranean, where no resistance had been established even to contagions such as the measles. The resulting diseases decimated the population. The population of Rome decreased from a million people to 250,000. Economic life worsened in consequence. Recruitment of troops became more difficult, so the empire was increasingly reduced to hiring Germanic soldiers to guard its frontiers. The need to pay troops added to the demands on the state's budget, just as declining production cut into tax revenues.

Here, perhaps, is the key to the process of decline: a set of general problems, triggered by a cycle of plagues that could not be prevented, resulting in a rather mechanistic spiral that steadily worsened. However, there is another side to Rome's downfall, although whether as a cause or result of the initial difficulties is hard to say. Rome's upper classes became steadily more pleasure-seeking, turning away from the political devotion and economic vigor that had characterized the republic and early empire. Cultural life decayed. Aside from some truly creative Christian writers—the fathers of Western theology—there was very little sparkle to the art or literature of the later empire. Many Roman scholars contented themselves with writing textbooks that rather mechanically summarized earlier achievements in science, mathematics, and literary style. Writing textbooks is not, of course, proof of absolute intellectual incompetence—at least, not in all cases—but the point was that new knowledge or artistic styles were not being generated, and even the levels of previous accomplishment began to slip. The later Romans wrote textbooks about rhetoric instead of displaying rhetorical talent in actual political life; they wrote simple compendiums, for example, about animals or geometry, that barely captured the essentials of what earlier intellectuals had known, and often added superstitious beliefs that previous generations would have scorned.

This cultural decline, finally, was not clearly due to disease or economic collapse, for it began in some ways before these larger problems surfaced. Something was happening to the Roman elite, perhaps because of the deadening effect of authoritarian political rule, perhaps because of a new interest in luxuries and sensual indulgence. Revealingly, the upper classes no longer produced many offspring, for bearing and raising children seemed incompatible with a life of pleasure-seeking.

Rome's fall, in other words, can be blamed on large, impersonal forces that would have been hard for any society to control or a moral and political decay that reflected growing corruption among society's leaders. Probably elements of both were involved. Thus, the plagues would have weakened even a vigorous society, but they would not necessarily have produced an irreversible downward spiral had not the morale of the ruling classes already been sapped by an unproductive lifestyle and superficial values.

Regardless of precise causes, the course of Roman decay is quite clear. As the quality of imperial rule declined, as life became more dangerous and economic survival more precarious, many farmers clustered around the protection of large landlords, surrendering full control over their plots of land in the hope of military and judicial protection. The decentralization of political and economic authority, which was greatest in the western, or European, portions of the empire, foreshadowed the manorial system of Europe in the Middle Ages. The system of estates gave great political power to landlords and did provide some local stability. But, in the long run, it weakened the power of the emperor and also tended to move the economy away from the elaborate and successful trade patterns of Mediterranean civilization in its heyday. Many estates tried to be self-sufficient. Trade and production declined further as a result, and cities shrank in size. The empire was locked in a vicious circle, in which responses to the initial deterioration merely lessened the chances of recovery.

Some later emperors tried vigorously to reverse the tide. Diocletian, who ruled from 284 to 305 C.E., tightened up the administration of the empire and tried to improve tax collection. Regulation of the dwindling economy increased. Diocletian also attempted to direct political loyalties to his own per-

the borders of Rome's holdings along the Mediterranean. Parthian conquerors had taken over this portion of Alexander the Great's empire. They produced little culture of their own, being content to rely on Persian styles, but they long maintained an effective military and bureaucratic apparatus. Then, around 227 C.E., a Persian rebellion displaced the Parthians and created a new Sassanid empire that more directly revived the glories of the earlier Persian empire. Persian religious ideas, including the religion of Zoroastrianism, revived, although there was some conversion to Christianity as well. Persian styles in art and manufacturing experienced a brilliant resurgence.

Both the Parthian and the Sassanid empires served as bridges between the Mediterranean and the East, transmitting goods and some artistic and literary styles between the Greek-speaking world and India and China. As the Roman Empire weakened, the Sassanids joined the attack, at times pushing into parts of southeastern Europe. Ultimately, however, the Byzantine Empire managed to create a stable frontier. The Sassanid empire preserved the important strain of Persian culture in the eastern part of the Middle East, and this continued to influence this region as well as India. The Sassanids themselves, however, were finally overthrown by the surge of Arab conquest that followed the rise of Islam, in the 7th century C.E.

Rome's fall, then, did not disrupt the northern Middle East—the original cradle of civilization—as much as might have been expected. Persian rule simply continued in one part of the region, until the Arab onslaught, which itself did not destroy Persian culture. Byzantium maintained many of the traditions of the later Roman Empire, plus Christianity, in the western part of the Middle East and in Greece and other parts of southeastern Europe.

The second zone that devolved from Rome's fall consisted of north Africa and the southeastern shores of the Mediterranean. Here, a number of regional kingdoms briefly succeeded the empire. While Christianity spread into the area—indeed, one of the greatest Christian theologians, **Augustine,** was a bishop in north Africa—its appearance was not so uniformly triumphant as in the Byzantine Empire or western Europe. Furthermore, separate beliefs and doctrines soon split north African Christianity from the larger branches, producing most notably the **Coptic** church in Egypt, which still survives as a Christian minority in that country. Soon this region would be filled with the still newer doctrines of Islam and a new Arab empire.

Finally, there was the western part of the empire—Italy, Spain, and points north. Here is where Rome's fall not only shattered unities but also reduced the level of civilization itself. Crude, regional Germanic kingdoms developed in parts of Italy, France, and elsewhere. Cities shrank still further, and, especially outside Italy, trade almost disappeared. The only clearly vital forces in this region emanated not from Roman traditions but from the spread of Christianity. Even Christianity could not sustain a sophisticated culture of literature or art, however. In the mire of Rome's collapse, this part of the world forgot for several centuries what it had previously known.

In this western domain, what we call the fall of Rome was scarcely noted at the time, for decay had been progressing for so many decades that the failure to name a new emperor meant little. There was some comprehension of loss, some realization that the present could not rival the past. Thus, Christian scholars were soon apologizing for their inability to write well or to understand some of the doctrines of the earlier theologians like Augustine. This sense of inferiority to classical achievements would long mark the culture of this western zone, even as times improved.

The New Religious Map

 The period of classical decline saw the rapid expansion of Buddhism and Christianity. This religious change had wider culture, social, and political implications. Islam would soon be added to the new map of world religions.

The end of the classical period is not simply the story of decay and collapse. This same period, from 200 to 600 C.E., saw the effective rise of many of the world's major religions. The devastating plagues caused new interest in belief systems that could provide solace amid rising death rates. From Spain to China, growing political instability clearly prompted many people to seek solace in joys of the spirit, and while the religious surge was not entirely new, the resulting changes in the religious map of Europe and Asia and the nature and intensity of religious interests were significant new forces. Christianity, born two centuries before Rome's collapse began, became a widespread religion throughout the Mediterranean region as the empire's political strength weakened. Buddhism, although launched still earlier, saw its surge into eastern Asia furthered by the growing problems of classical China. Thus, two major faiths,

Document

The Popularization of Buddhism

Chinese Buddhism, unlike most Chinese beliefs, spread among all regions and social groups. Although it divided into many sects that disagreed over details of theology and rituals by commenting on earlier Buddhist scriptures (the Sutras), many ordinary Chinese believers cared little for such details and were more concerned with direct spiritual benefits. Often they arranged to have Buddhist sermons copied, as a means of obtaining merit, while adding a note of their own. The following passages come from such notes, written mainly in the 6th century. They suggest the various reasons people might go through the challenging process of converting to a new religion.

> Recorded on the 15th day of the fourth month of 531.
>
> The Buddhist lay disciple Yuan Jung—having lived in this degenerate era for many years, fearful for his life, and yearning for home—now makes a donation of a thousand silver coins to the Three Jewels [the Buddha, the Law, and the Monastic Order]. This donation is made in the name of the Celestial King Vaisravana. In addition, he makes a donation of a thousand to ransom himself and his wife and children [from their earthly existence], a thousand more to ransom his servants, and a thousand more to ransom his domestic animals. This money is to be used for copying sutras. It is accompanied by the prayer that the Celestial King may attain Buddhahood; that the disciple's family, servants, and animals may be blessed with long life, may attain enlightenment, and may all be permitted to return to the capital.
>
> Dated the 29th day of the fourth month of 550.
>
> Happiness is not fortuitous: Pray for it and it will respond. Results are not born of thin air: Pay heed to causes and results will follow. This explains how the Buddhist disciple and nun Tao-jung—because her conduct in her previous life was not correct—came to be born in her present form, a woman, vile and unclean.
>
> Now if she does not honor the awesome decree of Buddha, how can future consequences be favorable for her? Therefore, having cut down her expenditures on food and clothing, she reverently has had the Nirvana Sutra copied once. She prays that those who read it carefully will be exalted in mind to the highest realms and that those who communicate its meaning will cause others to be so enlightened.

different in many ways but similar in their emphasis on spiritual life and the importance of divine power, reshaped major portions of Europe and Asia precisely as the structures of the classical period declined or disappeared. Finally, shortly after 600 C.E., an entirely new religion, Islam, surfaced and became the most dynamic force in world history during the next several centuries. In sum, the religious map of the world, although by no means completed by 500 C.E., was beginning to take on dramatic new contours. This means that while civilization in many ways declined, it was also being altered, taking new directions as well as losing some older strengths. Never before had single religions spread so widely, crossing so many cultural and political boundaries.

The newly expanding religions shared some general features. Christianity, Buddhism, and Hinduism (as well as Islam later on) all emphasized intense devotion and piety, stressing the importance of spiritual concerns beyond the daily cares of earthly life. All three offered the hope of a better existence after this life had ended, and each one responded to new political instability and to the growing poverty of people in various parts of the civilized world.

The spread of the major religions meant that hundreds of thousands of people, in Asia, Europe, and Africa, underwent a conversion process as the classical period drew to a close. Radically changing beliefs is an unusual human experience, symptomatic in this case of the new pressures on established political structures and on ordinary life. At the same time, many people blended new beliefs with the old, in a process called *syncretism*. This meant that the religions changed too, sometimes taking on the features of individual civilizations even while maintaining larger religious claims.

Despite these important common features, the major religions were themselves very different. Hinduism, as we have seen, retained its belief in reincarnation and its combination of spiritual interest in union with the divine essence and extensive rituals and ceremonies. The religion did experience greater popular appeal after the fall of the Guptas, associated

She also prays that in her present existence she will have no further sickness or suffering, that her parents in seven other incarnations (who have already died or will die in the future) and her present family and close relatives may experience joy in the four realms [earth, water, fire, and air], and that whatever they seek may indeed come to pass. Finally, she prays that all those endowed with knowledge may be included within this prayer.

Recorded on the 28th day of the fifth month of 583.

The Army Superintendent, Sung Shao, having suffered the heavy sorrow of losing both his father and mother, made a vow on their behalf to read one section each of [many] sutras. He prays that the spirits of his parents will someday reach the Pure Land [paradise] and will thus be forever freed from the three unhappy states of existence and the eight calamities and that they may eternally listen to the Buddha's teachings.

He also prays that the members of his family, both great and small, may find happiness at will, that blessings may daily rain down upon them while hardships disperse like clouds. He prays that the imperial highways may be open and free of bandits, that the state may be preserved from pestilence, that wind and rain may obey their proper seasons, and that all suffering creatures may quickly find release. May all these prayers be granted!

The preceding incantation has been translated and circulated.

If this incantation is recited 7, 14, or 21 times daily (after having cleansed the mouth in the morning with a willow twig, having scattered flowers and incense before the image of Buddha, having knelt and joined the palms of the hands), the four grave sins, the five wicked acts, and all other transgressions will be wiped away. The present body will not be afflicted by untimely calamities; one will at last be born into the realm of immeasurably long life; and reincarnation in the female form will be escaped forever.

Now, the Sanskrit text has been reexamined and the Indian Vinaya monk Buddhasangha and other monks have been consulted; thus we know that the awesome power of this incantation is beyond comprehension. If it is recited 100 times in the evening and again at noon, it will destroy the four grave sins and five wicked acts. It will pluck out the very roots of sin and will ensure rebirth in the Western Regions. If, with sincerity of spirit, one is able to complete 200,000 recitations, perfect intelligence will be born and there will be no relapses. If 300,000 recitations are completed, one will see Amita Buddha face to face and will certainly be reborn into the Pure Land of tranquility and bliss.

Copied by the disciple of pure faith Sun Szu-chung on the 8th day of the fourth month of 720.

Questions: Why did Buddhism spread widely in China by the 6th century? How did popular Buddhism compare with original Buddhist teachings (see Chapter 2)? How did Chinese Buddhists define holy life? How do these documents suggest some of the troubles China faced after the collapse of the Han dynasty?

---

with the expanded use of popular languages and with the worship of the mother goddess Devi.

Buddhism

Buddhism was altered more substantially than Hinduism as it traveled mainly beyond India's borders, becoming only a small minority faith in India itself. The chief agents of Buddhist expansion and leadership were monks, for Buddhism tended to divide the faithful among a minority who abandoned earthly life in favor of spiritual dedication and the larger number who continued to work in the world while doing the best they could to meet their spiritual obligations. Some centuries after Buddha's death, a doctrine of **bodhisattvas** developed, which held that some people could attain nirvana through their own meditation while choosing to remain in the world as saints and to aid others by prayer and example. Buddhism increasingly shifted from an original emphasis on ethics to become a more emotional cult stressing the possibility of popular salvation. The role of the bodhisattvas, in broadening the prospects of salvation for ordinary people by leading them in prayer and advising on spiritual matters, was crucial in this transformation.

Buddhism evolved further as the religion spread seriously to China after the fall of the Han dynasty, when the idea of a celestial afterlife proved almost irresistible. Monasteries in India and the Himalaya Mountains continued to serve as spiritual centers for Chinese Buddhism, but the religion developed strong roots in east Asia directly, spreading through China and from there to Korea and Japan. The east Asian form of Buddhism, called **Mahayana,** or the Greater Vehicle, retained basic Buddhist beliefs. However, the emphasis on Buddha himself as a divine savior increased in the Mahayana version. Statues devoted to Buddha as god countered the earlier Buddhist hostility to religious images. And the religion improved its organization, with priests, temples, creeds, and rituals. Buddhist holy men, bodhisattvas, remained important. Their souls after death resided in a kind of superheaven, where they could receive prayers and aid people. Intense spirituality continued to inform Buddhist faith as well. But prayers and rituals could now help ordinary people to become holy. Buddha became a god to whom one could appeal for solace, "the great physician for a sick and impure world." East Asian Buddhism also spurred new artistic interests in China and, later, in Japan, including the pagoda style of temple design and the statues devoted to Buddha.

Buddhism had a fascinating impact on women in China, largely among families who converted. On the face of things, Buddhism should have disrupted China's firm belief in patriarchal power, because Buddhists believed that women, like men, had souls. Indeed, some individual women in China captured great attention because of their spiritual accomplishments. But Chinese culture generated changes in Buddhism within the empire. Buddhist phrases like "husband supports wife" were changed to "husband controls his wife," whereas "the wife comforts the husband"—another Buddhist phrase from India—became "the wife reveres her husband." Here was a vital case of cultural blending, or syncretism. Finally, many men valued pious Buddhist wives, because they might benefit the family's salvation and because Buddhist activity would keep their wives busy, calm, and out of mischief. Buddhism was perhaps appealing to Chinese women because it led to a more meaningful life, but it did not really challenge patriarchy. A biography of one Buddhist wife put it this way: "At times of crisis she could be tranquil and satisfied with her fate, not letting outside things agitate her mind."

Buddhism was not popular with all Chinese. Confucian leaders, particularly, found in Buddhist beliefs in an afterlife a diversion from appropriate political interests. They disliked the notion of such intense spirituality and also found ideas of the holy life incompatible with proper family obligations. More important, Buddhism was seen as a threat that might distract ordinary people from loyalty to the emperor. When imperial dynasties revived in China, they showed some interest in Buddhist piety for a time, but ultimately they attacked the Buddhist faith, driving out many missionaries. Buddhism remained a minority current in China, and many villages worshipped in Buddhist shrines. Thus, China's religious composition became increasingly complex, but without overturning earlier cultural directions. Daoism reacted to Buddhism as well, by improving its organization and emphasizing practical benefits obtainable through magic. It was at this point that Daoism developed a clear hold on many peasants, incorporating many of their beliefs in the process. Buddhism

had a greater lasting influence in the religious experience of other parts of east Asia, notably Japan, Korea, and Vietnam, than in China itself. Buddhism had also spread to significant parts of southeast Asia, where it remained somewhat truer to earlier Buddhist concepts of individual meditation and ethics.

In the world today, some 500 million people count themselves as Buddhists. Most live in the areas of east and southeast Asia, where the religion had taken root by 500 C.E. Buddhism did not, by itself, dominate any whole civilization; rather, it lived alongside other faiths. However, it provided major additions to Asia's religious map and an important response to changing conditions in the troubled centuries after the classical period had ended.

Christianity

Christianity moved westward, from its original center in the Middle East, as Buddhism was spreading east from India. Although initially less significant than Buddhism in terms of the number of converts, Christianity would ultimately prove to be one of the two largest faiths worldwide. And it would play a direct role in the formation of two postclassical civilizations, those of eastern and western Europe. Despite important similarities to Buddhism in its emphasis on salvation and the guidance of saints, Christianity differed in crucial ways. It came to place more emphasis on church organization and structure, copying from the example of the Roman Empire. Even more than Buddhism, it placed a premium on missionary activity and widespread conversions. More, perhaps, than any other major religion, Christianity stressed the exclusive nature of its truth and was intolerant of competing beliefs. Such fierce confidence was not the least of the reasons for the new religion's success.

Christianity began in reaction to rigidities that had developed in the Jewish priesthood during the two centuries before the birth of Jesus Christ. A host of reform movements sprang up, some of them preaching the coming of a Messiah, or savior, who would bring about a Last Judgment on humankind. Many of these movements also stressed the possibility of life after death for the virtuous, which was a new element in Judaism. **Jesus of Nazareth,** believed by Christians to be the son of God sent to earth to redeem human sin, crystallized this radical reform movement. Combining extraordinary gentleness of spirit and great charisma, Jesus preached widely in Israel and gathered a group of loyal disciples around him. Initially, there seems to have been no intent on his or his followers' part to found a new religion. After Jesus' crucifixion, the disciples expected his imminent return and with it the end of the world. Only gradually, when the Second Coming did not transpire, did the disciples begin to fan out and, through their preaching, attract growing numbers of supporters in various parts of the Roman Empire.

The message of Jesus and his disciples seemed clear: There was a single God who loved humankind despite earthly sin. A virtuous life was one dedicated to the worship of God and fellowship among other believers; worldly concerns were secondary, and a life of poverty might be most conducive to holiness. God sent Jesus (called "Christ" from the Greek word for "God's anointed") to preach his holy word and through his sacrifice to prepare his followers for the widespread possibility of an afterlife and heavenly communion with God. Belief, good works, and the discipline of fleshly concerns would lead to heaven; rituals, such as commemorating Christ's Last Supper with wine and bread, would promote the same goal.

Christianity's message spread at an opportune time. The official religion of the Greeks and Romans had long seemed rather sterile, particularly to many of the poor. The Christian emphasis on the beauty of a simple life and the spiritual equality of all people, plus the fervor of the early Christians and the satisfying rituals they created, captured growing attention. The great reach of the Roman Empire made it relatively easy for Christian missionaries to travel widely in Europe and the Middle East, to spread the new word, although as we have seen, they also reached beyond, to Persia, Axum, and Ethiopia. Then when conditions began to deteriorate in the empire, the solace this otherworldly religion provided resulted in its even wider appeal. Early Christian leaders made several important adjustments to maximize their conversions. Under the guidance of **Paul,** not one of the original disciples but an early convert, Christians began to see themselves as part of a new religion, rather than part of a Jewish reform movement, and they welcomed non-Jews. Paul also encouraged more formal organization within the new church, with local groups selecting elders to govern them; soon, a single leader, or bishop, was appointed for each city. This structure paralleled the provincial government of the empire. Finally, Christian doctrine became increasingly organized, as the writings of several disciples and others were collected into what became known as the New Testament of the Christian Bible.

During the first three centuries after Christ, the new religion competed among a number of eastern mystical religions. It also faced, as we have seen, periodic persecution from the normally tolerant imperial government. Even so, by the time Constantine converted to Christianity and accepted it as the one true legitimate faith, perhaps 10 percent of the empire's population had accepted the new religion. Constantine's conversion brought new troubles to Christianity, particularly some interference by the state in matters of doctrine. However, it became much easier to spread Christianity with official favor, and the continued deterioration of the empire added to the impetus to join this amazingly successful new church. In the eastern Mediterranean, where imperial rule remained strong from its center in Constantinople, state control of the church became a way of life. But in the West, where conditions were far more chaotic, bishops had a freer hand. A centralized church organization under the leadership of the bishop of Rome, called **pope** from the word *papa*, or father, gave the Western church unusual strength and independence.

By the time Rome collapsed, Christianity had thus demonstrated immense spiritual power and developed a solid organization, although one that differed from East to West. The new church faced a number of controversies over doctrine but managed to promote certain standard beliefs as against several heresies. A key tenet involved a complex doctrine of the Trinity, which held that the one God had three persons—the Father, the Son (Christ), and the Holy Ghost. Experience in fighting heresies promoted Christian interest in defending a single belief and strengthened its resistance to any competing doctrine or faith. Early Christianity also produced an important formal theology, through formative writers such as Augustine. This theology incorporated many elements of classical philosophy with Christian belief and aided the church in its attempts to gain respectability among intellectuals. Theologians like Augustine grappled with such problems as freedom of the will: If God is all-powerful, can mere human beings have free will? And if not, how can human beings be justly punished for sin? By working out these issues in elaborate doctrine, the early theologians, or church fathers, provided an important role for formal, rational thought in a religion that continued to emphasize the primary importance of faith.

Finally, Christianity was willing to accommodate some earlier polytheistic traditions among the common people. The celebration of Christ's birth was thus moved to coincide with the winter solstice, a classic example of syncretism, which allowed the new faith to benefit from the power of selective older rituals.

Like all successful religions, Christianity combined a number of appeals. It offered deep devotion to an all-powerful God. Christianity also developed its own complex intellectual system. Mystical holy men and women flourished under Christian banners, particularly in the Middle East. In the West, soon after the empire's collapse, this impulse was partially disciplined through the institution of monasticism, first developed in Italy under **Benedict,** who started a monastery among Italian peasants whom he lured away from the worship of the sun god Apollo. The Benedictine Rule, which soon spread to many other monasteries and convents, urged a disciplined life, with prayer and spiritual fulfillment alternating with hard work in agriculture and study. Thus, Christianity attempted to encourage but also to discipline intense piety, and to avoid a complete gulf between the lives of saintly men and women and the spiritual concerns of ordinary people.

Christianity's success and organizational strength obviously appealed to political leaders. But the new religion never became the creature of the upper classes alone. Its popular message of salvation and satisfying rituals continued to draw the poor, more than most of the great classical belief systems; in this regard, it was somewhat like Hinduism in India. Christianity also provided some religious unity among different social groups. It even held special appeal for women. Christianity did not create equality among men and women, but it did preach the equal importance of male and female souls. And, it encouraged men and women to worship together, unlike many other faiths.

Christianity promoted a new culture among its followers. The rituals, the otherworldly emphasis, the interest in spiritual equality—these central themes were far different from those of classical Mediterranean civilizations. Christianity modified classical beliefs in the central importance of the state and of political loyalties. Although Christians accepted the state, they did not put it first. Christianity also worked against other classical institutions, such as slavery, in the name of brotherhood (although later Christians would accept slavery in other contexts). Christianity may have fostered greater respectability for disciplined work than had been the case in the

Mediterranean civilization, where an aristocratic ethic dominated. Western monasteries, for example, set forth rigid work routines for monks. Certainly, Christianity sought some changes in classical culture beyond its central religious message, including greater emphasis on sexual restraint. But Christianity preserved important classical values as well, in addition to an interest in solid organization and some of the themes of classical philosophy. Church buildings retained Roman architectural styles, although often with greater simplicity if only because of the poverty of the later empire and subsequent states. Latin remained the language of the church in the West, Greek the language of most Christians in the eastern Mediterranean. Through the patient librarianship of monks, monasticism played an immensely valuable role in preserving classical as well as Christian learning.

When the Roman Empire fell, Christian history was still in its infancy. The Western church would soon spread its missionary zeal to northern Europe, and the Eastern church would reach into the Slavic lands of the Balkans and Russia. By then, Christianity was already established as a significant world religion—one of the few ever generated. A world religion is defined as a faith of unusual durability and drawing power, one whose complexity wins the devotion of many different kinds of people. Major world religions, like Christianity and Buddhism, do indeed show some ability to cut across different cultures, to win converts in a wide geographic area and amid considerable diversity.

Islam

Islam, launched early in the 7th century, would initially surpass Christianity as a world faith and has remained Christianity's most tenacious rival. With Islam, the roster of world religions was essentially completed. Changes would follow, but no totally new religion of major significance arose—unless one counts some of the secular faiths, like communism, that appeared in the last century. The centuries after Christianity's rise, the spread of Buddhism, and the inception of Islam would see the conversion of most of the civilized world to one or another of the great faiths, producing a religious map that, in Europe and Asia and even parts of Africa, would not alter greatly until our own time. The table in the Visualizing the Past box shows the distribution of religions in the world today.

Visualizing the Past

Religious Geography

The distribution of the world's major religions calls for knowledge both of numerical data and geography. This map and table, using contemporary data, also suggest which aspects of the world's religious distribution were beginning to solidify at the end of the late classical period and which aspects depended on developments yet to come.

Questions: Where are the greatest concentrations of the four major religions today? Which religions affect the largest landmasses? Which affect the largest numbers of people? Which aspects of modern religious geography follow from the patterns of religious dissemination under way by the end of the classical period? Which cannot be explained by these late-classical developments? If you had been well informed about world religions and classical history in the 5th century, and magically gained knowledge about religions' distribution in the 21st century, which features would you find most surprising in light of logical 5th-century predictions?

Religions and Their Distribution in the World Today

Religion	Distribution*
Christianity	1.9 billion
Roman Catholic	(1 billion)
Protestant	(458 million)
Eastern Orthodox	(173 million)
Other	(195 million)
Islam	1 billion
Hinduism	751 million
Buddhism	334 million
Shintoism	3 million
Daoism	31 million
Judaism	18 million

*Figures for several religions have been reduced over the past 50 years by the impact of communism in eastern Europe and parts of Asia.

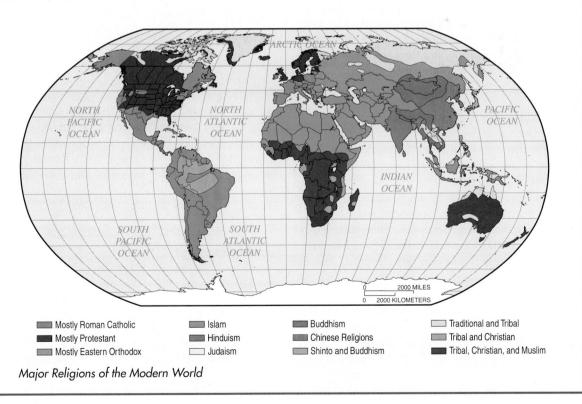

Mostly Roman Catholic · Islam · Buddhism · Traditional and Tribal
Mostly Protestant · Hinduism · Chinese Religions · Tribal and Christian
Mostly Eastern Orthodox · Judaism · Shinto and Buddhism · Tribal, Christian, and Muslim

Major Religions of the Modern World

The spread of major religions—Hinduism in India, Buddhism in east and southeast Asia, a more popular Daoism in China, Christianity in Europe and parts of the Mediterranean world, and ultimately Islam—was a vital result of the changes in classical civilizations brought on by attack and decay. Despite the important diversity among these great religions, which included fierce hatreds, particularly between Christian and Muslim, their overall development suggests the way important currents could run through the civilized world, crossing political and cultural borders—thanks in part to the integrations and contacts built by the classical civilizations. Common difficulties, including invading forces that journeyed from central Asia and contagious epidemics that knew no boundaries, help explain parallel changes in separate civilizations. Trade and travel also provided common bonds. Chinese travelers learned of Buddhism through trading expeditions to India, whereas Ethiopians learned about Christianity from Middle Eastern traders. The new religions spurred a greater interest in spiritual matters and resulted in a greater tendency to focus on a single basic divinity instead of a multitude of gods. Polytheistic beliefs and practices continued to flourish as part of popular Hinduism and popular Daoism, and they were not entirely displaced among ordinary people who converted to Christianity, Buddhism, or Islam. But the new religious surge reduced the hold of literal **animism** in much of Asia and Europe, and this too was an important development across boundaries.

The World Around 500 c.e.

Developments in many parts of the world by 500 C.E. produced three major themes for world history in subsequent centuries. First, and particularly in the centers of classical civilization, there was a response to the collapse of classical forms. Societies in China, India, and around the Mediterranean faced the task of reviving or reworking their key institutions and values after internal decline and external invasion. Second, in these areas but also in other parts of Africa, Europe, and Asia, was the need to react to the new religious map that was taking shape, to integrate new religious institutions and values into established civilizations or, as in northern Europe, to use them as the basis for a civilization that had previously been lacking. Finally, increased skill in agriculture and the cre-

ation of early civilizations or new contacts—like the Japanese import of writing—prepared parts of Europe, Africa, Asia, and the Americas for new developments in the centuries to come. The centers of classical civilization would still hold a dominant position in world history after 500 C.E., but their monopoly would be increasingly challenged by the spread of civilization to other areas.

GLOBAL CONNECTIONS: The Late Classical Period and the World

During most of the classical period, key developments often focused within civilizations. We have seen that there were wider contacts. Each civilization radiated trade and other influences to a larger region; thus India had contacts with other parts of south-southeast Asia, and China with Korea and Vietnam. Trade along the silk roads through central Asia, conducted mainly by nomadic merchants, was another key connection.

As the classical civilizations began to fail, contacts in some ways accelerated—but they also encountered new difficulties. Overland travel between China and Rome became more dangerous, because government protection faltered in both empires. This placed a new premium on using shipping connections, particularly in the Indian Ocean. On the other hand, traders, missionaries, and of course nomadic invaders began to reach out in new ways, as borders became more porous. The end of the classical period thus witnessed important new cultural exchanges across regions. These included the spread of Buddhism from India to China and to other parts of east Asia, and the spread of Christianity beyond the Roman Empire into parts of northeast Africa and into Armenia. These developments set new bases for connections among various societies in Afro-Eurasia.

Further Readings

The fall of the Roman Empire has generated rich and interesting debate. For recent interpretations and discussion of earlier views, see A. H. M. Jones, *The Decline of the Ancient World* (1966); J. Vogt, *The Decline of Rome* (1965); and F. W. Walbank, *The Awful Revolution—The Decline of the Roman Empire in the West* (1960). On India and China in decline, worthwhile sources include R. Thapar, *History of India*, Vol. 1 (1966); R. C. Majumdar, ed., *The Classical Age* (1966); Raymond Dawson, *Imperial China* (1972); J. A. Harrison, *The Chinese Empire* (1972); and Twitchett and Fairbanks, eds., *The Cambridge History of China*, Vol. 3, Part 1 (1979). On Africa, see K. Shillington, *History of Africa* (1989); Graham Connal, *African Civilizations: Precolonial Cities and States in Tropical Africa, an Archeological Perspective* (1987). On the role of disease, W. McNeill, *Plagues and Peoples* (1977), is useful. For the rise or spread of new religions, consult Geoffrey Parinder, ed., *World Religions* (1971); Jamail Ragi al Farugi, ed., *Historical Atlas of the Religions of the World* (1974); and Lewis M. Hopke, *Religions of the World* (1983). Important recent works on the world religions include N. C. Chaudhuri, *Hinduism, a Religion to Live By* (1979); S. Renko, *Pagan Rome and the Early Christians* (1986); M. Hengel, *Acts and the History of Earliest Christianity* (1986); A. Sharma, ed., *Women in World Religions* (1987); D. Carmody, *Women and World Religions* (1985); G. Clark, *Women in Late Antiquity: Pagan and Christian* (1993); and B. Witherington, *Women in the Earliest Churches* (1988). The causes of the rise and fall of civilizations are addressed in Jared Diamond, *Guns, Germs and Steel: The Fate of Human Societies* (1997); Christopher Chase-Dunn and Thomas D. Hall, *Rise and Demise: Comparing World-Systems* (1997); H. M. Jones, *The Decline of the Ancient World* (1966); Joseph A. Tainter, *The Collapse of Complex Societies* (1988); and Norman Yoffee and George L. Cowgill, *The Collapse of Ancient States and Civilizations* (1991).

On the Web

On Kushite civilization, see http://library.thinkquest. org/22845/kush/meroiticroyal.shtml; on Benedict, the early Christian monk, and his monastic rule, see http:// www.worth.org.uk/guides/m6.htm.

Web sites devoted to the fall of the Roman West include http://ancienthistory.about.com/library/weekly/aa061 599.htm and http://www.fordham.edu/halsall/source/ gibbon-fall.html. The new "religious map" of the later classical period can be explored at sites devoted to the Council of Nicea (http://www.columbia.edu/cu/ augustine/arch/sbrandt/nicea/htm), to the Hindu concept of the female aspect of the devine (http://www.asia. si.edu/devi/interpretingdevi.htm), to Mahayana Buddhism (http://www.geocities.com/Athens/8916/ index2.html), and to Islam (http://islamicity.com/ mosque/Intro_Islam.htm), all of which leave little doubt that the world of antiquity was fraught with portent for succeeding eras.

PART III

The Postclassical Era

CHAPTERS

6 The First Global Civilization: The Rise and Spread of Islam

7 Abbasid Decline and the Spread of Islamic Civilization to South and Southeast Asia

8 African Civilizations and the Spread of Islam

9 Civilization in Eastern Europe: Byzantium and Orthodox Europe

10 A New Civilization Emerges in Western Europe

11 The Americas on the Eve of Invasion

12 Reunification and Renaissance in Chinese Civilization: The Era of the Tang and Song Dynasties

13 The Spread of Chinese Civilization: Japan, Korea, and Vietnam

14 The Last Great Nomadic Challenges: From Chinggis Khan to Timur

15 The West and the Changing World Balance

Introduction

The next 10 chapters concentrate on the time period that runs from the 5th to the 15th century c.e., or from about 450 to about 1450. Most of the chapters deal with specific civilizations; many changes were occurring in old civilization centers (in the aftermath of the decline of the great classical empires) and in newer ones. Before we turn to individual cases, however, it is vital to get a sense of some overall patterns in this 1000-year period. The postclassical period witnessed the emergence of a coherent interregional framework. Instead of the parallelisms and tentative contacts between individual civilizations of the classical period, a genuine world historical dynamic was taking shape. From this point onward, regular, explicit exchange became a standard part of world history.

The Chronology of the Postclassical Period

 As with the classical period, there are two ways to define the postclassical age: in terms of the events that opened and closed it, and in terms of coherent trends that emerged between the beginning and the end.

The stage for the postclassical era was set by the same developments that ended its predecessor: the collapse of the Roman Empire and thus the end of Mediterranean unity, and the decline of classical empires in Asia. The 5th century saw most of these developments draw together, although the fall of the Guptas in India occurred slightly later and China's period of chaos

500 C.E.	**600** C.E.	**700** C.E.	**800** C.E.	**900** C.E.
527–565 Justinian, Eastern Roman (Byzantine) emperor	**610–613** Origins of Islam	**711** First Islamic attack in India	**800–814** Charlemagne Empire in western Europe	**960–1127** Song dynasty (China)
570–632 Muhammad	**618–907** Tang dynasty	**718** Byzantines defeat Arab attack on Constantinople	**c. 855** Russian kingdom around Kiev	**968** Tula established by Toltecs (Mesoamerica)
589–618 Sui dynasty (China)	**634–750** Arab invasions in Middle East; spread of Islam in North Africa	**750** Abbasid caliphate	**864** Cyril and Methodius missionaries in eastern Europe	**980–1015** Conversion of Vladimir I of Russia
	661–750 Ummayad Caliphate	**777** Independent Islamic kingdoms begin in North Africa	**878** Last Japanese embassy to China	
	668 Korea becomes independent from China			

occurred a bit earlier. Capped by invasions of nomadic peoples, the classical decline produced huge changes in the map of the world's civilizations.

The end of the postclassical era was heralded by another set of invasions from central Asia, even more powerful than the surge of the Huns that had helped close the classical period. During the 13th and 14th centuries, nomadic Mongol invaders poured through much of Asia and eastern Europe, ending or changing many governments. By 1400, much of Asia was beginning to recover from the Mongol onslaught, but a series of new changes was taking shape, including the beginning of western Europe's explorations into the wider world. These developments spanned about two centuries, from the early 13th to the mid-15th century; as before, the end of a world history period was not an overnight affair. The postclassical period closes with Mongol invasions and subsequent realignments. The realignments included the collapse of two key political units in the Middle East: the Arab caliphate and the Byzantine Empire.

The Postclassical Millennium and the World Network

 One of the most striking developments in the postclassical period was the formation of more regular connections among major societies in Asia, Africa, and Europe. This world network focused on a series of trade routes. Major routes ran east-west, but a series of north-south routes linked in as well.

Four overarching developments define the postclassical centuries, affecting most individual civilizations in different ways. The expanding influence of the Arabs and Islam, within their Middle Eastern base and well beyond, is one basic feature. The spread of civilization to additional regions of the world is another. A widespread shift in basic belief systems, from polytheism to several great world religions, is a third. The fourth general theme is the development of a world network consisting of increasingly regular and influential relations among most of the individual civilizations.

The Rise of Islam

Soon after the period began, a "leading civilization" emerged in terms of its expansionist capacity and ability to influence other civilizations. Islamic civilization, initially spread by the Arabs, spearheaded the creation of a new empire in the Middle East and north Africa as well as important political initiatives in India, Africa, southern Europe, and central Asia. Its religious outreach brought conversions to Islam in other parts of Africa and Asia. Arab commerce spread across the Indian Ocean to the western Pacific, down the east coast of Africa, and across the Sahara desert. In the classical period, the three major civilization areas had been roughly balanced, although India's outreach was particularly impressive. The postclassical era reshuffled the balance of power and created a definite world leader. Correspondingly, the decline of the Islamic imperial system was one of the key features leading to the end of this period and the emergence of a new era in world history.

The Expansion of Civilization

In the postclassical era, civilization began to spread geographically, covering many parts of the world not previously embraced by this kind of human organization. During these centuries the structures of civilization, including great regional trading kingdoms, spread across

1000 C.E.	1100 C.E.	1200 C.E.	1300 C.E.	1400 C.E.
1000 Ghana Empire at its height (Africa)	**c. 1100** Invention of explosive powder (China)	**1200** Rise of empire of Mali	**1320s** Europeans first use cannon in war	**1400** End of Polynesian expeditions
1054 Schism between Eastern and Western Christianity	**1150** Disintegration of Toltec Empire	**1206** Delhi sultanate in India	**1320–1340** Bubonic plague breaks out in Gobi desert and spreads to other parts of Asia	**1405–1433** Chinese trading expeditions
1055 Seljuk Turks control Abbasid caliphate	**1150–1350** Spread of Gothic style; scholasticism in western Europe	**1231–1392** Mongols rule Korea	**1325** Rise of Aztec Empire	**1439** Portugal acquires Azores
1066 Norman conquest of England; rise of feudal monarchy in western Europe	**1185–1333** Kamakura Shogunate (Japan)	**1236** Capture of Russia by Mongols	**1338–1453** Hundred Years' War in Europe	**1453** Turks capture Constantinople; end of Byzantine Empire
1096–1099 First Christian Crusade to Palestine		**1258** Capture of Baghdad by Mongols; end of Abbasid caliphate	**1350** Rise of Incas (Andes)	**1471–1493** Peak of Inca Empire
		1260 Death of Sundiata	**1392–1910** Yi dynasty (Korea)	
		1265 First English parliament		
		1279–1368 Mongol Empire in China		
		1290s Islam begins to spread to southeast Asia		

The Postclassical World Takes Shape, c. 900 C.E.

sub-Saharan Africa, in contrast to the previous concentration in a few centers such as the upper Nile River basin. Civilization also spread widely in northern Europe, both east and west, and became more fully established in Japan. The zones of civilization expanded in the Americas. The civilization map of the world was much larger in 1450 than it had been a thousand years before. At least seven diverse areas command attention in the postclassical era: the Middle East and north Africa, China and east Asia, eastern Europe, western Europe, sub-Saharan Africa, India and southeast Asia (where influences from several other civilizations intermingled), and the Americas.

The rise of new civilization centers meant new opportunities to define key characteristics. But several of the new civilizations shared certain features; for example, both eastern and western Europe, though different in many respects, were predominantly Christian. Many new centers actively imitated other areas, as parts of sub-Saharan Africa did with Islam and western Europe with the eastern Mediterranean. In dealing with the expanded civilization roster, defining separate identities raises some complexities. In addition, civilization areas continued to interact with potent nomadic societies, which took on new importance in the postclassical period.

The World Religions

The postclassical era was also defined by the spread of major religions across much of Asia, Europe, and Africa. Although this process had already begun in the late classical era, it defined the new period far more

clearly. While Hinduism took fuller shape as the majority religion in India and a few pockets in southeast Asia, Buddhism spread to China and other parts of central and east Asia, including Japan, and also to much of southeast Asia. Islam ran across the Middle East and north Africa and became an important minority religion in India, western China, and parts of sub-Saharan Africa. It also began to make inroads in southeast Asia toward the end of the period. Finally, Christianity spread northward in Europe, both east and west. The major world religions differed widely in many respects, but they did bring a new focus on issues of spirituality and an afterlife. People began to move away from a belief in multiple nature spirits or gods and toward a greater concentration on an overriding divinity or single supernatural force. The world religions shared an ability to extend beyond local cultures and win the adherence of diverse peoples to a core of beliefs and rituals. In this crucial sense, they and their mutual rivalries became part of the new set of international exchanges. In other words, the postclassical era saw widespread and fundamental shifts in religious belief and practices that included elites and ordinary people alike. In many cases, this huge change brought new institutions to the fore, such as the leading Christian churches, Buddhist monasteries, and the religious and legal experts of Islam.

Why did so many people in different areas change their basic beliefs? Pressed by political confusion after the fall of the classical empires, many people looked for new religious meaning. Islam, Christianity, and Buddhism were active propagating faiths. Many groups were converted to one of the new religions by the persuasion

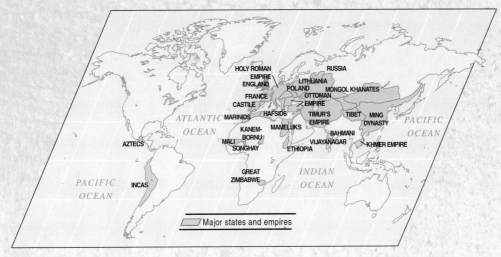

The Postclassical World in Transition, c. 1400 C.E.

of missionaries or other emissaries such as the Muslim Sufis or by the powerful example of political and commercial splendor in the seats of the new religious authority. Thus, Russia moved toward Christianity in part because of its leaders' awe at the civilized power of the Byzantine Empire and in part because of missionary influence. A growth in international trade also encouraged religious change, for local gods made less sense to people who exchanged goods with diverse and distant areas. The result was no agreement on belief—several of the new religions competed fiercely, with mutual hatred—but a vital underlying pattern nonetheless.

The World Network

The fourth major characteristic of the postclassical period, emerging with great force by about 1000 C.E., was ultimately the most important of all. An increasing level of interchange developed among the major civilizations of Asia, Europe, and Africa. Interregional trade grew. This particularly followed from the surge of Arab commerce but also resulted from continued activity by Indian merchants, Chinese exchanges with other parts of eastern and southeastern Asia, the development of new north-south trading connections in eastern and western Europe, and the rise of African merchant routes along the eastern coast and through the Sahara. With growing trade and periodic military encounters as civilizations new and old redefined their boundaries, other kinds of exchanges occurred across civilizations: Technology spread. Thus, the knowledge of paper, developed earlier in China, was gained by Muslim troops fighting

on China's western border in the 9th century. Paper production in the Middle East resulted. As western Europeans gained new links with this region through trade and religious wars, they learned of the new product. The first European paper manufacture was set up in Italy in the 13th century. Technological spread of this sort was hardly speedy, but it occurred at a more rapid pace than innovations in previous epochs had. Cultural exchange was another vital source of contact. In addition to religions, other kinds of ideas spread. Arabs gained knowledge of Indian mathematics, including the number system. Later in the period, western Europeans began to learn Arab mathematics, including the same number system, and they elaborated their philosophy by using and reacting to Arab thought.

In contrast to the very limited interregional trade of the classical period, the great trading system of the Indian Ocean, which stretched from east Africa to south China, expanded dramatically. At the far end of the system, wealthy Europeans in 1300 bought silks and other goods from Asia. World trade continued to involve luxury products, for the most part, but compared to the classical period the volume was higher, the geographic range was farther, and the impact on regional economies was greater. The spread of disease accelerated as well, and in the 14th century a new international epidemic of bubonic plague (the "Black Death") brought home the downside of more fluid international exchange.

The world network was a phenomenon of the Old World, extending an active framework of exchange among the various societies of Asia, Europe, and northern, central, and eastern Africa. However, it was not yet

115

global because the Americas, Polynesia, Australia, and several other regions were not included.

The postclassical era was not a time of fundamental technological innovation, although important advances occurred, particularly in China (such as printing and explosive powder) and at the end of the period in western Europe. But existing technical knowledge spread more widely. Developments such as the compass and lateen sail (vital to expanding Arab commerce) promoted the extension of intensified oceanic trade.

The postclassical era also witnessed a great variety of political forms but no dominant political definition. Empire declined as a common political form, partly because religious ties became more important in holding civilizations together.

World History Themes

 Because of new interregional connections and the spread of world religions, several world history themes took on new features during the postclassical period. Changes in the role of nomadic societies and new opportunities for human agency headed the list. Social inequality changed less, though religions created a more complex cultural context for it.

Basic characteristics of the postclassical period had various effects on leading world history themes. For example, this was not a period of massive environmental change. Agriculture claimed additional territory—there was considerable deforestation in Europe, for example—but the kind of soil depletion that had occurred in Roman days was less common. The spread of agriculture and population growth in central America did cause environmental problems that weakened this civilization by the 15th century. Overall, however, given the fact that few fundamental new technologies were introduced, environmental change reflected mainly population expansion. Nor did basic structures of social and gender inequality shift greatly, although new religious emphases highlighted spiritual equality. Slavery declined in some places but not all, and several societies introduced important new constraints on women. The role of nomads in history peaked with the Mongol invasions. After this, the impact of nomadic groups began to lessen. Even in the postclassical era itself, nomads began to play a lesser role in interregional trade, compared to organized merchants from the Middle East, India, Africa, China, and Europe. Trading companies, with regular representatives in dis-

tant ports, became the leading innovators in formal interregional relations.

Expanding civilizations and new religions also provided opportunities for human agency. Ordinary people could attain religious leadership through piety and organizational skill, reshaping religious ideas and practices in the process. Trade also called for creative people whose efforts would accumulate to solidify new trading patterns. Purely political leaders made their mark as well, but with states more loosely organized than in the classical period, few kings really changed the course of history even within a single civilization. Finally, the classic tension between individual civilizations and interregional contacts and forces was redefined in the postclassical centuries, as interregional exchanges grew in range and intensity.

Exchange and Imitation in the Postclassical World

 Three characteristics of the postclassical period highlight the importance of imitating established centers. Growing trade intensified contacts between outlying regions and the most prosperous established civilizations. Missionary activity did the same. Finally, the expansion of civilization as an organized form built on the possibility of explicit imitation.

The best-developed manufacturing centers and largest bureaucracies of the postclassical centuries continued to be located in places where classical civilizations had originally developed. These areas also contained the greatest cities: Constantinople, Baghdad, Zhangan, and Hangzhou. Thus, the Middle East (now dominated by Arabs), China, India, and the Byzantine Empire remained widely influential. Clustered around them were areas where civilization was newer: Japan, northern Europe, much of southeast Asia, and much of sub-Saharan Africa. These areas traded with the major centers but at some disadvantage, sending more raw materials in return for manufactured products. They imitated actively, although there were some features, most notably in centralized government, that they usually did not reproduce successfully. Cultural spread through contact was one of the leading features of the period, although the specific timing varied widely.

The chapters dealing with the postclassical millennium are arranged according to the major themes outlined here. Chapters 6 through 8 explore the emergence of the Arabs as major historical actors, the rise of Islam,

116

and the spread of this new religion to key regions such as India, southeast Asia, and Africa. The parts of the world particularly influenced by Islam illustrate all the overriding themes of the period: the rise of a world-class civilization, the expansion of civilization, changes in belief systems, and the impact of international exchange. Civilization expansion, religious change, and complex links to the world network are the focus of Chapters 9 and 10, on eastern and western Europe. The separate expansion of civilizations in the Americas is covered in Chapter 11. Chapter 12 turns to China, which was linked to larger patterns and the world network, but in distinctive ways. The expansion of east Asian civilization—another example of the spread-of-civilization theme—and the rise of the Mongol Empire (Chapters 13 and 14) lead to a final chapter on the changing world balance at the end of the postclassical period in the 15th century, Chapter 15.

I. In the postclassical period, what kind of principles did several major societies and religions develop concerning the proper treatment of women? What additional types of documents might help assess ideas about women?

1. Islam: The Koran 7th Century C.E.

O men, fear your Lord; who created you from a single cell, and from it created its mate, and from the two of them dispersed men and women in multitudes.

Do not covet what God has favoured some with more than He has some others. Men have a share in what they earn, and women have theirs in what they earn.

Men are the support of women as God gives some more means than others, and because men spend of their wealth (to provide for women). Women who are virtuous are obedient to God. As for wives whom you feel are hostile, talk to them persuasively, then leave them alone in bed, and go to bed with them (when they are willing). If they open out to you, do not seek an excuse for blaming them.

2. Western Europe: Jewish Commentary on Women Reciting the Grace after Meals c. 1200 C.E.

We learn that women sometimes join to form [an invitation to say grace] by themselves. However, in general, this is not the practice.

Further investigation is needed to determine whether women's obligation is fulfilled by the prayers of men, since they [women] do not understand [the words of Grace]. There are those who offer as a proof that their obligation is fulfilled from what it says below, "if a scholar makes the blessing, an ignoramus has his obligation fulfilled;" from this it appears that even the obligation of women for grace is fulfilled. As for our own [women] however, it is possible to rebut that proof, since there is a difference between an ignoramus, who understands Hebrew and some of what is said [in Grace but just does not know how to say Grace himself], but as for women, who do not understand at all, it could be said that they are not satisfied. . . .

3. Legal Code from the Byzantine Empire c. 900 C.E.

I do not know why the ancient authorities, without having considered the subject, conferred upon women the right of acting as witnesses. It was, indeed, well known, and they themselves could not fail to be aware that it was dishonorable for them to appear frequently before the eyes of men, and that those who were modest and virtuous should avoid doing so. For this reason, as I have previously stated, I do not understand why they permitted them to be called as witnesses, a privilege which resulted in their frequently being associated with great crowds of men.

And, indeed, the power to act as witnesses in the numerous assemblies of men with which they mingle, as well as taking part in public affairs, gives them the habit of speaking more freely than they ought, and, depriving them of the morality and reserve of their sex. For is it not an insult, and a very serious one, for women to be authorized to do something which is especially within the province of the male sex?

4. On Women's Problems, from Yuan Cai's Book of Advice for Family Heads China c. 1140–1195.

Some wives with stupid husbands are able to manage the family's finances, calculating the outlays of receipts of money and grain, without being cheated by anyone. Of those with degenerate husbands, there are also some who are able to manage the finances with the help of their sons without ending in bankruptcy. Even among those whose husbands have died and whose sons are young, there are occasionally women able to raise and educate their sons, keep the affection of all their relatives, manage the family business, and even prosper. All of these are worthy and wise women. But the most remarkable are the women who manage a household after their husbands have died leaving them with young children.

When wives themselves can read and do arithmetic . . . then things will usually work out all right.

5. Muslim Traveler Ibn Battuta in Mali c. 1352 C.E.

The condition of these people is strange and their manners outlandish. . . .

With regard to their women, they are not modest in the presence of men, they do not veil themselves in spite of their perseverance in the prayers. The women there have friends and companions amongst men outside the prohibited degrees of marriage [other than brothers, fathers, etc.]. Likewise for the men, there are companions from amongst women outside the prohibited degrees. One of them would enter his house to find his wife with her companion and would not disapprove of that conduct. . . .

Among the bad things which they do-their serving women, slave women and little daughters appear before people naked, exposing their private parts. Every leader of them has his food carried in to him by twenty or more slave girls and they are naked, every one.

II. According to the following documents, how did the expansion of trade in the postclassical period conflict, or not conflict with the dominant religious and philosophical systems? What was the relationship between trade and culture during the postclassical period? What additional types of documents would aid in assessing degrees of conflict?

1. From the Hadith (Islamic legal code) c. 8th Century C.E.

'Ukaz, Majanna and Dhul-Majaz were market-places in the Pre-Islamic period of ignorance. When Islam came, Muslims felt that marketing there might be a sin. So, the Divine Inspiration came: "There is no harm for you to seek the bounty of your Lord, (even in the seasons of the pilgrimage)." (2.198) Ibn 'Abbas recited the Verse in this way.

Allah's Apostle said, "The seller and the buyer have the right to keep or return goods; and if both parties spoke the truth and described the defects and qualities (of the goods), then they would be blessed in their transaction, and if they told lies or hid something, then the blessings of their transaction would be lost."

2. A Muslim View of the Characteristics of Traders: Ibn Khaldun c. 14th Century

The manners of tradesmen are inferior to those of rulers, and far removed from manliness and uprightness. We have already stated that traders must buy and sell and seek profits. This necessitates flattery, and evasiveness, litigation and disputation, all of which are characteristics of this profession. And these qualities lead to a decrease and weakening in virtue.

As for Trade, although it be a natural means of livelihood, yet most of the methods it employs are tricks aimed at making a profit by securing the difference between the buying and selling prices, and by appropriating the surplus. This is why [religious] Law allows the use of such methods, which, although they come under the heading of gambling, yet do not constitute the taking without return of other people's goods. . . .

3. Depiction of Saint Godric, a British merchant, by his Christian biographer, Reginald of Durham
c. 12th Century

When the boy had passed his childish years quietly at home; then, as he began to grow to manhood, he began to follow more prudent ways of life, and to learn carefully and persistently the teachings of worldly forethought. Wherefore he chose to study, learn and exercise the rudiment of more subtle conceptions. For this reason, aspiring to the merchant's trade, he began to follow the peddler's way of life, first learning how to gain in small bargains and things of insignificant price; and thence, while yet a youth, his mind advanced little by little to buy and sell and gain from things of great expense. . . . [H]e gradually associated himself by compact with city merchants. Hence, within a brief space of time . . . did [he] so profit by his increase of age and wisdom as to travel with associates of his own age through towns and boroughs, fortresses and cities, to fairs and to all the various booths of the market-place, in pursuit of his public commerce. He went along the high-way, neither puffed up by the good testimony of his conscience nor downcasting the nobler part of his soul by the reproach of poverty. . . .

In his travels he often (visited) the homes of past Saints and meditated on their lives with abundant tears. As a result he began to yearn for solitude and to hold his merchandise in less esteem than heretofore. . . . And after he had lived sixteen years as a merchant, he began to think of spending on charity, and he made a pilgrimage to Jerusalem, and turned against merchants who stole from others, but since he did not accuse them publicly he would later, when he had given himself entirely to God's service, weep for his unknowing transgressions.

4. Pope Innocent III: License to Venice to trade with the Saracens 1198

Following the example of Pope Gregory, we have placed under sentence of excommunication all those who in future consort with the Saracens [i.e., Muslims], directly or indirectly, or who attempt to give or send aid to them by sea, as long as the war between them and us shall last.

But our beloved sons Andreas Donatus and Benedict Grilion, your messengers, recently came to the apostolic see and were at pains to explain to us that by this decree your city was suffering no small loss, for she is not devoted to agriculture but rather to shipping and to commerce. We, therefore, induced by the paternal affection we have for you, and commanding you under pain of anathema not to aid the Saracens by selling or giving to them or exchanging with them iron, flax, pitch, pointed stakes, ropes, arms, helmets, ships, and boards, or unfinished wood, do permit for the present, until we issue further orders, the taking of goods, other than those mentioned, to Egypt and Babylon [areas controlled by Muslims], whenever necessary.

5. Humbert de Romans: An account of Medieval European fairs and markets c. 1250

Though markets and fairs are terms often used indiscriminately, there is a difference between them, for fairs deal with larger things and only once in the year, or at least rarely in the same place, and to them come men from afar. But markets are for lesser things, the daily necessaries of life; they are held weekly and only people from near at hand come. Hence markets are usually morally worse than fairs. They are held on feast days, and men miss thereby the divine office and the sermon and even disobey the precept of hearing Mass, and attend these meetings against the Church's commands. Sometimes, too, they are held in graveyards and other holy places. Frequently you will hear men swearing there: "By God I will not give you so much for it," or "By God I will not take a smaller price," or "By God it is not worth so much as that."

Sometimes again the lord is defrauded of market dues, which is perfidy and disloyalty. . . . Sometimes, too, quarrels happen and violent disputes. . . . Drinking is occasioned. . . . Christ, you may note, was found in the market-place, for Christ is justice and justice should be there. . . . Thus the legend runs of a man who, entering an abbey, found many devils in the cloister but in the market-place found but one, alone on a high pillar. This filled him with wonder. But it was told him that in the cloister all is arranged to help souls to God, so many devils are required there to induce monks to be led astray, but in the market-place, since each man is a devil to himself, only one other demon suffices.

6. China: Zhang Han's Essay on Merchants
16th Century

Money and profit are of great importance to men. They seek profit, then suffer by it, yet they cannot forget it. They exhaust their bodies and spirits, run day and night, yet they still regard what they have gained as insufficient.

Those who become merchants eat fine food and wear elegant clothes. They ride on beautifully caparisoned, double-harnessed horses-dust flying as they race through the streets and the horses'—precious sweat falling like rain. Opportunistic persons attracted by their wealth offer to serve them. Pretty girls in beautiful long-sleeved dresses and delicate slippers play string and wind instruments for them and compete to please them.

Merchants boast that their wisdom and ability are such as to give them a free hand in affairs. They believe that they know all the possible transformations in the universe and therefore can calculate all the changes in the human world, and that the rise and fall of prices are under their command. They are confident that they will not make one mistake in a hundred in their calculations. These merchants do not know how insignificant their wisdom and ability really are. As the Confucian classic says: "Great understanding is broad and unhurried; little understanding is cramped and busy."

CHAPTER 6

THE FIRST GLOBAL CIVILIZATION: THE RISE AND SPREAD OF ISLAM

The graceful "horseshoe" arches of the Alhambra palace in southern Spain provide a striking example of the sophistication and beauty attained by Islamic art and architecture. Because Spain was on the western fringe of the Islamic world, the superb creations of its Muslim era also remind us of the global reach of a vast civilization.

- Desert and Town: The Arabian World and the Birth of Islam
- The Life of Muhammad and the Genesis of Islam
- The Arab Empire of the Umayyads
- IN DEPTH: Civilization and Gender Relationships
- From Arab to Islamic Empire: The Early Abbasid Era
- DOCUMENT: *The Thousand and One Nights* as a Mirror of Elite Society in the Abbasid Era
- GLOBAL CONNECTIONS: Early Islam and the World
- VISUALIZING THE PAST: The Mosque as a Symbol of Islamic Civilization

Although there were important contacts between the civilized centers of the classical world, no single civilization had bound together large portions of the ancient world in either the Western or the Eastern Hemisphere. But in the 7th century C.E., the followers of a new religion, **Islam** (which literally means "submission, the self-surrender of the believer to the will of the one, true God, **Allah**"), spread from the Arabian peninsula and began a sequence of conquest and conversion that would forge the first truly global civilization. Until then, Arabia had been a nomadic backwater on the periphery of the civilizations of the eastern Mediterranean. Within decades, the **Muslims** (as the followers of the new faith and its prophet, **Muhammad,** were called) had conquered an empire extending from Spain in the west to central Asia in the east—an empire that combined the classical civilizations of Greece, Egypt, and Persia.

In succeeding centuries, Islamic civilization was spread by merchants, wandering mystics, and warriors across Africa, Asia, and southern Europe (Map 6.1). It spread throughout the steppes of central Asia (including most of what is today southern Russia) to western China and into south Asia. Islam also spread along the oceanic trade routes to maritime southeast Asia and down the eastern coast of Africa. It followed the overland trade routes across north Africa and down through the Sahara desert to west Africa (see Map 6.1). In addition, Muslim conquerors captured Asia Minor and advanced into the European heartland of Islam's great rival, Christendom.

During most of the millennium after the 7th century C.E., Islamic civilization provided key links and channels for exchange among what had been the main civilized centers of the classical era in the Eastern Hemisphere. Muslim merchants, often in cooperation with Jewish, Armenian, Indian, and other regional commercial groups, became key links in the trade between civilizations from the western Mediterranean to the South China Sea. Muslim traders and conquerors became the prime agents for the transfer of food crops, technology, and ideas among the many centers of civilization in the Eastern Hemisphere. Muslim scholars studied, preserved, and improved on the learning of these ancient civilizations, especially those of Greece, Persia, Egypt, and south Asia.

For several centuries, Muslim works in philosophy, literature, mathematics, and the sciences elevated Arabic (the language of the **Qur'an,** the holy book containing Allah's revelations to Muhammad) to the status of the international language of the educated and informed. Thus, building on the achievements of earlier civilizations, Muslim peoples forged a splendid

600 C.E.	620 C.E.	640 C.E.	660 C.E.	680 C.E.
c. 570–632 Lifetime of the prophet Muhammad **597–626** Wars between the Byzantine and Sasanian (Persian) empires **610** Muhammad's first revelations **613** Muhammad begins to preach the new faith	**622** Muhammad's flight *(hijra)* from Mecca to Medina **624–627** Wars between the followers of Muhammad and the Quraysh of Mecca **628** Muslim–Meccan truce **630** Muhammad enters Mecca in triumph **632** Death of Muhammad **632–634** Caliph Abu Bakr **633–634** Ridda Wars in Arabia **634–643** Early Muslim conquests in the Byzantine Empire **634–644** Caliph Umar **637** Arab invasion and destruction of Sasanian Empire	**644–656** Caliph Uthman **656–661** Caliph Ali; first civil war	**661–680** Mu'awiya **661–750** Umayyad caliphate	**680** Karbala, death of Ali's son Husayn **680–692** Second civil war **744–750** Third civil war; Abbasid revolt **750** Abbasid caliphate

new civilization that excelled in most areas of human endeavor, from poetry and architecture to the sciences and urban development.

The rise of the Arabs and of Islam defined much of the Middle East and north Africa from the postclassical period onward. It also defined much of the postclassical period itself, in its larger impact on other regions and on trading patterns throughout Afro-Eurasia. Innovations in the Arab tradition were central to the new developments, but the larger legacy of the classical Mediterranean and of Rome's collapse helped set the stage as well.

Desert and Town: The Arabian World and the Birth of Islam

 In the 7th century C.E., a new religion arose in the Arabian peninsula. Built on the revelations received by the prophet Muhammad, originally a trader from the town of Mecca, the new faith won over many of the camel-herding tribes of the peninsula within decades. Though initially an Arab religion, in both beliefs and practices Islam contained a powerful appeal that eventually made it one of the great world religions.

The Arabian peninsula (see Map 6.2) was a very unlikely birthplace for the first global civilization. Much of the area is covered by some of the most inhospitable desert in the world. An early traveler wrote of the region,

All about us is an iron wilderness; a bare and black shining beach of heated volcanic stones … a vast bed and banks of rusty and basaltic bluish rocks … stubborn as heavy matter, as iron and sounding like bell metal; lying out eternally under the sand-driving desert wind.

In the scrub zones on the edges of the empty quarters, or uninhabitable desert zones, a wide variety of **bedouin,** or nomadic, cultures had developed over the centuries, based on camel and goat herding. In oases like that pictured in Figure 6.1, which dotted the dry landscape, towns and agriculture flourished on a limited scale. Only in the coastal regions of the far south had extensive agriculture, sizeable cities, and regional kingdoms developed in ancient times. Over much of the rest of the peninsula, the camel nomads, organized in tribes and clans, were dominant. Yet in the rocky regions adjacent to the Red Sea, several trading towns had developed that played pivotal roles in the emergence of Islam.

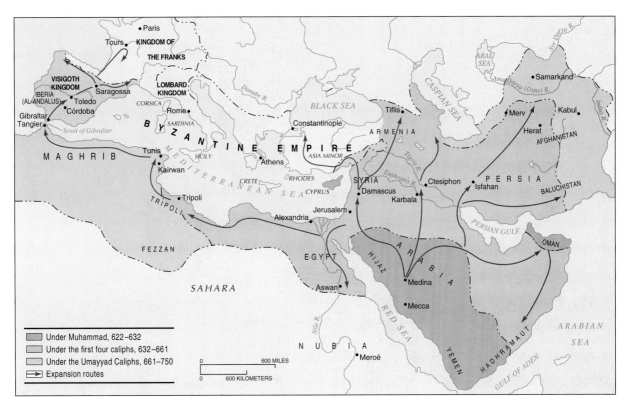

Map 6.1 *The Expansion of Islam in the 7th and 8th Centuries*

Although the urban roots of Islam have often been stressed by writers on Muslim civilization, the bedouin world in which the religion arose shaped the career of its prophet, his teachings, and the spread of the new beliefs. In fact, key towns such as Mecca and Medina were largely extensions of the tribal culture of the camel nomads. Their populations were linked by kinship to bedouin peoples. For example, Mecca had been founded by bedouins and at the time of Muhammad was ruled by former bedouin clans. The safety of the trade routes on which the towns depended was in the hands of the nomadic tribes that lived along the vulnerable caravan routes to the north and south. In addition, the town dwellers' social organization, which focused on clan and family, as well as their culture, including language and religion, were much like those of the nomads.

Clan Identity, Clan Rivalries, and the Cycle of Vengeance

The harsh desert and scrub environment of Arabia gave rise to forms of social organization and a lifestyle that were similar to those of other nomadic peoples. Bedouin herders lived in kin-related clan groups in highly mobile tent encampments. Clans, in turn, were clustered in larger tribal groupings, but these were rarely congregated together and then only in times of war or severe crisis. The struggle for subsistence in the unforgiving Arabian environment resulted in a strong dependence on and loyalty to one's family and clan. Survival depended on cooperation with and support from kin. To be cut off from them or expelled from the clan encampment was in most cases fatal. The use of watering places and grazing lands, which were essential to maintaining the herds on which bedouin life depended, was regulated by clan councils. But there could be wide disparities of wealth and status within clan groups and between clans of the same tribe. Though normally elected by councils of elder advisors, the **shaykhs,** or leaders of the tribes and clans, were almost always men with large herds, several wives, many children, and numerous retainers. The shaykhs' dictates were enforced by bands of free warriors, whose families made up a majority of a given clan group. Beneath the warriors

Figure 6.1 *With their supply of water, shade, and date palms, oases like this one in central Arabia have long been key centers of permanent settlement and trade in the desert. Major towns usually grew around the underground springs and wells or small rivers that fed the oases. Travelers' and traders' caravans stopped at the oases to water their camels and horses and to rest and eat after their arduous treks through the desert. As points of concentration of wealth, food, and precious water, oases were tempting targets for raids by bedouin bands.*

were slave families, often the remnants of rival clans defeated in war, who served the shaykhs or the clan as a whole.

Clan cohesion was reinforced by fierce interclan rivalries and struggles to control vital pasturelands and watering places. If the warriors from one clan found those from another clan drawing water from one of their wells, they were likely to kill them. Wars often broke out as a result of one clan encroaching on the pasture areas of another clan. In a culture in which one's honor depended on respect for one's clan, the flimsiest pretexts could lead to interclan violence. For instance, an insult to a warrior in a market town, the theft of a prize stallion, or one clan's defeat in a horse race by another clan could end in battles between clan groups. All the men of a given clan joined in these fights, which normally were won by the side that could field several champions who were famed for their strength and skill with spears or bows and arrows.

These battles were fought according to a code of chivalry that was quite common in early cultures. Although battles usually were small in terms of the numbers involved, they were hard-fought and often bloody affairs. Almost invariably the battles either initiated or perpetuated clan feuds, which could continue for hundreds of years. The deaths of the warriors of one clan required that revenge be taken on the clan that had killed them. Their deaths led in turn to reprisals. This constant infighting weakened the bedouins in relation to the neighboring peoples and empires and allowed them to be manipulated and set against each other.

Towns and Long-Distance Trade

Although bedouin herders occupied most of the habitable portions of Arabia, farmers and town dwellers carved out small communities in the western and southern parts of the peninsula in the classical era. Foreign invasions and the inroads of bedouin peoples had all but destroyed these civilizations centuries before the birth of Muhammad. But a number of cities had developed farther north as links in the transcontinental trading system that stretched from the Mediterranean to east Asia. The most important of these cities was **Mecca,** located in the mountainous region along the Red Sea on the western coast of Arabia (see Map 6.2). The town had been founded by the **Umayyad** clan of the **Quraysh** bedouin tribe, and members of the clan dominated its politics and commercial economy.

The wealth and status of Mecca and its merchant elite were enhanced by the fact that the city was the

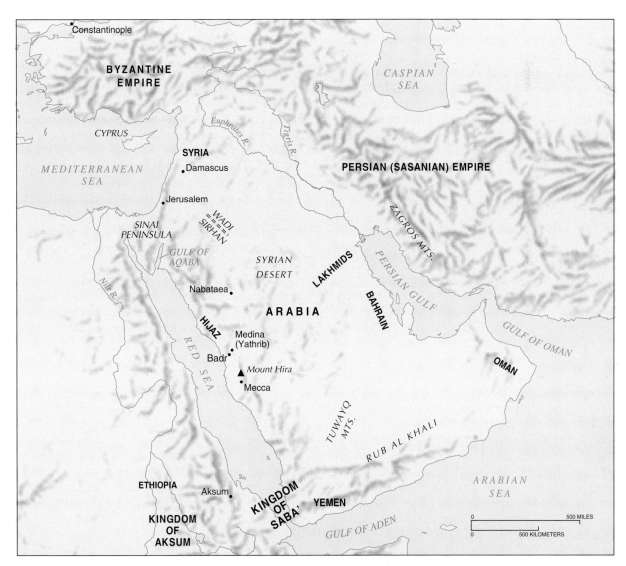

Map 6.2 *Arabia and Surrounding Areas Before and During the Time of Muhammad*

site of the **Ka'ba,** one of the most revered religious shrines in pre-Islamic Arabia. Not only did the shrine attract pilgrims and customers for Mecca's bazaars, but at certain times of the year it was the focus of an obligatory truce in the interclan feuds. Freed from fears of assault by rival groups, merchants and bedouins flocked to the town to trade, exchange gossip, and taste the delights of city life.

Northeast of Mecca was a town named Yathrib (see Map 6.2) that later came to be known as **Medina,** or the city of the prophet (Muhammad). Like most of the other towns in the peninsula, Medina was established in an oasis. Wells and springs made sedentary agriculture possible. In addition to wheat and other staples, Medina's inhabitants grew date palms, whose fruit and seeds (which were fed to camels) they traded to the bedouins. Medina was also engaged, though on a much smaller scale than Mecca, in the long-distance caravan trade that passed through Arabia. In contrast to Umayyad-dominated Mecca, control in Medina was contested by two bedouin and three Jewish clans. Their quarrels left the city a poor second to Mecca as a center of trade, and these divisions proved critical to the survival of the prophet Muhammad and the Islamic faith.

Marriage and Family in Pre-Islamic Arabia

Although the evidence is scant, there are several indications that women in pre-Islamic Arabian bedouin culture enjoyed greater freedom and higher status than those who lived in neighboring civilized centers, such as the Byzantine and Sasanian empires that then dominated the Middle East (Map 6.2). Women played key economic roles, from milking camels and weaving cloth to raising children. Because the men of the clan were often on the move, many tribes traced descent through the mother rather than the father. In some tribes, both men and women were allowed multiple marriage partners. To seal a marriage contract, the man was required to pay a bride-price to his prospective wife's family, rather than the woman's father sending a dowry or gift to the prospective husband. Unlike the women (especially those of elite status) in neighboring Syria and Persia, women in pre-Islamic Arabia were not secluded and did not wear veils. Their advice was highly regarded in clan and tribal councils, and they often wrote poems that were the focus of bedouin cultural life in the pre-Islamic era.

Despite these career outlets, women were not by any means considered equal to men. They could not gain glory as warriors, the most prized occupation of the bedouins, and often they were little more than drudge laborers. Their status depended on the custom of individual clans and tribes rather than on legal codes. As a result, it varied widely from one clan or family to the next. Customary practices of property control, inheritance, and divorce heavily favored men. In the urban environment of trading centers such as Mecca, the rise of a mercantile elite and social stratification appear to have set back the position of women on the whole. The more stable family life of the towns led to the practice of tracing descent through the male line, and while men continued to practice polygamy, women were expected to be monogamous.

Poets and Neglected Gods

Because of the isolation of Arabia in the pre-Islamic age and the harshness and poverty of the natural environment, Arab material culture was not highly developed. Except in the far south, there was little art or architecture of worth. Even Mecca made little impression on the cosmopolitan merchants who passed through the city in caravans from the fabled cities of the ancient civilizations farther north. The main focus of bedouin cultural creativity in the pre-Islamic era was poetry, which was composed and transmitted orally because there was as yet no written language. Clan and tribal bards narrated poems that told of their kinsmen's heroics in war and the clan's great deeds. Some poets were said to have magical powers or to be possessed by demons. More than any other source, their poems provide a vision of life and society in pre-Islamic Arabia. They tell of lovers spurned and passion consummated, war and vendettas, loyalty, and generosity.

Bedouin religion was for most clans a blend of animism and polytheism, or the worship of many gods and goddesses. Some tribes, such as the Quraysh, recognized a supreme god named Allah. But they seldom prayed or sacrificed to Allah, concentrating instead on less abstract spirits who seemed more relevant to their daily lives. Both spirits and gods (for example, the moon god, Hubal) tended to be associated with night, a cool period when dew covered the earth, which had been parched by the blaze of the desert sun. Likewise, the worship of nature spirits focused on sacred caves, pure springs, and groves of trees—places where the bedouins could take shelter from the heat and wind. Religion appears to have had little to do with ethics. Rather, standards of morality and proper behavior were rooted in tribal customs and unwritten codes of honor.

How seriously the bedouins took their gods is also a matter of some doubt. Their lukewarm adherence is illustrated by the famous tale of a bedouin warrior who had set out to avenge his father's death at the hands of a rival clan. He stopped at an oracle along the way to seek advice by drawing arrows that indicated various courses of action he might take. Three times he drew arrows that advised him to abandon his quest for revenge. Infuriated by this counsel, he hurled the arrows at the idol of the oracle and exclaimed, "Accursed one! Had it been thy father who was murdered, thou would not have forbidden my avenging him."

The Life of Muhammad and the Genesis of Islam

 By the 6th century C.E., the camel nomads were dominant throughout much of Arabia. The civilized centers to the south were in ruins, and trading centers such as Mecca and Medina depended on alliances with neighboring bedouin tribes to keep the caravan routes open. The constricted world of clan and kin, nomadic camp, blood feud, and local gods persisted despite the lure of the empires and cosmopolitan urban centers that stretched in a great arc to the north and east of the Arabian peninsula. But pressures for change were mounting. Both the Byzantine and Sasanian empires struggled to assert greater control over the nomadic tribes of the peninsula. In addition, Arab peoples migrated into Mesopotamia and other areas to the north, where they came increasingly under foreign influence. From these regions, the influence of established monotheistic religions, especially Judaism and Christianity, entered Arabia. These new currents gave rise to a number of Arab prophets who urged the bedouin tribes to renounce idol worship and rely on a single, almighty god. The prophet Muhammad and the new religion that his revelations inspired in the early decades of the 7th century responded both to these influences flowing into Arabia and to related social dislocations that were disrupting Arab life.

The hardships of Muhammad's early life underscore the importance of clan ties in the Arabian world. He was born around 570 C.E. into a prominent clan of the Quraysh tribe, the Banu Hashim, in a bedouin encampment where he spent the first six years of his life. Because his father died before he was born, Muhammad was raised by his father's relatives. The loss of his father was compounded by the death of Muhammad's mother shortly after he went to live with her some years later. Despite these early losses, Muhammad had the good fortune to be born into a respected clan and powerful tribe. His paternal uncle, Abu Talib, was particularly fond of the boy and served as his protector and supporter through much of his early life. Muhammad's grandfather, who like other leading members of the clan was engaged in commerce, educated the young man in the ways of the merchant. With Abu Talib, Muhammad made his first caravan journey to Syria, where on this and later trips he met adherents of the Christian and Jewish faiths, whose beliefs and practices had a great impact on his teachings.

In his adolescence, Muhammad took up residence in Mecca. By his early 20s he was working as a trader for **Khadijah** (the widow of a wealthy merchant), whom he married some years later. His life as a merchant in Mecca and on the caravan routes exposed Muhammad to the world beyond Arabia and probably made him acutely aware of the clan rivalries that had divided the peoples of the region for millennia. He would also have become increasingly concerned about new forces undermining solidarity within the clans. The growth of the towns and trade had enriched some clan families and left others behind, often in poverty. It had also introduced a new source of tension between clan and tribal groupings because some clans, such as the Umayyads, grew rich on the profits from commerce, whereas others maintained their herding lifestyle.

As a trader and traveler, Muhammad would almost certainly have been aware of the new religious currents that were sweeping Arabia and surrounding areas in the early 7th century. Particularly notable among these was the spread of monotheistic ideas and a growing dissatisfaction with the old gods that had been venerated by the bedouin peoples. In Muhammad's time, several prophets had arisen, proclaiming a new faith for the Arabs.

Though socially prominent, economically well off, and widely admired for his trading skills and trustworthiness, Muhammad grew increasingly distracted and dissatisfied with a life focused on material gain. He spent increasing amounts of time in meditation in the hills and wilderness that surrounded Mecca. In 610 or earlier, he received the first of many revelations, which his followers believe Allah transmitted to him through the angel Gabriel. These revelations were later written in Arabic and collected in the Qur'an. The teachings and injunctions of the Qur'an formed the basis of the new religion that Muhammad began to preach to his clan and the people of Mecca.

Persecution, Flight, and Victory

At first Muhammad's following was small, consisting mainly of his wife, several clanspeople, and some servants and slaves. As his message was clarified with successive revelations, the circle of the faithful grew so that the Umayyad notables who dominated Meccan life saw him as a threat to their own wealth and power. Above all, the new faith threatened to supplant the gods of the Ka'ba, whose shrines had done so much to establish the city as a center of commerce and bedouin interchange. Although he was protected for a time by his own clan, Muhammad was increasingly threatened by the Umayyads, who plotted with other clans to murder him. It was clear that Muhammad must flee Mecca, but where was he to find refuge? Muhammad's reputation as a skillful and fair negotiator prepared the way for his successful flight from Umayyad persecution. The quarrels between the clans in the nearby city of Medina had set off increasingly violent clashes, and the oasis community was on the verge of civil war. Leaders of the bedouin clans in Medina sent a delegation to invite Muhammad, who was related to them on his mother's side, to mediate their disputes and put an end to the strife that had plagued the town. Clever ruses and the courage of his clansman **Ali,** who at one point took Muhammad's place and thus risked becoming the target of assassins, secured in 622 the safe passage of Muhammad and a small band of followers from Mecca to Medina—the *hijra*, or flight to Medina, which marks the first year of the Islamic calendar. In Medina (where he is depicted in Figure 6.2 working with his followers), he was given a hero's welcome. He soon justified this warm reception by deftly settling the quarrels between the bedouin clans of the town. His wisdom and skill as a political leader won him new followers, who joined those who had accompanied him from Mecca as the core believers of the new faith.

Figure 6.2 *In this miniature painting, Muhammad, surrounded by the flaming halo, joins his disciples in laying the brick foundation for the large house where he lived with his family after his flight to Medina three years after Khadijah's death. The house also served the Muslim faithful as their main mosque until Mecca was captured in 629. After that date, the former pagan shrine called the Ka'ba was gradually transformed into a magnificent mosque. The Ka'ba soon became the central point for Muslims throughout the world, who were enjoined to always face Mecca when they offered their prayers to Allah.*

In the eyes of the Umayyad notables, Muhammad's successes made him a greater threat than ever. Not only was he preaching a faith that rivaled their own, but his leadership was strengthening Mecca's competitor, Medina. Muslim raids on Meccan caravans provided yet another source of danger. Determined to put an end to these threats, the Quraysh launched a series of attacks in the mid-620s on Muhammad and his followers in Medina. These attacks led to several battles. In these clashes, Muhammad proved an able leader and courageous fighter.

The ultimate victory for Muhammad and his followers was signaled by a treaty with the Quraysh in 628, which included a provision granting the Muslims permission to visit the shrine at Ka'ba in Mecca during the season of truce. By then Muhammad's community had won many bedouin allies, and more than 10,000 converts accompanied him on his triumphal return to his hometown in 629. After proving the power of Allah, the single god he proclaimed, by smashing the idols of the shrine, Muhammad gradually won over the Umayyads and most of the other inhabitants of Mecca to the new faith.

Arabs and Islam

Although Islam was soon to become one of the great world religions, the beliefs and practices of the prophet Muhammad were initially adopted only by the Arab town dwellers and bedouins among whom he had grown up. There is a striking parallel here with early Christianity, which focused on Jewish converts. The new religion preached by Muhammad had much to offer the divided peoples of Arabia. It gave them a form of monotheism that belonged to no single tribe and transcended clan and class divisions. It provided a religion that was distinctly Arab in origin and yet the equal of the monotheistic faiths held by the Christians and Jews, who lived in the midst of the bedouin tribes. If anything, the monotheism preached by Muhammad was even more uncompromising than that of the Christians because it allowed no intermediaries between the individual and God. God was one; there were no saints, and angels were nothing more than messengers. In addition, there were no priests in the Christian or Jewish sense of the term.

Islam offered the possibility of an end to the vendettas and feuds that had so long divided the peoples of Arabia and undermined their attempts to throw off the domination of neighboring empires. The **umma,** or community of the faithful, transcended old tribal boundaries, and it made possible a degree of political unity undreamed of before Muhammad's time. The new religion provided a single and supernaturally sanctioned source of authority and discipline. With unity, the skills and energies that the bedouins had once channeled toward warring with each other were turned outward in a burst of conquest that is perhaps unmatched in human history in its speed and extent. From vassals, march warriors, or contemptible "savages" of the desert waste, the Arab bedouins were transformed into the conquerors and rulers of much of the Middle Eastern world.

The new religion also provided an ethical system that did much to heal the deep social rifts within Arabian society. Islam stressed the dignity of all believers and their equality in the eyes of Allah. It promoted a moral code that stressed the responsibility of the well-to-do and strong for the poor and weak, the aged and infirm. Payment of the **zakat,** a tax for charity, was obligatory in the new faith. In both his revelations and his personal behavior, Muhammad enjoined his followers to be kind and generous to their dependents, including slaves. He forbade the rich to exploit the poor through exorbitant rents or rates of interest for loans.

The prophet's teachings and the revelations of the Qur'an soon were incorporated into an extensive body of law that regulated all aspects of the lives of the Muslim faithful. Held accountable before Islamic law on earth, they lived in a manner that would prepare them for the Last Judgment, which in Islam, as in Christianity, would determine their fate in eternity. A stern but compassionate God and a strict but socially minded body of law set impressive standards for the social interaction between adherents of the new faith.

Universal Elements in Islam

Although only Arabs embraced the religion of Islam in its early years, from the outset it contained beliefs and practices that would give it a strong appeal to peoples at virtually all stages of social development and in widely varying cultural settings. Some of these beliefs—Islam's uncompromising monotheism, highly developed legal codes, egalitarianism, and strong sense of community—were the same as the attributes that had won it support among the peoples of Arabia. Its potential as a world religion was enhanced by the fact that most of the attributes of Islam were to some degree anticipated by the other Semitic religions, particularly Judaism and Christianity, with which Muhammad had contact for much of his life. He accepted the validity of the earlier divine revelations that had given rise to the Jewish and Christian faiths. He taught that the revelations he had received were a refinement of these earlier ones and that they were the last divine instructions for human behavior and worship.

In addition to the beliefs and practices that have given Islam a universal appeal, its **five pillars,** principles that must be accepted and followed by all believers, provided the basis for an underlying religious unity. (1) The confession of faith was simple and powerful: "There is no God but Allah, and Muhammad is his Prophet." The injunctions (2) to pray, facing the holy city of Mecca, five times a day and (3) to fast during the month of **Ramadan,** enhanced community solidarity and allowed the faithful to demonstrate their fervor. (4) The zakat, or tithe for charity, also strengthened community cohesion and won converts from those seeking an ethical code that stressed social responsibility and the unity of all believers. (5) The **hajj,** or pilgrimage to the holy city of Mecca, to worship Allah at the Ka'ba, shown in Figure 6.3, drew together the faithful from Morocco to China. No injunction did more to give Islam a universal character.

The Arab Empire of the Umayyads

Muhammad's victory over the Umayyads and the resulting allegiance of many of the bedouin tribes of Arabia created a new center of power in the Middle Eastern cradle of civilization. A backward, nonagrarian area outside the core zones of Egypt, Mesopotamia, and Persia suddenly emerged as the source of religious and political forces that would eventually affect the history of much of the known world. But when the prophet Muhammad died suddenly in 632, it appeared that his religion might disappear. Despite internal disputes, the Muslim community held together and soon expanded beyond Arabia. Muhammad's old adversaries, the Umayya clan, emerged after several years' struggle as the dominant force in the Islamic community. Under Umayyad rule, the Arabs rapidly built a vast empire, which had established the foundations for an enduring Islamic civilization by the time of its fall in the mid-8th century C.E.

Many of the bedouin tribes that had converted to Islam renounced the new faith in the months after Muhammad's death, and his remaining followers quarreled over who should succeed him. Although these quarrels were never fully resolved,

Figure 6.3 *The Ka'ba in Mecca, with masses of pilgrims. Each year tens of millions of the Muslim faithful make the journey to the holy sites of Arabia from all around the world. The rituals associated with Mecca and Medina are key religious duties for all who can afford to travel to the holy cities.*

the community managed to find new leaders who directed a series of campaigns to force those who had abandoned Islam to return to the fold. Having united most of Arabia under the Islamic banner by 633, Muslim military commanders began to mount serious expeditions beyond the peninsula, where only probing attacks had occurred during the lifetime of the prophet and in the period of tribal warfare after his death. The courage, military prowess, and religious zeal of the warriors of Islam, and the weaknesses of the empires that bordered on Arabia, resulted in stunning conquests in Mesopotamia, north Africa, and Persia, which dominated the next two decades of Islamic history. The empire built from these conquests was Arab rather than Islamic. Most of it was ruled by a small Arab warrior elite, led by the Umayyads and other prominent clans. These groups had little desire to convert the subject populations, either Arab or otherwise, to the new religion.

Consolidation and Division in the Islamic Community

The leadership crisis brought on by Muhammad's death in 632 was compounded by the fact that he had not appointed a successor or even established a procedure by which a new leader would be chosen. Opinion within the Muslim community was deeply divided as to who should succeed him. In this moment of extreme danger, a strong leader who could hold the Islamic community together was urgently needed. On the afternoon Muhammad died, one of the clans that remained committed to the new faith called a meeting to select a leader who would be designated as the **caliph,** the political and religious successor to Muhammad. Several choices were possible, and a deadlock between the clans appeared likely—a deadlock that would almost certainly have been fatal to a community threatened by enemies on all sides. One of the main candidates, Ali, the cousin and son-in-law of Muhammad, was passed over because he was considered too young to assume a position of such great responsibility. This decision later proved to be a major source of division in the Islamic community. But in 632, it appeared that a difficult reconciliation had been won by the choice of one of Muhammad's earliest followers and closest friends, **Abu Bakr** (caliph from 632 to 634). In addition to his courage, warmth, and wisdom, Abu Bakr was well versed in the genealogical histories of the bedouin tribes, which meant that he knew which tribes could be turned against each other and which ones could be enticed into alliances. Initially, at least, his mandate was very limited. He received no financial support from the Muslim community. Thus, he had to continue his previous occupation as a merchant on a part-time basis, and he only loosely controlled the military commanders.

These commanders turned out to be very able. After turning back attacks on Mecca, the Islamic faithful routed one after another of the bedouin tribes. The defeat of rival prophets and some of the larger clans in what were known as the **Ridda Wars** soon brought about the return of the Arabian tribes to the Islamic fold. Emboldened by the proven skills of his generals and the swelling ranks of the Muslim faithful, Abu Bakr oversaw raids to the north of Arabia into the sedentary zones in present-day Iraq and Syria and eastward into Egypt (see Map 6.2).

The unified bedouin forces had originally intended to raid for booty and then retreat back into the desert. But their initial probes revealed the vulnerability of the Byzantine and Persian empires, which dominated or ruled the territories into which the Muslim warriors rode. The invaders were also encouraged by the growing support of the Arab bedouin peoples who had been migrating into the Fertile Crescent for centuries. These peoples had long served as the vassals and frontier guardians of the Byzantine and Persian empires. Now they joined their brethren in a combined assault on the two empires.

Motives for Arab Conquests

The Arab warriors were driven by many forces. The unity provided by the Islamic faith gave them a new sense of common cause and strength. United, they could stand up to the non-Arab rulers who had so long played them against each other and despised them as unwashed and backward barbarians from the desert wastelands. It is also probable that the early leaders of the community saw the wars of conquest as a good way to release the pent-up energies of the martial bedouin tribes they now sought to lead. Above all, the bedouin warriors were drawn to the campaigns of expansion by the promise of a share in the booty to be won in the rich farmlands raided and the tribute that could be exacted from towns that came under Arab rule. As an early Arab writer observed, the bedouins forsook their life as desert nomads not out of a promise of religious rewards, but because of a "yearning after bread and dates."

The chance to glorify their new religion may have been a motive for the Arab conquests, but they were not driven by a desire to win converts to it. In fact, other than fellow bedouin tribes of Arab descent, the invaders had good reason to avoid mass conversions. Not only would Arab warriors have to share the booty of their military expeditions with ever larger numbers if converts were made, but Muslims were exempted from some of the more lucrative taxes levied on Christian, Jewish, and other non-Muslim groups. Thus, the vision of **jihads,** or holy wars launched to forcibly spread the Muslim faith, which has long been associated with Islam in the Christian West, misrepresents the forces behind the early Arab expansion.

Weaknesses of the Adversary Empires

Of the two great empires that had once fought for dominance in the Fertile Crescent transit zone, the Sasanian Empire of Persia proved the more vulnerable. Power in the extensive Sasanian domains was formally concentrated in the hands of an autocratic emperor. By the time of the Arab explosion, the emperor was manipulated by a landed, aristocratic class that harshly exploited the farmers who made up most of the population of the empire. Zoroastrianism, the official religion of the emperor, lacked popular roots. By contrast, the religion of a visionary reformer named Mazdak, which had won considerable support among the peasants, had been brutally suppressed by the Sasanian rulers in the period before the rise of Islam. At first, the Sasanian commanders had contempt for the Arab invaders and set out against them with poorly prepared forces. By the time the seriousness of the Islamic threat was made clear by decisive Arab victories in the Fertile Crescent region and the defection of the Arab tribes on the frontier, Muslim warriors had broken into the Sasanian heartland. Further Muslim victories brought about the rapid collapse of the vast empire. The Sasanian rulers and their forces retreated eastward in the face of the Muslim advance. The capital was taken, armies were destroyed, and generals were slain. When in 651 the last of the Sasanian rulers was assassinated, Muslim victory and the destruction of the empire were ensured.

Despite an equally impressive string of Muslim victories in the provinces of their empire, the Byzantines proved a stronger adversary (see Chapter 9). However, their ability to resist the Muslim onslaught was impeded by both the defection of their own frontier Arabs and the support the Muslim invaders received from the Christians of Syria and Egypt. Members of the Christian sects dominant in these areas, such as the **Copts** and **Nestorians,** had long resented the rule of the Orthodox Byzantines, who

taxed them heavily and openly persecuted them as heretics. When it became clear that the Muslims would not only tolerate the Christians but tax them less heavily than the Byzantines did, these Christian groups rallied to the Arabs.

Weakened from within and exhausted by the long wars fought with Persia in the decades before the Arab explosion, the Byzantines reeled from the Arab assaults. Syria, western Iraq, and Palestine were quickly taken by the Arab invaders, and by 640 a series of probes had been made into Egypt, one of the richest provinces of the empire (see Map 6.1). In the early 640s, the ancient center of learning and commerce, Alexandria, was taken, most of Egypt was occupied, and Arab armies extended their conquests into Libya to the west. Perhaps even more astounding from the point of view of the Byzantines, by the mid-640s the desert bedouins were putting together war fleets that increasingly challenged the long-standing Byzantine mastery of the Mediterranean. The rise of Muslim naval supremacy in the eastern end of the Mediterranean sealed the loss of Byzantium's rich provinces in Syria and Egypt. It also opened the way to further Muslim conquests in north Africa, the Mediterranean islands, and even southern Italy (see Map 6.1). For a time the Byzantines managed to rally their forces and stave off further inroads into their Balkan and Asia Minor heartlands. But the early triumphs of the Arab invaders had greatly reduced the strength of the Byzantine Empire. Although it survived for centuries, it was henceforth a kingdom under siege.

The Problem of Succession and the Sunni–Shi'a Split

The stunning successes of Muslim armies and the sudden rise of an Arab empire diverted attention, for a time at least, from continuing divisions within the community. Although these divisions were often generations old and the result of personal animosities, resentments had also begun to build over how the booty from the conquests should be divided among the tribal groups that made up the Islamic community. In 656, just over two decades after the death of the prophet, the growing tensions broke into open violence. The spark that began the conflict was the murder of the third caliph, **Uthman,** by mutinous warriors returning from Egypt. His death was the signal for the supporters of Ali to proclaim him as caliph. Uthman's unpopularity among many of the tribes, particularly those from Medina and the prophet's earliest followers, arose in part from the fact that he was the first caliph to be chosen from Muhammad's early enemies, the Umayyad clan. Already angered by Uthman's murder, the Umayyads rejected Ali's claims and swore revenge when he failed to punish Uthman's assassins. Warfare erupted between the two factions.

Ali was a famous warrior and experienced commander, and his deeply committed supporters soon gained the upper hand. After his victory at the Battle of the Camel in late 656, most of the Arab garrisons shifted to his side against the Umayyads, whose supporters were concentrated in the province of Syria and the holy city of Mecca. Just as Ali was on the verge of defeating the Umayyad forces at the **Battle of Siffin** in 657, he was won over by a plea for mediation. His decision to accept mediation was fatal to his cause. Some of his most fervent supporters renounced his leadership and had to be suppressed violently. While representatives of both parties tried unsuccessfully to work out a compromise, the Umayyads regrouped their forces and added Egypt to the provinces backing their claims. In 660, **Mu'awiya,** the new leader of the Umayyads, was proclaimed caliph in Jerusalem, directly challenging Ali's position. A year later, Ali was assassinated, and his son, Hasan, was pressured by the Umayyads into renouncing his claims to the caliphate.

In the decades after the prophet's death, the question of succession generated deep divisions in the Muslim community. The split between the **Sunnis,** who backed the Umayyads, and the **Shi'a,** or supporters of Ali, remains to this day the most fundamental in the Islamic world. Hostility between these two branches of the Islamic faithful was heightened in the years after Ali's death by the continuing struggle between the Umayyads and Ali's second son, Husayn. After being abandoned by the clans in southern Iraq, who had promised to rise in a revolt supporting his claims against the Umayyads, Husayn and a small party were overwhelmed and killed at **Karbala** in 680. From that point on, the Shi'a mounted sustained resistance to the Umayyad caliphate.

Over the centuries, factional disputes about who had the right to succeed Muhammad, with the Shi'a recognizing none of the early caliphs except Ali, have been compounded by differences in belief, ritual, and law that have steadily widened the gap between Sunnis and Shi'a. These divisions have been further complicated by the formation of splinter sects within the Shi'a community in particular, beginning with those who defected from Ali when he agreed to arbitration.

The Umayyad Imperium

After a pause to settle internal disputes over succession, the remarkable sequence of Arab conquest was renewed in the last half of the 7th century. Muslim armies broke into central Asia, inaugurating a rivalry with Buddhism in the region that continues to the present day (see Map 6.1). By the early 8th century, the southern prong of this advance had reached into northwest India. Far to the west, Arab armies swept across north Africa and crossed the Straits of Gibraltar to conquer Spain and threaten France. Although the Muslim advance into western Europe was blocked by the hard-fought victory of Charles Martel and the Franks at Poitiers in 732, the Arabs did not fully retreat beyond the Pyrenees into Spain until decades later. Muslim warriors and sailors dominated much of the Mediterranean, a position that was solidified by the conquest of key islands such as Crete, Sicily, and Sardinia in the early decades of the 9th century. By the early 700s, the Umayyads ruled an empire that extended from Spain in the west to the steppes of central Asia in the east. Not since the Romans had there been an empire to match it; never had an empire of its size been built so rapidly.

Although Mecca remained the holy city of Islam, under the Umayyads the political center of community shifted to **Damascus** in Syria, where the Umayyads chose to live after the murder of Uthman. From Damascus a succession of Umayyad caliphs strove to build a bureaucracy that would bind together the vast domains they claimed to rule. The empire was very much an Arab conquest state. Except in the Arabian peninsula and in parts of the Fertile Crescent, a small Arab and Muslim aristocracy ruled over peoples who were neither Arab nor Muslim. Only Muslim Arabs were first-class citizens of this great empire. They made up the core of the army and imperial administration, and only they received a share of the booty derived from the ongoing conquests. They could be taxed only for charity. The Umayyads sought to keep the Muslim warrior elite concentrated in garrison towns and separated from the local population. It was hoped that isolation would keep them from assimilating to the subjugated cultures because intermarriage meant conversion and the loss of taxable subjects.

Converts and "People of the Book"

Umayyad attempts to block extensive interaction between the Muslim warrior elite and their non-Muslim subjects had little chance of succeeding. The citified bedouin tribes were soon interacting intensively with the local populations of the conquered areas and intermarrying with them. Equally critical, increasing numbers of these peoples were voluntarily converting to Islam, despite the fact that conversion did little to advance them socially or politically in the Umayyad period. In this era Muslim converts, **mawali,** still had to pay property taxes and in some cases the **jizya,** or head tax, levied on nonbelievers. They received no share of the booty and found it difficult, if not impossible, to get important positions in the army or bureaucracy. They were not even considered full members of the umma but were accepted only as clients of the powerful Arab clans.

As a result, the number of conversions in the Umayyad era was low. By far the greater portion of the population of the empire were the **dhimmi,** or "people of the book." As the name suggests, it was originally applied to Christians and Jews who shared the Bible with the Muslims. As Islamic conquests spread to other peoples, such as the Zoroastrians of Persia and the Hindus of India, the designation dhimmi was necessarily stretched to accommodate the majority groups within these areas of the empire. As the early illustration of Jewish worship in Muslim Spain in Figure 6.4 shows, the Muslim overlords generally tolerated the religions of dhimmi. Although they had to pay the jizya and both commercial and property taxes, their communities and legal systems were left intact, and they were allowed to worship as they pleased. This approach made it a good deal easier for these peoples to accept Arab rule, particularly because many had been oppressed by their pre-Muslim overlords.

Family and Gender Roles in the Umayyad Age

Broader social changes within the Arab and widening Islamic community were accompanied by signif-

Figure 6.4 *Jews worshiping in a synagogue. As dhimmi, or "people of the book," Jews were allowed to build impressive synagogues and worship freely throughout the Muslim world. Jewish merchant families amassed great wealth, often as partners of Muslim counterparts, and Jewish scholars were revered for their many contributions to learning from Spain to Baghdad.*

icant shifts in the position of women, both within the family and in society at large. In the first centuries of Arab expansion, the greatly strengthened position of women under Islam prevailed over the seclusion and subordination that were characteristic features of women's lives through much of the rest of the Middle East. Muhammad's teachings and the dictates of the Qur'an stressed the moral and ethical dimensions of marriage. The kindness and concern the prophet displayed for his own wives and daughters did much to strengthen the bonds between husband and wife and the nuclear family in the Islamic community. Muhammad encouraged marriage as a replacement for the casual and often commercial sexual liaisons that had been widespread in pre-Islamic Arabia. He vehemently denounced adultery on the part of both husbands and wives, and he forbade female infanticide, which apparently had been widely practiced in Arabia in pre-Islamic times. Men were allowed to marry up to four wives. But the Qur'an forbade multiple marriages if the husband could not support more than one wife or treat all of his wives equally. Women could not take more than one husband. But Muhammad gave his own daughters a say as to whom they would marry and greatly strengthened the legal rights of women in inheritance and divorce. He insisted that the bride-price paid by the husband's family be given to his future wife rather than to her father.

The prophet's teachings proclaimed the equality of men and women before God and in Islamic worship. Women, most notably his wife Khadijah, were some of Muhammad's earliest and bravest followers. They accompanied his forces to battle (as did the wives of their adversaries) with the Meccans, and a woman was the first martyr for the new faith. Many of the **hadiths,** or traditions of the prophet, which have played such a critical role in Islamic law and ritual, were recorded by women. In addition, Muhammad's wives and daughters played an important role in compiling the Qur'an.

Although women were not allowed to lead prayers, they played an active role in the politics of the early community. Muhammad's widow, Aisha, actively promoted the claims of the Umayyad party against Ali, while Zainab, Ali's daughter, went into battle with the ill-fated Husayn. Through much of the Umayyad period, little is heard of veiled Arab women, and women appear to have pursued a wide range of occupations, including scholarship, law, and commerce. Perhaps one of Zainab's nieces best epitomizes the independent-mindedness of Muslim women in the early Islamic era. When chided for going about without a veil, she replied that Allah in his wisdom had chosen to give her a beautiful face and that she intended to make sure that it was seen in public so that all might appreciate his grace.

Umayyad Decline and Fall

The ever-increasing size of the royal harem was just one manifestation of the Umayyad caliphs' growing addiction to luxury and soft living. Their legitimacy had been disputed by various Muslim factions since their seizure of the caliphate. But the Umayyads fur-

ther alienated the Muslim faithful as they became more aloof in the early 8th century and retreated from the dirty business of war into their pleasure gardens and marble palaces. Their abandonment of the frugal, simple lifestyle followed by Muhammad and the earliest caliphs—including Abu Bakr, who made a trip to the market the day after he was selected to succeed the prophet—enraged the dissenting sects and sparked revolts throughout the empire. The uprising that proved fatal to the short-lived dynasty began among the frontier warriors who had fought and settled in distant Iran.

By the mid-8th century, more than 50,000 warriors had settled near the oasis town of Merv in the eastern Iranian borderlands of the empire. Many of them had married local women, and over time they had come to identify with the region and to resent the dictates of governors sent from distant Damascus. The warrior settlers were also angered by the fact that they were rarely given the share of the booty, now officially tallied in the account books of the royal treasury, that they had earned by fighting the wars of expansion and defending the frontiers. They were contemptuous of the Umayyads and the Damascus elite, whom they saw as corrupt and decadent. In the early 740s, an attempt by Umayyad palace officials to introduce new troops into the Merv area touched off a revolt that soon spread over much of the eastern portions of the empire (see Map 6.1).

Marching under the black banners of the **Abbasid** party, which traced its descent from Muhammad's uncle, al-Abbas, the frontier warriors openly challenged Umayyad armies by 747. Deftly forging alliances with dissident groups that resisted the Umayyads throughout the empire, their leader, Abu al-Abbas, the great-great-grandson of the prophet's uncle, led his forces from victory to victory. Among his most important allies were the Shi'a, who, as we have seen, had rejected Umayyad authority from the time of Ali. Also critical were the mawali, or non-Arab converts to Islam. The mawali felt that under Umayyad rule they had never been recognized as fully Muslim. In supporting the Abbasids, the mawali hoped to attain full acceptance in the community of believers.

This diverse collection of Muslim rebels made short work of what remained of the Umayyad imperium. Persia and then Iraq fell to the rebels. In

In Depth

Civilization and Gender Relationships

Within a century of Muhammad's death, the strong position women had enjoyed as a result of the teachings and example of the prophet had begun to erode. We do not fully understand all the forces that account for this decline. Ambiguities in the Qur'an provide part of the answer. Muhammad was concerned about good treatment for women and defined certain rights, for example to property. He also, however, stipulated women's inferiority to men in key legal rights (differential punishments for adultery were a case in point). And, like Christianity, Islam argued that women were more likely than men to be sinners. But more critical were the beliefs and practices of the urbanized, sedentary peoples in the areas the Arabs conquered and where many of them settled from the mid-7th century onward. The example of these ancient and long-civilized peoples increasingly influenced the Arab bearers of Islam. They developed a taste for city life and the superior material and artistic culture of the peoples they ruled. In terms of gender roles, most of these influences weakened the position of women. We have seen this apparent connection between increasing political centralization and urbanization and the declining position of women in many of the ancient and classical civilizations treated thus far. In China, India, Greece, and the Middle East, women enjoyed broader occupational options and a stronger voice within the family, and in society as a whole, before the emergence of centralized polities and highly stratified social systems. In each case, the rise of what we have called civilizations strengthened paternal control within the family, inheritance through the male line, and male domination of positions of power and the most lucrative occupations. Women in these societies became more and more subjected to men—their fathers and brothers, husbands and sons—and more and more confined to the roles of homemakers and bearers of children. Women's legal rights were reduced, often sharply. In many civilizations, various ways were devised to shut women off from the world.

As we have seen, women played active and highly valued roles in the bedouin tribes of pre-Islamic Arabia. Particularly in towns such as Mecca, they experienced considerable freedom in terms of sexual and marriage partners, occupational choices (within the limited range available in an isolated pastoral society), and opportunities to influence clan decisions. The position of Muhammad's first wife,

Khadijah, is instructive. Her position as a wealthy widow in charge of a thriving trading enterprise reveals that women were able to remarry and to own and inherit property. They could also pursue careers, even after their husbands died. Khadijah employed Muhammad. After he had successfully worked for her for some time, she asked him to marry her, which apparently neither surprised nor scandalized her family or Meccan society. It is also noteworthy that Khadijah was 10 to 15 years older than the prophet, who was 25 at the time of their betrothal.

The impact of the bedouin pattern of gender roles and relationships is also clear in the teachings and personal behavior of Muhammad. Islam did much to legalize the strong but by no means equal status of women. In addition, it gave greater uniformity to their position from one tribe, town, or region to the next. For a century or two after the prophet's death, women in the Islamic world enjoyed unprecedented opportunities for education, religious expression, and social fulfillment.

Then the influences of the cultures into which the Arabs had expanded began to take hold. The practices of veiling and female seclusion that were long followed by the non-Arab dwellers of Syria and Persia were increasingly adopted by or imposed upon Muslim women. Confined more and more to the home, women saw their occupational options decrease, and men served as their go-betweens in legal and commercial matters.

Ironically, given the earlier status of women such as Khadijah, the erosion of the position of women was especially pronounced among those who lived in the cities that became the focus of Islamic civilization. Upper-class women, in particular, felt growing restrictions on their movement and activities. In the great residences that sprang up in the wealthy administrative centers and trading towns of the Middle East, the women's quarters were separate from the rest of the household and set off by high walls and gardens. In the palaces of Islamic rulers and provincial governors, this separation was marked by the development of the *harem*, or forbidden area. In the harem, the notables' wives and concubines lived in seclusion. They were constantly guarded by the watchful eyes and sharp swords of corps of eunuchs, men castrated specifically to qualify them for the task.

When upper-class women went into the city, they were veiled from head to toe and often were carried in covered sedan chairs by servants who guarded them from the glances of the townsmen and travelers. In their homes, upper-class women were spared the drudgery of domestic chores by large numbers of female slaves. If we are to judge from stories such as those related in the *Arabian Nights* (from which excerpts are included in the Document box), female slaves and servants were largely at the mercy of their male masters. Although veiling, seclusion, and other practices that limited the physical and occupational mobility of women also spread to the lower urban classes and rural areas, they were never as strictly observed there as in urban, upper-class households. Women from poorer families had to work to survive. Thus, they had to go out "veiled but often unchaperoned" to the market or to work as domestic servants. Lower-class women also worked hard at home, not just at housekeeping but at weaving, rugmaking, and other crafts that supplemented the family income. In rural areas and in towns distant from the main urban centers, veiling and confinement were observed less strictly. Peasant women worked the family or local landlord's fields, planted their own gardens, and tended the livestock.

Because of Islamic religion and law, in all locales and at all class levels the position of women in the Middle East never deteriorated to the same extent as in India, China, and many other civilized centers. Because of the need to read the Qur'an, women continued to be educated, family resources permitting, even if they rarely were able to use their learning for scholarship or artistic expression. Islamic law preserved for women property, inheritance, divorce, and remarriage rights that often were denied in other civilized societies. Thus, the strong position women had enjoyed in bedouin cultures, and that in many respects had been built into Islam, was never entirely undone by the customs and practices Muslims encountered as they came to rule the civilized centers in the rest of the Middle East.

The fact that the position of women has also been strong in other cultural areas where authority is decentralized and social organization not highly stratified, such as those in west Africa (see Chapter 8), suggests that at least in certain stages of its development, civilization works against the interests of women. Women in decentralized societies have often been able to own their own property, to engage in key economic activities, and to play important roles in religious ceremonies. The positions and status they have achieved in decentralized societies, such as those in early Arabia or much of sub-Saharan Africa and southeast Asia, suggest factors that may help explain the greater balance in gender roles and power in less centralized societies. The very immediate connection between women and agriculture or stock-raising, which are central to survival in these societies, may also account for the greater respect accorded them and for their often prominent roles in fertility rituals and religious cults. Whatever the explanation, until the present era, higher degrees of centralization and social stratification—both characteristic features of civilized societies—have almost always favored men in the allotment of power and career opportunities.

Questions: Compare the position of upper-class women in classical Indian, Chinese, Greek, and Roman societies with regard to their ability to hold property, opportunity to pursue careers outside the home, rights in marriage and divorce, and level of education. In which of these societies were women better off, and why? Were differences in the position of women at lower-class levels similar between these societies? In what ways were women better off in decentralized pastoral or forest-farming societies? What advantages have they enjoyed in highly urbanized and more centralized civilizations?

750, the Abbasid forces met an army led by the Umayyad caliph himself in a massive **Battle on the River Zab** near the Tigris. The Abbasid victory opened the way for the conquest of Syria and the capture of the Umayyad capital.

Wanting to eliminate the Umayyad family altogether to prevent recurring challenges to his rule, Abu al-Abbas invited many members of the clan to what was styled as a reconciliation banquet. As the Umayyads were enjoying the feast, guards covered them with carpets and they were slaughtered by Abbas's troops. An effort was then made to hunt down and kill all the remaining members of the family throughout the empire. Most were slain, but the grandson of a former caliph fled to Spain and founded there the Caliphate of Córdoba, which lived on for centuries after the rest of the Umayyads' empire had disappeared.

From Arab to Islamic Empire: The Early Abbasid Era

The sudden shift from Umayyad to Abbasid leadership reflected a series of fundamental transformations within an evolving Islamic civilization. The revolts against the Umayyads were a product of growing regional identities and divisions. As Islamic civilization spread even farther under the Abbasids, these regional interests and religious divisions made it increasingly difficult to hold together the vast areas the Arabs had conquered. They also gave rise to new divisions within the Islamic community that have sapped its strength from Abbasid times to the present. In addition, the victory of the Abbasids led to bureaucratic expansion, absolutism, and luxury on a scale beyond the wildest dreams of the Umayyads. The Abbasids also championed a policy of active conversion and the admission of converts as full members of the Islamic community. As a result, Islam was transformed from the religion of a small, Arab warrior elite into a genuinely universal faith with tens of millions of adherents from Spain to the Philippine islands.

The rough treatment the Umayyad clan had received at the hands of the victorious Abbasids should have forewarned their Shi'a and mawali allies of what was to come. But the Shi'a and other dissenting groups continued the support that allowed the Abbasids to level all other centers of political rivalry. Gradually, the Abbasids rejected many of their old allies, becoming more and more righteous in their defense of Sunni Islam and increasingly less tolerant of what they called the heretical views of the various sects of Shi'ism. With the Umayyads all but eliminated and their allies brutally suppressed, the way was clear for the Abbasids to build a centralized, absolutist imperial order.

The fact that they chose to build their new capital, **Baghdad,** in Iraq near the ancient Persian capital of Ctesiphon was a clear sign of things to come. Soon the Abbasid caliphs were perched on jewel-encrusted thrones, reminiscent of those of the ancient Persian emperors, gazing down on the great gatherings of courtiers and petitioners who bowed before them in their gilt and marble audience halls. The caliphs' palaces and harems expanded to keep pace with their claims to absolute power over the Islamic faithful as well as the non-Muslim subjects of their vast empire.

The ever-expanding corps of bureaucrats, servants, and slaves who strove to translate Abbasid political claims into reality lived and worked within the circular walls of the new capital at Baghdad. The bureaucratization of the Islamic Empire was reflected above all in the growing power of the **wazir,** or chief administrator and head of the caliph's inner councils. It was also embodied in a more sinister way in the fearful guise of the royal executioner, who stood close to the throne in the public audiences of the Abbasid rulers. The wazirs oversaw the building of an administrative infrastructure that allowed the Abbasids to project their demands for tribute to the most distant provinces of the empire. Sheer size, poor communication, and collusion between Abbasid officials and local notables meant that the farther the town or village was from the capital, the less effectively royal commands were carried out. But for more than a century, the Abbasid regime was fairly effective at collecting revenue from its subject peoples and preserving law and order over much of the empire.

Islamic Conversion and Mawali Acceptance

The Abbasid era saw the full integration of new converts, both Arab and non-Arab, into the Islamic community. In the last decades of the Umayyad period, there was a growing acceptance of the mawali, or non-Arab Muslims, as equals. There were also efforts to win new converts to the faith, particularly among Arab peoples outside the Arabian peninsula, such as those at prayer in Figure 6.5. In the Abbasid era, when the practice of dividing booty between the believers had long been discarded, mass conversions to Islam were encouraged for all peoples of the empire, from the Berbers of north Africa to the Persians and Turkic peoples of central Asia. Converts were admitted on an equal footing with the first generations of believers, and over time the distinction between mawali and the earlier converts all but disappeared.

Most converts were won over peacefully through the great appeal of Islamic beliefs and the advantages they enjoyed over non-Muslim peoples in the empire. Not only were converts exempt from paying the head tax, but they had greater opportunities to get advanced schooling and launch careers as administrators, traders, or judges. No group demonstrated the

Figure 6.5 *Massed Muslim worshipers. Whether in a nearby mosque or in their homes and shops, Muslims are required to pray five times a day, facing the holy city of Mecca. Those congregating in the mosque, as in this photo, are oriented to Mecca by the qibla wall, which is marked by a highly ornamented inset built into it, which indicates the direction of the holy city. Men congregate in the open spaces in the center of the mosque, while women pray in areas on the sides or in the back, or sometimes in balconies above, that are usually screened off by pillars or carved panels from the areas where the men worship.*

new opportunities open to converts as dramatically as the Persians, who, in part through their bureaucratic skills, soon came to dominate the upper levels of imperial administration. In fact, as the Abbasid rulers became more dissolute and less interested in affairs of state, several powerful Persian families close to the throne became the real locus of power in the imperial system.

Town and Country: Commercial Boom and Agrarian Expansion

The rise of the mawali was paralleled in the Abbasid era by the growth in wealth and social status of the merchant and landlord classes of the empire. The Abbasid age was a time of great urban expansion that was linked to a revival of the Afro-Eurasian trading network, which had declined with the fall of the Han dynasty in China in the early 3rd century C.E. and the slow collapse of the Roman Empire in the 4th and 5th centuries. The Abbasid domains in the west and the great Tang and Song empires in the east became the pivots of the revived commercial system.

From the western Mediterranean to the South China Sea, Arab **dhows,** or sailing vessels with lateen (triangular) sails, which later influenced European ship design, carried the goods of one civilized core to

be exchanged with those of another. Muslim merchants, often in joint ventures with Christians and Jews (which, because each merchant had a different Sabbath, meant that the firm could do business all week), grew rich by supplying the cities of the empire with provisions. Mercantile concerns also took charge of the long-distance trade that specialized in luxury products for the elite classes. The great profits from trade were reinvested in new commercial enterprises, the purchase of land, and the construction of the great mansions that dominated the central quarters of the political and commercial hubs of the empire. Some wealth also went to charity, as required by the Qur'an. A good deal of the wealth was spent on building and running mosques and religious schools, baths, and rest houses for weary travelers (Figure 6.6). Large donations were also made to hospitals, which in the numbers of their patients and the quality of their medical care surpassed those of any other civilization of that time.

The growth of Abbasid cities was also fed by a great increase in handicraft production. Both government-run and privately owned workshops expanded or were established to produce a wide range of products, from necessities such as furniture and carpets to luxury items such as glassware, jewelry, and tapestries. Although the artisans often were poorly paid and

Figure 6.6 *The rulers and nobility of the Abbasid capital in Baghdad frequented baths like that shown in this Persian miniature painting. Here the caliph, Haroun al-Rashid, receives a haircut while servants prepare the steam rooms. At the baths, the Abbasid elite could relax, exchange gossip, and enjoy expert massages.*

some worked in great workshops, they were not slaves or drudge laborers. They owned their own tools and were often highly valued for their skills. The most skilled of the artisans formed guildlike organizations, which negotiated wages and working conditions with the merchants and supported their members in times of financial difficulty or personal crisis.

In towns and the countryside, much of the unskilled labor was left to slaves, often attached to prominent families as domestic servants. Large numbers of slaves also served the caliphs and their highest advisors. It was possible for the more clever and

ambitious slaves to rise to positions of great power, and many eventually were granted their freedom or were able to buy it. Less fortunate were the slaves forced into lives of hard labor under the overseer's whip on rural estates and government projects, such as those devoted to draining marshlands, or into a lifetime of labor in the nightmare conditions of the great salt mines in southern Iraq. Most of these drudge laborers were non-Muslims captured on slaving raids in east Africa.

In the countryside, a wealthy and deeply entrenched landed elite called the **ayan** emerged in

Document

The Thousand and One Nights as a Mirror of Elite Society in the Abbasid Era

The luxurious lifestyle of the Abbasid rulers and their courtiers reflected the new wealth of the political and commercial elites of the Islamic Empire. At the same time, it intensified sectarian and social divisions in the Islamic community. As the compilation of folktales from many parts of the empire titled *The Thousand and One Nights* testifies, life for much of the elite in Baghdad and other major urban centers was luxurious and oriented to the delights of the flesh. Caliphs and wealthy merchants lived in palatial residences of stone and marble, complete with gurgling fountains and elaborate gardens, which served as retreats from the glare and heat of the southern Mediterranean climate. In the Abbasid palaces, luxurious living and ostentation soared to fantastic heights. In the Hall of the Tree, for example, there was a huge artificial tree, made entirely of gold and silver and filled with gold mechanical birds that chirped to keep the caliph in good cheer.

Because the tales were just that—tall tales—there is some exaggeration of the wealth, romantic exploits, and sexual excesses of the world depicted. But for some members of the elite classes, the luxuries, frivolities, and vices of the Abbasid age were very real. The following passages are taken from an English translation of *The Thousand and One Nights*. Each is selected to reveal a different facet of high society in the Abbasid era. The first, which describes the sumptuous interior of a mansion in Baghdad, indicates that conspicuous material consumption existed far beyond the palace:

They reached a spacious ground-floor hall, built with admirable skill and beautified with all manner of colors and carvings, with upper balconies and groined [sharply curved] arches and galleries and cupboards and recesses whose curtains hung before them. In the midst stood a great basin full of water surrounding a fine fountain, and at the upper end on the raised dais was a couch of juniper wood set with gems and pearls, with a canopy-like mosquito curtain of red satin-silk looped up with pearls as big as filberts [hazelnuts] and bigger.

In another tale, a fallen prince details the proper upbringing and education for a person of substance:

I am a king, son of a king, and was brought up like a prince. I learned intoning the Koran [Qur'an] according [to] the seven schools and I read all manner [of] books,

and held disputations on their contents with the doctors and men of science. Moreover, I studied star lore and the fair sayings of poets, and I exercised myself in all branches of learning until I surpassed the people of my time. My skill in calligraphy [writing, in this case Arabic and perhaps Persian] exceeded that of all of the scribes, and my fame was bruited abroad over all climes and cities, and all the kings learned to know my name.

In the following passage, a stylishly dressed woman from the elite classes is described in great detail:

There stood before him an honorable woman in a mantilla [veil] of Mosul silk broidered with gold and bordered with brocade [a rich cloth with a raised design, often of gold or silver]. Her walking shoes were also [bordered] with gold, and her hair floated in long plaits. She raised her face veil … showing two black eyes fringed with jetty lashes, whose glances were soft and languishing and whose perfect beauty was ever blandishing.

The woman leads a porter to a marketplace, which again reflects the opulence accessible to the rich and powerful of Abbasid society:

She stopped at the fruiter's shop and bought from him Shami apples and Osmani quinces and Omani peaches, and cucumbers of Nile growth, and Egyptian limes and Sultani oranges and citrons, besides Aleppine jasmine, scented myrtle berries, Damascene nenuphars [water lilies], flower of privit and camomile, blood-red anemones, violets, and pomegranate bloom, eglantine [wild rose], and narcissus, and set the whole in the porter's crate.

Questions: What objects are key symbols of wealth in Abbasid society? In what ways do these descriptions convey the cosmopolitan nature of Baghdad elite life? What attainments are highly valued for upper-class men? What do they tell us about occupations and talents that brought high status in Abbasid society, and how do they compare with career aspirations in our own? In comparison, what attributes of women are stressed in these passages? How do they compare with the preoccupations of the "jet-setters" of the late 20th century?

the early decades of Abbasid rule. Many of these landlords had been long established. Others were newcomers: Arab soldiers who invested their share of the booty in land or merchants and administrators who funneled their profits and kickbacks into sizeable estates. In many regions, most peasants did not own the land they worked. They occupied it as tenants, sharecroppers, or migrant laborers who were required to give the greater portion of the crops they harvested to the estate owners.

The First Flowering of Islamic Learning

When the Arabs first came out of the desert, they were for the most part illiterate and ignorant of the wider world. Their cultural backwardness was no better revealed than when the victorious Muslim armies came within sight of the city of Alexandria in Egypt. Chroniclers of the great conquests wrote that the veteran Arab warriors halted and sat on their horses, mouths open in wonderment, before the great walls of the city that stretched across the horizon from the Pharos lighthouse in the north to perhaps the greatest library in the ancient world in the south. As this confrontation suggests, the Arab conquerors burst suddenly into some of the most ancient and highly developed centers of civilization in human history. Within the confines of the Islamic domains were located the centers of the Hellenistic, Persian, Indian, Egyptian, and Mesopotamian civilizations as well as the widely dispersed Christian and Jewish traditions of thought and learning. The sparse cultural tradition of the Arabs made them receptive to influences from the subject peoples and remarkably tolerant of the great diversity of their styles and approaches to thought and artistic creativity.

In the first phase of Abbasid rule, the Islamic contribution to human artistic expression focused on the great mosques, such as those featured in the Visualizing the Past box, and great palaces. In addition to advances in religious, legal, and philosophical discourse, the Islamic contribution to learning focused on the sciences and mathematics. In the early Abbasid period, the main tasks were recovering and preserving the learning of the ancient civilizations of the Mediterranean and Middle East. Beyond the works of Plato, for example, much of Greek learning had been lost to the peoples of western Europe. Thanks to Muslim and Jewish scholars, the priceless writings of the Greeks on key subjects such as medicine, algebra, geometry, astronomy, anatomy, and ethics were saved, recopied in Arabic, and dispersed throughout the empire. From Spain, Greek writings found their way into Christendom. Among the authors rescued in this manner were Aristotle, Galen, Hippocrates, Ptolemy, and Euclid.

In addition, scholars working in Arabic transmitted ideas that paralleled the rise of Arab traders and merchants as the carriers of goods and inventions. For example, Muslim invaders of south Asia soon learned of the Indian system of numbers. From India they were carried by Muslim scholars and merchants to the Middle Eastern centers of Islamic civilization. Eventually the Indian numerical system was transmitted across the Mediterranean to Italy and from there to northern Europe. Along with Greek and Arab mathematics, Indian numbers later proved critical to the early modern Scientific Revolution in western Europe.

GLOBAL CONNECTIONS: Early Islam and the World

The rise of Islamic civilization from the 7th to 9th centuries C.E. was a stunning development without precedent in human history. Not only had the largely nomadic peoples from an Arabian backwater built one of the greatest empires of the preindustrial world, but they had laid the basis for the first truly global civilization if one excludes the Americas, which were unknown to the peoples of the Eastern Hemisphere. Building on earlier religious traditions, especially Christianity and Judaism, Arab culture had nurtured Islam, one of the great universal religions of humankind. The mosques, the prayer rituals and pilgrimages of the faithful, and the influence of Islamic law proclaimed the pervasive effects of this new creed on societies from Spain to eastern Indonesia and from central Asia to the savannas of west Africa.

Islamic and Arab commitment to trade and merchant activity was crucial in setting up wider connections among Asia, Africa, and Europe, with the Middle East as hub. The region's earlier functions in commerce, in and between the Indian Ocean and Mediterranean Sea, expanded greatly.

Visualizing the Past

The Mosque as a Symbol of the Islamic Civilization

From one end of the Islamic world to the other, Muslim towns and cities can be readily identified by the domes and minarets of the mosques where the faithful are called to prayer five times daily. The following illustrations trace the development of the mosque and the refinement of mosque architecture, the crowning glory of Islamic material culture, during the early centuries of Muslim expansion. As you look at these pictures and follow the development of the mosque, consider what the functions of the mosque and the evolving style of mosque architecture can tell us about Muslim beliefs and values and the impact of earlier religions, such as Judaism and Christianity, on Islam.

Given the low level of material culture in pre-Islamic Arabia, it is not surprising that the earliest prayer houses were simple in design and construction. In fact, these first mosques were laid out along the lines suggested by Muhammad's own house. They were square enclosures with a shaded porch on one side, a columned shelter on the other, and an open courtyard in between. The outer perimeter of the earliest mosques was made of reed mats,

but soon more permanent stone walls surrounded the courtyard and prayer areas. After Mecca was taken and the Ka'ba became the central shrine of the new faith, each mosque was oriented to the qibla, or Mecca wall, which always faced in the direction of the holy city.

In the last years of the prophet, his chair was located so that the faithful could see and hear him during prayer sessions. During the time of the first caliphs, the raised area became the place from which sermons were delivered. From the mid-8th century, this space evolved into a genuine pulpit. Somewhat earlier, the practice of build-

(continued)

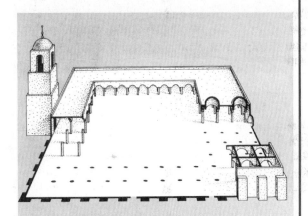

Domes and Minarets of Persian Mosques

Dome of the Rock

Pulpit

ing a special and often elaborately decorated niche in the qibla had developed.

Over time mosques became more elaborate. Very often the remains of Greek or Roman temples or abandoned Christian churches formed the core of major mosques, or the ruins of these structures were mined for stone for mosque construction. In the larger cities, the courtyards of the great mosques were surrounded by columns and arches, and eventually they were enclosed by great domes such as that at the Dome of the Rock in Jerusalem.

The first minarets, or towers from which the faithful were called to prayer, were added in the early 8th century and soon became a key feature of the mosque complex. As mosques grew larger and more architecturally refined, elaborate decoration in brightly colored ceramic tiles, semiprecious stones, and gold and silver filigree adorned their sides and domes. Because human and animal images were forbidden, geometric designs, passages from the Qur'an in swirling Arabic, and flower and plant motifs were favored. Nowhere were these decorations more splendid than in the great mosques of Persia. Thus, in the early centuries of Islam, these great houses of worship became the focal points of Islamic cities, key places of community worship and socialization, and, with the schools that were often attached, vital intellectual and educational centers of the Islamic world.

Questions: What do the design and decoration of Muslim mosques tell us about the Islamic view of God and the relationship between God and humans? Discuss the Christian and Jewish influences you detect in mosque design and the pattern of religious worship conducted there. What do you think is the significance of the lavish application of color and the frequent use of floral and plant motifs and Arabic verses from the Qur'an in the decoration of mosques through much of the Muslim world?

Qibla Wall with Decorated Section Facing Mecca

In the arts and sciences, the Muslims initially relied heavily on the achievements of the classical civilizations of Greece and Mesopotamia. But the work of preserving and combining the discoveries of earlier peoples soon led to reformulation and innovation. As in religion and politics, Muslim peoples were soon making important contributions to learning, invention, and artistic creativity, which were carried by their armies and religious teachers to other civilizations in Europe, Africa, and Asia.

Never before had a civilization spanned so many different cultures and combined such a patchwork of linguistic groups, religions, and ethnic types. Never before had a single civilization mediated so successfully between the other centers of civilized life. Never had a civilized lifestyle so deeply affected so many of the nomadic cultures that surrounded the pools of sedentary agriculture and urban life. Ironically, the contacts Islamic mediation made possible between the civilized cores of the Eastern Hemisphere contributed much to the transformations in technology and organization that increasingly tilted the balance of power against the Muslim peoples. But those reversals were still far in the future. In the short run, Islamic conversion and contact ushered in an age of unparalleled nomadic intervention in and dominance over global history.

Further Readings

There are many accounts of Muhammad's life and the rise of Islam. The most readable is Karen Armstrong's *Muhammad: A Biography of the Prophet* (1992). A sense of the very different interpretations that have been offered to explain these pivotal developments in global history can be gained by comparing W. Montgomery Watt's *Muhammad: Prophet and Statesman* (1961); Tor Andrae's *Muhammad: The Man and His Faith* (1960); Maxime Rodinson's *Mohammed* (1971); and the more recent revisionist (and somewhat less accessible) writings of Elizabeth Crone and Michael Cook.

H. A. R. Gibb's *Mohammedism* (1962) remains a useful introduction to Islam as a religion. John Esposito's *Islam: The Straight Path* (1991) and Karen Armstrong's *Islam: A Short History* (2000) also provide good and updated overviews of the faith. On early Islamic expansion and civilization through the first centuries of the Abbasid caliphate, see G. E. von Grunebaum's *Classical Islam* (1970); M. A. Shaban's *Islamic History: An Interpretation* (1971); and *The Abbasid Revolution* (1970). On nearly all of these topics, it is difficult to surpass Marshall G. S. Hodgson's brilliant analysis, *The Venture of Islam* (1974, vol. 1), but some grounding in the history and beliefs of the Muslims is recommended before one

attempts this sweeping and provocative work. More accessible but still authoritative and highly interpretive are Ira M. Lapidus' *A History of Islamic Societies* (1988) and Albert Hourani's *A History of the Arab Peoples* (1991).

On early Islamic society generally, see M. M. Ahsan's *Social Life Under the Abbasids* (1979). On women in Islam specifically, there is a superb essay by Guity Nashat, "Women in the Middle East, 8000 B.C.–A.D. 1800," in the collection titled *Restoring Women to History*, published in 1988 by the Organization of American Historians. See also the relevant portions of the essays in Lois Beck and Nikki Keddi, eds., *Women in the Muslim World* (1978), and the early chapters of Leila Ahmed, *Women and Gender in Islam* (1992). For a broad treatment of the roles and position of women in ancient civilizations more generally, see Sarah and Brady Hughes, *Women in Ancient Global History* (1998). For insights into Islamic culture and civilization from a literary perspective, a good place to begin is Eric Schroeder's delightful *Muhammad's People: A Tale by Anthology* (1955) and N. J. Dawood's translation of *Tales from the Thousand and One Nights* (1954). Of the many works on Muslim architecture, John D. Hoag's *Western Islamic Architecture* (1963) gives a good overview, but K. A. Creswell's *Early Muslim Architecture*, 2 vols. (1932–1940) and the more recent Markus Hattstein and Peter Delius, eds., *Islam: Art and Architecture* (2000), provide greater detail and far better illustrations.

On the Web

The religion and society of Islam (http://islamicity.com/mosque/Intro_Islam.htm), Islam's revealed text, the Qur'an (http://www.usc.edu/dept/MSA/quran), and its arts (http://islamicart.com/) set new standards for civilization for much of the world. Islam sought submission to the will of God, Allah (http://www.usc.edu/dept/MSA/fundamentals/tawheed/), through the message vouchsafed to the Prophet Muhammad (http://www.bbc.co.uk/worldservice/people/features/world_religions/islam_life.shtml and http://www.pbs.org/muhammad/timeline_html.shtml), whose immediate successor as leader of the fledgling Muslim community, Abu Bakr (http://i-cias.com/e.o/abubakr.htm), proved equal to the task of ensuring its survival.

The evolution of Islamic art from its Arab roots, its capacity to influence non-Islamic art, and its capacity for synthesis of non-Arab themes can be traced at http://www.islamicart.com/main/architecture/impact.html and http://www.lacma.org/islamic_art/intro.htm. The golden age of Islamic science, literature, and scholarship, as well as religious philosophy, can be studied at http://islamicity.com/mosque/IGC/knowledge.htm. A gorgeous site explicating the Muslim pilgrimage to Mecca can be found at http://www.the-webplaza.com/hajj/index.html.

CHAPTER 7

ABBASID DECLINE AND THE SPREAD OF ISLAMIC CIVILIZATION TO SOUTH AND SOUTHEAST ASIA

The richness and depth attained by Muslim civilizations in the far-flung regions in which they were found is illustrated by this 17-century, miniature painting of a scholar-poet in an imagined nighttime garden in Kashmir in northern India. The meditative figure with book in hand and framed by the flowering tree in the background captures the commitment to learning and refined aesthetic sense that was cultivated by members of the elite classes throughout the Islamic world.

- The Islamic Heartlands in the Middle and Late Abbasid Eras
- **DOCUMENT**: Ibn Khaldun on the Rise and Decline of Empires
- An Age of Learning and Artistic Refinements
- **VISUALIZING THE PAST**: The Patterns of Islam's Global Expansion
- The Coming of Islam to South Asia
- The Spread of Islam to Southeast Asia
- **IN DEPTH**: Conversion and Accommodation in the Spread of World Religions
- **GLOBAL CONNECTIONS**: Islam: A Bridge Between Worlds

By the mid-9th century C.E., the Abbasid dynasty had begun to lose control over the vast Muslim empire that had been won from the Umayyads a century earlier (Map 7.1). From north Africa to Persia, rebellious governors and new dynasties arose to challenge the Abbasid caliphs' claims to be the rightful overlords of all Islamic peoples. Paradoxically, even as the political power of the Abbasids declined, Islamic civilization reached new heights of creativity and entered a new age of expansion. In architecture and the fine arts, in literature and philosophy, and in mathematics and the sciences, the centuries during which the Abbasid Empire slowly came apart were an era of remarkable achievement.

At the same time, political fragmentation did little to slow the growth of the Islamic world through political conquest and, more importantly, enduring peaceful conversion. From the 10th to the 14th century, Muslim warriors, traders, and wandering mystics carried the faith of Muhammad into the savanna and desert of west Africa, down the coast of east Africa, to the Turks and many other nomadic peoples of central Asia, and into south and southeast Asia. For more than five centuries, the spread of Islam played a central role in the rise, extension, or transformation of civilization in much of the Afro-Asian world. The Islamic world also became a great conduit for the exchange of ideas, plants and medicines, commercial goods, and inventions both between centers of urban and agrarian life and between these core regions of civilization and the areas dominated by nomadic peoples that still encompassed much of the globe.

The Islamic Heartlands in the Middle and Late Abbasid Eras

The vast Abbasid empire gradually disintegrated between the 9th and 13th centuries. Revolts spread among the peasants, slavery increased, and the position of women was further eroded. Divisions within the empire opened the way for Christian crusaders from western Europe to invade and, for a short time, establish warrior kingdoms in the Muslim heartlands. Political decline and social turmoil were offset for many by the urban affluence, inventiveness, and artistic creativity of the Abbasid age.

As early as the reign of the third Abbasid caliph, **al-Mahdi** (775–785), the courtly excesses and political divisions that eventually contributed to the decline of the empire were apparent. Al-Mahdi's efforts to reconcile the moderates among the Shi'a opposition to Abbasid rule ended in failure. This meant that Shi'a revolts and assassination attempts against Abbasid officials would plague the dynasty to the end of its days. Al-Mahdi also abandoned the frugal ways of his predecessor. In the brief span of his reign, he established a taste for luxury and monumental building and surrounded himself

700 C.E.	800 C.E.	900 C.E.	1000 C.E.	1200 C.E.
661–750 Umayyad caliphate (Damascus)	**800** Independent dynasty established in Tunisia	**945** Persian Buyids capture Baghdad; caliphs made into puppet rulers	**c. 1020** Death of Firdawsi, author of the *Shah-Nama*	**1206** Establishment of the Delhi sultanate in India
711–713 First Muslim raids into India	**809** First war of succession between Abbasid princes	**973–1050** Life of al-Biruni, scientist	**1055** Seljuk Turks overthrow Buyids, control caliphate	**1290s** Beginning of the spread of Islam in southeast Asia
750 Establishment of the Abbasid caliphate (Baghdad)	**813–833** Reign of al-Ma'mun; first mercenary forces recruited	**998** Beginning of Ghanzi raids into western India	**1096–1099** First Christian Crusade in Palestine	**1291** Fall of Acre; last Crusader stronghold in Middle East
775–785 Reign of al-Mahdi	**865–925** Life of al-Razi, physician and scientist		**1111** Death of al-Ghazali, philosopher and scientist	**1258** Fall of Baghdad to Mongols; end of Abbasid caliphate
777 Independent dynasty established in Algeria			**1123** Death of Omar Khayyam, scientist and poet	
786–809 Reign of al-Rashid				
788 Independent dynasty established in Morocco				

with a multitude of dependant wives, concubines, and courtiers. These habits would prove to be an ever greater financial drain in the reigns of later caliphs.

Perhaps most critically, al-Mahdi failed to solve the vexing problem of succession. Not only did he waver between which of his older sons would succeed him, but he allowed his wives and concubines, the mothers of different candidates, to become involved in the palace intrigues that became a standard feature of the transfer of power from one caliph to the next. Although a full-scale civil war was avoided after al-Mahdi's death, within a year his eldest son and successor was poisoned. That act cleared the way for one of the most famous and enduring of the Abbasid caliphs, **Harun al-Rashid** (786–809), to ascend the throne.

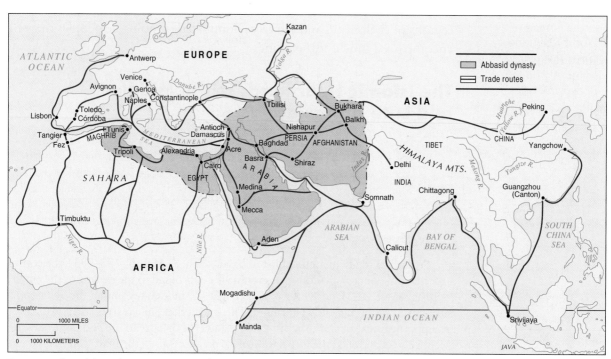

Map 7.1   *The Abbasid Empire at Its Peak*

Figure 7.1 *The richness and vitality of urban life in the Islamic world in the Abbasid age and later eras are wonderfully captured in this 16th-century Persian illustration from the* Khamsah (Five Poems) *of Nizami. Nizami gives us a bird's-eye view of a rather typical night in one of the great palaces of Baghdad. The multiple scenes vividly capture the bustle and high artistry of the splendidly decorated rooms and gardens, from a group of musicians serenading a man who is presumably the lord of the mansion to kitchen servants buying food and preparing to serve it to the lord and his guests.*

Imperial Extravagance and Succession Disputes

Emissaries sent in the early 9th century to Baghdad from Charlemagne, then the most powerful monarch in Christian Europe, provide ample evidence that Harun al-Rashid shared his father's taste for sumptuous living. Harun al-Rashid dazzled the Christians with the splendor of Baghdad's mosques, palaces, and treasure troves, which is reflected in the painting of nightlife in a palace in Figure 7.1. He also sent them back to Charlemagne with presents, including an intricate water clock and an elephant, that were literally worth a king's ransom.

The luxury and intrigue of Harun's court have also been immortalized by the tales of *The Thousand and One Nights* (see the Document in Chapter 6), set in the Baghdad of his day. The plots and maneuvers of the courtesans, eunuchs, and royal ministers related in the tales suggest yet another source of dynastic weakness. Partly because he was only 23 at the time of his accession to the throne, Harun became heavily dependant, particularly in the early years of his reign, on a family of Persian advisors. Although he eventually resisted their influence, the growth of the power of royal advisors at the expense of the caliphs became a clear trend in succeeding reigns. In fact, from the mid-9th century onward, most caliphs were pawns in the power struggles between different factions at the court.

Harun al-Rashid's death prompted the first of several full-scale civil wars over succession. In itself, the precedent set by the struggle for the throne was deeply damaging. But it had an additional consequence that would all but end the real power of the caliphs. The first civil war convinced the sons of al-Ma'mun (813–833), the winner, that they needed to build personal armies in anticipation of the fight for the throne that would break out when their father died. One of the sons, the victor in the next round of succession struggles, recruited a "bodyguard" of some 4000 slaves, mostly Turkic-speaking nomads from central Asia. On becoming caliph, he increased this mercenary force to more than 70,000.

Not surprisingly, this impressive force soon became a power center in its own right. In 846, slave mercenaries murdered the reigning caliph and placed one of his sons on the throne. In the next decade, four more caliphs were assassinated or poisoned by the mercenary forces. From this time onward, the leaders of the slave mercenary armies were often the real power behind the Abbasid throne and were major players in the struggles for control of the capital and empire. The mercenaries also became a major force for violent social unrest. They were often the catalyst for the food riots that broke out periodically in the capital and other urban centers.

Imperial Breakdown and Agrarian Disorder

In the last decades of the 9th century, the dynasty brought the slave armies under control for a time, but at a great cost. Constant civil violence drained the treasury and alienated the subjects of the Abbasids. A further strain was placed on the empire's dwindling revenues by some caliphs' attempts to escape the turmoil of Baghdad by establishing new capitals near the original one. The construction of palaces, mosques, and public works for each of these new imperial centers added to the already exorbitant costs of maintaining the court and imperial administration. Of course, the expense fell heavily on the already hard-pressed peasantry of the central provinces of the empire, where some imperial control remained. The need to support growing numbers of mercenary troops also increased the revenue demands on the peasantry.

Spiraling taxation and outright pillaging led to the destruction or abandonment of many villages in the richest provinces of the empire. The great irrigation works that had for centuries been essential to agricultural production in the fertile Tigris–Euphrates basin fell into disrepair, and in some areas they collapsed entirely. Some peasants perished through flood, famine, or violent assault; others fled to wilderness areas beyond the reach of the Abbasid tax collectors to neighboring kingdoms. Some formed bandit gangs or joined the crowds of vagabonds that trudged the highways and camped in the towns of the imperial heartland. In many cases, dissident religious groups, such as the various Shi'a sects, instigated peasant uprisings. Shi'a participation meant that these movements sought not only to correct the official abuses that had occurred under the Abbasid regime but to destroy the dynasty itself.

The Declining Position of Women in the Family and Society

The harem and the veil became the twin emblems of women's increasing subjugation to men and confinement to the home in the Abbasid era. Although the seclusion of women had been practiced by some Middle Eastern peoples since ancient times, the harem was a creation of the Abbasid court. The wives and the concubines of the Abbasid caliphs were restricted to the forbidden quarters of the imperial palace. Many of the concubines were slaves, who could win their freedom and gain power by bearing healthy sons for the rulers. The growing wealth of the Abbasid elite created a great demand for female and male slaves, who were found by the tens of thousands in Baghdad and other large cities. Most of these urban slaves continued to perform domestic services in the homes of the wealthy. One of the 10th-century caliphs is said to have had 11,000 eunuchs among his slave corps; another is said to have kept 4000 slave concubines.

Most of the slaves had been captured or purchased in the non-Muslim regions surrounding the empire, including the Balkans, central Asia, and Sudanic Africa. They were purchased in the slave markets found in all of the larger towns of the empire. Female and male slaves were prized for both their beauty and their intelligence. Some of the best-educated men and women in the Abbasid Empire were slaves. Consequently, caliphs and high officials often spent more time with their clever and talented slave concubines than with their less well-educated wives. Slave concubines and servants often had more personal liberty than freeborn wives. Slave women could go to the market, and they did not have to wear the veils and robes that were required for free women in public places.

Although women from the lower classes farmed, wove clothing and rugs, or raised silkworms to help support their families, rich women were allowed almost no career outlets beyond the home. Often married at puberty (legally set at age 9), women were raised to devote their lives to running a household and serving their husbands. But at the highest levels of society, wives and concubines cajoled their husbands and plotted with eunuchs and royal advisors to advance the interests of their sons and win for them the ruler's backing for succession to the throne. Despite these brief incursions into power politics, by the end of the Abbasid era, the freedom and influence—both within the family and in the wider world—that women had enjoyed in the first centuries of Islamic expansion had been severely curtailed.

Nomadic Incursions and the Eclipse of Caliphal Power

Preoccupied by struggles in the capital and central provinces, the caliphs and their advisors were powerless to prevent further losses of territory in the outer reaches of the empire. In addition, areas as close to the capital as Egypt and Syria broke away from Abbasid rule (see Map 7.1). More alarmingly, by the mid-10th century, independent kingdoms that had formed in areas that were once provinces of the empire were moving to supplant the Abbasids as lords of the Islamic world. In 945, the armies of one of these regional splinter dynasties, the **Buyids** of Persia, invaded the heartlands of the Abbasid Empire and captured Baghdad. From this point onward, the caliphs were little more than puppets controlled by families such as the Buyids. Buyid leaders took the title of *sultan* ("victorious" in Arabic), which came to designate Muslim rulers, especially in the West.

The Buyids controlled the caliph and the court, but they could not prevent the further disintegration of the empire. In just over a century, the Buyids' control over the caliphate was broken, and they were supplanted in 1055 by another group of nomadic invaders from central Asia via Persia, the **Seljuk Turks**. For the next two centuries, Turkic military leaders ruled the

remaining portions of the Abbasid Empire in the name of caliphs, who were usually of Arab or Persian extraction. The Seljuks were staunch Sunnis, and they moved quickly to purge the Shi'a officials who had risen to power under the Buyids and to rid the caliph's domains of the Shi'a influences the Buyids had tried to promote. For a time, the Seljuk military machine was also able to restore political initiative to the much reduced caliphate. Seljuk victories ended the threat of conquest by a rival Shi'a dynasty centered in Egypt. They also humbled the Byzantines, who had hoped to take advantage of Muslim divisions to regain some of their long-lost lands. The Byzantines' crushing defeat also opened the way to the settlement of Asia Minor, or Anatolia, by nomadic peoples of Turkic origins, some of whom would soon begin to lay the foundations of the **Ottoman Empire**.

The Impact of the Christian Crusades

Soon after seizing power, the Seljuks faced a very different challenge to Islamic civilization. It came from Christian crusaders, knights from western Europe (see Chapter 10) who were determined to capture the portions of the Islamic world that made up the Holy Land of biblical times. Muslim political divisions and the element of surprise made the first of the crusaders' assaults, between 1096 and 1099, by far the most successful. Much of the Holy Land was captured and divided into Christian kingdoms. In June 1099, the main objective of the Crusade, Jerusalem, was taken, and its Muslim and Jewish inhabitants were massacred by the rampaging Christian knights.

For nearly two centuries, the Europeans, who eventually mounted eight **Crusades** that varied widely in strength and success, maintained their precarious hold on the eastern Mediterranean region. But they posed little threat to the more powerful Muslim princes, whose disregard for the Christians was demonstrated by the fact that they continued to quarrel among themselves despite the intruders' aggressions. When united under a strong leader, as they were under Salah-ud-Din (known as **Saladin** in Christian Europe) in the last decades of the 12th century, the Muslims rapidly reconquered most of the crusader outposts. Saladin's death in 1193 and the subsequent breakup of his kingdom gave the remaining Christian citadels some respite. But the last of the crusader kingdoms was lost with the fall of Acre in 1291.

Document

Ibn Khaldun on the Rise and Decline of Empires

Although he lived in the century after the Abbasid Caliphate was destroyed in 1258, **Ibn Khaldun** was very much a product of the far-flung Islamic civilization that the Abbasids had consolidated and expanded. He was also one of the greatest historians and social commentators of all time. After extensive travels in the Islamic world, he served as a political advisor at several of the courts of Muslim rulers in north Africa. With the support of a royal patron, Ibn Khaldun wrote a universal history that began with a very long philosophical preface called *The Muqaddimah*. Among the subjects he treated at length were the causes of the rise and fall of dynasties. The shifting fortunes of the dynasties he knew well in his native north Africa, as well as the fate of the Abbasids and earlier Muslim regimes, informed his attempts to find persistent patterns in the confusing political history of the Islamic world. The following passages are from one of the most celebrated sections of *The Muqaddimah* on the natural life span of political regimes.

We have stated that the duration of the life of a dynasty does not as a rule extend beyond three generations. The first generation retains the desert qualities, desert toughness, and desert savagery. [Its members are used to] privation and to sharing their glory [with each other]; they are brave and rapacious. Therefore, the strength of group feeling continues to be preserved among them. They are sharp and greatly feared. People submit to them.

Under the influence of royal authority and a life of ease, the second generation changes from the desert attitude to sedentary culture, from privation to luxury and plenty, from a state in which everybody shared in the glory to one in which one man claims all the glory for himself while the others are too lazy to strive for [glory], and from proud superiority to humble subservience. Thus, the vigor of group feeling is broken to some extent. People become used to lowliness and obedience. But many of [the old virtues] remain in them, because they had direct personal contact with the first generation and its conditions.

The third generation, then, has [completely] forgotten the period of desert life and toughness, as if it had never existed. They have lost [the taste for] group feeling, because they are dominated by force. Luxury reaches its peak among them, because they are so much given to a life of prosperity and ease. They become dependent on the dynasty and are like women and children who need to be defended [by someone else]. Group feeling disappears completely. People forget to protect and defend themselves and to press their claims. With their emblems, apparel, horseback riding, and [fighting] skill, they deceive people and give them the wrong impression. For the most part, they are more cowardly than women upon their backs. When someone comes and demands something from them, they cannot repel him. The ruler, then, has need of other, brave people for his support. He takes many clients and followers. They help the dynasty to some degree, until God permits it to be destroyed, and it goes with everything it stands for.

Three generations last one hundred and twenty years. As a rule, dynasties do not last longer than that many years, a few more, a few less, save when, by chance, no one appears to attack [the dynasty]. When senility becomes preponderant [in a dynasty], there may be no claimant [for its power, and then nothing will happen] but if there should be one, he will encounter no one capable of repelling him. If the time is up [the end of the dynasty] cannot be postponed for a single hour, no more than it can be accelerated.

Questions: What does this passage reveal about Ibn Khaldun's views of the contrasts between nomads and urban dwellers? Why does he see the former as a source of military power and political strength? What forces undermine dynasties in later generations? How well do these patterns correspond to the history of the Umayyad and Abbasid dynasties we have been studying? How well do they work for other civilizations we have examined? Can elements of Ibn Khaldun's theory be applied to today's political systems? If so, which and how? If not, why not?

Undoubtedly, the impact of the Crusades was much greater on the Christians who launched them than on the Muslim peoples who had to fend them off. Because there had long been so much contact between western Europe and the Islamic world through trade and through the Muslim kingdoms in Spain and southern Italy, it is difficult to be sure which influences to attribute specifically to the Crusades. But the crusaders' firsthand experiences in the eastern Mediterranean certainly intensified European borrowing from the Muslim world that had been going on for centuries. Muslim weapons, such as the famous damascene swords (named after the city of Damascus), were highly prized and sometimes copied by the Europeans, who were always eager to improve on their methods of making war. Muslim techniques of building fortifications were adopted by many Christian rulers, as can be seen in the castles built in Normandy and coastal England by William the Conqueror and his successors in the 11th and 12th centuries. Richard the Lionhearted's legendary preference for Muslim over Christian physicians was but one sign of the Europeans' avid centuries-old interest in the superior scientific learning of Muslim peoples.

From Muslims and Jews in Spain, Sicily, Egypt, and the Middle East, the Europeans recovered much of the Greek learning that had been lost to northern Europe during the waves of nomadic invasions after the fall of Rome. They also mastered Arabic (properly Indian) numerals and the decimal system, and they benefited from the great advances Arab and Persian thinkers had made in mathematics and many of the sciences. The European demand for Middle Eastern rugs and textiles is demonstrated by the Oriental rugs and tapestries that adorned the homes of the European upper classes in Renaissance and early modern paintings. It is also reflected in European (and our own) names for different kinds of cloth, such as *fustian*, *taffeta*, *muslin*, and *damask*, which are derived from Persian terms or the names of Muslim cities where the cloth was produced and sold.

Muslim influences affected both the elite and popular cultures of much of western Europe in this period. These included Persian and Arabic words, games such as chess (like numbers, passed on from India), chivalric ideals and troubadour ballads, as well as foods such as dates, coffee, and yogurt. Some of these imports, namely the songs of the troubadours, can be traced directly to the contacts the crusaders made in the Holy Land. But most were part of a process of exchange that extended over centuries, and was largely a one-way process. Though Arab traders imported some manufactures, such as glass and cloth, and raw materials from Europe, Muslim peoples in this era showed little interest in the learning or institutions of the West. Nevertheless, the Italian merchant communities, which remained after the political and military power of the crusaders had been extinguished in the Middle East, contributed a good deal more to these ongoing interchanges than all the forays of Christian knights.

An Age of Learning and Artistic Refinements

 The avid interest in Muslim ideas and material culture displayed by European knights and merchants in this era cautions us against placing too great an emphasis on the political divisions and struggles that were so prominent in the later Abbasid era. It also invites comparison with neighboring civilizations, such as those of India and western Europe, that were much more fragmented and racked by warfare in late Abbasid times. In the midst of the political turmoil and social tensions of the Abbasid age, Muslim thinkers and artisans living in kingdoms from Spain to Persia created, refined, and made discoveries in a remarkable range of fields. Their collective accomplishments mark one of the great ages of human ingenuity and creativity.

Although town life became more dangerous, the rapid growth and increasing prosperity that characterized the first centuries of Muslim expansion continued until late in the Abbasid era. Despite the declining revenue base of the caliphate and deteriorating conditions in the countryside, there was a great expansion of the professional classes, particularly doctors, scholars, and legal and religious experts. Muslim, Jewish, and in some areas Christian entrepreneurs amassed great fortunes supplying the cities of the empire with staples such as grain and barley, essentials such as cotton and woolen textiles for clothing, and luxury items such as precious gems, citrus fruits, and sugar cane. Long-distance trade between the Middle East and Mediterranean Europe and between coastal India and island southeast Asia, in addition to the overland caravan trade with China, flourished through much of the Abbasid era (see Map 7.1).

Among the chief beneficiaries of the sustained urban prosperity were artists and artisans, who continued the great achievements in architecture and the crafts that had begun in the Umayyad period. Mosques and palaces grew larger and more ornate in most parts of the empire. Even in outlying areas, such as Córdoban Spain, which is pictured in Figure 7.2, Muslim engineers and architects created some of the great architectural treasures of all time. The tapestries and rugs of Muslim peoples, such as the Persians, were in great demand from Europe to China. To this day, Muslim rugs have rarely been matched for their exquisite designs, their vivid colors, and the skill with

Figure 7.2 *A forest of graceful arches fills the interior of the mosque at Córdoba in Spain. This style of architecture (only one of many variants in the Islamic world, as we saw in the Visualizing the Past box in Chapter 6) can be seen over a large area that includes the entire Iberian peninsula and much of north Africa. Such an architectural feat in an area on the furthest fringe of the Islamic world illustrates the depth and expansive power of Muslim civilization. It also dramatically demonstrates the engineering skill and refined aesthetic sensibilities of Muslim architects and their wealthy patrons.*

which they are woven. Muslim artisans also produced fine bronzes and superb ceramics.

The Full Flowering of Persian Literature

As Persian wives, concubines, advisors, bureaucrats, and—after the mid-10th century—Persian caliphs came to play central roles in imperial politics, Persian gradually replaced Arabic as the primary written language at the Abbasid court. Arabic remained the language of religion, law, and the natural sciences. But

Persian was favored by Arabs, Turks, and Muslims of Persian descent as the language of literary expression, administration, and scholarship. In Baghdad and major cities throughout the Abbasid Empire and in neighboring kingdoms, Persian was the chief language of "high culture," the language of polite exchanges between courtiers as well as of history, poetic musings, and mystical revelations.

Written in a modified Arabic script and drawing selectively on Arabic vocabulary, the Persian of the Abbasid age was a supple language as beautiful to look at when drafted by a skilled calligrapher as it was to read aloud (see Figure 7.3). Catch phrases ("A jug of wine, a loaf of bread—and Thou") from the *Rubaiyat* of Omar Khayyam are certainly the pieces of Persian literature best known in the West. But other writers from this period surpassed Khayyam in profundity of thought and elegance of style. Perhaps the single most important work was the lengthy epic poem **Shah-Nama** (Book of Kings), written by Firdawsi in the late 10th and early 11th centuries. The work relates the history of Persia from the beginnings of time to the Islamic conquests, and it abounds in dramatic details of battles, intrigues, and illicit love affairs. Firdawsi's Persian has been extolled for its grand, musical virtuosity, and portions of the *Shah-Nama* and other Persian works were read aloud to musical accompaniment. Brilliantly illustrated manuscripts of Firdawsi's epic history are among the most exquisite works of Islamic art.

In addition to historical epics, Persian writers in the Abbasid era wrote on many subjects, from doomed love affairs and statecraft to incidents from everyday life and mystical striving for communion with the divine. One of the great poets of the age, Sa'di, fuses an everyday message with a religious one in the following relation of a single moment in his own life:

> Often I am minded, from the days of my
>   childhood,
> How once I went out with my father on
>   a festival;
> In fun I grew preoccupied with all the
>   folk about,
> Losing touch with my father in the popular
>   confusion;
> In terror and bewilderment I raised up a cry,
> Then suddenly my father boxed my ears:
> "You bold-eyed child, how many times, now,

Figure 7.3 *As the intricate details of this vividly illuminated book of tales of the prophet Muhammad illustrates, Muslim scripts, whether Arabic, Persian, or Turkish, were viewed as works of art in themselves. Artists were expected to be masters of writing and pictorial representation, and books such as this were usually produced in workshops, at times employing several master painters and hundreds of artisans. Verses from the Qur'an, exquisitely rendered in porcelain tiles, were frequently used to decorate mosques and other public buildings.*

Have I told you not to lose hold of my skirt?"

A tiny child cannot walk out alone,

For it is difficult to take a way not seen;

You too, poor friend, are but a child upon endeavour's way:

Go, seize the skirts of those who know the way!

This blend of the mystical and commonplace was widely adopted in the literature of this period. It is epitomized in the *Rubaiyat*, whose author is much more concerned with finding meaning in life and a path to union with the divine than with extolling the delights of picnics in the garden with beautiful women.

Achievements in the Sciences

From preserving and compiling the learning of the ancient civilizations they had conquered in the early centuries of expansion, Muslim peoples—and the Jewish scholars who lived peacefully in Muslim lands—increasingly became creators and inventors in their own right. For several centuries, which spanned much of the period of Abbasid rule, Islamic civilization outstripped all others in scientific discoveries, new techniques of investigation, and new technologies. The many Muslim accomplishments in these areas include major corrections to the algebraic and geometric theories of the ancient Greeks and great advances in the use of basic concepts of trigonometry: the sine, cosine, and tangent.

Two discoveries in chemistry that were fundamental to all later investigation were the creation of the objective experiment and al-Razi's scheme of classifying all material substances into three categories: animal, vegetable, and mineral. The sophistication of Muslim scientific techniques is indicated by the fact that in the 11th century, al-Biruni was able to calculate the specific weight of 18 major minerals. This sophistication was also manifested in astronomical instruments such as those in Figure 7.4, developed through cooperation between Muslim scholars and skilled artisans. Their astronomical tables and maps of the stars were in great demand among scholars of other civilizations, including those of Europe and China.

As these breakthroughs suggest, much of the Muslims' work in scientific investigation had very practical applications. This practical bent was even greater in other fields. For example, Muslim cities such as Cairo boasted some of the best hospitals in the world. Doctors and pharmacists had to follow a regular course of study and pass a formal examination before they were allowed to practice. Muslim scientists did important work on optics and bladder ailments. Muslim traders introduced into the Islamic world and Europe many basic machines and techniques—namely, papermaking, silk-weaving, and ceramic firing—that had been devised earlier in China. In addition, Muslim scholars made some of

Figure 7.4 *This 15th-century Persian miniature of a group of Arab scientists testing and working with a wide variety of navigational instruments conveys a strong sense of the premium placed on scientific investigation in the Muslim world in the Abbasid age and the centuries thereafter. Muslim prototypes inspired European artisans, cartographers, and scientists to develop instruments and maps, which were essential to European overseas expansion from the 14th century onward.*

the world's best maps, which were copied by geographers from Portugal to Poland.

Religious Trends and the New Push for Expansion

The contradictory trends in Islamic civilization—social strife and political divisions versus expanded

trading links and intellectual creativity—were strongly reflected in patterns of religious development in the later centuries of the caliphate. On one hand, a resurgence of mysticism injected Islam with a new vibrancy. On the other, orthodox religious scholars, such as the **ulama,** grew increasingly suspicious of and hostile to non-Islamic ideas and scientific thinking. The Crusades had promoted the latter trend. This was particularly true regarding Muslim borrowing from ancient Greek learning, which the ulama associated with the aggressive civilizations of Christian Europe. Many orthodox scholars suspected that the questioning that characterized the Greek tradition would undermine the absolute authority of the Qur'an. They insisted that the Qur'an was the final, perfect, and complete revelation of an all-knowing divinity. Brilliant thinkers such as **al-Ghazali,** perhaps the greatest Islamic theologian, struggled to fuse the Greek and Qur'anic traditions. Their ideas were often rejected by orthodox scholars.

Much of the religious vitality in Islam in the later Abbasid period was centered on the Sufist movement. Like the Buddhist and Hindu ascetics earlier in India, **Sufis** (whose title was derived from the woolen robes they wore) were wandering mystics who sought a personal union with Allah. In its various guises—including both Sunni and Shi'a manifestations—Sufism was a reaction against the impersonal and abstract divinity that many ulama scholars argued was the true god of the Qur'an. Like the Indian mystics, the Sufis and their followers tried to see beyond what they believed to be the illusory existence of everyday life and to delight in the presence of Allah in the world. True to the strict monotheism of Islam, most Sufis insisted on a clear distinction between Allah and humans. But in some Sufist teachings, Allah permeated the universe in ways that appeared to compromise his transcendent status.

Some Sufis gained reputations as great healers and workers of miracles; others led militant bands that tried to spread Islam to nonbelievers. Some Sufis used asceticism or bodily denial to find Allah; others used meditation, songs, drugs, or (in the case of the famous dervishes) ecstatic dancing. Most Sufis built up a sizeable following, and the movement as a whole was a central factor in the continuing expansion of the Muslim religion and Islamic civilization in the later centuries of the Abbasid caliphate.

Visualizing the Past

The Patterns of Islam's Global Expansions

The table shows the present-day distribution of Muslims in key countries from Africa to Asia. It indicates the total number of Muslims in each of the countries represented, the percentage of Muslims in the total population of that area, and the numbers and percentages of other religious groups. The table also indicates the manner in which Islam was spread to each of these areas and the key agents of that diffusion. After using the table to compare the patterns of Islamization in different areas, answer the questions that follow.

Questions: Which areas have the highest absolute numbers of Muslims in the present day? Is this distribution what you would have expected or is it surprising? What factors might explain these distribution patterns? What were the main ways that Islam was transmitted to most areas? and to the areas with the largest number of Muslims? What does this say about the popular notion that Islam was historically a militant religion spread primarily by forcible conversion? Does Islam appear to be able to coexist with other faiths?

Comparative Statistics of Modern States with a Sizeable Muslim Population

	Total Population (2000 est.)	Total Number of Muslims	Percentage of Muslims	Total Number of Non-Muslims	Percentages of Other Religious Groups	Principle Agents/Modes of Conversion
Nigeria	114 million	57 million	50	57 million	40–Christian; 10–Other (African religions)	Trading Contacts Sufi Missionaries
Egypt	67 million	63 million	94	4 million	4–Christian; 2–Other	Arab Migration Voluntary Mass Conversion
Iraq	22.5 million	21.8 million	97: Shi'a: 60–65; Sunni: 32–37	700,000	3–Other (Zoroastrian, Christian, Jewish)	Arab Migration Voluntary Mass Conversion
Iran	65 million	64.35 million	99: Shi'a: 89; Sunni: 10	650,000	1–Other (Zoroastrian, Bahai, Christian, Jewish)	Arab Migration Voluntary Mass Conversion
Pakistan	138 million	133.85 million	97: Shi'a: 20; Sunni: 77	4.15 million	3–Other (Hindu, Christian, Buddhist)	Sufi Missionaries Voluntary Mass Conversion
India	1.001 billion	140.1 million	14	860.9 million	80–Hindu; 6–Other (Buddhist, Sikh, Christian)	Sufi Missionaries Trading Contacts Voluntary Mass Conversion

(continued)

	Total Population (2000 est.)	Total Number of Muslims	Percentage of Muslims	Total Number of Non-Muslims	Percentages of Other Religious Groups	Principle Agents/Modes of Conversion
Indonesia	216 million	188 million	87	28 million	6–Protestant; 7–Other (Catholic, Buddhist, etc.)	Sufi Missionaries Trading Contacts
The Philippines	79.5 million	4 million	5	75.5 million	83–Catholic; 9–Protestant; 3–Other	Trading Contacts Sufi Missionaries
Morocco	30 million	29.7 million	99	300,000	1–Other	Voluntary Mass Conversion Sufi Missionaries

Note: Numbers based on information from Wiesenfeld and Famighetti et al., eds., *The World Almanac and Book of Facts 2000* (Mahwah, NJ: World Almanac Books, 1999).

New Waves of Nomadic Invasions and the End of the Caliphate

As we have seen, in the 10th and 11th centuries the Abbasid domains were divided by ever growing numbers of rival successor states. In the early 13th century, a new threat arose at the eastern edge of the original Abbasid domains. Another central Asian nomadic people, the **Mongols,** united by their great war commander, **Chinggis Khan,** first raided in the 1220s and then smashed the Turko-Persian kingdoms that had developed in the regions to the east of Baghdad. Chinggis Khan died before the heartlands of the Muslim world were invaded, but his grandson, **Hulegu,** renewed the Mongol assault on the rich centers of Islamic civilization in the 1250s. In 1258, the Abbasid capital at Baghdad was taken by the Mongols, and much of it was sacked. The 37th and last Abbasid caliph was put to death by the Mongols. They then continued westward until they were finally defeated by the **Mamluks,** or Turkic slaves, who then ruled Egypt. Baghdad never recovered from the Mongol attacks. In 1401, it suffered a second capture and another round of pillaging by the even fiercer forces of Tamerlane. Baghdad shrank from the status of one of the great cities of the world to a provincial backwater. It was gradually supplanted by Cairo to the west and then Istanbul to the north.

The Coming of Islam to South Asia

 From the 7th century onward, successive waves of Muslim invaders, traders, and migrants carried the Islamic faith and elements of Islamic civilization to much of the vast south Asian subcontinent. By the 12th and 13th centuries, Muslim dynasties ruled much of north and central India. Muslim conquests and growing numbers of conversions provoked a variety of Hindu responses. They also prompted efforts on the part of some followers of both religions to reconcile their differences. Although these measures resulted only in an uneasy standoff between the two communities, Islamic influences had clearly become a major force in south Asian historical development.

All through the millennia when a succession of civilizations from Harappa to the brahmanic empire of the Guptas developed in south Asia, foreigners had entered India in waves of nomadic invaders or as small bands of displaced peoples seeking refuge. Invariably, those who chose to remain were assimilated into the civilizations they encountered in the lowland areas. They converted to the Hindu or Buddhist religion, found a place in the caste hierarchy, and adopted the dress, foods, and lifestyles of the farming and city-dwelling peoples of the many regions of the subcontinent. This capacity to absorb peoples moving into the area resulted from the strength and flexibility of India's civilizations and from the fact that India's peoples usually enjoyed a higher level of material culture than migrant groups entering the subcontinent. As a result, the persistent failure of Indian rulers to unite against aggressors meant periodic disruptions and localized destruction but not fundamental challenges to the existing order. All of this changed with the arrival of the Muslims in the last years of the 7th century C.E. (see Map 7.2).

With the coming of the Muslims, the peoples of India encountered for the first time a large-scale influx of bearers of a civilization as sophisticated, if not as ancient, as their own. They were also confronted by a religious system that was in many ways the very opposite of the ones they had nurtured. Hinduism, the predominant Indian religion at that time, was open, tolerant, and inclusive of widely varying forms of religious devotion, from idol worship to meditation in search of union with the spiritual source of all creation. Islam was doctrinaire, proselytizing, and committed to the exclusive worship of a single, transcendent god.

Socially, Islam was highly egalitarian, proclaiming all believers equal in the sight of God. In sharp contrast, Hindu beliefs validated the caste hierarchy. The latter rested on the acceptance of inborn differences between individuals and groups and the widely varying levels of material wealth, status, and religious purity these differences were believed to produce. Thus, the faith of the invading Muslims was religiously more rigid than that of the absorptive and adaptive Hindus. But the caste-based social system of India was much more compartmentalized and closed than the society of the Muslim invaders, with their emphasis on mobility and the community of believers.

Because growing numbers of Muslim warriors, traders, Sufi mystics, and ordinary farmers and herders entered south Asia and settled there, extensive interaction between invaders and the indigenous peoples was

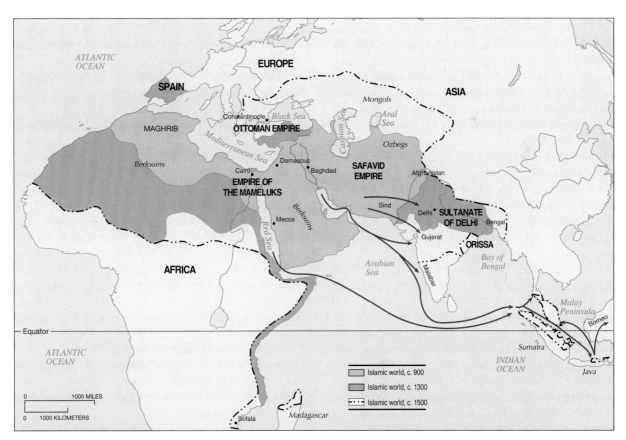

Map 7.2   *The Spread of Islam, 10th–16th Centuries. Arrows indicate the routes by which Islam spread to south and southeast Asia.*

inevitable. In the early centuries of the Muslim influx, conflict, often violent, predominated. But there was also a good deal of trade and even religious interchange between them. As time passed, peaceful (if wary) interaction became the norm. Muslim rulers employed large numbers of Hindus to govern the largely non-Muslim populations they conquered, mosques and temples dominated different quarters within Indian cities, and Hindu and Muslim mystics strove to find areas of agreement between their two faiths. Nonetheless, tensions remained, and periodically they erupted into communal rioting or warfare between Hindu and Muslim lords.

Political Divisions and the First Muslim Invasions

The first and least enduring Muslim intrusion, which came in 711, resulted indirectly from the peaceful trading contacts that had initially brought Muslims into contact with Indian civilization. Since ancient times, Arab seafarers and traders had been major carriers in the vast trading network that stretched from Italy in the Mediterranean to the South China Sea. After converting to Islam, these traders continued to visit the ports of India, particularly those on the western coast. An attack by pirates sailing from Sind in western India (see Map 7.2) on ships owned by some of these Arab traders prompted the viceroy of the eastern provinces of the Umayyad Empire to launch a punitive expedition against the king of Sind. An able Arab general, **Muhammad ibn Qasim,** who was only 17 years old when the campaign began, led more than 10,000 horse- and camel-mounted warriors into Sind to avenge the assault on Arab shipping. After victories in several fiercely fought battles, Muhammad ibn Qasim declared the region, as well as the Indus valley to the northeast, provinces of the Umayyad Empire.

In these early centuries, the coming of Islam brought little change for most inhabitants of the Indian subcontinent. In fact, in many areas, local leaders and the populace surrendered towns and districts willingly to the conquerors because they promised lighter taxation and greater religious tolerance. The Arab overlords decided to treat both Hindus and Buddhists as protected "people of the book," despite the fact that their faiths had no connection to the Bible, the book in question. This meant that although they were obliged to pay special taxes, non-Muslims, like Jews and Christians, enjoyed the freedom to worship as they pleased.

As in other areas conquered by the Arabs, most of the local officials and notables retained their posi-

tions, which did much to reconcile them to Muslim rule. The status and privileges of the brahman castes were respected. Nearly all Arabs, who made up only a tiny minority of the population, lived in cities or special garrison towns. Because little effort was expended in converting the peoples of the conquered areas, they remained overwhelmingly Hindu or Buddhist.

Indian Influences on Islamic Civilization

Although the impact of Islam on the Indian subcontinent in this period was limited, the Arab foothold in Sind provided contacts by which Indian learning was transmitted to the Muslim heartlands in the Middle East. As a result, Islamic civilization was enriched by the skills and discoveries of yet another great civilization. Of particular importance was Indian scientific learning, which rivaled that of the Greeks as the most advanced of the ancient world. Hindu mathematicians and astronomers traveled to Baghdad after the Abbasids came to power in the mid-8th century. Their works on algebra and geometry were translated into Arabic, and their instruments for celestial observation were copied and improved by Arab astronomers.

Most critically, Arab thinkers in all fields began to use the numerals that Hindu scholars had devised centuries earlier. Because these numbers were passed on to the Europeans through contacts with the Arabs in the early Middle Ages, we call them Arabic numerals today, but they originated in India. Because of the linkages between civilized centers established by the spread of Islam, this system of numerical notation has proved central to two scientific revolutions. The first in the Middle East was discussed earlier in this chapter. The second, discussed in Chapter 17, occurred in Europe some centuries later. From the 16th century to the present, it has brought fundamental transformations to both Europe and much of the rest of the world.

In addition to science and mathematics, Indian treatises on subjects ranging from medicine to music were translated and studied by Arab scholars. Indian physicians were brought to Baghdad to run the well-endowed hospitals that the Christian crusaders found a source of wonderment and a cause for envy. On several occasions, Indian doctors were able to cure Arab rulers and officials whom Greek physicians had pronounced beyond help. Indian works on statecraft, alchemy, and palmistry were also translated into Arabic, and it is believed that some of the tales in the *Arabian Nights* were based on ancient Indian stories. Indian musical instruments and melodies made their way into the repertoires of Arab performers, and the Indian game of chess became a favorite of both royalty and ordinary townspeople.

Arabs who emigrated to Sind and other Muslim-ruled areas often adopted Indian dress and hairstyles, ate Indian foods, and rode on elephants as the Hindu *rajas* (kings) did. As Figure 7.5 illustrates, the conquerors also adopted Indian building styles and artistic motifs. In this era, additional Arab colonies were established in other coastal areas, such as Malabar to the south and Bengal in the east (see Map 7.2). These trading enclaves later provided the staging areas from which Islam was transmitted to island and mainland southeast Asia.

From Booty to Empire: The Second Wave of Muslim Invasions

After the initial conquests by Muhammad ibn Qasim's armies, little territory was added to the Muslim foothold on the subcontinent. In fact, disputes between the Arabs occupying Sind and their quarrels with first the Umayyad and later the Abbasid caliphs gradually weakened the Muslim hold on the area. This was reflected in the reconquest of parts of the lower Indus valley by Hindu rulers. But the gradual Muslim retreat was dramatically reversed by a new series of military invasions, this time launched by a Turkish slave dynasty that in 962 had seized power in Afghanistan to the north of the Indus valley. The third ruler of this dynasty, **Mahmud of Ghazni,** led a series of expeditions that began nearly two centuries of Muslim raiding and conquest in northern India. Drawn by the legendary wealth of the subcontinent and a zeal to spread the Muslim faith, Mahmud repeatedly raided northwest India in the first decades of the 11th century. He defeated one confederation of Hindu princes after another, and he drove deeper and deeper into the subcontinent in the quest of ever richer temples to loot.

Figure 7.5 *Built in 1626 at Agra, this exquisite tomb of white marble encrusted with semiprecious stones is a superb example of the blending of Islamic and Hindu architectural forms, building materials, and artistic motifs. Although this structure was built centuries after the first Muslims entered India, from the outset this blending of traditions was evident.*

The raids mounted by Mahmud of Ghazni and his successors gave way in the last decades of the 12th century to sustained campaigns aimed at seizing political control in north India. The key figure in this transition was a tenacious military commander of Persian extraction, **Muhammad of Ghur.** After barely surviving several severe defeats at the hands of Hindu rulers, Muhammad put together a string of military victories that brought the Indus valley and much of north central India under his control. In the following years, Muhammad's conquests were extended along the Gangetic plain as far as Bengal, and into west and central India, by several of his most gifted subordinate commanders. After Muhammad was assassinated in 1206, **Qutb-ud-din Aibak,** one of his slave lieutenants, seized power.

Significantly, the capital of the new Muslim empire was at Delhi along the Jumna River on the Gangetic plain. Delhi's location in the very center of northern India graphically proclaimed that a Muslim dynasty rooted in the subcontinent itself, not an extension of a Middle Eastern central Asian empire, had been founded. For the next 300 years, a succession of dynasties ruled much of north and central India. Alternately of Persian, Afghan, Turkic, and mixed descent, the rulers of these imperial houses proclaimed themselves the *sultans of Delhi* (literally, princes of the heartland). They fought each other, Mongol and Turkic invaders, and the indigenous Hindu princes for control of the Indus and Gangetic heartlands of Indian civilization.

Patterns of Conversion

Although the Muslims fought their way into India, their interaction with the indigenous peoples soon came to be dominated by accommodation and peaceful exchanges. Over the centuries when much of the north was ruled by dynasties centered at Delhi, sizeable Muslim communities developed in different areas of the subcontinent. The largest of these were in Bengal to the east and in the northwestern areas of the Indus valley that were the points of entry for most of the Muslim peoples who migrated into India.

Few of these converts were won forcibly. The main carriers of the new faith often were merchants, who played a growing role in both coastal and inland trade, but were most especially Sufi mystics. The lat-

ter shared much with Indian gurus and wandering ascetics in both style and message. Belief in their magical and healing powers enhanced the Sufis' stature and increased their following. Their mosques and schools often became centers of regional political power. Sufis organized their devotees in militias to fend off bandits or rival princes, oversaw the clearing of forests for farming and settlement, and welcomed low-caste and outcaste Hindu groups into Islam. After their deaths, the tombs of Sufi mystics became objects of veneration for Indian Muslims as well as Hindu and Buddhist pilgrims.

Most of the indigenous converts, who came to form a majority of the Muslims living in India, were drawn from specific regions and social groups. Surprisingly small numbers of converts were found in the Indo-Gangetic centers of Muslim political power, a fact that suggests the very limited importance of forced conversions. Most Indians who converted to Islam were from Buddhist or low-caste groups. In areas such as western India and Bengal, where Buddhism had survived as a popular religion until the era of the Muslim invasions, esoteric rituals and corrupt practices had debased Buddhist teachings and undermined the morale of the monastic orders.

This decline was accelerated by Muslim raids on Buddhist temples and monasteries, which provided vulnerable and lucrative targets for the early invaders. Without monastic supervision, local congregations sank further into orgies and experiments with magic. All of these trends opposed the Buddha's social concerns and religious message. Disorganized and misdirected, Indian Buddhism was no match for the confident and vigorous new religion the Muslim invaders carried into the subcontinent. This was particularly true when those who were spreading the new faith had the charisma and organizing skills of the Sufi mystics.

Buddhists probably made up the majority of Indians who converted to Islam. But untouchables and low-caste Hindus, as well as animistic tribal peoples, were also attracted to the more egalitarian social arrangements promoted by the new faith. As was the case with the Buddhists, group conversions were essential because those who remained in the Hindu caste system would have little to do with those who converted. Some conversions resulted from the desire of Hindus or Buddhists to escape the head tax the Muslim rulers levied on unbelievers. It was also prompted by intermarriage between local peoples and

Muslim migrants. In addition, Muslim migrants swelled the size of the Islamic community in the subcontinent. This was particularly true in periods of crisis in central Asia. In the 13th and 14th centuries, for example, Turkic, Persian, and Afghan peoples retreated to the comparative safety of India in the face of the Mongol and Timurid conquests that are examined in detail in Chapter 14.

Patterns of Accommodation

Although Islam won many converts in certain areas and communities, it initially made little impression on the Hindu community as a whole. Despite military reverses and the imposition of Muslim political rule over large areas of the subcontinent, high-caste Hindus in particular saw the invaders as the bearers of an upstart religion and as polluting outcastes. Al-Biruni, one of the chief chroniclers of the Muslim conquests, complained openly about the prevailing Indian disdain for the newcomers:

> The Hindus believe that there is no country but theirs, no nation like theirs, no kings like theirs, no religion like theirs, no science like theirs. They are haughty, foolishly vain, self-conceited and stolid.

Many Hindus were willing to take positions as administrators in the bureaucracies of Muslim overlords or as soldiers in their armies and to trade with Muslim merchants. But they remained socially aloof from their conquerors. Separate living quarters were established everywhere Muslim communities developed. Genuine friendships between members of high-caste groups and Muslims were rare, and sexual liaisons between them were severely restricted.

During the early centuries of the Muslim influx, the Hindus were convinced that like so many of the peoples who had entered the subcontinent in the preceding millennia, the Muslims would soon be absorbed by the superior religions and more sophisticated cultures of India. Many signs pointed to that outcome. Hindus staffed the bureaucracies and made up a good portion of the armies of Muslim rulers. In addition, Muslim princes adopted regal styles and practices that were Hindu-inspired and contrary to the Qur'an. Some Muslim rulers proclaimed themselves to be of divine descent, and others minted coins decorated with Hindu images such as Nandi, the bull associated with a major Hindu god, Shiva.

More broadly, Muslim communities became socially divided along caste lines. Recently arrived Muslims generally were on top of the hierarchies that developed, and even they were divided depending on whether they were Arab, Turk, or Persian. High-caste Hindu converts came next, followed by "clean" artisan and merchant groups. Lower-caste and untouchable converts remained at the bottom of the social hierarchy. This may help to explain why conversions in these groups were not as numerous as one would expect given the original egalitarian thrust of Islam. Muslims also adopted Indian foods and styles of dress and took to chewing *pan*, or limestone wrapped with betel leaves.

The Muslim influx had unfortunate consequences for women in both Muslim and Hindu communities. The invaders increasingly adopted the practice of marrying women at the earlier ages favored by the Hindus and the prohibitions against the remarriage of widows found especially at the high-caste levels of Indian society. Some upper "caste" Muslim groups even performed the ritual of **sati,** the burning of widows on the same funeral pyres as their deceased husbands, which was found among some high-caste Hindu groups.

Islamic Challenge and Hindu Revival

Despite a significant degree of acculturation to Hindu lifestyles and social organization, Muslim migrants to the subcontinent held to their own distinctive religious beliefs and rituals. The Hindus found Islam impossible to absorb and soon realized that they were confronted by an actively proselytizing religion with great appeal to large segments of the Indian population. Partly in response to this challenge, the Hindus placed greater emphasis on the devotional cults of gods and goddesses that earlier had proved so effective in neutralizing the challenge of Buddhism.

Membership in these **bhaktic** cults was open to all, including women and untouchables. In fact, some of the most celebrated writers of religious poetry and songs of worship were women, such as **Mira Bai.** Saints from low-caste origins were revered by warriors and brahmans as well as by farmers, merchants, and outcastes. One of the most remarkable of these mystics was a Muslim weaver named **Kabir.** In plain and direct verse, Kabir played down the significance of religious differences and proclaimed that all could provide a path to spiritual fulfillment. He asked,

> O servant, where do thou seek Me?
>
> Lo! I am beside thee.
>
> I am neither in temple nor in mosque:
>
> Neither am I in rites and ceremonies, nor in Yoga and renunciation.

Because many songs and poems, such as those by Mira Bai and Kabir, were composed in regional languages, such as Bengali, Marathi, and Tamil, they were more accessible to the common people and became prominent expressions of popular culture in many areas.

Bhakti mystics and gurus stressed the importance of a strong emotional bond between the devotee and the god or goddess who was the object of veneration. Chants, dances, and in some instances drugs were used to reach the state of spiritual intoxication that was the key to individual salvation. Once one had achieved the state of ecstasy that came through intense emotional attachment to a god or goddess, all past sins were removed and caste distinctions were rendered meaningless. The most widely worshiped deities were the gods Shiva and Vishnu, the latter particularly in the guise of Krishna the goatherder, depicted in the folk painting in Figure 7.6. The goddess Kali was also venerated in a number of different manifestations. By increasing popular involvement in Hindu worship and by enriching and extending the modes of prayer and ritual, the bhakti movement may have done much to stem the flow of converts to Islam, particularly among low-caste groups.

Stand-Off: The Muslim Presence in India at the End of the Sultanate Period

The attempts of mystics such as Kabir to minimize the differences between Hindu and Islamic beliefs and worship won over only small numbers of the followers of either faith. They were also strongly repudiated by the guardians of orthodoxy in each religious community. Sensing the long-term threat to Hinduism posed by Muslim political dominance and conversion efforts, the brahmans denounced the Muslims as infidel destroyers of Hindu temples and polluted meat-eaters. Later Hindu mystics, such as the 15th-century holy man Chaitanya, composed songs that focused on love for Hindu deities and set

Figure 7.6 *This Indian miniature painting of milkmaids serving the Hindu god Krishna reflects the highly personalized devotional worship that was characteristic of the bhakti movement. The eroticism in the milkmaids' songs, in praise of Krishna's great beauty, reveals a blending of sacred and secular, carnal and spiritual that is a recurring motif in Hindu worship and art.*

out to convince Indian Muslims to renounce Islam in favor of Hinduism.

For their part, Muslim ulama, or religious experts, grew increasingly aware of the dangers Hinduism posed for Islam. Attempts to fuse the two faiths were rejected on the grounds that although Hindus might argue that specific rituals and beliefs were not essential, they were fundamental for Islam. If one played down the teachings of the Qur'an, prayer, and the pilgrimage, one was no longer a true Muslim. Thus, contrary to the teachings of Kabir and like-minded mystics, the ulama and even some Sufi saints stressed the teachings of Islam that separated it from Hinduism. They worked to promote unity within the Indian Muslim community and to strengthen its contacts with Muslims in neighboring lands and the Middle Eastern centers of the faith.

After centuries of invasion and migration, a large Muslim community had been established in the Indian subcontinent. Converts had been won, political control had been established throughout much of the area, and strong links had been forged with Muslims in other lands such as Persia and Afghanistan. But non-Muslims, particularly Hindus, remained the overwhelming majority of the population of the vast and diverse lands south of the Himalayas. Unlike the Zoroastrians in Persia or the animistic peoples of the Maghrib and the Sudan, most Indians showed little inclination to convert to the religion of the Muslim conquerors. After centuries of Muslim political dominance and missionary activity, south Asia remained one of the least converted and integrated of all the areas Muhammad's message had reached.

The Spread of Islam to Southeast Asia

 The spread of Islam to various parts of coastal India set the stage for its further expansion to island southeast Asia. Arab traders and sailors regularly visited the ports of southeast Asia long before they converted to Islam. From the 13th century, these traders, and the Sufi mystics they sometimes carried aboard their ships, spread Islam to Java and much of the rest of island southeast Asia. As was the case in India, conversion was generally peaceful, and the new believers combined Islamic teachings and rituals with elements of the animist, Hindu, and Buddhist religions that had spread throughout the area in preceding centuries.

From a world history perspective, island southeast Asia had long been mainly a middle ground. It was the zone where the Chinese segment of the great Euro-Asian trading complex met the Indian Ocean trading zone to the west. At ports on the coast of the Malayan peninsula, east Sumatra, and somewhat later north Java, goods from China were transferred from east Asian vessels to Arab or Indian ships. In these same ports, products from as far west as Rome were loaded into the emptied Chinese ships to be carried to east Asia. By the 7th and 8th centuries C.E., sailors and ships from areas of southeast Asia, particularly Sumatra and Malaya, had become active in the seaborne trade of the region. Southeast Asian products had also become important exports to China, India, and the Mediterranean region. Many of these products were luxury items, such as aromatic woods from the rain forests of Borneo and Sumatra and spices such as cloves, nutmeg,

and mace from the far end of the Indonesian archipelago. These trading links were to prove even more critical to the expansion of Islam in southeast Asia than they had earlier been to the spread of Buddhism and Hinduism.

From the 8th century onward, the coastal trade of India came increasingly to be controlled by Muslims from such regions as Gujarat in western India and various parts of south India. As a result, elements of Islamic culture began to filter into island southeast Asia. But only in the 13th century, after the collapse of the far-flung trading empire of **Shrivijaya,** centered on the Strait of Malacca between Malaya and the northeast of Sumatra (see Map 7.2), was the way open for the widespread introduction of Islam. Indian traders, Muslim or otherwise, were welcome to trade in the chain of ports controlled by Shrivijaya. But because the rulers and officials of Shrivijaya were devout Buddhists, there was little incentive for the traders and sailors of southeast Asian ports to convert to Islam, the religion of growing numbers of the merchants and sailors from India. With the fall of Shrivijaya, incentives increased for the establishment of Muslim trading centers and efforts to preach the faith to the coastal peoples.

Trading Contacts and Conversion

As in most of the areas to which Islam spread, peaceful contacts and voluntary conversion were far more important than conquest and force in spreading the faith in southeast Asia. Throughout the islands of the region, trading contacts paved the way for conversion. Muslim merchants and sailors introduced local peoples to the ideas and rituals of the new faith and impressed on them how much of the known world had already been converted. Muslim ships also carried Sufis to various parts of southeast Asia, where they played as vital a role in conversion as they had in India. The first areas to be won to Islam in the late 13th century were several small port centers on the northern coast of Sumatra. From these ports, the religion spread in the centuries that followed across the Strait of Malacca to Malaya.

On the mainland, the key to widespread conversion was the powerful trading city of **Malacca,** whose smaller trading empire had replaced the fallen Shrivijaya. From Malacca, Islam spread along the coasts of Malaya to east Sumatra and to the trading center of **Demak** on the north coast of Java. From Demak, the most powerful of the trading states on north Java,

In Depth

Conversion and Accommodation in the Spread of World Religions

Although not all great civilizations have produced world religions, the two tend to be closely associated throughout human history. World religions are those that spread across many cultures and societies, forge links between civilized centers, and bring civilized lifestyles to nomadic pastoral or shifting-cultivating peoples. Religions with these characteristics appeared before the rise of Islam. As we have seen, India alone produced two of these faiths in ancient times: Hinduism, which spread to parts of southeast and central Asia, and Buddhism, which spread even more widely in the Asian world. At the other end of the Eastern Hemisphere, Christianity spread throughout the Mediterranean region before claiming northern and western Europe as its core area. Judaism spread not because it won converts in non-Jewish cultures but because the Jewish people were driven from their homeland by Roman persecution and scattered throughout the Middle East, north Africa, and Europe.

Because religious conversion affects all aspects of life, from the way one looks at the universe to more mundane decisions about whom to marry or how to treat others, a world religion must be broad and flexible enough to accommodate the existing culture of potential converts. At the same time, its core beliefs and practices must be well enough defined to allow its followers to maintain a clear sense of common identity despite their great differences in culture and society. These beliefs and practices must be sufficiently profound and sophisticated to convince potential converts that their own cultures can be enriched and their lives improved by adopting the new religion.

In most instances, until the 16th century, when Christianity spread through the Western Hemisphere, no world religion could match Islam in the extent to which it spread across the globe and in the diversity of peoples and cultures that identified themselves as Muslims. Given its uncompromising monotheism, very definite doctrines, and elaborate rituals and principles of social organization, Islam's success at winning converts from very different cultural backgrounds is surprising at first glance. This is particularly true if it is compared with the much more flexible beliefs and ceremonial patterns of earlier world religions such as Buddhism and Hinduism. However, closer examination reveals that Islamic beliefs and social practices, as written in the Qur'an and interpreted by the ulama, proved quite flexible and adaptable when the religion was introduced into new, non-Islamic cultures.

The fact that Islam won converts overwhelmingly through peaceful contacts between long-distance traders and the preaching and organizational skills of Sufis exemplifies this capacity for accommodation. Those adopting the new religion did not do so because they were pressured or forced to convert but because they saw Islam as a way to enhance their understanding of the supernatural, enrich their ceremonial expression, improve the quality of their social interaction, and establish ongoing links to a transcultural community beyond their local world.

Because Islam was adopted rather than imposed, those who converted had a good deal to say about how much of their own cultures they would change and which aspects of Islam they would emphasize or accept. Certain beliefs and practices were obligatory

the Muslim faith spread to other Javanese ports. After a long struggle with a Hindu-Buddhist kingdom in the interior, the rest of the island was eventually converted. From Demak, Islam was also carried to the Celebes and the spice islands in the eastern archipelago, and from the latter to Mindanao in the southern Philippines.

This progress of Islamic conversion shows that port cities in coastal areas were particularly receptive to the new faith. Here trading links were critical.

Once one of the key cities in a trading cluster converted, it was in the best interest of others to follow suit to enhance personal ties and provide a common basis in Muslim law to regulate business deals. Conversion to Islam also linked these centers, culturally as well as economically, to the merchants and ports of India, the Middle East, and the Mediterranean.

Islam made slow progress in areas such as central Java, where Hindu-Buddhist dynasties contested its spread. But the fact that the earlier conversion to these

for all true believers—the worship of a single god, adherence to the prophet Muhammad and the divine revelations he received as recorded in the Qur'an, and the observance of the five pillars of the faith. But even these were subject to reinterpretation. In virtually all cultures to which it spread, Islamic monotheism supplanted but did not eradicate the animistic veneration of nature spirits or person and place deities. Allah was acknowledged as the most powerful supernatural force, but people continued to make offerings to spirits that could heal, bring fertility, protect their homes, or punish their enemies. In such areas as Africa and western China, where the veneration of ancestral spirits was a key aspect of religious life, the spirits were retained not as powers in themselves but as emissaries to Allah. In cultures such as those found in India and southeast Asia, Islamic doctrines were recast in a heavily mystical, even magical mode.

The flexibility of Islam was exhibited in the social as well as the religious sphere. In Islamic southeast Asia and, as we shall see in Chapter 8, in sub-Saharan Africa, the position of women remained a good deal stronger in critical areas, such as occupation and family law, than it had become in the Middle East and India. In both regions, the male-centric features of Islam that had grown more pronounced through centuries of accommodation in ancient Middle Eastern and Persian cultures were played down as Islam adapted to societies where women had traditionally enjoyed more influence, both within the extended family and in occupations such as farming, marketing, and craft production. Even the caste system of India, which in principle is opposed to the strong egalitarian strain in Islam, developed among Muslim groups that migrated into the subcontinent and survived in indigenous south Asian communities that converted to Islam.

Beyond basic forms of social organization and interaction, Islam accommodated diverse aspects of the societies into which it spread. For example, the African solar calendar, which was essential for coordinating the planting cycle, was retained along with the Muslim lunar calendar. In India, Hindu-Buddhist symbols of kingship were appropriated by Muslim rulers and acknowledged by both their Hindu and Muslim subjects. In island southeast Asia, exquisitely forged knives, called *krises*, which were believed to have magical powers, were among the most treasured possessions of local rulers both before and after they converted to Islam.

There was always the danger that accommodation could go too far—that in winning converts, Islamic principles would be so watered down and remolded that they no longer resembled or actually contradicted the teachings of the Qur'an. Sects that came to worship Muhammad or his nephew Ali as godlike, for example, clearly violated fundamental Muslim principles. This danger was a key source of the periodic movements for purification and revival that have been a notable feature of nearly all Islamic societies, particularly those on the fringes of the Islamic world. But even these movements, which were built around the insistence that the Muslim faith had been corrupted by alien ideas and practices and that a return to Islamic fundamentals was needed, were invariably cast in the modes of cultural expression of the peoples who rallied to them.

Questions: Can you think of ways in which world religions, such as Christianity, Hinduism, and Buddhism, changed to accommodate the cultures and societies to which they spread? Do these religions strike you as more or less flexible than Islam? Why?

Indian religions had been confined mainly to the ruling elites in Java and other island areas left openings for mass conversions to Islam that the Sufis eventually exploited. The island of Bali, where Hinduism had taken deep root at the popular level, remained largely impervious to the spread of Islam. The same was true of most of mainland southeast Asia, where centuries before the coming of Islam, Buddhism had spread from India and Ceylon and won the fervent adherence of both the ruling elites and the peasant masses.

Sufi Mystics and the Nature of Southeast Asian Islam

Because Islam came to southeast Asia primarily from India and was spread in many areas by Sufis, it was often infused with mystical strains and tolerated earlier animist, Hindu, and Buddhist beliefs and rituals. Just as they had in the Middle East and India, the Sufis who spread Islam in southeast Asia varied widely in personality and approach. Most were believed by those who followed them to have magical powers, and nearly all Sufis established mosque and school centers from which they traveled in neighboring regions to preach the faith.

In winning converts, the Sufis were willing to allow the inhabitants of island southeast Asia to retain pre-Islamic beliefs and practices that ortho-dox scholars would have found contrary to Islamic doctrine. Pre-Islamic customary law remained important in regulating social interaction, whereas Islamic law was confined to specific sorts of agree-ments and exchanges. Women retained a much stronger position, both within the family and in society, than they had in the Middle East and India. For example, trading in local and regional markets continued to be dominated by small-scale female buyers and sellers. In such areas as western Sumatra, lineage and inheritance continued to be traced through the female line after the coming of Islam, despite its tendency to promote male dominance and descent. Perhaps most tellingly, pre-Muslim reli-gious beliefs and rituals were incorporated into Muslim ceremonies. Indigenous cultural staples, such as the brilliant Javanese puppet shadow plays that were based on the Indian epics of the brah-manic age, were refined, and they became even more central to popular and elite beliefs and prac-tices than they had been in the pre-Muslim era.

GLOBAL CONNECTIONS: Islam: A Bridge Between Worlds

Although problems of political control and succes-sion continued to plague the kingdoms and empires that divided the Muslim world, the central position of Islamic civilization in global history was solidified during the centuries of Abbasid rule. Its role as the go-between for the more ancient civilizations of the Eastern Hemisphere grew as Arab trading networks expanded into new areas. More than ever, it enriched the lives of nomadic peoples, from the Turks and Mongols of central Asia to the Berbers of north Africa and the camel herders of the Sudan. Equally critically, Islam's original contributions to the growth and refinement of civilized life greatly increased. From its great cities and universities and the accomplishments they generated in the fine arts, sciences, and literature to its vibrant religious and philosophical life, Islam

pioneered patterns of organization and thinking that would affect the development of human societies in major ways for centuries to come.

In the midst of all this achievement, however, there were tendencies that would put the Muslim peoples at a growing disadvantage, particularly in relation to their long-standing European rivals. Mus-lim divisions would leave openings for political expan-sion that the Europeans would eagerly exploit, beginning with the island southeast Asian extremities of the Islamic world and then moving across north India. The growing orthodoxy and intolerance of the ulama, as well as the Muslim belief that the vast Islamic world contained all requirements for civilized life, caused Muslim peoples to grow less receptive to outside influences and innovations. These tendencies became increasingly pronounced at precisely the time when their Christian rivals were entering a period of unprecedented curiosity, experimentation, and explo-ration of the world beyond their own heartlands.

Further Reading

M. A. Shaban's *Islamic History: An Interpretation*, 2 vols. (1971), contains the most readable and thematic survey of early Islam, concentrating on the Abbasid period. Although Philip Hitti's monumental *History of the Arabs* (1967) and J. J. Saunders' *A History of Medieval Islam* (1965) are now somewhat dated, they contain much valuable information and some fine insights into Arab history. Also useful are the works of G. E. von Gruenenbaum, especially *Classical Islam* (1970), which covers the Abbasid era. On changes in Islamic religion and the makeup of the Muslim community, Marshall Hodgson's *Venture of Islam* (1974, vol. 2) is indis-pensable, but it should not be tackled by the beginner. *The Cambridge History of Islam*, 2 vols. (1970); Ira Lapidus' *A History of Islamic Societies* (1988); and Albert Hourani's *A History of the Islamic Peoples* (1991) are excellent reference works for the political events of the Abbasid era and Mus-lim achievements in various fields. D. M. Dunlop's *Arab Civilization to A.D. 1500* (1971) also contains detailed essays on Islamic culture as well as an article on the accom-plishments of Muslim women in this era.

On social history, B. F. Musallam's *Sex and Society in Islam* (1983) has material on the Abbasid period, and Ira Lapidus' *Muslim Cities in the Later Middle Ages* (1967) remains the standard work on urban life in the premodern era. Two essential works on the spread of Islam to India are S. M. Ikram's *Muslim Civilization in India* (1964) and Aziz Ahmad's *Studies in Islamic Cul-ture in the Indian Environment* (1964). For the role of the Sufis in Islamic conversion, Richard Eaton's *Sufis of Bijapur* (1978) and *The Rise of Islam and the Bengal Frontier* (1993) are particularly revealing. The best introduction to the pattern of Islamic conversion in southeast Asia is H. J. de Graaf's essay in *The Cambridge History of Islam* (1976, vol. 2). Clifford Geertz's *Islam Observed* (1968) provides a sweeping and provocative interpretation of the process of conversion in general and of the varying forms Islam takes in Java and Morocco in particular. Toby Huff's *The Rise of Early Modern Science: Islam, China, and the West* (1993) is a stimulating account of the ways in which science and technology were transmitted between these key centers of the Eastern Hemisphere and the effects of these exchanges on global history.

On the Web

Abbasid Baghdad is examined at http://www.fordham. edu/halsall/source/1000baghdad.html. Oman Khayyam was no mere writer of verses, but a leading scientist (http://www-gap.dcs.st-and.ac.uk/~history/ Mathematicians/Khayyam.html), as were many Abbasid intellectuals (http://cyberistan.org/islamic/places1. html).

A Turkic people's homepage (http://www.ee.surrey.ac. uk/Societies/turksoc/intro/r_who.html) provides an introduction to Turkish history, including the empire of the Seljuk Turks. It also contains information about the status of women in Turkey, past and present.

The Seljuk Turks had to confront both the Crusades (http://www.islamset.com/islam/civil/seljuk.html) and the Mongol warriors of Chinggis Khan (http://www. pma.edmonton.ab.ca/vexhibit/genghis/intro.htm), but they succeeded in helping to preserve the Islamic heartland, while Islam spread even further into Africa and south and southeast Asia and China (http://users.erols. com/zenithco/indiamus.htm), a process that owed much to Sufism (http://www.geocities.com/Athens/5738/ intro.htm).

Islam could arrive via the sword, but it was more often than not spread by Muslim mystics seeking cultural synthesis, such as the Muslim Indian bhakti poet, Kabir (http://www.upanishad.org/kabir/index.htm, http:// www.boloji.com/kabir/, and http://www.cs.colostate. edu/~malaiya/kabir.html), whose message is sufficiently universal that he is claimed by adherents of many religions as one of their own.

CHAPTER 8

AFRICAN CIVILIZATIONS AND THE SPREAD OF ISLAM

In 1324, Mali ruler Mansa Musa made a pilgrimage to Mecca that brought the attention of the Muslim world to the wealth of the Mali kingdom. Cartographer Abraham Cresques depicted the trip more than 50 years later in the map shown below, where Mansa Musa is drawn holding a golden sceptre and nugget.

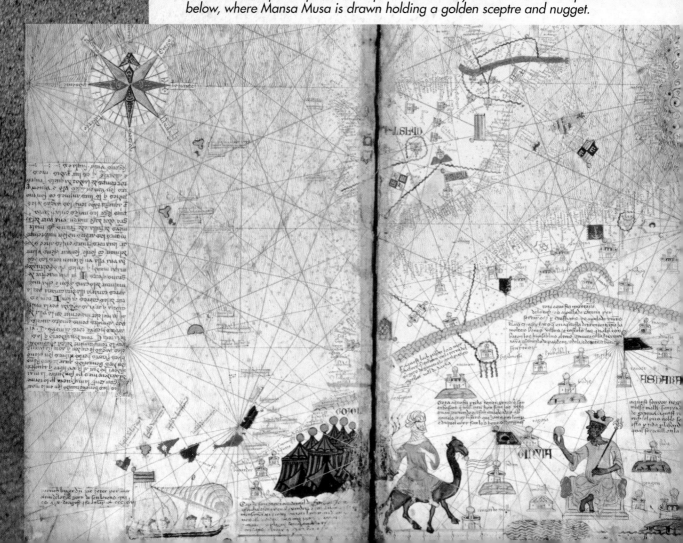

- African Societies: Diversity and Similarities
- Kingdoms of the Grasslands
- DOCUMENT: The Great Oral Tradition and the Epic of Sundiata
- The Swahili Coast of East Africa
- IN DEPTH: Two Transitions in the History of World Population
- Peoples of the Forest and Plains
- GLOBAL CONNECTIONS: Internal Development and Global Contacts

In 1324, a great caravan of hundreds of camels and slaves crossed the arid Sahara desert and wended its way into Cairo on the banks of the Nile. Mansa Musa, lord of the African empire of Mali, was making the *hajj*, the pilgrimage to Mecca, distributing gold with an open hand. His wealth and prodigality dazzled all who witnessed it and his fame spread throughout the Islamic world and beyond. Mansa Musa's caravan symbolized the wealthy potential of Africa, but even by the time he made his trip, west African gold was already well-known in the world economy and Africa was already involved in contacts of various kinds with other areas of the world.

Africa below the Sahara was never totally isolated from the centers of civilization in Egypt, west Asia, or the Mediterranean, but for long periods the contacts were difficult and intermittent. At the time of the Roman Empire, sub-Saharan Africa, like northern Europe, was on the edge of the major centers of civilization. After the fall of Rome, the civilizations of Byzantium and the Islamic world provided a link between the civilizations of the Middle East and the Mediterranean as well as the areas on their frontiers, such as northern Europe and Africa. In Africa, between roughly 800 and 1500 C.E., contacts with the outside world increased as part of the growing international network. Social, religious, and technological changes took place. Chief among these changes was the arrival of the followers of the prophet Muhammad. The spread of Islam from its heartland in the Middle East and north Africa to India and southeast Asia revealed the power of the religion and its commercial and sometimes military attributes. Civilizations were changed by Islam but retained their individuality. A similar pattern developed in sub-Saharan Africa as Islam provided new influences and contacts without uniting African culture as a whole with the Middle Eastern core. New religious, economic, and political patterns developed in relation to the Islamic surge, but great diversity remained.

The spread of Islam across much of the northern third of Africa produced profound effects on both those who converted and those who resisted the new faith. Islamization also linked Muslim Africa even more closely to the outside world through trade, religion, and politics. Trade and long-distance commerce were carried out in many parts of the continent and linked regions beyond the Muslim world. Until about 1450, however, Islam provided the major external contact between sub-Saharan Africa and the world.

State-building took place in many areas of the continent under a variety of conditions. For example, west Africa experienced both the cultural influence of Islam and its own internal civilization developments that produced great artistic accomplishments in some places. The formation of some powerful states, such as Mali and Songhay, depended more on military power

100 C.E.	600 C.E.	1000 C.E.	1200 C.E.	1400 C.E.
100–200 Camels introduced for trade in the Sahara **300** Origins of the kingdom of Ghana	**600–700** Islam spreads across North Africa	**1000** Ghana at height of its power **1100** Almoravid movement in the Sahara	**1200** Rise of the empire of Mali **1260** Death of Sundiata; earliest stone buildings at Zimbabwe; Lalibela rules in Ethiopia; Yoruba culture flourishes at Ile-Ife **1300** Mali at its height; Kanem Empire as a rival **1324** Pilgrimage of Mansa Musa	**1400** Flourishing of cities of Timbuktu and Jenne; Ethiopian Christian kingdom; Swahili cities flourish on East Africa coast **1417, 1431** Last Chinese trade voyages to East Africa **1500** Songhay Empire flourishes; Benin at height of power

and dynastic alliances than on ethnic or cultural unity. In this aspect and in the process of state formation itself, Africa paralleled the roughly contemporaneous developments of western Europe. The development of city-states, with strong merchant communities in west Africa and on the Indian Ocean coast of east Africa, bore certain similarities to the urban developments of Italy and Germany in this period. However, disparities between the technologies and ideologies of Europeans and Africans by the end of this period also created differences in the ways in which their societies developed. The arrival of western Europeans—the Portuguese—in the 15th century prompted a series of exchanges that drew Africans increasingly into the world economy and created a new set of relationships that characterized African development for centuries to come.

Several features characterize the history of Africa in the postclassical centuries. Northern Africa and the east African coast became increasingly incorporated into the Arab Muslim world, but even other parts of the continent reflected the power of Islamic thought and institutions. New centers of civilization and political power arose in several parts of sub-Saharan Africa, illustrating the geographic diffusion of civilization. African civilizations built somewhat less clearly on prior societies than did other postclassical civilizations. Some earlier themes, such as the Bantu migration and the formation of large states in the western Sudan, persisted. Overall, sub-Saharan Africa remained a varied and distinctive setting; parts of it were drawn into new contacts with the growing world network, but much of it retained a certain isolation.

African Societies: Diversity and Similarities

 African societies developed diverse forms, from large centralized states to stateless societies organized around kinship or age sets rather than central authority. Within this diversity were many shared aspects of language and beliefs. Universalistic faiths penetrated the continent and served as the basis for important cultural developments in Nubia and Ethiopia.

Like most continents, Africa is so vast and its societies so diverse that it is almost impossible to generalize about them. Differences in geography, language, religion, politics, and other aspects of life contributed to Africa's lack of political unity over long periods of time. Unlike in many parts of Asia, Europe, and north Africa, neither universal states nor universal religions characterized the history of sub-Saharan Africa. Yet universal religions, first Christianity and later Islam, did find adherents in Africa and sometimes contributed to the formation of large states and empires.

Stateless Societies

Some African societies had rulers who exercised control through a hierarchy of officials in what can be called states, but others were **stateless societies,** organized around kinship or other forms of obligation and lacking the concentration of political power and authority we normally associate with the state. Sometimes the stateless societies were larger and more extensive than the neighboring states. Stateless societies had forms of government, but the authority and power normally exercised by a ruler and his court in a kingdom could be held instead by a council of families or by the community, with no need to tax the population to support the ruler, the bureaucrats, the army, or the nobles, as was usually the case in state-building societies. Stateless societies had little concentration of authority, and that authority affected only a small part of the peoples' lives. In these societies, government was rarely a full-time occupation.

Other alternatives to formal government were possible. Among peoples of the west African forest, secret societies of men and women controlled customs and beliefs and were able to limit the authority of rulers. Especially among peoples who had sharp rivalries between lineages or family groupings, secret societies developed that cut across the lineage divisions. Members' allegiance to these groups transcended their lineage ties. The secret societies settled village disputes. They acted to maintain stability within the community, and they served as an alternative to the authority of state institutions.

Throughout Africa many stateless societies thrived, perhaps aided by the fact that internal social pressures or disputes often could be resolved by allowing dissidents to leave and establish a new village in the sparsely populated continent. Still, stateless societies found it difficult to resist external pressures, mobilize for warfare, organize large building projects, or create stable conditions for continuous long-distance trade with other peoples. All these needs or goals contributed to the formation of states in sub-Saharan Africa.

Common Elements in African Societies

Even amid the diversity of African cultures, certain similarities in language, thought, and religion provided some underlying unities. The spread of the Bantu-speaking peoples provided a linguistic base across much of Africa, so that even though specific languages differed, structure and vocabulary allowed some mutual understanding between neighboring Bantu speakers.

The same might be said of the animistic religion that characterized much of Africa. The belief in the power of natural forces personified as spirits or gods and the role of ritual and worship—often in the form of dancing, drumming, divination, and sacrifice—in influencing their actions was central to the religion of many African peoples. Africans, like Europeans, believed that some evil, disasters, and illnesses were produced by witchcraft. Specialists were needed to combat the power of evil and eliminate the witches. This led in many societies to the existence of a class of diviners or priests who guided religious practice and helped protect the community. Above all, African religion provided a cosmology—a view of how the universe worked—and a guide to ethics and behavior.

Many African peoples shared an underlying belief in a creator deity whose power and action were expressed through spirits or lesser gods and through the founding ancestors of the group. The ancestors often were viewed as the first settlers and thus the "owners" of the land or the local resources, and through them the fertility of the land, game, people, and herds could be ensured. Among some groups, working the land took on religious significance, so the land itself had a meaning beyond its economic usefulness.

Religion, economics, and history were thus closely intertwined. The family, lineage, or clan around which many African societies were organized also had an important role in dealing with the gods. Deceased ancestors often were a direct link between their living relatives and the spirit world. Veneration of the ancestors and gods was part of the same system of belief. Such a system was strongly linked to specific places and people. It showed remarkable resiliency even in the face of contact with monotheistic religions such as Islam and Christianity.

The economies of Africa are harder to describe in general terms than some basic aspects of politics and culture. North Africa, fully involved in the Mediterranean and Arab economic world, stands clearly apart. Sub-Saharan Africa varied greatly from one region to the next. In many areas, settled agriculture and skilled ironwork had been established before or advanced rapidly during the postclassical period. Specialization encouraged active local and regional trade, the basis for many lively markets and the many large cities that grew in both the structured states and the decentralized areas. The bustle and gaiety of market life were important ingredients of African society, and women as well as men participated actively. Professional merchants, in many cases in hereditary kinship groupings, often controlled trade. Participation in international trade increased in many regions in this period, mainly with the Islamic world and often through Arab traders.

Finally, one of the least known aspects of early African societies is the size and dynamics of their populations. This is true not only of Africa but of much of the world. Archeological evidence, travelers' reports, and educated guesses are used to estimate the population of early African societies, but in truth, our knowledge of how Africa fits into the general trends of the world population is very slight. By 1500, Africa may have had 30 to 60 million inhabitants.

The Arrival of Islam in North Africa

Africa north of the Sahara had long been part of the world of classical antiquity, where Phoenicians, Greeks, Romans, and Vandals traded, settled, built, battled, and destroyed. The Greek city of Cyrene (c. 600 B.C.E.) in modern Libya and the great Phoenician outpost at Carthage (founded c. 814 B.C.E.) in Tunisia attest to the part north Africa played in the classical world. After the age of the pharaohs, Egypt (conquered by Alexander in 331 B.C.E.) had become an important part of the Greek world and then later a key province in the Roman Empire, valued especially for its grain. Toward the end of the Roman Empire, Christianity had taken a firm hold in Mediterranean Africa, but in the warring between the Vandals and the Byzantines in north Africa in the 5th and 6th centuries C.E., great disruption had taken place. During that period, the Berber peoples of the Sahara had raided the coastal cities. As we have seen with Egypt, north Africa was linked across the Sahara to the rest of Africa in many ways. With the rise of Islam, those ties became even closer.

Between 640 and 700 C.E., the followers of Muhammad swept across north Africa from Suez to Morocco's Atlantic shore. By 670 C.E., Muslims ruled Tunisia, or **Ifriqiya**—what the Romans had called Africa. (The Arabs originally used this word as the name for eastern north Africa and **Maghrib** for lands

to the west.) By 711, Arab and Berber armies had crossed into Spain. Only their defeat in France by Charles Martel at Poitiers in 732 brought the Muslim advance in the West to a halt. The message of Islam found fertile ground among the populations of north Africa. Conversion took place rapidly within a certain political unity provided by the Abbasid dynasty. This unity eventually broke down, and north Africa divided into several separate states and competing groups.

In opposition to the states dominated by the Arabic rulers, the peoples of the desert, the Berbers, formed states of their own at places such as Fez in Morocco and at Sijilmasa, the old city of the trans-Saharan caravan trade. By the 11th century, under pressure from new Muslim invaders, a great puritanical reformist movement, whose followers were called the **Almoravids,** grew among the desert Berbers of the western Sahara. Launched on the course of a *jihad*—a holy war waged to purify, spread, or protect the faith—the Almoravids moved south against the African kingdoms of the savanna and west into Spain. In 1130 another reformist group, the **Almohadis,** followed the same pattern. These north African and Spanish developments were an essential background to the penetration of Islam into sub-Saharan Africa.

Islam offered many attractions within Africa. Its fundamental teaching that all Muslims are equal within the community of believers made the acceptance of conquerors and new rulers easier. The Islamic tradition of uniting the powers of the state and religion in the person of the ruler or caliph appealed to some African kings as a way of reinforcing their authority. The concept that all members of the umma, or community of believers, were equal put the newly converted Berbers and later Africans on an equal footing with the Arabs, at least in law. Despite these egalitarian and somewhat utopian ideas within Islam, practices differed considerably at local levels. Social stratification remained important in Islamicized societies, and ethnic distinctions also divided the believers. Despite certain teachings on the equality between men and women, the fine for killing a man was twice that for killing a woman. The disparity between law and practice—between equality before God and inequality within the world—sometimes led to utopian reform movements. Groups such as the Almohadis are characteristic within Islamic history, often developing in peripheral areas and dedicated to purifying society by returning to the original teachings of Muhammad.

The Christian Kingdoms: Nubia and Ethiopia

Islam was not the first universalistic religion to take root in Africa, and the wave of Arab conquests across northern Africa had left behind it islands of Christianity. Christian converts had been made in Egypt and Ethiopia even before the conversion of the Roman Empire in the 4th century C.E. In addition to the Christian kingdom of Axum, Christian communities thrived in Egypt and Nubia, further up the Nile. The Christians of Egypt, the Copts, developed a rich tradition in contact with Byzantium, translating the gospels and other religious literature from Greek to Coptic, their own tongue, which was based on the language of ancient Egypt. On doctrinal and political issues they eventually split from the Byzantine connection. When Egypt was conquered by Arab armies and then converted to Islam, the Copts were able to maintain their faith; Muslim rulers recognized them as followers of a revealed religion and thus entitled to a certain tolerance. The Coptic influence had already spread up the Nile into Nubia, the ancient land of Kush. Muslim attempts to penetrate Nubia were met with such stiff resistance in the 9th century that the Christian descendants of ancient Kush were left as independent Christian kingdoms until the 13th century.

The Ethiopian kingdom that grew from Axum was perhaps the most important African Christian outpost. Cut off from Christian Byzantium by the Muslim conquest of Egypt and the Red Sea coast, surrounded by pagan neighbors, and probably influenced by pagan and Jewish immigrants from Yemen, the Christian kingdom turned inward. Its people occupied the Ethiopian highlands, living in fortified towns and supporting themselves with agriculture on terraced hillsides. Eventually, through a process of warfare, conversion, and compromise with non-Christian neighbors, a new dynasty appeared, which under King Lalibela (d. 1221) sponsored a remarkable building project in which 11 great churches were sculpted from the rock in the town that bore his name (Figure 8.1).

In the 13th and 14th centuries, an Ethiopian Christian state emerged under a dynasty that traced its origins back to the biblical marriage of Solomon and Sheba. Using the Geez language of Axum as a religious language and Amharic as the common speech, this state maintained its brand of Christianity in isolation while facing constant pressure from its increasingly Muslim neighbors.

The struggle between the Christian state in the Ethiopian highlands and the Muslim peoples in Somalia and on the Red Sea coast shaped much of the history of the region and continues to do so today.

Figure 8.1 *The 13th-century churches of Lalibela, some cut from a single rock, represent the power of early Christianity in Ethiopia.*

When one of these Muslim states, with help from the Ottoman Turks, threatened the Ethiopian kingdom, a Portuguese expedition arrived in 1542 at Massawa on the Red Sea and turned the tide in favor of its Christian allies. Portuguese attempts thereafter to bring Ethiopian Christianity into the Roman Catholic church failed, and Ethiopia remained isolated, Christian, and fiercely independent.

Kingdoms of the Grasslands

 In the sahel grasslands, several powerful states emerged that combined Islamic religion and culture with local practices. The kingdoms of Mali and Songhay and the Hausa states were African adaptations of Islam and its fusion with African traditions.

As the Islamic wave spread across north Africa, it sent ripples across the Sahara, not in the form of invading armies but at first in the merchants and travelers who trod the dusty and ancient caravan routes toward the savanna. Africa had three important "coasts" of contact: the Atlantic, the Indian Ocean, and the savanna on the southern edge of the Sahara.

On the edge of the desert, where several resource zones came together, African states such as Ghana had already formed by the 8th century by exchanging gold from the forests of west Africa for salt or dates from the Sahara or for goods from Mediterranean north Africa. Camels, which had been introduced from Asia to the Sahara between the 1st and 5th centuries C.E., had greatly improved the possibilities of trade, but these animals, which thrived in arid and semiarid environments, could not live in the humid forest zones because of disease. Thus, the **sahel,** the extensive grassland belt at the southern edge of the Sahara, became a point of exchange between the forests to the south and north Africa—an active "coast" where ideas, trade, and people from the Sahara and beyond arrived in increasing numbers. Along that coast, several African states developed between the trading cities, taking advantage of their position as intermediaries in the trade. But their location on the open plains of the dry sahel also meant that these states were subject to attack and periodic droughts.

Founded probably in the 3rd century C.E., Ghana rose to power by taxing the salt and gold exchanged within its borders. By the 10th century, its rulers had converted to Islam, and Ghana was at the height of its power. At a time when William the Conqueror could muster perhaps 5000 troops for his invasion of England, Muslim accounts reported that the king of Ghana could field an army many times that size. Eventually, however, Almoravid armies invaded Ghana from north Africa in 1076, and although the kingdom survived, its power was in decline, so that by the beginning of the 13th century, new states had risen in the savanna to take its place of leadership.

Sudanic States

There were several Sudanic kingdoms, and even during the height of Ghana's power, neighboring and competing states persisted, such as Takrur on the Senegal River to the west and Gao (Kawkaw) on the Niger River to the east. Before we deal with the most important kingdoms that followed Ghana, it is useful to review some of the elements these states had in common.

The **Sudanic states** often had a patriarch or council of elders of a particular family or group of lineages as leaders. Usually these states had a territorial core area in which the people were of the same linguistic or ethnic background, but their power extended over subordinate communities. These were conquest states, which drew on the taxes, tribute, and military support of the subordinate areas, lineages, and villages. The effective control of subordinate societies and the legal or informal control of their sovereignty are the usual definition of empires. The Sudanic states of Ghana, Mali, and Songhay fit that definition (Map 8.1).

The rulers of these states were considered sacred and were surrounded by rituals that separated them from their subjects. With the conversion of the rulers of Ghana and Takrur after the 10th century, Islam was used to reinforce indigenous ideas of kingship, so that Islam became something of a royal cult. Much of the population never converted, and the Islamicized ruling families also drew on their traditional powers to fortify their rule.

Several savanna states rose among the various peoples in the Sudan. We can trace the development and culture of two of the most important, Mali and Songhay, as an example of the fusion of Islamic and

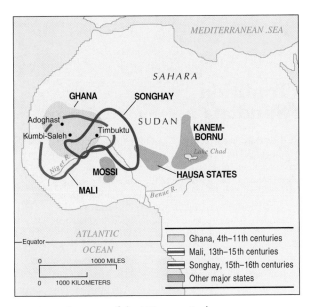

Map 8.1 *Empires of the Western Sudan*

indigenous African cultures within the context of trade and military expansion.

The Empire of Mali and Sundiata, the "Lion Prince"

The empire of **Mali,** centered between the Senegal and Niger rivers, was the creation of the Malinke peoples, who in the 13th century broke away from the control of Ghana, which was by then in steady decline. In Mali the old forms of kingship were reinforced by Islam. As in many of the Sudanic states, the rulers supported Islam by building mosques, attending public prayers, and supporting preachers. In return, sermons to the faithful emphasized obedience and support of the king. Mali became a model of these Islamicized Sudanic kingdoms. The economic basis of society in the Mali Empire was agriculture. This was combined with an active tradition of trade in many products, although like Ghana Mali also depended on its access to gold-producing areas to the south. Malinke merchants, or **juula,** formed small partnerships and groups to carry out trade throughout the area. They spread beyond the borders of the empire and throughout all of west Africa. The beginning of Malinke expansion is attributed to **Sundiata** (sometimes written Sunjata), a brilliant leader whose exploits were celebrated in a great oral tradition. The **griots,** professional oral historians who also served as keepers of traditions and advisors to kings, began their epic histories of Mali with Sundiata, the "Lion Prince."

> Listen then sons of Mali, children of the black people, listen to my word, for I am going to tell you of Sundiata, the father of the Bright Country, of the savanna land, the ancestor of those who draw the bow, the master of a hundred vanquished kings.... He was great among kings, he was peerless among men; he was beloved of God because he was the last of the great conquerors.

After a difficult childhood, Sundiata emerged from a period of interfamily and regional fighting to create a unified state. Oral histories ascribed to him the creation of the basic rules and relationships of Malinke society and the outline of the government of the empire of Mali. He became the mansa, or emperor. It was said that Sundiata "divided up the world," which meant that he was considered the originator of social arrangements. Sixteen clans of free people were entitled to bear arms and carry the bow and quiver of arrows as the symbol of their status, five clans were devoted to religious duties, and four clans were specialists such as blacksmiths and griots. Division and grouping by clans apparently represented traditional patterns among the peoples of the savanna in ancient Ghana as well, but Sundiata as the hero of origins was credited with creating this social arrangement. Although he created the political institutions of rule that allowed for great regional and ethnic differences in the federated provinces, he also stationed garrisons to maintain loyalty and security. Travel was secure and crime was severely punished, as **Ibn Batuta,** the Arab traveler, reported: "Of all peoples," he said, "the Blacks are those who most hate injustice, and their emperor pardons none who is guilty of it." The security of travelers and their goods was an essential element in a state where commerce played so important a role.

Sundiata died about 1260, but his successors expanded the borders of Mali until it controlled most of the Niger valley almost to the Atlantic coast. A sumptuous court was established and hosted a large number of traders. Mali grew wealthy from the trade. Perhaps the most famous of Sundiata's successors was Mansa Kankan Musa (c. 1312–1337), who made a pilgrimage to Mecca in 1324 and brought the attention of the Muslim world to Mali. The trip caused a

Document

The Great Oral Tradition and the Epic of Sundiata

Oral traditions take various forms. Some are simply the shared stories of a family or people, but in many west African societies, the mastery of oral traditions is a skill practiced by *griots*. Although today's griots are professional musicians and bards, historically they held important places at the courts of west African kingdoms. The epic of Sundiata, the great ruler of Mali, has been passed down orally for centuries. In the following excerpts from a version collected among the Mandingo (Malinke) people of Guinea by the African scholar D. T. Niane, the role of the griot and the advantages of oral traditions are outlined.

We are now coming to the great moments in the life of Sundiata. The exile will end and another sun will rise. It is the sun of Sundiata. Griots know the history of kings and kingdoms and that is why they are the best counsellors of kings. Every king wants to have a singer to perpetuate his memory, for it is the griot who rescues the memories of kings from oblivion, as men have short memories. Kings have prescribed destinies just like men, and seers who probe the future know it. They have knowledge of the future, whereas we griots are depositories of the knowledge of the past. But whoever knows the history of a country can read its future.

Other peoples use writing to record the past, but this invention has killed the faculty of memory among them. They do not feel the past any more, for writing lacks the warmth of the human voice. With them everybody thinks he knows, whereas learning should be a secret. The prophets did not write and their words have been all the more vivid as a result. What paltry learning is that which is concealed in dumb books!

The following excerpt describes the preparation for a major battle fought by Sundiata against the forces of Soumaoro, king of the Sossos, who had taken control of Mali and who is called an evil sorcerer in the epic. Note the interweaving of proverbs, the presence of aspects of Muslim and animist religion, the celebration of Sundiata's prowess, the recurring references to iron, and the high value placed on the cavalry, the key to military power in the savanna. Note how the story of Alexander the Great inspires this "African Alexander."

Every man to his own land! If it is foretold that your destiny should be fulfilled in such and such a land, men can do nothing against it. Mansa Tounkara could not keep Sundiata back because the destiny of Songolon's son was bound up with that of Mali. Neither the jealousy of a cruel stepmother, nor her wickedness could alter for a moment the course of great destiny.

The snake, man's enemy, is not long-lived, yet the serpent that lives hidden will surely die old. Djata (Sundiata) was strong enough now to face his enemies. At the age of eighteen he had the stateliness of the lion and the strength of the buffalo. His voice carried authority, his eyes were live coals, his arm was iron, he was the husband of power.

Moussa Tounkara, king of Mema, gave Sundiata half of his army. The most valiant came forward of their own free will to follow Sundiata in the great adventure. The cavalry of Mema, which he had fashioned himself, formed his iron squadron. Sundiata, dressed in the Muslim fashion of Mema, left the town at the head of his small but redoubtable army. The whole population sent their best wishes with him. He was surrounded by five messengers from Mali, and Manding Bory [Sundiata's brother] rode proudly at his side. The horsemen of Mema formed behind Djata a bristling iron squadron. The troop took the direction of Wagadou, for Djata did not have enough troops to confront Soumaoro directly, and so the king of Mema advised him to go to Wagadou and take half the men of the king, Soumaba Cissé. A swift messenger had been sent there and so the king of Wagadou came out in person to meet Sundiata and his troops. He gave Sundiata half of his cavalry and blessed the weapons. Then Manding Bory said to his brother, "Djata, do you think yourself able to face Soumaoro now?"

"No matter how small a forest may be, you can always find there sufficient fibers to tie up a man. Numbers mean nothing; it is worth that counts. With my cavalry I shall clear myself a path to Mali."

Djata gave out his orders. They would head south, skirting Soumaoro's kingdom. The first objective to be reached was Tabon, the iron-gated town in the midst of the mountains, for Sundiata had promised Fran Kamara that he would pass Tabon before returning to Mali. He hoped to find that his childhood companion had become king. It was a forced march and during the halts the divines, Singbin Mara Cissé and Mandjan Bérété, related to Sundiata the history of Alexander the Great and several other heroes, but of all of them Sundiata preferred Alexander, the king of gold and silver, who crossed the world from west to east. He wanted to outdo his prototype both in the extent of his territory and in the wealth of his treasury.

Questions: Can oral traditions be used like other sources? Even if they are not entirely true, do they have historical value? Judging from this epic, how did people of the Sudan define the qualities of a king? What aspects of the epic reveal contacts between this part of Africa and the wider world?

sensation across the Sudan and into Egypt, where it was said that so much gold was distributed by his retinue that a general devaluation of currency took place. The trip and the ruler became almost legendary. In 1375, Abraham Cresques, a Jewish mapmaker in Spain, illustrated a map of Africa with an image of the ruler of Mali holding a golden sceptre (see Chapter 8 opening photo). Mansa Musa's trip had other consequences as well. From Mecca he brought back poet and architect Ishak al-Sahili, who came from Muslim Spain. The architect directed the building of several important mosques, and eventually a distinctive form of Sudanic architecture developed that made use of beaten clay. This can still be seen in the great mosque of Jenne (Figure 8.2). Mali's contact with the outer world brought change and innovation.

City Dwellers and Villagers

The cities of the western Sudan began to resemble those of north Africa, but with a distinctive local architectural style. The towns were commercial and often included craft specialists and a resident foreign merchant community. The military expansion of states such as Ghana, Mali, and later Songhay contributed to their commercial success because the power of the state protected traders. A cosmopolitan court life developed as merchants and scholars were attracted by the power and protection of Mali. Mandinka traders ranged across the Sudan and exploited their position as intermediaries. "Port" cities flourished, such as Jenne and **Timbuktu,** which lay just off the flood plain on the great bend in the Niger River. Timbuktu was reported to have a population of 50,000, and by the 14th century, its great Sankore mosque contained a library and an associated university where scholars, jurists, and Muslim theologians studied. The book was the symbol of civilization in the Islamic world, and it was said that the book trade in Timbuktu was the most lucrative business.

For most people in the empire of Mali and the other Sudanic states, life was not centered on the

Figure 8.2   *The spread of Islam and the importance of trade in Africa are represented by the great mosque at Jenne on the Niger River in the modern Republic of Mali.*

royal court, the great mosque, or long-distance trade but rather on the agricultural cycle and the village. Making a living from the land was the preoccupation of most people, and about 80 percent of the villagers lived by farming. This was a difficult life. The soils of the savanna were sandy and shallow. Plows were rarely used. The villagers were people of the hoe who looked to the skies in the spring for the first rains to start their planting. Rice in the river valleys, millet, sorghums, some wheat, fruits, and vegetables provided the basis of daily life in the village and supplied the caravan trade. Even a large farm rarely exceeded 10 acres, and most were much smaller. Clearing land often was done communally, accompanied by feasts and competition, but the farms belonged to families and were worked by them. A man with two wives and several unmarried sons could work more land than a man with one wife and a smaller family. Polygamy, the practice of having multiple wives, was common in the region, and it remains so today.

Given the difficulties of the soil, the periodic droughts, insect pests, storage problems, and the limitations of technology, the farmers of the Sudanic states—by the methods of careful cultivation, crop rotation, and, in places such as Timbuktu, the use of irrigation—were able to provide for their people the basic foods that supported them and the imperial states on which they were based. The hoe and the bow became symbols of the common people of the savanna states.

The Songhay Kingdom

As the power of Mali began to wane, a successor state from within the old empire was already beginning to emerge. The people of **Songhay** dominated the middle areas of the Niger valley. Traditionally, the society of Songhay was made up of "masters of the soil," that is, farmers, herders, and "masters of the waters," or fishers. Songhay had begun to form in the 7th century as an independent kingdom, perhaps under a Berber dynasty. By 1010, a capital was established at Gao on the Niger River, and the rulers had become Muslims, although the majority of the population remained pagan. Dominated by Mali for a while, by the 1370s Songhay had established its independence again and began to thrive as new sources of gold from the west African forests began to pass through its territory. Gao became a large city with a resident foreign merchant community and several mosques. Under a

dynamic leader, Sunni Ali (1464–1492), the empire of Songhay was forged.

Sunni Ali was a great tactical commander and a ruthless leader. His cavalry expanded the borders and seized the traditional trading cities of Timbuktu and Jenne. The middle Niger valley fell under his control, and he developed a system of provincial administration to mobilize recruits for the army and rule the far-flung conquests. Although apparently a Muslim, he met any challenge to his authority even when it came from the Muslim scholars of Timbuktu, whom he persecuted. A line of Muslim rulers who took the military title *askia* succeeded him. These rulers, especially **Muhammad the Great,** extended the boundaries of the empire so that by the mid-16th century Songhay dominated the central Sudan.

Life in the Songhay Empire followed many of the patterns established in the previous savanna states. The fusion of Islamic and pagan populations and traditions continued. Muslim clerics and jurists sometimes were upset by the pagan beliefs and practices that continued among the population, and even more by the local interpretation of Islamic law. They wanted to impose a strict interpretation of the law of Islam and were shocked that men and women mixed freely in the markets and streets, that women went unveiled.

Songhay remained the dominant power in the region until the end of the 16th century. In 1591, a Muslim army from Morocco, equipped with muskets, crossed the Sahara and defeated the vastly larger forces of Songhay. This sign of weakness stimulated internal revolts against the ruling family, and eventually the parts of the old empire broke away.

The demise of the Songhay imperial structure did not mean the end of the political and cultural tradition of the western Sudan. Other states that combined Muslim and pagan traditions rose among the **Hausa** peoples of northern Nigeria, based on cities such as Kano and Katsina. The earliest Muslim ruler of Kano took control in the late 14th century and turned the city into a center of Muslim learning. In Kano and other Hausa cities of the region, an urbanized royal court in a fortified capital ruled over the animistic villages, where the majority of the population lived. With powerful cavalry forces these states extended their rule and protected their active trade in salt, grains, and cloth. Although these later Islamicized African states tended to be small and their goals were local, they reproduced many of the social, political, and religious forms of the great empires of the grasslands.

Beyond the Sudan, Muslim penetration came in various forms. Merchants became established in most of the major trading cities, and religious communities developed in each of these, often associated with particular families. Networks of trade and contact were established widely over the region as merchants and groups of pastoralists established their outposts in the area of Guinea. Muslim traders, herders, warriors, and religious leaders became important minorities in these segmented African societies, composed of elite families, occupational groups, free people, and slaves. Intermarriage often took place, but Muslim influence varied widely from region to region. Nevertheless, families of traders and lineages that became known as specialists in Muslim law spread widely through the region, so that by the 18th century Muslim minorities were scattered widely throughout west Africa, even in areas where no Islamicized state had emerged.

Political and Social Life in the Sudanic States

We can generalize from these brief descriptions of Mali and Songhay about the nature of the Sudanic states. The village communities, clans, and various ethnic groups continued to organize many aspects of life in the savanna. The development of unified states provided an overarching structure that allowed the various groups and communities to coexist. The large states usually represented the political aims and power of a particular group and often of a dominant family. Many states pointed to the immigrant origins of the ruling families, and in reality the movement and fusion of populations were constant features in the Sudan. Islam provided a universalistic faith that served the interests of many groups. Common religion and law provided solidarity and trust to the merchants who lived in the cities and whose caravans brought goods to and from the savanna. The ruling families used Islamic titles, such as *emir* or *caliph*, to reinforce their authority, and they surrounded themselves with literate Muslim advisors and scribes, who aided in government administration. The Muslim concept of a ruler who united civil and religious authority reinforced traditional ideas of kingship. It is also important to note that in Africa, as elsewhere in the world, the formation of states heightened social differences and made these societies more hierarchical.

In all the Sudanic states, Islam was fused with the existing traditions and beliefs. Rulership and authority were still based on the ability to intercede with local spirits, and although Sundiata and Sunni Ali were nominally Muslim, they did not ignore the traditional basis of their rule. For this reason, Islam in these early stages in the Sudan tended to accommodate pagan practice and belief. Large proportions of the populations of Mali and Songhay never converted to Islam, and those who did convert often maintained many of the old beliefs as well.

We can see this fusion of traditions clearly in the position of women. Several Sudanic societies were matrilineal, and some recognized the role of women within the lines of kinship, contrary to the normal patrilineal customs inscribed in the **Sharia,** or Islamic law. As in the case of Songhay, north African visitors to the Sudan were shocked by the easy familiarity between men and women and the freedom enjoyed by women.

Finally, slavery and the slave trade between black Africa and the rest of the Islamic world had a major impact on women and children in these societies. Various forms of slavery and dependant labor had existed in Africa before Islam was introduced. Although we know little about slavery in central Africa in this period, slavery had been a marginal aspect of the Sudanic states. Africans had been enslaved by others before, and Nubian (African) slaves had been known in the classical world, but with the Muslim conquests of north Africa and commercial penetration to the south, slavery became a more widely diffused phenomenon, and a slave trade in Africans developed on a new scale.

In theory, Muslims viewed slavery as a stage in the process of conversion—a way of preparing pagans to become Muslims—but in reality, conversion did not guarantee freedom. Slaves in the Islamic world were used in a variety of occupations, as domestic servants and laborers, but they were also used as soldiers and administrators who, having no local ties and affiliations, were considered to be dependant and thus trustworthy by their masters. Slaves were also used as eunuchs and concubines, hence the emphasis on enslaving women and children. The trade caravans from the sahel across the Sahara often transported slaves as well as gold, and as we shall see, other slave trade routes developed from the African interior to the east African coast. The tendency for the children of slave mothers to be freed and integrated into Muslim society, though positive in one sense, also meant a constant demand for more slaves. Estimates of the volume of this trade vary widely. One scholar places the total in the trans-Saharan trade at 4.8 million, with another 2.4 million sent to the Muslim ports on the Indian Ocean coast. Actual figures may have been considerably lower, but the trade extended over 700 years and affected a large area. In a way, it was one more way in which Islamic civilization changed sub-Saharan Africa.

The Swahili Coast of East Africa

A string of Islamicized African ports tied to the trade across the Indian Ocean dotted the east African coast. Although these cities were Islamicized, African customs and the Bantu Swahili language remained so strong that they represented a cultural fusion, mostly limited to the coast.

While the kingdoms of west Africa came under the influence of Islam from across the Sahara, another center of Islamic civilization was developing on the seaboard and offshore islands of Africa's Indian Ocean coast (Map 8.2). Along that coast, extending south from the horn of Africa to modern-day Mozambique, a string of Islamicized trading cities developed that reflected their cosmopolitan contacts with trading partners from Arabia, Persia, India, and China. Islam provided the residents of these towns a universal set of ethics and beliefs that made their maritime contacts easier, but in east Africa, as in the savanna kingdoms of west Africa, Islamization was slow to reach the general population. When it did, the result often was a compromise between indigenous ways and the new faith.

The Coastal Trading Ports

A 1st-century Greek account of the Indian Ocean, *The Periplus of the Erythraean Sea*, mentioned some ports in east Africa but was vague about whether the inhabitants were Africans or immigrants from the Arabian peninsula. From that century to the 10th century, the wave of Bantu migration had clearly reached the east African interior. Bantu-speaking herders in the north and farmers in the south mixed with older populations in the region. Other peoples were also moving to the African coast. Contact across the Indian Ocean dated back to at least the 2nd century B.C.E. From Indonesia or Malaya, seaborne immigrants settled on the large island of Madagascar

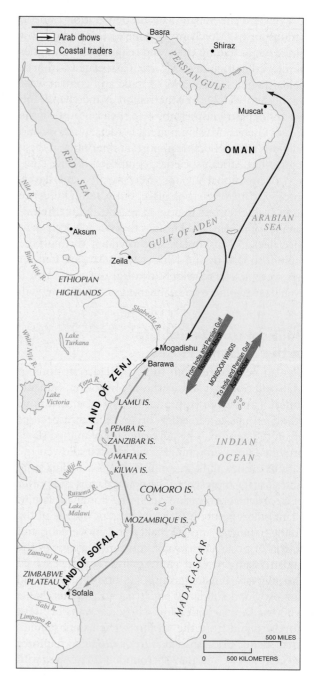

Map 8.2 *The Swahili Coast; African Monsoon Routes and Major Trade Routes*

and from there introduced foods such as bananas and coconuts to the African coast. These were widely adopted and spread rapidly along the coast and into central Africa. Small coastal villages of fishers and farmers, making rough pottery and working iron, dotted this coast. By the 8th and 9th centuries, visitors and refugees from Oman and the Persian Gulf had established themselves at some of these villages, attracted by the possibilities of trade with the land of **Zenj,** the Arabic term for the east African coast.

By the 13th century, a string of urbanized east African trading ports had developed along the coast. These towns shared the common Bantu-based and Arabic-influenced Swahili (which means "coastal") language and other cultural traits, although they were governed by separate Muslim ruling families. Towns such as Mogadishu, Mombasa, Malindi, Kilwa, Pate, and Zanzibar eventually contained mosques, tombs, and palaces of cut stone and coral. Ivory, gold, iron, slaves, and exotic animals were exported from these ports in exchange for silks from Persia and porcelain from China for the ruling Muslim families. The Arab traveler Ibn Batuta was impressed with the beauty and refinement of these towns. He described Kilwa as "one of the most beautiful and well-constructed towns in the world" and was also impressed by the pomp and luxury of its ruler. Kilwa was particularly wealthy because it controlled the southern port of Sofala, which had access to the gold produced in the interior (near Great Zimbabwe), and because of its location as the farthest point south at which ships from India could hope to sail and return in a single monsoon season.

From the 13th to the 15th centuries, Kilwa flourished in the context of international trade, but it was not alone. As many as 30 of these port towns eventually dotted the coast. They were tied to each other by an active coastal commerce and, in a few places, to the interior by a caravan trade, although it was usually Africans who brought the goods to the coast. Some Chinese ports sent goods directly to Africa in the 13th century, and as late as 1417 and 1431, large, state-sponsored expeditions sailing directly from China stopped at the east African coast to load ivory, gold, and rare woods. The Chinese discontinued such contact after 1431, and goods from China came to the coast thereafter in the ships of Arab or Indian traders.

The Mixture of Cultures on the Swahili Coast

The Islamic influence in these towns promoted long-distance commerce. The 13th century was a period of great Islamic expansion, and as that faith spread eastward to India and Indonesia, it provided a religious bond of trust and law that facilitated trade throughout

ports of the Indian Ocean. The ruling families in the east African trading ports built mosques and palaces; the mosque at Mogadishu was begun in 1238. Many of these ruling families claimed to be descendants of immigrants from Shiraz in Persia—a claim intended to legitimize their position and orthodoxy. In fact, some evidence indicates that the original Muslim families had emigrated to the Somali coast and from there to other towns farther south. The institutions and forms of the Muslim world operated in these cities. Whereas the rulers and merchants tended to be Muslim, the majority of the population on the east African coast, and perhaps even in the towns themselves, retained their previous beliefs and culture.

African culture remained strong throughout the area. The Swahili language was essentially a Bantu language containing a large number of Arabic words, although many of these words were not incorporated until the 16th century. The language was written in an Arabic script some time before the 13th century; the ruling families could also converse in Arabic. Islam itself penetrated very little into the interior among the hunters, pastoralists, and farmers. Even the areas of the coast near the trading towns remained largely unaffected. In the towns, the mud and thatch houses of the non-Muslim common peoples surrounded the stone and coral buildings of the Muslim elite. Islamization was to some extent class based. Still, a culture developed that fused Islamic and traditional elements. For example, family lineage was traced both through the maternal line, which controlled property (the traditional African practice), and through the paternal line, as was the Muslim custom. Swahili culture was a dynamic hybrid, and the Swahili people spread their language and culture along the coast of east Africa.

By the time the Portuguese arrived on this coast around 1500, the Swahili culture was widely diffused. Kilwa was no longer the predominant city, and the focus of trade had shifted to Malindi and Mombasa on the Kenya coast, but the commerce across the Indian Ocean continued. Eventually, the Portuguese raided Kilwa and Mombasa in an attempt to take control of trade. Their outpost on Mozambique Island and their control of Sofala put much of the gold trade in their hands. Although the Portuguese built a major outpost at Fort Jesus in Mombasa in 1592, they were never able to control the trade on the northern Swahili coast. The east African patterns, as established by 1500, persisted even more than those of the Sudanic kingdoms.

In Depth

Two Transitions in the History of World Population

Africa and the ancient Americas are two regions that make clear the difficulty of establishing the past size and structure of populations. Estimates based on fragmentary sources, the amount of available resources, and analysis of agricultural or hunting techniques have been used as rough guesses about population size. The results often are inadequate or controversial, but historians believe that the question is important. **Demography,** the study of population, has increasingly become a valued tool of historical inquiry. Clearly, unless we know the size, density, age structure, health, and reproductive capacity of a population, it is difficult to understand many aspects of its society, politics, and economy. In the contemporary world, most nations conduct periodic censuses to assess the present situation of their populations and to plan for the future. Before the mid-18th century, when census-taking became a regular procedure, population estimates and counts were sporadic and usually inaccurate. Estimating populations in the past, especially in nonliterate societies, is a highly speculative exercise in which archeological evidence and estimates of productive capacity of agricultural practices and technology are used. The earliest date for a population estimate with a margin of error less than 20 percent is probably 1750.

The history of human population can be divided into two basic periods: a long era—almost all of human history—of very slow growth and a very short period—about 250 years from 1750 to the present—of very rapid growth. For most of this history, the human population was very small and grew very slowly. Before agriculture was developed, the hunting-and-gathering economies of the world's populations supported 5 to 10 million people, if modern studies of such populations can be used as a guide. After about 8000 B.C.E., when plants and animals were domesticated, population began to increase more rapidly but still at a modest level. Agriculture provided a more secure and larger food supply, but population concentration in villages and towns may have made people more susceptible to disease and thus reduced their numbers. Other historians believe that the settled agricultural life also led to intensified warfare (because of the struggle for land and water) and increasing social stratification within societies. Still, the Neolithic revolution and the development of agriculture stimulated population growth. It was the first major transition in the history of world pop-

ulation. One estimate, based on Roman and Chinese population counts and some informed guesses about the rest of the world, is an annual growth rate of about 0.36 per million. By 1 C.E., the world population may have been about 300 million people. It increased between 1 C.E. and 1750 C.E. to about 500 million people. We should bear in mind that during this period of general increase, there were always areas that suffered decline, sometimes drastic, because of wars, epidemics, or natural catastrophes. The disastrous decline of American Indian populations after contact with Europeans, caused by disease, conquest, and social disruption, is a case in point. The effect of the slave trade on Africa, though still debated, is another. Sharp population changes usually resulted in profound social and cultural adjustments. Some scholars argue that the slave trade had just such an impact on social and political patterns in Africa.

A second and extremely important transition took place between the mid-17th and the mid-18th centuries. Initially based on new food resources, this transition often is associated with the Industrial Revolution, when new sources of energy were harnessed. The growth rate greatly increased during this period in the countries most affected. Between 1750 and 1800, the world population grew at a rate of more than 4 percent a year to more than a billion people. By the mid-20th century, the world growth rate had tripled, and by 1990 world population had risen to more than 5 billion.

This **demographic transition** took place first in Europe and is still more characteristic of the developed world. Most premodern agrarian economies were characterized by a balance between the annual number of births and deaths; both were high. Life expectancy usually was less than 35 years, and the high mortality was compensated by high fertility; that is, women had many children. Improvements in medicine, hygiene, diet, and the general standard of living contributed to a decrease in mortality in the 18th century. This allowed populations to begin to grow at a faster rate. By the 19th century in most of western Europe, the decline in mortality was followed by a decline in fertility brought about by contraception. In some countries such as France, these two transitions took place at about the same time, so population growth was limited. In much of Europe, however, the decline in fertility lagged behind the decrease in mortality, so there was a period of rapid population growth. Until the 1920s, population growth in western Europe and the United States was higher than in the rest of the world, especially in the less industrialized countries. In recent times, that situation has been reversed.

Some demographers believe that demographic transition is part of the process of shifting from a basically agrarian society to an industrial, urbanized one and that the improvements in medicine, technology, and higher standards of living will necessarily result in a change to a modern demographic structure. They believe that a decreasing need for children as part of the family economic unit, laws against child labor, and state intervention in family planning will eventually lower the world birth rate and decrease the pressure of population on economic growth. This assumption remains to be proved, and responses may vary greatly from one region of the world to another because of economic conditions and cultural attitudes about proper family size.

Finally, we should also note that responses to demographic transition can vary greatly according to historical conditions. In the 18th and 19th centuries, Europe resolved the problem of population growth with an enormous wave of emigration to the Americas, Australia, and various colonies around the globe. Present-day political circumstances make this solution less possible, although the new waves of migration in the global economy may indicate that the process is continuing.

Still, it is clear that a demographic transition has begun to take place in the developing world of Latin America, Africa, and Asia. Mortality has dropped very rapidly since 1950 because of modern medical technology, and life expectancy has doubled. To cite a single example, in Sri Lanka the mortality rate was almost cut in half between 1945 and 1952 simply by eliminating malarial mosquitoes. Fertility has declined in many places in Asia and Latin America, but in Africa, where children continue to have an important economic and social role in the extended family, it remains high. It is difficult to project what demographic transitions will take place in these areas of the world. However, all countries are faced with the problem of balancing their population's growth against the ability of the society to feed and provide an adequate standard of living to the people.

At present, the world's population is growing because of a moderate rate of growth in the industrialized nations and a high rate in the developing countries. In the 1970s, demographer Ansley Coale pointed out that the rate of growth, about 2 percent a year, is 100 times greater than it had been for most of human history. At this rate the world's population would be multiplied by 1000 every 350 years. The results of such growth would be disastrous. Coale concluded that the present period of growth is transitory. Some people who are concerned with rapid population growth believe that the solution is to limit population growth in the developing nations by state intervention, through incentives to have smaller families and education about birth control. Others believe that a redistribution of resources from rich nations to poor nations would alleviate the human misery created by population pressure and eventually lead to political and social conditions that would contribute to a gradual lowering of the birth rates. Clearly, demographic questions must always be set in political, economic, and social contexts.

Questions: Why do nations differ in their need to control population growth? Why has the rate of population growth varied in different areas of the world? Is overpopulation essentially a biological, social, or political problem?

Peoples of the Forest and Plains

 Across central Africa, kingdoms developed that were supported by complex agrarian societies capable of great artistic achievements. At Benin, in the Kongo, in the Yoruba city-states, and at Great Zimbabwe, royal authority—often considered divinely inspired—led to the creation of powerful states.

As important as the Islamic impact was on the societies of the savanna and the east African coast, other African peoples in the continent's interior and in the forests of west Africa were following their own trajectories of development. By 1000 C.E., most of these societies were based on a varied agriculture, sometimes combined with herding, and most societies used iron tools and weapons. Many were still organized in small village communities. In various places, however, states had formed. Some of them began to resolve the problems of integrating large territories under a single government and ruling subject peoples. Whereas Egypt, Kush, and Ethiopia had developed writing and other areas borrowed the Arabic script, many sub-Saharan African societies were preliterate and transmitted their knowledge, skills, and traditions by oral methods and direct instruction. The presence or absence of writing has often been used as a measure of civilization by Western observers, but as in pre-Columbian Peru, various African societies made great strides in the arts, building, and statecraft, sometimes in the context of highly urbanized settings, without a system of writing.

Artists and Kings: Yoruba and Benin

In the forests of central Nigeria, terra-cotta objects of a realistic and highly stylized form have been discovered near the village of **Nok**. These objects, most of which date from about 500 B.C.E. to 200 C.E., reveal considerable artistic skill. The inhabitants of ancient Nok and its region practiced agriculture and used iron tools. They remain something of a mystery, but it appears that their artistic traditions spread widely through the forest areas and influenced other peoples. Nevertheless, there is a long gap in the historical and archeological record between the Nok sculptures and the renewed flourishing of artistic traditions in the region after about 1000 C.E.

Among the Yoruba-speaking peoples of Nigeria, at the city of Ile-Ife, remarkable terra-cotta and bronze portrait heads of past rulers were produced in the period after 1200 C.E. The lifelike quality of these portraits and the skill of their execution place them among the greatest achievements of African art (Figure 8.3). The artists of Ile-Ife also worked in wood and ivory. Much of the art seems to be associated with kings and the authority of kingship. Ile-Ife, like other **Yoruba** states, seems to have been an agricultural society supported by a peasantry and dominated by a ruling family and an aristocracy. Ile-Ife was considered by many peoples in the region to be the original cultural center, and many of them traced their own beginnings to it.

Yoruba origins are obscure. Ile-Ife was seen as the holiest city of the Yoruba, their place of birth. Another legend maintained by the royal historians was that Oduduwa, a son of the king of Mecca, migrated from the east and settled in Yoruba. Modern historians have suggested that the real origins were perhaps Meroë and Nubia, or at least in the savanna south of the Sahara. In any case, the Yoruba spoke a non-Bantu language of the west African Kwa

Figure 8.3 *In the 13th and 14th centuries, Ife artists worked in terra-cotta as well as bronze and produced personalized portraits.*

family and recognized a certain affinity between themselves and neighboring peoples, such as the Hausa, who spoke Afro-Asian languages.

The Yoruba were organized in small city-states, each controlling a radius of perhaps 50 miles. The Yoruba were highly urbanized, although many of the town inhabitants farmed in the surrounding countryside. These city-states developed under the strong authority of regional kings, who were considered divine. A vast royal court that included secondary wives, musicians, magicians, and bodyguards of soldier-slaves surrounded the king. His rule was not absolute, however. We can use the example of the Yoruba state of Oyo, which had emerged by the 14th century. Its king, the alafin, controlled subject peoples through "princes" in the provinces, drawn from local lineages, who were allowed to exercise traditional rule as long as they continued to pay tribute to Oyo. In the capital, a council of state, made up of nobles from the seven city districts, advised the ruler and limited his power, and the Ogboni, or secret society of religious and political leaders, reviewed decisions of the king and the council. The union of civil and supernatural powers in the person of the ruler was the basis of power. The highly urbanized nature of Yoruba society and the flourishing of artisan traditions within these towns bear some similarity to those of the city-states of medieval Italy or Germany.

Patterns similar to those in the Yoruba city-states could be found among Edo peoples to the east of Yoruba. A large city-state called **Benin** was formed sometime in the 14th century. Under Ewuare the Great (r. 1440–1473), Benin's control extended from the Niger River to the coast near modern Lagos. Benin City was described by early European visitors in the 16th century as a city of great population and broad avenues. The Oba, or ruler, lived in a large royal compound surrounded by a great entourage, and his authority was buttressed by ritual and ceremony.

That authority was also the theme of the magnificent artistic output in ivory and cast bronze that became characteristic of Benin. Tradition had it that Iguegha, an artisan in bronze casting, was sent from Ile-Ife to introduce the techniques of making bronze sculptures. Benin then developed its own distinctive style, less naturalistic than that of Ile-Ife but no less impressive. Celebration of the powers and majesty of the royal lineage as well as objects for the rituals surrounding kingship were the subjects of much of this art. When the first Europeans, the Portuguese, visited Benin in the 1480s, they were impressed by the power of the ruler and the extent of his territory. Similarly, the artists of Benin were impressed with the Portuguese, and Benin bronzes and ivories began to include representations of Portuguese soldiers and other themes that reflected the contact with outsiders (Figure 8.4).

Figure 8.4 *Copper plaque of Benin ruler and retainers with Portuguese soldiers.*

Central African Kingdoms

South of the rain forest that stretched across Africa almost to Lake Victoria lay a broad expanse of savanna and plain, cut by several large rivers such as the Kwango and the Zambezi. From their original home in Nigeria, the Bantu peoples had spread into the southern reaches of the rain forest along the Congo River, then southward onto the southern savannas, and eventually to the east coast. By the 5th century C.E., Bantu farmers and fishers had reached beyond the Zambezi, and by the 13th century they were approaching the southern end of the continent. Mostly beyond the influence of Islam, many of these central African peoples had begun their own process of state formation by about 1000 C.E., replacing the pattern of kinship-based societies with forms of political authority based on kingship. Whether the idea of kingship developed in one place and was diffused elsewhere or had multiple origins is unknown, but the older system based on seniority within the kinship group was replaced with rule based on the control of territory and the parallel development of rituals that reinforced the ruler's power. Several important kingdoms developed. In Katanga, the Luba peoples modified the older system of village headmen to a form of divine kinship in which the ruler and his relatives were thought to have a special power that ensured fertility of people and crops; thus, only the royal lineage was fit to rule. A sort of bureaucracy grew to administer the state, but it was hereditary, so that brothers or male children succeeded to the position. In a way, this system was a half step toward more modern concepts of bureaucracy, but it provided a way to integrate large numbers of people in a large political unit.

The Kingdoms of Kongo and Mwene Mutapa

Beginning about the 13th century, another kingdom was forming on the lower Congo River. By the late 15th century this kingdom, **Kongo,** was flourishing. On a firm agricultural base, its people also developed the skills of weaving, pottery, blacksmithing, and carving. Individual artisans, skilled in the working of wood, copper, and iron, were highly esteemed. There was a sharp division of labor between men and women. Men took responsibility for clearing the forest and scrub, producing palm oil and palm wine, building houses, hunting, and long-distance trade. Women took charge of cultivation in all its aspects,

the care of domestic animals, and household duties. On the seacoast, women made salt from seawater, and they also collected the seashells that served as currency in the Kongo kingdom. The population was distributed in small family-based villages and in towns. The area around the capital, Mbanza Kongo, had a population of 60,000 to 100,000 by the early 16th century.

The kingship of the Kongo was hereditary but local chieftainships were not, and this gave the central authority power to control subordinates. In a way, the Kongo kingdom was a confederation of smaller states brought under the control of the manikongo, or king, and by the 15th century it was divided into eight major provinces. The word *mani* means "blacksmith," and it demonstrated the importance of iron and the art of working it in its association with political and ritual power.

Farther to the east, another large Bantu confederation developed among the farming and cattle-herding Shona-speaking peoples in the region between the Zambezi and Limpopo rivers. Beginning in the 9th century C.E., migrants from the west began to build royal courts in stone, to which later immigrants added more polished constructions. There were many of these zimbabwe, or stone house, sites (about 200 have been found) that housed local rulers and subchiefs, but the largest site, called **Great Zimbabwe,** was truly impressive (Figure 8.5). It was the center of the kingdom and had a religious importance, associated with the bird of God, an eagle that served as a link between the world and the spirits. The symbol of the bird of God is found at the ruins of Great Zimbabwe and throughout the area of its control. Great Zimbabwe (not to be confused with the modern nation of Zimbabwe) included several structures, some with strong stone walls 15 feet thick and 30 feet high, a large conical tower, and extensive cut-stone architecture made without the use of mortar to join the bricks together. Observers in the 19th century suspected that Phoenicians or Arabs had built these structures, mostly because their prejudices prevented them from believing that Africans were capable of erecting such structures, but archeologists have established that a Bantu kingdom had begun construction in stone by the 11th century C.E. and had done its most sophisticated building in the 14th and 15th centuries.

By the 15th century, a centralized state ruled from Great Zimbabwe had begun to form. It con-

Figure 8.5 *Great Zimbabwe was one of several stone settlement complexes in southeastern Africa. Added to at different times, it served as the royal court of the kingdom.*

trolled a large portion of the interior of southeast Africa all the way to the Indian Ocean. Under a king who took the title *Mwene Mutapa* (which the Portuguese later pronounced "Mono-motapa"), this kingdom experienced a short period of rapid expansion in the late 15th and 16th centuries. Its dominance over the sources of gold in the interior eventually gave it great advantages in commerce, which it developed with the Arab port of Sofala on the coast. Evidence of this trade is found in the glass beads and porcelain unearthed by archeologists at Great Zimbabwe. By the 16th century, internal divisions and rebellion had split the kingdom apart, and perhaps an emphasis on cattle as a symbol of wealth led to soil exhaustion. Control of the gold fields still provided a source of power and trade. Representatives of the Mwene Mutapa called at the east coast ports to buy Indian textiles, and their regal bearing and fine iron weapons impressed the first Europeans

who saw them. As late as the 19th century, a much smaller kingdom of Mwene Mutapa survived in the interior and provided some leadership against European encroachment, but pastoralism had come to play a central role in the lives of the Shona people who descended from the great tradition.

 GLOBAL CONNECTIONS: Internal Development and Global Contacts

This chapter has concentrated on the Sudanic states and the Swahili coast, where the impact of Islam was the most profound and where, because of the existence of written sources, it is somewhat easier to reconstruct the region's history. Sub-Saharan Africa had never been totally isolated from the Mediterranean world or other outside contacts, but the spread of Islam obviously brought large areas of Africa into more intensive contact with the global community, even though Africa remained something of an Islamic frontier. Still, the fusion of Islamic and indigenous African cultures created a synthesis that restructured the life of many Africans. Sudanic kingdoms and the Swahili coast participated in extensive borrowing and interactions with north Africa and the Middle East, similar to imitation efforts by several other societies in the postclassical period. Islamic contacts were also heavily involved in the growing integration of several parts of sub-Saharan Africa with global trade.

Although the arrival of Islam in Africa in the period from 800 to 1500 was clearly a major event, it would be wrong to see Africa's history in this period exclusively in terms of the Islamic impact. Great Zimbabwe and the Kongo kingdom, to cite only two examples, represented the development of Bantu concepts of kingship and state-building independently of trends taking place elsewhere on the continent. Similar processes and accomplishments could also be seen in Benin and among the Yoruba of west Africa. Meanwhile in Ethiopia, east Africa, and the eastern Sudan, the impact of the pre-Islamic Mediterranean world had been long felt. The dynamic relationship between the impact of the civilizations and peoples external to Africa and the processes of development within the continent itself was a major theme in Africa's history.

By the late 15th century, when the first Europeans, the Portuguese, began to arrive on the west and east coasts of Africa, in many places they found well-developed, powerful kingdoms that were able to deal with the Portuguese as equals. This was even truer in the parts of Africa that had come under the influence of Islam and through it had established links with other areas of Muslim civilization. In this period, Africa had increasingly become part of the general cultural trends of the wider world. Moreover, the intensified export trade in ivory, slaves, and especially gold from Africa drew Africans, even those far from the centers of trade, into a widening network of global relations. With the arrival of Europeans in sub-Saharan Africa in the late 15th century, the pace and intensity of the cultural and commercial contacts became even greater, and many African societies faced new and profound challenges.

Further Readings

Several books are also useful in relation to this chapter. The period covered in this chapter is summarized in Roland Oliver and Anthony Atmore's *The African Middle Ages, 1400–1800* (1981). Basil Davidson has produced many excellent popular books that provide a sympathetic view of African development. A good example, prepared to accompany a television series, is *The Story of Africa* (1984). A readable book that gives an overview of African history and emphasizes broad common themes and everyday life is Robert W. July's *Precolonial Africa* (1975). Essential reading on central Africa is Jan Vansina, *Paths in the Rainforests* (1990). On the Swahili craft, see A. Mazrui and I. Shariff, *The Swahili: Idiom and Identity of an African People* (1994).

A very good survey of the early history of Africa with interesting comments on the Nok culture is Susan Keech McIntosh and Roderick J. McIntosh's "From Stone to Metal: New Perspectives on the Later Prehistory of West Africa," *Journal of World History*, vol. 2, no. 1 (1988), 89–133. Basil Davidson and F. K. Buah, *A History of West Africa* (1966), is a good introduction for that region. More detailed, however, is J. F. Ade Ajayi and Michael Crowder's *History of West Africa*, 2 vols. (2nd ed., 1987), which contains excellent review chapters by specialists. N. Levtzion's *Ancient Ghana and Mali* (1973) is still the best short introduction to these kingdoms of the sahel. For the east African coast, an excellent survey and introduction are provided by Derek Nurse and Thomas Spear in *The Swahili: Reconstructing the History and Language of an African Society* (1985).

Two good books on the Kongo kingdom are Anne Hilton's *The Kingdom of the Kongo* (1985), which shows how African systems of thought accommodated the arrival of Europeans and their culture, and Georges Balandier's *Daily Life in the Kingdom of the Kongo* (1969), which makes good use of travelers' reports and other documents to give a rounded picture of Kongo society. David Birmingham and Phyllis Martin's *History of Central Africa*, 2 vols. (1983), is an excellent regional history.

Two multivolume general histories of Africa that provide synthetic articles by leading scholars on many of the topics discussed in this chapter are *The Cambridge History of Africa*, 8 vols. (1975–1986) and the UNESCO *General History of Africa*, 7 vols. to date (1981–).

Some important source materials on African history for this period are D. T. Niane, *Sundiata, an Epic of Old Mali* (1986); G. R. Crone, ed., *The Voyages of Cadamosto*, 2nd series, vol. 80 (1937), which deals with Mali, Cape Verde, Senegal, and Benin; and Ross Dunn, *The Adventures of ibn Batuta, A Muslim Traveler of the 14th Century* (1986).

On the Web

Excellent brief descriptions of various African civilizations are provided on the Internet at http://www.bbc.co.uk/worldservice/africa/features/storyofafrica/index.shtml. Virtual visits and overviews of Great Zimbabwe are provided at http://www.mc.maricopa.edu/~reffland/anthropology/lost_tribes/zimbabwe/ and http://www.campus.northpark.edu/history/WebChron/Africa/Great Zimbabwe.html.

Nubia and sub-Saharan Timbuktu are explored at http://i-cias.com/private/abubakr/nubia/ and http://www.pbs.org/wonders/fr_e5.htm. The art of the sub-Saharan empire of Benin can be explored at http://www.nmafa.si.edu/pubaccess/acrobat/benin.pdf and http://www.metmuseum.org/toah.hd/zimb/hd_zim.htm.

Web sites are devoted to the trans-Saharan empires of Mali and Songhay (http://www.learner.org/exhibits/collapse/mali.html and http://www.ucalgary.ca/applied_history/tutor/islam/fractured/westAfrica.html).

The life of the founder of the empire of Mali, Sundiata, is explored at http://www.mrdowling.com/609-sundiata.html and http://ias.berkeley.edu/orias/sundiata.html. The background to the famous epic story of his life is provided at http://courses.wcupa.edu/jones/his311/notes/sundiata.htm. The career of his most famous successor, Mansa Musa, is examined at http://www.mrdowling.com/609-mansamusa.html, a site that also offers both a gateway to the study of North Africa and also a virtual visit to Timbuktu.

CHAPTER 9

CIVILIZATION IN EASTERN EUROPE: BYZANTIUM AND ORTHODOX EUROPE

Just as theologians through the centuries have worked to understand Christ's message, so too have artists struggled to capture his image. This powerful mosaic of Christ at the Church of Chora in Istanbul was created in the first part of the 14th century.

- The Byzantine Empire
- **VISUALIZING THE PAST:** Women and Power in Byzantium
- The Spread of Civilization in Eastern Europe
- **DOCUMENT:** Russia Turns to Christianity
- **IN DEPTH:** Eastern and Western Europe: The Problem of Boundaries
- **GLOBAL CONNECTIONS:** Eastern Europe and the World

During the postclassical period, in addition to the great civilizations of Asia and Africa, two major Christian civilizations took shape in Europe. One was anchored in the Byzantine Empire, which straddled western Asia and southeastern Europe and sponsored the spread of Orthodox Christianity to eastern Europe. The other was defined above all by the beliefs and institutions of Catholicism in western and central Europe. Both European civilizations were influenced by Islamic dynamism, but they operated according to different principles. The Byzantine Empire maintained particularly high levels of political, economic, and cultural life during much of the period from 500 to 1450 C.E. It controlled an important but fluctuating swath of territory in the Balkans, the northern Middle East, and the eastern Mediterranean. Its leaders saw themselves as Roman emperors, and their government was in many ways a direct continuation of the eastern portion of the late Roman Empire. Byzantium particularly built on traditions of late Roman emperors like Diocletian and Constantine. This was not really Rome moved eastward. The term *Byzantine*, though not used at the time, accurately suggests the distinction from Rome itself: This was a political heir to Rome, but with geography and focus of its own.

The real significance of the Byzantine Empire goes well beyond its ability to keep Rome's memory alive. The empire lasted for almost a thousand years, between Rome's collapse in the West and the final overthrow of the regime by Turkish invaders. The empire's capital, Constantinople, was one of the truly great cities of the world, certainly the most opulent and important city in Europe in this period. From Constantinople radiated one of the two major branches of Christianity: the Orthodox Christian churches that became dominant throughout most of eastern Europe.

Like the other great civilizations of the period, the Byzantine Empire spread its cultural and political influence to parts of the world that had not previously been controlled by any major civilization. Just as Muslim influence helped shape civilization in parts of Africa south of the Sahara, the Byzantines began to create a new civilization area in the Balkans and particularly in western Russia (present-day Ukraine and Belarus as well as western Russia proper). This was a major expansion of the civilization map, contributing to one of the key characteristics of the early centuries of the postclassical millennium.

Ultimately, the empire's most important stepchild was Russia, whose rise as a civilized area relied heavily on influences from the Byzantines to the south. Russia took many initial cultural and political characteristics from the

100 C.E.	600 C.E.	800 C.E.	1000 C.E.	1200 C.E.	1400 C.E.
1st century C.E.–650 Slavic migrations into eastern Europe **330s** Constantinople made capital of Eastern Roman Empire **527–565** Justinian	**718** Defeat of Arab attack on Constantinople	**855** According to legend, Rurik king of Kievan Russia **864** Beginning of missionary work of brothers Cyril and Methodius in Slavic lands **870** First kingdom in what is now Czech and Slovak republics **896** Magyars settle in Hungary **c. 960** Emergence of Polish state **980–1015** Conversion of Vladimir I of Russia to Christianity	**1018** Defeat of first Bulgarian Empire, taken over by Byzantines **1019–1054** Yaroslav king of Rus' **1054** Schism between Eastern and Western Christianity **1100–1453** Byzantine decline; growing Turkish attack	**1203–1204** Capture of Constantinople during the Fourth Crusade **1237–1241** Capture of Russia by Mongols (Tatars)	**1453** Capture of Constantinople by Ottoman Turks; end of Byzantine Empire **1480** Expulsion of Tatars from Russia

Byzantine Empire and ultimately claimed to inherit the mantle of the empire itself. This heritage blended with other developments after the postclassical period, when Russia emerged from its tentative beginnings.

Studying civilization in eastern Europe requires an understanding of the relationship between the two Christian churches in postclassical Europe. There were many commonalities between developments in eastern Europe and those of the Christian West. In both cases, civilization spread northward because of the missionary appeal of the religion itself. In both cases, polytheism gave way to monotheism, although important compromises were made, particularly at the popular level. In both cases, more northerly political units, such as Russia, Poland, Germany, and France, struggled for political definition without being able to rival the political sophistication of the more advanced civilization areas in Asia and north Africa or in Byzantium itself. In both cases, new trading activities brought northern regions into contact with the major centers of world commerce, including Constantinople. In both cases, newly civilized areas looked back to the Greco-Roman past, as well as to Christianity, for cultural inspiration, using some of the same political ideas and artistic styles.

Yet with all these shared ingredients, the civilizations that expanded in the East and developed in the West operated largely on separate tracks. They produced different versions of Christianity, which culturally as well as organizationally were separate, even hostile. The civilizations had little mutual contact, until late in this period; commercial patterns in both cases ran south to north rather than east to west. During most of the postclassical millennium, major portions of eastern Europe were significantly more advanced than the West in political sophistication, cultural range, and economic vitality. When the two civilizations did meet, in this period and later, they met as distant cousins, related but not close kin.

The Byzantine Empire

 The Byzantine Empire unfolded initially as part of the greater Roman Empire. Then, as this framework shattered with Roman decline, it took on a life of its own, particularly from the reign of the Emperor Justinian onward. It centered on a territory different from and smaller than the eastern Mediterranean as Rome had defined it. This was the result of new pressures, particularly the surge of Islam throughout north Africa and the bulk of the Middle East. Despite many attacks, the empire flourished until the 11th century.

Origins of the Empire

The Byzantine Empire in some senses began in the 4th century C.E., when the Romans set up their eastern capital in Constantinople. This city quickly became the most vigorous center of the otherwise fading imperial structure. Emperor Constantine constructed a host of elegant buildings, including Christian churches, in his new city, which was built on the foundations of a previously modest town called Byzantium. Soon, separate eastern emperors ruled from the new metropolis, even before the western portion of the empire fell to the Germanic invaders. They warded off invading Huns and other intruders while enjoying a solid tax base in the peasant agriculture of the eastern Mediterranean. Constantinople was responsible for the Balkan peninsula, the northern Middle East, the Mediterranean coast, and north Africa. Although for several centuries Latin was the court language of the eastern empire, Greek was the common tongue, and after Emperor Justinian in the 6th century, it became the official language as well. Indeed, in the eyes of the easterners, Latin became an inferior, barbaric means of communication. Knowledge of Greek enabled the scholars of the eastern empire to read freely in the ancient Athenian philosophical and literary classics and in the Hellenistic writings and scientific treatises.

The new empire benefited from the high levels of commerce long present in the eastern Mediterranean. New blood was drawn into administration and trade as Hellenized Egyptians and Syrians, long excluded from Roman administration, moved to Constantinople and entered the expanding bureaucracy of the Byzantine rulers. The empire faced many foreign enemies, although the pressure was less severe than that provided by the Germanic tribes in the West. It responded by recruiting armies in the Middle East itself, not by relying on barbarian troops. Complex administration around a remote emperor, who was surrounded by elaborate ceremonies, increasingly defined the empire's political style.

Justinian's Achievements

The early history of the Byzantine Empire was marked by a recurrent threat of invasion. Eastern emperors, relying on their local military base plus able generalship by upper-class Greeks, beat off attacks by the Sassanian Empire in Persia and by Germanic invaders. Then, in 533 C.E., with the empire's borders reasonably secure, a new emperor, Justinian, tried to reconquer western territory in a last futile effort to restore an empire like that of Rome. He was somber, autocratic, and prone to grandiose ideas. A contemporary historian named Procopius described him as "at once villainous and amenable; as people say colloquially, a moron. He was never truthful with anyone, but always guileful in what he said and did, yet easily hoodwinked by any who wanted to deceive him." The emperor was also heavily influenced by his wife Theodora, a courtesan connected with Constantinople's horse-racing world, who was eager for power. Theodora stiffened Justinian's resolve in response to popular unrest and pushed the plans for expansion.

Justinian's positive contributions to the Byzantine Empire lay in rebuilding Constantinople, ravaged by earlier riots against high taxes, and systematizing the Roman legal code. Extending later Roman architecture, with its addition of domes to earlier classical styles, Justinian's builders created many new structures, the most inspiring of which was the huge new church, the **Hagia Sophia,** long one of the wonders of the Christian world. This was an achievement in engineering as well as architecture, for no one had previously been able to build the supports needed for a dome of its size. Justinian's codification of Roman law reached a goal earlier emperors had sought but not achieved, summing up and reconciling many prior edicts and decisions. Unified law not only reduced confusion but also united and organized the new empire, paralleling the state's bureaucracy. Updated by later emperors, the code ultimately helped spread Roman legal principles in various parts of Europe.

Justinian's military exploits had more ambiguous results. The emperor wanted to recapture the old Roman Empire itself. With the aid of a brilliant general, **Belisarius,** new gains were made in north Africa and Italy. The Byzantines hoped to restore north Africa to its role as grain producer for the Mediterranean world, and Italy would be the symbol of past imperial glories. Unable to hold Rome against the Germans, Justinian's forces made their temporary capital, Ravenna, a key artistic center, embellished by some of the most beautiful Christian mosaics known anywhere in the world (Figure 9.1). But the major Italian holdings were short-lived, unable to withstand Germanic pressure, and north African territory was soon besieged as well.

Furthermore, Justinian's westward ambitions had weakened the empire in its own sphere. Persian forces attacked in the northern Middle East, while new Slavic groups, moving into the Balkans, pressed on another front (Map 9.1). Justinian finally managed to create a new line of defense and even pushed Persian forces back again, but some Middle Eastern territory was lost. Furthermore, all these wars, offensive and defensive alike, created new tax pressures on the government and forced Justinian to exertions that contributed to his death in 565 C.E.

Arab Pressure and the Empire's Defenses

After some hesitations and setbacks, Justinian's successors began to concentrate on defending the eastern empire itself. Persian successes in the northern Middle East were reversed in the 7th century, and the

Figure 9.1 *Mosaics in Ravenna, Italy, from the early period of the Byzantine Empire, illustrate some of the highest achievements of Byzantine religious art and provide a dazzling, ornate environment for worship. This mosaic features a rather militant Christ the Redeemer. Notice the characteristic Christian assertion of human dominance over nature.*

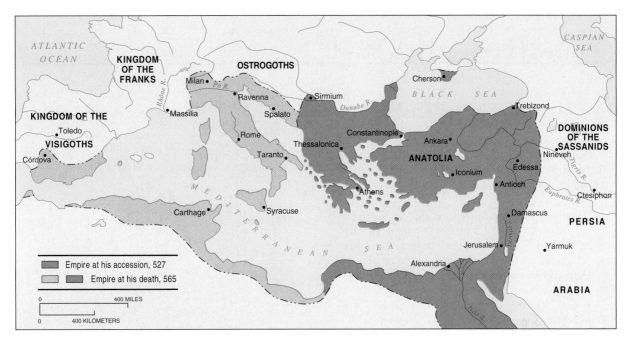

Map 9.1   *The Byzantine Empire Under Justinian. Justinian's expansion exhausted his treasury, and the empire had retreated to the northeastern Mediterranean within 50 years after his death.*

population was forcibly reconverted to Christianity. The resultant empire, centered in the southern Balkans and the western and central portions of present-day Turkey, was a far cry from Rome's greatness. However, it was sufficient to amplify a rich Hellenistic culture and blend it more fully with Christianity while advancing Roman achievements in engineering and military tactics as well as law.

The Byzantine Empire was also strong enough to withstand the great new threat of the 7th century, the surge of the Arab Muslims, though not without massive losses. By the mid-7th century, the Arabs had built a fleet that challenged Byzantine naval supremacy in the eastern Mediterranean while repeatedly attacking Constantinople. They quickly swallowed the empire's remaining provinces along the eastern seaboard of the Mediterranean and soon cut into the northern Middle Eastern heartland as well. Arab cultural and commercial influence also affected patterns of life in Constantinople.

The Byzantine Empire held out nevertheless. A major siege of the capital in 717–718 C.E. was beaten back, partly because of a new weapon, a kind of napalm called **Greek fire** (a petroleum, quicklime, and sulfur mixture) that devastated Arab ships. The

Arab threat was never removed entirely. Furthermore, wars with the Muslims had added new economic burdens to the empire, as invasions and taxation, weakening the position of small farmers, resulted in greater aristocratic estates and new power for aristocratic generals. The free rural population that had served the empire during its early centuries—providing military recruits and paying the bulk of the taxes—was forced into greater dependence. Greater emphasis was given to organizing the army and navy.

After the greatest Arab onslaughts had been faced, the empire was run by a dizzying series of weak and strong emperors. Periods of vigor alternated with seeming decay. Arab pressure continued. Conquest of the island of Crete in the 9th century allowed the Muslims to harass Byzantine shipping in the Mediterranean for several centuries. Slavic kingdoms, especially **Bulgaria,** periodically pressed Byzantine territory in the Balkans, although at times military success and marriage alliances brought Byzantine control over the feisty Bulgarian kingdom. Thus, while a Bulgarian king in the 10th century took the title of *tsar,* a Slavic version of the word *Caesar,* steady Byzantine pressure through war eroded the regional kingdom. In the 11th century, the Byzantine emperor

Visualizing the Past

Women and Power in Byzantium

This mosaic, developed between 1034–1042, portrays the Empress Zoë, her consort, and Christ (in the center). This was a period of unusual power for two women at the head of the empire, as the struggle between Zoë and her sister Theodora suggests.

Questions: What evidence does this mosaic provide about the political relationship between Zoë and her husband? What does it suggest about the relationship between church and state in Byzantium and about ways religion might be used to bolster political power? (Interpreting the haloes is a good start in answering this question.) Why, in terms of the appropriation of Christian tradition, are three figures represented? Can this picture be used to comment on women's conditions in the empire? What sense of history and religion made it reasonable to show Christ between two 11th-century people?

Istanbul, St. Sophia, Mosaic in the South Tribune: *Empress Zoë, Her Consort, and Christ, 1034–1042* (Dumbarton Oaks, Center for Byzantine Studies).

Basil II, known as *Bulgaroktonos*, or slayer of the Bulgarians, used the empire's wealth to bribe many Bulgarian nobles and generals. He defeated the Bulgarian army in 1014, blinding as many as 15,000 captive soldiers. The sight of this tragedy brought on the Bulgarian king's death. Bulgaria became part of the empire, its aristocracy settling in Constantinople and merging with the leading Greek families.

Thus, despite all its problems, the imperial core had real strength, governing a territory about half the size of the previous eastern portion of the Roman Empire and withstanding a series of enemies. Briefly, at the end of the 10th century, the Byzantine emperor may have been the most powerful monarch on earth, with a capital city whose rich buildings and abundant popular entertainments awed visitors from western Europe and elsewhere.

Byzantine Society and Politics

The Byzantine political system had remarkable similarities to the earlier patterns in China. The emperor was held to be ordained by God, head of church as well as state. He appointed church bishops and passed religious and secular laws. The elaborate court rituals symbolized the ideals of a divinely inspired, all-powerful ruler, although they often immobilized rulers and inhibited innovative policy.

At key points, women held the imperial throne while maintaining the ceremonial power of the office. The experiences of Empress Theodora (981–1056), namesake of Justinian's powerful wife, illustrate the complex nature of Byzantine politics and the whims of fate that affected women rulers. Daughter of an emperor, Theodora was strong and austere; she refused to marry the imperial heir, who then wed her sister Zoë. Zoë was afraid of Theodora's influence and had her confined to a monastery. A popular rebellion against the new emperor installed Theodora and Zoë jointly (and one assumes uneasily) as empresses. Theodora soon yielded power to Zoë's new husband. When he died, however, Theodora reasserted her rights, at age 70. After brief turmoil, she checked unruly nobles and limited bureaucratic corruption, although her severe retaliation against personal enemies brought criticism. Theodora also had trouble building a reliable staff and was attacked for her reliance on "menials."

Supplementing the centralized imperial authority was one of history's most elaborate bureaucracies. Trained in Greek classics, philosophy, and science in a secular school system that paralleled church education for the priesthood, Byzantine bureaucrats could be recruited from all social classes. As in China, aristocrats predominated, but talent also counted among this elite of highly educated scholars. Bureaucrats were specialized into various offices, and officials close to the emperor were mainly eunuchs. Provincial governors were appointed from the center and were charged with keeping tabs on military authorities. An elaborate system of spies helped preserve loyalty while creating intense distrust even among friends. It is small wonder that the word *Byzantine* came to refer to complex institutional arrangements. At the same time, the system successfully supported the longest-lived single government structure the Mediterranean world has ever known.

Careful military organization arose as well, as Figure 9.2 suggests. Byzantine rulers adapted the later Roman system by recruiting troops locally and rewarding them with grants of land in return for their military service. The land could not be sold, but sons inherited its administration in return for continued military responsibility. Many outsiders, particularly Slavs and Armenian Christians, were recruited for the army in this way. Increasingly, hereditary military leaders assumed regional power, displacing more traditional and better-educated aristocrats. One emperor, Michael II, was a product of this system and was notorious for his hatred of Greek education and his overall personal ignorance. On the other hand, the military system had obvious advantages in protecting a state recurrently under attack from Muslims of various sorts—Persians, Arabs, and later Turks—as well as nomadic intruders from central Asia. Until the 15th century, the Byzantine Empire effectively blocked the path to Europe for most of these groups.

Socially and economically, the empire depended on Constantinople's control over the countryside, with the bureaucracy regulating trade and controlling food prices. The large peasant class was vital in supplying goods and providing the bulk of tax revenues. Food prices were kept artificially low, to content the numerous urban lower classes, in a system supported largely by taxes on the hard-pressed peasantry. Other cities were modest in size—for example, Athens dwindled—

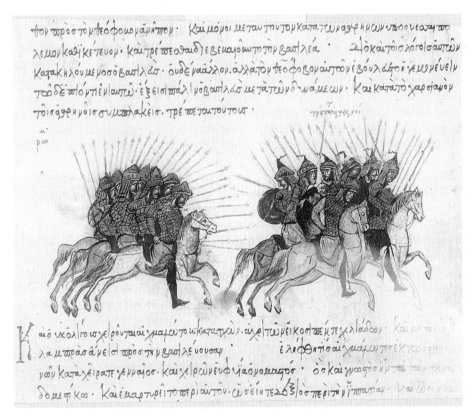

Figure 9.2 *Imperial cavalry, detail from "Chronicle" of John Scylitzes, 14th century. The painting shows the stylized representation characteristic of Byzantine art and suggests the importance of well-organized military activity.*

because the focus was on the capital city and its food needs. The empire developed a far-flung trading network with Asia to the east and Russia and Scandinavia to the north. Silk production expanded in the empire, with silkworms and techniques initially imported from China, and various luxury products, including cloth, carpets, and spices, were sent north. This gave the empire a favorable trading position with less sophisticated lands. Only China produced luxury goods of comparable quality. The empire also traded actively with India, the Arabs, and east Asia while receiving simpler products from western Europe and Africa. At the same time, the large merchant class never gained significant political power, in part because of the elaborate network of government controls. In this, Byzantium again resembled China and differed notably from the looser social and political networks of the West, where merchants were gaining greater voice.

Byzantine cultural life centered on the secular traditions of Hellenism, so important in the education of bureaucrats, and on the evolving traditions of Eastern, or Orthodox, Christianity. Although a host of literary and artistic creations resulted from this mixture, there was little innovation. The Byzantine strength lay in preserving and commenting on past forms more than in developing new ones. Art and architecture were exceptions; a distinct Byzantine style developed fairly early. The adaptation of Roman domed buildings, the elaboration of powerful and richly colored religious mosaics, and a tradition of **icon** painting—paintings of saints and other religious figures, often richly ornamented—expressed this artistic impulse and its marriage with Christianity. The blue and gold backgrounds set with richly dressed religious figures were meant to represent the unchanging brilliance of heaven. An important controversy over religious art arose in the 8th century, when a new emperor attacked the use of religious images in worship (probably responding to Muslim claims that Christians were idol worshipers). This attack, called **iconoclasm** (the breaking of images), roused huge protest from Byzantine monks, which briefly threatened a split between church and state. After a long and complex battle, the use of icons was gradually restored, and the tradition of state control over church affairs also resumed.

The Split Between East and West

Byzantine culture and politics, as well as the empire's economic orientation toward Asia and northeastern Europe, helped explain the growing break between its Eastern version of Christianity and the Western version headed by the pope in Rome. There were many milestones in this rift. Different rituals developed as the West translated the Greek Bible into Latin in the 4th century. Later, Byzantine emperors deeply resented papal attempts to interfere in the iconoclastic dispute, for the popes, understandably enough, hoped to loosen state control over the Eastern church to make it conform more fully to their own idea of church–state relations. There was also scornful hostility to efforts by a Frankish ruler, Charlemagne, to proclaim himself a Roman emperor in the 9th century. Byzantine officials believed that they were the true heirs of Rome and that Western rulers were crude and unsophisticated. However, they did extend some recognition to the "Emperor of the Franks." Contact between the two branches of Christianity trailed off, though neither East nor West cared to make a definitive break. The Eastern church acknowledged the pope as first among equals, but papal directives had no hold in the Byzantine church, where state control loomed larger. Religious art conveyed different styles and beliefs, as Figures 9.3 and 9.4 suggest. Even monastic movements operated according to different rules.

Then, in 1054, an ambitious church patriarch in Constantinople raised a host of old issues, including a quarrel over what kind of bread to use for the celebration of Christ's last supper in the church liturgy. (The bread quarrel was an old one, relating to ritual use of bread in Christ's day, that Patriarch Michael now revived: Must bread used for communion be baked without yeast?) The patriarch also attacked the Roman Catholic practice, developed some centuries earlier, of insisting on celibacy for its priests; Eastern Orthodox priests could marry. Delegations of the two churches discussed these disputes, but this led only to new bitterness. The Roman pope finally excommunicated the patriarch and his followers; that is, he banished them from Christian fellowship and the sacraments. The patriarch responded by excommunicating all Roman Catholics. Thus, the split between the Roman Catholic church and Eastern Orthodoxy—the Byzantine or Greek, as well as the Russian Orthodox, Serbian Orthodox, and others—became formal and has endured to this day. A late-12th-century church patriarch in Constantinople even argued that Muslim rule would be preferable to that of the pope: "For if I am subject to the Muslim, at least he will not force me to share his faith. But if I have to be

Figure 9.3 *In this mosaic of Christ, dating from about 1100 C.E., notice the difference from the images of Christ common in Western Christianity, which place more emphasis on suffering and less on divine majesty.*

under the Frankish rule and united with the Roman Church, I may have to separate myself from God."

The East-West split fell short of complete divorce. A common Christianity with many shared or revived classical traditions and frequent commercial and cultural contacts continued to enliven the relationship between the two European civilizations. The division did reflect the different patterns of development the two civilizations followed during the postclassical millennium.

The Empire's Decline

Shortly after the split between East and West, the Byzantine Empire entered a long period of decline (Map 9.2). Turkish invaders who had converted to Islam in central Asia began to press on its eastern bor-

ders, having already gained increasing influence in the Muslim caliphate. In the late 11th century, Turkish troops, the Seljuks, seized almost all the Asiatic provinces of the empire, thus cutting off the most prosperous sources of tax revenue and the territories that had supplied most of the empire's food. The Byzantine emperor lost the battle of Manzikert in 1071, his larger army was annihilated, and the empire never recovered. It staggered along for another four centuries, but its doom, at least as a significant power, was sealed. The creation of new, independent Slavic kingdoms in the Balkans, such as Serbia, showed the empire's diminished power.

Eastern emperors appealed to Western leaders for help against the Turks, but their requests were largely ignored. The appeal helped motivate Western Crusades to the Holy Land, but this did not help the

Figure 9.4 *The Byzantine Empire developed a distinctively stylized religious art, adapted from earlier Roman painting styles and conveying the solemnity of the holy figures of the faith. This 11th-century miniature features the holy women at the sepulchre of Christ.*

Byzantines. At the same time, Italian cities, blessed with powerful navies, gained increasing advantages in Constantinople, such as special trading privileges—a sign of the shift in power between East and West. One Western Crusade, in 1204, ostensibly set up to conquer the Holy Land from the Muslims, actually turned against Byzantium. Led by greedy Venetian merchants, the Crusade attacked and conquered Constantinople, briefly unseating the emperor and weakening the whole imperial structure. But the West was not yet powerful enough to hold this ground, and a small Byzantine Empire was restored, able through careful diplomacy to survive for another two centuries.

Turkish settlements pressed ever closer to Constantinople in the northern Middle East—in the area that is now Turkey—and finally, in 1453, a Turkish sultan brought a powerful army, equipped with artillery purchased from the West, against the city, which fell after two months. By 1461, the Turks had conquered remaining pockets of Byzantine control, including most of the Balkans, bringing Islamic power farther into eastern Europe than ever before. The great eastern empire was no more.

The fall of Byzantium was one of the great events in world history, and we will deal with its impact in several later chapters. It was a great event because the Byzantine Empire had been so durable and important, anchoring a vital corner of the Mediterranean even amid the rapid surge of Islam. The empire's trading contacts and its ability to preserve and spread classical and Christian learning made it a vital unit throughout the postclassical period. After its demise, its influence affected other societies, including the new Ottoman Empire.

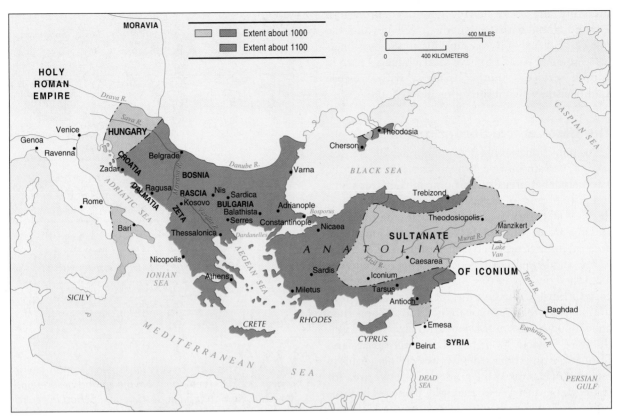

Map 9.2 *The Byzantine Empire, 1000–1100. The Byzantine Empire went from a major to a minor power in the century and a half portrayed on this map. After the Turkish defeat at Manzikert in 1071, the Byzantines maintained effective control of only a small fringe of Anatolia. In the Balkans, the new Serbian, Bulgarian, and Hungarian states grew powerful, even though the Byzantines claimed control over the region.*

The Spread of Civilization in Eastern Europe

Missionary attempts to spread Christianity, new Byzantine conquests in the Balkans (particularly Bulgaria), and trade routes running north and south through western Russia and Ukraine created abundant contacts with key portions of eastern Europe. A number of regional states formed. Kievan Rus', in a territory including present-day Ukraine, Belarus, and western Russia, developed some of the formative features of Russian culture and politics. Mongol invasions ended this period of early Russian history, redividing parts of eastern Europe.

Long before the Byzantine decline after the 11th century, the empire had been the source of a new northward surge of Christianity. Orthodox missionaries sent from Constantinople busily converted most people in the Balkans to their version of Christianity, and some other trappings of Byzantine culture came in their wake. In 864, the Byzantine government sent the missionaries **Cyril** and **Methodius** to the territory that is now the Czech and Slovak republics. Here the venture failed, in that Roman Catholic missionaries were more successful. But Cyril and Methodius continued their efforts in the Balkans and in southern Russia, where their ability to speak the Slavic language greatly aided their efforts. The two missionaries devised a written script for this language, derived from Greek letters; to this day, the Slavic alphabet is known as Cyrillic. Thus, the possibility of literature and some literacy developed in eastern Europe along with Christianity, well beyond the political borders of Byzantium. Byzantine missionaries were quite willing to have local languages used in church services—another contrast with Western Catholicism, which insisted on church Latin.

The East Central Borderlands

Eastern missionaries did not monopolize the borderlands of eastern Europe. Roman Catholicism and the Latin alphabet prevailed not only in the Czech area but also in most of Hungary (which was taken over in the 9th century by a Turkic people, the Magyars) and in Poland. Much of this region would long be an area of competition between Eastern and Western political and intellectual models. During the centuries after the conversion to Christianity, this stretch of eastern Europe north of the Balkans was organized in a series of regional monarchies, loosely governed amid a powerful, land-owning aristocracy. The kingdoms of Poland, Bohemia (Czechoslovakia), and Lithuania easily surpassed most western kingdoms in territory. This was also a moderately active area for trade and industry. For example, ironworking was more developed than in the West until the 12th century. Eastern Europe during these centuries also received an important influx of Jews, who were migrating away from the Middle East but also fleeing intolerance in western Europe. Poland gained the largest single concentration of Jews. Eastern Europe's Jews, largely barred from agriculture and often resented by the Christian majority, gained strength in local commerce while maintaining their own religious and cultural traditions (Figure 9.5). A strong emphasis on extensive education and literacy, though primarily for males, distinguished Jewish culture not only from the rest of eastern Europe but also from most other societies in the world at this time.

The Emergence of Kievan Rus'

Russia shared many features with the rest of northeastern Europe before the 15th century, including hesitant advances in economy and politics. A full-fledged Russian civilization had yet to emerge; this was the beginning of a society that would become more important after 1450. As in much of eastern Europe, the centuries of Byzantine influence were an important formative period that would influence later developments. Slavic peoples had moved into the

Figure 9.5 *This 14th-century illustrated German Jewish prayer book is a remnant from the spread of Jews and Jewish culture during the postclassical period in central and east-central Europe.*

sweeping plains of Russia and eastern Europe from an Asian homeland during the time of the Roman Empire (Map 9.3). They mixed with and incorporated some earlier inhabitants and some additional invaders, such as the Bulgarians, who adopted Slavic language and customs. The Slavs already used iron, and they extended agriculture in the rich soils of what is now Ukraine and western Russia, where no durable civilization had taken root. Slavic political organization long rested in family tribes and villages. The Slavs maintained an animist religion with gods for the sun, thunder, wind, and fire. The early Russians also had a rich tradition of folk music and oral legends, and they developed some very loose regional kingdoms.

During the 6th and 7th centuries, traders from Scandinavia began to work through the Slavic lands, moving along the great rivers of western Russia, which run south to north, particularly the Dnieper. Through this route the Norse traders were able to reach the Byzantine Empire, and a regular, flourishing trade developed between Scandinavia and Constantinople. Luxury products from Byzantium and the Arab world

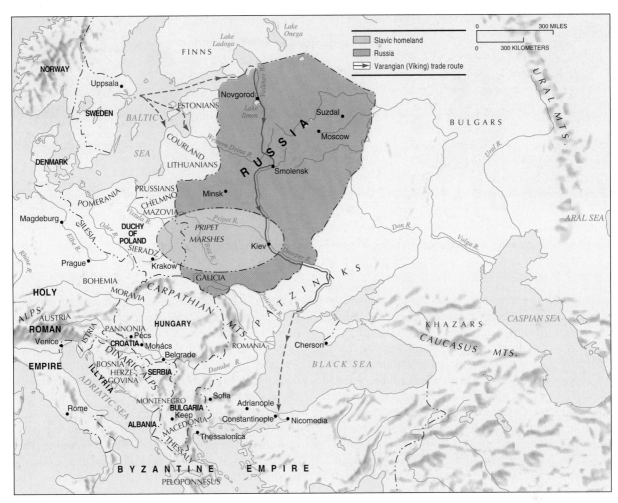

Map 9.3 *East European Kingdoms and Slavic Expansion by c. 1000. Beginning around the 5th century C.E., the Slavs moved in all directions from their lands around the Pripet River. Their migrations took them from the Baltic Sea to the Oder River and down to the Adriatic and Aegean seas. The arrival of the Hungarians in the 9th and 10th centuries prevented the Slavs from unifying.*

traveled north in return for furs and other crude products. The Scandinavian traders, militarily superior to the Slavs, gradually set up some governments along their trade route, particularly in the city of **Kiev.** A monarchy emerged, and according to legend a man named **Rurik,** a native of Denmark, became the first prince of what came to be called Kievan Rus' about 855 C.E. This principality, though still loosely organized through alliances with regional, landed aristocrats, flourished until the 12th century. It was from the Scandinavians that the word *Russia* was coined, possibly from a Greek word for "red," for the hair

color of many of the Norse traders. In turn, the Scandinavian minority gradually mingled with the Slavic population, particularly among the aristocracy.

Contacts between Kievan Rus' and Byzantium extended steadily. Kiev, centrally located, became a prosperous trading center, and from there many Russians visited Constantinople. These exchanges led to growing knowledge of Christianity. Prince **Vladimir I,** a Rurik descendant who ruled from 980 to 1015, finally took the step of converting to Christianity, not only in his own name but on behalf of all his people (Figure 9.6). He was eager to avoid the papal

Figure 9.6 *This painting shows the Russian king Vladimir I accepting Christianity.*

influence that came with Roman Catholicism, which he knew about through the experiences of the Polish kingdom. Orthodox Christianity was a valid alternative to the prevailing animism. Islam was rejected, according to one account, because Vladimir could not accept a religion that forbade alcoholic drink. Russian awe at the splendor of religious services in Constantinople also played a role. Having made his decision, Vladimir organized mass baptisms for his subjects, forcing conversions by military pressure. Early church leaders were imported from Byzantium, and they helped train a literate Russian priesthood. As in Byzantium, the king characteristically controlled major appointments, and a separate **Russian Orthodox** church soon developed.

As Kievan Rus' became Christian, it was the largest single state in Europe, though highly decentralized. Rurik's descendants managed for some time to avoid damaging battles over succession to the throne. Following Byzantine example, they issued a formal law code that reduced the severity of traditional punishments and replaced community vendettas with state-run courts, at least in principle. The last of the great Kievan princes, **Yaroslav,** issued the legal codification while building many churches and arranging the translation of religious literature from Greek to Slavic.

Institutions and Culture in Kievan Rus'

Kievan Rus' borrowed much from Byzantium, but it was in no position to replicate major institutions such as the bureaucracy or an elaborate educational system. Major princes were attracted to Byzantine ceremonials and luxury and to the concept (if not yet the reality) that a central ruler should have wide powers. Many characteristics of Orthodox Christianity gradually penetrated Russian culture. Fervent devotion to the power of God and to many Eastern saints helped organize worship. Churches were ornate, filled with icons and the sweet smell of incense. A monastic movement developed that stressed prayer and charity. Traditional practices, such as polygamy, gradually yielded to the Christian practice of monogamy. The emphasis on almsgiving long described the sense of obligation felt by wealthy Russians toward the poor.

The Russian literature that developed, which used the Cyrillic alphabet, featured chronicles that described a mixture of religious and royal events and showered praises on the saints and the power of God. Disasters were seen as expressions of the just wrath of God against human wickedness, and success in war followed from the aid of God and the saints in the name of Russia and the Orthodox faith. This tone also was common in Western Christian writing during these centuries, but in Kievan Rus' it monopolized formal culture; a distinct philosophical or scientific current did not emerge in the postclassical period.

Russian and Ukrainian art focused on the religious also, with icon painting and illuminated religious manuscripts becoming a Kievan specialty. Orthodox churches, built in the form of a cross surmounted by a dome, similarly aped Byzantine mod-

Document

Russia Turns to Christianity

This document from a monk's chronicle, describing King Vladimir's conversion policy, indicates what was officially believed about the power of Russian princes, Russian social structure, and the relationship between Christianity and earlier animism. These official claims are important, but they may not reflect the whole reality of this important transition in Russia history. Here is a classic case of the need to understand a particular mindset and genre of writing, to understand why particular explanations are offered without accepting their reality.

For at this time the Russes were ignorant pagans. The devil rejoiced threat, for he did not know that his ruin was approaching. He was so eager to destroy the Christian people, yet he was expelled by the true cross even from these very lands....Vladimir was visited by Bulgars of the Mohammedan faith....[He] listened to them for he was fond of women and indulgence, regarding which he heard with pleasure. But...abstinence from pork and wine were disagreeable to him. "Drinking," said he, "is the joy of the Russes. We cannot exist without that pleasure." [Russian envoys sent to Constantinople were astonished by the beauty of the churches and the chanting], and in their wonder praised the Greek ceremonial....

[Later, Vladimir was suffering from blindness; a Byzantine bishop baptized him] and as the bishop laid his hand upon him, he straightway recovered his sight. Upon experiencing this miraculous cure, Vladimir glorified God, saying, "I have now perceived the one true God." When his followers beheld this miracle, many of them were also baptized....Thereafter Vladimir sent heralds throughout the whole city to proclaim that if any inhabitant, rich or poor, did not betake himself to the river [for mass baptism] he would risk the Prince's displeasure. When the people heard these words, they wept for joy and exclaimed in their enthusiasm, "If this were not good, the Prince and his nobles would not have accepted it."... There was joy in heaven and upon earth to behold so many souls saved. But the devil groaned, lamenting, "Woe is me. How am I driven out hence ... my reign in these regions is at an end."...

He [Vladimir] ordered that wooden churches should be built and established where [pagan] idols have previously stood. He founded the Church of Saint Basil on the hill where the idol of Perun and the other images had been set, and where the prince and the people had offered their sacrifices. He began to found churches, to assign priests throughout the cities and towns, and to bring people in for baptism from all towns and villages. He began to take the children of the best families and send them for instruction from books.

Questions: In what ways might the account be simplistic in describing royal powers and popular response? What explanations does this religious chronicler offer for the conversion of Russians to Christianity? Which of the explanations are most likely, and which are the results of some kind of bias? What kind of church–state relationship did this kind of conversion predict?

els, although the building materials often were wood rather than stone. Domed structures, as Figure 9.7 shows, adapted Byzantine themes to Russian conditions, in what proved to be a durable regional style. Religious art and music were rivaled by popular entertainments in the oral tradition, which combined music, street performances, and some theater. The Russian church unsuccessfully tried to suppress these forms, regarding them as pagan.

Just as Russia's religious culture developed separately from western Europe's, Russian social and economic patterns took distinctive shape. Russian peasants were fairly free farmers, although an aristocratic landlord class existed. Russian aristocrats, called **boyars,** had less political power than their counterparts in western Europe, although the Kievan princes had to negotiate with them.

For all its distinctiveness, Russia was not unaware of other parts of Europe. The greatest ruler of the period, Yaroslav the Wise (1019–1054), used marriages to create ties. He arranged over 30 marriages with central European royalty, including 11 with Germany, pressing six Russian princes to take German wives while inducing five German nobles to accept Russian brides. Even here, however, Yaroslav kept his main focus on Byzantium, promoting Byzantine styles in the great cathedral of Kiev and using Byzantine example as the basis for Russia's first law code.

Figure 9.7 *Cathedral of St. Dimitry, built in the late 12th century in Kiev, at the height of Russia's postclassical prosperity in trade and interactions with Byzantium. The church used a Byzantine classical style but adapted it to Russian conditions, including fewer resources and possibly less architectural experience. Although the towers were topped by characteristic Orthodox domes, there was no major central dome, as in the great churches in Constantinople.*

Kievan Decline

The Kievan principality began to fade in the 12th century. Rival princes set up regional governments, and the royal family often squabbled over succession to the throne. Invaders from Asia whittled at Russian territory. The rapid decline of Byzantium reduced Russian trade and wealth, for the kingdom had always depended heavily on the greater prosperity and sophisticated manufacturing of its southern neighbor. A new kingdom was established briefly around a city

near what is now Moscow, but by 1200 Russia was weak and disunited. The final blow in this first chapter of Russian history came in 1237–1238 and 1240–1241, when two invasions by Mongols from central Asia moved through Russia and into other parts of eastern Europe (see Chapter 14). The initial Mongol intent was to add the whole of Europe to their growing empire. The Mongols easily captured the major Russian cities, but they did not penetrate much farther west because of political difficulties in their Asian homeland. Called **Tatars** in the Russian tradition (from a Turkish word) the invaders were quickly despised but also feared—"the accursed raw-eating Tatars," as one chronicle put it.

For over two centuries much of Russia remained under Tatar control. This control further separated the dynamic of Russian history from that of western Europe. Russian literature languished under Tatar supervision. Trade lapsed in western Russia, and the vigorous north-south commerce of the Kievan period never returned. At the same time, loose Tatar supervision did not destroy Russian Christianity or a native Russian aristocratic class. As long as tribute was paid, Tatar overlords left day-to-day Russian affairs alone. For a time, Tatar control created some new harmony among various Russian social classes: The word *Christian* (*Kirstianin*) was adapted as an accepted term for Russian peasants, which showed their religious commitment but also a common bond with other groups. Thus, when Tatar control was finally forced out in the second half of the 15th century, a Russian cultural and political tradition could reemerge, serving as a partial basis for the further, fuller development of Russian society.

Russian leaders retained an active memory of the glories of Byzantium. When Constantinople fell to the Turks in 1453, just as Russia was beginning to assert its independence from the Tatars, it was logical to claim that the mantle of east European leadership had fallen on Russia. A monk, currying favor, wrote the Russian king in 1511 that whereas heresy had destroyed the first Roman Empire and the Turks had cut down the second, Byzantium—a "third, new Rome"—under the king's "mighty rule" "sends out the Orthodox Christian faith to the ends of the earth and shines more brightly than the sun." "Two Romes have fallen, but the third stands, and there will be no fourth." This sense of an Eastern Christian mission, inspiring a Russian resurgence, was just one result of

In Depth

Eastern and Western Europe: The Problem of Boundaries

Deciding where one civilization ends and another begins is not always easy, particularly when many political units and some internal cultural differences are involved. Defining the territory of the two related civilizations that developed in Europe is particularly difficult. A number of states sat, and still sit, on the borders of the two civilizations, sharing some characteristics of each. Furthermore, political disputes and nationalist attachments, fierce in this border territory of east central Europe during the past two centuries, make territorial definitions an emotional issue. So the question of defining Europe's civilizations is a particularly thorny case of a larger problem.

If a civilization is defined simply by its mainstream culture, then east and west Europe in the postclassical period divide logically according to Orthodox and Catholic territories (and use of the Cyrillic and Greek or of the Latin alphabets). By this reckoning, Poland, the Czech areas, and the Baltic states (these latter did not convert to Catholicism until the 14th century) are western, and Hungary is largely so. South Slavs are mainly but not entirely Orthodox, a regional division that can provoke recurrent violence. Russia and Ukraine are decidedly Orthodox in tradition. Religion matters. Poland and other Catholic regions have long maintained much more active ties with western Europe than Russia has. At the end of the postclassical period, a Czech religious dissenter, named Hus, even foreshadowed the later Protestant Reformation in his attacks on the Catholic church.

Politically, the case is more complicated. Poland, Hungary, and Lithuania formed large regional kingdoms at various times during and after the postclassical period. But these kingdoms were very loosely organized, much more so than the feudal monarchies that were developing in western Europe. Exceptionally large aristocracies in Poland and Hungary (by western or by Russian standards) helped limit these states.

Trade patterns also did not closely unite Poland or Hungary with western Europe until much later, when the two regions were clearly different in economic structure. Also, Polish and Hungarian societies often shared more features with Russia than with western Europe.

Russian expansion later pulled parts of eastern Europe, including Poland, into its orbit, although it never eliminated strong cultural identities. It is also important to remember that borders can change. The Mongol invasions that swept through Russia also conquered Poland and Hungary, but the armies did not stay there. Part of the Ukraine was also free from direct Mongol control, which helped differentiate it from Russia proper. For two centuries, at the end of the postclassical period, the divisions within eastern Europe intensified. Since 1989, many east European countries have again achieved full independence from Russia, and they want to claim their distinctive pasts. Not an easy border area to characterize in terms of a single civilization, east central Europe has also been a victim of many conquests interspersed with periods of proud independence.

Questions: What were the main characteristics of Russian civilization as it first emerged in the postclassical period? In what ways did Poland, Hungary, and the Czech lands differ from these characteristics? Are there other civilization border areas, in the postclassical period or later, that are similarly difficult to define because of their position between two other areas?

this complicated formative period in the emergence of a separate European civilization in the Slavic lands.

The End of an Era in Eastern Europe

With Byzantium and Russia both under siege, east European civilization fell on hard times at the end of the postclassical era. These difficulties confirmed the largely separate trajectories of West and East in Europe, for western Europe remained free from outside control and, despite some new problems, maintained a clearer vigor in politics, economy, and culture. When eastern Europe did reemerge, it was at some disadvantage to the West in terms of power and economic and cultural sophistication—a very different balance from that of the glory days of Byzantium and the vigor of Kievan Russia.

Tatar invasion and Byzantine collapse were profoundly disruptive. Key features of Kievan social structure disappeared in the later development of imperial Russia. Yet continuity was not entirely lost. Not only Christianity but also the east European assumptions about political rulers and church–state relations and the pride in a lively artistic culture served as organizing threads when Russia and other Slavic societies turned to rebuilding.

 ## GLOBAL CONNECTIONS: Eastern Europe and the World

The Byzantine Empire participated actively in interregional trade. Constantinople had become one of the world's great trading cities, a connecting point between Europe and Asia. The Byzantine import of a silk industry from China was a sign of their active awareness of the world beyond their borders. The empire served as an active link in the postclassical global system, between northern Europe and the Mediterranean.

The situation was somewhat different for Russia. Russia's geographical position inevitably encouraged awareness both of Europe and of western Asia. Vladimir I reflected this when he pondered his religious choices, among Western Christianity, Orthodox Christianity, or Islam. But Russia became dependant on Byzantium as its main trading contact with the wider world. When Byzantium declined, and when the Mongols conquered Russia, this led to a period of unusual isolation. Russia was not able to benefit from wider relationships during the Mongol centuries, though the Mongol influence itself left a mark. When, by the 15th century, Russia began to regain independence, it faced decisions about what kind of broader contacts to foster, and how.

Further Readings

J. M. Hussey's *The Byzantine World* (1982) is a useful overview. Byzantine Christianity is studied in G. Every's *The Byzantine Patriarchate, 451–1204* (1978) and S. Runciman's *The Byzantine Theocracy* (1977); see also D. M. Nicol's *Church and Society in the Last Centuries of Byzantium* (1979). On culture, see William Brumfield, ed., *Christianity and the Arts in Russia* (1991); Helen Evans and

William Wixom, *The Glory of Byzantium: Art and Culture of the Middle Byzantine Era A.D. 843–1261* (1997); and E. Kitzinger's *Byzantine Art in the Making* (1977). Byzantine relations with the West are the main topic in H. J. Magoulias' *Byzantine Christianity: Emperor, Church and the West* (1982). On Byzantine influence in eastern Europe, D. Obolensky's *The Byzantine Commonwealth: Eastern Europe, 500–1453* (1971) remains an excellent analysis. See also A. P. Kazhdan and A. W. Epstein, *Changes in Byzantine Culture in the Eleventh and Twelfth Centuries* (1985).

On Russian history, the best survey is Nicholas Riasanovsky's *A History of Russia* (5th ed., 1992), which has a good bibliography. Books dealing with early Russian culture include Mary Charmot, *Russian Painting and Sculpture* (1963), N. P. Kondakov's *The Russian Icon* (1927), J. H. Billington's *The Icon and the Axe: An Interpretive History of Russian Culture* (1966), and Arthur Voyce's *The Art and Architecture of Medieval Russia* (1967). Vladimir Volkoff, *Vladimir the Russian Viking, 960–1015* (1985), offers a unique glimpse of early Russia. Two collections are also very helpful on early Russian history: Thomas Riha, ed., *Readings in Russian Civilization*, vol. 1, *Russia Before Peter the Great, 900–1700* (1970); and especially S. A. Zenkovsky, ed. and trans., *Medieval Russia's Epics, Chronicles and Tales* (1963). The impact of the Mongols on the shaping of Russian history is examined in Robert Marshall, *Storm From the East: From Genghis Khan to Khubilai Khan* (1993), and in an older, but still serviceable work, M. N. Thompson, *The Mongols and Russia* (1966).

On the Web

Useful overviews and assessments of Byzantine Civilization and links to related sites are provided at http://www.adams.edu/academics/art_letters/hgp/civ/110/4easternorthodox.html and http://www.fordham.edu/halsall/byzantium/. It is possible to wander the streets of Byzantine Jerusalem via http://www.american.edu/projects/mandala/TED/hpages/jerusalem/byzantin.htm. A virtual visit to one of the oldest cities of Kievan Rus', Novgorod, is offered by that city at its official Web site, http://www.novgorod.ru/english/city/history, http://emuseum.mnsu.edu/history/russia/kievanrus.html and also at http://www.neva.ru/EXPO96/book/chap1-1.html.

The ruler who converted Kievan Rus' to Orthodox Christianity, Vladimir I (http://elvis.rowan.edu/~kilroy/JEK/07/15.html) and the church leaders who converted the Balkans and southern Russia to that faith, including Cyril and Methodius (http://www.newadvent.org/cathen/04592a.htm), can be studied on the Web. Just as interesting are the lives of the women who rose to positions of power and authority at that time.

The Great Schism that came to separate and define Western Catholicism and Eastern Orthodoxy is examined from the Orthodox perspective at http://orthodoxphotos. com/readings/Orthodox_Church/schism.shtml. The Catholic perspective is offered at http://www. newadvent.org/cathen/13535a.htm.

The Emperor Justinian (http://www.historyguide.org/ ancient/justinian.html and http://www.newadvent.org/ cathen/08578b.htm) influenced much of the history of the Mediterranean world with Theodora as coruler (http://womenshistory.about.com/library/bio/ biblio-theodora.htm and http://campus.northpark.edu/ history/Webchron/EastEurope/Theodora.html). Anna Comnena, a politically ambitious daughter of a Byzantine Emperor and also an historian, is revealed at http:// womeninworldhistory.com/heroine5.html, http://www. fordham.edu/halsall/source/comnena-cde.html, and http://www.wsu.edu:8080/~wldciv/world_civ_reader/ world_civ_reader_1/comnena.html. One of the centerpieces of Byzantine architecture, Hagia Sophia, can be visited at http://www.patriarchate.org/ecumenical_ patriarchate/chapter_4/html/hagia_sophia.html.

CHAPTER 10

A NEW CIVILIZATION EMERGES IN WESTERN EUROPE

This scene showing peasants at work in the fields near a grand palace is from an illuminated manuscript that was produced in the early 1400s for the Duc de Berry, an art patron and the brother of the king of France. The manuscript depicts a variety of scenes from the daily life of both peasants and the aristocracy in the 15th century.

- Stages of Postclassical Development
- IN DEPTH: Western Civilization
- Western Culture in the Postclassical Era
- Changing Economic and Social Forms in the Postclassical Centuries
- VISUALIZING THE PAST: Peasant Labor
- DOCUMENT: Changing Roles for Women
- The Decline of the Medieval Synthesis
- GLOBAL CONNECTIONS: Medieval Europe and the World

The postclassical period in western Europe began with the decline and fall of the Roman Empire and extended until the 15th century. The period is known as the **Middle Ages** in European history (the adjective form is *medieval*). The period featured gradual recovery from the shock of Rome's collapse and growing interaction with other societies, particularly around the Mediterranean. Key characteristics of western European civilization emerged from this dynamic process.

Developments in Western civilization during the Middle Ages reflected many of the larger themes of postclassical world history. The spread of civilization underlay medieval history. Although western Europe had been touched by the Roman Empire at its height, contacts had been superficial outside the Mediterranean zone. Much of the north—most of Germany, northern Britain, and Scandinavia—had been entirely beyond Roman reach. During the Middle Ages, civilization extended gradually to the whole of western Europe.

Western Europe also witnessed the spread of new religious beliefs. The missionary activity of Christianity led most western Europeans to convert from polytheistic faiths in the initial postclassical centuries. Many produced an amalgam in which beliefs in magic and supernatural spirits coexisted with often fervent Christianity.

Finally, medieval western Europe participated in the network of expanding contacts among major societies in Asia, Europe, and parts of Africa. From such contacts medieval Europeans learned new technologies. New tools introduced by invaders from Asia helped spur medieval agriculture from the 10th century onward. New crops from Africa increased food production. Trade in the Mediterranean, bringing contacts with the Arabs, yielded other technological gains, such as the first European paper factory. Medieval culture was at least as powerfully shaped by connections with the wider world. From the Byzantines and the Arabs, Western scholars by the 11th and 12th centuries learned new lessons in mathematics, science, and philosophy. The medieval West unquestionably took more from the emerging world network than it contributed, but it was also challenged by its international position to seek new world roles. The theme of contacts is central to explaining developments in postclassical western Europe.

Two Images

Muslim writers who encountered Europeans, for example during the Crusades in the 12th century, viewed them as tragically backward. One wrote, "Their bodies are large, their manners harsh, their understanding dull and their tongues heavy. Those who are farthest to the north are the most

213

500 c.e.	800 c.e.	1000 c.e.	1150 c.e.	1300 c.e.	1450 c.e.
500–900 Recovery period after Rome's fall; missionary work in northern Europe	**800–814** Charlemagne's empire	**1018** Beginning of Christian reconquest of Spain	**1150–1300** Gothic style spreads	**1303** Seizure of papacy by French king	**1469** Formation of single Spanish monarchy
732 Franks defeat Muslims in France	**900–1000** Spread of new plows; use of horses in agriculture, transport	**1066** Norman conquest of England, strong feudal monarchy	**1180** University of Paris	**1338–1453** Hundred Years' War	
	962 Germanic kings "revive" Roman Empire	**1070–1141** Peter Abelard	**1200–1274** Thomas Aquinas and flowering of scholasticism	**1348** Black Death (bubonic plague)	
		1073–1085 Gregory VII, reform pope	**1215** Magna Carta		
		1096–1270 Crusades	**1226–1270** Louis IX of France		
			1265 First English parliament		

subject to stupidity, grossness, and brutishness." The comment reflected obvious prejudice. But it also picked up on the fact that Europeans were newer to civilization than many Middle Easterners were, their economy was less advanced, and their manners were less polished.

Thomas Aquinas, an Italian churchman at the University of Paris, was one of the most intelligent thinkers in European history. He dictated his books to secretaries and was so smart that he could juggle three or four sections of a complex argument at the same time, turning first to one secretary, then to another as the first caught up with his words. Working to blend rational knowledge and Christian faith, Aquinas thought he could sum up all essential understanding about man, God, and nature—something that no single individual has thought possible since then.

How, at about the same point in time, could Europe seem backward yet produce such flashes of intellectual brilliance?

Stages of Postclassical Development

 Medieval European development unfolded in two subperiods up to about 1300. Between the 6th and the 10th centuries, chaotic conditions prevailed, despite gains made by the church and Charlemagne's brief empire. Then, improvements in trade and agriculture brought new strength and diversity. Feudal monarchy developed as a stronger political form. During this period, western Europe also developed expansionist tendencies, particularly in the Crusades.

From about 550 c.e. until about 900, western Europe suffered from a number of problems. Rome's decline had left Italy fragmented, its cities and commerce shrinking, and its intellectual life in tatters.

Rome continued to serve as the center of the growing Catholic church, in turn the most powerful institution in the West. But Italy was divided politically. Spain, another key region of the Roman Empire in the West, lay in the hands of the Muslims through much of the Middle Ages. A vibrant intellectual and economic life was focused there, and it would have an important influence on Western developments later on, but it was for the time being out of the Western mainstream. The center of the postclassical West lay in France, the Low Countries, and southern and western Germany, with England increasingly drawn in—areas where civilization, as a form of human organization, was new.

Frequent invasions reflected and prolonged the West's weakness, making it difficult to develop durable government or economic forms. Raids by the seagoing **Vikings** from Scandinavia periodically disrupted life from Ireland to Sicily. With weak rulers and little more than subsistence agriculture, it was small wonder that intellectual activity almost ground to a halt. The few who could read and write were concentrated in the hierarchy and the monasteries of the Catholic church, where they kept learning alive. But they could do little more than copy older manuscripts, including those of the great Christian thinkers of the later Roman Empire. By their own admission, they could not understand much of the philosophy involved, and they often apologized for their inability to write good Latin.

The Manorial System: Obligations and Allegiances

Between Rome's fall and the 10th century, effective political organization was largely local, although Germanic kings ruled some territories, such as a portion of what is France today. **Manorialism** was the system of economic and political relations between landlords and their peasant laborers. Most people were **serfs,** living on self-sufficient agricultural estates called manors. Serfs were agricultural workers who received some protection, including the administration of justice, from the landlords; in return, they were obligated to turn over part of their goods and to remain on the land. The manorial system had originated in the later Roman Empire. It was strengthened by the decline of trade and the lack of larger political structures. Serfs needed the military forces the landlords could muster for their security. Without much market economy to stimulate production and specialization, these same landlords used the serfs' produce and labor to support their own modest establishments.

Life for most serfs was difficult. Agricultural equipment was limited, and production was low. The available plows, copied from Mediterranean models, were too light to work the heavy soils of France and Germany effectively. In the 9th century a better plow, the **moldboard** (a curved iron plate), was introduced that allowed deeper turning of the soil. Most Western peasants early in the postclassical period also left half their land uncultivated each year to restore nutrients. This again limited productivity, although by the 9th century a new **three-field system** improved the situation. Here, only a third of the land was left unplanted each year, to regain fertility.

The obligations of the manorial system bore as heavily on most serfs as did the technological limitations. Serfs had to give their lord part of their crops in return for grazing their animals on his land or milling their grain. They also provided many days of labor repairing the lord's castle or working the lands under his control. Serfs were not slaves: They could not be bought or sold, and they retained essential ownership of their houses and lands as long as they kept up with their obligations; they could also pass their property rights on through inheritance. Nevertheless, life remained hard, particularly in the early postclassical centuries. Some serfs escaped landlord control, creating a host of wanderers who added to the disorder of the early Middle Ages.

The Church: Political and Spiritual Power

During the centuries of recovery after the Roman Empire's collapse in the 6th century, the Catholic church was the only extensive example of solid organization. In theory, and to an extent in fact, the church copied the government of the Roman Empire to administer Christendom. The pope in Rome was the top authority. Regional churches were headed by bishops, who were supposed to owe allegiance to the church's central authority; bishops, in turn, appointed and to some degree supervised local priests. The popes did not always appoint the bishops, for monarchs and local lords often claimed this right, but they did send directives and receive information. The popes also regulated doctrine, beating back several heresies that threatened a unified Christian faith. Moreover, they sponsored extensive missionary activity. Papal missionaries converted the English to Christianity. They brought the religion to northern and eastern Germany, beyond the borders of the previous Roman Empire, and, by the 10th century, to Scandinavia. They were active in the border regions of eastern Europe (see Chapter 9), sometimes competing directly with Orthodox missionaries. The interest of early Germanic kings in Christianity was a sign of the political as well as spiritual power of the church. A warrior chieftain, **Clovis,** converted to Christianity about 496 C.E. to gain greater prestige over local rivals, who were still pagan. This authority, in turn, gave him a vague dominion over the Franks, a Germanic tribe located in much of what is France today. Conversion of this sort also strengthened beliefs by Western religious leaders, particularly the popes, that they had a legitimate authority separate from and superior to the political sphere. As Figure 10.1 suggests, religious commitments continued to expand to many people.

The church also developed an important chain of monasteries during the Dark Ages—the centuries immediately after Rome's fall. Western monasteries helped discipline the intense spirituality felt by some individual Christians, people who wanted to devote themselves to prayer and religious discipline and escape the limits of ordinary material life. The most important set of monastic rules was developed by Benedict of Nursia (in Italy) in the 6th century; the spread of Benedictine monasteries promoted Christian unity in western Europe. Monasteries also served ordinary people as examples of a holy life, adding to the spiritual focus that formed part of the fabric of medieval society. Many monasteries helped improve the cultivation of the land at a time when agricultural techniques were at a low ebb. Monasteries also provided some education and promoted literacy.

Charlemagne and His Successors

One significant development occurred during the early postclassical centuries in the more strictly political sphere. The royal house of the Franks grew in strength during the 8th century. A new family, the **Carolingians,** took over this monarchy, which was based in northern France, Belgium, and western Germany. One founder of the Carolingian line, **Charles Martel,** or "Charles the Hammer," was responsible for defeating the Muslims in the battle of Tours in 732, although his victory had more to do with Arab exhaustion and an overextended invasion force than Carolingian strength. This defeat helped confine the Muslims to Spain and, along with the Byzantine defeat of the Arabs in the same period, preserved Europe for Christianity.

Figure 10.1   Anxiety for Salvation: The Resurrection. *This picture was part of materials to be read in religious services in the 11th century in Germany. The dead are rising from their tombs for the Last Judgment, summoned by angels escorted by the winds. The picture illustrates the goals Christians were urged to make paramount, focusing on life after death.*

A later Carolingian ruler in this same royal line, Charles the Great, or **Charlemagne,** established a substantial empire in France and Germany around the year 800 (see Figure 10.2). Briefly, it looked as if a new Roman Empire might revive in the West; indeed, Charlemagne's successors in Germany continued to use the title of emperor. Charlemagne helped to restore some church-based education in western Europe, and the level of intellectual activity began a slow recovery, in part because of these efforts. When Charlemagne died in 814, however, this empire did not long survive him. Rather, it was split into three portions as inheritance for his three grandsons: the outlines of modern France, Germany, and a middle strip consisting of the Low Countries, Switzerland, and northern Italy (Map 10.1). Several of Charlemagne's successors, with nicknames such as "the Bald" and "the Fat," were not great leaders even in their regional kingdoms.

From this point onward, the essential political history of western Europe consisted of the gradual emergence of regional monarchies; a durable empire proved impossible, given competing loyalties and the absence of a strong bureaucracy. Western Europe proved to have strong cultural unity, initially centered in Catholic Christianity, but with pronounced political divisions. No single language united this civilization, any more than did a single government. Intellectuals and the church officials used Latin, but during the Middle Ages separate spoken languages evolved, usually merging Germanic and Latin elements. These separate languages, such as French and English, in turn helped form the basis of halting national identities when political and national boundaries roughly

Figure 10.2 *The pope's coronation of the emperor Charlemagne was a vital precedent for the idea that church approval was essential for a legitimate state in western Europe, although in fact Charlemagne's power greatly exceeded the pope's.*

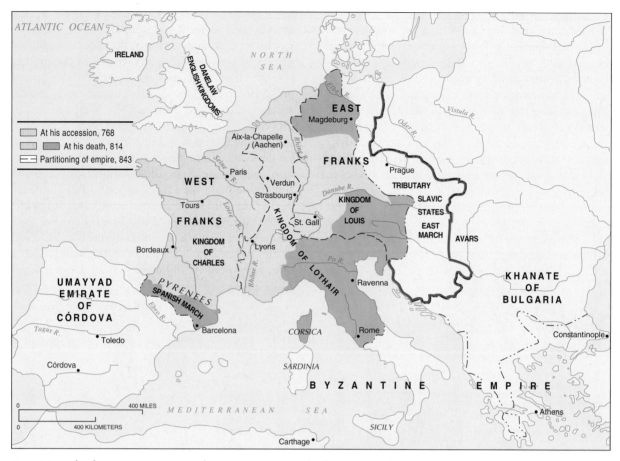

Map 10.1 *Charlemagne's Empire and Successor States. Charlemagne gathered a wide section of western Europe under his sway, but the empire was divided among his three grandsons after his death.*

coincided, which is what began to happen in key cases after the 9th century.

The royal houses of several lands gained new visibility soon after Charlemagne's empire split. At first, the rulers who reigned over Germany and northern Italy were in the strongest position. It was they who claimed the title *emperor*, beginning around the 10th century. Later they called themselves **Holy Roman emperors,** merging Christian and classical claims. By this time, however, their rule had become increasingly hollow, precisely because they relied too much on their imperial claims and did not build a solid monarchy from regional foundations. Local lords often went their own way in Germany, and city-states showed independence in northern Italy. The future lay elsewhere, with the rise of monarchies in individual states—states that ultimately would become nations.

New Economic and Urban Vigor

By 900, a series of developments began to introduce new sources of strength into Western society that ultimately had clear political and cultural repercussions. New agricultural techniques developed from contacts with eastern Europe and with Asian raiders into central Europe. The new moldboard plow and the three-field system were crucial gains; so was a new horse collar that allowed horses to be yoked without choking. The use of horse collars and stirrups also confirmed the military dominance of the lords, who monopolized fighting on horseback. The European nobility became defined by land ownership and military power. But better plows helped the ordinary people by allowing deeper working of heavy soil and the opening of new land. Monasteries also promoted better agricultural methods (in contrast to the less worldly orientation of monks in eastern Europe). During the 10th century, Viking raids began to taper off, partly because regional governments became stronger (sometimes when the Vikings themselves took over, as in the French province of Normandy) and partly because the Vikings, now Christianized, began to settle down. Greater regional political stability and improved agriculture promoted population growth, an important fact of Western history from the 10th through the 13th centuries.

Population growth encouraged further economic innovation. More people created new markets. There was a wedge here for growing trade, which in turn encouraged towns to expand, another source of demand. Landlords and serfs alike began to look to lands that had not previously been converted to agriculture. Whole regions, such as northeastern Germany, became colonized by eager farmers, and new centers sprang up throughout settled regions such as France. To woo labor to the new farms, landlords typically had to loosen the bonds of serfdom and require less outright labor service, sometimes simply charging a money rent. Harsh serfdom still existed, but most serfs gained greater independence, and some free peasants emerged. Contacts with other countries brought knowledge of new crops, such as durum wheat (from north Africa), the vital ingredient for pasta, and alfalfa (from Persia). The pace of economic life created a less rigid social structure, and more commercial, market-oriented economic motives began to coexist with earlier military and Christian ideals.

The growth of towns reflected the new vigor of western Europe's agriculture. In parts of Italy and the Low Countries, where trade and urban manufacturing were especially brisk, urban populations soared to almost 20 percent of the total by the 13th century. Overall, the townspeople made up about 5 percent of the West's population—a significant figure, though below the often 15 percent levels of the advanced Asian civilizations. Few European cities approached a population level of 100,000 people (in contrast, China had 52 larger cities), but the rise of modest regional centers was an important development. Literacy spread in the urban atmosphere, spurring the popular languages; professional entertainers introduced new songs as well as dazzling tricks such as fire-eating and bear-baiting; urban interests spurred new forms of religious life, including city-based monastic orders dedicated to teaching or hospital work. Merchant activity and craft production expanded.

Europe's economic and urban surge helped feed formal cultural life, which had already gained some-

what under Charlemagne's encouragement. By the 9th and 10th centuries, schools began to form around important cathedrals, training children who were destined for church careers. By the 11th century, there was enough demand for educated personnel to sustain the first universities. Italy offered universities to train students in medicine and law; the legal faculties profited from a growing revival in knowledge of Roman law, and medicine benefited from new learning imported from the Arabs and from revived Greek and Hellenistic science. By the 12th century, a more characteristic university was forming in Paris. It specialized in training clergy, with theology as the culminating subject but with faculties in other subjects as well. The Parisian example inspired universities in England (Oxford and Cambridge), Germany, and elsewhere. Solid educational institutions, though destined for only a small minority of Europe's population, supported increasingly diverse and sophisticated efforts in philosophy and theology. At the same time, medieval art and architecture reached a new high point, spurred by the same prosperity.

Feudal Monarchies and Political Advances

Prosperity also promoted political change, influenced by structures established in more unstable times. From the 6th century onward, the key political and military relationships in western Europe had evolved in a system called **feudalism.** Feudal relationships linked military elites, mostly landlords, who could afford the horses and iron weaponry necessary to fight. Greater lords provided protection and aid to lesser lords, called **vassals;** vassals in turn owed their lords military service, some goods or payments, and advice. Early feudalism after Rome's fall was very local; many landlords had armed bands of five or ten local vassals, easily converted into raiding parties. But feudal relationships could be extended to cover larger regions and even whole kingdoms. Charlemagne's empire boosted this more stable version of feudalism. He could not afford to pay his own bureaucracy, so he rewarded most of his military leaders with estates, which they quickly converted into family property in return for pledges of loyalty and service. Many German duchies were created by powerful lords with their own armies of vassals, ostensibly deferring to the Holy Roman emperor. On the whole, European feudalism inhibited the development of strong central states, but it also gradually reduced purely local warfare.

Furthermore, kings could use feudalism to build their own power. Kings of France began to win growing authority, from the 10th century onward, under the Capetian royal family. At first they mainly exploited their position as regional feudal lords in the area around Paris. They controlled many serf-stocked manors directly, and they held most other local landlords as vassals. More attentive administration of this regional base produced better revenues and armies. The kings also formed feudal links with great lords in other parts of France, often through marriage alliances, gradually bringing more territory under their control. They experimented with the beginnings of bureaucratic administration by separating their personal accounts from government accounts, thus developing a small degree of specialization among the officials who served them. Later Capetian kings sent out officials to aid in regional administration.

The growth of a strong feudal monarchy in France took several centuries. By the early 14th century, the process of cautious centralization had gone so far in France that a king could claim rights to make the church pay taxes (an issue that caused great conflict). The king could mint money and employ some professional soldiers apart from the feudal armies that still did most of the fighting.

Feudal monarchy in England was introduced more abruptly. The Duke of Normandy, of Viking descent, who had already built a strong feudal domain in his French province, invaded England in 1066. The duke, now known as **William the Conqueror,** extended his tight feudal system to his new kingdom. He tied the great lords of England to his royal court by bonds of loyalty, giving them estates in return for their military service. But he also used some royal officials, called sheriffs, to help supervise the administration of justice throughout the kingdom. In essence, he and his successors merged feudal principles with a slightly more centralized approach, including more standardized national law codes issued by the royal court.

The growth of feudal monarchy unknowingly duplicated measures taken earlier in other centralizing societies, such as China. Developing an explicit bureaucracy, with some specialized functions, and sending emissaries to outlying provinces are examples. In Europe, kings often chose urban business or professional people to staff their fledgling bureaucracies, because unlike the feudal nobles they would be loyal to the ruler who appointed them. Government functions expanded modestly, as kings tried to tax subjects directly and hire a small professional army to supplement feudal forces.

Limited Government

Stronger monarchies did not develop evenly throughout Europe. The West remained politically divided and diverse. Germany and Italy, though nominally controlled by the Holy Roman emperor, were actually split into regional states run by feudal lords and city-states. The pope directly ruled the territory of central Italy. The Low Countries, a vigorous trade and manufacturing region, remained divided into regional units. Equally important were the limitations over the most successful feudal monarchies. The power of the church continued to limit political claims, for the state was not supposed to intrude on matters of faith except in carrying out decisions of the popes or bishops.

Feudalism created a second limitation, for aristocrats still had a powerful independent voice and often their own military forces. The growth of the monarchy cut into aristocratic power, but this led to new statements of the limits of kings. In 1215, the unpopular English King John faced opposition to his taxation measures from an alliance of nobles, townspeople, and church officials. Defeated in his war with France and then forced down by the leading English lords, John was compelled to sign the Great Charter, or **Magna Carta,** which confirmed feudal rights against monarchical claims. John promised to observe restraint in his dealings with the nobles and the church, agreeing, for example, not to institute new taxes without the lords' permission or to appoint bishops without the church's permission.

Late in the 13th century, this same feudal balance led to the creation of **parliaments** as bodies representing not individual voters but privileged groups such as the nobles and the church. (Even earlier, in 1000, the regional kingdom of Catalonia created a parliament.) The first full English parliament convened in 1265, with the House of Lords representing the nobles and the church hierarchy, and the Commons made up of elected representatives from wealthy citizens of the towns. The parliament institutionalized the feudal principle that monarchs should consult with their vassals. In particular, parliaments gained the right to rule on any proposed changes in taxation; through this power, they could also advise the crown on other policy issues. Although the parliamentary tradition became strongest in England, similar institutions arose in France, Spain, Scandinavia, and several of the regional governments in Germany. Here too, parliaments represented the **key three estates:** church, nobles, and urban leaders. They were not widely elected.

Feudal limited government was not modern limited government. People had rights according to the estate into which they were born; nobles transmitted membership in their estate to their children. There was no general concept of citizenship and certainly no democracy. Still, by creating the medieval version of representative institutions, Western feudal monarchy produced the beginnings of a distinctive political tradition. This tradition differed from the political results of Japanese feudalism, which emphasized group loyalty more than checks on central power.

Even with feudal checks, European monarchs did develop more capacity for central administration during the later Middle Ages. The results clearly were uneven and by Asian standards still woefully limited. European rulers also continued to see war as a key purpose. Local battles gave way to larger wars, such as the conflicts between the proud rulers of France and England. In the 14th century, a long battle began—the **Hundred Years' War,** between the national monarchies of France and England—over territories the English king controlled in France and over feudal rights versus the emerging claims of national states.

The West's Expansionist Impulse

During the period of political development and economic advance, western Europe began to show its muscle beyond its initial postclassical borders. Population growth spurred the expansionist impulse, as did the memory of Rome's lost greatness and the righteous zeal provided by Christianity. The most concrete expansion took place in east central Europe from the 11th century onward. Germanic knights and agricultural settlers poured into sparsely settled areas in what is now eastern Germany and Poland, changing the population balance and clearing large areas of forest. A different kind of expansionist surge occurred in Spain. Small Christian states remained in northern Spain by the 10th century, and they gradually began to attack the Muslim government that held most of the peninsula. The "reconquest" escalated by the 11th century, as Christian forces, swelled by feudal warriors from various areas, pushed into central Spain, conquering the great Muslim center of Toledo. Full expulsion of Muslim rulers occurred only at the end of the Middle Ages in 1492, but the trend of the Christian offensive was clear even earlier. During the 15th century regional Spanish monarchies fused through the marriage of Ferdinand and Isabella. At Europe's other extreme, Viking voyagers had pushed out into the northern Atlantic, establishing settlements in Iceland. By the 11th century, other voyages had pushed to Greenland and the Hudson Bay area in what is now Canada, where short-lived outposts were created. By the 13th century, Spanish and Italian seafarers entered the Atlantic from the Mediterranean, though without much initial result except several lost expeditions.

The most dramatic expansionist move involved the great Crusades against the Muslim control of the Holy Land. Pope **Urban II** called for the First Crusade in 1095, appealing to the piety of the West's rulers and common people. Crusaders were promised full forgiveness of sins if they died in battle, ensuring their entry to heaven, which obviously enhanced the religious motivations involved. The idea of attacking Islam had great appeal, as Figure 10.3 suggests. The attraction of winning spoils from the rich Arab lands

Figure 10.3 *This imaginary duel between the noble Christian champion King Richard of England and the Muslim leader Saladin clearly shows the difference between "good guys" and "bad guys."*

added to the inducement, as did the thirst for excitement among the West's feudal warriors. Internal wars were declining in Europe, and the military values of feudalism sought outlets elsewhere. Three great armies, with tens of thousands of crusaders from various parts of the West, assembled in Constantinople in 1097, much to the distress of the Byzantine government. The Western crusaders moved toward Jerusalem, winning it from the Turkish armies that held the area by that time. For almost a century, Western knights ruled the "kingdom of Jerusalem," losing it to a great Muslim general, Saladin, during the 12th century. Several later Crusades attempted to win back the Holy Land, but many later efforts turned toward other goals or toward pure farce. The Third Crusade at the end of the 12th century led to the death of the German emperor and the imprisonment of the English king, although it did produce a brief truce with Saladin that facilitated Christian pilgrims' visits to Jerusalem. The Fourth Crusade was manipulated by merchants in Venice, who turned it into an attack on their commercial rivals in Constantinople.

The Crusades did not demonstrate a new Western superiority in the wider world, despite brief successes. But in expressing a combination of religious zeal and growing commercial and military vigor on the part of the knights and merchants who organized the largest efforts, the Crusades unquestionably showed the aggressive spirit of the Western Middle Ages at their height. They also helped expose the West to new cultural and economic influences from the Middle East, a major spur to further change and to the West's interaction with the larger world, including a greater thirst for trade. Simply visiting the thriving urban center of Constantinople during the Crusades could open European eyes to new possibilities. One crusader exclaimed, "Oh, what a great and beautiful city is Constantinople! How many churches and palaces it contains, fashioned with wonderful skill! Their tradesmen at all times bring by boat all the necessities of man."

Religious Reform and Evolution

As medieval society developed, the Catholic church went through several periods of decline and renewal. At times, church officials and the leading monastic groups became preoccupied with their land holdings and their political interests. The church was a wealthy institution; it was tempting for many priests and monks to behave like ordinary feudal lords in pursuit of greater worldly power. Several reform movements fought this secularism, such as the 13th-century flowering that created orders such as the Franciscans, devoted to poverty and service in Europe's bustling cities. St. Clare of Assisi (1194–1253) exemplified this new spirit of purity and dedication to the church (Figure 10.4). She was deeply influenced by St. Francis, also from Assisi, who had converted to a life of piety and preaching in 1205 and who founded a new monastic order around him. Clare refused to marry, as her parents wanted, but rather founded a women's Franciscan order (later known as the Order of St. Clare, or the Poor Clares) with Francis' backing. Like many women in Europe, Clare found in monasticism a vital means of personal expression. She composed rules of severe piety for her order, and many women, including her mother and sister, joined her. People believed that her prayers turned two invading armies away from Assisi, and she was credited with many other miracles in her life and after death. She was can-

Figure 10.4 *St. Clare of Assisi*

In Depth

Western Civilization

For some time, Americans have talked about "Western civilization." The concept of the West was actively used in the cold war with the Soviet Union, yet it is hard to define. We have seen that the classical Mediterranean did not directly identify a "Western" civilization, and this classical heritage was used most selectively by postclassical western Europe. Further, the consistent absence of political unity in western Europe complicates any definition of common structures.

Western Europeans could not have identified Western civilization in the postclassical period, but they would have recognized the concept of Christendom, along with some difference between their version of this religion and that of eastern Europe. The first definition of this civilization was primarily religious, although artistic forms associated with religion also figured in this definition. Regional cultures varied, of course, and there was no linguistic unity, but cultural developments in one area—for example, the creation of universities, which started in Italy—surfaced elsewhere fairly quickly. Supplementing culture were some reasonably common social structures—like manors and guilds—and trade patterns that increasingly joined northern and much of southern Europe. The resulting civilization was by no means as coherent as Chinese civilization; many of its members detested each other, like the English and French, who were often in conflict and sometimes engaged in name-calling (the English were "les goddams," because they swore so much, and the French were "frogs" because of what they ate). Until very recently, Europeans thought in terms of distinctive national histories, not European ones. But it is possible to define some common features that differed from those of neighboring civilizations. Even as the civilization began to change, late in the postclassical period, it preserved some common directions. Debate continues about the balance between the Western and more purely national features.

Defining Western civilization is also complicated in the postclassical period because Western leaders copied so much from other societies. They eagerly learned of new technologies from Asia. They benefited from Arab mathematics and philosophy, and they imitated Muslim commercial law on how to treat tradespeople from outside the locality. But even in imitating, most Europeans were keenly conscious of their distinctiveness as Christians. They sometimes resented the societies they copied from. Toward the end of the Middle Ages, as Europeans began to seek a new role in the world at large, the openness to imitation also began to decline, as part of the further definition of a Western or European identity.

Questions: Was there a Western civilization before the postclassical period? What were the defining features of Western civilization by the end of the postclassical period? Was it separate from eastern Europe, in terms of major features? How does the definition of Western civilization today compare to that of the postclassical period?

onized in 1255, and in 1958 Pope Pius XII declared her the patron saint of television, for during her last illness she miraculously heard and saw a Christmas mass being performed on the other side of Assisi.

In addition to monastic leaders, reform-minded popes, such as **Gregory VII** (1073–1085), tried to purify the church and free it from interference by feudal lords. One technique was insistence on the particularly holy character of the priesthood. Reformers stipulated that all priests remain unmarried, to separate the priesthood from the ordinary world of the flesh. Gregory also tried to free the church from any trace of state control. He quarreled vigorously with Holy Roman Emperor Henry IV over the practice of state appointment, or **investiture,** of bishops in Germany. Ultimately, by excommunicating the emperor from the church, Gregory won his point. The emperor appealed to the pope for forgiveness on his knees in the snow of a northern Italian winter, and the investiture controversy ended, apparently in the church's favor. Gregory and several later popes made clear their beliefs that the church not only was to be free from state interference but was superior to the state in its function as a direct channel of God's word. These claims were not entirely accurate because governments still influenced religious affairs, but they were not hollow. Independently of the state, a network of church courts developed to rule on matters of religious law and to bring heretics to trial and occasionally to execution. This was the origin of recurrent Western beliefs in church–state separation.

The High Middle Ages

The postclassical version of Western civilization reached its high mark in the 12th and 13th centuries. Fed by the growing dynamism of western Europe's population, agriculture, and cities, the High Middle Ages were characterized by a series of creative tensions. Feudal political structures, derived from local and personal allegiances, were balanced by emerging central monarchies. The unquestionable authority of the church and the cultural dominance of Christianity jostled with the intellectual vitality and diversity that formed part of university life. A social order and economy, based primarily on agriculture and the labor of serfs, now had to come to terms with important cities, merchants, and some new opportunities even for ordinary farmers.

Western Culture in the Postclassical Era

 Christian culture formed the clearest unifying element in western Europe during the postclassical centuries, although it changed as European society matured. Theologians and artists developed distinctive expressions, although there were other philosophical and artistic currents as Europe's cultural creativity increased.

Theology: Assimilating Faith and Reason

During the centuries before about 1000, a small number of clergy continued the efforts of preserving and interpreting past wisdom, particularly the writings of church fathers such as Augustine, but also the work of some non-Christian Latin authors. During Charlemagne's time, a favorite practice was to gather quotations from ancient writers around key subjects. Efforts of this sort showed little creativity, but they gradually produced a fuller understanding of past thought as well as improvements in Latin writing style. Interest in classical principles of rhetoric, particularly logic, reflected the concern for coherent organization; Aristotle, known to the Middle Ages as *the* philosopher, was valued because of his clear exposition of rational thought.

From 1000 onward, a series of outstanding clerics advanced the logical exposition of philosophy and theology to new levels. They stressed the importance of absolute faith in God's word, but they believed that human reason could move toward an understanding of some aspects of religion and the natural order as well. Thus, according to several theologians, it was possible to prove the existence of God. Fascination with logic led some intellectuals to a certain zeal in pointing out inconsistencies in past wisdom, even in the writings of the church fathers. In the 12th century, **Peter Abelard** in Paris wrote a treatise called *Yes and No* in which he showed several logical contradictions in established interpretations of doctrine. Although Abelard protested his faith, saying, "I would not be an Aristotle if this were to part me from Christ," he clearly took an impish delight in suggesting skepticism. Here was a fascinating case of an individual's role in history. Abelard was clearly working in an established logical tradition, but his personality helped move the tradition to a new critical level. At the same time, his defiant attitudes may have drawn more attack than a softer approach would have done, which had consequences too.

The logical–rationalist current in Western philosophy was hardly unopposed. Apart from the fact that most ordinary Christians knew nothing of these debates, seeing their religion as a matter of received belief and appointed sacraments that would remove sin and promote salvation, many church leaders emphasized the role of faith alone. A powerful monk, **Bernard of Clairvaux,** successfully challenged Abelard. Bernard, an intellectual of a different sort, stressed the importance of mystical union with God, attainable even on this earth in brief blissful glimpses, rather than rationalist endeavor. Bernard believed that reason was dangerous and proud and that God's truth must be received through faith alone.

The debates over how and whether to combine the classical Mediterranean philosophical and scientific tradition with revealed religious faith had much in common with debates among Arab intellectuals during the 10th and 11th centuries. Both Christianity and Islam relied heavily on faith in a revealed word, through the Bible or Qur'an, respectively, but some intellectuals in both cultures strained to include other approaches.

Combining rational philosophy and Christian faith was the dominant intellectual theme in the post-classical West, showing the need to come to terms with both Christian and classical heritages. This combination of rational philosophy and Christian faith also posed formidable and fascinating problems. By the 12th century, the zeal for this kind of knowledge produced several distinctive results. It explained the intellectual vitality of most of the emerging universities, where students flocked to hear the latest debates by leading theologians. Higher education certainly benefited students through resulting job opportunities; for example, trained lawyers could hope for advancement in the growing bureaucracies of church or state. In contrast to China's institutions, however, the new universities were not directly tied into a single bureaucratic system, and the excitement they engendered during the Middle Ages did not follow from opportunism alone. A large number of students, from the whole of western Europe, sought out the mixture of spiritual and rational understanding that leading thinkers were trying to work out. Many early universities had their students pay the teachers directly if they were interested in attending a given set of lectures, and the eagerness for learning could make this system work.

The postclassical intellectual drive also motivated a growing interest in knowledge newly imported from the classical past and from the Arab world, and this knowledge fed the highest achievements of medieval learning. By the 12th century, Western scholars were reading vast amounts of material translated from Greek in centers in the Byzantine Empire, Italy, and Muslim Spain. They gained familiarity with the bulk of ancient Greek and Hellenistic philosophy and science. They also read translations of Arab and Jewish learning, particularly the works in which Middle Eastern scholars had wrestled with the problems of mixing human reasoning with truths gained by faith.

With much fuller knowledge of Aristotelian and Hellenistic science, plus the work of Arab rationalists such as Ibn-Rushd (known in the West as Averroës), Western philosopher–theologians in the 13th century proceeded to the final great synthesis of medieval learning. The leading figure was **Thomas Aquinas,** the Italian-born monk who taught at the University of Paris. Aquinas maintained the basic belief that faith came first, but he greatly expanded the scope given to reason. Through reason alone, humans could know much of the natural order, of moral law, and of the nature of God. Thomas had complete confidence that all essential knowledge could be organized coherently, and he produced a host of *Summas*, or highest works, that used careful logic to eliminate all possible objections to truth as revealed by reason and faith. Essentially, this work restated in Christian terms the Greek efforts to seek a rationality in nature that would correspond to the rational capacities of the human mind. To be sure, a few philosophers carried the interest in logic to absurd degrees. After the 13th century, **scholasticism**—as the dominant medieval philosophical approach was called because of its base in the schools—sometimes degenerated into silly debates such as the one about how many angels could dance on the head of a pin. But at its height, and particularly with Aquinas, scholasticism demonstrated an unusual confidence in the logical orderliness of knowledge and in human ability to know.

Medieval philosophy did not encourage a great deal of new scientific work. The emphasis on mastering past learning and organizing it logically could lead to overemphasis on previous discoveries rather than empirical research. Thus, university-trained doctors stressed memorization of Galen, the Hellenistic authority, rather than systematic practical experience. Toward the end of the 13th century, a current of practical science developed. In Oxford, members of the clergy, such as Roger Bacon, did experimental work with optics, pursuing research done earlier by Muslim scholars. An important by-product of this interest was the invention of eyeglasses. During the 14th and 15th centuries, experimenters also advanced knowledge in chemistry and astronomy. This early work set the stage for the flourishing of Western science.

Popular Religion

Far less is known about popular beliefs than about formal intellectual life in the Middle Ages. Christian devotion undoubtedly ran deep and may well have increased with time among many ordinary people. At least in the early medieval centuries, many people diligently followed Christian rituals yet seemed unaware of how many of their actions might contradict Christian morality. For example, Raoul de Cambrai, hero of a French epic written down in the late 12th century but orally transmitted earlier, sets fire to a convent filled with nuns, then asks a servant to bring him some food. The servant berates him for burning the convent, then reminds him that it is Lent, a time of fasting and repentance before Easter. Raoul denies that his deed was unjust, for the nuns deserved it for insulting his knights, but admits that he had forgotten Lent and goes off to distract himself from his hunger by playing chess.

Whether popular morality improved or not, popular means of expressing religious devotion expanded over time. The rise of cities saw the formation of lay groups to develop spirituality and express their love of God. The content of popular belief evolved as well. Enthusiasm for the veneration of Mary, the mother of Jesus, expanded by the 12th century, showing a desire to stress the merciful side of Christianity, rather than the supposed sternness of God the Father, and new hopes for assistance in gaining salvation. The worship of various saints showed a similar desire for intermediaries between humanity and God. At the same time, ordinary people continued to believe in various magical rituals, and they celebrated essentially pagan festivals, which often involved much dancing and merriment. They blended their version of Christianity with great earthiness and spontaneity, some of which was conveyed by late medieval authors such as English writer Geoffrey Chaucer.

Religious Themes in Art and Literature

Christian art in many ways reflected both the popular outlook and the more formal religion of theologians and church leaders. Religious art was another cultural area in which the medieval West came to excel, as was the case in other societies where religious enthusiasm ran strong, such as the Islamic Middle East or Hindu India. Like philosophy, medieval art and architecture were intended to serve the glory of God. Western painters used religious subjects almost exclusively. Painting mainly on wooden panels, artists in most parts of western Europe depicted Christ's birth and suffering and the lives of the saints, using stiff, stylized figures. By the 14th and 15th centuries, artists improved their ability to render natural scenes realistically and portrayed a host of images of medieval life as backdrops to their religious subjects. Stained glass designs and scenes for churches were another important artistic expression.

Medieval architecture initially followed Roman models, particularly in church building, using a rectangular, or Romanesque, style sometimes surmounted by domes. During the 11th century, however, a new style took hold that was far more original, though it

benefited from knowledge of Muslim design plus advances in structural engineering in the West itself. **Gothic** architects built soaring church spires and tall arched windows, as Figure 10.5 illustrates. Although their work focused on creating churches and great cathedrals, some civic buildings and palaces also picked up the Gothic motif. It is not far-fetched to see the Gothic style as representative of Western postclassical culture more generally. Its spiritual orientation showed in the towers cast up to the heavens. It built also on growing technical skills and deep popular devotion, expressed in the money collected to build the huge monuments and the patient labor needed for construction that often lasted many decades. The originality of Gothic styles reflected the growing Western ability to find suitable new means of expression, just as use of Gothic styles in the later Western world showed the ongoing power of medieval models.

Figure 10.5 *Gothic architecture was one of the creative expressions of postclassical western Europe and was used particularly in churches. This major cathedral in Amiens, France, was built over many centuries and dwarfs the surrounding buildings.*

Medieval literature and music reflected strong religious interests. Most Latin writing dealt with points of philosophy, law, or political theory. However, alongside writing in Latin came the development of a growing literature in the spoken languages, or vernaculars, of western Europe. The pattern was not unlike that of India a few centuries earlier after the fall of the Gupta empire, when Sanskrit served as a scholarly language but increasing power was given to popular languages such as Hindi. Vernacular literature helped develop separate European languages and focused largely on secular themes. Several oral sagas, dealing with the deeds of great knights and mythic figures in the past, were written down. From this tradition came the first known writing in early English, *Beowulf*, and in French, *The Song of Roland*. Late in the Middle Ages, a number of writers created adventure stories, comic tales, and poetry in the vernacular tongues, such as Chaucer's *Canterbury Tales*. Much of their work, and also plays written for performance in the growing cities, reflected the tension between Christian values and a desire to portray the richness and coarseness of life on earth. Chaucer's narrative shows a fascination with bawdy behavior, a willingness to poke fun at the hypocrisy of many Christians, and an ability to capture some of the tragedies of human existence. In France, a long poem called *The Romance of the Rose* used vivid sexual imagery, and the poet Villon wrote, in largely secular terms, of the terror and poignancy of death. Finally, again in vernacular language, a series of courtly poets, or troubadours, based particularly in southern France in the 14th century, wrote hymns to the love that could flourish between men and women. Although their verses stressed platonic devotion rather than sexual love and paid homage to courtly ceremonies and polite behavior, their concern with love was the first sign of a new valuation of this emotional experience in the Western tradition.

In sum, medieval intellectual and artistic life created a host of important themes. Religion was the centerpiece, but it did not preclude a growing range of interests, from science to romantic poetry. Medieval culture was a rich intellectual achievement in its own right. It also set in motion a series of developments—in rationalist philosophy, science, artistic representations of nature, and vernacular literature—that would be building blocks for later Western thought and art.

Changing Economic and Social Forms in the Postclassical Centuries

 With the revival of trade and agriculture, commercial ties spread through most of western Europe. Urban merchants gained unusual power, but early capitalism was disputed by the different economic values of the guilds.

Although culture provided the most obvious cement for Western society during the Middle Ages, common features also described economic activity and social structure. Here too, the postclassical West demonstrated impressive powers of innovation, for classical patterns had little hold. As trade revived by the 10th century, the West became a common commercial zone. Most regions produced primarily for local consumption, as was true in agricultural societies generally. But Italian merchants actively sought cloth manufactured in the Low Countries (present-day Belgium and the Netherlands), and merchants in many areas traded for wool grown in England or timber supplies and furs brought from Scandinavia and the Baltic lands. Great ports and trading fairs, particularly in the Low Countries and northern France, served as centers for Western exchange as well as markets for a few exotic products such as spices brought in from other civilizations.

New Strains in Rural Life

The improvements in agriculture after 800 C.E. brought important new ingredients to rural life. Some peasants were able to shake off the most severe constraints of manorialism, becoming almost free farmers with only a few obligations to their landlords, although rigid manorialism remained in place in many areas. Noble landlords still served mainly military functions, for ownership of a horse and armor were prerequisites for fighting until the end of the medieval period. Although most nobles shunned the taint of commerce—like aristocrats in many societies, they found too much money-grubbing demeaning—they did use trade to improve their standard of living and adopt more polished habits. The courtly literature of the late Middle Ages reflected this new style of life.

As many lords sought improved conditions they were often tempted to press their serfs to pay higher

Visualizing the Past

Peasant Labor

This scene, from an illuminated (illustrated) manuscript of the 15th century, shows peasant labor and tools in France, near a stylized great palace.

Questions: What kind of social and gender structure does the picture suggest? What kind of tools were used in farming, and how productive would they be? (The picture clearly indicates what kind of farming activity was being performed.) Interpretation of the picture must also involve the art itself: Is it realistic? What features seem most different from probable rural conditions, and what accounts for the differences? The picture should be compared to earlier medieval representations, such as the representation of Charlemagne's coronation: What were the trends in medieval artistic styles, in terms of dealing with human figures and nature? The manuscript was part of a seasonal book for a French aristocrat. What do the symbols at the top of the picture suggest about developments in medieval science and calendars?

rents and taxes, even as serfs were gaining a new sense of freedom and control over their own land. From the late Middle Ages until the 19th century, this tension produced a recurrent series of peasant–landlord battles in Western society. Peasants sought what they viewed as their natural and traditional right to the land, free and clear. They talked of Christian equality, turning such phrases as "When Adam delved and Eve span, Who was then a gentleman?" A more complex economy clearly brought new social strains, similar to the recurrent wave of popular unrest in China or the rural uprisings in the Middle East, where religion helped prompt egalitarian sentiments as well. The gap between lord and peasant was the crucial social inequality in Europe, but it was open to change and it generated some egalitarian ideas in response.

On the whole, the lives of Western peasants improved during the most dynamic part of the Middle Ages. Landlord controls were less tight than they had become in other societies, such as the Middle East. Western agriculture was not yet particularly advanced technologically (compared with east Asia, for example), but it had improved notably over early medieval levels.

Growth of Trade and Banking

Gains in agriculture promoted larger changes in medieval economic life. Urban growth allowed more specialized manufacturing and commercial activities, which in turn promoted still greater trade. Spearheaded by Italian businesspeople, banking was introduced to the West to facilitate the long-distance exchange of money and goods (Figure 10.6). The use of money spread steadily, to the dismay of many Christian moralists and many ordinary people who preferred the more direct, personal ways of traditional society. The largest trading and banking operations, not only in Italy but in southern Germany, the Low Countries, France, and Britain, were clearly capitalistic. Big merchants invested funds in trading ships and the goods they carried, hoping to make large profits on this capital. Profitmaking was not judged kindly by Christian thinkers such as Thomas Aquinas, who urged that all prices should be "just," reflecting only the labor put into the goods.

Rising trade took several forms. There were exchanges between western Europe and other parts of the known world. Wealthy Europeans developed a taste for some of the luxury goods and spices of Asia. The latter were not used merely to flavor food but were vital in preserving perishable items such as meat. Spice extracts also had great medicinal value. The Crusades played a role in bringing these products to wider attention. A Mediterranean trade redeveloped, mainly in the hands of Italian merchants, in which European cloth and some other products were exchanged for the more polished goods of the East. Commerce within Europe involved exchanges of timber and grain from the north for cloth and metal products manufactured in Italy and the Low Countries. At first an exporter of raw wool, England developed some manufactured goods for exchange by the later Middle Ages. Commercial alliances developed. Cities in northern Germany and southern Scandinavia grouped together in the **Hanseatic League** to encourage trade. With growing banking facilities, it became possible to organize commercial transactions throughout much of western Europe. Bankers, including many Jewish businesspeople, were valued for their service in lending money to monarchs and the papacy.

The growth of trade and banking in the Middle Ages served as the origin of capitalism in Western civilization. The greater Italian and German bankers, the long-distance merchants of the Hanseatic cities, were clearly capitalistic in their willingness to invest in trading ventures with the expectation of profit. Given the dangers of trade by land and sea, the risks in these investments were substantial, but profits of 100 percent or more were possible. In many cities, such as London, groups of powerful merchants banded together to invest in international trade, each buying shares in the venture and profiting or losing accordingly.

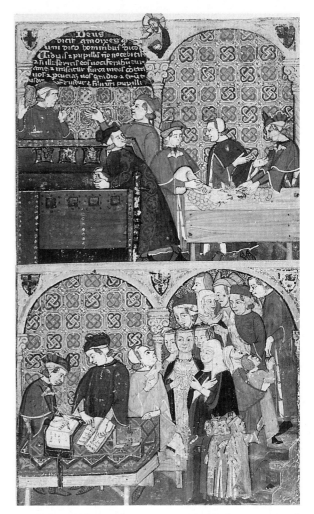

Figure 10.6 *This 14th-century miniature shows views of a banking house.*

Individual merchants could amass—and lose—great fortunes. Jacques Coeur (c. 1395–1456), one of Europe's most extraordinary merchants, demonstrated the opportunities and risks of new forms of trade (Figure 10.7). Son of a furrier, he married the daughter of a royal official and served as a tax official until he was caught minting coins with less valuable metals. He then founded a trading company that competed with Italians and Spaniards in dealing with the Middle East. He visited Damascus to buy spices, setting up a regular trade in rugs, Chinese silk, and Indonesian spices and sugar. He also became financial advisor and supplier to the French king and was ennobled. With the largest fleet ever

Figure 10.7 *Jacques Coeur*

owned by a French subject, Coeur surrounded himself with splendor, even arranging with the pope for his 16-year-old son to become an archbishop. But he had enemies, many of them nobles in debt to him, and they turned the king against him. Tortured, he admitted to various crimes, including supplying weapons to Muslims. His property was confiscated, but, adventurer to the last, he died on a Greek island while serving in a papal fleet against the Turks.

By world standards this was not a totally unprecedented merchant spirit. European traders were still less venturesome and less wealthy than some of their Muslim counterparts. Nor was Western society as tolerant of merchants as Muslim or Indian societies were. Yet Western commercial endeavors clearly were growing. Because Western governments were weak, with few economic functions, merchants had a freer hand than in many other civilizations. Many of the growing cities were ruled by commercial leagues. Monarchs liked to encourage the cities as a counterbalance to the power of the landed aristocracy, and in the later Middle Ages and beyond, traders and kings typically were allied. However, aside from taxing merchants and using them as sources of loans, royal governments did not interfere much with trading activities. Merchants even developed their own codes of commercial law, administered by city courts. Thus, the rising merchant class, though not unusual in strength or venturesomeness, was staking out an unusually powerful and independent role in European society.

Capitalism was not yet typical of the Western economy, even aside from the moral qualms fostered by the Christian tradition. Most peasants and landlords had not become enmeshed in the market system. In the cities, the dominant economic ethic stressed group protection, not profitmaking. The characteristic institution was not the international trading firm but the merchant or artisan guild. **Guilds** grouped people in the same business or trade in a single city, sometimes with loose links to similar guilds in other cities. These organizations were new in western Europe, although they resembled guilds in various parts of Asia but with greater independence from the state. They stressed security and mutual control. Merchant guilds thus attempted to give all members a share in any endeavor. If a ship pulled in loaded with wool, the clothiers' guild of the city insisted that all members participate in the purchase so that no one member would monopolize the profits.

Artisan guilds were made up of the people in the cities who actually made cloth, bread, jewelry, or furniture. These guilds tried to limit their membership so that all members would have work. They regulated apprenticeships to guarantee good training but also to ensure that no member would employ too many apprentices and so gain undue wealth. They discouraged new methods because security and a rough equality, not maximum individual profit, were the goals; here was their alternative to the capitalistic approach. Guilds also tried to guarantee quality so that consumers would not have to worry about shoddy quality on the part of some unscrupulous profit-seeker. Guilds played an important political and social role in the cities, giving their members recognized status and often a voice in city government. Their statutes were in turn upheld by municipal law and often backed by the royal government as well.

Despite the traditionalism of the guilds, manufacturing and commercial methods improved in medieval Europe. Western Europe was not yet as advanced as Asia in ironmaking and textile manufacture, but it was beginning to catch up. In a few areas, such as clockmaking—which involved both

Document

Changing Roles for Women

A late-14th-century Parisian manual titled *The Good Wife* revealed the kind of thinking about gender that became more pronounced as medieval society developed in the West. It invites comparison with patriarchal views you have studied in other agricultural civilizations. Is any room left for initiatives by women?

> Wherefore I counsel you to make such cheer to your husband at all his comings and stayings, and to persevere therein; and also be peaceable with him, and remember the rustic proverb, which saith that there be three things which drive the goodman from home, to wit, a leaking roof, a smoky chimney, and a scolding woman. And therefore, fair sister, I beseech you that you keep yourself in the love and good favour of your husband, you be unto him gentle, and amiable, and debonair. Do unto him what the good simple women of our country say hath been done to their sons, when these have set their love elsewhere and their mothers cannot wean them therefrom.
>
> Wherefore, dear sister, I beseech you thus to bewitch and bewitch again your husband that shall be, and beware of roofless house and of smoky fire, and scold him not,

but be unto him gentle and amiable and peaceable. Have a care that in winter he have a good fire and smokeless and let him rest well and be well covered between your breasts, and thus bewitch him....

And thus shall you preserve and keep your husband from all discomforts and give him all the comforts whereof you can bethink you, and serve him and have him served in your house, and you shall look to him for outside things, for if he be good he will take even more pains and labour therein than you wish, and by doing what I have said, you will cause him ever to miss you and have his heart with you and your loving service and he will shun all other houses, all other women, all other services and households.

Questions: Is this a distinctively Christian view of women? How does it compare with Muslim or Chinese views of women in the postclassical period? Why might postclassical values about women have become more rigorous in the late medieval centuries in the West?

---

sophisticated technology and a concern for precise time initially linked to the schedule of church services—European artisans led the world. Furthermore, some manufacturing spilled beyond the bounds of guild control. Particularly in the Low Countries and parts of Italy, groups of manufacturing workers were employed by capitalists to produce for a wide market. Their techniques were simple, and they worked in their own homes, often alternating manufacturing labor with agriculture. Their work was guided not by the motives of the guilds but by the inducements of merchant capitalists, who provided them with raw materials and then paid them for their production.

Thus, by the later Middle Ages western Europe's economy and society embraced many contradictory groups and principles. Commercial and capitalist elements jostled against the slower pace of economic life in the countryside and even against the dominant group protectionism of most urban guilds. Most people remained peasants, but a minority had escaped to the cities, where they found more excitement, along

with increased danger and higher rates of disease. Medieval tradition held that a serf who managed to live in the city for a year and a day became a free person. A few prosperous capitalists flourished, but most people operated according to very different economic values, directed toward group welfare rather than individual profit. This was neither a static society nor an early model of a modern commercial society. It had its own flavor and its own tensions—the fruit of several centuries of economic and social change.

Limited Sphere for Women

The increasing complexity of medieval social and economic life may have had one final effect, which is familiar from patterns in other agricultural societies: new limits on the conditions of women. Women's work remained vital in most families. The Christian emphasis on the equality of all souls and the practical importance of women's monastic groups in providing an alternative to marriage continued to have distinctive effects on women's lives in Western society.

The veneration of Mary and other female religious figures gave women real cultural prestige, counterbalancing the biblical emphasis on Eve as the source of human sin. In some respects, women in the West had higher status than their sisters under Islam: They were less segregated in religious services (although they could not lead them) and were less confined to the household. Still, women's voice in the family may have declined in the Middle Ages. Urban women often played important roles in local commerce and even operated some craft guilds, but they found themselves increasingly hemmed in by male-dominated organizations. By the late Middle Ages, a literature arose that stressed women's roles as the assistants and comforters to men, listing supplemental household tasks and docile virtues as women's distinctive sphere. Patriarchal structures seemed to be taking deeper root.

The Decline of the Medieval Synthesis

 Amid new problems of overpopulation and disease, the postclassical version of Western civilization declined after 1300. This decline was evident in the feudal aristocracy, the church, and theology.

After about 1300, some of the characteristics of medieval life at its height began to give way. The international community was affected as strong monarchies consolidated their holdings and adjusted state boundaries (Map 10.2). One problem, both a symptom and a cause of larger issues, was the major war that engulfed France and England during the 14th and 15th centuries. The Hundred Years' War, which sputtered into the mid-15th century, lasted even longer than its name and initially went very badly for France—a sign of new weakness in the French monarchy (Figure 10.8). Not very bloody, the war ultimately demonstrated the futility of some of the military and organizational methods attached to feudalism. As the war dragged on, kings reduced their reliance on the prancing forces of the nobility in favor of paid armies of their own. New military methods challenged the key monopoly of the feudal lords, as ordinary paid archers learned how to unseat armored knights with powerful bows and arrows and

with crossbows. The war ended with a French victory, sparked in part by the heroic leadership of the inspired peasant woman Joan of Arc, but both its devastation and the antifeudal innovations it encouraged suggested a time of change.

Concurrently, from about 1300 onward, key sources of Western vitality threatened to disappear. Medieval agriculture could no longer keep pace with population growth: The readily available new lands had been used up, and there were no major new technological gains to compensate. The result included severe famines and a decline in population levels until the end of the century. A devastating series of plagues that persisted for several centuries, beginning with the **Black Death** in 1348, further challenged Europe's population and social structure (Figure 10.9). New social disputes arose, heightening some of the tensions noted earlier between peasants and landlords, artisans and their employees. Not until the 16th century would the West begin to work out a new social structure. The West's economy did not go into a tailspin; in some respects, as in manufacturing and mining technology, progress may even have accelerated. The 150 to 200 years after 1300 form in Western history a transition period in which the features of the Middle Ages began to blur while new problems and developments began to take center stage. Western civilization was not in a spiral of decline, but the postclassical version of this civilization was.

Signs of Strain

The decline of medieval society involved increasing challenges to several typical medieval institutions. Decline was not absolute but rather a sign of change, as Western society began to shed part of its earlier skin only to emerge, with renewed dynamism, in somewhat different garb by the middle of the 15th century. During the 14th century, the ruling class of medieval society, the land-owning aristocracy, began to show signs of confusion. It had long staked its claim to power on its control of land and its military prowess, but its skill in warfare was now open to question. The growth of professional armies and new weaponry such as cannon and gunpowder made traditional fighting methods, including fortified castles, increasingly irrelevant. The aristocracy did not simply disappear, however. Rather, the nobility chose to emphasize a rich ceremonial style of life, featuring

Map 10.2 *Western Europe Toward the End of the Middle Ages, c. 1360 C.E. Near the end of the postclassical period, strong monarchies had consolidated their holdings, and boundaries between states were coming into sharper focus.*

tournaments in which military expertise could be turned into competitive games. The idea of chivalry—carefully controlled, polite behavior, including behavior toward women—gained ground. The upper class became more cultivated. We have seen similar transformations in the earlier Chinese and Muslim aristocracy. Yet at this transitional point in Europe, some of the elaborate ceremonies of chivalry seemed rather hollow, even a bit silly—a sign

that medieval values were losing hold without being replaced by a new set of purposes.

Another key area involved decisive shifts in the balance between church and state that had characterized medieval life. For several decades in the aftermath of the taxation disputes in the early 14th century, French kings wielded great influence on the papacy, which they relocated from Rome to Avignon, a town surrounded by French territory. Then rival

Figure 10.8 *In the Hundred Years' War, English archers fought France's feudal cavalry; this was the beginning of the end of feudal warfare in Europe. This 14th-century battle of Crécy was a resounding defeat for France's noble army, although it outnumbered the English army. Why did this kind of warfare threaten feudalism?*

claimants to the papacy confused the issue further. Ultimately a single pope was returned to Rome, but the church was clearly weakened. Moreover, the church began to lose some of its grip on Western religious life. Church leaders were so preoccupied with their political involvement that they tended to neglect the spiritual side. Religion was not declining; indeed, signs of intense popular piety continued to blossom, and new religious groups formed in the towns. But devotion became partially separated from the institution of the church. One result, again beginning in the

14th century, was a series of popular heresies, with leaders in places such as England and Bohemia (the present-day Czech Republic) preaching against the hierarchical apparatus of the church in favor of direct popular experience of God. Another result was an important new series of mystics, many of them women, who claimed direct, highly emotional contacts with God.

A third area in which medievalism faded was the breakdown of the intellectual and even artistic synthesis. After the work of Aquinas, the sterile philo-

Figure 10.9 *Burying plague victims in coffins at Tournai before mass burial became the only way to keep up with the deaths. The 14th-century Black Death was a massive shock to European society.*

sophical pursuits of the later scholastics seemed petty. Church officials became less tolerant of intellectual daring, and they even declared some of Aquinas's writings heretical. The earlier blend of rationalism and religion no longer seemed feasible. Ultimately, this turned some thinkers away from religion, but this daring development took time. In art, growing interest in realistic portrayals of nature, though fruitful, suggested the beginnings of a shift away from medieval artistic standards. Religious figures became less stylized as painters grew more interested in human features for their own sake. The various constraints on forms of postclassical culture prompted many Western intellectuals to look for different emphases. In Italy most clearly, new kinds of literature and art took shape that differed from the styles and subjects of the postclassical centuries.

The Postclassical West and Its Heritage

Medieval Europe had several faces. The term *Middle Ages* implies a lull, between the glories of Rome and the glitter of more modern Europe. There is some truth to this, for medieval Europe did grapple with backwardness and vulnerability.

But the Middle Ages were also a period of growing dynamism. Particularly after 900 C.E., gains in

population, trade and cities, and intellectual activity created a vigorous period in European history. Key developments set a tone that would last even after the specifically medieval centuries had ended. Universities and Gothic art (often intertwined, as in the many American campuses that revived the Gothic style for their buildings) were an enduring legacy to Western society. Distinctive ideas about government, building on Christian and feudal traditions, constituted another medieval contribution.

The medieval period was also a special moment in the relationship between Europe and the regions around it. Significant change in the relationship occurred during the period, as Europe gained strength. But the opportunities to advance by imitation were particularly striking, from technology to science to trade and consumption. Even the medieval university may have had Arab origins, in the higher schools of the Muslim world. Imitation, indeed, unites the themes of the medieval period: the relative weakness but also the dynamism and the capacity to contribute durable themes to later periods in world history.

Medieval Europe warrants a particular comparison with other areas in which civilization was partially new during the postclassical period and where change and imitation proceeded rapidly. Divided political rule in Europe resembled conditions in west Africa and Japan (the only other feudal society in the period). Imitation targets can be compared among Europe, Africa, Japan, and Russia. But the Crusades suggest a distinctive expansionist spirit in Europe that also warrants attention, in suggesting a more aggressive interest in the wider world than the other emerging societies.

GLOBAL CONNECTIONS: Medieval Europe and the World

Western Europe in the Middle Ages developed something of a love-hate relationship with the world around it. During the early centuries of the Middle Ages, Europe seemed at the mercy of invasions, from the Vikings in the north or various nomadic groups pushing in from central Asia. European leaders were also keenly aware of the power of Islam, which controlled most of the Mediterranean including Spain. Most Europeans saw Islam as a dangerously false religion and an obvious threat.

At the same time, there was much to be learned from this wider world. During the Middle Ages Europeans actively copied a host of features from Islam, from law to science and art. They imported products and technologies from Asia. This process of imitation accelerated during the centuries of Mongol control, when European traders and travelers eagerly pushed into eastern Asia. A key question for Europe at the end of the Middle Ages involved how to gain greater control over the benefits that came from world contacts, while reducing the sense of threat. Partly through weakness, partly because of the advantages that Europeans learned from contact, the new civilization developed an active sense of global awareness.

Further Readings

For the Middle Ages generally, Joseph Strayer's *Western Europe in the Middle Ages* (1982) is a fine survey with an extensive bibliography. Key topics are covered in R. S. Lopez's *The Commercial Revolution of the Middle Ages, 950–1350* (1976) and C. H. Lawrence's *Medieval Monasticism: Forms of Religious Life in Western Europe in the Middle Ages* (1984). National histories are important for the period, particularly on political life; see J. W. Baldwin's *The Government of Philip Augustus: Foundations of French Royal Power in the Middle Ages* (1986); G. Barraclough's *The Origins of Modern Germany* (1984); and M. Chibnall's *Anglo-*

Norman England, 1066–1166 (1986). R. Barlett, *The Making of Medieval Europe* (1992), suggests that Western civilization was the product of cross-cultural fertilization.

Social history has dominated much recent research on the period. See P. Ariès and G. Duby, eds., *A History of Private Life*, vol. 2 (1984), and Barbara Hanawalt, *The Ties That Bound: Peasant Families in Medieval England* (1986), for important orientation in this area. David Herlihy's *Medieval Households* (1985) is a vital contribution, as is J. Chapelot and R. Fossier's *The Village and House in the Middle Ages* (1985). J. Kirshner and S. F. Wemple, eds., *Women of the Medieval World* (1985), is a good collection. On tensions in popular religion, see C. Bynum's *Jesus as Mother: Studies in the Spirituality of the High Middle Ages* (1982) and L. Little's *Religious Poverty and the Profit Economy in Medieval Europe* (1978). A highly readable account of medieval life is E. Leroy Ladurie's *Montaillou: The Promised Land of Error* (1979).

Several excellent studies take up the theme of technological change: J. Gimpel's *The Medieval Machine: The Industrial Revolution of the Middle Ages* (1977); Lynn White Jr.'s *Medieval Technology and Social Change* (1962); and David Landes' *Revolution in Time: Clocks and the Making of the Modern World* (1985). On environmental impact, see Roland Bechmann, *Trees and Man: The Forest in the Middle Ages* (1990).

On intellectual and artistic life, E. Gilson's *History of Christian Philosophy in the Middle Ages* (1954) is a brilliant sketch, and his *Reason and Revelation* (1956) focuses on key intellectual issues of the age. S. C. Ferruolo's *The Origins of the University* (1985) and N. Pevsner's *An Outline of European Architecture* (1963) deal with other important features; see also H. Berman's *Law and Revolution: The Formation of the Western Legal Tradition* (1983). On contacts, see Khalil Semaan, *Islam and the Medieval West: Aspects of Intercultural Relations* (1980). An intriguing classic, focused primarily on culture, is J. Huizinga's *The Waning of the Middle Ages* (1973).

On the Web

The postclassical period of the West witnessed the beginning of a new world order as well as the decline and collapse of the old one. This was visible in the patterns of daily life examined at http://www.learner.org/exhibits/middleages/.

New political systems were emerging to meet new conditions, as exemplified by the career of Charlemagne (http://www.humnet.ucla.edu/santiago/histchrl.html), and by the writing of the later English Magna Carta (http://www.archives.gov/exhibit_hall/featured_documents/magna_carta/ and http://www.yale.edu/lawweb/avalon/medieval/magframe.htm).

Manorial life underwent changes and new economic relations emerged as the monetization of labor (http://www1.enloe.wake.k12.nc.us/enloe/CandC/showme/trading.html) undermined the tradition of serfdom in Western Europe (http://www.fordham.edu/halsall/source/manumission.html and http://courses.washington.edu/balt/SCAND344/celms.htm).

The value, nature, and sources of human knowledge were also being reevaluated in the works of men such as Peter Abelard (http://www.fordham.edu/halsall/source/abelard-sel.html and http://justus.anglican.org/resources/bio/142.html), Thomas Aquinas (http://www.utm.edu/research/iep/a/aquinas.htm), and those pursuing new avenues in both European and Islamic medicine and science (http://members.aol.com/McNelis/medsci_index.html).

This was not a period that witnessed the advancement of the position of women, but insight into the lives of medieval women, ordinary and extraordinary, can be found at http://www.womeninworldhistory.com/heroine3.html, http://www.umilta.net/, http://library.thinkquest.org/12834/text/distaffside.html, http://www.smu.edu/ijas/ and http://www2.sunysuffolk.edu/westn/essaymedieval.html#Women%20in%20Childbirth.

The Black Death had an impact on all facets of life in the Middle Ages. It can be explored at http://www.iath.virginia.edu/osheim/intro.html, http://www.nytimes.com/books/first/o/oldstone-viruses.html, http://www.brown.edu/Departments/Italian_Studies/dweb/plague/origins/spread.shtml, http://www.byu.edu/ipt/projects/middleages/LifeTimes/Plague.html, and http://www.fidnet.com/~weid/plague.htm.

CHAPTER 11

THE AMERICAS ON THE EVE OF INVASION

The Toltec political and cultural influence spread from its capital at Tula in northern Mexico (shown here as it looks today) to places as far south as Chichén Itzá in Yucatan. The warriors shown here served as columns to support the roof of this large temple.

- Postclassic Mesoamerica, 1000–1500 C.E.
- Aztec Society in Transition
- DOCUMENT: Aztec Women and Men
- IN DEPTH: The "Troubling" Civilizations of the Americas
- Twantinsuyu: World of the Incas
- VISUALIZING THE PAST: Archeological Evidence of Political Practices
- The Other Indians
- GLOBAL CONNECTIONS: The Americas and the World

In central Mexico on the last day of the year and the end of the 52-year cycle of the religious calendar, all the fires in the land, in every temple and in every humble home, were extinguished. At a small temple, not far from today's Mexico City, a prisoner was sacrificed and a new fire kindled on his body. If the gods honored their prayers and the fire took hold, runners would then light their torches in the new flames and carry the fire to every town and village. Life would continue at least for another 52-year cycle, until at some point the gods would create a great cataclysm to destroy the world, as had happened four times in the past.

Some of these concepts and practices of the Aztec peoples of central Mexico were widely shared by many peoples in the Americas. They represent the distinctive cultural processes of the Americas that had continued to develop in the postclassic period after 900 C.E.

By 1500, the Americas were densely populated in many places by Indian peoples long indigenous to the New World. Of course, the term **Indian** is derived from a mistake Columbus made when he thought he had reached the Indies, what Europeans called India and the lands beyond, but the label is also misleading because it implies a common identity among the peoples of the Americas that did not exist until after the arrival of Europeans. *Indian* as a term to describe all the peoples of the Americas could have a meaning only when there were non-Indians from which to distinguish them. Still, the term has been used for so long—and is still in use by many Native Americans today—that we will continue to use it.

As should already be clear, there were many Indian peoples with a vast array of cultural achievements. The variety of cultural patterns and ways of life of pre-Columbian civilizations makes it impossible to discuss each in detail here, but we can focus on a few areas where major civilizations developed, based on earlier achievements. By concentrating on these regions, we can demonstrate the continuity of civilization in the Americas. We shall examine in some detail Mesoamerica, especially central Mexico, and the Andean heartland. In both these areas great imperial states were in place when European expansion brought them into direct contact with the Old World. We shall also discuss in less detail a few areas influenced by the centers of civilization—and some whose development seems to have been independent of them—to provide an overview of the Americas on the eve of invasion.

239

900 C.E.	1150 C.E.	1300 C.E.	1450 C.E.
900 End of Intermediate Horizon and decline of Tihuanaco and Huari	**1150** Fall of Tula, disintegration of Toltec Empire	**1325** Aztecs established in central Mexico; Tenochtitlan founded	**1471–1493** Inca Topac Yupanqui increases areas under control
900–1465 Chimor Empire based on Chan Chan on north coast	**1200–1500** Mississipian culture flourishes	**1350** Incas established in Cuzco area	**1493–1527** Huayna Capac expands into Ecuador; his death results in civil war
968 Tula established by Toltecs		**1434** Creation of triple alliance	**1502–1520** Moctezuma II
1000 Toltec conquest of Chichén Itzá and influence in Yucatan		**1434–1471** Great expansion under Inca Pachacuti	
		1434–1472 Rule of Nezhualcoyotl at Texcoco	
		1438 Incas dominate Cuzco and southern highlands	
		1440–1469 Moctezuma I	

Postclassic Mesoamerica, 1000–1500 C.E.

 Chief among the civilizations that followed the collapse of Teotihuacan and the abandonment of the classic Maya cities in the 8th century C.E. were the Toltecs and later the Aztecs, who built on the achievements of their predecessors but rarely surpassed them except in political and military organization. The Toltecs created a large empire whose influence extended far beyond central Mexico. In the 15th century, the Aztecs rose from humble beginnings to create an extensive empire organized for war, motivated by religious zeal, and based on a firm agrarian base.

With the collapse of Teotihuacan in central Mexico and the abandonment of the classical Maya cities in the 8th century C.E., Mesoamerica experienced significant political and cultural change. In central Mexico, nomadic peoples from the north took advantage of the political vacuum to move into the richer lands. Among these peoples were the Toltecs, who established a capital at Tula about 968. **Toltec culture** adopted many features from the sedentary peoples and added a strongly militaristic ethic. This included the cult of sacrifice and war that is often portrayed in Toltec art. Later Mesoamerican peoples, such as the Aztecs, had some historical memory of the Toltecs and thought of them as the givers of civilization. However, the archeological record indicates that Toltec accomplishments often were fused or confused with those of Teotihuacan in the memory of the Toltecs' successors.

The Toltec Heritage

Among the legends that survived about the Toltecs were those of **Topiltzin,** a Toltec leader and apparently a priest dedicated to the god **Quetzalcoatl** (the Feathered Serpent) who later became confused with the god himself in the legends. Apparently, Topiltzin, a religious reformer, was involved in a struggle for priestly or political power with another faction. When he lost, Topiltzin and his followers went into exile, promising to return to claim his throne on the same date, according to the cyclical calendar system. Supposedly, Topiltzin and his followers sailed for Yucatan; there is much evidence of Toltec influence in that region. The legend of Topiltzin–Quetzalcoatl was well known to the Aztecs and may have influenced their response when the Europeans arrived.

The Toltecs created an empire that extended over much of central Mexico, and their influence spread from their capital, Tula, to areas as far away as Guatemala. About 1000 C.E., Chichén Itzá in Yucatan was conquered by Toltec warriors, and it and several other cities were ruled for a long time by central Mexican dynasties or by Maya rulers under Toltec influence.

Toltec influence spread northward as well. Obsidian was mined in northern Mexico, and the Toltecs may have traded for turquoise in the American Southwest. It has been suggested that the great Anasazi adobe town at Chaco Canyon in New Mexico was abandoned when the Toltec Empire fell and the trade in local turquoise ended.

How far eastward Toltec influence spread is a matter of dispute. Was there contact between Mesoamerica and the elaborate culture and concentrated towns of the Hopewell peoples of the Ohio and Mississippi valleys? Scholars disagree. Eventually, in the lower Mississippi valley from about 700 C.E., elements of Hopewell culture seem to have been enriched by external contact, perhaps with Mexico. This Mississippian culture, which flourished between 1200 and 1500 C.E., was based on maize and bean agriculture. Towns, usually located along rivers, had stepped temples made of earth, and sometimes large burial mounds. Some of the burials include well-produced pottery and other goods and seem to be accompanied by ritual executions or sacrifices of servants or wives. This indicates social stratification in the society. Cahokia, near East St. Louis, Illinois, covered 5 square miles and may have had more than 30,000 people in and around its center. Its largest earthen pyramid, now called Monk's Mound, covers 15 acres and is comparable in size to the largest pyramids of the classic period in Mexico. Many of these cultural features seem to suggest contact with Mesoamerica.

The Aztec Rise to Power

The Toltec Empire lasted until about 1150, when it apparently was destroyed by nomadic invaders from the north, who also seem to have sacked Tula about that time. The center of population and political power in central Mexico shifted to the valley of Mexico and especially to the shores of the large chain of lakes in that basin. These provided a rich aquatic environment. The shores of the lakes were dotted with settlements and towns and supported a dense population. Of the approximately 3000 square miles in the basin of the valley, about 400 square miles were under water. The lakes became the cultural heartland and population center of Mexico in the postclassic period. In the unstable world of post-Toltec Mesoamerica, various peoples and cities jockeyed for control of the lakes. The winners of this struggle, the Aztecs (or, as they called themselves, the *Mexica*), eventually built a great empire, but when they emerged on the historical scene they were the most unlikely candidates for power.

The Aztec rise to power and formation of an imperial state was as spectacular as it was rapid. According to some of their legends, the Mexica had once inhabited the central valley and had known agriculture and the "civilized" life but had lived in exile to the north in a place called Aztlan (from whence we get the name *Aztec*). This may be an exaggeration by people who wanted to lay claim to a distinguished heritage. Other sources indicate that the Aztecs were simply one of the nomadic tribes that used the political anarchy, after the fall of the Toltecs, to penetrate the area of sedentary agricultural peoples. Like the ancient Egyptians, the Aztecs rewrote history to suit their purposes.

What seems clear is that the Aztecs were a group of about 10,000 people who migrated to the shores of Lake Texcoco (Map 11.1) in the central valley of Mexico around 1325. After the fall of the Toltec Empire, the central valley was inhabited by a mixture of peoples: Chichimec migrants from the northwest and various groups of sedentary farmers. In this period, the area around the lake was dominated by several tribes or peoples organized into city-states. Much like medieval Europe, this was a world of political maneuver and state marriages, competing powers and shifting alliances. These political units claimed authority on the basis of their military power and

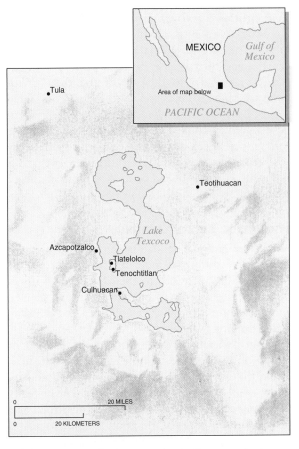

Map 11.1 *Central Mexico and Lake Texcoco. An aquatic environment at the heart of the Aztec empire.*

their connections to Toltec culture. Many of these peoples spoke Nahuatl, the language the Toltecs had spoken. The Aztecs also spoke this language, a fact that made their rise to power and their eventual claims to legitimacy more acceptable.

An intrusive and militant group, the Aztecs were distrusted and disliked by the dominant powers of the area, but their fighting skills could be put to use, and this made them attractive as mercenaries or allies. For about a century the Aztecs wandered around the shores of the lake, being allowed to settle for a while and then driven out by more powerful neighbors.

In a period of warfare, the Aztecs had a reputation as tough warriors and fanatical followers of their gods, to whom they offered human sacrifices. This reputation made them both valued and feared. Their own legends held that their wanderings would end when they saw an eagle perched on a cactus with a serpent in its beak. Supposedly, this sign was seen on a marshy island in Lake Texcoco, and there, on that island and one nearby, the Mexica settled. The city of **Tenochtitlan** was founded about 1325.

From this secure base the Aztecs began to take a more active role in regional politics. Serving as mercenaries and then as allies brought prosperity to the Aztecs, especially to their ruler and the warrior nobles, who took lands and tribute from conquered towns. By 1428 Aztecs had emerged as an independent power. In 1434, Tenochtitlan created an alliance with two other city-states that controlled much of the central plateau. In reality, Tenochtitlan and the Aztecs dominated their allies and controlled the major share of the tribute and lands taken.

The Aztec Social Contract

Aztec domination extended from the Tarascan frontier about a hundred miles north of present-day Mexico City southward to the Maya area. Subject peoples were forced to pay tribute, surrender lands, and sometimes do military service for the growing Aztec Empire.

Aztec society had changed in the process of expansion and conquest. From a loose association of clans, the Mexica had become a stratified society under the authority of a supreme ruler. The histories were rewritten and the Mexica were described as a people chosen to serve the gods. Human sacrifice, long a part of Mesoamerican religion, greatly expanded into an enormous cult in which the military class played a central role as suppliers of war cap-

tives to be used as sacrificial victims. A few territories were left unconquered so that periodic "flower wars" could be staged in which both sides could obtain captives for sacrifice. Whatever the religious motivations of this cult, the Aztec rulers manipulated it as an effective means of political terror. By the time of Moctezuma II, the Aztec state was dominated by a king who represented civil power and served as a representative of the gods on earth. The cult of human sacrifice and conquest was united with the political power of the ruler and the nobility.

Religion and the Ideology of Conquest

Aztec religion incorporated many features that had long been part of the Mesoamerican belief system. Religion was a vast, uniting, and sometimes oppressive force in which little distinction was made between the world of the gods and the natural world. The traditional deities of Mesoamerica—the gods of rain, fire, water, corn, the sky, and the sun, many of whom had been worshiped as far back as the time of Teotihuacan—were venerated among the Aztecs. There were at least 128 major deities, but there seemed to be many more: Each deity had a female consort or feminine form because a basic duality was recognized in all things. Moreover, gods might have different forms or manifestations, somewhat like the avatars of the Hindu deities. Each god had at least five aspects, each associated with one of the cardinal directions and the center. Certain gods were thought to be the patrons of specific cities, ethnic groups, or occupations.

This extensive pantheon was supported by a round of yearly festivals and ceremonies that involved feasting and dancing along with penance and sacrifice. This complex array of gods can be organized into three major themes or cults. The first were the gods of fertility and the agricultural cycle, such as **Tlaloc,** the god of rain (called *Chac* by the Maya), and the gods and goddesses of water, maize, and fertility. A second group centered on the creator deities, the great gods and goddesses who had brought the universe into being. The story of their actions played a central role in Aztec cosmography. Much Aztec abstract and philosophical thought was devoted to the theme of creation. Finally, the cult of warfare and sacrifice built on the preexisting Mesoamerican traditions that had been expanding since Toltec times and, under the militaristic Aztec state, became the cult of the state. **Huitzilopochtli,** the Aztec tribal patron, became the central figure of this cult.

The Aztecs revered the great traditional deities—such as Tlaloc and Quetzalcoatl, the ancient god of civilization—so holy to the Toltecs, but their own tribal deity, Huitzilopochtli, was paramount. The Aztecs identified him with the old sun god, and they saw him as a warrior in the daytime sky fighting to give life and warmth to the world against the forces of the night. To carry out that struggle, the sun needed strength, and just as the gods had sacrificed themselves for humankind, the nourishment the gods needed most was that which was most precious: human life in the form of hearts and blood. The great temple of Tenochtitlan was dedicated to both Huitzilopochtli and Tlaloc. The tribal deity of the Aztecs and the ancient agricultural god of the sedentary peoples of Mesoamerica were thus united.

In fact, although human sacrifice had long been a part of Mesoamerican religion, it expanded considerably in the postclassic period of militarism. Warrior cults and the militaristic images of jaguars and eagles devouring human hearts were characteristic of Toltec art. The Aztecs simply took an existing tendency and carried it further. Both the types and frequency of sacrifice increased, and a whole symbolism and ritual, which included ritual cannibalism, developed as part of the cult (Figure 11.1). How much of Aztec sacrifice was the result of religious conviction and how much was a tactic of terror and political control by the rulers and priests is still open to debate.

Beneath the surface of this polytheism, there was also a sense of spiritual unity. **Nezhualcoyotl,** the king of Texcoco, wrote hymns to the "lord of the close vicinity," an invisible creative force that supported all the gods. Yet his conception of a kind of monotheism, much like that of Pharaoh Akhnaten in Egypt, appears to have been too abstract and never gained great popularity.

Although the bloody aspects of Aztec religion have gained much attention, we must also realize that the Aztecs concerned themselves with many of the great religious and spiritual questions that have preoccupied other civilizations: Is there life after death? What is the meaning of life? What does it mean to live a good life? Do the gods really exist?

Nezhualcoyotl, whose poetry survived in oral form and was written down in the 16th century, wondered about life after death:

> Do flowers go to the land of the dead?
>
> In the Beyond, are we dead or do we still live?
>
> Where is the source of light, since that which gives life hides itself?

Figure 11.1 *Human sacrifice was practiced by many Mesoamerican peoples, but the Aztecs apparently expanded its practice for political and religious reasons.*

As in the Vedas of ancient India, he also wondered about the existence of the gods:

Are you real, are you fixed?

Only You dominate all things

The Giver of Life.

Is this true?

Perhaps, as they say, it is not true.

Aztec religious art and poetry are filled with images of flowers, birds, and song, all of which the Aztecs greatly admired, as well as human hearts and blood, the "precious water" needed to sustain the gods. This mixture of images makes the symbolism of Aztec religion difficult for modern observers to appreciate.

Aztec religion depended on a complex mythology that explained the birth and history of the gods and their relationship to peoples, and on a religious symbolism that infused all aspects of life. As we have seen, the Mesoamerican calendar system was religious, and many ceremonies coincided with particular points in the calendar cycle. Moreover, the Aztecs also believed in a cyclical view of history, and that the world had been destroyed four times before and would be destroyed again. Thus, there was a certain fatalism in Aztec thought and a premonition that eventually the sacrifices would be insufficient and the gods would again bring catastrophe.

Tenochtitlan: The Foundation of Heaven

The Aztecs considered their capital city a sacred space, or as they called it, the "foundation of Heaven." The city-state with its ruler–spokesman was a key central Mexican concept, and it applied to Tenochtitlan. It became a great metropolis, with a central zone of palaces and whitewashed temples, as shown in Figure 11.2. This zone was surrounded by adobe brick residential districts, smaller palaces, and markets. The design and construction were outstanding. Hernán Cortés, the Spanish conqueror who viewed the city, reported, "The stone masonry and the woodwork are equally good; they could not be bettered anywhere." There were gardens, and a zoo was kept for the ruler's enjoyment. The nobility had houses two stories high, sometimes with gardens on the roofs. Tlatelolco also had impressive temples and palaces, and its large market was the most important place of trade and exchange. By 1519, the city covered about 5 square miles. It had a population of 150,000, larger than contemporary European cities such as Seville and Paris.

Its island location gave Tenochtitlan a peculiar character. Set in the midst of a lake, the city was connected to the shores by four broad causeways and was crisscrossed by canals that allowed the constant canoe traffic on the lake access to the city. Each city ward, controlled by a **calpulli,** or kin group, maintained its

Figure 11.2 *The great Aztec capital of Tenochtitlan was dominated by the pyramid and twin temples of Huitzilopochtli, shown here in a modern miniature reconstruction.*

neighborhood temples and civic buildings. The structural achievement was impressive. A Spanish foot soldier who saw it in 1519 wrote,

> Gazing on such wonderful sights, we did not know what to say, or whether what appeared before us was real, for on one side, on the land, there were great cities, and in the lake ever many more, and the lake was crowded with canoes, and in the causeway were many bridges at intervals, and in front of us stood the great city of Mexico.

Tenochtitlan was the heart of an empire and drew tribute and support from its allies and dependents, but in theory it was still just a city-state ruled by a headman, just like the 50 or more other city-states that dotted the central plateau. Present-day Mexico City rises on the site of the former Aztec capital.

Feeding the People: The Economy of the Empire

Feeding the great population of Tenochtitlan and the Aztec confederation in general depended on traditional forms of agriculture and on innovations developed by the Aztecs. Lands of conquered peoples often were appropriated, and food sometimes was demanded as tribute. In and around the lake, however, the Aztecs adopted an ingenious system of irrigated agriculture by building **chinampas** for agriculture. These were beds of aquatic weeds, mud, and earth that had been placed in frames made of cane and rooted to the lake floor. They formed artificial floating islands about 17 feet long and 100 to 330 feet wide. This narrow construction allowed the water to reach all the plants, and willow trees were also planted at intervals to give shade and help fix the roots. Much of the land of Tenochtitlan itself was chinampa in origin, and in the southern end of the lake, more than 20,000 acres of chinampas were constructed. The yield from chinampa agriculture was high: Four corn crops a year were possible. Apparently, this system of irrigated agriculture had been used in preclassic days, but a rise in the level of the lakes had made it impossible to continue. After 1200, however, lowering water levels once again stimulated chinampa construction, which the Aztecs carried out on a grand scale.

Production by the Aztec peasantry, whom we see at work in Figure 11.3, and tribute provided the basic foods. In each Aztec community, the local clan apportioned the lands, some of which were also set

Figure 11.3 *Agriculture was the basis of Aztec society, and a diet centered on maize sustained the dense populations of the Valley of Mexico. The plow was unknown, and planting was done with a digging stick.*

aside for support of the temples and the state. In addition, individual nobles might have private estates, which were worked by servants or slaves from conquered peoples. Each community had periodic markets—according to various cycles in the calendar system, such as every 5 and 13 days—in which a wide variety of goods were exchanged. Cacao beans and gold dust sometimes were used as currency, but much trade was done as barter. The great market at Tlatelolco operated daily and was controlled by the special merchant class, or **pochteca,** which specialized in long-distance trade in luxury items such as plumes of tropical birds and cacao. The markets were highly regulated and under the control of inspectors and special judges. Despite the importance of markets, this was not a market economy as we usually understand it.

The state controlled the use and distribution of many commodities and redistributed the vast amounts of tribute received from subordinate peoples. Tribute levels were assigned according to whether the subject peoples had accepted Aztec rule or had fought against it. Those who surrendered paid less. Tribute payments, such as food, slaves, and sacrificial victims, served political and economic ends. More than 120,000 mantles of cotton cloth alone were collected as tribute each year and sent to Tenochtitlan. The Aztec state redistributed these goods. After the original conquests, it rewarded its nobility richly, and the commoners received far less.

Aztec Society in Transition

 Aztec society became more hierarchical as the empire grew and social classes with different functions developed, although the older organization based on the calpulli never disappeared. Tribute was drawn from subject peoples, but Aztec society confronted technological barriers that made it difficult to maintain the large population of central Mexico.

Widening Social Gulf

During their wanderings, the Aztecs had been divided into seven calpulli, or clans, a form of organization that they later expanded and adapted to their imperial position. The calpulli were no longer only kinship groups but also residential groupings, which might include neighbors, allies, and dependants. Much of Aztec local life was based on the calpulli, which performed important functions such as distributing land to heads of households, organizing labor gangs and military units in times of war, and maintaining a temple and school. Calpulli were governed by councils of family heads, but not all families were equal, nor were all calpulli of equal status.

The calpulli obviously had been the ancient and basic building block of Aztec society. In the origins of Aztec society every person, noble and commoner, had belonged to a calpulli, but Aztec power increased and the rule of the empire expanded. The calpulli had been transformed, and other forms of social stratification had emerged. As Aztec power expanded, a class of nobility emerged, based on certain privileged families in the most distinguished calpulli. Originating from the lineages that headed calpulli and from marriages, military achievements, or service to the state, this group of nobles accumulated high offices, private lands, and other advantages. The most prominent families in the calpulli, those who had dominated leadership roles and formed a kind of local nobility, eventually were overshadowed by the military and administrative nobility of the Aztec state.

Although some commoners might be promoted to noble status, most nobles were born into the class. Nobles controlled the priesthood and the military leadership. In fact, the military was organized into various ranks based on experience and success in taking captives (Figure 11.4). Military virtues were linked to the cult of sacrifice and infused the whole society; they became the justification for the nobility's status. The "flowery death," or death while taking prisoners for the sacrificial knife, was the fitting end to a noble life and ensured eternity in the highest heaven—a reward also promised to women who died in childbirth. The military was highly ritualized. There were orders of warriors: The Jaguar and Eagle "Knights" and other groups each had a distinctive uniform and ritual and fought together as units. Banners, cloaks, and other insignia marked off the military ranks.

The social gulf that separated the nobility from the commoners was widening as the empire grew. Egalitarian principles that may have existed in Aztec life disappeared, as happened among the warring German tribes of early medieval Europe. Social distinctions were made apparent by the use of and restrictions on clothing, hairstyles, uniforms, and other symbols of rank. The imperial family became the most distinguished of the pipiltin families.

As the nobility broke free from their old calpulli and acquired private lands, a new class of workers almost like serfs was created to serve as laborers on these lands. Unlike the commoners attached to the land-controlling calpulli, these workers did not control land and worked at the will of others. Their status was low, but it was still above that of the slaves, who might have been war captives, criminals, or peo-

Figure 11.4 *In the militarized society of the Aztec Empire, warriors were organized into regiments and groups distinguished by their uniforms. They gained rank and respect by capturing enemies for sacrifice. Note the symbolic gripping of the defeated captives' hair as a sign of military success.*

ple who had sold themselves into bondage to escape hunger. Finally, there were other social groups. The scribes, artisans, and healers all were part of an intermediate group that was especially important in the larger cities. The long-distance merchants formed a sort of calpulli with their own patron gods, privileges, and internal divisions. They sometimes served as spies or agents for the Aztec military, but they were subject to restrictions that hindered their entry into or rivalry with the nobility.

It is possible to see an emerging conflict between the nobility and the commoners and to interpret this as a class struggle, but some specialists emphasize that to interpret Aztec society on that basis is to impose Western concepts on a different reality. Corporate bodies such as the calpulli, temple maintenance associations, and occupational groups cut across class and remained important in Aztec life. Competition between corporate groups often was more apparent and more violent than competition between social classes.

Overcoming Technological Constraints

Membership in society was defined by participation in various wider groups, such as the calpulli or a specific social class, and by gender roles and definitions. Aztec women assumed a variety of roles. Peasant women helped in the fields, but their primary domain was the household, where child-rearing and cooking took up much time. Above all, weaving skill was highly regarded. The responsibility for training young girls fell on the older women. Marriages often were arranged between lineages, and virginity at marriage was highly regarded for young women. Polygamy existed among the nobility, but the peasants were monogamous. Aztec women could inherit property and pass it to their heirs. The rights of Aztec women seem to have been fully recognized, but in political and social life their role, though complementary to that of men, remained subordinate.

The technology of the Americas limited social development in a variety of ways. Here we can see a significant difference between the lives of women in Mesoamerica and in the Mediterranean world. In the maize-based economies of Mesoamerica, women spent six hours a day grinding corn by hand on stone boards, or *metates*, to prepare the household's food. Although similar hand techniques were used in ancient Egypt, they were eventually replaced by animal- or water-powered mills that turned wheat into flour. The miller or baker of Rome or medieval Europe could do the work of hundreds of women. Maize was among the simplest and most productive cereals to grow but among the most time-consuming to prepare. Without the wheel or suitable animals for power, the Indian civilizations were unable to free women from the 30 to 40 hours a week that went into preparing the basic food.

Finally, we must consider the size of the population of the Aztec state. Estimates have varied widely, from as little as 1.5 million to more than 25 million, but there is considerable evidence that population density was high, resulting in a total population that was far greater than previously suspected. Some historical demographers estimate that the population of central Mexico under Aztec control reached over 20

Document

Aztec Women and Men

In the mid-16th century, Bernardino de Sahagún, a Spanish missionary, prepared an extraordinary encyclopedia of Aztec culture. His purpose was to gather this information to learn the customs and beliefs of the Indians and their language in order to better convert them. Although Sahagún hated the Indian religion, he came to admire many aspects of their culture. His work, *The General History of the Things of New Spain*, is one of the first ethnographies and a remarkable compendium of Aztec culture. Sahagún used many Indian informants to tell him about the days before the European arrival, and even though this work dates from the postconquest era, it contains much useful information about earlier Aztec life.

In the following excerpts, the proper behavior for people in different roles in Aztec society are described by the Aztecs themselves.

Father

One's father is the source of lineage. He is the sincere one. One's father is diligent, solicitous, compassionate, sympathetic, a careful administrator of his household. He rears, he teaches others, he advises, he admonishes one. He is exemplary; he leads a model life. He stores up for himself; he stores up for others. He cares for his assets; he saves for others. He is thrifty; he saves for the future, teaches thrift. He regulates, distributes with care, establishes order.

The bad father is incompassionate, negligent, unreliable. He is unfeeling ... a shirker, a loafer, a sullen worker.

Mother

One's mother has children; she suckles them. Sincere, vigilant, agile, she is an energetic worker—diligent, watchful, solicitous, full of anxiety. She teaches people; she is attentive to them. She caresses, she serves others; she is apprehensive for their welfare; she is careful, thrifty—constantly at work.

The bad mother is evil, dull, stupid, sleepy, lazy. She is a squanderer, a petty thief, a deceiver, a fraud. Unreliable, she is one who loses things through neglect or anger, who heeds no one. She is disrespectful, inconsiderate, disregarding, careless. She shows the way to disobedience; she expounds nonconformity.

The Rulers

The ruler is a shelter—fierce, revered, famous, esteemed, well-reputed, renowned.

The good ruler is a protector: one who carries his subjects in his arms, who unites them, who brings them together. He rules, he takes responsibilities, assumes burdens. He carries his subjects in his cape; he bears them in his arms. He governs; he is obeyed. To him as a shelter, as refuge, there is recourse....

The bad ruler is a wild beast, a demon of the air, an ocelot, a wolf—infamous, avoided, detested as a respecter of nothing. He terrifies with his gaze; he makes the earth rumble; he implants; he spreads fear. He is wished dead.

The Noble

The noble has a mother, a father. He resembles his parents. The good noble is obedient, cooperative, a follower of his parents' ways, a discreet worker; attentive, willing. He follows the ways of his parents; he resembles his father; he becomes his father's successor; he assumes his lot.

One of noble lineage is a follower of the exemplary life, a taker of the good example of others, a seeker, a follower of the exemplary life. He speaks eloquently; he is soft-spoken, virtuous, deserving of gratitude. He is noble of heart, gentle of word, discreet, well-reared, well-taught. He is moderate, energetic, inquiring, inquisitive. He scratches the earth with a thorn. He is one who fasts, who starves his entrails, who parches his lips. He provides nourishment to others. He sustains one, he serves food, he provides comfort. He is a concealer [of himself], a belittler of himself. He magnifies and praises others. He is a mourner for the dead, a doer of penances, a gracious speaker, devout, godly, desirable, wanted, memorable.

The bad noble is ungrateful and forgetful, a debaser, a disparager of things, contemptuous of others, arrogant, bragging. He creates disorder, glories over his lineage, extols his own virtues.

The Mature Common Woman

The good mature woman is candid. She is resolute, firm of heart, constant—not to be dismayed; brave like a man; vigorous, resolute, persevering—not one to falter. She is long-suffering; she accepts reprimands calmly—endures things like a man. She becomes firm—takes courage. She is intent. She gives of herself. She goes in humility. She exerts herself.

The bad woman is thin, tottering, weak—an inconstant companion, unfriendly. She annoys others, chagrins them, shames, oppresses one. She becomes impatient; she loses hope, becomes embarrassed—chagrined. Evil is her life; she lives in shame.

The Weaver of Designs

She concerns herself with using thread, works with thread. The good weaver of designs is skilled—a maker of varicolored capes, an outliner of designs, a blender of colors, a joiner of pieces, a matcher of pieces, a person of good memory. She does things dexterously. She weaves designs. She selects. She weaves tightly. She forms borders. She forms the neck....

The bad weaver of designs is untrained—silly, foolish, unobservant, unskilled of hand, ignorant, stupid. She tangles the thread, she harms her work—she spoils it.

The Physician

The physician is a knower of herbs, of roots, of trees, of stones; she is experienced in these. She is one who conducts examinations; she is a woman of experience, of trust, of professional skill: a counselor.

The good physician is a restorer, a provider of health, a relaxer—one who makes people feel well, who envelops one in ashes. She cures people; she provides them health; she lances them; she bleeds them ... pierces them with an obsidian lancet.

Questions: In what ways do the expectations for men and women differ in Aztec society? To what extent do the roles for men and women in Aztec society differ from our own? Did the Aztecs value the same characteristics as our own and other historical societies?

million, excluding the Maya areas. This underlines the extraordinary ability of the Aztec state to intimidate and control such vast numbers of people.

A Tribute Empire

Each city-state was ruled by a speaker chosen from the nobility. The Great Speaker, the ruler of Tenochtitlan, was first among supposed equals. He was in effect the emperor, with great private wealth and public power, and was increasingly considered a living god. His court was magnificent and surrounded with elaborate rituals. Those who approached him could not look him in the eye and were required to throw dirt upon their heads as a sign of humility. In theory he was elected, but his election was really a choice between siblings of the same royal family. The prime minister held a position of tremendous power and usually was a close relative of the ruler. There was a governing council; in theory, the rulers of the other cities in the alliance also had a say in government, but in reality most power was in the hands of the Aztec ruler and his chief advisor.

During a century of Aztec expansion, a social and political transformation had taken place. The position and nature of the old calpulli clans had changed radically, and a newly powerful nobility with a deified and nearly absolute ruler had emerged. The ancient cult of military virtues had been elevated to a supreme position as the religion of the state, and the double purpose of securing tribute for the state and obtaining victims for Huitzilopochtli drove further Aztec conquests.

The empire was never integrated, and local rulers often stayed in place to act as tribute collectors for the Aztec overlords. In many ways the Aztec Empire was

simply an expansion of long-existing Mesoamerican concepts and institutions of government, and it was not unlike the subject city-states over which it gained control. These city-states, in turn, were often left unchanged if they recognized Aztec supremacy and met their obligations of labor and tribute. Tribute payments served both an economic and a political function, concentrating power and wealth in the Aztec capital. Archeologists at the recent excavations of the Great Temple beneath the center of Mexico City have been impressed by the large number of offerings and objects that came from the farthest ends of the empire and beyond. At the frontiers, neighboring states such as the Tarascans of Michoacan preserved their freedom, while within the empire independent kingdoms such as Tlaxcala maintained a fierce opposition to the Aztecs. There were many revolts against Aztec rule or a particular tribute burden, which the Aztecs often put down ruthlessly.

In general, the Aztec system was a success because it aimed at exerting political domination and not necessarily direct administrative or territorial control. In the long run, however, the increasing social stresses created by the rise of the nobles and the system of terror and tribute imposed on subject peoples were internal weaknesses that contributed to the Aztec Empire's collapse.

The Aztecs were a continuation of the long process of civilization in Mesoamerica. The civilizations of the classic era did not simply disappear in central Mexico or among the Maya in Yucatan and Central America, but they were reinterpreted and adapted to new political and social realities. When Europeans arrived in Mexico, they assumed that what they found was the culmination of Indian civilization, when in fact it was the militarized afterglow of earlier achievements.

In Depth

The "Troubling" Civilizations of the Americas

From the first encounter with the peoples of the Americas, European concepts and judgments about civilization, barbarism, morality, power, politics, and justice were constantly called into question. The American Indian societies had many religious ideas and practices that shocked Christian observers, and aspects of their social and familial arrangements clashed with European sensibilities. Those sensibilities often were influenced by religious and political considerations. Many of those who most condemned human sacrifice, polygamy, or the despotism of Indian rulers were also those who tried to justify European conquest and control, mass violence, and theft on a continental scale. Other European voices also were heard. Not long after the Spanish conquests in the 16th century, defenders of Indian rights came forward to argue that despite certain "unfortunate" habits, Indian civilization was no less to be admired than that of the ancient (and pagan) Romans and Greeks.

For Western civilization, evaluating and judging non-Western or past societies has always been a complex business that has mixed elements of morality, politics, religion, and self-perception along with the record of what is observed or considered to be reality. That complexity is probably just as true for Chinese, Persian, or any culture trying to understand another. Still, Western society seems to have been particularly troubled by the American civilizations, with their peculiar combination of Neolithic technology and imperial organization. At times this has led to abhorrence and rejection—as of Aztec sacrifice—but at other times it has led to a kind of utopian romanticism in which the accomplishments of the Indian past are used as a critique of the present and a political program for the future.

The existence of **Inca socialism** is a case in point. Some early Spanish authors portrayed Inca rule as despotic, but others saw it as a kind of utopia. Shortly after the conquest of Peru, Garcilaso de la Vega, the son of a Spaniard and an Indian noblewoman, wrote a glowing history of his mother's people in which he presented an image of the Inca Empire as a carefully organized system in which every community contributed to the whole and the state regulated the distribution of resources on the basis of need and reciprocity. There was some truth in this view, but it ignored some aspects of exploitation as well. In the 20th century, Peruvian socialists, faced with underdevelopment and social inequality in their country, used this utopian view of Inca society as a possible model for their own future. Their interpretation and that of historians who later wrote of Inca socialism tended to ignore the hierarchy in the Inca Empire and the fact that the state extracted labor and goods from the subject communities to support the nobles, who held extensive power. The utopian view of the Incas was no less political than the despotic view. Perhaps the lesson here is that what we see in the past often depends on what we think about the present or what we want for the future.

But if Inca socialism and despotism have fascinated students of the past, Aztec religion has caught the imagination of historians and the general public. It causes us to ask how a civilization as advanced as this could engage in a practice so cruel and, to us, so morally reprehensible. Perhaps nothing challenges our appreciation of the American civilizations more than the extensive evidence of ritual torture and human sacrifice, which among the Aztecs reached staggering proportions. On some occasions thousands of people were slain, usually by having their hearts ripped out.

First, we must put these practices in perspective. Cruelty and violence can be found in many cultures, and to a world that has seen genocide, mass killings, and atomic warfare, the Aztec practices are not so different from what our own age has seen. Certain customs in many past civilizations and present cultures seem to us strange, cruel, and immoral. We find Aztec human sacrifice particularly abhorrent, but such practices also were found among the ancient Canaanites and the Celtic peoples, and the Old Testament story of Abraham and Isaac, though its message is against such sacrifice, reflects a known practice. Human sacrifice was practiced in pre-Christian Scandinavia and ancient India. Although by the time of Confucius human sacrifice of wives and retainers at the burial of a ruler was no longer practiced in China, the custom had been known. The issue of sati, the Hindu ritual suicide of the widow on the funeral pyre of her husband, raged in India in the 19th century. The Aztecs certainly were not alone in taking human life as a religious rite. Whatever our moral judgments about such customs, it remains the historian's responsibility to understand them in the context of their own culture and time.

How have historians tried to explain or understand Aztec human sacrifice? Some defenders of

Aztec culture have seen it as a limited phenomenon, greatly exaggerated by the Spanish for political purposes. Many scholars have seen it as a religious act central to the Aztec belief that humans must sacrifice that which was most precious to them—life—to receive the sun, rain, and other blessings of the gods that make life possible. Others have viewed Aztec practice as the intentional manipulation and expansion of a widespread phenomenon that had long existed among many American peoples. In other words, the Aztec rulers, priests, and nobility used the cult of war and large-scale human sacrifice for political purposes, to terrorize their neighbors and subdue the lower classes. Another possible explanation is demographic. If central Mexico was as densely populated as we believe, then the sacrifices may have been a kind of population control.

Other interpretations have been even more startling. Anthropologist Marvin Harris has suggested that Aztec sacrifice, accompanied by ritual cannibalism, was a response to a lack of protein. He argued that in the Old World, human sacrifice was replaced by animal sacrifice, but in Mesoamerica, which lacked cattle and sheep, that transformation never took place. Harris called the Aztec Empire a "cannibal kingdom." Other scholars have strongly objected to Harris' interpretation of the evidence, which gave little attention to the ritual aspects of these acts. Still, human sacrifice shades all assessments of Aztec civilization.

These debates ultimately raise important questions about the role of moral judgments in historical analysis and the way in which our vision of the past is influenced by our own political, moral, ethical, and social programs. We cannot and perhaps should not abandon those programs, but we must always try to understand other times and other peoples in their own terms.

Questions: What special features of Aztec civilization must be explained? Are they really distinctive? What explanations are most persuasive in terms of historical sensitivity and contemporary standards? Are there features of 21st-century society that are similar to those of Aztec civilization and that later generations will need to explain?

Twantinsuyu: World of the Incas

 After about 1300 C.E. in the Andean cultural hearth, a new civilization emerged and eventually spread its control over the whole region. The Inca empire, or **Twantinsuyu**, was a highly centralized system that integrated various ethnic groups into an imperial state. Extensive irrigated agriculture supported a state religion and a royal ancestor cult. With notable achievements in architecture and metallurgy, the Incas, like the Aztecs, incorporated many elements of the civilizations that preceded them.

Almost at the same time that the Aztecs extended their control over much of Mesoamerica, a great imperial state was rising in the Andean highlands, and it eventually became an empire some 3000 miles in extent (Map 11.2). The Inca Empire incorporated many aspects of previous Andean cultures but fused them together in new ways. With a genius for state organization and bureaucratic control over peoples of different cultures and languages, it achieved a level of integration and domination previously unknown in the Americas.

Throughout the Andean cultural hearth, after the breakup of the large "intermediate horizon" states of Tihuanaco and Huari (c. 550–1000 C.E.), several smaller regional states continued to exercise some power. Unlike the breakdown of power that took place in postclassic Mesoamerica, in the Andean zone many large states continued to be important. Some states in the Andean highlands on the broad open areas near Lake Titicaca and the states along rivers on the north coast, such as those in the Moche valley, remained centers of agricultural activity and population density. This was a period of war between rival local chiefdoms and small states and in some ways was an Andean parallel to the post-Toltec militaristic era in Mesoamerica. Of these states, the coastal kingdom of Chimor, centered on its capital of Chan-Chan, emerged as the most powerful. Between 900 and its conquest by the Incas in 1465, it gained control of most of the north coast of Peru.

The Inca Rise to Power

While Chimor spread its control over 600 miles of the coast, in the southern Andean highlands, where there were few large urban areas, ethnic groups and

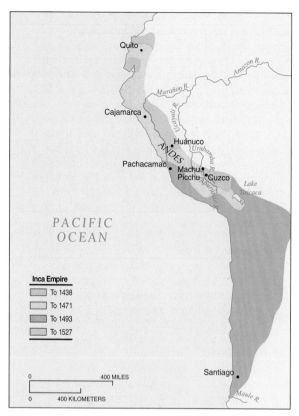

Map 11.2 *Inca Expansion. Each ruler expanded the empire in a series of campaigns to increase wealth and political control.*

politics struggled over the legacy of Tihuanaco. Among these groups were several related Quechua-speaking clans, or ayllus, living near Cuzco, an area that had been under the influence of Huari but had not been particularly important. Their own legends stated that 10 related clans emerged from caves in the region and were taken to Cuzco by a mythical leader. Wherever their origins, by about 1350 C.E. they lived in and around Cuzco, and by 1438 they had defeated their hostile neighbors in the area. At this point under their ruler, or *inca*, **Pachacuti** (r. 1438–1471), they launched a series of military alliances and campaigns that brought them control of the whole area from Cuzco to the shores of Lake Titicaca.

Over the next 60 years, Inca armies were constantly on the march, extending control over a vast territory. Pachacuti's son and successor, Topac Yupanqui, conquered the northern coastal kingdom of Chi-

mor by seizing its irrigation system, and he extended Inca control into the southern area of what is now Ecuador. At the other end of the empire, Inca armies reached the Maule River in Chile against stiff resistance from the Araucanian Indians. The next ruler, Huayna Capac (r. 1493–1527) consolidated these conquests and suppressed rebellions on the frontiers. By the time of his death, the Inca Empire—or, as they called it, Twantinsuyu—stretched from what is now Colombia to Chile and eastward across Lake Titicaca and Bolivia to northern Argentina. Between 9 and 13 million people of different ethnic backgrounds and languages came under Inca rule, a remarkable feat, given the extent of the empire and the technology available for transportation and communication.

Conquest and Religion

What impelled the Inca conquest and expansion? The usual desire for economic gain and political power that we have seen in other empires is one possible explanation, but there may be others more in keeping with Inca culture and ideology. The cult of the ancestors was extremely important in Inca belief. Deceased rulers were mummified and then treated as intermediaries with the gods, paraded in public during festivals, offered food and gifts, and consulted on important matters by special oracles. From the Chimor kingdom the Incas adopted the practice of royal **split inheritance,** whereby all the political power and titles of the ruler went to his successor but all his palaces, wealth, land, and possessions remained in the hands of his male descendants, who used them to support the cult of the dead Inca's mummy for eternity. To ensure his own cult and place for eternity, each new Inca needed to secure land and wealth, and these normally came as part of new conquests. In effect, the greater the number of past Inca rulers, the greater the number of royal courts to support and the greater the demand for labor, lands, and tribute. This system created a self-perpetuating need for expansion, tied directly to ancestor worship and the cult of the royal mummies, as well as tensions between the various royal lineages. The cult of the dead weighed heavily on the living.

Inca political and social life was infused with religious meaning. Like the Aztecs, the Incas held the sun to be the highest deity and considered the Inca to be the sun's representative on earth. The magnif-

Visualizing the Past

Archeological Evidence of Political Practices

The Inca system of split inheritance probably originated in the Chimu kingdom. Chimu king lists recorded 10 rulers' names. Excavations at Chan-Chan, the Chimu capital, have revealed 10 large walled structures. Archeologists believe that each of these palatial compounds was a different king's residence and that each became a mausoleum for his mummy upon his death.

Questions: To what extent does such evidence indicate the composite nature of Inca culture? What are some of the possible problems of archeological interpretation? To what extent can material remains be used to explain or illustrate social phenomena?

City of Chan-Chan

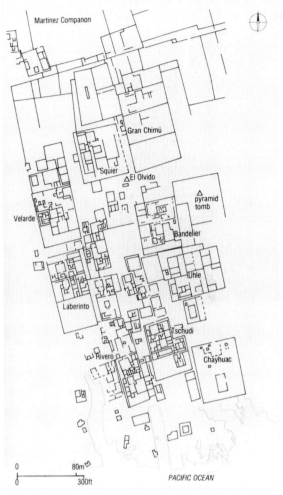

Chan-Chan covered more than 2 square miles. It contained palace compounds, storehouses, residences, markets, and other structures.

icent **Temple of the Sun** in Cuzco was the center of the state religion, and in its confines the mummies of the past Incas were kept. The cult of the sun was spread throughout the empire, but the Inca did not prohibit the worship of local gods.

Other deities were also worshiped as part of the state religion. Viracocha, a creator god, was a favorite of Inca Pachacuti and remained important. Popular belief was based on a profound animism that endowed many natural phenomena with spiritual power. Mountains, stones, rivers, caves, tombs, and

temples were considered to be **huacas,** or holy shrines. At these places, prayers were offered and animals, goods, and humans were sacrificed. In the Cuzco area, imaginary lines running from the Temple of the Sun organized the huacas into groups for which certain ayllus took responsibility. The temples were served by many priests and women dedicated to preparing cloth and food for sacrifice. The temple priests were responsible mainly for the great festivals and celebrations and for the divinations on which state actions often depended.

The Techniques of Inca Imperial Rule

The Inca were able to control their vast empire by using techniques and practices that ensured cooperation or subordination. The empire was ruled by the inca, who was considered almost a god. He ruled from his court at Cuzco, which was also the site of the major temple; the high priest usually was a close relative. Twantinsuyu was divided into four great provinces, each under a governor, and then divided again. The Incas developed a state bureaucracy in which almost all nobles played a role. Although some chroniclers spoke of a state organization based on decimal units of 10,000, 1000, 100, and smaller numbers of households to mobilize taxes and labor, recent research reveals that many local practices and variations were allowed to continue under Inca rule. Local rulers, or **curacas,** were allowed to maintain their positions and were given privileges by the Inca in return for their loyalty. The curacas were exempt from tribute obligations and usually received labor or produce from those under their control. For insurance, the sons of conquered chieftains were taken to Cuzco for their education.

The Incas intentionally spread the Quechua language as a means of integrating the empire. The Incas also made extensive use of colonists. Sometimes Quechua-speakers from Cuzco were settled in a newly won area to provide an example and a garrison. On other occasions, the Incas moved a conquered population to a new home. Throughout the empire, a complex system of roads was built, with bridges and causeways when needed (Map 11.3). Along these roads, way stations, or **tambos,** were placed about a day's walk apart to serve as inns, storehouses, and supply centers for Inca armies on the move. Tambos also served as relay points for the system of runners who carried messages throughout the empire. The Inca probably maintained more than 10,000 tambos.

The Inca Empire extracted land and labor from subject populations. Conquered peoples were enlisted in the Inca armies under Inca officers and were rewarded with goods from new conquests. Subject peoples received access to goods not previously available to them, and the Inca state undertook large building and irrigation projects that formerly would have been impossible. In return, the Incas demanded loyalty and tribute. The state claimed all resources and redistributed them. The Incas divided conquered

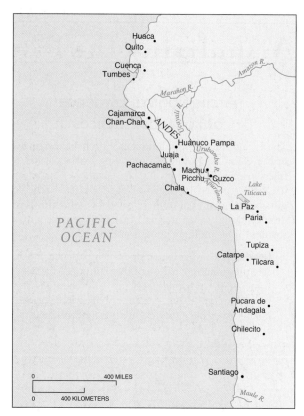

Map 11.3   *The Ancient Cities of Peru. The Inca system of roads, with its series of tambos, linked major towns and cities and allowed rapid communication and troop movement.*

areas into lands for the people, lands for the state, and lands for the sun—that is, for religion and the support of priests. Also, some nobles held private estates.

With few exceptions the Incas, unlike the Aztecs, did not demand tribute in kind but rather exacted labor on the lands assigned to the state and the religion. Communities were expected to take turns working on state and church lands and sometimes on building projects or in mining. These labor turns, or **mita,** were an essential aspect of Inca control. In addition, the Inca required women to weave high-quality cloth for the court and for religious purposes. The Incas provided the wool, but each household was required to produce cloth. Woven cloth, a great Andean art form, had political and religious significance. Some women were taken as concubines for the Inca; others were selected as servants at the temples, the so-called Virgins of the Sun. In all this, the Inca had an overall imperial system but remained sensitive to local variations, so that its application accommodated regional and ethnic differences.

In theory, each community aimed at self-sufficiency and depended on the state for goods it could not acquire easily. The ayllus of each community controlled the land, and the vast majority of the men were peasants and herders. Women worked in the fields, wove cloth, and cared for the household. Roles and obligations were gender specific and theoretically equal and interdependent. Andean peoples recognized parallel descent, so that property rights within the ayllus and among the nobility passed in both the male and female lines. Women passed rights and property to daughters, men to sons. Whether in pre-Inca times women may have served as leaders of ayllus is open to question, but under the Incas this seems to have been uncommon. The Inca emphasis on military virtues reinforced the inequality of men and women.

The concept of close cooperation between men and women was also reflected in the Inca view of the cosmos. Gods and goddesses were worshiped by men and women, but women felt a particular affinity for the moon and the goddesses of the earth and corn: the fertility deities. That special link was recognized in rituals such as that illustrated in Figure 11.5. The inca queen, the inca's senior wife (usually also a sister of the inca), was seen as a link to the moon. Queen and sister of the sun, she represented imperial authority to all women. But despite an ideology of gender equality, Inca practice created a gender hierarchy that paralleled the dominance of the Inca state over subject peoples. This fact is supported, and the power of the empire over local ethnic groups is demonstrated, by the Incas' ability to select the most beautiful young women to serve the temples or be given to the inca.

The integration of imperial policy with regional and ethnic diversity was a political achievement. Ethnic headmen were left in place, but over them were administrators drawn from the Inca nobility in Cuzco. Reciprocity and hierarchy continued to characterize Andean groups as they came under Inca rule; reciprocity between the state and the local community was simply an added level. The Inca state could provide roads, irrigation projects, and hard-to-get goods. For example, maize usually was grown on irrigated land and was particularly important as a ritual crop. State-sponsored irrigation added to its cultivation. The Inca state manipulated the idea of reciprocity to extract labor power, and it dealt harshly

Figure 11.5 *The role of women in Inca agriculture is emphasized in this 17th-century drawing of the symbolic irrigation of the fields. Complex Inca irrigation systems permitted the farming of steep hillsides and marginal lands.*

with resistance and revolt. In addition to the ayllu peasantry, there was also a class of people, the **yanas**, who were removed from their ayllus and served permanently as servants, artisans, or workers for the Inca or the nobility.

Members of the Inca nobility were greatly privileged, and those related to the inca himself held the highest positions. The nobility were all drawn from the 10 royal ayllus. In addition, the residents of Cuzco were given noble status to enable them to serve in high bureaucratic posts. The nobles were distinguished by dress and custom. Only they were entitled to wear the large ear spools that enlarged the ears and caused the Spaniards to later call them *orejones*, or "big ears." Noticeably absent in most of the Inca Empire was a distinct merchant class. Unlike in Mesoamerica, where long-distance trade was so important, the Incas' emphasis on self-sufficiency and state regulation of production and surplus limited trade. Only in the northern areas of the empire, in the chiefdoms of Ecuador, the last region brought under Inca control, did a specialized class of traders exist.

The Inca imperial system, which controlled an area of almost 3000 miles, was a stunning achievement of statecraft, but like all other empires it lasted only as long as it could control its subject populations and its own mechanisms of government. A system of royal multiple marriages as a way of forging alliances created rival claimants for power and the possibility of civil war. That is exactly what happened in the 1520s, just before the Europeans arrived. When the Spanish first arrived in Peru, they saw an empire weakened by civil strife.

Inca Cultural Achievements

The Incas drew on the artistic traditions of their Andean predecessors and the skills of subject peoples. Beautiful pottery and cloth were produced in specialized workshops. Inca metalworking was among the most advanced in the Americas, and Inca artisans worked gold and silver with great skill. The Incas also used copper and some bronze for weapons and tools. Like the Mesoamerican peoples, the Incas made no practical use of the wheel, but unlike them, they had no system of writing. However, the Incas did use a system of knotted strings, or **quipu,** to record numerical and perhaps other information. It worked like an abacus, and with it the Incas took censuses and kept financial records. The Incas had a passion for numerical order, and the population was divided into decimal units from which population, military enlistment, and work details could be calculated. The existence of so many traits associated with civilization in the Old World combined with the absence of a system of writing among the Incas illustrates the variations of human development and the dangers of becoming too attached to certain cultural characteristics or features in defining civilizations.

The Incas' genius was best displayed in their land and water management, extensive road system, statecraft, and architecture and public buildings. They developed ingenious agricultural terraces on the steep slopes of the Andes, using a complex technology of irrigation to water their crops. The empire was linked together by almost 2500 miles of roads, many of which included rope suspension bridges over mountain gorges and rivers. Inca stonecutting was remark-

ably accurate; the best buildings were built of large fitted stones without the use of masonry. Some of these buildings were immense. These structures, the large agricultural terraces and irrigation projects, and the extensive system of roads were among the Incas' greatest achievements, displaying their technical ability as well as their ability to mobilize large amounts of labor.

Comparing Incas and Aztecs

The Inca and the Aztec cultures were based on a long development of civilization that preceded them. Although in some areas of artistic and intellectual achievement earlier peoples had surpassed their accomplishments, both cultures represented the success of imperial and military organization. Both empires were based on intensive agriculture organized by a state that accumulated surplus production and then controlled the circulation of goods and their redistribution to groups or social classes. In both states, older kinship-based institutions, the ayllu and the calpulli, were transformed by the emergence of a social hierarchy in which the nobility was increasingly predominant. In both areas, these nobles also were the personnel of the state, so that the state organization was almost an image of society.

Although the Incas tried to create an overarching political state and to integrate their empire as a unit (the Aztecs did less in this regard), both empires recognized local ethnic groups and political leaders and allowed variation from one group or region to another as long as Inca or Aztec sovereignty was recognized and tribute paid. Both the Aztecs and the Incas, like the Spaniards who followed them, found that their military power was less effective against nomadic peoples who lived on their frontiers. Essentially, the empires were created by the conquest of sedentary agricultural peoples and the extraction of tribute and labor from them.

We cannot overlook the great differences between Mesoamerica and the Andean region in terms of climate and geography or the differences between the Inca and Aztec civilizations. Trade and markets were far more developed in the Aztec Empire and earlier in Mesoamerica in general than in the Andean world. There were differences in metallurgy, writing systems, and social definition and hierarchy. But within the context of world civilizations, it is probably best to view these two empires and the cultural areas they represent as variations of similar patterns and processes, of which sedentary agriculture is the most important. Basic similarities underlying the variations can also be seen in systems of belief and cosmology and in social structure. Whether similar origins, direct or indirect contact between the areas, or parallel development in Mesoamerica and the Andean area explains the similarity is unknown. But the American Indian civilizations shared much with each other; that factor and their isolation from external cultural and biological influences gave them their peculiar character and their vulnerability. At the same time, their ability to survive the shock of conquest and contribute to the formation of societies after conquest demonstrates much of their strength. Long after the Aztec and Inca empires had ceased to exist, the peoples of the Andes and Mexico continued to draw on these cultural traditions.

The Other Indians

 The civilizations of Mesoamerica and the Andes, and the imperial states in place at the moment of contact with the wider world, were high points of an Indian cultural achievement cut short by contact and conquest. However, the Americas continued to be occupied by a wide variety of peoples who lived in different ways, ranging from highly complex sedentary agricultural empires to simple kin-based bands of hunters and gatherers.

Rather than a division between "primitive" and "civilized" Indians, it is more useful to consider gradations of material culture and social complexity. Groups such as the Incas had many things in common with the tribal peoples of the Amazon basin, such as the division into clans or halves—that is, a division of villages or communities into two major groupings with mutually agreed-upon roles and obligations. Moreover, as we have seen, the diversity of ancient America forces us to reconsider ideas of human development based on Old World examples. If social complexity is seen as dependant on an agricultural base for society, that theory is not supported by the existence in the Americas of some groups of fishers and hunters and gatherers, such as the Indians of the northwest coast of the United States and

British Columbia, who developed hierarchical societies. For those who see control of water for agriculture as the starting point for political authority and the state, such societies as the Pimas of Colorado and some of the chiefdoms of South America, who practiced irrigated agriculture but did not develop states, provide exceptions.

How Many Indians?

A major issue that has fascinated students of the Americas for centuries is the question of population size. For many years after the European conquests, many people discounted the early descriptions of large and dense Indian populations as the exaggeration of conquerors and missionaries who wanted to make their own exploits seem more impressive. In the early 20th century, the most repeated estimate of Indian population about 1492 was 8.4 million (4 million in Mexico, 2 million in Peru, and 2.4 million in the rest of the hemisphere). Since that time, new archeological discoveries, a better understanding of the impact of disease on indigenous populations, new historical and demographic studies, and improved estimates of agricultural techniques and productivity have led to major revisions. Estimates still vary widely, and some have gone as high as 112 million at the time of contact. Most scholars agree that Mesoamerica and the Andes supported the largest populations. Table 11.1 summarizes one of the most careful estimates, which places the total figure at more than 67

TABLE 11.1
A Population Estimate for the Western Hemisphere, 1492

Area	Population (thousands)
North America	4,400
Mexico	21,400
Central America	5,650
Caribbean	5,850
Andes	11,500
Lowland South America	18,500
Total	67,300

Sources: William M. Deneven, *The Native Population of the Americas in 1492* (1976), 289–292; John D. Durand, "Historical Estimates of World Population," *Population and Development Review* vol. 3 (1957), 253–296; Russell Thornton, *American Indian Holocaust and Survival* (1987).

million, although an American Indian demographer has increased this figure to 72 million. Other scholars are unconvinced by these estimates.

These figures should be considered in a global context. In 1500, the population of the rest of the world was probably about 500 million, of which China and India each had 75 to 100 million people and Europe had 60 to 70 million, a figure roughly equivalent to the population of the Americas (Table 11.2). If the modern estimates are valid, the peoples of the Americas clearly made up a major segment of humanity.

Differing Cultural Patterns

Although it is impossible to summarize the variety of cultural patterns and lifeways that existed in the Americas on the eve of contact, we can describe the major patterns outside the main civilization areas. Northern South America and part of Central America were an intermediate area that shared many features with the Andes and some with Mesoamerica and perhaps served as a point of cultural and material exchange between the two regions. In fact, with the exception of monumental architecture, the intermediate zone chieftainships resembled the sedentary agriculture states in many ways.

TABLE 11.2
World Population, c. 1500

Area	Population (thousands)
China	100,000–150,000
Indian subcontinent	75,000–150,000
Southwest Asia	20,000–30,000
Japan	15,000–20,000
Rest of Asia (except Russia)	15,000–30,000
Europe (except Russia)	60,000–70,000
Russia (USSR)	10,000–18,000
Northern Africa	6,000–12,000
Rest of Africa	30,000–60,000
Oceania	1,000–2,000
Americas	57,000–72,000
Total	389,000–614,000

Sources: William M. Deneven, *The Native Population of the Americas in 1492* (1976), 289–292; John D. Durand, "Historical Estimates of World Population," *Population and Development Review* vol. 3 (1957), 253–296; Russell Thornton, *American Indian Holocaust and Survival* (1987).

Similar kinds of chieftainships based on sedentary agriculture were found elsewhere in the Americas. There is strong evidence of large chieftainships along the Amazon, where the rich aquatic environment supported complex and perhaps hierarchical societies. The island Arawaks, encountered by Columbus on the Caribbean island of Hispaniola, were farmers organized in a hierarchical society and divided into chiefdoms. These Indian chiefdom-level societies strongly resemble the societies of Polynesia. On the bigger Caribbean islands, such as Hispaniola and Puerto Rico, chieftainships ruled over dense populations, which lived primarily on manioc.

Agriculture was spread widely throughout the Americas by 1500. Some peoples, such as those of the eastern North American woodlands and the coast of Brazil, combined agriculture with hunting and fishing. Techniques such as slash and burn farming led to the periodic movement of villages when production declined. Social organization in these societies often remained without strong class divisions, craft specializations, or the demographic density of people who practiced permanent, intensive agriculture. Unlike Europe, Asia, and Africa, the Americas lacked nomadic herders. However, throughout the Americas, from Tierra del Fuego to the Canadian forests, some people lived in small, mobile, kin-based groups of hunters and gatherers. Their material culture was simple and their societies were more egalitarian.

Nowhere is American Indian diversity more apparent than in North America. In that vast continent, by 1500, perhaps as many as 200 languages were spoken, and a variety of cultures reflected Indian adaptation to different ecological situations. By that time, most concentrated towns of the Mississippian mound-builder cultures had been abandoned, and only a few groups in southeastern North America still maintained the social hierarchy and religious ideas of those earlier cultures. In the Southwest, descendants of the Anasazi and other cliff dwellers had taken up residence in the adobe pueblos along the Rio Grande (Figure 11.6), where they practiced terracing and irrigation to support their agriculture. Their rich religious life, their artistic ceramic and weaving traditions, and their agricultural base reflected their own historical traditions.

Elsewhere in North America, most groups were hunters and gatherers or combined those activities with some agriculture. Sometimes an environment

Figure 11.6   *The pueblos of the Rio Grande valley like Taos or Acoma seen here reflected a number of the cultural traditions of the older Native American cultures of the southwestern United States.*

was so rich that complex social organization and artistic specialization could develop without an agricultural base. This was the case among the Indians of the northwest coast, who depended on the rich resources of the sea. In other cases, technology was a limiting factor. The tough prairie grasses could not be farmed easily without metal plows, nor could the buffalo be hunted effectively before Europeans introduced the horse. Thus, the Great Plains were only sparsely occupied.

Finally, we should note that although there was great variation among the Indian cultures, some aspects stood in contrast to contemporary societies in Europe and Asia. With the exception of the state systems of Mesoamerica and the Andes, most Indian societies were strongly kin based. Communal action and ownership of resources, such as land and hunting grounds, were emphasized, and material wealth often was disregarded or placed in a ritual or religious context. It was not that these societies were necessarily egalitarian but rather that ranking usu-

ally was not based on wealth. Although often subordinate, women in some societies held important political and social roles and usually played a central role in crop production. Indians tended to view themselves as part of the ecological system and not in control of it. These attitudes stood in marked contrast to those of many contemporary European and Asian civilizations.

American Indian Diversity in World Context

By the end of the 15th century, two great imperial systems had risen to dominate the two major centers of civilization in Mesoamerica and the Andes. Both empires were built on the achievements of their predecessors, and both reflected a militaristic phase in their area's development. These empires proved to be fragile, weakened by internal strains and the conflicts that any imperial system creates but also limited by their technological inferiority.

The Aztec and Inca empires were one end of a continuum of cultures that went from the most simple to the most complex. The Americas contained a broad range of societies, from great civilizations with millions of people to small bands of hunters. In many of these societies, religion played a dominant role in defining the relationship between people and their environment and between the individual and society. How these societies would have developed and what course the American civilizations might have taken in continued isolation remain interesting and unanswerable questions. The first European observers were simultaneously shocked by the "primitive" tribespeople and astounded by the wealth and accomplishments of civilizations such as that of the Aztecs. Europeans generally saw the Indians as curiously backward. In comparison with Europe and Asia, the Americas did seem strange—more like ancient Babylon or Egypt than contemporary China or Europe—except that without the wheel, large domesticated animals, the plow, and to a large extent metal tools and written languages, even that comparison is misleading. The isolation of the Americas had remained important in physical and cultural terms, but that isolation came to an end in 1492, with disastrous results.

GLOBAL CONNECTIONS: The Americas and the World

Conditions in the Americas before 1492 reveal the importance of global connections in Afro-Eurasia and of their absence in the Americas. American isolation from effective global connections shows in the absence of key technologies, like ironworking and the wheel, that would have been easily transmitted had contacts been available. It shows in the absence of the standard range of domesticated animals. It shows in the absence of any trace of any of the great world religions. It would show, tragically, in the absence of any immunity to some of the standard contagious diseases of Afro-Eurasia.

The absence of several features that had become normal in Afro-Eurasia must be stated carefully. It should not detract from the impressive economic, cultural, and political achievements of the key American Indian civilizations, including their ability (particularly in Mesoamerica) to sustain dense populations. It

should not obscure the heritage of these societies to later patterns in the Americas. The comparative distinctions that resulted from lack of wider contact would count only when the Americas were forced into new global connections after 1492—but then they mattered greatly.

Further Readings

Alvin M. Josephy, Jr.'s *The Indian Heritage of America* (2nd revised ed., 1991) is a broad, comprehensive history that deals with North and South America and provides much detail without being tedious. It is a logical starting point for further study. Freiderich Katz's *The Ancient Civilizations of the Americas* (2nd revised ed., 1997) provides the best overall survey that compares Mesoamerica and Peru. It traces the rise of civilization in both areas. Michael Coe et al., *Atlas of Ancient America* (1986), includes excellent maps, illustrations, and an intelligent and comprehensive text.

The literature on the Aztecs is growing rapidly. Sahagún's *Florentine Codex: The General History of the Things of New Spain*, Charles Dibble and Arthur J. O. Anderson, eds. and trans., 2 vols. (1950–1968) is a fundamental source. A good overview is Jacques Soustelle's *Daily Life of the Aztecs* (1961), but more recent is Frances Berdan's *The Aztecs of Central Mexico: An Imperial Society* (1982) and Inga Clendinnin, *Aztecs: An Interpretation* (1995). Miguel Leon-Portilla's *Aztec Thought and Culture* (1963) and *Fifteen Aztec Poets* (1992) deal with religion and philosophy in a sympathetic way. Burr Cartwright Brundage has traced the history of the Aztec rise in several books such as *A Rain of Darts* (1972); his *The Jade Steps* (1985) provides a good analysis of religion. Nigel Davies' *The Aztec Empire* (1987) is a political and social analysis. Susan D. Gillespie's *The Aztec Kings* (1989) views Aztec history in terms of myth.

On Peru, a good overview through solid scholarly articles is provided in Richard W. Keatinge, ed., *Peruvian Prehistory* (1988). The article on Inca archeology by Craig Morris is especially useful. Alfred Metraux's *The History of the Incas* (1970) is an older but still useful and very readable book. John Murra's *The Economic Organization of the Inca State* (1980) is a classic that has influenced much thinking about the Incas. J. Hyslop's *The Inca Road System* (1984) examines the building and function of the road network. The series of essays in John V. Murra, Nathan Wachtel, and Jacques Revel, eds., *Anthropological History of Andean Polities* (1986), shows how new approaches in ethnohistory are deepening our understanding of Inca society. Interesting social history is now being done. Irene Silverblatt's *Moon,*

Sun, and Witches: Gender Ideologies and Class in Inca and Colonial Peru (1987) is a controversial book on the position of women before, during, and after the Inca rise to power.

In Geoffrey W. Conrad and Arthur A. Demerest's *Religion and Empire: The Dynamics of Aztec and Inca Expansionism* (1984), two archeologists compare the political systems of the two empires and the motivations for expansion. The authors find more similarities than differences. Excellent studies on specific themes on Mexico and Peru are found in George A. Collier et al., eds., *The Inca and Aztec States, 1400–1800* (1982).

On the Web

The still vibrant, but soon to perish, worlds of the Aztecs (http://www.taisei.co.jp/cg_e/ancient_world/azteca/aazteca.html), Toltecs (http://emuseum.mnsu.edu/ prehistory/latinamerica/meso/cultures/toltec.html), Inca (http://loki.stockton.edu/~gilmorew/consorti/1fcenso.htm), and Maya (http://mayaruins.com/, http://mysteriousplaces.com/mayan/TourEntrance.html, and http://emuseum.mnsu.edu/prehistory/latinamerica/meso/cultures/maya.html) are well represented on the Internet. One of the last Mayan cities, Tulum, can be visited at http://www.geocities.com/RainForest/Vines/4273/index1.htm and http://www.d.umn.edu/cla/faculty/troufs/anth3618/matulum.html. Recent discoveries in ancient MesoAmerican culture are offered at http://www.archaeolink.com/central_american_archaeology.htm.

Child marriage and the complex family structure of the ancient Aztecs (Nahua) can be explored at http://www.hist.umn.edu/~rmccaa/index.html (scroll down to "Nahua Calli" and to "child marriage").

CHAPTER 12

REUNIFICATION AND RENAISSANCE IN CHINESE CIVILIZATION: THE ERA OF THE TANG AND SONG DYNASTIES

Manufacturing silk was a laborious process that involved several steps. Here a woman and a small girl are at work on a roll of embroidered cloth. Textile weaving, sewing, and finishing were often done in the household in family workshops. In this way, women and young girls were income-earning members of the family.

- Rebuilding the Imperial Edifice in the Sui–Tang Era
- DOCUMENT: Ties That Bind: Paths to Power
- Tang Decline and the Rise of the Song
- Tang and Song Prosperity: The Basis of a Golden Age
- IN DEPTH: Artistic Expression and Social Values
- GLOBAL CONNECTIONS: China's World Role

The postclassical period saw a vital consolidation of Chinese civilization. Although less fundamental changes occurred in China than those experienced in eastern and western Europe, the Americas, and certainly the Middle East, Chinese civilization developed in important new ways. Some of these innovations, especially the technological ones, soon affected the wider world.

Attention to postclassical China means returning to one of the core civilization areas of Asia and to the network of relationships that had been developing for millennia among societies from Iberia in the west to Japan in the east. China also established its own orbit of influence in eastern Asia through ongoing exchanges with Japan, Korea, Vietnam, and other parts of southeast Asia. More isolated than the Islamic world and India, China nevertheless contributed vitally to other areas as it flourished under two vigorous dynasties, the Tang and Song, in the postclassical era.

In the era of political division and civil strife after the breakdown of the Han dynasty in the late 2nd century C.E., most of the advances of the Qin–Han era (221 B.C.E. to 220 C.E.) appeared to have been lost. Writers in the Era of Division that followed (220–589 C.E.) feared that the basis for maintaining civilization in China had been swept away by a new series of nomadic invasions and the seemingly endless wars fought by the regional kingdoms that vied for the imperial throne of the fallen Han. The bureaucratic apparatus of the empire collapsed, although many of the successor states aspired to the Qin–Han ideal of state centralization. In most kingdoms the position of the scholar-gentry declined sharply as landed families with aristocratic pretensions dominated regional rulers.

The reemergence of bickering and self-serving aristocratic elites reminded the scholars who recorded China's history of the chaos and suffering of the Warring States period before the rise of the Qin. In the centuries after the fall of the Han, non-Chinese nomads ruled much of China, and a foreign religion, Buddhism, eclipsed Confucian teachings as the prime force in Chinese political and cultural life. The Great Wall was divided between kingdoms and usually poorly defended as nomadic peoples raided and conquered across the north China plain. Trade and city life declined, technology stagnated, and with mainly Buddhist exceptions, thought degenerated into the quest for magical cures and immortality.

Given the magnitude of these reverses and the fact that Chinese civilization was battered for nearly four centuries, its revival at the very end of the 6th century C.E. appears abrupt at first glance. But the reestablishment of a centralized empire under the short-lived Sui dynasty, and then the restoration and growth of Chinese civilization during the 300-year Tang

200 c.e.	600 c.e.	800 c.e.	950 c.e.	1100 c.e.	1250 c.e.
220 End of the Han dynasty **220–589** Era of Division; political division in China; time of greatest Buddhist influence **589–618** Sui dynasty; building of the Grand Canal	**618–626** Gaozu emperor **618–907** Tang dynasty **627–649** Tang Taizong emperor **688** Korean conquest; vassal state of Silla **690–705** Empress Wu; Buddhist influence in China peaks **712–756** Xuanzong emperor	**840s** Period of Buddhist persecution **907** End of the Tang dynasty	**960–1279** Song dynasty; Neo-Confucian revival **c. 1050** Invention of block printing with movable type **1067–1085** Shenzong emperor; reforms of Wang Anshi	**c. 1100** Invention of gunpowder **1115** Jurchen (Qin) kingdom in North China **1119** First reference to use of compass for sea navigation **1127–1279** Southern Song dynasty	**1279–1368** Mongol (Yuan) dynasty rules all China

reign (618–907) that followed, demonstrated the great strength of the patterns of civilized life that had coalesced in the Qin–Han era. The rapid revival under the Tang was also made possible by the preservation, in the kingdoms that carved up the Han Empire, of the Confucian institutions and ideas that had been so central to the development of civilization in China. Particularly in thought and the arts, the revival begun in the Tang was continued and in some ways brought to full fruition under the Song dynasty (960–1279) that followed.

Rebuilding the Imperial Edifice in the Sui–Tang Eras

 The emergence at the end of the 6th century C.E. of the Sui dynasty from the patchwork of warring states that had dominated Chinese history for nearly four centuries signaled a return to strong dynastic control. In the Tang era that followed the Sui interlude, the bureaucratic institutions begun under the Han were restored, improved, and greatly expanded. A Confucian revival enhanced the position of the scholar-gentry administrators and provided the ideological basis for a return to highly centralized rule under an imperial dynasty.

The initial rise of the Sui dynasty in the early 580s appeared to be just another factional struggle of the sort that had occurred repeatedly in the splinter states fighting for control of China in the centuries after the fall of the Han. **Wendi,** a member of a prominent north Chinese noble family that had long been active in these contests, struck a marriage alliance between his daughter and the ruler of the northern Zhou empire. The Zhou monarch had recently defeated several rival rulers and united much of the north China plain. After much intrigue, Wendi seized the throne of his son-in-law and proclaimed himself emperor. Although Wendi was Chinese, he secured his power base by winning the support of neighboring nomadic military commanders. He did this by reconfirming their titles and showing little desire to favor the Confucian scholar-gentry class at their expense. With their support, Wendi extended his empire across north China. In 589, Wendi's armies attacked and conquered the weak and divided Chen kingdom, which had long ruled much of the south. With his victory over the Chen, Wendi reunited the traditional core areas of Chinese civilization for the first time in three and a half centuries.

Wendi won widespread support by lowering taxes and establishing granaries throughout his domains. These bins for storing grain were built in all of the large cities and in each village of the empire to ensure that there would be a reserve food supply in case floods or drought destroyed the peasants' crops and threatened the people with famine. Large landholders and poor peasants alike were taxed a portion of their crop to keep the granaries filled. Beyond warding off famine, the surplus grain was brought to market in times of food shortages to hold down the price of the people's staple food.

Sui Excesses and Collapse

The foundations Wendi laid for political unification and economic prosperity were at first strengthened even further by his son **Yangdi,** who murdered his father to reach the throne. Yangdi extended his father's conquests and drove back the nomadic intruders who threatened the northern frontiers of the empire. He established a milder legal code and devoted resources to upgrading Confucian education. Yangdi also sought to restore the examination system for regulating entry into the bureaucracy. These legal and educational reforms were part of a broader policy of promoting the scholar-gentry in the imperial administration. But their advancement often worked to the detriment of the great aristocratic families and nomadic military commanders.

Yangdi was overly fond of luxury and extravagant construction projects. He forcibly conscripted hundreds of thousands of peasants to build palaces, a new capital city at Loyang (see Map 12.1), and a series of great canals to link the various parts of his empire. His demands on the people seemed limitless. In his new capital, Yangdi had an extensive game park laid out. Because there was not enough forest on the site chosen, tens of thousands of laborers were forced to dig up huge trees in the nearby hills and cart them miles to be replanted in the artificial mounds that tens of thousands of other laborers had built.

Even before work on his many construction projects had been completed, Yangdi led his exhausted and angry subjects into a series of unsuccessful wars to bring Korea back under Chinese rule. His failures in the Korean campaigns between 611 and 614 and the near-fatal reverse he suffered in central Asia at the hands of Turkic nomads in 615 set in motion widespread revolts throughout the empire. Provincial governors declared themselves independent rulers, bandit gangs raided at will, and nomadic peoples again seized large sections of the north China plain. Faced with a crumbling empire, the increasingly deranged emperor retreated to his pleasure palaces in the city of Hangzhou on the Yangtze River to the south. When Yangdi was assassinated by his own ministers in 618, it looked as if China would return to the

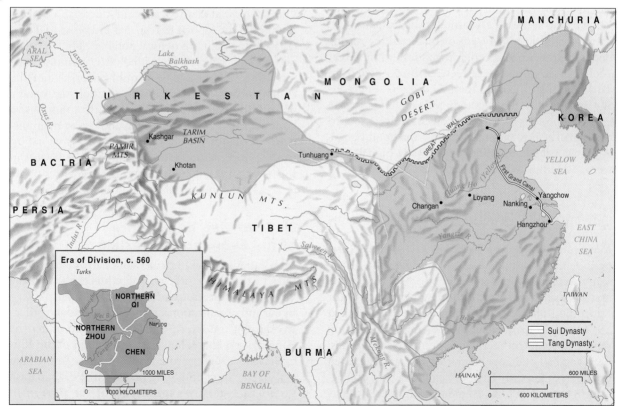

Map 12.1 *China During the Era of Division, the Sui Dynasty, and the Tang Dynasty*

state of political division and social turmoil it had endured in the preceding centuries.

The Emergence of the Tang and the Restoration of the Empire

The dissolution of the imperial order was averted by the military skills and political savvy of one of Yangdi's officials, **Li Yuan,** the Duke of Tang. Of noble and mixed Chinese-nomadic origins, Li Yuan was for many years a loyal supporter of the Sui ruler. In fact, on one occasion Li Yuan rescued Yangdi, whose forces had been trapped by a far larger force of Turkic cavalry in a small fort that was part of the Great Wall defenses. But as Yangdi grew more and more irrational and unrest spread from one end of the empire to another, Li Yuan was convinced by his sons and allies that only rebellion could save his family and the empire. From the many-sided struggle for the throne that followed Yangdi's death and continued until 623, Li Yuan emerged the victor. Together with his second son, Tang Taizong, in whose favor he abdicated in 626, Li Yuan laid the basis for the golden age of the Tang.

Tang armies conquered deep into central Asia as far as present-day Afghanistan. These victories meant that many of the nomadic peoples who had dominated China in the Six Dynasties era had to submit to Tang rule. Tang emperors also completed the repairs begun by the Sui and earlier dynasties on the Great Wall and created frontier armies. Partly recruited from Turkic nomadic peoples, these frontier forces gradually became the most potent military units in the empire. The sons of Turkic tribal leaders were sent to the capital as hostages to guarantee the good behavior of the tribe in question. At the Tang capital, they were also educated in Chinese ways in the hope of their eventual assimilation into Chinese culture.

The empire was also extended to parts of Tibet in the west, the Red River valley homeland of the Vietnamese in the south (see Chapter 13), and Manchuria in the north (see Map 12.1). In the Tang period, the Yangtze River basin and much of the south were fully integrated with north China for the first time since the Han. In 668, under the emperor Kaozong, Korea was overrun by Chinese armies, and a vassal kingdom called Silla was established that long remained loyal to the Tang. In a matter of decades, the Tang had built an empire that was far larger than even that of the early Han—an empire whose boundaries in many directions extended beyond the borders of present-day China.

Rebuilding the Bureaucracy

Crucial for the restoration of Chinese unity were the efforts of the early Tang monarchs to rebuild and expand the imperial bureaucracy. A revived scholar-gentry elite and reworked Confucian ideology played central roles in the process. From the time of the second Sui emperor, Yangdi, the fortunes of the scholar-gentry had begun to improve. This trend continued under the early Tang emperors, who desperately needed loyal and well-educated officials to govern the vast empire they had put together in a matter of decades. The Tang rulers also used the scholar-gentry bureaucrats to offset the power of the aristocracy. As the aristocratic families' control over court life and administration declined, their role in Chinese history was reduced. From the Tang era onward, political power in China was shared by a succession of imperial families and the bureaucrats of the civil service system. Members of the hereditary aristocracy continued to occupy administrative positions, but the scholar-gentry class staffed most of the posts in the secretariats and executive department that oversaw a huge bureaucracy.

This bureaucracy reached from the imperial palace down to the subprefecture, or district level, which was roughly equivalent to an American county. One secretariat drafted imperial decrees; a second monitored the reports of regional and provincial officials and the petitions of local notables. The executive department, which was divided into six ministries—including war, justice, and public works—ran the empire on a day-to-day basis. In addition, there was a powerful Bureau of Censors whose chief task was to keep track of officials at all levels and report their misdeeds or failings. Finally, there was a very large staff to run the imperial household, including the palaces in the new capital at **Changan** and the residences of the princes of the imperial line and other dignitaries.

The Growing Importance of the Examination System

Like Yangdi, the Tang emperors patronized academies to train state officials and educate them in the Confucian classics, which were thought to teach moral and organizational principles essential to effective administrators. In the Tang era, and under the Song dynasty that followed, the numbers of the educated scholar-gentry rose far above those in the Han era. In the Tang and Song periods, the examination system was greatly expanded, and the pattern of advancement in the civil service was much more regularized. Several different kinds of examinations were administered by the **Ministry of Rites** to students from government schools or to those recommended by distinguished scholars.

The highest offices could be gained only by those who were able to pass exams on the philosophical or legal classics and the even more difficult exams on Chinese literature. Those who passed the latter earned the title of **jinshi.** Their names were announced throughout the empire, and their families' positions were secured by the prospect of high office that was opened up by their success. Overnight they were transformed into dignitaries whom even their former friends and fellow students addressed formally and treated with deference. Success in exams at all levels won candidates special social status. This meant that they gained the right to wear certain types of clothing and were exempt from corporal punishment. They gained access to the higher level of material comfort and the refined pleasures that were enjoyed by members of this elite, some of whom are shown at play in Figure 12.1.

Even though a much higher proportion of Tang bureaucrats won their positions through success in civil service examinations than had been the case in the Han era, birth and family connections continued to be important in securing high office. Some of these relationships are clearly illustrated by the peti-tioner's letter printed in the Document section. Established bureaucrats not only ensured that their sons and cousins got into the imperial academies but could pull strings to see that even failed candidates from their families received government posts. Ethnic and regional ties also played a role in staffing bureaucratic departments. This meant that although bright commoners could rise to upper-level positions in the bureaucracy, the central administration was overwhelmingly dominated by a small number of established families. Sons followed fathers in positions of power and influence, and prominent households bought a disproportionate share of the places available in the imperial academies. Many positions were reserved for members of the old aristocracy and the low-ranking sons and grandsons of lesser wives and concubines belonging to the imperial household. Merit and ambition counted for something, but birth and family influence often counted for a good deal more.

State and Religion in the Tang–Song Era

Increasing state patronage for Confucian learning threatened not only the old aristocratic families but also the Buddhists monastic orders, which had become a major force in Chinese life in the Six

Figure 12.1 *As shown in this ink drawing of Chinese philosophers of the Song dynasty, board games and musical recitals were highly esteemed leisure activities for the scholar-gentry class. Members of the scholar-gentry elite might also attend poetry reading or writing parties, travel to mountains to meditate amid scenic splendors, or paint the blossoming plum trees in their gardens. As in their work, members of this highly educated elite admired those who at leisure pursued a diverse array of activities.*

Document

Ties That Bind: Paths to Powers

The following letter was included in a short story by Tang author Niu Su. It was sent by a local functionary named Wu Bao to a high official to whom Wu hoped to attach himself and thus win advancement in the imperial bureaucracy. What can this letter tell us about the ways in which the Chinese bureaucracy worked in the Tang and Song eras?

> To my great good fortune, we share the same native place, and your renown for wise counsel is well known to me. Although, through gross neglect, I have omitted to prostrate myself before you, my heart has always been filled with admiration and respect. You are the nephew of the Prime Minister, and have made use of your outstanding talents in his service. In consequence of this, your high ability has been rewarded with a commission. General Li is highly qualified both as a civil and a military official, and he has been put in full command of the expedition [to put down "barbarian" rebellions in the southern parts of the empire]. In his hands he unites mighty forces, and he cannot fail to bring these petty brigands to order. By the alliance of the General's heroic valor and your own talent and ability, your armies' task of subjugation will be the work of a day. I, in my youth, devoted myself to study.
>
> Reaching manhood, I paid close attention to the [Confucian] classics. But in talent I do not compare with other men, and so far I have held office only as an officer of the guard. I languish in this out-of-the-way corner beyond the Chien [mountains], close to the haunts of the barbarians. My native place is thousands of miles away, and many passes and rivers lie between. What is more, my term of office here is completed, and I cannot tell when I shall receive my next appointment. So lacking in talent, I fear I am but poorly fitted to be selected for an official post; far less can I entertain the hope of some meager salary. I can only retire, when old age comes, to some rustic retreat, and "turn aside to die in a ditch." I have heard by devious ways of your readiness to help those in distress. If you will not overlook a man from your native place, be quick to bestow your special favour on me, so that I may render you service "as a humble groom." Grant me some small salary, and a share however slight in your deeds of merit. If by your boundless favor I could take part in this triumphal progress, even as a member of the rear-most company, the day would live engraved on my memory.

Questions: What techniques does Wu use to win the high official's favor? How does Wu expect the official to help him? What does he promise in return? Does birth or merit appear to be more important in his appeals? What does this suggest about the place of the examinations in the political system? What dangers to the imperial system are contained in the sorts of ties that Wu argues bind him to the high official?

Dynasties era. Many of the rulers in the pre-Tang era, particularly those from nomadic origins, were devout Buddhists and strong patrons of the Buddhist establishment. In the centuries after the fall of the Han, Buddhist sects proliferated in China. The most popular were those founded by Chinese monks, in part because they soon took on distinctively Chinese qualities. Among the masses, the salvationist **pure land** strain of Mahayana Buddhism won widespread conversions because it seemed to provide a refuge from an age of war and turmoil. Members of the elite classes, on the other hand, were more attracted to the **Chan** variant of Buddhism, or **Zen** as it is known in Japan and the West. With its stress on meditation and the appreciation of natural and artistic beauty, Zen had great appeal for the educated classes of China.

The goal of those who followed Zen was to come to know the ultimate wisdom, and thus find release from the cycle of rebirth, through introspective meditation. The nature of this level of consciousness often was expressed in poetic metaphors and riddles, such as those in the following lines from an 8th century C.E. treatise called the *Hymn to Wisdom*:

> The power of wisdom is infinite.
> It is like moonlight reflected in a thousand waves; it can see, hear, understand, and know.
> It can do all these and yet is always empty and tranquil.
> Being empty means having no appearance.
> Being tranquil means not having been created.

One will then not be bound by good and evil,
   or be seized by quietness or disturbance.

One will not be wearied by birth and death or
   rejoice in Nirvana.

The combination of royal patronage and widespread conversion at both the elite and mass levels made Buddhism a strong social, economic, and political force by the time of the Tang unification. The early Tang rulers continued to patronize Buddhism while trying to promote education in the Confucian classics. Emperors such as Taizong endowed monasteries, built in the style of those pictured in Figure 12.2. They also sent emissaries to India to collect texts and relics and commissioned Buddhist paintings and statuary. However, no Tang ruler matched **Empress Wu** (r. 690–705) in supporting the Buddhist establishment. At one point she tried to elevate Buddhism to the status of a state religion.

Empress Wu also commissioned many Buddhist paintings and sculptures. The sculptures are noteworthy for their colossal size. She had statues of the Buddha, which were as much as two and three sto-ries high, carved from stone or cast in bronze. Some of these statues, such as those pictured in Figure 12.3, were carved out of the rock in the great caves near her capital at Loyang; for cast figures at other locations, Wu had huge pagodas built. With this sort of support, it is not surprising that Buddhism flourished in the early centuries of Tang rule. By the mid-9th century, there were nearly 50,000 monasteries and hundreds of thousands of Buddhist monks and nuns in China.

The Anti-Buddhist Backlash

Buddhist successes aroused the envy of Confucian and Daoist rivals. Some of these attacked the religion as alien, even though the faith followed by most of the Chinese was very different from that originally preached by the Buddha or that practiced in India or southeast Asia. Daoist monks tried to counter Buddhism's appeals to the masses by stressing their own magical and predictive powers. Most damaging to the fortunes of Buddhism was the growing campaign of Confucian scholar-administrators to convince the Tang

Figure 12.2 *Because many of the great Buddhist temples and monasteries in China were destroyed in various waves of persecution, some of the best surviving examples of east Asian Buddhist architecture, such as this monastery in present-day Kyoto, are found in Japan. Some of the most characteristic features of this splendid style of construction are its steeply sloping tiled roofs with upturned corners, the extensive use of fine wood in floors, walls, and ceilings, and the sliding panels that covered doors and windows in inclement weather and opened up the temples or monasteries to the natural world on pleasant days.*

Figure 12.3   *At sites such as Lungmen near the Tang capital of Loyang on the Yellow River and Yunkang far to the north, massive statues of the Buddha were carved out of rocky cliffsides beginning in the 6th century* C.E. *Before the age of Buddhist predominance, sculpture had not been highly developed in China, and the art at these centers was strongly influenced by that of central and even west Asia. Known more for their sheer size than for artistic refinement, the huge Buddhas of sites such as Lungmen attest to the high level of skill the Chinese had attained in stone- and metalworking.*

rulers that the large Buddhist monastic establishment posed a fundamental economic challenge to the imperial order. Because monastic lands and resources were not taxed, the Tang regime lost huge amounts of revenue as a result of imperial grants or the gifts of wealthy families to Buddhist monasteries. The state was also denied labor power because it could neither tax nor conscript peasants who worked on monastic estates.

By the mid-8th century, state fears of Buddhist wealth and power led to measures to limit the flow of land and resources to the monastic orders. Under Emperor **Wuzong** (r. 841–847), these restrictions grew into open persecution of Buddhism. Thousands of monasteries and Buddhist shrines were destroyed, and hundreds of thousands of monks and nuns were forced to abandon their monastic orders and return to civilian lives. They and the slaves and peasants who worked their lands were again subject to taxation, and monastery lands were parceled out to taxpaying landlords and peasant smallholders.

Although Chinese Buddhism survived this and other bouts of repression, it was weakened. Never again would the Buddhist monastic orders have the political influence and wealth they had enjoyed in the first centuries of Tang rule. The great age of Buddhist painting and cave sculptures gave way to art dominated by Daoist and Confucian subjects and styles in the late Tang and the Song dynastic era that followed. The Zen and pure land sects of Buddhism continued to attract adherents, with those of the latter numbering in the millions. But Confucianism emerged as the central ideology of Chinese civilization for most of the period from the 9th to the early 20th century. Buddhism left its mark on the arts, the Chinese language, and Chinese thinking about things such as heaven, charity, and law, but it ceased to be a dominant influence. Buddhism's fate in China contrasts sharply with its ongoing and pivotal impact on the civilizations of mainland southeast Asia, Tibet, and parts of central Asia.

Tang Decline and the Rise of the Song

After several centuries of strong rule, the Tang dynasty fell on hard times. Beset by internal rebellions and nomadic incursions, the Tang gave way to the Song in the early 10th century. Although the Song domains were smaller than the Tang, the Confucian revival flourished under the successor dynasty. Following new waves of nomadic invasions, in the mid-12th century the Song lost control of north China. A century and a half later, their empire in south China fell, after a prolonged struggle, to the Mongols under Kubilai Khan.

The motives behind the mid-9th-century Tang assault on the Buddhist monastic order were symptomatic of a general weakening of imperial control that had begun almost a century earlier. After the controversial but strong rule between 690 and 705 by Empress Wu, who actually tried to establish a new dynasty, a second attempt to control the throne was made by a high-born woman who had married into the imperial family. Backed by her powerful relatives and a group of prominent courtiers, Empress Wei poisoned her husband, the son of Empress Wu, and placed her own small child on the throne. But Empress Wei's attempt to seize power was thwarted by another prince, who led a palace revolt that ended with the destruction of Wei and her supporters. The early decades of the long reign of this prince, who became the emperor **Xuanzong** (r. 713–756), marked the peak of Tang power and the high point of Chinese civilization under the dynasty.

Initially, Xuanzong took a strong interest in political and economic reforms, which were pushed by the very capable officials he appointed to high positions. Increasingly, his interest in running the vast empire waned. More and more he devoted himself to patronizing the arts and enjoying the pleasures available within the confines of the imperial city. These diversions included music, which he played himself and also had performed by the many musicians he patronized. Thousands of concubines vied in the imperial apartments for the attention of the monarch. After the death of his second wife, the aged and lonely emperor became infatuated with **Yang Guifei,** a beautiful young woman from the harem of one of the imperial princes (Figure 12.4).

Figure 12.4 *This painting of Yang Guifei gives a vivid impression of the opulence and refinement of Chinese court life in the late Tang era. Here a very well-dressed Yang Guifei is helped by some of her servants onto a well-fed horse, presumably for a trot through the palace grounds. Two fan-bearers stand ready to accompany the now powerful concubine on her sedate ride while other attendants prepare to lead the horse through the confined space of the royal enclosure.*

Their relationship was one of the most famous and ill-fated romances in all of Chinese history. Xuanzong promenaded in the imperial gardens and gave flute lessons to Yang. Soon she was raised to the status of royal concubine, and she used her new power to pack the upper levels of the government with her greedy relatives. They and Yang assumed an ever greater role in court politics. The arrogance and excessive ambition of Yang Guifei and her family angered members of the rival cliques at court, who took every opportunity to turn Yang's excesses into a cause for popular unrest. Xuanzong's long neglect of state affairs resulted in economic distress, which fed this discontent. It also led to chronic military weaknesses, which left the government unable to deal with the disorders effectively. The deepening crisis came to a head in 755 when one of the emperor's main military leaders, a general of nomadic origins named An Lushan, led a widely supported revolt with the aim of founding a new dynasty to supplant the Tang.

Although the revolt was crushed and the Tang dynasty preserved, victory was won at a very high cost. Early in the rebellion, Xuanzong's retreating and demoralized troops mutinied, first killing several members of the Yang family and then forcing the emperor to have Yang Guifei executed. Xuanzong lived on for a time, but his grief and disillusionment rendered him incapable of continuing as emperor. None of the Tang monarchs who followed him could compare with the able leaders that the dynasty had consistently produced in the first century and a half of its rule.

Equally critical, to defeat the rebels the Tang had sought alliances with nomadic peoples living on the northern borders of the empire. They had also delegated resources and political power to regional commanders who remained loyal to the dynasty. As had happened so often in the past, in the late 8th and 9th centuries the nomads used political divisions within China to gain entry into and eventually assert control over large areas of the north China plain. At the same time, many of the allied provincial governors became in effect independent rulers. They collected their own taxes, passing little or none on to the imperial treasury. These regional lords raised their own armies and bequeathed their titles to their sons without asking for permission from the Tang court. Worsening economic conditions led to a succession of revolts in the 9th century, some of which were popular uprisings led by peasants.

The Founding of the Song Dynasty

By the end of the 9th century, little remained of the once-glorious Tang Empire. By 907, when the last emperor of the Tang dynasty was forced to resign, China appeared to be entering another phase of nomadic dominance, political division, and social strife. In 960, however, a military commander emerged to reunite China under a single dynasty. **Zhao Kuangyin** had established a far-flung reputation as one of the most honest and able of the generals of the last of the Five Dynasties that had struggled to control north China after the fall of the Tang. Though a fearless warrior, Zhao was a scholarly man who collected books rather than booty while out campaigning. Amid the continuing struggles for control in the north, Zhao's subordinates and regular troops insisted that he proclaim himself emperor. In the next few years, Zhao, renamed Emperor Taizu, routed all his rivals except one, thus founding the Song dynasty that was to rule most of China for the next three centuries.

The one rival Taizu could not overcome was the northern **Liao dynasty,** which had been founded in 907 by the nomadic **Khitan** peoples from Manchuria. This failure set a precedent for weakness on the part of the Song rulers in dealing with the nomadic peoples of the north. This shortcoming plagued the dynasty from its earliest years to its eventual destruction by the Mongols in the late 13th century. Beginning in 1004, the Song were forced by military defeats at the hands of the Khitans to sign a series of humiliating treaties with their smaller but more militarily adept northern neighbors. These treaties committed the Song to paying a very heavy tribute to the Liao dynasty to keep it from raiding and possibly conquering the Song domains. The Khitans, who had been highly *Sinified*, or influenced by Chinese culture, during a century of rule in north China, seemed content with this arrangement. They clearly saw the Song Empire as culturally superior—an area from which they could learn much in statecraft, the arts, and economic organization.

Song Politics: Settling for Partial Restoration

A comparison of the boundaries of the early Song Empire (see Map 12.2) with that of the Tang domains (see Map 12.1) reveals that the Song never matched its predecessor in political or military strength. The weakness of the Song resulted in part

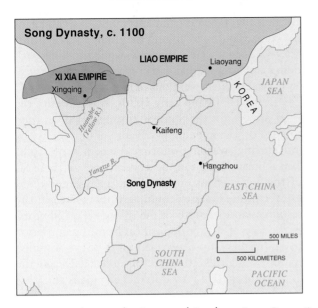

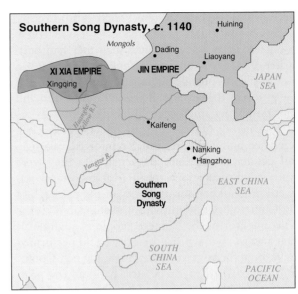

Map 12.2   *China in the Song and Southern Song Dynastic Periods*

from imperial policies that were designed to ward off the conditions that had destroyed the Tang Empire. From the outset, the military was subordinated to the civilian administrators of the scholar-gentry class. Only civil officials were allowed to be governors, thereby removing the temptation of regional military commanders to seize power. In addition, military commanders were rotated to prevent them from building up a power base in the areas where they were stationed.

At the same time, the early Song rulers strongly promoted the interests of the Confucian scholar-gentry, who touted themselves as the key bulwark against the revival of warlordism. Officials' salaries were increased, and many perks—including additional servants and payments of luxury goods such as silk and wine—made government posts more lucrative. The civil service exams were fully routinized. They were given every three years at three levels: district, provincial, and imperial. Song examiners passed a far higher percentage of those taking the exams than the Tang examiners had, and these successful candidates were much more likely to receive an official post than their counterparts in the Tang era. As a result, the bureaucracy soon became bloated with well-paid officials who often had little to do. In this way, the ascendancy of the scholar-gentry class over its aristocratic and Buddhist rivals was fully secured in the Song era.

The Revival of Confucian Thought

The great influence of the scholar-gentry in the Song era was mirrored in the revival of Confucian ideas and values that dominated intellectual life. Many scholars tried to recover long-neglected texts and decipher ancient inscriptions. New academies devoted to the study of the classical texts were founded, and impressive libraries were established. The new schools of philosophy propounded rival interpretations of the teachings of Confucius and other ancient thinkers. They also sought to prove the superiority of indigenous thought systems, such as Confucianism and Daoism, over imported ones, especially Buddhism.

The most prominent thinkers of the era, such as **Zhu Xi,** stressed the importance of applying philosophical principles to everyday life and action. These **neo-Confucians,** or revivers of ancient Confucian teachings, believed that cultivating personal morality was the highest goal for humans. They argued that virtue could be attained through knowledge gained by book learning and personal observation as well as through contact with men of wisdom and high morality. In these ways, the basically good nature of humans could be cultivated, and superior men, fit to govern and teach others, could be developed. Neo-Confucian thinking had a great impact on Chinese intellectual life during the eras of all the dynasties that followed the Song. Its hostility to foreign philosophical systems, such as Buddhism, made Chinese rulers and bureaucrats less receptive to outside ideas and influences than they had been earlier. The neo-Confucian emphasis on tradition and hostility to outside influences was one of a number of forces that eventually stifled innovation and critical thinking among the Chinese elite.

The neo-Confucian emphasis on rank, obligation, deference, and traditional rituals reinforced class, age, and gender distinctions, particularly as they were expressed in occupational roles. Great importance was given to upholding the authority of the patriarch of the Chinese household, who was compared to the male emperor of the Chinese people as a whole. If men and women kept to their place and performed the tasks of their age and social rank, the neo-Confucians argued, there would be social harmony and prosperity. If problems arose, the best solutions could be found in examples drawn from the past. They believed that historical experience was the best guide for navigating the uncertain terrain of the future.

Roots of Decline: Attempts at Reform

The means by which the Song emperors had secured their control over China undermined their empire in the long run. The weakness they showed in the face of the Khitan challenge encouraged other nomadic peoples to carve out kingdoms on the northern borders of the Song domains. By the mid-11th century, **Tangut** tribes, originally from Tibet, had established a kingdom named **Xi Xia** to the southwest of the Khitan kingdom of Liao (see Map 12.2). The tribute that the Song had to pay these peoples for "protection" of their northern borders was a great drain on the resources of the empire and a growing burden for the Chinese peasantry. Equally burdensome was the cost of the army—numbering nearly 1 million soldiers by the mid-11th century—that the Song had to maintain to guard against invasion from the north. But the very size of the army was a striking measure of the productivity and organizational ability of Chinese civilization. It dwarfed its counterparts in other civilizations from Japan to western Europe. The emphasis on civil administration and the scholar-gentry and the growing disdain among the Song elite for the military also took their toll. Although Song armies were large, their commanders rarely were the most able men available. In addition, funds needed to upgrade weapons or repair fortifications often were diverted to the schol-

arly pursuits and entertainments of the court and gentry. At the court and among the ruling classes, painting and poetry were cultivated, while the horseback riding and hunting that had preoccupied earlier rulers and their courtiers went out of fashion.

In the 1070s and early 1080s, **Wang Anshi,** the chief minister of the Song Shenzong emperor, tried to ward off the impending collapse of the dynasty by introducing sweeping reforms. A celebrated Confucian scholar, Wang ran the government on the basis of the Legalist assumption that an energetic and interventionist state could greatly increase the resources and strength of the dynasty. For 20 years, in the face of strong opposition from the conservative ministers who controlled most of the administration, Wang tried to correct the grave defects in the imperial order. He introduced cheap loans and government-assisted irrigation projects to encourage agricultural expansion. He taxed the landlord and scholarly classes, who had regularly exempted themselves from military service. Wang used the increased revenue to establish well-trained mercenary forces to replace armies that had formerly been conscripted from the untrained and unwilling peasantry. Wang even tried to reorganize university education and reorient the examination system. His reforms stressed analytical thinking rather than the rote memorization of the classics that had long been key to success among the scholar-gentry.

Reaction and Disaster: The Flight to the South

Unfortunately, Wang's ability to propose and enact reforms depended on continuing support from the Shenzong emperor. In 1085 that emperor died, and his successor favored the conservative cliques that had long opposed Wang's changes. The neo-Confucians came to power, ended reform, and reversed many of Wang's initiatives. As a result, economic conditions continued to deteriorate, and peasant unrest grew throughout the empire. Faced by banditry and rebellion from within, an unprepared military proved no match for the increasing threat from beyond the northern borders of the empire. In 1115, a new nomadic contender, the **Jurchens,** overthrew the Liao dynasty of the Khitans and established the **Jin** kingdom north of the Song Empire (see Map 12.2). After successful invasions of Song territory, the Jurchens annexed most of the Yellow River basin to what had become the Qin Empire. These conquests forced the Song to flee to the south. With the Yangtze River basin as their anchor and their capital transferred to Hangzhou, the Song dynasty survived for another century and a half. Politically the **Southern Song** dynasty (1127–1279) was little more than a rump state carved out of the much larger domains ruled by the Tang and northern-based Song. Culturally, its brief reign was to be one of the most glorious in Chinese history—perhaps in the history of humankind.

Tang and Song Prosperity: The Basis of a Golden Age

◈ The Tang and Song period was a time of major transitions in Chinese history. Shifts in the population balance within China, new patterns of trade and commerce, renewed urban expansion, novel forms of artistic and literary expression, and a series of technological breakthroughs contributed to new directions in the development of Chinese civilization.

The attention given to canal building by the Sui emperors and the Tang rulers who followed them was driven by a major shift in the population balance within Chinese civilization. The **Grand Canal,** which Yangdi risked his throne to have built, was designed to link the original centers of Chinese civilization on the north China plain with the Yangtze river basin more than 500 miles to the south (see Maps 12.1 and 12.2). Because the great river systems that were essential to China's agrarian base ran from west to east—from the mountains of central Asia to the sea— the movement of people and goods in that direction was much easier than from north to south. Although no major geographic barriers separated the millet-growing areas of northern China from the rice-producing Yangtze basin, overland travel was slow and difficult. The transport of bulk goods such as millet and rice was prohibitively expensive. The great increase of the Chinese population in the southern regions in the later Han and Six Dynasties periods made it necessary to improve communications between north and south once the two regions were joined by the Sui conquests. Not only did more and more of the emperor's subjects live in the southern regions, but the Yangtze basin and other rice-growing areas in the south were fast becoming the major food-producing areas of the empire. By late Tang and early Song times, the south had surpassed the north in both crop production and total population.

Yangdi's Grand Canal was intended to facilitate control over the southern regions by courts, bureaucracies, and armies centered in ancient imperial centers such as Changan and Loyang in the north. The canal made it possible to transport to the capital revenue collected in the form of grain from the fertile southern regions and to transfer food from the south to districts threatened by drought and famine in the north. No wonder that Yangdi was obsessed with canal construction. By the time the Grand Canal was finished, more than a million forced laborers had worked, and many had died, on its locks and embankments. The completed canal system was an engineering achievement every bit as impressive as the Great Wall. Most stretches of the canal, which was nearly 1200 miles long, were 40 paces wide, and imperial highways lined with willow trees ran along the banks on both sides.

A New Phase of Commercial Expansion

Tang conquests in central Asia and the building of the canal system did much to promote commercial expansion in the Tang and Song eras. The extension of Tang control deep into central Asia meant that the overland silk routes between China and Persia were reopened and protected. This intensified international contacts in the postclassical period. Tang control promoted exchanges between China and Buddhist centers in the nomadic lands of central Asia as well as with the Islamic world farther west. Horses, Persian rugs, and tapestries passed to China along these routes, while fine silk textiles, porcelain, and paper were exported to the centers of Islamic civilization. As in the Han era, China exported mainly manufactured goods to overseas areas, such as southeast Asia, while importing mainly luxury products such as aromatic woods and spices. Trading ships for ocean, canal, and river transport improved dramatically, and their numbers multiplied many times in the Tang and Song eras. In late Tang and Song times, Chinese merchants and sailors increasingly carried Chinese trade overseas instead of being content to let foreign seafarers come to them. Along with the dhows of the Arabs, Chinese **junks** were the best ships in the world in this period. They were equipped with watertight bulkheads, sternpost rudders, oars, sails, compasses, bamboo fenders, and gunpowder-propelled rockets for self-defense. With such vessels, Chinese sailors and merchants became the dominant force in the Asian seas east of the Malayan peninsula.

The heightened role of commerce and the money economy in Chinese life was readily apparent in the market quarters found in all cities and major towns (Figure 12.5). These were filled with shops and stalls that sold products drawn from local farms, regional centers of artisan production, and trade centers as distant as the Mediterranean. The Tang and Song governments supervised the hours and marketing methods in these centers, and merchants specializing in products of the same kind banded together in guilds to promote their interests with local officials and to regulate competition.

This expansion in scale was accompanied by a growing sophistication in commercial organization and forms of credit available in China. The proportion of exchanges involved in the money economy expanded greatly, and deposit shops, an early form of the bank, were found in many parts of the empire. The first use of paper money also occurred in the Tang era. Merchants deposited their profits in their hometowns before setting out on trading caravans to distant cities. They were given credit vouchers, or what the Chinese called **flying money,** which they could then present for reimbursement at the appropriate office in the city of destination. This arrangement greatly reduced the danger of robbery on the often perilous journeys merchants made from one market center to another. In the early 11th century, the government began to issue paper money when an economic crisis made it clear that the private merchant banks could no longer handle the demand for the new currency.

The World's Most Splendid Cities

The expansion of commerce and artisan production was complemented by a surge in urban growth in the Tang and Song eras. At nearly 2 million, the population of the Tang capital and its suburbs at Changan was far larger than that of any other city in the world at the time. The imperial city, an inner citadel within the walls of Changan, was divided into a highly restricted zone dominated by the palace and audience halls and a section crowded with the offices of the ministries and secretariats of the imperial government. Near the imperial city but outside Changan's walls, elaborate gardens and a hunting park were laid out for the amusement of the emperors and favored courtiers. The spread of commerce and the increasing population also fed urban growth in the rest of China. In the north and especially the south, old cities mushroomed as suburbs spread in all directions from the original city walls. Towns grew rapidly into cities, and the proportion of the empire's population living in urban centers grew steadily. The number of people living in large cities in China, which may have been as high as 10 percent, was also far greater than that found in any civilization until after the Industrial Revolution.

Of all China's remarkable urban centers in this era, perhaps none surpassed the late Song capital of **Hangzhou** in size, beauty, and sophistication. Located between a large lake and a river in the Yangtze delta, Hangzhou was crisscrossed by canals and bridges. The city's location near the Yangtze and the coast of the East China Sea allowed its traders and artisans to prosper through the sale of goods or the manufacture of products from materials drawn from both north and south China as well as overseas. By late Song times, Hangzhou had more than a million and a half residents and was famed for its wealth, cleanliness, and the number and variety of diversions it offered.

A visitor to Hangzhou could wander through its 10 great marketplaces, each stocked with products from much of the known world. The less consumption-minded visitor could enjoy the city's many parks and delightful gardens, or go boating on the great Western Lake. There the pleasure craft of the rich mingled with special barges for gaming, dining, or listening to Hangzhou's famous "singing-girls." By late afternoon, one could visit the bath houses that were found throughout the city. At these establishments, one could also get a massage and sip a cup of tea or rice wine. In the evening, one might dine at one of the city's many fine restaurants, which specialized in the varied and delicious cuisines of the different regions of China. After dinner, there was a variety of entertainments from which to choose. One could take in the pleasure parks, where acrobats, jugglers, and actors performed for the passing crowds. Other options included one of the city's ornate tea houses, an opera performance by the lake, or a viewing of landscape paintings by artists from the city's famed academy. Having spent such a day, it would be hard for a visitor to disagree with Marco Polo—who himself hailed from another beautiful city of canals, Venice—that Hangzhou was "the most noble city and the best that is in the world."

Figure 12.5 *One of the many urban scenes painted in the Song era provides a panoramic view of the bustling city of Kaifeng (once an imperial capital) on the Grand Canal. The broad-hulled riverboats pictured here were ideal for transporting bulk goods, such as rice or cloth, between north and south China. But they were no match for the great junks that ventured into the seas to trade with Japan and southeast Asia. The riverfront is dominated by markets and open-air restaurants that spread throughout China in this era of prosperity.*

Expanding Agrarian Production and Life in the Country

The movement of the population southward to the fertile valleys of the Yangtze and other river systems was part of a larger process of agrarian expansion in the Tang and Song period. The expansion of Chinese settlement and agricultural production was promoted by the rulers of both dynasties. Their officials actively encouraged peasant groups to migrate to uncultivated areas or those occupied by shifting cultivators

or peoples of non-Chinese descent. The state also supported military garrisons in these areas to protect the new settlements and to complete the task of subduing non-Chinese peoples. State-regulated irrigation and embankment systems advanced agrarian expansion. For example, the great canals made it possible for peasants who grew specialized crops, such as tea, or those who cultivated silkworms to market their produce over much of the empire. The introduction of new seeds, such as the famed Champa rice from Vietnam; better use of human, animal, and silt manures; more thorough soil preparation and weeding; and multiple cropping and improved water control techniques increased the yields of peasant holdings. Inventions such as the wheelbarrow eased the plowing, planting, weeding, and harvesting tasks that occupied much of the time of most Chinese people. The engraving shown in Figure 12.6 gives us a glimpse of rural scenes that were reproduced hundreds of thousands of times across China all through the Tang and Song centuries and much of the millennium that followed.

The rulers of both the Sui and Tang dynasties had adopted policies aimed at breaking up the great estates of the old aristocracy and distributing land more equitably among the free peasant households of the empire. These policies were designed in part to reduce or eliminate the threat that the powerful aristocracy posed for the new dynasties. They were also intended to bolster the position of the ordinary peasants, whose labors and well-being had long been viewed by Confucian scholars as essential to a prosperous and stable social order. To a point, these agrarian measures succeeded. For a time the numbers of the free peasantry increased, and the average holding size in many areas rose. The fortunes of many of the old aristocratic families also declined, thus removing many of them as independent centers of power. They were supplanted gradually in the rural areas by the gentry side of the scholar-gentry combination that dominated the imperial bureaucracy.

The extended-family households of the gentry that were found in rural settlements in the Han era increased in size and elegance in the Tang and Song. The widespread use of the graceful curved roofs with upturned corners that one associates with Chinese civilization dates from the Tang period. By imperial

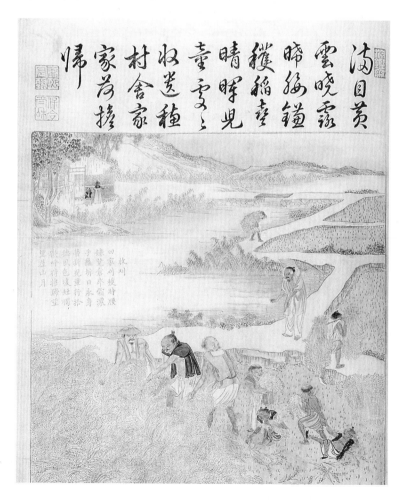

Figure 12.6 *The farming methods developed in the Song era are illustrated by this 17th-century engraving. Note the overseer, protected by an umbrella from the hot sun. Improved productivity, particularly of staple crops such as irrigated rice, meant that China's long-held advantages over other civilizations in terms of the population it could support increased in this era. By the early 14th century, as much as a quarter of humanity may have lived in the Chinese empire.*

decree, curved roofs were reserved for people of high rank, including the gentry families. With intricately carved and painted roof timbers topped with glazed tiles of yellow or green, the great dwellings of the gentry left no doubt about the status and power of the families who lived in them. At the same time, their muted colors, wood and bamboo construction, and simple lines blended beautifully with nearby gardens and groves of trees.

Family and Society in the Tang–Song Era

Chinese family organization at various class levels in the Tang and Song centuries closely resembled that found in earlier periods. Nonetheless, the position of women showed signs of improving under the Tang and early Song eras, and then deteriorated steadily in the late Song. As in the classical age, extended-family households were preferred, but normally they could be afforded only by the upper classes. The male-dominated hierarchy promoted by Confucius and other early thinkers held sway at all class levels. In the Tang period, the authority of elders and males within the family was buttressed by laws that prescribed beheading as a punishment for children who struck their parents or grandparents in anger, and two and one-half years of hard labor for younger brothers or sisters who hit their older siblings. Over the centuries, a very elaborate process of forging marriage alliances developed. Professional go-betweens, almost always women, helped both families to negotiate such prickly issues as matching young men and women and the amount of the dowry to be paid to the husband's family. Brides and grooms in China, in contrast to those in India, generally were about the same age, probably because of the Confucian reluctance to mix generations.

Both within the family and in society at large, women remained clearly subordinate to men. But some evidence suggests that at least for women of the upper classes in urban areas, the opportunities for personal expression increased in the Tang and early Song. As the example of the empresses Wu and Wei and the concubine Yang Guifei make clear, Tang women could wield considerable power at the highest levels of Chinese society. That they also enjoyed access to a broad range of activities, if not career possibilities, is indicated by a surviving pottery figure from the early Tang period of a young woman playing polo.

Tang and Song law allowed divorce by mutual consent of both husband and wife. There were also laws prohibiting a husband from setting aside his wife if her parents were dead or if he had been poor when they were married and later became rich. These suggest that Chinese wives had more defenses against capricious behavior by their husbands than was the case in India at this time. A remarkable degree of independence is also indicated by the practice, reported in late Song times, of wealthy women in large cities such as Hangzhou taking lovers (or what were politely called "complementary husbands") with the knowledge of their husbands.

The Neo-Confucian Assertion of Male Dominance

Evidence of the independence and legal rights enjoyed by a small minority of women in the Tang–Song era is all but overwhelmed by the worsening condition of Chinese women in general. The assertion of male dominance was especially pronounced in the thinking of the neo-Confucian philosophers, who, as we have seen, became a major force in the later Song period. The neo-Confucians stressed the woman's role as homemaker and mother, particularly as the bearer of sons to continue the patrilineal family line. They advocated confining women and emphasized the importance of virginity for young brides, fidelity for wives, and chastity for widows. Like their counterparts in India, widows were discouraged from remarrying.

At the same time, men were permitted to have premarital sex without scandal, to take concubines if they could afford them, and to remarry if one or more of their wives died. The neo-Confucians attacked the Buddhists for promoting career alternatives for women, such as scholarship and the monastic life, at the expense of marriage and raising a family. They drafted laws that favored men in inheritance, divorce, and familial interaction. They also excluded women from the sort of education that would allow them to enter the civil service and rise to positions of political power.

No practice exemplifies the degree to which women in Chinese civilization were constricted and subordinated as dramatically as **footbinding.** This counterpart of the veil and seclusion in Islam may have had its origins in the delight one of the Tang emperors took in the tiny feet of his favorite dancing girl. Whatever its origins, by the later Song era, upper-class men had developed a preference for small feet for women. This preference later spread to lower-class groups, including the peasantry. In response to male demands, on which the successful negotiation of a young woman's marriage contract might hinge, mothers began to bind the feet of their daughters as early as age five or six. The young girl's toes were turned under and bound with silk, as shown by the illustration in Figure 12.7, which was wound more tightly as she grew. By the time she reached marriageable age, her foot had been transformed into the "lotus petal" or "golden lily" shapes that were presumably preferred by prospective husbands.

Bound feet were a constant source of pain for the rest of a woman's life, and they greatly limited her mobility by making it very difficult to walk even short distances. Limited mobility made it easier for husbands to confine their wives to the family compound. It also meant that women could not engage in occupations except ones that could be pursued within the family compound, such as textile production (see chapter opening illustration). For this reason, the

lower classes, whose households often depended on women's labor in the fields, markets, or homes of the wealthy to make ends meet, were slow to adopt the practice. But once it was in fashion among the scholar-gentry and other elite classes, footbinding became vital to winning a husband. Because a good marriage for their daughters was the primary goal of Chinese mothers, the practice was unquestioningly passed from one generation of women to the next. Foot-binding epitomized the extent to which elite women's possibilities for self-fulfillment had been constricted by the later Song period.

A Glorious Age: Invention and Artistic Creativity

Perhaps even more than for political and economic transformations, the Tang and Song eras are remembered as a time of remarkable Chinese accomplishments in science, technology, literature, and the fine arts. Major technological breakthroughs and scientific discoveries were made under each dynasty. Some of them, particularly those involving the invention of new tools, production techniques, and weapons, gradually spread to other civilizations and fundamentally changed the course of human development. Until recent centuries, the arts and literature of China were not well known beyond its borders. Their impact was confined mainly to areas such as central Asia, Japan, and Vietnam, where Chinese imports had long been a major impetus for cultural change. But the poetry and short stories of the Tang and the landscape paintings of the Song are some of the most splendid artistic creations of all human history.

As we have seen, new agricultural tools and innovations such as banks and paper money contributed a great deal to economic growth and social prosperity in the Tang–Song era. In this respect, the engineering feats of the period are particularly noteworthy. In addition to building the Grand Canal, Tang and Song engineers made great advances in building dikes and dams and regulating the flow of water in complex irrigation systems. They also devised ingenious new ways to build bridges, long a major focus of engineering efforts in a land dominated by mountains and waterways. From arched and segmented to suspension and trussed, most of the basic bridge types known to humans were pioneered in China.

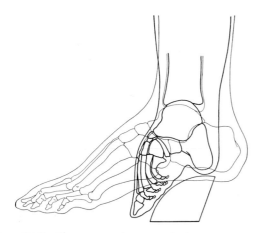

Figure 12.7 *The contrast between the bone structure of a normal foot and that of a Chinese woman whose foot has been bound since she was a young girl is illustrated in this diagram. Young girls with bound feet needed special footwear as they matured. As the diagram shows, most of the foot rested on a thick heel. Little or no sole was needed, and the outer covering came to a point in front where the toes would have been had the foot been allowed to grow normally.*

In Depth

Artistic Expression and Social Values

Studying artistic creativity is one of the most effective ways of probing the beliefs and values of a civilization. In some cases in which the civilization in question did not develop writing, or at least writing that we can now decipher, art and architecture provide much of the evidence by which we can learn about the attitudes and lifestyles of vanished peoples. Some of the most notable examples include the ancient Indus civilization of south Asia and many of the high civilizations of the Americas and sub-Saharan Africa. Even in civilizations for which written records have survived, we can learn a good deal about social structure by discovering who produced the art and for whom it was created, about technology by studying artistic techniques and materials, and about worldviews by exploring the messages the art was intended to convey. In comparing some of the major forms of artistic expression of the great civilizations, we can also identify underlying similarities and differences in the values by which the peoples who developed them organized their societies and responded to the natural and supernatural worlds.

The fact that members of the ruling political elite produced many of the landscape paintings of the Song era is unusual in the history of civilization. The sculptures that adorned the temples of India and the statues, paintings, and stained glass that graced the cathedrals of medieval Europe were created mainly by specialized and highly trained artisans whose skills were passed down over many generations. By contrast, the Song artists were often amateurs who painted in their leisure time. Even the most talented, who won enough patronage to devote themselves to painting full time, began as Confucian scholars and very often administrators. It is not just the amateur and "master of all fields" ideals that are remarkable here but the fact that so much art was produced by the men who also ran the country. In most of the other civilizations we have studied, political life has been dominated by warrior and priestly classes, not artistic scholar-bureaucrats like those who governed China.

Even in civilizations such as those of medieval Europe and Islam, where priests and religious teachers produced fine art in the form of manuscript illu-minations, the people involved seldom had political responsibilities or power. Thus, the artistic creativity of China's political elite underscores the importance of the preference for civil over military leaders in Chinese society. It also tells us a good deal about the qualities the Chinese associated with a truly civilized and superior person—a person who was deemed worthy to rule the Middle Kingdom.

Song landscapes expressed the reactions and ideals of individual people, whom we can identify by the distinctive seals with which they stamped their paintings. The paintings clearly were intended for the pleasure and edification of the Chinese educated classes, not for museum viewing or mass consumption. Landscape painting reinforced the identity and values of this scholarly elite across the vast spaces of the Chinese empire as well as across time. In a famous incident, the Confucian philosopher Ju Xi remarked on the nobility and loyalty that he saw so clearly in the calligraphy of scholars from the Warring States era.

This individualism and elitism in Chinese art can be contrasted with the anonymous creation of sculptures and religious paintings in Hindu and Buddhist civilizations and medieval Europe or the mosaic decorations of the mosques of Islam. In each of these other civilizations, artistic works that adorned temples, cathedrals, and mosques were intended for a mass audience. The moral instruction for the scholarly few that was contained in the Song landscapes had a very different purpose than the religious sculptures or mosaics of other civilizations. The sculptures and mosaics were created to convey a religious message, to remind the viewers of a key event in the life of Christ or the Buddha, or to impress upon them the horrors of hell or the delights of heaven.

Thus, the highest art forms, linked to a common religion, bridged the gulf between elites and the masses in Hindu, Buddhist, Christian, and Muslim civilizations. Imported Buddhist art forms performed this function in some periods in Chinese history. But the more enduring Confucian-Daoist artistic creativity, best exemplified by landscape painting, accentuated the differences that separated the educated scholar-gentry and the common people.

(continued)

Questions: What do you think the small size of the people in Chinese landscape paintings can tell us about Chinese views on the relationship between humans and the natural world? What political functions might be served by monumental art such as that of Hindu, Islamic, and Christian civilizations beyond reminding the masses of their religious ties to the elite? Which forms of artistic expression exact the highest toll from the mass of the people, and which best serve their interests? Can you think of American or European politicians who have created great works of art? Do we expect this sort of creativity from our elected officials? If not, what does this tell us about the values of our own civilization?

One of the most important of the many technological advances made in the Tang era, the invention of explosive powder, at first had little impact on warfare. For centuries, the Chinese used these potent chemical mixtures mainly for fireworks, which delighted emperors and the masses alike. By the late Song, however, explosive powder was widely used by the imperial armies in a variety of grenades and bombs that were hurled at the enemy by catapults. Song armies and warships also were equipped with naphtha flamethrowers, poisonous gases, and rocket launchers. These projectiles were perhaps the most effective weapons the dynasty used in its losing struggle to check nomadic incursions. On the domestic scene, chairs—modeled on those found in India—were introduced into the household, the habit of drinking tea swept the empire, coal was used for fuel for the first time, and the first kite soared into the heavens.

Although the number of major inventions in the Song era was lower than in the Tang, several were pivotal for the future of all civilizations. Compasses, which had been used since the last centuries B.C.E. by Chinese military commanders and magicians, were applied to sea navigation for the first time in the Song period. The abacus, the ancestor of the modern calculator, was introduced to help merchants count their profits and tax collectors keep track of revenues. In the mid-11th century, a remarkable artisan named Bi Sheng devised the technique of printing with movable type. Although block printing had been perfected in China in the preceding centuries, the use of movable type was a great advance in the production of written records and scholarly books. Combined with paper, which the Chinese had invented in the Han period, printing made it possible for them to attain a level of literacy that excelled that of any preindustrial civilization.

Scholarly Refinement and Artistic Accomplishment

The reinvigorated scholar-gentry elite was responsible for much of the artistic and literary creativity of the Tang–Song era. Buddhist art and architecture had been heavily patronized by the court, prosperous merchants, and wealthy monasteries in the Tang period. But scholar-administrators and Confucian teachers wrote much of the literature for which the Tang is best remembered, and they painted the landscapes that were the most sublime cultural productions of the Song. Confucian thinkers valued skillful writing and painting, and educated people were expected to practice these arts. The Chinese educational establishment was geared to turning out generalists rather than the specialists who are so revered in our own society. A well-educated man dabbled with varying degrees of success in many fields. Thus, after a hard day at the Ministry of Public Works, a truly accomplished official was expected to spend the evening composing songs on his lute, admiring a new painting or creating his own, or sipping rice wine while composing a poem to the harvest moon. Thus, talented and often well-trained amateurs wrote most of the poems, composed much of the music, and painted the landscapes for which the Tang–Song era is renowned (Figure 12.8).

As the Confucian scholar-gentry supplanted the Buddhists as the major producers of art and literature, devotional objects and religious homilies gave way to a growing fixation on everyday life and the delights of the natural world. Much of the short story literature was focused on the lives of the common people, popular beliefs in witchcraft and demons, ill-fated romances, and even detective stories about brutal murders. Tang poetry moved from early verses that dwelt on the "pleasant breezes that envelope[d]

Figure 12.8 *The simplicity of composition, the use of empty space, and the emphasis on nature are all characteristic of Chinese landscape painting at its height in the Song era. The colors used tended to be muted; often only brown or black ink was used. Most artists stamped their work with signature seals, and poems describing scenes related to those in the painting floated in the empty space at the top or sides.*

the emperor's chair" to a seemingly endless variety of ways of celebrating the natural world. No one was better at the latter than the most famous poet of the Tang era, **Li Bo.** His poems, like those of the great Persian authors, blend images of the everyday world with philosophical musings:

> The rain was over, green covered the land.
>
> One last cloudlet melted away in the clear sky.
>
> The east wind came home with the spring
>
> Bearing blossoms to sprout on the branches.
>
> Flowers are fading now and time will end.
>
> All mortal men perceive it and their sighs are deep.
>
> But I will turn to the sacred hills
>
> And learn from Tao [Dao] and from magic how to fly.

This intense interest in nature came to full artistic fruition in the landscape paintings of the Song era. Most of them were produced by the cultivated men of the scholar-gentry class, and they pulled together diverse aspects of Chinese civilization. The brushes and techniques used were similar to those used in writing the Chinese language, which itself was regarded as a high art form. The paintings were symbolic, intended to teach moral lessons or explore philosophical ideas. The objects depicted were not only beautiful in themselves but stood for larger concepts: A crane and a pine tree, for example, represented longevity; bamboo shoots were associated with the scholar-gentry class; and a dragon could call to mind any number of things, including the emperor, the cosmos, or life-giving rain.

There was an abstract quality to the paintings that gives them a special appeal in the present day.

The artists were not concerned with depicting nature accurately but rather with creating a highly personal vision of natural beauty. A premium was placed on subtlety and suggestion. For example, the winner of an imperial contest painted a lone monk drawing water from an icy stream to depict the subject announced by the emperor: a monastery hidden deep in the mountains during the winter. Song landscapes often were painted on scrolls that could be read as the viewer unfolded them bit by bit. Most were accompanied by a poem, sometimes composed by the painter, that complemented the subject matter and was aimed at explaining the artist's ideas.

GLOBAL CONNECTIONS: China's World Role

By retreating to the south, the Song rulers managed to survive the assaults of the nomads from the north. But as the dynasty weakened, enduring patterns of nomadic incursions resurfaced and built to the apex of pastoral military and political expansion under the Mongols. The Song emperors could not retreat far enough to escape the onslaught of the most brilliant nomadic commander of them all, Chinggis Khan, who directed perhaps the most powerful military machine the world had seen up to that time. The Song rulers bought time by paying tribute to the Mongol Khan and making alliances with him against their common enemies. But another Mongol leader, Kubilai Khan, who was ready to launch a sustained effort to conquer the southern refuge of the Song dynasty, later emerged as the paramount Mongol lord. He was soon ready to launch a sustained effort to conquer the southern refuge of the Song dynasty, which was completed by 1279.

The long Tang–Song era was truly pivotal in Chinese and world history. Centralized administration and the great Chinese bureaucracy were not only restored but strengthened. The scholar-gentry elite, which had for so long been the critical binding force for Chinese civilization, triumphed over its aristocratic, nomadic, and Buddhist monastic rivals. Under nomadic and indigenous dynasties, the scholar-gentry continued to define and direct Chinese civilization for the next six and a half centuries. During the nearly seven centuries of Tang and Song rule, the area of Chinese civilization had grown dramatically as the south was fully integrated with the north.

From the Tang era until the 18th century, the Chinese economy was one of the world's most advanced in terms of market orientation, volume of overseas trade, productivity per acre, and sophistication of its tools and techniques of craft production. Production of luxury craft goods drew attention from merchants and upper-class consumers in many other regions, feeding expanding Afro-Eurasian trade. Chinese inventions such as paper, printing, and gunpowder, also spreading widely, fundamentally changed the course of development in all other human civilizations. Until the 18th century, the imperial dynasties of China had political power and economic resources unmatched by those of any other civilization.

Further Readings

In addition to the general histories of China suggested in Chapter 5, several important works cover the Tang and Song eras. The volume, edited by Denis Twitchett, devoted to the Tang and Song in the *Cambridge History of China* is an essential reference work. There are detailed works on the founding of the Tang dynasty by C. P. Fitzgerald (1970) and Woodbridge Bingham (1940), but these should be read in conjunction with the more recent *Mirror to the Son of Heaven* (1974), which provides valuable correctives to the interpretations of these earlier authors. Useful insights into political and cultural life in the Tang era can be gleaned from the specialized essays in the volume *Perspectives on the Tang* (1973), edited by Arthur Wright and Denis Twitchett. On social patterns in the Tang era, see Charles Benn, *Daily Life in Traditional China: The Tang Dynasty* (2002). Until recently, the most accessible work on society and politics in the Song era was Jacques Gernet's *Daily Life in China on the Eve of the Mongol Invasion, 1250–1276* (1962), which is highly entertaining and informative. On the great social and economic transitions of the Song era, Mark Elvin's *The Pattern of the Chinese Past* (1973) is insightful, provocative, and controversial. These standard accounts can now be supplemented by P. B. Ebry, *The Aristocratic Families of Early Imperial China* (1978); Heng Chye Kiang, *Cities of Aristocrats and Bureaucrats: The Development of Medieval Chinese Cities* (1999); and D. McMullen, *State and Scholars in T'ang China* (1988). Bret Hinsch's *Women in Early Imperial China* (2002) provides a useful introduction to this subject, which is closely examined in Kathryn Bernhardt, *Women and Property in China, 960-1949* (1999) and Bettine Birge, *Women, Property and Confucian Reaction in Sung and Yüan China, 960-1368* (2002).

Of the numerous works on Chinese art and painting, perhaps the best place to start is with the standard work by Mai-mai Sze, *The Way of Chinese Painting* (1956), which quotes extensively from Chinese manuals. Of more recent works, the general survey by Laurence Sickman and Alexander Soper, as well as James Cahill's study of landscape painting, stand out. And they can be supplemented by Alfreda Murch's recent study of *Poetry and Painting in Song China* (2000). A wonderful sampler of Li Bo's poetry can be found in a volume titled *Bright Moon, Perching Bird* (1987), edited by J. P. Seaton and James Cryer.

On the Web

The art of Six Dynasties, including calligraphy, is the subject of a virtual exhibit at http://www.artsmia.org/arts-of-asia/china/dynasties/six.cfm, http://cla.calpoly.edu/~jwetzel/Study/SECULA~1.HTM and http://depts.washington.edu/chinaciv/callig/7calsixd.htm. Changan, the capital of the most culturally brilliant of these dynasties, the Tang, is presented visually at http://suntzu.larc.calpoly.edu/mrc/320-2002/China%20Tang%20Changan/Home.html and set in the context of Chinese urban history at http://www.owlnet.rice.edu/~arch343/lecture8.html. The remarkable technological achievements of this period of Chinese history, which included the development of explosives and paper, are presented at http://www.silkroadcn.com/chinainfo/fourinvention.htm, and http://geocities.com/Athens/oracle/2793/china.html. Mahayana and Chan Buddhism (http://www.ciolek.com/WWWVL-Buddhism.html) survived the nativist revival that also characterized this era. The prosperity of the times stimulated the spread of the practice of the foot binding of women, the results of which are graphically shown and http://academic.brooklyn.cuny.edu/core9/phalsall/studpages/vento.html, http://www-ec.njit.edu/~jkc1763/fb.htm, and http://www.amonline.net.au/bodyart/shaping/footbinding.htm.

CHAPTER 13

THE SPREAD OF CHINESE CIVILIZATION: JAPAN, KOREA, AND VIETNAM

Buddhist temples and gardens provided havens for peace in the turbulent centuries of warlord domination in Japanese history. Although Chinese motifs and architectural styles were employed by the Japanese, the Vietnamese, and the Koreans, each people evolved its own distinctive style. The Japanese in particular excelled in garden design, producing one of the most emulated traditions of landscape design in human history.

- Japan: The Imperial Age
- The Era of Warrior Dominance
- IN DEPTH: Comparing Feudalisms
- Korea: Between China and Japan
- Between China and Southeast Asia: The Making of Vietnam
- VISUALIZING THE PAST: What Their Portraits Tell Us: Gatekeeper Elites and the Persistence of Civilizations
- DOCUMENT: Literature as a Mirror of the Exchanges Between Civilized Centers
- GLOBAL CONNECTIONS: In the Orbit of China: The East Asian Corner of the Global System

The splendid achievements of the Chinese in nearly all areas of human endeavor were readily apparent to neighboring peoples in east and central Asia. It was perhaps inevitable that surrounding peoples would try to emulate China as a model of civilized development. As we have seen, Japan, the most important of these neighbors in terms of its impact on global history, began to borrow heavily from China in the critical 5th and 6th centuries C.E., when its own pattern of civilization started to coalesce. China's influence on the nomadic peoples to the north and west and on areas such as Tibet has been noted in earlier chapters. By the last centuries B.C.E., Vietnam and Korea were also drawn into the orbit of Chinese civilization.

This chapter focuses on the interaction and exchanges between China and the three agrarian neighbors it so strongly influenced: Japan, Korea, and Vietnam. In each of these societies, Chinese influences blended with local conditions, preferences, and creativity to produce related but distinctive patterns of civilized development. In the case of the Japanese, we examine the strategies they adopted to build on the foundations laid in the first centuries C.E. For Korea and Vietnam, we begin with the first contacts between the Chinese and the peoples of these areas and then examine the different paths to civilization each followed.

In each of these areas, Buddhism played key roles in the transmission of Chinese civilization and the development of the indigenous cultures. Because Buddhism originated in India, the layers of cross-cultural interaction in these processes are all the more complex and profound. In each case, ideas and rituals originating in India were filtered through Chinese society and culture before being passed on to Japan, Korea, and Vietnam. Buddhism also provided a critical link between the civilizations developing in Korea and Japan.

Japan: The Imperial Age

Chinese influence on Japan peaked in the 7th and 8th centuries as Japanese rulers and their courtiers tried to build a Chinese-style bureaucracy and army and to emulate Chinese etiquette and art. But the isolated and ultracivilized court centers at Nara and later Heian lost political control to powerful aristocratic families and local warlords. Intensifying rivalries between these regional military leaders eventually plunged Japan into a long series of civil wars from the 12th to the 17th century.

By the 7th and 8th centuries C.E., the Japanese court at Nara (see Map 13.1) was awash in Chinese imports. Indigenous cultural influences, particularly those linked to Shinto views of the natural and supernatural world, remained central to Japanese cultural development. But in the Taika (645–710), Nara (710–784), and

200 B.C.E.	600 C.E.	800 C.E.	1000 C.E.	1200 C.E.	1400 C.E.
206 B.C.E.–220 C.E. Reign of Han dynasty in China	**618–907** Tang dynasty in China	**838** Last Japanese embassy to China	**1160–1185** Taira clan dominant in Japan	**1231–1392** Mongol rule in Korea	**1467–1477** Onin War in Japan
111 Vietnam conquered by Chinese	**646** Taika reforms in Japan	**857–1160** Period of Fujiwara dominance in Japan	**1180–1185** Gempei Wars in Japan	**1279–1368** Mongol rule in China	**1500** Nguyen dynasty in central/south Vietnam founded
109 Choson (Korea) conquered by Chinese	**668** Korea wins independence from Tang conquerors	**918–1392** Koryo dynasty in Korea	**1185–1333** Kamakura Shogunate in Japan	**1392–1910** Yi dynasty in Korea	**1539–1787** Trinh dynasty in Vietnam/Red River area
39 C.E. Trung sisters revolt in Vietnam	**668–918** Silla kingdom in Korea	**939** Vietnam wins its independence from China			**1600** Founding of the Tokugawa Shogunate in Japan
222–589 Era of Division in China	**710–784** Imperial Japanese capital at Nara	**960–1279** Song dynasty in China			
589–618 Sui dynasty in China	**794** Japanese capital shifts to Heian (Kyoto)	**980–1009** Le dynasty in Vietnam			

Heian (794–857) periods, Japanese borrowing from China—though selective—peaked. This borrowing touched nearly all aspects of Japanese life, particularly at the level of the elites and among the people of the court towns.

In 646, the emperor and his advisors introduced the far-reaching **Taika reforms,** aimed at completely revamping the imperial administration along Chinese lines. Japanese court scholars struggled to master thousands of Chinese characters, which bore little relationship to the language they spoke. They wrote dynastic histories patterned after those commissioned by the emperors of China, and followed an elaborate court etiquette that somewhat uneasily combined Chinese protocol with ancient Japanese ideas about politeness and decorum. The Japanese aristocracy struggled to master Confucian ways, worshiped in Chinese-style temples, and admired Buddhist art that was Chinese in subject matter and technique.

Even the common people were affected by the steady flow of influence from the mainland. In the towns they stared in awe at the great Buddhist temples and bowed to passing aristocrats trying to present themselves as Confucian scholars. The peasants turned to Buddhist monks for cures when they were sick or to Buddhist magic when they needed a change of luck. They had begun to mesh the worship of Buddhist deities with that of the ancient *kami,* or nature spirits, of Japan.

Crisis at Nara and the Shift to Heian (Kyoto)

If they had succeeded, the Taika reforms of 646 would have represented the culmination of cen-

turies of Japanese borrowing from China. The central objectives of the proposed changes were to remake the Japanese monarch into an absolutist Chinese-style emperor (even to the point of adding "Son of Heaven" to the Japanese ruler's many titles). The reforms also were intended to create a genuine professional bureaucracy and peasant conscript army in Japan to match those of Han and Tang China. But the changes necessary for these goals to be achieved were frustrated by the resistance of the aristocratic families and the Buddhist monastic orders, who dominated both the emperor and the capital as a whole.

A century after the reforms were introduced, the Buddhist monks in particular had grown so bold and powerful that the court and aristocracy lived in fear of street demonstrations by "rowdy monks" and of the escalating demands of the heads of the monastic orders. Their influence even threatened to engulf the throne in the 760s, when a clever Buddhist prelate worked his way into the inner circle of the empress Koken. His schemes to marry her and become emperor were uncovered and foiled. But it was clear to the emperor's advisors that measures had to be taken to ensure that women could never rule Japan and to check the growing influence of the monastic orders at court.

The emperor, Koken's husband, fled and established a new capital city at Heian (see Map 13.1), or what was later called Kyoto, about 28 miles away. The Buddhists were forbidden to build monasteries in the new capital. But to get around this restriction, the monks established monasteries in the hills surrounding Heian, and they soon reemerged as a potent force at court as royal advisors.

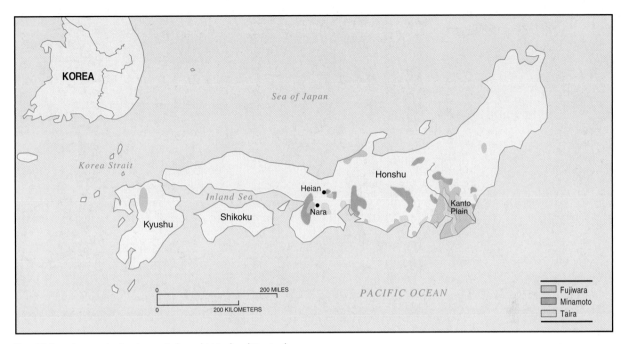

Map 13.1 *Japan in the Imperial and Warlord Periods*

In addition to trying to control the Buddhist monks, the emperor abandoned all pretense of continuing the Taika reforms, which had long been stalled by aristocratic and popular opposition. He fully restored the great aristocratic families, whose power the reforms had been intended to curb. The elaborate system of ranks into which the aristocrats were divided (patterned after that in China) was maintained. But like the Koreans, the Japanese broke with Chinese precedent in determining rank by birth and by allowing little mobility between the various orders. The aristocrats had already taken over most of the positions in the central government. Now, their formal right to build up rural estates was restored as well. The emperor also gave up an ambitious scheme to build a peasant conscript army. In its place, local leaders were ordered to organize militia forces, which would soon play a critical role in further eroding the control of the imperial household.

Ultracivilized: Court Life in the Heian Era

Although the basis of imperial political power had been severely eroded within decades of the shift to Heian, court culture soared to new levels of refine-ment. For several centuries more, the Japanese emperors and their courtiers continued to inhabit a closed world of luxury and aesthetic delights. Men and women of the aristocratic classes lived their lives in accordance with strict codes of polite behavior, under the constant scrutiny of their peers and superiors. In this hothouse atmosphere, social status was everything, love affairs were a major preoccupation, and gossip was rampant. By our standards, life in this constricted and very artificial world was false and suffocating. Yet rarely in human history has so much energy been so focused on the pursuit of beauty or has social interaction—on the surface at least—been so gracious and well mannered.

At the Heian court, members of the imperial household and the leading aristocratic families lived in a complex of palaces and gardens, a section of which is depicted in the painting in Figure 13.1. The buildings were of unpainted wood, which the Japanese found the most appealing, with sliding panels, matted floors, and wooden walkways running between the separate residences where the many dignitaries lived. Fish ponds, artificial lakes with water-falls, and fine gardens were scattered among the courtiers' living quarters. Writing verse was perhaps the most valued art at the court. The poems were

Figure 13.1 *From this artist's impression of the elaborate dress and studied poses of Heian courtiers, as well as the carefully cultivated trees and the tasteful decor, one gains a vivid sense of the formality and attention to aesthetic pleasures that dominated the lives of the Japanese elite in this era. As the prominence of women in the painting suggests, the hothouse world of the Heian court provided a tiny minority of Japanese women with outlets for expressing emotion and creativity that have been denied to most women through much of civilized history.*

often written on painted fans or scented paper, and sometimes they were sent in little boats down the streams that ran through the palace grounds. The verse was brief and full of allusions to Chinese and Japanese classical writings. In the following couplet, a young courtier expresses his disappointment at being denied access to a pretty young girl:

Having come upon an evening blossom

The mist is loath to go with the morning sun.

Partly to accommodate the need for literary expression of this type, the written script the Japanese had borrowed from the Chinese was simplified, making it more compatible with spoken Japanese. One result of these changes was an outpouring of poetic and literary works that were more and more distinctively Japanese. The most celebrated of these was Lady Murasaki's *The Tale of Genji.* None of the works on court life captured its charm and its underlying tensions and sadness as wonderfully as Lady Murasaki's,

which was the first novel in any language (Figure 13.2). In the story, she relates the life history of a prominent and amorous son of the emperor and the fate of his descendants. As the story makes clear, Genji's life is almost wholly devoted to the pursuit of aesthetic enjoyment, whether in affairs with beautiful women or in musical entertainments in a garden scented with blooming flowers. Uncouth commoners and distasteful things, such as dirt, cheap pottery, and rough popular entertainments, are to be avoided at all costs. When her rivals at the court want to insult Genji's mother, for example, they leave spoiled fruit in the passages where she or her maidservants must pass. An encounter with a shriveled piece of fruit contributes to the illness that leads to her premature death.

Everyone who matters in Genji's world is obsessed with the social conventions that govern everything, from which gown is proper for a given ceremony to the composition of a suitable poem to woo a potential lover or win the emperor's favor. Although women rivaled men as poets, artists, and

In addition to novels such as Lady Murasaki's, some of the most elegant poetry in the Japanese language was written in this era. Again, it is sparing in words but rich in imagery and allusions to the natural world:

This perfectly still

Spring Day bathed in the soft light

From the spread-out sky,

Why do the cherry blossoms so restlessly scatter down?

Although I am sure

That he will not be coming

In the evening light

When the locusts shrilly call

I go to the door and wait.

As the female authorship of this poem and *The Tale of Genji* clearly illustrate, women at the Heian court were expected to be as poised and cultured as men. Because they were less involved, however, with Chinese cultural imports (presumed to be a superior male preserve) they actually, for a time, played an unusually creative role in Japanese productions. They wrote poems, played flutes or stringed instruments in informal concerts, and participated in elaborate schemes to snub or disgrace rivals. Like their counterparts in China and the Islamic world, they also became involved in palace intrigues and power struggles.

The Decline of Imperial Power

While the emperor and his courtiers admired the plum blossoms and the newest fashions in court dress, some of the aristocratic families at court were busy running the rapidly shrinking imperial bureaucracy. By the mid-9th century, one of these families, the **Fujiwara,** exercised exceptional influence over imperial affairs. Not only did they pack the upper administration with family members and shape imperial policy, but they also increasingly married Fujiwaras into the imperial family. By the middle of the 10th century, one aged Fujiwara chief minister had seen four of his daughters married to emperors.

Families such as the Fujiwara used the wealth and influence of their high office to build up large estates that provided a stable financial base for their growing power. Especially in the vicinity of the capital, they had to compete in these purchases with the Buddhist

Figure 13.2   *The prominent roles played by women at the Japanese imperial court centers are evident in this painting illustrating one of the episodes in Lady Murasaki's* The Tale of Genji. *The painting also captures the intensely inward-looking character of court life that gradually cut the emperor and his entourage off from the warriors, townspeople, and peasants they ruled. The growing isolation of the court provided opportunities for regional lords with a more military orientation and more effective links to the population as a whole to eventually seize effective control of Japan.*

musicians and in their pervasive cultivation of aesthetic pleasure, it was unseemly for them to openly pursue lovers. Nonetheless, as Lady Murasaki's poignant novel makes clear, some women did court prospective lovers with great guile and passion. It was not uncommon for a high-born woman to spurn a suitor and humiliate him in front of her maidservants.

monasteries. But both could work together in the steady campaign to whittle down imperial control and increase their own. As the lands under their control expanded, both the monks and the court nobility greatly increased the number of peasants and artisans they in effect ruled. Cooperation between monastic orders and court aristocrats was promoted by the introduction of the secret texts and ceremonies of esoteric Buddhism in this period. These teachings and techniques to achieve salvation through prayers and meditation, which were focused by mystical diagrams and special hand positions, were the rage among the Heian elite. As aristocrats and monks steadily built up their own power in the capital, however, they failed to reckon with the growing power of the local lords.

The Rise of the Provincial Warrior Elites

The pursuit of landed estates that increasingly preoccupied the court aristocracy was also taken up by elite families in the provinces. Some of these families had aristocratic origins, but most had risen to power as landowners, estate managers, or local state officials. These families came to control land and labor and to deny these resources to the court. They gradually carved out little kingdoms, ruled by "house" governments, in various parts of the islands. They dominated their mini-states within the larger Japanese realm from small fortresses surrounded by wooden or earthen walls and moatlike ditches. The local lord and his retainers were housed within the fortress, constantly on the alert for an attack by a neighboring lord or the forces of one of the powerful families at court. Granaries for storing the rice provided by local peasants, blacksmith forges and stables, wells for water, and even armories made the fortresses self-contained worlds.

Within the mini-states ruled from the forts, the warrior leaders, or **bushi,** administered law, supervised public works projects, and collected revenue—mainly for themselves, not the court. The failure of the court's plans to build conscript armies also allowed the bushi to build up their own armies. These soon became the most effective military forces in the land. Although these mounted troops, or **samurai,** were loyal to the local lords, not to the court or high aristocratic officials, they were increasingly called in to protect the emperor and his retainers and to keep

the peace in the capital. As the imperial government's control over the country weakened in the 11th and 12th centuries, bandits freely roamed the countryside and the streets of the capital. Buddhist monasteries employed armed toughs to protect them and attack rival sects. In this atmosphere of rampant crime and civil strife, the court and high officials hired provincial lords and their samurai retainers to serve as bodyguards and to protect their palaces and mansions from robbery and arson.

These trends proved critical to the emergence of a warrior class, a characteristically fierce member of which is depicted in Figure 13.3. Counting on peasant dependants to supply them with food and other necessities, the bushi and samurai devoted their lives to hunting, riding, archery practice, and other activities that sharpened their martial skills. Until the 12th century, the main weapons of the mounted warriors

Figure 13.3 *The imposing presence of a fully armed samurai warrior is captured in this pen-and-ink drawing. The slats that make up the warrior's armor were crafted of fine steel braided together with leather, giving him protection against enemy arrows and sword thrusts and some freedom of movement. Note the two finely forged swords, his major weapons, and the flag attached to his armor, which identifies both the lord he serves and the unit to which he is attached.*

were powerful longbows, although they also carried straight swords. From the 12th century on, they increasingly relied on the superbly forged, curved steel swords that we commonly associate with the Japanese samurai. The bushi and the samurai warriors who served them rode into battles that increasingly hinged on the duels of great champions. These combats represented heroic warfare in the extreme. The time and location of battles were elaborately negotiated beforehand, and each side tried to demonstrate the justice of its cause and the treachery of its enemies. Before charging into battle, Japanese warriors proudly proclaimed their family lineage and its notable military exploits to their adversaries, who often missed the details because they were shouting back their own.

A warrior code developed that stressed family honor and death rather than retreat or defeat. Beaten or disgraced warriors turned to ritual suicide to prove their courage and restore their family's honor. They called this practice **seppuku,** which meant disembowelment. But it has come to be known in the West by the more vulgar expression *hara-kiri*, or belly splitting. Battles were chaotic—lots of shouting and clashing but few fatalities—that were won or lost depending on the performance of the champions on each side. Although a full chivalric code did not develop until some centuries later, Japan was steadily moving toward a feudal order that was remarkably similar to that developing in western Europe in this same postclassical period.

The rise of the samurai frustrated all hopes of creating a free peasantry. In fact, Japanese peasants were reduced in the next centuries to the status of serfs, bound to the land they worked and treated as the property of the local lord. They were also separated by rigid class barriers from the warrior elite, which was physically set off by its different ways of dressing and by prohibitions against the peasants carrying swords or riding horses. In their growing poverty and powerlessness, the peasants turned to popular Buddhism in the form of the salvationist pure land sect. The teachings of the pure land offered the promise of bliss in heaven for those who lived upright lives on earth. Colorful figures, such as the dancing monk Kuya, were intended to make Buddhist teachings comprehensible and appealing to both the peasantry and the artisans, who were concentrated in the fortress towns. Buddhist shrines and images became popular destinations for pilgrimages and objects of veneration.

The Era of Warrior Dominance

 From the 12th century onward, Japanese history was increasingly dominated by civil wars between shifting factions of the court aristocracy and local warlords. Chinese influence declined steadily in the centuries that followed. But in the midst of strife and social dislocation, the warrior elite and the artisan classes that served them managed to produce sublime creations in fields as diverse as ceramics, landscape architecture, and religious poetry. However, this creativity was obscured by continuing civil strife, which peaked in the late 15th and 16th centuries and ended only with the rise of the Tokugawa warlord family in the early 1600s.

As the power of the provincial lords grew, that of the imperial household and court aristocracy declined. Powerful families at the court, such as the Fujiwara, increasingly depended on alliances with regional lords to support them in disputes with their rivals. By the 11th and 12th centuries, the provincial families had begun to pack the court bureaucracy and compete for power. By the mid-12th century, competition turned to open feuding between the most powerful of these families, the **Taira** and the **Minamoto.** For a time, the Taira gained the upper hand by controlling the emperor and dominating at court. But when rivalry turned to open warfare in the early 1180s, the Minamoto commanders and their powerful network of alliances with provincial lords in various parts of the country proved superior to the leaders or allies the Taira could muster. More importantly, the Tairas' concentration of their power-grabbing efforts in the capital led to the breakdown of critical links with rural notables, who often sided with the Minamoto in the factional struggles.

The Declining Influence of China

As the power of the imperial house weakened, the relevance of Chinese precedents and institutions diminished for the Japanese. Pretensions to a heavenly mandate and centralized power became ludicrous; the emergence of a scholar-gentry elite was stifled by the reassertion of aristocratic power and prerogatives. Grand designs for an imperial bureaucracy never materialized. Buddhism was increasingly transformed by both aristocrats and peasants into a distinctively Japanese religion. With the decline of the Tang and a return to decades of political uncertainty and social turmoil in China, the Chinese model seemed even less relevant to the Japanese. As early as 838, the Japanese court decided to discontinue its embassies to the much-reduced Tang court. Japanese monks and traders still made the dangerous sea crossing to China, but the emperor's advisors no longer deemed official visits and groveling before the Son of Heaven to be worth all the bother.

For five years, the **Gempei Wars** raged in the heartland of the main island of Honshu (see Map 13.1). This conflict brought great suffering to the peasantry, whose farmlands were ravaged. At the same time, they were compelled to fight against each other. Often large numbers of poorly trained peasants were cut down by the better-armed, professional samurai warriors, who met these hapless rivals in the course of their seemingly endless ritual combats. By 1185, the Taira house faction had been destroyed. The Minamoto then established the **bakufu** (which literally means "tent"), or military government. The Minamoto capital was located at Kamakura in their base area on the Kanto plain, far to the east of the old court center at Heian (see Map 13.1). The emperor and his court were preserved, but real power now rested with the Minamoto and their samurai retainers. The feudal age in Japan had begun.

The Breakdown of Bakufu Dominance and the Age of the Warlords

Yoritomo, the leader of the victorious Minamoto, gravely weakened the Kamakura regime because of his obsessive fear of being overthrown by members of his own family. Close relatives, including his brother Yoshitsune, whose courage and military genius had much to do with the Minamoto triumph over the Taira, were murdered or driven into exile. Fear of spies lent an element of paranoia to elite life under the first of the Kamakura **shoguns,** or the military leaders of the bakufu. Although Yoritomo's rule went unchallenged, the measures he adopted to protect his throne left him without an able heir. His death and the weakness of those who succeeded him led to a scramble on the part of the bushi lords to build up their own power and enlarge their domains. The **Hojo,** one of the warrior families that had long been

closely allied to the Minamoto, soon dominated the Kamakura regime, although they were content to leave the Minamoto as the formal rulers. Thus, a curious and confusing three-tiered system arose. Real power rested in the Hojo family, who manipulated the Minamoto shoguns, who in turn claimed to rule in the name of the emperor who lived at Kyoto.

In the early 14th century, the situation became even murkier when the head of one of the branches of the Minamoto family, **Ashikaga Takuaji,** led a revolt of the bushi that overthrew the Kamakura regime and established the **Ashikaga Shogunate** (1336–1573) in its place. Because the emperor at the time of Ashikaga's seizure of power refused to recognize the usurper and tried to revive imperial power, he was driven from Kyoto to the mountain town of Yoshino. There, with the support of several warlords, the exiled emperor and his heirs fought against the Ashikaga faction and the puppet emperors they placed on the throne at Kyoto for much of the rest of the 14th century.

Although the Ashikaga were finally successful in destroying the rival Yoshino center of imperial authority, the long period of civil strife seriously undermined whatever authority the emperor had left as well as that of the shogunate. The bushi vassals of the warring factions were free to crush local rivals and to seize the lands of the peasantry, the old aristocracy, and competing warlords. As the power of the bushi warlords grew, the court aristocracy, which was impoverished by its inability to defend its estates, was nearly wiped out. The lands the warlords acquired were parceled out to their samurai retainers, who in turn pledged their loyalty and were expected to provide military support whenever their lord called on them.

The collapse of centralized authority was sharply accelerated by the outbreak of full-scale civil war, which raged from 1467 to 1477. Rival heirs to the Ashikaga Shogunate called on the warlord chiefs to support their claims. Samurai flocked to rival headquarters in different sections of Kyoto, where feuding soon broke into all-out warfare. Within a matter of years, the old imperial capital had been reduced to rubble and weed-choked fields. While the shogunate self-destructed in the capital, the provincial lords continued to amass power and plot new coalitions to destroy their enemies. Japan was divided into nearly 300 little kingdoms, whose warlord rulers were called **daimyos** rather than bushi.

In Depth

Comparing Feudalisms

In one sense, the existence of feudalism is easily explained. Many societies generated only weak central government structures simply because they lacked the resources, shared political values, and bureaucratic experience to develop alternatives. China under the Zhou dynasty is sometimes called feudal. The Russian kings from Rurik onward exercised only loose control over powerful landlords. Kings in the divine monarchy systems of sub-Saharan Africa, which flourished from about the 9th to the 19th century in various parts of the continent, similarly relied on deals and compromises with local and regional leaders. Indeed, African historians have often noted that kingdoms such as Ghana and Mali were ruled about as effectively as were Western monarchies during the Middle Ages.

A comparison of this sort reminds us that feudal systems were in many ways early, less sophisticated versions of political societies that were gradually moving from purely local toward more centralized organization. Indeed, almost all civilizations have experienced long periods of semicentralized rule. In all such cases, including feudal ones, the claims of central authorities are not matched by effective power. Regional leaders have armies of their own and do much of the effective administration of their localities. Kings have to make deals with such leaders, relying on personal negotiation and pledges of mutual respect, marriage alliances, negotiation, and a willingness to give the local princes free rein in practice.

The feudal systems that arose in the West and Japan differed in some respects from the many other decentralized systems they resemble. These differences make it desirable not to call all such systems feudal, thus diluting an extremely useful term beyond recognition. For example, Russia was often decentralized and often saw its rulers, whatever their grandiose claims, make concessions to regional nobles because the tsars depended on the loyalty and service of these subordinate lords. But Russia never developed a genuinely feudal political hierarchy, which is one of the features that distinguished it from the West. The same holds true for Zhou China or even the Sudanic empires of Africa.

Japan and the medieval West developed feudal systems grounded in a set of political values that embraced, however imperfectly, most of the participants in the system. The most important of these participants were the aristocratic lords, who effectively controlled the mass of the peasants. The idea of mutual ties and obligations, and the rituals and institutions that expressed them, went beyond the more casual local deals and compromises characteristic of ancient China or medieval and early modern Russia.

In both western Europe and Japan, feudalism was highly militaristic. Both the medieval West and Japan went through long centuries of unusually frequent and bitter internal warfare, based in large part on feudal loyalties and rivalries. Although this warfare was more confined to the warrior-landlord class in Europe than in Japan, in both instances feudalism summed up a host of elite military virtues that long impeded the development of more stable, centralized government. These values included physical courage, personal or family alliances, loyalty, ritualized combat, and often contempt for nonwarrior groups such as peasants and merchants.

The military aura of feudalism survived the feudal era in both cases. It left Japan with serious problems in controlling its samurai class after the worst periods of internal conflict had passed the early 17th century. In the West, the warrior ethic of feudalism persisted in the prominent belief that a central purpose of the state was to make war, thereby providing opportunities for military leaders to demonstrate their prowess. But the legacy of feudalism was not simply military. For example, the idea of personal ties between leaders or among elite groups as a foundation for political activity continued to affect political life and institutions in both the West and Japan, long after the feudal period ended.

The characteristics of feudalism in Japan and in the West were not identical. Western feudalism emphasized contractual ideas more strongly than did Japanese. Although mutual ties were acknowledged by members of the European warrior elite, feudal loyalties were sealed by negotiated contracts, in which the parties involved obtained explicit assurances of the advantages each would receive from the alliance. Japanese feudalism relied more heavily on group and individual loyalties, which were not confirmed by contractual agreements. Probably for this reason, the clearest ongoing legacy of feudalism in the West proved to be parliamentary institutions, where individual aristocrats (as well as townsmen and clergy)

(continued)

could join to defend their explicitly defined legal interests against the central monarch. (Western feudalism also helped encourage the emergence of lawyers, who have never played a comparable role in Japan.) In Japan, the legacy of feudalism involved a less institutionalized group consciousness. This approach encouraged individuals to function as part of collective decision-making teams that ultimately could be linked to the state.

Can the common fact of a feudal heritage be used to explain another similarity between the West and Japan that emerged clearly in the 20th century? Both societies have been unusually successful in industrial development. Both have also proven adept at running capitalist economies. It is certainly tempting to point to feudalism, the medieval feature the two societies uniquely shared, as a partial explanation for these otherwise unexpected 19th- and 20th-century resemblances. The feudal legacy may also help to account for less positive aspects of western European and Japanese development in these centuries, especially their propensity for imperialist expansion and the fact that they frequently resorted to war to solve conflicts with foreign powers. In the case of Japan and Germany, recent historians have established intriguing connections between the persistence of

feudalism late into the early modern era and the rise of right-wing militarist regimes in the 1930s.

When the Japanese talent for group cohesion is identified so strikingly as an ingredient in 20th-century economic success, or when Western nations win political stability through use of parliamentary forms, it surely seems legitimate to point to some persistent threads that run through the experience of the two societies. Whether the common experience of feudalism is a basis for later economic dynamism is a matter for speculation. However, it need not be excluded from a list of provocative uses of comparative analysis simply because the links are challenging.

Questions: Do you think the characteristics of feudalism help explain the later success of Western and Japanese societies? If so, in what ways? If not, why not? Which aspects of feudalism do you think had the greatest effect on these outcomes? If feudalism had persisted in each area, would the outcomes have been as positive as they have been? What other factors should be taken into account if we want to fully analyze these trends? Why might Arab or Chinese historians be skeptical about any claims for feudalism's special importance in world history?

Toward Barbarism? Military Division and Social Change

Although the rituals became more elaborate, the armor heavier, and the swords more superbly forged, the chivalrous qualities of the bushi era deteriorated noticeably in the 15th and 16th centuries. In the place of mud-walled forts, there arose the massive wood and stone castles, such as that at Himeji pictured in Figure 13.4. These imposing structures dominated the Japanese landscape in the centuries that followed. Spying, sneak attacks, ruses, and timely betrayals became the order of the day. The pattern of warfare was fundamentally transformed as large numbers of peasants armed with pikes became a critical component of daimyo armies. Battles hinged less and less on the outcome of samurai combat. Victory depended on the size and organization of a warlord's forces and on how effectively his commanders used them in the field. The badly trained and poorly fed peasant forces became a major source of the growing misery of the common people. As they marched

about the countryside to fight the incessant wars of their overlords, they looted and pillaged. The peasantry in different areas sporadically rose up in hopeless but often ferocious revolts, which fed the trend toward brutality and destruction. It is no wonder that contemporary accounts of the era, as well as those written in later centuries, are dominated by a sense of pessimism and foreboding, a conviction that Japan was reverting from civilized life to barbarism.

Despite the chaos and suffering of the warlord period, there was much economic and cultural growth. Most of the daimyos clearly recognized the need to build up their petty states if they were to survive in the long run. The more able daimyos tried to stabilize village life within their domains by introducing regular tax collection, supporting the construction of irrigation systems and other public works, and building strong rural communities. Incentives were offered to encourage the settlement of unoccupied areas. New tools, the greater use of draft animals, and new crops—especially soybeans—contributed to the well-being of the peasantry in the bet-

Figure 13.4 *Himeji Castle was one of the most formidable of the many fortresses that dominated the Japanese landscape in the age of the warlords. Although the inner buildings were often made of wood, these more vulnerable structures were defended by walls and long, fortified passageways made of stone. Like those of medieval Europe, each castle had wells and granaries for the storage of food that allowed its defenders to withstand long sieges by the forces of rival warlords.*

ter-run domains. Peasants were also encouraged to produce items such as silk, hemp, paper, dyes, and vegetable oils, which were highly marketable and thus potential sources of household income. Daimyos vied with each other to attract merchants to their growing castle towns. Soon a new and wealthy commercial class emerged as purveyors of goods for the military elite and intermediaries in trade between Japan and overseas areas, especially China. As in medieval Europe, guild organizations for artisans and merchants were strong in this era. They helped provide social solidarity and group protection in a time of political breakdown and insecurity.

Evidence reveals that the growth of commerce and the handicraft industries gave some Japanese women opportunities to avoid the sharp drop in status that most experienced in the age of the warring daimyos. Women in merchant and artisan families apparently exercised a fair degree of independence. This was reflected in their participation in guild organizations and business management and by the fact that their positions were sometimes inherited by their daughters. But the status of women in the emerging commercial classes contrasted sharply with that of women in the warrior elites. In earlier centuries, the wives and daughters of the provincial bushi households learned to ride and to use a bow

and arrow, and they often joined in the hunt. By the 14th and 15th centuries, however, the trend among the daimyo families toward primogeniture, or limiting inheritance to the eldest son, dealt a heavy blow to women of the elite classes. The wives and daughters of warrior households, who had hitherto shared in the division of the family estate, now received little or no land or income.

Disinheritance was part of a larger pattern that saw women increasingly treated as defenseless appendages of their warrior fathers or husbands. They were given in marriage to cement alliances between warrior households and reared to anticipate their warrior husband's every desire. They were also taught to slay themselves rather than dishonor the family line by being raped by illicit suitors or enemy soldiers. Japanese women of all classes lost the role of the celebrant in village religious ceremonies and were replaced in Japanese theatrical performances by men specially trained to impersonate women.

Artistic Solace for a Troubled Age

Fears that the constant wars between the swaggering samurai might drag Japan back to barbarism were somewhat mollified by continuing cultivation of the arts. Zen Buddhism, which because of its stress on simplicity and discipline had a special appeal to the warrior elite, played a critical role in securing the place of the arts in an era of strife and destruction. Zen monasteries provided key points of renewed diplomatic and trade contacts with China, which in turn led to a revival of Chinese influence in Japan, at least at the cultural level. Although much painting of the era imitated earlier Chinese work of the Song period, the monochrome ink sketches of Japanese artists were both brilliant and original. Also notable were screen and scroll paintings, such as the one in Figure 13.5, that capture the natural beauty of Japan; others provide us with invaluable glimpses into Japanese life in this period. Zen sensibilities are also prominent in some of the splendid architectural works of this period, including the Golden and Silver Pavilions that Ashikaga shoguns had built in Kyoto (Figure 13.6). Each pavilion was designed to blend into the natural setting in which it was placed to create a pleasing shelter that would foster contemplation and meditation.

This contemplative mood is also evident in the design of some of the more famous gardens of this era. One of these, at the Ryoanji Temple, consisted entirely of islands of volcanic rock set amid white pebbles, which were periodically raked into varying patterns. The influence of Shintoism and Zen Buddhism on such gardens, and the related Japanese ability to find great beauty in the rough and simple, were also present in the tea ceremony that developed in the era of warrior dominance. The graceful gestures, elaborate rituals, and subtly shaped and glazed pots and cups associated with the service of tea on special occasions all lent themselves to composure and introspection.

Figure 13.6 *The Golden Pavilion, also called the Kinkaku-ji Pavilion, is one of the great architectural treasures of the age of the warring houses in Japan. Built on a small lake near Kyoto in the 15th century, the wooden, tile-roofed structure reflects the Zen and Shinto stress on simplicity typical of almost all Japanese artistic production in the centuries of the warring states. Interestingly, its gold-painted exterior and the reflecting pond enhance these sensibilities.*

Figure 13.5 *Patronage of landscape painting and the other fine arts in Japan allowed artistic expression to survive in the long centuries of political division and civil war. In paintings such as the one pictured here, Chinese aesthetic preferences and techniques were strong. In fact, Japanese artists consciously imitated the monochrome (one-colored) paintings of Song China, which they regarded as the apex of the genre. Japanese artists not only concentrated on the same themes, such as landscapes with tiny human figures, but imitated the brushstrokes that they believed had been used by the Song masters.*

Korea: Between China and Japan

Of all the areas to which the Chinese formula for civilized development spread, Korea was the most profoundly influenced for the longest period of time. Because the Korean peninsula is an extension of the Chinese mainland, and because historically Korean kingdoms were dwarfed by their giant neighbor to the west, most observers have treated Korea as little more than an appendage of China. But lumping Korea together with China overlooks the fact that the peninsula was ruled by indigenous dynasties through most of its history, even though these dynasties often paid tribute to the reigning Chinese emperor. Equally important, the Korean people, like the Vietnamese and Japanese, developed a separate identity that was expressed in distinctive forms of dress, cuisine, and a class system that differed significantly from China's.

The peoples who occupied the Korean peninsula represented quite a different ethnic blend from those who, centuries earlier, had come to identify themselves as Chinese. The Koreans descended from the hunting and herding peoples of eastern Siberia and Manchuria rather than the Mongolian- and Turkic-speaking tribes to the west. By the 4th century B.C.E., the peoples who moved into the Korean peninsula had begun to acquire sedentary farming and metalworking techniques from the Chinese. From this point onward, the Koreans played a role in the dynastic struggles that preoccupied the peoples of the north China plain. In 109 B.C.E., the earliest Korean kingdom, **Choson,** was conquered by the Han emperor Wudi. Thereafter, parts of Korea were colonized by Chinese settlers, who remained for nearly four centuries. These colonies soon became a channel by which Chinese influences began to filter into Korean culture in the critical centuries of its early development. A small Japanese enclave in the southeast of the peninsula provided contact with the islands as well, although cultural influences in this era ran overwhelmingly eastward, from China to Korea and then on to Japan.

Despite conquest and colonization under the Han, the tribal peoples of the peninsula, particularly the **Koguryo** in the north, soon resisted Chinese rule. As Chinese control weakened, the Koguryo established an independent state in the northern half of the peninsula that was soon at war with two southern rivals, **Silla** and **Paekche** (see Map 13.2). Contacts between the splinter kingdoms that ruled north China after the fall of the Han and the Koguryo kingdom resulted in the first wave of **Sinification**—that is, the extensive adoption of Chinese culture—in Korea. As was the case in Japan, Buddhism supplied the key links between Korea and the successors of the Han dynasty in northeast China. Korean rulers patronized Buddhist artists and financed the building of monasteries and pagodas. Korean scholars traveled to China, and a select few went to the source of the Buddhist faith, India.

In addition to Sinified variants of Buddhism, Chinese writing was introduced, even though the spoken Korean language was as ill suited for adaptation to the Chinese characters as the Japanese language had been. The Koguryo monarch imposed a unified law code patterned after that of Han China. He established universities, where Korean youths struggled to master the Confucian classics and their teachers wrote histories of China rather than their

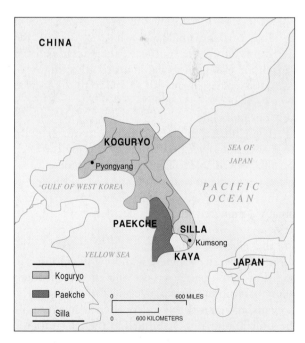

Map 13.2 *The Korean Peninsula During the Three Kingdoms Era*

own land. To expand his power and improve revenue collection, the Koguryo ruler also tried to put together a Chinese-style bureaucracy. But the noble families who supported him had little use for a project that posed such an obvious threat to their own power. Without their support, the monarch did not have the resources for such an ambitious undertaking. Thus, full implementation of these policies had to wait for a more powerful dynasty to emerge some centuries later.

Tang Alliances and the Conquest of Korea

Centuries of warfare between the three Korean kingdoms weakened each without giving paramount power in the peninsula to any. Internal strife also left Korea vulnerable to further attacks from the outside. In addition to the unsuccessful campaigns of the Sui (see Chapter 12), the founders of the more lasting Tang dynasty included Korea in the territories they staked out for their empire. But it was several decades before one of them could finally mount a successful invasion. The stubborn warriors of the Koguryo kingdom bore the brunt of the Tang assaults, just as they had borne those of the Sui rulers. Finally, Tang strategists hit on the idea of taking advantage of Korean divisions to bring the troublesome region into line. Striking an alliance with the rulers of the Silla kingdom to the southeast, they destroyed the Paekche kingdom and then defeated the Koguryo. Thus, the Chinese finally put an end to the long-lived dynasty that had played such a key role in Korea's early development.

The Chinese conquerors began to quarrel with their Silla allies over how to divide the spoils. When the Silla proved able to fight the larger Chinese forces in the peninsula to a standstill and revolts broke out in the former Paekche and Koguryo territories already conquered, the Tang decided it was time to strike a deal. In return for regular tribute payments and the Silla monarch's submission as a vassal of the Tang emperor, the Chinese withdrew their armies in 668. In so doing, they left the Silla the independent rulers of a united Korea. Despite brief lapses, the Koreans maintained this independence and roughly the same boundaries established by the Silla until the occupation of their land by the Japanese in the early 20th century.

Sinification: The Tributary Link

Under the Silla monarchs, who ruled from 668 until the late 9th century, and the Koryo dynasty (918–1392) that followed, Chinese influences peaked and Korean culture achieved its first full flowering. The Silla rulers consciously strove to turn their kingdom into a miniature of the Tang Empire. They regularly sent embassies and tribute to the Tang court, where Korean scholars collected Chinese texts and noted the latest fashions in court dress and etiquette. The Koreans' regular attendance on the Chinese emperors was a key sign of their prominent and enduring participation in the Chinese *tribute system*. At various times, the participants in the system included nomads from central and north Asia, the Tibetans, many of the kingdoms of southeast Asia, and the emperors of Japan. None of these participants were more committed to the tributary arrangements than the Koreans. Rather than try to conquer the Koreans and other surrounding peoples, most Chinese emperors were content to receive their embassies. These emissaries offered tribute in the form of splendid gifts and acknowledged the superiority of the Son of Heaven by their willingness to kowtow to him (kowtowing involved a series of ritual bows in which the supplicant prostrated himself before the throne).

To most of the peoples involved, this seemed a small price to pay for the benefits they received from the Middle Kingdom. Not only did submission and tribute guarantee continuing peace with the Chinese, but it brought far richer gifts than the tribute bearers offered to the Chinese ruler. In addition, the tributary system provided privileged access to Chinese learning, art, and manufactured goods. Tribute missions normally included merchants, whose ability to buy up Chinese manufactures and sell their own goods in the lucrative Chinese market hinged on their country's participation in the Chinese system. Missions from heavily Sinified areas, such as Japan, Korea, and Vietnam, also included contingents of scholars. They studied at Chinese academies or Buddhist monasteries and busily purchased Chinese scrolls and works of art to fill the libraries and embellish the palaces back home. Thus, the tribute system became the major channel of trade and intercultural exchange between China and its neighbors.

The Sinification of Korean Elite Culture

The Silla rulers rebuilt their capital at Kumsong on the Kyongju plain to look like its Tang counterpart. The streets were laid out on a regular grid; there were central markets, parks, lakes, and a separate district to house the imperial family. Fleeing the tedium of the backward rural areas and provincial capitals, the aristocratic families who surrounded the throne and dominated imperial government crowded their mansions into the areas around the imperial palace. With their large extended families and hundreds of slaves and hangers-on, they made up a large portion of the capital's population. Some aristocrats studied in Chinese schools, and a minority even submitted to the rigors of the Confucian examination system introduced under the Silla rulers. Most of the aristocracy opted for the artistic pursuits and entertainments available in the capital. They could do so because most positions in the government continued to be occupied by members of the aristocratic families by virtue of their birth and family connections rather than their knowledge of the Confucian classics.

Partly out of self-interest, the Korean elite continued to favor Buddhism over Confucianism. They and the Korean royal family lavishly endowed monasteries and patronized works of religious art, which became major forms of Korean cultural creativity. The capital at Kumsong soon became crowded with Buddhist temples, which usually were made of wood. Buddhist monks were constantly in attendance on the ruler as well as on members of the royal family and the more powerful aristocratic households. But the schools of Buddhism that caught on among the elite were Chinese. Korean artwork and monastic design reproduced, sometimes splendidly, Chinese prototypes. Even the location of monasteries and pagodas in high places followed Chinese ideas about the need to mollify local spirits and balance supernatural forces.

Sometimes the Koreans borrowed from the Chinese and then outdid their teachers. Most notable in this regard was the pottery produced in the Silla and Koryo eras. The Koreans first learned the techniques of porcelain manufacture from the Chinese. But in the pale green-glazed celadon bowls and vases of the late Silla and Koryo, they created masterworks that even Chinese connoisseurs admired and collected.

They also pioneered in making oxide glazes that were used to make the black- and rust-colored stoneware of this era, which is pictured in Figure 13.7. Both the celadon porcelains and the black stoneware are still recognized as some of the finest pottery ever crafted.

Civilization for the Few

With the exception of Buddhist sects such as the pure land that had strong appeal for the ordinary people, imports from China in this and later eras were all but monopolized by the tiny elite. The aristocratic families were divided into several ranks that neither intermarried nor socialized with each other, much less the rest of the population. They not only filled most of the posts in the Korean bureaucracy but also dominated the social and economic life of

Figure 13.7 *Although all of the major civilized centers of east Asia produced refined ceramics, perhaps nowhere was this art as highly developed as in Korea. As the simple, yet elegant, pitcher in this photo illustrates, Korean pottery was initially crafted for household use. That which has survived from earlier periods of Korean history has become the object of collectors of fine arts and is prominently displayed in major museums.*

the entire kingdom. Much of Korea's trade with the Chinese and Japanese was devoted to providing these aristocrats with the fancy clothing, special teas, scrolls, and artwork that occupied such an important place in their idle lives. In return, Korea exported mainly raw materials, such as forest products and metals such as copper, which was mined by near-slaves who lived in horrendous conditions.

Members of the royal family and the aristocratic households often financed artisan production for export or to supply the court. In addition, some backed mercantile expeditions and even engaged extensively in moneylending. All of this limited the activities of artisans and traders. The former were usually considered low in status and were poorly paid for their talents and labor. The latter were so weak that they did not really form a distinct class.

The aristocrats were the only people who really counted for anything in Korean society. The classes beneath them were oriented to their service. These included government functionaries, who were recognized as a separate social category; commoners, who were mainly peasants; and near-slaves, who were known as the "low born" and ranged from miners and artisans to servants and entertainers. Buddhist festivals periodically relieved the drudgery and monotony of the lives of the common people, and Buddhist salvationist teachings gave them hope for bliss in the afterlife.

Koryo Collapse, Dynastic Renewal

Periodically, the common people and the low born found their lot too much to bear and rose up against a ruling class that was obviously much more devoted to pursuing its own pleasures than to their well-being. Most of these uprisings were local affairs and were ruthlessly repressed by armies of the ruling class. But collectively they weakened both the Silla and Koryo regimes, and in combination with quarrels between the aristocratic households and outside invasions, they contributed to the fall of both dynasties. In the absence of real alternatives, the aristocratic families managed to survive these crises and elevated one of their number to the royal throne. After nearly a century and a half of conflict and turmoil triggered by the Mongol invasion in 1231, the **Yi** dynasty was established in 1392. Remarkably, it ruled Korea until 1910. Although there were some modifications, the Yi quickly restored the aristocratic dominance and links to China that had predominated under their prede-

cessors. Of all of the peoples who received higher civilization from China, none were as content to live in the shadow of the Middle Kingdom as the Koreans.

Between China and Southeast Asia: The Making of Vietnam

 From the Chinese point of view, the Red River valley, which became the heartland of the Vietnamese people in the 1st millennium C.E., was just another rice-growing area to be annexed to their ever-expanding civilization. So much territory and so many peoples had already been absorbed in the fertile southern regions that it was natural to anticipate the same fate for the Red River area and its inhabitants. But the Viets, who lived there, differed in critical ways from the other "southern barbarians" the Chinese had encountered. For one thing, their homeland was farther away from the main centers of Chinese political power on the northern plains than that of any people whom the Chinese had sought to absorb up to that point. For another, the Viets had already developed a sophisticated and, as it turned out, resilient culture of their own—a culture that shared much with the other peoples of southeast Asia.

The preconquest culture of the Vietnamese gave them a strong sense of themselves as a distinct people with a common heritage that they did not want to see overwhelmed by an expanding China. The Viets were well aware of the benefits they derived from the superior technology, modes of political organization, and ideas they received from China. But their gratitude was tempered by their fear of losing their own identity and becoming just another part of China's massive civilization.

Ironically, the Viets first appear in recorded history as a group of "southern barbarians" mentioned by Chinese scholars in accounts of Qin raids in south China in the 220s B.C.E. At that time, their kingdom, which the Chinese called Nam Viet, meaning "people in the south," extended along the southern coastal area of what is now China (see Map 13.3). The initial raids by Qin forces left little lasting Chinese presence. But they probably gave a boost to the lively trade that had been conducted between the

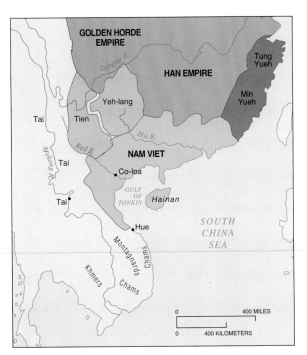

Map 13.3   *South China and Vietnam on the Eve of the Han Conquest*

Viets and the peoples of south China for centuries. In exchange for silk manufactured by the Chinese, the Viets traded ivory, tortoise shells, pearls, peacock feathers, aromatic woods, and other exotic products drawn from the sea and tropical forests. Some decades after the Qin raids, the Viet rulers defeated the feudal lords who controlled the Red River valley and brought their lands under the control of the Viet kingdom. In the centuries that followed, the Viets intermarried and blended with the Mon-Khmer- and Tai-speaking peoples who occupied the Red River area. This proved to be a crucial step in the formation of the Vietnamese as a distinct ethnic group.

As the Viets' willingness to intermarry with ethnic groups such as the **Khmers** (today's Cambodians) and the Tais suggests (see Map 13.3), before their conquest by the Han their culture had many features characteristic of southeast Asia. Their spoken language was not related to Chinese. They enjoyed a strong tradition of village autonomy, physically symbolized by the bamboo hedges that surround northern Vietnamese villages to the present day. The Vietnamese favored the nuclear family to the extended household preferred by the Chinese, and they never developed the clan networks that have been such a prominent

feature of south Chinese society. Vietnamese women have historically had greater freedom and more influence, both within the family and in society at large, than their Chinese counterparts.

Vietnamese customs and cultural forms also differed very significantly from Chinese. The Vietnamese dressed very differently. For example, women preferred long skirts to the black pants that nonelite women wore in China. The Vietnamese delighted in the cockfight, a typical southeast Asian pastime; they chewed betel nut, which the Chinese found disgusting; and they blackened their teeth, which the Chinese also considered repulsive. In the centuries when they were dominated by the Chinese politically, the Vietnamese managed to preserve most of these features of their society. They also became much more fervently attached at the grassroots level to Buddhism, and they developed art and literature, especially poetry, that was refined and distinct from that of the Chinese.

Conquest and Sinification

As the Han rulers who succeeded the Qin tried to incorporate south China into their empire, they came into conflict with the Viets. The Han emperor initially settled for the Viet ruler's admission of his vassal status and periodic payments of tribute. But by 111 B.C.E., the Han thought it best to conquer the feisty Viets outright and to govern them directly using Chinese officials. The Red River area was garrisoned by Chinese troops, and Chinese administrators set to work co-opting the local lords and encouraging them to adopt Chinese culture. Because the Viet elite realized that they had a great deal to learn from their powerful neighbors to the north, they cooperated with the agents of the new regime. Sensing that they had found another barbarian people ripe for assimilation, the Chinese eagerly introduced essential elements of their own culture into the southern lands.

In the centuries after the Chinese conquest, the Vietnamese elite was drawn into the bureaucratic machine that the Han emperors and the shi had developed to hold together the empire won by the Qin. They attended Chinese-style schools, where they wrote in the Chinese script and read and memorized the classical Chinese texts of Confucius and Mencius. They took exams to qualify for administrative posts, whose responsibilities and privileges were defined by Chinese precedents. They introduced Chinese cropping techniques and irrigation technology,

Visualizing the Past

What Their Portraits Tell Us: Gatekeeper Elites and the Persistence of Civilizations

Some decades ago, a distinguished historian of ancient China called the scholar-gentry elite the gatekeepers of Chinese civilization. In his usage, gatekeepers are pivotal elite groups that have emerged in all civilizations and proved critical to their persistence over time. Although they usually shared power with other social groups and often did not rule in their own right, gatekeepers played vital roles in shaping the dominant social values and worldviews of the cultures in which they appeared. In everything from the positions they occupied

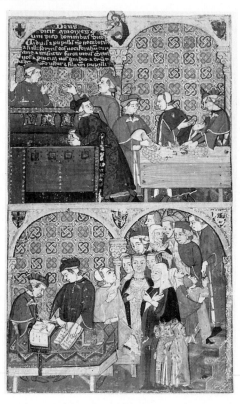

A Samurai Warrior

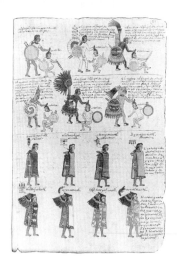

Warrior Ranks from the Aztec Empire

Bankers and Merchants from Western Europe

which soon made Vietnamese agriculture the most productive in southeast Asia. This meant that Vietnamese society, like that of China, could support larger numbers of people. The result was the high population density characteristic of the Red River valley and the lowland coastal areas to the south.

The Vietnamese also found that Chinese political and military organization gave them a decisive edge over the peoples to the west and south, who had adopted Indian patterns of kingship and warfare, and with whom they increasingly clashed over the control of lands to settle and cultivate. Over time, the Vietnamese elite also adopted the extended family model

and took to venerating their ancestors in the Confucian manner. Their Chinese overlords had every reason to assume that the Vietnamese "barbarians" were well on their way to becoming civilized—that is, like the Chinese themselves.

Roots of Resistance

Sporadic revolts led by members of the Vietnamese aristocracy, and the failure of Chinese cultural imports to make much of an impression on the Vietnamese peasantry, ultimately frustrated Chinese hopes for assimilating the Viets. Although they had learned

to their manners and fashions in dress, gatekeepers defined the norms and served as role models for much of the rest of society. Some gatekeeper elites, such as the scholar-gentry in China and the brahmans in India, promoted norms and ideals in written treatises on good government or the proper social order. Other gatekeepers, such the samurai of Japan and the Aztec warriors of Tenochtitlan, embodied these ideals in their public personas and military enterprises, which at times were immortalized in songs, legends, and epics.

The illustrations shown here provide portraits of people belonging to gatekeeper elites from four of the civilizations we have considered in depth thus far. Because each of these portraits was produced by artists from the same society as the gatekeeper elite depicted here, we can assume that the portraits capture the values, symbols of legitimacy, and demeanor that these people intended to project to the viewer. Carefully examine each of these portraits, paying special attention to clothing, poses adopted, objects included in the portraits, backgrounds selected, and activities depicted.

For historical background of the civilizations that each exemplifies, see the relevant sections of Chapters 10, 11, 12, and 13. Compare each of the portraits to the others, and then answer the questions that follow.

Questions: What do the dress, poses, and settings of each of these portraits tell you about the values, ideals, and worldviews that each gatekeeper elite group is intended to represent? To what extent were these elite groups politically and socially dominant in the societies to which they belonged? With which elite groups did they share power? How did they legitimize their power and privileges and to what degree is this reflected in the portraits? What occupational roles and ideals bolstered the efforts of each group to perpetuate the civilizations for which they served as gatekeepers? Which elite exercised the greatest control or influence, and why? Are there comparable gatekeeper elite groups in the contemporary United States? If so, which group or groups play this role? If not, why not?

Chinese Scholars Enjoying Their Leisure Time

much from the Chinese, the Vietnamese lords chafed under their rule, in part because the Chinese often found it difficult to conceal their disdain for local customs in what they considered a backward and unhealthy outpost of the empire. Vietnamese literature attests to the less than reverent attitudes felt by Vietnamese collaborators toward Chinese learning and culture. In the following poem, a teacher mocks himself and doubts his usefulness to the people he serves:

I bear the title "Disciple of Confucius."
Why bother with blockheads, wearing such a label?

I dress like a museum piece:
I speak only in learned quotations (poetry and prose); Long since dried out, I still strut like a peacock; Failed in my exams, I've been dropped like a shrivelled root.

Doctorate, M.A.: all out of reach,
So why not teach school, and beat the devil out of my students.

Elsewhere in Vietnamese writings, self-doubt and mockery turn to rage and a fierce determination to resist Chinese dominance, whatever the cost. The following sentiments of a Vietnamese caught up in resistance to the reimposition of rule from China by the Mongols in the 13th century provide a dramatic case in point:

> I myself often forget to eat at mealtime, and in the middle of the night I wake up and caress my pillow. My intestines hurt me incessantly, as if they had been cut off, and tears flow abundantly from my eyes. My only grief is that I have not yet succeeded in hacking apart the enemy's body, peeling off his skin, swallowing his liver, drinking his blood.

The intensity and ferocity of this passage give some sense of why the Chinese failed to assimilate the Vietnamese. They also failed because the peasantry rallied again and again to the call of their own lords to rise up and drive off the alien rulers. The fact that the most famous of these uprisings was led in 39 C.E. by the **Trung sisters,** who were children of a deposed local leader, points to the importance of the more favored position of women in Vietnamese society, in contrast to the Chinese, as a source of resistance.

Vietnamese women were understandably hostile to the Confucian codes and family system that would have confined them to the household and subjected them to male authority figures. We do not know whether this resentment figured in the Trung sisters' decision to revolt. But poetry written in later centuries by female authors leaves little doubt about the reactions of Vietnamese women to Confucian norms or male dominance. One of the most famous of these writers, Ho Xuan Huong, flouts Confucian decorum in the following ribald verse and mocks her male suitors:

> Careful, careful where are you going:
>
> You group of know-nothings!
>
> Come here and let your older sister teach you to write poems.
>
> Young bees whose stingers itch rub them in wilted flowers.
>
> Young goats who have nothing to do with their horns butt them against sparse shrubbery.

In another poem, "Sharing a Husband," Huong ridicules those who advocate polygamy, a practice favored by any self-respecting Confucian:

> One wife is covered by a quilted blanket, while one wife is left in the cold.

> Cursed be this fate of sharing a common husband. Seldom do you have an occasion to possess your husband,
>
> Not even twice in one month.
>
> You toil and endure hardships in order to earn your steamed rice, and then the rice is cold and tasteless. It is like renting your services for hire, and then receiving no wages.
>
> How is it that I have turned out this way,
>
> I would rather suffer the fate of remaining unmarried and living alone by myself.

Winning Independence and Continuing Chinese Influences

In addition to a strong sense of identity and motives for resistance that crossed class and gender barriers, the Vietnamese struggle for independence was assisted by the fragility of the links that bound them to China. Great distances and mountain barriers created nightmare conditions for Chinese administrators responsible for supplying military expeditions to the far south. Only small numbers of Chinese—mostly bureaucrats, soldiers, and merchants—lived in the Red River area, and few of them did so permanently. Most critically, Chinese control over the distant Vietnamese depended on the strength of the ruling dynasties in China itself. The Vietnamese were quick to take advantage of political turmoil and nomadic incursions in northern China to assert their independence. After failing to completely free themselves on several occasions, they mounted a massive rebellion during the period of chaos in China after the fall of the Tang dynasty in 907. By 939, they had won political independence from their northern neighbors. Although both the Mongol and Ming rulers of China later tried to reassert control over the Vietnamese, both efforts ended in humiliating retreats. From 939 until the conquests by the French in the 19th century, the Vietnamese were masters of their own land.

Although the Chinese political hold was broken, Chinese cultural exports continued to play central roles in Vietnamese society. A succession of Vietnamese dynasties beginning with the Le (980–1009), which became the source of legitimacy for the rest, built Chinese-style palaces as in Figure 13.8, in the midst of forbidden cities patterned after those in Changan and Beijing. They ruled through a bureau-

Figure 13.8 *As this view of the moat and part of the palace of the Vietnamese emperors at Hue illustrates, Chinese taste and architectural styles strongly influenced the construction and decoration of Vietnamese court centers. Not only were the upturned, tiled roofs and long galleries built in conscious imitation of prototypes in Changan or Beijing, but they were set amid moats, ponds, and gardens patterned after those Vietnamese envoys had seen in China. Despite this imitation, however, Vietnamese rulers were more accessible to their subjects, and their palaces and capital city made little impression on Chinese visitors, who disparaged the informality and lack of grandeur at the Hue court.*

cracy that was a much smaller copy of the Chinese administrative system, with secretariats, six main ministries, and a bureau of censors to keep graft and corruption in check. Civil service exams were reintroduced, and an administrative elite schooled in the Confucian classics sought the emperor's favor and commanded deference from the common people.

But the Vietnamese equivalent of the Chinese scholar-gentry never enjoyed as much power. For one thing, their control at the village level was much less secure than that of their Chinese counterparts. Much more than those in China, local Vietnamese officials tended to identify with the peasantry rather than with the court and higher administrators. To a much greater degree, they looked out for local interests and served as leaders in village uprisings against the ruling dynasty when its demands on the common people became too oppressive.

The power of the scholar-bureaucrats in Vietnam was also limited in the reign of many dynasties by competition from well-educated Buddhist monks. The fact that the Buddhists had much stronger links with the Vietnamese peasantry than the monastic orders had in China strengthened them in their struggles with the Confucian scholars. The high esteem in which women were held in Buddhist teachings and institutions also enhanced the popularity of the monks in Vietnam. Thus, competing centers of power and influence prevented most Vietnamese dynasties from enjoying the authority of their Chinese counterparts.

The Vietnamese Drive to the South

However watered down, the Chinese legacy gave the Vietnamese great advantages in the struggles within

Document

Literature as a Mirror of the Exchanges Between Civilized Centers

The following passages from Lady Murasaki's classic Japanese account of court life, *The Tale of Genji* (Vintage Press, 1985 edition), and from perhaps the most popular and beloved work of Vietnamese literature, Nguyen Du's *The Tale of Kieu* (Vintage Press, 1973 edition), are superb examples of the important and far-reaching exchanges between the civilizations of south and east Asia. Not surprisingly, Chinese influences, including many allusions to Chinese writings and historical events, are paramount, but Buddhist (hence originally Indian) themes are pervasive in both works. There is also evidence in one of these passages of significant exchanges between the satellite civilizations of China.

[Kieu] dreamed a girl appeared hard by her side and murmured: "Kieu! Your Karma's still undone. How can you shirk your debt of grief to fate? You yet have to play out your woman's role."

The moderator was a man of considerable learning. There was much of interest in his exchanges with the Korean. There were also exchanges of Chinese poetry, and in one of his poems the Korean succeeded most skillfully in conveying his joy at having been able to observe such a countenance on this the eve of his return to his own land.... Summoning an astrologer of the Indian school, the emperor was pleased to learn that the Indian view coincided with the Japanese and the Korean; and so he concluded that the boy should become a commoner with the name of Minamoto or Genji.

Looking at the keepsakes Myobu had brought back, [Genji] thought what a comfort it would be if some wizard were to bring him, like that Chinese emperor, a comb from the world where his lost love was dwelling....There are limits to the powers of the most gifted artist. The Chinese lady in the paintings did not have the luster of life. Yang Kuei-fei was said to have resembled the lotus of the Sublime Pond, the willows of

the Timeless Hall. No doubt she was very beautiful in her Chinese finery.

"You are well-famed as a lute-player," he said. "Like Chung Tzu-ch'i I've longed to hear you play."... Now [Kieu] began to play. A battle scene—oh how they clashed and clanged, Han and Chu swords! The Ssu-ma tune, A Phoenix Seeks His Mate—it sounded like an outburst of pure grief. Then Hsi K'ang's masterpiece, Kuangling, was heard: it rushed on like a stream or flew like clouds. Next came what Chao-chin played—she mourned her Prince and all her kinsfolk she must leave behind as she crossed the Great Wall to wed a Hun.

The [abbot] talked of this ephemeral world and of the world to come. His own burden of sin was heavy, thought Genji, that he had been lured into an illicit and profitless affair. He would regret it all his life and suffer even more terribly in the life to come. What a joy to withdraw to such a place [a mountain monastery] as this!

When one must weigh and choose between one's love and filial duty, which will turn the scale? Kieu brushed aside her solemn vows to [the young student] Kim— she'd pay a daughter's debt before all else. Resolved on what to do, she spoke her mind: "Hands off my father, please! I'll sell myself and ransom him."

Questions: From these passages can you identify Chinese precedents in terms of place names and historical personages, allusions to Chinese literary works, and attitudes toward gender or social organization that can be traced to Chinese models? Can you detect passages that convey Buddhist ideas about the nature of the world and human existence? Are additional Indian influences suggested? Are there ideas that are distinctively Japanese or Vietnamese, or are the authors totally caught up in Chinese precedents?

Indochina that became a major preoccupation of independent Vietnamese rulers. Because the Vietnamese refused to settle in the malarial highlands that fringed the Red River area and rose abruptly from the coastal plains farther south, their main adversaries were the **Chams** and Khmers, who occupied the lowland areas to the south that the Vietnamese sought to settle themselves (see Map 13.3). The Vietnamese launched periodic expeditions to retaliate for raids on their villages by the hill peoples. They also regularly traded with the hill dwellers for forest products. But the Vietnamese tried to minimize cultural exchange with these hunters and shifting cultivators, whom they saw as "nude savages."

As they moved out in the only direction left to them—south along the narrow plain between the mountains and the sea—the Vietnamese made good use of the larger population and superior bureaucratic and military organization that the Chinese connection had fostered. From the 11th to the 18th century, they fought a long series of generally successful wars against the Chams, an Indianized people living in the lowland areas along the coast. Eventually most of the Chams were driven into the highlands, where their descendants, in much smaller numbers, live to the present day. Having beaten the Chams and settled on their former croplands, the Vietnamese next clashed with the Khmers, who had begun to move into the Mekong delta region during the centuries of the Vietnamese drive south. Again, Indianized armies proved no match for the Chinese-inspired military forces and weapons of the Vietnamese. By the time the French arrived in force in the Mekong area in the late 18th century, the Vietnamese had occupied much of the upper delta and were beginning to push into territory that today belongs to Cambodia.

Expansion and Division

As Vietnamese armies and peasant colonists moved farther and farther from the capital at Hanoi, the dynasties centered there found it increasingly difficult to control the commanders and peasants fighting and living in the frontier areas. As the southerners intermarried with and adopted some of the customs of the Chams and Khmers, differences in culture and attitude developed between them and the northerners. Although both continued to identify themselves as Vietnamese, the northerners (much like their counterparts in the United States) came to see the Vietnamese who settled in the frontier south as less energetic and slower in speech and movement. As the hold of the Hanoi-based dynasties over the southern regions weakened, regional military commanders grew less and less responsive to orders from the north and slower in sending taxes to the court. Bickering turned to violent clashes, and by the end of the 16th century a rival, the **Nguyen,** had emerged to challenge the claims of legitimacy of the **Trinh** family that ruled the north.

The territories of the Nguyen at this time were centered on the narrow plains that connected the two great rice bowls of present-day Vietnam along the Red and Mekong rivers. Their capital was at Hue (see Map 13.3), far north of the Mekong delta region that in this period had scarcely been settled by the Vietnamese. For the next two centuries, these rival houses fought for the right to rule Vietnam. Neither accepted the division of Vietnam as permanent; each sought to unite all of the Vietnamese people under a single monarch. This long struggle not only absorbed much of the Vietnamese energies but also prevented them from recognizing the growing external threat to their homeland. For the first time in history, the danger came not from the Chinese giant to the north but from a distant land and religion about which the Vietnamese knew and cared nothing—France and the conversion-minded Roman Catholic church.

 GLOBAL CONNECTIONS: In the Orbit of China: The East Asian Corner of the Global System

The first millennium C.E. was a pivotal epoch in the history of the peoples of east Asia. The spread of ideas, organizational models, and material culture from a common Chinese center spawned the rise of three distinct patterns of civilized development in Japan, Korea, and Vietnam. In contrast to the lands of the nomadic peoples who had long been in contact with China from the north and west, each of these regions contained fertile and well-watered lowland areas that were suited to sedentary cultivation, which was essential to the spread of the Chinese pattern of civilized development. In fact, each provided an ideal environment for the cultivation of wet rice, which was increasingly replacing millet and other grains as the staple of China.

Common elements of Chinese culture, from modes of writing and bureaucratic organization to religious teachings and art, were transmitted to each of these three areas. In all three cases, Chinese imports, with the important exception of popular Buddhism, were all but monopolized by court and provincial elite groups, the former prominent in Japan and Korea, the latter in Vietnam. In all three cases, Chinese thought patterns and modes of social organization were actively and willingly cultivated by these local elites, who knew that they were the key to a higher level of development.

Thus, for a time at least, all three areas shared prominent aspects of political organization, social development, and intellectual creativity. But the differing ways in which Chinese influences were transmitted to each of these peoples resulted in very different outcomes. The various combinations of Chinese-derived and indigenous elements produced distinctive variations on a common pattern of civilized life. In Korea, the period of direct Chinese rule was brief, but China's physical presence and military power were all too apparent. Thus, the need for symbolic political submission was obvious and the desire for long-term cultural dependence firmly implanted. In Vietnam, where Chinese conquest and control lasted more than a thousand years, a hard-fought struggle for political independence gave way to a growing attachment to Chinese culture as a counterbalance to the Indian influences that had brought civilization to the southeast Asian rivals of the Vietnamese.

In Japan, where all attempts by Chinese dynasties to assert direct control had failed, Chinese culture was emulated by the courtly elite that first brought civilization to the islands. But the rise of a rival aristocratic class, which was based in the provinces and championed military values that were fundamentally opposed to Chinese Confucianism, led to the gradual limitation of Chinese influence in Japan and the reassertion of Japanese traditional ways. Japanese political patterns, in particular, formed a marked contrast with the predominance of rule by a centralized bureaucracy in China. Nonetheless, in Japan as in the rest of east Asia, China remained the epitome of civilized development; Chinese ways were the standard by which all peoples in this far-flung region were judged.

Despite different patterns, the power of the Chinese model had one other important result for Korea, Japan, and to a large extent Vietnam. Contacts with other parts of the world were slight to nonexistent, because there was no sense that any other place had examples worth emulating. The intensity of interactions within the east Asian region generated a degree of isolation from the world beyond.

Further Readings

There are many good secondary works on early Japanese and Vietnamese history. Some older but accessible works on Korea are William Heathorn's *History of Korea* (1971), which gives some attention to the arts, and Hatada

Takashi's *A History of Korea* (1969). The best new short introduction to the history owf Korea is C. J. Eckert, *Korea Old and New: A History* (1980). K. B. Lee, (trans. by E. Wagner et. al.) *A New History of Korea* (1984) is quite comprehensive, while L. Kendall, *Shahmans, Housewives and Other Restless Spirits: Women in Korean Ritual Life* (1985) offers a fresh perspective on Korean social history. The best introductory works on Japanese history and culture are the writings of Reischauer, J. W. Hall's *Japan from Prehistory to Modern Times* (1970), and Mikisio Hane's superb overview, *Japan: A Historical Survey* (1972). H. Paul Varley's *Japanese Culture: A Short History* (1973) has fine sections on the arts, religion, and literature of the warlord era. Also good on this period are Peter Duus' *Japanese Feudalism* (1969); Varley's *Samurai* (1970), which was coauthored with Ivan Morris and Nobuko Morris; and the first and second volumes of George Sansom's *A History of Japan* (1958, 1960).

For an understanding of the Chinese impact on Vietnam, there is no better place to begin than Alexander Woodsides' *Vietnam and the Chinese Model* (1971). The best works on the earliest period in Vietnamese history are translations of the writings of French scholar Georges Coedes and the superspecialized *Birth of Vietnam* (1983) by Keith Taylor. Thomas Hodgkin's survey of Vietnamese history is highly readable and makes extensive use of Vietnamese literature. Troung Buu Lam's edited volume, *Patterns of Vietnamese Response to Foreign Intervention* (1967), along with the Genji and Kieu tales cited in the Document of this chapter, provide wonderful ways for the student to get inside Japanese and Vietnamese culture.

On the Web

The history of Japan during what for Europe was the Middle Ages is traced at http://www.wsu.edu:8080/ ~dee/FEUJAPAN/CONTENTS.HTM. A brief history of successive Japanese Shogunates, the art and literature of the period, and the lore, weapons, and code of the samurai (Bushido) can be examined at http://victorian. fortunecity.com/duchamp/410/main.html and http://www.samurai-archives.com/. The women warriors and leaders of Japan are discussed at http://www. koryubooks.com/Library/wwj1.html, http://www. samurai-archives.com/women.html, and http://www. womeninworldhistory.com/sample-08.html. The life of Lady Murasaki and her world is illuminated at http://www.reconstructinghistory.com/ Japanese/fujiwara.htm and http://mcel.pacificu.edu/as/ students/genji/culture.html. *The Tale of Genji* is analyzed at http://www.taleofgenji.org/, http://mcel. pacificu.edu/as/students/genji/homepage.html, and http://webworld.unesco.org/genji/en/index.shtml.

The myths and legends of the people of Korea helped sustain their identity over the centuries of interaction with Chinese civilization and successive independent Korean kingdoms of Koguryo, Packche, and Silla (http://www. asd.k12.ak.us/Schools/West/Countries/Korea/ KoreaHistory.html and http://www.asianinfo.org/ asianinfo/korea/history.htm) retained their identity while adapting facets of Chinese culture. The Queens of Silla receive treatment at http://www. womeninworldhistory.com/heroine7.html. Chinese-influenced Korean court music can be sampled at http:// www.asiasound.com/pages/learn/time/korea.htm. The Korean family structure is explored at http://www. askasia.org/Korea/soc6.html. Korean art in its historical context is displayed at http://asiasocietymuseum.org/ default/asp (scroll to bottom of page and click on "Korea"). Korean technology as expressed via its mechanical toy production is at http://www.askasia.org/Korea/ math1.html

The origin myths of the Vietnamese also performed a sustaining function during their long encounter with Chinese civilization (http://www.askasia.org/frclasrm/ readings/r000061.htm). The lands of present day Vietnam had a long history prior to the coming of the Chinese. An imperial kingdom, Champa, whose society had absorbed ancient Indian, rather than Chinese tradition (http://www.viettouch.com/champa/), had long ruled the southern portion of the country.

In the North, the Vietnamese development of and trade in bronze drums linked it to the wider world prior to the Chinese efforts to conquer them (http://www.viettouch. com/pre-hist/dongson_drums.html).

Vietnam absorbed much Chinese culture, but also sought to retain its own values even within the Chinese model government they adopted, such as by politically constructing a relatively un-Chinese tradition of heroic women warriors like the Trung sisters (http://www. womeninworldhistory.com/heroine10.html, http:// www.fortunecity.com/victorian/postmodern/428/ goddessheart1a4.html, and http://www.richmond.edu/ ~ebolt/history398/TrungSisters.html) and by incorporating nativist ideals in uprisings against the Chinese model Vietnamese state, such as the Tayson Rebellion (http://www.humnet.ucla.edu/humnet/ealc/ faculty/dutton/TSHome.html) during which women also took to the field of battle. The latter, together with profiles of Vietnam's most prominent precolonial rulers, is discussed at http://greenfield.fortunecity.com/ crawdad/204/nguyenhue.html. The Vietnamese admiration for Chinese culture and hostility to Chinese political domination and their equally ambivalent approach to other external forces is examined at http://www.cseas. kyoto-u.ac.jp/seas/40/4/nguyen.pdf. This process can also be seen in images of traditional Vietnam provided at http://www2.centenary.edu/vietnam/lairson/images. html and http://www.sweb.uky.edu/~mnguy2/ histofVN.htm.

CHAPTER 14

THE LAST GREAT NOMADIC CHALLENGES: FROM CHINGGIS KHAN TO TIMUR

A 14th-century miniature painting from Rashid al-Din's History of the World depicts Mongol cavalry charging into battle against retreating Persians. The speed and endurance of Mongol cavalry made it difficult for routed foes to retreat and live to fight another day. As the painting suggests, surrender or death were often the only options for those overrun by Mongol units.

- The Mongol Empire of Chinggis Khan
- DOCUMENT: A European Assessment of the Virtues and Vices of the Mongols
- The Mongol Drive to the West
- VISUALIZING THE PAST: The Mongol Empire as a Bridge Between Civilizations
- The Mongol Interlude in Chinese History
- IN DEPTH: The Eclipse of the Nomadic War Machine
- GLOBAL CONNECTIONS: The Mongol Linkages

From the first explosion of Mongol military might from the steppes of central Asia in the early 13th century to the death of Timur in 1405, the nomads of central Asia made a stunning return to center stage in world history. Mongol invasions ended or interrupted many of the great empires of the postclassical period and also extended the world network that had increasingly defined the period. Under Chinggis Khan, the Mongols and their many nomadic neighbors were forged into the mightiest war machine the world had seen to that time. With stunning rapidity his Mongol forces conquered central Asia, northern China, and eastern Persia (see Map 14.1). Under Chinggis Khan's sons and grandsons, the rest of China, Tibet, Persia, Iraq, much of Asia Minor, and all of southern Russia were added to the vast Mongol imperium.

Although the empire was divided between Chinggis Khan's sons after his death in 1227, the four **khanates** or kingdoms, which emerged in the struggles for succession, dominated most of Asia for the next one and a half centuries. The Mongol conquests and the empires they produced were the most formidable nomadic challenge to the growing global dominance of the sedentary peoples of the civilized cores since the great nomadic migrations in the first centuries C.E. Except for Timur's devastating but short-lived grab for power at the end of the 14th century, nomadic peoples would never again mount a challenge as massive and sweeping as that of the Mongols.

In most histories until quite recently, the Mongol conquests have been depicted as a savage assault by backward and barbaric peoples on many of the most ancient and developed centers of human civilization. Depending on the civilization from whose city walls a historian recorded the coming of the Mongol "hordes," they were depicted as the scourge of Islam, devils bent on destroying Christianity, persecutors of the Buddhists, or defilers of the Confucian traditions of China. They were indeed fierce fighters and capable of terrible acts of retribution against those who dared to defy them, but the Mongols' conquests brought much more than death and devastation. At the peak of their power, the domains of the Mongol *khans*, or rulers, made up a vast realm in which once-hostile peoples lived together in peace and most religions were tolerated. From the Khanate of Persia in the west to the empire of the fabled Kubilai Khan in the east, the law code first promulgated by Chinggis Khan gave order to human interaction. Like the Islamic expansion that preceded it, the Mongol explosion laid the foundations for more human interaction on a global scale, extending and intensifying the world network that had been building since the classical age.

313

900 C.E.	**1100 C.E.**	**1200 C.E.**	**1250 C.E.**	**1300 C.E.**
907–1118 Khitan conquest of North China	**1115–1234** Jurchens (Qin dynasty) rule north China	**1206** Temujin takes the name of Chinggis Khan; Mongol state is founded	**1253** Mongol victory over Seljuk Turks; rise of Ottoman Turks in Middle East	**1336–1405** Life of Timur
1037–1194 Seljuk Turks dominant in the Middle East	**1126** Song dynasty flees to south China	**1215** First Mongol attacks on north China; Beijing captured	**1258** Mongol destruction of Baghdad	**mid-14th century** Spread of Black Death in Eurasia
	1130–c. 1250 Almohads rule North Africa and Spain	**1219–1223** First Mongol invasions of Russia and the Islamic world	**1260** Mamluk (slave) rulers of Egypt defeat Mongols at Ain Jalut; end of drive west	
		1227 Death of Chinggis Khan; Ogedei named successor	**1260–1294** Reign of Kubilai Khan in China	
		1234 Mongols take all of north China; end of Qin dynasty	**1271–1295** Journey of Marco Polo to central Asia, China, and southeast Asia	
		1235–1279 Mongol conquest of south China; end of southern Song dynasty	**1271–1368** Reign of the Yuan (Mongol) dynasty in China	
		1236–1240 Mongol conquest of Russia	**1274–1280** Failed Mongol invasions of Japan	
		1240–1241 Mongol invasion of western Europe	**1290s** First true guns used in China	

The Mongol Empire of Chinggis Khan

The Mongols had long been one of the nomadic peoples that intervened periodically in Chinese history. But tribal divisions and rivalries with neighboring ethnic groups, particularly Turkic peoples, had long blunted the expansive potential of Mongol warrior culture. In the early 13th century, these and other obstacles to Mongol expansion were overcome, primarily because of the leadership of an astute political strategist and brilliant military commander who took the title Chinggis Khan. Within decades, the Mongols and allied nomadic groups built an empire that stretched from the Middle Eastern heartlands of the Islamic world to the China Sea.

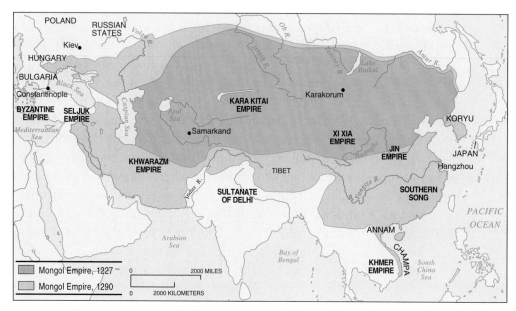

Map 14.1   *The Mongol Empire of Chinggis Khan*

In most ways, the Mongols epitomized nomadic society and culture. Their survival depended on the well-being of the herds of goats and sheep they drove from one pasture area to another according to the cycle of the seasons. Their staple foods were the meat and milk products provided by their herds, supplemented in most cases by grain and vegetables gained through trade with sedentary farming peoples. They also traded hides and dairy products for jewelry, weapons, and cloth made in urban centers. They dressed in sheepskins, made boots from tanned sheep hides, and lived in round felt tents made of wool sheared from their animals (Figure 14.1). The tough little ponies they rode to round up their herds, hunt wild animals, and make war were equally essential to their way of life. Mongol boys and girls could ride as soon as they were able to walk. Mongol warriors could ride for days on end, sleeping and eating in the saddle.

Like the early Arabs and other nomadic peoples we have encountered, the basic unit of Mongol society was the tribe, which was divided into kin-related clans whose members camped and herded together on a regular basis. When threatened by external enemies or preparing for raids on other nomads or invasions of sedentary areas, clans and tribes could be combined in great confederations. Depending on the skills of their leaders, these confederations could be held together for months or even years. But when the threat had passed or the raiding was done, clans and tribes drifted back to their own pasturelands and campsites. At all organizational levels, leaders were elected by the free men of the group. Although women exercised influence within the family and had the right to be heard in tribal councils, men dominated leadership positions.

Courage in battle, usually evidenced by bravery in the hunt, and the ability to forge alliances and attract

Figure 14.1 *This sketch of a Mongol household on the move illustrates the diversity and mobility of one of the nomadic societies that has shaped global history. The Mongols depended on sheep for food, clothing, and shelter, and they rode both horses and camels. As the drawing shows, they also used oxen when they needed animal power for key tasks such as transporting their housing for seasonal or longer-term migrations. This obviously was a cumbersome process, but the Mongols mounted the tents on huge wagons, which were pulled by large teams of oxen. This combination of animal transport and comfortable but movable shelters made the Mongols one of the most mobile preindustrial societies.*

dependants were vital leadership skills. A strong leader could quickly build up a large following of chiefs from other clans and tribal groups. If the leader grew old and feeble or suffered severe reverses, his subordinates would quickly abandon him. He expected this to happen, and the subordinates felt no remorse. Their survival and that of their dependants hinged on attaching themselves to a strong tribal leader.

The Making of a Great Warrior: The Early Career of Chinggis Khan

Since the early millennia of recorded history, nomadic peoples speaking Mongolian languages had enjoyed moments of power and had actually carved out regional kingdoms in north China in the 4th and 10th centuries C.E. In the early 12th century, Chinggis Khan's great-grandfather, Kabul Khan, led a Mongol alliance that had won glory by defeating an army sent against them by the Qin kingdom of north China. Soon after this victory, Kabul Khan became ill and died. His successors could neither defeat their nomadic enemies nor hold the Mongol alliance together. Divided and beaten, the Mongols fell on hard times.

Chinggis Khan, who as a youth was named Temujin, was born in the 1170s into one of the splinter clans that fought for survival in the decades after the death of Kabul Khan (see Figure 14.2). Temujin's father was an able leader who built up a decent following and negotiated a promise of marriage between

Figure 14.2 *In this miniature from a Persian history, Chinggis Khan is shown acknowledging the submission of a rival prince. Though he conquered a vast empire, Chinggis Khan did not live long enough to build a regular bureaucracy to govern it. His rule was dependant on vassal chieftains such as the one shown in the painting, whose loyalty in turn depended on the maintenance of Mongol military might. When the military strength of the Mongol Empire began to decline, subject princes soon rose up to establish the independence of their domains.*

Document

A European Assessment of the Virtues and Vices of the Mongols

As we have seen, much of what we know about the history of nomadic peoples is based on the records and reactions of observers from sedentary cultures that were their mortal enemies. Some of the most famous observers were those, including Marco Polo, who visited the vast Mongol domains at the height of the khans' power in the 12th and 13th centuries. Many tried to assess the strengths and weaknesses of these people, who were suddenly having such a great impact on the history of much of the known world. One of the most insightful of these observers was a Franciscan friar named Giovanni de Piano Carpini. In 1245, Pope Innocent IV sent Piano Carpini as an envoy to the "Great Khan" to protest the recent assaults by his Mongol forces on Christian Europe. The pope's protest had little effect on the Mongol decision to strike elsewhere in the following years. But Piano Carpini's extensive travels produced one of the most detailed accounts of Mongol society and culture to be written in the mid-13th century. As the following passages suggest, like other visitors from sedentary areas, he gave the Mongols a very mixed review:

> In the whole world there are to be found no more obedient subjects than the Tartars [Mongols]....They pay their lords more respect than any other people, and would hardly dare lie to them. Rarely do they revile each other, but if they should, the dispute hardly ever leads to blows. Wars, quarrels, the infliction of bodily harm, and manslaughter do not occur among them, and there are no large-scale thieves or robbers among them....
>
> They treat one another with due respect; they regard each other almost as members of one family, and, although they do not have a lot of food, they like to share it with one another....When riding they can endure extreme cold and at times also fierce heat; they are neither soft, nor sensitive [to the weather]. They do not seem to feel in any way envious of one another, and no public trials occur among them. No one holds his fellow in con-

tempt, but each helps and supports the other to the limits of his abilities.

They are extremely arrogant toward other people and look down on all others with disdain. In fact, they regard them, both noble and humble people alike, as little better than nothing....Toward other people the Tartars tend to anger and are easily roused....They are the greatest liars in the world in dealing with other people [than the Tartars], and hardly a true word escapes from their mouths. Initially they flatter but in the end they sting like scorpions. They are crafty and sly, and wherever possible they try to get the better of everybody else by false pretenses....

They are messy in their eating and drinking and in their whole way of life. Drunkenness is honorable among them....At the same time they are mean and greedy, and if they want something, they will not stop begging and asking for it, until they have got it. They cling fiercely to what they have, and in making gifts they are extremely miserly. They have no conscience about killing other people. In short, if one tried to enumerate all their bad characteristics there would be too many to put on paper.

Questions: What might the qualities of the Mongols that Piano Carpini emphasizes tell us about his own society and its values or shortcomings? How are the Mongol virtues he extols linked to the achievements of Chinggis Khan and the stunning Mongol wars of conquest? To what extent would they be typical of nomadic societies more generally? In what ways might his account of Mongol vices be simply dismissed as "sour grapes" resulting from European defeats? In what ways might these vices be linked to the hardships of Mongol life? How useful do you think this stereotyping is? Why have observers from nearly all cultures resorted to these sorts of generalizations when describing other peoples and societies?

---

his eldest son and the daughter of a stronger Mongol chief. According to Mongol accounts, just when the family fortunes seemed to be on the upswing, Temujin's father was poisoned by the agents of a rival nomadic group. Suddenly, Temujin, who was still a teenager, was thrust into a position of leadership. But most of the chiefs who had attached themselves to his

father refused to follow a mere boy, whose prospects of survival appeared to be slim.

In the months that followed, Temujin's much-reduced encampment was threatened and finally attacked by a rival tribe. He was taken prisoner in 1182, locked into a wooden collar, and led in humiliation to the camp of his enemies. After a daring midnight escape, Temujin rejoined his mother and brothers and found refuge for his tiny band of followers deep in the mountains. Facing extermination, Temujin did what any sensible nomad leader would have done: He and his people joined the camp of a more powerful Mongol chieftain who had once been aided by Temujin's father. With the support of this powerful leader, Temujin avenged the insults of the clan that had enslaved him and another that had taken advantage of his weakness to raid his camp for horses and women.

These successes and Temujin's growing reputation as a warrior and military commander soon won him allies and clan chiefs eager to attach themselves to a leader with a promising future. Within a decade, the youthful Temujin had defeated his Mongol rivals and routed the forces sent to crush him by other nomadic peoples. In 1206, at a **kuriltai,** or meeting of all of the Mongol chieftains, Temujin—renamed Chinggis Khan—was elected the **khagan,** or supreme ruler, of the Mongol tribes. United under a strong leader, the Mongols prepared to launch a massive assault on an unsuspecting world.

Building the Mongol War Machine

The men of the Mongol tribes that had elevated Chinggis Khan to leadership were natural warriors. Trained from youth not only to ride but also to hunt and fight, they were physically tough, mobile, and accustomed to killing and death. They wielded a variety of weapons, including lances, hatchets, and iron maces. None of their weapons was as devastating as their powerful short bows. A Mongol warrior could fire a quiver of arrows with stunning accuracy without breaking the stride of his horse. He could hit enemy soldiers as distant as 400 yards (the range for the roughly contemporary English longbow was 250 yards) while ducking under the belly of his pony, or leaning over the horse's rump. The fact that the Mongol armies were entirely cavalry meant that they moved so rapidly that their advances alone could be demoralizing to enemy forces.

To a people whose very lifestyle bred mobility, physical courage, and a love of combat, Chinggis Khan and his many able subordinate commanders brought organization, discipline, and unity of command. The old quarrels and vendettas between clans and tribes were overridden by loyalty to the khagan. Thus, energies once devoted to infighting were now

directed toward conquest and the forcible exaction of tribute, both in areas controlled by other nomadic groups and in the civilized centers that fringed the steppes on all sides. The Mongol forces were divided into armies made up of basic fighting units called **tumens,** each consisting of 10,000 warriors. Each tumen was further divided into units of 1000, 100, and 10 warriors. Commanders at each level were responsible for training, arming, and disciplining the cavalrymen under their charge. The tumens were also divided into heavy cavalry, which carried lances and wore some metal armor, and light cavalry, which relied primarily on the bow and arrow and leather helmets and body covering. Even more lightly armed were the scouting parties that rode ahead of Mongol armies and, using flags and special signal fires, kept the main force informed of the enemy's movements.

Chinggis Khan also created a separate messenger force whose bodies were tightly bandaged to allow them to remain in the saddle for days, switching from horse to horse to carry urgent messages between the khagan and his commanders. Military discipline had long been secured by personal ties between commanders and ordinary soldiers. Mongol values, which made courage in battle a prerequisite for male self-esteem, were buttressed by a formal code that dictated the immediate execution of a warrior who deserted his unit. Chinggis Khan's swift executions left little doubt about the fate of traitors to his own cause or turncoats who abandoned enemy commanders in his favor. His generosity to brave foes was also legendary. The most famous of the latter, a man named Jebe, nicknamed "The Arrow," won the khagan's affection and high posts in the Mongol armies by standing his ground after his troops had been routed and fearlessly shooting Chinggis Khan's horse out from under him.

A special unit supplied Mongol armies with excellent maps of the areas they were to invade. These were drawn largely according to the information supplied by Chinggis Khan's extensive network of spies and informers. New weapons, including a variety of flaming and exploding arrows, gunpowder projectiles, and later bronze cannons, were also devised for the Mongol forces. By the time Chinggis Khan's armies rode east and west in search of plunder and conquest in the second decade of the 13th century, they were among the best armed and trained and the most experienced, disciplined, and mobile soldiers in the world.

Conquest: The Mongol Empire Under Chinggis Khan

When he was proclaimed the khagan in 1206, Temu-jin probably was not yet 40 years old. At that point, he was the supreme ruler of nearly one-half million Mongols and the overlord of 1 to 2 million more nomads who had been defeated by his armies or had allied themselves with this promising young com-mander. But Chinggis Khan had much greater ambi-tions. He once said that his greatest pleasure in life was making war, defeating enemies, forcing "their beloved [to] weep, riding on their horses, embracing their wives and daughters." He came to see himself and his sons as men marked for a special destiny: war-riors born to conquer the known world. In 1207, he set out to fulfill this ambition. His first campaigns humbled the Tangut kingdom of Xi Xia in northwest China (see Map 14.1), whose ruler was forced to declare himself a vassal of the khagan and pay a hefty tribute. Next, the Mongol armies attacked the much more powerful Qin Empire, which the Manchu-related Jurchens had established a century earlier in north China.

In these campaigns, the Mongol armies were confronted for the first time with large, fortified cities whose inhabitants assumed that they could easily withstand the assaults of these uncouth nomads from the steppes. Indeed, the Mongol invaders were thwarted at first by the intricate defensive works that the Chinese had perfected over the centuries to deter nomadic incursions. But the adaptive Mongols, with the help of captured Chinese artisans and military commanders, soon devised a whole arsenal of siege weapons. These included battering rams, catapults that hurled rocks and explosive balls, and bamboo rockets that spread fire and fear in besieged towns.

Chinggis Khan and the early Mongol comman-ders had little regard for these towns, whose inhabi-tants they saw as soft. Therefore, when they met resistance, the Mongols adopted a policy of terrifying retribution. Although the Mongols often spared the lives of famous scholars—whom they employed as advisors—and artisans with particularly useful skills, towns that fought back were usually sacked once they had been taken. The townspeople were slaughtered or sold into slavery; their homes, palaces, mosques, and temples were reduced to rubble. Towns that sur-rendered without a fight were usually spared this fate, although they were required to pay tribute to their Mongol conquerors as the price of their deliverance.

First Assault on the Islamic World: Conquest in China

Once they had established a foothold in north China and solidified their empire in the steppes, the Mon-gol armies moved westward against the Kara Khitai Empire, which had been established by a Mongolian-speaking people a century earlier (see Map 14.1). Having overwhelmed and annexed the Kara Khitai by 1219, Chinggis Khan dispatched envoys to demand the submission of **Muhammad Shah II,** the Turkic ruler of the Khwarazm Empire to the west. Outraged by the audacity of the still little-known Mongol com-mander, one of Muhammad's subordinates had some of Chinggis Khan's later envoys killed and sent the rest with shaved heads back to the khagan. These insults meant war—a war in which the Khwarazm were overwhelmed. Their great cities fell to the new siege weapons and tactics the Mongols had perfected in their north China campaigns.

Again and again, the Mongols used their favorite battle tactic in these encounters. Cavalry were sent to attack the enemy's main force. Feigning defeat, the cavalry retreated, drawing the opposing forces out of formation in the hope of a chance to slaughter the flee-ing Mongols. Once the enemy's pursuing horsemen had spread themselves over the countryside, the main force of Mongol heavy cavalry, until then concealed, attacked them in a devastating pincer formation.

Within two years, his once-flourishing cities in ruin and his kingdom in Mongol hands, Muhammad Shah II, having retreated across his empire, died on a desolate island in the Caspian Sea. In addition to greatly enlarging his domains, Chinggis Khan's vic-tories meant that he could bring tens of thousands of Turkic horsemen into his armies. By 1227, the year of his death, the Mongols ruled an empire that stretched from eastern Persia to the North China Sea.

Life Under the Mongol Imperium

Despite their aggressiveness as warriors and the destruction they could unleash on those who resisted their demands for submission and tribute, the Mon-gols were remarkably astute and tolerant rulers. Chinggis Khan himself set the standard. He was a complex man, capable of gloating over the ruin of his enemies but also open to new ideas and committed to building a world where the diverse peoples of his empire could live together in peace. Though illiter-ate, Chinggis Khan was neither the ignorant savage nor the cultureless vandal often depicted in the accounts of civilized writers—usually those who had never met him. Once the conquered peoples had been subdued, he took a keen interest in their arts and learning, although he refused to live in their cities. Instead, he established a new capital at **Karakorum** on the steppes and summoned the wise and clever from all parts of the empire to the lavish palace of tents with gilded pillars where he lived with his wives and closest advisors.

At Karakorum, Chinggis Khan consulted with Confucian scholars about how to rule China, with Muslim engineers about how to build siege weapons and improve trade with the lands farther west, and with Daoist holy men, whom he hoped could give him an elixir that would make him immortal. Although he himself followed the *shamanistic* (focused on nature spirits) beliefs of his ancestors, all religions were tolerated in his empire. An administrative framework that drew on the advice and talents of both Muslim and Chinese bureaucrats was created. A script was devised for the Mongolian language to facilitate recordkeeping and the standardization of laws.

The Mongol conquests brought a peace to much of Asia that in some areas persisted for generations. In the towns of the empire, handicraft production and scholarship flourished and artistic creativity was allowed free expression. Secure trade routes made for prosperous merchants and wealthy, cosmopolitan cities. One Muslim historian wrote of the peoples within the Mongol Empire that they "enjoyed such a peace that a man might have journeyed from the land of sunrise to the land of sunset with a golden platter upon his head without suffering the least violence from anyone." Paradoxically, Mongol expansion, which sedentary chroniclers condemned as a "barbarian" orgy of violence and destruction, also became a major force for economic and social development and the enhancement of civilized life.

The Death of Chinggis Khan and the Division of the Empire

In 1226, his wars to the west won, Chinggis Khan turned east with an army of 180,000 warriors to complete the conquest of China that he regretted having left unfinished more than a decade earlier. After routing a much larger Tangut army in a battle fought on the frozen waters of the Yellow River, the Mongol armies overran the kingdom of Xi Xia, plundering, burning, and mercilessly hunting down Tangut survivors. As his forces closed in on the Tangut capital and last refuge, Chinggis Khan, who had been injured in a skirmish some months earlier, fell grievously ill. After lecturing his sons on the dangers of quarreling among themselves for the spoils of the empire, the khagan died in August 1227.

With one last outburst of wrath, this time directed against death itself, the Mongols carried his body back to Mongolia for burial. The Mongol forces escorting the funeral procession hunted down and killed every human and animal in its path. The vast pasturelands the Mongols now controlled were divided between Chinggis Khan's three remaining sons and **Batu,** a grandson and heir of the khagan's recently deceased son, Jochi. Towns and cultivated areas such as those in north China and parts of Persia were considered the common property of the Mongol ruling family. A kuriltai was convened at Karakorum, the Mongol capital, to select a successor to the great conqueror. In accordance with Chinggis Khan's preference, **Ogedei,** his third son, was elected grand khan. Though not as capable a military leader as his brothers or nephews, Ogedei was a crafty diplomat and deft manipulator. As it turned out, these skills were much needed to keep the ambitious heads of the vast provinces of the empire from each other's throats.

For nearly a decade, Ogedei directed Mongol energies into further campaigns and conquests. The areas targeted by this new round of Mongol expansion paid the price for peace within the Mongol Empire. The fate of the most important victims—Russia and eastern Europe, the Islamic heartlands, and China—will be the focus of much of the rest of this chapter.

The Mongol Drive to the West

 While pursuing the Khwarazm ruler, Muhammad Shah II, the Mongols had made their first contacts with the rich kingdoms to the west of the steppe heartlands of Chinggis Khan's empire. Raids into Georgia and across the Russian steppe convinced the Mongol commanders that the Christian lands to the west were theirs for the taking.

Russia and Europe were added to the Mongols' agenda for world conquest. Subjugating these regions became the project of the armies of the **Golden Horde,** named after the golden tent of the early

Visualizing the Past

The Mongol Empire as a Bridge Between Civilizations

Chinggis Khan and his successors actively promoted the growth of trade and travelers by protecting the caravans that made their way across the ancient Asian silk routes. The Mongols also established rest stations for weary merchants and fortified outposts for those harassed by bandits. These measures transformed the Mongol imperium into a massive conduit between the civilizations of Europe, the Middle East, and the rest of Asia. The map below illustrates a wide variety of marketable goods and inventions, as well as the agents and objects of several religions, between areas within the empire and along its lengthy borders. Study these patterns and then answer the questions that follow.

Questions: Discuss some of the major ways in which the Mongol Empire facilitated exchanges and interaction between civilizations and culture areas. What were the main centers of different kinds of products? What were the main directions in which ideas, goods, and new inventions flowed? Based on the discussions in the preceding chapters, who were some of the key agents of these exchanges? Why were the networks of exchange established by the Mongols so short-lived?

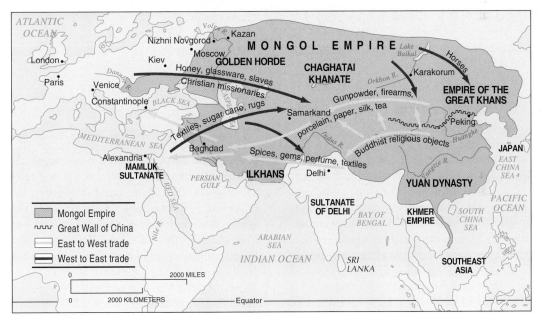

The Mongol Empire and the Global Exchange Network

khans of the western sector of the Mongol Empire. The territories of the Golden Horde made up one of the four great khanates into which the Mongol Empire was divided at the time of Chinggis Khan's death (Map 14.2). Under the rule of Chinggis Khan's grandson Batu, they began an invasion of Russia in 1236. In a very real sense, the Mongol assault on

Russia was a side campaign, a chance to fine-tune the war machine and win a little booty on the way to the real prize: western Europe.

As we saw in Chapter 9, in the first half of the 13th century when the Mongol warriors first descended, Russia had been divided into numerous petty kingdoms, centered on trading cities such as

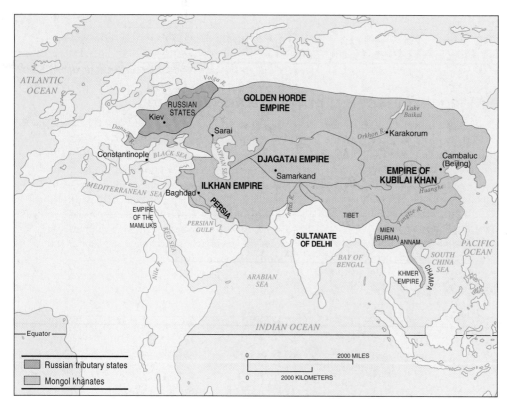

Map 14.2 *The Four Khanates of the Divided Mongol Empire*

Novgorod and Kiev (see Maps 9.3 and 14.2). By this time, Kiev, which originally dominated much of central Russia, had been in decline for some time. As a result, there was no paramount power to rally Russian forces against the invaders. Despite the warnings of those who had witnessed the crushing defeats suffered by the Georgians in the early 1220s, the princes of Russia refused to cooperate. They preferred to fight alone, and they were routed individually.

In 1236, Batu led a Mongol force of more than 120,000 cavalrymen into the Russian heartlands. From 1237 to 1238 and later in 1240, these Tatars, or Tartars (meaning people from hell), as the Russians called them, carried out the only successful winter invasions in Russian history. In fact, the Mongols preferred to fight in the winter. The frozen earth provided good footing for their horses, and frozen rivers gave them access to their enemies. One after another, the Mongol armies defeated the often much larger forces of local nomadic groups and Russian princes. Cities such as Ryazan, Moscow, and Vladimir, which

resisted the Mongol command to surrender, were destroyed; their inhabitants were slaughtered or led into slavery. As a contemporary Russian chronicler observed, "No eye remained to weep for the dead." Just as it seemed that all of Russia would be ravaged by the Mongols, whom the Russians compared to locusts, Batu's armies withdrew. The largest cities, Novgorod and Kiev, appeared to have been spared. Russian priests thanked God; the Mongol commanders blamed the spring thaw, which slowed the Mongol horsemen and raised the risk of defeat in the treacherous mud.

The Mongols returned in force in the winter of 1240. In this second campaign, even the great walled city of Kiev, which had reached a population of more than 100,000 by the end of the 12th century, fell. Enraged by Kievan resistance—its ruler had ordered the Mongol envoys thrown from the city walls—the Mongols reduced the greatest city in Russia to a smoldering ruin. The cathedral of Saint Sophia was spared, but the rest of the city was looted and destroyed, and its inhabitants were smoked out and slaughtered. Novgorod braced itself for the Mongol onslaught. Again, according to the Russian chroniclers, it was "miraculously" spared. In fact, it was saved largely because of the willingness of its prince, Alexander Nevskii, to submit, at least temporarily, to Mongol demands. In addition, the Mongol armies were eager to move on to the main event: the invasion of western Europe, which they perceived as a far richer but equally vulnerable region.

Russia in Bondage

The crushing victories of Batu's armies initiated nearly two and a half centuries of Mongol dominance in Russia. Russian princes were forced to submit as vassals of the khan of the Golden Horde and to pay tribute. Mongol demands fell particularly heavily on the Russian peasantry, who had to give their crops and labor to both their own princes and the Mongol overlords. Impoverished and ever fearful of the lightning raids of Mongol marauders, the peasants fled to remote areas or became, in effect, the serfs (see Chapter 9) of the Russian ruling class in return for protection. Some Russian towns made profits on the increased trade made possible by the Mongol links. Sometimes the gains exceeded the tribute they paid to the Golden Horde. No town benefited from the Mongol presence more than Moscow. Badly plundered and partially burned in the early Mongol assaults, the city was gradually rebuilt, and its ruling princes steadily swallowed up nearby towns and surrounding villages. After 1328, Moscow also profited from its status as the tribute collector for the Mongol khans. Its princes not only used their position to fill their own coffers but also annexed other towns as punishment for falling behind on tribute payments.

As Moscow grew in strength, the power of the Golden Horde declined. Mongol religious toleration benefited both the Orthodox church and Moscow. The choice of Moscow as the seat of the Orthodox leaders brought new sources of wealth to its princes and buttressed its claims to be Russia's leading city. In 1380, those claims got an additional boost when the princes of Moscow shifted from being tribute collectors to being the defenders of Russia. In alliance with other Russian vassals, they raised an army that defeated the forces of the Golden Horde at the **Battle of Kulikova.** Their victory and the devastating blows

Timur's attacks dealt the Golden Horde two decades later effectively broke the Mongol hold over Russia.

Although much of the Mongols' impact was negative, their conquest was a turning point in Russian history in several ways. In addition to their importance to Moscow and the Orthodox church, Mongol contacts led to changes in Russian military organization and tactics and in the political style of Russian rulers. Claims that the Tatars were responsible for Russian despotism, either tsarist or Stalinist, are clearly overstated. Still, the Mongol example may have influenced the desire of Russian princes to centralize their control and reduce the limitations placed on their power by the landed nobility, clergy, and wealthy merchants. By far the greatest effects of Mongol rule were those resulting from Russia's isolation from Christian lands farther west. On one hand, the Mongols protected a divided and weak Russia from the attacks of much more powerful kingdoms such as Poland, Lithuania, and Hungary (see Map 14.2). On the other hand, in the period of Mongol rule, Russia was cut off from key transformations in western Europe that were inspired by the Renaissance and led ultimately to the Reformation.

Mongol Incursions and the Retreat from Europe

Until news of the Mongol campaigns in Russia reached European peoples such as the Germans and Hungarians farther west (see Map 14.2), Christian leaders had been quite pleased by the rise of a new military power in central Asia. Rumors and reports from Christians living in the area, chafing under what they saw as persecution by their Muslim overlords, convinced many in western Europe that the Mongol khan was none other than **Prester John.** Prester John was the name given to a mythical rich and powerful Christian monarch whose kingdom had supposedly been cut off from Europe by the Muslim conquests of the 7th and 8th centuries. Sometimes located in Africa, sometimes in central Asia, Prester John loomed large in the European imagination as a potential ally who could strike the Muslim enemy from the rear and join up with European Christians to destroy their common adversary. The Mongol assault on the Muslim Khwarazm Empire appeared to confirm the speculation that Chinggis Khan was indeed Prester John.

The assault on Christian, though Orthodox, Russia made it clear that the Mongol armies were neither the legions of Prester John nor more partial to Christians than to any other people who stood in their way. The rulers of Europe were nevertheless slow to realize the magnitude of the threat the Mongols posed to western Christendom. When Mongol envoys, one of whom was an Englishman, arrived at the court of King Bela of Hungary demanding that he surrender a group of nomads who had fled to his domains after being beaten by the Mongols in Russia, the king contemptuously dismissed them. King Bela also rebuffed Batu's demand that he submit to Mongol rule. The Hungarian monarch reasoned that he was the ruler of a powerful kingdom, whereas the Mongols were just another ragtag band of nomads in search of easy plunder. His refusal to negotiate provided the Mongols with a pretext to invade. Their ambition remained the conquest and pillage of all western Europe. That this goal was clearly attainable was demonstrated by the sound drubbing they gave to the Hungarians in 1240 and later to a mixed force of Christian knights led by the German ruler, King Henry of Silesia.

These victories left the Mongols free to raid and pillage from the Adriatic Sea region in the south to Poland and the German states of the north. It also left the rest of Europe open to Mongol conquest. Just as the kings and clergy of the western portions of Christendom were beginning to fear the worst, the Mongol forces disappeared. The death of the khagan Ogedei, in the distant Mongol capital at Karakorum, forced Batu to withdraw in preparation for the struggle for succession. The campaign for the conquest of Europe was never resumed. Perhaps Batu was satisfied with the huge empire of the Golden Horde that he ruled from his splendid new capital at Sarai on the Volga river in what is southern Russia today (see Map 14.2). Most certainly the Mongols had found richer lands to plunder in the following decades in the Muslim empires of the Middle East. Whatever the reason, Europe was spared the full fury of the Mongol assault. Of the civilizations that fringed the steppe homelands of the Mongols, only India was as fortunate.

The Mongol Assault on the Islamic Heartland

After the Mongol conquest of the Khwarazm Empire, it was only a matter of time before they struck west- ward against the far wealthier Muslim empires of Mesopotamia and north Africa (see Maps 7.2 and 14.2). The conquest of these areas became the main project of Hulegu, another grandson of Chinggis Khan and the ruler of the Ilkhan portions of the Mongol Empire. As we saw in Chapter 7, one of the key results of Hulegu's assaults on the Muslim heartlands was the capture and destruction of Baghdad in 1258 (Figure 14.3). The murder of the Abbasid caliph, one of some 800,000 people who were reported to have been killed in Mongol retribution for the city's resistance, ended the dynasty that had

Figure 14.3 *The Abbasid capital at Baghdad had long been in decline when the Mongols besieged it in 1258. The Mongols' sack of the city put an end to all pretense that Baghdad was still the center of the Muslim world. The Mongol assault on Baghdad also revealed how vulnerable even cities with high and extensive walls were to the artillery and other siege weapons that the Mongols and Chinese had pioneered. In the centuries that followed, major innovations in fortifications, many introduced first in Europe, were made to counter the introduction of gunpowder and the new siege cannon.*

ruled the core regions of the Islamic world since the mid-8th century.

Given the fate of Baghdad, it is understandable that Muslim historians treated the coming of the Mongols as one of the great catastrophes in the history of Islam. The murder of the caliph and his family left the faithful without a central authority. The sack of Baghdad and many other cities from central Asia to the shores of the Mediterranean devastated the focal points of Islamic civilization. One contemporary Muslim chronicler, Ibn al-Athir, found the violence the Mongols had done to his people so horrific that he apologized to his readers for recounting it and wished that he had not been born to see it. He lamented,

> In just one year they seized the most populous, the most beautiful, and the best cultivated part of the earth whose inhabitants excelled in character and urbanity. In the countries that have not yet been overrun by them, everyone spends the night afraid that they may yet appear there, too….Thus, Islam and the Muslims were struck, at that time by a disaster such as no people had experienced before.

Given these reverses, one can imagine the relief the peoples of the Muslim world felt when the Mongols were finally defeated in 1260 by the armies of the Mamluk, or slave, dynasty of Egypt. Ironically, **Baibars,** the commander of the Egyptian forces, and many of his lieutenants had been enslaved by the Mongols some years earlier and sold in Egypt, where they rose to power through military service. The Muslim victory was won with the rare cooperation of the Christians, who allowed Baibars' forces to cross unopposed through their much-diminished crusader territories in Palestine. Christian support demonstrated how far the former crusader states had gone in accommodating their more powerful Muslim neighbors.

Hulegu was in central Asia, engaged in yet another succession struggle, when the battle occurred. Upon his return, he was forced to reconsider his plans for conquest of the entire Muslim world. The Mamluks were deeply entrenched and growing stronger; Hulegu was threatened by his cousin **Berke,** the new khan of the Golden Horde to the north, who had converted to Islam. After openly clashing with Berke and learning of Baibars' overtures for an alliance with the Golden Horde, Hulegu decided to settle for the kingdom he already ruled, which stretched from the frontiers of Byzantium to the Oxus River in central Asia (see Map 14.2).

The Mongol Interlude in Chinese History

 Of all the areas the Mongols conquered, perhaps none was administered as closely as China. After decades of hard campaigning in the mid-13th century, the Mongol interlude in Chinese history lasted only about a century. Although the age-old capacity of the Chinese to assimilate their nomadic conquerors was evident from the outset, the Mongols managed to retain a distinct culture and social separateness until they were driven back beyond the Great Wall in the late 1360s. They also opened China to influences from Arab and Persian lands, and even to contacts with Europe, which came to full fruition in the centuries of indigenous Chinese revival that followed under the Ming dynasty.

Soon after Ogedei was elected as the great khan, the Mongol advance into China was resumed. Having conquered the Xi Xia and Qin empires, the Mongol commanders turned to what remained of the Song empire in south China (see Maps 14.1 and 14.2). In the campaigns against the Song, the Mongol forces were directed by **Kubilai Khan** (Figure 14.4). Kubilai was one of the grandsons of Chinggis Khan, and he would play a pivotal role in Chinese history for the next half century. Even under a decadent dynasty that had long neglected its defenses, south China was one of the toughest areas for the Mongols to conquer. From 1235 to 1279, the Mongols were constantly on the march; they fought battle after battle and besieged seemingly innumerable, well-fortified Chinese cities. In 1260, Kubilai assumed the title of the great khan, much to the chagrin of his cousins who ruled other parts of the empire. A decade later, in 1271, on the recommendation of Chinese advisors, he changed the name of his Mongol regime to a Chinese-language dynastic title, the Yuan. Although he was still nearly a decade away from fully defeating the last-ditch efforts of Confucian bureaucrats and Chinese generals to save the Song dynasty, Kubilai ruled most of China. He now set about the task of establishing more permanent Mongol control.

As the different regions of China came under Mongol rule, Kubilai passed many laws to preserve the distinction between Mongol and Chinese. He

Figure 14.4 *This portrait of Kubilai Khan, by far the most important Mongol ruler of China, emphasizes his Mongol physical features, beard and hair styles, and dress. But Kubilai was determined to "civilize" his Mongol followers according to Chinese standards. Not only did he himself adopt a Chinese lifestyle, but he had his son educated by the best Confucian scholars to be a proper Chinese emperor. Kubilai also became a major patron of the Chinese arts and a promoter of Chinese culture.*

the culture of the defeated, Kubilai Khan had long been fascinated by Chinese civilization. Even before beginning the conquest of the Song Empire, he had surrounded himself with Chinese advisors, some Buddhist, others Daoist or Confucian. His capital at **Tatu** in the north (present-day Beijing) was built on the site occupied by earlier dynasties, and he introduced Chinese rituals and classical music into his own court. Kubilai also put the empire on the Chinese calendar and offered sacrifices to his ancestors at a special temple in the imperial city. But he rebuffed the pleas of his Confucian advisors to reestablish the civil service exams, which had been discontinued by the Qin rulers.

In the Yuan era, a new social structure was established in China, with the Mongols on top and their central Asian nomadic and Muslim allies right below them in the hierarchy. These two groups occupied most offices at the highest levels of the bureaucracy. Beneath them came the north Chinese; below them, the ethnic Chinese and the minority peoples of the south. Thus, ethnic Chinese from both north and south ran the Yuan bureaucracy at the regional and local levels, but they could exercise power at the top only as advisors to the Mongols or other nomadic officials. At all levels, their activities were scrutinized by Mongol functionaries from an enlarged and much-strengthened censors' bureau.

Gender Roles and the Convergence of Mongol and Chinese Culture

Mongol women remained aloof from Chinese culture—at least Chinese culture in its Confucian guise. They refused to adopt the practice of footbinding, which so limited the activities of Chinese women. They retained their rights to property and control within the household as well as the freedom to move about the town and countryside. No more striking evidence of their independence can be found than contemporary accounts of Mongol women riding to the hunt, both with their husbands and at the head of their own hunting parties. The daughter of one of Kubilai's cousins went to war, and she refused to marry until one of her many suitors was able to throw her in a wrestling match.

The persisting influence of Mongol women after the Mongols settled down in China is exemplified by **Chabi,** the wife of Kubilai Khan (Figure 14.5). She was one of Kubilai's most important confidants on

forbade Chinese scholars to learn the Mongol script, which was used for records and correspondence at the upper levels of the imperial government. Mongols were forbidden to marry ethnic Chinese, and only women from nomadic families were selected for the imperial harem. Even friendships between the two peoples were discouraged, and Mongol military forces remained separate from the Chinese. Mongol religious ceremonies and customs were retained, and a tent encampment in the traditional Mongol style was set up in the imperial city even though Kubilai usually lived in a Chinese-style palace.

Despite his measures to ensure that the conquering Mongol minority was not completely absorbed by

Figure 14.5 *A portrait of Chabi, the energetic and influential wife of Kubilai Khan. Kubilai's determination to adopt Chinese culture without being overwhelmed by it was bolstered by the advice and example of Chabi. Displaying the independent-mindedness and political savvy of many Mongol women, Chabi gave Kubilai critical advice on how to counter the schemes of his ambitious brother and how to handle the potentially hostile scholar-gentry elite and peasantry that came to be ruled by Mongol overlords.*

political and diplomatic matters, and she promoted Buddhist interests in the highest circles of government. Chabi played a critical role in fostering policies aimed at reconciling the majority ethnic Chinese population of the empire to Mongol rule. She convinced Kubilai that the harsh treatment of the survivors of the defeated Song imperial family would only anger the peoples of north China and make them more dif-

ficult to rule. On another occasion, she demonstrated that she shared Kubilai's respect for Chinese culture by frustrating a plan to turn cultivated lands near the capital into pasturelands for the Mongols' ponies. Thus, the imperial couple were a good match of astute political skills and cosmopolitanism, tempered by respect for their own traditions and a determination to preserve those they found the most valuable.

Mongol Tolerance and Foreign Cultural Influence

Like Chinggis Khan and other Mongol overlords, Kubilai and Chabi had unbounded curiosity and very cosmopolitan tastes. Their generous patronage drew scholars, artists, artisans, and office-seekers from many lands to the splendid Yuan court. Some of the most favored came from Muslim kingdoms to the east that had come under Mongol rule. Muslims were included in the second highest social grouping, just beneath the Mongols themselves. Persians and Turks were admitted to the inner circle of Kubilai's administrators and advisors. Muslims designed and supervised the building of his Chinese-style imperial city and proposed new systems for more efficient tax collection. Persian astronomers imported more advanced Middle Eastern instruments for celestial observations, corrected the Chinese calendar, and made some of the most accurate maps the Chinese had ever seen. Muslim doctors ran the imperial hospitals and added translations of 36 volumes on Muslim medicine to the imperial library.

In addition to the Muslims, Kubilai welcomed travelers and emissaries from many foreign lands to his court. Like his grandfather, Kubilai had a strong interest in all religions and insisted on toleration in his domains. Buddhists, Nestorian Christians, Daoists, and Latin Christians made their way to his court. The most renowned of the latter were members of the Polo family from Venice in northern Italy, who traveled extensively in the Mongol Empire in the middle of the 13th century. Marco Polo's account of Kubilai Khan's court and empire, where he lived and served as an administrator for 17 years, is perhaps the most famous travel account written by a European (Figure 14.6). Marco accepted fantastic tales of grotesque and strange customs, and he may have taken parts of his account from other sources. Still, his descriptions of the palaces, cities, and wealth of Kubilai's empire enhanced European interest in Asia

Figure 14.6 *This 15th-century manuscript illumination depicts Marco Polo and his uncle offering homage to the Great Khan. The Polos were Venetian merchants, and Marco's elders had already traveled extensively in Asia in the decade before they set off with Marco. Marco had a great facility with languages, which served him well in his journeys through Asia by land and sea. On his way home in the mid-1290s, he related his many adventures to a writer of romances while both were prisoners of the Genoese, who were fierce rivals of the Venetians. Eventually published under the title* Description of the World, *Polo's account became one of a handful of definitive sources on the world beyond Europe for the explorers of the coming age of overseas expansion.*

and helped to inspire efforts by navigators such as Columbus to find a water route to these fabled lands.

Social Policies and Scholar-Gentry Resistance

Kubilai's efforts to promote Mongol adaptation to Chinese culture were overshadowed in the long run by measures to preserve Mongol separateness. The ethnic Chinese who made up the vast majority of his subjects, particularly in the south, were never really reconciled to Mongol rule. Despite Kubilai's cultivation of Confucian rituals and his extensive employment of Chinese bureaucrats, most of the scholar-gentry saw the Mongol overlord and his successors as uncouth barbarians whose policies endangered Chinese traditions. As it was intended to do, Kubilai's refusal to reinstate the examination route to administrative office prevented Confucian scholars from dominating politics. The favoritism he showed Mongol and other foreign officials further alienated the scholar-gentry.

To add insult to injury, Kubilai went to great lengths to bolster the position of the artisan classes, who had never enjoyed high standing, and the merchants, whom the Confucian thinkers had long dismissed as parasites. From the outset the Mongols had shown great regard for artisans and because of their useful skills had often spared them while killing their fellow city dwellers. During the Yuan period in China, merchants also prospered and commerce boomed, partly because of Mongol efforts to improve transportation and expand the supply of paper money. With amazing speed for a people who had no prior experience with seafaring, the Mongols developed a substantial navy, which played a major role in the conquest of the Song Empire. After the conquest of China was completed, the great Mongol war fleets were used to put down pirates, who threatened river and overseas commerce. Toward the end of Kubilai's reign, the navy also launched a number of overseas expeditions of exploration and conquest, which led to attacks on Japan and a brief reoccupation of Vietnam.

Ironically, despite the Mongols' suspicion of cities and sedentary lifestyles, both flourished in the Yuan era. The urban expansion begun under the Tang and Song dynasties continued, and the Mongol elite soon became addicted to the diversions of urban life. Traditional Chinese artistic endeavors, such as poetry and essay writing, languished under the Mongols in comparison with their flowering in the Tang and Song eras. But popular entertainments, particularly musical dramas, flourished. Perhaps the most famous Chinese dramatic work, *The Romance of the West Chamber*, was written in the Yuan period. Dozens of major playwrights wrote for the court, the rising merchant classes, and the Mongol elite. Actors and actresses, who had long been relegated by the Confucian scholars to the despised status of "mean people," achieved celebrity and social esteem. All of this rankled the scholar-gentry, who waited for the chance to restore Confucian decorum and what they believed to be the proper social hierarchy for a civilized people.

Initially, at least, Kubilai Khan pursued policies toward one social group, the peasants, that the scholarly class would have heartily approved. He forbade Mongol cavalrymen from turning croplands into pasture and restored the granary system for famine relief that had been badly neglected in the late Song. Kubilai also sought to reduce peasant tax and forced-labor burdens, partly by redirecting peasant payments from local nonofficial tax farmers directly to government officials. He and his advisors also developed a revolutionary plan to establish elementary education in the villages. Although the level of learning they envisioned was rudimentary, such a project, if it had been

enacted, would have been a major challenge to the educational system centered on the elite that long had dominated Chinese civilization.

The Fall of the House of Yuan

Historians often remark on the seeming contradiction between the military prowess of the Mongol conquerors and the short life of the dynasty they established in China. Kubilai Khan's long reign encompassed a good portion of the nine decades in which the Mongols ruled all of China. Already by the end of his reign, the dynasty was showing signs of weakening. Song loyalists raised revolts in the south, and popular hostility toward the foreign overlords was expressed more and more openly. The Mongol aura of military invincibility was badly tarnished by Kubilai's rebuffs at the hands of the military lords of Japan and the failure of the expeditions that he sent to punish them, first in 1274 and again in a much larger effort in 1280. The defeats suffered by Mongol forces engaged in similar expeditions to Vietnam and Java during this same period further undermined the Mongols' standing.

Kubilai's dissolute lifestyle in his later years, partly brought on by the death of his most beloved wife, Chabi, and five years later the death of his favorite son, led to a general softening of the Mongol ruling class as a whole. Kubilai's successors lacked his capacity for leadership and cared little for the tedium of day-to-day administrative tasks. Many of the Muslim and Chinese functionaries to whom they entrusted the imperial finances enriched themselves through graft and corruption. This greatly angered the hard-pressed peasantry, who bore the burden of rising taxes and demands for forced labor. The scholar-gentry played on this discontent by calling on the people to rise up and overthrow the "barbarian" usurpers.

By the 1350s, the signs of dynastic decline were apparent. Banditry and piracy were widespread, and the government's forces were too weak to curb them. Famine hit many regions and spawned local uprisings, which engulfed large portions of the empire. Secret religious sects, such as the **White Lotus Society,** were dedicated to overthrowing the dynasty. Their leaders' claims that they had magical powers to heal their followers and confound their enemies helped encourage further peasant resistance against the Mongols. As in the past, rebel leaders quarreled and fought with each other. For a time, chaos reigned as

The Eclipse of the Nomadic War Machine

As the shock waves of the Mongol and Timurid explosions amply demonstrate, nomadic incursions into the civilized cores have had an impact on global history that far exceeds what one would expect, given the small numbers of nomadic peoples and the limited resources of the regions they inhabited. From the time of the great Indo-European migrations in the formative epoch of civilized development in the 3rd and 2nd millennia B.C.E. through the classical and postclassical eras, nomadic peoples periodically emerged from their steppe, prairie, and desert fringe homelands to invade, often build empires, and settle in the sedentary zones of Eurasia, Africa, and the Americas. Their intrusions have significantly changed political history by destroying existing polities and even—as in the case of Assyria and Harappa—whole civilizations. They have also generated major population movements, sparked social upheavals, and facilitated critical cultural and economic exchanges across civilizations. As the Mongols' stunning successes in the 13th century illustrate, the ability of nomadic peoples to break through the defenses of the much more populous civilized zones and to establish control over much richer and more sophisticated peoples arose primarily from the nomads' advantages in waging war.

A reservoir of battle-ready warriors and mobility have proved to be the keys to success for expansion-minded nomads. Harsh environments and ongoing intertribal and interclan conflicts for survival within them produced tough, resourceful fighters who could live off the land on the march and who saw combat as an integral part of their lives. The horses and camels on which pastoral peoples in Eurasia and Sudanic Africa relied gave them a degree of mobility that confounded the sedentary peoples who tried to ward off their incursions. The mounted warriors of nomadic armies had the advantages of speed, surprise, and superior intelligence, gathered by mounted patrols. The most successful nomadic invaders, such as the Mongols, also were willing to experiment with and adapt to technological innovations. Some of these, such as the stirrup and various sorts of harnesses, were devised by the nomads themselves. Others, such as gunpowder and the siege engines—both Muslim and Chinese—that the Mongols used to smash the defenses of walled towns were borrowed from sedentary peoples and adapted to the nomads' fighting styles.

Aside from the military advantages of the nomads' lifestyles and social organization, their successes in war owed much to the weaknesses of their adversaries in the sedentary, civilized zones. Even in the best circumstances, the great empires that provided the main defense for agricultural peoples against nomadic incursions were diverse and overextended polities. Imperial control and protection diminished steadily as one moved away from the capital and core provinces. Imperial boundaries were usually fluid, and the outer provinces were vulnerable to nomadic raids and conquest.

Classical and postclassical empires, such as the Egyptian and Han and the Abbasid, Byzantine, and Song, enjoyed great advantages over the nomads in terms of the populations and resources they controlled. But their armies, almost without exception, were too slow, too low on firepower, and too poorly trained to resist large and well-organized forces of nomadic intruders. In times of dynastic strength in the sedentary zones, well-defended fortress systems and ingenious weapons—such as the crossbow, which the peasant conscripts could master fairly easily—were quite effective against nomadic incursions. Nonetheless, even the strongest dynasties depended heavily on protection payments to nomad leaders and the divisions between the nomadic peoples on their borders for their security. Even the strongest sedentary empires were shaken periodically by nomadic raids into the outer provinces. When the empires weakened or when large numbers of nomads were united under able leaders, such as Muhammad and his successors or Chinggis Khan, nomadic assaults made a shambles of sedentary armies and fortifications.

In many ways, the Mongol and Timurid explosions represented the apex of nomadic power and influence on world history. After these remarkable interludes, age-old patterns of interaction between nomads and town-dwelling peoples were transformed. These transformations resulted in the growing ability of sedentary peoples to first resist and then dominate nomadic peoples, and they mark a watershed in the history of the human community. Some of the causes of the shift were immediate and specific. The most critical of these was the devastation wrought by the Black Death on the nomads of central Asia in the 14th century. Although the epidemic was catastrophic for large portions of the civilized zones as well, it dealt the sparse nomadic populations a blow from which they took centuries to recover.

In the centuries after the Mongol conquests, the rulers of sedentary states found increasingly effective ways to centralize their political power and mobilize the labor and resources of their domains for war. The rulers of China and the empires of the Islamic belt made some improvements, but the sovereigns of the emerging states of western Europe surpassed all others in this regard. Stronger control and better organization allowed a growing share of steadily increasing national wealth to be channeled toward military ends. The competing rulers of Europe also invested heavily in technological innovations with military applications, from improved metalworking techniques to more potent gunpowder and firearms. From the 15th and 16th centuries, the discipline and training of European armies also improved. With pikes, muskets, fire drill, and trained commanders, European armies were more than a match for the massed nomad cavalry that had so long terrorized sedentary peoples.

With the introduction early in the 17th century of light, mobile field artillery into the armies of the warring states of central and western Europe, the nomads' retreat began. States such as Russia, which had centralized power on the western European model, as well as the Ottoman Empire in the eastern Mediterranean and the Qing in China, which had shared many of the armament advances of the Europeans, moved steadily into the steppe and desert heartlands of the horse and camel nomads. Each followed a conscious policy of settling part of its rapidly growing peasant population in the areas taken from the nomads. Thus, nomadic populations not only were brought under the direct rule of sedentary empires but saw their pasturelands plowed and planted wherever the soil and water supply permitted.

These trends suggest that the nomadic war machine had been in decline long before the new wave of innovation that ushered in the Industrial Revolution in the 18th century. But that process sealed its fate. Railways and repeating rifles allowed sedentary peoples to penetrate even the most wild and remote nomadic refuges and subdue even the most determined and fierce nomadic warriors, from the Plains Indians of North America to the bedouin of the Sahara and Arabia. The periodic nomadic incursions into the sedentary zones, which had recurred for millennia, had come to an end.

Questions: What are some of the major ways in which nomadic peoples and their periodic expansions have affected global history? Which of their movements and conquests do you think were the most important? Why were the Mongols able to build a much greater empire than any previous nomadic contender? Why did the Mongol Empire collapse so rapidly, and what does its fall tell us about the underlying weaknesses of the nomadic war machine?

the Yuan regime dissolved, and the Mongols who could escape the fury of the mob retreated into central Asia. The restoration of peace and order came from an unexpected quarter. Rather than a regional military commander or an aristocratic lord, a man from a poor peasant family, **Ju Yuanzhang,** emerged to found the **Ming dynasty,** which ruled China for most of the next three centuries.

Aftershock: The Brief Ride of Timur

Just as the peoples of Europe and Asia had begun to recover from the upheavals caused by Mongol expansion, a second nomadic outburst from central Asia plunged them again into fear and despair. This time the nomads in question were Turks, not Mongols, and their leader, **Timur-i Lang,** or Timur the Lame, was from a noble land-owning clan, not a tribal, herding background (Figure 14.7). Timur's personality was complex. On one hand, he was a highly cultured person who delighted in the fine arts, lush gardens, and splendid architecture and who could spend days conversing with great scholars such as Muslim historian Ibn Khaldun (see the Document in Chapter 7). On the other, he was a ruthless conqueror, apparently indifferent to human suffering and capable of commanding his troops to commit atrocities on a scale that would not be matched in the human experience until the 20th century. Beginning in the 1360s, his armies moved out from his base at Samarkand to conquests in Persia, the Fertile Crescent, India, and southern Russia.

Although his empire did not begin to compare with that of the Mongols in size, he outdid them in the ferocity of his campaigns. In fact, Timur is remembered for little more than barbaric destruction:

Figure 14.7 *In 1398, Timur-i Lang's central Asian armies left Delhi completely destroyed and India politically fragmented. Most of the rest of Timur's conquests were in central Asia, so they had much less of an effect on the Islamic heartlands, Europe, or China than Mongol expansion, which extended to these areas but ironically did not include India. Perhaps Timur's most lasting legacy was through his distant descendant Babur, who founded the last and most splendid Muslim dynasty in south Asia, the Mughals, who ruled much of India from the early 16th until the late 18th century.*

the pyramids of skulls he built with the heads of the tens of thousands of people slaughtered after the city of Aleppo in Asia Minor was taken or the thousands of prisoners he had massacred as a warning to the citizens of Delhi, in north India, not to resist his armies. In the face of this wanton slaughter, the fact that he

spared artisans and scientists to embellish his capital city at Samarkand counts for little. Unlike that of the Mongols, his rule brought neither increased trade and cross-cultural exchanges nor internal peace. Fortunately, his reign was as brief as it was violent. After his death in 1405, his empire was pulled apart by his warring commanders and old enemies anxious for revenge. With his passing, the last great challenge of the steppe nomads to the civilizations of Eurasia came to an end.

GLOBAL CONNECTIONS: The Mongol Linkages

Although much of what the Mongols did was destructive, their forays into Europe, China, and the Muslim heartlands brought some lasting changes that were often beneficial. They taught new ways of making war and impressed on their Turkic and European enemies the effectiveness of gunpowder. Mongol conquests facilitated trade between the civilizations at each end of Eurasia, making possible the exchange of foods, tools, and ideas on an unprecedented scale. The revived routes brought great wealth to traders, such as those from north Italy, who set up outposts in the eastern Mediterranean, along the Black Sea coast, and as far east as the Caspian Sea. Because the establishment of these trading empires by the Venetians and Genoese provided precedents for the later drives for overseas expansion by peoples such as the Portuguese and English, they are of special significance in global history.

Perhaps the greatest long-term impact of the Mongol drive to the west was indirect and unintended. In recent years, a growing number of historians have become convinced that the Mongol conquests played a key role in transmitting the fleas that carried bubonic plague from south China and central Asia to Europe and the Middle East. The fleas may have hitched a ride on the livestock the Mongols drove into the new pasturelands won by their conquests or on the rats that nibbled the grain transported by merchants along the trading routes the Mongol rulers fostered between east and west. Whatever the exact connection, the Mongol armies unknowingly paved the way for the spread of the dreaded Black Death across the steppes to much of China, to the Islamic heartlands, and from there to most of Europe in the mid-14th century. In so doing, they unleashed possibly the most fatal epidemic in all human history. From mortality rates higher than 50 percent in some areas of Europe and the Middle East to the economic and social adjustments that the plague forced wherever it spread, this accidental but devastating side effect of the Mongol conquests influenced the course of civilized development in Europe, Asia, and north Africa for centuries.

The Mongol framework for Asian-European interactions, though brief, also facilitated other exchanges. Europeans, particularly, gained new knowledge of Chinese products and technologies that they would quickly adapt back home. Explosive powder and printing were the most important examples. Regions more remote from the Mongols, such as Africa, lacked this kind of stimulus. Even the collapse of the Mongol network had an impact. Many societies had an interest in maintaining contacts, though China grew more wary of outsiders. But the Mongol decline made land-based travel more dangerous, which quickly turned attention toward sea routes. Again, the legacy of the Mongol period was both complex and durable.

Further Readings

A substantial literature has developed on the Mongol interlude in global history. The most readable and reliable biography of Chinggis Khan is René Grousset's *Conqueror of the World* (1966). Grousset has also written a broader history of central Asia, *The Empire of the Steppes* (1970). Peter Brent's more recent *The Mongol Empire* (1976) provides an updated overview and wonderful illustrations. Berthold Spuler's *The Mongols in History* (1971) attempts to gauge their impact on world history, and his *History of the Mongols* (1968) supplies a wide variety of firsthand accounts of the Mongols from the founding of the empire to life in its successor states. Robert S. Marshall's *Storm From the East: from Genghis Khan to Khubilai Khan* (1993) and Charles J. Halperin, *Russia and the Golden Horde: The Mongol Impact on Medieval Russian History, 1581-1990* (1996) examine the Mongol impact on Russia. While George Vernadsky's *The Mongols in Russia* (1953) remains the standard work on that subject, some of its views are now contested. Morris Rossabi's *Kubilai Khan: His Life and Times* (1988) is by far the best work on the Mongols in China. George James Chambers' *The Devil's Horsemen* (1979) and Denis Sinor's *History of Hungary* (1957) contain good accounts of the Mongol incursions into eastern and central Europe. T. Allsen's *Mongol Imperialism* (1987) is the best account of the rise and structure of the empires built by Chinggis Khan and his successors. The fullest and most accessible summary of the links between Mongol expansion and the spread of the Black Death can be found in William H. McNeill's *Plagues and Peoples* (1976).

On the Web

The last great empire of the steppe, the Mongol Empire, can be virtually toured at http://www.kiku.com/electric_samurai/virtual_mongol/history.html. Its founder, Chinggis Khan, receives close attention at http://www.fsmitha.com/h3/h11mon.htm and http://www.angelfire.com/mo/QBranch/. An excellent summary of the strategic and tactical elements of Mongol warfare can be found at http://www.humanities.ualberta.ca/history111/jan15/jan15/sld003.htm. The life of Chinggis Khan's grandson, Kubilai Khan, who continued his grandfather's unbroken string of victories with his conquest of China, is described at http://www.1upinfo.com/country-guide-study/mongolia/mongolia27.html.

Two other virtual exhibits (http://www.pma.edmonton.ab.ca/vexhibit/intro.htm and http://www.nationalgeographic.com/features/97/genghis/index.html illuminate the world of inner Asia under Mongol control.

CHAPTER 15

THE WEST AND THE CHANGING WORLD BALANCE

This Persian-style painting depicts the Ottoman Turks as they attack the Hungarians with troops and cannons in a battle in 1526.

- The Decline of the Old Order
- The Rise of the West
- **VISUALIZING THE PAST:** Population Trends
- **DOCUMENT:** Italian Renaissance Culture
- Western Expansion: The Experimental Phase
- Outside the World Network
- **IN DEPTH:** The Problem of Ethnocentrism
- **GLOBAL CONNECTIONS:** 1450 and the World

The world in 1400 was in fundamental transition. This chapter highlights the main features of this transition. The principal focus is on shifts in the balance of power between civilizations in Asia, Africa, and Europe and related changes in the nature of international contact.

This period of transition began with the decline of Arab strength—symbolized by the fall of the last Arab caliphate in 1258—and the disruptions that Mongol incursions caused elsewhere in Asia and eastern Europe. These developments created new opportunities in the international network that had been established in the postclassical centuries, initially under Arab sponsorship. Various candidates emerged to take a new international role, including for a short time China in its new Ming dynasty.

The most dynamic new contender for international power ultimately proved to be western Europe, and the conditions that propelled Western civilization toward a new position around 1400 are the second key theme of this chapter. The West was not yet the world's major power; it did not replace the Arabs as international leaders quickly or easily. The first stages of the rise of the West were accompanied by important changes in Western civilization itself, also taking shape by about 1400. At this point, Italy, Spain, and Portugal took a new leadership role in western European outreach, which they would hold for about two centuries.

It is also vital to note changes in the societies outside the international network, in the Americas and Polynesia. New difficulties in the great American empires, in particular, inadvertently reduced the ability to respond to a European challenge that was about to arrive.

Focusing on new frameworks for international contacts, this chapter inevitably deals with the question of why individual civilizations reacted differently to key forces. This was a vital period of redefinition, comparable to the centuries that led from the classical to postclassical periods but with developments that had even wider sweep.

The Decline of the Old Order

 The first steps in the new world order that was beginning to emerge by 1400 involved major reshuffling in the Middle East and north Africa.

In 1200, the Middle East was still dominated by two powerful empires, the Byzantine in the northwest and the Islamic caliphate through much of the Middle Eastern heartland. By 1400, this structure was in disarray. The Byzantine Empire still existed, but it was in decline, pressed by invading Ottoman Turks. The imperial capital, Constantinople, fell to the Turks in 1453, effectively ending the empire. Two centuries earlier, the caliphate, long sapped by increasing reliance on foreign

1250 C.E.	1300 C.E.	1350 C.E.	1400 C.E.	1450 C.E.
1258 Mongol conquest of Baghdad; fall of Abbasid caliphate **c. 1266–1337** Giotto **1275–1292** Marco Polo in China **1290–1317** New famines in Europe **1291** First Italian expedition seeks route to Indies	**1304–1374** Petrarch; development of Italian Renaissance **1320s** Spread of bubonic plague in Gobi desert **1320s** First European use of cannon in warfare **1330s** Black Death reaches China **1347** Plague reaches Sicily **1348** Peak of Black Death in Middle East **1348–1375** Plague spreads in Europe, including Russia	**1368** Mongols expelled from China; Ming dynasty	**1400** End of Polynesian migrations **1405** Chinese trading expeditions begin **1433** End of Chinese expeditions **1439** Portugal takes over Azores; increasing expeditions into Atlantic, along northwest African coast	**1453** Ottomans capture Constantinople, fall of Byzantine Empire **1469** Union of Aragon and Castile; rise of Spanish monarchy

troops and advisors, including the Turks, had fallen to Mongol invasion. Arabs have never since been able to unite all of their region under their own rule.

Social and Cultural Change in the Middle East

By about 1300, religious leaders in the Islamic Middle East gained the upper hand over poets, philosophers, and scientists. An earlier tension between diverse cultural elements yielded to the predominance of the faith. The new piety associated with the rising Sufi movement, discussed in Chapter 7, was both the cause and the result of this development. In literature, emphasis on secular themes, such as the joys of feasting and hunting, gave way to more strictly religious ideas. Persian poets, writing in their own language instead of Arabic, led the way, and religious poetry—not poetry in general—became part of the education of upper-class children. In philosophy, the rationalistic current encountered new attack. In Muslim Spain, philosopher Ibn Rushd (Averroës) espoused Greek rationalism, but his efforts were largely ignored in the Middle East. In fact, European scholars were more heavily influenced by his work. In the Middle East proper, a more typical philosopher now claimed to use Aristotle's logic to show that it was impossible to discover religious truth by human reason, in a book revealingly titled *The Destruction of Philosophy*. Many Sufi scholars wrote excitedly of their mystical contacts with God and the stages of their religious passion, which led to dramatic new statements of Islam. Islamic science continued, but its role diminished.

Changes in society and the economy were as telling as the shifts in politics and intellectual life. As the authority of the caliphate declined, landlords seized power over the peasantry. As a result, from about 1100 onward, Middle Eastern peasants increasingly lost their freedom, becoming serfs on large estates, providing the labor and produce landlords now sought. This loss was not the peasants' alone, for agricultural productivity suffered as a result. Landlords turned to sucking what they could from their estates rather than trying to develop a more vital agriculture. Tax revenues declined, and Arab and other Middle Eastern traders began to lose ground. Few Arab coins have been found in Europe dating from later than 1100. European merchants began to control their own turf and challenge the Arabs in other parts of the Mediterranean; initiative in this vital trading area was passing to their hands. Arab and Persian commerce remained active in the Indian Ocean, but the time was not too distant when it would face new competition there as well.

The decline of the Islamic caliphate and its economy was gradual and incomplete. It cannot be compared with the dramatic fall of the Roman Empire in the West many centuries before. A more subtle model is needed. The reduced dynamism in trade did not take the Arabs out of major world markets, for example. Indeed, Middle Eastern commerce rebounded somewhat by 1400.

Finally, the political fragmentation of the Arab world did not produce prolonged confusion in the Middle East. The emerging Ottoman Turkish state soon mastered most of the lands of the old caliphate as well as the Byzantine corner, expanding into southeastern Europe. (See Chapter 21 for the development of the new Ottoman Empire.) It is important to realize that the empire was far more powerful, politically and militarily, than the caliphate had been for many centuries. It was thus more frightening to observers in neighboring civilizations such as western Europe.

A Power Vacuum in International Leadership

Even the rise of the Ottoman Empire did not restore the full international vigor that the Islamic caliphate had at the height of its powers. The empire was not the sole hub of an international network, as the Arab caliphate had been a few centuries before.

The Mongols developed the first alternative global framework, with their interlocking holdings that included central Asia, China, and Russia, with thrusts into the Middle East and south Asia. Here was a system that actively encouraged interregional travelers and provided unprecedented opportunities for exchanges of technology and ideas—exchanges that particularly benefited western Europe through contacts with Asia. The Mongol decline, first in China, then gradually elsewhere, raised again the question of domination of international contacts and trade. The end of the Mongol empires also turned attention to seaborne trade, as the overland Asian trade routes were disrupted. Two societies, successively, stepped up to the challenge.

Chinese Thrust and Withdrawal

For a brief time China took full advantage of the new opportunities in international trade. Rebellions in China drove out the deeply resented Mongol overlords in 1368. A rebel leader from a peasant family seized the Mongol capital of Beijing and proclaimed a new Ming—meaning "brilliant"—dynasty that was to last until 1644. This dynasty began with a burst of unusual expansionism. The initial Ming rulers pressed to secure the borders of the Middle Kingdom. This meant pushing the Mongols far to the north, to the plains of what is now Mongolia. It meant reestablishing influence over neighboring governments and winning tribute payments from states in Korea, Vietnam, and Tibet, reviving much of the east Asian regional structure set up by the Tang dynasty. Far more unusual was a new policy, adopted soon after 1400, of mounting huge, state-sponsored trading expeditions to southern Asia and beyond.

A first fleet sailed in 1405 to India, with 62 ships carrying 28,000 men. Later voyages reached the Middle East and the eastern coast of Africa, bringing chinaware and copper coinage in exchange for local goods. Chinese shipping at its height consisted of 2700 coastal vessels, 400 armed naval ships, and at least as many long-distance ships. Nine great treasure ships, the most sophisticated in the world at the time, explored the Indian Ocean, the Persian Gulf, and the Red Sea, establishing regular trade all along the way.

Between 1405 and their termination in 1433, these expeditions were commanded by the admiral **Zhenghe.** A Muslim from western China, Zhenghe was well suited to deal with Muslims in southeast Asia on his trade route. Zhenghe was also a eunuch, castrated for service at the royal court. China's Ming emperors retained a large harem of wives to ensure succession, and eunuchs were needed to guard them without threat of sexual rivalry; many gained bureaucratic powers well beyond this service. Zhenghe's expeditions usually hugged the coastline, but he had an improved compass and excellent maps as well as huge vessels that contained ample supplies—even gardens—as well as goods for trade. His fleets must have impressed, even terrified, the local rulers around the Indian Ocean, many of whom paid tribute to the emperor. For while Zhenghe brought gifts, he also had 28,000 well-armed troops on his expeditions. Several missions visited China from the Middle East and Africa. From Africa also came ostriches, zebras, and giraffes for the imperial zoo; the latter became the unicorns of Chinese fable. But Zhenghe was resented by the Confucian bureaucrats, who refused even to write much about him in their chronicles.

There is no question that the course of world history might have been changed dramatically had the Chinese thrust continued, for the tiny European expeditions that began to creep down the western coast of Africa at about the same time would have been no match for this combination of merchant and military organization. Indeed, historians wonder if one expedition might have rounded Africa to at least glimpse the Atlantic. But China's emperors called the expeditions to a halt in 1433. The bureaucrats had long opposed the new trade policy, out of rivalry with other officials such as Zhenghe, but there were deeper reasons as well. The costs seemed unacceptable, given the continuing expenses of the campaigns against the Mongols and establishing a luxurious new capital city in Beijing.

This assessment was not inevitable and it must be explained. It reflected a preference for traditional expenditures rather than distant foreign involvements.

Chinese merchant activity continued to be extensive in southeast Asia. Chinese trading groups established permanent settlements in the Philippines, Malaysia, and Indonesia, where they added to the cultural diversity of the area and maintained a disproportionate role in local and regional trading activities into the 20th century. Nonetheless, China's chance to become a dominant world trading power was lost, at least for several centuries.

To Western eyes, accustomed to judging a society's dynamism by its ability to reach out and gain new territories or trade positions, China's decision may seem hard to understand—the precursor to decline. But to the Chinese, it was the brief trading flurry that was unusual, not its end. China had long emphasized internal development, amid considerable international isolation and concern over protection against invasion from central Asia. Its leaders were suspicious of any policy that would unduly elevate commercial activity. Ming emperors consolidated their rule over the empire's vast territory. Internal economic development continued as well, with no need for foreign products. Chinese goods continued to be highly valued in the world market. Industry expanded, with growth in the production of textiles and porcelain; ongoing trade with southeast Asia enriched the port cities; agricultural production and population increased.

The shift in Chinese policy unintentionally cleared the way for another, in most ways less organized civilization to work toward a new international position. With the Arabs in partial eclipse and with China briefly moving into the resulting trade vacuum but then retreating, hesitant Western expansionism, ventured before 1400, began to take on new significance. Within a century, Western explorers and traders had launched an attempt to seize international trading dominance and had expanded the international network to include parts of the Americas for the first time.

The Rise of the West

 Western Europe began to undergo important changes in the 14th and 15th centuries. Some involved new problems; others created new opportunities. Examining the various strengths and weaknesses of this once backward region sets the stage for Europe's new ventures in world trade.

The West's gradual emergence into larger world contacts during the 15th century was surprising in many respects. Westerners remained awed by the powerful bureaucracies and opulent treasuries of empires in the traditional civilization centers such as Constantinople. Furthermore, the West was changing in some painful ways. The staples of medieval culture at its height were under new question by 1400. The church, which had long been one of the organizing institutions of Western civilization, was under new attack. Medieval philosophy had passed its creative phase. Warrior aristocrats, long a key leadership group in feudal society, softened their style of life, preferring court rituals and jousting tournaments and adopting military armor so cumbersome that real fighting was difficult.

Even more strikingly, the lives and economic activities of ordinary Europeans were in disarray. This was a time of crisis, and Europe's expanding world role could not reverse the fundamental challenges to its internal economic and demographic structure. Europeans began to suffer from recurrent famine after 1300 because population outstripped the food supply and no new food production techniques were discovered. Famine reduced disease resistance, making Europe more vulnerable to the bubonic plagues that spread from Asia.

Bubonic plague, or Black Death, surfaced in various parts of Asia in the 14th century. In China it reduced the population by nearly 30 percent by 1400. Following trade routes, it then spread into India and the Middle East, causing thousands of deaths per day in the larger cities. The plague's worst European impact occurred between 1348 and 1375, by which time 30 million people, one-third of Europe's population, died. The resulting economic dislocation produced bitter strikes and peasant uprisings.

Sources of Dynamism: Medieval Vitality

How could the West be poised for a new international role? The answer to that question is complex. First, several key advances of medieval society were not really reversed by the troubles of the decades around 1400. For example, the strengthening of feudal monarchy provided more effective national or regional governments for much of the West. The Hundred Years' War between Britain and France stimulated innovations in military organization,

Visualizing the Past

Population Trends

Questions: What do these population charts show about relationships in population size, and comparative trends in population size, among the major inhabited regions of the world? Population pressure did not drive European expansion in the 15th century, because population was falling temporarily, but were there longer-term trends, from the year 1000, that might have encouraged the expansionist effort? What societies show the greatest changes in population levels between 1000 and 1800? What might have caused these changes? Finally, what do the charts suggest about the demographic position of Europe in the 20th century compared to the world as a whole?

Reading population statistics provides vital information, but it also raises questions, including ones about causation, which numbers alone cannot answer. What other data would be most helpful to put these figures in appropriate world history contexts? Which figures are more revealing: absolute numbers or percentages? Why?

Population Levels (Millions)

Continents	Years				
	1000	1700	1800	1900	1975
Europe	36	120	180	390	635
Asia (includes Middle East)	185	415	625	970	2300
Africa	33	61	70	110	385
Americas	39	13	24	145	545
Oceania (includes Australia)	1.5	2.25	2.5	6.75	23
Totals	294.5	611.25	901.5	1621.75	3888

Note: Earlier figures are only estimates; they are fairly accurate indicators of relative size.

Source: Adapted from Dennis H. Wrong, ed., *Population and Society* (1977).

Percentages or Proportions of Total World Population

Continents	Years				
	1000	1700	1800	1900	1975
Europe	12.2	19.6	19.7	24	16.3
Asia	62.9	67.6	69.3	59.8	59.2
Africa	11.2	10.0	7.8	6.8	9.9
Americas	13.4	2.1	2.7	8.9	14.0
Oceania	0.4	0.4	0.3	0.3	0.6

Source: Adapted from Dennis H. Wrong, ed., *Population and Society* (1977).

including nonaristocratic soldiers recruited and paid directly by the royal government, that enhanced central political power. Strong regional monarchies took hold in parts of Spain and in Portugal as Christian leaders drove back the Muslim rulers of this region. The growth of cities and urban economies continued to spur the commercial side of Western society. Even the church had made its peace with such key principles of capitalism as profit-seeking. Technology continued to advance, particularly in ironwork—used for bells and weapons—and timekeeping.

In short, explaining the new Western vigor involves an understanding that some of the gains the West achieved during the Middle Ages continued even as certain characteristic medieval forms wavered.

Imitation and International Problems

Two additional causes involved western Europe's international position. New opportunities for imitation were an obvious advantage. The Mongol Empire established in Asia and eastern Europe in the late 13th and early 14th centuries provided new access to Asian knowledge and technology. Political stability and an openness to foreign visitors by the great khans helped

Westerners learn of Asian technologies, ranging from printing to the compass and explosive powder. Western Europe had ideal access in the Mongol period. It was not disrupted by the Mongols, as eastern Europe and so many parts of Asia were, but it was in active contact, unlike sub-Saharan Africa. Internal European warfare and merchant zeal made western Europe an eager learner, for the Asian technologies promised to meet existing military and commercial needs.

The second international factor was the intensification of European problems in the existing world market and international arena. From the Crusades onward, Western elites had become used to increasing consumption of Asian luxury products, including spices such as cinnamon and nutmeg, silks, sugar, perfumes, and jewels. In exchange for the luxury items, Europeans mainly had cruder goods to offer: wool, tin, copper, honey, and salt. The value of European exports almost never equaled the value of what was imported from Asia. The resulting unfavorable balance of trade had to be made up in gold, but western Europe had only a limited gold supply. By 1400, the constant drain to Asia was creating a gold famine that threatened the whole European economy with collapse.

Furthermore, there were legitimate fears of a new Muslim threat. The Ottoman Empire was taking shape, and Europeans began to fear a new Muslim surge. Even before this, the Muslim capture of the last crusader stronghold (the city of Acre in the Middle East) in 1291 gave Muslim traders, particularly Egyptians, new opportunities to act as intermediaries in the Asian trade, for there were no Western-controlled ports left in the eastern Mediterranean. One response to this was a series of conquests by the city-state of Venice along the eastern coast of the Adriatic. A more important response was to begin exploring alternative routes to Asia that would bypass the Middle East and the feared and hated Muslim realms altogether.

Secular Directions in the Italian Renaissance

The final major ingredient of the West's surge involved changes within the West itself, starting with Italy, where medieval forms had never fully taken hold. In 1400, Italy was in the midst of a vital cultural and political movement known as the **Renaissance,** or rebirth. The early phases of the Renaissance stressed more secular subjects in literature and art. Religious art remained dominant but used more realistic portrayals of people and nature, and some nonreligious themes surfaced outright (Figure 15.1). The doings of human beings deserved attention for their own sake, in the Renaissance view, not as they reflected a divine plan. Artists and writers became more openly ambitious for personal reputation and glory.

Italy was the center of initial Renaissance culture because it had more contact with Roman tradition than did the rest of Europe and because by the 14th century it led the West in banking and trade. Active commerce and urban manufacturing gave Italian cities the wealth to sponsor new cultural activities, and contacts with some foreign scholars, particularly in Byzantium, helped revive Greco-Roman styles. Finally, the attention to government and diplomacy by the competitive governments of Italy's city-states led intellectuals and political leaders to emphasize worldly culture.

Human Values and Renaissance Culture

Despite its political and commercial roots, the Renaissance was first and foremost a cultural movement, launched in Florence and manifesting itself in literature and various arts. The Renaissance focused on a new interest in stylistic grace and a concern for practical ethics and codes of behavior for urban gentlemen. One leading 14th-century writer, **Francesco Petrarch,** not only took pride in his city and his age but explored the glories of personal achievement with new confidence.

Innovation flourished in the visual arts and music as well. The subject matter of art moved toward nature and people, including cityscapes and portraits of the rich and powerful, whether the themes were religious or secular. Florentine painter Giotto led the way, departing from medieval formalism and stiffness. While still a young apprentice to the painter Cimabue, Giotto painted a fly on the nose of one of Cimabue's portrait subjects, and it was so realistic that Cimabue repeatedly tried to swat it off before going back to work on the canvas. Other painters, beginning later in the 14th century, started to introduce perspective while using new colors and other materials. In architecture, favor shifted away from the Gothic to a classicism derived from the styles of

Figure 15.1   *Europe's new spirit amid old values. Dante, Italian writer of the 14th century, holds a copy of his great work, the* Divine Comedy, *with both religious (souls tormented in hell) and Renaissance (the solid, classical-style urban buildings of the city of Florence) symbolism greeting him. The painting was designed by Domenico di Michelina for the cathedral of Florence in 1465.*

Greece and Rome. Vivid, realistic statues complemented the new palaces and public buildings.

The impact of the early Renaissance must not be exaggerated. It had little influence outside of Italy. Even in Italy, it focused on high culture, not popular culture, and on the arts; there was little initial interest in science. And although it built on distinctive political and economic forms, it was not a full break from medieval tendencies.

Nevertheless, these new cultural currents were an important innovation in Western history. The full ramifications of the Renaissance feed into the next period of both world and Western history (see Chapter 17). The movement was only getting started by 1400. The wide range of Italian commerce and shipping proved to be one of the building blocks of European outreach. By the 14th century, ships, particularly from the western Italian city of Genoa, which was less well placed than Venice for eastern Mediterranean trade and the resultant links to Asia, were ready for new roles. Ambitious city-state governments encouraged new ventures, eager to collect more tax money

Document

Italian Renaissance Culture

Writers in the first phase of the Italian Renaissance were aware that they were defining a culture quite different from that of medieval theologians and philosophers. In the passages that follow, Petrarch (1304–1374) writes about his priorities in literature, including the kind of classical examples he revered, first in a letter to another major writer, Boccaccio, and then in a poem. Petrarch's cultural interests and his definition of personal goals form part of a movement called humanism (see Chapter 17). Judging by the following documents, what defined a Renaissance humanist?

From Petrarch, Letter to Boccaccio (1362)

Neither exhortations to virtue nor the argument of approaching death should divert us from literature; for in a good mind it excites the love of virtue, and dissipates, or at least diminishes, the fear of death. To desert our studies shows want of self-confidence rather than wisdom, for letters do not hinder but aid the properly constituted mind which possesses them; they facilitate our life, they do not retard it…. If it were otherwise, surely the zeal of certain persons who persevered to the end could not have roused such admiration. Cato, I never forget, acquainted himself with Latin literature as he was growing old, and Greek when he had really become an old man. Varro, who reached his hundredth year still reading and writing, parted from life sooner than from his love of study. Livius Drusus, although weakened by age and afflicted with blindness, did not give up his interpretation of the civil law, which he carried on to the great advantage of the state….

Besides these and innumerable others like them, have not all those of our own religion whom we should wish most to imitate devoted their whole lives to literature, and grown old and died in the same pursuit? Some, indeed, were overtaken by death while still at work reading or writing. To none of them, so far as I know, did it prove a disadvantage to be noted for secular learning….

While I know that many have become famous for piety without learning, at the same time I know of no one who has been prevented by literature from following the path of holiness. The apostle Paul was, to be sure, accused of having his head turned by study, but the world has long ago passed its verdict upon this accusation. If I may be allowed to speak for myself, it seems to me that, although the path to virtue by the way of ignorance may be plain, it fosters sloth. The goal of all good people is the same, but the ways of reaching it are many and various. Some advance slowly, others with more spirit; some obscurely, others again conspicuously. One takes a lower path, another takes a higher path. Although all alike are on the road to happiness, certainly the more elevated path is the more glorious. Hence ignorance, however devout, is by no means to be put on a plane with the enlightened devoutness of one familiar with literature. Nor can you pick me out from the whole array of unlettered saints, an example so holy that I cannot match it with a still holier one from the other group.

From Petrarch, the Sonnets (c. 1535)

To a Friend, Encouraging Him to Pursue Poetry

Torn is each virtue from its earthy throne
By sloth, intemperance, and voluptuous ease;
Far hence is every light celestial gone,
That guides mankind through life's perplexing maze….
Who now would laurel, myrtle-wreaths obtain?
Let want, let shame, Philosophy attend!
Cries the base world, intent on sordid gain.
What though thy favourite path be trod by few;
Let it but urge thee more, dear gentle friend,
Thy great design of glory to pursue.

Questions: What are the key purposes of intellectual activity, according to Petrarch? How can these purposes be reconciled with Christianity? How do Petrarch's arguments compare with Cicero's defense of Greek culture? To what extent does Petrarch's humanism suggest a more modern outlook than that of medieval Western culture? Does this Renaissance spirit suggest factors that might explain Europe's new expansion? Did the Renaissance encourage human agency? How important were individuals in this major development, compared to the larger causes?

and promote commerce as one of their explicit functions. A general "Renaissance spirit" could also spur innovation. Whereas people such as Petrarch defined human ambition mainly in cultural terms, other urban and commercial leaders, including seafaring men such as Genoa's Christopher Columbus, might apply some of the same confidence and desire for personal glory to different areas, such as exploration or conquest.

The Iberian Spirit of Religious Mission

Along with Italy, a key center for change by the 14th century was the Iberian peninsula, where Christian military leaders had for several centuries been pressing back the boundaries of the Muslim state in Spain. Soon after 1400, major regional monarchies had been established in the provinces of **Castile** and **Aragon,** which would be united through royal marriage in 1469.

Even before the marriage between Ferdinand and Isabella, Spanish and Portuguese rulers had developed a vigorous military and religious agenda. They supported effective armies, including infantry and feudal cavalry. And they believed that government had a mission to promote Christianity by converting or expelling Arabs and Jews and by maintaining doctrinal purity within the church. Close links between church and state, portrayed in art, provided revenues and officials for the royal government. In return, the government supported church courts in their efforts to enforce moral and doctrinal purity. Later in the 15th century, this interaction led to the reestablishment of the church-run courts of the Inquisition in Spain, designed to enforce religious orthodoxy. In other words, Spain and Portugal were developing effective new governments with a special sense of religious mission and religious support. These changes promoted the West's expansion into wider world contacts.

Western Expansion: The Experimental Phase

Specific European attempts to explore the Atlantic (beyond the earlier Viking voyages in the North Atlantic) began in the later 13th century. Early discoveries increased Europeans' interest in setting up a new colonial system.

Early Explorations

As early as 1291, two Italian brothers, the **Vivaldis** from Genoa, sailed with two galleys through the Straits of Gibraltar, seeking a Western route to the "Indies," the spice-producing areas of south and southeast Asia. They were never heard from again. Although they were precursors of a major Western thrust into the southern Atlantic, it is not even entirely clear what they meant by the "Indies." Early

in the 14th century, other explorers from Genoa rediscovered the Canary Islands, in the Atlantic, populated by a hunting-and-gathering people. These islands had been known vaguely since classical times but had never been explored by Europeans. Genoese sailors also visited the Madeiras and probably reached the more distant Azores by 1351. Soon after this, ships from northeastern Spain, based in the port of Barcelona, sailed along the African coast as far south as present-day Sierra Leone.

Until 1430, technological barriers prevented further exploration for alternative routes. Without adequate navigation instruments, Europeans could not risk wider ventures into the Atlantic. They also needed better ships than the shallow-drafted, oar-propelled Mediterranean galleys. However, efforts were under way to develop an oceangoing sailing vessel. At the same time, the crucial navigational problems were met by the compass and the astrolabe, used to determine latitude at sea by reckoning from the stars. Contacts with Arab merchants (who had learned from the Chinese) provided knowledge of these devices. European mapmaking, improving steadily during the 14th century, was also a key innovation. Because of these advances, as well as mistaken geographic assumptions shown on the map in Figure 15.2, Europeans were ready in the decades after 1400 to undertake voyages impossible just a century before. In 1498, the Portuguese explorer **Vasco da Gama** was the first European to reach India by sea, preparing Portuguese entry into the Indian Ocean (Figure 15.3).

Colonial Patterns

Even as these wider-ranging voyages began, Westerners led by the Spanish and Portuguese had begun to take advantage of the new lands they had already discovered. A driving force behind both the further expeditions and the efforts to make already-discovered areas economically profitable was Prince Henry of Portugal, known as **Henry the Navigator.** A student of astronomy and nautical science, Henry sponsored about a third of Portuguese voyages of exploration before his death in 1460. His mixture of motivation—scientific and intellectual curiosity, desire to spread the name of Christ to unfamiliar lands, and financial interest—reflected some of the key forces in late postclassical Europe.

Portugal by 1439 had taken control of the Azores and had granted land to colonists. Soon Spaniards and Portuguese had conquered and colonized the

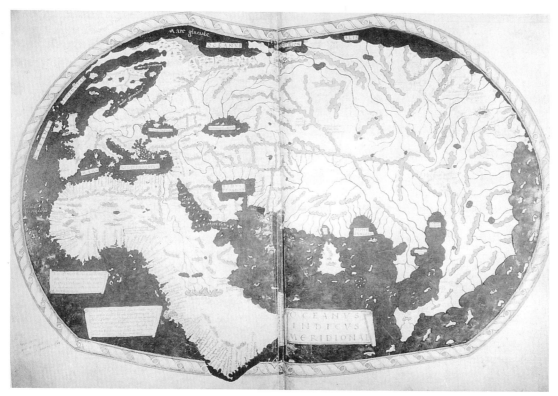

Figure 15.2 *Columbus is supposed to have had a copy of this world map in Spain. The map, dating from about 1489, shows the Old World as Europeans were increasingly coming to know it. Note how reachable India looked to Europeans using this map.*

Madeiras and Canaries, bringing in Western plants, animals, weapons, and diseases. The result was something of a laboratory for the larger European colonialism that would soon take shape, particularly in the Americas. European colonists quickly set up large agricultural estates designed to produce cash crops that could be sold on the European market. First they introduced sugar, an item once imported from Asia but now available in growing quantities from Western-controlled sources. Ultimately, other crops such as cotton and tobacco were also introduced to the Atlantic islands. To produce these market crops the new colonists brought in slaves from northwestern Africa, mainly in Portuguese ships—the first examples of a new, commercial version of slavery and the first sign that Western expansion could have serious impact on other societies as well.

These developments about 1400 remained modest, even in their consequences for Africa. They illustrate mainly how quickly Western conquerors decided what to do with lands and peoples newly in their grasp. The ventures were successful enough to motivate more extensive probes into the southern Atlantic as soon as technology permitted. Indeed, voyages of exploration down the coast of Africa and across the Atlantic began to occur as the island colonies were being fully settled. The ventures summed up the swirl of forces that were beginning to reshape the West's role in the world: inferiorities and fears, particularly with regard to the Muslims; new energies of Renaissance merchants and Iberian rulers; economic pressures; and a long-standing population surge.

Outside the World Network

 The international framework that had developed during the postclassical period embraced most of Asia, Europe, and Africa. This network left out important groups and regions that had their own vigorous histories.

Figure 15.3 *This 18th-century engraving portrays Vasco da Gama's audience with the Indian ruler of Calicut in 1498.*

Developments in the Americas and Polynesia were not affected by the new international exchange. During the next period of world history, these regions all were pulled into a new level of international contact, but a world balance sheet in 1400 must emphasize their separateness.

At the same time, several of the societies outside the international network were experiencing some new problems during the 15th century that would leave them vulnerable to outside interference thereafter. Such problems included new political strains in the leading American civilizations and a fragmentation of the principal island groups in Polynesian culture.

Political Issues in the Americas

As we discussed in Chapter 11, the Aztec and Inca empires ran into increasing difficulties not long after 1400. Aztec exploitation of subject peoples for gold, slaves, and religious sacrifices roused great resentment. What would have happened to the Aztec Empire if the Spaniards had not intervened after 1500 is not clear, but it is obvious that disunity created opportunities for outside intervention that might not have existed otherwise. The Inca system, though far less brutal than that of the Aztecs, provided ongoing tension between central leadership and local initiative. This complicated effective control of the vast expanse of the Inca domains. Here too, overextension made change likely by the 1500s—indeed, the empire was already receding somewhat—even without European intervention. At the same time, other cultures were developing in parts of the Americas that might well have been candidates for new political leadership, if American history had proceeded in isolation.

Expansion, Migration, and Conquest in Polynesia

A second culture that was later pulled into the expanding world network was that of Polynesia. Here, as in the Americas, important changes took place during the postclassical era but with no relationship to developments in societies elsewhere in the world. The key Polynesian theme from the 7th century to 1400 was expansion, spurts of migration, and conquest that implanted Polynesian culture well beyond the initial base in the Society Islands, as Tahiti, Samoa, and Fiji are called collectively (Map 15.1).

One channel of migration pointed northward to the islands of Hawaii. The first Polynesians reached these previously uninhabited islands before the 7th century, traveling in great war canoes. From the 7th century until about 1300 or 1400, recurrent contacts remained between the Hawaiian islands and the larger Society Islands group, allowing periodic new migration. From about 1400 until the arrival of European explorers in 1778, Hawaiian society was cut off even from Polynesia.

Polynesians in Hawaii spread widely across the islands in agricultural clusters and fishing villages amid the volcanic mountains. Hawaiians were inventive in using local vegetation, weaving fabrics as well as making materials and fishing nets from grass. They also imported pigs from the Society Islands—a vital source of meat but a source of devastation to many plant species unique to Hawaii. Politically, Hawaii

In Depth

The Problem of Ethnocentrism

Many cultures encourage an ethnocentric outlook, and the culture of the West is certainly one of them. Ethnocentrism creates problems in interpreting world history. The dictionary definition of *ethnocentrism* is "a habitual disposition to judge foreign peoples or groups by the standards and practices of one's own culture or ethnic group"—and often finding them inferior. Most of us take pride in many of our own institutions and values, and it is tempting to move from this pride to a disapproval of other peoples when they clearly do not share our behaviors and beliefs. Many Americans have a difficult time understanding how other peoples have failed to establish the stable democratic political structure of our own country. Even liberals who pride themselves on a sophisticated appreciation of different habits in some areas may adopt an ethnocentric shock at the oppression (by current American standards) of women that is visible in certain societies today or in the past. Indeed, unless a person is almost totally alienated from his or her own society, some ethnocentric reactions are hard to avoid.

Nevertheless, unexamined ethnocentrism can be a barrier in dealing with world history. We will grasp other times and places better, and perhaps use our own values more intelligently, if we do not too readily dismiss cultures in which "objectionable" practices occur.

Ethnocentrism is not just an issue for modern Westerners. Civilized peoples in the past routinely accused outsiders of barbaric ways, as in the Islamic characterizations of the Mongols described in Chapter 14. But the current power of Western standards makes our own ethnocentric potential a real issue today in dealing with world history, as in the tendency to dismiss any people who did not exploit the latest available military technology as somehow inferior.

Controlling ethnocentrism does not mean abandoning all standards, as if any social behavior were as good as any other. It does involve a certain open-mindedness and sophistication. Reducing distracting levels of ethnocentrism can be aided by some specific procedures. It is important to realize that few cultures behave irrationally over long periods of time. They may differ from our taste, but their patterns respond to valid causes and problems. Our own values are not without complexity. We sometimes believe things about our own society that are not as true as we want, or, in judging other societies, we forget about drawbacks in our own surroundings. Perspective on our own habits, including awareness of how other cultures might judge us, helps us restrain our ethnocentrism.

However, ethnocentrism may become a particularly strong impulse in dealing with some of the changes in world history taking shape about 1400. The West was gaining strength. Because many Americans identify with Western civilization, it is tempting to downplay some of the subtleties and disadvantages of this process or to exaggerate the extent to which the West began to organize world history more generally.

The balance of power among civilizations was beginning to shift about 1400, and it is legitimate—not simply ethnocentric—to note that the West's rise was one of the leading forces of this change. It is unnecessary to ignore the many other patterns continuing or emerging—including new vigor in several other societies—or to gloss over the motives and results that the West's rise entailed. The rise of the West was not just "good." It did not result simply from a triumph of progressive values. At the same time, avoiding ethnocentric impulses in evaluating this crucial transition period in world history does not require an anti-Western approach. Balance and perspective are essential—easy to say, not always easy to achieve.

Questions: Why can ethnocentrism complicate interpretations of world history? How can one balance disapproval and understanding in dealing with practices such as female infanticide? What are some nonethnocentric ways to interpret initial European expansion?

was organized into regional kingdoms, which were highly warlike. Society was structured into a caste system with priests and nobles at the top, who reserved many lands for their exclusive use. Commoners were viewed almost as a separate people, barred from certain activities.

Thus, with a Neolithic technology and no use of metals, the Hawaiians created a complex culture on their islands. Without a written language, their legends and oral histories, tracing the genealogies of chiefly families back to the original war canoes, provided a shared set of stories and values.

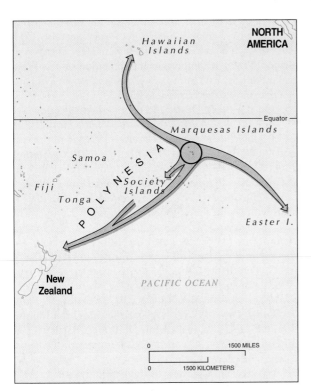

Map 15.1 *Polynesian Expansion. Starting in the 7th century, the Polynesians expanded north and south of their starting point in the Society Islands.*

Isolated Achievements by the Maori

Another group of Polynesians migrated thousands of miles to the southwest of the Society Islands, perhaps as early as the 8th century, when canoe or raft crews discovered the two large islands that today make up New Zealand. The original numbers of people were small but were supplemented over the centuries that followed by additional migrations from the Polynesian home islands. The Polynesians in New Zealand, called the Maori, successfully adapted to an environment considerably colder and harsher than that of the home islands. They developed the most elaborate of all Polynesian art and produced an expanding population that may have reached 200,000 people by the 18th century, primarily on the northern of the two islands. As in Hawaii, tribal military leaders and priests held great power in Maori society; each tribe also included a group of slaves drawn from prisoners of war and their descendants.

All these achievements were accomplished in total isolation from the rest of the world and, par-

ticularly after 1400, substantial isolation of each major island grouping from the rest of the Polynesian complex. Polynesians would be the last of the major isolated cultures to encounter the larger world currents brought forcefully by European explorers in the 18th century. When this encounter did come, it produced the same effects that it had in the Americas: vulnerability to disease, weakness in the face of superior weaponry and technology, and cultural disintegration.

Adding Up the Changes

It is tempting to see some sort of master plan in the various changes that began to occur around 1400. People who emphasize an ethnocentric approach to world history, stressing some inherent superiorities in Western values, might be tempted to simplify the factors involved. However, a series of complex coincidences provides a more accurate explanation, as in other cases in which the framework of world history changed substantially.

Independent developments in the Americas and elsewhere figured in, as did crucial policy decisions in places such as China. Each of the separate steps can be explained, but their combination was partly accidental.

Several elements of the world history transition deserve particular attention. Technology played a role, as opportunities to copy Asian developments were supplemented by European initiative, particularly in gunnery and ship design. The role of individuals, such as Prince Henry, must be compared with the impact of more general forces such as Europe's international trade woes.

The overall result of change affected even societies where existing patterns persisted. Sub-Saharan Africa, for example, was not experiencing great political or cultural shifts around 1400. Regional kingdoms fell and rose: The empire of Mali fell to regional rivals, but another Muslim kingdom, Songhay, soon arose in its stead, flourishing between 1464 and 1591. African political and religious themes persisted for several centuries, but the context for African history was shifting. The decline of the Arabs reduced the vitality of Africa's key traditional contact with the international network. In contrast to the Europeans, Africans had no exchange with the Mongols. Even as Africa enjoyed substantial continuity, its power relationship with western Europe was beginning to change, and this became a source of further change.

GLOBAL CONNECTIONS: 1450 and the World

The end of the postclassical period saw both change and continuity in the contacts that affected so many societies in Asia, Africa, and Europe. Change came in the procession of societies that served as active agents for contacts. Muslim traders and missionaries from the Middle East continued to be active, particularly in the Indian Ocean and in dealing with Africa. But the period of Mongol consolidation had introduced a new set of contacts, many of them land-based and involving Asia and Europe. Mongol overlords turned out to be delighted to encounter different ideas and to use officials from many different places and cultures. Mongol decline returned attention to sea-based contacts, particularly in the Indian Ocean. For a time, China took an unusually active role. The question of leadership in global contacts was a vital one, and by 1450 it was in flux.

The key continuity involved the interest and dependence of many societies on interregional trade and other contacts. African merchants and leaders continued to rely heavily on interactions with the Middle East. Western Europe's involvement in contacts was intensifying. Southeast Asia was increasingly drawn in, not only to trade but also to Muslim missionary efforts. The Middle East, India, and China continued to assume the availability of goods and merchant activities beyond their own borders. The diverse advantages of Afro-Eurasian contacts were widely realized, even amid changes in trade routes and regional initiatives.

Further Readings

On the world network, see Jerry Bentley, *Old World Encounters: Cross Cultural Contacts and Exchanges in Pre-Modern Times* (1993). Crucial changes in the Middle East are covered in F. Babinger's *Mehmed the Conqueror and His Times* (1978) on the Ottoman leader who captured Constantinople, and Bernard Lewis' *The Arabs in History* (4th ed., 1958), which offers a brisk interpretation of Arab decline. See also H. Islamoglu-Inan, ed., *The Ottoman Empire and the World Economy* (1987). On China under the early Ming dynasty, see Charles O. Hucker's *The Ming Dynasty: Its Origins and Evolving Institutions* (1978).

An important, highly readable interpretation of the West's rise in a world context is C. Cipolla's *Guns, Sails and Empires: Technological Innovation and the Early Phases of European Expansion, 1400–1700* (1985). See also J. H. Parry's *Age of Reconnaissance* (1963) and *The Discovery of the Sea* (1981). An important interpretation of new Western interests is S. W. Mintz's *Sweetness and Power: The Place of Sugar in Modern History* (1985).

On the Black Death and economic dislocation, see M. W. Dols' *The Black Death in the Middle East* (1977); W. H. McNeill's *Plagues and Peoples* (1976); and the very readable B. Tuchman's *A Distant Mirror: The Calamitous 14th Century* (1979). A provocative study of relevant Western outlook is P. Ariès's *The Hour of Our Death* (1981).

J. Huizinga's *The Waning of the Middle Ages* (1973) deals with the decline of medieval forms in Europe. The early Renaissance is treated in D. Hay's *The Italian Renaissance* (1977); see also C. Hibbert, *Florence: The Biography of a City* (1993). For more cultural emphasis, see C. Trinkhaus' *The Scope of Renaissance Humanism* (1983). On Spain, see F. Braudel's *The Mediterranean and the Mediterranean World* (2 vols., 1978), and see E. Paris' *The End of Days* (1995) on Spanish Jews and the Inquisition. On expansion in general, see Robert Bartlett's *The Making of Europe: Conquest, Colonization and Cultural Change* (1993).

An excellent overview of the period is Janet L. Abu-Lughod's *Before European Hegemony: The World System A.D. 1250–1350* (1989).

On the Web

This transitional age in human history saw the rise of two great state systems, China's Ming Dynasty (http://www.wsu.edu:8080/~dee/MING/MING1.HTM) and the Ottoman Empire (http://www.friesian.com/turkia.htm and http://www.naqshbandi.org/ottomans/). It witnessed the rise of new navigational technologies that led up to European explorations, (http://www.ucalgary.ca/applied_history/tutor/eurvoya/ship.html and http://www.chenowith.k12.or.us/tech/subject/social/explore.html). It also witnessed the voyages of two of the world's greatest explorers, Cheng Ho (http://chinapage.com/zhenghe.html) and Christopher Columbus (http://www1.minn.net/~keithp/), and the publication of the fabled travel literature of Marco Polo (http://www.korcula.net/mpolo/index.html). It marked the climax of Muslim philosophy and science (http://www.muslimphilosophy.com/) as evidenced by the work of Ibn Rushd (http://users.erols.com/zenithco/rushd.html, http://www.aljadid.com/classics/0320raslan.html and http://www.fordham.edu/halsall/source/1190averroes.html). That Ibn Rushd's work and those of other Muslim scientists helped stimulate the Renaissance in Europe is an issue addressed at http://www.isesco.org.ma/pub/Eng/Arabiculture/page

4.htm, http://www.xmission.com/~dderhak/index/ moors.htm, and http://cyberistan.org/islamic/.

The art and daily life of the period (http://history. evansville.net/renaissa.html) is reflected in the life and work of painters such as Giotto (http://www.kfki.hu/ ~arthp/tours/giotto/, http://www.ibiblio.org/wm/ paint/auth/giotto/, and http://www.artchive.com/ artchive/G/giotto.html), da Vinci, Raphael and Michelangelo (http://www.artcyclopedia.com/ artists/leonardo_da_vinci.html, http://www.kausal. com/leonardo/, http://www.kfki.hu/~arthp/bio/r/ raphael/biograph.html, and http://www.michelangelo. com/buonarroti.html), and in the work of writers such as

Francesco Petrarch (http://latter-rain.com/eccle/ petrarch.htm). However, it also witnessed the Hundred Years War (http://www.ku.edu/kansas/medieval/108/ lectures/hundred_years_war.html), the Inquisition (http://es.rice.edu/ES/humsoc/Galileo/Things/ inquisition.html), and the persistence of the Black Death (http://history.boisestate.edu/westciv/plague/ and http://www.iath.virginia.edu/osheim/intro.html). War and disease, however, could not dim the civic pride, commercial zeal, and artistic achievements of the residents of Renaissance Florence, whose city can be virtually visited at the height of its glory at http://es.rice.edu/ES/ humsoc/Galileo/Student_Work/Florence96/FlorTour. html, http://mega.it/eng/egui/epo/refio.htm and http://www.english.firenze.net/groups/6/29/87/.

PART IV

The World Shrinks, 1450–1750

CHAPTERS

16 The World Economy

17 The Transformation of the West, 1450–1750

18 The Rise of Russia

19 Early Latin America

20 Africa and the Africans in the Age of the Atlantic Slave Trade

21 The Muslim Empires

22 Asian Transitions in an Age of Global Change

Introduction

Many developments highlighted world history between 1450 and 1750, which marked a major new period—the early modern—in the global experience. As in most new world history periods, the balance of power among major civilizations shifted; western Europe became the most dynamic force worldwide. Contacts among many civilizations intensified. The world became smaller as international trade affected diverse societies and the speed and range of sailing ships increased. This growth of commerce affected western Europe and areas under its economic influence, such as Africa and the Americas, but commerce grew in China and Japan as well. Partly on the basis of innovations in weaponry, particularly gunpowder, new or revamped empires formed important regional political units in many parts of the world. These developments were especially significant in Asia. In addition to European colonial empires in various parts of the world, land-based empires formed in Russia, Persia, the Middle East and the Mediterranean, and India.

The early modern period was launched during the 15th century when European countries, headed by Portugal and Spain, began new explorations and soon new colonization efforts in Africa, Asia, and the Americas. It was launched also by the formation of the powerful Ottoman Empire in the Middle East, the Mughal and Ming empires in Asia, and the emergence of Russia from two centuries of Mongol control.

1300 C.E.	**1400** C.E.	**1500** C.E.	**1550** C.E.
1281 Founding of Ottoman dynasty	**1405–1433** Chinese expedition period	**1500–1600** Europe's commercial revolution	**1552** Russia begins expansion in central Asia and western Siberia
1350s Ottoman invasion of south-eastern Europe	**1434–1498** Portuguese expeditions down west African coast	**1501–1510** Safavid conquest of Iran	**1570** Portuguese colony of Angola (Africa)
1368 Ming dynasty in China	**1441** Beginning of European slave trade in Africa	**1509** Spanish colonies on American mainland	**1571** Ottoman naval defeat at Lepanto
1390 Ming restrictions on overseas trade	**1453** Ottoman conquest of Constantinople	**1510–1511** Portugal conquers Goa (India), Malacca (Malaysia)	**1590** Hideyoshi unifies Japan
	1480 Moscow region free of Mongol control	**1517–1541** Protestant Reformation (Europe)	**1591** Fall of Songhay (Africa)
	1492 Columbus expeditions	**1519–1521** Magellan circumnavigates globe	
	1498–1499 Vasco da Gama expedition opens seas to Asia	**1519–1524** Cortés conquers Mexico	
		1520–1566 Suleiman the Magnificent (Ottoman)	
		1526 Babur conquest in northern India (Mughal)	
		1533 Pizarro wins Peru	
		1548 Portuguese government in Brazil	

On the Eve of the Early Modern Period: The World Around 1450

A number of societies had expanded during the postclassical period. Russia was one, as a Russian monarchy formed. Western Europe failed to gain political unity but slowly recovered from the 5th-century collapse of the Roman Empire. Western Europeans built important regional kingdoms while expanding the role of urban commerce and establishing an elaborate culture around Catholic Christianity. In sub-Saharan Africa, another set of regional kingdoms formed, although vital areas there were organized more loosely. African trade and artistic expression gained ground steadily. Finally, areas in contact with China built increasingly elaborate societies. Japan, like western Europe, emphasized a decentralized feudal system in politics. But it copied many aspects of Chinese culture and some social forms, including a more patriarchal approach to the status of women.

Other areas of the world featured civilizations or elaborate cultures developing in isolation from any global contacts. This was true of the expanding Polynesian zone in the Pacific Islands and of the populous civilizations of the Americas, focused in Mesoamerica, under the Aztecs, and in the Andes, which by the 15th century were under the vast Inca realm.

The structure of the postclassical world began to shift between the 13th and 15th centuries, setting the stage for a new period in world history. The great Aztec and Inca empires were showing signs of strain and overextension by the later 15th century. In Asia, Africa, and Europe, the key development was the decline of Arab political power and cultural dynamism. Islam continued to expand, but its political and commercial units fragmented. At the same time, there was a new round of invasions from central Asia, launched by the Mongols. In the 13th century, they attacked China, the Middle East, and eastern Europe, toppling established kingdoms and allowing new contacts between Asia and Europe.

By 1400 the Mongol surge was receding, though only slowly in Russia. A new empire emerged in China. The Arab caliphate had perished. But a new Islamic political force, under the Ottoman Turks, was taking shape. The Ottomans unified much of the Middle East and positioned themselves to destroy the venerable Byzantine Empire. Using their growing commercial vigor but also terrified by the emergence of a new Islamic power, western Europeans looked for ways to gain greater control over international trade. The Chinese briefly experimented with a series of mighty trading expeditions across the Indian Ocean. But a shift in emperors led to a retreat, with a decision to concentrate on traditions of internal political, cultural, and commercial development. As it turned out, this left the way

1600 C.E.	1650 C.E.	1700 C.E.	1750 C.E.
1600 Dutch and British merchants begin activity in India	**1652** Dutch colony South Africa	**1713** New Bourbon dynasty, Spain	**1756–1763** Seven Years' War
1600–1690 Scientific Revolution (Europe)	**1658–1707** Aurangzeb reign, beginning of Mughal decline	**1722** Fall of Safavid dynasty (Iran)	**1763** Britain acquires "New France"
1603 Tokugawa shogunate	**1682–1699** Turks driven from Hungary	**1759–1788** Reforms of Latin American colonial administration	**1764** British East India Company controls Bengal (India)
1607 First British colonies in North America	**1689–1725** Peter the Great (Russia)		**1770s** European–Bantu conflicts in southern Africa
1608 First French North American colonies			**1772–1795** Partition of Poland
1637 Russian pioneers to Pacific			**1775–1783** American Revolution
1640s Japan moves into isolation			**1781** Indian revolts in New Grenada and Peru (Latin America)
1641 Dutch colonies in Indonesia			**1792** Slave uprising in Haiti
1642–1727 Isaac Newton			
1644 Qing dynasty, China			

open for the western European overseas expeditions. Western explorers and merchants benefited from technologies newly learned from China and the Islamic world, such as the compass and triangular sail, while adding important innovations such as guns and faster oceangoing ships.

The Rise of the West

 Between 1450 and 1750, western Europe, headed initially by Spain and Portugal and then by Holland, Britain, and France, gained control of the key international trade routes. It established colonies in the Americas and, on a much more limited basis, in Africa and parts of Asia.

At the same time, partly because of its new international position, the West itself changed rapidly, becoming an unusual kind of agricultural civilization. Commerce began to change the social structure and also affected basic attitudes toward family life and the natural environment. A host of new ideas, some of them springing from religious reformers, created a novel cultural climate in which scientific principles were increasingly valued. The Scientific Revolution gradually reshaped Western culture as a whole. More effective political structures emerged by the 17th century, as Western monarchs began to introduce bureaucratic principles similar to those pioneered long before in China.

A vital facet of the early modern period, then, was the West's expansion as an international force and its internal transformation. Like the previous global civilization, Arab Islam, the West developed a diverse and dynamic culture and society, which was both a result and a cause of its rising international prominence.

The World Economy and Global Contacts

 Fed by new naval technologies, the world network intensified and took on new dimensions. The change involved more than the fact that the Europeans, not the Muslims, dominated international trade. It featured an expansion of the world network to global proportions, well beyond previous international linkages. The

Americas were brought into contact with other cultures and included in global exchanges for the first time. At the end of the period, in the 18th century, Polynesian and Australian societies began to undergo the same painful integrating experience.

By 1750 there were no fully isolated societies of any great size. The new globalism of human contacts had a host of consequences that ran through early modern centuries. The human disease pool became fully international for the first time, and peoples who had previously been isolated from the rest of the world suffered greatly from exposure to diseases for which they had developed no immunities. The global network also permitted a massive exchange of plants and animals. Cows and horses were introduced to the Americas, prompting significant changes in Native American societies and economies. American food crops were spread around the world, bringing sweet potatoes, corn, and manioc to China, corn to Africa, and potatoes and tobacco to Europe. One result through most of the world, beginning in Asia as well as western Europe, was rapid population expansion.

As part of this new globalization, highly unequal relationships were established among many civilizations. During the postclassical millennium, 450–1450 C.E., a few areas had contributed inexpensive raw materials (including labor power in the form of slaves) to more advanced societies, notably China and the Islamic world. These supply areas included western Europe and parts of Africa and southeast Asia. Although economic relationships in these instances were unequal, they did not affect the societies that produced raw materials too severely because international trade was not sufficient to do so. After 1450 or 1500, as Western commerce expanded internationally, the West began to set up unequal relationships with a number of areas. Areas such as Latin America depended heavily on exports of cheap raw materials, on imports of processed goods, and on Western ships and merchants to handle international trade. Dependence of this sort skewed labor relations by encouraging commercial exploitation of slaves and serfs. It is vital to stress that much of the world, particularly in the great Asian civilizations, was not developed by this set of relationships, as they benefited from global trade on their own terms. But the global network spread: Western overseas expansion began to engulf India and parts of Indonesia by the 18th century.

World Boundaries

The period of 1450–1750 saw an unusual number of boundary changes in world history. The spread of Western colonies was the most obvious development, but the establishment or extension of a number of large land-based empires was almost as significant.

Compare the two maps by tracing the areas of Western penetration. You will see the different forms this penetration took in different parts of the world. Note also what parts of the world offered particular opportunities for rivalries among the leading Western colonial powers and what parts were immune to Western expansion.

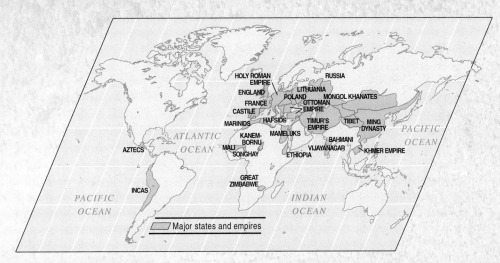

World Boundaries, c. 1453

World Boundaries, c. 1700. Compare with the 1453 map. What were the main changes? What areas were most stable? Why did Western colonies spread in some parts of the world and not in others?

353

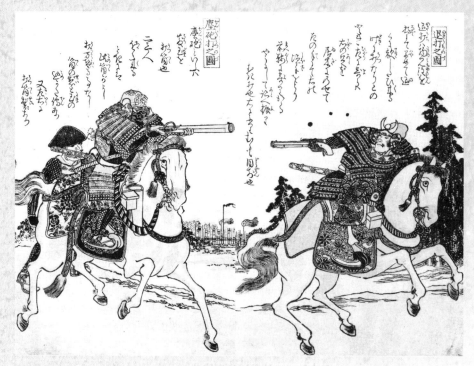

The power of gunpowder. The gun was introduced into Japan in 1542 by the Portuguese. By 1562, 10,000 Japanese soldiers carried muskets. The scenes depicted here are from a military manual written by one of the greatest generals of the period, Nobunaga.

The Gunpowder Empires

The rise of western Europe and its growing dominance of world trade was not the only major theme of early modern world history. The centuries after 1450 could also be called the age of the gunpowder empires. The development of cannons and muskets in the 15th and 16th centuries, through the combination of Western technology and previous Chinese invention, spurred the West's expansion. Ship-based artillery was fundamental to the West's mastery of international sea lanes and many ports and islands. But gunnery was picked up by other societies as well. The Ottoman Turks used huge cannons in their successful siege of Constantinople in 1453. The subsequent Ottoman Empire relied heavily on field guns to supplement trained cavalry. The rise of a new Russian Empire after 1480 was also built on the growing use of guns, and the

Russian economy was later reshaped to ensure the manufacture of the new military hardware. Three other key empires—the Mughal in India, the Safavid in Persia, and the 17th-century Qing dynasty in China—relied on the new strength of land armies armed with guns. Guns also played a role in Japanese and African history during the period.

Guns supported the forging of new land empires throughout much of Asia and eastern Europe and, to some extent, in Africa. These developments were largely independent of Western influence, and they counterbalanced the growth of Western power. The rise of the Russian Empire ran through the whole period, and though not as important as the expansion of the West, it was certainly a vital theme. The rise of the Ottomans, Safavids, and Mughals was a bit shorter-lived but echoed through the first two centuries of the period and, in the case of the Ottomans, created one of the most durable empires in world history.

354

Themes

 Many of the key themes of world history changed during the early modern centuries. Most strikingly, the impact of nomadic societies—once vital to world history dynamics—declined dramatically after the Mongol incursions. The new gunpowder empires, particularly Russia and China, conquered many of the old nomad strongholds. In many areas nomadic intermediaries were replaced by more direct relations among states or merchant groups. For example, European governments began regular diplomatic contacts, recognizing the importance of consistent interchange. China had received foreign representatives for centuries. In Europe, the practice started among Italian city-states in the Renaissance and then spread more widely. Representation to governments in Africa and Asia was a bit more haphazard, but formal emissaries were sent out to negotiate on trade and other matters.

Developments in the changing world economy had major effects on patterns of inequality. Gender relations did not change greatly in most areas, but labor systems were transformed throughout much of the world. The massive expansion of slavery and harsh serfdom in key parts of the world created new social hierarchies. The same developments also reduced human agency for millions of people who were captured or otherwise forced into slavery or serfdom. Growing wealth and new cultural currents, including the rise of science, created new opportunities for a small number of Europeans, and individual genius in art, trade, science, or military organization ultimately had global effects. Conquests created opportunities for human agency elsewhere as well, as with the imaginative leaders who first established the Mughal Empire in India.

Finally, the early modern centuries saw drastic environmental change, though more because of the exchanges of foods, animals, and diseases with the Americas than because of new technology. Imported horses, sheep, and cattle, reproducing rapidly, had great effects on American grasslands and densely settled Native American farmlands. Imported diseases such as measles and smallpox had even more devastating results. Soil conditions were changed in some places by the introduction of new crops such as sugar, which often replaced native vegetation. From North America to China, settlers in search of land to farm began clearing temperate forests. In a number of regions, the clearing of the world's great rain forests began.

Civilizations and Larger Trends

 As in earlier times, many developments during these early modern centuries occurred within individual civilizations, with little or no relationship to more general world trends. Only the Americas came close to being overwhelmed by outside influences. Nevertheless, the impact of the three international trends—Western expansion, intensification and globalization of the world commercial network, and the military and political results of gunpowder—affected patterns in the separate societies in many ways. Each civilization had to respond to these trends. Reactions were diverse, ranging from the eager embrace of new international currents to forced compliance or deliberate isolation.

International pressures increased with time. By 1700 western Europe's activities were looming larger, not just in key areas such as the Americas, the Asian island groups, and the coast of west Africa, but in mainland Asia and eastern Europe as well. A new Russian urge to selectively copy aspects of the West, and the establishment of growing British control in parts of India, were two facets of this shift. Even Japan, which initially responded to the new world economy by effective isolation, began to show a new but modest openness, exemplified by the end of a long-standing ban on translating Western books.

The first two chapters in this section focus on the emergence of Western colonies and Western-dominated world trade and on changes within the West. Then, two chapters deal with two societies that had particular links with the West: Russia, whose expansion was an important theme in its own right, and a new kind of emerging civilization in Latin America. The last three chapters deal with major societies in Asia and Africa, where contacts with the West and the new world economy were significant, particularly as the early modern period wore on, but where separate patterns of activity remained vital.

I. What can these documents tell us about the motives of the Europeans and the consequences of their encounters with the indigennous peoples of the Americas? What additional types of documents might be helpful in answering these questions?

1. Letter of Amerigo Vespucci: his first voyage to the New World c. 1497

Amongst those people we did not learn that they had any law, nor can they be called Moors nor Jews, and (they are) worse than pagans: because we did not observe that they offered any sacrifice: nor even had they a house of prayer: their manner of living I judge to be Epicurean: their dwellings are in common: and their houses (are) made in the style of huts, but strongly made, and constructed with very large trees, and covered over with palm-leaves, secure against storms and winds: and in some places (they are) of so great breadth and length, that in one single house we found there were 600 souls . . . every eight or ten years they change their habitations: and when asked why they did so: (they said it was) because of the soil which, from its filthiness, was already unhealthy and corrupted, and that it bred aches in their bodies, which seemed to us a good reason: their riches consist of bird's plumes of many colours, or of rosaries which they make from fishbones, or of white or green stones which they put in their cheeks and in their lips and ears, and of many other things which we in no wise value: they use no trade, they neither buy nor sell. In fine, they live and are contended with that which nature gives them. The wealth that we enjoy in this our Europe and elsewhere, such as gold, jewels, pearls, and other riches, they hold as nothing; and although they have them in their own lands, they do not labour to obtain them, nor do they value them. They are liberal in giving, for it is rarely they deny you anything: and on the other hand, liberal in asking, when they shew themselves your friends. . . .

2. Dr. Diego Alverez Chanca, participant in Columbus's second voyage, on the Caribe Indians, in a published account c. 1500

The way of life of these *caribe* people is bestial. . . .

These people raid the other islands and carry off the women whom they can take, especially the young and beautiful ones, whom they keep to serve them and have as concubines, and they carry off so many that in fifty houses nobody was found, and of the captives more than twenty were young girls. These women also say that they are treated with a cruelty which seems incredible, for sons whom they have from them are eaten and they only rear those whom they have from their native women. The men whom they are able to take, those who are alive they bring to their houses to butcher for meat, and those who are dead are eaten there and then. They say that men's flesh is so good that there is nothing like it in the world, and it certainly seems so for the bones which we found in these houses had been gnawed of everything they could gnaw, so that nothing was left on them except what was much too tough to be eaten.

3. Spanish explorer Hernando Cortés in Mexico, writing to the Spanish government c. 1520

Captain Hernando Cortés . . . decided . . . to depart; and so hoisting sail they left that Island of Cozumel . . . very peaceably inclined, so much so that if it were proposed to found a colony there the natives would be ready without coercion to serve their Spanish masters. The chiefs in particular were left contented and at ease with what the Captain had told them on behalf of your Majesties and with the numerous articles of finery which he had given them for their own persons. I think there can be no doubt that all Spaniards who may happen to come to this Island in the future will be as well received as if they were arriving in a land which had been long time colonized.

Your Majesties must know that when the Captain told the chiefs in his first interview with them that they must live no longer in the pagan faith which they held they begged him to acquaint them with the law under which they were henceforth to live. The Captain accordingly informed them to the best of his ability in the Catholic Faith . . . and gave them to understand very fully what they must do to be good Christians, all of which they manifestly received with very good will, and so we left them very happy and contented. . . .

4. French explorer Samuel de Champlain in North America, reporting to his government c. 1632

All these savages from the Island Cape wear neither robes nor furs, except very rarely. . . . They have only the sexual parts concealed with a small piece of leather; so likewise the women, with whom it comes down a little lower behind than with the men, all the rest of the body being naked. . . . Their bodies are well-proportioned. I cannot tell what government they have, but I think that in this respect they resemble their neighbors, who have none at all. They know not how to worship or pray; yet, like the other savages, they have some superstitions, which I shall describe in the place. . . . Even a slight intercourse with them gives you at once a knowledge of them. They are great thieves and, if they cannot lay hold of any thing with their hands, they try to do so with their feet, as we have oftentimes learned by experience. I am of opinion that, if they had any thing to exchange with us, they would not give themselves to thieving. They bartered away to us their bows, arrows, and quivers, for pins and buttons; and if they had had any thing else better they would have done the same with it. It is necessary to be on one's guard against this people, and live in a state of distrust with them, yet without letting them perceive it.

5. Aztec reactions to the European encounter
16th Century

The messengers [of the Aztec leader Motecuhzoma, returning from the Spanish explorer Hernando Cortés] also said: "Their trappings and arms are all made of iron. They dress in iron and wear iron casques on their heads. Their swords are iron; their bows are iron; their shields are iron, their spears are iron. Their deer carry them on their backs wherever they wish to go. These deer, our lord, are as tall as the roof of a house.

"The strangers' bodies are completely covered, so that only their faces can be seen. Their skin is white, as if it were made of lime. They have yellow hair, though some of them have black. Their beards are long and yellow, and their moustaches are also yellow. Their hair is curly, with very fine strands."

When Motecuhzoma heard this report, he was filled with terror. It was as if his heart had fainted, as if it had shriveled. It was as if he were conquered by despair.

While the Spaniards were in Tlaxcala, a great plague broke out in Tenochtitlan. It began to spread . . . striking everywhere in the city and killing a vast number of our people. Sores erupted on our faces, our breasts, our bellies; we were covered with agonizing sores from head to foot.

II. Evaluate the cultural, economic, and political calculations that were made by Russians, Asians, and Africans as a result of the sudden increase in the West European role in world trade. What additional types of documents might assist in addressing this question?

1. Russia: Decree of Tsar Peter the Great Regarding the Study of Navigation Abroad c. 1714

3. Discover as much as possible how to put ships to sea during a naval battle. Those who cannot succeed in this effort must diligently ascertain what action should be taken by the vessels that do and those that do not put to sea during such a situation [naval battle]. Obtain from [foreign] naval officers written statements, bearing their signatures and seals, of how adequately you [Russian students] are prepared for [naval] duties.

4. If, upon his return, anyone wishes to receive [from the Tsar] greater favors for himself, he should learn, in addition to the above enumerated instructions, how to construct those vessels aboard which he would like to demonstrate his skills.

5. Upon his return to Moscow, every [foreign-trained Russian] should bring with him at his own expense, for which he will later be reimbursed, at least two experienced masters of naval science.

2. China: Memorial of bureaucrat Hsu Kuang-Chi (to the Emperor) c. 1617

Knowing full well that the arts and sciences of the foreigners are in a high degree correct, your majesty's humble servant earnestly begs of his sacred Intelligence, the illustrious honor of issuing a manifesto on their behalf. . . .

As your servant for years past has been thus accustomed to engage in discussions and investigations with these [European] courtiers, he has become well acquainted with them, and knows that they are not only in deportment and in heart wholly free from anything which can excite suspicion, but that they are indeed worthies and sages; that their doctrines are most correct; their regimen most strict, their learning most extensive; their knowledge most refined; their hearts most true; their views most steady. . . . Now the reason of their coming thousands of miles eastward, is because hearing that the teachers, the sages and worthies of China, served Heaven by the cultivation of personal virtue . . . they desired, notwithstanding the difficulties and dangers by land and by sea, to give their seal to the truth. . . .

3. Muslim Indian reactions: Abu Taleb Khan's book about his travels to England 18th Century

The first and greatest defect I observed in the English is their want of faith in religion, and their great inclination to philosophy [atheism]: The effect of these principles, or rather want of principle, is very conspicuous in the lower orders of people, who are totally devoid of honesty. They are, indeed, cautious how they transgress against the laws, from fear of punishment; but whenever an opportunity offers of stealing anything without the risk of detection, they never pass it by. . . .

Their third defect is a passion for acquiring money and their attachment to worldly affairs. Although these bad qualities are not so reprehensible in them as in countries more subject to the vicissitudes of fortune, (because, in England, property is so well protected by the laws that every person reaps the fruits of his industry, and, in his old age, enjoys the earnings or economy of his youth,) yet sordid habits are generally found to accompany avarice; on the contrary, generosity, if it does not launch into prodigality, but is guided by the hand of prudence, will render a man respected and esteemed. . . .

4. Reactions to the first Portuguese arrivals in East Africa, from a Swahili chronicle c. 1520

During al-Fudail's reign there came news from the land of Mozambique that men had come from Europe. They had three ships, and the name of their captain was al-Mirati [Dom Vasco da Gama]. After a few days there came word that the ships had passed Kilwa and had gone on to Mafia. The lord of Mafia rejoiced, for they thought that [the Europeans] were good and honest men. But those who knew the truth confirmed that they were corrupt and dishonest persons who had only come to spy out the land in order to seize it. And they determined to cut the anchors of their ships so that they should drift ashore and be wrecked by the Muslims. The Europeans learnt of this and went on to Malindi. When the people of Malindi saw them, they knew they were bringers of war and corruption, and were troubled with very great fear. They gave them all they asked, water, food, firewood, and everything else. And the Europeans asked for a pilot to guide them to India, and after that back to their own land—God curse it!

5. Japanese exclusion of the Portuguese c. 1639

1. The matter relating to the banning of Christianity is known [to the Portuguese]. However, heretofore they have secretly transported those who are going to propagate that religion.

2. If those who believe in that religion band together in an attempt to do evil things, they must be subjected to punishment.

3. While those who believe in the preaching of the priests are in hiding, there are incidents in which that country [Portugal] has sent gifts to them for their sustenance.

In view of the above, hereafter entry by the Portuguese ships is forbidden. If they insist on coming [to Japan], the ships must be destroyed and anyone aboard those ships must be beheaded. We have received the above order and are thus transmitting it to you accordingly.

The above concerns our disposition with regard to the *galeota*.

CHAPTER 16

THE WORLD ECONOMY

In this 16th-century Japanese painting, the artist depicted the Europeans and their African slaves as exotic and unfamiliar.

- The West's First Outreach: Maritime Power
- IN DEPTH: Causation and the West's Expansion
- Toward a World Economy
- VISUALIZING THE PAST: West Indian Slaveholding
- Colonial Expansion
- DOCUMENT: Western Conquerors: Tactics and Motives
- GLOBAL CONNECTIONS: The World Economy—And the World

This chapter deals with the consequences of some key developments long celebrated in American school texts: the voyages of Columbus and the explorers and the empires built by European conquerors and missionaries. The result was a power shift in world affairs, but another set of crucial developments in world history also resulted: the redefinition of interchanges among major societies in the world.

Previous periods had seen important steps toward greater diffusion of goods and ideas. During the classical era, most attention was given to developing larger regional economies and cultural zones, such as the Chinese Middle Kingdom and the Mediterranean basin. Wider international contacts existed, but they were not of fundamental importance to the societies involved. The level and significance of contacts increased in the postclassical era. Missionary religions spilled across civilization boundaries, as with Buddhism in eastern and southeast Asia and above all with Islam. For the Middle East, parts of Africa and Europe, and much of India, interregional trade became an important feature of the basic economic structure, with some regions dominating trade in particular goods.

Despite these important precedents, the global relationships that developed after 1450, mainly but not exclusively sponsored by western Europe, spelled a new period in world history. New areas of the world were for the first time brought into the global complex, particularly the Americas. The rate of global trade also increased in some portions of the Old World, such as the islands of southeast Asia. Furthermore, global trade became so significant that it forged different relationships between key societies, based on the kind of goods and amount of control contributed to the surging world economy. The emergence of this new kind of global economy was the most important development in world history during the early modern centuries.

Various nations in western Europe were the key agents in the world economy. As profits flowed in, other changes within western Europe accelerated. Close connections developed between Western changes, discussed in the next chapter, and the world economy. Several parts of the world became increasingly dependent on Western economic control.

But the world economy remained complex, and many Asian societies continued their own strong economic performance. Europe was now able to use New World goods, particularly silver, to help pay for the luxury products still sought in China and India. China, particularly, accumulated more American silver than any other society as a result. Europeans were still trying to improve their role in trading with the big Asian powers at the end of the 18th century.

1400 C.E.	1500 C.E.	1600 C.E.	1700 C.E.
1394–1460 Prince Henry the Navigator	**1509** First Spanish colonies on Latin American mainland	**1607** First British colony in Virginia	**1744** French–British wars in India
1433 China ends great expeditions	**1514** Expedition to Indonesia	**1608** First French colonies in Canada; first trading concession in India to England	**1756–1763** Seven Years' War in Europe, India, and North America
1434 Portugal extends expeditions down west African coast	**1519–1521** Magellan circumnavigates globe	**1641** Dutch begin conquests on Java, in Indonesia	**1763** British acquire New France
1488 Portuguese round Cape of Good Hope	**1534** First French explorations in Canada	**1652** Dutch launch colony in southern Africa	**1775–1783** American Revolution
1492 Columbus' first expedition	**1542** Portuguese reach Japan		**1756** "Black hole" of Calcutta
1497–1498 Vasco da Gama to India	**1562** Britain begins its slave trade		**1764** East India Company control of Bengal
	1571 Ottoman fleet defeated in Battle of Lepanto		
	1588 British defeat Spanish Armada		
	1597 Japan begins isolation policy		

This chapter begins with a discussion of the West's emergence as the world's leading commercial and colonial power. We then turn to the larger world system that the West helped create, which turned out to have a life of its own. New exchanges of goods, ideas, and diseases followed the emergence of the new system. Finally, we sort out the different kinds of reactions that the world economy generated, from substantial isolation to outright subjugation.

Foods

About 30 percent of the foods consumed in the world today come from plants of American origin. These plants—corn and the potato are the most important among them—began to be spread after 1500. China and Africa, encountering American foods through contacts with European traders, adopted them eagerly. Corn became a staple in the African diet. Europeans, ironically, were more conservative. Rumors spread that American foods spread the plague. The foods were not mentioned in the Bible. Only later did the potato begin to gain ground, with fried potatoes (French fries) sold on Paris streets in the 1680s.

The West's First Outreach: Maritime Power

 Between 1450 and 1650, various western European nations gained unprecedented mastery of the world's oceans. Trading patterns and colonial expansion focused on Europe's maritime power. Pioneering efforts by Spain and Portugal were followed by the surge of Britain, Holland, and France.

Various European leaders, particularly merchants but also some princes and clergy, had become increasingly aware of the larger world around them since 1100. The Crusades brought knowledge of the Islamic world's superior economy and the goods that could be imported from Asia. The Mongol Empire, which sped up exchanges between the civilizations of Asia, also spurred European interest. The fall of the khans in China disrupted this interchange, as China became once again a land of mystery to Europeans. Europe's upper classes had by this time become accustomed to imported products from southeast Asia and India, particularly spices. These goods were transported to the Middle East in Arab ships, then brought overland, where they were loaded again onto vessels (mainly from Genoa and Venice, in Italy) for the Mediterranean trade.

Europeans entered into this era of growing contacts with several disadvantages. They remained ignorant of the wider world. Viking adventurers from Scandinavia had crossed the Atlantic in the 10th century, reaching Greenland and then North America, which they named Vinland. However, they quickly lost interest beyond establishing settlements on Greenland and Iceland, in part because they encountered indigenous warriors whose weaponry was good enough to cause them serious problems. And many Europeans continued to believe that the earth was flat, although scientists elsewhere knew otherwise; this belief made them fearful of distant voyages lest they fall off the world's edge.

As Europeans launched a more consistent effort at expansion from 1291 onward, they were pressed by new problems: fear of the strength of the emerging Ottoman Empire and the lack of gold to pay for Asian imports. Initial settlements in island groups in the south Atlantic fed their hopes for further gains. However, the first expeditions were limited by the small, oar-propelled ships used in the Mediterranean trade, which could not travel far into the oceans.

New Technology: A Key to Power

During the 15th century, a series of technological improvements began to change the equation. Europeans developed deep-draft, round-hulled sailing ships for the Atlantic, capable of carrying heavy armaments. They also began to use the compass for navigation (an instrument they copied from the Arabs, who had learned it from the Chinese). Mapmaking and other navigational devices improved as well. Finally, European knowledge of explosives, another Chinese invention, was adapted into gunnery. European metalwork, steadily advancing in sophistication, allowed Western metalsmiths to devise the first guns and cannons. Though not very accurate, these weapons were awesome by the standards of the time (and terrifying to many Europeans, who had reason to fear the new destructive power of their own armies and navies). The West began to forge a military advantage over all other civilizations of the world, at

first primarily on the seas—an advantage it would retain into the 20th century. With an unprecedented ability to kill and intimidate from a distance, western Europe was ready for its big push.

Portugal and Spain Lead the Pack

The specific initiative came from the small kingdom of Portugal, whose Atlantic location made it well-suited for new initiatives. Portugal's rulers were drawn by the excitement of discovery, the harm they might cause to the Muslim world, and a thirst for wealth—a potent mix. A Portuguese prince, Henry the Navigator (Figure 16.1), organized a series of expeditions along the African coast and also outward to islands such as the Azores. Beginning in 1434 the Portuguese began to press down the African coast, each expedition going a little farther than its predecessor. They brought back slaves, spices such as pepper, and many stories of gold hoards they had not yet been able to find.

Later in the 15th century, Portuguese sailors ventured around the **Cape of Good Hope** in an attempt to find India, where direct contact would give Europeans easier access to luxury cloths and spices. They rounded the cape in 1488, but weary sailors forced the expedition back before it could reach India.

Figure 16.1 *Prince Henry the Navigator, of Portugal, sent annual expeditions down the western coast of Africa. He was not a sailor, but his sponsorship was essential.*

Then, after news of Columbus's discovery of America for Spain in 1492, Portugal redoubled its efforts, hoping to stave off the new Spanish competition. Vasco da Gama's fleet of four ships reached India in 1498, with the aid of a Hindu pilot picked up in east Africa. The Portuguese mistakenly believed that the Indians were Christians, for they thought the Hindu temples were churches. They faced the hostility of Muslim merchants, who had long dominated trade in this part of the world, and they brought only crude goods for sale, like iron pots. But fortunately they had a lot of gold as well. They managed to return with a small load of spices. A later trip involved more violence. Da Gama used ships' guns to intimidate, and his forces killed or tortured many Indian merchants to set an example.

Da Gama's success set in motion an annual series of Portuguese voyages to the Indian Ocean, outlined in Map 16.1. One expedition, blown off course, reached Brazil, where it proclaimed Portuguese sovereignty (Figure 16.2). Portugal began to set up forts on the African coast and also in India—the forerunners of such Portuguese colonies as Mozambique, in east Africa, and Goa, in India. By 1514 the Portuguese had reached the islands of Indonesia, the center of spice production, and China. In 1542 one Portuguese expedition arrived in Japan, where a missionary effort was launched that met with some success for several decades.

Meanwhile, only a short time after the Portuguese quest began, the Spanish reached out with even greater force. Here also was a country only recently freed from Muslim rule, full of missionary zeal and a desire for riches. The Spanish had traveled into the Atlantic during the 14th century. Then in 1492, the same year that the final Muslim fortress was captured in Spain, the Italian navigator **Christopher Columbus,** operating in the name of the newly united Spanish monarchy, set sail for a westward route to India, convinced that the round earth would make his quest possible. As is well known he failed, reaching the Americas instead and mistakenly nam-

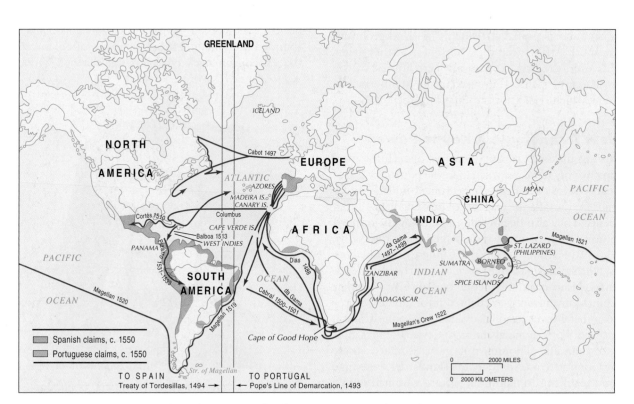

Map 16.1 *Spain and Portugal: Explorations and Colonies, c. 1600. In the early years of new exploration, Spanish and Portuguese voyages surveyed much of the coast of South America and some choice ports in Africa and Asia.*

Figure 16.2 *This is the earliest European sketch of Native Americans at the time of a Portuguese expedition to northern South America about 1500. "The people are thus naked, handsome, brown....They also eat each other...and hang the flesh of them in the smoke. They become a hundred and fifty years of age, and have no government."*

ing their inhabitants "Indians." Although Columbus believed to his death that he had sailed to India, later Spanish explorers realized that they had voyaged to a region where Europeans, Africans, and Asians had not traveled previously. One expedition, headed by Amerigo Vespucci, gave the New World its name. Spain, eager to claim this new land, won papal approval for Spanish dominion over most of what is now Latin America, although a later treaty awarded Brazil to Portugal.

Finally, a Spanish expedition under **Ferdinand Magellan** set sail westward in 1519, passing the southern tip of South America and sailing across the Pacific, reaching the Indonesian islands in 1521 after incredible hardships. It was on the basis of this voyage, the first trip around the world, that Spain claimed the Philippines, which it held until 1898.

Portugal emerged from this first round of exploration with coastal holdings in parts of Africa and in the Indian port of Goa, a lease on the Chinese port of Macao, short-lived interests in trade with Japan, and, finally, the claim on Brazil. Spain asserted its hold on the Philippines, various Pacific islands, and the bulk of the Americas. During the 16th century, the Spanish backed up these claims by military expeditions to Mexico and South America. The Spanish also held Florida and sent expeditions northward from Mexico into California and other parts of what later became the southwestern United States.

Northern European Expeditions

Later in the 16th century, the lead in exploration passed to northern Europe, as newly strong monarchies, such as France and England, got into the act and zealous Protestants in Britain and Holland strove to rival Catholic gains (Map 16.2). In part this shift in dynamism occurred because Spain and Portugal were busy digesting the gains they had already made; in part it was because northern Europeans, particularly the Dutch and the British, improved the design of oceanic vessels, producing lighter, faster ships than those of their Catholic adversaries. Britain won a historic sea battle with Spain in 1588, routing a massive Spanish Armada. From this point onward, the British, the Dutch, and to some extent the French vied for dominance on the seas, although in the Americas they aimed mainly northward because they could not challenge the Spanish and Portuguese colonies. Only in the sugar-rich West Indies did northern Europe seize islands initially claimed by Spain.

The new adventurers, like their Spanish and Portuguese predecessors, appreciated the economic potential of such voyages. Two 16th-century English explorers, trying to find an Arctic route to China, were told to keep an eye out for any native populations en route, for such people would provide a perfect market for warm English woolens. And if the territory was unpopulated, it might be put to use as

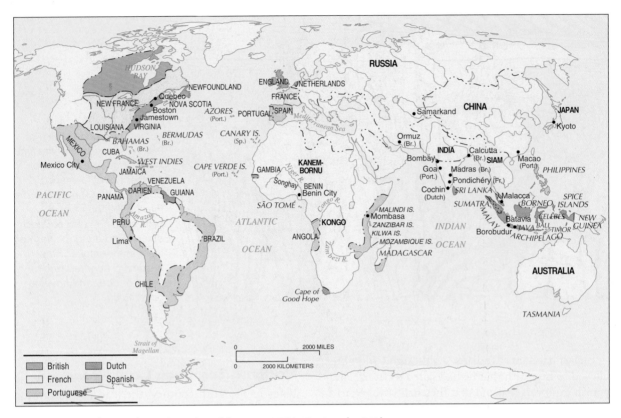

Map 16.2 *French, British, and Dutch Holdings, c. 1700. During the 17th century, northwestern Europe took the initiative in explorations, venturing into North America and seeking convenient trading stations elsewhere.*

a source of fish for Britain. A quest for profit had become a dominant policy motive.

French explorers crossed the Atlantic first in 1534, reaching Canada, which they claimed. In the 17th century, various expeditions pressed down from Canada into the Great Lakes region and the Mississippi valley.

The British also turned their attention to North America, starting with a brief expedition as early as 1497. The English hoped to discover a northwest passage to spice-rich India, but accomplished little beyond exploration of the Hudson Bay area of Canada during the 16th century. England's serious work began in the 17th century, with the colonization of the east coast of North America. Holland also had holdings in North America and, for a time, in Brazil.

The Dutch entered the picture after winning independence from Spain, and Holland quickly became a major competitor with Portugal in southeast Asia. The Dutch sent many sailors and ships to the region, oust-

ing the Portuguese from the Indonesian islands by the early 17th century. Voyagers from the Netherlands explored the coast of Australia, though without much immediate result. Finally, toward the mid-17th century, Holland established a settlement on the southern tip of Africa, mainly to provide a relay station for its ships bound for the East Indies.

The Netherlands, Britain, and France all chartered great trading companies, such as the **Dutch East India Company** and the British firm of similar name. These companies were given government monopolies of trade in the regions designated, but they were not rigorously supervised by their own states. They had rights to raise armies and coin money on their own. Thus, semiprivate companies, amassing great commercial fortunes, long acted almost like independent governments in the regions they claimed. For some time, a Dutch trading company effectively ruled the island of Taiwan off the coast of China; the **British East India Company** played a

In Depth

Causation and the West's Expansion

Because of their interest in social change, historians inevitably deal with causation. What prompted the fall of Rome? Why did Islam spread so widely? What factors explain why most agricultural civilizations developed patriarchal family structures?

Historical causation differs from the kinds of causation many scientists test. When experiments or observations can be repeated, scientists can gain a fairly precise understanding of the factors that produce a phenomenon: Remove an ingredient and the product changes. Historical causation is more complex. Major developments may resemble each other, but they never happen the same way twice. Definitive proof that factor X explains 40 percent of the spread of Buddhism in east Asia is impossible. This is why historians often disagree about causation. But if precision is impossible, high probability is not. We can get a fairly good sense of why things happen, and sloppy causation claims can be disproved. Furthermore, probing causation helps us explore the phenomenon itself. We know more about the nature of Western expansion in the 15th and 16th centuries if we discuss what caused it.

Some historians and other social scientists look to a single kind of cause as the explanation of a variety of circumstances. Some anthropologists are cultural determinists. They judge that a basic set of cultural factors, usually assumed to be very durable, causes the ongoing differences between societies: Chinese and Greeks, on average, respond differently to emotional stimuli because of their different cultural conditioning. More common is a technological or economic determinism. Some historians see technological change as setting other changes in motion. Others, including Marxists, argue that economic arrangements—how the economy is structured and what groups control it—produce at least the basic framework for innovations. At another pole, some historians used to claim "great men" as the prime movers in history. The causes of change thus became Chinggis Khan or Ashoka, with no need to look much farther.

Various approaches to causation have been applied to the West's explorations and colonial conquests in the early modern period. There is room for a "great man" analysis. Many descriptive accounts that dwell on explorers and conquerors (Vasco da Gama and Cortés, for example) and on leaders who sponsored them (such as Henry the Navigator) suggest that the key cause of the West's new role stemmed from the daring and vision of exceptional individuals.

Cultural causation can also be invoked. Somehow, Europe's expansion must relate to the wonders of innovation introduced by the Renaissance. The link with Christian culture is even easier to prove, for a missionary spirit quickly supplemented the efforts of early explorers, leading to more voyages and settlements in Asia and the Americas.

Political causation enters in, if not in causing the initial surge, at least in confirming it. Starting in the 16th century, rivalries between the nation-states motivated a continuing quest for new trade routes and colonies.

There is also room for a simpler, technologically determinist approach. In this view, Europe's gains came from a handful of new inventions. Benefiting from knowledge of advances in China and the Middle East, Europeans introduced naval cannons. Along with steady improvements in navigation and ship design, new techniques explain why Europe gained as it did. Except in the Americas, where they had larger technical and organizational advantages, Europeans advanced in areas they could reach by sea and dominate by ships' guns—port cities, islands, and trade routes—and not elsewhere. Put simply, Europe gained because of these few technological edges.

Like all determinisms, however, this technological approach raises as many questions as it answers. Why were Europeans so ready to adopt new inventions? (What caused the cause?) Why did other societies that were aware of Europe's innovations, such as China, deliberately scorn any adoption of Western naval techniques? Here a different culture determined a reaction different from that of the West. Technology and culture went hand in hand. Clearly, some combined causal framework is needed in this case.

We cannot expect uniform agreement on a precise ordering of causation. However, we can expect fruitful debate—the kind of debate that has already moved our understanding beyond surface causes, such as the powerful personalities of a few people, to a grasp of more underlying contexts.

Questions: If you had to choose a single determinism (cultural, technological, or economic) as basic to social change, which one would you pick? Why? In what ways might the professed motives of Western explorers and colonists have differed from their real motives? Would they necessarily have been aware of the discrepancy?

similar role in parts of India during much of the 18th century. The companies in North America traded actively in furs.

No matter where in Europe they came from, explorers and their crews faced many hardships at sea. The work was tiring and uncertain, with voyages lasting many months or years, and diseases such as scurvy were rampant. One expedition accepted only bachelors for its crew because married men would miss their families too much. A sailor on another trip complained that "he was tired of being always tired, that he would rather die once than many times, and that they might as well shut their eyes and let the ship go to the bottom."

Toward a World Economy

 Europe's maritime dominance and the opening of the Atlantic and Pacific oceans had three major consequences in world history. They created a new international pool for basic exchanges of foods, diseases, and a few manufactured products. They created a new world economy, involving the first embrace of the Americas in international trade but setting a different framework even for Europe and Asia. And they created the conditions for direct Western penetration of some parts of the world through colony formation.

The "Columbian Exchange" of Disease and Food

The impact of wider exchange became visible quickly. The extension of international contacts spread disease (see Chapter 19). The victims were millions of Native Americans who had not previously been exposed to Afro-Eurasian diseases such as smallpox and measles and who therefore had no natural immunities (Figure 16.3). During the 16th and 17th centuries, they died in huge numbers. Overall, in North and South America, more than half the native population would die; some estimates run as high as 80 percent. Whole island populations in the West Indies were wiped out. This was a major blow to earlier civilizations in the Americas as well as an opportunity for Europeans to forge a partially new population of their own citizens and slaves imported from Africa. The devastation occurred over a 150-year period, although in some

Figure 16.3 *A 16th-century print of Aztecs suffering from smallpox during the Cortés invasion (1518–1519).*

areas it was more rapid. When Europeans made contact with Polynesians and Pacific Coast peoples in the 18th century, the same dreadful pattern played out, again devastating vibrant cultures.

Other exchanges were less dire. New World crops were spread rapidly via Western merchants. American corn and sweet potatoes were taken up widely in China (where merchants learned of them from Spaniards in the Philippines), the Mediterranean, and parts of Africa. In some cases these productive new crops, along with local agricultural improvements, triggered large population increases. For example, China began to experience long-term population pressure in the 17th century, and new crops played a key role. When Europeans introduced the potato around 1700, major population upheaval occurred there as well.

Animal husbandry became more similar across the world as European and Asian animals, such as horses and cattle, were introduced to the New World. The spread of basic products and diseases formed an important backdrop to world history from the 16th century on, with varying effects on population structures in diverse regions.

The West's Commercial Outreach

Europeans did not displace all Asian shipping from the coastal waters of China and Japan, nor did they completely monopolize the Indian Ocean (see Chapter 22). Along the east African coast, while a few European bases were established, Muslim traders remained active, and commerce continued to move toward the Middle East. Generally, however, western Europe dominated a great deal of oceanic shipping, even muscling in on trade between other societies, as between India and southeast Asia. This greatly increased Europe's overall profits, and disproportionate control by the great merchant companies increased the European ability to determine the framework for international trade. In the eastern Mediterranean, for example, a Spanish-directed fleet defeated the navy of the Ottoman Empire in the battle of **Lepanto** in 1571. With this setback, any hope of successful Muslim rivalry against European naval power ended. The Turks rebuilt their fleet and continued their activity in the eastern Mediterranean, but they could not challenge the Europeans on the larger international routes.

Although western Europe did not conquer much inland territory in Africa or Asia, it did seek a limited network of secure harbors. Led by Spain and Portugal, then followed by the various northern powers, European ports spread along the west coast of Africa, several parts of the Indian subcontinent, and the islands of southeast Asia by the 17th century. Even in China, where unusually strong governments limited the Europeans' ability to seize harbors outright, the Portuguese won effective control over the island port of Macao. European-controlled ports served as areas for contact with overland traders (usually local merchants) and provided access to inland goods not directly within the reach of the West.

Where direct control was not feasible, European influence led to the formation of special Western enclaves in existing cities, where Western traders won special legal rights. This was the pattern in the Ottoman Empire, where Western merchants set up colonies within Constantinople, and in Russia, where Western factors (shipping agents) set up first in Moscow and then in St. Petersburg. Elements of this system even emerged in Japan after a firm isolationist policy was launched about 1600, as Dutch traders had some special access to the port of Nagasaki. The point was obvious: International trade gained growing importance in supplementing regional economies. Because western Europe now ran this trade, it won special rights of access.

Imbalances in World Trade

The most active competition in world trade emerged between European nations themselves. Spain briefly dominated, thanks to its imports of silver from the Americas. But it lacked a good banking system and could not support a full commercial surge. England, France, and Holland, where merchants had firmer status, soon pulled in the lion's share of profits from world trade.

Western Europe quickly expanded its manufacturing operations, so that it could export expensive finished goods, such as guns and cloth, in return for unprocessed goods, such as silver and sugar, traded by other societies. Here was another margin for profit.

The dominant **core nations** in the new world system supplemented their growing economic prowess by self-serving political policies. The doctrines of **mercantilism,** which urged that a nation-state not import goods from outside its own empire but sell exports as widely as possible in its own ships, both reflected and encouraged the new world system. Tariff policies discouraged manufacturing in colonial areas and stimulated home-based manufacturing.

Beyond western Europe lay areas that were increasingly enmeshed in the world economy but on a strictly dependant basis. These areas produced low-cost goods: precious metals and cash crops such as sugar, spice, tobacco, and later cotton. Human labor was a vital item of exchange. Parts of sub-Saharan Africa entered the new world economy mainly as suppliers of slaves. The earlier west African patterns of trade across the Sahara yielded to a dominant focus on the Atlantic and therefore to activities organized by Western shippers. In return for slaves and unprocessed goods, Europeans traded their manufactured items, including guns, while profiting from their control of commercial and shipping services.

Visualizing the Past

West Indian Slaveholding

The following table describes the rise of the plantation system, and attendant slaveholding, on the British West Indian island of Antigua, where sugar growing for export gained increasing hold. Trends of the sort indicated in this table raise further analytical issues about cause and effect. What might have caused the main changes in Antigua's estate system? How might the changes have related to the larger framework of the world economy? What do the trends suggest about the European demand for sugar and about production methods used to meet this demand?

What impact would the trends have had on slaves themselves? Laws in the British Caribbean soon began to enforce the estate system, exempting masters from murder charges when slaves died from beatings administered as punishment and fining groups such as the Quakers for daring to bring slaves to religious meetings. How do the statistical trends help explain the imposition of new laws of this sort?

Questions: What main trends in the social and economic structure of this part of Antigua during the

	1688	1706	1767
Taxables	53	36	65
Slaveholders	16	30	65
Planters with 20+ slaves	6	16	46
Planters with 100+ slaves	0	4	22
Slaves	332	1,150	5,610
Acreage	5,811	5,660	12,350

18th century do these figures suggest? What were the main changes in the relationship of slaveholding to property ownership? In the size of estates? In the comparative growth rates of owner and slave populations? Did the estate economy become more or less labor intensive, given the acreage involved? What do the trends suggest about the nature of the European-born or European-derived elite of Antigua?

A System of International Inequality

The new world economic relationships proved highly durable. Most of the areas established as dependant by the 17th century still carry some special burdens in world trade today. The core–dependant system should not be exaggerated, in part because most of the world, including most of Asia and much of Africa, was not yet fully embraced by it. In dependant areas such as Latin America and the slave-supplying parts of Africa, not all people were mired in poverty. African slave traders and princes who taxed the trade might grow rich. In Latin America the silver mines and commercial estates required regional merchants and farmers to supply food. Furthermore, many peasants in Latin America and even more in Africa were not yet involved in a market economy at all—whether regional or international—but rather produced for local subsistence with traditional motives and methods. However, significant minorities were involved in production for the world market. Also, most African and Latin American merchants and landlords did not fully control their own terms of trade. They might prosper, but their wealth did not stimulate much local manufacturing or general economic advance. Rather, they tended to import European-made goods, including (in the case of American planters) art objects and luxury items.

Coercive labor systems spread. Because dependent economies relied on cheap production of unprocessed goods, there was a tendency to build a system of forced labor that would cost little even when the overall labor supply was precarious. In the Americas, given the population loss from disease, this led to the massive importation of African slaves. Also, for many Native Americans and **mestizos** (people of mixed European and Native American blood), systems of estate management developed that demanded large amounts of labor. More limited examples of estate agriculture, in which peasants were forced into labor without the legal freedom to leave, arose for spice production in the Dutch East Indies and, by the 18th century, in British-dominated agricultural operations in India.

How Much World in the World Economy?

Huge areas of the world were not yet caught up in contact with the world economy. The societies that remained outside the world system did not gain ground as rapidly as the core areas of Europe because they did not have the profit opportunities in international trade. Their technologies changed less rapidly. But until the 18th century or beyond, they did not face great international problems.

China clearly benefited from the world economy, while participating less actively than Europe did. The Chinese government, having renounced large-scale international trade of its own early in the 15th century, deliberately avoided involvement with international trade on someone else's terms. It did copy some firearms manufacturing from the Europeans, but at a fairly low level. Beyond this it depended on extensive government regulation, backed up by a coastal navy, to keep European activities in check. Most of the limited trade that existed was channeled through Macao. European visitors wrote scornfully of China's disdain for military advances. A Jesuit wrote that "the military... is considered mean among them." The Chinese were also disparaged for adhering to tradition. One Western missionary in the 17th century described how, in his opinion, the Chinese could not be persuaded "to make use of new instruments and leave their old ones without an especial order from the Emperor to that effect. They are more fond of the most defective piece of antiquity than of the most perfect of the modern, differing much in that from us who are in love with nothing but what is new."

So China managed to avoid trying to keep up with European developments but also avoided subservience to European merchants. The world economy played only a subordinate role in Chinese history through the 18th century. Chinese manufacturing gains led to a strong export position, which is why Europeans sent a great deal of American silver to China to pay for the goods they wanted. But official isolation persisted. Indeed, at the end of the 18th century, a famous British mission, appealing to the government to open the country to greater trade, was rebuffed. The imperial court, after insisting on extreme deference from the British envoy, haughtily informed him that the Chinese had no need for outside goods. European eagerness for Chinese goods—attested to by the habit adopted in the 17th century of calling fine porcelain "china"—was simply not matched by Chinese enthusiasm, but a trickle of trade continued. Westerners compensated in part by developing their own porcelain industry by the 18th century, which contributed to the early Industrial Revolution, particularly in Britain. Still, there were hopes for commercial entry to China that remained unfulfilled.

Japan, though initially attracted by Western expeditions in the 16th century, also more fully pulled back. So did Korea. The Japanese showed some openness to Christian missions, and they were fascinated by Western advances in gunnery and shipping. Artists captured the interest in exotic foreigners. Guns had particular relevance to Japan's ongoing feudal wars, for there was no disdain here for military life. Yet Japanese leaders soon worried about undue Western influence and the impact this could have on internal divisions among warring lords, as well as the threat guns posed to samurai military dominance. They encouraged a local gunmaking industry that matched existing European muskets and small cannon fairly readily, but having achieved this they cut off most contact with any world trade. Most Japanese were forbidden to travel or trade abroad, the small Christian minority was suppressed, and from the 17th until the 19th centuries Japan entered a period of almost complete isolation except for some Chinese contact and trading concessions to the small Dutch enclave near Nagasaki.

Several other societies were not deeply affected by new world trade, participating at levels too low to have significant impact. The rulers of India's new Mughal Empire in the 16th century were interested in Western traders and even encouraged the establishment of small port colonies. India also sold goods in return for New World silver. Most attention, however, was riveted on internal development and land-based expansion and commerce; world trade was a sideline. The same held true for the Ottoman and Safavid empires in the Middle East through the 17th century, despite the presence of small European enclaves in key cities. Russia also lay outside the world economic orbit until the 18th century. A largely agricultural society, Russia conducted much of its trade with nomadic peoples in central Asia, which further insulated it from west European demands. Finally, much of Africa, outside the slave-trading orbit in western regions, was untouched by world trade patterns.

The Expansionist Trend

The world economy was not stationary; it tended to gain ground over time. South America, the West Indies, a part of North America, and some regions in west Africa were first staked out as dependencies beginning in the 16th century, and the list later expanded. Portions of southeast Asia that produced for world markets, under the dominance of the great Western trading companies, were brought into the orbit by the 17th century.

By the late 17th century, Western traders were advancing in India as the Mughal Empire began to fall apart. The British and French East India Companies staked out increasing roles in internal trade and administration. Early in the 18th century, Britain passed tariffs against the import of cotton cloth made in India as a means of protecting Britain's own cotton industry. The intent was to use India as a market for British-processed goods and a source of outright payments of gold, which the British were requiring by the late 18th century. Indian observers were aware of the shifting balance. An 18th century account noted,

> But such is the little regard which they [the British] show to the people of this kingdom, and such their apathy and indifference for their welfare, that the people under their dominion groan everywhere, and are reduced to poverty and distress.

India maintained a complex regional economy still, with much internal manufacturing and trade; it was not forced into such complete dependency as Latin America, for example. However, what had initially been a position outside the world economy was changing, to India's disadvantage. Manufacturing began to decline.

Eastern Europe also was brought into a growing relationship with the world economy and the west European core. The growth of cities in the West created a growing market for imported grains by the 18th century. Much of this demand was met by east European growers, particularly in Prussia and Poland but also in Russia. Export grains, in turn, were pro-duced mainly on large estates by serfs, who were subjected to prolonged periods of labor service. This relationship was similar to that which prevailed in Latin America, with one exception: Outside of Poland, east European governments were much stronger than their Latin American counterparts.

Colonial Expansion

 Along with the larger world economic system, a new wave of colonialism took shape after the early Spanish and Portuguese explorations. Key European nations developed direct overseas empires. Two sets of American colonies developed, one in Latin America and the Caribbean, one in parts of North America. The Americas hosted the largest colonies, but colonialism also spread to Africa and Asia.

The Americas: Loosely Controlled Colonies

Opportunities to establish colonies were particularly inviting in the Americas, where European guns, horses, and iron weapons offered special advantages and where political disarray and the population losses provided openings in many cases (see Chapter 19). Spain moved first. The Spanish colonized several West Indian islands soon after Columbus's first voyage, starting with Hispaniola and then moving into Cuba, Jamaica, and Puerto Rico. Only in 1509 did they begin settlement on the mainland, in search of gold; the first colony was established in what is now Panama, under an able but unscrupulous adventurer, **Vasco de Balboa.** Several expeditions fanned out in Central America, and then a separate expedition from Cuba launched the Spanish conquest of the Aztecs in Mexico. Another expedition headed toward the Inca realm in the Andes in 1531, where hard fighting was needed before ultimate victory. From this base several colonial expeditions spread to Colombia, other parts of the Andes, and portions of Argentina.

Expansion resulted from the efforts of a motley crew of adventurers, many of them violent and treacherous, like **Francisco Pizarro** (1478?–1541), admittedly one of the more successful examples (Figure 16.4). Pizarro first came to the Americas in 1502 and settled on the island of Hispaniola. Later, he joined Balboa's colony in Panama, where he received a cattle ranch. Learning of wealth in Peru, he joined

Figure 16.4 *Francisco Pizarro*

with an illiterate soldier and a priest, mounting two expeditions that failed. In 1528 he returned to Spain to gain the king's support and also his agreement that he would be governor of the new province. With these pledges and a force of about 180 men, he attacked the divided Inca empire. Capturing Emperor Atahuallpa, he accepted a large ransom and then strangled him. Several revolts followed during Pizarro's rule from Lima, a coastal city he founded. But the Spanish king ennobled Pizarro for his success. At a dinner in 1541, Pizarro was assassinated by a group of Inca rebels.

Early colonies in the Americas typically were developed by small bands of gold-hungry Europeans, often loosely controlled by colonial administrations back home. Colonial rulers often established only loose controls over native populations at first, content to exact tribute without imposing detailed administration and sometimes leaving existing leaders in place. Gradually, more formal administration spread as agricultural settlements were established and official colonial systems took shape under control of bureaucrats sent from Spain and Portugal. Active missionary efforts, designed to Christianize the native peoples, added another layer of detailed administration throughout the Spanish holdings in North and South America.

France, Britain, and Holland, though latecomers to the Americas, also staked out colonial settlements. French explorations along the St. Lawrence River in Canada led to small colonies around Quebec, from 1608 onward, and explorations in the Mississippi river basin. Dutch and English settlers moved into portions of the Atlantic coastal regions early in the 17th century. Also in the 17th century, all three countries seized and colonized several West Indian islands, which they soon involved in the growing slave trade.

British and French North America: Backwater Colonies

Colonies of European settlers developed in North America, where patterns differed in many respects from those in Latin America and the Caribbean. English colonies along the Atlantic received religious refugees, such as the Calvinists who fled religious tensions in Britain to settle in New England. Government grants of land to major proprietors such as William Penn led to explicit efforts to recruit settlers. New York began as a Dutch settlement but was taken over easily by an English expedition in 1664.

In Canada, the first substantial European settlements were launched by the French government under Louis XIV. The initial plan involved setting up manorial estates under great lords whose rights were carefully restricted by the state. French peasants were urged to emigrate, although it proved difficult to develop an adequate labor force. However, birth rates were high, and by 1755 **New France** had about 55,000 settlers in a peasant society that proved extremely durable as it fanned out around the fortress of Quebec. Strong organization by the Catholic church completed this partial replica of French provincial society. Britain attacked the French strongholds (Figure 16.5) as part of a worldwide colonial struggle

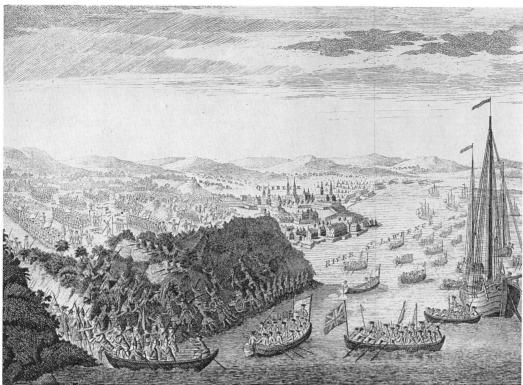

View of the Taking of QUEBECK by the English Forces Commanded by Gen.ˡ Wolfe Sep: 13ᵗʰ 1759

Figure 16.5 *British naval power allowed the light infantry to scale the French fort from the St. Lawrence River and capture Quebec in 1759. The attack nullified the cannon in the French fort in what turned out to be a crucial event in Canada's history.*

between the two powers, the **Seven Years' War.** France lost its colony under the terms of the **Treaty of Paris,** which in 1763 settled the war. France eagerly regained its West Indian sugar islands, along with trading posts in Africa, and Britain took control of Canada and the Mississippi basin. Relations between British officials and the French Canadian community remained strained as British settlements developed in eastern Canada and in Ontario. The flight of many American loyalists after the 1776 revolution added to the English-speaking contingent in Canada.

Colonial holdings along the Atlantic and in Canada were generally of modest interest to Western colonial powers in the 17th and even the 18th centuries. The Dutch were more attached to their Asian colonies. British and French leaders valued their West Indian holdings much more than their North American colonies. The value of North American products, such as timber and furs, was not nearly as great as

profits from the Caribbean or Latin America, so much less attention was given to economic regulation. As a result, some merchant and manufacturing activities emerged among new Americans themselves.

However, the American colonies that would become the United States had a population of a mere 3 million, far smaller than the powerful colonies in Latin America. Southern colonies that produced tobacco and sugar, and then cotton, became important. Patterns there were similar to those of Latin America, with large estates based on imported slave labor, a wealthy planter class bent on importing luxury products from western Europe, and weak formal governments. Still, in world historical terms the Atlantic colonies in North America were a backwater amid the larger colonial holdings staked out in the early modern centuries.

Yet European settlers did arrive. Driven by religious dissent, ambition, and other motives, Euro-

Document

Western Conquerors: Tactics and Motives

In the first passage quoted here, Columbus writes to the Spanish monarchy on his way home from his 1492 expedition. In the second passage, the brother of Francisco Pizarro, the Spanish conqueror of Peru, describes in 1533 how the Inca ruler, Atahuallpa, was defeated.

Columbus's 1492 Expedition

Sir, believing that you will take pleasure in hearing of the great success which our Lord has granted me in my voyage, I write you this letter, whereby you will learn how in thirty-three days' time I reached the Indies with the fleet which the most illustrious King and Queen, our Sovereigns, gave to me, where I found very many islands thickly peopled, of all which I took possession without resistance for their Highnesses by proclamation made and with the royal standard unfurled. To the first island that I found I gave the name of *San Salvador*, in remembrance of His High Majesty, who hath marvelously brought all these things to pass; the Indians call it *Guanaham*....

Espanola is a wonder. Its mountains and plains, and meadows, and fields, are so beautiful and rich for planting and sowing, and rearing cattle of all kinds, and for building towns and villages. The harbours on the coast, and the number and size and wholesomeness of the rivers, most of them bearing gold, surpass anything that would be believed by one who had not seen them. There is a great difference between the trees, fruits, and plants of this island and those of *Juana*. In this island there are many spices and extensive mines of gold and other metals. The inhabitants of this and of all the other islands I have found or gained intelligence of, both men and women, go as naked as they were born, with the exception that some of the women cover one part only with a single leaf of grass or with a piece of cotton, made for that purpose. They have neither iron, nor steel, nor arms, nor are they competent to use them, not that they are not well-formed and of handsome stature, but because they are timid to a surprising degree....

Although I have taken possession of all these islands in the name of their Highnesses, and they are all more abundant in wealth than I am able to express...yet there was one large town in *Espanola* of which especially I took possession, situated in a locality well adapted for the working of the gold mines, and for all kinds of commerce, either with the main land on this side, or with that beyond which is the land of the great Khan, with which there is great profit....

I have also established the greatest friendship with the king of that country, so much so that he took pride in calling me his brother, and treating me as such. Even should these people change their intentions towards us and become hostile, they do not know what arms are, but, as I have said, go naked, and are the most timid people in the world; so that the men I have left could, alone, destroy the whole country, and this island has no danger for them, if they only know how to conduct themselves.... Finally, and speaking only of what has taken place in this voyage, which has been so hasty, their Highnesses may see that I shall give them all the gold they require, if they will give me but a very little assistance; spices also, and cotton, as much as their Highnesses shall command to be shipped; and mastic, hitherto found only in Greece...slaves, as many of these idolators as their Highnesses shall command to be shipped....

But our Redeemer hath granted this victory our illustrious King and Queen and their kingdoms, which have acquired great fame by an event of such high importance, in which all Christendom ought to rejoice, and which it ought to celebrate with great festivals and the offering of solemn thanks to the Holy Trinity with many solemn prayers, both for the great exaltation which may accrue to them in turning so many nations to our holy faith, and also for the temporal benefits which will bring great refreshment and gain, not only to Spain, but to all Christians.

Why and How Atahuallpa Was Defeated

The messengers came back to ask the Governor to send a Christian to Atahuallpa, that he intended to come at once, and that he would come unarmed. The Governor sent a Christian, and presently Atahuallpa moved, leaving the armed men behind him. He took with him about five or six thousand Indians without arms, except that under their shirts they had small darts and slings with stones.

He came in a litter, and before went three or four hundred Indians in liveries, cleaning straws from the road and singing. Then came Atahuallpa in the midst of his chiefs and principal men, the greatest among them being also borne on men's shoulders.... A Dominican Friar, who was with the Governor, came forward to tell him, on the part of the Governor, that he waited for him in his lodgings, and that he was sent to speak with him. The Friar then told Atahuallpa that he was a Priest, and that he was sent there to teach the things of the Faith, if they should desire to be Christians. He showed Atahuallpa a book ... and told him that book contained the things of God. Atahuallpa asked for the book, and threw it on the ground, saying: "I will not leave this place until you have restored all that you have taken in my land. I know well who you are, and what you have come for."...The Friar went to the Governor and reported what was being done, and that no time was to be lost. The Governor sent to me; and I had arranged with the Captain of the artillery that, when a sign was given, he

(continued)

should discharge his pieces, and that, on hearing the reports, all the troops should come forth at once. This was done, and as the Indians were unarmed, they were defeated without danger to any Christian. Those who carried the litter, and the chiefs who surrounded Atahuallpa, were all killed, falling around him. The Governor came out and seized Atahuallpa, and in protecting him, he received a knife cut from a Christian in the hand. The troops continued the pursuit as far as the place where the armed Indians were stationed, who made no resistance whatever, because it was night. All were brought into town, where the Governor was quartered.

Next morning the Governor ordered us to go to the camp of Atahuallpa, where we found forty thousand pesos worth of gold and two or three pounds of silver....The Governor said that he had not come to make war on the Indians, but that our Lord the Emperor, who was Lord of the whole world, had ordered him to come that he might see the land, and let Atahuallpa know the things of our Faith....The Governor also told him that that land, and all other lands, belonged to the Emperor, and that he must acknowledge him as his Lord. He replied that he was content, and, observing that the Christians had collected some gold, Atahuallpa said to the Governor that

they need not take such care of it, as if there was so little; for that he could give them ten thousand plates, and that he could fill the room in which he was up to a white line, which was the height of a man and a half from the floor.

Questions: What were the main bases for initial European judgments about the characteristics of Native American? How might the native peoples have judged the Europeans? What motives does Columbus appeal to in trying to interest Spanish rulers in the new land?

These documents raise obvious problems of interpretation. They interpret interactions with another, very foreign culture from the European standpoint only. They also attribute motives to the adventurers that may or may not have been predominant. Figuring out how to gain useful, valid information from documents of this sort, which are undeniably revealing of key passages in world history, is a major challenge. What parts of the accounts seem most reliable, and what criteria can be used to sort out degrees of accuracy?

peans, many from the British Isles, colonized the Atlantic coastal region, where native populations were quickly reduced by disease and war. The society that developed in the British colonies was far closer to west European forms than was that of Latin America. The colonies operated their own assemblies, which provided the people with political experience. Calvinist and Quaker church assemblies gave governing power to groups of elders or wider congregations. Many colonists thus had reason to share with some west Europeans a sense of the importance of representative institutions and self-government.

Colonists were also avid consumers of political theories written in Europe, such as the parliamentary ideas of John Locke. There was also wide reading and discussion of Enlightenment materials. Institutions such as the 18th-century American Philosophical Society deliberately imitated European scientific institutes, and hundreds of North Americans contributed scientific findings to the British Royal Society. The colonies remained modest in certain cultural attainments. Art was rather primitive, although many stylistic cues came from Europe. There was no question that in formal culture, North American leaders saw themselves as part of a larger Western world.

By the late 18th century, some American merchants were trading with China, their ships picking up medicinal herbs along the Pacific coast and exchanging them for Chinese artifacts and tea. Great Britain tried to impose firmer limits on this modestly thriving local economy after the Seven Years' War. It hoped to win greater tax revenues and to guarantee markets for British goods and traders, but the effort came too late and helped encourage rebellion in key colonies. Unusual among the colonies, North America developed a merchant class and some stake in manufacturing in a pattern similar to that taking shape in western Europe itself.

The spread of Western values in the Atlantic colonies and in British and French settlements in Canada was facilitated by the modest impact of Native Americans in these settled areas (Figure 16.6). The native population of this part of North America had always been less dense than in Central America or the Andes region. Because few Native American groups in these regions practiced settled agriculture, instead combining hunting with slash and burn corn growing, European colonists found it easy to displace them from large stretches of territory. The ravages of European-imported disease reduced the indigenous population greatly. Many forest peoples were pushed

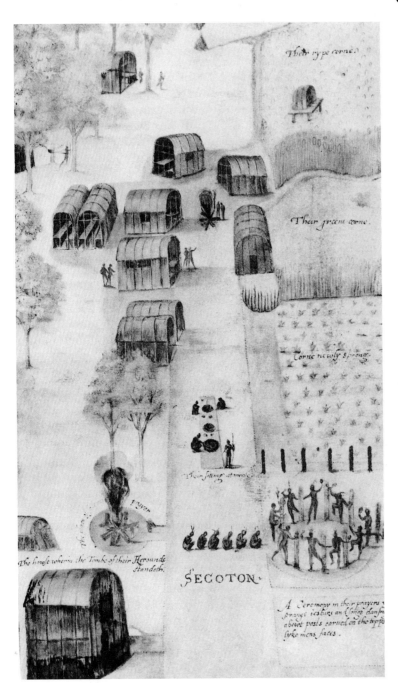

Figure 16.6 *Watercolor by John White (c. 1590) of the Native American settlement of Secoton, Virginia. White was one of the pioneer settlers on Roanoke Island, North Carolina, and was also a pioneer of straightforward observation.*

westward. Some abandoned agriculture, turning to a new horse-based hunting economy on the plains (the horse was brought to Mexico by the Spaniards). Many territorial wars further distracted the Native American groups. The net result of these factors was that although European colonists interacted with Native Americans, learned from them, and feared and mistreated them, the colonists did not combine with them to forge new cultural groups like those emerging in much of Latin America.

By 1700, the importation of African slaves proved to be a more important addition to the

North American experience, particularly in the southern colonies. The practice of slaveholding and interactions with African culture distinguished North American life from its European counterpart. By the 18th century, 23 percent of the population of the English colonies was of African origin.

North America and Western Civilization

On balance, most white settlers intended to transplant key Western habits into their new setting. For example, family patterns were similar. American colonists were able to marry slightly earlier than ordinary western Europeans because of the greater abundance of land, and they had larger families. Still, they reproduced most features of the European-style family, including the primary emphasis on the nuclear unit. The new Americans did have unusual concern for children, if only because they depended so heavily on their work in a labor-scarce environment. European visitors commented on the child-centeredness of American families and the freedom of children to speak up. These variations, though significant, played on trends also becoming visible in Europe, such as the new emphasis on family affection.

Even when key colonies rebelled against European control, as they did in 1776, they moved in the name of Western political ideas and economic goals against the dependency the British tried to impose. They established a government that responded to the new Western political theories, implementing some key ideas for the first time.

Africa and Asia: Coastal Trading Stations

Europeans for the most part contented themselves with small coastal fortresses in Africa, negotiating with African kings and merchants but not trying to claim large territories on their own. Generally, Europeans were deterred by climate, disease, and nonnavigable rivers from trying to reach into the interior. There were two important exceptions. From initial coastal settlements, Portugal sent expeditions into Angola in search of slaves. These expeditions had a more direct and more disruptive impact in this part of southwestern Africa than elsewhere along the Atlantic coast. More important still was the **Cape Colony** planted by the Dutch on the Cape of Good Hope in 1652. The intent was to form another coastal station to supply Dutch ships bound for Asia. But some Dutch farmers were sent, and these **Boers** (the Dutch word for farmers) began to fan out on large farms in a region still lightly populated by Africans. They clashed with local hunting groups, enslaving some of them. Only after 1770 did the expanding Boer settlements directly conflict with Bantu farmers, opening a long battle for control of southern Africa that raged until the late 20th century in the nation of South Africa.

European colonies in Asia were also exceptional. Spain set up an administration for the Philippines and sent active Catholic missionaries. The Dutch East India company administered portions of the main islands of present-day Indonesia and also (for a time) Taiwan, off the China coast.

Colonization in Asia entered a new phase as the British and French began to struggle for control of India, beginning in the late 17th century when the Mughal Empire weakened. Even before the Mughals faltered after the death in 1707 of their last great emperor, Aurangzeb, French and British forts dotted the east and west coasts, along with Portuguese Goa. As Mughal inefficiency increased, with a resultant surge of regional states ruled by Indians, portions of the subcontinent became an arena for the growing international rivalry between Britain and France.

The British East India Company had two advantages in this competition. Through negotiation with local princes, it had gained a station at **Calcutta,** which gave it some access to the great wealth of the Ganges valley. Furthermore, the company had enormous influence over the British government and, through Britain's superior navy, excellent communication on the ocean routes. Its French rivals, in contrast, had less political clout at home, where the government often was distracted by European land wars. The French also were more interested in missionary work than the British, for Protestants became deeply committed to colonial missions only in the 19th century. Before then, the British were content to leave Hindu customs alone and devote themselves to commercial profits.

French–British rivalry raged bitterly through the mid-18th century. Both sides recruited Indian princes and troops as allies. Outright warfare erupted in 1744 and then again during the Seven Years' War. In 1756, an Indian ruler in Bengal attacked and captured the British base at Calcutta. In the aftermath of the battle, English prisoners were placed in their own jail, where humidity and overcrowding led to perhaps as many as 120 deaths before Indian officials became aware of their plight and released them. The English used this incident, which they dubbed the "black hole" of Calcutta, to rally their forces. The East India Company's army recaptured Calcutta and then seized additional Indian and French territory, aided by abundant bribes to many regional princes. French power in India was destroyed, and the East India Company took over administration of the Bengal region, which stretched inland from Calcutta. Soon after this, the British also gained the island of Ceylon (Sri Lanka) from the Dutch.

The full history of British India did not begin until late in the 18th century, when the British government took a more active hand in Indian administration, supplementing the unofficial government of the East India Company (Figure 16.7). Indeed, British control of the subcontinent was incomplete. The Mughal Empire remained, although it was increasingly weak and it controlled scant territory, as did other regional kingdoms, including the Sikh state. Britain gained some new territories by force but was also content to form alliances with local princes without disturbing their internal administration.

In most colonies, European administration long remained fairly loose. Few settlers arrived, except in South Africa and the Americas. Outside the Americas, cultural impositions were slight. Missionary activity won many converts in the Philippines but not elsewhere in Asia or in Africa at this point. The main impact of colonies supplemented the more general development of the world economy: Colonial administrations pressed for economic advantage for the home country by opening markets and prompting commercial production of cheap foods and raw materials. Here, of course, the consequences to colonial peoples were very real.

Figure 16.7 *This Indian portrait of two women in European dress illustrates the English influence in 18th-century India.*

Impact on Western Europe

Western Europe was hugely affected by its own colonial success, not only economically but also diplomatically. Colonial rivalries and wars added to the existing hostilities between key nation-states. England and Holland early turned against Spanish success, with great effect. The Dutch and the English competed, engaging in many skirmishes in the 17th century. Then attention turned to the growing competition between the British and the French. This contest had extensive geographic scope: The Seven Years' War (1756–1763), fought in Europe, India, and North America, has been called the first world war.

There were also lesser effects on European society. For example, from the mid-17th century onward, the use of colonially produced sugar spread widely. Previously, sugar had been a costly, upper-class item. Now for the first time, except for salt, a basic product available to ordinary people was being traded over long distances. The spread of sugar had cultural as well as social and economic significance in giving ordinary Europeans the ability to obtain pleasurable sensations in quick doses—an interesting foreshadowing of later features of Western consumer behavior. It also promoted a growing role for dentists by the 18th century.

More broadly, the profits Europeans brought in from world trade, including the African slave trade, added wealth and capital. Many Europeans turned to manufacturing operations, as owners and workers, partly because of opportunities for export in world trade. These developments enhanced Europe's commercial character, while reducing dependence on agriculture alone. They provided additional tax revenues for growing governments and their military ambitions.

The Impact of a New World Order

The development of the world economy and European colonialism had immense impact. The imposition of unfree labor systems, to supply goods for world trade, was increasingly widespread. Slavery and serfdom deeply affected Latin America and eastern Europe, while the slave trade disrupted west Africa, and millions of individual lives as well.

Yet the world economy brought benefits as well as hardships, quite apart from the profits to Europe. New foods and wider trade patterns helped some societies deal with scarcity. Individual merchants and landowners gained new wealth virtually everywhere. China prospered from the imports of silver, though rapid population growth checked gains overall. The mixture of profits and compulsion brought more and more people and regions into the world economy network.

GLOBAL CONNECTIONS: The World Economy—And the World

Buoyed by its growing role in the world, western Europe unquestionably saw its economy and military power increase more rapidly than those of any other society during the early modern period. As the next chapter shows, Europe changed internally as well, often in dramatic ways. Because of these facts, it is tempting to see the early modern centuries as a European drama in which other regions either played supporting roles or watched in awe.

Yet the relationships to the world economy were in fact quite complex. They ranged from conscious isolation to controlled participation to undeniable dependency. Many societies retained vibrant political systems and internal economies. Some, although attracted to certain Western features, wanted to stand apart from the values and institutions that world economic success seemed to involve.

Even societies that had changes thrust upon them, like Latin America, were hardly passive. Pressed by missionaries, Latin Americans did not simply adopt European-style Christianity, but rather blended in traditional beliefs and practices and many distinctive artistic forms. The world was growing closer, but it was not necessarily becoming simpler.

Further Readings

Excellent discussions of Western exploration and expansion are Carlo Cipolla's *Guns, Sails and Empires: Technological Innovation and the Early Phases of European Expansion 1400–1700* (1997); J. H. Parry's *The Age of Reconnaissance* (1982); Richard S. Dunn's *Sugar and Slaves: The Rise of the Planter Class in the English West Indies, 1624–1713* (1972); and D. Boorstin's *The Discoverers* (1991). Recent works include Alan K. Smith's *Creating a World Economy: Merchant Capital, Colonialism and World Trade 1460–1825* (1991) and James Tracy, ed., *The Rise of Merchant Empires* (1986) and *The Political Economy of Merchant Empires* (1991). Somewhat more specific facets are treated in D. K. Fieldhouse's *The Colonial Empires* (1971); J. H. Parry's *The Discovery of South America* (1979); and S. Subrahmanyam's *The Portuguese Empire in Asia, 1500–1700* (1993). A vital treatment of the international results of new trading patterns of foods and disease is Alfred Crosby's *The Columbian Exchange: Biological and Cultural Consequences of 1492* (1972); see also Elinor G. Melville's *A Plague of Sheep: Environmental Consequences of the Conquest of Mexico* (1994). For a stimulating reemphasis on Asia, see Andre Geuder Frank's *ReOrient: Global Economy in the Asian Age* (1998).

On slavery and its trade, see Eric Williams' *Capitalism and Slavery* (1964); Orlando Patterson's *Slavery and Social Death: A Comparative Study* (1982); and D. B. Davis' *Slavery and Human Progress* (1984); the last two are important comparative and analytical statements in a major field of recent historical study. See also Philip D. Curtin's *Atlantic Slave Trade* (1972) and his edited volume, *Africa Remembered: Narratives by West Africans from the Era of the Slave Trade* (1967). A good recent survey of developments in Africa and in the period is Paul Bohannan and Philip Curtin's *Africa and Africans* (3rd ed., 1988).

New world trading patterns, including Asia's role in them, are discussed in K. N. N. Shanduri, *Trade and Civilization in the Indian Ocean* (1985); Stephan Frederic Dale, *Indian Merchants and Eurasia Trade: 1600–1750* (1994); and Philip Curtin, *Cross-Cultural Trade in World History* (1984). A controversial theoretical statement about new trade relationships and their impact on politics and social structure is Immanuel Wallerstein's *The Modern World System: Capitalist Agriculture and the Origins of the European World Economy in the Sixteenth Century* (1974) and *The Modern World System: Mercantilism and the Consolidation of the European World Economy 1600–1750* (1980); see also his *Politics of the World Economy: The States, the Movements and the Civilizations* (1984).

For discussions on where colonial North America fits in this period of world history, see Jack Greene and J. R. Pole, eds., *Colonial British America: Essays on the New History of the Early Modern Era* (1984); William J. Eccles, *France in America* (rev. ed., 1990); and Gary Nash, *Red, White and Black: The Peoples of Early America* (rev. ed., 1982).

On the Web

Biographies of leaders of the European age of discovery, from Henry the Navigator to Vasco De Gama, are offered at http://www.win.tue.nl/cs/fm/engels/discovery/. This site also traces the lives of the world's great explorers of every region and era.

Links to the most valuable sites examining the contact between conquistadors and Indians in North America and its aftermath can be found at http://www.nhc.rtp.nc. us:8080/tserve/nattrans/ntecoindian/ecolinksce.htm/. Though seemingly a lesson plan, http://www.yale.edu/ynhti/curriculum/units/1992/2/92.02.01.x.html#a offers excellent overviews of Euro-American contacts and a superb bibliography.

A virtual version of an exhibit mounted by the Library of Congress and other materials that look at the multicultural dimensions of the events of 1492, the life of Christopher Columbus, and the Colombian exchange his voyages initiated can be found at http://www.loc.gov/exhibits/1492/. Other such exhibits and analyses of his career can be found at http://www.ibiblio.org/expo/1492.exhibit/c-Columbus/columbus.html and http://xroads.virginia.edu/~CAP/COLUMBUS/col3.html.

Most discussions on the nature of that exchange rightly focus on the material outcomes of the Atlantic slave trade, such as the development of plantation economies and the exchange of crops, animals, and diseases. However, one site, http://daphne.palomar.edu/scrout/colexc.htm, also examines what it admits to be the controversial notion that the indigenous peoples of the Americas may have contributed toward the evolution of important modern ideas, including Western conceptions of liberty, ecology, and even corporate structure. At the very least, such speculation reminds us that the relationship between the indigenous people of the Americas and their European conquerors was complex.

The relationship between conquistador Hernando Cortez and Donna Maria/La Malinche, his female Nahuatl-speaking translator, certainly was as complicated as Cortez's relations with his Aztec-hating Mesoamerica allies. Both relationships are discussed at http://thedagger.com/conquest.html. Another site, http://www.fordham.edu/halsall/mod/aztecs1.html, offers a text of the discussions between Cortez and Montezuma, that Malinche facilitated as a translator, that foreshadowed the end of the Aztec empire. Malinche's role in the Columbian exchange is examined at http://www.mexconnect.com/mex_/history/malinche.html and http://thedagger.com/archive/conquest/malinche.html.

Francisco Pizarro's encounter with Inca leaders and the imposition of Spanish rule over their empire is presented at http://www.ucalgary.ca/applied_history/tutor/eurvoya/inca.html.

The controversy over the demographic catastrophe that accompanied the conquest of Mexico is analyzed from the perspective of contemporary Spanish and Nahuatl records at http://www.hist.umn.edu/~rmccaa/vircatas/vir6.htm (or scroll down to this subject in 1998 files at http://www.hist.umn.edu/~rmccaa/).

Dutch and British traders soon outstripped their Iberian competitors in the new global economy, a process described at http://www.theeastindiacompany.com/, http://65.107.211.206/post/india/hohenthal/3.1.html, and http://www.fordham.edu/halsall/mod/modsbook03.html. The latter site also contains the chief primary documentation for the early modern world system and includes a summary of Immanuel Wallerstein's World System Theory (http://www.fordham.edu/halsall/mod/wallerstein.html). The pattern of the then emerging new world order can be glimpsed through a visit to the Dutch factory at Batavia at http://batavia.rug.ac.be/index.html.

CHAPTER 17

THE TRANSFORMATION OF THE WEST, 1450–1750

Anatomy as science and as art: The anatomical sketches and notes by Leonardo da Vinci demonstrate his study of the human form. In keeping with the scientific spirit of the age, artists of the late Renaissance sometimes turned to science in order to portray the human body as realistically as possible.

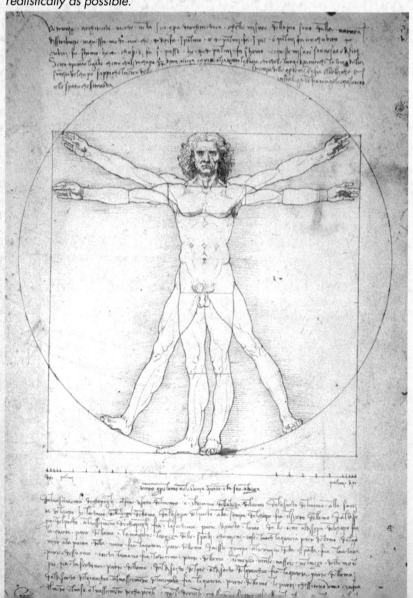

- The First Big Changes: Culture and Commerce
- Science and Politics: The Next Phase of Change
- VISUALIZING THE PAST: Versailles
- IN DEPTH: Elites and Masses
- The West by 1750
- DOCUMENT: Controversies About Women
- GLOBAL CONNECTIONS: Europe and the World

During the three centuries after 1450, Western civilization changed in dramatic ways. Still a largely agricultural society in 1750, the West had become unusually commercially active and had laid out a growing manufacturing sector. Government powers had expanded, and new political ideas complicated the picture. Beliefs had changed. Science came to form the center of Western intellectual life for the first time in the history of any society. Popular beliefs, including ideas about family and nature, also had shifted. In some respects, the West in this period was following a path that other civilizations had already laid out, such as increased bureaucratization in government. But in other areas, such as popular belief and family structure, the West was striking out in new directions.

Changes within western Europe resulted in part from overseas expansion and growing dominance in international trade. In turn, Europe's evolution furthered this international role.

Europe's internal changes unfolded amid much internal conflict. A host of terms, such as *Renaissance* and *Enlightenment*, describe key phases of change. Although there was no master plan, there were focal points: Europe's transformation centered on commerce, the state, and culture, with some support from technology. Between 1450 and 1650, a series of cultural shifts held center stage along with the rise in trade. Thereafter, the scientific revolution and the advent of new political forms introduced additional changes, which were amplified in the 18th-century Enlightenment.

A New Spirit

The Italian writer Francesco Petrarch (1304–1374) once climbed a mountain, Ventoux, in southern France. He wrote of his ascent, proud of his own skill and using the climb as a symbol of what he could achieve. There was a new spirit in this work, intended to be published, compared to the more religious Middle Ages. But Petrarch did not abandon religion, and in later life he talked about how he had given up poetry in favor of reading Christian texts, finding "hidden sweetness which I had once esteemed but lightly."

1300 c.e.	1450 c.e.	1500 c.e.	1550 c.e.	1650 c.e.	1750 c.e.
1300–1450 Italian Renaissance	**1450–1519** Leonardo da Vinci	**1500–1600** "Commercial revolution"	**1550–1649** Religious wars in France, Germany, and Britain	**1670–1692** Decline of witchcraft trials	**1756–1763** Seven Years' War; France, Britain, Prussia, and Austria
	1450–1600 Northern Renaissance	**1515–1547** Francis I of France	**1555–1603** Elizabeth I, England	**1682–1699** Hapsburgs drive Turks from Hungary	**1776** Adam Smith's *Wealth of Nations*
	1455 First European printing press in Mainz, Germany	**1517** Luther's 95 theses; beginning of Protestant Reformation	**1564–1642** Galileo	**1688–1690** Glorious Revolution in Britain; parliamentary monarchy; some religious toleration; political writing of John Locke	**1780–1790** Joseph II, Austria and Hungary
	1469–1527 Machiavelli	**1534** Beginning of Church of England	**1588** Defeat of Spanish Armada by English		**1792** Mary Wollstonecraft's *Vindication of the Rights of Women*
	1475–1514 Michelangelo	**1541–1564** Calvin in Geneva	**17th century** Scientific Revolution		
	1490s France and Spain invade Italian city-states; beginning of Italian decline	**1543** "Copernican revolution"; Copernicus' work on astronomy	**1609** Independence of Netherlands	**18th century** Enlightenment	
			1618–1648 Thirty Years' War	**1712–1786** Frederick the Great of Prussia; enlightened despotism	
			1642–1649 English civil wars	**1730–1850** European population boom	
			1642–1727 Isaac Newton	**1733** James Kay invents flying shuttle loom	
			1643–1715 Louis XIV in France; absolute monarchy	**1736** Beginnings of Methodism	
			1647–1648 Culmination of popular rebellion		

The First Big Changes: Culture and Commerce

 During the 15th century the Renaissance emphasized new styles and beliefs. This was followed by even more sweeping cultural and political change in the 16th century, with the Protestant Reformation and the Catholic response to it. A new commercial and social structure grew up as well, creating new opportunities and intense new grievances.

The Italian Renaissance

The move away from earlier patterns began with the Renaissance, which first developed in Italy during the 14th and 15th centuries. Largely an artistic movement, the Renaissance challenged medieval intellectual values and styles. It also sketched a new, brasher spirit that may have encouraged a new Western interest in exploring strange waters or urging that old truths be reexamined.

Italy was already well launched in the development of Renaissance culture by the 15th century, based on its unusually extensive urban, commercial economy and its competitive city-state politics. Writers such as Petrarch and Boccaccio had promoted classical literary canons against medieval logic and theology, writing in Italian as well as the traditional Latin and emphasizing secular subjects such as love and pride. Painting turned to new realism and classical and human-centered themes. Religion declined as a central focus. The Italian Renaissance blossomed further in the 15th and early 16th centuries. This was a great age of Western art, as Leonardo da Vinci advanced the realistic portrayal of the human body and Michelangelo applied classical styles in painting and sculpture. In political theory, **Niccolo Machiavelli** emphasized realistic discussions of how to seize and maintain power. Like the artists, Machiavelli bolstered his realism with Greek and Roman examples.

Overall, Italian Renaissance culture stressed themes of **humanism:** a focus on humankind as the center of intellectual and artistic endeavor. Religion was not attacked, but its principles were no longer predominant. Historians have debated the reasons for this change. Italy's more urban, commercial environment was one factor, but so was the new imitation of classical Greek and Roman literature and art.

These Renaissance themes had some bearing on politics and commerce. Renaissance merchants improved their banking techniques and became more openly profit-seeking than their medieval counterparts had been. City-state leaders experimented with new political forms and functions. They justified their rule not on the basis of heredity or divine guidance but more on the basis of what they could do to advance general well-being and their city's glory. Thus, they sponsored cultural activities and tried to improve the administration of the economy. They also developed more professional armies, for wars among the city-states were common, and gave new attention to military tactics and training. They also rethought the practice of diplomacy, introducing the regular exchange of ambassadors for the first time in the West. Clearly, the Renaissance encouraged innovation, although it also produced some dependence on classical models.

The Renaissance Moves Northward

Italy began to decline as a Renaissance center by Isaac about 1500. French and Spanish monarchs invaded the peninsula, reducing political independence. At the same time, new Atlantic trade routes reduced the importance of Mediterranean ports, a huge blow to the Italian economy.

As Renaissance creativity faded in its Italian birthplace, it passed northward. The **Northern Renaissance**—focused in France, the Low Countries, Germany, and England—began after 1450. Renaissance styles also affected Hungary and Poland in east central Europe. Classical styles in art and architecture became the rage. Knowledge of Greek and Latin literature gained ground, although many northern humanists wrote in their own languages (English, French, and so on). Northern humanists were more religious than their Italian counterparts, trying to blend secular interests with continued Christian devotion. Renaissance writers such as Shakespeare in England and Rabelais in France also mixed classical themes with an earthiness—a joy in bodily functions and human passions—that maintained elements of medieval popular culture. Renaissance literature established a new set of classics for literary traditions in the major Western languages, such as the writings of Shakespeare in England and Cervantes in Spain.

The Northern Renaissance produced some political change, providing another move toward greater state powers. As their revenues and operations expanded, Renaissance kings increased their pomp and ceremony. Kings such as **Francis I** in France became patrons of the arts, importing Italian sculp-

tors and architects to create their classical-style palaces. By the late 16th century, many monarchs were sponsoring trading companies and colonial enterprises. Interest in military conquest was greater than in the Middle Ages. Francis I was even willing to ally with the Ottoman sultan, the key Muslim leader. His goal was to distract his main enemy, the Habsburg ruler of Austria and Spain. In fact, it was an alliance in name only, but it illustrated how power politics was beginning to abandon the feudal or religious justifications that had previously clothed it in the West.

Yet the impact of the Renaissance should not be overstated, particularly outside Italy. Renaissance kings were still confined by the political powers of feudal landlords. Ordinary people were little touched by Renaissance values; the life of most peasants and artisans went on much as before. Economic life also changed little, particularly outside the Italian commercial centers. Even in the upper classes, women sometimes encountered new limits as Renaissance leaders touted men's public bravado over women's domestic roles.

Changes in Technology and Family

More fundamental changes were brewing in Western society by 1500, beneath the glittering surface of the Renaissance. Spurred by trading contacts with Asia, workers in the West improved the quality of pulleys and pumps in mines and learned how to forge stronger iron products. Printing was introduced in the 15th century when the German **Johannes Gutenberg** introduced movable type, building on Chinese printing technology. Soon books were distributed in greater quantities in the West, which helped expand the audience for Renaissance writers and disseminated religious ideas. Literacy began to gain ground and became a fertile source of new kinds of thinking.

Family structure was also changing. A **European-style family** pattern came into being by the 15th century. This pattern involved a late marriage age and a primary emphasis on nuclear families of parents and children rather than the extended families characteristic of most agricultural civilizations. The goal was to limit family birth rates. By the 16th century, ordinary people usually did not marry until their late 20s—a marked contrast to most agricultural societies. These changes emphasized the importance of husband–wife relations. They also closely linked the family to individual property holdings, for most people could not marry until they had access to property.

The Protestant and Catholic Reformations

In the 16th century, religious upheaval and a new commercial surge began to define the directions of change more fully. In 1517, a German monk named **Martin Luther** nailed a document containing 95 *theses*, or propositions, to the door of the castle church in Wittenberg. He was protesting claims made by a papal representative in selling *indulgences*, or grants of salvation, for money, but in fact his protest went deeper. Luther's reading of the Bible convinced him that only faith could gain salvation. Church sacraments were not the path, for God could not be manipulated. Luther's protest, which was rebuffed by the papacy, soon led him to challenge many Catholic beliefs, including the authority of the pope himself. Luther would soon argue that monasticism was wrong, that priests should marry (as he did), and that the Bible should be translated from Latin so ordinary people could have direct access to its teachings. Luther did not want to break Christian unity, but the church he wanted should be on his terms (or, as he would have argued, the terms of the true faith).

Luther picked up wide support for his views during the mid-16th century and beyond. Many Germans, in a somewhat nationalist reaction, resented the authority and taxes of the Roman pope. German princes saw an opportunity to gain more power because their nominal leader, the Holy Roman emperor, remained Catholic. Princes who turned Protestant could increase their independence and seize church lands. The Lutheran version of **Protestantism** (as the general wave of religious dissent was called) urged state control of the church as an alternative to papal authority, and this had obvious political appeal.

There were reasons for ordinary people to shift their allegiance as well. Some German peasants saw Luther's attack on authority as a sanction for their own social rebellion against landlords, although Luther specifically renounced this reading. Some townspeople were drawn to Luther's approval of work in the world. Because faith alone gained salva-

tion, Lutheranism could sanction moneymaking and other earthly pursuits more wholeheartedly than did traditional Catholicism. Unlike Catholicism, Lutherans did not see special vocations as particularly holy; monasteries were abolished, along with some of the Christian bias against moneymaking.

Once Christian unity was breached, other Protestant groups sprang forward. In England, Henry VIII began to set up an **Anglican church,** initially to challenge papal attempts to enforce his first marriage, which had failed to produce a male heir. (Henry ultimately had six wives in sequence, executing two of them, a particularly graphic example of the treatment of women in power politics.) Henry was also attracted to some of the new doctrines, and his most durable successor, his daughter Elizabeth I, was Protestant outright. Still more important were the churches inspired by **Jean Calvin,** a Frenchman who established his base in the Swiss city of Geneva. Calvinism insisted on God's *predestination*, or prior determination, of those who would be saved. Calvinist ministers became moral guardians and preachers of God's word. Calvinists sought the participation of all believers in local church administration, which promoted the idea of a wider access to government. They also promoted broader popular education so that more people could read the Bible. Calvinism was accepted not only in part of Switzerland but also in portions of Germany, in France (where it produced strong minority groups), in the Netherlands, in Hungary, and in England and Scotland. By the early 17th century, Puritan exiles brought it to North America.

The Catholic church did not sit still under Protestant attack. It did not restore religious unity, but it defended southern Europe, Austria, Poland, much of Hungary, and key parts of Germany for the Catholic faith. Under a **Catholic Reformation,** a major church council revived Catholic doctrine and refuted key Protestant tenets such as the idea that priests had no special sacramental power and could marry. They also attacked popular superstitions and remnants of magical belief, which meant that Catholics and Protestants alike were trying to find new ways to shape the outlook of ordinary folk. A new religious order, the **Jesuits,** became active in politics, education, and missionary work, regaining some parts of Europe for the church. Jesuit fervor also sponsored Catholic missionary activity in Asia and the Americas.

The End of Christian Unity in the West

The Protestant and Catholic Reformations had several results in Europe during the late 16th and early 17th centuries. Most obvious was an important series of religious wars. France was a scene of bitter battles between Calvinist and Catholic forces. These disputes ended only with the granting of tolerance to Protestants through the **edict of Nantes** in 1598, although in the next century French kings progressively cut back on Protestant rights. In Germany, the **Thirty Years' War** broke out in 1618, pitting German Protestants and allies such as Lutheran Sweden against the Holy Roman emperor, backed by Spain. The war was so devastating that it reduced German power and prosperity for a full century, cutting population by as much as 60 percent in some regions (Figure 17.1). It was ended only by the 1648 **Treaty of Westphalia,** which agreed to the territorial toler-

ance concept: Some princely states and cities chose one religion, some another. This treaty also finally settled a rebellion of the Protestant Netherlands against Spain, giving the former its full independence.

Religious fighting punctuated British history, first before the reign of Elizabeth in the 16th century, then in the **English Civil War** in the 1640s. Here too, religious issues combined with other problems, particularly in a battle between the claims of parliament to rights of control over royal actions and some rather tactless assertions of authority by a new line of English kings. The civil war ended in 1660 (well after King Charles I had been beheaded; Figure 17.2), but full resolution came only in 1688–1689, when limited religious toleration was granted to most Protestant (but not Catholic) faiths.

Religious issues thus dominated European politics for almost a century. The religious wars led to a grudging and limited acceptance of the idea of religious pluralism: Christian unity could not be restored, although in most individual countries the idea of full religious liberty was still in the future. The religious wars persuaded some people that religion itself was suspect; if there was no dominant single truth, why all the cruelty and carnage? Finally, the wars affected the political balance of Europe, as Map 17.1 shows. After a period of weakness during its internal strife, France was on the upswing. The Netherlands and Britain were galvanized toward a growing international role. Spain, briefly ascendant, fell back. Internally, some kings and princes benefited from the decline of papal authority by taking a stronger role in religious affairs. This was true in many Catholic and Protestant domains. In some cases, however, Protestant dissent encouraged popular political movements and enhanced parliamentary power.

The impact of religious change went well beyond politics. Popular beliefs changed most in Protestant areas, but Catholic reform produced new impulses as well. Western people gradually became less likely to see an intimate connection between God and nature. Protestants resisted the idea of miracles or other interventions in nature's course. Religious change also promoted greater concentration on family life. Religious writers encouraged love between husband and wife. As one English Protestant put it, "When love is absent between husband and wife, it is like a bone out of joint: there is no ease, no order." This promotion of the family had ambiguous implications

Figure 17.1 *Hans Holbein's* The Dance of Death *illustrated social upheaval encouraged by the continuing plague as well as religious conflict.*

Figure 17.2   *Civil war resulted in the execution of Charles I in London, England, in 1649.*

for women. Protestantism, abolishing religious convents, made marriage more necessary for women than before; there were fewer alternatives for women who could not marry. Fathers were also responsible for the religious training of the children. On the other hand, women's emotional role in the family improved with the new emphasis on affection.

Religious change accompanied and promoted growing literacy along with the spread of the printing press. In the town of Durham, England, around 1570, only 20 percent of all people were literate, but by 1630 the figure had climbed to 47 percent. Growing literacy opened people to additional new ideas and ways of thinking.

The Commercial Revolution

Along with religious upheaval during the 16th century, the economic structure of the West was fundamentally redefined. The level of European trade rose sharply, and many Europeans had new goods available to them. Involvement with markets and merchants increased. Here was the clearest impact of the new world economy in western Europe.

A basic spur to greater commercialization was the price inflation that occurred throughout western Europe during the 16th century. The massive import of gold and silver from Spain's new colonies in Latin America forced prices up. The availability of more money, based on silver supply, generated this price rise. New wealth heightened demand for products to sell, both in the colonies and in Europe, but Western production could not keep pace, hence the price inflation. Inflation encouraged merchants to take new risks, for borrowing was cheap when money was losing value. A sum borrowed one year would be worth less, in real terms, five years later, so it made sense to take loans for new investments.

Inflation and the new colonial opportunities led to the formation of the great trading companies, often with government backing, in Spain, England, the Netherlands, and France. Governments granted regional monopolies to these giant concerns; thus, the Dutch East Indies Company long dominated trade with the islands of Indonesia. European merchants brought new profits back to Europe and developed new managerial skills and banking arrangements.

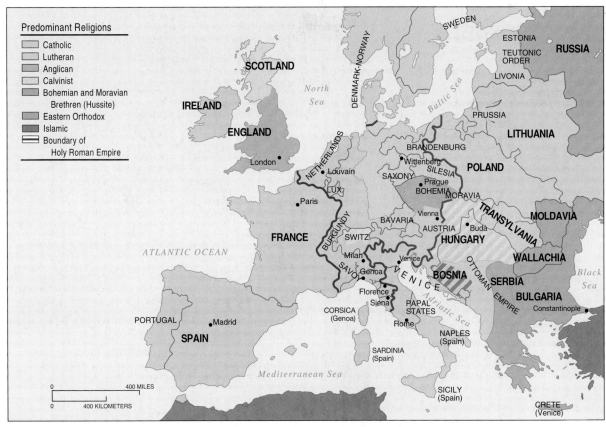

Map 17.1   *Western Europe During the Renaissance and Reformation. Different Protestant denominations made inroads in much of northwestern Europe with the Reformation, but Catholicism maintained its hold on significant portions of the continent.*

Colonial markets stimulated manufacturing. Most peasants continued to produce mainly for their own needs, but agricultural specialty areas developed in the production of wines, cheeses, wool, and the like. Some of these industries favored commercial farming and the use of paid laborers on the land. Shoemaking, pottery, metalworking, and other manufacturing specializations arose in both rural villages and the cities. Technical improvements followed in many branches of manufacture, particularly in metals and mining.

Prosperity increased for many ordinary people as well as for the great merchants. One historian has estimated that by about 1600 the average Western peasant or artisan owned five times as many "things" as his or her counterpart in southeastern Europe. A 16th-century Englishman noted that whereas in the past a peasant and his family slept on the floor and had only a pan or two as kitchenware, by the final decades of the century a farmer might have "a fair garnish of pewter in his cupboard, three or four feather beds, so many coverlets and carpets of tapestry, a silver salt, a bowl for wine ... and a dozen spoons." It was about this time that French peasants began to enjoy wine fairly regularly rather than simply at special occasions—the result of higher productivity and better trade and transport facilities.

Social Protest

There were victims of change as well, however. Growing commercialization created the beginnings of a new **proletariat** in the West—people without access to wealth-producing property. Population growth and rising food prices hit hard at the poor, and many people had to sell their small plots of land. Some proletarians became manufacturing workers, depending on orders from merchant capitalists to keep their tools busy in their cottages. Others became paid laborers on agricultural estates, where landlords were eager for a more manipulable workforce to take advantage of business opportunities in the cities. Others pressed into the cities, and a growing problem of beggars and wandering poor began to affect Western society. By blaming the poor for moral failings, a new, tough attitude toward poverty took shape that has lasted to some extent to the present day.

Not surprisingly, the shifts in popular economic and cultural traditions provoked important outcries. A huge wave of popular protest in western Europe developed at the end of the 16th century and extended until about 1650. Peasants and townspeople alike rose for greater protection from poverty and loss of property. The uprisings did not deflect the basic currents of change, but they revealed the massive insecurity of many workers.

The popular rebellions of the 17th century revealed social tension and new ideas of equality. Peasant songs voiced such sentiments as this: "The whole country must be overturned, for we peasants are now to be the lords, it is we who will sit in the shade." Uprisings in 1648 produced demands for a popular political voice; an English group called the Levelers gained 100,000 signatures on a petition for political rights. Elsewhere, common people praised the kings while attacking their "bad advisors" and high taxes. One English agitator said that "we should cut off all the gentlemen's heads....We shall have a merrier world shortly." In France, Protestant and Catholic peasants rose together against landlords and taxes: "They seek only the ruin of the poor people for our ruin is their wealth."

An unprecedented outburst against suspected witches arose in the same decades in various parts of western Europe and also in New England. Although attacks on witches had developed before, the new scale reflected intense social and cultural upheaval. Between 60,000 and 100,000 suspected witches were accused and killed. The **witchcraft persecution** reflected new resentments against the poor, who were often accused of witchcraft by communities unwilling to accept responsibility for their poverty. The hysteria also revealed new tensions about family life and the role of women, who were the most common targets of persecution. A few of the accused witches actually believed they had magical powers, but far more were accused by fearful or self-serving neighbors. The whole witchcraft experience revealed a society faced with forces of unusual complexity.

Science and Politics: The Next Phase of Change

 As the impact of the Reformation and commercialization continued, new scientific discoveries and political forms took shape from 1600 onward. These two forces shaped a new round of change that continued into the 18th century.

The revolution in science, culminating in the 17th century, set the seal on the cultural reorientation of the West. Although the **Scientific Revolution** most obviously affected formal intellectual life, it also promoted changes in popular outlook.

At the same time, after the political upheavals of the Reformation, a more decisive set of new government forms arose in the West, centering on the emergence of the nation-state. The functions of the state expanded. The Western nation-state was not a single form, because key variants such as absolute monarchies and parliamentary regimes emerged, but there were some common patterns beneath the surface.

Did Copernicus Copy?

This is a chapter about big changes in western Europe during the early modern period. Big changes are always complex. One key development was the rise of science in intellectual life. A key first step here was the discovery by the Polish monk **Copernicus,** in the 16th century, that the planets moved around the sun rather than the earth, as the Greeks had thought. This discovery set other scientific advances in motion, and more generally showed that new thinking could improve on tradition. Copernicus is usually taken as a quiet hero of Western science and rationalism.

Copernicus based his findings on mathematics, understanding that the Greek view of earth as central raised key problems in calculating planetary motion. Historians have recently uncovered similar geometrical findings by two Arabs, al-Urdi and al-Tusi, from the 13th and 14th centuries. Did Copernicus copy, as Westerners had previously done from the Arabs, while keeping quiet because learning from Muslims was now unpopular? Or did he discover independently? It's also worth noting that scientists in other traditions, such as Chinese, Indian, and Mayan, had already realized the central position of the sun. Change, again, is complicated.

What is certain is that based on discoveries like that of Copernicus, science began to take on more importance in Western intellectual life than had ever been the case in the intellectual history of other societies, including classical Greece. Change may be complicated but it does occur.

Science: The New Authority

During the 16th century, scientific research quietly built on the traditions of the later Middle Ages. After Copernicus, Johannes Kepler (1571–1630; Figure 17.3) was another important early figure in the study of planetary motion. Unusual for a major researcher, Kepler was from a poor family; his father abandoned the family outright, and his mother, once tried for

Figure 17.3 *Johannes Kepler*

witchcraft, was unpleasant. But Kepler made his way to university on scholarship, aiming for the Lutheran ministry but drawn to astronomy and mathematics. Using the work of Copernicus and his own observations, he resolved basic issues of planetary motion. He also worked on optics and, with the mixed interests so common in real intellectual life, also practiced astrology, casting horoscopes for wealthy patrons. Also around 1600, anatomical work by the Belgian Vesalius gained greater precision. These key discoveries not only advanced knowledge but also implied a new power for scientific research in its ability to test and often overrule accepted ideas.

A series of empirical advances and wider theoretical generalizations extended the possibilities of science from the 1600s onward. New instruments such as the microscope and improved telescopes allowed gains in biology and astronomy. The Italian **Galileo** publicized Copernicus' discoveries while adding his own basic findings about the laws of gravity and planetary motion. Condemned by the Catholic church for his innovations, Galileo proved the inadequacy of traditional ideas about the universe. He also showed the new pride in scientific achievement, writing modestly how he, "by marvelous discoveries and clear demonstrations, had enlarged a thousand times" the knowledge produced by "the wise men of bygone ages." Chemical research advanced understanding of the behavior of gasses. English physician **William Harvey** demonstrated the circular movement of the blood in animals, with the heart as the "central pumping station."

These advances in knowledge were accompanied by important statements about science and its impact. Francis Bacon urged the value of careful empirical research and predicted that scientific knowledge could advance steadily, producing improvements in technology as well. **René Descartes** established the importance of a skeptical review of all received wisdom, arguing that human reason could develop laws that would explain the fundamental workings of nature.

The capstone to the 17th-century scientific revolution came in 1687, when **Isaac Newton** published his *Principia Mathematica*. This work drew the various astronomical and physical observations and wider theories together in a neat framework of natural laws. Newton set forth the basic principles of all motion (for example, that a body in motion maintains uniform momentum unless affected by outside forces such as friction). Newton defined the forces of gravity in great mathematical detail and showed that the whole universe responded to these forces, which among other things explained the planetary orbits described by Kepler. Finally, Newton stated the basic scientific method in terms of a mixture of rational hypothesis and generalization and careful empirical observation and experiment. Here was a vision of a natural universe that could be captured in simple laws (although increasingly complex mathematics accompanied the findings). Here was a vision of a method of knowing that might do away with blind reliance on tradition or religious faith.

The scientific revolution was quickly popularized among educated Westerners. Here was a key step in the cultural transformation of western Europe in the early modern period. New scientific institutes were set up, often with government aid, to advance research and disseminate the findings. Lectures and easy-to-read manuals publicized the latest advances and communicated the excitement that researchers shared in almost all parts of Europe. Attacks on beliefs in witchcraft became more common, and magistrates grew increasingly reluctant to entertain witchcraft accusations in court. Public hysteria began to die down after about 1670. There were growing signs of a new belief that people could control and calculate their environment. Insurance companies sprang up to help guard against risk. Doctors increased their attacks on popular healers, promoting a more scientific diagnosis of illness. Newsletters, an innovation by the late 17th century, began to advertise "lost and found" items, for there was no point leaving this kind of problem to customary magicians, called cunning men, who had poked around with presumably enchanted sticks.

By the 1680s writers affected by the new science, though not themselves scientists, began to attack traditional religious ideas such as miracles, for in the universe of the Scientific Revolution there was no room for disruption of nature's laws. Some intellectuals held out a new conception of God, called **Deism,** arguing that although there might be a divinity, its role was simply to set natural laws in motion. In England, **John Locke** argued that people could learn everything they needed to know through their senses and reason; faith was irrelevant. Christian beliefs in human sinfulness crumbled in the view of these intellectuals, for they saw human nature as basically good.

Finally, scientific advances created wider assumptions about the possibility of human progress. If knowledge could advance through concerted human effort, why not progress in other domains? Even literary authorities joined this parade, and the idea that past styles set timeless standards of perfection came under growing criticism.

Science had never before been central to intellectual life. Science had played important roles in other civilizations, as in China, classical Greece, central America, and Islam. Generally, however, wider religious or philosophical interests predominated. In China most notably, despite some real interest in generalizations about the physical universe derived from Daoism, science continued to be construed mainly in terms of practical, empirical advances. The Western passion for combining empiricism with more sweeping rational formulations—the idea of general laws of nature—clearly built on traditions that had come from Greek thought as mediated by Christian theology and Islamic philosophy during the postclassical period. In sum, the West was not alone in developing crucial scientific data, but it now became the leading center for scientific advance, and its key thinkers stood alone for some time in seeing science as the key to gaining and defining knowledge.

Absolute and Parliamentary Monarchies

The feudal monarchy—the balance between king and nobles—that had defined Western politics since the late postclassical period finally came undone in the 17th century. In most countries, after the passions of religious wars finally cooled, monarchs gained new powers, curtailing the tradition of noble pressure or revolt. At the same time, more ambitious military organization, in states that defined war as a central purpose, required more careful administration and improved tax collection.

The model for this new pattern was France, now the West's most important nation. French kings steadily built up their power in the 17th century. They stopped convening the medieval parliament and passed laws as they saw fit, although some provincial councils remained strong. They blew up the castles of dissident nobles, another sign that gunpowder was undercutting the military basis of feudalism. They appointed a growing bureaucracy drawn from the

Visualizing the Past

Versailles

This picture shows Louis XIV's grand 17th-century palace at Versailles. It displays the sheer opulence of this absolute monarchy, in what was Europe's richest and most populous and influential nation. It also shows the renewed hold of a classical style, seen to be most prestigious for public buildings. What else does it suggest?

Architecture is sometimes thought to be the most socially and historically revealing of all the arts because it depends most heavily on public support; it is harder for architects, particularly dealing with public buildings, to be as idiosyncratic as painters or poets may be.

Questions: What kinds of intentions on the part of Louis and his advisors does this building represent? How can Versailles be interpreted as a statement of absolute monarchy in addition to its obvious showiness? What are the relationships to nature and to spatial arrangement? What would the palace represent to an ordinary French person? To an aristocrat?

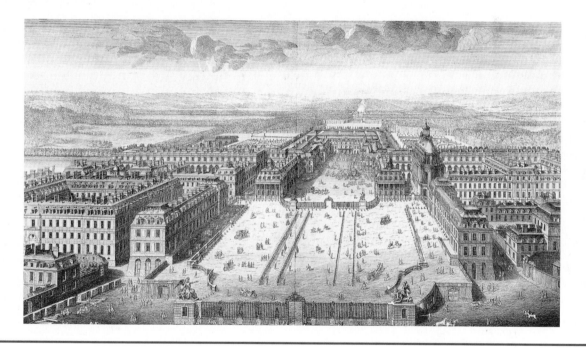

merchants and lawyers. They sent direct representatives to the outlying provinces. They professionalized the army, giving more formal training to officers, providing uniforms and support, and creating military hospitals and pensions.

So great was the power of the monarch, in fact, that the French system became known as **absolute monarchy.** Its most glorious royal proponent, King **Louis XIV,** summed up its principles succinctly: "I am the state." Louis became a major patron of the arts, giving government a cultural role beyond any previous levels in the West. His academies not only encouraged science but also worked to standardize the French language. A sumptuous palace at Versailles was used to keep nobles busy with social functions so that they could not interfere with affairs of state.

Using the new bureaucratic structure, Louis and his ministers developed additional functions for the state. They reduced internal tariffs, which acted as barriers to trade, and created new, state-run manufacturing. The reigning economic theory, mercantilism, held that governments should promote the internal economy to improve tax revenues and to limit imports from other nations, lest money be lost to enemy states. Therefore, absolute monarchs such as Louis XIV set tariffs on imported goods, tried to encourage their merchant fleets, and sought colonies to provide raw materials and a guaranteed market for manufactured goods produced at home.

The basic structure of absolute monarchy developed in other states besides France (see Map 17.2). Spain tried to imitate French principles in the 18th century, which resulted in efforts to tighten control over its Latin American colonies. However, the most important spread of absolute monarchy occurred in the central European states that were gaining in importance. A series of kings in Prussia, in eastern Germany, built a strong army and bureaucracy. They promoted economic activity and began to develop a state-sponsored school system. Habsburg kings in Austria-Hungary, though still officially rulers of the Holy Roman Empire, concentrated increasingly on developing a stronger monarchy in the lands under

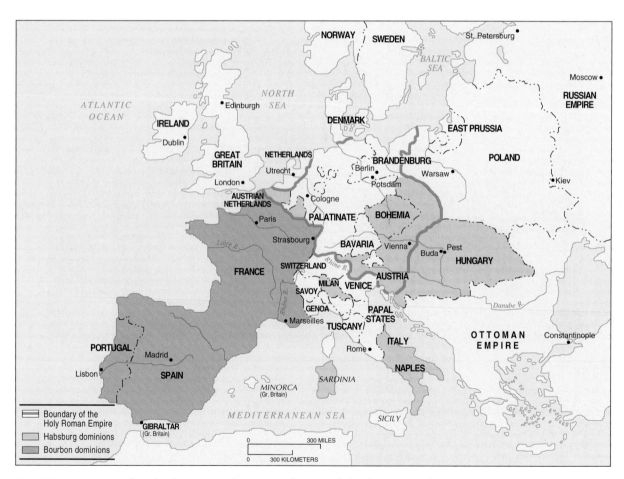

Map 17.2 *Europe Under Absolute Monarchy, 1715. The rise of absolute monarchies led to consolidation of national borders as states asserted full control of areas within their boundaries. For example, a recent study shows that villages that straddled the French–Spanish border were undifferentiated before 1600, but by 1700 they showed marked national differences because of different state policies and the greater impact of belonging to one state or another.*

In Depth

Elites and Masses

What caused the end of witchcraft hysteria in the West by the later 17th century? Did wise rulers calm a frenzied populace or did ordinary people themselves change their minds? One explanation focuses on new efforts by elites, such as local magistrates, to discipline mass impulses. Authorities stopped believing in demonic disruptions of natural processes, and so forced an end to persecutions. But many ordinary people were also thinking in new ways. Without converting fully to a scientific outlook, they became open to new ideas about how to handle health problems, reducing their belief in magical remedies; they needed witches less. Potential "witches" may have become more cautious. Older women, threatened by growing community suspicion, learned to maintain a lower profile and to emphasize benign, grandmotherly qualities rather than seeking a more independent role. Without question, there was a decline both in witchcraft beliefs, once a key element in the Western mentality, and in the hysteria specifically characteristic of the 16th and 17th centuries. This decline reflected new ways of thinking about strangeness and disruption. It involved complex interactions between various segments of Western society: magistrates and villagers, scientists and priests, husbands and widows.

The transformation of Western society after 1450 raises fascinating questions about the role of elites—particularly powerful groups and creative individuals—versus the ordinary people in causing change. The growing importance of social history has called attention to ordinary people, as we have seen, but it has not answered all the questions about their actual role. This role varies by place and time, of course. Some social historians tend to see ordinary people as victims of change, pushed around by the power groups. Others tend to stress the positive historical role of ordinary people in partly shaping the context of their own lives and affecting the larger course of history.

It is easy to read the early modern transformation of western Europe as an operation created by elites, with the masses as passively watching or futilely protesting. Not only the Renaissance and Reformation, but also the commercial revolution, required decisive action by key leadership groups. Leading merchants spurred economic change, and they ultimately began to farm out manufacturing jobs. The resultant rise of dependant wage labor, which tore a growing minority of western Europeans away from property and so from economic control of their lives, illustrates the power disparities in Western society. Ordinary people knuckled under or protested, but they were reacting, not initiating.

The rise of science rivets our attention on the activities of extraordinarily creative individuals, such as Newton, and elite institutions, such as the scientific academies. Some historians have suggested that the rise of science opened a new gap between the ways educated upper classes and masses thought.

Yet the ordinary people of western Europe were not passive, nor did they simply protest change in the name of tradition. Widespread shifts came from repeated decisions by peasants and artisans, not just from those at the top. The steady technological improvements in manufacturing thus flowed upward from practicing artisans, not downward from formal scientists. The European-style family that had taken shape by the 16th century was an innovation by ordinary people long ignored by the elite. It encouraged new parent–child relations and new tensions between young adults and the old that might spur other innovations, including a willingness to settle distant colonies in search of property. The fact that young people often had to wait to marry until their property-owning fathers died could induce many to seek new lands or new economic methods. In other words, ordinary people changed their habits too, and these changes had wide impact.

Questions: Did elites gain new power over the masses in early modern Western society? Are ordinary people more conservative by nature, more suspicious of change, than groups at the top? Can you describe at least two other historical cases in which it is important to determine whether change was imposed on ordinary people from above or whether ordinary people themselves produced important innovations?

their direct control. The power of these Habsburg rulers increased after they pushed back the last Turkish invasion threat late in the 17th century and then added the kingdom of Hungary to their domains.

Most absolute monarchs saw a strong military as a key political goal, and many hoped for territorial expansion. Louis XIV used his strong state as the basis for a series of wars from the 1680s onward. The wars yielded some new territory for France but finally attracted an opposing alliance system that blocked further advance. Prussian kings, though long cautious in exposing their proud military to the risk of major war, turned in the 18th century to a series of conflicts that won new territory.

Britain and the Netherlands, both growing commercial and colonial powers, stood apart from the trend toward absolute monarchy in the 17th century. They emphasized the role of the central state, but they also built parliamentary regimes in which the kings shared power with representatives selected by the nobility and upper urban classes. The English civil wars produced a final political settlement in 1688 and 1689 (the so-called **Glorious Revolution**) in which parliament won basic sovereignty over the king. The English parliament no longer depended on the king to convene, for regular sessions were scheduled. Its rights to approve taxation allowed it to monitor or initiate most major policies.

Furthermore, a growing body of political theory arose in the 17th century that built on these parliamentary ideas. John Locke and others argued that power came from the people, not from a divine right to royal rule. Kings should therefore be restrained by institutions that protected the public interest, including certain general rights to freedom and property. A right of revolution could legitimately oppose unjust rule.

Overall, western Europe developed important diversity in political forms, between absolute monarchy and a new kind of **parliamentary monarchy.** It maintained a characteristic tension between government growth and the idea that there should be some limits to state authority. This tension was expressed in new forms, but it recalled some principles that had originated in the Middle Ages.

The Nation-State

The absolute monarchies and the parliamentary monarchies shared important characteristics as nation-states. Unlike the great empires of many other civilizations, they ruled peoples who shared a common culture and language, some important minorities apart. They could appeal to a certain loyalty that linked cultural and political bonds. This was as true of England, where the idea of special rights

of Englishmen helped feed the parliamentary movement, as it was of France. Not surprisingly, ordinary people in many nation-states, even though not directly represented in government, increasingly believed that government should act for their interests. Thus, Louis XIV faced recurrent popular riots based on the assumption that when bad harvests drove up food prices, the government was obligated to help people out.

In sum, nation-states developed a growing list of functions, particularly under the banner of mercantilism, whose principles were shared by monarchists and parliamentary leaders alike. They also promoted new political values and loyalties that were very different from the political traditions of other civilizations. They kept the West politically divided and often at war.

The West by 1750

 The three great currents of change—commercialization, cultural reorientation, and the rise of the nation-state—continued to operate in the West after 1700, along with the growing international influence of the West. Each current produced new changes that furthered the overall transformation of the West.

Political Patterns

Many of the key changes in modern Europe drew together by the mid-18th century. Political changes were least significant. During much of the century, English politics settled into a bloated parliamentary routine in which key political groups competed for influence without major policy differences. Absolute monarchy in France changed little institutionally, but it became less effective. It could not force changes in the tax structure that would give it more solid financial footing because aristocrats refused to surrender their traditional exemptions.

Political developments were far livelier in central Europe. In Prussia, **Frederick the Great,** building on the military and bureaucratic organization of his predecessors, introduced greater freedom of religion while expanding the economic functions of the state.

His government actively encouraged better agricultural methods; for example, it promoted use of the American potato as a staple crop. It also enacted laws promoting greater commercial coordination and greater equity; harsh traditional punishments were cut back. Rulers of this sort claimed to be enlightened despots, wielding great authority but for the good of society at large.

Enlightened or not, the policies of the major Western nation-states produced recurrent warfare. France and Britain squared off in the 1740s and again in the Seven Years' War (1756–1763); their conflicts focused on battles for colonial empire. Austria and Prussia also fought, with Prussia gaining new land. Wars in the 18th century were carefully modulated, without devastating effects, but they demonstrated the continued linkage between statecraft and war that was characteristic of the West.

Enlightenment Thought and Popular Culture

In culture, the aftermath of the Scientific Revolution spilled over into a new movement known as the **Enlightenment,** centered particularly in France but with adherents throughout the Western world. Enlightenment thinkers continued to support scientific advance. Although there were no Newton-like breakthroughs, chemists gained new understanding of major elements, and biologists developed a vital new classification system for the natural species.

The Enlightenment also pioneered in applying scientific methods to the study of human society, sketching the modern social sciences. The basic idea was that rational laws could describe social as well as physical behavior and that knowledge could be used to improve policy. Thus, criminologists wrote that brutal punishments failed to deter crime, whereas a decent society would be able to rehabilitate criminals through education. Political theorists wrote about the importance of carefully planned constitutions and controls over privilege, although they disagreed about what political form was best. A new school of economists developed. In his classic book *Wealth of Nations*, Scottish philosopher **Adam Smith** set forth a number of principles of economic behavior. He argued that people act according to their self-interest but, through competition, promote general eco-

nomic advance. Government should avoid regulation in favor of the operation of individual initiative and market forces. This was an important statement of economic policy and an illustration of the growing belief that general models of human behavior could be derived from rational thought.

Single individuals could sum up part of the Enlightenment's impressive range. Denis Diderot (1713–1784; Figure 17.4) was a multifaceted leader of the French Enlightenment, best known for his editorial work on the *Encyclopédie* that compiled scientific and social scientific knowledge. Trained initially by the Jesuits, Diderot also wrote widely on philosophy, mathematics, and the psychology of deaf-mutes and also tried his hand at literature. An active friend

Figure 17.4 *Denis Diderot*

Document

Controversies About Women

Changes in family structure and some shifts in the economic roles of women, as well as ambivalent Protestant ideas about women that emphasized the family context but urged affection and respect between wives and husbands, touched off new gender tensions in Western society by the 17th century. Some of these tensions showed in witchcraft trials, so disproportionately directed against women. Other tensions showed in open debate about women's relationships to men; women not content with a docile wifeliness vied with new claims of virtue and prowess by some women. Although the debate was centered in the upper class of Protestant nations such as England, it may have had wider ramifications. Some of these ramifications, though quieter during the 18th century, burst forth again in arguments about inequality and family confinement in the 19th century, when a more durable feminist movement took shape in the West. In the selections here, the antiwoman position is set forth in a 1615 pamphlet by Joseph Swetham; the favorable view implicitly urging new rights is in a 1640 pamphlet pseudonymously authored by "Mary Tattle-Well and Ioane Hit-Him-Home, spinsters."

Swetham's "Arraignment of Women"

Men, I say, may live without women, but women cannot live without men: for Venus, whose beauty was excellent fair, yet when she needed man's help, She took Vulcan, a clubfooted Smith....

For women have a thousand ways to entice thee and ten thousand ways to deceive thee and all such fools as are suitors unto them: some they keep in hand with promises, and some they feed with flattery, and some they delay with dalliances, and some they please with kisses. They lay out the folds of their hair to entangle men into their love; betwixt their breasts in the vale of destruction; and in their beds there is hell, sorrow and repentance. Eagles eat not men till they are dead, but women devour them alive....

It is said of men that they have that one fault, but of women it is said that they have two faults: that is to say, they can neither say well nor do well. There is a saying that goeth thus: that things far fetched and dear bought are of us most dearly beloved. The like may be said of women; although many of them are not far fetched, yet they are dear bought, yea and so dear that many a man curseth his hard pennyworths and bans his own heart. For the pleasure of the fairest woman in the world lasteth but a honeymoon; that is, while a man hath glutted his affections and reaped the first fruit, his pleasure being past, sorrow and repentance remaineth still with him.

Tattle-Well and Hit-Him-Home's "Women's Sharp Revenge"

But it hath been the policy of all parents, even from the beginning, to curb us of that benefit by striving to keep us under and to make us men's mere Vassals even unto all posterity. How else comes it to pass that when a Father hath a numerous issue of Sons and Daughters, the sons forsooth they must be first put to the Grammar school, and after perchance sent to the University, and trained up in the Liberal Arts and Sciences, and there (if they prove not Blockheads) they may in time be book-learned?...

When we, whom they style by the name of weaker Vessels, though of a more delicate, fine, soft, and more pliant flesh therefore of a temper most capable of the best Impression, have not that generous and liberal Education, lest we should be made able to vindicate our own injuries, we are set only to the Needle, to prick our fingers, or else to the Wheel to spin a fair thread for our own undoing, or perchance to some more dirty and debased drudgery. If we be taught to read, they then confine us within the compass of our Mother Tongue, and that limit we are not suffered to pass; or if (which sometimes happeneth) we be brought up to Music, to singing, and to dancing, it is not for any benefit that thereby we can engross unto ourselves, but for their own particular ends, the better to please and content their licentious appetites when we come to our maturity and ripeness. And thus if we be weak by Nature, they strive to make us more weak by our Nurture; and if in degree of place low, they strive by their policy to keep us more under.

Now to show we are no such despised matter as you would seem to make us, come to our first Creation, when man was made of the mere dust of the earth. The woman had her being from the best part of his body, the Rib next to his heart, which difference even in our complexions may be easily decided. Man is of a dull, earthy, and melancholy aspect, having shallows in his face and a very forest upon his Chin, when our soft and smooth Cheeks are a true representation of a delectable garden of intermixed Roses and Lilies.... Man might consider that women were not created to be their slaves or vassals; for as they had not their Original out of his head (thereby to command him), so it was not out of his foot to be trod upon, but in a medium out of his side to be his fellow feeler, his equal, and companion....

Thus have I truly and impartially proved that for Chastity, Charity, Constancy, Magnanimity, Valor, Wisdom, Piety, or any Grace or Virtue whatsoever, women have always been more than equal with men, and that for Luxury, Surquidant obscenity, profanity, Ebriety, Impiety, and all that may be called bad we do come far short of them.

Questions: What are the main disagreements in these 17th-century texts? What kind of approach was more novel, judging by the Western gender tradition to that point? What conditions prompted a more vigorous public debate about gender in the 17th century? How does it connect to religious, commercial, and political change? How does the favorable argument compare with more modern views about women? What kinds of change does it advocate? Did the new arguments about women's conditions suggest that these conditions were improving?

of other philosophers, Diderot also traveled to foreign courts as advisor and visiting intellectual. A visit to Catherine the Great of Russia in 1773–1774, to thank her for generous patronage, harmed his health, but he maintained his relationship with his mistress, Sophie Volland.

More generally still, the Enlightenment produced a set of basic principles about human affairs: Human beings are good, at least improvable, and they can be educated to be better; reason is the key to truth, and religions that rely on blind faith or refuse to tolerate diversity are wrong. Enlightenment thinkers attacked the Catholic church with particular vigor. Progress was possible, even inevitable, if people could be set free. Society's goals should center on improving material and social life.

Although it was not typical of the Enlightenment's main thrust, a few thinkers applied these general principles to other areas. A handful of socialists argued that economic equality and the abolition of private property must become important goals. A few feminist thinkers, such as **Mary Wollstonecraft** in England, argued—against the general male-centered views of most Enlightenment thinkers—that new political rights and freedoms should extend to women. Several journals written by women for women made their first appearance during this extraordinary cultural period. Madame de Beaumere took over the direction of the French *Journal des Dames* from a man, and in Germany, Marianne Ehrmann used her journal to suggest that men might be partly to blame for women's lowly position.

The popularization of new ideas encouraged further changes in the habits and beliefs of many ordinary people. Reading clubs and coffeehouses allowed many urban artisans and businessmen to discuss the latest reform ideas. Leading writers and compilations of scientific and philosophical findings, such as the *Encyclopaedia Britannica*, won a wide audience and, for a few people, a substantial fortune from the sale of books.

Other changes in popular outlook paralleled the new intellectual currents, although they had deeper sources than philosophy alone. Attitudes toward children began to shift in many social groups. Older methods of physical discipline were criticized in favor of more restrained behavior that would respect the goodness and innocence of children. Swaddling—wrapping infants in cloth so they could not move or harm themselves—began to decline as parents became interested in freer movement and greater interaction for young children. Among wealthy families, educational toys and books for children reflected the idea that childhood should be a stage for learning and growth.

Family life generally was changed by a growing sense that old hierarchies should be rethought and revised toward greater equality in the treatment of women and children in the home. Love between family members gained new respect, and an emotional bond in marriage became more widely sought. Parents grew more reluctant to force a match on a son or daughter if the emotional vibrations were not right. Here was a link not only with Enlightenment ideas of proper family relations but with the novels such as Richardson's *Pamela* that poured out a sentimental view of life.

Ongoing Change in Commerce and Manufacturing

Ongoing economic change paralleled changes in popular culture and intellectual life. Commerce continued to spread. Ordinary Westerners began to buy processed products, such as refined sugar and coffee or tea obtained from Indonesia and the West Indies, for daily use. This was a sign of the growing importance of Europe's new colonies for ordinary life and of the beginnings of mass consumerism in Western society. Another sign of change was the growing use of paid professional entertainment as part of popular leisure, even in rural festivals. Circuses, first introduced in France in the 1670s, began to redefine leisure to include spectatorship and a taste for the bizarre.

Agriculture began to change. Until the late 17th century, western Europe had continued to rely largely on the methods and techniques characteristic of the Middle Ages—a severe economic constraint in an agricultural society. The three-field system still meant that a full third of all farmland was left unplanted each year to restore fertility. First in the Netherlands and then elsewhere, new procedures for draining swamps added available land. Reformers touted nitrogen-fixing crops to reduce the need to leave land idle. Stockbreeding improved, and new techniques such as seed-drills and the use of scythes instead of sickles for harvesting increased productivity. Some changes spread particularly fast on large estates, but other changes affected ordinary peasants as well. Particularly vital in this category was the spread of the potato from the late 17th century onward.

A New World crop, the potato had long been shunned because it was not mentioned in the Bible and was held to be the cause of plagues. Enlightened government leaders, and the peasants' desire to win greater economic security and better nutrition, led to widespread use of this crop. In sum, the West improved its food supply and agricultural efficiency, leaving more labor available for other pursuits.

These changes, along with the steady growth of colonial trade and internal commerce, spurred increased manufacturing. Capitalism—the investment of funds in hopes of larger profits—also spread from big trading ventures to the production of goods. The 18th century witnessed a rapid spread of household production of textiles and metal products, mostly by rural workers who alternated manufacturing with some agriculture. Here was a key use of labor that was no longer needed for food. Hundreds of thousands of people were drawn into this domestic system, in which capitalist merchants distributed supplies and orders and workers ran the production process for pay (Figure 17.5). Although manufacturing tools were still operated by hand, the spread of domestic manufacturing spurred important technological innovations designed to improve efficiency. In 1733, John Kay in England introduced the flying shuttle, which permitted automatic crossing of threads on looms; with this, an individual weaver could do the work of two. Improvements in spinning soon followed as the Western economy began to move toward a full-fledged Industrial Revolution (see Chapter 23).

Human changes accompanied and sometimes preceded technology. Around 1700, most manufacturers who made wool cloth in northern England were artisans, doing part of the work themselves. By 1720, a group of loom owners were becoming outright manufacturers with new ideas and behaviors. How were manufacturers different? They spent their time organizing production and sales rather than doing their own work. They moved work out of their homes. They stopped drinking beer with their workers. And they saw their workers as market commodities, to be treated as the conditions of trade demanded. In 1736, one such manufacturer coolly wrote that because of slumping sales, "I have turned off [dismissed] a great many of my makers, and keep turning more off weekly."

Finally, agricultural changes, commercialism, and manufacturing combined, particularly after about 1730, to produce a rapidly growing population in the West. With better food supplies, more people survived, particularly with the aid of the potato. Furthermore, new manufacturing jobs helped landless people support themselves, promoting earlier marriage and sexual relationships. Population growth, in turn, promoted further economic change, heightening competition and producing a more manipulable labor force. The West's great population revolution, which continued into the 19th century, both caused and reflected the civilization's dynamism, although it also produced great strain and confusion.

Innovation and Instability

By the 18th century, the various strands of change were increasingly intertwined in Western civiliza-

Figure 17.5   *A family of woolmakers at home.*

tion. Stronger governments promoted agricultural improvements, which helped prod population growth. Changes in popular beliefs were fed by new economic structures; both encouraged a reevaluation of the family and the roles of children. New beliefs also raised new political challenges. Enlightenment ideas about liberty and fundamental human equality could be directed against existing regimes. New family practices might have political implications as well. Children, raised with less adult restraint and encouraged to value their individual worth through parental love and careful education, might see traditional political limitations in new ways.

There was no perfect fit, no inevitable match, in the three strands of change that had been transforming the West for two centuries or more: the commercial, the cultural, and the political. However, by 1750 all were in place. The combination had already produced an unusual version of an agricultural civilization, and it promised more upheaval in the future.

GLOBAL CONNECTIONS: Europe and the World

In 1450, Europeans were convinced that their Christianity made them superior to other people. But they also understood that many societies were impressive in terms of cities and wealth and the strength of their governments.

As Europe changed and prospered, its outlook toward the world changed as well. We saw in the previous chapter how Europeans began to use technology as a measure of society, arguing that other societies that were less interested in technological change were inferior. By the 18th century, criticisms of the superstitions of other people began to surface among Europeans proud of their science and rationalism.

The wider world could still provide a sense of wonder, but increasingly this was focused on natural phenomena and the strange animals being imported to European zoos. The Enlightenment generated the idea of a "noble savage"—a person uncorrupted by advanced civilization and urban ways. But this was largely a fiction designed to comment on Europe itself, not a source of real admiration for other peoples. Increasingly, European power and the rapid changes within Western civilization led to a sense that most other societies were backward, perhaps not even civilized. The idea had powerful impact, not only on European attitudes but also on the ways other societies perceived themselves and reacted.

Further Readings

For an overview of developments in Western society during this period, with extensive bibliographies, see Sheldon Watts' *A Social History of Western Europe, 1450–1720* (1984); Michael Anderson's *Approaches to the West European Family* (1980); and Peter N. Stearns' *Life and Society in the West: The Modern Centuries* (1988). Charles Tilly's *Big Structures, Large Processes, Huge Comparisons* (1985) offers an analytical framework based on major change; see also Tilly's edited volume, *The Formation of National States in Western Europe* (1975).

On more specific developments and periods, J. R. Hale's *The Civilization of Europe in the Renaissance* (1994); J. H. Plumb's *The Italian Renaissance* (1986); F. H. New's *The Renaissance and Reformation: A Short History* (1977); O. Chadwick's *The Reformation* (1983); and Steven Ozment's *The Age of Reform, 1520–1550* (1980) and his *Protestants: The Birth of a Revolution* (1992) are fine introductions to early changes. See also Hubert Jedin and John Dolan, eds., *Reformation and Counter Reformation* (1980). H. Baron, *The Crisis of the Early Italian Renaissance* (1996), examines the place of civic life in Italian humanism. E. Amt, ed., *Women's Lives in the Medieval Europe: A Source-Book* (1992), and A. Vickery, *The Gentleman's Daughter: Women's Lives in Georgian England* (1998), survey the growth or retreat of opportunities for women over time.

Later changes are sketched in Thomas Munck's *Seventeenth Century Europe: 1598–1700* (1990) and Jeremy Black's *Eighteenth Century Europe: 1700–1789* (1990). On England in the civil war period, see Christopher Hill, *A Nation of Change and Novelty* (1990).

Key aspects of social change in this period can be approached through Peter Burke's *Popular Culture in Early Modern Europe* (1978); Robin Biggs' *Communities of Belief: Cultural and Social Tensions in Early Modern France* (1989); Keith Thomas' *Religion and the Decline of Magic* (1971); Lawrence Stone's *The Family, Sex and Marriage in England 1500–1800* (1977); and James Sharpe's *Instruments of Darkness: Witchcraft in Early Modern England* (1997). On popular protest, see Charles Tilly's *The Contentious French* (1986) and H. A. F. Kamen's *The Iron Century: Social Change in Europe 1550–1660* (1971).

On science, A. R. Hall's *From Galileo to Newton, 1630–1720* (1982) is a fine introduction. Relations between science and technology are covered in C. Cipolla's *Before the Industrial Revolution* (1976).

On the Web

Daily life in Renaissance Italy is examined at http://history.evansville.net/renaissa.html. The lives and art of Leonardo da Vinci (http://www.mos.org/leonardo/), Michelangelo (http://www.michelangelo.com/buonarroti.html), and Raphael (http://www.theartgallery.com.au/ArtEducation/greatartists/Raphael/about/) were closely intertwined with the city of Florence, whose history is addressed at http://www.mega.it/eng/egui/epo/secrepu.htm.

Martin Luther's life (http://www.iclnet.org/pub/resources/text/wittenberg/wittenberg-luther.html and http://www.wittenberg.de/e/seiten/personen/luther.html) and the course of the Protestant Reformation/Catholic Reformation are discussed at http://mars.acnet.wnec.edu/~grempel/courses/wc2/lectures/catholicreform.html, http://old.jccc.net/~jjackson/refo.html, and http://www.fordham.edu/halsall/sbook1y.html. The art and literature of the Northern Renaissance is examined at http://www.urtonart.com/history/Renaissance/northrenaiss.htm, http://www.msu.edu/~cloudsar/nrweb.htm, while http://communication.ucsd.edu/bjones/Books/luther.html illustrates the role of the printing press in the Reformation.

The Web provides insight into the role of two of the leading absolute monarchs of Europe, Frederick the Great (http://members.tripod.com/~Nevermore/king7.html) and Louis XIV (http://www.louis-xiv.de/, http://history.hanover.edu/texts/louisxiv.htm, and http://www.chateauversailles.fr/).

Isaac Newton's life and letters can be examined at http://www.cannylink.com/historyissacnewton.htm, while other leading figures of the Scientific Revolution can be explored at http://www.fordham.edu/halsall/mod/SCIREV.html.

The development of modern political and economic theory can be traced through the lives of Niccolo Machiavelli (http://sol.brunel.ac.uk/~jarvis/bola/ethics/mach.html), the Medici family (http://es.rice.edu/ES/humsoc/Galileo/People/medici.html), Adam Smith (http://www.socserv.mcmaster.ca/econ/ugcm/3ll3/smith/index.html), and through the study of the Glorious Revolution of 1688 (http://65.107.211.206/history/Glorious_Revolution.html and http://www.thegloriousrevolution.com). Sites addressing Renaissance women and their texts can be found at http://www.yesnet.yk.ca/schools/projects/renaissance/renaissancewomen.html, http://www.allsands.com/History/People/womanoftheren_vzp_gn.htm, http://womenshistory.miningco.com/cs/medieval/, and http://www.wwp.brown.edu/texts/rwoentry.html.

CHAPTER 18

THE RISE OF RUSSIA

Peter I of Russia (1672–1725), commonly known as Peter the Great, is shown here in a heroic pose. An autocrat who put down revolts against his rule with great cruelty, he was also a reformist who traveled widely in the West and took many steps toward westernizing Russia.

- Russia's Expansionist Politics Under the Tsars
- Russia's First Westernization, 1690–1790
- DOCUMENT: The Nature of Westernization
- Themes in Early Modern Russian History
- VISUALIZING THE PAST: Oppressed Peasants
- IN DEPTH: Multinational Empires
- GLOBAL CONNECTIONS: Russian and the World

Russia's great land empire was formed between 1450 and 1750. Unlike Western colonial empires, Russia's expansion involved only limited commercial exchange. Nevertheless, it fundamentally altered power balances from Europe to Asia.

Russian leaders, casting off Tatar (Mongol) domination between 1450 and 1480, proceeded on a fairly steady course of expansion. Much of the new territory was Asian, but Russia also gained the leading role in eastern Europe by the 17th century. Regional kingdoms remained in eastern Europe, and many of them differed from Russia in important ways. Poland and Lithuania continued to rival Russia into the 17th century. But Russia was increasingly the focal point as it became a significant force in world history.

Russia's evolution after 1450 draws our attention not just because of territorial expansion and growing importance but because of the fascinating changes the nation underwent as part of its surge onto the world scene. Building on a strong sense of separate identity, the Russians also entered into new contacts with Western society. Controversy over Western influence—whether to embrace it, select from it, or shun it—has continued in Russian culture to this day.

Russia's Expansionist Politics Under the Tsars

 Between 1450 and 1650, Russia began its process of territorial expansion while working to strengthen the tsarist state in what proved to be the first phase of the empire's early modern development.

Russia's emergence as a new power in eastern Europe and central Asia initially depended on its gaining freedom from Mongol (Tatar) control. The Duchy of Moscow was the center for the liberation effort beginning in the 14th century. Local princes began to carve out greater autonomy, and the effectiveness of Mongol control began to diminish. Ironically, the Moscow princes initially gained political experience as tax collectors for the Mongols, but gradually they moved toward regional independence. Under **Ivan III**—Ivan the Great, who claimed succession from the Rurik dynasty and the old Kievan days—a large part of Russia was freed after 1462. Ivan organized a strong army, giving the new government a military emphasis it would long retain. He also used loyalties to the Orthodox Christian faith and to Russia to win support for his campaigns. By 1480, Moscow had been freed from any payment to the Mongols and had gained a vast territory running from the borders of the Polish Lithuanian kingdom to the Ural mountains.

1450 C.E.	1600 C.E.	1750 C.E.
1462 Much of Russia freed from Tatars by Ivan III (Ivan the Great)	**1604–1613** Time of Troubles	**1762–1796** Catherine the Great
1480 Moscow region free; Russian expansion presses south	**1613–1917** Romanov dynasty	**1773–1775** Pugachev revolt
1533–1584 Ivan IV (Ivan the Terrible), first to emphasize the title of tsar, boyar power reduced	**1637** Russian pioneers to Pacific	**1772, 1793, 1795** Partition of Poland
1552–1556 Russian expansion in central Asia, western Siberia	**1649** Law enacted making serfdom hereditary	**1785** Law enacted tightening landlord power over serfs
	1689–1725 Peter the Great	
	1700–1721 Wars with Sweden	
	1703 Founding of St. Petersburg	

The Need for Revival

Mongol control never reshaped basic Russian values, for the rulers were interested in tribute, not full government. Many Russian landlords adopted Mongol styles of dress and social habits. However, most Russians remained Christians, and most local administrative issues remained in the hands of regional princes, landlords, or peasant villages. In these senses, Russia was set to resume many of its earlier patterns when full independence was achieved. On the other hand, the Mongol period reduced the vigor of Russian cultural life, lowering the levels of literacy among the priesthood, for example. Economic life deteriorated as well: With trade down and manufacturing limited, Russia had become a purely agricultural economy dependant on peasant labor. In these senses, independence brought a challenge for revival and reform.

Ivan the Great claimed an earlier tradition of centralized rule, which went back to the Rurik dynasty and Byzantine precedents, and added to it a new sense of imperial mission. He married the niece of the last Byzantine emperor, which gave him the chance to assert control over all Orthodox churches whether in Russia or not.

Encouraged by his advisors, Ivan also insisted that Russia had succeeded Byzantium as a **third Rome,** with all that this implied in terms of grandeur and expansionist potential. Ivan accordingly called himself tsar, or Caesar, the "autocrat of all the Russias."

The next important tsar, **Ivan IV,** justly called Ivan the Terrible, continued the policy of Russian expansion. He also placed greater emphasis on controlling the tsarist autocracy, earning his nickname by killing many of the Russian nobles, or **boyars,** whom he suspected of conspiracy. Russian aristocrats lacked the tradition of political assertion of their counterparts in western Europe, and Ivan's policies of terror confirmed this fact.

Patterns of Expansion

The territorial expansion policy focused particularly on central Asia. It was motivated by a desire to push the former Mongol overlords farther back. Russia was a country of vast plains, with few natural barriers to invasion. The early tsars turned this drawback to an advantage by pushing southward toward the Caspian Sea; they also moved east into the Ural mountains and beyond. Both Ivan III and Ivan IV recruited peasants to migrate to the newly seized lands, particularly in the south. These peasant-adventurers, or **cossacks,** were Russian pioneers, combining agriculture with daring military feats on horseback. The expansion territories long had a rough-and-ready frontier quality, only gradually settling down to more regular administration. The cossack spirit provided volunteers for further expansion, for many of the pioneers—like their American counterparts in the 19th century—chafed under detailed tsarist control and were eager to move on to new settlements. During the 16th century, the cossacks not only conquered the Caspian Sea area but also moved into western Siberia, across the Urals, beginning the gradual takeover and settlement of these vast plains, which previously had been sparsely inhabited by nomadic Asian peoples (Map 18.1).

Expansion also offered tsars a way to reward loyal nobles and bureaucrats by giving them estates in new territories. This practice provided new agricultural areas and sources of labor; Russia used slaves for certain kinds of production work into the 18th century. Although Russia never became as dependant on expansion for social control and economic advance as the later Roman Empire or the Ottoman Empire had, it certainly had many reasons to continue the policy. Russia also created trading connections with its new Asian territories and their neighbors.

Russia's early expansion, along with that of the Ottoman Empire to the south, eliminated indepen-

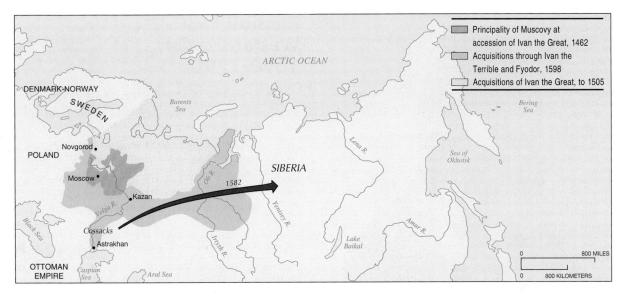

Map 18.1   *Russian Expansion Under the Early Tsars, 1462–1598. From its base in the Moscow region, Russia expanded in three directions; the move into Siberia involved pioneering new settlements and political control.*

dent central Asia—that age-old source of nomadic cultures and periodic invasions in both the east and the west. The same expansion, though driven by the movement of Russian peasants and landlords to new areas, also added to Russia diverse new peoples, making this a multicultural empire, like that of the Mughals and Ottomans. Particularly important was the addition of a large Muslim minority, overseen by the tsarist government but not pressed to integrate with Russian culture.

Western Contact and Romanov Policy

Along with expansion and enforcement of tsarist primacy, the early tsars added one element to their overall approach: carefully managed contacts with western Europe. The tsars realized that Russia's cultural and economic subordination to the Mongols had put them at a commercial and cultural disadvantage. Ivan III was eager to launch diplomatic missions to the leading Western states. During the reign of Ivan IV, British merchants established trading contacts with Russia, selling manufactured products in exchange for furs and other raw materials. Soon, Western merchants established outposts in Moscow and other Russian centers.

The tsars also imported Italian artists and architects to design church buildings and the magnificent royal palace in the Kremlin in Moscow. The foreign architects modified Renaissance styles to take Russian building traditions into account, producing the ornate, onion-shaped domes that became characteristic of Russian (and other east European) churches and creating a distinctive form of classicism. A tradition of looking to the West, particularly for emblems of upper-class art and status, was beginning to emerge by the 16th century, along with some reliance on Western commercial initiative (Figure 18.1).

Ivan IV died without an heir. This led to some new power claims by the boyars—the **Time of Troubles**—plus Swedish and Polish attacks on Russian territory. In 1613, however, an assembly of boyars chose a member of the Romanov family as tsar. This family, the **Romanov dynasty,** was to rule Russia until the great revolution of 1917. Although many individual Romanov rulers were weak, and tensions with the claims of nobles recurred, the Time of Troubles did not produce any lasting constraints on tsarist power.

The first Romanov, Michael, reestablished internal order without great difficulty. He also drove out the foreign invaders and resumed the expansionist policy of his predecessors. A successful war against Poland

Figure 18.1 *This icon, from the early 15th century, depicts Mary and the Christ Child. The Russian icon tradition used styles derived from Byzantine art that under Western influence became more naturalistic by the 17th century.*

brought Russia part of the Ukraine, including Kiev; in the south, Russia's boundaries expanded to meet those of the Ottoman Empire. Expansion at this point was beginning to have new diplomatic implications as Russia encountered other established governments.

Alexis Romanov, Michael's successor, abolished the assemblies of nobles and gained new powers over the Russian church. He was eager to purge the church of many superstitions and errors that, in his judgment, had crept in during Mongol times. His policies resumed the Orthodox tradition of state control over the church. Dissident religious conservatives, called **Old Believers,** were exiled to Siberia or to southern Russia, where they maintained their religion and extended Russia's colonizing activities.

Russia's First Westernization, 1690–1790

 By the late 17th century, Russia was poised for dramatic, if selective, internal change. Peter the Great led the first westernization effort in history, changing Russia permanently and providing a model for later westernization attempts elsewhere. Peter and his successors used westernization to bolster Russia's expansionist empire, without intending to become a truly Western society.

By the end of the 17th century Russia had become one of the great land empires, but it remained unusually agricultural by the standards of the West and the great Asian civilizations. The reign of **Peter I,** the son of Alexis and known with some justice as Peter the Great, built many new features into this framework between 1689 and 1725. In essence, Peter extended his predecessors' policies of building up tsarist control and expanding Russian territory (Map 18.2). He added a more definite interest in changing selected aspects of Russian economy and culture by imitating Western forms.

Peter the Great was a vigorous leader of exceptional intelligence and ruthless energy. A giant, standing 6 feet 8 inches, he was eager to move his country more fully into the Western diplomatic and cultural orbit without making it fully Western. He traveled widely in the West, incognito, seeking Western allies for a crusade against Turkish power in Europe—for which he found little enthusiasm. He also visited many Western manufacturing centers, even working as a ship's carpenter in Holland; through these activities he gained an interest in Western science and technology. He brought scores of Western artisans back with him to Russia.

Tsarist Autocracy of Peter the Great

In politics, Peter was clearly an autocrat. He put down revolts against his rule with great cruelty, in one case executing some of the ringleaders personally. He had no interest in the parliamentary features of Western centers such as Holland, seizing instead on the absolutist currents in the West at this time. Peter enhanced the power of the Russian state by

Map 18.2 *Russia Under Peter the Great. From 1696 to 1725, Peter the Great allowed his country only one year of peace. For the rest of this time he radically changed the form of his government to pursue war. By the end, he had established his much-desired "Windows on the West" on the Baltic.*

using it as a reform force, trying to show that even aristocratic habits could be modified by state decree. Peter also extended an earlier policy of recruiting bureaucrats from outside aristocratic ranks and giving them noble titles to reward bureaucratic service. Here was a key means of freeing the state from exclusive dependence on aristocratic officials. Peter imitated Western military organization, creating a specially trained fighting force that put down local militias. Furthermore, Peter the Great set up a secret police to prevent dissent and to supervise the bureaucracy. Here he paralleled an earlier Chinese innovation but went well beyond the bureaucratic control impulses of Western absolutists at that time. Peter's

Chancery of Secret Police survived, under different names and with changing functions, to the 1990s; it was reinstituted after 1917 by a revolutionary regime that in other respects worked to undo key features of the tsarist system.

Peter's foreign policy maintained many well-established lines. He attacked the Ottoman Empire, but he won no great victories. He warred with Sweden, at the time one of the leading northern powers in Europe, and gained territory on the eastern coast of the Baltic Sea, thus reducing Sweden to second-rate military status. Russia now had a window on the sea, including a largely ice-free port. From this time onward, Russia became a major factor in European diplomatic and military alignments. The tsar commemorated Russia's shift of interests westward by moving his capital from Moscow to a new Baltic city that he named St. Petersburg.

What Westernization Meant

Overall, Peter concentrated on improvements in political organization, on selected economic development, and on cultural change. He tried to streamline Russia's small bureaucracy and alter military structure by using Western organizational principles. He created a more well-defined military hierarchy while developing functionally specialized bureaucratic departments. He also improved the army's weaponry and, with aid from Western advisors, created the first Russian navy. He completely eliminated the old noble councils, creating a set of advisors under his control. Provincial governors were appointed from St. Petersburg, and although town councils were elected, a tsar-appointed town magistrate served as final authority. Peter's ministers systematized law codes to extend through the whole empire and revised the tax system, with taxes on ordinary Russian peasants increasing steadily. New training institutes were established for aspiring bureaucrats and officers—one way to bring talented nonnobles into the system.

Peter's economic efforts focused on building up metallurgical and mining industries, using Russia's extensive iron holdings to feed state-run munitions and shipbuilding facilities. Without urbanizing extensively or developing a large commercial class, Peter's reforms changed the Russian economy. Landlords were rewarded for using serf labor to staff new manufacturing operations. This was a limited goal but a very important one, giving Russia the internal economic means to maintain a substantial military presence for almost two centuries.

Finally, Peter was eager to make Russia culturally respectable in Western eyes. Before Peter the Great, it was a custom in upper-class marriages for the father of the bride to pass a small whip to the groom. This symbolized the transfer of male power over women. Peter, knowing that upper-class women had greater freedom in the West, abolished this practice. He also encouraged upper-class women to wear Western-style clothing and attend public cultural events. He found support among women as a result. He also reduced a source of embarrassment among Westerners in Russia, who otherwise could easily point to uncivilized

treatment of women. But, as with most of his reforms, he made no move to change gender relations among the masses of Russian peasants.

Peter was eager to cut the Russian elite off from its traditions, to enhance state power, and to commit the elite to new identities. He required male nobles to shave off their beards (Figure 18.2) and also wear Western clothes; in symbolic ceremonies he cut off the long, Mongol-type sleeves and pigtails that were characteristic of the boyars. Thus, traditional appearance was forcibly altered as part of Western-oriented change, although only the upper class was involved.

Cultural change supplemented bureaucratic training. Of greater substance were attempts to provide more education in mathematics and other technical subjects for the nobility. Peter and his successors founded scientific institutes and academies along Western lines, and serious discussion of the latest scientific and technical findings became common. At the elite level, Peter built Russia into a Western cultural zone, and Western fads and fashions extended easily into the glittering new capital city. Ballet, ini-

Figure 18.2 *This contemporary Russian cartoon lampoons Peter the Great's order to his nobility to cut off their beards.*

tially encouraged in the French royal court, was imported and became a Russian specialty. The use of Christmas trees came from Germany.

This westernization effort had several features that can be compared with imitation processes in other societies later on. In the first place, the changes were selective. Peter did not try to touch the ordinary people of Russia or to involve them in the technological and intellectual aspects of westernization. New manufacturing involved serf labor that was partially coerced, not the wage-labor spreading in the West. There was no interest in building the kind of worldwide export economy characteristic of the West. Peter wanted economic development to support military strength rather than to achieve wider commercial goals. Finally, westernization was meant to encourage the autocratic state, not to challenge it with some of the new political ideas circulating in the West. This was real change, but it did not fold Russia into Western civilization outright. Selectivity was crucial, and there was no interest in abandoning particularly Russian goals.

Furthermore, the westernization that did occur brought hostile responses. Many peasants resented the westernized airs and expenses of their landlords, some of whom no longer even knew Russian but spoke only French. Elements of the elite opposed Peter's thirst for change, arguing that Russian traditions were superior to those of the West. As one priest wrote to Tsar Alexis, "You feed the foreigners too well, instead of bidding your folk to cling to the old customs." This tension continued in Russian history from this point forward, leading to important cycles of enthusiasm and revulsion toward Western values.

Consolidation Under Catherine the Great

The death of Peter the Great in 1724 was followed by several decades of weak rule, dominated in part by power plays among army officers who guided the selection of several ineffective emperors and empresses. The weakness of tsardom in these years encouraged new grumblings about undue westernization and some new initiatives by church officials eager to gain more freedom of maneuver, but no major new policy directions were set. Russian territorial expansion continued, with several clashes with the Ottoman Empire and further exploration and settlement in Siberia. In 1761, Peter III, nephew of

Peter the Great's youngest daughter, reached the throne. He was retarded, but his wife, a German-born princess who changed her name to Catherine—and was later known as **Catherine the Great**—soon took matters in hand and continued to rule as empress after Peter III's death (see Figure 18.3). Catherine resumed Peter the Great's interests in several respects. She defended the powers of the central monarch. She put down a vigorous peasant uprising, led by Emelian Pugachev, butchering Pugachev himself. She used the **Pugachev rebellion** as an excuse to extend the powers of the central government in regional affairs.

Catherine II (the Great) (1729–1796) is one of the fascinating women leaders of history. Born a Prussian princess, she converted to the Orthodox faith after her marriage to the heir to the Russian throne was arranged. Her married life was miserable, with frequent threats of divorce from her husband. She also disliked her son, the future tsar Paul I.

Figure 18.3 *Catherine the Great. Test your stereotypes: Does her appearance correspond to your expectations as you read about what Catherine did?*

Carefully cultivating the Russian court, Catherine benefited from a plot to dethrone her husband, Peter III, after an unpopular foreign policy move. Officers of the palace guard installed her as empress in 1762. The tsar was later murdered, possibly with Catherine's consent. Catherine's reign combined genuine Enlightenment interests with her need to consolidate power as a truly Russian ruler—a combination that explains the complexities of her policies. Like many male rulers, Catherine maintained an active personal life and had a succession of lovers, some of them politically influential.

Like Peter the Great, Catherine was also a selective westernizer, as her "instruction of 1767" (see the Document section) clearly demonstrated. She flirted with the ideas of the French Enlightenment, importing several French philosophers for visits and patronizing the arts and sciences. She summoned various reform commissions to discuss new law codes and other Western-style measures, including reduction of traditionally severe punishments.

Catherine's image was not always consistent with her policies, however. She was a centralizer and certainly an advocate of a strong tsarist hand. But Catherine also gave new powers to the nobility over their serfs, maintaining a trade-off that had been developing over the previous two centuries in Russia. In this trade-off, nobles served a strong central government and staffed it as bureaucrats and officers. They were in this sense a service aristocracy, not an independent force. They also accepted into their ranks newly ennobled officials chosen by the tsars. In return, however, most of the actual administration over local peasants, except for those on government-run estates, was wielded by the noble landlords. These landlords could requisition peasant labor, levy taxes in money and goods, and even impose punishments for crimes because landlord-dominated courts administered local justice. Catherine increased the harshness of punishments nobles could decree for their serfs.

Catherine patronized Western-style art and architecture, continuing to build St. Petersburg in the classical styles popular at the same time in the West and encouraging leading nobles to tour the West and even send their children to be educated there. But she also tried to avoid cultural influence from the West. When the great French Revolution broke out in 1789, Catherine was quick to close Russia's doors to the "seditious" writings of liberals and democrats. She also censored a small but emerging band of Russian intellectuals who urged reforms along Western lines. One of the first Western-inspired radicals, a noble named Radishev, who sought abolition of serfdom and more liberal political rule, was vigorously harassed by Catherine's police, and his writings were banned.

Catherine pursued the tradition of Russian expansion with energy and success. She resumed campaigns against the Ottoman Empire, winning new territories in central Asia, including the Crimea, bordering the Black Sea. The Russian–Ottoman contest became a central diplomatic issue for both powers, and Russia became increasingly ascendant. Catherine accelerated the colonization of Russia's holdings in Siberia and encouraged further exploration, claiming the territory of Alaska in Russia's name. Russian explorers also moved down the Pacific coast of North America into what is now northern California, and tens of thousands of pioneers spread over Siberia.

Finally, Catherine pressed Russia's interests in Europe, playing power politics with Prussia and Austria, though without risking major wars. She increased Russian interference in Polish affairs. The Polish government was extremely weak, almost paralyzed by a parliamentary system that let members of the nobility veto any significant measure, and this invited interest by more powerful neighbors. Russia was able to win agreements with Austria and Prussia for the **partition of Poland.** Three partitions, in 1772, 1793, and 1795, eliminated Poland as an independent state, and Russia held the lion's share of the spoils. The basis for further Russian involvement in European affairs had obviously been created, and this would show in Russia's ultimate role in putting down the French armies of Napoleon after 1812—the first time Russian troops moved into the heartland of western Europe.

By the time of Catherine's death in 1796, Russia had passed through three centuries of extraordinary development. It had won independence and constructed a strong central state, though one that had to maintain a balance with the local political and economic interests of a powerful nobility. It had brought new elements into Russia's culture and economy, in part by borrowing from the West. And it had extended its control over the largest land empire in the world (Map 18.3). In the east it bordered China, where an 18th-century Amur River agreement set new frontiers. A tradition of careful but successful military aggrandizement had been established, along with a real pioneering spirit of settlement. It is no wonder that not long after 1800, a perceptive French observer, Alexis

Document

The Nature of Westernization

Peter the Great and Catherine the Great were the two chief reformist rulers in Russia before 1800. In the first of the following edicts, Peter focuses on educational change; his approach reflected a real desire for innovation, Russia's autocratic tradition in government, and its hierarchical social structure. Catherine's "Instruction" borrowed heavily from Western philosophers and was hailed by one French intellectual as "the finest monument of the century." This document also showed distinctively Russian traditions and problems. However, the reforms in law and punishment were not put into practice, and the document itself was banned as subversive by Catherine's successor, as Russia's rulers began to fear the subversive qualities of Western influence after the French Revolution.

Decrees on Compulsory Education of the Russian Nobility, January 12 and February 28, 1714

Send to every *gubernia* [region] some persons from mathematical schools to teach the children of the nobility—except those of freeholders and government clerks—mathematics and geometry; as a penalty [for evasion] establish a rule that no one will be allowed to marry unless he learns these [subjects]. Inform all prelates to issue no marriage certificates to those who are ordered to go to schools….

The Great Sovereign has decreed: in all *gubernias* children between the ages of ten and fifteen of the nobility, of government clerks, and of lesser officials, except those of freeholders, must be taught mathematics and some geometry. Toward that end, students should be sent from mathematical schools [as teachers], several into each *gubernia*, to prelates and to renowned monasteries to establish schools. During their instruction these teachers should be given food and financial remuneration of three altyns and two dengas per day from *gubernia* revenues set aside for that purpose by personal orders of His Imperial Majesty. No fees should be collected from students. When they have mastered the material, they should then be given certificates written in their own handwriting. When the students are released they ought to pay one ruble each for their training.

Without these certificates they should not be allowed to marry or receive marriage certificates.

The "Instruction" of 1767

6. Russia is a European State.

7. This is clearly demonstrated by the following Observations: The Alterations which Peter the Great undertook in Russia succeeded with the greater Ease, because the Manners, which prevailed at that Time, and had been introduced amongst us by a Mixture of different Nations, and the Conquest of foreign Territories, were quite unsuitable to the Climate. Peter the First, by introducing the Manners and Customs of Europe among the European People in his Dominions, found at that Time such Means as even he himself was not sanguine enough to expect.

8. The Possessions of the Russian Empire extend upon the terrestrial Globe to 32 Degrees of Latitude, and to 165 of Longitude.

9. The Sovereign is absolute; for there is no other Authority but that which centers in his single Person, that can act with a Vigour proportionate to the Extent of such a vast Dominion.

10. The Extent of the Dominion requires an absolute Power to be vested in that Person who rules over it. It is expedient so to be, that the quick Dispatch of Affairs, sent from distant Parts, might make ample Amends for the delay occasioned by the great Distance of the Places.

11. Every other Form of Government whatsoever would not only have been prejudicial to Russia, but would even have proved its entire Ruin.

12. Another Reason is: That it is better to be subject to the Laws under one Master, than to be subservient to many.

13. What is the true End of Monarchy? Not to deprive People of their natural Liberty; but correct their Actions, in order to attain the supreme Good….

272. The more happily a People live under a government, the more easily the Number of the Inhabitants increases….

519. It is certain, that a *high* opinion of the *Glory* and *Power* of the Sovereign, would *increase* the *Strength* of his Administration; but a *good Opinion of his Love of Justice, will increase it at least as much.*

520. All this will never please those flatterers, who are daily instilling this pernicious Maxim into all the Sovereign on Earth, That their People are created for them only. But We think, and esteem it Our Glory to declare, "That We are created for Our People; and, of this Reason, We are obliged to Speak of Things just as they ought to be." For God forbid! That, after this Legislation is finished, any Nation on Earth should be more just; and, consequently, should flourish, more than Russia; otherwise the Intention of Our Laws would be totally frustrated; an Unhappiness which I do not wish to survive.

Questions: In what sense did reformist measures strengthen Russian autocracy? Why might 18th-century Western thinkers admire reformist tsars? What relationships to the West did the reform measures suggest? What do the documents suggest about the motivations of leaders such as Peter and Catherine? Were they similar? Which westernizer maintained a closer match between their claims and appearances and Russia's real conditions?

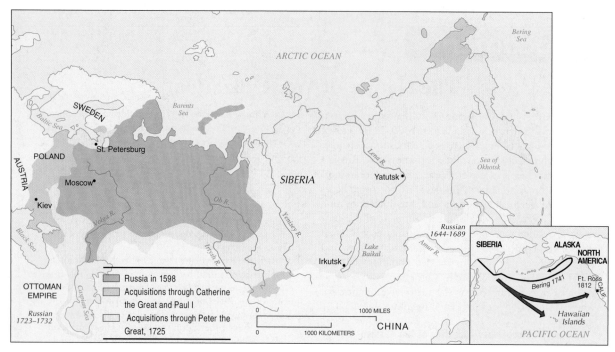

Map 18.3   *Russia's Holdings by 1800. Expansion fluctuated from one decade to the next but persisted, bringing Russia into encounters with three other civilization areas.*

de Tocqueville, likened the expanded and increasingly important Russia to the new country emerging in the Western Hemisphere, the United States of America, as the two new giants of future world history.

Themes in Early Modern Russian History

Russian society differed greatly from that of the West. It focused on serfdom and a deep-rooted peasant culture. The gap between Russia's traditional economic and social structure and its westernization efforts at the top set up some durable tensions on the nation's history, visible even today. Although Russian serfdom was particularly severe, a similar social system developed in other east European areas.

Because of its great estates, its local political power, and its service to the state, the Russian nobility maintained a vital position in Russian society. In Russia and in eastern Europe generally, landed nobles

tended to be divided between a minority of great magnates, who lived in major cities and provided key cultural patronage, and smaller landowners, whose culture was less westernized and whose lifestyle was much less opulent.

Serfdom: The Life of East Europe's Masses

During the 17th and 18th centuries, the power of the nobility over the serfs increased steadily. Before the Mongol conquest, Russian peasants had been largely free farmers with a legal position superior to that of their medieval Western counterparts. After the expulsion of the Tatars, however, increasing numbers of Russian peasants fell into debt and had to accept servile status to the noble landowners when they could not repay. They retained access to much of the land, but not primary ownership. The Russian government actively encouraged this process from the 16th century onward. Serfdom gave the government a way to satisfy the nobility and regulate peasants when the government itself lacked the bureaucratic means to extend direct controls over the common people. As new territories were added to the empire, the system of serfdom was extended accordingly, sometimes after a period of free farming.

By 1800, half of Russia's peasantry was enserfed to the landlords, and much of the other half owed comparable obligations to the state. Laws passed during the 17th and 18th centuries tied the serfs to the land and increased the legal rights of the landlords. An act in 1649 fixed the hereditary status of the serfs, so that people born to that station could not legally escape it.

Russia was setting up a system of serfdom very close to outright slavery in that serfs could be bought and sold, gambled away, and punished by their masters. The system was a very unusual case in which a people essentially enslaved many of its own members, in contrast to most slave systems, which focused on "outsiders."

Rural conditions in many other parts of eastern Europe were similar. Nobles maintained estate agriculture in Poland, Hungary, and elsewhere. They used the system to support their political control and distinctive lifestyle, as in Russia.

The intensification of estate agriculture and serf labor also reflected eastern Europe's growing economic subordination to the West; in this sense the systems should be compared with developments in Latin America, despite very different specific origins (see Chapter 19). Coerced labor was used to produce grain surpluses sold to Western merchants for the growing cities of western Europe. In return, Western merchants brought in manufactured goods, including the luxury furnishings and clothing essential to the aristocratic lifestyle.

Serfs on the estates of eastern Europe were taxed and policed by their landlords. In Russia, whole villages were sold as manufacturing labor—a process Peter the Great actively encouraged. Peasants were not literally slaves. They continued to use village governments to regulate many aspects of their lives, relying more heavily on community ties than their counterparts in the Western countryside. Yet most peasants were illiterate and quite poor. They paid high taxes or obligations in kind, and they owed extensive labor service to the landlords or the government—a source not only of agricultural production but also of mining and manufacturing. The labor obligation tended to increase steadily. Both the economic and the legal situation of the peasantry continued to deteriorate. Although Catherine the Great sponsored a few model villages to display her enlightenment to Western-minded friends, she turned the government of the serfs over to the landlords more completely than ever before. A law of 1785 allowed landlords to punish harshly any serfs convicted of major crimes or rebellion.

Trade and Economic Dependence

In between serfs and landlords, there were few layers of Russian society. Cities were small, and 95 percent of the population remained rural. (Most manufacturing took place in the countryside, so there was no well-defined artisan class.) Government growth encouraged some nonnoble bureaucrats and professionals. Small merchant groups existed as well, although most of Russia's European trade was handled by Westerners posted to the main Russian cities and relying on Western shipping. The nobility, concerned about this potential social competition, prevented the emergence of a substantial merchant class.

Russia's social and economic system worked well in many respects. It produced enough revenue to support an expanding state and empire. Russia was able to trade in furs and other commodities with areas in central Asia outside its boundaries, which meant that its export economy was not totally oriented toward the more dynamic West. It underwrote the aristocratic magnates and their glittering, westernized culture. The system, along with Russia's expansion, yielded significant population growth: Russia's population doubled during the 18th century to 36 million. For an empire burdened by a harsh climate in most regions, this was no small achievement. Despite periodic famines and epidemics, there was no question that the overall economy had advanced.

Yet the system suffered from important limitations. Most agricultural methods were highly traditional, and there was little motivation among the peasantry for improvement because increased production usually was taken by the state or the landlord. Landlords debated agricultural improvements in their academies, but when it came time to increase production, they concentrated on squeezing the serfs. Manufacturing lagged behind

Visualizing the Past

Oppressed Peasants

This painting is from the early 20th century (1907), when revolutionary currents were swirling in Russia and the status of the peasantry was widely discussed. This raises obvious issues of interpretation. The subject of the painting, tax collection and the poor material conditions of 17th-century peasants, is accurate.

Questions: Does this painting suggest early 20th-century rather than 17th-century sympathies in Russian culture? If so, in what ways? Does the painting include any glaring inaccuracies? Given the lack of popular art from the 17th century itself, except religious art, does the painting provide useful material for understanding peasant conditions? What elements were probably guesswork on the artist's part? What aspects of the tax collector's appearance suggest that the artist was striving for an accurate rendition of the ways officials looked *before* the reforms of Peter the Great?

Western standards, despite the important extension developed under Peter the Great.

Social Unrest

Russia's economic and social system led to protest. By the end of the 18th century, a small but growing number of Western-oriented aristocrats such as Radishev were criticizing the regime's backwardness, urging measures as far-reaching as the abolition of serfdom. Here were the seeds of a radical intelligentsia that, despite government repression, would grow with time. More significant still were the recurring peasant rebellions. Russian peasants for the most part were politically loyal to the tsar, but they harbored bitter resentments against their landlords, whom they accused of taking lands that were rightfully theirs. Periodic rebellions saw peasants destroy manorial records, seize land, and sometimes kill landlords and their officials.

Peasant rebellions had occurred from the 17th century onward, but the Pugachev rebellion of the 1770s was particularly strong. Pugachev (Figure 18.4), a cossack chieftain who claimed to be the legitimate tsar, promised an end to serfdom, taxation, and military conscription along with the abolition of the landed aristocracy. His forces roamed over southern Russia until they were finally defeated. Pugachev was brought to Moscow in a case and cut into quarters in a public square. The triumph of Catherine and the nobility highlighted the mutual dependence of government and the upper class but did not end protest. Radishev, finding peasants barely able to work their own plots of land and sometimes tortured to work harder, thought he saw the handwriting on the wall: "Tremble, cruel hearted landlord! On the brow of each of your peasants I see your condemnation written."

Russia and Eastern Europe

Russian history did not include the whole of eastern Europe after the 15th century. Regions west of Russia continued to form a fluctuating borderland between west European and east European influences. Even in the Balkans, under Ottoman control, growing trade with the West sparked some new cultural exchange by the 18th century, as Greek merchants, for example, picked up many Enlightenment ideas.

Areas such as present-day Poland or the Czech and Slovak regions operated more fully within the Western cultural orbit. The Polish scientist Copernicus was an early participant in fundamental discoveries in what became the Scientific Revolution. Western currents such as the Reformation also echoed in parts of east central Europe such as Hungary.

At the same time, many smaller east European nationalities lost political autonomy during the early modern era. Hungary, freed from the Ottomans, became part of the German-dominated Habsburg Empire. This empire also took over the Czech lands,

Figure 18.4 *After the great serf revolt, its cossack leader, Emelian Pugachev, was imprisoned and then executed.*

then called Bohemia. Prussian territory pushed eastward into Polish areas.

The decline of Poland was particularly striking. In 1500, Poland, formed in 1386 by a union of the regional kingdoms of Poland and Lithuania, was the largest state in eastern Europe aside from Russia. Polish cultural life, linked with the West through shared Roman Catholicism, flourished in the 16th century. By 1600, however, economic and political setbacks mounted. Polish aristocrats, charged with electing the king, began deliberately choosing weak figures. As in Russia, urban centers, and thus a merchant class, were lacking. The aristocratic parliament vetoed any reform efforts until late in the 18th century, after Poland began to be partitioned by its more powerful neighbors. The eclipse of Poland highlighted Russian emergence on the European as well as the Eurasian stage.

In Depth

Multinational Empires

Of all the new multinational empires created in the early modern period, Russia's was the most successful, lasting until 1991 and to an extent beyond. In contrast, India's Mughal Empire disappeared completely by the mid-19th century, and the Ottoman and Habsburg empires flickered until after World War I. All the multinational empires were reasonably tolerant of internal diversity (like the Roman and Arab empires of the past, two other multinational entities). The Russian tsar, for example, called himself "Khan of the north" to impress central Asian people and took oaths of loyalty from this region on the Qur'an. However, Russia differed from Asian empires and the Habsburgs in having a larger core of ethnic groups ready to fan out to the frontiers and establish pioneer settlements that sometimes developed into larger Russian enclaves. Russia also benefited from its willingness and ability to copy the West selectively, in contrast most obviously to the Ottoman Empire in the same period. This copying provided access to new military technologies and some new organizational forms.

Ironically, the same period that saw the creation of so many new empires also confirmed the importance of the culturally more cohesive nation-state, the dominant form in western Europe. England and France, prototypical nation-states, were not culturally homogeneous; they had important pockets of minorities who differed linguistically or religiously from the majority culture. But both maintained a clear basis for joining the political unit to the cultural one to foster loyalty. Efforts by the 17th-century French kings to purify and standardize the French language, or by English parliamentarians to claim empowerment from the "rights of freeborn Englishmen," were early signs that politics and national culture were coming together.

The clash between national loyalties and multinational empires did not become serious until the 19th century, and it has continued into the 21st. In the long run, most multinational states have not been able to sustain themselves in the face of increasing demands from individual national groups. The collapse of several multinational units in the 20th century—the Ottomans in the Middle East, the Habsburgs in east central Europe, and the Russians—created new diplomatic trouble spots quite obvious in the world today, for stable nation-states have had a hard time developing in these regions.

Questions: Why have nation-states been more successful, as political units, in modern world history than multinational empires have been? In what ways did the Russian Empire develop some nation-state characteristics? What were its principal multinational features? Amid new needs for international economic coordination in the 21st century, is it possible to build multinational organizations on some new basis?

 ## GLOBAL CONNECTIONS: Russia and the World

From a world history standpoint, Russia's emergence as a key player both in Europe and in Asia was a crucial development in the early modern period. Today, Russia spans 10 time zones, and much of this territory had been acquired by the late 18th century. By this point, Russia was affecting diplomatic and military developments in Europe, in the Middle East (through its frequent battles with the Ottoman Empire), and in east Asia. It had gained a direct hold in central Asia. The spread of Russian claims to Alaska, and expeditions even to Hawaii, hinted at an even larger role. This was a different kind of empire from those Western nations were building, but it had huge impact.

Further Readings

For excellent survey coverage on this period, as well as additional bibliography, see Nicholas Riasanovsky's *History of Russia* (5th ed., 1992). Two excellent source collections for this vital period of Russian history are T. Riha, ed., *Readings in Russian Civilization, Vol. 2, Imperial Russia 1700–1917* (1969), and Basil Dmytryshyn, *Imperial Russia: A Sourcebook 1700–1917* (1967).

On important regimes, see P. Dukes, *The Making of Russian Absolutism: 1613–1801* (1982); J. L. I. Fennell, *Ivan the Great of Moscow* (1961); L. Hughes, *Russia in the Age of*

Peter the Great (1998); R. Massie, *Peter the Great* (1981); and N. V. Riasanovsky, *The Image of Peter the Great in Russian History and Thought* (1985). This last book is a very interesting interpretive effort. On Catherine, see I. de Madariaga's *Russia in the Age of Catherine the Great* (1981).

Three good studies deal with cultural history: H. Rogger, *National Consciousness in Eighteenth Century Russia* (1963); Marc Raeff, *Origins of the Russian Intelligentsia: The Eighteenth Century Nobility* (1966); and Marc Raeff, ed., *Russian Intellectual History* (1986).

For economic and social history, A. Kahan's *The Knout and the Plowshare: Economic History of Russia in the 18th Century* (1985) is an important treatment. For the vital peasant question, see Jerome Blum's *Lord and Peasant in Russia from the Ninth to the Nineteenth Century* (1961); see also Richard Hellie's *Slavery in Russia, 1450–1725* (1982). For an analytical overview, see Marc Raeff's *Understanding Imperial Russia: State and Society in the Old Regime* (1984). A very revealing comparison is Peter Kolchin, *Unfree Labor: American Slavery and Russian Serfdom* (1987). A fine recent survey on military and diplomatic strategy is William Fuller, *Strategy and Power in Russia, 1600–1914* (1992).

On the Web

A vivid introduction to Russian history is offered at http://www.departments.bucknell.edu/russian/index. html. Russia before the Romanovs is examined at http://geographica.com/russia/rushis 4.htm and http://www.alexanderpalace.org/. Peter the Great's maritime interests are examined at http://www. maritimeheritage.org/ports/europe/russia.html. The lives of Peter the Great and Catherine the Great are seen against the backdrop of early modern Russia at http://emuseum.mnsu.edu/history/russia/peter.html and http://emuseum.mnsu.edu/history/russia/catherine. html. A virtual tour of their capital is available at http://www.cityvision2000.com/city_tour/index.htm. A colorful slice of Czarist life is revealed by a virtual exhibit on the snuffboxes of Catherine the Great at http://www. hermitage.museum.org/html_En/03/hm3_6_4.html.

Cossack life is presented at http://www.sfu.ca/ archaeology/museum/russia/cossack.htm, http://www.stanford.edu/~gfreidin/courses/147/ cossack.htm and http://www.cossackweb.com/ cossacks/hst_all.htm. Catherine the Great's response to the rebellion led by a Don Cossack, Emelian Pugachev, and how it illuminated the differences in the political landscape of revolutionary France and absolutist Russia, is described at http://mars.acnet.wnec.edu/~grempel/ courses/russia/lectures/16catherine.html. An overview of Pugachev's Rebellion can be supplemented by reading his *ukaz* or order recorded at http://artsci.shu.edu/ reesp/documents/pugachev.htm.

CHAPTER 19

EARLY LATIN AMERICA

The arrival of the Spaniards in Mexico brought Europeans into contact for the first time with the great civilizations of Mesoamerica. This depiction of the Spaniards by a Native American artist, drawn after the conquest, demonstrates a fusion of European and indigenous forms of representation.

- Spaniards and Portuguese: From Reconquest to Conquest
- DOCUMENT: A Vision from the Vanquished
- The Destruction and Transformation of American Indian Societies
- IN DEPTH: The Great Exchange
- Colonial Economies and Governments
- Brazil: The First Plantation Colony
- Multiracial Societies
- VISUALIZING THE PAST: Race or Culture? A Changing Society
- The 18th-Century Reforms
- GLOBAL CONNECTIONS: Latin American Civilization and the World Context

When Hernán Cortés, the Spanish conquistador, first gazed upon the Aztec capital of Tenochtitlan he was almost struck dumb by its beauty. The whitewashed walls and roof gardens of its houses, the gold of its temples shining so brightly in the sun that he thought the entire city might be roofed with precious metals, dazzled him and his men. He was also overwhelmed by the city's size that dwarfed most European cities of the time. But what impressed him most was its setting. Seeming to float on the surface of a great lake, the city was crisscrossed by canals teeming with boats. The Spaniards thought that it could only be compared with Venice, whose own canals traversed one the richest and most beautiful cities of Europe. Later, w hen the Spaniards first saw the Inca cities of Peru like Cuzco, they were similarly impressed.

In the initial conquests, these cities were sacked, the temples destroyed, and the rubble used as the foundation for the conquerors' own houses of worship. Eventually, the new arrivals would attempt to assume the mantle of Aztec and Inca glory and even to exploit some of the same practices like forced labor used by their Native American predecessors. But this pattern of conquest and continuity and rebuilding on the ruins of the past was not new. The Aztecs had once been newcomers in the valley of Mexico, inheriting the mantle of leadership from the Toltecs, who in turn had absorbed the way of life of the earlier civilization of Teotihuacan. The Incas of Peru had also conquered, but then incorporated the peoples around them, adopting from them and following ancient customs. The Americas on the eve of conquest was but one layer of a centuries old cultural base, much of which survived even after the jolt of invasion by the newcomers from across the sea.

Still, the Europeans' arrival was a shock, which would be amplified in the decades that followed. According to later Aztec accounts (possibly embellished by the Spaniards), Moctezuma, emperor of the Aztecs, grew alarmed when news of strange ships and men reached him in 1519. He heard stories of hills that moved on the waves carrying bearded white men who came mounted on stags or on eagles. In fact, within four years, Moctezuma was dead and his empire destroyed by the new overlords who ruled in his place.

The European conquest of the Americas was a process with tremendous impact on those peoples and on the world in general. During the 15th and 16th centuries, Spain and Portugal created empires in the Americas by conquest and settlement. These lands, what became Latin America, were immediately drawn into a new world economy, providing silver, gold, new crops,

1450 C.E.	1500 C.E.	1600 C.E.	1750 C.E.
1493–1520 Exploration and settlement in the Caribbean **1494** Treaty of Tordesillar **1492** Fall of Granada, last Muslim kingdom in Spain; expulsion of the Jews; Columbus landfall in the Caribbean **1493** Columbus's second expedition; beginnings of settlement in the Indies	**1500** Cabral lands in Brazil **1519–1524** Cortés leads conquest of Mexico **1533** Cuzco, Peru, falls to Francisco Pizarro **1541** Santiago, Chile, founded **1540–1542** Coronado explores southwestern United States **1549** Royal government established in Brazil **1580–1640** Spain and Portugal united under same rulers	**1630–1654** Dutch capture northeastern Brazil **1654** English take Jamaica **1695** Gold discovered in Brazil **1702–1713** War of the Spanish succession; Bourbon dynasty rules Spain	**1755–1776** Marquis of Pombal, prime minister of Portugal **1759** Jesuits expelled from Brazil **1756–1763** Seven Years' War **1759–1788** Carlos III rules Spain; Bourbon reforms **1763** Brazilian capital moved to Rio de Janeiro **1767** Jesuits expelled from Spanish America **1781** Comunero revolt in New Granada; Tupac Amaru rebellion in Peru **1788** Conspiracy for independence in Minas Gerais, Brazil

and other goods. The emerging hierarchy of world economic relationships shaped conditions in this new civilization for several centuries.

The societies of Latin America also created important new political and cultural forms. The Spaniards and Portuguese, often called Iberians because they came from the Iberian peninsula in Europe, mixed with Native Americans and their earlier civilization forms and were influenced by imported African slaves. The formative period for Latin American civilization extended from initial contacts in the 1490s through the 18th century, when colonial structures began to decline. This period spanned a number of stages, from raw conquest to growing economic and political complexity by the 18th century.

New societies, created by the intrusion of Spaniards and Portuguese and by the incorporation or destruction of Native American cultures, arose throughout the American continents. Both Europeans and Native Americans drew heavily on their previous experiences as they grappled with the problems created by their encounter with one other. Much of what the Iberians did in the Americas followed the patterns and examples of their European traditions. The Native Americans who survived, although they were battered and profoundly transformed, showed a vitality and resiliency that shaped later societies in many ways. What resulted drew on European and Native American precedents, but it was something new: the world's latest addition to the list of distinctive civilizations.

Various European peoples sought the same ends in the New World: economic gain and social mobility. The Portuguese, English, Spanish, Dutch, and French all created large landed estates, or plantations, worked by coerced laborers—ultimately African slaves—wherever tropical conditions and European demand made such enterprises feasible. The Europeans exploited precious metals when they were discovered, and those who did not find the metals followed rumors of gold or emeralds.

Spaniards and Portuguese: From Reconquest to Conquest

 The Spaniards and Portuguese came from societies long in contact with peoples of other faiths and cultures in which warfare and conquest were well-established activities. American realities and the resistance of indigenous peoples modified these traditions, first in the Caribbean and then on the mainland as Spaniards and Portuguese with the backing of the state moved to conquer and settle. By the 1570s, much of the Americas had been brought under Iberian control.

The peoples that inhabited the Iberian peninsula, Spain and Portugal, had long lived at the frontier of Mediterranean Europe. During the Middle Ages their lands had become a cultural frontier between Christianity and Islam. Conflicts created a strong tradition of military conquest and rule over peoples of other beliefs and customs. Christian kingdoms had emerged, such as Portugal on the Atlantic coast, Aragon in eastern Spain, and in the center of the peninsula, Castile, the largest of all. By the mid-15th century, the rulers **Ferdinand of Aragon** and his wife **Isabella of Castile** carried out a program of unification that sought to eliminate the religious and ethnic diversity in their kingdoms. With the fall in 1492 of Granada, the last Muslim kingdom, the cross had triumphed throughout the peninsula. Moved by political savvy and religious fervor, Isabella ordered the Jews of her realm to convert or leave the country. As many as 200,000 people may have left, severely disrupting some aspects of the Castilian economy. It was also in 1492, with the Granada War at an end and religious unification established, that Isabella and Ferdinand were willing to support the project of a Genoese mariner named Christopher Columbus, who hoped to reach the East Indies by sailing westward around the globe.

Iberian Society and Tradition

Like many Mediterranean peoples, the Spanish and Portuguese were heavily urban, with many peasants living in small towns and villages. The desire to live in an urban setting helped set up a pattern of Spanish cities amid a largely American Indian countryside.

Many commoners who came to America as conquerors sought to recreate themselves as a new nobility, with native peoples as their serfs. The patriarchal family was readily adapted to Latin America, where large estates and grants of American Indian laborers, or **encomiendas,** provided the framework for relations based on economic dominance. The Iberian peninsula had maintained a tradition of holding slaves—part of its experience as an ethnic frontier—in contrast to most of medieval Europe, and African slaves had been imported from the trans-Sahara trade. The extension of slavery to America built on this tradition.

The political centralization of both Portugal and Castile depended on a professional bureaucracy, usually made up of men trained as lawyers and judges. This system is worthy of comparison with China and other great empires. Religion and the church served as the other pillar of Iberian politics; close links between church and state resulted from the reconquest of the peninsula from the Muslims, and these links, including royal nomination of church officials, were also extended to the New World.

Spanish and particularly Portuguese merchants also shaped traditions that became relevant in the American colonies. Portugal had been moving down the African coast since 1415, establishing trading posts rather than outright colonies. In the Atlantic islands, however, more extensive estates were established, leading to a slave trade with Africa and a highly commercial agricultural system based on sugar. Brazil would extend this pattern, starting out as a trade factory but then shifting, as in the Atlantic islands, to plantation agriculture.

The Chronology of Conquest

The Spanish and Portuguese conquest and colonization of the Americas falls roughly into three periods during the early modern centuries: first, an era of conquest from 1492 to about 1570 (Map 19.1), during which the main lines of administration and economy were set out; second, a phase of consolidation and maturity from 1570 to about 1700 in which the colonial institutions and societies took their definite form; and finally, during the 18th century, a period of reform and reorganization in both Spanish America and Portuguese Brazil that intensified the colonial relationship and planted the seeds of dissatisfaction and revolt.

The period from 1492 to about 1570 witnessed a remarkable spurt of human destruction and creation.

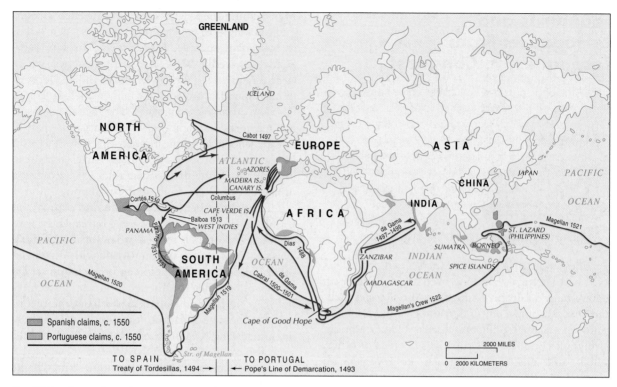

Map 19.1   *Spanish and Portuguese Explorations, 1400–1600*

During roughly a century, vast areas of two continents and millions of people were brought under European control. Immigration, commerce, and exploitation of native populations linked these areas to an emerging Atlantic economy. These processes were accompanied and made possible by the conquest and destruction of many American Indian societies and the transformation of others, as well as by the introduction in some places of African slaves. Mexico and Peru, with their large sedentary populations and mineral resources, attracted the Spaniards and became the focus of immigration and institution building. Other conquests radiated outward from the Peruvian and Mexican centers.

The Caribbean Crucible

The **Caribbean** experience served Spain as a model for its actions elsewhere in the Americas. After Columbus' original voyage in 1492, a return expedition in the next year established a colony on the island of Santo Domingo, or **Hispaniola** (Figure 19.1). From there and from Spain, expeditions car-

ried out new explorations and conquests. Puerto Rico (1508) and Cuba (1511) fell under Spanish control, and by 1513 settlements existed in Panama and on the northern coast of South America.

In the Caribbean, the agricultural Taino people of the islands provided enough surplus labor to make their distribution to individual Spaniards feasible, and thus began what would become the encomienda, or grant of indigenous people to individual Spaniards in a kind of serfdom. The holder of an encomienda, an **encomendero,** was able to use the people as workers or to tax them. Gold hunting, slaving, and European diseases rapidly depopulated the islands, and within two decades little was left there to hold Spanish attention. A few strongly fortified ports, such as Havana, San Juan, and Santo Domingo, guarded Spain's commercial lifeline, but on the whole the Caribbean became a colonial backwater for the next two centuries, until sugar and slaves became the basis of its resurgence.

In the 40 years between the first voyage of Columbus and the conquest of Mexico, the Caribbean served as a testing ground. The Spaniards established Iberian-style cities but had to adapt them to American

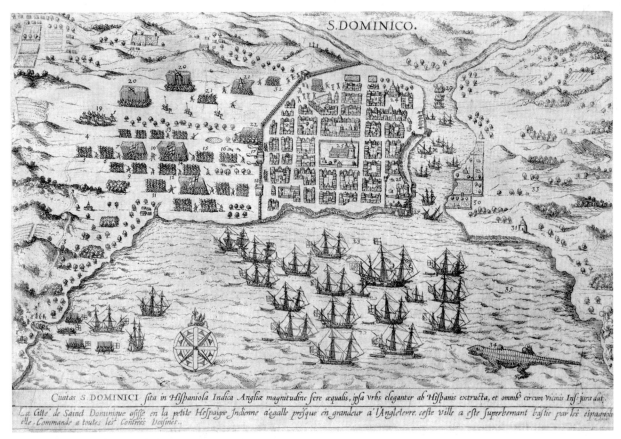

S.DOMINICO.

Ciutas S.DOMINICI sita in Hispaniola Indica Angliæ magnitudine fere æqualis, ipsa vrbs eleganter ab Hispanis extructa, et omnib circum vicinis Insʳ iura dat.*

La Citté de Saind Dominique assise en la petite Hespaigne Indienne ægalle presque en grandeur a l'Angleterre, ceste ville a este superbemant bastie par les espagnols elle Commande a toutes les Contrees Voisines.

Figure 19.1 *The city and port of Santo Domingo was the principal Spanish settlement in the Caribbean in the 16th century.*

realities. Hurricanes and the native peoples' resistance caused many towns to be moved or abandoned, but the New World also provided opportunities to implant new ideas and forms. Unlike cities in Europe, Spanish American cities usually were laid out according to a grid plan or checkerboard form with the town hall, major church, and governor's palace in the central plaza (Figure 19.2). Spaniards applied Roman models and rational town planning ideas to the new situation. Conquest came to imply settlement.

To rule, Spain created administrative institutions: the governorship, the treasury office, and the royal court of appeals staffed by professional magistrates. Spanish legalism was part of the institutional transfer. Notaries accompanied new expeditions, and a body of laws was developed based on those of Spain and augmented by American experience. The church, represented at first by individual priests and then by missionaries such as the Dominicans, participated in

the enterprise. By 1530, a cathedral was being built on Hispaniola, and a university soon followed.

Rumors and hopes stimulated immigration from Spain, and by the 1510s the immigrants included larger numbers of Spanish women. Also, Spanish and Italian merchants began to import African slaves to work on the few sugar plantations that operated on the islands. The arrival of both Spanish women and African slaves represented a shift from an area of conquest to one of settlement. The gold-hunting phase had given out in the islands by the 1520s and was replaced by the establishment of ranches and sugar plantations. The adventurous, the disappointed, and the greedy repeated the pattern as expeditions spun off in new directions.

Disease and conquest virtually annihilated the native peoples of the Caribbean. Depopulation of the laboring population led to slaving on other islands, and in 30 years or so, most of the indigenous

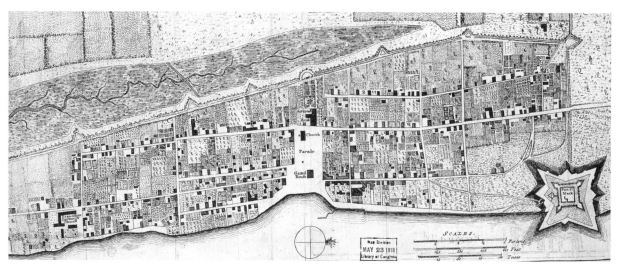

Figure 19.2 *St. Augustine, Florida, the oldest city in the United States (founded in 1565), reflects its Spanish heritage in the central plaza and the checkerboard layout that can be seen in this 18th-century engraving.*

population had died or been killed. The people of the lesser Antilles, or "Caribs," whom the Spanish accused of cannibalism and who were thus always subject to enslavement, held out longer because their islands were less attractive to European settlement. To meet the labor needs of the islands, African slaves were imported.

As early as 1510, the mistreatment and destruction of the American Indians led to attempts by clerics and royal administrators to end the worst abuses. The activities of men such as Dominican friar **Bartolomé de Las Casas** (1484–1566; Figure 19.3), a conquistador turned priest, initiated the struggle for justice.

Expeditions leaped from island to island. Where the native peoples and cultures were more resilient, their impact on the societies that emerged was greater than in the Caribbean, but the process of contact was similar.

By the time of the conquest of Mexico in the 1520s and Peru in the 1530s, all the elements of the colonial system of Latin America were in place. Even in Brazil, which the Portuguese began to exploit after 1500, a period of bartering with the Native Americans was slowly replaced by increasing royal control and development of a sugar plantation economy. There, as in the Caribbean, resistance and subsequent depopulation of the native peoples led to the importation of African laborers.

Figure 19.3 *Father Bartolomé de Las Casas*

Document

A Vision from the Vanquished

History usually is written by the victors, so it is rare to find a detailed statement from the vanquished. In the 17th century, Guaman Poma de Ayala, an acculturated Peruvian Indian who claimed to trace his lineage to the provincial nobility of Inca times, composed a memorial outlining the history of Peru under the Incas and reporting on the current conditions under Spanish rule. Guaman Poma was a Christian and a loyal subject. He hoped that his report would reach King Philip III of Spain, who might then order an end to the worst abuses, among which were the Spanish failure to recognize the rank and status of Indian nobles. His book was not published in his lifetime and was not recovered until the 20th century.

Guaman Poma was an educated, bilingual Indian who spoke Quechua as well as Spanish and who had a profound understanding of Andean culture. His book is remarkable for its revelations of Indian life, for its detailed criticism of the abuses suffered by the Indians, and especially because Guaman Poma illustrated his memorial with a series of drawings that give his words a visual effect. The illustrations also reveal the worldview of this interesting man. The drawings and text offer a critical inside view not of the laws, but of the workings of Spain's empire in America from an Indian point of view.

Miners

At the mercury mines of Huancavelica the Indian workers are punished and ill-treated to such an extent that they die like flies and our whole race is threatened with extermination. Even the chiefs are tortured by being suspended by their feet. Conditions in the silver-mines of Potosí and Chocllococha, or at the gold-mines of Carabaya are little better. The managers and supervisors, who are Spaniards or mestizos, have virtually absolute power. There is no reason for them to fear justice, since they are never brought before the courts.

Beatings are incessant. The victims are mounted for this purpose on a llama's back, tied naked to a round pillar or put in stocks. Their hair is cut off and they are deprived of food and water during detention.

Any shortage in the labor gangs is made an excuse for punishing the chiefs as if they were common thieves or traitors instead of the nobility of the country. The work itself is so hard as to cause permanent injury to many of those who survive it. There is no remuneration for the journey to the mines and a day's labor is paid at the rate for half a day.

Proprietors

Your Majesty has granted large estates, including the right to employ Indian labor, to a number of individuals of whom some are good Christians and the remainder are very bad ones. These encomenderos, as they are termed, may boast about their high position, but in reality they are harmful both to the labor force and to the surviving Indian nobility. I therefore propose to set down the details of their life and conduct.

They exude an air of success as they go from their card games to their dinners in fine silk clothes. Their money is squandered on these luxuries, as well it may, since it costs them no work or sweat whatever. Although the Indians ultimately pay the bill, no concern is ever felt for them or even for Your Majesty or God himself.

Official posts like those of royal administrator and judge ought not to be given to big employers or mine-owners or to their obnoxious sons, because these peoples

(continued)

have enough to live on already. The appointments ought to go to Christian gentlemen of small means, who have rendered some service to the Crown and are educated and humane, not just greedy.

Anybody with rights over Indian labor sees to it that his own household is well supplied with servant girls and indoor and outdoor staff. When collecting dues and taxes, it is usual to impose penalties and detain Indians against their will. There is no redress since, if any complaint is made, the law always favors the employer.

The collection of tribute is delegated to stewards, who make a practice of adding something in for themselves. They too consider themselves entitled to free service and obligatory presents, and they end up as bad as their masters. All of them, and their wives as well, regard themselves as entitled to eat at the Indians' expense.

The Indians are seldom paid the few reales a day which are owed to them, but they are hired out for the porterage of wine and making rope or clothing. Little rest is possible either by day or night and they are usually unable to sleep at home.

It is impossible for servant girls, or even married women, to remain chaste. They are bound to be corrupted and prostituted because employers do not feel any scruple about threatening them with flogging, execution, or burial alive if they refuse to satisfy their master's desires.

The Spanish grandees and their wives have borrowed from the Inca the custom of having themselves conveyed in litters like the images of saints in processions. These Spaniards are absolute lords without fear of either God or retribution. In their own eyes they are judges over our people, whom they can reserve for their personal service or their pleasure, to the detriment of the community.

Great positions are achieved by favour from above, by wealth or by having relations at Court in Castile. With some notable exceptions, the beneficiaries act without consideration for those under their control. The encomenderos call themselves conquerors, but their Conquest was achieved by uttering the words: Ama mancha noca Inca, or "Have no fear. I am Inca." This false pretense was the sum total of their performance.

Questions: What are the main abuses Guaman Poma complains about? What remedies does he recommend? What relationship do his views have to traditional Inca values? How might a white landlord or colonial official have answered his attacks?

The Paths of Conquest

No other race can be found that can penetrate through such rugged lands, such dense forests, such great mountains and deserts and cross such broad rivers as the Spaniards have done ... solely by the valor of their persons and the forcefulness of their breed.

These words, written by Pedro Cieza de Leon, one of the conquistadors of Peru, underlined the Spaniards' pride in their accomplishments. In less than a century, a large portion of two continents and islands in an inland sea, inhabited by millions of people, was brought under Spanish control. Spanish expeditions, usually comprising 50 to 500 men, provided the spearhead of conquest, and in their wake followed the women, missionaries, administrators, and artisans who began to form civil society.

The conquest was not a unified movement but rather a series of individual initiatives that usually operated with government approval. The conquest of the Americas was two-pronged: One prong was directed toward Mexico, and the other aimed at South America.

We can use the well-documented campaign in Mexico as an example of a conquest. In 1519, **Hernán Cortés,** an educated man with considerable ability as a leader, led an expedition of 600 men to the coast of Mexico. After hearing rumors of a great kingdom in the interior, he began to strike inland. Pitched battles were fought with towns subject to the Aztec Empire, but after gaining these victories, Cortés was able to enlist the defeated peoples' support against their overlords. With the help of the Indian allies, Cortés eventually reached the great Aztec island capital of Tenochtitlan. By a combination of deception, boldness, ruthlessness, and luck, the Aztec emperor **Moctezuma II** was captured and killed. Cortés and his followers were forced to flee the Aztec capital and retreat toward the coast, but with the help of the Aztecs' traditional enemies, they cut off and besieged Tenochtitlan. Although the Aztec confederacy put up a stiff resistance, disease, starvation, and battle brought the city down in 1521. Tenochtitlan was replaced by **Mexico City.** The Aztec poets later remembered,

We are crushed to the ground,
we lie in ruins.
There is nothing but grief and suffering
in Mexico and Tlatelolco,
where once we saw beauty and valor.

By 1535, most of central Mexico, with its network of towns and its dense, agricultural populations, had been brought under Spanish control as the kingdom of **New Spain.** From there, the Spanish pushed their conquest southward into Central America and northward into the area of the nomadic peoples of north central Mexico.

The second trajectory of conquests led from the Caribbean outposts to the coast of northern South America and Panama. From Panama, the Spaniards followed rumors of a rich kingdom to the south. In 1532, after a false start, Francisco Pizarro led his men to the conquest of the Inca Empire, which was already weakened by a long civil war. Once again, using guile and audacity, fewer than 200 Spaniards and their Indian allies brought down a great empire. The Inca capital of Cuzco, high in the Andes, fell in 1533, but the Spanish decided to build their major city, Lima, closer to the coast. By 1540, most of Peru was under Spanish control, although an active resistance continued in remote areas for another 30 years.

From the conquests of densely populated areas, such as Mexico and Peru, where there were surpluses of food and potential laborers, Spanish expeditions spread out in search of further riches and strange peoples. Spanish expeditions penetrated the zones of semisedentary and nomadic peoples, who often offered stiff resistance. From 1540 to 1542, in one of the most famous expeditions, **Francisco Vázquez de Coronado,** searching for mythical cities of gold, penetrated what is now the southwestern United States as far as Kansas. At the other end of the Americas, **Pedro de Valdivia** conquered the tenacious Araucanians of central Chile and set up the city of Santiago in 1541, although the Araucanians continued to fight long after. Buenos Aires, in the southern part of the continent, founded by an expedition from Spain in 1536, was abandoned because of resistance and was not refounded until 1580. Other expeditions penetrated the Amazon basin, and explored the tropical forests of Central and South America during these years, but there was little there to attract permanent settlement to those areas. By 1570, there were 192 Spanish cities and towns throughout the Americas, one-third of which were in Mexico and Central America.

The Conquerors

The Spanish captains led by force of will and personal power. "God in the sky, the king in Spain, and me here" was the motto of one captain, and sometimes, absolute power could lead to tyranny. The crown received one-fifth of all treasure. Men signed up on a shares basis; those who brought horses or who had special skills might get double shares. Rewards were made according to the contract, and premiums were paid for special service and valor. There was a tendency for leaders to reward their friends, relatives, and men from their home province more liberally than others, so that after each conquest there was always a group of unhappy and dissatisfied conquerors ready to organize a new expedition. As one observer put it, "if each man was given the governorship, it would not be enough."

Few of the conquerors were professional soldiers; they represented all walks of Spanish life, including a scattering of gentlemen. Some of the later expeditions included a few Spanish women such as Ines Suárez, the heroine of the conquest of Chile, but such cases were rare. In general, the conquerors were men on the make, hoping to better themselves and serve God by converting the heathen at the same time. Always on the lookout for treasure, most conquerors were satisfied by encomiendas. These adventurous men, many of humble origins, came to see themselves as a new nobility entitled to dominion over a new peasantry: the American Indians.

The reasons for Spanish success were varied. Horses, firearms, and more generally steel weapons gave them a great advantage over the stone technology of the native peoples. This technological edge, combined with effective and ruthless leadership, produced remarkable results. Epidemic disease also proved to be a silent ally of the Europeans. Finally, internal divisions and rivalries within American Indian empires, and their high levels of centralization, made the great civilizations particularly vulnerable. It is no accident that the peoples who offered the stiffest and most continuous resistance were usually the mobile, tough, nomadic tribes rather than the centralized states of sedentary peasants.

By about 1570, the age of the conquest was coming to a close. Bureaucrats, merchants, and colonists replaced the generation of the conquerors as institutions of government and economy were created. The transition was not easy. In Peru a civil war erupted in the 1540s, and in Mexico there were grumblings from the old followers of Cortés. But the establishment of viceroys in the two main colonies and the creation of law courts in the main centers signaled that Spanish America had become a colony rather than a conquest.

Conquest and Morality

Conquest involved violence, domination, and theft. The Spanish conquest of the Americas created a series of important philosophical and moral questions for Europeans. Who were the Indians? Were they fully human? Was it proper to convert them to Christianity? Was the conquest of their lands justified? Driven by greed, many of the conquistadors argued that conquest was necessary to spread the gospel and that control of Indian labor was essential for Spain's rule. In 1548 Juan Gines de Sépulveda, a noted Spanish scholar, basing his arguments on Aristotle, published a book claiming that the conquest was fully justified. The Spaniards had come to free the Indians from their unjust lords and to bring the light of salvation. Most importantly, he argued, the Indians were not fully human, and that some peoples "were born to serve."

In 1550, the Spanish king suspended all further conquests and convoked a special commission in Valladolid to hear arguments for and against this position. Father Bartolomé de Las Casas—former conqueror and encomendero, Dominican priest, bishop of Chiapas, untiring defender of the Indians, and critic of Spanish brutality—presented the contrary opinion against Sépulveda. Las Casas had long experience in the West Indies, and he believed that the inhabitants were rational people who, unlike the Muslims, had never done harm to Christians. Thus, the conquest of their lands was unjustified. The Indians had many admirable customs and accomplishments, he said. He argued that "the Indians are our brothers and Christ has given his life for them." Spanish rule in order to spread the Christian faith was justified, but conversion should take place only by peaceful means.

The results of the debate were mixed. The crown had reasons to back Las Casas against the dangerous ambitions of the Spanish conquerors. Sépulveda's book was censored, but the conquests nevertheless continued. Although some of the worst abuses were moderated, in reality the great period of conquest was all over by the 1570s. It was too little, too late. Still, the Spanish government's concern with the legality and morality of its actions and the willingness of Spaniards such as Las Casas to speak out against abuses are also part of the story. One of the last surviving conquerors of Peru, Mancio Sierra de Legizamon, as he lay dying in 1589, wrote in his will that he was

ashamed of what the Spaniards had destroyed "by their evil behavior." He pointed out, "there was not a thief, or a scoundrel nor an adulteress among them … nor were they an immoral people, but satisfied and honest in their labors." For the peace of his conscience and that of his king, he asked that the abuses and bad examples be ended and that the Indians be treated fairly. The interests of many other conquerors and officials, however, ran in the opposite direction.

The Destruction and Transformation of American Indian Societies

 To varying degrees, all the indigenous societies suffered the effects of the conquest. Demographic loss was extreme in many areas. The Spanish created institutions such as the encomienda and later the mita to tax the native population or make them work. These policies disrupted indigenous societies.

The various American peoples responded in many different ways to the invasion of their lands and the transformation of their societies. All of them suffered a severe decline of population—a demographic catastrophe (Figure 19.4). On the main islands of the Caribbean, the indigenous population had nearly disappeared by 1540 as the result of slaving, mistreatment, and disease. In central Mexico, war, destruction, and above all disease brought the population from an estimated 25 million in 1519 to less than 2 million in 1580. In Peru, a similar process brought a loss from 10 million to 1.5 million between 1530 and 1590. Elsewhere in the Americas a similar but less well documented process took place. Smallpox, influenza, and measles wreaked havoc on the American Indian population, which had developed no immunities against these diseases.

Although epidemic was the major cause of depopulation, the conquest and the weakening of indigenous societies contributed to the losses. Population declines of this size disrupted Indian societies in many ways. For example, in central Mexico the contraction of the Indian population led the Spanish to concentrate the remaining population in fewer towns, and this led in turn to the seizure of former communal farming lands by Spanish landowners. Demographic collapse made maintaining traditional social and economic structures very difficult.

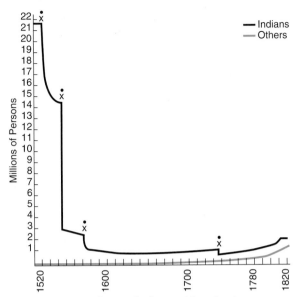

Figure 19.4 *Population decline in New Spain.*

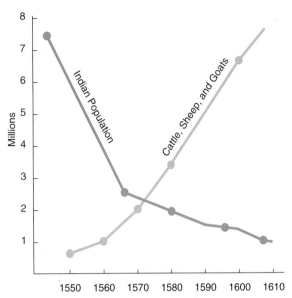

Figure 19.5 *A comparison of human and livestock populations in central Mexico.*

The case of Mexico is particularly stark. The tremendous decline of the Indian population was matched by the rapid increase in European livestock. Cattle, sheep, and horses flourished on the newly created Spanish farms or on unclaimed lands. In a way, European livestock replaced the Indian population of Mexico (Figure 19.5).

Exploitation of the Indians

The Spaniards did not interfere with aspects of American Indian life that served colonial goals or at least did not openly conflict with Spanish authority or religion. Thus, in Mexico and Peru, while the old Indian religion and its priestly class were eliminated, the traditional Indian nobility remained in place, supported by Spanish authority, as middlemen between the tax and labor demands of the new rulers and the majority of the population.

The enslavement of Indians, except those taken in war, was prohibited by the mid-16th century in most of Spanish America. Instead, different forms of labor or taxation were imposed. At first, encomiendas were given to the individual conquerors of a region. The holders of these grants were able to use their Indians as workers and servants or to tax them. Whereas commoners had owed tribute or labor to the state in the Inca and Aztec empires, the new demands were arbitrary, often excessive, and usually without the reciprocal obligation and protection characteristic of the Indian societies. In general, the encomiendas were destructive to Indian societies. The Spanish crown, unwilling to see a new nobility arise in the New World among the conquerors with their grants of Indian serfs, moved to end the institution in the 1540s. The crown limited the inheritability of encomiendas and prohibited the right to demand certain kinds of labor from the Indians. Although encomiendas continued to exist in marginal regions at the fringes of the empire, they were all but gone by the 1620s in the central areas of Mexico and Peru. Colonists increasingly sought grants of land rather than Indians as the basis of wealth.

Meanwhile, the colonial government increasingly extracted labor and taxes from native peoples. In many places, communities were required to send groups of laborers to work on state projects, such as church construction or road building, or in labor gangs for mining or agriculture. This forced labor, called the *mita* in Peru, mobilized thousands of Indians to work in the mines and on other projects. Although the Indians were paid a wage for this work, there were many abuses of the system by the local officials, and community labor requirements often were disruptive and destructive to Indian life. By the 17th century, many Indians left their villages to avoid

In Depth

The Great Exchange

The arrival of the Spaniards and the Portuguese in the Americas began one of the most extensive and profound changes in the history of humankind. The New World, which had existed in isolation since the end of the last ice age, was now brought into continual contact with the Old World. The peoples and cultures of Europe and Africa came to the Americas through voluntary or forced immigration. Between 1500 and 1850, perhaps 10 to 15 million Africans and 5 million Europeans crossed the Atlantic and settled in the Americas as part of the great migratory movement. Contact also initiated a broader biological and ecological exchange that changed the face of both the Old World and the New World—the way people lived, what they ate, and how they died, indeed how many people there were in different regions—as the animals, plants, and diseases of the two hemispheres were transferred. We have seen that these biological contacts were a vital aspect of the establishment of the new world economy.

It was historian Alfred Crosby who first called this process the **Columbian exchange,** and he has pointed out its profound effects as the first stage of the "ecological imperialism" that accompanied the expansion of the West. In this chapter we have discussed the devastating impact of Old World disease on Native American peoples. Long separated from the populations of the Old World and lacking immunities to diseases such as measles and smallpox, populations throughout the Americas suffered disastrous losses after initial contact. Not only among the dense populations in Peru and Mexico, but in the forests of Brazil and the woodlands of North America, contact with Europeans and Africans resulted in epidemics that devastated the indigenous populations. Only after many generations did immunities build up in the remaining populations that allowed them to withstand the diseases.

Disease may have also moved in the other direction. Some authorities believe that syphilis had an American origin and was brought to Europe only after 1492. In general, however, forms of life in the Old World—diseases, plants, and animals—were

more complex than those in the Americas and thus displaced the New World varieties in open competition. The diseases of Eurasia and Africa had a greater impact on America than American diseases had on the Old World.

With animals also, the major exchange was from the Old World to the New World. From the beginning of contact, Europeans noted with curiosity the strange fauna of America, so different from that of Europe. The birds were a hit. Parrots were among the first creatures brought to Europe from America. Many early observers commented on the smaller size of the mammals in the New World and the absence of certain types, not realizing that mastodons, horses, camels, and other animals that had once roamed the Americas had long since disappeared. Native American had domesticated dogs, guinea pigs, some fowl, and llamas, but in general domesticated animals were far less important in the Americas than in the Old World. Protein resources were thus also more restricted. The absence of cattle and horses had also left the peoples of the Americas without beasts of burden except for the llamas of the Andes.

In the first years of settlement in the Caribbean, the Spanish introduced horses, cattle, sheep, chickens, and domestic goats and pigs, all of which were considered essential for civilized life as the Iberians understood it. Some of these animals thrived in the New World. In the scrub brush and prairies of North America, in the tropical grasslands of Venezuela and on the South American pampas, vast herds of cattle began to roam freely. A hundred head of cattle abandoned by the Spanish in the Rio de la Plata area in 1587 had become 100,000 head 20 years later. Both for the consumption of meat, tallow, and hides in the Americas and eventually for the export of hides and meat to Europe and the rest of the world, the arrival of cattle in the Americas was a revolutionary occurrence. In Mexico, livestock and Spanish haciendas grew as rapidly as the Native American populations declined and their communities contracted. The replacement of Native Americans by cattle became a metaphor of the conquest of Mexico.

the labor and tax obligations, preferring instead to work for Spanish landowners or to seek employment in the cities. This process eventually led to the growth of a wage labor system in which Indians, no longer

resident in their villages, worked for wages on Spanish-owned mines and farms or in the cities.

In the wake of this disruption, Native American culture also demonstrated great resiliency in the face

The success of other European livestock was no less impressive. In the Andes and in Mexico, sheep thrived and supported an active textile industry, which eventually supplied most of the local needs. Horses were adopted quickly by the nomadic peoples of North and South America. This adaptation transformed their societies and gave them added mobility, allowing them to meet the Europeans on an almost equal basis. With horses, the Apaches of Arizona and the Indians of the Argentine pampas were able to hold off the Europeans for 300 years.

European livestock, even pigs and chickens, transformed indigenous life in America. Native Americans acquired some animals, such as oxen, slowly, but other animals, such as horses and sheep, had obvious benefits and were acquired more rapidly. The chieftain in Panama who answered that the greatest benefit Spain had brought to his people was the chicken egg may have disappointed his questioner, but his statement reflected a keen appreciation of the importance of the interchange. The newly introduced animals changed the ecological balance in the New World. Not only animals that were purposefully introduced, but species such as the sparrow and the brown rat, whose arrival was unplanned, changed the nature of life in the Americas.

The Europeans also brought their crops and their weeds. It was hard for Iberians to live without the Mediterranean necessities: wheat bread, olive oil, and wine. Columbus on his second voyage in 1499 introduced wheat, peas, melons, onions, grapes, and probably olives as well as sugar cane. Some crops, such as sugar cane, thrived and provided the basis for the rise of plantation economies; other crops such as wheat, olives, and grapes needed cooler or drier environments and had to wait until the Spanish reached the more temperate zones before they flourished. Later, Europeans introduced all of their own crops and even some crops such as bananas, coconut trees, coffee, and breadfruit that they had found in Africa, Asia, and the Pacific. They also inadvertently introduced other plants, such as tumbleweed, which spread quickly.

In the exchange of foods and stimulants, the contribution of America probably outweighed that of Europe, however. It is difficult today to imagine the diet of the Old World before the discovery of America. New World plants, such as tomatoes, squash, sweet potatoes, types of beans, and peppers, became essential foods in Europe. Tobacco and cacao, or chocolate, both American in origin, became widely distributed throughout the world.

Even more important were basic crops, such as the potato, maize, and manioc, all of which yielded more calories per acre than all the Old World grains except rice. The high yield of calories per acre of maize and potatoes had supported the high population densities of the American civilizations. After the Columbian voyages, these foods began to produce similar effects in the rest of the world. Manioc, or casava (we know it as tapioca), was a basic Indian food in the Caribbean and tropical South America. Particularly well suited to the tropics, manioc was never popular in Europe, but it spread widely in Asia and Africa, where it became a basic food by the 18th century. The potato, a staple of the Andean civilizations, was easy to grow and yielded large numbers of calories. By the 18th century it was well known from Ireland to Russia. Maize was a great success. It yielded as many calories per acre as rice, but it was easier to grow and could flourish in a wide variety of situations. By the 17th century it had spread to Spain and France, and by the 18th century it was found in Italy, Turkey, Greece, and Russia. The Europeans also introduced it to west Africa and China. Maize became a staple across the globe. At present, at least one-third of the crops raised to feed the world's population are of New World origin.

After 1750, the world population experienced a dramatic rise. The reasons for this expansion were many, but the contribution of the American foodstuffs with their high yields was a central one. Manioc, potatoes, sweet potatoes, and maize—to say nothing of peanuts, beans, and tomatoes—greatly expanded the food resources available throughout the world and continue to do so today. The balance sheet of the Columbian exchange was mixed, but the world was undeniably different after it began.

Questions: Why and in what ways was the Columbian exchange a particularly significant case of global contact? Was western Europe the chief beneficiary of the exchange? What balance was there between the economic dependency of the Americas and the ideas, technology, and goods they received from Europe?

of Spanish institutions and forms, adapting and modifying them to indigenous ways. In Peru and Mexico, native peoples learned to use the Spanish legal system and the law courts so that litigation became a way of life. At the local level, many aspects of Native American life remained, and Native Americans proved to be selective in their adaptation of European foods, technology, and culture.

Colonial Economies and Governments

Agriculture and mining were the basis of the Spanish colonial economy. Eventually, Spanish farms and ranches competed with Native American villages, but they also depended on Native Americans as laborers. Over this economy Spain built a bureaucratic empire in which the church was an essential element and a major cultural factor.

Spanish America was an agrarian society in which perhaps 80 percent of the population lived and worked on the land. Yet in terms of America's importance to Spain, mining was the essential activity and the basis of Spain's rule in the West Indies. It was precious metals that first began to fit Latin America into the developing world economy.

Although the booty of conquest provided some wealth, most of the precious metal sent across the Atlantic came from the postconquest mining industry. Gold was found in the Caribbean, Colombia, and Chile, but it was silver far more than gold that formed the basis of Spain's wealth in America.

The Silver Heart of Empire

The major silver discoveries were made in Mexico and Peru between 1545 and 1565. Great silver mining towns developed. **Potosí** in upper Peru (in what is now Bolivia) was the largest mine of all, producing about 80 percent of all the Peruvian silver. In the early 17th century, more than 160,000 people lived and worked in the town and its mine. Peru's Potosí and Mexico's Zacatecas became wealthy mining centers with opulent churches and a luxurious way of life for some, but as one viceroy of Peru commented, it was not silver that was sent to Spain "but the blood and sweat of Indians."

Mining labor was provided by a variety of workers. The early use of American Indian slaves and encomienda workers in the 16th century gradually was replaced by a system of labor drafts. By 1572 the mining mita in Peru was providing about 13,000 workers a year to Potosí alone. Similar labor drafts were used in Mexico, but by the 17th century the mines in both places also had large numbers of wage workers willing to brave the dangers of mining in return for the good wages.

Although indigenous methods were used at first, most mining techniques were European in origin.

After 1580, silver mining depended on a process of amalgamation with mercury to extract the silver from the ore-bearing rock. The Spanish discovery of a mountain of mercury at **Huancavelica** in Peru aided American silver production. Potosí and Huancavelica became the "great marriage of Peru" and the basis of silver production in South America.

According to Spanish law, all subsoil rights belonged to the crown, but the mines and the processing plants were owned by individuals, who were permitted to extract the silver in return for paying one-fifth of production to the government, which also profited from its monopoly on the mercury needed to produce the silver (Figure 19.6).

Mining stimulated many other aspects of the economy, even in areas far removed from the mines. Workers had to be fed and the mines supplied. In Mexico, where most of the mines were located beyond the area of settled preconquest Indian population, large Spanish-style farms developed to raise cattle, sheep, and wheat. The Peruvian mines high in the Andes were supplied from distant regions with mercury, mules, food, clothing, and even coca leaves, used to deaden hunger and make the work at high altitudes less painful. From Spain's perspective, mining was the heart of the colonial economy.

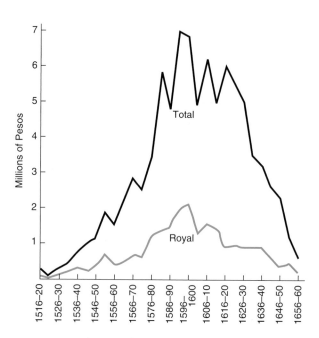

Figure 19.6 *Silver production in Spanish America, 1516–1660.*

Haciendas and Villages

Spanish America remained predominantly an agrarian economy, and wherever large sedentary populations lived, Indian communal agriculture of traditional crops continued. As populations dwindled, Spanish ranches and farms began to emerge. The colonists, faced with declining Indian populations, also found land ownership more attractive. Family-owned rural estates, which produced grains, grapes, and livestock, developed throughout the central areas of Spanish America. Most of the labor force on these estates came from Native Americans who had left the communities and from people of mixed Native American and European heritage. These rural estates, or **haciendas,** producing primarily for consumers in America, became the basis of wealth and power for the local aristocracy in many regions. Although some plantation crops, such as sugar and later cacao, were exported to Europe from Spanish America, they made up only a small fraction of the value of the exports in comparison with silver. In some regions where Native American communities continued to hold traditional farming lands, an endemic competition between haciendas and village communities emerged.

Industry and Commerce

In areas such as Ecuador, New Spain, and Peru, sheep raising led to the development of small textile sweatshops, where common cloth was produced, usually by women. America became self-sufficient for its basic foods and material goods and looked to Europe only for luxury items not locally available.

Still, from Spain's perspective and that of the larger world economy taking shape in the early modern centuries, the American "kingdoms" had a silver heart, and the whole Spanish commercial system was organized around that fact. Spain allowed only Spaniards to trade with America and imposed tight restrictions. All American trade from Spain after the mid-16th century passed through the city of Seville and, later, through the nearby port of Cadiz. A Board of Trade in Seville controlled all commerce with America, registered ships and passengers, kept charts, and collected taxes. It often worked in conjunction with a merchant guild, or **consulado,** in Seville that controlled goods shipped to America and handled much of the silver received in return. Linked to branches in Mexico City and Lima, the consulados kept tight control over the trade and were able to keep prices high in the colonies.

Other Europeans looked on the West Indies trade with envy. To discourage foreign rivals and pirates, the Spanish eventually worked out a convoy system in which two fleets sailed annually from Spain, traded their goods for precious metals, and then met at Havana, Cuba, before returning to Spain.

The fleet system was made possible by the large, heavily armed ships, called **galleons,** that were used to carry the silver belonging to the crown. Two great galleons a year also sailed from Manila in the Philippines to Mexico loaded with Chinese silks, porcelain, and lacquer. These goods were then shipped on the convoy to Spain along with the American silver. In the Caribbean, heavily fortified ports, such as Havana and Cartagena (Colombia), provided shelter for the treasure ships, while coast guard fleets cleared the waters of potential raiders. Although cumbersome, the convoys (which continued until the 1730s) were successful. Pirates and enemies sometimes captured individual ships, and some ships were lost to storms and other disasters, but only one fleet was lost—to the Dutch in 1627.

In general, the supply of American silver to Spain was continuous and made the colonies seem worth the effort, but the reality of American treasure was more complicated. Much of the wealth flowed out of Spain to pay for Spain's European wars, its long-term debts, and the purchase of manufactured goods to be sent back to the West Indies. Probably less than half of the silver remained in Spain itself. The arrival of American treasure also contributed to a sharp rise in prices and a general inflation, first in Spain and then throughout western Europe during the 16th century. At no time did the American treasure make up more than one-fourth of Spain's state revenues, which is to say that the wealth of Spain depended more on the taxes levied on its own population than it did on the exploitation of its Native American subjects. However, the seemingly endless supply of silver stimulated bankers to continue to lend money to Spain because the prospect of the great silver fleet was always enough to offset the falling credit of the Spanish rulers and the sometimes bankrupt government. As early as 1619, Sancho de Moncada wrote that "the poverty of Spain resulted from the discovery of the Indies," but there were few who could see the long-term costs of empire.

Ruling an Empire: State and Church

Spain controlled its American empire through a carefully regulated bureaucratic system. Sovereignty rested with the crown, based not on the right of conquest but on a papal grant that awarded the West Indies to Castile in return for its services in bringing those lands and peoples into the Christian community. Some Native Americans found this a curious idea, and European theologians agreed, but Spain was careful to bolster its rule in other ways. The **Treaty of Tordesillas** (1494) between Castile and Portugal clarified the spheres of influence and right of possession of the two kingdoms by drawing a hypothetical north–south line around the globe and reserving to Portugal the newly discovered lands (and their route to India) to the east of the line and to Castile all lands to the west. Thus, Brazil fell within the Portuguese sphere. Other European nations later raised their own objections to the Spanish and Portuguese claims.

The Spanish Empire became a great bureaucratic system built on a juridical core and staffed to a large extent by **letrados,** university-trained lawyers from Spain. The modern division of powers was not clearly defined in the Spanish system, so that judicial officers also exercised legislative and administrative authority. Laws were many and contradictory at times, but the **Recopilación** (1681) codified the laws into the basis for government in the colonies.

The king ruled through the **Council of the Indies** in Spain, which issued the laws and advised him. Within the West Indies, Spain created two **viceroyalties** in the 16th century, one based in Mexico City and the other in Lima. Viceroys, high-ranking nobles who were direct representatives of the king, wielded broad military, legislative, and, when they had legal training, judicial powers. The viceroyalties of New Spain and Peru were then subdivided into 10 judicial divisions controlled by superior courts, or **audiencias,** staffed by professional royal magistrates who helped to make law as well as apply it. At the local level, royally appointed magistrates applied the laws, collected taxes, and assigned the work required of American Indian communities. It is little wonder that they often were highly criticized for bending the law and taking advantage of the Indians under their control. Below them were many minor officials who made bureaucracy both a living and a way of life.

To some extent, the clergy formed another branch of the state apparatus, although it had other functions and goals as well. Catholic religious orders such as the Franciscans, Dominicans, and Jesuits carried out the widespread conversion of the Indians,

establishing churches in the towns and villages of sedentary Indians and setting up missions in frontier areas where nomadic peoples were forced to settle.

Taking seriously the pope's admonition to Christianize the peoples of the new lands as the primary justification for Spain's rule, some of the early missionaries became ardent defenders of Indian rights and even admirers of aspects of Indian culture. For example, Franciscan priest Fray Bernardino de Sahagún (1499–1590) became an expert in the Nahuatl language and composed a bilingual encyclopedia of Aztec culture, which was based on methods very similar to those used by modern anthropologists. Other clerics wrote histories, grammars, and studies of Indian language and culture. Some were like Diego de Landa, Bishop of Yucatán (1547), who admired much about the culture of the Maya but who so detested their religion that he burned all their ancient books and tortured many Maya suspected of backsliding from Christianity. The recording and analysis of Indian cultures were designed primarily to provide tools for conversion.

In the core areas of Peru and New Spain, the missionary church eventually was replaced by an institutional structure of parishes and bishoprics. Archbishops sat in the major capitals, and a complicated church hierarchy developed. Because the Spanish crown nominated the holders of all such positions, the clergy tended to be major supporters of state policy as well as a primary influence on it.

The Catholic church profoundly influenced the cultural and intellectual life of the colonies in many ways. The construction of churches, especially the great baroque cathedrals of the capitals, stimulated the work of architects and artists, usually reflecting European models but sometimes taking up local themes and subjects. The printing presses, introduced to America in the early 16th century, always published a high percentage of religious books as well as works of history, poetry, philosophy, law, and language. Much intellectual life was organized around religion. Schools—such as those of Mexico City and Lima, founded in the 1550s—were run by the clergy, and universities were created to provide training primarily in law and theology, the foundations of state and society. Eventually, more than 70 universities flourished in Spanish America. A stunning example of colonial intellectual life was the nun **Sor Juana Inés de la Cruz** (1651–1695; Figure 19.7), author, poet, musician, and social thinker. Sor Juana was welcomed at the court of the viceroy in Mexico City, where her beauty and intelligence were

Figure 19.7 *Sor Juana Inés de la Cruz was the remarkable Mexican poet and writer whose talents won her recognition rarely given to women for intellectual achievements in colonial Latin America.*

celebrated. She eventually gave up secular concerns and her library, at the urging of her superiors, to concentrate on purely spiritual matters.

To control the morality and orthodoxy of the population, the tribunal of the Inquisition set up offices in the major capitals. Although American Indians usually were exempt from its jurisdiction, Jews, Protestants, and other religious dissenters were prosecuted and sometimes executed in an attempt to impose orthodoxy. Overall, church and state combined to create an ideological and political framework for the society of Spanish America.

Brazil: The First Plantation Colony

In Brazil, the Portuguese created the first great plantation colony of the Americas, growing sugar with the use of Native American and then African slaves. In the 18th century, the discovery

of gold opened up the interior of Brazil to settlement and the expansion of slavery. Whereas Spanish America seemed to fulfill dreams of mineral wealth, Brazil—Portugal's American colony—became the first major plantation zone, organized to produce a tropical crop, sugar, in great demand and short supply in Europe.

The first official Portuguese landfall on the South American coast took place in 1500 when **Pedro Alvares Cabral,** leader of an expedition to India, stopped briefly on the tropical Brazilian shore. There was little at first to attract European interest except for the dyewood trees that grew in the forests, and thus the Portuguese crown paid little attention to Brazil for 30 years, preferring instead to grant licenses to merchants who agreed to exploit the dyewood. Pressure from French competitors finally moved the Portuguese crown to military action. The coast was cleared of rivals and a new system of settlement was established in 1532. Minor Portuguese nobles were given strips of land along the coast to colonize and develop. The nobles who held these **capitaincies** combined broad, seemingly feudal powers with a strong desire for commercial development. Most of them lacked the capital needed to carry out the colonization, and some had problems with the indigenous population. In a few places, towns were established, colonists were brought over, relations with the Native Americans were peaceful, and, most importantly, sugar plantations were established using first Native American, then African slaves.

In 1549, the Portuguese king sent a governor general and other officials to create a royal capital at Salvador. The first Jesuit missionaries also arrived. By 1600, indigenous resistance had been broken in many places by military action, missionary activity, or epidemic disease. A string of settlements extended along the coast, centered on port cities such as Salvador and Rio de Janeiro. These served roughly 150 sugar plantations, a number that doubled by 1630. The plantations were increasingly worked by African slaves. By 1600, the Brazilian colony had about 100,000 inhabitants: 30,000 Europeans, 15,000 black slaves, and the rest Native Americans and people of mixed origin.

Sugar and Slavery

During most of the next century, Brazil held its position as the world's leading sugar producer. Sugar cane had to be processed in the field. It was cut and pressed in large mills, and the juice was then heated to crystallize into sugar. This combination of agriculture and industry in the field demanded large amounts of capital for machinery and large quantities of labor for the backbreaking work (Figure 19.8). Although there were always some free workers who had skilled occupations, slaves did most of the work. During the 17th century, about 7000 slaves a year were imported from Africa. By the end of the century, Brazil had about 150,000 slaves—about half its total population.

On the basis of a single crop produced by slave labor, Brazil became the first great plantation colony and a model that later was followed by other European nations in their own Caribbean colonies. Even after the Brazilian economy became more diverse, Brazil's social hierarchy still reflected its plantation and slave origins. The white planter families became an aristocracy linked by marriage to resident merchants and to the few Portuguese bureaucrats and officials, and they dominated local institutions. At the bottom of society were the slaves, distinguished by their color and their status as property. However, a growing segment of the population was composed of people of mixed origins, the result of miscegenation between whites, Indians, and Africans who—alongside poorer whites, freed blacks, and free Indians—served as artisans, small farmers, herders, and free laborers. In many ways, society as a whole reflected the hierarchy of the plantation.

Like Spain, Portugal created a bureaucratic structure that integrated this colony within an imperial system. A governor general ruled from Salvador, but the governors in each capitaincy often acted independently and reported directly to the overseas council in Lisbon. The missionary orders were particularly important in Brazil, especially the Jesuits. Their extensive cattle ranches and sugar mills supported the construction of churches and schools as well as a network of missions with thousands of Native American residents.

As in Spanish America, royal officials trained in the law formed the core of the bureaucracy. Unlike the Spanish Empire, which except for the Philippines was almost exclusively American, the Portuguese Empire included colonies and outposts in Asia, Africa, and Brazil. Only gradually, in the 17th century, did Brazil become the predominant Portuguese colony. Even then, Brazil's ties to Portugal were in some ways stronger and more dependant than those between Spanish America and Spain. Unlike Spanish America, Brazil had neither universities nor printing presses. Thus, intellectual life was always an extension of Portugal, and Brazilians seeking higher education

Figure 19.8 *Sugar was introduced to the Caribbean in 1493, and Brazil became the greatest producer by the next century. Sugar plantations using slave labor characterized Brazil and the Caribbean. This early European engraving is wrong in some details, but it does convey an image of the almost factorylike conditions in the sugar mills.*

and government offices or hoping to publish their works always had to turn to the mother country. The general economic dependency of Latin America was matched by an intellectual subordination more intense in Brazil than in Spanish America.

Brazil's Age of Gold

As overseas extensions of Europe, the American colonies were particularly susceptible to changes in European politics. For 60 years (1580–1640), the Habsburg kings of Spain also ruled Portugal, a situation that promoted their cooperation and gave these rulers a truly worldwide empire. From 1630 to 1654, as part of a global struggle against Spain, the Dutch seized a portion of northeastern Brazil and controlled its sugar production. Although the Dutch were expelled from Brazil in 1654, by the 1680s the Dutch, English, and French had established their own plantation colonies in the Caribbean and were producing sugar, once again with slave laborers. This competition, which led to a rising price for slaves and a falling world price for sugar, undercut the Brazilian sugar industry, and the colony entered into hard times. Eventually, each European nation tried to establish an integrated set of colonies that included plantations (the Caribbean, Brazil), slaving ports (Africa), and food-producing areas (New England, southern Brazil).

Although Brazil's domination of the world sugar market was lost, throughout the 17th century **Paulistas,** hardy backwoodsmen from São Paulo (an area with few sugar plantations), had been exploring the interior, capturing Indians, and searching for precious metals. These expeditions not only established Portuguese claims to much of the interior of the continent but eventually were successful in their quest for wealth. In 1695, gold strikes were made in the mountainous interior in a region that came to be called **Minas Gerais** (General Mines), and the Brazilian colony experienced a new boom.

A great gold rush began. People deserted coastal towns and plantations to head for the gold washings, and they were soon joined by waves of about 5000 immigrants a year who came directly from Portugal. Slaves provided labor in the mines, as in the plantations. By 1775, there were over 150,000 slaves (out of a total population of 300,000 for the region) in Minas Gerais. Wild mining camps and a wide-open society eventually coalesced into a network of towns such as the administrative center of Ouro Prêto, and the government, anxious to control the newfound

wealth, imposed a heavy hand to collect taxes and rein in the unruly population. Gold production reached its height between 1735 and 1760 and averaged about 3 tons a year in that period, making Brazil the greatest source of gold in the Western world.

The discovery of gold—and later of diamonds—was a mixed blessing in the long run. It opened the interior to settlement, once again with disastrous effects on the indigenous population and with the expansion of slavery. The early disruption of coastal agriculture caused by the gold strikes was overcome by government control of the slave trade, and exports of sugar and tobacco continued to be important to the colony. Mining did stimulate the opening of new areas to ranching and farming, to supply the new markets in the mining zone. **Rio de Janeiro,** the port closest to the mines, grew in size and importance. It became capital of the colony in 1763. In Minas Gerais, a distinctive society developed. The local wealth was used to sponsor the building of churches, which in turn stimulated the work of artists, architects, and composers. Like the rest of Brazil, however, the hierarchy of color and the legal distinctions of slavery marked life in the mining zones, which were populated by large numbers of slaves and free persons of color.

Finally, gold allowed Portugal to continue economic policies that were detrimental in the long run. With access to gold, Portugal could buy the manufactured goods it needed for itself and its colonies, as few industries were developed in the mother country. Much of the Brazilian gold flowed from Portugal to England to pay for manufactured goods and to compensate for a trade imbalance. After 1760, as the supply of gold began to dwindle, Portugal was again in a difficult position—it had become in some ways an economic dependency of England.

Multiracial Societies

 The mixture of whites, Africans, and Indians created the basis of multiracial societies in which hierarchies of color, status, and occupation all operated. By the 18th century, the castas, people of mixed origin, began to increase rapidly and had become a major segment of the population.

The conquest and settlement of Latin America created the conditions for the formation of multiethnic societies on a large scale. The three major groups—Indians, Europeans, and Africans—had been brought together under very different conditions: the

Europeans as conquerors and voluntary immigrants, the Indians as conquered peoples, and the Africans as slaves. This situation created hierarchies of masters and servants, Christians and pagans, that reflected the relationships of power and the colonial condition. In central Mexico, where an Indian nobility had existed, aspects of preconquest social organization were maintained because they served the ends of Spanish government. In theory, there was a separation between the "republic of the Spaniards," which included all non-Indians, and the "republic of the Indians," which was supposed to have its own social rankings and its own rules and laws. This separation was never a reality, however, and the "republic of the Indians" always formed the base on which all society rested. Indians paid tribute, something not required of others in society.

The Society of Castas

Spaniards had an idea of society drawn from their own medieval experience, but American realities soon altered that concept. The key was miscegenation. The conquest had involved the sexual exploitation of Indian women and occasional alliances formed by the giving of concubines and female servants. Marriages with indigenous women, especially of the Indian nobility, were not unknown. With few European women available, especially in frontier regions, mixed marriages and informal unions were common. The result was the growth of a large population of mixed background, the so-called mestizos. Although they were always suspected of illegitimacy, their status, especially in the early years, was higher than that of Indians. More acculturated than the Indians and able to operate in two worlds, mestizos became members of an intermediate category, not fully accepted as equals to Spaniards and yet expected to live according to the standards of Spanish society and often acting as auxiliaries to it. A similar process took place in areas such as Brazil and the Caribbean coasts, where large numbers of African slaves were imported. Slave owners exploited their female slaves or took slave women as mistresses, and then sometimes freed their mulatto children. The result was the growth of a large population of mixed background.

Throughout the Spanish Indies, European categories of noble, priest, and commoner continued, as did hierarchies based on wealth and occupation. But American realities created new distinctions in which race and place of birth also played a crucial role. This was the **sociedad de castas,** based on racial origins, in which Europeans or whites were at the top, black slaves or Native Americans were at the bottom, and the many kinds of mixes filled the intermediate categories. This accompanied the great cultural fusion in the formation of Latin America.

From the three original ethnic categories, many combinations and crosses were possible: mestizo, mulatto, and so on. By the 18th century, this segment of the population had grown rapidly, and there was much confusion and local variation in terminology. A whole genre of painting developed simply to identify and classify the various combinations. Together, the people of mixed origins were called the castas, and they tended to be shopkeepers and small farmers. In 1650, the castas made up perhaps 5 to 10 percent of the population of Spanish America, but by 1750 they made up 35 to 40 percent (see Visualizing the Past). In Brazil, still dominated by slavery, free people of color made up about 28 percent of the population—a proportion equal to that of whites. Together, however, free and slave blacks and mulattos made up two-thirds of the inhabitants of Brazil in the late 18th century.

As the mixed population grew in Spanish America, increasing restrictions were placed on them, but their social mobility could not be halted. A successful Indian might call himself a mestizo; a mestizo who married a Spanish woman might be called white. The ranks of the castas were also swelled by former slaves who had been given or had bought their freedom and by Indians who left their communities, spoke Spanish, and lived within the orbit of the Hispanic world. Thus, physical characteristics were only one criterion of rank and status, but color and ethnicity mattered, and they created a pseudoracial hierarchy. European or white status was a great social advantage. Not every person of European background was wealthy, but most of the wealthy merchants, landowners, bureaucrats, and miners were white. As one visitor wrote, "In America, every white is a gentleman."

Originally, all whites had shared the privileged status of Spaniards regardless of the continent of their birth, but over time distinctions developed between **peninsulares,** or those actually born in Spain, and **Creoles,** or those born in the New World. Creoles thought of themselves as loyal American Spaniards, but with so many mestizos around, the shadow of a

Visualizing the Past

Race or Culture? A Changing Society

The process of marriage or sexual contact between Spaniards, Indians, and Africans began to complicate the demographic and the social structures of the American colonies. The rise of a significant number of people of mixed origin could be noted in both Peru and Mexico. These graphs point out the differences in the two areas and may imply something about the situation of the indigenous communities as well as that of the castas. We should also remember that these categories were not nec-

essarily biological and that Indians might be classified as castas if they spoke Spanish or wore Spanish-style clothes. What seems to be precise demographic measurement, may, in fact, be imprecise social definition.

Question: Do modern censuses that use cultural or "racial" labels face the same problems of definition that the early censuses in the colonial Americas confronted?

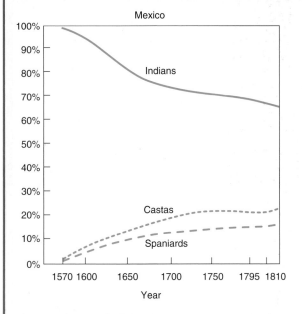

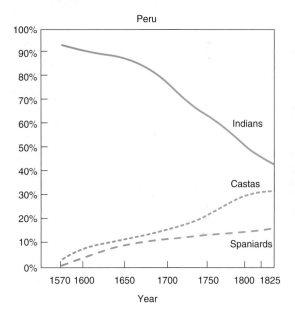

Changing Ratios of Ethnic Categories in Mexico and Peru

possible Indian ancestor and illegitimacy always made their status suspect as far as the Europeans were concerned. Still, Creoles dominated the local economies, held sway over large numbers of dependents at their haciendas and mines, and stood at the top of society, second only to the peninsulares. Increasingly, they developed a sense of identity and pride in their accomplishments, and they were sensitive to any suggestion of inferiority or to any discrimination because of their American birth. That growing sense of self-

identity eventually contributed to the movements for independence in Latin America.

The hierarchy of race intersected with traditional Iberian distinctions based on gender, age, and class. The father of a family had legal authority over his children until they were 25. Women were in a subordinate position; they could not serve in government and were expected to assume the duties of motherhood and household (Figure 19.9). After marriage, women came under the authority of their husbands,

Figure 19.9 *Women in colonial Latin America engaged in agriculture and manufacturing, especially in textile workshops, but social ideology still reserved the household and the kitchen as the proper sphere for women, as seen in this scene of a kitchen in a large Mexican home.*

but many a widow assumed the direction of her family's activities. Lower-class women often controlled small-scale commerce in towns and villages, worked in the fields, and labored at the looms of small factories. Marriages often were arranged and accompanied by the payment of a dowry, which remained the property of the woman throughout the marriage. Women also had full rights to inheritance. Upper-class women who did not marry at a young age were placed in convents to prevent contacts or marriages with partners of unsuitable backgrounds.

The 18th-Century Reforms

 Increasing attacks on the Iberian empires by foreign rivals led to the Bourbon reforms in Spanish America and the reforms of Pombal in Brazil. These changes strengthened the two empires but also generated colonial unrest that eventually led to movements for independence.

No less than in the rest of Europe, the 18th century was a period of intellectual ferment in Spain and Portugal as well as in their empires. In Spain and its colonies, small clubs and associations, calling themselves **amigos del país,** or friends of the country, met in many cities to discuss and plan all kinds of reforms. Their programs were for material benefits and improvements, not political changes. In Portugal, foreign influences and ideas created a group of progressive thinkers and bureaucrats open to new ideas in economy, education, and philosophy. Much of the change that came in both empires resulted as much from the changing European economic and demographic realities as from new ideas. The expansion of population and economy in Europe, and the increased demands for American products, along with the long series of wars in the 18th century, gave the American colonies a new importance. Both the Spanish and Portuguese empires revived, but with some long-term results that eventually led to the fall of both.

The Shifting Balance of Politics and Trade

By the 18th century, it was clear that the Spanish colonial system had become outmoded and that Spain's exclusive hold on the Indies was no longer secure. To some extent the problem lay in Spain itself. Beset by foreign wars, increasing debt, declining population, and internal revolts, a weakened Spain was threatened by a powerful France and by the rising mercantile strength of England and Holland, whose Protestantism also made them natural rivals of Catholic Spain. Since the 16th century, French, Dutch, and English ship captains had combined contraband trade with raiding in the Spanish Empire, and although Spain's European rivals could not seize Mexico or Peru, the sparsely populated islands and coasts of the Caribbean became likely targets. Buccaneers, owing allegiance to no nation, raided the Caribbean ports in the late 17th century. Meanwhile, the English took Jamaica in 1654, the French took control of western Hispaniola (Haiti) by 1697, and other islands fell to the English, French, and Dutch. Many of the islands turned to sugar production and the creation of slave and plantation colonies much like those in Brazil. These settlements were part of a general process of colonization, of which the English settlement of eastern North America and the French occupation of Canada and the Mississippi valley were also part.

Less apparent than the loss of territories, but equally important, was the failure of the Spanish mercantile and political system. The annual fleets became irregular. Silver payments from America declined, and most goods shipped to the West Indies and even the ships that carried them were non-Spanish in origin. The colonies became increasingly self-sufficient in basic commodities, and as central government became weaker, local aristocrats in the colonies exercised increasing control over the economy and government of their regions, often at the expense of the Native American and the lower-class populations. Graft and corruption were rampant in many branches of government. The empire seemed to be crumbling. What is most impressive is that Spain was able to retain its American possessions for another century.

Even with Spain in decline, the West Indies still seemed an attractive prize coveted by other powers, and the opportunity to gain them was not long in coming. A final crisis was set in motion in 1701 when the Spanish king, Charles II, died without an heir. Other European nations backed various claimants to the Spanish throne, hoping to win the prize of the Spanish monarchy and its American colonies. Philip of Anjou, a Bourbon and thus a relative of the king of France, was named successor to the Spanish throne. The **War of the Spanish Succession** (1702–1713) ensued, and the result at the Treaty of Utrecht (1713) was recognition of a branch of the Bourbon family as rulers of Spain; the price was some commercial concessions that allowed French merchants to operate in Seville and permitted England to trade slaves in Spanish America (and even to send one ship per year to trade for silver in the Americas). Spain's commercial monopoly was now being broken not just by contraband trade but by legal means as well.

The Bourbon Reforms

The new and vigorous Bourbon dynasty in Spain launched a series of reforms aimed at strengthening the state and its economy. In this age of "enlightened despotism," the Spanish Bourbon monarchs, especially **Charles III** (r. 1759–1788), were moved by economic nationalism and a desire for strong centralized government to institute economic, administrative, and military reforms in Spain and its empire. The goal of these rulers and their progressive ministers was to revive Spain within the framework of its traditional society. Their aim was to make government more effective, more powerful, and better able to direct the economy. Certain groups or institutions that opposed these measures or stood in the way might be punished or suppressed. The Jesuit order, with its special allegiance to Rome, its rumored wealth, and its missions in the New World (which controlled almost 100,000 Indians in Paraguay alone), was a prime target. The Jesuits were expelled from Spain and its empire in 1767, as they had been from the Portuguese empire in 1759. In general, however, the entrenched interests of the church and the nobility were not frontally attacked as long as they did not conflict with the authority of the crown. The reforms were aimed at material improvements and a more powerful state, not social or political upheaval. French bureaucratic models were introduced. The system of taxation was tightened. The navy was reformed, and new ships were built. The convoy fleet system was abandoned, and in 1778 new ports were opened in Spain and America for the West Indies trade, although trade still was restricted to Spaniards or to ships sailing under Spanish license.

In the West Indies, the Bourbons initiated a broad program of reform. New viceroyalties were created in

New Granada (1739) and the Rio de la Plata (1778) to provide better administration and defense to the growing populations of these regions. Royal investigators were sent to the Indies. The most important of them, **José de Gálvez,** spent six years in Mexico before returning to Spain to become Minister of the Indies and a chief architect of reform. His investigations, as well as reports by others, revealed the worst abuses of graft and corruption, which implicated the local magistrates and the Creole landowners and aristocracy. Gálvez moved to eliminate the Creoles from the upper bureaucracy of the colonies. New offices were created. After 1780, the *corregidores,* or local magistrates, were removed from the Indian villages, and that office was replaced by a new system of intendants, or provincial governors, based on French models. This intendancy system was introduced throughout the Indies. Such measures improved tax collection and made government more effective, but the reforms also disrupted the patterns of influence and power, especially among the Creole bureaucrats, miners, and landowners as their political power declined.

Many of the reforms in America were linked directly to defense and military matters. During the century, Spain often was allied with France, and the global struggle between England and France for world hegemony made Spain's American possessions a logical target for English attack. During the Seven Years' War (1756–1763), the loss of Florida and the English seizure of Havana shocked Spain into action, particularly because when England held Havana in 1762, Cuban trade boomed. Regular Spanish troops were sent to New Spain, and militia units, led by local Creoles who were given military rank, were created throughout the empire. Frontiers were expanded, and previously unoccupied or loosely controlled regions, such as California, were settled by a combination of missions and small frontier outposts. In the Rio de la Plata, foreign competitors were resisted by military means. Spain sought every means to strengthen itself and its colonies.

During the Bourbon reforms, the government took an active role in the economy. State monopolies were established for items the government considered essential, such as tobacco and gunpowder. Whole new areas of Spanish America were opened to development. Monopoly companies were granted exclusive rights to develop certain colonial areas in return for developing the economies of those regions.

The commerce of the Caribbean greatly expanded under the more liberal trading regulations. Cuba became another full-scale plantation and slave colony, exporting sugar, coffee, and tobacco and importing large numbers of Africans. Buenos Aires, on the Rio de la Plata, proved to be a great success story. Its population had grown rapidly in the 18th century, and by 1790 it had a booming economy based on ranching and the export of hides and salted beef. A newly prosperous merchant community in Buenos Aires dominated the region's trade.

The commercial changes were a double-edged sword. As Spanish and English goods became cheaper and more accessible, they undercut locally produced goods so that some regions that had specialized in producing cloth or other goods were unable to compete with the European imports. Links to international trade tightened as the diversity of Latin America's economy decreased. Later conflicts between those who favored free trade and those who wanted to limit imports and protect local industry often were as much about regional interests as about economic philosophy.

Finally, and most importantly, the major centers of the Spanish Empire also experienced rapid growth in the second half of the 18th century. Mining inspectors and experts had been sent to Peru and New Spain to suggest reforms and introduce new techniques. These improvements, as well as the discovery of new veins, allowed production to expand, especially in New Spain, where silver output reached new heights. In fact, silver production in Mexico far outstripped that of Peru, which itself saw increased production.

All in all, the Bourbon reforms must be seen from two vantage points: Spain and America. Undoubtedly, in the short run, the restructuring of government and economy revived the Spanish Empire. In the long run, the removal of Creoles from government, the creation of a militia with a Creole officer corps, the opening of commerce, and other such changes contributed to a growing sense of dissatisfaction among the elite, which only their relative well-being and the existing social tensions of the sociedad de castas kept in check.

Pombal and Brazil

The Bourbon reforms in Spain and Spanish America were paralleled in the Portuguese world during the administration of the **Marquis of Pombal** (1755–1776), Portugal's authoritarian prime minister. Pombal had lived as ambassador in England and had observed the benefits of mercantilism at firsthand. He hoped to use these same techniques, along with state intervention in the economy, to break England's hold on the Portuguese economy, especially on the flow of Brazilian gold from Portugal to England. This became crucial as the production of Brazilian gold began to decline after 1760. In another example of "enlightened despotism," Pombal brutally suppressed any group or institution that stood in the way of royal power and his programs. He developed a particular dislike for the Jesuits because of their allegiance to Rome and their semi-independent control of large areas in Brazil. Pombal expelled the Jesuits from the Portuguese Empire in 1759.

Pombal made Brazil the centerpiece of his reforms. Vigorous administrators were sent to the colony to enforce the changes. Fiscal reforms were aimed at eliminating contraband, gold smuggling, and tax evasion. Monopoly companies were formed to stimulate agriculture in older plantation zones and were given the right to import large numbers of slaves. New crops were introduced. Just as in Spanish America, new regions in Brazil began to flourish. Rio de Janeiro became the capital, and its hinterland was the scene of agricultural growth. The undeveloped Amazonian region, long dominated by Jesuit missionaries, received new attention. A monopoly company was created to develop the region's economy, and it stimulated the development of cotton plantations and the export of wild cacao from the Amazonian forests. These new exports joined the traditional sugar, tobacco, and hides as Brazil's main products.

Pombal was willing to do some social tinkering as part of his project of reform. He abolished slavery in Portugal to stop the import of slaves there and to ensure a steady supply to Brazil, the economic cornerstone of the empire. Because Brazil was vast and needed to be both occupied and defended, he removed Indians from missionary control in the Amazon and encouraged whites to marry them. Immigrant couples from Portugal and the Azores were sent to colonize the Amazon basin and the plains of southern Brazil, which began to produce large quantities of wheat and cattle. Like the Bourbons in Spain, Pombal hoped to revitalize the colonies as a way of strengthening the mother country. Although new policies were instituted, little changed within the society. Brazil was just as profoundly based on slavery in the late 18th century as it had ever been: The levels of slave imports reached 20,000 a year.

Even in the long run, Pombal's policies were not fully effective. Although he reduced Portugal's trade imbalance with England during this period, Brazilian trade suffered because the demand for its products on the world market remained low. This was a classic problem for the American colonies. Their economies were so tied to the sale of their products on the European market and so controlled by policies in the metropolis that the colonies' range of action was always limited. Although Pombal's policies were not immediately successful, they provided the structure for an economic boom in the last 20 years of the 18th century that set the stage for Brazilian independence.

Reforms, Reactions, and Revolts

By the mid-18th century, the American colonies of Spain and Portugal, like the rest of the world, were experiencing rapid growth in population and productive capacity. By the end of the century, Spanish America had a population of almost 13 million. Between 1740 and 1800, the population of Mexico, the most populous area, increased from 3.5 million to almost 6 million, about half of whom were Indians. In Brazil, the population reached about 2 million by the end of the century. This overall increase resulted from declining mortality rates, increasing fertility levels, increasing immigration from Europe, and the thriving slave trade. The opening of new areas to development and Europe's increasing demand for American products accompanied the population growth. The American colonies were experiencing a boom in the last years of the 18th century.

Reformist policies, tighter tax collection, and the presence of a more activist government in both Spanish America and Brazil disrupted old patterns of power and influence, raised expectations, and sometimes provoked violent colonial reactions. Urban riots, tax revolts, and Indian uprisings were not unknown before 1700, but serious and more protracted rebellions broke out after that date. In New Granada (present-day Colombia), popular complaints against the government's control of tobacco and liquor consumption, and rising prices as well as new taxes, led to the widespread **Comunero Revolt** in 1781. A royal army was defeated, the viceroy fled from Bogota, and a rebel army almost took the capital. Only tensions between the various racial and social groups, and concessions by the government, brought an end to the rebellion.

At the same time, in Peru, an even more threatening revolt erupted. A great Indian uprising took place under the leadership of Jose Gabriel Condorcanqui, known as **Tupac Amaru.** A mestizo with a direct link to the family of the Incas, Tupac Amaru led a rebellion against "bad government." For almost three years the whole viceroyalty was thrown into turmoil while more than 70,000 Indians, mestizos, and even a few Creoles joined in rebellion against the worst abuses of the colonial regime. Tupac Amaru was captured and brutally executed, but the rebellion smoldered until 1783. It failed mostly because the Creoles, although they had their own grievances against the government, feared that a real social upheaval might take place if they upset the political balance.

This kind of social upheaval was not present in Brazil, where a government attempt to collect back taxes in the mining region led in 1788 to a plot against Portuguese control. A few bureaucrats, intellectuals, and miners planned an uprising for independence, but their conspiracy was discovered. The plotters were arrested, and one conspirator, a militia officer nicknamed Tiradentes, was hanged.

Despite their various social bases, these movements indicated that activism by governments increased dissatisfaction in the American colonies. The new prosperity of the late 18th century contributed to a sense of self-confidence and economic interest among certain colonial classes, which made them sensitive to restrictions and control by Spain and Portugal. Different groups had different complaints, but the sharp social and ethnic divisions within the colonies acted as a barrier to cooperation for common goals and tended to undercut revolutionary movements. Only when the Spanish political system was disrupted by a crisis of legitimacy at the beginning of the 19th century did real separation and independence from the mother countries become a possibility.

GLOBAL CONNECTIONS: Latin American Civilization and the World Context

In three centuries, Spain and Portugal created large colonial empires in the Americas. These American colonies provided a basis of power to their Iberian mother countries and took a vital place in the expanding world economy as suppliers of precious minerals and certain crops to the growing economy of Europe. By the 18th century, the weakened positions of Spain and Portugal within Europe allowed England and France to benefit directly from the Iberian trade with American colonies. To their American colonies, the Iberian nations transferred and imposed their language, laws, forms of government, religion, and institutions. Large numbers of immigrants, first as conquerors and later as settlers, came to the colonies. Eventually, the whole spectrum of Iberian society was recreated in the New World as men and women came to seek a better life, bringing with them their customs, ideas, religion, laws, and ways of life. By government and individual action, a certain homogeneity was created, both in Spanish America and in Brazil. That seeming unity was most apparent among the Europeanized population.

In fact, despite the apparent continuity with Spain and Portugal and homogeneity among the various colonies, there were great variations. Latin America, with its distinct environments, its various economic possibilities, and its diverse indigenous peoples, imposed new realities. In places such as Mexico and Peru, Native American cultures emerged from the shock of conquest, battered but still vibrant. Native American communities adapted to the new colonial situation. A distinctive multiethnic and multiracial society developed, drawing on Iberian precedents but also dependant on the native population, the imported Africans, and the various mixed racial categories. Argentina with few Native Americans, Cuba with its slaves and plantations, and Mexico with its large rural indigenous populations all shared the same Hispanic traditions and laws, and all had a predominantly white elite, but their social and economic realities made them very different places. Latin America developed as a composite civilization—distinct from the West but related to it—combining European and Native American culture and society or creating the racial hierarchies of slave societies in places such as Brazil.

The empires of Spain and Portugal in Latin America bear comparison with the Russian Empire that had been formed at about the same time. While Iberian expansion had been maritime and Russian expansion over land, the process of colonization and the conquest of indigenous peoples created many parallels, including the development of coerced labor. The creation of all of these empires also demonstrated the impact of gunpowder. The cultural impact of the West was different in the Iberian and Russian empires. Whereas the Russian rulers had decided, quite selectively, what aspects of Western culture to adopt, in Latin America Western forms were often simply imposed on the populations, but not without resistance.

From the perspective of the world economy, despite the ultimate decline in production of precious metals, Latin American products remained in great demand in Europe's markets. As Latin Americans began to seek political independence in the early 19th century, they were confronted by this basic economic fact and by their continued dependence on trade with the developing global economy. Latin America's world economic position, with its dependant and coerced labor force and outside commercial control, revealed its colonial status, but in its often bitter history of cultural clash and accommodation a new civilization had been born.

Further Readings

James Lockhart and Stuart B. Schwartz's *Early Latin America* (1983) provides an interpretation and overview. Lyle N. Macalister's *Spain and Portugal in the New World* (1984) is particularly good on the Iberian background and the formation of societies in Latin America. The relevant chapters of Leslie Bethell, ed., *The Cambridge History of Latin America*, vols. 1 & 2 (1985) are a good starting point for a discussion of commerce and government. On the conquest period there are excellent regional studies. Geographer Carl O. Sauer's *The Early Caribbean* (1966) describes the discovery, settlement, and conquest of that region, with much attention to Indian culture. James Lockhart's *Spanish Peru* (1968) is a model reconstruction of conquest society, The conquest of Mexico can be seen from two different angles in Bernal Díaz del Castillo's *The Discovery and Conquest of Mexico*, trans. A. P. Maudsley (1956), and in James Lockhart's edition of the Aztec testimony gathered after the conquest by Bernardino de Sahagún, published as *We Peoples Here* (1962). Many sources are collected in S. Schwartz, ed. *Victors and Vanquished* (2000).

The transformation of Indian societies has been studied in books such as Steve J. Stern's *Peru's Indian Peoples and the Challenge of Spanish Conquest* (1982) on the early colonial era, and Ward Stavig, *The World of Tupac Amaru* (1999) on 18th century Peru, and in Matthew Restall, *The Maya World* (1997) on Yucatan. Another approach to the impact of conquest is presented in Noble David Cook's *Born to Die: Disease and New World Conquest, 1492-1650* (1998), and Murdo MacLeod's *Spanish Central America* (1973) presents an integrated regional study of society and economy. Particularly sensitive to Indian views is Nancy Farriss' *Maya Society Under Colonial Rule* (1984).

Social and economic history have received considerable attention. The establishment of colonial economies has been studied in detail in books such as Eric Van Young's *Hacienda and Market in Eighteenth-Century Mexico* (1981); Stuart Schwartz's *Sugar Plantations and the Formation of Brazilian Society* (1985); and Peter J. Bakewell's *Silver Mining and Society in Colonial Mexico* (1971). Very good social history is now being written. For example, Susan Socolow's *Women in Colonial Latin America* (2000) examines the changing role of women. In Louisa Schell Hoberman and Susan Migden Socolow, eds., *Cities and Society in Colonial Latin America* (1986), urban social types are examined. A different kind of social history that examines popular thought can be seen in Serge Gruzinski, *The Conquest of Mexico* (1993).

The best starting place on the Bourbon reforms is David Brading's *Miners and Merchants in Bourbon Mexico* (1971), and John L. Phelan's study, *The Comunero Revolt: The People and the King* (1978) examines the Bourbon reforms' unintended effects. The revolt of Tupac Amaru is analyzed in Sinclair Thomson, *We Alone Will Rule* (2002). Dauril Alden's *Royal Government in Colonial Brazil* (1968) and Kenneth Maxwell, *Conflicts and Conspiracies* (1973) show Pombal's effects on Brazil.

On the Web

The methods by which Europeans extracted wealth from Latin America by the manipulation of old or imposition of new patterns of mining, labor, and land ownership (the mita and encomendero systems) and the impact these new patterns of economic life had on both the indigenous population and the imported African slave population is collectively examined at http://www.emory.edu/COLLEGE/CULPEPER/BAKEWELL/index.html, http://www.hist.umn.edu/~rmccaa/colonial/potosi/, http://history.smsu.edu/jchuchiak/HSt%20350--/Theme%2017--Colonial_silver_mining. htm, and http://www.cla.sc.edu/hist/faculty/seardaville/hist420/doe114.htm. These sites also illuminate the efforts of Portugal's Marquis of Pombal and the Spanish throne to control the economies of Latin America.

Indigenous resistance to Latin America's dependant economic position is given a human face through a discussion of the rebellions of Tupac Amaru and Juan Santos Atahualpa at http://www.dickshovel.com/500.html. Some of the syncretic or composite elements of modern Latin American civilization is revealed in its celebration of the "Day of the Dead" http://www.public.iastate.edu/~rjsalvad/scmfaq/muertos.html and http://teacherlink. ed.usu.edu/tlresources/units/Byrnes-celebrations/Day.html. A traditional Day of the Dead altar can be constructed using guidelines provided at http://www.mexweb.com/muertos.htm.

CHAPTER 20

AFRICA AND THE AFRICANS IN THE AGE OF THE ATLANTIC SLAVE TRADE

African slave market

- The Atlantic
  Slave Trade
- African Societies,
  Slavery, and the
  Slave Trade
- VISUALIZING THE PAST:
  Symbols of African
  Kingship
- White Settlers
  and Africans in
  Southern Africa
- IN DEPTH: Slavery and
  Human Society
- The African
  Diaspora
- DOCUMENT: An
  African's
  Description
  of the Middle
  Passage
- GLOBAL CONNECTIONS:
  Africa and the
  African Diaspora
  in World Context

Sometimes a single, extraordinary life can represent the forces and patterns of a whole historical era. Mahommah Gardo Baquaqua was a young man from the trading town of Djougou in the north of what is now the modern Benin Republic in west Africa. A Muslim, he could speak Arabic, Hausa, and a number of other languages, as was common among the trading peoples from which he came. At a young age, Baquaqua was captured and enslaved during internal wars in Africa; after gaining his freedom, he was enslaved again, and around 1845 sold into the Atlantic slave trade. He was taken first to northeastern Brazil and from there was purchased by a ship captain from Rio de Janeiro. After voyages along the Brazilian coast, his ship eventually sailed for New York. There, in 1847, after an attempt to use the courts to gain his freedom, Baquaqua with the help of local abolitionists fled to Boston. Befriended by American Baptist missionaries, Baquaqua sailed for Haiti with them. Eventually he learned French and English and studied at a college in upstate New York, in order to prepare for missionary work in his native Africa. Racial incidents eventually moved him to immigrate to Canada, and although he left the Baptist college, he continued to seek ways to return to Africa. In 1854, hoping for funding that would help him realize his dream, and with the help of abolitionist friends, he published his autobiography, *An Interesting Narrative: Biography of Mahommah G. Baquaqua*. We do not know if he returned to the land of his birth. The life of this African—caught up in the historical currents of his age while singular in many aspects—still represents the stories of millions of Africans in the age of the slave trade, and these make up an important part of world history.

Sub-Saharan Africa, previously linked to the Muslim world in many ways, moved at its own pace even as it was pulled in new directions during the early modern centuries. Islam remained important, and in eastern Africa so did trade with western Asia, but the rise of the West and of the Western-dominated world economy proved to be a powerful force in recasting the framework of African history. The strength of earlier African cultural and political traditions persisted in many places, but the impact of the West was the newest influence in Africa and in some respects an immensely powerful one. African history had its own pace and rhythm, and this chapter therefore exceeds the chronological boundaries of the early modern period. The influences of Islam and the West initiated or intensified processes of religious conversion, political reorganization, and social change that persisted in some cases into the 19th century. The distinctive nature and chronology of African history should not blind us to its role in world history.

1400 C.E.	1500 C.E.	1600 C.E.	1700 C.E.	1800 C.E.
1415 Portuguese capture Ceuta (Morocco); beginning of European expansion **1441** First shipment of African slaves brought directly from Africa to Portugal **1481** Portuguese fort established at El Mina	**1562** Beginnings of English slave trade **1570** Portuguese establish colony in Angola **1591** Fall of Songhay Empire	**1652** Dutch establish colony at Cape of Good Hope	**1700–1717** Osei Tutu unifies the Asante kingdom **1713** English get right to import slaves to Spanish Empire **1720s** Rise of the kingdom of Dahomey **1790s** Abolitionist movement gains strength in England **1792** Slave uprising in Haiti	**1804** Usuman Dan Fodio leads Hausa expansion **1815** Cape colony comes under formal British control **1818–1828** Shaka forges Zulu power and expansion; *Mfecane* under way **1833** Great Britain abolishes slavery in the West Indies **1834** Boers make "Great Trek" into Natal

During the age of European maritime and commercial expansion, large areas of Africa were brought into the orbit of the expanding world economy and were influenced by the transformation taking place. Not all parts of Africa were influenced in the same way or at the same time. After 1450, the growing and often bitter contacts between Europeans and Africans, primarily through the slave trade, linked the destiny of Africa to the broader external trends of the emerging world economy. These contacts also resulted in a diaspora of millions of Africans to the Middle East, Europe, and especially the Americas. Not all European contact with Africa was centered on the slave trade, nor was the desire for slaves the only impulse behind European explorations, but the slave trade after 1600 overshadowed other activities until the mid-19th century. Along with Latin America and Europe itself, sub-Saharan Africa was most deeply affected by the world economy during the early modern period, but its patterns, including its involvements with the West, remained distinctive.

Changing global interactions had a direct impact on certain areas of Africa, and it also made Africans an important element in the shifting balance of world civilizations. The forced movement of Africans as captive laborers and the creation of slave-based societies in the Americas were major aspects of the formation of the modern world and the growth of the economies of western Europe. This forced migration was part of the international exchange of foods, diseases, animals, and ideas that marked the era and had a profound influence on the indigenous peoples in various regions, as we saw in the case of the Americas. Moreover, in large areas of the Americas colonized by Europeans, where slavery came to be the predominant form of labor, African culture was transferred, contributing to the creation of new cultural forms. In this chapter we examine the history of parts of Africa in the age of the slave trade and the creation of slave societies in the Atlantic world as part of the general process of European expansion and the creation of a world economy.

Although much of the analysis in this chapter emphasizes the increasing linkage between Africa and the wider world, it should be made clear at the outset that many fundamental processes of African development continued throughout this period. Almost all of Africa remained independent of outside political control, and most cultural development was autonomous as well. Africa differed profoundly from Latin America in these respects during the early modern centuries.

A variety of trends affected various parts of the sub-Saharan region. Islam consolidated its position in east Africa and the Sudan. In Ethiopia, the Christian kingdom of the highlands continued to hold off its Muslim rivals. In many places in Africa, as in Europe, independent states continued to form and expand, perhaps as a result of a population expansion that followed the spread of iron tools and improved agriculture. Kingdoms spread to new areas. Scholars disagree on the extent to which these long-term developments were affected by Europeans and the rise of the Atlantic slave trade. Some argue that the enlarged political scale—the growth of large kingdoms through much of the subcontinent—was the dominant theme of the period and that slavery was one of its by-products. Others see European demand as a major impulse in political expansion. In this chapter we emphasize the impact of slavery and the slave trade because our focus is not simply the geographic region of Africa but the African peoples who, like Baquaqua, were swept into the expanding international economy.

The Atlantic Slave Trade

 Early Portuguese contacts set the patterns for contact with the African coast. The slave trade expanded to meet the demand for labor in the new American colonies, and millions were exported in an organized commerce that involved Europeans and Africans.

Portuguese ships pushed down the west African coast and finally reached the Cape of Good Hope in 1487 (Map 20.1). Along the coast, the Portuguese established **factories:** forts and trading posts with resident merchants. The most important of these was **El Mina** (1482) in the heart of the gold-producing region of the forest zone. These forts allowed the Portuguese to exercise some control with few personnel. Although the early voyagers carried out some raids, once out of range of their cannons, the Portuguese simply were not powerful enough to enforce their will on the larger west African states. Therefore, most forts were established with the consent of local rulers, who benefited from access to European commodities and sometimes from the military support the Portuguese provided in local wars.

Africans acquired goods from the Portuguese, who sometimes provided African rulers with slaves brought from other stretches of the coast. In return, the Portuguese received ivory, pepper, animal skins, and gold. From El Mina, Accra, and other trade forts, routes led directly into the gold-producing regions of the interior, so that the Portuguese eventually traded with Mande and Soninke merchants from Mali and Songhay. Much of the Portuguese success resulted from their ability to penetrate the existing African trade routes, to which they could also add specialized items. Portuguese and African-Portuguese mulatto traders struck out into the interior to establish trade contacts and collection points.

Trade was the basis of Portuguese relations with Africans, but in the wake of commerce came political, religious, and social relations. The small states of the Senegambian coast did not impress the Portuguese who were particularly suspicious of Muslims, their traditional enemies. When they reached the Gold Coast (modern Ghana) and found the kingdom of Benin, they were impressed both by the power of

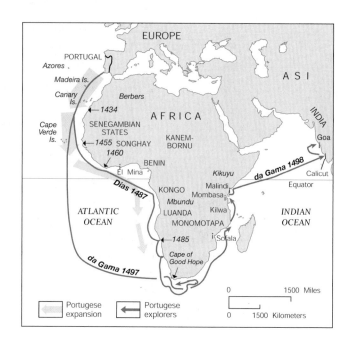

Map 20.1 *Portuguese Expansion and Major African Kingdoms*

the ruler and by the magnificence of his court. Other large African states also provoked similar responses.

Missionary efforts were made to convert the rulers of Benin, Kongo, and other African kingdoms. The Portuguese contacted the Kongo kingdom south of the Zaire River about 1484. The missionaries achieved a major success in Kongo, where members of the royal family were converted. The ruler, **Nzinga Mvemba** (r. 1507–1543), with the help of Portuguese advisors and missionaries, brought the whole kingdom to Christianity. Attempts were made to "Europeanize" the kingdom. Portugal and Kongo exchanged ambassadors and dealt with each other with a certain equality in this early period, but eventually enslavement of his subjects led Nzinga Mvemba to try to end the slave trade and limit Portuguese activities. He was only partially successful because of Portugal's control of Kongo's ability to communicate with the outside world and its dominance over Kongo's trade.

These first contacts were marked by cultural preconceptions as well as by appreciation and curiosity. Africans found the newcomers strange and at first tried to fit them into their existing concepts of the spiritual and natural world. Images of Portuguese soldiers and traders began to appear in the bronzes of Benin and the carved ivory sculptures of other African peoples (Figure 20.1). The Portuguese tended to

look on Africans as savages and pagans who were also capable of civilized behavior and conversion.

Portuguese exploration continued southward toward the Cape of Good Hope and beyond in the 16th century. Early contacts were made with the Mbundu peoples south of Kongo in the 1520s, and a more permanent Portuguese settlement was established there in the 1570s with the foundation of **Luanda** on the coast. This became the basis for the Portuguese colony of Angola. As we have already seen, the Portuguese tried to dominate the existing trading system of the African ports in the Indian Ocean and Red Sea. They established a base on Mozambique Island and then secured bases at Kilwa, Mombasa, Sofala, and other ports that gave them access to the gold trade from Monomotapa (Mwenemutapa) in the interior. In east Africa, as on the west African coast, the number of permanent Portuguese settlers was minimal. The Portuguese effort was primarily commercial and military, although it was always accompanied by a strong missionary effort.

The patterns of contact established by the Portuguese were followed by others. In the 17th century, the Dutch, English, French, and others competed with the Portuguese and displaced them to some extent, but the system of fortified trading stations, the combination of force and diplomacy, alliances with local rulers, and the predominance of commercial

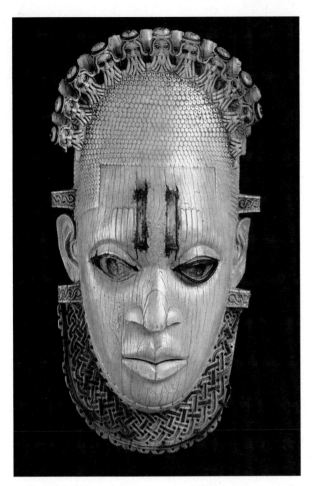

Figure 20.1 *African artists were impressed by Europeans and sometimes incorporated them in their own work, as can be seen in the headpiece of this beautifully carved ivory head of a Benin monarch. Europeans in turn employed African artisans to produce decorative luxury goods.*

relations continued as the principal pattern of European contact with Africa.

Although for a long time Portugal's major interest was in gold, pepper, and other products, a central element in this pattern was the slave trade. Slavery as an institution had been extensive in the Roman Empire but had greatly declined in most of Europe during the Middle Ages, when it was replaced by serfdom. In the Mediterranean and in Iberia, however, where there was an active military frontier between Christians and Muslims, it had remained important. Moreover, the trans-Saharan slave trade had brought small numbers of black Africans into the Mediterranean throughout the period. The Portuguese voyages now opened a direct channel to sub-Saharan Africa. The first slaves brought directly to Portugal from Africa arrived in 1441, and after that date slaves became a common trade item. The Portuguese and later other Europeans raided for slaves along the coast, but the numbers acquired in this way were small. After initial raids, Europeans found that trade was a much more secure and profitable way to get these human cargoes. For example, the Portuguese sent about 50 slaves per year to Portugal before 1450, when raiding was prevalent, but by 1460 some 500 slaves per year arrived in Portugal as a trade with African rulers developed. Whether the victims were acquired by raiding or by trade, the effects on them were similar. An eyewitness to the unloading of slaves in Portugal in 1444 wrote,

> But what heart could be so hard as not to be pierced with piteous feelings to see that company? For some kept their heads low and their faces bathed in tears, looking one upon another; others stood groaning very dolorously, looking up to the height of heaven, fixing their eyes upon it, crying out loudly, as if asking help of the Father of Nature.

The slave trade was given added impetus when the Portuguese and the Spanish began to develop sugar plantations on the Atlantic islands of Madeira (Portugal) and the Canaries (Spain) and off the African coast on Portuguese Sao Tomé. Sugar production demanded many workers and constant labor under difficult conditions, usually in a tropical or subtropical environment. The plantation system of organization associated with sugar, in which managers were able to direct and control laborers over long periods with little restraint, was later extended to America and then to other crops. Although the system did not depend only on Africans, they became the primary plantation laborers in the Atlantic world. The slave trade grew significantly in volume and complexity after 1550 as the American plantation colonies, especially Brazil, began to develop. By 1600, the slave trade predominated over all other kinds of commerce on the African coast.

Trend Toward Expansion

Although debate and controversy surround many aspects of the history of slavery, it is perhaps best to start with the numbers. Estimates of the volume of the trade vary widely, and scholars still debate the figures and their implications, but the range of calculations has been narrowed by recent research. Between 1450 and 1850, it is estimated that about 12 million

TABLE 20.1
Slave Exports from Africa, 1500-1900 (in thousands)

	1500–1600 (%)	1600–1700 (%)	1700–1800 (%)	1800–1900 (%)	Total
Red Sea	200 (17)	200 (7)	200 (3)	450 (8)	1050 (6)
Trans-Sahara	550 (47)	700 (24)	700 (9)	1200 (22)	3150 (19)
East Africa and Indian Ocean	100 (9)	100 (4)	400 (5)	442 (8)	1042 (6)
Trans-Atlantic	325 (28)	1868 (65)	6133 (83)	3330 (61)	11,656 (69)
					16,898

Source: Adapted from Paul Lovejoy, *Transformations in Slavery: A History of Slavery in Africa* (1983).

Africans were shipped across the Atlantic (Table 20.1). With a mortality rate of 10 to 20 percent on the ships, about 10 or 11 million Africans actually arrived in the Americas. How many people died in Africa as a result of the slaving wars or in the forced marches to the coast is unknown, but estimates have been as high as one-third of the total captured. The volume changed over time. In the 16th century, the numbers were small, but they increased to perhaps 16,000 per year in the 17th century. The 18th century was the great age of the Atlantic slave trade; probably more than 7 million slaves, or more than 80 percent of all those embarked, were exported between 1700 and 1800. By the latter date, about 3 million slaves lived in the Americas. Even in the 19th century, when slavery was under attack, the trade to some places continued. Cuba received some 700,000 slaves, and Brazil took more than 1 million in that century alone.

The high volume of the slave trade was necessary to the slave owners because, in most of the slave regimes in the Caribbean and Latin America, slave mortality was high and fertility was low (partly because more men than women were imported). Thus, over time there was usually a loss of population. The only way to maintain or expand the number of slaves was by importing more from Africa. The one exception to this pattern was the southern United States, where the slave population grew, perhaps because of the temperate climate and the fact that few worked in the most dangerous and unhealthy occupations, such as sugar growing and mining. By 1860, almost 6 million slaves worked in the Americas, about 4 million of them in the southern United States, an area that depended more on natural population growth than on the Atlantic slave trade. In terms of total population, however, slaves in British North America were never more than one-fourth of the whole population, whereas in the British and French Caribbean they made up 80 to 90 percent of the population.

The dimensions of the trade varied over time, reflecting the economic and political situation in the Americas. From 1530 to 1650, Spanish America and Brazil received the majority of African slaves, but after the English and French began to grow sugar in the Caribbean, the islands of Jamaica, Barbados, and St. Domingue (Haiti) became important terminals for the slavers. By the 18th century, Virginia and the Carolinas in North America had also become major destinations, although they never rivaled the Caribbean or Brazil (Table 20.2).

Between 1550 and 1850, Brazil alone received 3.5 to 5 million Africans, or about 42 percent of all those who reached the New World. The Caribbean islands, dedicated to sugar production, were the other major destination of Africans. The island colonies of St. Domingue and Jamaica each received more than 1 million slaves in the 18th century alone.

TABLE 20.2
Destinations of African Slaves in the Atlantic Slave Trade

	Thousands	Percentage
British North America	523	5
Spanish America	1687	15
British Caribbean	2443	21
French Caribbean	1655	15
Dutch Caribbean	500	4
Danish Caribbean	50	0.4
Brazil	4190	37
Old World	297	2.6
	11,345	

Source: James Rawley, *The Transatlantic Slave Trade* (1981), 428.

It should be emphasized that these figures represent only the volume in the Atlantic slave trade. The older trans-Sahara, Red Sea, and east African slave trades in the hands of Muslim traders continued throughout the period and added another 3 million people to the total of Africans exported as slaves in this period (see Table 20.1).

The Atlantic slave trade drew slaves from across the continent, and its concentration shifted over time. In the 16th century, the majority of slaves were exported from the Senegambia region, but by the 17th century, west central Africa (modern Zaire and Angola) was the major supplier. That area was joined by the areas of the Gold Coast and the Slave Coast—Dahomey and Benin—at the end of the century, when Benin alone was exporting more than 10,000 slaves per year. In the century that followed, wars for control of the interior created the large states of Asante among the Akan peoples of the Gold Coast and Dahomey among the Fon peoples. These wars were both the cause and the result of increasing slave exports from these regions.

Demographic Patterns

The majority of the trans-Saharan slave trade consisted of women to be used as concubines and domestic servants in north Africa and the Middle East, but the Atlantic slave trade concentrated on men. To some extent this was because planters and mine owners in the Americas were seeking workers for heavy labor and were not eager to risk buying children because of the high levels of mortality. Also, African societies that sold captives into slavery often preferred to sell the men and keep the women and children as domestic slaves or to extend existing kin groups.

The Atlantic trade seems to have had a demographic impact on at least certain parts of west and central Africa. One estimate is that the population of about 25 million in 1850 in those regions was about one-half what it would have been had there been no slave trade. It is true that the trans-Atlantic trade carried more men than women and more women than children, but captive women and children who remained in Africa swelled the numbers of enslaved people and skewed the proportion of women to men in the African enslaving societies. Finally, as the Atlantic trade developed, new crops, such as maize and manioc, were introduced to Africa that provided new food resources for the population and helped it recover from the losses to the slave trade.

Organization of the Trade

The patterns of contact and trade established by the Portuguese at first were followed by rival Europeans on the African coast. Control of the slave trade or a portion of it generally reflected the political situation in Europe. For one and a half centuries, until about 1630, the Portuguese controlled most of the coastal trade and were the major suppliers of their own colony of Brazil and the Spanish settlements in America. The growth of slave-based plantation colonies in the Caribbean and elsewhere led other Europeans to compete with the Portuguese. The Dutch became major competitors when they seized El Mina in 1637. By the 1660s, the English were eager to have their own source of slaves for their growing colonies in Barbados, Jamaica, and Virginia. The **Royal African Company** was chartered for that purpose. The French made similar arrangements in the 1660s, but not until the 18th century did France become a major carrier. Like other small European nations, even Denmark had its agents and forts on the African coast.

Each nation established merchant towns or trade forts at places such as Axim, Nembe, Bonny, Whydah, and Luanda from which a steady source of captives could be obtained. For the Europeans stationed on the coast, Africa was also a graveyard because of the tropical diseases they encountered. Fewer than 10 percent of the employees of the Royal Africa Company who went to Africa ever returned to England, and the majority died in the first year out. European mortality among the crews of slave ships was also very high because of tropical diseases such as malaria. The slave trade proved deadly to all involved, but at least some of the Europeans had a choice, whereas for the enslaved Africans there was none.

European agents for the companies often had to deal directly with local rulers, paying a tax or offering gifts. Various forms of currency were used, such as iron bars, brass rings, and cowrie shells. The Spanish developed a complicated system in which a healthy man was called an **Indies piece,** and children and women were priced at fractions of that value. Slaves were brought to the coast by a variety of means. Sometimes, as in Angola, European military campaigns produced captives for slaves, or African and mulatto agents purchased captives at interior trade centers. In Dahomey, a royal monopoly was established to control the flow of slaves. Some groups used their position to tax or control the movement of slaves from the interior to the coast. Although African and European states tried to establish monopolies over the trade, private merchants often circumvented restrictions.

Clearly, both Europeans and Africans were actively involved in the slave trade. It was not always clear which side was in control. One group of English merchants on the Gold Coast complained of African insolence in 1784 because in negotiations the Africans had emphasized that "the country belongs to them." In any case, the result of this collaboration was to send millions of Africans into bondage in foreign lands.

Historians have long debated the profitability of the slave trade. Some argue that the profits were so great and constant that they were a major element in the rise of commercial capitalism and, later, the origins of the Industrial Revolution. Undoubtedly, many people profited from the trade in African slaves. A single slaving voyage might make a profit of as much as 300 percent, and merchants in the ports that specialized in fitting out ships for the slave trade, such as Liverpool, England, or Nantes, France—as well as African suppliers—derived a profit from the slave trade. But the slave trade also involved risks and costs, so that in the long run, profitability levels did not remain so high. In the late 18th century, profitability in the English slave trade probably ran from 5 to 10 percent on average, and in the French and Dutch trades it was slightly lower. The slave trade was little more profitable in the long run than most business activities of the age, and by itself was not a major source of the capital needed in the Industrial Revolution.

However, it is difficult to calculate the full economic importance of slavery to the economies of Europe because it was so directly linked to the plantation and mining economies of the Americas. During some periods, a **triangular trade** existed in which slaves were carried to the Americas; sugar, tobacco, and other goods were then carried to Europe; and European products were sent to the coast of Africa to begin the triangle again. Were profits from the slave trade accumulated in Liverpool invested in the textile industry of England? And if so, how important were these investments for the growth of that industry? We would need to calculate the value of goods produced in Europe for exchange in the slave trade as well as the profits derived from the colonies to measure the importance of slavery to the growth of the European economies. Still, the very persistence of the slave trade indicates its viability. The slave trade surely contributed to the formation of emerging capitalism in the Atlantic world. In Africa itself, the slave trade often drew economies into dependence on trade with Europeans and suppressed the growth of other economic activities.

It is clear that by the late 18th century, the slave trade and slavery were essential aspects of the economy of the Atlantic basin, and their importance was increasing. More than 40 percent of all the slaves that crossed the Atlantic embarked during the century after 1760, and the plantation economies of Brazil, the Caribbean, and the southern United States were booming in the early 19th century. The slave trade was profitable enough to keep merchants in it, and it contributed in some way to the expanding economy of western Europe. It was also the major way in which Africa was linked to the increasingly integrated economy of the world.

African Societies, Slavery, and the Slave Trade

 The slave trade influenced African forms of servitude and the social and political development of African states. Newly powerful states such as Asante and Dahomey emerged in west Africa, and in the Sudan and east Africa, slavery also produced long-term effects.

Europeans in the age of the slave trade sometimes justified the enslavement of Africans by pointing out that slavery already existed on that continent. However, although forms of bondage were ancient in Africa, and the Muslim trans-Sahara and Red Sea trades already were established, the Atlantic trade interacted with and transformed these earlier aspects of slavery.

African societies had developed many forms of servitude, which varied from a peasant status to something much more like chattel slavery, in which people were considered things: "property with a soul," as Aristotle put it. African states usually were nonegalitarian, and because in many African societies all land was owned by the state or the ruler, the control of slaves was one of the few ways, if not the only way, in which individuals or lineages could increase their wealth and status. Slaves were used as servants, concubines, soldiers, administrators, and field workers. In some cases, as in the ancient empire of Ghana and in Kongo, there were whole villages of enslaved dependants who were required to pay tribute to the ruler. The Muslim traders of west Africa who linked the forest region to the savanna had slave porters as well as villages of slaves to supply their caravans. In many situations, these forms of servitude were fairly benign and were an extension of lineage and kinship systems. In others, however, they were exploitive economic and social relations that reinforced the hierarchies of various African societies and allowed the nobles, senior lineages, and rulers to exercise their power. Among the forest states of west Africa, such as Benin, and in the Kongo kingdom in central Africa, slavery was already an important institution before the European arrival, but the Atlantic trade opened up new opportunities for expansion and intensification of slavery in those societies.

Despite great variation in African societies and the fact that slaves sometimes attained positions of command and trust, in most cases slaves were denied choice about their lives and actions. They were placed in dependant or inferior positions, and they were often considered aliens. It is important to remember that the enslavement of women was a central feature of African slavery. Although slaves were used in many ways in African societies, domestic slavery and the extension of lineages through the addition of female members remained a central feature in many places. Some historians believe that the excess of women led to polygyny (having more than one wife at a time) and the creation of large harems by rulers and merchants, whose power was increased by this process, and the position of women was lowered in some societies.

In the Sudanic states of the savanna, Islamic concepts of slavery had been introduced. Slavery was viewed as a legitimate fate for nonbelievers but was illegal for Muslims. Despite the complaints of legal scholars such as Ahmad Baba of Timbuktu (1556–1627) against the enslavement of Muslims, many of the Sudanic states enslaved their captives, both pagan and Muslim. In the Niger valley, slave communities produced agricultural surpluses for the rulers and nobles of Songhay, Gao, and other states. Slaves were used for gold mining and salt production and as caravan workers in the Sahara. Slavery was a widely diffused form of labor control and wealth in Africa.

The existence of slavery in Africa and the preexisting trade in people allowed Europeans to mobilize the commerce in slaves quickly by tapping existing routes and supplies. In this venture they were aided by the rulers of certain African states, who were anxious to acquire more slaves for themselves and to supply slaves to the Europeans in exchange for aid and commodities. In the 16th-century Kongo kingdom, the ruler had an army of 20,000 slaves as part of his household, and this gave him greater power than any Kongo ruler had ever held. In general,

African rulers did not enslave their own people, except for crimes or in other unusual circumstances; rather, they enslaved their neighbors. Thus, expanding, centralizing states often were the major suppliers of slaves to the Europeans as well as to societies in which slavery was an important institution.

Slaving and African Politics

As one French agent put it, "The trade in slaves is the business of kings, rich men, and prime merchants." European merchants and royal officials were able to tap existing routes, markets, and institutions, but the new and constant demand also intensified enslavement in Africa and perhaps changed the nature of slavery itself in some African societies.

In the period between 1500 and 1750, as the gunpowder empires and expanding international commerce of Europe penetrated sub-Saharan Africa, existing states and societies often were transformed. As we saw in Chapter 8, the empire of Songhay controlled a vast region of the western savanna until its defeat by a Moroccan invasion in 1591, but for the most part the many states of central and western Africa were small and fragmented. This led to a situation of instability caused by competition and warfare as states tried to expand at the expense of their neighbors or to consolidate power by incorporating subject provinces. The warrior or soldier emerged in this situation as an important social type in states such as the Kongo kingdom and Dahomey as well as along the Zambezi River. The endless wars promoted the importance of the military and made the sale of captives into the slave trade an extension of the politics of regions of Africa. Sometimes, as among the Muslim states of the savanna or the Lake Chad region, wars took on a religious overtone of believers against nonbelievers, but in much of west and central Africa that was not the case. Some authors see this situation as a feature of African politics; others believe it was the result of European demand for new slaves. In either case, the result was the capture and sale of millions of human beings. Although increasing centralization and hierarchy could be seen in the enslaving African societies, a contrary trend of self-sufficiency and antiauthoritarian ideas developed among the peoples who bore the brunt of the slaving attacks.

One result of the presence of Europeans on the coast was a shift in the locus of power within Africa. Just as states such as Ghana and Songhay in the savanna took advantage of their position as intermediaries between the gold of the west African forests and the trans-Saharan trade routes, the states closer to the coast or in contact with the Europeans could play a similar role. Those right on the coast tried to monopolize the trade with Europeans, but European meddling in their internal affairs and European fears of any coastal power that became too strong blocked the creation of centralized states under the shadow of European forts. Just beyond the coast it was different. With access to European goods, especially firearms, iron, horses, cloth, tobacco, and other goods, western and central African kingdoms began to redirect trade toward the coast and to expand their influence. Some historians have written of a gun and slave cycle in which increased firepower allowed these states to expand over their neighbors, producing more slaves, which they traded for more guns. The result was unending warfare and the disruption of societies as the search for slaves pushed ever farther into the interior.

Asante and Dahomey

Perhaps the effects of the slave trade on African societies are best seen in some specific cases. Several large states developed in west Africa during the slave trade era. Each represented a response to the realities of the European presence and the process of state formation long under way in Africa. Rulers in these states grew in power and often surrounded themselves with ritual authority and a luxurious court life as a way of reinforcing the position that their armies had won (Figures 20.2 and 20.3).

In the area called the Gold Coast by the Europeans, the empire of **Asante** (Ashanti) rose to prominence in the period of the slave trade. The Asante were members of the Akan people (the major group

Figure 20.2   *The annual yam harvest festival was an occasion when the power and authority of the Asante ruler could be displayed. The English observers who painted this scene were impressed by the might of this west African kingdom.*

Figure 20.3   *The size of African cities and the power of African rulers often impressed European observers. Here the city of Loango, capital of a kingdom on the Kongo coast, is depicted as a bustling urban center. At this time it was a major port in the slave trade.*

of modern Ghana) who had settled in and around Kumasi, a region of gold and kola nut production that lay between the coast and the Hausa and Mande trading centers to the north. There were at least 20 small states, based on the matrilineal clans that were common to all the Akan peoples, but those of the Oyoko clan predominated. Their cooperation and their access to firearms after 1650 initiated a period of centralization and expansion. Under the vigorous **Osei Tutu** (d. 1717), the title **asantehene** was created to designate the supreme civil and religious leader. His golden stool became the symbol of an Asante union that was created by linking the many Akan clans under the authority of the asantehene but recognizing the autonomy of subordinate areas. An

all-Asante council advised the ruler, and an ideology of unity was used to overcome the traditional clan divisions. With this new structure and a series of military reforms, conquest of the area began. By 1700, the Dutch on the coast realized that a new power had emerged, and they began to deal directly with it.

With control of the gold-producing zones and a constant supply of prisoners to be sold as slaves for more firearms, Asante maintained its power until the 1820s as the dominant state of the Gold Coast. Although gold continued to be a major item of export, by the end of the 17th century, slaves made up almost two-thirds of Asante's trade.

Farther to the east, in the area of the Bight of Benin (between the Volta and Benin rivers on what

Visualizing the Past

Symbols of African Kingship

In many African societies, the symbols of authority and kingship had a ritual power. African kings were sacred, or sacredness resided in the symbols of their authority. Art and design, by creating impressive ritual and civil objects, were often used to emphasize the power and prestige of the ruler and the links between the community and the king. In Dahomey, for example, royal treasures were paraded by the people as a way of creating a sense of pride and awe among the viewers. Among the Fante people, young males of the chief's family carry staffs and decorative swords, each of which carries a message or symbolic meaning. Such ceremonies solidify the image of the king and link the generations. Arts can serve kingship, and by mobilizing artists and by defining the images and messages to be conveyed, rulers help to create culture. This was a technique of rule in no way limited to Africa.

Fante Boys in Ghana Holding Symbolic Swords

the Europeans called the Slave Coast), several large states developed. The kingdom of Benin was at the height of its power when the Europeans arrived. It traced its origins to the city of Ife and to the Yoruba peoples that were its neighbors, but it had become a separate and independent kingdom with its own well-developed political and artistic traditions, especially in the casting of bronze. As early as 1516, the ruler, or *oba*, limited the slave trade from Benin, and for a long time most trade with Europeans was controlled directly by the king and was in pepper, textiles, and ivory rather than slaves. Eventually, European pressure and the goals of the Benin nobility combined to generate a significant slave trade in the 18th century, but Benin never made the slave trade its primary source of revenue or state policy.

The kingdom of **Dahomey,** which developed among the Fon (or Aja) peoples, had a different response to the European presence. It began to emerge as a power in the 17th century from its center at Abomey, about 70 miles from the coast. Its kings ruled with the advice of powerful councils, but by the 1720s access to firearms allowed the rulers to create an autocratic and sometimes brutal political regime based on the slave trade. In the 1720s, under

King Agaja (1708–1740), the kingdom of Dahomey moved toward the coast, seizing in 1727 the port town of Whydah, which had attracted many European traders. Although Dahomey became to some extent a subject of the powerful neighboring Yoruba state of Oyo, whose cavalry and archers made it strong, Dahomey maintained its autonomy and turned increasingly to the cycle of firearms and slaves. The trade was controlled by the royal court, whose armies (including a regiment of women) were used to raid for more captives. As Dahomey expanded it eliminated the royal families and customs of the areas it conquered and imposed its own traditions. This resulted in the formation of a unified state, which lasted longer than some of its neighbors. Well into the 19th century, Dahomey was a slaving state, and dependence on the trade in human beings had negative effects on the society as a whole. More than 1.8 million slaves were exported from the Bight of Benin between 1640 and 1890.

This emphasis on the slave trade should not obscure the creative process within many of the African states. The growing divine authority of the rulers paralleled the rise of absolutism in Europe. It led to the development of new political forms, some of which had the power to limit the role of the king. In the Yoruba state of Oyo, for example, a governing council shared power with the ruler. In some states, a balance of offices kept central power in check. In Asante, the traditional village chiefs and officials whose authority was based on their lineage were increasingly challenged by new officials appointed by the asantehene as a state bureaucracy began to form.

The creativity of these societies was also seen in traditional arts. In many places, crafts such as bronze casting, woodcarving, and weaving flourished. Guilds of artisans developed in many societies, and their specialization produced crafts executed with great skill. In Benin and the Yoruba states, for example, remarkable and lifelike sculptures in wood and ivory continued to be produced. Often, however, the best artisans labored for the royal court, producing objects designed to honor the ruling family and reinforce the civil and religious authority of the king. This was true in architecture, weaving, and the decorative arts as well. Much of this artistic production also had a religious function or contained religious symbolism; African artists made the spiritual world visually apparent.

Europeans came to appreciate African arts and skills. In the 16th century the Portuguese began to employ African artists from Benin, Sierra Leone, and Kongo to work local ivory into ladles, saltcellars (containers), and other decorative objects that combined African and European motifs in beautifully carved designs (Figure 20.4). Although commissioned by Europeans and sometimes including European religious and political symbols, African artists found ways to incorporate traditional symbols and themes from motherhood to royal power. Many of these objects ended up in the collections of nobles and kings throughout Renaissance Europe. They demonstrated the growing contact between Africa and the wider world.

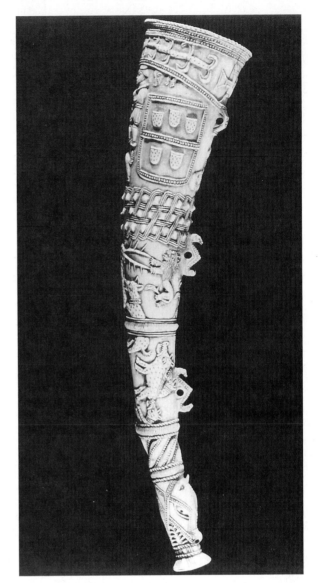

Figure 20.4 *Ivory hunting horn*

East Africa and the Sudan

West Africa obviously was the region most directly influenced by the trans-Atlantic slave trade, but there and elsewhere in Africa, long-term patterns of society and economy continued and intersected with the new external influences. On the east coast of Africa, the Swahili trading cities continued their commerce in the Indian Ocean, adjusting to the military presence of the Portuguese and the Ottoman Turks. Trade to the interior continued to bring ivory, gold, and a steady supply of slaves. Many of these slaves were destined for the harems and households of Arabia and the Middle East, but a small number were carried away by the Europeans for their plantation colonies. The Portuguese and Indo-Portuguese settlers along the Zambezi River in Mozambique used slave soldiers to increase their territories, and certain groups in interior east Africa specialized in supplying ivory and slaves to the east African coast. Europeans did establish some plantation-style colonies on islands such as Mauritius in the Indian Ocean, and these depended on the east African slave trade.

On Zanzibar and other offshore islands, and later on the coast itself, Swahili, Indian, and Arabian merchants followed the European model and set up clove-producing plantations using African slave laborers. Some of the plantations were large, and by the 1860s Zanzibar had a slave population of about 100,000. The sultan of Zanzibar alone owned more than 4000 slaves in 1870. Slavery became a prominent feature of the east African coast, and the slave trade from the interior to these plantations and to the traditional slave markets of the Red Sea continued until the end of the 19th century.

Much less is known about the interior of eastern Africa. The well-watered and heavily populated region of the great lakes of the interior supported large and small kingdoms. Bantu speakers predominated, but many peoples inhabited the region. Linguistic and archeological evidence suggests that pastoralist peoples from the upper Nile valley with a distinctive late Iron Age technology moved southward into what is today western Kenya and Uganda, where they came into contact with Bantu speakers and with the farmers and herders who spoke another group of languages called Cushitic. The Bantu states absorbed the immigrants, even when the newcomers established ruling dynasties. Later Nilotic migrations, of people who spoke languages of the Nilotic group, especially of the **Luo** peoples, resulted in the construction of related dynasties among the states in the area of the large lakes of east central Africa. At Bunyoro, the Luo eventually established a ruling dynasty among the existing Bantu population. This kingdom exercised considerable power in the 16th and 17th centuries. Other related states formed in the region. In Buganda, near Lake Victoria, a strong monarchy ruled a heterogeneous population and dominated the region in the 16th century. These developments in the interior, as important as they were for the history of the region, were less influenced by the growing contact with the outside world than were other regions of Africa.

Across the continent in the northern savanna at the end of the 18th century, the process of Islamization, which had been important in the days of the Mali and Songhay empires, entered a new and violent stage that not only linked Islamization to the external slave trade and the growth of slavery in Africa but also produced other long-term effects in the region. After the breakup of Songhay in the 16th century, several successor states had developed. Some, such as the Bambara kingdom of Segu, were pagan. Others,

such as the Hausa kingdoms in northern Nigeria, were ruled by Muslim royal families and urban aristocracies but continued to contain large numbers of animist subjects, most of whom were rural peasants. In these states the degree of Islamization was slight, and an accommodation between Muslims and animists was achieved.

Beginning in the 1770s, Muslim reform movements began to sweep the western Sudan. Religious brotherhoods advocating a purifying Sufi variant of Islam extended their influence throughout the Muslim trade networks in the Senegambia region and the western Sudan. This movement had an intense impact on the **Fulani** (Fulbe), a pastoral people who were spread across a broad area of the western Sudan.

In 1804, Usuman Dan Fodio, a studious and charismatic Muslim Fulani scholar, began to preach the reformist ideology in the Hausa kingdoms. His movement became a revolution when in 1804, seeing himself as God's instrument, he preached a jihad against the Hausa kings, who, he felt, were not following the teachings of Muhammad. A great upheaval followed in which the Fulani took control of most of the Hausa states of northern Nigeria in the western Sudan. A new kingdom, based on the city of Sokoto, developed under Dan Fodio's son and brother. The Fulani expansion was driven not only by religious zeal but by political ambitions, as the attack on the well-established Muslim kingdom of Bornu demonstrated. The result of this upheaval was the creation of a powerful Sokoto state under a caliph, whose authority was established over cities such as Kano and Zaria and whose rulers became emirs of provinces within the Sokoto caliphate.

By the 1840s, the effects of Islamization and the Fulani expansion were felt across much of the interior of west Africa. New political units were created, a reformist Islam that tried to eliminate pagan practices spread, and social and cultural changes took place in the wake of these changes. Literacy became more widely dispersed, and new centers of trade, such as Kano, emerged in this period. Later jihads established other new states along similar lines. All of these changes had long-term effects on the region of the western Sudan.

These upheavals, moved by religious, political, and economic motives, were affected by the external pressures on Africa. They fed into the ongoing processes of the external slave trade and the development of slavery within African societies. Large numbers of captives resulting from the wars were exported down to the coast for sale to the Europeans, while another stream of slaves crossed the Sahara to north Africa. In the western and central Sudan, the level of slave labor rose, especially in the larger towns and along the trade routes. Slave villages, supplying royal courts and merchant activities as well as a plantation system, developed to produce peanuts and other crops. Slave women spun cotton and wove cloth for sale, slave artisans worked in the towns, and slaves served the caravan traders, but most slaves did agricultural labor. By the late 19th century, regions of the savanna contained large slave populations—in some places as much as 30 to 50 percent of the whole population. From the Senegambia region of Futa Jallon, across the Niger and Senegal basins, and to the east of Lake Chad, slavery became a central feature of the Sudanic states and remained so through the 19th century.

White Settlers and Africans in Southern Africa

 In southern Africa, a Dutch colony eventually brought Europeans into conflict with Africans, especially the southern Bantu-speaking peoples. One of these groups, the Zulu, created under Shaka a powerful chiefdom during the early 19th century in a process of expansion that affected the whole region.

One area of Africa little affected by the slave trade in the early modern period was the southern end of the continent. As we saw in Chapter 8, this region was still occupied by non-Bantu hunting peoples, the San (Bushmen); by the Khoikhoi (Hottentots), who lived by hunting and sheep herding; and, after contact with the Bantu, by cattle-herding peoples. Peoples practicing farming and using iron tools were living south of the Limpopo River by the 3rd century C.E. Probably Bantu speakers, they spread southward and established their villages and cattle herds in the fertile lands along the eastern coast, where rainfall was favorable to their agricultural and pastoral way of life. The drier western regions toward the Kalahari Desert were left to the Khoikhoi and San. Mixed farming and pastoralism spread throughout the region in a complex process that involved migration, peaceful contacts, and warfare.

By the 16th century, Bantu-speaking peoples occupied much of the eastern regions of southern Africa. They practiced agriculture and herding; they

worked iron and copper into tools, weapons, and adornments; and traded with their neighbors. They spoke related languages such as Tswana and Sotho as well as the Nguni languages such as Zulu and Xhosa. Among the Sotho, villages might have contained as many as 200 people; the Nguni lived in hamlets made up of a few extended families. Men worked as artisans and herders; women did the farming and housework, and sometimes organized their labor communally.

Politically, chiefdoms of various sizes—many of them small, but a few with as many as 50,000 inhabitants—characterized the southern Bantu peoples. Chiefs held power with the support of relatives and with the acceptance of the people, but there was great variation in chiefly authority. The Bantu-speaking peoples' pattern of political organization and the splitting off of junior lineages to form new villages created a process of expansion that led to competition for land and the absorption of newly conquered groups. This situation became intense at the end of the 18th century, either because of the pressures and competition for foreign trade through the Portuguese outposts on the east African coast or because of the growth of population among the southern Bantu. In any case, the result was farther expansion southward into the path of another people who had arrived in southern Africa.

In 1652, the Dutch East India Company established a colony at the Cape of Good Hope to serve as a provisioning post for ships sailing to Asia. Large farms developed on the fertile lands around this colony. The Cape Colony depended on slave labor brought from Indonesia and Asia for a while, but it soon enslaved local Africans as well. Expansion of the colony and its labor needs led to a series of wars with the San and Khoikhoi populations, who were pushed farther to the north and west. By the 1760s, the Dutch, or Boer, farmers had crossed the Orange River in search of new lands. They saw the fertile plains and hills as theirs, and they saw the Africans as intruders and a possible source of labor. Competition and warfare resulted. By about 1800 the Cape Colony had about 17,000 settlers (or Afrikaners, as they came to be called), 26,000 slaves, and 14,000 Khoikhoi.

As the Boers were pushing northward, the southern Bantu were extending their movement to the south. Matters were also complicated by European events when Great Britain seized the Cape Colony in 1795 and then took it under formal British control in 1815. While the British government helped the settlers to clear out Africans from potential farming lands, government attempts to limit the Boer settlements and their use of African labor were unsuccessful. Meanwhile, competition for farming and grazing land led to a series of wars between the settlers and the Bantu during the early 19th century.

Various government measures, the accelerating arrival of English-speaking immigrants, and the lure of better lands caused groups of Boers to move to the north. These *voortrekkers* moved into lands occupied by the southern Nguni, eventually creating a number of autonomous Boer states. After 1834, when Britain abolished slavery and imposed restrictions on landholding, groups of Boers staged a **great trek** far to the north to be free of government interference. This movement eventually brought them across the Orange River and into Natal on the more fertile east coast, which the Boers believed to be only sparsely inhabited by Africans. They did not realize or care that the lack of population resulted from a great military upheaval taking place among the Bantu peoples of the region.

The Mfecane and the Zulu Rise to Power

Among the Nguni peoples, major changes had taken place. A unification process had begun in some of the northern chiefdoms, and a new military organization

had emerged. In 1818, leadership fell to Shaka, a brilliant military tactician, who reformed the loose forces into regiments organized by lineage and age. Iron discipline and new tactics were introduced, including the use of a short stabbing spear to be used at close range. The army was made a permanent institution, and the regiments were housed together in separate villages. The fighting men were allowed to marry only after they had completed their service.

Shaka's own Zulu chiefdom became the center of this new military and political organization, which began to absorb or destroy its neighbors (Figure 20.5). Shaka demonstrated talent as a politician, destroying the ruling families of the groups he incorporated into the growing Zulu state. He ruled with an iron hand, destroying his enemies, acquiring their cattle, and crushing any opposition. His policies brought power to the Zulu, but his erratic and cruel behavior also earned him enemies among his own people. Although he was assassinated in 1828, Shaka's reforms remained in place, and his successors built on the structure he had created. Zulu power was still growing in the 1840s, and the Zulu remained the most impressive military force in black Africa until the end of the century.

The rise of the Zulu and other Nguni chiefdoms was the beginning of the **mfecane,** or wars of crushing and wandering. As Zulu control expanded, a

Figure 20.5 *This Zulu royal kraal, drawn in the 1830s, gives some idea of the power of the Zulu at the time that Shaka was forging Zulu dominance during the mfecane.*

In Depth

Slavery and Human Society

Slavery is a very old and widespread institution. It has been found at different times all over the globe, among simple societies and in the great centers of civilization. In some of these societies, it has been a marginal or secondary form of labor, whereas in others it became the predominant labor form or "mode of production" (in the jargon of Marxist analysis). The need for labor beyond the capacity of the individual or the family unit is very old, and as soon as authority, law, or custom could be established to set the conditions for coercion, the tribe, the state, the priests, or some other group or institution extracted labor by force. Coerced labor could take different forms. There are important distinctions between indentured servants, convict laborers, debt-peons, and chattel slaves.

Although most societies placed some limits on the slaveholder's authority or power, the denial of the slave's control over his or her own labor and life choices was characteristic of this form of coercion throughout history. In most societies that had a form of chattel slavery, the slave was denied a sense of belonging in the society—the idea of kinship. The honor associated with family or lineage was the antithesis of slavery. Joseph in Egypt, and the viziers of the sultans of Turkey, might rise to high positions, but the fact that they were slaves meant that they were instruments of their masters' will. In fact, because they were slaves and thus unconstrained by kinship or other ties and obligations, they could be trusted in positions of command.

Because slaves became nonpersons—or, as one modern author has put it, because they suffered a "social death"—it was always easier to enslave "others" or "outsiders": those who were different in some way. Hebrews enslaved Canaanites, Greeks enslaved "barbarians," and Muslims made slaves of nonbelievers. If the difference between slave and master was readily seen, it made enforcement of slave status that much easier. Racism as such did not cause modern slavery, but differences in culture, language, color, and other physical characteristics always facilitated enslavement. The familiarity of Europeans and Muslims with black Africans in an enslaved status contributed to the development of modern racism. To paraphrase English historian Charles Boxer, no people can enslave another for 400 years without developing an attitude of superiority.

Slavery was not only a general phenomenon that existed in many societies. Rarely questioned on any grounds, it was seen as a necessary and natural phenomenon. Slavery is accepted in the texts of ancient India, the Old Testament, and the writings of 5th-century Greece. Aristotle specifically argued that some people were born to rule and others to serve. In Christian theology, although all people might be free in spirit in the kingdom of God, servitude was a necessary reality in the real world. Voices might be raised arguing for fair treatment or against the enslavement of a particular group, but the condition of servitude itself usually was taken as part of the natural order of the world.

In this context, the attack on slavery in Western culture that grew from the Enlightenment and the social and economic changes in western Europe and its Atlantic colonies at the end of the 18th century was a remarkable turning point in world history. Whether one believes that slavery was an outdated labor form that was incompatible with industrial capitalism and was therefore abolished or that it was destroyed because its immorality became all too obvious, its demise was quick. In about a century and a half, the moral and religious underpinning of chattel slavery was cut away and its economic justifications were questioned seriously. Although slavery lingered in at least a few places well into the 20th century, few people were willing to defend the institution publicly.

Although slavery historically existed in many places, it has become intimately associated with Africa because of the scope of the Atlantic slave trade and the importance of slavery in forming the modern world system. There was nothing inevitable about Africa's becoming the primary source of slaves in the modern world. Europeans did use Native American and European indentured workers when they could, but historical precedents, maritime technology, and availability combined to make Africa the source of labor for the expanding plantation colonies of Europe.

African slavery obviously played an important role in shaping the modern world. The African slave trade was one of the first truly international trades, and it created an easy access to labor that enabled Europeans to exploit the Americas. Some have argued that it was an important, even a necessary feature in the rise of capitalism and the international division of labor. Others disagree. In this question, as in nearly every other question about modern slavery, controversies still abound.

(continued)

In the context of African history, the interpretation of slavery is still changing rapidly. A recent and careful estimate of the volume involved in the Atlantic trade (10–12 million) has been questioned seriously, especially by African scholars, who see this new figure as an attempt to downplay the exploitation of Africa. Another debate centers on the impact of the trade on the population and societies within Africa. The slave trade was important to the economy of the Atlantic, but how important was this external trade in Africa itself? Reacting to the preabolitionist European self-justifications that the slave trade was no great crime because Africans had long become familiar with slavery and were selling already enslaved people, early researchers argued that African slavery often was an extension of kinship or other forms of dependency and was quite unlike the chattel slavery of western Europe. But further research has demonstrated that in many African societies, slavery was an integral part of the economy and that although specific conditions sometimes differed greatly from those in the Americas, the servile condition in Africa had much in common with chattel slavery. For example, the Sokoto caliphate in the 19th century had a proportion of slaves similar to that in Brazil and the southern United States. Slave societies did exist in Africa.

Now, controversy rages over the extent to which the development of African slavery resulted from the long-term impact of the slave trade and the European demand for captive labor. African societies did not live in isolation from the pressures and examples of the world economy into which they were drawn. The extent to which that contact transformed slavery in Africa is now in question. These controversies among historians reflect current concerns and a realization that the present social and political situation in Africa and in many places in the Americas continues to bear the burden of a historical past in which slavery played an essential role. In evaluating slavery, as in all other historical questions, what we think about the present shapes our inquiry and our interpretation of the past.

Questions: Why did Africa become the leading source of slaves in the early modern world economy? What are some of the leading issues in interpreting African slavery? What were the roles of Africans and Europeans in the early modern slave trade?

series of campaigns and forced migrations led to constant fighting as other peoples sought to survive by fleeing, emulating, or joining the Zulu. Groups spun off to the north and south, raiding the Portuguese on the coast, clashing with the Europeans to the south, and fighting with neighboring chiefdoms. New African states, such as the **Swazi,** that adapted aspects of the Zulu model emerged among the survivors. One state, **Lesotho,** successfully resisted the Zulu example. It combined Sotho and Nguni speakers and defended itself against Nguni armies. It eventually developed as a kingdom far less committed to military organization, one in which the people had a strong influence on their leaders.

The whole of the southern continent, from the Cape Colony to Lake Malawi, had been thrown into turmoil by raiding parties, remnants, and refugees. Superior firepower allowed the Boers to continue to hold their lands, but it was not until the Zulu Wars of the 1870s that Zulu power was crushed by Great Britain, and even then only at great cost. During that process, the basic patterns of conflict between Africans and Europeans in the largest settler colony on the continent were created. These patterns included competition between settlers and Africans for land, the expanding influence of European government control, and the desire of Europeans to use Africans as laborers.

The African Diaspora

 The slave trade and the horrifying Middle Passage carried millions of Africans from their original homelands. In the Americas, especially in plantation colonies, they became a large segment of the population, and African cultures were adapted to new environments and conditions. Africans also resisted enslavement.

The slave trade was the means by which the history of the Americas and Africa became linked and a principal way in which African societies were drawn into the world economy. The import into Africa of European firearms, Indian textiles, Indonesian cowrie shells, and American tobacco in return for African ivory, gold, and especially slaves demonstrated Africa's integration into the mercantile structure of the world. Africans involved in the trade learned to

Document

An African's Description of the Middle Passage

During the era of the slave trade, enslaved Africans by one means or another succeeded in telling their stories. These accounts, with their specific details of the injustice and inhumanities of slavery, became particularly useful in the abolitionist crusade. The autobiography of Frederick Douglass is perhaps the most famous of these accounts. The biography of Olaudah Equiano, an Ibo from what is today eastern Nigeria on the Niger River, presents a personal description of enslavement in Africa and the terrors of the Middle Passage. Equiano and his sister were kidnapped in 1756 by African slave hunters and sold to British slave traders. Separated from his sister, Equiano was carried to the West Indies and later to Virginia, where he became servant to a naval officer. He traveled widely on his master's military campaigns and was later sold to a Philadelphia Quaker merchant, who eventually allowed him to buy his freedom. Later, he moved to England and became an active member in the movement to end slavery and the slave trade. His biography was published in 1789. The political uses of this kind of biography and Equiano's association with the abolitionists should caution us against accepting the account at face value, but it does convey the personal shock and anguish of those caught in the slave trade.

The first object which saluted my eyes when I arrived on the coast was the sea, and a slaveship, which was riding at anchor, and waiting for its cargo. These filled me with astonishment, which was soon converted into terror, which I am yet at a loss to describe, nor the then feelings of my mind. When I was carried on board I was immediately handled, and tossed up, to see if I were sound, by some of the crew; and I was now persuaded that I had got into a world of bad spirits, and that they were going to kill me. Their complexions too differing so much from ours, their long hair, and the language they spoke, which was very different from any I had ever heard, united to confirm me in this belief. Indeed, such were the horrors of my views and fears at that moment, that if ten thousand worlds had been my own, I would have freely parted with them all to have exchanged my condition with that of the meanest slave in my own country. When I looked round the ship too, and saw a large furnace or copper boiler, and a multitude of black people of every description chained together, every one of their countenances expressing dejection and sorrow, quite overpowered with horror and anguish, I fell motionless on the deck and fainted. When I recovered a little, I found some black people about me, who I believed were some of those who brought me on board, and had been receiving their pay; they talked to me in order to cheer me, but all in vain. I asked them if we were not to be eaten by those white men with horrible looks, red faces, and long hair. They told me I was not.... I now saw myself deprived of all chance of returning to my native country, or even the least glimpse of hope of gaining the shore, which I now considered as friendly; and I even wished for my former slavery, in preference to my present situation, which was filled with horrors of every kind, still heightened by my ignorance of what I was to undergo. I was not long suffered to indulge my grief; I was soon put down under decks, and there I received such a salutation in my nostrils as I had never experienced in my life; so that with the loathsomeness of the stench, and the crying together, I became so sick and low that I was not able to eat, nor had I the least desire to taste anything. I now wished for the last friend, death, to relieve me; but soon, to my grief two white men offered me eatables; and on my refusing to eat, one of them held me fast by the hands, and laid me across, I think, the windlass, and tied my feet while the other flogged me severely. I had never experienced anything of this kind before; and, although not being used to the water, I naturally feared that element the first time I saw it; yet, nevertheless, could I have got over the nettings, I would have jumped over the side; but I could not; and, besides the crew used to watch us very closely who were not chained down to the decks, lest we should leap into the water; and I have seen some of these poor African prisoners most severely cut for attempting to do so, and hourly whipped for not eating. This indeed was often the case with myself. In a little time after amongst the poor chained men, I found some of my own nation, which in a small degree gave ease to my mind. I inquired of them what was to be done with us? They gave me to understand we were to be carried to these white people's country to work for them. I then was a little revived, and thought, if it were no worse than working, my situation was not so desperate; but still I feared I should be put to death, the white people looked and acted, as I thought, in so savage a manner; for I had never seen among any people such instances of brutal cruelty; and this was not only shown to us blacks, but also to some of the whites themselves....

At last when the ship we were in had got in all her cargo, they made ready with many fearful noises, and we were all put under deck, so that we could not see how they managed the vessel. But this disappointment was the least of my sorrow. The stench of the hold while we were on the coast was so intolerably loathsome, that it was dangerous to remain there for any time, and some of us had been permitted to stay on deck for the fresh

(continued)

air; but now the whole ship's cargo was confined together, it became absolutely pestilential. The closeness of the place, and the heat of the climate, added to the number in the ship, which was so crowded that each had scarcely room to turn himself, almost suffocated us. This produced copious perspirations, so that the air soon became unfit for respiration, from a variety of loathsome smells, and brought on a sickness amongst the slaves, of which many died, thus falling victims to the improvident avarice, as I may call it, of their purchasers. This wretched situation was again aggravated by the galling of the chains, now become insupportable; and the filth of the necessary tubs, into which the children fell, and were almost suffocated. The shrieks of the women, and the groans of the dying, rendered the whole a scene of horror almost inconceivable.

Questions: In what ways does Equiano's description contradict a previous understanding of the slave trade? What opportunities existed for the captives to resist? What effect might the experience of Africans on the slave ships have had on their perceptions of each other and of the Europeans?

deal effectively with this situation. Prices of slaves rose steadily in the 18th century, and the terms of trade increasingly favored the African dealers. In many African ports, such as Whydah, Porto Novo, and Luanda, African or Afro-European communities developed that specialized in the slave trade and used this position to advantage.

Slave Lives

For the slaves themselves, slavery meant the destruction of their villages or their capture in war, separation from friends and family, and then the forced march to an interior trading town or to the slave pens at the coast. Conditions were deadly; perhaps as many as one-third of the captives died along the way or in the slave pens. Eventually the slaves were loaded onto the ships. Cargo sizes varied and could go as high as 700 slaves crowded into the dank, unsanitary conditions of the slave ships, but most cargoes were smaller. Overcrowding was less of a factor in mortality than the length of the voyage or the point of origin in Africa; the Bights of Benin and Biafra were particularly dangerous. The average mortality rate for slaves varied over time, but it ran at about 18 percent or so until the 18th century, when it declined somewhat. Still, losses could be catastrophic on individual ships, as on a Dutch ship in 1737, where 700 of the 716 slaves died on the voyage.

The **Middle Passage,** or slave voyage to the Americas, was traumatic. Taken from their homes, branded, confined, and shackled, the Africans faced not only the dangers of poor hygiene, dysentery, disease, and bad treatment but also the fear of being beaten or worse by the Europeans. Their situation sometimes led to suicide or resistance and mutiny on the ships. However traumatic, the Middle Passage certainly did not strip Africans of their culture, and they arrived in the Americas retaining their languages, beliefs, artistic traditions, and memories of their past.

Africans in the Americas

The slaves carried across the Atlantic were brought mainly to the plantations and mines of the Americas. Landed estates using large amounts of labor, often coerced, became characteristic of American agriculture, at first in sugar production and later for rice, cotton, and tobacco. The plantation system already used for producing sugar on the Atlantic islands of Spain and Portugal was transferred to the New World. After attempts to use Native American laborers in places such as Brazil and Hispaniola, Africans were brought in. West Africans, coming from societies in which herding, metallurgy, and intensive agriculture were widely practiced, were sought by Europeans for the specialized tasks of making sugar. In the English colonies of Barbados and Virginia, indentured servants from England eventually were replaced by enslaved Africans when new crops, such as sugar, were introduced or when indentured servants became less available.

In any case, the plantation system of farming with a dependant or enslaved workforce characterized the production of many tropical and semitropical crops in demand in Europe, and thus the plantation became the locus of African and American life. But slaves did many other things as well, from mining to urban occupations as artisans, street vendors, and household servants. In short, there was almost no occupation that slaves did not perform, although most were agricultural laborers (Figure 20.6).

American Slave Societies

Each American slave-based society reflected the variations of its European origin and its component African cultures, but there were certain similarities and common features. Each recognized distinctions between African-born **saltwater slaves,** who were almost invariably black (by European standards) and their American-born descendants, the **Creole slaves,** some of whom were mulattos as a result of the sexual exploitation of slave women or other forms of miscegenation. In all American slave societies, a hierarchy of status evolved in which free whites were at the top, slaves were at the bottom, and free people of color had an intermediate position. In this sense, color and "race" played a role in American slavery it had not

played in Africa. Among the slaves, slaveholders also created a hierarchy based on origin and color. Creole and especially mulatto slaves were given more opportunities to acquire skilled jobs or to work as house servants rather than in the fields or mines. They were also more likely to win their freedom by manumission, the voluntary freeing of slaves.

This hierarchy was a creation of the slaveholders and did not necessarily reflect perceptions among the slaves. There is evidence that important African nobles or religious leaders, who for one reason or another were sold into slavery, continued to exercise authority within the slave community. Still, the distinctions between Creole and African slaves tended to divide that community, as did the distinctions between different African groups whose members maintained their ties and affiliations in America. Many of the slave rebellions in the Caribbean and Brazil were organized along African ethnic and

1. Moulin. 2. Fourneaux et Chaudieres. 3. Formes. 4. Vinaigrerie. 5. Cannes de Sucre   SVCRERIE. 6. Gros Cocos. p. 155. 7. Latanir. p. 111. 8. Pajomirioba. p. 92. 9. Choux Caraibes. 10. Cafes de Negres. 11 Figuir. p. 132.

Figure 20.6 *Africans performed all kinds of labor in the Americas, from domestic service to mining and shipbuilding. Most worked on plantations like this sugar mill in the Caribbean.*

political lines. In Jamaica, there were several Akan-led rebellions in the 18th century, and the largest escaped slave community in 17th-century Brazil apparently was organized and led by Angolans.

Although economic factors imposed similarities, the slave-based societies also varied in their composition. In early 17th-century Lima, Peru, the capital of Spain's colony in South America, blacks outnumbered Europeans. In the 18th century, on the Caribbean islands where the indigenous population had died out or had been exterminated and where few Europeans settled, Africans and their descendants formed the vast majority. In Jamaica and St. Domingue, slaves made up more than 80 percent of the population, and because mortality levels were so high, a large proportion were African-born. Brazil also had large numbers of imported Africans, but its more diverse population and economy, as well as a tradition of manumitting slaves and high levels of miscegenation, meant that slaves made up only about 35 percent of the population. However, free people of color, the descendants of former slaves, made up about another one-third, so that together slaves and free colored people made up two-thirds of the total population.

North American cities such as Charleston and New Orleans also developed a large slave and free African population. But the southern colonies of British North America differed significantly from the Caribbean and Brazil, by depending less on imported Africans because of natural population growth among the slaves. In North America, Creole slaves predominated, but manumission was less common, and free people of color made up less than 10 percent of the total Afro-American population. The result was that slavery in North America was less influenced by Africa. By the mid-18th century, the slave population in most places in North America was reproducing itself. By 1850, fewer than 1 percent of the slaves there were African-born. The combination of natural growth and the small direct trade from Africa reduced the degree of African cultural reinforcement.

The People and Gods in Exile

Africans brought as slaves to the Americas faced a peculiar series of problems. Working conditions were exhausting, and life for most slaves often was difficult and short. Family formation was made difficult because of the general shortage of female slaves; the ratio of men to women was as much as three to one in some places. To this was added the insecurity of slave status: Family members might be separated by sale or by a master's whim. Still, most slaves lived in family units, even though their marriages were not always sanctioned by the religion of their masters. Throughout the Americas, wherever Africans were brought, aspects of their language, religion, artistic sensibilities, and other cultural elements survived. To some extent, the amount of continuity depended on the intensity and volume of the slave trade from a particular area. Some slaveholders tried to mix up the slaves on their plantations so that strong African identities would be lost, but colonial dependence on slavers who consistently dealt with the same region tended to undercut such policies. In the Americas, African slaves had to adapt and to incorporate other African peoples' ideas and customs into their own lives. Moreover, the ways and customs of the masters were also imposed. Thus, what emerged as Afro-American culture reflected specific African roots adapted to a new reality. Afro-American culture was dynamic and creative in this sense.

Religion was an obvious example of continuity and adaptation. Slaves were converted to Catholicism by the Spaniards and the Portuguese, and they showed fervent devotion as members of Black Catholic brotherhoods, some of which were organized by African origins. In North America and the British Caribbean they joined Protestant denominations. Still, African religious ideas and practices did not die out. In the English islands, **obeah** was the name given to the African religious practices, and the men and women knowledgeable in them were held in high regard within the community. In Brazilian **candomble** (Yoruba) and Haitian **vodun** (Aja), fully developed versions of African religions flourished and continue today, despite attempts to suppress them.

The reality of the Middle Passage meant that religious ideas were easier to transfer than the institutional aspects of religion. Without religious specialists or a priestly class, aspects of African religions were changed by contact with other African peoples as well as with colonial society. In many cases, slaves held their new faith in Christianity and their African beliefs at the same time, and tried to fuse the two. For Muslim Africans this was more difficult. In 1835 in Bahia, the largest slave rebellion in Brazil was organized by Muslim Yoruba and Hausa slaves and directed against the whites and against nonbelievers.

Resistance and rebellion were other aspects of African-American history. Recalcitrance, running away, and direct confrontation were present wherever slaves were held. As early as 1508, African runaways disrupted communications on Hispaniola, and in 1527, a plot to rebel was uncovered in Mexico City. Throughout the Americas, communities of runaway slaves formed. In Jamaica, Colombia, Venezuela, Haiti, and Brazil, runaway communities were persistent. In Brazil, during the 17th century, **Palmares,** an enormous runaway slave kingdom with many villages and a population of perhaps 8000 to 10,000 people, resisted Portuguese and Dutch attempts to destroy it for a century. In Jamaica, the runaway Maroons were able to gain some independence and a recognition of their freedom. So-called ethnic slave rebellions organized by a particular African group were common in the Caribbean and Brazil in the 18th century. In North America, where reinforcement from the slave trade was less important, resistance was also important, but it was based less on African origins or ethnicities.

Perhaps the most remarkable story of African-American resistance is found in the forests of **Suriname,** a former Dutch plantation colony. There, large numbers of slaves ran off in the 18th century and mounted an almost perpetual war in the rain forest against the various expeditions sent to hunt them down. Those captured were brutally executed, but eventually a truce developed. Today about 50,000 Maroon descendants still live in Suriname and French Guiana. The Suriname Maroons maintained many aspects of their west African background in terms of language, kinship relations, and religious beliefs, but these were fused with new forms drawn from European and American Indian contacts resulting from their New World experience. From this fusion based on their own creativity, a truly Afro-American culture was created (Figure 20.7).

The End of the Slave Trade and the Abolition of Slavery

The end of the Atlantic slave trade and the abolition of slavery in the Atlantic world resulted from economic, political, and religious changes in Europe and its overseas American colonies and former colonies. These changes, which were manifestations of the Enlightenment, the age of revolution, Christian revivalism, and perhaps the Industrial Revolution,

Figure 20.7 *African, American, or both? In Suriname, descendants of escaped slaves maintain many aspects of African culture but have adapted, modified, and transformed them in many ways. This wooden door shows the imaginative skills of African-American carvers.*

were external to Africa, but once again they determined the pace and nature of change within Africa.

Like much else about the history of slavery, there is disagreement about the end of the slave trade. It is true that some African societies began to export other commodities, such as peanuts, cotton, and palm oil, which made their dependence on the slave trade less important, but the supply of slaves to European merchants was not greatly affected by this development. In general, the British plantation economies were booming in the period from 1790 to 1830, and plantations in Cuba, Brazil, and the southern United States flourished in the decades that followed. Thus, it is difficult to find a direct and simple link between economic self-interest and the movement to suppress the slave trade.

Opponents of slavery and the brutality of the trade had appeared in the mid-18th century, in relation to new intellectual movements in the West. Philosopher Jean-Jacques Rousseau in France and political economist Adam Smith in England both wrote against it. Whereas in ancient Rome during the spread of Christianity and Islam, and in 16th-century Europe, the enslavement of "barbarians" or nonbelievers was seen as positive—a way to civilize others—slavery during the European Enlightenment and bourgeois revolution came to be seen as backward and immoral. The slave trade was particularly criticized. It was the symbol of slavery's inhumanity and cruelty.

England, as the major maritime power of the period, was the key to the end of the slave trade. Under the leadership of religious humanitarians, such as John Wesley and **William Wilberforce,** an abolitionist movement gained strength against the merchants and the West Indies interests. After much parliamentary debate, the British slave trade was abolished in 1807. Having set out on this course, Britain tried to impose abolition of the slave trade on other countries throughout the Atlantic. Spain and Portugal were pressured to gradually suppress the trade, and the British navy was used to enforce these agreements by capturing illegal slave ships. By the 19th century, the moral and intellectual justifications that had supported the age of the slave trade had worn thin and the movement to abolish slavery was growing in the Atlantic world. The full end of slavery in the Americas did not occur until 1888, when it was abolished in Brazil.

GLOBAL CONNECTIONS: Africa and the African Diaspora in World Context

Africa was drawn into the world economy in the era of the slave trade, at first slowly, but with increasing intensity after 1750. Its incorporation produced differing effects on African societies, reinforcing author-

ity in some places, creating new states in others, and sometimes provoking social, religious, and political reactions. Although many aspects of African life followed traditional patterns, contact with the world economy forced many African societies to adjust in ways that often placed them at a disadvantage and facilitated Europe's colonization of Africa in the 19th century. Well into the 20th century, as forced labor continued in Africa under European direction, the legacy of the slave trade era proved slow to die.

Part of that legacy was the movement of millions of Africans far from their continent. Taken against their will, they and their descendants drew on the cultures and practices of Africa as they coped with slavery. Eventually, they created vibrant new cultural forms, which along with their labor and skills contributed to the growth of new societies.

Further Readings

Aside from the general books on Africa already mentioned in the Further Readings for previous chapters, some specific readings are particularly useful. Martin Hall's *The Changing Past: Farmers, Kings, and Traders in Southern Africa* (1987) discusses the use of archeological evidence in African history. D. Birmingham and Phyllis Martin, eds., *History of Central Africa*, 2 vols. (1983) presents extended essays on a number of regions. On west Africa in the age of the slave trade, a good introduction is J. F. A. Ajayi and Michael Crowder, eds., *History of West Africa*, 2 vols. (1975), especially volume 2. On southern Africa, Leonard Thompson's *A History of South Africa* (1990) presents a broad survey, and J. D. Omer-Cooper's *The Zulu Aftermath* (1969) is a classic account.

There are many histories of the slave trade, but Herbert S. Klein's *The Atlantic Slave Trade* (1999) provides an up-to-date and intelligent overview. On the quantitative aspects of the slave trade, Philip Curtin's *The Atlantic Slave Trade: A Census* (1969) is the proper starting point, while David Eltis' *The Rise of African Slavery in the Americas* (2000) is an important new study. All new quantitative studies will depend on the CD-ROM edited by David Eltis et al. entitled *The Atlantic Slave Trade* (1998). Roger Anstey's *The Atlantic Slave Trade and British Abolition* (1975) deals with the economic and religious aspects of the end of the slave trade.

On Africa, Paul Lovejoy's *Transformations in Slavery: A History of Slavery in Africa* (1983) and Patrick Manning's *Slavery and African Life* (1990) provide comprehensive overviews, and J. E. Inikori's *Forced Migration: The Impact of the Export Slave Trade on African Societies* (1982) brings together essays by leading scholars. Robert Harme,

The Diligent: Voyage Through the Worlds of the Slave Trade (2002) uses one voyage to examine the whole system of the Atlantic slave.

Joseph Miller's *Way of Death* (1989) is a detailed study of the effects of the slave trade on Angola and a fine example of an in-depth study of one region.

John K. Thornton, *Africa and Africans in the Making of the Atlantic World* (1994) is an excellent argument for the centrality of slavery in Africa, and Walter Rodney's essay "Africa in Europe and the Americas," in *Cambridge History of Africa*, vol. 4, 578–622, is a succinct overview of the African diaspora. Herbert Klein's *African Slavery in Latin America and the Caribbean* (1987) is an up-to-date survey. Excellent overviews based on the best secondary literature are Robin Blackburn's *The Making of New World Slavery* (1997), and his *The Overthrow of Colonial Slavery* (1988).

On the general theoretical issues of slavery, Orlando Patterson's *Slavery and Social Death* (1982) is a broad comparative sociological study. David B. Davis' *Slavery and Human Progress* (1984) takes a historical approach to many of the same questions and then places the abolitionist movement in context.

On the Web

A full account of slavery from the perspective of one of its African victims, Olaudah Equiano, is provided on-line at http://history.hanover.edu/texts/equiano/equiano_contents.html. Other accounts of the slave trade as described by the slaves themselves can be found at http://vi.uh.edu/pages/mintz/primary.htm, http://www.fordham.edu/halsall/africa/africasbook.html (scroll down

to "Enslaved People"). Narratives of slaves who lived in the American South can be encountered at http://memory.loc.gov/ammem/snhtml/snhome.html.

The role of the Royal African Company in the slave trade is described at http://www.pbs.org/wgbh/aia/part1/1p269.html. The career of the Amistad, a slave schooner which became the subject of a major film, is closely analyzed at http://www.law.umkc.edu/faculty/projects/ftrials/amistad/AMISTD.HTM and http://www.archives.gov/digital_classroom/lessons/amistad_case/amistad_case.html.

The Asante of what is now the nation of Ghana (http://www.uiowa.edu/~africart/toc/people/Asante.html) built an empire out of the slave trade, while the people of Benin, less dependent upon it, were still able to maintain their rich artistic heritage and religious traditions (http://www.nmafa.si.edu/exhibits/benin.htm, http://www.dia.org/collections/aonwc/africanart/beninkings.html, and http://www.artareas.com/ArtAreas/home.nsf/Profiles/Royal+Benin+Art+Gallery).

At the same time, the Swahili states of East Africa (http://whc.unesco.org/exhibits/afr_rev/africa-k.htm, http://www.ucalgary.ca/applied_history/tutor/oldwrld/merchants/diaspora.html and http://www.wsu.edu:8080/~dee/CIVAFRCA/SWAHILI.HTM) joined with Arabs and Indians in establishing spice plantations in Zanzibar and Shaka Zulu built an empire in the southern regions of the continent. Biographies of Shaka can be found at http://campus.northpark.edu/history/WebChron/Africa/ShakaZulu.html and http://www.carpenoctem.tv/military/shaka.html.

CHAPTER 21

THE MUSLIM EMPIRES

A portrait of a Safavid notable, probably Shah Suleyman I (1667–1693), by a Persian court artist. He is surrounded by courtiers, including a European visitor bearing presents for the Persian leader. From the time of Abbas, Europeans of different nationalities vied fiercely with each other for influence at the Safavid court.

- The Ottomans: From Frontier Warriors to Empire Builders
- DOCUMENT: An Islamic Traveler Laments the Muslims' Indifference to Europe
- The Shi'a Challenge of the Safavids
- IN DEPTH: The Gunpowder Empires and the Shifting Balance of Global Power
- The Mughals and the Apex of Muslim Civilization in India
- VISUALIZING THE PAST: The Basis of Imperial Power in the Rival Muslim Empires
- GLOBAL CONNECTIONS: Gunpowder Empires and the Restoration of the Islamic Bridge Between Civilizations

The great nomadic invasions by the Mongols in the first half of the 13th century and by the armies of Timur in the last decades of the 14th century had made a shambles of much of the Muslim world. The pretense of Muslim unity, which had been preserved by the Seljuk sultans' retention of the powerless caliphs after 1055, was shattered in 1258 by the conquest and sacking of the Abbasid capital and the extinction of the long-lived caliphate. Regional dynasties in areas as distant as Asia Minor and India were also crushed by nomadic armies, and many splendid Islamic cities were laid to waste. But in the wake of the most powerful incursions of the nomadic peoples of central Asia into the civilized heartlands of Eurasia, three new Muslim dynasties arose. These produced a new flowering of Islamic civilization with major achievements in the arts and architecture in particular. Competition between them also led to important political divisions and periodic military clashes within the Muslim world.

The largest of the three empires, the **Ottoman,** stretched at its peak in the 17th century from north Africa to southern Russia, and from Hungary to the port of Aden on the southern end of the Red Sea (see Map 21.1). To the east in what is now Iran and Afghanistan, the **Safavid dynasty** arose to challenge the Ottomans for leadership of the Islamic world. Finally, yet another Muslim empire in India, centered like most of the earlier ones on the Delhi region of the Ganges plain, was built under the leadership of a succession of remarkable **Mughal** rulers. The combination of these three empires produced the greatest political and military power the Islamic world had yet attained.

The formation of new Muslim empires warrants comparison with Russia's new landed empire, which also included some Muslim peoples, and of course with the West's overseas expansion. All reflected the importance of new military technology on land as well as sea. The Muslim empires, in contrast to Russia, interacted far less with the West, and during most of the period they also retained control over their dealings with the world economy.

The Ottomans: From Frontier Warriors to Empire Builders

From the devastation that the Mongol invasions brought to much of the Islamic heartlands, a new power, the **Ottomans,** arose in the 13th and 14th centuries. Founded by yet another Turkic nomadic people migrating from the central Asian steppes, the Ottoman dynasty gradually built an empire in the eastern Mediterranean that rivaled the Abbasid imperium at its height. The Ottomans finally put an end to the long-besieged civilization of Byzantium and advanced deep into

1250 C.E.	1400 C.E.	1500 C.E.	1525 C.E.	1550 C.E.	1650 C.E.	1700 C.E.
1243 Mongol invasion of Asia Minor	**1402** Timur's invasion; Ottoman setbacks under Bayazid	**1501–1510** Safavid conquest of Persia (present-day Iran)	**1526** Battle of Panipat; Babur's conquest of India	**1556** Mughal Empire reestablished in north India	**1657–1658** Great war of succession between sons of Shah Jahan	**1722** First Turkish-language printing press founded
1281 Founding of the Ottoman dynasty	**c. 1450s** Shi'a influences enter Safavid teachings	**1507** Portuguese victory over Ottoman-Arab fleet at Diu in Indian Ocean	**1529** First Ottoman siege of Vienna	**1556–1605** Reign of Akbar	**1658–1707** Reign of Aurangzeb	**1722** Fall of the Safavid dynasty
1334 Death of the first Safavid Sufi master at Ardabil	**c. 1450s** Beginning of large-scale recruitment of Janissary troops	**1514** Ottoman victory over Safavids at Chaldiran	**1540** Babur's successor, Humayan, driven from India	**1571** Battle of Lepanto	**1683** Last Ottoman siege of Vienna	**1730** Ottoman armies are defeated by Persian forces under Nadir Khan (later Nadir Shah, emperor of Persia)
1350s Ottoman invasion of Europe; conquest of much of the Balkans and Hungary	**1453** Ottoman capture of Constantinople	**1517** Ottoman capture of Syria and Egypt	**1540–1545** Humayan in exile at the Safavid court	**1582** Akbar's proclamation of his new religion	**1680s** Rajput and peasant revolts in North India	**1730s** First Western-modeled military schools established
		1520–1566 Rule of Suleyman the Magnificent; construction of Suleymaniye mosque in Constantinople		**1588–1629** Reign of Abbas I (the Great) in Persia	**1699** Treaty of Carlowitz; Ottomans cede territories in Europe	**1736–1747** Reign of Nadir Shah
						1739 Nadir Shah invades India from Persia, sacks Mughal capital at Delhi

eastern and central Europe, where they came to rule large numbers of Christians. The Ottomans built much of their empire on the ideas and institutions of earlier Muslim civilizations. But in warfare, architecture, and engineering, they carried Islamic civilization in new directions.

For centuries before the rise of the Ottoman dynasty, Turkic-speaking peoples from central Asia had played key roles in Islamic civilization as soldiers and administrators, often in the service of the Abbasid caliphs. But the collapse of the Seljuk Turkic kingdom of Rum in eastern Anatolia in Asia Minor (see Map 21.2), after the invasion by the Mongols in 1243, opened the way for the Ottomans to seize power in their own right. The Mongols raided but did not directly rule Anatolia, which fell into a chaotic period of warfare between would-be successor states to the Seljuk sultans. Turkic peoples, both those fleeing the Mongols and those in search of easy booty, flooded into the region in the last decades of the 13th century. One of these peoples, called the Ottomans after an early leader named Osman, came to dominate the rest, and within decades they had begun to build a new empire based in Anatolia.

By the 1350s, the Ottomans had advanced from their strongholds in Asia Minor across the Bosporus straits into Europe. Thrace was quickly conquered, and by the end of the century large portions of the Balkans had been added to their rapidly expanding territories

(see Map 21.2). In moving into Europe in the mid-14th century, the Ottomans had bypassed rather than conquered the great city of Constantinople, long the capital of the once powerful Byzantine Empire. By the mid-15th century, the Ottomans, who had earlier alternated between alliances and warfare with the Byzantines, were strong enough to undertake the capture of the well-fortified city. For seven weeks in the spring of 1453, the army of the Ottoman sultan, **Mehmed II,** "The Conqueror," which numbered well over 100,000, assaulted the triple ring of land walls that had protected the city for centuries (Figure 21.1). The outnumbered forces of the defenders repulsed attack after attack until the sultan ordered his gunners to batter a portion of the walls with their massive siege cannon. Wave after wave of Ottoman troops struck at the gaps in the defenses that had been cut by the guns, quickly overwhelmed the defenders, and raced into the city to loot and pillage for the three days that Mehmed had promised as their reward for victory.

In the two centuries after the conquest of Constantinople, the armies of a succession of able Ottoman rulers extended the empire into Syria and Egypt and across north Africa, thus bringing under their rule the bulk of the Arab world (see Map 21.2). The empire also spread through the Balkans into Hungary in Europe and around the Black and Red seas. The Ottomans became a formidable naval power in the Mediterranean Sea. Powerful Ottoman galley fleets made possible the capture of major island bases on Rhodes, Crete, and Cyprus. The Ottoman armies also drove the Venetians and Genoese from much of the eastern Mediterranean and threatened southern Italy with invasion on several occasions. From their humble origins as frontier vassals, the Ottomans had risen to become the protectors of the Islamic heartlands and the scourge of Christian Europe. As late as 1683, Ottoman armies were able to lay siege to the capital of the Austrian Habsburg dynasty at Vienna. Even though the Ottoman Empire was in decline by this time, and the threat the assault posed to Vienna was far less serious than a previous attack in the early 16th century, the Ottomans remained a major force in European politics until the late 19th century.

A State Geared to Warfare

Military leaders played a dominant role in the Ottoman state, and the economy of the empire was geared to warfare and expansion. The Turkic cavalry, chiefly responsible for the Ottomans' early conquests from the 13th to the 16th centuries, gradually developed into a warrior aristocracy. They were granted control over land and peasant producers in annexed areas for the support of their households and military retainers. From the 15th century onward, members of the warrior class also vied with religious leaders and administrators drawn from other social groups for control of the expanding Ottoman bureaucracy. As the power of the warrior aristocracy shrank at the center, they built up regional and local bases of support. These inevitably competed with the sultans and the central bureaucracy for revenue and labor control.

From the mid-15th century, the imperial armies were increasingly dominated by infantry divisions made up of troops called **Janissaries.** Most of the Janissaries had been forcibly conscripted as adolescent

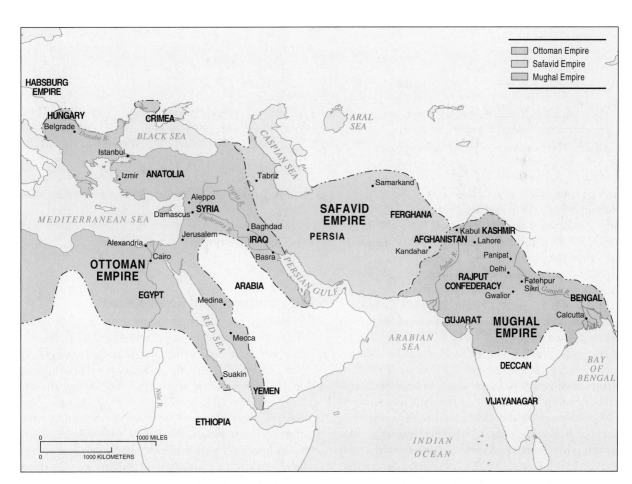

Map 21.1   *The Ottoman, Safavid, and Mughal Empires*

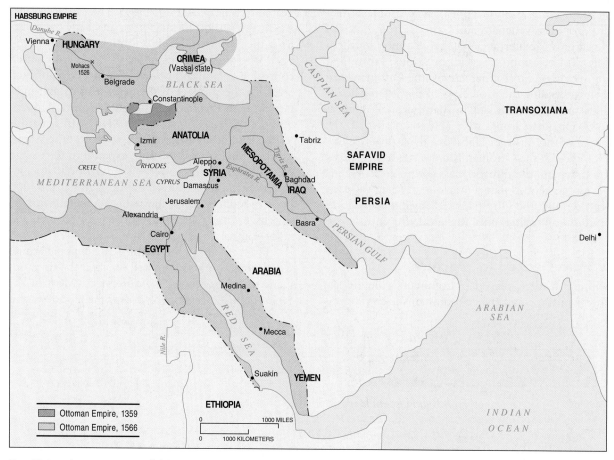

Map 21.2   *The Expansion of the Ottoman Empire*

boys in conquered areas, such as the Balkans, where the majority of the population retained its Christian faith. Sometimes the boys' parents willingly turned their sons over to the Ottoman recruiters because of the opportunities for advancement that came with service to the Ottoman sultans. Though legally slaves, the youths were given fairly extensive schooling for the time and converted to Islam. Some of them went on to serve in the palace or bureaucracy, but most became Janissaries.

Because the Janissaries controlled the artillery and firearms that became increasingly vital to Ottoman success in warfare with Christian and Muslim adversaries, they rapidly became the most powerful component in the Ottoman military machine. Their growing importance was another factor contributing to the steady decline of the role of the aristocratic cavalry. Just like the mercenary forces that had earlier served the caliphs of Baghdad, the Janissaries eventually tried to translate military service into

political influence. By the late 15th century they were deeply involved in court politics; by the mid-16th century they had the power to depose sultans and decide which one of a dying ruler's sons would mount the throne.

The Sultans and Their Court

Nominally, the Ottoman rulers were absolute monarchs. But even the most powerful sultan maintained his position by playing factions in the warrior elite off each other and pitting the warriors as a whole against the Janissaries and other groups. Chief among the latter were the Islamic religious scholars and legal experts, who retained many of the administrative functions they had held under the Arab caliphs of earlier centuries. In addition to Muslim traders, commerce within the empire was in the hands of Christian and Jewish merchants, who as dhimmis, or "people of the Book," were under the protection of the

Figure 21.1   *An illuminated French manuscript from the 15th century shows the Ottoman siege of Constantinople in 1453. The Muslim capture of the great eastern bastion of Christian Europe aroused fears throughout the continent, resulting in demands for new Crusades to recapture the city. The advance of the Ottomans in the east also provided impetus to the overseas expansion of nations such as Spain and Portugal on the western coasts of Europe. Both of these Catholic maritime powers saw their efforts to build overseas empires as part of a larger campaign to outflank the Muslim powers and bring areas that they controlled into the Christian camp.*

Ottoman rulers. Although they have often been depicted in Western writings as brutal and corrupt despots, some Ottoman sultans, especially in the early centuries of their sway, were very capable rulers. Ottoman conquest often meant effective administration and tax relief for the peoples of areas annexed to the empire.

Like the Abbasid caliphs, the Ottoman sultans grew more and more distant from their subjects as their empire increased in size and wealth. In their splendid marble palaces and pleasure gardens, surrounded by large numbers of slaves and the many wives and concubines of their harems, Ottoman rulers followed elaborate court rituals based on those of earlier Byzantine, Persian, and Arab dynasties. Day-to-day administration was carried out by a large bureaucracy headed by a grand **vizier** (*wazir* in Arabic).

The vizier was the overall head of the imperial administration, and he often held more real power than the sultan himself. Early sultans took an active role in political decisions and often personally led their armies into battle.

Like earlier Muslim dynasties, however, the Ottomans suffered greatly because they inherited Islamic principles of political succession that remained vague and contested. The existence of many talented and experienced claimants to the throne meant constant danger of civil strife. The death of a sultan could, and increasingly did, lead to protracted warfare among his sons. Defeated claimants sometimes fled to the domains of Christian or Muslim rulers hostile to the Ottomans, thereby becoming rallying points for military campaigns against the son who had gained the throne.

Constantinople Restored and the Flowering of Ottoman Culture

An empire that encompassed so many and such diverse cultures from Europe, Africa, and Asia naturally varied greatly from one province to the next in its social arrangements, artistic production, and physical appearance. But the Ottomans' ancient and cosmopolitan capital at Constantinople richly combined the disparate elements of their extensive territories. Like the Byzantine Empire as a whole, Constantinople had fallen on hard times in the centuries before the Ottoman conquest in 1453. Soon after Mehmed II's armies had captured and sacked the city, however, the Ottoman ruler set about restoring its ancient glory. He had the cathedral of Saint Sophia converted into one of the grandest mosques in the Islamic world, and new mosques and palaces were built throughout the city. This construction benefited greatly from architectural advances the Ottomans derived from the Byzantine heritage. Aqueducts were built from the surrounding hills to supply the growing population with water, markets were reopened, and the city's defenses were repaired.

Each sultan who ruled in the centuries after Mehmed strove to be remembered for his efforts to beautify the capital. The most prominent additions were further mosques that represent some of the most sublime contributions of the Ottomans to Islamic and human civilization. The most spectacular of these was the Suleymaniye, pictured in Figure 21.2. As its name suggests, the mosque was built at the behest of the most successful of the sultans, Suleyman the Magnificent (r. 1520–1566). Although it smacks of hometown pride, the following description by a 17th-century Ottoman chronicler of the reaction of some Christian visitors to the mosque conveys a sense of the awe that the structure still evokes:

> The humble writer of these lines once himself saw ten Frankish infidels skillful in geometry and architecture, who, when the door-keeper had changed their shoes for slippers, and had introduced them into the mosque for the purpose of showing it to them, laid their finger on their mouths, and each bit his finger from astonishment when they saw the minarets; but when they beheld the dome they tossed up their hats and cried Maria! Maria! and on observing the four arches which supported the dome...they could not find terms to express their admiration, and the ten...remained a full hour looking with astonishment on those arches. [One of them said] that nowhere was so much beauty, external and internal, to be found united, and that in the whole of Frangistan [Christian Europe] there was not a single edifice which could be compared to this.

Figure 21.2 *Built in the reign of Suleyman I in the 1550s and designed by the famous architect Sinan, the Suleymaniye mosque is among the largest domed structures in the world, and it is one of the great engineering achievements of Islamic civilization. The pencil-thin minarets flanking the great central dome are characteristic of Ottoman architecture, which was quite distinct from its Safavid and Mughal counterparts (shown in Figures 21.4 and 21.6).*

In addition to the mosques, sultans and powerful administrators built mansions, rest houses, religious schools, and hospitals throughout the city. Both public and private gardens further beautified the capital, which Ottoman writers compared to paradise itself. The city and its suburbs stretched along both sides of the Bosporus, the narrow strait that separates Europe from Asia (see Map 21.2). Its harbors and the Golden Horn, a triangular bay that formed the northern boundary of the city, were crowded with merchant ships from ports throughout the Mediterranean and the Black Sea. Constantinople's great bazaars were filled with merchants and travelers from throughout the empire and places as distant as England and Malaya. They offered the seasoned shopper all manner of produce, from the spices of the East Indies and the ivory of Africa to slaves and forest products from Russia and fine carpets from Persia. Coffeehouses—places where men gathered to smoke tobacco (introduced from America in the 17th century by English merchants), gossip, do business, and play chess—were found in all sections of the city. They were pivotal to the social life of the capital. The coffeehouses also played a major role in the cultural life of Constantinople as places where poets and scholars could congregate, read their latest works aloud, and debate about politics and the merits of each other's ideas.

Beneath the ruling classes, a sizeable portion of the population of Constantinople and other Ottoman cities belonged to the merchant and artisan classes. The Ottoman regime closely regulated commercial exchanges and handicraft production. Government inspectors were employed to ensure that standard weights and measures were used and to license the opening of new shops. They also regulated the entry of apprentice artisans into the trades and monitored the quality of the goods they produced. Like their counterparts in medieval European towns, the artisans were organized into guilds. Guild officers set craft standards, arbitrated disputes between their members, and provided financial assistance for needy members. They even arranged popular entertainments, often linked to religious festivals.

The early Ottomans had written in Persian, and Arabic remained an important language for works on law and religion throughout the empire's history. But by the 17th century, the Turkish language of the Ottoman court had become the preferred mode of expression for poets and historians as well as the language of the Ottoman bureaucracy. In writing, as in the fine arts, the Ottomans' achievements have been somewhat overshadowed by those of their contemporary Persian and Indian rivals. Nonetheless, the authors, artists, and artisans of the Ottoman Empire have left a considerable legacy, particularly in poetry, ceramics, carpet manufacturing, and above all in architecture.

The Problem of Ottoman Decline

Much of the literature on the Ottoman Empire concentrates on its slow decline from the champion of the Muslim world and the great adversary of Christendom to the "sick man" of Europe in the 18th and 19th centuries. This approach provides a very skewed view of Ottoman history as a whole. Traced from its origins in the late 13th century, the Ottoman state is one of the great success stories in human political history. Vigorous and expansive until the late 17th century, the Ottomans were able to ward off the powerful enemies that surrounded their domains on all sides for nearly four centuries. The dynasty endured for more than 600 years, a feat matched by no other in all human history.

From one perspective, the long Ottoman decline, which officials and court historians actively discussed from the mid-17th century onward, reflects the great strength of the institutions on which the empire was built. Despite internal revolts and periodic conflicts with such powerful foreign rivals as the Russian, Austrian, Spanish, and Safavid empires, the Ottomans ruled into the 20th century. Yet the empire had reached the limits of its expansive power centuries earlier, and by the late 17th century the long retreat from Russia, Europe, and the Arab lands had begun. In a sense, some contraction was inevitable. Even when it was at the height of its power, the empire was too large to be maintained, given the resource base that the sultans had at their disposal and the primitive state of transport and communications in the preindustrial era.

The Ottoman state had been built on war and steady territorial expansion. As possibilities for new conquests ran out and lands began to be lost to the Ottomans' Christian and Muslim enemies, the means of maintaining the oversized bureaucracy and army shrank. The decline in the effectiveness of the administrative system that held the empire together was signaled by the rampant growth of corruption among Ottoman officials. The venality and incompetence of state bureaucrats prompted regional and local officials to retain more revenue for their own purposes.

Poorly regulated by the central government, many local officials, who also controlled large landed estates, squeezed the peasants and the laborers who worked their lands for additional taxes and services. At times the oppressive demands of local officials and estate owners sparked rebellions. Peasant uprisings and flight resulted in the abandonment of cultivated lands and in social dislocations that further drained the resources of the empire.

From the 17th century onward, the forces that undermined the empire from below were compounded by growing problems at the center of imperial administration. The early practice of assigning the royal princes administrative or military positions, to prepare them to rule, died out. Instead, possible successors to the throne were kept like hostages in special sections of the palace, where they remained until one of them ascended the throne. The other princes and potential rivals were also, in effect, imprisoned for life in the palace. Although it might have made the reigning sultan more secure, this solution to the problem of contested succession produced monarchs far less prepared to rule than those in the formative centuries of the dynasty. The great warrior-emperors of early Ottoman history gave way, with some important exceptions, to weak and indolent rulers, addicted to drink, drugs, and the pleasures of the harem. In many instances, the later sultans were little more than pawns in the power struggles of the viziers and other powerful officials with the leaders of the increasingly influential Janissary corps. Because the imperial apparatus had been geared to strong and absolute rulers, the decline in the caliber of Ottoman emperors had devastating effects on the empire as a whole. Civil strife increased, and the discipline and leadership of the armies on which the empire depended for survival deteriorated.

Figure 21.3 *The clash of the galley fleets at Lepanto was one of the greatest sea battles in history. But despite devastating losses, the Ottomans managed to replace most of their fleet and go back on the offensive against their Christian adversaries within a year. Here the epic encounter is pictured in one of the many paintings devoted to it in the decades that followed. The tightly packed battle formations that both sides adopted show the importance of ramming rather than cannon fire in naval combat in the Mediterranean in this era. This pattern was reversed in the Atlantic and the other oceanic zones in which the Europeans had been expanding since the 14th century.*

Military Reverses and the Ottoman Retreat

Debilitating changes within the empire were occurring at a time when challenges from without were growing rapidly. The Ottomans had made very effective use of artillery and firearms in building their empire. But their reliance on huge siege guns, and the Janissaries' determination to block all military changes that might jeopardize the power they had gained within the state, caused the Ottomans to fall farther and farther behind their European rivals in the critical art of waging war. With the widespread introduction of light field artillery into the armies of the European powers in the 17th century, Ottoman losses on the battlefield multiplied rapidly, and the threat they posed for the West began to recede.

On the sea, the Ottomans were eclipsed as early as the 16th century. The end of their dominance was presaged by their defeat by a combined Spanish and Venetian fleet at Lepanto in 1571. The great battle is depicted in the painting in Figure 21.3. Although the Ottomans had completely rebuilt their war fleet within a year after Lepanto and soon launched an assault on north Africa that preserved that area for Islam, their control of the eastern Mediterranean had been lost. Even more ominously, in the decades before Lepanto, the Ottomans and the Muslim world had been outflanked by the Portuguese seafarers who sailed down

Document

An Islamic Traveler Laments the Muslims' Indifference to Europe

Although most of the travelers and explorers in this era were Europeans who went to Africa, Asia, and the Americas, a few people from these lands visited Europe. One of these, Abu Taleb, was a scholar of Turkish and Persian descent whose family had settled in India. At the end of the 18th century, Abu Taleb traveled in Europe for three years and later wrote an account in Persian of his experiences there. Although his was one of the few firsthand sources of information about Europe available to Muslim scholars and leaders, Abu Taleb was deeply disturbed by the lack of interest shown by other Muslims in his observations and discoveries. He wrote,

> When I reflect on the want of energy and the indolent dispositions of my countrymen, and the many erroneous customs which exist in all Mohammedan countries and among all ranks of Mussulmans, I am fearful that my exertions [in writing down his experiences in Europe] will be thrown away. The great and the rich intoxicated with pride and luxury, and puffed up with the vanity of their possessions, consider universal science as comprehended in the circle of their own scanty acquirements and limited knowledge; while the poor and common people, from the want of leisure, and overpowered by the difficulty of procuring a livelihood, have not time to attend to his personal concerns, much less to form desires for the acquirement of information of new discoveries and inventions, although such a person has been implanted by nature in every human breast, as an honour and an ornament to the species. I therefore despair of their reaping any fruit from my labours, being convinced that they will consider this book of no greater value than the volumes of tales and romances which they peruse merely to pass away their time, or are attracted thereto by the easiness of the style. It may consequently be concluded, that as they will find no pleasure in reading a work which contains a number of foreign names, treats on uncommon subjects, and alludes to other matters which cannot be understood at first glance, but require a little time for consideration, they will, under pretense of zeal for their religion, entirely abstain and refrain from perusing it.

Questions: What reasons does Abu Taleb give for his fellow Muslims' indifference to his travel reports on Europe? What other factors can be added as a result of our study of long-standing Islamic attitudes toward Europe and conditions in the Ottoman Empire in this period? In what ways might the Muslims' neglect of events in Europe have hindered their efforts to cope with this expansive civilization in the centuries that followed? Were there Western counterparts to Abu Taleb in these centuries, and how were their accounts of distant lands received in Europe?

and around the coast of Africa. The failure in the early 1500s of the Ottomans and their Muslim allies in the Indian Ocean to drive the Portuguese from Asian waters proved far more harmful in the long run than Ottoman defeats in the Mediterranean.

Portuguese naval victories in the Indian Ocean revealed the decline of the Ottoman galley fleets and Mediterranean-style warships more generally. The trading goods, particularly spices, that the Portuguese carried around Africa and back to Europe enriched the Ottomans' Christian rivals. In addition, the fact that a large portion of the flow of these products was no longer transmitted to European ports through Muslim trading centers in the eastern Mediterranean meant that merchants and tax collectors in the Ottoman Empire lost critical revenues. As if this were not enough, from the late 16th century on, large amounts of silver flowed into the Ottomans' lands from mines worked by Native American laborers in the Spanish empire in Peru and Mexico. This sudden influx of bullion into the rigid and slow-growing economy of the Ottoman empire set off a long-term inflationary trend that further undermined the finances of the empire.

Several able sultans took measures to shore up the empire in the 17th century. The collapse of the Safavid dynasty in Persia and conflicts between the European powers at this time also gave the Ottomans hope that their earlier dominance might be restored. But their reprieve was temporary. With the scientific, technological, and commercial transformations occurring in Europe (discussed in Chapter 15), the Ottomans were falling behind their Christian rivals in most areas. But the growing gap was most critical in trade and warfare. The Ottomans inherited from their Arab, Persian, and Turkic predecessors the conviction that little of what happened in Europe was important. This belief, which is seen as a major cause of Ottoman decline by the traveler Abu Taleb quoted in the Document, prevented them from taking seriously the revolutionary changes that were transforming western Europe. The intense conservatism of powerful groups such as the Janissaries, and to a lesser extent the religious scholars, reinforced this fatal attitude. Through much of the 17th and 18th centuries, these groups blocked most of the Western-inspired innovations that reform-minded sultans and their advisors tried to introduce. As a result of these narrow and potentially dangerous attitudes, the isolated Ottoman imperial system proved incapable of checking the forces that were steadily destroying it.

The Shi'a Challenge of the Safavids

 In the first years of the 16th century, after decades of warfare against established Muslim states, rival sects, and Christian communities in what is today southern Russia, the Safavids founded a dynasty and conquered the region that makes up the present-day nation of Iran. From that point onward, Iran has been one of the strongest and most enduring centers of Shi'ism within the Islamic world. Under the Safavid dynasty, which lasted until 1722, the Iranian region was also restored as a center of political power and cultural creativity at a level that it had rarely enjoyed since the collapse of the Sasanian Empire in the mid-7th century.

Like the Ottomans, the Safavid dynasty arose from the struggles of rival Turkic nomadic groups in the wake of the Mongol and Timurid invasions of the 13th and 14th centuries. Also like the Ottomans, the Safavids rose to prominence as the frontier warrior champions of a highly militant strain of Islam. But unlike the Ottomans, who became the champions of the Sunni majority of the Muslim faithful, the Safavids espoused the Shi'a variant of Islam. As we saw in Chapter 6, in the early decades of Muslim expansion a split developed in the community of the faithful between the Sunnis, who recognized the legitimacy of the first three successors to Muhammad (Abu Bakr, Umar, and Uthman), and the Shi'a, who believed that only the fourth successor (Ali, Mohammed's cousin and son-in-law) had the right to succeed the prophet. Over time, differences in doctrine, ritual, and law were added to the disagreements over succession that originally divided the Islamic community. Divisions have also arisen within both the Shi'a and Sunni groupings, but bitter hostility and violent conflict most often have developed along Sunni–Shi'a lines. The long rivalry between the Sunni Ottomans and the Shi'a Safavids proved to be one of the most pivotal episodes in the long history of these sectarian struggles.

The Safavid dynasty had its origins in a family of Sufi mystics and religious preachers, whose shrine center was at Ardabil near the Caspian Sea (see Map 21.3). In the early 14th century, one of these Sufis, **Sail al-Din,** who gave the dynasty its name, began a militant campaign to purify and reform Islam and spread Muslim teachings among the Turkic tribes of

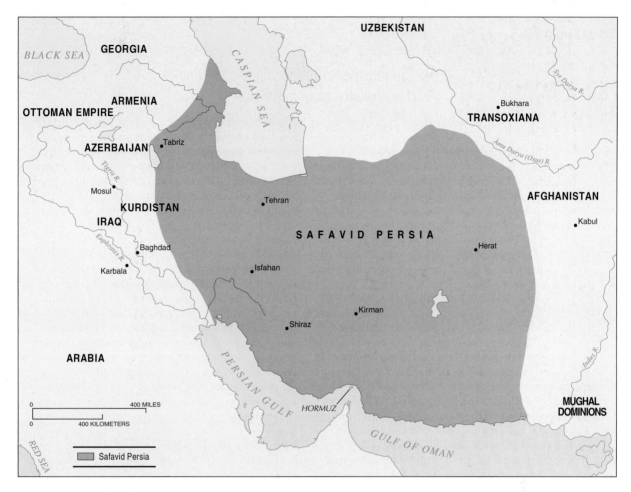

Map 21.3 *The Safavid Empire*

the region. In the chaos that followed the collapse of Mongol authority in the mid-14th century, Sail al-Din and other Safavid Sufi leaders gained increasing support. But as the numbers of the **Red Heads** (as the Safavids' followers were called because of their distinctive headgear) grew, and as they began in the mid-15th century to preach Shi'a doctrines, their enemies multiplied. After decades of fierce local struggles in which three successive Safavid leaders perished, a surviving Sufi commander, **Ismâ'il,** led his Turkic followers to a string of victories on the battlefield. In 1501, Ismâ'il's armies took the city of Tabriz, where he was proclaimed *shah*, or emperor.

In the next decade, Ismâ'il's followers conquered most of Persia, drove the Safavid's ancient enemies, the Ozbegs—a neighboring nomadic people of Turkic stock—back into the central Asian steppes, and advanced into what is now Iraq. The Safavid successes

and the support their followers received in the Ottoman borderlands from Turkic-speaking peoples brought them into conflict with Ottoman rulers. In August 1514, at **Chaldiran** in northwest Persia, the armies of the two empires met in one of the most fateful battles in Islamic history. Chaldiran was more than a battle between the two most powerful dynasties in the Islamic world at the time. It was a clash between the champions of the Shi'a and Sunni variants of Islam. The religious fervor with which both sides fought the battle was intensified by the long-standing Safavid persecutions of the Sunnis and the slaughter of Shi'a living in Ottoman territories by the forces of the Ottoman sultan, Selim.

The battle also demonstrated the importance of muskets and field cannon in the gunpowder age. Because his artillery was still engaged against enemies far to the east, Ismâ'il hoped to delay a decisive

In Depth

The Gunpowder Empires and the Shifting Balance of Global Power

Like so many of their predecessors, each of the great Muslim dynasties of the premodern era came to power with the support of nomadic warrior peoples. Each based the military forces that won and sustained its empire on massed cavalry. But in each case, there was a significant divergence from past conditions. As the outcome of the critical battle of Chaldiran between the Ottomans and Safavids made clear, by the 16th century firearms had become a decisive element in armed conflict—the key to empire building. In military and political terms, global history had entered a new phase.

Although the Chinese had invented gunpowder and were the first to use it in war, the Mongols were the first to realize the awesome potential of the new type of weaponry based on explosive formulas. The Mongols continued to build their armies around swift cavalry and their skill as mounted archers. But siege cannons became critical to Mongol conquests once they ventured into the highly urbanized civilizations that bordered on their steppe homelands. Mongol successes against intricately walled and heavily fortified cities in China, Russia, and the Islamic heartlands impressed their sedentary and nomadic adversaries with the power of the new weaponry and contributed much to its spread throughout the Eurasian world in the late 13th and 14th centuries.

Innovation in the use of gunpowder spread quickly to many areas, especially Europe and the Muslim Middle East. By the late 15th century, muskets and field cannons, however heavy and clumsy the latter might be, were transforming warfare from Europe to China. In the Middle East, Janissary musketeers and heavy artillery became the driving force of Ottoman expansion. The Safavids' lack of artillery was

critical to their defeat at Chaldiran. In Europe, armies were increasingly built around musket and artillery regiments. Rival states vied to attract gunsmiths who could provide them with the latest weaponry or, even better, invent guns that would give them decisive advantages over their rivals. In the Atlantic and the Mediterranean, handguns and cannons were introduced into sea warfare—an innovation that proved essential to the Europeans' ability to project their power overseas from the 16th century onward.

In many areas, the new military technology contributed to broader social and political changes. In feudal Europe and somewhat later in Japan, for example, siege cannons reduced feudal castles to rubble. In so doing, they struck a mortal blow at the warrior aristocracies that had dominated these societies for centuries. But the success of the new weaponry forced a revolution in the design of fortifications and defense strategies. The defense systems that resulted, which were expensive and elaborate, spawned corps of professional officers and engineers, vast military supply industries, and urban centers enclosed by low-lying walls and star-shaped bastions. The cost of the field artillery, siege weapons, and new defense industries promoted state centralization, as the experience of the Muslim empires and the history of Europe and Japan in the gunpowder age demonstrate. Rulers with national or imperial ambitions had the firepower to level the fortresses of regional lords and thus more effectively control the populations and resources of their domains.

Although the new weaponry was vital to the rise and sustenance of nation-states and empires, some political systems were more compatible than others with efforts to exploit and improve on it. At one

confrontation with the Ottoman forces under the Sultan Selim. When battle could not be avoided, Ismâ'il threw his cavalry against the cannon and massed muskets of the Ottoman forces. Despite desperate attempts to make up through clever maneuvers what he lacked in firepower, Ismâ'il's cavalry proved no match for the well-armed Ottomans.

The Safavids were dealt a devastating defeat. Thus, their victory at Chaldiran buttressed the

Ottomans' efforts to build the most powerful empire in the Islamic world. But the Ottomans could not follow up the battle with conquests that would have put an end to their Safavid rivals. The latter's capital at Tabriz was too far from Ottoman supply areas to be held through the approaching winter. The withdrawal of the Ottoman armies gave the Safavids the breathing space they needed to regroup their forces and reoccupy much of the territory they had origi-

extreme, the Chinese scholar-gentry limited innovations in gunpowder weaponry and its use in warfare because they feared that these changes would lead to the dominance of the military in Ming and later Qing society. After the early 1600s, the shoguns, or military leaders, of neighboring Japan virtually banned the firearms that had done so much to bring them to power. In this case, a military caste feared that the spread of firearms to the general populace would destroy what was left of the feudal order they had built centuries earlier.

The obstacles faced by nomadic peoples such as the Mongols were very different. Their sparse populations and arid lands simply did not generate the resources or sustained invention that would allow them to keep up with their sedentary neighbors in the expensive arms races that the new technology spawned. As the advantages of sedentary societies grew more pronounced in the 17th and 18th centuries, nomadic peoples found not only that they could no longer raid or conquer the agrarian cores but also that sedentary adversaries could advance into and occupy their homelands on the steppe and desert fringes.

Nomadic dynasties, such as the Ottomans, Safavids, and Mughals, who had won their empires in the early stages of the gunpowder revolution, did control the agrarian bases and skilled artisans needed to supply their armies with muskets and siege cannons. But they were confronted by internal conflicts and, perhaps more critically in the long run, formidable external rivals. To begin with, their military technology was far in advance of the transport and communication systems of their far-flung empires. This fact, and their failure to build effective imperial bureaucracies, left them at the mercy of the warrior elites who brought them to power. In each of the three empires, the regional bases of the warrior classes became increasingly independent of the ruling dynasty. This meant that the rulers were denied revenue and other resources that were vital to maintaining competitive military establishments. Their fragile

and overstretched administrative systems proved difficult to reform and more and more ineffective at administering the peasant populations in their charge. Internal revolts further sapped the resources of the hard-pressed Muslim dynasties.

In each Muslim empire, decline was hastened by the rise of European rivals, who proved more adept at taking advantage of the gunpowder revolution. The smaller but highly competitive nation-states of western Europe were better able to mobilize their smaller human and natural resources than their Muslim counterparts. Constant struggles for survival in the multistate European system also made the elites of Spain, England, and France more receptive to technological innovation, which became a central ingredient of political success in the gunpowder era. Emulating the more advanced states of western Europe, for example, Peter the Great forced social reforms and military innovations that transformed a weak and backward Russia into a powerful adversary of the Ottomans and the nomadic peoples of the steppes. Thus, although it began in China and was initially spread by the Mongol nomads, the gunpowder revolution eventually tipped the global balance of power in favor of the peoples of Christian Europe. This shift was an essential condition for Europe's rise to global power in the centuries that followed.

Questions: What advantages would gunpowder weaponry give to those who used it over those who did not in the early modern era? Were these advantages as decisive as they were later in the industrial age? Why would the use of muskets and early field cannons take a higher level of military organization and troop discipline and training than had been needed in earlier time periods? What made the new military technology so expensive? Why did the Europeans adopt it more readily than most other peoples, and why were they so intent on improving it?

nally conquered. Nonetheless, defeat at Chaldiran put an end to Ismâ'il's dreams of further westward expansion, and most critically it checked the rapid spread of conversions to Shi'a Islam in the western borderlands that had resulted from the Safavid's recent successes in battle. The outcome at Chaldiran determined that Shi'ism would be confined largely to Persia, or present-day Iran, and neighboring areas in what is today southern Iraq.

Politics and War Under the Safavid Shahs

After his defeat at Chaldiran, Ismâ'il, once a courageous warrior and a popular leader, retreated to his palace and tried to escape his troubles through drink. His seclusion, along with struggles between the factions backing each of his sons for the right to succeed him, left openings for subordinate Turkic chiefs to attempt to seize power. After years of turmoil, a new shah, Tahmasp I (r. 1534–1576), won the throne and set about restoring the power of the dynasty. The Turkic chiefs were foiled in their bid for supreme power, and the Ozbegs were again and again driven from the Safavid domains. Under Shah Abbas I (r. 1587–1629) the empire reached the height of its strength and prosperity, although the territories it controlled remained roughly equivalent to those ruled by Ismâ'il and Tahmasp I.

Under Tahmasp I and his successors, repeated efforts were made to bring the Turkic chiefs under control. They were gradually transformed into a warrior nobility comparable to that in the Ottoman domains. Like their Ottoman counterparts, the Safavid warrior nobles were assigned villages, whose peasants were required to supply them and their troops with food and labor. The most powerful of the warrior leaders occupied key posts in the imperial administration, and from the defeat at Chaldiran onward they posed a constant threat to the Safavid monarchs. To counterbalance this threat, Safavid rulers recruited Persians for positions at the court and in the rapidly expanding imperial bureaucracy. The struggle for power and influence between Turkic and Persian notables was further complicated by the practice, initiated by Ismâ'il's successor, Tahmasp I, of recruiting into the bureaucracy and army slave boys who were captured in campaigns in southern Russia. Like the Janissaries in the Ottoman Empire, many of these slaves rose to positions of power. Also like the Janissaries, the slave regiments soon became a major force in Safavid political struggles.

Of all of the Safavid shahs, Abbas I, known also as **Abbas the Great,** made the greatest use of the youths who were captured in Russia and then educated and converted to Islam. They not only came to form the backbone of his military forces but were granted provincial governorships and high offices at court. Like the Janissaries, "slave" regiments, which were wholly dependant on Abbas's support, monopolized the firearms that had become increasingly prominent in Safavid armies. The Persians had artillery and handguns long before the arrival of the Portuguese by sea in the early 16th century. But Abbas and his successors showed little reluctance to call on the knowledgeable but infidel Europeans for assistance in their wars with the Ottomans. Abbas turned to European advisors, such as the one portrayed in the illustration at the beginning of this chapter. Of special importance were the Sherley brothers

from England. They provided instruction in the casting of cannons and trained Abbas' slave infantry and a special regiment of musketeers recruited from the Iranian peasantry. By the end of his reign, Abbas had built up a standing army of nearly 40,000 troops and an elite bodyguard. These measures to strengthen his armies and his victories on the battlefield appeared to promise security for the Safavid domains for decades to come—a promise that was not fulfilled.

State and Religion

The Safavid family was originally of Turkic stock, and early shahs such as Ismâ'il wrote in Turkish, unlike their Ottoman rivals, who preferred to write in Persian. After Chaldiran, however, Persian gradually supplanted Turkish as the language of the court and bureaucracy. Persian influences were also felt in the organization of court rituals and in the more and more exalted position of the Safavid shahs. Abandoning all pretense of the egalitarian camaraderie that had marked their earlier dealings with the warrior chiefs, the Safavids took grand titles, such as *padishah*, or king of kings, often derived from those used by the ancient Persian emperors. Like the Ottoman rulers, the Safavids presided from their high thrones over opulent palace complexes crowded with servants and courtiers. The pattern of palace life was set by elaborate court rituals and social interaction governed by a refined sense of etiquette and decorum. Although the later Safavid shahs played down claims to divinity that had been set forth under Ismâ'il and his predecessors, they continued to claim descent from one of the Shi'a **imams,** or successors of Ali.

Changes in the status accorded to the Safavid rulers were paralleled by shifts in the religious impulses that had been so critical to their rise to power. The militant, expansive cast of Shi'a ideology was modified as the faith became a major pillar of dynasty and empire. The early Safavids imported Arabic-speaking Shi'a religious experts. But later shahs came to rely on Persian religious scholars who entered into the service of the state and were paid by the government. **Mullahs,** who were both local mosque officials and prayer leaders, were also supervised by the state and given some support from it. All religious leaders were required to curse the first three caliphs and mention the Safavid ruler in the Friday sermon. Teaching in the mosque schools was also planned and directed by state religious officials.

Through these agents, the bulk of the Iranian population was converted to Shi'ism during the centuries of Safavid rule. Sunni Muslims, Christians, Jews, Zoroastrians, and the followers of Sufi preachers were pressured to convert to Shi'ism. Shi'a religious festivals, such as that commemorating the martyrdom of Husayn (a son of Ali) and involving public flagellation and passion plays, and pilgrimages to Shi'a shrines, such as that at Karbala in central Iraq, became the focal points of popular religion in Iran. Thus, Shi'ism not only provided ideological and institutional support for the Safavid dynasty but also came to be an integral part of Iranian identity, setting the people of the region off from most of their Arab and Turkic neighbors.

Elite Affluence and Artistic Splendor

Although earlier rulers had built or restored mosques and religious schools and financed public works projects, Abbas I surpassed them all. After securing his political position with a string of military victories, Abbas I set about establishing his empire as a major center of international trade and Islamic culture. He

had a network of roads and rest houses built, and he strove to make merchants and travelers safe within his domains. He set up workshops to manufacture the silk textiles and splendid Persian carpets that were in great demand. Abbas I encouraged Iranian merchants to trade not only with their Muslim neighbors and India and China to the east but also with the Portuguese—and later the Dutch and English—whose war and merchant ships were becoming a familiar sight in the Persian Gulf and Arabian Sea.

Although Abbas I undertook building projects throughout his empire, he devoted special attention to his capital at **Isfahan.** The splendid seat of Safavid power was laid out around a great square, shown in Figure 21.4, which was lined with two-story shops interspersed with great mosques, government offices, and soaring arches that opened onto formal gardens. Abbas I founded several colleges and oversaw the construction of numerous public baths and rest houses. He patronized workshops where intricately detailed and brilliantly colored miniatures were produced by master painters and their apprentices.

Above all, the great mosques that Abbas I had built at Isfahan were the glory of his reign. The vividly colored ceramic tiles, which Iranian builders had

Figure 21.4 *The great square of the Safavid capital at Isfahan was built by Abbas I to project the splendor and power of his empire. The buildings of the square made up one of the most splendid architectural complexes of the early modern era.*

begun to use centuries earlier, turned the massive domes and graceful minarets of Safavid mosques and royal tombs into creations of stunning beauty. Geometric designs, floral patterns, and verses from the Qur'an written in stylized Arabic added movement and texture to the deep blue tiles that distinguished the monumental construction of the Safavid era. Gardens and reflecting pools were built near the mosques and rest houses. By combining graceful arches, greenery, and colorful designs, Persian architects and artisans created lush, cool refuges (perhaps duplicating heaven itself, as it is described in the Qur'an) in a land that is dry, dusty, and gray-brown for much of the year.

Society and Gender Roles: Ottoman and Safavid Comparisons

Although the Ottomans and Safavids were bitter political rivals and religious adversaries, the social systems that developed under the two dynasties had much in common. Both were dominated, particularly in their earliest phases, by warrior aristocracies, which shared power with the absolutist monarchs of each empire and enjoyed prestige and luxury in the capital and on rural estates. In both cases, the warrior aristocrats gradually retreated to the estates, making life increasingly difficult for the peasants on whom they depended for the support of their grand households and many retainers. As the real power of the rulers of each empire diminished and as population increases reduced the uncultivated lands to which peasants might flee, the demands of the landlord class grew harsher. Foreign invasions, civil strife, and the breakdown in vital services once provided by the state added to the growing misery of the peasantry. The resulting spread of banditry, peasant uprisings, and flight from the land further drained the resources of both empires and undermined their legitimacy.

The early rulers of both the Ottoman and the Safavid empires encouraged the growth of handicraft production and trade in their realms. Both dynasties established imperial workshops where products ranging from miniature paintings and rugs to weapons and metal utensils were manufactured. The rulers of each empire lavishly patronized public works projects that provided reasonably well-paid work for engineers, stonemasons, carpenters, and other sorts of artisans. Some of the more able emperors of these dynasties also pursued policies that they believed

would increase both internal and international trade. In these endeavors, the Ottomans gained in the short run from the fact that large-scale traders in their empire often were from minority groups, such as Christians and Jews, who had extensive contacts with overseas traders that the bazaar merchants of the Safavid realm normally lacked. Although Safavid cooperation with Portuguese traders remedied this shortcoming to some extent, the Safavid economy remained much more constricted, less market oriented, and more technically backward than that of their Ottoman rivals.

Women in Islamic societies under Ottoman or Safavid rule faced legal and social disadvantages comparable to those we have encountered in most civilized areas so far. Within the family, women were subordinated to their fathers and husbands. They seldom had political or religious power, and they had surprisingly meager outlets for artistic or scholarly expression. Even women of nomadic Turkic and Mongol backgrounds gradually lost their independence when they settled in the towns of conquered areas. There, the dictates of increasingly patriarchal codes and restrictive practices such as seclusion and veiling were imposed on women of all classes, but most strictly on those of the elite.

However, recent evidence suggests that many women in the Islamic heartlands in this era, perhaps clinging to the memory of the lives led by their nomadic predecessors, struggled against these restrictions. Travelers to Persia in the time of Abbas I remarked on the brightly colored robes worn by women in the capital and elsewhere, and noted that many women made no effort to cover their faces in public. At both the Ottoman and Safavid courts, the wives and concubines of the rulers and royal princes continued to exert influence behind the throne and remained deeply involved in palace conspiracies. More important for ordinary women in each of these societies was the fact that many were active in trade and some in money-lending. Court records also suggest that women often could invoke provisions in Islamic law that protected their rights to inheritance, decent treatment by their spouses, and even divorce in marital situations that had become intolerable.

How typical these instances of assertion and expression were is not clear. Although some women were a good deal better off than we had once thought, perhaps as well off as or even better off than their counterparts in China and India, most women probably lived unenviable lives. Limited largely to contacts with their own families and left with little more than household chores and domestic handicrafts such as embroidery to occupy their time, the overwhelming majority of women in effect disappeared from the history of two of the great centers of Islamic civilization.

The Rapid Demise of the Safavid Empire

Given the power and splendor the Safavid Empire had achieved by the end of the reign of Abbas I, its collapse was stunningly rapid. Abbas' fears of usurpation by one of his sons, which were fed by plots on the part of several of his closest advisors, had led during his reign to the death or blinding of all who could legitimately succeed him. A grandson, who was weak and thus thought by high state officials to be easily manipulated, was placed on the throne after Abbas' death. From this point, the dynasty's fortunes declined. As was true of the Ottomans, the practice of confining the princes to the atmosphere of luxury and intrigue that permeated the court led to a sharp fall in the quality of Safavid rulers. Able shahs, such as Abbas II (r. 1642–1666), were too few to halt the decline of the imperial administration or to deal effectively with the many foreign threats to the empire. Factional disputes and rebellions shook the empire from within, and nomadic raiders and Ottoman and Mughal armies steadily reduced the territory the Safavids could tap for labor and revenue.

By March 1722, Isfahan was besieged by Afghani tribes. In October, after over 80,000 of the capital's inhabitants had died of starvation and disease, the city fell and Safavid power was ended. One of those who fought for the throne in the decade of war and destruction that followed claimed descent from the Safavid line. But a soldier-adventurer named **Nadir Khan Afshar** eventually emerged victorious from these bloody struggles. Although he began as a champion of Safavid restoration, Nadir Khan proclaimed himself shah in 1736. Despite the title, his dynasty and those that followed were short-lived. The area that had once made up the Safavid Empire was reduced for generations to a battleground for its powerful neighbors and a tempting target for nomadic raiders.

The Mughals and the Apex of Muslim Civilization in India

 In the first decades of the 16th century, another wave of nomadic invaders established what was to become the most powerful of a succession of Muslim dynasties in south Asia. A warrior prince, Babur, and his remarkable descendants spread the power of the Mughal dynasty through much of the Indian subcontinent. Under their rule, Islam peaked as a force in south Asian history, and a blend of Hindu-Islamic civilization produced architecture and art as splendid as that created in Persia under the Safavids. By the early 17th century, however, a familiar pattern of dynastic decline took hold.

Despite the fact that the founder of the Mughal dynasty, **Babur,** traced his descent on one side from the Mongol khans, the Mughal in the dynasty's name was not derived from the earlier nomadic conquerors. Babur was also descended from Turkic warriors, like Timur, and most of his followers were from Turkic or mixed nomadic origins. Unlike the Ottomans and Safavids, Babur's motives for conquest and empire building had little to do with religious fervor. He led his followers into India in 1526 because he had lost his original kingdom, centered on Ferghana in central Asia, in the preceding decades (see Map 21.4).

After his father's death in 1498, Babur, then only a boy of 16, was thrown into a fierce struggle with the Ozbeg tribes for control of his ancestral realm. By 1504, Babur and his supporters had been driven back to Kabul in what is now Afghanistan. Originally, he directed raids into the fertile and heavily populated plains of India only to gain booty to support his campaigns to win back Ferghana. Although India had much greater potential as a base on which to build an empire, Babur cared little for the green and well-watered subcontinent. Even after he later conquered India, he continued to long for the arid steppe and blue-domed mosques of his central Asian birthplace. But after decades of wars that repeatedly ended in defeat, he was forced to give up his dream of reclaiming his homeland and to turn his full energies to the conquest of northern India.

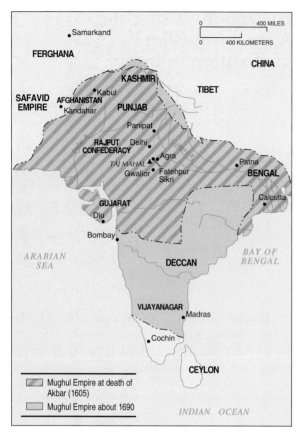

Map 21.4 *The Growth of the Mughal Empire, from Akbar to Aurangzeb*

In 1526, Babur—by then a seasoned military commander—entered India at the head of an experienced and well-organized army. At Panipat, north of Delhi, his army of 12,000 met the huge force of more than 100,000 sent to crush it by the last ruler of the Muslim Lodi dynasty, which then ruled much of northern India. Using gun carts, movable artillery, and cavalry tactics similar to those that had brought the Ottomans victory at Chaldiran, Babur routed the Lodi army. In addition to the superior firepower and mobility of his forces, their victory owed a great deal to the tactic of frightening the hundreds of war elephants that led the Lodi army into battle. The elephants stampeded, trampling thousands of Lodi infantrymen or sending them into flight. A year later, Babur's forces, again vastly outnumbered, defeated a confederation of Hindu warrior-kings at Khanua, a small village near Agra. Within two years, he had conquered large portions of the Indus and Ganges plains and established a dynasty that would last more than 300 years.

The founder of the Mughal dynasty was a remarkable man. A fine military strategist and fierce fighter who went into battle alongside his troops, in the decades when he was continually fighting for his very life, Babur also cultivated a taste for the arts and music. He wrote one of the great histories of India, was a fine musician, and designed wonderful gardens for his new capital at Delhi. But he was a better conqueror than administrator. He did little to reform the very ineffective Lodi bureaucracy he had taken over—a project that would have solidified the Mughals' hold on the empire he had conquered. In 1530, at the age of 48, Babur suddenly fell ill and died, leaving his son, **Humayan,** to inherit the newly founded kingdom.

Like his father, Humayan was a good soldier; in fact, he had won his first battle at age 18. But Babur's death was the signal for his enemies to strike from all sides. One of Humayan's brothers disputed his succession, and armies from Afghanistan and the Rajput states of western India marched on his capital. By 1540, with his armies shattered, Humayan was forced to flee to Persia. There he remained in exile, an embarrassed guest at the Safavid court, for nearly a decade. Having gained a foothold at Kabul in 1545, Humayan launched a series of campaigns into India that restored Mughal rule to the northern plains by 1556. But Humayan did not live to savor his victory. Shortly after entering Delhi in triumph, he was hurrying down his library steps, his arms full of books, to answer the call to prayer. He stumbled and fell, hitting his head. He died within days.

Akbar and the Basis for a Lasting Empire

Humayan's sudden death once again imperiled the Mughal dynasty. His son and successor, **Akbar,** was only 13 years old, and the Mughals' enemies moved quickly to take advantage of what they saw as a very favorable turn of events. Their expectations were soon dashed because Akbar proved to be one of the greatest leaders of all history. Interestingly, Akbar's reign was contemporaneous with those of several other remarkable monarchs, including Elizabeth I of England, Philip of Spain, and the Muslim rulers Suleyman the Magnificent and Abbas I. Akbar was a match for any one of these very formidable rivals.

Like his father and grandfather, Akbar was a fine military commander with great personal courage. But unlike his predecessors, Akbar also had a vision of empire and sense of mission that hinged on uniting

Visualizing the Past

The Basis of Imperial Power in the Rival Muslim Empires

The table below provides the vital statistics of each of the three great Muslim empires of the early modern era. Use the data to determine the relative strengths and weaknesses of each of the empires. Also make use of the maps provided throughout this chapter to include geographical factors and incorporate points from the text with relevance to the questions posed below.

Questions: Which of the rival empires has the largest resource base? On the basis of your impressions from the text discussion, which was the most for-

midable in terms of artisan production and external trade? Which empire did geography favor the most in terms of defending itself and projecting its power? Which was the most secure/most threatened by (a) rival powers? (b) internal enemies? Which of these threats proved the most powerful and why? How would you rank the three empires in terms of overall military strength? What long-term problems can you identify regarding the survival of these imperial systems in the changing global system of the early modern era?

Vital Statistics of the Gunpowder Empires

	Land Area	Approximate Population	Religious Composition	Estimated Size of Military Forces	Source of Cannon/Firearms
Ottoman Empire, c. 1566	c. 1,200,000 sq. mi.	30–35 million	Large majority Sunni Muslim; significant Jewish and Christian minorities	Largest army recorded: 200,000 cavalry, infantry, artillery; 90 warships+	Produced locally
Safavid Empire, 1600	c. 750,000 sq. mi.	No reliable consensus; perhaps 10–15 million	Majority Shi'a Muslim; small Sunni, Jewish, and Christian minorities	40,000–50,000 cavalry, infantry, artillery; no navy	Imported cannon not widely used, except by European mercenaries
Mughal Empire, c. 1600	c. 1,000,000 sq. mi.	105–110 million	10–15% Muslim (divided Sunni/ Shi'a); great majority Hindu and Sikh, Jewish, Christian minorities	Armies in hundreds of thousands reported; cavalry, infantry, artillery; no navy	Imported and produced locally

Note: c. = approximations or rough estimates.

India under his rule. A workaholic who seldom slept more than three hours a night, Akbar personally oversaw the building of the military and administrative systems that would form the backbone of the Mughal Empire for centuries. He also patronized the arts and entered into complex religious and philo-sophical discussions with learned scholars from throughout the Muslim, Christian, and Hindu worlds. In addition, Akbar found time to carry out social reforms and invent his own universalistic religion. Though illiterate—there had been little time for book learning when his father fought for survival in the wilderness—Akbar had an insatiable curiosity and an incredible memory. By having others read aloud to him, he became educated in many fields.

At first with the help of senior advisors, but soon on his own, Akbar routed the enemies who had hoped to capitalize on the Mughals' misfortunes. In the decades after 1560, when he took charge of the government, Akbar's armies greatly extended the empire with conquests throughout north and central India. But it was Akbar's social policies and administrative genius that made it possible to establish the foundations of a lasting dominion in the subcontinent. He pursued a policy of reconciliation and cooperation with the Hindu princes and the Hindu majority of the population of his realm. He encouraged intermarriage between the Mughal aristocracy and the families of the Hindu Rajput rulers. Akbar also abolished the much-hated *jizya*, or head tax, that earlier Muslim rulers had levied on Hindu unbelievers. He promoted Hindus to the highest ranks in the government, ended a long-standing ban on the building of new Hindu temples, and ordered Muslims to respect cows, which the Hindu majority viewed as sacred.

Despite the success of these policies in reconciling the Hindu majority to Muslim rule, Akbar viewed tolerance as merely the first stage in a longer strategy to put an end to sectarian divisions in the subcontinent. Blending elements of the many religions with which he was familiar, he invented a new faith, the **Din-i-Ilahi,** that he believed could be used to unite his Hindu and Muslim subjects. If the adherents of India's diverse religions could be convinced to embrace this common creed, Akbar reasoned, sectarian quarrels and even violent conflict could be brought to an end.

Like their counterparts in the Ottoman and Safavid empires, the Muslim and Hindu warrior aristocrats who formed the core of the supporters of the Mughal dynasty were granted peasant villages for their support. In turn, they were required to maintain a specified number of cavalry and to be on call if the emperor needed their services. The court and the central bureaucracy were supported by revenues drawn from the tribute paid by the military retainers and from taxes on lands set aside for the support of the imperial household. Because of a shortage of administrators, in most areas local notables, many of whom were Hindu, were left in place as long as they swore allegiance to the Mughal rulers and paid

their taxes on time. These arrangements left the control and welfare of the village population largely in the hands of the military retainers of the dynasty and local power brokers.

Social Reform and Social Change

In addition to his administrative reforms, Akbar pushed for social changes that he believed would greatly benefit his subjects. Beyond the public works typically favored by able Muslim rulers, Akbar sought to improve the calendar, to establish living quarters for the large population of beggars and vagabonds in the large cities, and to regulate the consumption of alcohol. Whatever success the latter campaign may have had in Indian society as a whole, it apparently failed in Akbar's own household, for one of his sons was reputed to drink 20 cups of double-distilled wine per day.

More than any of Akbar's many reform efforts, those involving the position of women demonstrated how far the Mughal ruler was in advance of his time. He encouraged widow remarriage, at that point taboo for both Hindus and Muslims, and discouraged child marriages. The latter were so widespread among the upper classes that he did not try to outlaw them, and it is doubtful that his disapproval did much to curb the practice. Akbar did legally prohibit sati, or the burning of high-caste Hindu women on their husbands' funeral pyres (Figure 21.5). Because this custom was deeply entrenched among the Rajput princes and warrior classes that were some of his most faithful allies, this was a risky move on Akbar's part. But he was so determined to eradicate sati, particularly in cases where the widow was pressured to agree to be burned alive, that he once personally rescued a young girl despite the protestations of her angry relatives. He also tried to provide relief for women trapped in purdah, or seclusion in their homes, by encouraging the merchants of Delhi and other cities to set aside special market days for women only.

Mughal Splendor and Early European Contacts

Despite his many successes and the civil peace and prosperity his reign brought to much of northern India, Akbar died a lonely and discouraged man. By 1605, he had outlived most of his friends and faced revolts by sons eager to claim his throne. Above all, he died knowing that Din-i-Ilahi, the religion he had

Figure 21.5 *This engraving from a late 16th-century German traveler's account of India shows a European artist's impression of an Indian widow committing sati. Not surprisingly, this practice of burning high-caste widows on their deceased husbands' funeral pyres often was described at great length by European visitors in this era. There was some disagreement in their accounts as to whether the women went willingly into the fire, as some early authors claimed. Later inquiries in the British period revealed that some of the widows had been drugged and others tied to the funeral pyre. It is likely that most simply caved in to the relentless pressure applied by their dead spouse's relatives and their own children.*

created to reconcile his Hindu and Muslim subjects, had been rejected by both.

Although neither of his successors, Jahangir (r. 1605–1627) or Shah Jahan (r. 1627–1658), added much territory to the empire Akbar had left them, in their reigns Mughal India reached the peak of its splendor. European visitors marveled at the size and opulence of the chief Mughal cities: Delhi, Agra, and Lahore. The huge Mughal armies, replete with elephant and artillery corps, dwarfed those of even the most powerful European rulers at the time. Some of the more perceptive European observers, such as François Bernier, also noted the poverty in which the lower classes in both town and country-side lived and the lack of discipline and training of most of the soldiers in the Mughal armies. Perhaps most ominously, Bernier added that in invention and the sciences, India had fallen far behind western Europe in most areas.

Nonetheless, by the late 17th century, Mughal India had become one of the major overseas destinations for European traders. They brought products from throughout Asia, though little from Europe itself, to exchange for a variety of Indian manufactures, particularly the subcontinent's famed cotton textiles. The trade gap that the demand for Indian cotton cloth and clothing had created in the West in Roman times persisted millennia later. The importance of the Indian textile trade to the West is suggested by the names we still use for different kinds of cotton cloth, from calico (after the Indian port city of Calicut) to chintz and muslin, as well as by our names for cotton clothes such as pajamas.

Because they were easily washed and inexpensive, Indian textiles first won a large market among the working and middle classes in Britain and elsewhere in Europe. In the reigns of Queen Mary and Queen Anne, fine Indian cloth came into fashion at the court as well. An incident from the reign of the Mughal emperor **Aurangzeb,** who succeeded Shah Jahan, suggests just how fine the cloth in question was. Aurangzeb, a religious zealot, scolded his favorite daughter for appearing in his presence in garments that revealed so much of her body. The daughter protested that she had on three layers of fine cotton clothing. It is thus no wonder that even after industrialization had revolutionized cotton textile manufacture in England, European visitors to India continued to observe and write in great detail about the techniques Indian artisans used to weave and dye cotton cloth. The popularity of madras cloth today demonstrates that this interest has not died out.

Artistic Achievement in the Mughal Era

Both Jahangir and Shah Jahan continued Akbar's policy of tolerance toward the Hindu majority and retained most of the alliances he had forged with Hindu princes and local leaders. They made little attempt to change the administrative apparatus they had inherited from Akbar, and they fought their wars in much the same way as the founders of the dynasty had. Both mounted campaigns to crush potential enemies and in some cases to enlarge the empire. But neither was as interested in conquest and politics as in enjoying the good life. Both were fond of drink, female dancers, and the pleasure gardens they had laid out from Kashmir to Allahabad. Both were delighted by polo matches (a game invented by the princes of India), ox and tiger or elephant fights, and games of pachisi, which they played on life-sized boards with palace dancers as chips. Both took great pleasure in the elaborate court ceremonies that blended Indian and Persian precedents, lavish state processions, their palaces and jewel-studded wardrobes, and the scented and sweetened ices that were rushed from the cool mountains in the north to their capitals on the sweltering plains.

Jahangir and Shah Jahan are best remembered as two of the greatest patrons of the fine arts in human history. They expanded the painting workshops that had been started by the early Mughals so that thousands of exquisite miniature paintings could be produced during their reigns. Both Jahangir and Shah Jahan also devoted massive resources to building some of the most stunning architectural works of all time. The best known of these is the **Taj Mahal** (Figure 21.6), which has become a symbol for India itself. But structures such as the audience hall in the Red Fort at Delhi, Akbar's tomb at Sikandra, and the tomb of Itimad al-Dowleh at Agra rival the Taj Mahal in design and perhaps surpass it in the beauty of their detail and decoration.

At its best, Mughal architecture blends what is finest in the Persian and Hindu traditions. It fuses the Islamic genius for domes, arches, and minarets and the balance between them with the Hindu love of ornament. In place of the ceramic tiles that the Persians used to finish their mosques and tombs, Indian artisans substituted gleaming white marble, inset with semiprecious stones arranged in floral and geometric patterns. Extensive use was also made of marble reflecting pools, the most famous of which mirrors the beauty of the Taj Mahal. When these pools were

Figure 21.6 *Perhaps no single building has come to symbolize Indian civilization more than the Taj Mahal. The grace and elegance of the tomb that Shah Jahan built in his wife's honor provide an enduring source of aesthetic delight. The white marble of the tomb is inlaid with flowers and geometric designs cut from semiprecious stones. The windows of the central chamber, which houses the tombs of Shah Jahan and Mumtaz Mahal, are decorated with carved marble screens, which add a sense of lightness and delicacy to the structure.*

inlaid with floral patterns and provided with fountains, the rippling water appeared to give life to the stone plant forms. Like the architects and artisans of the Ottoman Empire and Safavid Persia, those who served the Mughal rulers strove to create paradise on earth, an aspiration that was carved in marble on the audience hall of the Red Fort at Delhi. Around the ceiling of the great hall, it is written "If there is paradise on earth—It is here … it is here."

Court Politics and the Position of Elite and Ordinary Women

Not surprisingly, two rulers who were so absorbed in the arts and the pursuit of pleasure left most of the mundane tasks of day-to-day administration largely in the hands of subordinates. In both cases, strong-willed wives took advantage of their husbands' neglect of politics to win positions of power and influence at the Mughal court. Jahangir's wife, **Nur Jahan,** continually amassed power as he became more and more addicted to wine and opium. She packed the court with able male relatives, and her faction dominated the empire for most of the later years of Jahangir's reign. Nur Jahan was a big spender, but not only on pomp and luxury. She became a major patron of much-needed charities in the major cities. Despite her success at pursuits that were normally reserved for males, she was defeated in the end by the roles of wife and mother to which many felt she should confine herself. She died giving birth to her 19th child.

Shah Jahan's consort, **Mumtaz Mahal,** also became actively involved in court politics. But Shah Jahan was a much more engaged and able ruler than Jahangir, and thus her opportunities to amass power behind the throne were more limited. She is remembered not for her political acumen but for the love and devotion Shah Jahan bestowed upon her, a love literally enshrined in the Taj Mahal, the tomb where she is buried. Shah Jahan's plans to build a companion tomb for himself in black marble across the Jumna River were foiled by the revolt of his sons and by his imprisonment. He was buried next to his wife in the Taj Mahal, but her tomb is central and far larger than that of her husband.

Although the position of women at the Mughal court improved in the middle years of the dynasty's power, that of women in the rest of Indian society declined. Child marriage grew more popular, and the age limit was lowered. It was not unheard of for girls to be married at age nine. Widow remarriage among Hindus nearly died out. Seclusion was more and more strictly enforced for upper-caste women, both Hindu and Muslim. Muslim women rarely ventured forth from their homes unveiled, and those who did risked verbal and even physical abuse. The governor of one of the provinces of the Mughal Empire divorced his wife because she was seen scrambling for her life, unveiled, from a runaway elephant. Among upper-caste Hindus, the practice of sati spread despite Shah Jahan's renewed efforts to outlaw it. The dwindling scope of productive roles left to women, combined with the burden of the dowry that had to be paid to marry them off, meant that the birth of a girl was increasingly seen as an inauspicious event. At court as well as in the homes of ordinary villagers, only the birth of a son was greeted with feasting and celebrations.

The Beginnings of Imperial Decline

Aurangzeb, Shah Jahan's son and successor, seized control of an empire that was threatened by internal decay and growing dangers from external enemies. For decades, the need for essential administrative, military, and social reforms had been ignored. The Mughal bureaucracy had grown bloated and corrupt. The army was equally bloated and backward in weaponry and tactics. Peasants and urban workers had seen their productivity and living standards fall steadily. The Taj Mahal and other wonders of the Mughal artistic imagination had been paid for by the mass of the people at a very high price.

Though not the cruel bigot he is often portrayed as, Aurangzeb was not the man to restore the dynasty's declining fortunes. Courageous, honest, intelligent, and hard-working, he seemed an ideal successor to two rulers who had so badly neglected the affairs of state. But Aurangzeb was driven by two ambitions that proved disastrous to his schemes to strengthen the empire. He was determined to extend Mughal control over the whole of the Indian subcontinent, and he believed that it was his duty to purify Indian Islam and rid it of the Hindu influences he was convinced were steadily corrupting it.

The first ambition increased the number of the empire's adversaries, strained the allegiance of its vassals and allies, and greatly overextended its huge but obsolete military forces. By the time of his death in 1707, after a reign of nearly 50 years, Aurangzeb had conquered most of the subcontinent and extended Mughal control as far north as Kabul in what is now Afghanistan. But the almost endless warfare of his years in power drained the treasury and further enlarged an inefficient bureaucracy and army without gaining corresponding increases in revenues to support them.

Equally critically, the long wars occupied much of Aurangzeb's time and energies, diverting him from the administrative tasks and reforms essential to the dynasty's continued strength. While he was leading his massive armies in the south, there were peasant uprisings and revolts by Muslim and Hindu princes in the north. Perhaps even more harmful to the imperial system was the growing autonomy of local leaders, who diverted more and more revenue from the central administration into their own coffers. On the northern borders, incursions by Persian and Afghan warrior bands were increasing.

While Aurangzeb's military campaigns strained the resources of the empire, his religious policies gravely weakened the internal alliances and disrupted the social peace Akbar had so skillfully established. Aurangzeb continued to employ Hindus in the imperial service; in fact, he did not have the Muslim replacements to do without them. But non-Muslims were given far fewer posts at the upper levels of the bureaucracy, and their personal contact with the emperor was severely restricted. Aurangzeb also took measures that he and his religious advisors felt would help rid their Muslim faith and culture of the Hindu influences that had permeated it over the centuries. He forbade the building of new temples and put an end to Hindu religious festivals at court. Aurangzeb also reinstated the hated head tax on unbelievers—a measure he hoped might prod them to convert to Islam. The tax fell heavily on the Hindu poor and in some cases drove them to support sectarian movements that rose up to resist Aurangzeb.

By the end of Aurangzeb's reign, the Mughal Empire was far larger than it had been under any of the earlier emperors, but it was also more unstable. Internal rebellions, particularly those mounted by the **Marattas** in western India, put an end to effective Mughal control over large areas. The rise of new sects, such as the **Sikhs** in the northwest, further strained the declining resources of an imperial system that was clearly overextended. The early leaders of the Sikhs originally tried to bridge the differences between Hindu and Muslim. But Mughal persecution of the new sect, which was seen as religiously heretical and a political threat to the dynasty, eventually transformed Sikhism into a staunchly anti-Muslim force within the subcontinent. In addition, Muslim kingdoms in central and east India continued to resist Mughal hegemony, and Islamic invaders waited at the poorly guarded passes through the Himalayas to strike and plunder once it was clear that the Mughals could no longer fend them off.

GLOBAL CONNECTIONS: Gunpowder Empires and the Restoration of the Islamic Bridge Between Civilizations

The internal causes of decline discussed in this chapter for the early modern Muslim empires probably were sufficient to destroy the great gunpowder empires of Islam. But each was also undermined by further weaknesses that had profound significance for Islamic civilization as a whole. Captivated by their rivalries with each other and the problems of holding together their empires, none of the dynasties took the rising threat from Europe seriously. They called on Western travelers and missionaries for advice in casting cannons or military tactics, but none of these Islamic peoples systematically monitored technological advances in Europe.

This failure to take strong measures to meet the challenges that European overseas expansion was creating for Islamic civilization was also responsible for the weakening of the economic basis of each of the empires. Key tax revenues and merchant profits were drained off by the rise of European trading empires in Asia (see Chapters 15, 16, and 22). The Europeans' gains in ways to generate wealth and economic growth meant increasing losses for Muslim societies and political systems. These setbacks eventually proved critical to the failure of Muslim efforts to compete politically and militarily with their Christian rivals.

The changes in the position of key Islamic empires in the wider world were gradual and complex. The empires retained active programs of overseas trade. Arabs, for example, continued to interact with the east African coast and its trade in slaves and other goods. Europeans sought luxury products both in the Middle East and in India—India, indeed, gained important profits in American silver, which the Europeans used to pay for the spices and textiles they exported. But Europeans were increasingly assertive, setting up their own merchant groupings in Istanbul, for example, where they followed their laws rather than those of the Ottoman Empire. European disdain for the slower pace of scientific and technological change in the Muslim empires increased also. In India, finally, the decline of the Mughals opened the door for growing economic and military intervention by Europeans, particularly the British and French, who formed alliances with rival princes in an increasingly decentralized society. As discussed in Chapter 16, a British empire in India was actively forming by the end of the early modern centuries.

Further Readings

The Lapidus survey suggested in the earlier chapters on Islam provides a fine introduction to the empires that are the focus of this chapter. For a comparative look at the subject, see William H. McNeill, *The Age of Gunpowder Empires, 1450-1800* (1989).

The best detailed studies of the Ottoman Empire can be found in the works of Halil Inalcik, especially his chapters in *The Cambridge History of Islam* (1977). For a different perspective on the Ottomans, see Stanford Shaw's *History of the Ottoman Empire and Modern Turkey*, vol. I (1780–1808) (1976). Bernard Lewis's *Istanbul and the Civilization of the Ottoman Empire* (1963) provides internal perspectives of life at the center of the Ottoman Empire. For the most recent and approachable exploration of the origins of the Ottoman state, see C. Kafadar, *Between Two Worlds: The Construction of the Ottoman State* (1995). G. Necipoglu, *Architecture, Ceremonial, and Power: the Topkapi Palace in the Fifteenth and Sixteenth Centuries* (1991) illuminates the potent political symbolism embedded in the Ottoman Empire's greatest artistic achievement. S. S. Blair, and J. Bloom, *The Art and Architecture of Islam, 1250-1800* (1994), can be used to extend this analysis across the Muslim world. Peter F. Sugar's *Southeastern Europe Under Ottoman Rule, 1354–1804* (1977) is a fine account of life in the Christian portions of the empire. Afaf Lutfi al-Sayyid Marsot's *Women and Men in Late Eighteenth Century Egypt* (1995) explores gender roles in the age of the Ottomans.

R. M. Savory's writings, including *Iran under the Safavids* (1980), and his chapters in *The Cambridge History of Iran* (1986), are the most reliable of a very limited literature in English on the Safavid period. Though quite specialized, Michel Mazzaoui's *The Origins of the Safavids* (1972) provides the fullest account of the beginnings and rise of the Safavid dynasty. The contributions to the volume that Savory edited on *Islamic Civilization* (1976) include good discussions of the arts and society in the Turkic and Persian sectors of the Islamic heartland. The introductory sections of Nikki Keddi's *Roots of Revolution* (1981) provide a good discussion of the relationship between religion and the state in the Safavid period.

The Ikram and Ahmad books cited in Chapter 12 on expansion of Islam in India are also good on the Mughals. Though specialized, the works of Irfan Habib, M. Athar Ali, Richard Eaton, John F. Richards, and Douglas Streusand on the Mughal Empire are also critical, as is Muzzafar Alam's *The Crisis of the Empire in Mughal North India* (1993), one of many recent works reexamining the decline of the Mughal Empire. Of the many works on Mughal art and architecture, Gavin Hambly's *Mughal Cities* (1968) has some of the best color plates and an intelligent commentary.

The role of women in the Islamic Gunpowder Empires is addressed in several recent studies, many which take India's Nur Jahan as their touchstone. These include Stephen P. Blake, "Contributors to the Urban Landscape: Women Builders in Safavid Isfahan and Mughal Shahjahanabad," in Gavin Hambly, ed., *Women in the Medieval Islamic World* (1998); Ellison Banks Findly, *Nur Jahan: Empress of Mughal India* (1993); Stanley K. Freiberg, *Jahanara: Daughter of the Taj Mahal* (1999); and D. Fairchild Ruggles, eds. *Women, Patronage, and Self-Representation in Islamic Societies* (2000).

Trade between the Muslim gunpowder empires is one of the issues explored in Ashin Das Gupta and M. N. Pearson, eds., *Indian and the Indian Ocean; 1500-1800* (1987) and Michael Adas, *Islamic and European Expansion* (1993).

On the Web

Virtual visits to the palaces of the Ottomans (http://www.ee.bilkent.edu.tr/~history/topkapi.html), the Safavids (http://isfahan.anglia.ac.uk./glossary/hist8.htm and http://www.art-arena.cm/safavidart.htm), and the Mughals (http://rohini.ncst.ernet.in/fatehpur/, http://rubens.anu.edu.au/student.projects/tajmahal/home.html, http://ignca.nic.in/agra001.htm, and http://www.taj-mahal.net), provide clear evidence of the splendor of their empires.

A simulated interview with the Mughal Emperor Akbar (http://itihaas.com/medieval/akbar2.html) lends insight into his early struggles with his tutors, his skill as an empire-builder, and the wisdom of his policy of religious toleration as embodied in his Din-i-Illahi.

The brilliant art and literary record left by some Mughal and Ottoman emperors provides glimpses into the working of their regimes as is revealed by the Akbarnama (http://www.bampfa.berkeley.edu/exhibits/indian/u0300.html). Among the lavish illustrations that are included in this work is that illuminating the building of the Mughal city of Fatephur Sikri (http://rubens.anu.edu.au/htdocs/surveys/charlotte/bycountry/display00310.html). Further insight into war and slavery in gunpowder empires can be obtained at http://i-cias.com/e.o/janissaries.htm, http://www.fordham.edu/halsall/islam/1493janissaries.html, and http://www.fordham.edu/halsall/mod/1555busbecq.html.

CHAPTER 22

ASIAN TRANSITIONS IN AN AGE OF GLOBAL CHANGE

A number of the major forms of interaction between expansive European peoples and those of Asia are vividly illustrated in this panoramic Japanese silk screen painting from the early 1600s. The strong impression made by the size and power of the Portuguese ship that has just arrived in harbor is evident in the artist's exaggeration of the height of its fore and aft castles. The trade goods being unloaded, mainly Chinese silks, which are also being sold in the marketplace at the right of the painting, but also exotic products such as peacocks and tiger skins, demonstrate the ways in which the Portuguese had become carriers between different areas in Asia, including Japan. The cluster of black-robed missionaries waiting to greet the arriving Portuguese sea captain (under the umbrella in the center) suggest that efforts to convert the Japanese to Christianity were in full swing, at least in this area of the kingdom.

- The Asian Trading World and the Coming of the Europeans
- VISUALIZING THE PAST: Intruders: The Pattern of Early European Expansion into Asia
- Ming China: A Global Mission Refused
- DOCUMENT: Exam Questions as a Mirror of Chinese Values
- IN DEPTH: Means and Motives for Overseas Expansion: Europe and China Compared
- Fending Off the West: Japan's Reunification and the First Challenge
- GLOBAL CONNECTIONS: An Age of Eurasian Closure

When Vasco da Gama's ships returned to Lisbon in 1499, it was clear that tiny Portugal rather than mighty Spain had won the race to the fabled Indies. Columbus' voyages to the Americas, with the support of the Spanish rulers, opened up new worlds to the civilizations of Europe, Asia, and Africa. But da Gama's 1498 expedition accomplished the task that had been the ultimate aim of all the explorations launched by the Europeans as early as the 14th century. He and his sailors had found a sea link between an expansive and insecure Europe and the powerful and wealthy civilizations of Asia.

Although da Gama's voyage marked a major turning point for much of western Europe, its impact on most of Asia was much less decisive, at least in the 16th and 17th centuries. The Portuguese, and the Dutch, French, and English who followed them into Asia, soon found that they had little to offer the Indians, southeast Asians, or Chinese in exchange for the silks and spices they risked their lives to carry back to Europe. They were disappointed to find that few Asian peoples were interested in converting to Christianity. The Europeans also quickly realized that however feisty and well-armed they might be, they were far too few in numbers to make much headway against even the smaller kingdoms of Asia, such as Siam or Vietnam, much less against mighty empires such as those ruled by the Chinese or the Mughals.

1350 C.E.	1500 C.E.	1550 C.E.	1600 C.E.	1650 C.E.	1700 C.E.
1368 Ming dynasty comes to power in China **1368–1398** Reign of the Hongwu emperor **1390** Ming restrictions on overseas commerce **1403–1424** Reign of the Yunglo emperor in China **1405–1423** Zhenghe expeditions from China to southeast Asia, India, and East Africa **1498–1499** Vasco da Gama opens the sea route around Africa to Asia	**1507** Portuguese defeat combined Muslim war fleet near Diu off western India coast **1510** Portuguese conquest of Goa in western India **1511** Portuguese conquer Malacca on the tip of Malayan peninsula **1540s** Francis Xavier makes mass converts in India	**1573** End of the Ashikaga shogunate **1573–1620** Reign of the Wanli emperor **1580s** Jesuits arrive in China **1590** Hideyoshi unifies Japan **1592** First Japanese invasion of Korea **1597** Second Japanese invasion of Korea	**1600s** Dutch and British assault on Portuguese Empire in Asia; decline of Portuguese power **1603** Tokugawa shogunate established **1614** Christianity banned in Japan **1619–1620** Dutch East India Company established at Batavia on Java **1640s** Japan moves into self-imposed isolation **1641** Dutch capture Malacca from Portuguese; Dutch confined to Deshima Island off Nagasaki	**1644** Nomadic Manchus put an end to Ming dynasty; Manchu Qing dynasty rules China **1654–1722** Reign of the Kangxi emperor in China	**1755–1757** Dutch become paramount power on Java; Qing conquest of Mongolia

As was the case with the Mughal and Safavid empires (see Chapter 21), the central themes in the history of Asian civilizations in the 16th and 17th centuries often had little or nothing to do with European expansion. They emerged from long-term processes rooted in the inner workings of these ancient civilizations and their interaction with neighboring states and nomadic peoples. Although the European presence was felt in each of the areas considered in this chapter, the impact of Europe's global expansion was of secondary importance except in island southeast Asia, which was especially vulnerable to Western sea power.

The Asian Trading World and the Coming of the Europeans

 Several European seafaring nations were actively involved in south and southeast Asia in the centuries after Vasco da Gama rounded the Cape of Good Hope in 1498. Most European enterprise in the region was centered on trade, as all the European powers struggled to find the most profitable ways to obtain the many products they wanted from Asia. Some Europeans went to Asia in search of Christian converts rather than personal gain. Small numbers of Europeans also settled in coastal enclaves in both India and the Indonesian archipelago.

Vasco da Gama and his Portuguese crew received a rather rude shock soon after arriving in India in 1498. Still congratulating themselves on having found a sea route around Africa, which Portuguese explorers had been seeking for generations, they successfully made their way across the Arabian Sea to India. At Calicut, a prosperous commercial center on the southwest coast, they went ashore to trade for the spices, fine textiles, and other Asian products that were among the main objectives of the voyages of exploration. Reveling in the fine quality and abundance of the products from all over Asia that were available in the town's great marketplace, the Portuguese were startled to learn that the local merchants were not interested in the products they had brought to trade for Asian goods. In fact, their cast-iron pots, coarse cloth, and coral beads elicited little more than sneers from the merchants they approached. Suddenly da Gama and his crews faced the humbling prospect of returning home with little proof that they had reached Asia and begun to tap its fabled wealth. Reluctantly, they concluded that they had little choice but to use the small supply of silver bullion they had brought along for emergencies. They found that the Asian merchants were willing to take their precious metal. But they also discovered that their meager provision did not go very far toward filling the holds of their ships with Asian treasures.

Much of what the Europeans did in Asia in the 16th and 17th centuries was devoted to working out the implications of that first encounter in Calicut. The very fact of da Gama's arrival demonstrated both the needs and curiosity that had driven the Europeans halfway around the world as well as the seaworthiness of their **caravel** ships. Their stops at Calicut and ports on the eastern coast of Africa also made the Portuguese acutely aware of the fact that their old rivals, the Muslims, had arrived in east Africa and south and southeast Asia well ahead of them. This unpleasant discovery promised resistance to Portuguese trading and empire building in Asia. It also meant major obstacles to their plans for converting the peoples of the area to Roman Catholicism. But the Portuguese also observed that the Muslims and Asian peoples were deeply divided and that they rarely understood the potential threat posed by what was, after all, a handful of strangers from across the world.

Bonds of Commerce: The Asian Sea Trading Network, c. 1500

As later voyages by Portuguese fleets revealed, Calicut and the ports of east Africa, which da Gama had found on the initial foray into Asia, made up only a small segment of a larger network of commercial exchange and cultural interaction. This trading system stretched thousands of miles from the Middle East and Africa along all the coasts of the giant Asian continent. Both the products exchanged in this network and the main routes followed by those who sailed it had been established for centuries—in many cases, millennia.

In general, the **Asian sea trading network** can be broken down into three main zones, each of which was focused on major centers of handicraft manufacture (see Map 22.1). In the west was an Arab zone

anchored on the glass-, carpet-, and tapestry-making Islamic heartlands at the head of the Red Sea and the Persian Gulf. India, with its superb cotton textiles, dominated the central portions of the system, and China, which excelled in producing paper, porcelain, and silk textiles, formed the eastern pole. In between or on the fringes of the three great manufacturing centers were areas such as Japan, the mainland kingdoms and island states of southeast Asia, and the port cities of east Africa that fed mainly raw materials—precious metals, foods, and forest products—into the trading network.

Of the raw materials circulating in the system, the broadest demand and highest prices were paid for spices, which came mainly from Ceylon and the islands at the eastern end of what is today the Indonesian archipelago. Long-distance trade was largely in high-priced commodities such as spices, ivory from Africa, and precious stones. But silk and cotton textiles also were traded over long distances. Bulk items, such as rice, livestock, and timber, normally were exchanged between the ports within each of the main trading zones.

Since ancient times, monsoon winds and the nature of the ships and navigational instruments available to sailors had dictated the main trade routes in the Asian network. Much navigation was of the coasting variety, that is, sailing along the shoreline and charting distances and location with reference to towns and natural landmarks. The Arabs and Chinese, who had compasses and large, well-built ships, could cross large expanses of open water such as the Arabian and South China seas. But even they preferred established coastal routes rather than the largely uncharted and less predictable open seas. As the Portuguese quickly learned, there were several crucial points where segments of the trade converged or where geography funneled it into narrow areas. The mouths of the Red Sea and Persian Gulf were two of these points, as were the Straits of Malacca, which separated mainland from island southeast Asia (see Map 22.1).

Two general characteristics of the trading system at the time of the Portuguese arrival were critical to European attempts to regulate and dominate it. First, there was no central control. Second, military force was usually absent from commercial exchanges within it. Although Arab sailors and merchants were found in ports throughout much of the network, they had no sense of common cause. They sailed and

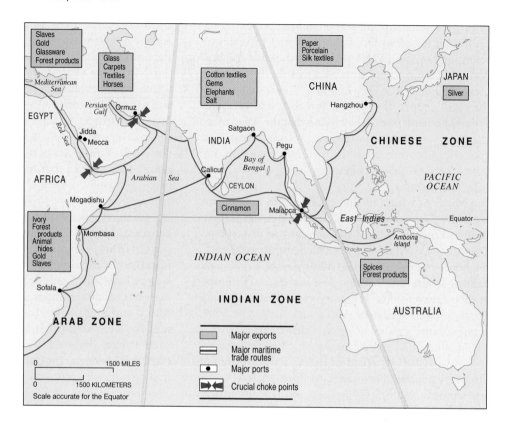

Map 22.1 *Routes and Major Products Exchanged in the Asian Trading Network, c. 1500*

traded to provide for their own livelihood and to make profits for the princes or merchants who financed their expeditions. The same was true for the Chinese, southeast Asian, and Indian merchants and sailors who were concentrated in particular segments of the trading complex. Because all the peoples participating in the network had something to trade for the products they wanted from others, exchanges within the system were largely peaceful. Trading vessels were lightly armed for protection against attack by pirates.

Trading Empire: The Portuguese Response to the Encounter at Calicut

The Portuguese were not prepared to abide by the informal rules that had evolved over the centuries for commercial and cultural exchanges in the great Asian trading complex. It was apparent after the trip to the market in Calicut that the Portuguese had little, other than gold and silver, to exchange with Asian peoples.

In an age in which prominent economic theorists, called *mercantilists*, taught that a state's power depended heavily on the amount of precious metals a monarch had in his coffers, a steady flow of bullion to Asia was unthinkable. It was particularly objectionable because it would enrich and thus strengthen merchants and rulers from rival kingdoms and religions, particularly the Muslims, whose position the Portuguese had set out to undermine through their overseas enterprises. Unwilling to forgo the possibilities for profit that a sea route to Asia presented, the Portuguese resolved to take by force what they could not get through fair trade.

The decision by the Portuguese to use force to extract spices and other goods from Asia resulted largely from their realization that they could offset their lack of numbers and trading goods with their superior ships and weaponry (see Figure 22.1). Except for the huge war fleets of Chinese junks, no Asian people could muster fleets able to withstand the firepower and maneuverability of the Portuguese squadrons. Their sudden appearance in Asian waters and their

Figure 22.1 *In the 15th and 16th centuries, the port of Lisbon in tiny Portugal was one of the great centers of international commerce and European overseas exploration. Although aspects of the early, streamlined caravel design can be detected in the ships pictured here, additional square sails, higher fore and aft castles, and numerous cannons projecting from holes cut in the ships' sides exemplify a later stage of naval development.*

interjection of sea warfare into a peaceful trading system gained the European intruders an element of surprise that kept their adversaries off balance in the critical early years of empire building. The Portuguese forces were small in numbers but united in their drive for wealth and religious converts. This allowed them to take advantage of the deep divisions that separated their Asian competitors and the Asians' inability to combine their forces effectively in battle. Thus, when da Gama returned for a second expedition to Asian waters in 1502, he was able to force ports on both the African and Indian coasts to submit to a Portuguese tribute regime. He also assaulted towns that refused to cooperate. When a combined Egyptian–Indian fleet was finally sent in reprisal in 1509, it was defeated off Diu on the western Indian coast. The Portuguese would not have to face so formidable an alliance of Asian sea powers again.

The Portuguese soon found that sea patrols and raids on coastal towns were not sufficient to control the trade in the items they wanted, especially spices. Thus, from 1507 onward they strove to capture towns and build fortresses at a number of strategic points on the Asian trading network (see map in Visualizing the Past). In that year they took **Ormuz** at the southern end of the Persian Gulf; in 1510 they captured **Goa** on the western Indian coast; most critical of all, in the next year they successfully stormed **Malacca** on the tip of the Malayan peninsula. These ports served both as naval bases for Portuguese fleets patrolling Asian waters and as *factories*, or points where spices and other products could be stored until they were shipped to Europe. Ships and naval stations became the key components of a Portuguese trading empire that was financed and directed by the kings of Portugal.

The aim of the empire was to establish Portuguese monopoly control over key Asian products, particularly spices, such as the cinnamon being processed in Figure 22.2. Ideally, all the spices produced were to be shipped in Portuguese galleons to Asian or European markets. There they would be sold at high prices, which the Portuguese could dictate because they controlled the supply of these goods. The Portuguese also sought, with little success, to impose a licensing system on all merchant ships that traded in the Indian Ocean from Ormuz to Malacca. The combination of monopoly and the licensing system, backed by force, was intended to give the Portuguese control of a sizeable portion of the Asian trading network.

Figure 22.2   *Sinhalese workers peeling the bark from the branches of cinnamon trees are depicted in this photo taken in the era of British rule on Ceylon. Similar techniques were used by cinnamon peelers in the pre-European, the Portuguese, and the Dutch periods to extract the cinnamon sticks and powder that were in great demand in Europe. Like the other spices European traders carried home from Asia, cinnamon had many uses that would seem strange to us today. It was mixed into medicines and used as an effective mouthwash and, of course, as a popular ingredient in pastries and other sweets.*

Portuguese Vulnerability and the Rise of the Dutch and English Trading Empires

The plans for empire that the Portuguese drew up on paper never became reality. They managed for some decades to control much of the flow of spices, such as nutmeg and mace, which were grown in very limited areas. But control of the market in key condiments, such as pepper and cinnamon, eluded them. At times the Portuguese resorted to severe punishments such as cutting off the hands of the rival traders and ships' crews caught transporting spices in defiance of their monopoly. But they simply did not have the soldiers or the ships to sustain their monopolies, much less the licensing system. The resistance of Asian rivals, poor military discipline, rampant corruption among crown officials, and heavy Portuguese shipping losses caused by overloading and poor design had taken a heavy toll on the empire by the end of the 16th century.

The overextended and declining Portuguese trading empire proved no match for the Dutch and English rivals, whose war fleets challenged it in the early 17th century. Of the two, the Dutch emerged, at least in the short term, as the victors. They captured the critical Portuguese port and fortress at Malacca and built a new port of their own in 1620 at **Batavia** on the island of Java. The latter location, which was much closer to the island sources of key spices, reflected the improved European knowledge of Asian geography. It also reflected the Dutch decision to concentrate on the monopoly control of certain spices rather than on Asian trade more generally. The English, who fought hard but lost the struggle for control of the spice islands, were forced to fall back to India.

The **Dutch trading empire** (see map in Visualizing the Past) was made up of the same basic components as the Portuguese: fortified towns and factories, warships on patrol, and monopoly control of a limited number of products. But the Dutch had more numerous and better armed ships and went about the business of monopoly control in a much more systematic fashion. To regulate the supply of cloves, nutmeg, and mace, for example, they uprooted the plants that produced these spices on islands they did not control. They also forcibly removed or wiped out island peoples who cultivated these spices without Dutch supervision and dared to sell them to their trading rivals.

Although the profits from the sale of these spices in Europe in the mid-17th century helped sustain Holland's golden age, the Dutch found that the greatest profits in the long run could be gained from peacefully working themselves into the long-established Asian trading system. The demand for spices declined and their futile efforts to gain control over crops such as pepper that were grown in many places became more and more expensive. In response, the Dutch came to rely mainly (as they had long done in Europe) on the fees they charged for transporting products from one area in Asia to another. They also depended on profits gained from buying Asian products, such as cloth, in one area and trading them in other areas for goods that could be sold in Europe at inflated prices. The English also adopted these peaceful trading patterns, although their enterprises were concentrated along the coasts of India and on the cloth trade rather than on the spices of southeast Asia.

Going Ashore: European Tribute Systems in Asia

Their ships and guns allowed the Europeans to force their way into the Asian trading network in the 16th and 17th centuries. But as they moved inland and away from the sea, their military advantages and their ability to dominate the Asian peoples rapidly disappeared. Because the vastly superior numbers of Asian armies offset the Europeans' advantage in weapons and organization for waging war on land, even small kingdoms such as those on Java and in mainland southeast Asia were able to resist European inroads into their domains. In the larger empires such as those in China, India, and Persia—and when confronted by martial cultures such as Japan's—the Euro-

peans quickly learned their place. That they were often reduced to kowtowing or humbling themselves before the thrones of Asian potentates is demonstrated by the instructions given by a Dutch envoy about the proper behavior for a visit to the Japanese court:

> Our ministers have no other instruction to take there except to look to the wishes of that brave, superb, precise nation in order to please it in everything, and by no means to think on anything which might cause greater antipathy to us....That consequently the Company's ministers frequenting the scrupulous state each year must above all go armed in modesty, humility, courtesy, and amity, always being the lesser.

In certain situations, however, the Europeans were drawn inland away from their forts, factories, and war fleets in the early centuries of their expansion into Asia. The Portuguese, and the Dutch after them, felt compelled to conquer the coastal areas of Ceylon to control the production and sale of cinnamon, which grew in the forests of the southern portions of that island. The Dutch moved slowly inland from their base at Batavia into the highlands of western Java. They discovered that this area was ideal for growing coffee, which was in great demand in Europe by the 17th century. By the mid-18th century, the Dutch not only controlled the coffee-growing areas but were the paramount power on Java.

The Spanish, taking advantage of the fact that the Philippine Islands lay in the half of the world the pope had given them to explore and settle in 1493, invaded the islands in the 1560s. The conquest of **Luzon** and the northern islands was facilitated by the fact that their animistic inhabitants lived in small states the Spanish could subjugate one by one. The repeated failure of Spanish expeditions to conquer the southern island of **Mindanao,** which was ruled by a single kingdom whose Muslim rulers were determined to resist Christian dominance, dramatically underscores the limits of the Europeans' ability to project their power on land in this era.

In each area where the Europeans went ashore in the early centuries of expansion, they set up tribute regimes that closely resembled those the Spanish imposed on the Native American peoples of the New World (see Chapter 19). The European overlords were content to let the indigenous peoples live in their traditional settlements, controlled largely by hereditary leaders drawn from their own communities. In most

Visualizing the Past

Intruders: The Pattern of Early European Expansion into Asia

Compare the map shown here with Map 22.1. Note the new routes, major port centers, and fortified factory centers added by the different European powers as they moved into Asia. Compare these with the traditional regions of spice growing, textile manufacture, and other industries.

Also note the areas where the different European powers began to establish substantial territorial empires and the dates when these areas were brought under Western control. Compare the routes favored by the Portuguese, Dutch, English, French, and Spanish, and the areas where their fortified outposts and territorial conquests are centered.

Questions: What do the shifting areas where European routes and fortified trading centers are located tell us about the main goals and relative power of each of the European countries? What advantages did those who entered later in the process have in this regard? On the basis of the discussion in Chapters 15 and 16, which of these states would you argue had the strongest power base in Europe itself? Why was the Spanish pattern of expansion so radically different from those of the other powers? Which areas of Asia were the most impervious to European expansionism in this period, and why?

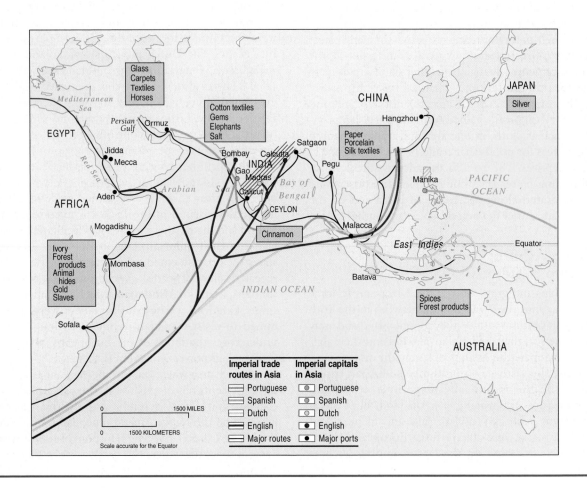

areas, little attempt was made to interfere in the daily lives of the conquered peoples as long as their leaders met the tribute quotas set by the European conquerors. The tribute was paid in the form of agricultural products grown by the peasantry under forced labor systems supervised by the peasants' own elites. In some cases, the indigenous peoples continued to harvest crops they had produced for centuries, such as the bark of the cinnamon plant (see Figure 22.2). In other areas new crops, such as coffee and sugar cane, were introduced. But in all cases, the demands for tribute took into account the local peasants' need to raise the crops on which they subsisted.

Spreading the Faith: The Missionary Enterprise in South and Southeast Asia

Although the Protestant Dutch and English were little interested in winning converts to Christianity during the early centuries of overseas expansion, the spread of Roman Catholicism was a fundamental part of the global mission of the Portuguese and Spanish. After the widespread conversion of Native American peoples, the meager returns from the Iberian missionary offensive in Asia were disappointing. The fact that Islam had arrived in much of maritime south and southeast Asia centuries before da Gama's arrival had much to do with the indifference or open hostility the Portuguese met when they tried to convert the peoples of these regions to Christianity. The dream of a Christian Asia joining the Iberian crusade against the Muslims was also dealt a setback by the discovery that the Hindus, whom da Gama and some of his entourage had originally believed to be Christians, had a sophisticated and deeply entrenched set of religious ideas and rituals.

Despite these setbacks, of all the Asian areas where European enclaves were established in the early centuries of expansion, India appeared to be one of the most promising fields for religious conversion. From the 1540s onward, Franciscan and Dominican missionaries, as well as the Jesuit **Francis Xavier,** who were willing to minister to the poor, low-caste fisherfolk and untouchables along the southwest coast, converted tens of thousands. But these missionary orders soon found that they were making little headway among high-caste groups. In fact, taboos against contact with untouchables and other low-caste groups made it nearly impossible for the missionaries to approach prospective upper-caste converts.

To overcome these obstacles, an Italian Jesuit named **Robert di Nobili** devised a different conversion strategy in the early 1600s. He learned several Indian languages, including Sanskrit, which allowed him to read the sacred texts of the Hindus. He donned the garments worn by Indian brahmans and adopted a vegetarian diet. All these measures were calculated to win over the upper-caste Hindus in south India, where he was based. Di Nobili reasoned that if he succeeded in Christianizing the high-caste Hindus, they would then bring the lower Hindu castes into the fold. But, he argued, because the ancient Hindu religion was sophisticated and deeply entrenched, Indian brahmans and other high-caste groups would listen only to those who adopted their ways. Meat eaters would be seen as defiling; those who were unfamiliar with the Hindus' sacred texts would be considered ignorant.

Despite some early successes, di Nobili's strategy was undone by the refusal of high-caste Hindu converts to worship with low-caste groups and to give up many of their traditional beliefs and religious rituals. Rival missionary orders, particularly the Dominicans and Franciscans, denounced his approach. In assimilating to Hindu culture, they claimed, di Nobili and his co-workers, not the Indians, were the ones who had been converted. His rivals also pointed out that the refusal of di Nobili's high-caste converts to worship with untouchable Christians defied one of the central tenets of Christianity: the equality of all believers before God. His rivals finally won the ear of the pope, and di Nobili was recalled to Rome. Deprived of his energy and knowledge of Indian ways, his mission in south India quickly collapsed.

Beyond socially stigmatized groups such as the untouchables, the conversion of the general populace in Asia occurred only in isolated areas. Perhaps the greatest successes of the Christian missions occurred in the northern islands of the Philippines, which had not previously been exposed to a world religion such as Islam or Buddhism. Because the Spanish had conquered the island of Luzon and the smaller islands to the south, and then governed them as part of their vast intercontinental empire, they were able to launch a major missionary effort. The *friars*, as the priests and brothers who went out to convert and govern the rural populace were called, became the main channel for transmitting European influences. The friars first converted local Filipino leaders. These leaders then directed their followers to build new settlements that were centered, like those in Iberia and the New World, on town squares where the local church, the residences of the missionary fathers, and government offices were located. Beyond tending to the spiritual needs of the villagers in their congregation, the friars served as government officials.

Like the Native Americans of Spain's New World empire, most Filipinos were formally converted to Catholicism. But also like the Native Americans, the Filipinos' brand of Christianity represented a creative blend of their traditional beliefs and customs and the religion preached by the friars. Because key tenets of the Christian faith were taught in Spanish for fear that they would be corrupted if put in the local languages, it is doubtful that most of the converts had a very good grasp of Christian beliefs. Many converted because Spanish dominance and their own leaders' conversion gave them little choice. Others adopted the new faith because they believed that the Christian God could protect them from illness or because they were taken with the notion that they would be equal to their Spanish overlords in heaven.

Almost all Filipinos clung to their traditional ways and in the process seriously compromised Christian beliefs and practices. The peoples of the islands continued public bathing, which the missionaries condemned as immodest, and refused to give up ritual drinking. They also continued to commune with deceased members of their families, often in sessions that were disguised as public recitations of the rosary. Thus, even in the Asian area where European control was the strongest and pressures for acculturation to European ways the greatest, much of the preconquest way of life and approach to the world was maintained.

Ming China: A Global Mission Refused

 With the restoration of ethnic Chinese rule and the reunification of the country under the Ming dynasty (1368–1644), Chinese civilization enjoyed a new age of splendor. Renewed agrarian and commercial growth supported a population that was the largest of any center of civilization at the time, probably exceeding that of all western Europe combined. Chinese goods remained very successful in the world market, with Europeans using American silver to pay for their growing exports (given the fact that European goods had no appeal for the Chinese). The Ming Empire's resources were vast, and it had some of the world's most advanced technology as well as large numbers of skilled engineers and artisans to put its rich soils and mineral wealth to productive use. China's centralized bureaucracy remained the best organized and most efficient in the world. Although the firearms of its armies began to fall somewhat behind those of the West, China still had a formidable military establishment in numbers, organization, and leadership.

Zhu Yuanzhang, a military commander of peasant origins who founded the Ming dynasty, had suffered a great deal under the Mongol yoke. Both his parents and two of his brothers had died in a plague in 1344, and he and a remaining brother were reduced to begging for the land in which to bury the rest of their family. Threatened with the prospect of starvation in one of the many famines that ravaged the countryside in the later, corruption-riddled reigns of the Mongols, Zhu alternated between begging and living in a Buddhist monastery to survive. When the neighboring countryside rose in rebellion in the late 1340s, Zhu left the monastery to join a rebel band. His courage in combat and his natural capacity as a leader soon made him one of the more prominent of several rebel warlords attempting to overthrow the Yuan dynasty. After protracted military struggles against rival rebel claimants to the throne and the Mongol rulers themselves, Zhu's armies conquered most of China. Zhu declared himself the **Hongwu** emperor in 1368. He reigned for 30 years.

Immediately after he seized the throne, Zhu launched an effort to rid China of all traces of the "barbarian" Mongols. Mongol dress was discarded, Mongol names were dropped by those who had adopted them and were removed from buildings and court records, and Mongol palaces and administrative buildings in some areas were raided and sacked. The nomads themselves fled or were driven beyond the Great Wall, where Ming military expeditions pursued them on several occasions.

Document

Exam Questions as a Mirror of Chinese Values

The subjects and specific learning tested on the Chinese civil service exams give us insight into the behavior and attitudes expected of the literate, ruling classes of what was perhaps the best-educated preindustrial civilization. Sample questions from these exams can tell us a good deal about what sorts of knowledge were considered important and what kinds of skills were necessary for those who aspired to successful careers in the most prestigious and potentially the most lucrative field open to Chinese youths: administrative service in the imperial bureaucracy. The very fact that such a tiny portion of the Chinese male population could take the exams and an even smaller number could successfully pass them says a lot about gender roles and elitism in Chinese society. In addition, the often decisive role of a student's calligraphy—the skill with which he was able to brush the Chinese characters—reflects the emphasis the Chinese elite placed on a refined sense of aesthetics.

Question 1: Provide the missing phrases and elaborate on the meaning of the following:

The Duke of She observed to Confucius: "Among us there was an upright man called Kung who was so upright that when his father appropriated a sheep, he bore witness against him." Confucius said …

[The missing phrases are, "The upright men among us are not like that. A father will screen his son and a son his father … yet uprightness is to be found in that."]

Question 2: Write an eight-legged essay [one consisting of eight sections] on the following:

Scrupulous in his own conduct and lenient only in his dealings with the people.

Question 3: First unscramble the following characters and then comment on the significance of this quotation from one of the classic texts:

Beginning, good, mutually, nature, basically, practice, far, near, men's

[The correct answer is, "Men's beginning nature is basically good. Nature mutually near. Practice mutually far."]

Questions: Looking at the content of these questions, what can we learn about Chinese society and attitudes? For example, where do the Chinese look for models to orient their social behavior? What kinds of knowledge are important to the Chinese? Do they stress specialist skills or the sort of learning that we associate with a broad liberal arts education? If we take SAT exams as equivalent gauges of our social values, how would you compare Ming China and modern America? What are the advantages and drawbacks of each system?

Another Scholar-Gentry Revival

Because the Hongwu emperor, like the founder of the earlier Han dynasty, was from a peasant family and thus poorly educated, he viewed the scholar-gentry with some suspicion. But he also realized that their cooperation was essential to the full revival of Chinese civilization. Scholars well versed in the Confucian classics were again appointed to the very highest positions in the imperial government. The generous state subsidies that had supported the imperial academies in the capital and the regional colleges were fully restored. Most critically, the civil service examination system, which the Mongols had discontinued, was reinstated and greatly expanded. In the Ming era and the Qing that followed, the examinations played a greater role in determining entry into the Chinese bureaucracy than had been the case under any earlier dynasty.

In the Ming era, the examination system was routinized and made more complex than before. Prefectural, or county, exams were held in two out of three years. The exams were given in large compounds, like the one depicted in Figure 22.3, surrounded by walls and watchtowers from which the examiners could keep an eye on the thousands of candidates. Each candidate was assigned a small cubicle where he struggled to answer the questions, slept, and ate over the several days that it took to complete the arduous exam. Those who passed and received the lowest

Figure 22.3   *A 19th-century engraving shows the cubicles in which Chinese students and bureaucrats took the imperial civil service examinations in the capital at Beijing. Candidates were confined to the cubicles for days and completed their exams under the constant surveillance of official proctors. They brought their own food, slept in the cubicles, and were disqualified if they were found talking to others taking the exams or going outside the compound where the exams were being given.*

degree were eligible to take the next level of exams, which were given in the provincial capitals every three years. Only the most gifted and ambitious went on because the process was fiercely competitive—in some years as many as 4000 candidates competed for 150 degrees. Success at the provincial level brought a rise in status and opened the way for appointments to positions in the middle levels of the imperial bureaucracy. It also permitted particularly talented scholars to take the imperial examinations, which were given in the capital every three years. Those who passed the imperial exams were eligible for the highest posts in the realm and were the most revered of all Chinese, except members of the royal family.

Reform: Hongwu's Efforts to Root Out Abuses in Court Politics

Hongwu was mindful of his dependence on a well-educated and loyal scholar-gentry for the day-to-day administration of the empire. But he sought to put clear limits on their influence and to institute reforms that would check the abuses of other factions at court. Early in his reign, Hongwu abolished the position of chief minister, which had formerly been the key link between the many ministries of the central government. The powers that had been amassed by those who occupied this office were transferred to the emperor himself. Hongwu also tried to impress all officials with the honesty, loyalty, and discipline he expected from them by introducing the practice of public beatings for bureaucrats found guilty of corruption or incompetence. Officials charged with misdeeds were paraded before the assembled courtiers and beaten a specified number of times on their bare buttocks. Many died of the wounds they received in the ordeal. Those who survived never recovered from the humiliation, which was to a certain extent shared by all the scholar-gentry by virtue of the very fact that such degrading punishments could be meted out to any of them.

Hongwu also introduced measures to cut down on the court factionalism and never-ending conspiracies that had eroded the power of earlier dynasties. He decreed that the emperor's wives should come only from humble family origins. This was intended to put an end to the power plays of the consorts from high-ranking families, who built palace cliques that were centered on their influential aristocratic relatives. He warned against allowing eunuchs to occupy positions of independent power and sought to limit their numbers within the Forbidden City. To prevent plots against the ruler and fights over succession, Hongwu established the practice of exiling all potential rivals to the throne to estates in the provinces, and he forbade them to become involved in political affairs. On the darker side, Hongwu condoned thought control, as when he had some sections from Mencius' writings that displeased him deleted forever from the writings included on the imperial exams. Although many of these measures went far to keep peace at court under Hongwu and his strong successor, the Yunglo emperor (r. 1403–1424), they were allowed to lapse under later, less capable, rulers, with devastating consequences for the Ming Empire.

A Return to Scholar-Gentry Social Dominance

Perhaps because his lowly origins and personal suffering made him sensitive to the plight of the peasantry, Hongwu introduced measures that would improve the lot of the common people. Like most strong emperors, he promoted public works projects, including dike building and the extension of irrigation systems aimed at improving the farmers' yields. To bring new lands under cultivation and encourage the growth of a peasant class that owned the lands it toiled so hard to bring into production, Hongwu decreed that unoccupied lands would become the tax-exempt property of those who cleared and cultivated them. He lowered forced labor demands on the peasantry by both the government and members of the gentry class. Hongwu also promoted silk and cotton cloth production and other handicrafts that provided supplemental income for peasant households.

Although these measures led to some short-term improvement in the peasants' condition, they were all but offset by the growing power of rural landlord families, buttressed by alliances with relatives in the imperial bureaucracy. Gentry households with members in government service were exempted from land taxes and enjoyed special privileges, such as permission to be carried about in sedan chairs and to use fans and umbrellas. Many gentry families engaged in moneylending on the side; some even ran lucrative gambling dens. Almost all added to their estates either by buying up lands held by peasant landholders or by foreclosing on loans made to farmers in times of need in exchange for mortgages on their family plots. Peasants displaced in these ways had little choice but to become tenants of large landowners or landless laborers moving about in search of employment.

More land meant ever larger and more comfortable households for the gentry class. They justified the growing gap between their wealth and the poverty of the peasantry by contrasting their foresight and industry with the lazy and wasteful ways of the ordinary farmers. The virtues of the gentry class were celebrated in stories and popular illustrations. The latter showed members of gentry households hard at work weaving and storing grain to see them through the cold weather, while commoners who neglected these tasks wandered during the winter, cold and hungry, past the walled compounds and closed gates of gentry households.

At most levels of Chinese society, the Ming period continued the subordination of youths to elders and women to men that had been steadily intensifying in earlier periods. If anything, neo-Confucian thinking was even more influential than under the late Song and Yuan dynasties. Some of its advocates proposed draconian measures to suppress challenges to the increasingly rigid social roles. For example, students were expected to venerate and follow the instructions of their teachers, no matter how muddle-headed or tipsy the latter might be. A terrifying lesson in proper decorum was drawn from an incident in which a student at the imperial academy dared to dispute the findings of one of his instructors. The student was beheaded, and his severed head was hung on a pole at the entrance to the academy. Not surprisingly, this rather unsubtle solution to the problem of keeping order in the classroom merely drove student protest underground. Anonymous letters critical of poorly prepared teachers continued to circulate among the student body.

Women were also driven to underground activities to ameliorate their subordination and, if they dared, expand their career opportunities. At the court, they continued, despite Hongwu's measures, to play strong roles behind the scenes. Even able rulers such as Hongwu were swayed by the advice of favorite wives or dowager mothers and aunts. On one occasion, Hongwu chided the empress Ma for daring to inquire into the condition of the common people. She replied that because he was the father of the people, she was the mother, and thus it was quite proper for her to be concerned for the welfare of her children.

Even within the palace, the plight of most women was grim. Hundreds, sometimes thousands of attractive young women were brought to the court in the hope that they would catch the emperor's fancy and become one of his concubines or perhaps even be elevated to the status of wife. Because few actually succeeded, many spent their lives in loneliness and inactivity, just waiting for the emperor to glance their way.

In society at large, women had to settle for whatever status and respect they could win within the family. As before, their success in this regard hinged largely on bearing male children and, when these children were married, moving from the status of daughter-in-law to mother-in-law. The daughters of upper-class families were often taught to read and write by their parents or brothers, and many composed poetry, painted, and played musical instruments (Figure 22.4).

For women from the nonelite classes, the main avenues for some degree of independence and self-expression remained becoming courtesans or entertainers. The former should be clearly distinguished from prostitutes because they served a very different clientele and were literate and often accomplished in painting, music, and poetry. Although courtesans often enjoyed lives of luxury, even the most successful made their living by gratifying the needs of upper-class men for uninhibited sex and convivial companionship.

An Age of Growth: Agriculture, Population, Commerce, and the Arts

The first decades of the Ming period were an age of buoyant economic growth in China that both was fed by and resulted in unprecedented contacts with other civilizations overseas. The territories controlled by the Ming emperors were never as extensive as those ruled by the Tang dynasty. But in the Ming era, the great commercial boom and population increase that had begun in the late Song were renewed and accelerated. The peopling of the Yangtze region and the areas to the south was given a great boost by the importation, through Spanish and Portuguese merchant intermediaries, of new food crops from the Americas, particularly root crops from the Andes highlands. Three plants—maize (or corn), sweet potatoes, and peanuts—were especially important. Because these crops could be grown on inferior soils without irrigation, their cultivation spread quickly through the hilly and marginal areas that bordered on the irrigated rice lands of southern China. They became vital supplements to the staple rice or millet diet of the Chinese people, particularly those of the rapidly growing southern regions.

Because these plants were less susceptible to drought, they also became an important hedge against famine. The introduction of these new crops was an important factor behind the great surge in population growth that was under way by the end of the Ming era. By 1600, the population of China had risen to about 120 million from 80 to 90 million in the 14th century. Two centuries later, in 1800, it had more than doubled and surpassed 300 million.

Agrarian expansion and population increase were paralleled in early Ming times by a renewal of commercial growth. The market sector of the domestic economy became ever more pervasive, and overseas trading links multiplied. Because China's advanced handicraft industries produced a wide variety of goods, from silk textiles and tea to fine ceramics and lacquerware, that were in high demand throughout Asia and in Europe, the terms of trade ran very much in China's favor. This is why China received more American silver (brought by European merchants) than any other single society in the world economy of the early modern period. In addition to the Arab and Asian traders, Europeans arrived in increasing numbers at the only two places—**Macao** and, somewhat later and more

Figure 22.4 *The varied diversions of the wives and concubines of Ming emperors are depicted in this scene of court life. In addition to court intrigues and maneuvers to win the emperor's favor, women of the imperial household occupied themselves with dance, music, games, and polite conversation. With eunuchs, officials, and palace guards watching them closely, the women of the palace and imperial city spent most of their lives in confined yet well-appointed spaces.*

sporadically, **Canton**—where they were officially allowed to do business in Ming China.

Not surprisingly, the merchant classes, particularly those engaged in long-distance trade, reaped the biggest profits from the economic boom. But a good portion of their gains was transferred to the state in the form of taxes and to the scholar-gentry in the form of bribes for official favors. Much of the merchants' wealth was invested in land rather than plowed back into trade or manufacturing, because land owning, not commerce, remained the surest route to social status in China.

Ming prosperity was reflected in the fine arts, which found generous patrons both at court and among the scholar-gentry class more generally. Although the monochromatic simplicity of the work of earlier dynasties was sustained by the ink brush paintings of artists such as Xuwei, much of the Ming output was busier and more colorful. Portraits and scenes of court, city, or country life were more prominent (see Figure 22.4). Nonetheless, the Chinese continued to delight in depicting individual scholars or travelers contemplating the beauty of mountains, lakes, and marshes, which dwarf the human observers.

Whereas the painters of the Ming era concentrated mainly on developing established techniques and genres, major innovation was occurring in literature. Most notable in this regard was the full development of the Chinese novel, which had had its beginnings in the writings of the Yuan era. The novel form was given great impetus by the spread of literacy among the upper classes in the Ming era. This was facilitated by the growing availability of books that had resulted from the spread of woodblock printing from the 10th century onward. Ming novels, such as *The Water Margin*, *Monkey*, and *The Golden Lotus*, were recognized as classics in their own time and continue to set the standard for Chinese prose literature today.

An Age of Expansion: The Zhenghe Expeditions

The seemingly boundless energy of the Chinese in early decades of Ming rule drove them far beyond the traditional areas of expansion in central Asia and the regions south of the Yangtze. In the reign of the third Ming emperor, Yunglo, they launched a series of expeditions that had no precedent in Chinese history. Between 1405 and 1423, as discussed in Chapter 15, the admiral Zhenghe, one of Yunglo's most trusted subordinates, led seven major expeditions overseas

(see Map 22.2). A mix of motives, including a desire to explore other lands and proclaim the glory of the Ming Empire to the wider world, prompted the voyages. The early expeditions were confined largely to southeast Asian seas and kingdoms. The last three expeditions reached as far as Persia, southern Arabia, and the east coast of Africa—distances comparable to those covered by the Portuguese in their early voyages around Africa.

The ships and fleets involved in each of the overseas missions were truly impressive. The initial fleet contained 62 ships (Columbus had three ships in 1492, and in 1498 da Gama had four) that carried nearly 28,000 sailors, merchants, and soldiers (da Gama had 150 for his first voyage around Africa). Some of the larger ships in Zhenghe's fleet were more than 400 feet long and displaced up to 1500 tons of water; the largest of da Gama's caravels could not have been much more than 60 feet long and displaced about 300 tons of water. Taken together, the expeditions led by Zhenghe leave little doubt that the Chinese had the capacity to expand on a global scale at least a century before the Europeans rounded the Cape of Good Hope and entered Asian waters.

Chinese Retreat and the Arrival of the Europeans

Just over a half century after the last of the Zhenghe expeditions, China had purposely moved from the position of a great power reaching out overseas to an

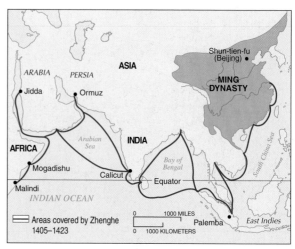

Map 22.2 *Ming China and the Zhenghe Expeditions, 1405–1423*

In Depth

Means and Motives for Overseas Expansion: Europe and China Compared

Given China's capacity for overseas expansion and the fateful consequences for global history that resulted from the fact that Europe, not China, eventually took the lead, the reasons for the Chinese failure to follow up on their early voyages of exploration merit serious examination. The explanations for the Chinese refusal to commit to overseas expansion can be best understood if they are contrasted with the forces that drove the Europeans with increasing determination into the outside world. In broad terms, such a comparison underscores the fact that although both the Europeans and the Chinese had the means to expand on a global scale, only the Europeans had strong motives for doing so.

The social and economic transformations that occurred in European civilization during the late Middle Ages and the early Renaissance had brought it to a level of development that compared favorably with China in many areas (see Chapters 15 and 16). Although the Chinese empire was far larger and more populous than tiny nation-states such as Portugal, Spain, and Holland, the European kingdoms had grown more efficient at mobilizing their more limited resources. Rivalries between the states of a fragmented Europe had also fostered a greater aggressiveness and sense of competition on the part of the Europeans than the Chinese rulers could even imagine. China's armies were far larger than those of any of the European kingdoms, but European soldiers were on the whole better led, armed, and disciplined. Chinese wet rice agriculture was more productive than European farming, and the Chinese rulers had a far larger population to cultivate their fields, build their dikes and bridges, work their mines, and make tools, clothing, and weapons. But on the whole, the technological innovations of the medieval period had given the Europeans an advantage over the Chinese in the animal and machine power they could generate—a capacity that did much to make up for their deficiencies in human power.

Despite their differences, both civilizations had the means for sustained exploration and expansion overseas, although the Chinese were ready to undertake such enterprises a few centuries earlier than the Europeans. As the voyages of da Gama, Columbus, and Zhenghe demonstrated, both civilizations had the shipbuilding and navigational skills and technology needed to tackle such ambitious undertakings.

Why, then, were the impressive Zhenghe expeditions a dead end, whereas the more modest probes of Columbus and da Gama were the beginning of half a millennium of European overseas expansion and global dominance?

The full answer to this question is as complex as the societies it asks us to compare. But we can learn a good deal by looking at the groups pushing for expansion within each civilization and the needs that drove them into the outside world. There was widespread support for exploration and overseas expansion in seafaring European nations such as Portugal, Spain, Holland, and England. European rulers financed expeditions they hoped would bring home precious metals and trade goods that could be sold at great profits. Both treasure and profits could be translated into warships and armies that would strengthen these rulers in their incessant wars with European rivals and, in the case of the Iberian kingdoms, with their Muslim adversaries.

European traders looked for much the same benefits from overseas expansion. Rulers and merchants also hoped that explorers would find new lands whose climates and soils were suitable for growing crops such as sugar that were in high demand and thus would bring big profits. Leaders of rival branches of the Christian faith believed that overseas expansion would give their missionaries access to unlimited numbers of heathens to be converted or would put them in touch with the legendary lost king, Prester John, who would ally with them in their struggle with the infidel Muslims.

By contrast, the Chinese Zhenghe expeditions were very much the project of a single emperor and a favored eunuch, whose Muslim family origins may go a long way toward accounting for his wanderlust. Yunglo appears to have been driven by little more than curiosity and the vain desire to impress his greatness and that of his empire on peoples whom he considered inferior. Although some Chinese merchants went along for the ride, most felt little need for the voyages. They already traded on favorable terms for all the products Asia, and in some cases Europe and Africa, could offer. The merchants had the option of waiting for other peoples to come to them, or, if they were a bit more ambitious, of going out in their own ships to southeast Asia.

(continued)

The scholar-gentry were actively hostile to the Zhenghe expeditions. The voyages strengthened the position of the much-hated eunuchs, who vied with the scholar-gentry for the emperor's favor and the high posts that went with it. In addition, the scholar-gentry saw the voyages as a foolish waste of resources that the empire could not afford. They believed it would be better to direct the wealth and talents of the empire to building armies and fortifications to keep out the hated Mongols and other nomads. After all, the memory of foreign rule was quite fresh.

As had happened so often before in their history, the Chinese were drawn inward, fixated on internal struggles and the continuing threat from central Asia. Scholar-gentry hostility and the lack of enthusiasm for overseas voyages displayed by Yunglo's successors after his death in 1424 led to their abandonment after 1430. As the Chinese retreated, the Europeans surged outward. It is difficult to exaggerate the magnitude of the consequences for both civilizations and all humankind.

Questions: How might history have been changed if the Chinese had mounted a serious and sustained effort to project their power overseas in the decades before da Gama rounded the Cape of Good Hope? Why did the Chinese fail to foresee the threat that European expansion would pose for the rest of Asia and finally for China itself? Did other civilizations have the capacity for global expansion in this era? What prevented them from launching expeditions similar to those of the Chinese and Europeans? In terms of motivation for overseas expansion, were peoples such as the Muslims, Indians, and Native Americans more like the Europeans or the Chinese?

increasingly isolated empire. In 1390, the first imperial edict aimed at limiting Chinese overseas commerce was issued. In the centuries that followed, the Ming war fleet declined dramatically in the number and quality of its ships, and strict limits were placed on the size and number of masts with which a seagoing ship might be fitted. As the Chinese shut themselves in, the Europeans probed ever farther across the globe and were irresistibly drawn to the most legendary of all overseas civilizations, the Middle Kingdom of China. In addition to the trading contacts noted earlier, Christian missionaries infiltrated Chinese coastal areas and tried to gain access to the court, where they hoped to curry favor with the Ming emperors. While religious orders such as the Franciscans and Dominicans toiled to win converts among the common people and made modest progress that could be counted in the tens of thousands, the Jesuits adopted the top-down strategy that di Nobili had pursued in India (Figure 22.5). In China, however, a single person, the Ming emperor, instead of a whole caste, sat at the top of the social hierarchy, and for that reason the rulers and their chief advisors became the prime targets of the Jesuit mission.

Some Chinese scholars showed interest in Christian teachings and Western thinking more generally. But the Jesuit missionaries who made their way to Beijing clearly recognized that their scientific knowledge and technical skills were the keys to maintaining a presence at the Ming court and eventually interesting the Chinese elite in Christianity. Beginning in the 1580s, a succession of brilliant Jesuit scholars, such as **Matteo Ricci** and **Adam Schall,** spent most of their time in the imperial city, correcting faulty calendars, forging cannons, fixing clocks imported from Europe, and astounding the Chinese scholar-gentry with the accuracy of their instruments and their ability to predict eclipses. They won a few converts among the elite. However, most court officials were suspicious of these strange-looking "barbarians" with large noses and hairy faces, and they tried to limit their contacts with the imperial family. Some at the court, especially the scholar-officials who were humiliated by the foreigners' corrections to their calendars, were openly hostile to the Jesuits. Despite serious harassment, however, the later Ming emperors remained sufficiently fascinated by these very learned and able visitors that they allowed a handful to remain.

Ming Decline and the Chinese Predicament

By the late 1500s, the Ming retreat from overseas involvement had become just one facet of a familiar pattern of dynastic decline. The highly centralized, absolutist political structure, which had been estab-

Figure 22.5 *Jesuits in Chinese dress at the emperor's court. The Jesuits believed that the best way to convert a great civilization such as China was to adopt the dress, customs, language, and manners of its elite. They reasoned that once the scholar-gentry elite had been converted, they would bring the rest of China's vast population into the Christian fold.*

lished by Hongwu and had been run well by able successors such as Yunglo, became a major liability under the mediocre or incompetent men who occupied the throne through much of the last two centuries of Ming rule. Decades of rampant official corruption, exacerbated by the growing isolation of weak rulers by the thousands of eunuchs who gradually came to dominate life within the Forbidden City, eventually eroded the foundations on which the empire was built.

Public works projects, including the critical dike works on the Yellow River, fell into disrepair, and floods, drought, and famine soon ravaged the land. Peasants in afflicted districts were reduced to eating the bark from trees or the excrement of wild geese.

Some peasants sold their children into slavery to keep them from starving, and peasants in some areas resorted to cannibalism. Rapacious local landlords built huge estates by taking advantage of the increasingly desperate peasant population. As in earlier phases of dynastic decline, farmers who had been turned off their land and tortured for taxes, or had lost most of the crop they had grown, turned to flight, banditry, and finally open rebellion to confiscate food and avenge their exploitation by greedy landlords and corrupt officials.

True to the pattern of dynastic rise and fall, internal disorder resulted in and was intensified by foreign threats and renewed assaults by nomadic peoples from beyond the Great Wall. One of the early signs of the seriousness of imperial deterioration was the inability of Chinese bureaucrats and military forces to put an end to the epidemic of Japanese (and ethnic Chinese) pirate attacks that ravaged the southern coast in the mid-16th century. Despite an official preoccupation with the Mongols early in the Ming era and with the Manchus to the northeast of the Great Wall in later times, the dynasty was finally toppled in 1644, not by nomads but by rebels from within. By that time, the administrative apparatus had become so feeble that the last Ming emperor, **Chongzhen,** did not realize how serious the rebel advance was until enemy soldiers were scaling the walls of the Forbidden City. After watching his wife withdraw to her chambers to commit suicide, and after bungling an attempt to kill his young daughter, the ill-fated Chongzhen retreated to the imperial gardens and hanged himself rather than face capture.

Fending Off the West: Japan's Reunification and the First Challenge

 Fortunately for the Japanese, their ability to defend their island home was not tested in the early centuries of expansion. In the decades just after the Europeans began to arrive in the islands in the 1540s, the Japanese found leaders who had the military and diplomatic skills and ruthlessness needed to restore the shogunate. To do so it was necessary to force the daimyo, or most powerful warlords, to acknowledge a supreme commander, if not a true sovereign. By the early 1600s, with the potential threat from the Europeans looming ever larger in the Japanese imagination, the new Tokugawa shoguns had gained sufficient control to let them gradually shut down contacts with outsiders. They succeeded in enveloping the islands in a state of isolation that lasted nearly two and a half centuries.

By the 16th century, the daimyo stalemate and the pattern of recurring civil war were so entrenched in Japanese society that a succession of three remarkable military leaders was needed to restore unity and internal peace. **Nobunaga,** the first of these leaders, was from a minor warrior household. But his skills as a military leader soon vaulted him into prominence in the ongoing struggles for power among the daimyo lords. As a leader Nobunaga combined daring, a willingness to innovate, and ruthless determination—some would say cruelty. He was not afraid to launch a surprise attack against an enemy that outnumbered him ten to one, and he was one of the first of the daimyos to make extensive use of the firearms that the Japanese had begun to acquire from the Portuguese in the 1540s.

In 1573, Nobunaga deposed the last of the Ashikaga shoguns, who had long ruled in name only. By 1580, he had unified much of central Honshu under his command (see Map 22.3). As his armies drove against the powerful western daimyo in 1582, Nobunaga was caught off guard by one of his vassal generals and was killed when the Kyoto temple where he had taken refuge was burned to the ground.

At first it appeared that Nobunaga's campaigns to restore central authority to the islands might be undone. But his ablest general, **Toyotomi Hideyoshi** (Figure 22.6), moved quickly to punish those who had betrayed Nobunaga and to renew the drive to break the power of the daimyos who had not yet submitted to him. Though the son of a peasant, Hideyoshi matched his master in military prowess but was far more skillful at diplomacy. A system of alliances and a string of victories over the last of the resisting daimyos made Hideyoshi the military master of Japan by 1590.

The ambitious overlord had much more grandiose schemes of conquest in mind. He dreamed of ruling China and even India, although he knew little about either place. Hideyoshi also threatened,

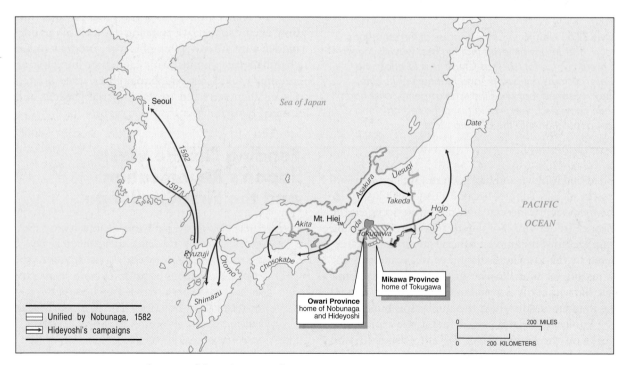

Map 22.3 *Japan During the Rise of the Tokugawa Shogunate*

Figure 22.6 *In this late 16th-century portrait, Hideyoshi (1536–1598) grasps the sword that catapulted him to power and exudes the discipline and self-confidence that impelled his campaigns to unify Japan. Although warrior skills were vital in his rise to power, he and other members of the samurai class were expected to be literate, well mannered by the conventions of the day, and attuned to the refined aesthetics of rock gardens and tea ceremonies.*

ily populated Kanto plain. Ieyasu soon emerged triumphant from the renewed warfare that resulted from Hideyoshi's death. Rather than continue Hideyoshi's campaigns of overseas expansion, Ieyasu concentrated on consolidating power at home. In 1603, he was granted the title of shogun by the emperor, an act that formally inaugurated centuries of rule by the **Tokugawa shogunate.**

Under Ieyasu's direction, the remaining daimyos were reorganized. Most of the lands in central Honshu either were controlled directly by the Tokugawa family, who now ruled the land from the city of **Edo** (later Tokyo), or were held by daimyos who were closely allied with the shoguns. Although many of the outlying or vassal daimyos retained their domains, they were carefully controlled and were required to pledge their personal allegiance to the shogun. It was soon clear that the Tokugawas' victory had put an end to the civil wars and brought a semblance of political unity to the islands.

Dealing with the European Challenge

All through the decades when the three unifiers were struggling to bring the feisty daimyos under control, they also had to contend with a new force in Japanese history: the Europeans. From the time in 1543 when shipwrecked Portuguese sailors were washed up on the shore of Kyushu island, European traders and missionaries had been visiting the islands in increasing numbers (see the Japanese depiction of their coming in the painting that opens this chapter). The traders brought the Japanese goods that were produced mainly in India, China, and southeast Asia and exchanged them for silver, copper, pottery, and lacquerware. Perhaps more important, European traders and the missionaries who followed them to the islands brought firearms, printing presses, and other Western devices such as clocks. The firearms, which the Japanese could themselves manufacture within years and were improving in design within a generation, revolutionized Japanese warfare and contributed much to the victories of the unifiers. Commercial contacts with the Europeans also encouraged the Japanese to venture overseas to trade in nearby Formosa and Korea and in places as distant as the Philippines and Siam.

Soon after the merchants, Christian missionaries, including Francis Xavier (Figure 22.7), arrived in the

among others, the Spanish in the Philippines. Apparently as the first step toward fulfilling this vision of empire building on a grand scale, Hideyoshi launched two attacks on Korea in 1592 and 1597, each of which involved nearly 150,000 soldiers. After initial successes, both campaigns stalled. The first ended in defeat; the second was still in progress when Hideyoshi died in 1598.

Although Hideyoshi had tried to ensure that he would be succeeded by his son, the vassals he had appointed to carry out his wishes tried to seize power for themselves after his death. One of these vassals, **Tokugawa Ieyasu,** had originally come from a minor daimyo house. But as an ally of Hideyoshi, he had been able to build up a powerful domain on the heav-

Figure 22.7 *The arrival of Francis Xavier and his entourage in Japan is depicted in this 16th-century screen painting. The painting wonderfully conveys Japanese perceptions of these strangers from distant lands as exotic, awkward, and curiously dressed. Other than differences in skin color, to which the Japanese were highly sensitive, all have rather similar facial features, perhaps because the Japanese thought that all the Westerners looked alike.*

islands and set to work converting the Japanese to Roman Catholicism. Beginning in the outlying daimyos' domains, the missionaries worked their way toward the political center that was beginning to coalesce around Nobunaga and his followers by the 1570s. Seeing Christianity as a counterforce to the militant Buddhist orders that were resisting his rise to power, Nobunaga took the missionaries under his protection and encouraged them to preach their faith to his people. The Jesuits, adopting the same top-down strategy of conversion that they had followed in India and China, converted many of the daimyos and their samurai retainers. Some of the Jesuits were also convinced that they were on the verge of winning over Nobunaga, who delighted in wearing Western clothes, encouraged his artists to copy Western paintings of the Virgin Mary and scenes from the life of Christ, and permitted the missionaries to build churches in towns throughout the islands. The missionaries were persuaded that Nobunaga's conversion would bring the whole of the Japanese people into the Christian fold. Even without it, they reported converts in the hundreds of thousands by the early 1580s.

In the late 1580s, quite suddenly, the missionaries saw their carefully mounted conversion campaign collapse. Nobunaga was murdered, and his successor, Hideyoshi, though not yet openly hostile, was lukewarm toward the missionary enterprise. In part, the missionaries' fall from favor resulted from the fact that the resistance of the Buddhist sects had been crushed. More critically, Hideyoshi and his followers were alarmed by reports of converts refusing to obey their overlords' commands when they believed them to be in conflict with their newly adopted Christian beliefs. Thus, the threat that the new religion posed for the established social order was growing more apparent. That threat was compounded by signs that the Europeans might follow up their commercial and missionary overtures with military expeditions aimed at conquering the islands. The Japanese had been strongly impressed with the firearms and pugnacity of the Europeans, and they did not take threats of invasion lightly.

Japan's Self-Imposed Isolation

Growing doubts about European intentions, and fears that both merchants and missionaries might subvert the existing social order, led to official measures to restrict foreign activities in Japan, beginning in the late 1580s. First, Hideyoshi ordered the Christian missionaries to leave the islands—an order that was not rigorously enforced, at least at the outset. By the mid-1590s, Hideyoshi was actively persecuting both Christian missionaries and converts. His successor, Ieyasu, continued this persecution and then officially banned the faith in 1614. European missionaries were driven out of the islands; those who remained underground were hunted down and killed or expelled. Japanese converts were compelled to renounce their faith; those who refused were imprisoned, tortured, and executed. By the 1630s, the persecutions, even against Christians who tried to practice their faith in secret, had become so intense that thousands of converts in the western regions joined in hard-fought but hopeless rebellions against the local daimyos and the forces of the shogun. With the suppression of these uprisings, Christianity in Japan was reduced to an underground faith of isolated communities.

Under Ieyasu and his successors, the persecution of the Christians grew into a broader campaign to isolate Japan from outside influences. In 1616, foreign traders were confined to a handful of cities; in the 1630s, all Japanese ships were forbidden to trade or even sail overseas. One after another, different European nations were either officially excluded from Japan (the Spanish) or decided that trading there was no longer worth the risk (the English). By the 1640s, only a limited number of Dutch and Chinese ships were allowed to carry on commerce on the small island of **Deshima** in Nagasaki Bay. The export of silver and copper was greatly restricted, and Western books were banned to prevent Christian ideas from reentering the country. Foreigners were permitted to live and travel only in very limited areas.

By the mid-17th century, Japan's retreat into almost total isolation was complete. Much of the next century was spent in consolidating the internal control of the Tokugawa shogunate by extending bureaucratic administration into the vassal daimyo domains throughout the islands. In the 18th century, a revival of neo-Confucian philosophy, which had marked the period of the Tokugawa's rise to power, increasingly gave way to the influence of thinkers who championed the **school of National Learning.** As its name implies, the new ideology laid great emphasis on Japan's unique historical experience and the revival of indigenous culture at the expense of Chinese imports such as Confucianism. In the centuries that followed, through contacts with the small Dutch community at Deshima, members of the Japanese elite also followed developments in the West. Their avid interest in European achievements contrasted sharply with the indifference of the Chinese scholar-gentry in this period to the doings of the "hairy barbarians" from Europe.

GLOBAL CONNECTIONS: An Age of Eurasian Closure

In 1700, after two centuries of European involvement in south and southeast Asia, most of the peoples of the area had been little affected by efforts to build trading empires and win Christian converts. European sailors had added several new routes to the Asian trading network. The most important of these were the link around the Cape of Good Hope between Europe and the Indian Ocean and the connection between the Philippine Islands and Mexico in the Americas. The Europeans' need for safe harbors and storage areas led to the establishment and rapid growth of trading centers such as Goa, Calicut, and Batavia. It also resulted in the gradual decline of existing indigenous commercial centers, especially the Muslim cities on the east coast of Africa and somewhat later the fortress town of Malacca. The Europeans introduced the principle of sea warfare into what had been a peaceful commercial world. But the Asian trading system as a whole survived the initial shock of this innovation, and the Europeans eventually concluded that they were better off adapting to the existing commercial arrangements rather than dismantling them.

Because exchanges had been taking place between Europe and Asia for millennia, few new inventions or diseases were spread in the early centuries of expansion. This low level of major exchanges was particularly striking compared with the catastrophic interaction between Europe and the Americas. But, as in Africa, European discoveries in the long-isolated Western Hemisphere did result in the introduction of important new food plants into India, China, and other areas from the 1600s onward. The import of silver was also an addition to wealth and adornment in China. Otherwise, Europeans died mainly of diseases that they contracted in Asia, such as new strains of malaria and dysentery. They spread diseases only to the more isolated parts of Asia, such as the Philippines, where the coming of the Spanish was accompanied by a devastating smallpox epidemic. The impact of European ideas, inventions, and modes of social organization was also very limited during the first centuries of expansion. Key European devices, such as clocks, were seen as toys by Asian rulers to whom they were given as presents.

During the early modern period in global history, the West's surge in exploration and commercial expansion touched most of Asia only peripherally. This was particularly true of east Asia, where the political cohesion and military strength of the vast Chinese empire and the Japanese warrior-dominated states blocked all hope of European advance. Promising missionary inroads in the 16th century were stifled by hostile Tokugawa shoguns in the early 17th century. They were also carefully contained by the Ming emperors and the nomadic Qing dynasty in the mid-1600s. Strong Chinese and Japanese rulers limited trading contacts with the aggressive Europeans and confined European merchants to a few ports— Macao and Canton in China, Deshima in Japan—that were remote from their respective capitals. In its early decades, the Ming dynasty also pursued a policy of overseas expansion that had no precedent in Chinese history. But when China again turned inward in the last centuries of the dynasty, a potentially formidable obstacle to the rise of European dominance in maritime Asia was removed. China's strong position in global trade continued, in marked contrast to Japan's greater isolation. But even China failed to keep pace with changes in European technology and merchant activity, with results that would show more clearly in the next stage of global interconnections.

Further Readings

C. G. F. Simkins' *The Traditional Trade of Asia* (1968) and Anthony Reid, *Southeast Asia in the Age of Commerce, 1450-1680* (1988) provide overviews of the Asian trading network from ancient times until about the 18th century. Much more detailed accounts of specific segments of the system, as well as the impact upon it of the Dutch and Portuguese, can be found in the works of J. C. van Leur, M. A. P. Meilink-Roelofsz, K. N. Chaudhuri, Ashin Das Gupta, Sanjay Subrahmanyam, and Michael Pearson. C. R. Boxer's *The Portuguese Seaborne Empire* (1969) and *The Dutch Seaborne Empire* (1965) are still essential reading, although the latter has little on the Europeans in Asia. Boxer's *Race Relations in the Portuguese Colonial Empire,*

1415–1852 (1963) provides a stimulating, if contentious, introduction to the history of European social interaction with overseas peoples in the early centuries of expansion. Important correctives to Boxer's work can be found in the more recent contributions of George Winius.

Louise Levathes, *When China Ruled the Seas: The Treasure Fleet of the Dragon Throne, 1405-33* (1994) is an entertaining account of China's global reach.

G. B. Sansom's *The Western World and Japan* (1968) includes a wealth of information on the interaction between Europeans and, despite its title, peoples throughout Asia, and it has good sections on the missionary initiatives in both China and Japan.

The period of the Ming dynasty has been the focus of broader and more detailed studies than the dynasties that preceded it. An important early work is Charles O. Hucker's *The Censorial System of Ming China* (1966). Two essential recent works are Albert Chan's *The Glory and Fall of the Ming Dynasty* (1982) and Edward Dreyer's more traditional political history, *Early Ming China, 1355–1435* (1982). See also the more recent F. Mote and D. Twitchett, eds., *The Cambridge History of China: The Ming Dynasty 1368-1644,* Vols. VI (1988) and VII (1998).

There are also wonderful insights into daily life at various levels of Chinese society in Roy Huang's very readable *1587: A Year of No Significance; The Ming Dynasty in Decline* (1981) and into the interaction between the Chinese and the Jesuits in Jonathan Spence's *The Memory Palace of Matteo Ricci* (1984). Frederic Wakeman Jr.'s *The Great Enterprise,* 2 vols. (1985), is essential to an understanding of the transition from Ming to Manchu rule. The early chapters of Spence's *The Search for Modern China* (1990) also provide an illuminating overview of that process.

Perhaps the best introductions to the situation in Japan in the early phase of European expansion are provided by G. B. Sansom's survey, *A History of Japan, 1615–1867* (1963), and Conrad Totman's *Politics in the Tokugawa Bakufu, 1600–1843* (1967). Numerous studies on the Europeans in Japan include those by Donald Keene, Grant Goodman, Noel Perrin, and C. R. Boxer. Intellectual trends in Japan in this era are most fully treated in H. D. Harootunian's *Toward Restoration: The Growth of Political Consciousness in Tokugawa Japan* (1970).

On the Web

The achievement of the Ming and later Qing Dynasties are on view at virtual tours of their versions of the Great Wall and Forbidden City offered at http://www. chinavista.com/travel/greatwall/greatwall.html and http://www.chinavista.com/beijing/gugong/map.html.

Perhaps the finest of all virtual tour sites on the Web is that which provides a glimpse into the rich cultural life of the Tokugawa capital of Edo at http://www.us-japan.

org/EdoMatsu/.This shogunate was established after a civil war that followed the reigns of Nobunaga Oda (http://ox.compsoc.net/~gemini/simons/historyweb/oda-nobunaga.html) and Toyotomi Hideyoshi, developer of the grand Osaka Castle (http://www.tourism.city.osaka.jp/en/castle/mainmenu.htm). It marked the ascension of Tokugawa Ieyasu (http://www.samurai-archives.com/ieyasu.html and http://www.japan-guide.com/e/e2128.html) whose shogunate paved the way for the construction of modern Japan.

The era that saw the rise and development of the Tokugawa witnessed much exchange between Asians and Christian missionaries elsewhere in Asia. An exceptional on-line study of these exchanges and the lives of Mateo Ricci, Adam Schall, and Robert DiNobili can be found at http://acc6.its.brooklyn.cuny.edu/~phalsall/texts/ric-jour.html and http://archive.ncsa.uiuc.edu/SDG/Experimental/vatican.exhibit/exhibit/i-rome_to_china/Rome_to_china.html.

These exchanges were made possible by earlier developments in seagoing transportation, trade, and exploration, such as the travels of Zhenghe or Chengho (http://chinapage.com/chengho.html), the development of the caravel (http://www.mariner.org/age/portuguese.html and http://www.pfri.hr/pov/pov07.html), and the development of Portuguese and Dutch trading empires (http://www.geocities.com/Athens/Styx/6497/).

Web pages devoted to the Dutch East Indian Company (http://batavia.rug.ac.be/index.html and http://batavia.UGent.be/) provide luminous virtual tours of both Batavia and Deshima that demonstrate the still peripheral role of Europeans in Asia at this time.

PART V

Industrialization and Western Global Hegemony, 1750–1914

CHAPTERS

23 The Emergence of Industrial Society in the West, 1750–1914

24 Industrialization and Imperialism: The Making of the European Global Order

25 The Consolidation of Latin America, 1830–1920

26 Civilizations in Crisis: The Ottoman Empire, the Islamic Heartlands, and Qing China

27 Russia and Japan: Industrialization Outside the West

Introduction

Between 1750 and 1914, world history was dominated by growing European imperialism. These were the decades in which Western civilization (embracing much of North America as well as western Europe) experienced the Industrial Revolution, which transformed the bases of production through new technology and new sources of power. European dominance in the world economy became almost overwhelming.

In contrast to the early modern period, when Western power on land was limited, no area could escape the possibility of extensive European or United States penetration. Africa, previously able to resist Western political and military power, was carved up into a patchwork of colonies. The West's new hegemony was also expressed through growing commercial penetration of areas such as China and the Ottoman Empire that were not held as colonies. Finally, Western hegemony was expressed in the need for leaders in every civilization to decide what Western institutions and values to imitate and how.

International commercial contacts increased steadily. They were enhanced by major technological innovations, notably the steamship, railroad, and telegraph. Cultural contacts reflected Western power as well. Just as Christianity and commercial penetration went hand in hand in Latin America during the early modern period, by the end of the 19th century religious conversion began to accompany imperialist entry into Africa's heartlands, and Western science and new ideas such as nationalism spread even more widely.

By the 1850s, the leading issues in all civilizations began to revolve around what to do about the West's new power: how and whether to resist, and what could or should be imitated. Common responses included growing interest in military reforms and in establishing new kinds of schools and, often, even parliaments and constitutions.

Chronology: From Industrial Revolution to the Beginnings of a Western Breakdown

The beginning of this new period, 1750, focuses on no particular event. The war that opened in that decade, which produced battles in Europe, North America, and India as well as on the seas, has some claim to being history's first global conflict. More important is the fact that during the 1750s, the forces that produced Europe's Industrial Revolution began to take shape: rapid population growth, expansion of manufacturing, and a surge of new inventions. The real Industrial Revolution is properly dated a few decades later, but the second half of the 18th century included its formative stages.

With Western industrialization under way, signs of its impact on the wider world followed quickly. In 1798, a modest French expeditionary force seized Egypt from its Muslim rulers—a clear sign of a new power balance in the eastern Mediterranean. In the 1820s, Britain's hold over India began to intensify. In the 1830s, the West forced open China's markets, using insistence on the right to sell opium in China as its entering wedge. In the 1850s, Britain and France defeated Russia in a war in its own Crimean backyard, while the United States and Britain pried open Japanese markets under threat of naval bombardment. The American Civil War (1861–1865) saw the industrial North prevail over the slaveholding South. Also in the 1860s, the scramble for new African colonies began. In the 1870s, a new level of commercial penetration started to transform the Latin American economy and social relationships. Between the 1850s and 1900, the islands of Polynesia were brought under Western control as colonies, and the Maoris of New Zealand were subjected to a government of European settlers.

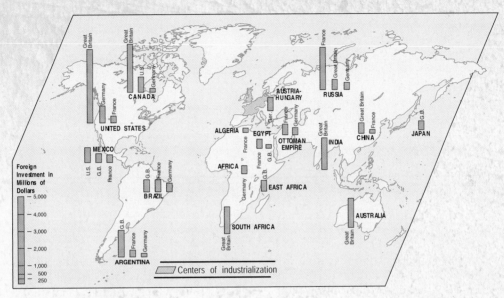

Industrial Development in Key Regional Centers, c. 1900

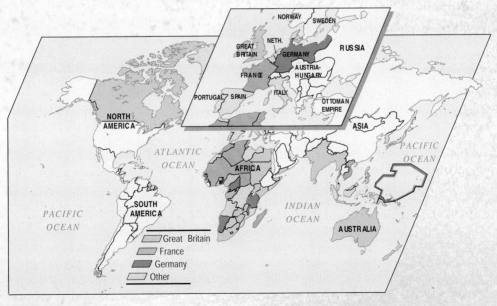

Main Colonial Holdings, c. 1914

1700 C.E.	**1800** C.E.	**1825** C.E.
1730–1850 Population boom in western Europe	**1805–1849** Muhammad Ali rules Egypt	**1825–1855** Repression in Russia
1770 James Watt's steam engine; beginning of Industrial Revolution	**1808–1825** Latin American wars of independence	**1826** New Zealand colonization begins
1776–1783 American Revolution	**1815** Vienna settlement	**1830, 1848** Revolutions in Europe
1786–1790 First British reforms in India	**1815** British annexation of Cape Town and region of southern Africa	**1835** English education in India
1788 Australian colonization begins	**1822** Brazil declares independence	**1838** Ottoman trade treaty with Britain
1789–1815 French Revolution and Napoleon	**1823** Monroe Doctrine	**1839–1841** Opium War between England and China
1798 Napoleon's invasion of Egypt		**1839–1876** Reforms in Ottoman Empire
		1840 Semiautonomous government in Canada
		1846–1848 Mexican-American War
		1848 ff. Beginnings of Marxism

The industrial–imperialist period drew to a close with the outbreak of World War I in 1914 simply because, in the wake of this massive conflict, the West's world hold began to recede. Revolutions in Russia, Japanese expansion, and the beginnings of colonial revolt signaled the end of the undisputed dominance of the industrial West.

The Industrial Revolution

 The Industrial Revolution restructured the economy first in Britain and then in the rest of western Europe and the United States. It featured dramatic new technology and a new organization of work.

The essence of the Industrial Revolution was technological change, particularly the application of coal-powered engines (or, later, engines powered by other fossil fuels) to production. The new engines replaced people and animals as the key sources of energy in many branches of production. They were joined by new production equipment that could apply power to manufacturing through more automatic processes. Thus, spindles were invented that wrapped fiber automatically into thread, and looms mixed threads automatically without direct human intervention. Engines were also used in sugar refining, printing, and other processes.

The British Industrial Revolution resulted from a host of factors, including favorable natural resources. Industrialization was fed also by the late 18th-century population crisis. Population pressure forced innovations at all social levels. The Industrial Revolution also built on previous trends in Western society, including the growth of the large manufacturing sector and the huge advantages in world trade. Prior development in science set a basis on which creative artisans could widen their efforts at technical innovation. Governments already committed to policies of economic growth also supported industrialization by instituting laws encouraging new inventions and new trading and banking systems. Finally, Europe's dominance in the world economy generated both investment capital, from profits on trade, and market opportunities.

Origins of Industrialization, 1770–1840

The key inventions of early industrialization developed in Britain during the 18th century. Automatic machinery in textiles initially was intended for manual

1850 C.E.	1875 C.E.	1900 C.E.
1850–1864 Taiping rebellion in China	**1877–1878** Ottomans out of most of Balkans; Treaty of San Stefano	**1901** Commonwealth of Australia
1853 Perry expedition to Edo Bay in Japan	**1879–1890s** Partition of west Africa	**1903** Construction of Panama Canal begins
1854–1856 Crimean War	**1882** British takeover of Egypt	**1904–1905** Russo-Japanese War
1867 Union of central and eastern Canada	**1884–1914** Russian industrialization	**1905–1906** Revolution in Russia; limited reforms
1858 British parliament assumes control over India	**1885** Formation of National Congress Party in India	**1908** Young Turk rising
1860–1868 Civil strife in Japan	**1886–1888** Slavery abolished in Cuba and Brazil	**1910** Japan annexes Korea
1861 Emancipation of serfs in Russia; reform era begins	**1890** Japanese constitution	**1911–1912** Revolution in China; end of empire
1861–1865 American Civil War	**1890s** Partition of east Africa	**1914–1918** World War I
1863 Emancipation of slaves in United States	**1890s** European leases in China	
1864–1871 German unification	**1894–1895** Sino Japanese War	
1868–1912 Meiji (reform) era in Japan	**1895** Cuban revolt against Spain	
1870 Establishment of Japanese Ministry of Industry	**1898** Formation of Marxist Social Democratic Party in Russia	
1870–1910 Acceleration of "demographic transition" in western Europe and the United States	**1898** Spanish–American War; United States acquires the Philippines, Puerto Rico, and Hawaii; United States intervenes in Cuba	
1870–1910 Expansion of commercial export economy in Latin America	**1898–1901** Boxer Rebellion in China	
1871–1912 High point of European imperialism		

use in the domestic system. Then, in the 1770s, Scottish artisan James Watt devised a steam engine that could be used for production, and the Industrial Revolution was off and running. Within a decade in Britain, the domestic production of key materials, such as cotton thread, was converted to factory-housed machines at the expense of thousands of home workers, mostly women.

Additional inventions followed, for a key feature of the Industrial Revolution was recurrent technological change. Early machine spindles were expanded, enabling a given worker to supervise even faster output. American inventors devised a production system of interchangeable parts, initially for rifles, that helped standardize and so mechanize the production of machinery itself. Metallurgy advanced by use of coal and coke, instead of charcoal, for smelting and refining, allowing the creation of larger furnaces and greater output.

Technological change was applied quickly to transportation and communication, which became essential because there were more goods to be moved and more distant markets to contact. The development of the telegraph, steam shipping, and the railway, all early in the 19th century, provided faster movement of information and goods.

The Industrial Revolution depended on improvements in agriculture. Industrialization concentrated increasing amounts of manufacturing in cities, where power sources could be brought together with labor. City growth was dizzying during the first decades of industrialization. Sleepy villages such as Manchester, England, grew to cities of several hundred thousand people. This kind of growth depended on better agricultural production, accomplished through improved equipment and seeds and the growing use of fertilizers.

Industrialization also meant a factory system. Steam engines had to be concentrated because their power could not be widely diffused until the later application of electricity. Factory labor separated work from the home—one of the basic human changes inherent in the Industrial Revolution. It also allowed manufacturers to introduce greater specialization of labor and more explicit rules and discipline, which along with the noisy machines permanently changed the nature of human labor.

Industrialization had profound and complex environmental impact. Use of coal and iron reduced pressure on Europe's remaining forests. But smoke pollution in factory areas was an early issue, and both factory wastes and growing cities quickly affected water quality. Industrial demands for raw materials created desolate slagheaps around mines, both in Europe and in areas where raw materials were produced. The Industrial Revolution, and particularly its new uses of energy, transformed human use of nature, with an accelerating impact that stretched through the 20th century.

The Disruptions of Industrial Life

The Industrial Revolution was not just a technological upheaval; indeed, the changing role of technology and work organizations reshaped human life. The process involved huge movements of people from countryside to city. Families were disrupted, as young adults proved to be the prime migrants. Cities themselves, poorly equipped to begin with and crowded beyond all precedent, became hellholes for many new residents. Health conditions worsened in poor districts because of packed housing and inadequate sanitation. Crime increased for a time. New social divisions opened up as middle-class families moved away from the city, beginning a pattern of suburbanization that continued into the late 20th century. Work became more unpleasant for many people. Not only was it largely separated from family, but the new machines and factory rules compelled a rapid pace and coordination that pulverized traditional values of leisurely, high-quality production. First in Britain, and then elsewhere, groups of workers responded to the new machines by outright attack; Luddite protests, named after a mythical British machine-breaker called Ned Ludd, failed to stop industrialization, but they showed the stress involved.

The early Industrial Revolution also forced new constraints on traditions of popular leisure. Factory owners, bent on getting as much work as possible from their labor force to help pay for expensive machines, tried to ban singing, napping, drinking, and other customary frivolities on the job. Punctuality and efficiency were cast as virtues, and anything that took time away from work was considered almost sinful. A typical tract, called "The Duty and Advantage of Early Rising," issued in 1786, warned workers that "by soaking . . . so long between warm sheets, the flesh is as it were parboiled, and becomes soft and flabby. The nerves, in the meantime, are quite unstrung."

Family life changed. Middle-class people quickly enhanced the redefinition of the family already begun in the early modern centuries. The family for them served as an image of affection and purity. Children and women were to be sheltered from the storms of the new work world. Women, traditionally active partners to merchants, now withdrew from formal jobs. They gained new roles in caring for children and the home, and their moral status in many ways improved, but their sphere was more separate from that of men than had been true before. Children also were redefined. The middle class came to see education, not work and apprenticeship, as the logical role for children to prepare them for a complex future.

The changes in family roles and values show how deeply the Industrial Revolution could reach into personal life. The confusion of change worried many people, even businesspeople actively building the new industrial world. As a leading French industrialist noted, "Progress is not necessarily progressive. If it were not inevitable, it might be better to stop it."

Industrialization, West, and World

The Industrial Revolution was a Western phenomenon for several decades, though it built on the West's preexisting position in the world economy. But the revolution quickly had world impact. It increased the West's military power by generating new weapons technology, the mass production of guns with standardized parts, and new forms of transportation, such as steamboats that could transport troops upriver into the interior of places like Africa and China. Here, in turn, was the key foundation for the burst of Western imperialism.

Industrialization also redefined the world economy. It increased Western dominance in the economy. It pushed dependant areas, like Latin America, to become even more dependant, in supplying cheap raw materials and foods for export while relying on cheap labor. Slavery and serfdom were increasingly repealed by law, but working conditions typically remained depressed. Areas that previously had profited from world trade while retaining some independence, like China, were now forced to open their economies. Places like India, China, and Latin America, which had previously had flourishing manufacturing sectors, now experienced a "deindustrialization," as Western factory goods flooded the market with cheaper wares.

In the longer run, however, industrialization also pushed many societies to additional kinds of change. Some tried to industrialize outright, in the Western image, and a few succeeded in launching this process before 1914. Others experienced changes in work and leisure patterns, inspired by industrial conditions, even when full industrialization remained elusive; modern European sports, for example, spread more widely than the Industrial Revolution did.

In the ways it transformed the West, in inspiring efforts to change, and in forcing new relationships on literally the entire world, the Industrial Revolution provided the context for most of the fundamental developments of the 1750–1914 period in world history.

Population Movements

 Western industrialization and imperialism led to huge shifts in the population structures of various parts of the world. Both basic dynamics and migration patterns were involved.

In the West, including the United States, the birth rate began to decline to historically low levels. This demographic transition to low birth rates reflected the fact that child labor was being displaced by machines; children were far less useful than they had been in agricultural societies. But high birth rates continued elsewhere in the world, and new public health measures began to reduce the death rates. The West's percentage of total world population began to slip by 1900 even as the West's world power reached its brief peak.

Industrialization drew workers from populous agricultural regions to the new factory centers. European areas that were slow to industrialize, especially in southern and eastern Europe, sent hundreds of thousands of immigrants to centers in Germany and France and especially to the United States, Australia, and Canada. Italian, Portuguese, and Spanish immigrants also flooded to the more prosperous Latin American nations in the late 19th century. The slave trade from Africa was ended under British leadership early in the 19th century; only a trickle continued, mainly to the Middle East. Humanitarian considerations, as well as the new ability of industrial factories to organize free workers more effectively for production, fed this development.

Various immigration patterns arose to replace the slave trade. Asian and European immigrants were recruited. New Asian minorities became important factors in various parts of the world, beginning a pattern that continued in the 20th century. Though not slaves, most immigrants were poorly paid and often were restricted by harsh contracts and forced to pay inflated prices at company-owned stores. Many Asian immigrants, replacing former slave labor, were signed to restrictive indentures. Others served as shopkeepers and other commercial agents in their new societies.

Diversity in the Age of Western Dominance

 Industrialization and Western power shaped the 19th century, but they did not homogenize it. Reactions varied, as did regional patterns and initiatives.

Western industrialization and imperialist expansion were not the only major developments in the world between 1750 and 1914. A major surge of popular conversion to Islam began in sub-Saharan Africa at the end of the 18th century, marking an important shift in the continent's religious map. Latin American nations, for the most part winning freedom from Spain and Portugal by the 1820s after a series of wars for independence, launched an important process of new nation building. Significant developments elsewhere echoed more traditional themes. Thus, in China, major social unrest in the mid-19th century recalled earlier periods of dynastic decline in which rural elements rose against the hardships caused by population pressure and unchecked control by landlords.

From the global standpoint, the principal complexity in describing the period from 1750 to 1914 lies in detailing the diverse reactions to the growth of Western military and industrial might. One reaction was incorporation into an expanded Western civilization. The West enlarged during the 19th century through the emergence of strong immigrant societies in the United States, Canada, Australia, and New Zealand, each with its own important modifications of basic Western patterns.

Two societies, Russia and Japan, underwent dramatic internal change, imitating key Western gains without becoming entirely Western. China and the Ottoman Empire both lost territories to Western imperialism but preserved a degree of independence amid growing weakness, outside interference, and agonizing indecision about the most effective way to counter the challenge from the West. Latin American nations that were newly independent also grappled with reform currents, but under intense economic constraints.

Most of the rest of the world, including north Africa, was colonized outright. Colonial rule was not a constant, having somewhat different effects in India, for example, than in Africa, where imperialism was a later arrival and where a harsher racism characterized Western policy.

The different reactions to the industrial, imperialist West affected traditional civilization alignments. The growing gap between Japan and China is a case in point. Increasingly, however, industrialization became the world's dividing force. Societies that industrialized at least to a significant extent gained in wealth. This included the West, but also settler societies like the United States and Australia. Societies that were impeded in industrialization, for whatever combination of factors, often saw wealth decline, pressed by new population growth and falling prices for raw materials. By 1914, a few societies hovered in the middle—notably, Japan and Russia—able to begin industrialization and maintain full independence, but not yet secure in new prosperity.

Major Themes Transformed

 One indication of the global power of industrialization was the recasting of some crucial human themes in world history. Humankind's relationship to nature shifted decisively.

New machines and higher population densities intensified human ability to change the environment, often for the worse. In addition to industrial and urban pollution, food needs prompted farmers and estate owners elsewhere to cut down forests and to plant crops not compatible with local soil conditions. Rubber trees, spread widely in Brazil from their native home in southeast Asia, caused massive erosion; so did the spread of palm plantations (used for vegetable oil) in Africa.

New transportation and worldwide trade and military pressures made isolation more difficult for any civilization (although renewed efforts surfaced after 1918). With contacts and growing Western dominance also came new forms of international relations. Independent nations began to exchange diplomatic representatives worldwide. Furthermore, from the 1860s onward, international agencies arose for the first time, setting rules for such matters as postal exchange and commercial licensing across national boundaries. These agencies, soon joined by other groups such as the Red Cross and a new Olympic committee, were long dominated by the West, but they created unprecedented conduits for relationships between states.

Industrialization had complex effects on social and economic inequality. Inequality between regions increased: the standard of living in Mexico was about two-thirds as high as that in the United States in 1800, and had dropped to one-third by 1900. Inequality within many societies also increased with the spread of wage labor. On the other hand, the most blatant forced labor systems, including slavery, were abolished in this period. Legal equality increased, but other, more complex forms of inequality persisted. Gender relations took on new dimensions, and they continued to vary between societies. Machines and male labor replaced or devalued women's work in many settings; one clear indicator was the worldwide rise of female domestic servants. Yet new Western beliefs began to idealize women in other respects, giving them unprecedented credit for beauty and moral purity.

The sweeping forces of industrialization and imperialism reduced human agency in some regards. Many people had to do work or accept rulers they neither liked nor chose. Even peasants were subjected to new taxes and pressure to change the ways they produced food. In some cases, technology gained supremacy over human agency. A French factory owner every week put a garland of flowers on the machine that had been most productive, offering the workers nothing at all. Yet human agency was not entirely crushed. Most groups of workers, immigrants, or colonial laborers managed to preserve or invent some rituals and values that gave them a certain identity. Nevertheless, the question of human agency for all but the very rich and powerful became more complex in the 19th century.

Globalization

 By the end of the 19th century, interconnections among all parts of the world had intensified to a level never before experienced in world history. No significant society was isolated from the forces involved.

New technologies—the telegraph, steamship, railroad, and, by 1900, radios and telephones linked by undersea cables—provided the basis for unprecedented speed and volume in global trade and communication. The opening of the Suez and then the Panama canals (1869 and 1914, respectively) added greatly to the speed of global travel. Many corporations, though based in western Europe or the United States, now had branch production outlets in Latin America, Russia, east Asia, and elsewhere. These international companies avidly sought both raw materials and markets around the world.

Political responses to globalization lagged behind technology and commerce. Nevertheless, key international agreements from the 1860s onward provided arrangements for worldwide postal service as well as international rules governing the treatment of civilians in wartime. An International Court was set up in the Netherlands to deal with disputes, though its effective powers were limited. The establishment of the International Red Cross and the revival of the Olympic games represented other organizational efforts to respond to globalization. Most efforts, to be sure, rested on Western initiative and control; other societies were pressed to join in with little or no voice in the process.

Cultural globalization involved the rapid imitation of European sports, particularly soccer football, which began to spread widely in Latin America, Asia, and Africa from the 1860s onward. By 1914, Hollywood was beginning to establish its role as international film capital, with branch offices around the world. Overall, spurred by Western industrialization and imperialism, an imposing network of global contacts and impacts was coming into play.

I. What was the relationship between national-ism on the one hand, and liberalism and conser-vatism on the other in the 18th and 19th centuries? What additional types of documents would help in understanding this relationship?

1. Decree of the revolutionary National Convention in France 1792

Henceforth the French nation proclaims the sovereignty of the people, the suppression of all civil and military authorities which have governed you up to the present, and of all taxes which you sustain, in whatever form they exist; the abolition of the tithe, of feudalism, of seigneurial [feudal] rights . . . of real and personal servitude, of aristocratic hunting and fish-ing privileges, [labor service and all manorial taxes], and gen-erally of every species of contributions with which you have been burdened by your usurpers; it proclaims also the aboli-tion among you of all prerogatives and privileges that are con-trary to equality. You are henceforth, brothers and friends, all citizens, all equal in rights, and all equally summoned to gov-ern, to serve, and to defend your *Patrie* [fatherland].

2. Prussian government proclamation rousing the people against Napoleon 1813

Brandenburgers, Prussians, Silesians, Pomeranians, Lithuani-ans! You know what you have borne for the past seven years; you know the sad fate that awaits you if we do not bring this war to an honorable end. Think of the times gone by,—of the Great Elector, the great Frederick! Remember the blessings for which your forefathers fought under their leadership and which they paid for with their blood,—freedom of conscience, national honor, independence, commerce, industry, learning.

Great sacrifices will be demanded from every class of the peo-ple, for our undertaking is a great one, and the number and resources of our enemies far from insignificant. But would you not rather make these sacrifices for the fatherland and for your own rightful king than for a foreign ruler, who, as he has shown by many examples, will use you and your sons and your uttermost farthing for ends which are nothing to you?

3. Speech of Simón Bolívar to the Legislature of Venezuela after Independence 1819

All our moral powers will not suffice to save our infant repub-lic from this chaos unless we fuse the mass of the people, the government, the legislation, and the national spirit into a uni-fied single body. Unity, unity, unity must be our motto in all things. The blood of our citizens is varied: let it be mixed for the sake of unity. Our constitution has divided our powers of government: let them be bound together to secure unity. Our laws are but a sad relic of ancient and modern despotism. Let this monstrous edifice crumble and fall; and, having removed even its ruins, let us erect a temple to Justice; and, guided, by its sacred inspiration, let us write a code of Venezuelan laws.

4. Speech of the Mexican intellectual Gabino Barreda c. 1867

Fellow citizens: in the future let our motto be Liberty, Order, and Progress; Liberty as means; Order as a base, and Progress as an end; it is a triple motto represented by the tricolor on our beautiful flag, that same flag which became in 1821 a blessed emblem of our independence . . . the emblem which . . . assured the future of America and the world by rescuing republican institutions.

In the future, may a complete freedom of conscience and an absolute freedom of expression permitting all ideas and inspir-ations, concede an enlightenment everywhere and make all disturbance not spiritual and all revolution which is not merely intellectual, unnecessary and impossible. May the physical order, conserved and maintained by all governors and respected by the governed, be a sure guarantor and the best way forever along the florid path of progress and civilization.

5. Slavic nationalist Nikolai Danilevsky c. 1869

In the socio-economic sphere, Russia is the only large state which has solid ground under its feet, in which there are no landless masses, and in which, consequently, the social edifice does not rest on the misery of the majority of the citizens and on the insecurity of their situation. In Russia only there can-not and does not exist any contradiction between political and economic ideals. This contradiction threatens disaster to Euro-pean life, a life which has embarked on its historical voyage in the dangerous seas between . . . military despotism and . . . social revolution. The factors that give such superiority to the Russian social structure over the European, and give it an unshakable stability, are the peasant's land and its common ownership. On this health of Russia's socio-economic struc-ture we found our hope for the great socio-economic signif-icance of the Slav cultural-historical type. This type has been able for the first time to create a just and normal system of human activity, which embraces not only human relations in the moral and political sphere, but also man's mastery of nature, which is a means of satisfying human needs and requirements. Thus it establishes not only formal equality in the relations between citizens, but a real and concrete equal-ity. Under the wise authority of our Emperor, Russians ben-efit from political order, not the corrupt agitation of Western politicians.

II. How did leaders in Europe, the United States, and Japan justify the expansion of educational opportunity in the 19th century? What additional types of documents would assist in this evaluation?

1. France: Writings of Albertine-Adrienne Necker de Saussure 838

But this part of our celestial nature which education should constantly seek to bring out, man has scarcely taken into account. He has had this life only in view, and has shut his eyes upon whatever limited his rights here. He has seen only the wife in the woman—in the young girl only the future wife. All the faculties, the qualities which have no immediate relation to his interests, have seemed to him worthless. Yet there are many of the gifts bestowed upon woman that have no relation to the state of a wife. This state, although natural, is not necessary—perhaps half the women who now exist, have not been, or are no longer, married. In the indigent classes, the girl who is able to maintain herself, quits her parents, and supports herself by industry for a long time, perhaps for life, without requiring aid from man. No social arrangements oblige her to become dependent. It is therefore important, that education should unfold in the young girl the qualities which give the surest promise of wisdom, happiness, usefulness, and dignity, whatever may be her lot. . . .

2. Reform leader Horace Mann's *The Goals of Education* c. 1840

One of the highest and most valuable objects, to which the influences of a school can be made conducive, consists in training our children to self-government. . . . So tremendous, too, are the evils of anarchy and lawlessness, that a government by mere force, however arbitrary and cruel, has been preferable to no-government. But self-government, self-control, a voluntary compliance with the laws of reason and duty, have been justly considered as the highest point of excellence attainable by a human being. No one, however, can consciously obey the laws of reason and duty, until he understands them. Hence the preliminary necessity of their being clearly explained, of their being made to stand out, broad, lofty, and as conspicuous as a mountain against a clear sky. There may be blind obedience without a knowledge of the law, but only of the will of the lawgiver; but the first step towards rational obedience is a knowledge of the rule to be obeyed, and of the reasons on which it is founded.

3. United States: Eliza Duffy on Education 1874

If there is really a radical mental difference in men and women founded upon sex, you *cannot* educate them alike, however much you try. If women *cannot* study unremittingly, why then they *will* not, and you *cannot make them*. But because they do, because they choose so to do, because they will do so in spite of you, should be accepted as evidence that they can, and, all other things being equal, can with impunity. Instead of our race dying out through these women, they are the hope of the country—the women with broad chests, large limbs and full veins, perfect muscular and digestive systems and harmonious sexual organs, who will keep pace with men either in a foot or an intellectual race, who know perfectly their own powers and are not afraid to tax them to their utmost, knowing as they do that action generates force. These are the mothers of the coming race. . . . The result will be truly "the survival of the fittest."

4. Japan: Imperial Rescript on Education 1890

Our Imperial Ancestors have founded Our Empire on a basis broad and everlasting, and have deeply and firmly implanted virtue; Our subjects ever united in loyalty and filial piety have from generation to generation illustrated the beauty thereof. This is the glory of the fundamental character of Our Empire, and herein also lies the source of Our education. Ye, Our subjects, . . . pursue learning and cultivate arts; and thereby develop intellectual faculties and perfect moral powers; furthermore advance public good and promote common interests; always respect the Constitution and observe the laws; should emergency arise, offer yourselves courageously to the State; and thus guard and maintain the prosperity of Our Imperial Throne coeval with heaven and earth. So shall ye not only be Our good and faithful subjects, but render illustrious the best traditions of our forefathers.

5. Japan: Educational reformer Yukichi Fukuzawa's *Autobiography* 1899

In the education of the East, so often saturated with Confucian teaching, I find two things lacking; that is to say, a lack of studies in the number and reason in material culture, and a lack of the idea of independence in spiritual culture. But in the West I think I see why their states then are successful in managing their national affairs, and the businessmen in theirs, and the people generally ardent in their patriotism and happy in their family circles.

I regret that in our country I have to acknowledge that people are not formed on these two principles, though I believe no one can escape the laws of number and reason, nor can anyone depend on anything but the doctrine of independence as long as nations are to exist and mankind is to thrive. Japan could not assert herself among the great nations of the world without full recognition of these two principles. And I reasoned that Chinese philosophy as the root of education was responsible for our obvious shortcomings.

CHAPTER 23

THE EMERGENCE OF INDUSTRIAL SOCIETY IN THE WEST, 1750–1914

Romantic painters delighted in evocative scenes and a mysterious Gothic presence, as depicted by John Constable in The Cornfields.

- The Age of Revolution
- **VISUALIZING THE PAST:** The French Revolution in Cartoon
- The Consolidation of the Industrial Order, 1850–1914
- **DOCUMENT:** Women in the Industrial Revolution
- Cultural Transformations
- Western Settler Societies
- **IN DEPTH:** The United States in World History
- Diplomatic Tensions and World War I
- **GLOBAL CONNECTIONS:** Industrial Europe and the World

Two themes dominate the complex history of Western society between 1750 and 1914, both operating within the unfolding of the **Industrial Revolution.** Political upheaval was most obvious, highlighted by the age of revolution, 1775–1848. The second theme involved the exportation of western European institutions and values to settler societies such as the United States and Australia, which expanded Western civilization's geographic range.

Change is measured by befores and afters. In 1750, western Europe consisted almost entirely of monarchies. By 1914 many monarchies had been overthrown, and everywhere powerful parliaments, based on extensive voting systems, defined much of the political apparatus. In 1750, North America was a minor player in Western and world history. By 1914, the United States and other settler societies made an increasing mark on the economy and politics of the West.

In the century and a half after 1750, Western society went through a dizzying series of disruptions. Dramatic new cultural styles developed, some challenging 18th-century Enlightenment thought and some building on it through scientific research or political theory. A host of diplomatic upheavals accompanied internal change. New states rose to power—Germany and the United States were particularly noteworthy—and at the end of the period, a new alliance system brought the West to a catastrophic war.

The best way to untangle the complexity of the Western transformation is to proceed historically—that is, to identify key subperiods within the longer span. These subperiods involve a growing crisis, late in the 18th century, that helped create changes in a variety of areas from sex to machinery; then a phase of experimentation, from roughly 1775 to 1850, in which political revolution vied for attention with the first phases of the industrialization process; and finally, from 1850 to 1914, a more mature stage in which the implications of industrial society were more fully worked out.

Optimism in Chaos

In 1793, a French aristocrat, the Marquis de Condorcet, was hiding from the dominant party of the French Revolution. He had not voted to execute the French king, and his life was in danger as a result. While in hiding, he wrote a book on the "Progress of the Human Mind," demonstrating that progress had become inevitable in the modern world because of growing education and wider literacy; mankind was on the verge of virtual perfection. After eight months of hiding, Condorcet was caught and put in jail, where he died. His last years testify to the harsh downside of political upheaval in modern Europe, but also to the firm hold of hope in better things to come.

1700 C.E.	1820 C.E.	1840 C.E.	1860 C.E.
1730 ff. Massive population rise	**1820** Revolutions in Greece and Spain; rise of liberalism and nationalism	**1840** Union act reorganizes Canada, provides elected legislature	**1860–1870** Second Maori War
c. 1770 James Watt's steam engine; beginning of Industrial Revolution	**1820s ff.** Industrialization in United States	**1843–1848** First Maori War in New Zealand	**1861–1865** American Civil War
1788 First convict settlement in Australia	**1823** First legislative council in Australia	**1846–1848** Mexican-American War	**1863** Emancipation of slaves
1789 Washington, first president of the United States	**1826–1837** Active European colonization begins in New Zealand	**1848 ff.** Writings of Karl Marx; rise of socialism	**1864–1871** German unification
1789–1799 French Revolution	**1829** Jackson, seventh president of United States	**1848–1849** European revolutions	**1867** British North America Act, unites eastern and central Canada
1790 ff. Beginning of per capita birthrate decline (United States)	**1830, 1848** Revolutions in several European countries	**1850** Australia's Colonies Government Act allows legislature and more autonomy	**1870–1879** Institution of French Third Republic
1793 First free European settlers in Australia	**1832** Reform Bill of 1832 (England)	**1852** New constitution in New Zealand; elected councils	**1870s ff.** Rapid birth rate decline
1793–1794 Radical phase	**1837** Rebellion in Canada	**1859** Darwin's *Origin of Species*	**1870s ff.** Spread of compulsory education laws
1799–1815 Reign of Napoleon	**1837–1842** United States–Canada border clashes	**1859–1870** Unification of Italy	**1871–1914** High point of European imperialism
1800–1850 Romanticism in literature and art	**1839** New British colonial policy allows legislature and more autonomy		**1879–1907** Alliance system: Germany-Austria (1879); Germany-Austria-Russia (1881); Germany-Italy-Austria (1882); France-Russia (1891); Britain-France (1904); Britain-Russia (1907)
1803 Louisiana Purchase (United States)			
1810–1826 Rise of democratic suffrage in United States.			
1815 Congress of Vienna; more conservative period			

The Age of Revolution

 Even before industrialization, new ideas and social pressures caused a series of political revolutions, beginning with the American Revolution in 1775. The French Revolution of 1789 had an impact throughout Europe and beyond and encouraged new movements of liberalism and nationalism. Lesser revolutions followed in 1820 and 1830.

Against the backdrop of intellectual challenge, commercial growth, and population pressure, the placid politics of the 18th century were shattered by the series of revolutions that took shape in the 1770s and 1780s. This was the eve of the **age of revolution,** a period of political upheaval beginning roughly with the American Revolution in 1775 and continuing through the French Revolution of 1789 and other movements for change up to 1848. The wave of revolutions caught up many social groups with diverse motives, some eager to use revolution to promote further change and some hoping to turn back the clock and recover older values.

Forces of Change

Three forces were working to shatter Europe's calm by the mid-18th century. The first of the forces was cultural, for intellectual ferment was running high.

Enlightenment thinkers challenged regimes that did not grant full religious freedom or that insisted on aristocratic privilege, and a few called for widespread popular voice in government. Jean-Jacques Rousseau argued for government based on a general will, and this could be interpreted as a plea for democratic voting. A gap had opened between leading intellectuals and established institutions, and this played a role in the revolutions that lay ahead. Enlightenment thinkers also encouraged economic and technological change and policies that would promote industry; manufacturers and political reformers alike could take inspiration from these ideas.

Along with cultural change, ongoing commercialization continued to stir the economy. Businesspeople, gaining new wealth, might well challenge the idea that aristocrats alone should hold the highest political offices. They certainly were growing interested in new techniques that might spur production. Commercial practices might also draw attack, from artisans or peasant villagers who preferred older economic values. This could feed revolution as well.

A final source of disruption was occurring more quietly at all social levels. Western Europe experienced a huge population jump after about 1730. Within half a century, the population of France rose by 50 percent; that of Britain and Prussia rose 100 percent. This **population revolution** was caused by better border policing by the efficient nation-state

1880 c.e.	**1900 c.e.**
1880s ff. High point of Impressionism in art	**1901** Commonwealth of Australia, creates national federation
1881–1914 Canadian Pacific Railway	**1907** New Zealand dominion status in British Empire
1881–1889 German social insurance laws enacted	**1912–1913** Balkan Wars
1882 United States excludes Chinese immigrants	**1914** Beginning of World War I
1891–1898 Australia and New Zealand restrict Asian immigration	**1917** United States enters World War I
1893 Women's suffrage in New Zealand	
1898 Spanish-American War; United States acquires Puerto Rico, Guam, Philippines	
1898 United States annexes Hawaii	
1899 United States acquires part of Samoa	

governments, which reduced the movement of disease-bearing animals. More important was improved nutrition resulting from the growing use of the potato. These factors reduced the death rate, particularly for children; instead of more than 40 percent of all children dying by age 2, the figure by the 1780s was closer to 33 percent. More children surviving also meant more people living to have children of their own, so the birth rate increased as well.

Population pressure at this level always has dramatic impact. Upper-class families, faced with more surviving children, tried to tighten their grip on existing offices. In the late 18th century, it became harder for anyone who was not an aristocrat to gain a high post in the church or state. This reaction helped feed demands for change by other groups. Above all, population pressure drove many people into the working class as they lost any real chance of inheriting property, creating new motives for protest.

The population growth of the 18th century prompted a rapid expansion of domestic manufacturing in western Europe and, by 1800, in the United States. Hundreds of thousands of people became full- or part-time producers of textile and metal products, working at home but in a capitalist system in which materials, work orders, and sales depended on urban merchants. This development has been called **proto-industrialization,** and it ultimately encouraged new technologies to expand production further because

of the importance of new market relationships and manufacturing volume.

Population upheaval and the spread of a propertyless class that worked for money wages had a sweeping impact on a variety of behaviors in Western society, including North America. Many villagers began to change their dress to more urban styles; this suggests an early form of new consumer interest. Premarital sex increased, and out-of-wedlock births rose to 10 percent of all births. Among groups with little or no property, parental authority began to decline because the traditional threat of denying inheritance had no meaning. Youthful independence became more marked, and although this was particularly evident in economic behavior as many young people looked for jobs on their own, the new defiance of authority might have had political implications as well.

The American Revolution

When Britain's Atlantic colonies rebelled in 1775, it was primarily a war for independence rather than a full-fledged revolution. A large minority of American colonists resisted Britain's attempt to impose new taxes and trade controls on the colonies after 1763. Many settlers also resented restrictions on movement into the frontier areas. The colonists also invoked British political theory to argue that they should not be taxed without representation. The Stamp Act of 1765, imposing taxes on documents and pamphlets, particularly roused protest against British tyranny. Other grievances were involved. Crowding along the eastern seaboard led some younger men to seek new opportunities, including political office, that turned them against the older colonial leadership. Growing commerce antagonized some farmers and artisans, who looked for ways to defend the older values of greater social equality and community spirit.

With the start of the **American Revolution,** colonial rebels set up a new government, which issued the Declaration of Independence in 1776 and authorized a formal army to pursue its war. The persistence of the revolutionaries was combined with British military blunders and significant aid from the French government, designed to embarrass its key enemy. After several years of fighting, the United States won its freedom and, in 1789, set up a new constitutional structure based on Enlightenment principles, with checks and balances between the legislature and the executive branches of government, and formal guarantees of individual liberties. Voting rights, though limited, were widespread, and the new regime was for a time the most advanced in the world. Socially, the revolution accomplished less; slavery was untouched.

Crisis in France in 1789

The next step in the revolutionary spiral occurred in France. It was the **French Revolution** that most clearly set in motion the political restructuring of western Europe. Several factors combined in the 1780s in what became a classic pattern of revolutionary causation. Ideological insistence on change won increasing attention from the mid-18th century onward, as Enlightenment thinkers urged the need to limit the powers of the Catholic church, the aristocracy, and the monarchy. Social changes reinforced the ideological challenge. Some middle-class people, proud of their business or professional success, wanted a greater political role. Many peasants, pressed by population growth, wanted fuller freedom from landlords' demands.

The French government and upper classes proved incapable of reform. Aristocrats tightened their grip in response to their own population pressure, and the government proved increasingly ineffective—a key ingredient in any successful revolution. Finally, a sharp economic slump in 1787 and 1788, triggered by bad harvests, set the seal on revolution.

The French king, **Louis XVI,** called a meeting of the traditional parliament to consider tax reform for his financially pinched regime. But middle-class representatives, inspired by Enlightenment ideals, insisted on turning this assembly (which had not met for a century and a half) into a modern parliament, with voting by head and with majority representation for nonnoble property owners. The fearful king caved in after some street riots in Paris in the summer of 1789, and the revolution was under way.

Events that summer were crucial. The new assembly, with its middle-class majority, quickly turned to devising a new political regime. A stirring *Declaration of the Rights of Man and the Citizen* proclaimed freedom of thought. Like the American Declaration of Independence, this law enacted natural rights to "liberty, property, security, and resistance to oppression" and specifically guaranteed free expression of ideas. A popular riot stormed a political prison, the Bastille, on July 14, in what became the revolution's symbol; ironically, almost no prison-

ers were there. Soon after this, peasants seized manorial records and many landed estates. This triggered a general proclamation abolishing manorialism, giving peasants clear title to much land and establishing equality under the law. Although aristocrats survived for some time, the principles of aristocratic rule were undercut. The privileges of the church were also attacked, and church property was seized. A new constitution proclaimed individual rights, including freedom of religion, press, and property. A strong parliament was set up to limit the king, and about one-half the adult male population—those with property—were eligible to vote.

The French Revolution: Radical and Authoritarian Phases

By 1792, the initial push for reform began to turn more radical. Early reforms provoked massive opposition in the name of church and aristocracy, and civil war broke out in several parts of France. Monarchs in Britain, Prussia, and Austria trumpeted their opposition to the revolution, and France soon moved toward European war as well. These pressures led to a takeover by radical leaders, who wanted to press the revolution forward and to set up firmer authority in the revolution's defense. The radicals abolished the monarchy. The king was decapitated on the **guillotine,** a new device introduced, Enlightenment-fashion, to provide more humane executions, but instead it became a symbol of revolutionary bloodthirst. The radicals also executed several thousand opponents in what was named the Reign of Terror, even though by later standards it was mild.

The leader of the radical phase was Maximilien Robespierre (1758–1794), a classic example of a revolutionary ideologue. Born into a family of lawyers, he gained his law degree in 1781 and soon was publishing Enlightenment-style political tracts. The new philosophies inspired passion in Robespierre, particularly the democratic ideas of Rousseau. Elected to all the initial revolutionary assemblies, Robespierre headed the prosecution of the king in 1792 and then took over the leadership of government. He put down many factions, sponsored the Terror, and worked to centralize the government. In 1794, he set up a civic religion, the "cult of the Supreme Being," to replace Catholicism. Personally incorruptible, Robespierre came to symbolize the single-minded revolutionary, although he shied away from significant social reforms that might have drawn

Visualizing the Past

The French Revolution in Cartoons

This cartoon, titled *The Former Great Dinner of the Modern Gargantua with His Family*, appeared in 1791 or 1792, as the French Revolution was becoming more radical. It pictures the king and his wife as latter-day Gargantuas, referring to a French literary figure who was a notoriously great eater.

Questions: How does the cartoon characterize the relationship between French society and economy and the monarchy? What social structure is implied? What conclusions might readers of the cartoon draw about what should happen to the monarchy? With improvements in printing and literacy, cartoons were becoming more available, and they have continued to be important into the present day. Why were they effective as a means of communicating ideas? Did they spur people to action, or might they deflect action by provoking a good laugh?

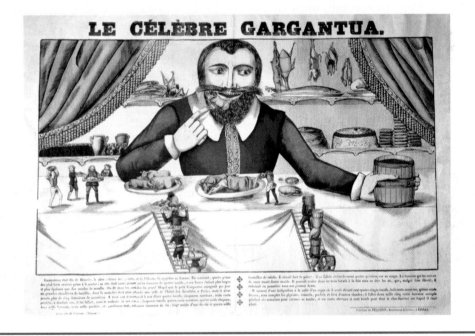

urban support. He was convinced that he knew the people's will, but opposition mounted, and when he called for yet another purge of moderate leaders he was arrested and guillotined on the same day, abandoned by the popular factions that had once spurred him on.

While in power, Robespierre and his colleagues pushed revolutionary reforms. A new constitution, never fully put into practice, proclaimed universal adult male suffrage. The radicals introduced a metric system of weights and measures, the product of the rationalizing genius of the Enlightenment. Slavery was abolished in the French colonies, though this measure was reversed after the radical regime collapsed. Robespierre and his allies also proclaimed universal military conscription, arguing that men who were free citizens owed loyalty and service to the government. And revolutionary armies began to win major success. Not only were France's enemies driven out, but the regime began to acquire new territory in the Low Countries, Italy, and Germany, spreading revolutionary gains farther in western Europe.

A new spirit of popular **nationalism** surfaced during the revolution's radical phase. Many French people felt an active loyalty to the new regime—to a state they believed they had helped create. A new symbol was a revolutionary national anthem (the world's first), with its rousing first lines, "Come, children of the nation, the day of glory has arrived." Nationalism could replace older loyalties to church or locality.

The fall of the radicals led to four years of moderate policies. Then in 1799 the final phase of the revolution was ushered in with the victory of **Napoleon Bonaparte,** a leading general who soon converted the revolutionary republic to an authoritarian empire. Napoleon reduced the parliament to a rubber stamp, and a powerful police system limited freedom of expression. However, Napoleon confirmed other liberal gains, including religious freedom, while enacting substantial equality—though for men, not women—in a series of new law codes. To train bureaucrats, Napoleon developed a centralized system of secondary schools and universities.

Driven by insatiable ambition, Napoleon devoted most of his attention to expansion abroad (Map 23.1). A series of wars brought France against all of Europe's major powers, including Russia. At its height, about 1812, the French Empire directly held or controlled as satellite kingdoms most of western Europe, and its success spurred some reform measures even in Prussia and Russia. The French Empire crumbled after this point. An attempt to invade Russia in 1812 failed miserably. French armies perished in the cold Russian winter even as they pushed deep into the empire. An alliance system organized by Britain crushed the emperor definitively in 1814 and 1815. Yet Napoleon's campaigns had done more than dominate European diplomacy for one and a half decades. They had also spread key revolutionary legislation—the idea of equality under the law and the attack on privileged institutions such as aristocracy, church, and craft guilds—throughout much of western Europe.

The revolution and Napoleon encouraged popular nationalism outside of France as well as within.

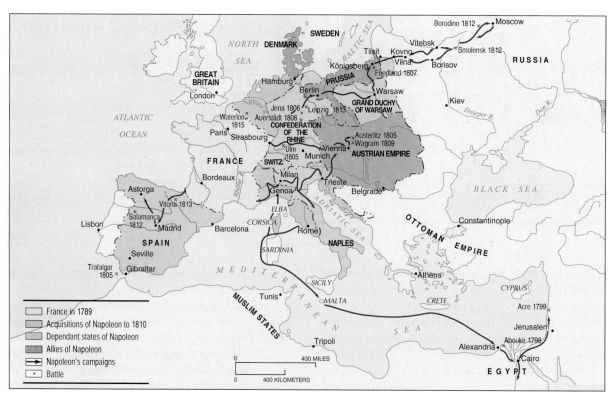

Map 23.1 *Napoleon's Empire in 1812. By this point, France dominated Europe to the borders of Russia, whose cold winters would weaken Napoleon's army. Napoleon's redrawing of satellite states stoked nationalist fervor, particularly in Italy and Germany.*

French military success continued to draw great excitement at home. Elsewhere, French armies tore down local governments, as in Italy and Germany, which whetted appetites there for greater national unity. And the sheer fact of French invasion made many people more conscious of loyalty to their own nations; popular resistance to Napoleon, in parts of Spain and Germany, played a role in the final French defeat.

A Conservative Settlement and the Revolutionary Legacy

The allies who had brought the proud French emperor down met at Vienna in 1815 to reach a peace settlement that would make further revolution impossible. Diplomats at the **Congress of Vienna** did not try to punish France too sternly, on the grounds that the European balance of power should be restored. Still, a series of stronger powers was established around France, which meant gains for Prussia within Germany and for the hitherto obscure nation of Piedmont in northern Italy. The old map was not restored, and the realignments ultimately facilitated national unifications. Britain gained new colonial territories, confirming its lead in the scramble for empire in the wider world. Russia, newly important in European affairs, maintained its hold over most of Poland.

These territorial adjustments kept Europe fairly stable for almost half a century—a major achievement, given the crisscrossed rivalries that had long characterized Western society. But the Vienna negotiators were much less successful in promoting internal peace. The idea was to restore monarchy in France and to link Europe's major powers in defense of churches and kings. This was a key statement of the growing movement of **conservatives** in Europe, who defined themselves in opposition to revolutionary goals.

But political movements arose to challenge conservatism. They involved concrete political agitation, but also an explosion of ideals. Many of the ideals would resonate in many parts of the world during the 19th and 20th centuries. **Liberals** focused primarily on issues of political structure. They looked for ways to limit state interference in individual life and urged representation of propertied people in government. Liberals touted the importance of constitutional rule and protection for freedoms of religion, press, and assembly. Largely representing the growing middle class, many liberals also sought economic reforms, including better education, which would promote industrial growth.

Radicals accepted the importance of most liberal demands, but they also wanted wider voting rights. Some advocated outright democracy. They also urged some social reforms in the interest of the lower classes. A smaller current of socialism urged an attack on private property in the name of equality and an end to capitalist exploitation of workers. Nationalists, often allied with liberalism or radicalism, urged the importance of national unity and glory.

Political protest found support among students and among urban artisans, concerned about economic changes that might displace craft skills. Revolutions broke out in several places in 1820 and again in 1830. The 1820 revolts involved a nationalist **Greek Revolution** against Ottoman rule—a key step in gradually dismantling the Ottoman Empire in the Balkans—and a rebellion in Spain. Another French Revolution of 1830 installed a different king and a somewhat more liberal monarchy. Uprisings also occurred in key states in Italy and Germany, though without durable result; the Belgian Revolution of 1830 produced a liberal regime and a newly independent nation.

Britain and the United States also participated in the process of political change, though without revolution. Key states in the United States granted universal adult male suffrage (except for slaves) and other political changes in the 1820s, leading to the election of a popular president, Andrew Jackson, in 1828. In Britain, the **Reform Bill of 1832,** a response to popular agitation, gave the parliamentary vote to most middle-class men. By the 1830s, regimes in France, Britain, Belgium, the United States, and several other countries had solid parliaments (Congress in the United States), some guarantees for individual rights against arbitrary state action, religious freedom not only for various Christian sects but also for Jews, and voting systems from democratic (for men) to the upper-middle class plus aristocracy alone.

Industrialization and the Revolutions of 1848

By the 1830s and 1840s, industrialization began to add pressures to Europe's revolutionary ferment. The 1832 Reform Bill in England, for example, responded in part to growing working-class agitation, though it did not extend the vote to workers and led to further political protest. By this time France, Belgium, and Germany, as well as the United States, were fully engaged in the early stages of the Industrial Revolution, based in part on copying British models.

These developments spurred some direct unrest among factory workers. They raised even more concerns among artisans, worried for the future of traditional skilled labor, and these groups provided much of the muscle that went into the final phase of the age of revolution.

Key lower-class groups turned to political protest as a means of compensating for industrial change. Artisans and workers in Britain generated a new movement to gain the vote in the 1830s and 1840s. This **Chartist movement** hoped that a democratic government would regulate new technologies and promote popular education.

The extraordinary wave of revolutions of 1848 and 1849 brought protest to a head. Paris was again the center. In the popular uprising that began in February 1848, the French monarchy was once again expelled, this time for good, and a democratic republic was established briefly. Urban artisans pressed for serious social reform—perhaps some version of socialism, and certainly government-supported jobs for the unemployed. Groups of women schoolteachers agitated for the vote and other rights for women. The social demands were far wider than those of the great uprising of 1789.

Revolution quickly spread to other centers. Major revolts occurred in Germany (Figure 23.1), Austria, and Hungary. Revolutionaries in these areas devised liberal constitutions to modify conservative monarchies, artisans pressed for social reforms that would restrain industrialization, and peasants sought a complete end to manorialism. Revolts in central Europe also pressed for nationalist demands: German nationalists worked for the unity of their country, and various nationalities in Austria–Hungary, including Slavic groups, sought greater autonomy. A similar liberal nationalist revolt occurred in various parts of Italy.

The revolutionary fires burned only briefly. The social demands of artisans and some factory workers were put down quickly; not only conservatives but middle-class liberals opposed these efforts. Nationalist agitation also failed for the moment, as the armies of Austria–Hungary and Prussia restored the status quo to central Europe and Italy. Democracy persisted in France, but a nephew of the great Napoleon soon

Figure 23.1 In 1848, crowds—mainly urban artisans—stormed the military arsenal in Berlin during the last great revolution in the industrial West.

replaced the liberal republic with an authoritarian empire that lasted until 1870. Peasant demands were met, and serfdom was fully abolished throughout western Europe. Many peasants, uninterested in other gains, supported conservative forces.

The substantial failure of the revolutions of 1848 drew the revolutionary era in western Europe to a close. Failure taught many liberals and working-class leaders that revolution was too risky; more gradual methods should be used instead. Improved transportation reduced the chance of food crises, the traditional trigger for revolution in Western history. Bad harvests in 1846 and 1847 had driven up food prices and helped promote insurgency in the cities, but famines of this sort did not recur in the West. Many governments also installed better riot control police.

By 1850, an industrial class structure had come to predominate. Earlier revolutionary gains had reduced the aristocrats' legal privileges, and the rise of business had eroded their economic dominance. With industrialization, social structure came to rest less on privilege and birth and more on money. Key divisions by 1850 pitted middle-class property owners against workers of various sorts. The old alliances that had produced the revolutions were now dissolved.

The Consolidation of the Industrial Order, 1850–1914

 Industrial society developed more fully after 1850 and contained new family and leisure patterns. Political consolidation brought national unifications in Italy and Germany and new constitutions. Governments developed new functions, and the rise of socialism changed the political spectrum.

In most respects, the 65 years after 1850 seemed calmer than the frenzied period of political upheaval and initial industrialization. Railroads and canals linked cities across Europe and spurred industrialization and urbanization (Map 23.2). City growth continued in the West; indeed, several countries, starting with Britain, passed the 50-percent mark in urbanization—the first time in human history that more than a minority of a population lived in cities. City governments began to gain ground on the pressing problems growth had created. Sanitation improved, and death rates fell below birth rates for the first time

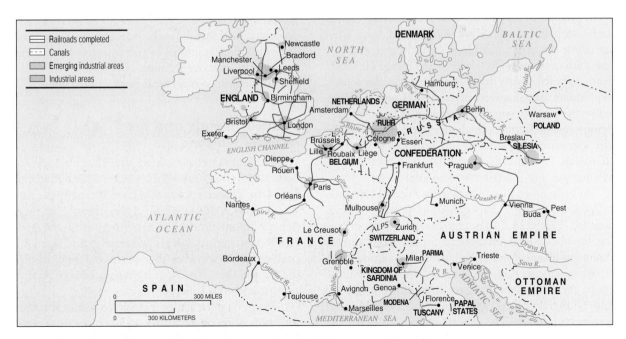

Map 23.2 *Industrialization in Europe, c. 1850. By the mid-19th century, industrialization had spread across Europe, aided by the development of railroad links and canals that brought resources to the new factories and transported their finished goods to world markets.*

in urban history. Parks, museums, effective regulation of food and housing facilities, and more efficient police forces all added to the safety and the physical and cultural amenities of urban life. Revealingly, crime rates began to stabilize or even drop in several industrial areas, a sign of more effective social control but also of a more disciplined population.

Adjustments to Industrial Life

Family life adjusted to industrialization. Birth rates began to drop as Western society began a demographic transition to a new system that promoted fairly stable population levels through a new combination of low birth rates and low death rates. Children were now seen as a source of emotional satisfaction and parental responsibility, not as workers contributing to a family economy. As the Document shows, arguments about women's special family duties gained ground.

Material conditions generally improved after 1850. By 1900, probably two-thirds of the Western population enjoyed conditions above the subsistence level. People could afford a few amenities such as newspapers and family outings, their diet and housing improved, and their health got better. The decades from 1880 to 1920 saw a real revolution in children's health, thanks in part to better hygiene during childbirth and better parental care. Infancy and death separated for the first time in human history: Instead of one-third or more of all children dying by age 10, child death rates fell to less than 10 percent and continued to plummet. The discovery of germs by **Louis Pasteur** led by the 1880s to more conscientious sanitary regulations and procedures by doctors and other health care specialists; this reduced the deaths of women in childbirth. Women began to outlive men by a noticeable margin, but men's health also improved.

In little more than a decade, between 1860 and 1873, the number of corporations in western Europe doubled (Figure 23.2). The rise of corporations, drawing on stockholder investment funds, was a major change in business and organizational life. Important labor movements took shape among industrial workers by the 1890s, with massive strike movements by miners, metalworkers, and others from the United States to Germany. The new trade union movement stressed the massed power of workers. Hosts of labor leaders sprang up amid detested work conditions and political repression. Many workers learned to bargain for better pay and shorter hours.

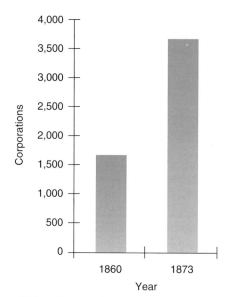

Figure 23.2 *Corporations in western Europe, 1860–1873: The expansion in numbers.*

In the countryside, peasant protests declined. Many European peasants gained a new ability to use market conditions to their own benefit. Some, as in Holland and Denmark, developed cooperatives to market goods and purchase supplies efficiently. Many peasants specialized in new cash crops, such as dairy products. Still more widely, peasants began to send their children to school to pick up new knowledge that would improve farming operations. The traditional isolation of rural areas began to decline.

Political Trends and the Rise of New Nations

Western politics consolidated after the failed revolutions of 1848. Quite simply, issues that had dominated the Western political agenda for many decades were largely resolved within a generation. The great debates about fundamental constitutions and government structure, which had emerged in the 17th century with the rise of absolutism and new political theory and then raged during the decades of revolution, at last grew quiet.

Many Western leaders worked to reduce the need for political revolution after 1850. Liberals decided that revolution was too risky and became more willing to compromise. Key conservatives strove to develop reforms that would save elements of the old regime, including power for the landed aristocracy

Document

Women in the Industrial Revolution

The West's Industrial Revolution changed the situation of women in many ways. Some of the changes have recurred more recently in other civilizations, and others were particularly characteristic of the 19th-century West. Industrialization cut into women's traditional work and protest roles (for example, in spearheading bread riots as attention shifted to work-based strikes), but it tended to expand the educational opportunities for women. Some new work roles and protest outlets, including feminism, developed by 1914. Important changes occurred in the home as well. New ideas and standards elevated women's position and set up more demanding tasks. Relationships between women were also affected by the growing use of domestic servants (the most common urban job for working-class women) and new attitudes of middle- and lower-class women. The first document that follows sketches the idealization of middle-class women; it comes from an American moral tract of 1837, written anonymously, probably by a man. The second document, written by a woman in an English women's magazine, shows new household standards of another sort, with a critical tone also common in middle-class literature. Finally, a British housewife discusses her servant problems, reflecting yet another facet of women's lives. How could women decide what their domestic roles were and whether they brought satisfaction?

Women as Civilizers (1837)

As a sister, she soothes the troubled heart, chastens and tempers the wild daring of the hurt mind restless with disappointed pride or fired with ambition. As a mistress, she inspires the nobler sentiment of purer love, and the sober purpose of conquering himself for virtue's sake. As a wife, she consoles him in grief, animates him with hope in despair, restrains him in prosperity, cheers him in poverty and trouble, swells the pulsations of his throbbing breast that beats for honorable distinction, and rewards his toils with the undivided homage of a grateful heart. In the important and endearing character of mother, she watches and directs the various impulses of unfledged genius, instills into the tender and susceptible mind the quickening seeds of virtue, fits us to brave dangers in time of peril, and consecrates to truth and virtue the best affections of our nature.

Motherhood as Power and Burden (1877)

Every woman who has charge of a household should have a practical knowledge of nursing, simple doctoring and physicianing. The professional doctor must be called in for real illness. But the Home Doctor may do so much to render professional visits very few and far between. And her knowledge will be of infinite value when it is necessary to carry out the doctor's orders....

The Mother Builder

It is a curious fact that architects who design and builders who carry out their plans must have training for this work. But the Mother Builder is supposed to have to know by instinct how to put in each tiny brick which builds up the "human." The result of leaving it to "instinct" is that the child starts out with bad foundations and a jerry-built constitution....

When one considers that one child in every three born dies before the age of five years, it is evident how widespread must be the ignorance as to the feeding and care of these little ones. It is a matter of surprise to those who understand the constitution and needs of infants that, considering the conditions under which the large number of them are reared, the mortality is not greater....

The Risks Babies Run

To begin with, the popular superstition that a young baby must be "hungry" because it lives on milk, and is on this plea the recipient of scraps and bits of vegetables, potato and gravy, crusts, and other heterogeneous articles of diet, has much to answer for. Then, the artistic sense of the mother which leads her to display mottled necks, dimpled arms, and chubby legs, instead of warmly covering these charming portions of baby's anatomy, goes hugely to swell the death-rate. Mistakes in feeding and covering have much to answer for in the high mortality of infants....

The Servant "Problem" (1860)

So we lost Mary, and Peggy reigned in her stead for some six weeks....

But Peggy differed greatly from her predecessor Mary. She was not clean in her person, and my mother declared that her presence was not desirable within a few feet. Moreover she had no notion of putting things in their places, but always left all her working materials in the apartment where they were last used. It was not therefore pleasant, when one wanted a sweeping brush, to have to sit down and think which room Peggy had swept the last, and so on with all the paraphernalia for dusting and scrubbing. But this was not the worst. My mother, accustomed to receive almost reverential respect from her old servants could not endure poor Peggy's familiar ways....

(continued)

Now, though I am quite willing to acknowledge the mutual obligation which exists between the employer and employed, I do not agree with my charwoman that she is the only person who ought to be considered as conferring a favor. I desire to treat her with all kindness, showing every possible regard to her comfort, and I expect from her no more work than I would cheerfully and easily perform in the same time. But when I scrupulously perform my part of the bargain, both as regards food and wages, not to mention much thought and care in order to make things easy for her and which were not in the agreement at all, I think she ought not only to keep faith with me if possible, but to abstain from hinting at the obligation she confers in coming.

It is not pleasant, as my mother says, to beg and pray for the help for which we also pay liberally. But it is worse for my kitchen helper to be continually reminding me that she need not go out unless she likes, and that it was only to oblige me she ever came at all. I do not relish this utter ignoring of her wages, etc., or her being quite deaf because I choose to offer a suggestion as to the propriety of dusting out the corners, or when I mildly hint that I should prefer her doing something in my way....

But if I were to detail all my experiences, I should never have done. I have had many good and willing workers; but few on whose punctuality and regularity I could rely.

Questions: In what ways did industrialization increase differences between women and men in the 19th-century West? What were the main changes in women's roles and ideals? How did middle-class and working-class women differ? These magazine articles were prescriptive, suggesting what women should be like. Middle-class audiences consumed vast amounts of this kind of prescriptive literature from the 19th century onward, as sources of both praise and constructive criticism. Did the women's images projected in these materials bolster or undermine women's position? Would they generate contentment or dissatisfaction among their readers? Finally, do they reflect real life or merely idealized standards (for wives, mothers, and servants)? What are the problems in using prescriptive materials to describe 19th-century women's history?

and the monarchy. A British conservative leader, **Benjamin Disraeli,** took the initiative of granting the vote to working-class men in 1867. **Count Camillo di Cavour,** in the Italian state of Piedmont, began even earlier to support industrial development and extend the powers of the parliament to please liberal forces. In Prussia a new prime minister, **Otto von Bismarck,** similarly began to work with a parliament and to extend the vote to all men (though grouping them in wealth categories that blocked complete democracy). Other Prussian reforms granted freedom to Jews, extended (without guaranteeing) rights to the press, and promoted mass education. The gap between liberal and conservative regimes narrowed in the West, although it remained significant.

The new conservatives also began to use the force of nationalism to win support for the existing social order. Previously, nationalism had been a radical force, challenging established arrangements in the name of new loyalties. Many liberals continued to defend nationalist causes. However, conservative politicians learned how to wrap themselves in the flag, often promoting an active foreign policy in the interest of promoting domestic calm. Thus, British conservatives became champions of expanding the

empire, while in the United States, by the 1890s, the Republican party became increasingly identified with imperialist causes.

The most important new uses of nationalism in the West occurred in Italy and Germany. After wooing liberal support, Cavour formed an alliance with France that enabled him to attack Austrian control of northern Italian provinces in 1858. The war set in motion a nationalist rebellion in other parts of the peninsula that allowed Cavour to unite most of Italy under the Piedmontese king (Map 23.3). This led to a reduction of the political power of the Catholic pope, already an opponent of liberal and nationalist ideas—an important part of the general reduction of church power in Western politics.

Following Cavour's example, Bismarck in Prussia staged a series of wars in the 1860s that expanded Prussian power in Germany. He was a classic diplomatic military strategist, a key example of an individual agent seizing on larger trends such as nationalism to produce results that were far from inevitable. For example, in 1863 Bismarck used the occasion of Danish incorporation of two heavily German provinces, Schleswig and Holstein, to justify the Prussian and Austrian defeat of Denmark. Then he maneuvered a

Map 23.3   *The Unification of Italy. The mid-19th century saw both Italy and Germany fused into single nations, as strong leaders brought together numerous small regional states.*

Map 23.4   *The Unification of Germany, 1815–1871*

pretext for Prussian declaration of war against Austria. In 1866, Prussia emerged as the supreme German power. A final war, against France, led to outright German unity in 1871 (Map 23.4). The new German Empire boasted a national parliament with a lower house based on universal male suffrage and an upper house that favored conservative state governments. This kind of compromise, combined with the dizzying joy of nationalist success, won support for the new regime from most liberals and many conservatives.

Other key political issues were resolved at about the same time. The bloody **American Civil War**—the first war based extensively on industrial weaponry and transport systems, carefully watched by European military observers—was fought between 1861 and 1865. The war resolved by force the simmering dispute over sectional rights between the North and South and also brought an end to slavery in the nation. France, after its defeat by Germany in 1870, overthrew its short-

lived echo of the Napoleonic Empire and established a conservative republic with votes for all men, a reduction of church power, and expansion of education, but no major social reform. Just as conservative Bismarck could be selectively radical, France proved that liberals could be very cautious.

Almost all Western nations now had parliamentary systems, usually democracies of some sort, in which religious and other freedoms were widely protected. In this system, liberal and conservative ministries could alternate without major changes of internal policy. Indeed, Italy developed a process called **trasformismo,** or transformism, in which parliamentary deputies, no matter what platforms they professed, were transformed once in Rome to a single-minded pursuit of political office and support for the status quo.

The Social Question and New Government Functions

The decline of basic constitutional disputes by the 1870s promoted the fuller development of an industrial-style state in the West. A new set of political movements emerged.

Government functions and personnel expanded rapidly throughout the Western world after 1870. All Western governments introduced civil service examinations to test applicants on the basis of talent rather than on connections or birth alone, thus unwittingly imitating Chinese innovations more than a thousand years before. With a growing bureaucracy and improved recruitment, governments began to extend their regulatory apparatus, inspecting factory safety, the health of prostitutes, hospital conditions, and even (through the introduction of passports and border controls) personal travel.

Schooling expanded, becoming generally compulsory up to age 12. Governments believed that education provided essential work skills and the basis for new levels of political loyalty. Many American states by 1900 began also to require high school education, and most Western nations expanded their public secondary school systems. Here was a huge addition to the ways in which governments and individuals interacted. The new school systems promoted literacy; by 1900, 90 to 95 percent of all adults in western Europe and the United States could read. Schools also encouraged certain social agendas. Girls were carefully taught about the importance of home and women's moral mission in domestic science programs. Schools also carefully propounded nationalism, teaching the superiority of the nation's language and history as well as attacking minority or immigrant cultures.

Governments also began to introduce wider welfare measures, replacing or supplementing traditional groups such as churches and families. Bismarck was a pioneer in this area in the 1880s as he tried to wean German workers from their attraction to socialism. His tactic failed, as socialism steadily advanced, but his measures had lasting importance. German social insurance began to provide assistance in cases of accident, illness, and old age. Some measures to aid the unemployed were soon added, initially in Britain. These early welfare programs were small and their utility limited, but they sketched a major extension of government power.

Accompanying the quiet revolution in government functions was a realignment of the political spectrum in the Western world during the late 19th century. Constitutional issues were replaced by social issues—what people of the time called the **social question**—as the key criteria for political partisanship. Socialist and feminist movements surged to the political fore, placing liberals and conservatives in a new defensive posture.

The rise of **socialism** depended above all on the power of grievance of the working class, with allies from other groups. It also reflected a redefinition of political theory by German theorist **Karl Marx.** Early socialist doctrine, from the Enlightenment through 1848, had focused on human perfectibility: Set up a few exemplary communities where work and rewards would be shared, and the evils of capitalism would end. Marx's socialism, worked out between 1848 and 1860, was tough-minded, and he blasted earlier theorists as giddy utopians. Marx saw socialism as the final phase of an inexorable march of history, which could be studied dispassionately and scientifically. History for Marx was shaped by the available means of production and who controlled those means, an obvious reflection of the looming role of technology in the industrial world forming at that time. According to Marx, class struggle always pitted a group out of power with the group controlling the means of production; hence, in the era just passed, the middle class had battled the feudal aristocracy and its hold on the land. Now the middle class had won; it dominated production and, through this, the state and the culture as well. But it had created a new class enemy, the propertyless proletariat, that would grow until revolution became inevitable. Then, after a transitional period in which proletarian dictatorship would clean up the remnants of the bourgeois social order, full freedom would be achieved. People would benefit justly and equally from their work, and the state would wither away; the historic class struggle would at last end because classes would be eliminated.

Marx's vision was a powerful one. It clearly identified capitalist evil. It told workers that their low wages were exploitive and unjust. It urged the need for violent action but also ensured that revolution was part of the inexorable tides of history. The result would be heaven on earth—ultimately, an Enlightenment-like vision of progress.

By the 1860s, when working-class activity began to revive, Marxist doctrine provided encouragement and structure. Marx himself continued to concentrate on ideological development and purity, but leaders in many countries translated his doctrine into practical political parties.

Germany led the way. As Bismarck extended the vote, socialist leaders in the 1860s and 1870s were the first to understand the implications of mass electioneering. Socialist movements provided fiery speakers who courted popular votes. By the 1880s, socialists in Germany were cutting into liberal support, and by 1900, the party was the largest single political force in the nation. Socialist parties in Austria, France, and elsewhere followed a roughly similar course, everywhere emerging as a strong minority force.

The rise of socialism terrified many people in Western society, who took the revolutionary message literally. In combination with major industrial strikes and unionization, it was possible to see social issues portending outright social war. But socialism itself was not unchanging. As socialist parties gained strength they often allied with other groups to achieve more moderate reforms. A movement called **revisionism** arose, which argued that Marx's revolutionary vision was wrong and that success could be achieved by peaceful democratic means. Many socialist leaders denounced revisionism but put their energies into building electoral victories rather than plotting violent revolution.

Socialism was not the only challenge to the existing order. By 1900, powerful **feminist movements** had arisen. These movements sought various legal and economic gains for women, such as equal access to professions and higher education as well as the right to vote. Feminism won support particularly from middle-class women, who argued that the very moral superiority granted to women in the home should be translated into political voice. Many middle-class women also chafed against the confines of their domestic roles, particularly as family size declined. In several countries, feminism combined with socialism, but in Britain, the United States, Australia, and Scandinavia, a separate feminist current arose that petitioned widely and even conducted acts of violence in order to win the vote. Several American states and Scandinavian countries extended the vote to women by 1914, in a pattern that would spread to Britain, Germany, and the whole United States after 1918.

The new feminism, like the labor movement, was no mere abstraction but the fruit of active, impassioned leadership, in this case, largely from the middle classes. Emmeline Pankhurst (1858–1928; Figure 23.3) was typical of the more radical feminist leadership both in background and tactics. Born to a

Figure 23.3 *Emmeline Goulden Pankhurst*

reform-minded English middle-class family, she was active in women's rights issues, as was her husband. She collaborated with Richard Pankhurst, whom she had married in 1879, to work for improvements in women's property rights, and she participated in the Socialist Fabian Society. But then she turned more radical. She formed a suffrage organization in 1903 to seek the vote for women, and with her daughter Christabel sponsored attention-getting public disturbances, including planting a bomb in St. Paul's Cathedral. Window-smashing, arson, and hunger strikes rounded out her spectacular tactical arsenal. Often arrested, she engaged in a huge strike in 1912. The suffragists' support of the war effort in 1914 gained them public sympathy. Pankhurst moved to Canada for a time, leaving the English movement to her daughter, but returned as a respected figure to run for parliament after women had gained the vote in 1928.

Cultural Transformations

 Western culture changed dramatically during the 19th century. Growing emphasis on consumers introduced new values and leisure forms. Science increased its hold but generated a new, complex view of nature, and new artistic movements demonstrated innovation and spontaneity.

Emphasis on Consumption and Leisure

Key developments in popular culture differentiated Western society after 1850 from the decades of initial industrialization. Better wages and the reduction of work hours gave ordinary people new opportunities (Figure 23.4). Alongside the working class grew a large white-collar labor force of secretaries, clerks, and salespeople, who served the growing bureaucracies of big business and the state. These workers, some of them women, adopted many middle-class values, but they also insisted on interesting consumption and leisure outlets. The middle class itself became more open to the idea that pleasure could be legitimate.

Furthermore, the economy demanded change. Factories could now spew out goods in such quantity that popular consumption had to be encouraged simply to keep pace with production. Widespread advertising developed to promote a sense of need where none had existed before. Product crazes emerged.

The bicycle fad of the 1880s, in which middle-class families flocked to purchase the new machine, was the first of many consumer fads in modern Western history. People just had to have them. Bicycles also changed previous social habits, as women needed less cumbersome garments and young couples could out-pedal chaperones during courtship.

Mass leisure culture began to emerge. Popular newspapers, with bold headlines and compelling human interest stories, won millions of subscribers in the industrial West. They featured shock and entertainment more than appeals to reason or political principle. Crime, imperialist exploits, sports, and even comics became the items of the day. Popular theater soared. Comedy routines and musical revues drew thousands of patrons to music halls; after 1900, some of these entertainment themes dominated the new medium of motion pictures. Vacation trips became increasingly common, and seaside resorts grew to the level of big business.

The rise of team sports readily expressed the complexities of the late 19th-century leisure revolution. Here was another Western development that soon had international impact. Soccer, American football, and baseball surged into new prominence at both amateur and professional levels. These new sports reflected industrial life. Though based on traditional games, they were organized by means of rules and umpires. They taught the virtues of coordination and discipline and could be seen as useful preparation for work or military life. They were suitably commercial: Sports equipment, based on the ability to mass-produce rubber balls, and professional teams and stadiums quickly became major businesses. But sports also expressed impulse and violence. They expressed irrational community loyalties and even, as the Olympic games were reintroduced in 1896, nationalist passions.

Overall, new leisure interests suggested a complex set of attitudes on the part of ordinary people in Western society. They demonstrated growing secularism. Religion still counted among some groups, but religious practice had declined as people increasingly looked for worldly entertainments. Many people would have agreed that progress was possible on this earth through rational planning and individual self-control. Yet mass leisure also suggested a more impulsive side to popular outlook, one bent on the display of passion or at least vicarious participation by spectators in emotional release.

Figure 23.4 *Middle-class and working-class families made trips to the seaside popular before appropriate clothing had been designed, as can be seen in this scene from Yarmouth, England.*

Advances in Scientific Knowledge

Science and the arts took separate paths, with influential developments in each area. The size of the intellectual and artistic community in the West expanded steadily with rising prosperity and advancing educational levels. A growing audience existed for various intellectual and artistic products. The bulk of the new activity was resolutely secular. Although new churches were built as cities grew, and missionary activity reached new heights outside the Western world, the churches no longer served as centers for the most creative intellectual life. Continuing advances in science kept alive the rationalist tradition. Universities and other research establishments increasingly applied science to practical affairs, linking science and technology in the popular mind under a general aura of progress. Improvements in medical pathology and the germ theory combined science and medicine, although no breakthrough therapies resulted yet. Science was applied to agriculture through studies of seed yields and chemical fertilizers, with Germany and then the United States in the lead.

The great advance in theoretical science came in biology with the evolutionary theory of **Charles Darwin,** whose major work was published in 1859. Darwin argued that all living species had evolved into their present form through the ability to adapt in a struggle for survival. Biological development could be scientifically understood as a process taking place over time, with some animal and plant species disappearing and others—the fittest in the survival struggle—evolving from earlier forms. Darwin's ideas clashed with traditional Christian beliefs that God had fashioned humankind as part of initial creation, and the resultant debate further weakened the hold of religion. Darwin also created a more complex picture of nature than Newton's simple physical laws had suggested. In this view, nature worked through random struggle, and people were seen as animals with large brains, not as supremely rational.

Developments in physics continued as well, with work on electromagnetic behavior and then, about 1900, increasing knowledge of the behavior of the atom and its major components. New theories arose, based on complex mathematics, to explain the behavior of planetary motion and the movement of electrical particles, where Newtonian laws seemed too simple. After 1900, **Albert Einstein** formalized this new work through his theory of relativity, adding time as a factor in physical measurement. Again, science seemed to be steadily advancing in its grasp of the physical universe, although it is also important to note that its complexity surpassed the understanding even of educated laypeople.

The social sciences also continued to use observation, experiment, and rationalist theorizing. Great efforts went into compiling statistical data about populations, economic patterns, and health conditions. Sheer empirical knowledge about human affairs had never been more extensive. At the level of theory, leading economists tried to explain business cycles and the causes of poverty, and social psychologists studied the behavior of crowds. Toward the end of the 19th century, Viennese physician **Sigmund Freud** began to develop his theories of the workings of the human subconscious. He argued that much behavior is determined by impulses but that emotional problems can be relieved if they are brought into the light of rational discussion.

New Directions in Artistic Expression

A second approach in Western culture developed in the 19th century. This approach emphasized artistic values and often glorified the irrational. To be sure, many novelists, such as Charles Dickens in England, bent their efforts toward realistic portrayals of human problems, trying to convey information that would inspire reform. Many painters built on the discoveries of science, using knowledge of optics and color. For example, French painter Georges Seurat was inspired by findings about how the eye processes color, applying tiny dots of paint to his canvasses so that they would blend into a coherent whole in a style aptly called pointillism.

Nevertheless, the central artistic vision, beginning with **romanticism** in the first half of the century, held that emotion and impression, not reason and generalization, were the keys to the mysteries of human experience and nature. Artists portrayed intense passions, even madness, not calm reflection. Romantic novelists wanted to move readers to tears, not philosophical debate; painters sought empathy with the beauties of nature (as in Constable's painting in the opening of this chapter) or the storm-tossed tragedy of shipwreck. Romantics and their successors after 1850 also deliberately tried to violate traditional Western artistic standards. Poetry did not have to rhyme; drama did not necessarily need plot; painting could be evocative, not literal (Figure 23.5). (For literal portrayals, painters could now argue, use a camera.) Each generation of artists proved more defiant than the last. By 1900, painters and sculptors were becoming increasingly abstract, and musical composers worked with atonal scales that defied long-established conventions. Some artists talked of art for art's sake, arguing essentially that art had its own purposes unrelated to the larger society around it.

At neither the formal nor the popular levels, then, did Western culture produce a clear synthesis in the 19th century. New scientific discipline and rationalism warred with impulse—even with evocations of violence. The earlier certainties of Christianity and even the Enlightenment gave way to greater debate. Some observers worried that this debate also expressed tensions between different facets of the same modern mind and that these tensions could become dangerous. Perhaps the Western world was not put together quite as neatly as the adjustments and consolidations after 1850 might suggest.

Western Settler Societies

 Western industrial growth and nationalist rivalry brought an explosion of imperialist expansion in the late 19th century (see Chapter 24). Along with this expansion, several societies, including the growing United States, extended many Western values and institutions to new areas. This expansion of the West to a number of vast settler societies was one of the crucial developments of the 19th century.

The Industrial Revolution prompted a major expansion of the West's power in the world. Western nations could pour out far more processed goods than before, which meant that they needed new markets. They also needed new raw materials and agricultural products, which spurred the development of more commercial agriculture in places such as Africa and

Figure 23.5 *Cézanne's The Large Bathers (1898–1905). This painting illustrates the artist's abandonment of literal pictorial realism to concentrate on what he considered fundamental. His use of nudity further alienated the "respectable" public.*

Latin America. The vast ships and communication networks created by industrial technology spurred the intensification of the Western-led world economy.

Industrialization also extended the West's military advantage in the wider world. Steamships could navigate previously impassable river systems, bringing Western guns inland as never before. The invention of the repeating rifle and machine gun gave small Western forces superiority over masses of local troops. These new means combined with new motives: European nations competed for new colonies as part of their nationalistic rivalry, businesspeople sought new chances for profit, and missionaries sought opportunities for conversion. Haltingly before 1860, then rapidly, Europe's empires spread through Africa, southeast Asia, and parts of China and the Middle East.

Many of the same forces, and also massive European emigration, created Western settler societies overseas in areas where indigenous populations were decimated by disease. Some settler societies maintained sizeable local populations, sometimes even a considerable majority. South Africa was a case in point, discussed in Chapter 24. But some societies filled with an overwhelming majority of immigrants, mostly of European origin, and also brought in so many institutions and beliefs from Europe that they gained a close link with Western history. Some, perhaps, were part of the West outright. The most important overseas Western nation, and the only one to become a major world force before 1914, was the United States.

Most of the older settler societies, and also Australia and New Zealand, were also influenced by the results of the age of political revolution. Revolution formed the United States directly. To avoid a repetition, Britain treated other settler societies, like Canada, with greater care, facilitating the spread of parliamentary governments and liberal constitutions.

Emerging Power of the United States

The country that was to become the United States did not play a substantial role in world history in its colonial period. Its export products were far less significant than those of Latin America and the Caribbean. The American Revolution caused a stir in Europe, but the new nation emphasized internal development through the early 19th century. The Monroe Doctrine (1823) warned against European meddling in the Americas, but it was British policy and naval power that kept the hemisphere free from new colonialism. American energies were poured into elaboration of the new political system, internal commercial growth and early industrialization, and westward expansion. The Louisiana Purchase, the acquisition of Texas, and the rush to California rapidly extended the United States beyond the Mississippi. The nation stood as a symbol of freedom to many Europeans, and it was often invoked in the revolutions of 1848, as in the earlier Latin American wars for independence. It began to receive a new stream of immigrants, particularly from Ireland and Germany, during the 1840s. Its industrialists also borrowed heavily from European investors to fund national expansion.

The crucial event for the United States in the 19th century was the Civil War, fought between 1861 and 1865. Profound differences separated the increasingly industrial North, with its growing farms, from the slaveholding South, with its export-oriented plantation economy and distinctive value system. Disputes over slaveholding led the Southern states to try secession; the North opposed these actions in the interests of preserving national unity and, somewhat hesitantly, ending the slavery system. The Civil War produced an anguishing level of casualties and maimings. The North's victory brought important gains for the freed slave minority, although by the late 1870s, white politicians in the South had begun to severely constrain the political and economic rights of African Americans.

The Civil War also accelerated American industrialization. Heavy industry boomed in a push to produce for the war effort. The completion of a rail link to the Pacific opened the west to further settlement, leading to the last bitter round of wars with Native Americans. Economic expansion brought the United States into the industrial big leagues, its growth rivaling that of Germany. After the Civil War, American armaments manufacturers began to seek export markets. Other industrial producers soon followed as the United States became a major competitor worldwide. American firms, such as the Singer sewing machine company, set up branches in other countries. American agriculture, increasingly mechanized, began to pour out exports of grain and meats (the latter thanks to the development of refrigerated shipping), particularly to European markets where peasant producers could not fully compete.

American diplomacy was not particularly influential outside the Western Hemisphere, although a wave of imperialist expansion from the late 1890s onward brought American interests to the Pacific and Asia. American culture was also seen as largely parochial. Despite increasingly varied art and literature, American work had little impact abroad. Many artists and writers, such as Henry James and James McNeill Whistler, sought inspiration in European centers, sometimes becoming expatriates. Even in technology, American borrowing from Europe remained extensive, and American scientific work gained ground only in the late 19th century, partly through the imitation of German-style research universities. These developments confirmed the role of the new giant in extending many larger Western patterns.

European Settlements in Canada, Australia, and New Zealand

During the 19th century, Canada, Australia, and New Zealand filled with immigrants from Europe and established parliamentary legislatures and vigorous commercial economies that aligned them with the dynamics of Western civilization (Map 23.5). Sparse and disorganized hunting-and-gathering populations (particularly in Canada and Australia) offered little resistance. Like the United States, these new nations looked primarily to Europe for cultural styles and intellectual leadership. They also followed common Western patterns in such areas as family life, the status of women, and the extension of mass education and culture. Unlike the United States, however, these nations remained part of the British Empire, though with growing autonomy.

Canada, won by Britain in wars with France in the 18th century, had remained apart from the American Revolution. Religious differences between French Catholic settlers and British rulers and settlers troubled the area recurrently, and several uprisings occurred early in the 19th century. Determined not to lose this colony as it had lost the United States, the British began in 1839 to grant increasing self-rule. Canada set up its own parliament and laws but remained attached to the larger empire. Initially, this system applied primarily to the province of Ontario, but other provinces were included, creating a federal system that describes Canada to this day. French hostilities were eased somewhat by the creation of a separate province, Quebec, where the majority of French speakers was located. Massive railroad building, beginning in the 1850s, brought settlement to the western territories and a great expansion of mining and commercial agriculture in the vast plains. As in

the United States, new immigrants from southern and particularly eastern Europe poured in during the last decades of the century, attracted by Canada's growing commercial development.

Britain's Australian colonies originated in 1788, when a ship deposited convicts to establish a penal settlement at Sydney. Australia's only previous inhabitants had been a hunting-and-gathering people called the aborigines, and they were in no position to resist European settlement and exploration. By 1840, Australia had 140,000 European inhabitants, engaged mainly in a prosperous sheep-raising agriculture that provided needed wool for British industries. The exportation of convicts ceased in 1853, by which time most settlers were free immigrants. The discovery of gold in 1851 spurred further pioneering, and by 1861 the population had grown to more than a million. As in Canada, major provinces were granted self-government with a multiparty parliamentary system. A unified federal nation was proclaimed on the first day of the 20th century. By this time, industrialization, a growing socialist party, and significant welfare legislation had taken shape.

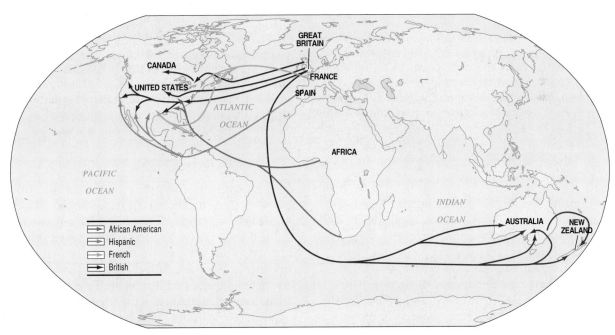

Map 23.5 *19th-Century Settlement and Consolidation in the United States, Canada, Australia, and New Zealand. Immigration led European settlers (and, in North America, enslaved Africans) to key areas previously populated by peoples vulnerable to imported diseases.*

In Depth

The United States in World History

Placing United States history in world history raises some important issues. Should the United States be treated as a separate civilization (perhaps along with Canada and other places that mixed dominant Western settlement with frontier conditions)? Latin America, because of its ongoing position in the world economy and its blending of European, Native American, and African influences, usually is not treated as part of Western civilization. Does the same hold true for the United States?

Because the United States is so often treated separately in history courses, there is a ready assumption of American uniqueness. The United States had purer diplomatic motives than did western Europe—look at the idealism of Woodrow Wilson. It had its own cultural movements, such as the religious "great awakening" of the 18th century and transcendentalism in the 19th. The United States had the unique experience of wave after wave of immigrants reaching its shores, contributing great cultural diversity but also promoting cultural and social integration under the banners of Americanization. Many thoughtful historians argue for American exceptionalism—that is, the United States as its own civilization, not as part of larger Western patterns. *American exceptionalists* do not contend that the United States was immune from contact with western Europe, which would be ridiculous, but they argue that this contact was incidental to the larger development of the United States on its own terms.

American exceptionalists can point to several factors that caused the development of a separate United States civilization. Although colonial immigrants often intended to duplicate European styles of life, the vastness and wealth of the new land quickly forced changes. As a result, American families gave greater voice to women and children, and abundant land created a class of independent farmers rather than a traditional peasantry with tight-knit villages. The successful revolution continued to shape a political life different from that of western Europe. The frontier, which lasted until the 1890s and had cultural impact even beyond that date, would continue to make Americans unusually mobile and restless while draining off some of the social grievances that arose in western Europe.

Distinctive causes produced distinctive results. There is no question that the United States, into the 20th century, had a different agricultural setup from that of western Europe. American politics, with the exception of the Civil War, emphasized small disagreements between two major political parties; third-party movements typically were pulled into the mainstream rather quickly. There was less political fragmentation and extremism than in western Europe and more stability (some would say boredom). No strong socialist movement took shape. Religion was more important in American than in European life by the late 19th century. Religion served immigrants as a badge of identity and helped all Americans, build-

Finally, New Zealand, visited by the Dutch in the 17th century and explored by the English in 1770, began to receive British attention after 1814. Here the Polynesian hunting-and-gathering people, the Maoris, were well organized politically (see Chapter 24). Missionary efforts converted many of them to Christianity between 1814 and the 1840s. The British government, fearful of French interest in the area, moved to take official control in 1840, and European immigration followed. New Zealand settlers relied heavily on agriculture (including sheep raising), selling initially to Australia's booming gold-rush popula-

tion and then to Britain. Wars with the Maoris plagued the settlers during the 1860s, but after the Maori defeat, generally good relations were established, and the Maoris won some representation in parliament. As in Canada and Australia, a parliamentary system was created that allowed the new nation to rule itself as a dominion of the British Empire without interference from the mother country.

Canada, New Zealand, and Australia each had distinct national flavors and national issues. These new countries were far more dependant on the European, particularly the British, economy than was the

ing a new society, retain some sense of their moorings. The absence of established churches in the United States kept religion out of politics, in contrast to Europe, where churches got caught up in more general attacks on the political establishment.

The American exceptionalist argument often appeals particularly to things Americans like to believe about themselves—more religious than people in other societies, less socialistic, full of the competence that came from taming a frontier—but it must embrace some less savory distinctiveness as well. The existence of slavery, and then the racist attitudes and institutions that arose after its abolition, created ongoing issues in American life that had no direct counterpart in western Europe. Correspondingly, Europe had less direct contact with African culture; jazz was one of the key products of this aspect of American life.

Yet from a world history standpoint, the United States must be seen also, and perhaps primarily, as an offshoot of Western civilization. The colonial experience and the revolution showed the powerful impact of Western political ideas, culture, and even family styles. American history in the 19th century followed patterns common in western Europe. The development of parliamentary life and the spread of democracy, though occurring unusually early in the United States, fit a larger Western pattern. American industrialization was a direct offshoot of that in Europe and followed a common dynamic. Labor strikes and trade unionism spread in similar ways in western Europe and the United States in the late 19th century. American intellectuals kept in close contact with European developments, and there were few purely American styles. Conditions for women and wider patterns of

family life, in areas such as birth control and disciplining children, were similar on both sides of the North Atlantic, which shows that the United States not only imitated western Europe but paralleled it.

In some important cases, because the United States was freer from peasant and aristocratic traditions, it pioneered developments that surfaced later in western Europe. This was true in the development of mass consumer culture and mass media (such as the popular press and popular films).

American exceptions remain, such as the Civil War, racial issues, and the absence of serious socialism. American distinctiveness remains in another respect: The United States was rising to world power just as key European nations, notably Britain, began to decline. The trajectory of American history is somewhat different from that of western Europe, and the 20th century revealed a growing American ability to play power politics in western Europe itself. Just as American exceptionalists must admit crucial western European influences, those who see the United States as part of the West must factor in special features and dynamics.

The main point is to analyze American history in careful comparative terms, removing the nation's history from the isolation in which it is so often taught and viewed.

Questions: Which argument has the greater strength in describing 19th-century history: the United States as a separate civilization or the United States as part of the West? Have the United States and western Europe become more or less similar in the 21st century? Why?

United States. Industrialization did not overshadow commercial agriculture and mining, even in Australia, so that exchanges with Europe remained important. Nevertheless, despite their distinctive features these countries followed the basic patterns of Western civilization, from political forms to key leisure activities. The currents of liberalism, socialism, modern art, and scientific education that described Western civilization to 1900 and beyond largely characterized these important new extensions.

It was these areas, along with the United States and part of Latin America, particularly Brazil and Argentina,

that received new waves of European emigrants during the 19th century. Although Europe's population growth rate slowed after 1800, it still advanced rapidly on the basis of previous gains as more children reached adulthood and had children of their own. Europe's export of people helped explain how Western societies could take shape in such distant areas.

The spread of the Western settler societies also reflected the new power of Western industrialization. Huge areas could be settled quickly, thanks to steamships and rails, while remaining in close contact with western Europe.

Diplomatic Tensions and World War I

 Diplomatic and military tensions within Europe began to increase, particularly from the 1890s onward. Rival alliance systems built up their military arsenals. A series of crises, particularly in the Balkans, accelerated the tension.

The unification of Germany and its rapid industrial growth profoundly altered the power balance within Europe. Bismarck was very conscious of this, and during the 1870s and 1880s, still a skilled manipulator, he built a complex alliance system designed to protect Germany and divert European attention elsewhere. France, Germany's deepest enemy, was largely isolated. But even the French concentrated on imperialist expansion in Africa and Asia.

By 1900, however, few parts of the world were available for Western seizure. Latin America was independent but under extensive United States influence, so that a new intrusion of colonialism was impossible. Africa was almost entirely carved up. The few final colonies taken after 1900—Morocco by France and Tripoli (Libya) by Italy—caused great diplomatic furor on the part of other colonial powers worried about the balance of forces. China and the Middle East were technically independent, but were in fact crisscrossed by rivalries between the Western powers and Russia (and in China's case, Japan). No agreement was possible on further takeovers.

Yet imperialist expansion had fed the sense of rivalry between key nation-states. Britain, in particular, grew worried about Germany's overseas drive and its construction of a large navy. Economic competition between a surging Germany and a lagging Britain added fuel to the fire. France, eager to escape the Bismarck-engineered isolation, was willing to play down its traditional rivalries with Britain. The French also took the opportunity to ally with Russia, when after 1890 Germany dropped this particular alliance because of Russian–Austrian enmity.

The New Alliance System

By 1907, most major European nations were paired off in two alliance systems: Germany, Austria–Hungary, and Italy formed the **Triple Alliance,** and Britain, Russia, and France formed the newer **Triple Entente.** Three against three seemed fair, but Ger-

many grew increasingly concerned about facing potential enemies to the east (Russia) and west (France). These powers steadily built up their military arsenals in what turned out to be the first of several arms races in the 20th century. All powers save Britain had instituted peacetime military conscription to provide large armies and even larger trained reserves. Artillery levels and naval forces grew steadily—the addition of a new kind of battleship, the dreadnought, was a key escalation—and discussions about reducing armament levels went nowhere. Each alliance system depended on an unstable partner. Russia suffered a revolution in 1905, and its allies worried that any further diplomatic setbacks might paralyze the eastern giant. Austria–Hungary was plagued by nationality disputes, particularly by minority Slavic groups; German leaders fretted that a diplomatic setback might bring chaos. Both Austria and Russia were heavily involved in maneuverings in the Balkans, the final piece in what became a nightmare puzzle.

Small Balkan nations had won independence from the Ottoman Empire during the 19th century; as Turkish power declined, local nationalism rose, and Russian support for its Slavic neighbors paid off. But the nations were intensely hostile to one another. Furthermore, **Balkan nationalism** threatened Austria, which had a large southern Slav population. Russia and Austria nearly came to blows on several occasions over Balkan issues. Then, in 1912 and 1913, the Balkan nations engaged in two internal wars, which led to territorial gains for several states but satisfied no one (Map 23.6). Serbia, which bordered Austria to the south, had hoped for greater stakes. At the same time, Austria grew nervous over the gains Serbia had achieved. In 1914, a Serbian nationalist assassinated an Austrian archduke on behalf of Serbian claims. Austria vowed to punish Serbia. Russia rushed to the defense of Serbia and mobilized its troops against Austria. Germany, worried about Austria and also eager to be able to strike against France before Russia's cumbersome mobilization was complete, called up its reserves and then declared war on August 1. Britain hesitated briefly, then joined its allies. World War I had begun, and with it came a host of new problems for Western society.

Diplomacy and Society

The tensions that spiraled into major war are not easy to explain. Diplomatic maneuverings can seem quite

Map 23.6 *The Balkan Wars, 1912–1913. Before and after the two regional wars.*

remote from the central concerns of most people, if only because key decisions—for example, with whom to ally—are made by a specialist elite. Even as the West became more democratic, few ordinary people placed foreign affairs high on their election agendas.

The West had long been characterized by political divisions and rivalries. In comparison with some other civilizations, this was an inherent weakness of the Western political system. In a sense, what happened by the late 19th century was that the nation-state system got out of hand, encouraged by the absence of serious challenge from any other civilizations. The rise of Germany and new tensions in the Balkans simply complicated the growing nationalist competition.

This diplomatic escalation also had some links to the strains of Western society under the impact of industrialization. Established leaders in the West continued to worry about social protest. They tended to seek diplomatic successes to distract the people. This procedure worked nicely for a few decades when imperialist gains came easily. But then it backfired: Around 1914 German officials, fearful of the power of the socialists, wondered whether war would aid national unity. British leaders, beset by feminist dissent and labor unrest, failed to think through their own diplomatic options. Leaders also depended on military buildups for economic purposes. Modern

industry, pressed to sell the soaring output of its factories, found naval purchases and army equipment a vital supplement. Mass newspapers, which fanned nationalist pride with stories of conquest and tales of the evils of rival nations, helped shape a belligerent popular culture.

Thus, just a few years after celebrating a century of material progress and peace, ordinary Europeans went to war almost gaily in 1914. Troops departed for the front convinced that war would be exciting, with quick victories. Their departure was hailed by enthusiastic civilians, who draped their trains with flowers. Four years later, almost everyone would have agreed that war had been unmitigated hell. However, the complexities of industrial society were such that war's advent seemed almost a welcome breath of the unexpected, a chance to get away from the disciplined stability of everyday life.

 GLOBAL CONNECTIONS: Industrial Europe and the World

Europe's growing power during the 19th century transformed the world. Imperialism and the redefinition of the world economy pushed European interests to every corner of the globe.

This same power made developments in 19th-century Europe something of a global model. Some leaders, aware of Europe's political and industrial change, found the example repellent. Russian conservatives, for example, warned against the divisiveness of parliamentary politics and the exploitation of modern industry.

Europe's revolutionary heritage, however, also won admiration, partly because it contained principles that could be used to counter European power. Liberalism, radicalism, and socialism began to spread beyond the boundaries of Europe and the settler societies. They could be directed against colonial controls or the exploitation of workers in the world economy. Nationalism spread rapidly as well, from its initial base in revolutionary Europe. Europe, in sum, was a global force in the 19th century as no society had ever been before, but its message was extremely complex.

Further Readings

Two excellent studies survey Europe's Industrial Revolution: Sidney Pollard's *Peaceful Conquest: The Industrialization of Europe* (1981) and David Landes' *The Unbound Prometheus: Technological Change and Industrial Development in Western Europe from 1700 to the Present* (1969). See also Phyllis Deane's *The First Industrial Revolution* (1980) on Britain. For a more general survey, see Peter N. Stearns' *The Industrial Revolution in World History* (1993). On the demographic experience, see Thomas McKeown's *The Modern Rise of Population* (1977).

For the French Revolution and political upheaval, Isser Woloch's *The New Regime: Transformations of the French Civic Order, 1789–1829* (1994) is a useful introduction. Lynn Hunt's *Politics, Culture and Class in the French Revolution* (1984) is an important recent study. Other revolutionary currents are treated in *The Crowd in History: Popular Disturbances in France and England* (1981) by George Rudé and *1848: The Revolutionary Tide in Europe* (1974) by Peter Stearns.

The impact of the Industrial Revolution on gender relations is analyzed in A. Clarke, *The Struggle for the Breeches: Gender and the Making of the British Working Class* (1995). Major developments concerning women and the family are covered in Louise Tilly and Joan Scott's *Women, Work and Family* (1978) and Steven Mintz and Susan Kellogg's *Domestic Revolutions: A Social History of American Family Life* (1989). See also R. Evans' *The Feminists: Women's Emancipation in Europe, America and Australia* (1979). An important age group is treated in John Gillis' *Youth and History* (1981). An influential generation receives its due in T. Hoppen's *The Mid-Victorian Generation, 1846-1886* (1998).

For an overview of social change, see Peter Stearns' and Herrick Chapman's *European Society in Upheaval* (1991). On labor history, see Michael Hanagan's *The Logic of Solidarity* (1981) and Albert Lindemann's *History of European Socialism* (1983). Eugen Weber's *Peasants into Frenchmen: The Modernization of Rural France* (1976) and Harvey Graff, ed., *Literacy and Social Development in the West* (1982) deal with important special topics.

On political and cultural history, see Gordon Wright's *France in Modern Times* (1981); Gordon Craig's *Germany, 1866–1945* (1978); and Louis Snyder's *Roots of German Nationalism* (1978); J. H. Randall's *The Making of the Modern Mind* (1976) is a useful survey; see also O. Chadwick's *The Secularization of the European Mind in the Nineteenth Century* (1976). On major diplomatic developments, see D. K. Fieldhouse's *Economics and Empire, 1830–1914* (1970) and David Kaiser's *Politics and War: European Conflict from Philip II to Hitler* (1990).

The impact of these winds of change as they swept across the American socio-political landscape is examined at W. Cronon, *Nature's Metropolis: Chicago and the Great West*, (1991); R. M. Utley, *The Indian Frontier and the American West, 1846-1890* (1984); Robert Dahl, *How Democratic is the American Constitution* (2002), S. M. Lipsett, *American Exceptionalism: A Double-Edged Sword* (1996); and T. Dublin, *Women at Work: The Transformation of Work and Community in Lowell, Massachusetts, 1826-1860* (1979).

On the Web

The sights, sounds, and songs of the French Revolution of 1789 are offered at http://otal.umd.edu/~fraistat/romrev/frbib.html, http://history.hanover.edu/modern/frenchrv.htm, http://userwww.port.ac.uk/andressd/frlinks.htm, http://chnm.gmu.edu/revolution/, http://marseillaise.org/english/, and http://www.admi.net/marseillaise.html.

One of the French Revolution's most lasting achievements, abolition of the feudal system in France, is recorded at http://history.hanover.edu/texts/abolfeud.htm.

The American Revolution and the Revolutionary War are explored in documents, site visits, and publications at http://www.revwar.com/links/document.html, http://www.nps.gov/revwar/, http://revolution.h-net.msu.edu/, http://www.pbs.org/ktca/liberty/, http://revolution.h-net.msu.edu/bib.html, and http://userpages.aug.com/captbarb/femvets.html.

A bibliography of the women of the American Revolution is provided at http://www.carleton.ca/~pking/

arbib/z.htm. Many Web pages offer insight into the personalities of the age of revolution, such as Marie Antoinette (http://www2.lucidcafe.com/lucidcafe/library/95nov/antoinette.html), Napoleon (http://www.napoleon.org/en/home.asp, http://www.napoleonseries.org/index.cfm, http://www.napoleonbonaparte.nl/), and http://www.pbs.org/empires/napoleon/, and Thomas Paine (http://odur.let.rug.nl/~usa/B/tpaine/paine.htm).

Also readily available are Web resources that can provide an overview of the Industrial Revolution (http://www.scholars.nus.edu.sg/victorian/technology/ir/irov.html) or surveys of the lives of key figures of that watershed in world history, such as James Watt (whose re-conception of the steam engine can be found at http://www.geocities.com/Athens/Acropolis/6914/watte.htm, http://www.spartacus.schoolnet.co.uk/SCwatt.htm, and http://homepages.westminster.org.uk/hooke/issue10/watt.htm), Eli Whitney (http://www.eliwhitney.org/ew.htm) and Ned Ludd (http://www.bigeastern.com/ludd/nl_whats.htm and http://www.spartacus.schoolnet.co.uk/PRluddites.htm), whose name became synonymous with resistance to technological change.

The life of industrial workers in 19th century England is examined at http://www.fordham.edu/halsall/mod/1844engels.html and http://dbhs.wvusd.k12.ca.us/Chem-History/Faraday-Letter.html.

Other Web sites illuminate the world of women workers (http://www.fordham.edu/halsall/mod/1842womenminers.html, http://www.womeninworldhistory.com/textile.html, http://www.fordham.edu/halsall/mod/robinson-lowell.html, and http://www.library.hbs.edu/hc/wes/collections/labor/textiles) and working children (http://www.spartacus.schoolnet.co.uk/Twork.htm). Domestic life in 19th century England is examined at http://artsci.washington.edu/drama-phd/kjdomest.html.

The impact of industrialization gave thrust to the writings of Karl Marx and others whose critiques and assessments of the future of capitalism were to usher in a new revolutionary period in human history. A brief essay at http://www.scholars.nus.edu.sg/victorian/philosophy/phil2.html manages to illuminate key forms of Marxian analysis, including the role of ideology in human society. Two of the best sites for accessing and comparing the ideas of Marxist writers are http://www.marxists.org/index.htm and http://www.anu.edu.au/polsci/marx/marx.html (which includes a very clear RealAudio file of the "Internationale" sung by an Irish folksinger accompanied on the guitar).

CHAPTER 24

INDUSTRIALIZATION AND IMPERIALISM: THE MAKING OF THE EUROPEAN GLOBAL ORDER

A romantic depiction of the 1879 battle of Isandhlwana in the Natal province of south Africa. The battle demonstrated that despite their superior firepower, the Europeans could be defeated by well-organized and determined African or Asian resistance forces.

- The Shift to Land Empires in Asia
- IN DEPTH: Western Education and the Rise of an African and Asian Middle Class
- Industrial Rivalries and the Partition of the World, 1870-1914
- Patterns of Dominance: Continuity and Change
- VISUALIZING THE PAST: Capitalism and Colonialism
- DOCUMENT: Contrary Images: The Colonizer Versus the Colonized on the "Civilizing Mission"
- GLOBAL CONNECTIONS: A European-Dominated World Order

The process of industrialization that began to transform western European societies in the last half of the 18th century fundamentally changed the nature and impact of European overseas expansion. In the industrial era, from roughly 1800 onward, the things that Europeans sought in the outside world as well as the source of the insecurities that drove them there changed dramatically. Not spices or manufactured goods but raw materials were the main products the Europeans sought overseas—metals, vegetable oils, dyes, cotton, and hemp were needed to feed the machines of Europe. Industrialization began to transform Europe into the manufacturing center of the world for the first time. As a result, overseas markets for machine-made European products became a key concern of those who pushed for colonial expansion. Changes in power relationships followed as well. It was only by around 1840, as a result of industrialization, that Europe began to be able to sell more goods to many Asian markets than it imported. It thus broke through the balance of payments imbalance that had affected its global trade for centuries.

Cultural and political connections changed in this context. Christian missionaries, by the 19th century as likely to be Protestant as Roman Catholic, still tried to win converts overseas. But unlike the rulers of Portugal and Spain in the early centuries of expansion, European leaders in the industrial age rarely took initiatives overseas to promote Christianity. In part, this reflected the fact that western Europe was no longer seriously threatened by the Muslims or any other non-European people. The fears that fueled European imperialist expansion in the industrial age arose from internal rivalries between the European powers themselves. Overseas peoples might resist the European advance, but different European national groups feared each other far more than even the largest non-European empires.

The contrast between European expansion in the preindustrial era and in the age of industrialization was also reflected in the extent to which the Europeans were able to build true empires overseas. Industrial technology and the techniques of organization and discipline associated with the increasing mechanization of the West gave the Europeans the ability to reach and infiltrate any foreign land. Few peoples were remote enough to be out of reach of the steamships and railways that carried the Europeans to and across all continents of the globe. No culture was strong enough to remain untouched by the European drive for global dominance in this era. None could long resist the profound changes unleashed by European conquest and colonization.

1600 C.E.	1700 C.E.	1750 C.E.	1800 C.E.
1619 Dutch established trading post at Batavia in Java	**1707** Death of Mughal emperor, Aurangzeb; beginning of imperial breakdown	**1750s** Civil war and division of Mataram; Dutch become the paramount power on Java	**1815** British annex Cape Town and surrounding area
1620s Sultan of Mataram's attacks on Batavia fail	**1739** Nadir Shah's invasion of India from Persia	**1756–1763** Seven Years' War, British–French global warfare	**1830** Start of the Boers' "Great Trek" in South Africa
1652 First Dutch settlement in South Africa at Cape Town	**1740–1748** War of Austrian Succession; global British–French struggle for colonial dominance	**1757** Battle of Plassey; British dominant power in Bengal	**1835** Decision to give support for English education in India; English adopted as the language of Indian law courts
1661 British port-trading center founded at Bombay		**1769–1770** Great Famine in Bengal	
1690 Calcutta established at center of British activities in Bengal		**1775–1782** War for independence by American colonists; another British–French struggle for global preeminence	
		1786–1790 Cornwallis' political reforms in India	
		1790–1815 Wars of the Revolution and Napoleonic era	
		1798 Napoleon's invasion of Egypt	

The Shift to Land Empires in Asia

 From the mid-18th century onward, the European powers began to build true empires in Asia similar to those they had established in the Americas beginning in the 16th century. Using divide-and-conquer tactics, first the Dutch on Java and then the British in India began the process of carving up Asia, Africa, and Oceania into colonial possessions. In this first phase of the colonization process, Europeans overseas were willing to adapt their lifestyles to the climates and cultures of the peoples they had gone out to rule.

Although we usually use the term *partition* to refer to the European division of Africa at the end of the 19th century, the Western powers had actually been carving up the globe into colonial enclaves for centuries (see Map 24.1). At first, this process was haphazard and often quite contrary to the interests and designs of those in charge of European enterprises overseas. For example, the directors who ran the Dutch and English East India companies (which were granted monopolies of the trade between their respective countries and the East in the 17th and 18th centuries) had little interest in territorial acquisitions. In fact, they were actively opposed to involvement in the political rivalries of the Asian princes. Wars were expensive, and direct administration of African or Asian possessions was even more so. Both cut deeply into the profits gained through participation in the Asian trading system, and profits—not empires—were the chief concern of the Dutch and English directors.

Whatever policies company directors may have instructed their agents in Africa and Asia to follow, these "men-on-the-spot" were often drawn into local power struggles. And before the Industrial Revolution produced the telegraph and other methods of rapid communication, company directors and European prime ministers had very little control over those who actually ran their trading empires. In the 18th century, a letter took months to reach Calcutta from London; the reply took many months more. Thus, commanders in the field had a great deal of leeway. They could conquer whole provinces or kingdoms before home officials even learned that their armies were on the move.

1850 c.e.	1900 c.e.
1850s Boer republics established in the Orange Free State and Transvaal	**1902** Anglo–Japanese Treaty
1853 First railway line constructed in India	**1904** Anglo–Russian crisis at Dogger Bank
1857 Calcutta, Madras, and Bombay universities founded	**1904–1905** The first Moroccan crisis
1857–1858 "Mutiny" or Great Rebellion in north India	**1911** The second Moroccan crisis
1858 British parliament assumes control over India from the East India Company	**1914** Outbreak of World War I
1867 Diamonds discovered in Orange Free State	
1869 Opening of the Suez Canal	
c. 1879–1890s Partition of west Africa	
1879 Zulu victory over British at Isandhlwana; defeat at Rourke's Drift	
1882 British invasion of Egypt	
1885 Indian National Congress Party founded in India; gold discovered in the Transvaal	
1890s Partition of east Africa	
1898 British–French crisis over Fashoda in the Sudan	
1899–1902 Anglo-Boer War in South Africa	

Prototype: The Dutch Advance on Java

One of the earliest empires to be built in this fashion was that pieced together in the late 17th and 18th centuries by the Dutch in Java (see Map 24.2). Java was then and is now the most populous of the chain of hundreds of islands that today makes up the country of Indonesia. In the early years after the Dutch established their Asian headquarters at Batavia on the northwest coast of the island in 1619, it was a struggle just to survive. The Dutch were content to become the vassals of and pay tribute to the sultans of **Mataram,** who ruled most of Java. In the decades that followed, the Dutch concentrated on gaining monopoly control over the spices produced on the smaller islands of the Indonesian archipelago to the east. But in the 1670s, the Dutch repeatedly intervened in the wars between rival claimants to the throne of Mataram, and they backed the side that eventually won. As the price for their assistance, the Dutch demanded that the territories around Batavia be turned over to them to administer.

This episode was the first of a long series of Dutch interventions in the wars of succession between the princes of Mataram. Dutch armies were made up mainly of troops recruited from the island peoples of the eastern Indonesian archipelago, led by Dutch commanders. Their superior organization and discipline, even more than their firearms, made the Dutch a potent ally of whichever prince won them to his side. But the price the Javanese rulers paid was very high. Each succession dispute and Dutch intervention led to more and more land being ceded to the increasingly land-hungry Europeans. By the mid-18th century, the sultans of Mataram controlled only the south central portions of Java (see Map 24.2). A failed attempt by Sultan Mangkubumi to restore Mataram's control over the Dutch in the 1750s ended with a Dutch-dictated division of the kingdom that signified Dutch control of the entire island. Java had been transformed into the core of an Asian empire that would last for 200 years.

Pivot of World Empire: The Rise of the British Rule in India

In many ways, the rise of the British as a land power in India resembled the Dutch capture of Java. The directors of the English East India Company were as hostile as the Dutch financiers to territorial expansion. But British agents of the company in India repeatedly meddled in disputes and conflicts between local princes. In these interventions, the British, adopting a practice pioneered by the French, relied heavily on Indian troops, called **sepoys** (some of whom are pictured in Figure 24.1) recruited from peoples throughout the subcontinent. As had been the case in Java, Indian princes regarded the British as allies whom they could use and control to crush competitors from within India or put down usurpers who tried to seize their thrones. As had happened in Java, the European pawns gradually emerged as serious rivals to the established Indian rulers and eventually dominated the region.

Partly because the struggle for India came later, there were also important differences between the patterns of colonial conquest in India and Java as well as between the global repercussions of each. In contrast to the Dutch march inland, which resulted largely from responses to local threats and opportunities, the rise of the **British Raj** (the Sanskrit-derived name for the British political establishment in India) owed much to the fierce global rivalry between the British and the French. In the 18th century, the two powers found themselves on opposite sides in five

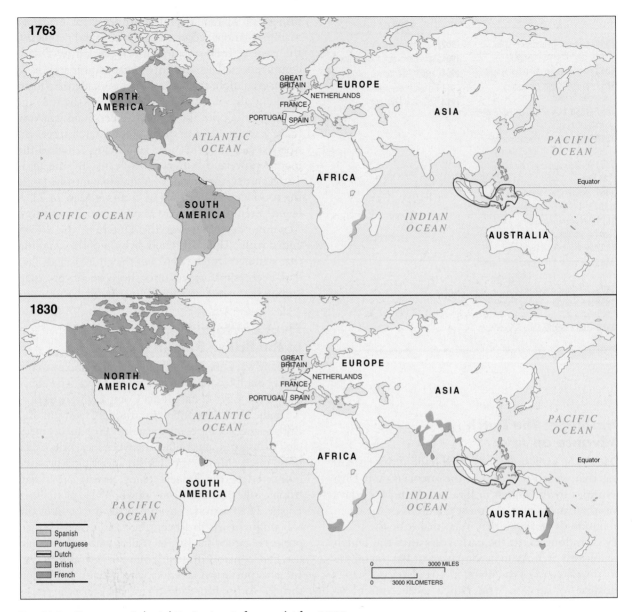

Map 24.1   *European Colonial Territories, Before and After 1800*

major wars. These struggles were global in a very real sense. On land and sea, the two old adversaries not only fought in Europe but also squared off in the Caribbean, where each had valuable plantation colonies; in North America; and on the coasts and bays of the Indian Ocean. With the exception of the American War of Independence (1775–1782), these struggles ended in British victories. The British loss of the American colonies was more than offset by earlier victories in the Caribbean and especially in India.

These triumphs gradually gave the British control of the entire south Asian subcontinent.

Although the first victories of the British over the French and the Indian princes came in the south in the late 1740s, their rise as a major land power in Asia hinged on victories won in Bengal to the northeast (see Map 24.3). The key battle at **Plassey** in 1757, in which fewer than 3000 British troops and Indian sepoys defeated an Indian army of nearly 50,000, is traditionally pictured as the heroic triumph of a hand-

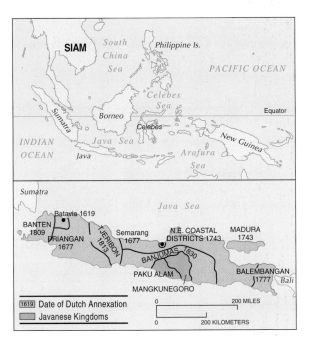

Map 24.2   *The Stages of Dutch Expansion in Java*

ful of brave and disciplined Europeans over a horde of ill-trained and poorly led Asians. The battle pitted Sirāj ud-daula, the teenage *nawab*, or ruler, of Bengal, against **Robert Clive,** the architect of the British victory in the south. The prize was control of the fertile and populous kingdom of Bengal. The real reasons for Clive's famous victory tell us a good deal about the process of empire building in Asia and Africa.

The numbers on each side and the maneuvers on the field had little to do with the outcome of a battle that in a sense was over before it had begun. Clive's well-paid Indian spies had given him detailed accounts of the divisions in Sirāj ud-daula's ranks in the months before the battle. With money provided by Hindu bankers who were anxious to get back at the Muslim prince for unpaid debts and for confiscating their treasure on several occasions, Clive bought off the nawab's chief general and several of his key allies. Even the nawab's leading spy was on Clive's payroll, which somewhat offset the fact that the main British spy had been bribed by Sirāj ud-daula. The backing Clive received from the Indian bankers also meant that his troops were well paid, whereas those of the nawab were not.

Thus, when the understandably nervous teenage ruler of Bengal rode into battle on June 23, 1757, his fate had already been sealed. The nawab's troops under French officers and one of his Indian commanders fought well. But his major Indian allies defected to the British or remained stationary on his flanks when the two sides were locked in combat. These defections wiped out the nawab's numerical advantage, and Clive's skillful leadership and the superiority of his

Figure 24.1   *Indian soldiers, or sepoys, made up a large portion of the rank-and-file troops in the armies of British India. Commanded by European officers and armed, uniformed, and drilled according to European standards, troops such as those pictured here were recruited from the colonized peoples and became one of the mainstays of all European colonial regimes. The European colonizers preferred to recruit these soldiers from subject peoples whom they saw as particularly martial. In India, these included the Sikhs (pictured here) and Marattas, as well as Gurkhas recruited from neighboring but independent Nepal.*

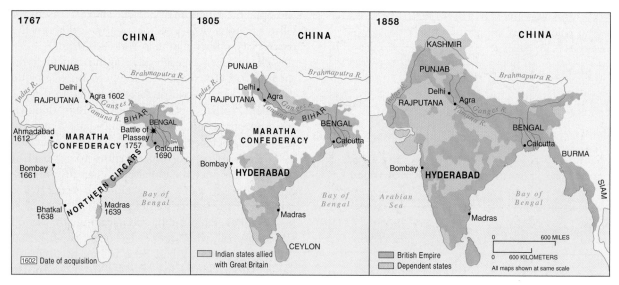

Map 24.3 *The Growth of the British Empire in India, from the 1750s to 1858*

artillery did the rest. The British victors had once again foiled their French rivals. As the nawab had anticipated, they soon took over the direct administration of the sizable Bengal-Bihar region. The foundations of Britain's Indian and global empire had been laid.

The Consolidation of British Rule

In the decades after Plassey, the British officials of the East India Company repeatedly went to war with Indian princes whose kingdoms bordered on the company's growing possessions (see Map 24.3). These entanglements grew stronger and stronger as the Mughal Empire broke down more fully in the last decades of the century. In its ruins, regional Indian princes fought to defend or expand their territories at the expense of their neighbors. Interventions in these conflicts or assaults on war-weakened Indian kingdoms allowed the British to advance steadily inland from their three trading towns on the Indian coast: Madras, Bombay, and Calcutta. These cities became the administrative centers of the three **presidencies** that eventually made up the bulk of the territory the British ruled directly in India. In many areas, the British were content to leave defeated or allied Indian princes on the thrones of their **princely states** and to control their kingdoms through agents stationed at the rulers' courts.

Because there was no sense of Indian national identity, it was impossible for Muslim or Hindu rulers to appeal to the defense of the homeland or the need for unity to drive out the foreigners. Indian princes continued to fear and fight with each other despite the ever-growing power of the British Raj. Old grudges and hatreds ran deeper than the new threat of the British. Many ordinary Indians were eager to serve in the British regiments, which had better weapons, brighter uniforms, and higher and more regular pay than all but a handful of the armies of the Indian rulers. By the mid-19th century, Indian soldiers in the pay of the British outnumbered British officers and enlisted men in India by almost five to one.

From the first decades of the 19th century, India was clearly the pivot of the great empire being built by Britain on a global scale. Older colonies with large numbers of white settlers, such as Canada and Australia, contributed more space to the total square miles of empire the British were so fond of calculating. But India had by far the greater share of colonized peoples. Britain's largest and most powerful land forces were the armies recruited from the Indian peoples, and these were rapidly becoming the policemen of the entire British Indian Empire. In the mid-19th century, Indian soldiers were sent to punish the Chinese and Afghans, conquer Burma and Malaya, and begin the conquest of south and east Africa. Indian ports were essential to British sea power east of the Cape of Good Hope. As the century progressed, India became the major outlet for British overseas investments and manufactured goods as well as a major source of key raw materials.

Early Colonial Society in India and Java

Although they slowly emerged as the political masters of Java and India, the Dutch and the British were at first content to leave the social systems of the peoples they ruled pretty much as they had found them. The small numbers of European traders and company officials who lived in the colonies for any length of time simply formed a new class atop the social hierarchies that already existed in Java and different parts of India. Beneath them, the aristocratic classes and often the old ruling families were preserved. They were left in charge of the day-to-day administration at all but the very highest levels. At the highest levels, the local rulers were paired with an agent of the imperial power (Figure 24.2).

To survive in the hot tropical environments of south and southeast Asia, the Dutch and English were forced to adapt to the ancient and sophisticated host cultures of their Asian colonies. After establishing themselves at Batavia, for example, the Dutch initially tried to create a little Holland in Java. They built high, close-packed houses overlooking canals, just like those they had left behind in Amsterdam and Rotterdam. But they soon discovered that the canals were splendid breeding grounds for insects and microbes that (though the Europeans did not make the connection until somewhat later) carried debilitating or lethal diseases such as malaria, dysentery, and typhoid. By the late 17th century, the prosperous merchants and officials of Batavia had begun to move away from the unhealthy center of the city to villas in the suburbs. Their large dwellings were set in gardens and separated by rice paddies and palm groves. The tall houses of the inner city gave way in the countryside to low, sprawling dwellings with many open spaces to catch the tropical breezes. Each was ringed with long porches with overhanging roofs to block the heat and glare of the sun. Similar dwellings, from which we get our term *bungalow*, came into fashion in India in the 18th century.

Europeans living in the tropical colonies also adopted, to varying degrees, the dress, the eating and work habits, and even the political symbols and styles of the Asian peoples they ruled. Some Englishmen refused to give up their tight-fitting woolen clothing, at least in public. But many (one suspects most of

Figure 24.2 *The close alliances that the European colonizers often struck with the "native" princes of conquered areas are graphically illustrated by this photo of the Susuhunan of Surakarta, a kingdom in central Java, standing arm-in-arm with a high Dutch official. At the upper levels of the administration, Dutch leaders were paired with Javanese rulers and aristocrats. The Dutch official always had the last say in joint decisions. But his Javanese "partner" was closely linked to subordinate administrators and often had a good deal more to say about how effectively the decision was carried out.*

those who survived) took to wearing looser-fitting cotton clothing. Dutch gentlemen even donned the long skirt-like sarongs of the Javanese aristocrats. British and Dutch officials learned to appreciate the splendid cuisines of India and Java—a taste that the Dutch would never lose and the British would revive at home in the postindependence era. Englishmen smoked

Indian *hookahs*, or water pipes, and delighted in performances of Indian dancing "girls." Adjusting to the heat of the colonies, both the Dutch and the English worked hard in the cool of the morning, took a long lunch break (often with a siesta), and then returned to the office for the late afternoon and early evening.

Because the Europeans who went to Asia until the mid-19th century were overwhelmingly male, Dutch and British traders and soldiers commonly had liaisons with Asian women. In some cases these involved little more than visits to the local brothel. But very often European men lived with Asian women, and sometimes they married them. Before the end of the 18th century, mixed marriages on the part of prominent traders or officers were widely accepted, particularly in Java. Examples of racial discrimination against the subject peoples on the basis of their physical appearance can certainly be found during the early decades of European overseas empire. But the frequency of liaisons that cut across racial boundaries suggests a social fluidity and a degree of interracial interaction that would be unthinkable by the last half of the 19th century, when the social distance between colonizers and colonized was consciously marked in a variety of ways.

Social Reform in the Colonies

Until the early 19th century, neither the Dutch nor the British had much desire to push for changes in the social or cultural life of their Asian subjects. The British enforced the rigid divisions of the Hindu caste system, and both the British and the Dutch made it clear that they had little interest in spreading Christianity among the Indians or the Javanese. In fact, for fear of offending Hindu and Muslim religious sentiments, the British refused to allow Christian missionaries to preach in their territories until the second decade of the 19th century.

Beginning in the 1770s, however, rampant corruption on the part of company officials forced the British parliament to enact significant reforms in the administration of the East India Company and its colonies. By that time most of those who served in India saw their brief tenure as a chance to strike it rich quickly. They made great fortunes by cheating the company and exploiting the Indian peasants and artisans. The bad manners and conspicuous consumption of these upstarts, whom their contemporaries scornfully called **nabobs,** were satirized by leading English novelists of the age.

When the misconduct of the nabobs resulted in the catastrophic Bengal famine of 1770, in which as much as one-third of the population of that once prosperous province died, their abuses could no longer be ignored. The British parliament passed several acts that restructured the company hierarchy and made it much more accountable to the British government. A succession of political reforms culminated in sweeping measures taken in the 1790s by the same **Lord Charles Cornwallis** whose surrender at Yorktown had sealed Britain's loss of the American colonies. By cleaning up the courts and reducing the power of local British administrators, Cornwallis did much to check widespread corruption. Because of his mistrust of Indians, his measures also severely limited their participation in governing the empire.

In this same period, forces were building, in both India and England, that caused a major shift in British policy toward social reform among the subject peoples. The Evangelical religious revival, which had seen the spread of Methodism among the English working classes, soon spilled over into Britain's colonial domains. Evangelicals were in the vanguard of the struggle to put an end to the slave trade, and their calls for reforms in India were warmly supported by Utilitarian philosophers such as Jeremy Bentham and James Mill. These prominent British thinkers believed that there were common principles by which human societies ought to be run if decent living conditions were to be attained by people at all class levels. Mill and other Utilitarians were convinced that British society, though flawed, was far more advanced than Indian society. Thus, they pushed for the introduction of British institutions and ways of thinking in India, as well as the eradication of what they considered Indian superstitions and social abuses.

Both Utilitarians and Evangelicals agreed that Western education was the key to revitalizing an ancient but decadent Indian civilization. Both factions were contemptuous of Indian learning. Influential British historian Thomas Babington Macaulay put it most bluntly when he declared in the 1830s that one shelf of an English gentleman's library was worth all the writings of Asia. Consequently, the Evangelicals and the Utilitarians pushed for the introduction of English-language education for the children of the Indian elite. These officials also pushed for major reforms in Indian society and advocated a large-scale infusion of Western technology.

At the center of the reformers' campaign was the effort to put an end to sati, the ritual burning of

In Depth

Western Education and the Rise of an African and Asian Middle Class

To varying degrees and for many of the same reasons as the British in India, all European colonizers educated the children of African and Asian elite groups in Western-language schools. The early 19th-century debate over education in India was paralleled by an equally hard-fought controversy among French officials and missionaries regarding the proper schooling for the peoples of Senegal in west Africa. The Dutch did not develop European-language schools for the sons of the Javanese elite until the mid-19th century, and many young Javanese men continued to be educated in the homes of the Dutch living in the colonies until the end of the century. Whatever their particular views on education, all colonial policymakers realized that they needed administrative assistants and postal clerks and that they could not begin to recruit enough Europeans to fill these posts. Therefore, all agreed that Western education for some segments of the colonized population was essential for the maintenance of colonial order.

One of the chief advantages of having Western-educated African and Asian subordinates—for they were always below European officials or traders—was that their salaries were much lower than what Europeans would have been paid for doing the same work. The Europeans had no trouble rationalizing this inequity. Higher pay for the Europeans was justified as compensation for the sacrifices involved in colonial service. Colonial officials also assumed that European employees would be more hard-working and efficient.

Beyond the need for government functionaries and business assistants, each European colonizer stressed different objectives in designing Western-language schools for the children of upper-class families. The transmission of Western scientific learning and production techniques was a high priority for the British in India. The goal of educational policymakers, such as Macaulay, was to teach the Indians Western literature and manners and to instill in them a Western sense of morality. As Macaulay put it, the British hoped that English-language schools would turn out brown English gentlemen, who would in turn teach their countrymen the ways of the West.

The French, at least until the end of the 19th century, went even further. Because they conceived of French nationalism as a matter of culture rather than birth, it was of prime importance that Africans and other colonial students master the French language and the subtleties of French cuisine, dress, and etiquette. The French also saw the process of turning colonial subjects into black, brown, and yellow French citizens as a way to increase their stagnant population to keep up with rival nations, especially Germany and Great Britain. Both of these rivals and the United States had much higher birth rates in this period.

When the lessons had been fully absorbed and the students fully assimilated to French culture, they could become full citizens of France, no matter what their family origins or skin color. Only a tiny minority of the population of any French colony had the opportunity for the sort of schooling that would qualify them for French citizenship. But by the early 20th century, there were thousands of Senegalese and hundreds of Vietnamese and Tunisians who could carry French passports, vote in French elections, and even run for seats in the French parliament. Other European colonial powers adopted either the British or the French approach to education and its aims. The Dutch and the Germans followed the British pattern, whereas the Portuguese pushed assimilation for even smaller numbers of the elite classes among the peoples they colonized.

Western education in the colonies succeeded in producing clerks and railway conductors, brown Indian gentlemen, and black French citizens. It also had effects that those who shaped colonial educational policy did not intend, effects that within a generation or two would produce major challenges to European colonial dominance. The population of most colonized areas was divided into many different ethnic, religious, and language groups with separate histories and identities. Western-language schools gave the sons (and, in limited instances, the daughters) of the leading families a common language in which to communicate. The schools also spread common attitudes and ideas and gave the members of diverse groups a common body of knowledge. In all European colonial societies, Western education led to similar occupational opportunities: in government service, with Western business firms, or as professionals (e.g., lawyers, doctors, journalists). Thus, within a generation after their introduction, Western-language schools had created a new middle class in

(continued)

the colonies that had no counterpart in precolonial African or Asian societies.

Occupying social strata and economic niches in the middle range between the European colonizers and the old aristocracy on one hand and the peasantry and urban laborers on the other, Western-educated Africans and Asians became increasingly aware of the interests and grievances they had in common. They often found themselves at odds with the traditional rulers or the landed gentry, who, ironically, were often their fathers or grandfathers. Members of the new middle class also felt alienated from the peasantry, whose beliefs and way of life were so different from those they had learned in Western-language schools.

For more than a generation they clung to their European tutors and employers. Eventually, however, they grew increasingly resentful of their lower salaries and of European competition for scarce jobs. They were also angered by their social segregation from the Europeans, which intensified in the heightened racist atmosphere of the late 19th century. European officials and business managers often made little effort to disguise their contempt for even the most accomplished Western-educated Africans and Asians. Thus, members of the new middle class in the colonies were caught between two worlds: the traditional ways and teachings of their fathers and the modern world of their European masters. Finding that they would be fully admitted to neither world, they rejected the first and set about supplanting the Europeans and building their own versions of the second, or modern, world.

Questions: Why did the Europeans continue to provide Western-language education for Africans and Asians once it was clear they were creating a class that might challenge their position of dominance? What advantages did Western-educated Africans and Asians have as future leaders of resistance to the European colonial overlords? Do you think the European colonial rule would have lasted longer if Western-language education had been denied to colonized peoples?

Hindu widows on the funeral pyres of their deceased husbands. This practice, which was clearly a corruption of Hindu religious beliefs, had spread fairly widely among upper-caste Hindu groups by the era of the Muslim invasions in the 11th and 12th centuries. In fact, the wives of proud warrior peoples, such as the Rajputs, had been encouraged to commit mass suicide rather than risk dishonoring their husbands by being captured and molested by Muslim invaders. By the early 19th century, some brahman castes and even lower-caste groups in limited areas had adopted the practice of sati.

In the 1830s, bolstered by the strong support and active cooperation of Western-educated Indian leaders, such as **Ram Mohun Roy,** the British outlawed sati. One confrontation between the British and those affected by their efforts to prevent widow burnings illustrates the confidence of the reformers in the righteousness of their cause and the sense of moral and social superiority over the Indians that the British felt in this era. A group of brahmans complained to a British official, Charles Napier, that his refusal to allow them to burn the widow of a prominent leader of their community was a violation of their social customs. Napier replied,

> The burning of widows is your custom. Prepare the funeral pyre. But my nation also has a custom.

When men burn women alive, we hang them and confiscate all their property. My carpenters shall therefore erect gibbets on which to hang all concerned when the widow is consumed. Let us all act according to our national customs.

The range and magnitude of the reforms the British enacted in India in the early 19th century marked a watershed in global history. During these years, the alien British, who had become the rulers of one of humankind's oldest centers of civilization, consciously began to transmit the ideas, inventions, modes of organization, and technology associated with western Europe's scientific and industrial revolutions to the peoples of the non-Western world. English education, social reforms, railways, and telegraph lines were only part of a larger project by which the British tried to remake Indian society along Western lines. India's crop lands were measured and registered, its forests were set aside for "scientific" management, and its people were drawn more and more into the European-dominated global market economy. British officials promoted policies that they believed would teach the Indian peasantry the merits of thrift and hard work. British educators lectured the children of India's rising middle classes on the importance of emulating their European masters in matters as diverse as being punctual, exercising their bodies, and mastering the literature and scientific learning of the West. Ironically, the very values and ideals that the British preached so earnestly to the Indians would soon be turned against colonizers by those leading India's struggle for independence from Western political domination.

Industrial Rivalries and the Partition of the World, 1870–1914

The spread of the Industrial Revolution from the British Isles to continental Europe and North America greatly increased the advantages the Western powers already enjoyed in manufacturing capacity and the ability to wage war, relative to all other peoples and civilizations. These advantages resulted in ever higher levels of European and American involvement in the outside world and culminated in the domination of the globe by Western powers by the late 19th century. Beginning in the 1870s, the Europeans indulged in an orgy of overseas conquests that reduced most of Africa, Asia, and the Pacific Ocean region to colonial possessions by the time of the outbreak of World War I in 1914.

Although science and industry gave the Europeans power over the rest of the world, they also heightened economic competition and political rivalries between the European powers. In the first half of the 19th century, industrial Britain, with its seemingly insurmountable naval superiority, was left alone to dominate overseas trade and empire building. By the last decades of the century, Belgium, France, and especially Germany and the United States were challenging Britain's industrial supremacy and actively building (or in the case of France, adding to) colonial empires of their own. Many of the political leaders of these expansive nations saw colonies as essential to states that aspired to status as great powers. Colonies were also seen as insurance against raw material shortages and the loss of overseas market outlets to European or North American rivals.

Thus, the concerns of Europe's political leaders were both political and economic. The late 19th century was a period of recurring economic depressions in Europe and the United States. The leaders of the newly industrialized nations had little experience in

handling the overproduction and unemployment that came with each of these economic crises. They were deeply concerned about the social unrest and, in some cases, what appeared to be stirrings of revolution that each phase of depression created. Some political theorists argued that as destinations to which unemployed workers might migrate and as potential markets for surplus goods, colonies could serve as safety valves to release the pressure built up in times of industrial slumps.

In the era of the scramble for colonial possessions, political leaders in Europe played a much more prominent role in decisions to annex overseas territories than they had earlier, even in the first half of the 19th century. In part, this was because of improved communications. Telegraphs and railways made it possible to transmit orders much more rapidly from the capitals of Europe to their representatives in the tropics. But more than politicians were involved in late 19th-century decisions to add to the colonial empires. The development of mass journalism and the extension of the vote to the lower middle and working classes in industrial Europe and the United States made public opinion a major factor in foreign policy. Although stalwart explorers might on their own initiative make treaties with local African or Asian potentates who assigned their lands to France or Germany, these annexations had to be ratified by the home government. In most cases, ratification meant fierce parliamentary debates, which often spilled over into press wars and popular demonstrations. Empires had become the property and pride of the nations of Europe and North America.

Unequal Combat: Colonial Wars and the Apex of European Imperialism

Industrial change not only justified the Europeans' grab for colonial possessions but made them much easier to acquire. By the late 19th century, scientific discoveries and technological innovations had catapulted the Europeans far ahead of all other peoples in the capacity to wage war. The Europeans could tap mineral resources that most peoples did not even know existed, and European chemists mixed ever more deadly explosives. Advances in metallurgy made possible the mass production of light, mobile artillery pieces that rendered suicidal the massed cavalry or infantry charges that were the mainstay of Asian and

African armies. Advances in artillery were matched by great improvements in hand arms. Much more accurate and faster firing, breech-loading rifles replaced the clumsy muzzle-loading muskets of the first phase of empire building. By the 1880s, after decades of experimentation, the machine gun had become an effective battlefield weapon. Railroads gave the Europeans the mobility of the swiftest African or Asian cavalry and the ability to supply large armies in the field for extended periods of time. On the sea, Europe's already formidable advantages (amply illustrated in Figure 24.3) were increased by industrial transformations. After the opening of the Suez Canal in 1869, steam power supplanted the sail, iron hulls replaced wood, and massive guns, capable of hitting enemy vessels miles away, were introduced into the fleets of the great powers.

The dazzling array of new weaponry with which the Europeans set out on their expeditions to the Indian frontiers or the African bush made the wars of colonial conquest very lopsided. This was particularly true when the Europeans encountered resistance from peoples such as those in the interior of Africa or the Pacific islands (see Maps 24.4 and 24.5). These areas had been cut off from most preindustrial advances in technology, and thus their peoples were forced to fight European machine guns with spears, arrows, and leather shields. One African leader, whose followers struggled with little hope to halt the German advance into east Africa, resorted to natural imagery to account for the power of the invaders' weapons:

> On Monday we heard a shuddering like Leviathan, the voice of many cannon; we heard the roar like waves of the rocks and rumble like thunder in the rains. We heard a crashing like elephants or monsters and our hearts melted at the number of shells. We knew that we were hearing the battle of Pangani; the guns were like a hurricane in our ears.

Not even peoples with advanced preindustrial technology and sophisticated military organization, such as the Chinese and the Vietnamese, could stand against, or really comprehend, the fearful killing devices of the Europeans. In advising the Vietnamese emperor to give in to European demands, one of his officials, who had led the fight against the

Figure 24.3 *An engraving from the popular* Illustrated London News *shows British warships and gunboats bombarding the east African port of Mombasa in 1874. As in the early centuries of European expansion, sea power remained a critical way for British and other colonizers to project their power throughout the 19th century. Raids, such as the one shown in the illustration, were so heavily relied upon to control local rulers that the term* gunboat diplomacy *became a staple of international parlance in the mid-19th century.*

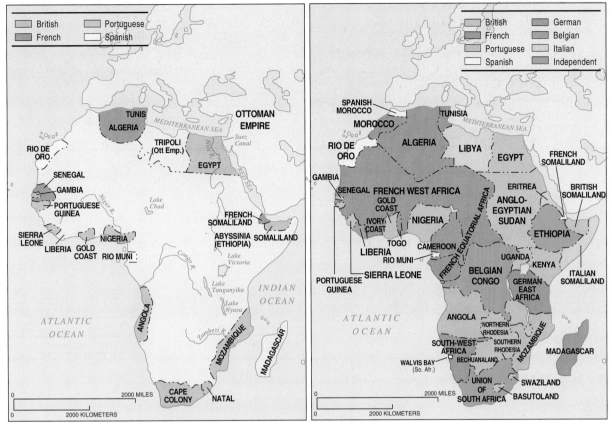

Map 24.4 *The Partition of Africa Between c. 1870 and 1914*

French invaders, warned, "Nobody can resist them. They go where they choose….Under heaven, everything is feasible to them, save only the matter of life and death."

Despite the odds against them, African and Asian peoples often fiercely resisted the imposition of colonial rule. West African leaders, such as Samory and Ahmadou Sekou, held back the European advance for decades. When rulers such as the Vietnamese emperors refused to fight, local officials organized guerrilla resistance in defense of the indigenous regime. Martial peoples such as the Zulus in south Africa had the courage and discipline to face and defeat sizeable British forces in conventional battles such as that at **Isandhlwana** in 1879 (depicted in the illustration that opens this chapter). But conventional resistance eventually ended in defeat. The guerrilla bands in Vietnam were eventually run to the ground. Even at

Isandhlwana, 3000 Zulus lost their lives in the massacre of 800 British and 500 African troops. In addition, within days of the Zulu victory, a tiny force of 120 British troops at a nearby outpost held off an army of thousands of Zulus.

Given European advantages in conventional battles, guerrilla resistance, sabotage, and in some cases banditry proved the most effective means of fighting the Europeans' attempts to assert political control. Religious leaders were often in the forefront of these struggles, which occurred across the globe, from the revivalist Ghost Dance religion in the late 19th-century American West to the Maji Maji uprisings in German East Africa in 1907 and the Boxer Rebellion in China in 1898. The magic potions and divine assistance they offered to protect their followers seemed to be the only way to offset the demoralizing killing power of the Europeans' weapons.

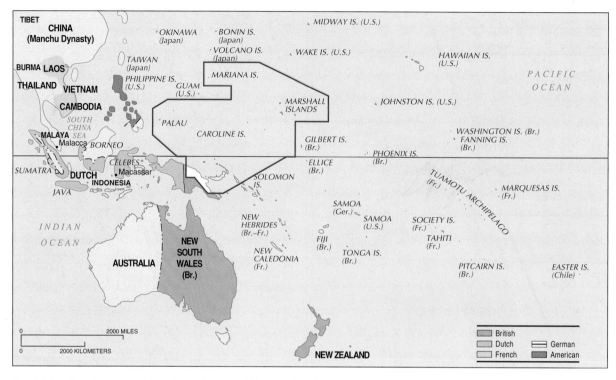

Map 24.5   *The Partition of Southeast Asia and the Pacific Islands to 1914*

Patterns of Dominance: Continuity and Change

 Widespread conquests were only the most dramatic manifestation of the great disparity in power that industrialization had created between the Europeans (including the North Americans) and all other peoples of the globe. The Europeans' sense of their own uniqueness and superiority, heightened by their unparalleled scientific and technological achievements, also led to major changes in their economic, social, and cultural relations with the colonized. Europeans living in the colonies increasingly distanced themselves from the peoples they ruled. Europe and North America became even more dominant in the world market system, with much of the rest of the globe supplying them with low-priced raw materials in return for the more highly priced, mass-produced consumer goods of the West. The demand for Western learning on the part of the elite and middle classes of colonized peoples in Africa and Asia rose sharply.

By the end of the 19th century, the European colonial order was made up of two different kinds of colonies. The greater portion of the European empires consisted of the so-called tropical dependencies in Africa, Asia, and the South Pacific. In these colonies, small numbers of Europeans ruled large populations of non-Western peoples. The tropical dependencies were a vast extension of the pattern of dominance the British, Dutch, and French had worked out earlier in India, Java, and African enclaves such as Senegal. Most of these colonies had been brought, often quite suddenly, under European rule in the late 19th and early 20th century.

Settlement colonies were the second major type of European overseas possession, but within this type there were different patterns of European occupation and indigenous response. One pattern was exhibited by colonies such as Canada and Australia, which the British labeled the **White Dominions** and are discussed in Chapter 23. White Dominions accounted for a good portion of the land area but only a tiny minority of the population of Britain's global empire. In these areas, as well as in some parts of Latin America, such as Chile and Argentina (see Chapter 25),

Visualizing the Past

Capitalism and Colonialism

In the century since the European powers divided up much of Africa, Asia, and the Pacific into their colonial fiefdoms, historians have often debated how much this process had to do with capitalism. They have also debated, perhaps even more intensely, over how much economic benefit the European colonial powers and the United States were able to garner from their colonies. The table shown here compares Great Britain, the premier industrialized colonial power, with Germany, Europe, the United States, and key areas of the British Empire. For each Western society and colonized area, various indices of the amount or intensity of economic interaction are indicated. A careful examination of each set of statistics and a comparison among them should enable you to answer the questions that follow on the connections between capitalism and colonialism.

Questions: To which areas did the bulk of British foreign investment flow? Which areas invested most heavily in Great Britain? With which areas did the British have the highest volume of trade? On which was it the most dependant for outlets for its manufactured goods? On which was it the most dependant for raw materials? On which for raw materials that had strategic importance? Do these patterns suggest that colonized areas were more or less important than independent nations; great power rivals, such as Germany and the United States; or settler colonies, such as Canada and Australia? On the basis of this information, would you say that Britain's "true" colonies (e.g., India, Malaya, sub-Saharan Africa) were vital to its economic well-being and defense? If so, which were the most important?

British Investment Abroad on the Eve of the First World War (1913)

Circa 1913	% of Total British Investment	% of Total British Imports	Main Products Exported to GB	% of Total British Exports	Main Products Imported fr. GB
Germany	0.17	8.98	Manufactures	9.82	Manufactures, Foodstuffs
Rest of Europe	5.64	27	Foodstuffs, Manufactures	30	Textiles, Machinery, Manufactures
"White" Dominions (ANZAC)	24.75	10.93	Wool, Foodstuffs, Ores, Textiles	12.28	Machinery, Textiles, Foodstuffs
United States of America	20.05	16.95	Manufactures, Foodstuffs	9.37	Manufactures
India (may include Ceylon)	10.07	6.30	Cotton, Jute, Narcotics, Tea, Other Comestibles	11.29	Machinery, Coal, Comestibles
Egypt	1.29	0.74	Cotton	1.25	Manufactures Textiles, Coal
West Africa	0.99		Foodstuffs, Plant Oils, Ores, Timber		Manufactures, Textiles, Machinery
South Africa	9.84	1.60	Diamonds, Gold, Wool, Other Ores	3.79	

descendants of European settlers made up most of the population in colonies in which small numbers of native inhabitants had been decimated by diseases and wars of conquest. These patterns of European settlement and the sharp decline of the indigenous population were also found in the portions of North America that came to form the United States, which won its independence in the late 18th century.

In some of the areas where large numbers of Europeans had migrated, a second major variation on the settlement colony developed. Both in regions that had been colonized as early as North America, such as south Africa, and in most of the areas Europeans and Americans had begun to occupy only in the mid- or late 19th century, such as Algeria, Kenya, Southern Rhodesia, New Zealand, and Hawaii, key characteristics of tropical dependencies and the settler colonies were combined. Temperate climates and mild disease environments in these areas made it possible for tens or hundreds of thousands of Europeans to settle permanently. Despite the Europeans' arrival, large indigenous populations survived and then began to increase rapidly. As a result, in these settlement colonies, which had been brought under colonial rule for the most part in the age of industrialization, Europeans and indigenous peoples increasingly clashed over land rights, resource control, social status, and cultural differences.

Colonial Regimes and Social Hierarchies in the Tropical Dependencies

As the Europeans imposed their rule over tens of millions of additional Africans and Asians in the late 19th century, they drew heavily on precedents set in older colonies, particularly India, in establishing administrative, legal, and educational systems. As in India (or in Java and Senegal), the Europeans exploited long-standing ethnic and cultural divisions between the peoples of their new African or Asian colonies to put down resistance and maintain control. In west and east Africa in particular, they used the peoples who followed animistic religions (those that focused on the proposition of nature or ancestral spirits) or those who had converted to Christianity against the Muslim communities that existed in most colonies. In official reports and censuses, colonial administrators strengthened existing ethnic differences by dividing the peoples in each colony into "tribes." The label itself, with its connotations of primitiveness and backwardness, says a great deal about general European

attitudes toward the peoples of sub-Saharan Africa. In southeast Asia, the colonizers attempted to use hill-dwelling "tribal" minorities against the majority populations that lived in the lowlands. In each colonial area, favored minorities, often Christians, were recruited into the civil service and police.

As had been the case in India, Java, and Senegal, small numbers of Europeans lived mainly in the capital city and major provincial towns. From these urban centers they oversaw the administration of the African and Asian colonies, which was actually carried out at the local level mainly by hundreds or thousands of African and Asian subordinates. Some of these subordinates, normally those in positions of the greatest authority, were Western educated. But the majority were recruited from indigenous elite groups, including village leaders, local notables, and regional lords (Figure 24.4). In Burma, Malaya, and east Africa, thousands of Indian administrators and soldiers helped the British to rule new additions to their empire.

In contrast to Java and India, where schools were heavily state supported, Western-language education in Africa was left largely to Protestant and Catholic missionaries. As a result of deep-seated racial prejudices held by nearly all the colonizers, higher education was not promoted in Africa. As a result, college graduates were few in Africa compared with India, the Dutch East Indies, or even smaller Asian colonies such as Burma and Vietnam. This policy stunted the growth of a middle class in black Africa, a consequence that European colonial officials increasingly intended. As nationalist agitation spread among the Western-educated classes in India and other Asian colonies, colonial policymakers warned against the dangers posed by college graduates. According to this argument, those with advanced educations among the colonized aspired to jobs that were beyond their capacity and were disgruntled when they could not find employment.

Changing Social Relations Between Colonizer and Colonized

In both long-held and newly acquired colonies, the growing tensions between the colonizers and the rising African and Asian middle classes reflected a larger shift in European social interaction with the colonized peoples. This shift had actually begun long before the scramble for colonies in the late 19th century. Its causes are complex, but the growing size and changing makeup of European communities in the colonies were critical factors. As more and more Europeans

Figure 24.4 *A dramatized engraving of the submission in 1896 of King Prempeh of the powerful Asante kingdom in present-day Ghana. The picture underscores the importance the European colonizers placed on alliances with (or the forced submission of) indigenous African rulers and local leaders. It also shows a rare case of the public humiliation of indigenous leaders, who in this instance had recently conspired to drive the British out by force. Normally, indigenous elites who cooperated with the colonizers were included in pageants celebrating the colonizers' power and were treated with respect, lest their hold over the mass of the colonized peoples be undermined.*

went to the colonies, they tended to keep to themselves on social occasions rather than mixing with the "natives." New medicines and increasingly segregated living quarters made it possible to bring to the colonies the wives and families of government officials and European military officers (but not of the rank and file until well into the 20th century). Wives and families further closed the social circle of the colonized, and European women looked disapprovingly on liaisons between European men and Asian or African women. Brothels were off limits for upper-class officials and officers, and mixed marriages or living arrangements met with more and more vocal disapproval within the constricted world of the colonial communities and back home in Europe. The growing numbers of missionaries and pastors for European congregations in the colonies obviously strengthened these taboos.

Historians of colonialism once put much of the blame on European women for the growing social gap between colonizer and colonized. But recent research has shown that male officials bore much of the responsibility. They established laws restricting or prohibiting miscegenation and other sorts of interracial liaisons. They also pushed for housing arrangements and police practices designed specifically to keep social contacts between European women and the colonized at a minimum. These measures locked European women in the colonies into an almost exclusively European world. They had many "native" servants and "native" nannies for their children. But they rarely came into contact with men or women of their own social standing from the colonized peoples. When they did, the occasions were highly public and strictly formal.

The trend toward social exclusivism on the part of Europeans in the colonies and their open disdain for the culture of colonized peoples were reinforced by notions of **white racial supremacy,** which peaked in acceptance in the decades before World War I. It was widely believed that the mental and moral superiority of whites over the rest of humankind, usually divided into racial types according to the crude criterion of skin color, had been demonstrated by what were then thought to be scientific experiments. Because the non-Europeans' supposedly inferior intelligence and weak sense of morality were seen as inherent and permanent, there seemed to be little motivation for Europeans to socialize with the colonized. There were also good reasons to fight the earlier tendency to adopt elements of the culture and lifestyle of subject peoples. As photos from the late 19th century reveal, stiff collars and ties for men and corsets and long skirts for women became obligatory for respectable colonial functionaries and their wives. The colonizers' houses were filled with the overstuffed furniture and bric-a-brac that the late Victorians loved so dearly. European social life in the colonies revolved around the infamous clubs, where the only "natives" allowed were the servants. In the heat of the summer, most of the administrators and nearly all of the colonizers' families retreated to hill stations, where the cool air and quaint architecture made it seem almost as if they were home again, or at least in a Swiss mountain resort.

Shifts in Methods of Economic Extraction

The relationship between the colonizers and the mass of the colonized remained much as it had been before. District officers, with the help of many "native" subordinates, continued to do their paternal duty to settle disputes between peasant villagers, punish criminals, and collect taxes. European planters and merchants still relied on African or Asian overseers and brokers to manage laborers and purchase crops and handicraft manufactures. But late 19th-century colonial bureaucrats and managers tried to instruct African and Asian peasants in scientific farming techniques and to compel the colonized peoples more generally to work harder and more efficiently. These efforts involved an important extension of dependant status in the Western-dominated world economy.

A wide range of incentives was devised to expand export production. Some of them benefited the colonized peoples, such as cheap consumer goods that could be purchased with cash earned by producing marketable crops or working on European plantations. In many instances, however, colonized peoples were simply forced to produce, for little or no pay, the crops or raw materials that the Europeans wanted. Head and hut taxes were imposed that could be paid only in ivory, palm nuts, or wages earned working on European estates. Under the worst of these forced-labor schemes, such as those inflicted on the peoples of the Belgian Congo in the late 19th century, villagers were flogged and killed if they failed to meet production quotas, and women and children were held hostage to ensure that the men would deliver the products demanded on time (Figure 24.5).

IN THE RUBBER COILS.

Figure 24.5 *As this political cartoon of a vicious snake with Leopold II's head squeezing the life out of a defenseless African villager illustrates, an international campaign developed in the 1890s in opposition to the brutal forced-labor regime in what became the Belgian king's personal fiefdom in the Congo after 1885. The much-publicized scandal compelled the Belgian government to take over the administration of the colony in 1906.*

Document

Contrary Images: The Colonizer Versus the Colonized on the "Civilizing Mission"

Each of the following passages from novels written in the colonial era expresses a different view of the reasons behind European colonization in Africa and Asia and its consequences. The first is taken from an adventure story written by John Buchan titled *Prester John*, a favorite in the pre–World War I decades among English schoolboys, many of whom would go out as young men to be administrators in the colonies. Davie, the protagonist in the story, is a "tall, square-set lad…renowned [for his] prowess at Rugby football." In the novel, Davie summarizes key elements of the "civilizing mission" credo by which so many European thinkers and political leaders tried to justify their colonization of most of the rest of the world.

> I knew then [after his struggle to thwart a "native" uprising in South Africa] the meaning of the white man's duty. He has to take all the risks, reck[on]ing nothing of his life or his fortunes and well content to find his reward in the fulfillment of his task. That is the difference between white and black, the gift of responsibility, the power of being in a little way a king; and so long as we know this and practise it, we will rule not in Africa alone but wherever there are dark men who live only for the day and their own bellies. Moreover the work made me pitiful and kindly. I learned much of the untold grievances of the natives and saw something of their strange, twisted reasoning.

The second passage is taken from René Maran's *Batouala*, which was first published in 1921 just after World War I. Though a French colonial official in west Africa, Maran was an African American, born in Martinique, who was highly sensitive to the plight of the colonized in Africa. Here his protagonist, a local African leader named Batouala, complains of the burdens rather than the benefits of colonial rule and mocks the self-important European agents of the vaunted civilizing mission.

> But what good does it do to talk about it? It's nothing new to us that men of white skin are more delicate than men of black skin. One example of a thousand possible. Everyone knows that the whites, saying that they are "collecting taxes," force all blacks of a marriageable age to carry voluminous packages from when the sun rises to when it sets.
>
> These trips last two, three, five days. Little matter to them the weight of these packages which are called "sandoukous." They don't sink under the burden. Rain, sun, cold? They don't suffer. So they pay no attention. And long live the worst weather, provided the whites are sheltered.
>
> Whites fret about mosquito bites….They fear mason bees. They are also afraid of the "prankongo," the scorpion who lives, black and venomous, among decaying roofs, under rubble, or in the midst of debris.
>
> In a word, everything worries them. As if a man worthy of the name would worry about everything which lives, crawls, or moves around him.

Questions: What sorts of roles does Davie assume that the Europeans must play in the colonies? What benefits accrue to colonized peoples from their rule? What impression does he convey of the thinking and behavior of the colonized peoples? In what ways do Batouala's views of the Europeans conflict with Davie's assumptions about himself and other colonizers? Does Batouala agree with Davie's conviction that colonial rule is beneficial for the Africans? What sorts of burdens does Batouala believe it imposes? According to Batouala, what advantages do Africans have over Europeans?

As increasing numbers of the colonized peoples were involved in the production of crops or minerals intended for export markets, the economies of most of Africa, India, and southeast Asia were reorganized to serve the needs of the industrializing European economies. Roads and railways were built primarily to move farm produce and raw materials from the interior of colonized areas to port centers from which they could be shipped to Europe. Benefiting from Europe's technological advances, mining sectors grew dramatically in most of the colonies. Vast areas that had previously been uncultivated or (more commonly) had been planted in food crops were converted to the production of commodities—such as cocoa, palm oil, rubber, and hemp—in great demand in the markets of Europe and, increasingly, the United States.

The profits from the precious metals and minerals extracted from Africa's mines or the rubber grown in Malaya went mainly to European merchants and industrialists. The raw materials themselves were shipped to Europe to be processed and sold or used to make industrial products. The finished products were intended mainly for European consumers. The African and Asian laborers who produced these products were generally poorly paid—if they were paid at all. The laborers and colonial economies as a whole were steadily reduced to dependence on the European-dominated global market. Thus, economic dependence complemented the political subjugation and social subordination of colonized African and Asian peoples in a world order loaded in favor of the expansionist nations of western Europe.

Settler Colonies in South Africa and the Pacific

The settlement colonies where large numbers of Europeans migrated intending to make permanent homes exhibited many of the patterns of political control and economic exploitation found in the tropical dependencies. But the presence of substantial numbers of European settlers *and* indigenous peoples considerably altered the dynamic of political and social domination in this type of colony in comparison with societies like India or the Belgian Congo, where settlers were few and overwhelmingly outnumbered by colonized peoples.

From Algeria to Argentina, settler colonies varied widely. But those settled in the 19th century, with the exception of Australia, tended to be quite different from those occupied in North and South America in the early centuries of European overseas expansion. In these early settler colonies, which included areas that eventually formed the nations of Canada, the United States, Argentina, and Chile, conquest and especially diseases transmitted unwittingly by incoming European migrants had devastating effects on the indigenous peoples, whose numbers in most of these regions were sparse to begin with. By the end of the 19th century in all of these areas, including Australia, which had been settled late but very thinly peopled when the Europeans arrived, the surviving indigenous peoples had been displaced to the margins both geographically and socially. As discussed in Chapter 23, several of these older settler societies—and particularly the United States, Canada, and Australia—imported so many people, institutions, and beliefs from Europe that they now became a part of Western history.

In most of the settler colonies established in the 19th century, the indigenous peoples were both numerous when the Europeans arrived and, in north and sub-Saharan Africa at least, largely resistant to the diseases the colonizers carried with them. Even Pacific islands, such as New Zealand and Hawaii, which had been largely isolated until their first sustained contacts with the Europeans in the late-18th century, were quite densely populated by peoples who were able over time to build up immunities to the diseases the Europeans transmitted. As a result, the history of the newer settler colonies that were formed as the result of large-scale migrations from industrializing societies has been dominated by enduring competition and varying degrees of conflict between European settlers and indigenous peoples. As these divisions were hardened by ethnic, racial, and national identities, settlers also clashed with local representatives of the European powers and in many instances sought to forcibly gain independence from meddling missionaries and transient colonial officials.

South Africa

The initial Dutch colony at Cape Town was established to provide a way station where Dutch merchant ships could take on water and fresh food in the middle of their long journey from Europe to the East Indies. The small community of Dutch settlers stayed near the coast for decades after their arrival. But the Boers (or farmers), as the descendants of the Dutch immigrants in south Africa came to be called, eventually began to move into the vast interior regions of the continent. There they found a temperate climate in which they could grow the crops and raise the livestock they were accustomed to in Europe. Equally important, they encountered a disease environment they could withstand.

Like their counterparts in North America and Australia, the Boers found the areas into which they moved in this early period of colonization sparsely populated. Boer farmers and cattle ranchers enslaved the indigenous peoples, the *Khoikhoi*, while integrating them into their large frontier homesteads. Extensive miscegenation between the Boers and Khoikhoi produced the sizeable "colored" population that exists in South Africa today. The coloreds have historically been seen as distinct from the black African majority.

The arrival of the British overlords in south Africa in the early 19th century made for major changes in the interaction between the Boers and the indigenous peoples and transformed the nature of the settlement colony in the region. The British captured

Cape Town during the wars precipitated by the French Revolution in the 1790s, when Holland was overrun by France, thus making its colonies subject to British attack. The British held the colony during the Napoleonic conflicts that followed, and they annexed it permanently in 1815 as a vital sea link to their prize colony India. Made up mainly of people of Dutch and French Protestant descent, the Boer community differed from the British newcomers in almost every way possible. The Boers spoke a different language, and they lived mostly in isolated rural homesteads that had missed the scientific, industrial, and urban revolutions that had transformed British society and attitudes. Most critically, the evangelical missionaries who entered south Africa under the protection of the new British overlords were deeply committed to eradicating slavery. They made no exception for the domestic pattern of enslavement that had developed in Boer homesteads and communities. By the 1830s, missionary pressure and increasing British interference in their lives drove a handful of Boers to open but futile rebellion, and many of the remaining Boers fled the Cape Colony.

In the decades of the Great Trek that followed, tens of thousands of Boers migrated in covered wagons pulled by oxen, first east across the Great Fish River and then over the mountains into the veld, or rolling grassy plains that make up much of the south African interior. In these areas, the Boers collided head-on with populous, militarily powerful, and well-organized African states built by Bantu peoples such as the Zulus and the Xhosa. The ever-multiplying contacts that resulted transformed the settler society in south Africa from one where the indigenous peoples were marginalized, typical of those founded in the early centuries of expansion, into a deeply contested colonial realm akin to those established in the age of industrialization. Throughout the mid-19th century, the migrating Boers clashed again and again with Bantu peoples, who were determined to resist the seizure of the lands where they pastured their great herds of cattle and grew subsistence foods. The British followed the Boer pioneers along the southern and eastern coast, eventually establishing a second major outpost at Durban in **Natal.** Tensions between the Boers and Britain remained high, but the imperial overlords were often drawn into frontier wars against the Bantu peoples, even though they were not always formally allied to the Boers.

In the early 1850s, the hard-liners among the Boers established two **Boer Republics** in the interior, named the Orange Free State and the Transvaal, which they tried to keep free of British influence. For more than a decade, the Boers managed to keep the British out of their affairs. But when diamonds were discovered in the Orange Free State in 1867, British entrepreneurs, including most famously **Cecil Rhodes,** and prospectors began to move in, and tensions between the Boers and the British began to build anew. In 1880–1881, these tensions led to a brief war in which the Boers were victorious. But the tide of British immigration into the republics rose even higher after gold was discovered in the Transvaal in 1885.

Although the British had pretty much left the Boers to deal as they pleased with the African peoples who lived in the republics, British miners and financiers grew more and more resentful of Boer efforts to limit their numbers and curb their civil rights. British efforts to protect these interlopers and bring the feisty and independent Boers into line led to the republics' declaration of war against the British in late 1899. Boer assaults against British bases in Natal, the Cape Colony, and elsewhere initiated the **Boer War** (1899–1902) that the British ultimately won but only at a very high cost in both lives and resources. British guilt over their brutal treatment of the Boers—men, women, and children—during the war also opened the way for the dominance of this settler minority over the black African majority that would prove to be the source of so much misery and violence in south African history through most of the 20th century.

Pacific Tragedies

The territories the Europeans, Americans, and Japanese claimed throughout the South Pacific in the 19th century were in some cases outposts of true empire and in others contested settler colonies. In both situations, however, the coming of colonial rule resulted in demographic disasters and social disruptions of a magnitude that had not been seen since the first century of European expansion into the Americas. Like the Native American peoples of the New World, the peoples of the South Pacific had long lived in isolation. This meant that, like the Native Americans, they had no immunities to many of the diseases European explorers and later merchants, missionaries, and settlers carried to their island homes from the 1760s onward. In addition, their cultures were extremely vulnerable to the corrosive effects of outside influences, such as new religions, different sexual mores, more lethal weapons, and sudden influxes of cheap consumer goods. Thus, whatever the intentions of the incoming Europeans and Americans—and they were by no means always benevolent—their contacts with the peoples of the Pacific islands almost invariably ushered in periods of social disintegration and widespread human suffering.

Of the many cases of contact between the expansive peoples of the West and the long-isolated island cultures of the South Pacific, the confrontations in New Zealand and Hawaii are among the most informative. As we have seen in Chapter 16, sophisticated cultures and fairly complex societies had developed in each of these areas. In addition, at the time of the European explorers' arrivals, the two island groups contained some of the largest population concentrations in the whole Pacific region. Both areas were subjected to European influences carried by a variety of agents, from whalers and merchants to missionaries and colonial administrators. With the great expansion of European settlement after the first decades of contact, the peoples of New Zealand and Hawaii experienced a period of crisis so severe that their continued survival was in doubt. In both cases, however, the threatened peoples and cultures rebounded and found enduring solutions to the challenges from overseas. Their solutions combined accommodation to outside influences, usually represented by the large numbers of European settlers living in their midst, with revivals of traditional beliefs and practices.

New Zealand The Maori of New Zealand actually went through two periods of profound disruption and danger. The first began in the 1790s, when timber merchants and whalers established small settlements on the New Zealand coast. Maori living near these settlements were afflicted with alcoholism and the spread of prostitution. In addition, they traded wood and food for European firearms, which soon revolutionized Maori warfare—in part by rendering it much more deadly—and upset the existing balance between different tribal groups. Even more devastating was the impact of diseases, such as smallpox, tuberculosis, and even the common cold, that ravaged Maori communities throughout the north island. By the 1840s, only 80,000 to 90,000 Maori remained of a population that had been as high as 130,000 less than a century earlier. But the Maori survived these calamities and began to adjust to the imports of the foreigners. They took up farming with European implements, and they grazed cattle purchased from European traders. They cut timber, built windmills, and traded extensively with the merchants who visited their shores. Many were even converted to Christianity by the missionaries, who established their first station in 1814.

The arrival of British farmers and herders in search of land in the early 1850s, and the British decision to claim the islands as part of their global empire, again plunged the Maori into misery and despair. Backed by the military clout of the colonial government, the settlers occupied some of the most fertile areas of the north island. The warlike Maori fought back, sometimes with temporary successes, but they were steadily driven back into the interior of the island. In desperation, in the 1860s and 1870s they flocked to religious prophets who promised them magical charms and supernatural assistance in their efforts to drive out the invaders. When the prophets also failed them, the Maori seemed for a time to face extinction. In fact, some British writers predicted that within generations the Maori would die out entirely.

The Maori displayed surprising resilience. As they built up immunities to new diseases, they also learned to use European laws and political institutions to defend themselves and preserve what was left of their ancestral lands. Because the British had in effect turned the internal administration of the islands over to the settlers' representatives, the Maori's main struggle was with the invaders who had come to stay. Western schooling and a growing ability to win British colonial officials over to their point of view eventually enabled the Maori to hold their own in their ongoing legal contests and daily exchanges with the settlers. Though New Zealand was included in the White Dominions of the British Empire, it was in fact a multiracial society in which a reasonable level of European and Maori accommodation and interaction has been achieved. Over time the Maori have also been able to preserve much of value in their pre-contact culture.

Hawaii The conversion of Hawaii to settler colony status followed familiar basic imperialist patterns but with specific twists. Hawaii did not become a colony until the United States proclaimed annexation in 1898, although an overzealous British official had briefly claimed the islands for his nation in 1843. Hawaii came under increasing Western influence from the late 18th century onward—politically at the hands of the British, and culturally and economically from the United States, whose westward surge quickly spilled into the Pacific Ocean.

Although very occasional contact with Spanish ships during the 16th and 17th centuries probably occurred, Hawaii was effectively opened to the West through the voyages of **Captain James Cook** from

1777 to 1779 (Figure 24.6). Cook was first welcomed as a god, partly because he had the good luck to land during a sacred period when war was forbidden. A later and less well-timed visit brought Cook's death as Hawaiian warriors tried to take over his ship for its metal nails. These humble objects were much prized by a people whose elaborate culture rested on a Neolithic technology and thus was without iron or steel. The Cook expedition and later British visits convinced a young Hawaiian prince, **Kamehameha,** that some imitation of Western ways could produce a unified kingdom under his leadership, replacing the small and warring regional units that had previously prevailed. A series of vigorous wars, backed by British weapons and advisors, won Kamehameha his kingdom between 1794 and 1810. The new king and his successors promoted economic change, encouraging Western merchants to establish export trade in Hawaiian goods in return for increasing revenues to the royal treasury.

Hawaiian royalty began to imitate Western habits, in some cases traveling to Britain and often building Western-style palaces. Two powerful queens advanced the process of change by insisting that traditional taboos subordinating women be abandoned. In this context, vigorous missionary efforts from Protestant New England, beginning in 1819, brought extensive conversions to Christianity. As with other conversion processes, religious change had wide implications. Missionaries railed against traditional Hawaiian costumes, insisting that women cover their breasts, and a new garment, the muumuu, was made from homespun American nightgowns with the sleeves cut off. Backed by the Hawaiian monarchy, missionaries quickly established an extensive school system, which by 1831 served 50,000 students from a culture that had not previously developed writing.

The combination of Hawaiian interest and Western intrusion produced creative political and cultural changes, though at the expense of previous values. Demographic and economic trends had more insidious effects. Western-imported diseases, particularly sexually transmitted diseases and tuberculosis, had the usual tragic consequences for a previously isolated people. By 1850 only about 80,000 Hawaiians remained of a prior population of about half a million. Because of the Hawaiian population decline, it

Figure 24.6 *One of the most famous, but ultimately tragic, cross-cultural encounters of the late 18th century was between Captain James Cook and the crew of the ship he commanded and the peoples of Hawaii. In this painting depicting his arrival in the islands, Cook, a renowned English explorer, is welocmed enthusiastically by the Hawaiians, who may have believed he was the god, Lono, whose festival had just begun. When Cook was later killed due to less fortunate timing and misunderstandings with the Hawaiians, he was lamented throughout Europe as one of the great lost heroes of his age.*

was necessary to import Asian workers to staff the estates. The first Chinese contract workers had been brought in before 1800; after 1868, a larger current of Japanese arrived. Westerners began to more systematically exploit the Hawaiian economy. Whalers helped create raucous seaport towns. Western settlers from various countries (called *haoles* by the Hawaiians) experimented with potential commercial crops, soon concentrating on sugar. Many missionary families, impatient with the subsistence habits of Hawaiian commoners, turned to leasing land or buying it outright. Most settlers did not entirely forget their religious motives for migrating to the islands, but many families who came to Hawaii to do good ended by doing well.

Literal imperialism came as an anticlimax. The abilities of Hawaiian monarchs declined after 1872, in one case because of disease and alcoholism. Under a weakened state, powerful planter interests pressed for special treaties with the United States that would promote their sugar exports, and the American government claimed naval rights at the Pearl Harbor base by 1887. As the last Hawaiian monarchs turned increasingly to promoting culture, writing a number of lasting Hawaiian songs but also spending money on luxurious living, American planters concluded that their economic interests required outright United States control. An annexation committee persuaded American naval officers to "protect American lives and property" by posting troops around Honolulu in 1893. The Hawaiian ruler was deposed, and an imperialist-minded United States Congress formally took over the islands in 1898.

As in New Zealand, Western control was combined with respect for Polynesian culture. Because Hawaiians were not enslaved and soon ceased to threaten those present, Americans in Hawaii did not apply the same degree of racism found in earlier relations with African slaves or Native Americans. Hawaii's status as a settler colony was further complicated by the arrival of many Asian immigrants. Nevertheless, Western cultural and particularly economic influence extended steadily, and the ultimate political seizure merely ratified the colonization of the islands.

GLOBAL CONNECTIONS: A European-Dominated World Order

The Industrial Revolution not only gave the Europeans and North Americans the motives, but it also provided the means for them to become the agents of the first civilization to dominate the entire world. By the end of the 19th century, the Western industrial powers had directly colonized most of Asia and Africa, and (as we shall see in Chapter 25) indirectly controlled the remaining areas through the threat of military interventions or the manipulation of local elites. Political power made it possible for the Europeans to use their already well-established position in world trade to build a global economic order oriented to their industrial societies. In many ways the first phase of globalization in the most meaningful sense of the term occurred in the four or five decades before the outbreak of World War I in 1914. The communications and commercial networks that undergirded the European colonial order made possible an unprecedented flow of foods and minerals from Africa, Asia, and Latin America to Europe and North America. Western industrial societies provided investment capital and machines to run the mines, plantations, and processing plants in colonized areas. European dominance also made it possible to extract cheap labor and administrative services from subject populations across the globe. Western culture, especially educational norms—but also manners, fashions, literary forms, and modes of entertainment—also became the first to be extensively exported to the rest of the world.

The European colonizers assumed that it was their God-given destiny to remake the world in the image of industrial Europe. But in pushing for change within colonized societies that had ancient, deeply rooted cultures and patterns of civilized life, the Europeans often aroused resistance to specific policies and to colonial rule more generally. The colonizers were able to put down protest movements led by displaced princes and religious prophets. But much more enduring and successful challenges to their rule came, ironically, from the very leaders their social reforms and Western-language schools had done so much to nurture. These Asian and African *nationalists* reworked European ideas and resurrected those of their own cultures. They borrowed European organizational techniques and used the communication systems and common language the Europeans had introduced into the colonies to mobilize the resistance to colonial domination that became one of the dominant themes of global history in the 20th century.

Further Readings

The literature on various aspects of European imperialism is vast. Useful general histories on the different empires include Bernard Porter's *The Lion's Share: A Short History of British Imperialism 1850–1970* (1975); Raymond Betts' *Tricouleur* (1978); James J. Cooke's *The New French Imperialism, 1880–1910* (1973); and Woodruff D. Smith's *The German Colonial Empire* (1978). For the spread of Dutch power in Java and the "outer islands," see Merle Ricklets' *A History of Modern Indonesia* (1981). There is no satisfactory general history of the growth of British Empire in India, but Edward Thompson and G. T. Garratt provide a lively chronology in *The Rise and Fulfillment of British Rule in India* (1962), which can be supplemented by the essays in R. C. Majumdar, ed., *British Paramountcy and Indian Renaissance, Part I* (1963). More recent accounts of specific aspects of the rise of British power in India are available in C. A. Bayley's *Indian Society and the Making of the British Empire* (1988), and P. J. Marshall's *Bengal: The British Beachhead, 1740–1828* (1987), both part of *The New Cambridge History of India*.

Of the many contributions to the debate over late 19th-century imperialism, some of the most essential are those by D. C. M. Platt, Hans-Ulrich Wehler, William Appleman Williams, Jean Stengers, D. K. Fieldhouse, and Henri Brunschwig, as well as the earlier works by Lenin and J. A. Hobson. Winfried Baumgart's *Imperialism* (1982) provides a good overview of the literature and conflicting arguments. Very different perspectives on the partition of Africa can be found in Jean Suret-Canale's *French Colonialism in Tropical Africa, 1900–1945* (1971), and Ronald Robinson and John Gallagher's *Africa and the Victorians* (1961).

Most of the better studies on the impact of imperialism and social life in the colonies are specialized monographs, but Percival Spear's *The Nabobs* (1963) is a superb place to start on the latter from the European viewpoint, and the works of Frantz Fanon, Albert Memmi, and O. Mannoni provide many insights into the plight of the colonized. The impact of industrialization and other changes in Europe on European attitudes toward the colonized are treated in several works, including Philip Curtin's *The Image of Africa* (1964); William B. Cohen's *The French Encounter with Africans* (1980); and Michael Adas' *Machines as the Measure of Men* (1989). Ester Boserup's *Women's Role in Economic Development* (1970) provides a good overview of the impact of colonization on African and Asian women and families, but it should be supplemented by more recent monographs on the position of women in colonial settings. One of the best of these is Jean Taylor's *The Social World of Batavia* (1983).

On the Web

The causes of imperialism in the nineteenth century are explored at http://mars.acnet.wnec.edu/~grempel/courses/wc2/lectures/imperialism.html and http://www.fordham.edu/halsall/mod/modsbook34.html. The nature and scope of British imperialism is examined at http://www.scholars.nus.edu.sg/victorian/history/empire/empireov.html and http://www.britishempire.co.uk. The Web also provides gateways for the study of German imperialism in China (http://www2.h-net.msu.edu/~german/gtext/kaiserreich/china.html) and Africa (http://web.jjay.cuny.edu/~jobrien/reference/ob22.html, http://www.cusd.chico.k12.ca.us/~bsilva/projects/imperialism/schuller.htm, and http://www.fordham.edu/halsall/mod/1901kaiser.html), American imperialism in the Philippines and the rest of Asia (http://www.smplanet.com/imperialism/toc.html), and Japanese imperialism in Korea (http://csf.colorado.eda/bcas/sample/comfdoc.htm), which included the use of chôngshindae ("Comfort Women") (http://www.koreanet/learnaboutkorea/hello/Generalinfo_25html and http://www.kimsoft.com/korea/jp-hist1.htm).

The onset of British imperialism in India, including studies of key personalities such as Robert Clive and key events such as the Battle of Plassey, receives careful treatment at http://www.sscnet.ucla.edu/southasia/History/British/Plassey.html. The life of Tipu Sultan, the Indian Muslim ruler who tried to defeat the British on their own terms, is examined at http://www.kamat.com/kalranga/itihas/tippu.htm.

The British debacle at Isandhlwana and the Zulu wars are given fulsome treatment at http://www.rorkesdriftvc.com/isandhlwana/isandhlwana.htm and http://schwartz.eng.auburn.edu/zulu/zulu.html. An African nationalist perspective of these anti-colonial struggles is offered at http://www.anc.org.za/ancdocs/history/misc/isandhlwana.html.

The "white man's burden" carried by Rudyard Kipling's prose and poetry is examined at http://www.geocities.com/Athens/Aegean/1457/, http://www.cwrl.utexas.edu/~benjamin/316kfall/316ktexts/whiteburden.html, and http://www.selfknowledge.com/238au.htm. The American anti-imperialist attack on Kipling's famous poem on race and empire is presented at http://www.boondocksnet.com/ai/kipling/kipling.html.

CHAPTER 25

THE CONSOLIDATION OF LATIN AMERICA, 1830–1920

Benito Juárez, an American Indian from southern Mexico, rose to the presidency and began a series of sweeping reforms. His uncompromising resistance to foreign intervention and monarchy made him a symbol of Mexican sovereignty and independence. That symbolism as a nationalist and a man of law is portrayed in a mural by Mexican artist Diego Rivera.

- From Colonies to Nations
- New Nations Confront Old and New Problems
- DOCUMENT: Confronting the Hispanic Heritage: From Independence to Consolidation
- Latin American Economies and World Markets, 1820–1870
- Societies in Search of Themselves
- IN DEPTH: Explaining Underdevelopment
- The Great Boom, 1880–1920
- GLOBAL CONNECTIONS: New Latin American Nations and the World

On a rainy morning in 1867, on a hill outside the Mexican city of Queretaro, the tall and handsome figure of the last emperor of Mexico, flanked by his loyal generals, bravely faced a firing squad. Maximilian I was an Austrian duke by birth, but European scheming and Mexican politics had led him to take the crown of Mexico. He had been well intentioned, had tried to bring reforms to his adopted country, and had even invited his political opponents to join in his government, but his authority rested on foreign bayonets, and his very presence was an insult to the Mexicans who sought to maintain the political independence that had been won after a long and bitter struggle. He died a tragic figure with the words "Long live Mexico, long live independence" on his lips. Even more tragically, by the time of his death hundreds of thousands of Mexicans had already perished in the civil wars that had brought him to, and finally toppled him from, the throne. His main political opponent, the Mexican Indian who had become president of Mexico, Benito Juárez, remained unmoved by the pleas sent by foreign governments to spare Maximilian. Mexico's sovereignty was not to be compromised. Juárez, like many Latin American leaders of the period, understood that Latin America needed to resolve its own problems without foreign intervention. Doing so would be a difficult task.

In the early 19th century, the various regions of Latin America had struggled and fought for their political independence, and had created new nations, often based on the old colonial administrative units. But what kind of nations were these to be? The form of government, the kind of society, the role of religion, and the nature of the economy all had to be defined in each of the new countries, and the deep divisions over these questions, and others, created sharp and bitter political struggles. Then too, there was always the shadow of foreign threat from the old colonial powers, from new imperialist regimes, and from neighbors seeking territory or economic advantages. Latin America in the 19th century was shaped both by the internal struggles over these questions and by the dominant international forces of the day.

The former American colonies of Spain and Portugal were swept by the same winds of change that transformed Europe's society and economy and led to the separation of England's North American colonies. Although at present Latin America is sometimes considered part of the developing nations along with many Asian and African nations, in reality its political culture was formed in the 18th century by the ideas of the Western Enlightenment. Thus, Latin American leaders in the 19th century, despite their many differences, often shared with Western political figures a firm belief in

1800 C.E.	1820 C.E.	1840 C.E.	1860 C.E.	1880 C.E.	1900 C.E.
1792 Slave rebellion in St. Domingue (Haiti)	**1821** Mexico declares independence; empire under Iturbide lasts to 1823	**1846–1848** Mexican–American War	**1862–1867** French intervention in Mexico	**1886–1888** Cuba and Brazil finally abolish slavery	**1903** Panamanian independence; beginning of Panama Canal (opens in 1914)
1804 Haiti declares independence	**1822** Brazil declares independence; empire established under Dom Pedro I	**1847–1855** Caste War in Yucatan	**1865–1870** War of the Triple Alliance (Argentina, Brazil, and Uruguay against Paraguay)	**1889** Fall of Brazilian Empire; republic established	
1808–1825 Spanish–American wars of independence	**1823** Monroe Doctrine indicates U.S. opposition to European ambitions in the Americas	**1850s** Beginnings of railroad construction in Cuba, Chile, and Brazil	**1868–1878** Ten-year war against Spain in Cuba	**1895–1898** Cuban Spanish–American War; United States acquires Puerto Rico and Philippines	
1808 Portuguese court flees Napoleon, arrives in Brazil; French armies invade Spain	**1829–1852** Juan Manuel de Roses rules Rio de la Plata	**1854** Benito Juárez leads reform in Mexico	**1869** First school for girls in Mexico		
1810 In Mexico, Father Hidalgo initiates rebellion against Spain	**1830** Bolívar dies; Gran Colombia dissolves into separate countries of Venezuela, Colombia, and Ecuador		**1876–1911** Porfirio Díaz rules Mexico		

the virtues of progress, reform, representational and constitutional government, and private property rights. At the same time, Latin American leaders often faced insurmountable problems different from those of Europe and the United States. The colonial heritage had left little tradition of participatory government among the majority of the Latin American population. A highly centralized colonial state had intervened in many aspects of life and had created both dependence on central authority and resentment of it. Class and regional interests deeply divided the new nations, and wealth was very unequally distributed. Finally, the rise of European industrial capitalism created an economic situation that often placed the new nations in a weak or dependant position. These problems and tensions are the focus of our examination of Latin America in the 19th century.

From Colonies to Nations

 Internal developments and the international situation of the Napoleonic wars set the independence movements in motion. Hidalgo in Mexico, Bolívar in northern South America, and San Martín in the Rio de la Plata led the successful revolutions. In Brazil, an independent monarchy was created.

By the late 18th century, the elites of American-born whites or Creoles (*criollos*) expressed a growing self-consciousness as they began to question the policies of Spain and Portugal. At the same time, these elites were joined by the majority of the population in resenting the increasingly heavy hand of government, as demonstrated by the new taxes and administrative reforms of the 18th century. But the shared resentment was not enough to overcome class conflicts and divisions. Early movements for independence usually failed because of the reluctance of the colonial upper classes to enlist the support of the American Indian, mestizo, and mulatto masses, who, they thought, might later prove too difficult to control. The actual movements were set in motion only when events in Europe precipitated actions in America.

Causes of Political Change

Latin American political independence was achieved as part of the general Atlantic revolution of the late 18th and early 19th centuries, and Latin American leaders were moved by the same ideas as those seeking political change elsewhere in the Atlantic world. Four external events had a particularly strong impact on political thought in Latin America. The American Revolution, from 1775 to 1783, provided a model of how colonies could break with the mother country. The French Revolution of 1789 provoked great interest in Latin America, and its slogan, "liberty, equality, and fraternity," appealed to some sectors of the population. As that revolution became increasingly radical, however, it was rejected by the Creole elites, who could not support regicide, rejection of the church's authority, and the social leveling implied by the *Declaration of the Rights of Man.*

The third external event was partially an extension of the French Revolution but had its own dynamic. Torn by internal political conflict during the turmoil in France, the whites and free people of color in St. Domingue, France's great sugar colony in the Caribbean, became divided. The slaves seized the moment in 1791 to stage a general rebellion under able leadership by **Toussaint L'Overture.** Various attempts to subdue the island were defeated, and in 1804 the independent republic of Haiti was proclaimed. For Latin American elites, Haiti was an example to be avoided. It was not accidental that neighboring Cuba and Puerto Rico, whose elites had plantations and slaves and were acutely aware of events in Haiti, were among the last of Spain's colonies to gain independence. For slaves and free people of color throughout the Americas, however, Haiti became a symbol of freedom and hope.

What eventually precipitated the movements for independence in Latin America was the confused Iberian political situation caused by the French Revolution and its aftermath. France invaded Portugal and Spain, and a general insurrection erupted in 1808, followed by a long guerrilla war. During the fighting, a central committee, or junta central, ruled in the Spanish king's name in opposition to Napoleon's brother, whom Napoleon appointed king.

Who was the legitimate ruler? By 1810, the confusion in Spain had provoked a crisis in the colonies. In places such as Caracas, Bogotá, and Mexico, local elites, pretending to be loyal to the deposed king Ferdinand, set up juntas to rule in his name, but they ruled on their own behalf. Soon the more conservative elements of the population—royal officials and those still loyal to Spain—opposed the movements for autonomy and independence. A crisis of legitimacy reverberated throughout the American colonies.

Spanish American Independence Struggles

The independence movements divided into three major theaters of operation. In Mexico, a conspiracy among leading Creoles moved one of the plotters, the priest **Father Miguel de Hidalgo,** to call for help from the American Indians and mestizos of his region in 1810. He won a number of early victories but eventually lost the support of the Creoles, who feared social rebellion more than they desired independence. Hidalgo was captured and executed, but the insurgency smoldered in various parts of the country. Eventually, after 1820 when events in Spain weakened the king and the central government, conservative Creoles in Mexico were willing to move toward independence by uniting with the remnants of the insurgent forces. **Augustín de Iturbide,** a Creole officer at the head of an army that had been sent to eliminate the insurgents, drew up an agreement with them instead, and the combined forces of independence occupied Mexico City in September 1821. Soon thereafter, with the support of the army, Iturbide was proclaimed emperor of Mexico.

This was a conservative solution. The new nation of Mexico was born as a monarchy, and little recognition was given to the social aspirations and programs of Hidalgo and his movement. Central America was briefly attached to the Mexican Empire, which collapsed in 1824. Mexico became a republic, and the Central American states, after attempting union until 1838, split apart into independent nations.

In South America and the Caribbean, the chronology of independence was a mirror image of the conquest of the 16th century. Formerly secondary areas such as Argentina and Venezuela were among the first to opt for independence and the best able to achieve it. The old colonial center in Peru was among the last to break with Spain. The Caribbean islands of Cuba and Puerto Rico, fearful of slave rebellion and occupied by large Spanish garrisons, remained loyal until the end of the 19th century.

In northern South America, a movement for independence centered in Caracas had begun in 1810. After early reverses, **Simon Bolívar,** a wealthy Creole officer, emerged as the leader of the revolt against Spain (Figure 25.1). With considerable military skill and a passion for independence, he eventually mobilized support, and between 1817 and 1822 he won a series of victories in Venezuela, Colombia, and Ecuador. Until 1830, these countries were united into a new nation called **Gran Colombia.** Political differences and regional interests led to the breakup of Gran Colombia. Bolívar became disillusioned and fearful of anarchy. "America is ungovernable," he said, and "those who have served the revolution have plowed the sea." To his credit, however, Bolívar rejected all attempts to crown him as king, and he remained until his death in 1830 firmly committed to the cause of independence and republican government.

Meanwhile, in southern South America, another movement had coalesced under **José de San Martín** in the Rio de la Plata. Buenos Aires had become a booming commercial center in the late 18th century, and its residents, called *porteños,* particularly resented Spanish trade restrictions. Pushing for freedom of trade, they opted for autonomy in 1810 but tried to keep the outlying areas, such as Paraguay, under their control. The myth of autonomy rather than independence was preserved for a while. By 1816, however, the independence of the United Provinces of the Rio de la Plata had been proclaimed, although the provinces were far from united. Upper Peru (Bolivia) remained under Spanish control, Paraguay declared independence in 1813, and the Banda Oriental (Uruguay) resisted the central authority of Buenos Aires.

In Buenos Aires, San Martín had emerged as a military commander willing to speak and act for independence. From Argentina his armies crossed the Andes to Chile to help the revolutionary forces in that colony. After winning victories there, the patriot forces looked northward. Peru was still under Spanish control. Its upper class was deeply conservative and not attracted to the movements for indepen-

Figure 25.1 *Simon Bolívar led the struggle for political independence in northern South America. Son of a wealthy Creole family, he became an ardent proponent of independence and a firm believer in the republican form of government.*

dence. San Martín's forces entered Peru, and Creole adherence was slowly won after major victories like the battle of Ayacucho in 1824, where royalist forces were defeated. By 1825, all of Spanish South America had gained its political independence. Despite various plans to create some form of monarchy in many of the new states, all of them emerged as independent republics with representative governments. The nations of Spanish America were born of the Enlightenment and the ideas of 19th-century liberalism. The wars of independence became the foundational moments of their heroic birth.

Brazilian Independence

Although the movement for independence in Brazil was roughly contemporaneous with those in Spanish America, and many of the causes were similar, independence there was achieved by a very different process. By the end of the 18th century, Brazil had grown in population and economic importance. The growth of European demand for colonial products, such as sugar, cotton, and cacao, contributed to that growth and to the increase in slave imports to the colony. Although Brazilian planters, merchants, and miners sometimes longed for more open trade and fewer taxes, they feared that any upsetting of the political system might lead to a social revolution or a Haitian-style general slave uprising. Thus, incipient movements for independence in Minas Gerais in 1788 and Bahia in 1798 were unsuccessful. As one official said, "Men established in goods and property were unwilling to risk political change."

The Napoleonic invasions provoked an outcome in Portugal different from that in Spain. When in 1807 French troops invaded Portugal, the whole Portuguese royal family and court fled the country and, under the protection of British ships, sailed to Brazil. Rio de Janeiro now became the capital of the Portuguese Empire. Brazil was raised to equal status with Portugal, and all the functions of royal government were set up in the colony. As a partial concession to England and to colonial interests, the ports of Brazil were opened to world commerce, thus satisfying one of the main desires of the Brazilian elites. Unlike Spanish America, where the Napoleonic invasions provoked a crisis of authority and led Spanish Americans to consider ruling in their own name, in Brazil the transfer of the court brought royal government closer and reinforced the colonial relationship.

Until 1820, the Portuguese king, Dom **João VI,** lived in Brazil and ruled his empire from there. Rio de Janeiro was transformed into an imperial city with a public library, botanical gardens, and other improvements. Printing presses began to operate in the colony for the first time, schools were created, and commerce, especially with England, boomed in the newly opened ports. The arrival of many Portuguese bureaucrats and nobles with the court created jealousy and resentment, however. Still, during this period Brazil was transformed into the seat of empire, a fact not lost on its most prominent citizens.

Matters changed drastically in 1820 when, after the defeat of Napoleon in Europe and a liberal revolution in Portugal, the king was recalled and a parliament convoked. João VI, realizing that his return was inevitable, left his young son Pedro as regent, warning him that if independence had to come, he should lead the movement. Although Brazilians were allowed representation at the Portuguese parliament, it became clear that Brazil's new status was doomed and that it would be recolonized. After demands that the prince regent also return to Europe, Pedro refused, and in September 1822 he declared Brazilian independence. He became Dom **Pedro I,** constitutional emperor of Brazil. Fighting against Portuguese troops lasted a year, but Brazil avoided the long wars of Spanish America. Brazil's independence did not upset the existing social organization based on slavery, nor did it radically change the political structure. With the brief exception of Mexico, all of the former Spanish American colonies became republics, but Brazil became a monarchy under a member of the Portuguese ruling house.

New Nations Confront Old and New Problems

 The new nations confronted difficult problems: social inequalities, political representation, the role of the church, and regionalism. These problems led to political fragmentation. Personalist leaders, representing various interests and their own ambitions, rose to prominence.

By 1830, the former Spanish and Portuguese colonies had become independent nations. The roughly 20 million inhabitants of these nations looked hopefully to the future. Many of the leaders of independence had shared ideals: representative government, careers open to talent, freedom of commerce and trade, the right to private property, and a belief in the individual as the basis of society. There was a general belief that the new nations should be sovereign and independent states, large enough to be economically viable and integrated by a common set of laws.

On the issue of freedom of religion and the position of the church, however, there was less agreement. Roman Catholicism had been the state religion and the only one allowed by the Spanish crown. While most leaders attempted to maintain Catholicism as the official religion of the new states, some tried to end the exclusion of other faiths. The defense of the church became a rallying cry for the conservative forces.

The ideals of the early leaders of independence often were egalitarian. Bolívar had received aid from Haiti and had promised in return to abolish slavery in the areas he liberated. By 1854, slavery had been abolished everywhere except Spain's remaining colonies, Cuba and Puerto Rico, as well as in Brazil; all were places where the economy was profoundly based on it. Despite early promises, an end to American Indian tribute and taxes on people of mixed origin came much more slowly, because the new nations still needed the revenue such policies produced. Egalitarian sentiments often were tempered by fears that the mass of the population was unprepared for self-rule and democracy. Early constitutions attempted to balance order and popular representation by imposing property or literacy restrictions on voters. Invariably, voting rights were reserved for men. Women were still disenfranchised and usually were not allowed to hold public office. The Creole elite's lack of trust of the popular classes was based on the fact that in many places the masses had not demonstrated a clear preference for the new regimes and had sometimes fought in royalist armies mobilized by traditional loyalties and regional interests.

Although some mestizos had risen to leadership roles in the wars of independence, the old color distinctions did not disappear easily. In Mexico, Guatemala, and the Andean nations, the large Indian population remained mostly outside national political life. The mass of the Latin American population— American Indians and people of mixed origins—waited to see what was to come, and they were suspicious of

the new political elite, who were often drawn from the old colonial aristocracy but were also joined by a new commercial and urban bourgeoisie.

Political Fragmentation

The new Latin American nations can be grouped into regional blocks (Map 25.1). Some of the early leaders for independence had dreamed of creating a unified nation in some form, but regional rivalries, economic competition, and political divisions soon made that hope impossible. Mexico emerged as a short-lived monarchy until a republic was proclaimed in 1823, but its government remained unstable until the 1860s because of military coups, financial failures, foreign intervention, and political turmoil. Central America broke away from the Mexican monarchy and formed a union, but regional antagonisms and resentment of Guatemala, the largest nation in the region,

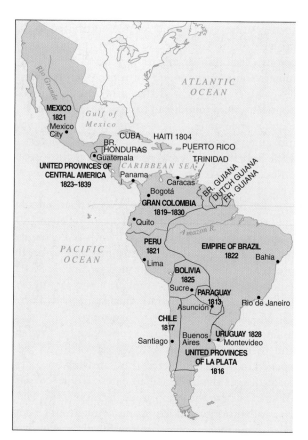

Map 25.1 *Independent States of Latin America*

eventually led to dissolution of the union in 1838. Spain's Caribbean colonies, Cuba and Puerto Rico, suppressed early movements for independence and remained outwardly loyal. The Dominican Republic was occupied by its neighbor Haiti, and after resisting its neighbor as well as France and Spain, it finally gained independence in 1844.

In South America, the old colonial viceroyalty of New Granada became the basis for Gran Colombia, the large new state created by Bolívar that included modern Ecuador, Colombia, Panama, and Venezuela. The union, made possible to some extent by Bolívar's personal reputation and leadership, disintegrated as his own standing declined, and it ended in 1830, the year of his death. In the south, the viceroyalty of the Rio de la Plata served as the basis for a state that the peoples of Argentina hoped to lead. Other parts of the region resisted. Paraguay declared and maintained its autonomy under a series of dictators. Modern Uruguay was formed by a revolution for independence against the dominant power of its large neighbors, Argentina and Brazil. It became an independent buffer between those two nations in 1828. The Andean nations of Peru and Bolivia, with their large Indian populations and conservative colonial aristocracies, flirted with union from 1829 to 1839 under the mestizo general **Andrés Santa Cruz,** but once again regional rivalries and the fears of their neighbors undermined the effort. Finally, Chile, somewhat isolated and blessed by the opening of trade in the Pacific, followed its own political course in a fairly stable fashion.

Most attempts at consolidation and union failed. Enormous geographic barriers and great distances separated nations and even regions within nations. Roads were poor and transportation rudimentary. Geography, regional interests, and political divisions were too strong to overcome. The mass of the population remained outside the political process. The problems of national integration were daunting. What is striking is not that Spanish America became 18 separate nations but that it did not separate into even more.

Caudillos, Politics, and the Church

The problems confronting the new nations were many. More than a decade of warfare in places such as Venezuela, Colombia, and Mexico had disrupted the economies and devastated wide areas. The mobi-lization of large armies whose loyalty to regional commanders was often based on their personal qualities, rather than their rank or politics, led to the rise of **caudillos,** independent leaders who dominated local areas by force and sometimes seized the national government itself. In times of intense division between civilian politicians, a powerful regional army commander became the arbiter of power, and thus the army sometimes made and unmade governments. Keeping the army in the barracks became a preoccupation of governments, and the amount of money spent on the military far exceeded the needs. The military had become important in the 18th century as Spain tried to shore up the defense of its empire, but it became a preserver of order.

Military commanders and regional or national caudillos usually were interested in power for their own sake, but they could represent or mobilize different groups in society. Many often defended the interests of regional elites, usually landowners, but others were populists who mobilized and claimed to speak for American Indians, peasants, and the poor and sometimes received their unquestioning support. A few, such as the conservative Rafael Carrera, who ruled Guatemala from 1839 to 1865, sincerely took the interest of the American Indian majority to heart, but other personalist leaders disregarded the normal workings of an open political system and the rule of law.

Other common issues confronted many of the new nations. Most political leaders were agreed on the republic as the basic form of government, but they could not agree on what kind of republic. A struggle often developed between **centralists,** who wanted to create strong, centralized national governments with broad powers, and **federalists,** who wanted tax and commercial policies to be set by regional governments. Other tensions developed between liberals and conservatives. Liberals stressed the rights of the individual and attacked the corporate (based on membership in a group or organization) structure of colonial society. They dreamed of a secular society and looked to the United States and France as models. Often they wanted a decentralized, or federalist, form of government. Conservatives usually believed in a strong centralized state, and they often wanted to maintain aspects of colonial society. They believed that a structure in which corporate groups (such as the American Indians), artisan guilds, or institutions (such as the church) provided the most

Document

Confronting the Hispanic Heritage: From Independence to Consolidation

Simon Bolívar (1783–1830), "The Liberator," was a man of determination and perception. His campaigns for independence were defeated on several occasions, yet he did not despair. In 1815, while in exile on the island of Jamaica, he penned a letter to a newspaper that gave his evaluation of Latin America's situation and his vision for the future for its various parts. He advocated a republican form of government and rejected monarchy, but he warned against federalism and against popular democracies that might lead to dictatorships: "As long as our countrymen do not acquire the abilities and political virtues that distinguish our brothers to the north, wholly popular systems, far from working to our advantage, will, I greatly fear, bring about our downfall." Spain had left America unprepared, and in this letter Bolívar summarized many of the complaints of Latin Americans against Spanish rule and underlined the difficulty of the tasks of liberation—political, social, and economic. The famous "Letter of Jamaica" is one of the most candid writings by a leader of Latin American independence. The following excerpts suggest its tone and content.

Bolívar's "Jamaica Letter" (1815)

We are young people. We inhabit a world apart, separated by broad seas. We are young in the ways of almost all the arts and sciences, although, in a certain manner, we are old in the ways of civilized society. I look upon the present state of America as similar to that of Rome after its fall. Each part of Rome adopted a political system conforming to its interest and situation or was led by the individual ambitions of certain chiefs, dynasties, or associations. But this important difference exists: those dispersed parts later reestablished their ancient nations, subject to the changes imposed by circumstances or extent. But we scarcely retain a vestige of what once was; we are, moreover, neither Indian nor European, but a species midway between the legitimate proprietors of this country and the Spanish usurpers. In short, although Americans by birth we derive our rights from Europe, and we have to assert these rights against the rights of the natives, and at the same time we must defend ourselves against the invaders. This places us in a most extraordinary and involved situation....

The role of the inhabitants of the American hemisphere has for centuries been purely passive. Politically they were nonexistent. We are still in a position lower than slavery, and therefore it is more difficult for us to rise to the enjoyment of freedom.... States are slaves because of either the nature or the misuse of their constitutions; a people is therefore enslaved when the government, by its nature or its vices infringes on and usurps the rights of the citizen or subject. Applying these principles, we find that America was denied not only its freedom but even an active and effective tyranny....

We have been harassed by a conduct which has not only deprived us of our rights but has kept us in a sort of permanent infancy with regard to public affairs. If we could have at least managed our domestic affairs and our internal administration, we could have acquainted ourselves with the processes and mechanics of public affairs. We should also have enjoyed a personal consideration, thereby commanding a certain unconscious respect from the people, which is so necessary to preserve amidst revolutions. That is why I say we have even been deprived of an active tyranny, since we have not been permitted to exercise its functions.

Americans today, and perhaps to a greater extent than ever before, who live within the Spanish system occupy a position in society no better than that of serfs destined to labor, or at best they have no more status than that of mere consumers. Yet even this status is surrounded with galling restrictions, such as being forbidden to grow European crops, or to store products which are royal monopolies, or to establish factories of a type the Peninsula (Spain) itself does not possess. To this add the privileges, even in articles of prime necessity, and the barriers between the American provinces, designed to prevent all exchange of trade, traffic, and understanding. In short, do you wish to know what our future held?—simply the cultivation of the fields of indigo, grain, coffee, sugar cane, cacao, and cotton; cattle raising on the broad plains, hunting wild game in the jungles; digging in the earth to mine its gold—but even these limitations could never satisfy the greed of Spain. So negative was our existence that I can find nothing comparable in any other civilized society.

By mid-century, Latin American political leaders were advocating "progress" and attempting to bring Latin America closer to the norms of life set by Europe. For liberals such as Argentine soldier, statesman, and author Domingo F. Sarmiento (1811–1888), his nation's task was to overcome the "barbarism" of rural life and implant the "civilization" of the Europeanized cities. Sarmiento saw in the bands of mounted rural workers, or *gauchos*, and their caudillo leaders an anachronistic way of life that held the nation back. His comparison of the gauchos to the Berbers of north Africa demonstrates the ancient hostility of "civilized" urban-dwellers to the nomadic way of life. In a way, Sarmiento saw the dictatorship of Juan Manuel de Rosas as a result of the persistence of the gauchos and the manipulation of the lower classes—a sort of living example of what Bolívar had warned against. The following excerpt from Sarmiento's classic *Life in the Argentine Republic in the Days of the Tyrants or Civilization and Barbarism* (1868) demonstrates his admiration for European culture, including that of Spain, and his desire to model his nation on it. That such a program might involve economic and cultural dependency did not concern Sarmiento and others like him.

The Search for Progress

Before 1810 two distinct, rival, and incompatible forms of society, two differing kinds of civilization existed in the Argentine Republic: one being Spanish, European, and cultivated, the other barbarous, American, and almost wholly of native growth. The revolution which occurred in the cities acted only as the cause, the impulse, which set these two distinct forms of national existence face to face, and gave occasion for a contest between them, to be ended, after lasting many years, by the absorption of one into the other.

I have pointed out the normal form of association, or want of association, of the country people, a form worse a thousand times, than that of a nomad tribe. I have described the artificial associations formed in idleness, and the sources of fame among the gauchos—bravery, daring, violence and opposition to regular law, to the civil law, that is, of the city. These phenomena of social organization existed in 1810, and still exist, modified in many points, slowly changing in others, and yet untouched in several more. These foci about which were gathered the brave, ignorant, free, and unemployed peasantry, were found by thousands through the country. The revolution of 1810 carried everywhere commotion and the sound of arms. Public life, previously wanting in this Arabo-Roman society, made its appearance in all the taverns, and the revolutionary movement finally brought about provincial, warlike associations, called montoneras [mounted gaucho guerrilla bands], legitimate offspring of the tavern and the field, hostile to the city and to the army of revolutionary patriots. As events succeed each other, we shall see the provincial montoneras headed by their chiefs; the final triumph, in Facundo Quiroga [a caudillo leader], of the country over the cities throughout the land; and by their subjugation in spirit, government, and civilization, the final formation of the central consolidated despotic government of the landed proprietor, Don Juan Manuel de Rosas, who applied the knife of the gaucho to the culture of Buenos Aires, and destroyed the work of centuries—of civilization, law, and liberty....

They [revolutions for independence] were the same throughout America, and sprang from the same source, namely, the progress of European ideas. South America pursued that course because all other nations were pursuing it. Books, events, and the impulses given by these, induced South America to take part in the movement imparted to France by North American demands for liberty, and to Spain by her own and French writers. But what my object requires me to notice is that the revolution—except in its external symbolic independence of the king—was interesting and intelligible only to the Argentine cities, but foreign and unmeaning to the rural districts. Books, ideas, municipal spirit, courts, laws, statues, education, all points of contact and union existing between us and the people of Europe, were to be found in the cities, where there was a basis of organization, incomplete and comparatively evil, perhaps, for the very reason it was incomplete, and had not attained the elevation which it felt itself capable of reaching, but it entered into the revolution with enthusiasm. Outside the cities, the revolution was a problematical affair, and [in] so far [as] shaking off the king's authority was shaking off judicial authority, it was acceptable. The pastoral districts could only regard the question from this point of view. Liberty, responsibility of power, and all the questions that the revolution was to solve, were foreign to their mode of life and to their needs. But they derived this advantage from the revolution, that it tended to confer an object and an occupation upon the excess of vital force, the presence of which among them has been pointed out, and was to add a broader base of union than that to which throughout the country districts the men daily resorted.

The Argentine Revolutionary War was twofold: first, a civilized warfare of the cities against Spain; second, a war against the cities on the part of the country chieftains with the view of shaking off all political subjugation and satisfying their hatred of civilization. The cities overcame the Spaniards, and were in their turn overcome by the country districts. This is the explanation of the Argentine Revolution, the first shot of which fired in 1810, and the last is still to be heard.

Questions: To what extent did the leaders of independence see their problems as a result of their Hispanic heritage? What would have been the reaction of the mass of the population to Sarmiento's idea of progress? Were the leaders naive about Latin America's possibilities for political democracy?

equitable basis of social action should be recognized in law. To the conservatives, society was not based on open competition and individualism but was organic: Each group was linked to the others like parts of a body whose health depended on the proper functioning of each part. Not all conservatives resisted change, and some—such as Mexican intellectual and politician Lucas Alamán—were among the most enlightened leaders in terms of economic and commercial reforms, but as a group the conservatives were skeptical of secularism and individualism and strove to keep the Catholic Iberian heritage alive.

The role of the church became a crucial issue in politics. It divided conservatives from the more secular liberals. In Mexico, for example, the church had played a major role in education, the economy, and politics. Few questioned its dogma, but liberals tried to limit its role in civil life. The church fought back with the aid of its pro-clerical supporters and with the power of the papacy, which until the 1840s refused to fill vacant positions in the hierarchy or to cooperate with the new governments.

Political parties, often calling themselves Liberal or Conservative, sprang up throughout Latin America. They struggled for power and tried to impose their vision of the future on society. However, their leaders usually were drawn from the same social class of landowners and urban bourgeoisie, with little to differentiate them except their position in the church or on the question of federalism versus centralization. The general population might be mobilized by the force and personality of a particular leader such as **Juan Manuel de Rosas** in Argentina or **Antonio López de Santa Anna** in Mexico, but political ideology rarely was an issue for most of the population.

The result was political turmoil and insecurity in much of Latin America in the first 50 years after independence. Presidents came and went quickly. Written constitutions, which both liberals and conservatives thought were a positive thing, were often short-lived and were overturned with a change in government because the margin for interpretation of the constitution was slight. Great efforts were made to make constitutions precise, specific, and definitive, but this resulted in an attempt to change them each time there was a change in government. Some nations avoided the worst aspects of instability. After enacting a constitution in 1833 that gave the president broad powers, Chile established a functioning political system that allowed compromise. Brazil, with its monarchical rule, despite a period of turmoil from 1832 to 1850, was able to maintain a political system of compromise, although it was dominated by the Conservatives, who were favored by the emperor. Its 1824 constitution remained in force until 1889.

It is fair to say that in much of Latin America the basic questions of government and society remained unresolved after independence. Some observers attributed these problems to personalism, a lack of civic responsibility, and other defects in the "Latin" character. Nevertheless, the parallel experience of later emerging nations in the 20th century suggests that these problems were typical of former colonial dependencies searching for order and economic security in a world in which their options were constrained by their own potential and by external conditions.

Latin American Economies and World Markets, 1820–1870

 In the mid-19th century, Latin American economies stagnated in the aftermath of the wars of independence. Dependence on exports created neocolonial ties. Toward mid-century, a new prosperity began as some nations found new markets for their exports. The revenues thus earned allowed liberal governments to advocate a variety of social and political changes. The examples of Mexico, Argentina, and Brazil illustrate the general pattern from political instability or economic stagnation to the emergence of stable liberal regimes by the end of the century.

The former colonies of Spain and Portugal now entered the world of diplomatic relations and international commerce. The new nations sought diplomatic recognition and security. In the 1820s, while Europe was undergoing the post-Napoleonic conservative reaction and monarchies were being restored, various plans to help Spain recolonize Latin America were put forward. Great Britain generally opposed those ideas, and because Great Britain was the dominant power at sea, its recognition of Latin American sovereignty was crucial. Moreover, the newly independent United States also felt an affinity and sympathy for the new nations to the south. The **Monroe Doctrine** of 1823 stated clearly that any attempt by a European power to colonize in the Americas would be considered an unfriendly act by the United States. The United States at the time probably could have done little to prevent such actions, but Britain could, and its support of Latin American independence provided needed protection.

There was a price for this support. During the turmoil of the 1820s, British foreign minister Lord Canning had once said, "Spanish America is free and if we do not mismanage our affairs sadly, she is English." He was referring to the broad economic and commercial advantages that the new nations offered. British commerce had legally penetrated the area in the 18th century, and Britain had profited from illegal trade as well. Now it could afford to offer its diplomatic recognition in exchange for the freedom to trade with the new nations. Although little capital had been invested directly in Latin America before 1850, Latin American governments now turned to foreign governments and banks for loans. Meanwhile, Britain became a major consumer of Latin American products. In return Britain sold about £5 million worth of manufactured goods to the new nations each year, about half of which went to Brazil, where British merchants were especially strong. Although some historians argue that this was a small portion of Britain's overseas trade, it was crucial for Latin America. In some ways, Britain replaced Spain as a dominant economic force over the area in a sort of neocolonial commercial system. Although other nations, notably France and the United States, also traded with Latin America, Britain remained predominant before 1860.

Open ports and the influx of foreign goods, often of better quality and cheaper than local products, benefited the port cities that controlled customhouses and the large landowners whose hides, sugar, and other products were exported. But these policies tended to damage local industries or regions that had specialized in producing for internal markets. Latin America became increasingly dependant on foreign markets and foreign imports and thereby reinforced the old colonial economic heritage in which land was the basis of wealth and prestige.

Mid-Century Stagnation

From about 1820 to 1850, the economy of Latin America was stagnant. Wars had destroyed many industries, roads were poor, and much money was still tied up in land. Only Cuba, with its booming sugar economy, expanded, but Cuba was still a colony of Spain. After 1850, however, this situation began to change as the expansion of the European economy created new demands for Latin American products. Coffee in Brazil, hides and beef in Argentina, and minerals and grains in Chile provided the basis of growth and allowed some Latin American governments to address social issues. For example, Peru exploited enormous **guano** (bird droppings) deposits on islands off

its coast. Between 1850 and 1880, exports of this fertilizer earned Peru more than £10 million, and this income allowed the government to end American Indian tribute and to abolish slavery by compensating the owners. Latin American cities began to grow and provide good internal markets, and the introduction of steamships and railroads began to overcome the old problems of transportation. By the 1840s, steamship lines improved communication within countries and opened up new possibilities for international commerce, and by the 1860s, railroads like the one in Figure 25.2 were being built, usually to link export-producing regions to the ports. Landed wealth and exports continued to characterize the economies of the region, as they had in the colonial era. As the levels of exports and the governments' dependence on them increased, Latin America's vulnerability to the vagaries of the world economy increased as well.

Without detailing all the complex changes within the Latin American nations during the 19th century, we can discern a few general patterns. After the turmoil of independence, liberal reformers tried to institute a series of programs in the 1820s and 1830s intended to break the patterns of the colonial heritage and to follow the main social and economic trends of western Europe. These ideas often were imposed on societies and economies unprepared for drastic change, especially because the strength of opposing institutions, such as the church and the army, remained intact. By the 1840s, conservatives had returned to power in many places to slow or stop the reform measures. Some of them tried to speak for the lower classes or the American Indians, who wanted to see the paternal aspects of the old colonial state reimposed to protect them from the reforms of the liberals. In some ways, an alliance between the landowners and the peasantry emerged in opposition to the changes suggested by the middle-class, urban modernizers.

Economic Resurgence and Liberal Politics

By the last quarter of the century, as the world economy entered a phase of rapid expansion, there was a shift in attitude and possibilities in Latin America. Liberals returned to power in many places in Latin America and initiated a series of changes that began to transform their nations. The ideological basis of the new liberal surge was also changing. Based on the ideas

Figure 25.2 *The drive for progress made Latin American nations anxious to accept foreign investment. Railroads were important for economic growth in that they often linked key exports to the ports and were designed principally to serve the needs of foreign capital. However, railroad workers often proved to be the most radical segment of the Latin American workforce.*

of **positivism** of the French philosopher **Auguste Comte,** who stressed observation and a scientific approach to the problems of society, Latin American politicians and intellectuals found a guiding set of principles and a justification of their quest for political stability and economic growth.

This shift was caused in large part by the general economic expansion of the second industrial revolution and the age of imperialism. The application of science to industry created new demands for Latin American products, such as copper and rubber, to accompany the increasing demand for its consumer products such as wheat, sugar, and coffee. The population of Latin America doubled to more than 43 million inhabitants in the 60 years between 1820 and 1880. After 1850, economies grew rapidly; the timing varied greatly, but the expansion of exports in places such as Colombia, Argentina, and Brazil stim-

ulated prosperity for some and a general belief in the advantages of the liberal programs. The desire to participate in the capitalist expansion of the Western economy dominated the thinking of Latin American leaders. Foreign entrepreneurs and bankers joined hands with philosophical liberals, landowners, and urban merchants in Latin America to back the liberal programs, which now became possible because of the increased revenues generated by exports.

The leaders of the post-1860 governments were a new generation of politicians who had matured during the chaotic years of postindependence politics. Their inspiration came from England, France, and the United States. They were firm believers in progress, education, and free competition within a secular society, but they were sometimes distrustful of the mass of their own people, who seemed to represent an ancient "barbarism" in contrast to the "civilization" of progress. That distrust and their sometimes insensitive application of foreign models to a very different reality in their own countries—what one Brazilian author has called "ideas out of place"—prevented many from achieving the progress they so ardently desired.

Economic growth and progress were costly. Responding to international demand, landowners increased their holdings, often aided by the governments they controlled or influenced. Peasant lands were expropriated in Chile, Peru, and Bolivia; small farmers were displaced in Brazil and Costa Rica; church lands were seized in Mexico. Labor was needed. Immigrants from Europe flooded into Argentina and Brazil, and in other countries new forms of tenancy, peonage, and disguised servitude developed.

Mexico: Instability and Foreign Intervention

After the short monarchical experiment, a Mexican republic was established. Its constitution of 1824, based on the examples of France, the United States, and Spain, was a federalist document that guaranteed basic civil rights. Nevertheless, this constitution did not address the nation's continuing social problems and needs: the maldistribution of land, the status of the American Indians, the problems of education, and the situation of vast numbers of poor people among the approximately 7 million people in Mexico, the most populous of the new nations. Politics soon became a complicated struggle between the conservative centralists and the liberal federalists and was made even more complicated by jockeying for advantage by commercial agents of Great Britain and the United States. For a short period from 1832 to 1835, the liberals were in control and tried to institute a series of sweeping social and economic reforms, but their attack on the church led to violent reaction and the assumption of power by General Antonio López de Santa Anna.

The mercurial Santa Anna remained until his death the maker of Mexican politics. He was a typical caudillo, a personalist, autocratic leader. But Mexico's instability resulted not only from his personality. Santa Anna was merely the symptom of deeper problems.

Mexico's instability and financial difficulties made it a target for various foreign interventions. Even more threatening to the nation, Anglo-American settlers were occupying Texas, the vast area of

Mexico's northern frontier. They brought their language, customs, and religion despite restrictions on the latter. Although the Texans at first sought more autonomy as federalists within the Mexican nation, as had been done in Yucatan and other Mexican provinces, ethnic and religious differences as well as Santa Anna's attempts to suppress the Texans in 1836 led to widespread fighting and the declaration of Texan independence. Santa Anna, captured for a while by the Texans, returned to dominate Mexican politics, but the question of Texas festered and became acute when in 1845 the United States, with its eye on California and moved by **manifest destiny**—a belief that it was destined to rule the continent from coast to coast—voted to annex Texas.

The result was war. A border dispute and the breakdown of negotiations over California led to hostilities in 1846. Santa Anna, who had been in exile, returned to lead the Mexican forces, but United States armies seized California, penetrated northern Mexico, and eventually occupied the Mexican capital. Mexico was forced to sign the disadvantageous **Treaty of Guadalupe-Hidalgo** (1848), in which the United States acquired about one-half of Mexico's national territory but less than 5 percent of its population. The **Mexican-American War** and the treaty left a bitter legacy of distrust of the northern neighbor, not only in Mexico but throughout the region. For Mexico there was also a serious loss of economic potential, but the heroic battle against the better-equipped Americans produced a sense of nationalism and a desire to confront the nation's serious internal problems, which also bore some responsibility for the war and the defeat.

Politics could not return to the prewar situation. Santa Anna did return to office for a while, more mercurial and despotic than ever, but now he was opposed by a new generation of liberals: intellectuals, lawyers, and some rural leaders, many of them from middle-class backgrounds, some of them mestizos and even a few American Indians. Perhaps the most prominent of them was **Benito Juárez** (1806–1872), a humble American Indian who had received a legal education and had eventually become the governor of his state. He shared the liberal vision of a secular society based on the rule of law in which the old privileges of the church and the army would be eliminated as a way of promoting economic change and growth.

The liberal revolt, called **La Reforma,** began in 1854 and triumphed within a year. In a series of laws integrated into a new constitution in 1857, the liberals set the basis for their vision of society. Military and clerical privileges were curtailed, and church property was placed on sale. Indian communal lands also were restricted, and the government forced the sale of these lands to individuals—to American Indians, it was hoped. The goal of these programs was to create a nation of small independent farmers. However, speculators or big landowners often bought up the lands and the result was that the peasants and American Indians lost what land they had. By 1910, about half of Mexico's rural population was landless. Good intentions had brought disastrous results.

The liberal program produced the expected conservative reaction. The church threatened to excommunicate those who upheld the new constitution. Civil war erupted, and in reaction, Juárez, now president, pushed forward even more radical measures. Losing ground in the war, the conservatives turned to Europe and convinced Napoleon III of France to intervene. Attracted by possible economic advantage, dreams of empire, and a desire to please Catholics in France, Napoleon III justified French intervention by claims of a shared "Latin" culture (this was the origin of the term *Latin America*). French forces landed in 1862 and soon took the capital. At the urging of the French, **Maximilian von Habsburg,** an Austrian archduke, was convinced to take the throne of Mexico. Well-intentioned but ineffective, Emperor Maximilian tried to get the support of Juárez and the liberals and even kept many of the laws of the Reforma in place, to the dismay of his conservative supporters. But Juárez absolutely rejected the idea of a foreign prince ruling Mexico. French troops and the United States' preoccupation with its own Civil War allowed Emperor Maximilian and his Empress Carlota to rule. When French troops were withdrawn, the regime crumbled. It was then, in 1867, that Maximilian and his loyal generals were captured and executed. Maximilian's death shocked Europeans. The famous painter Eduard Manet commemorated the event (see Figure 25.3). Juárez had sent a message to Europe: "hands off Mexico."

Juárez returned to office, but his administration was increasingly autocratic—a reality that he felt was unavoidable after so long a period of instability. By his death in 1872, the force of his personality, his concern for the poor, and his nationalist position against foreign intervention had identified liberalism with nationalism in Mexico and made Juárez a symbol of the nation. By 1880, Mexico was poised on the edge of a period of strong central government and relative political stability. One of Juárez's generals, Porfirio Díaz, became president and then virtual dictator. His government witnessed rapid economic growth, penetration of the economy by foreign capital, the expansion of the large landed estates, political repression, and eventually a revolution.

Argentina: The Port and the Nation

Whereas Mexico and its silver had been the core of Spain's empire in America, the rolling plains, or pampas, of the Rio de la Plata in southern South America had been a colonial backwater until the 18th century, when direct trade had begun to stimulate its economy. The port of Buenos Aires and its merchants dominated the Rio de la Plata, but the other areas of the region had their own interests and resented the power and growth of the port city and its surrounding countryside. The United Provinces of the Rio de la Plata, which declared their independence in 1816, soon split apart, and local caudillos, able to call on the support of gauchos, dominated each region. In Buenos Aires, the liberals gained control in the 1820s, and instituted a series of broad reforms in education, finance, agriculture, and immigration. These included a program of public land sales, which stimulated the growth of cattle ranches and the power of the rancher class.

As in Mexico, liberal reforms including freedom of religion produced a similar negative reaction from conservatives and the church. But the liberals' main sin was centralism, a desire to create a strong national government. Centralists (called *unitarians* in the Argentine context) provoked the reaction of the federalists, who by 1831 had taken power under Juan Manuel de Rosas, who commanded the loyalty of the gaucho employees of the ranchers.

Under Rosas, the federalist program of a weak central government and local autonomy was instituted, but Rosas' federalism favored the ranchers of the Buenos Aires province and the merchants of the great port. He campaigned against the American Indians to the south to open new lands to the cattle ranchers. Exports of hides and salted meat increased,

Figure 25.3 *Emperor Maximilian was finally captured after his attempt, with French help, to reestablish a monarchy in Mexico. Well-meaning, he eventually lost the support of the conservatives. Juárez refused to spare his life, as a warning to other ambitious nations that Mexico would remain independent.*

but the revenues collected at the port were not shared with the other provinces. Although popular with the gauchos and the urban poor and remembered today as a nationalist who resisted British and French economic pressure, Rosas proved to be a despotic leader, crushing his opponents and forcing people to display his slogan: "Death to the savage, filthy unitarians." His brand of populist, authoritarian, personalist politics drove liberal opponents into exile, where they plotted his overthrow. Eventually, the liberal exiles joined forces with the caudillos jealous of the advantages Rosas's brand of federalism had given Buenos Aires province. In 1852, this coalition defeated Rosas and drove him from power.

There followed a confused decade of rival governments because the questions of federalism and the role of Buenos Aires within the nation remained unresolved. A new constitution was issued in 1853 under the influence of Juan Bautista Alberdi, an able and progressive journalist who was also a strong believer in the need to encourage immigration. This constitution incorporated the programs of the federalists but guaranteed national unity through the power of the presidency over the provincial governors. By 1862, after considerable fighting, a compromise was worked out and the new, unified nation, now called the **Argentine Republic,** entered into a period of prosperity and growth under a series of liberal presidents whose programs paralleled the Reforma in Mexico. The age of the liberals was now in full swing.

Between 1862 and 1890, able and intelligent presidents like **Domingo F. Sarmiento** (1811–1888) initiated a wide series of political reforms and economic measures designed to bring progress to Argentina. Sarmiento was an archetype of the liberal reformers of the mid-century. A great admirer of England and the United States, a firm believer in the value of education, and an ardent supporter of progress, Sarmiento had been a constant opponent of Rosas and had been driven into exile. During that time, he wrote *Facundo*, a critique of the caudillo politics of the region, in which the "barbarism" of the gauchos and their leaders was contrasted to the "civilization" of the liberal reformers. (See the Document in this chapter.)

Now in power, Sarmiento and the other liberal leaders were able to put their programs into practice. They were aided by several factors. Political stability made investment more attractive to foreign banks and merchants. The expansion of the Argentine economy, especially exports of beef, hides, and wool, created the basis for prosperity. Foreign trade in 1890 was five times as great as it had been in 1860. The population tripled to more than 3 million as the agricultural expansion, high wages, and opportunities for mobility attracted large numbers of European immigrants. Buenos Aires became a great, sprawling metropolis (Figure 25.4). With increased revenues, the government could initiate reforms in education, transportation, and other areas, often turning to foreign models and foreign investors. There was also an increased feeling of national unity. A long and bloody war waged by Argentina, Brazil, and Uruguay against their neighbor Paraguay from 1865 to 1870 created a sense of unity and national pride.

That sense was also heightened by the final defeat of the American Indians south of Buenos Aires by 1880 as more land was opened to ranching and agriculture. At about the same time as in the United States, the railroad, the telegraph, and the repeating

Figure 25.4 *The tremendous boom in the Argentine economy was reflected in the growth of Buenos Aires, the so-called Paris of the Americas, as a cosmopolitan urban center.*

rifle brought an end to the American Indians' resistance and opened their lands to settlement. The American Indians, who were pushed far to the south, and the gauchos, whose way of life was displaced by the tide of immigrants, received little sympathy from the liberal government. By 1890, Argentina seemed to represent the achievement of a liberal program for Latin America.

The Brazilian Empire

It was sometimes said that despite its monarchical form, Brazil was the only functioning republic in South America in the 19th century. At first glance it seemed that Brazil avoided much of the political instability and turmoil found elsewhere in the continent and that through the mediation of the emperor a political compromise was worked out. However, problems and patterns similar to those in Spanish America lay beneath that facade. The transition to nationhood was smooth, and thus the basic foundations of Brazilian society—slavery, large landholdings, and an export economy—remained securely in place, reinforced by a new Brazilian nobility created for the new empire.

Brazilian independence had been declared in 1822, and by 1824 a liberal constitution had been issued by Dom Pedro I, the young Brazilian monarch, although not without resistance from those who wanted a republic or at least a very weak constitutional monarchy. But Dom Pedro I was an autocrat. In 1831, he was forced to abdicate in favor of his young son, Pedro (later to become Dom Pedro II), but the boy was too young to rule, and a series of regents directed the country in his name. What followed was an experiment in republican government, although the facade of monarchy was maintained.

The next decade was as tumultuous as any in Spanish America. The conflict between liberalism and conservatism was complicated by the existence of monarchist and antimonarchist factions in Brazil. A series of regional revolts erupted, some of which took on aspects of social wars as people of all classes were mobilized in the fighting. The army suppressed these movements. By 1840, however, the politicians were willing to see the young Dom Pedro II begin to rule in his own name.

Meanwhile, Brazil had been undergoing an economic transformation brought about by a new export crop: coffee. Coffee provided a new basis for agricultural expansion in southern Brazil. In the provinces of Rio de Janeiro and then São Paulo, coffee estates, or **fazendas,** began to spread toward the interior as new lands were opened. By 1840, coffee made up more than 40 percent of Brazil's exports, and by 1880, that figure reached 60 percent.

Along with the expansion of coffee growing came an intensification of slavery, Brazil's primary form of labor. For a variety of humanitarian and economic reasons, Great Britain pressured Brazil to end the slave trade from Africa during the 19th century, but the slave trade continued on an enormous scale up to 1850. More than 1.4 million Africans were imported to Brazil in the last 50 years of the trade, and even after the trans-Atlantic slave trade ended, slavery continued. At mid-century, about one-fourth of Brazil's population were still enslaved. Although some reformers were in favor of ending slavery, a real abolitionist movement did not develop in Brazil until after 1870. Brazil did not finally abolish slavery until 1888.

As in the rest of Latin America, the years after 1850 saw considerable growth and prosperity in Brazil. Dom Pedro II proved to be an enlightened man of middle-class habits who was anxious to reign over a tranquil and progressive nation, even if that tranquility was based on slave labor. The trappings of a monarchy, a court, and noble titles kept the elite attached to the regime. Meanwhile, railroads, steamships, and the telegraph began to change communication and transportation. Foreign companies invested in these projects as well as in banking and other activities. In growing cities such as Rio de Janeiro and São Paulo, merchants, lawyers, a middle class, and an urban working class began to exert pressure on the government. Less wedded to landholding and slavery, these new groups were a catalyst for change, even though the right to vote was still very limited. Moreover, the nature of the labor force was changing.

After 1850, a tide of immigrants, mostly from Italy and Portugal, began to reach Brazil's shores, increasingly attracted by government immigration schemes. Between 1850 and 1875, more than 300,000 immigrants arrived in Brazil; more than two-thirds of them went to work in the coffee estates of southern Brazil. Their presence lessened the dependence on slavery, and by 1870 the abolitionist movement was gaining strength. A series of laws freeing children and the aged, the sympathy of Dom Pedro II, the agitation by abolitionists (both black and white), and the efforts of the slaves (who began to resist and run away in large numbers) brought in 1888 an end to slavery in Brazil, the last nation in the Western Hemisphere to abolish it.

Support for the monarchy began to wither. The long war of the triple alliance against Paraguay (1865–1870) had become unpopular, and the military began to take an active role in politics. Squabbles with the church undercut support from the clergy. The planters now turned increasingly to immigrants for their laborers, and some began to modernize their operations. The ideas of positivism, a modernizing philosophy that attempted to bring about material progress by applying scientific principles to government and society, attracted many intellectuals and key members of the army. Politically, a Republican party formed in 1871 began to gather support in urban areas from a wide spectrum of the population. The Brazilian monarchy, long a defender of the planter class and its interests, could not survive the abolition of slavery. In 1889, a nearly bloodless military coup deposed the emperor and established a republic under military men strongly influenced by positivist intellectuals and Republican politicians.

But such "progress" came at certain costs in many nations in Latin America. In the harsh backlands of northeastern Brazil, for example, the change to a republic, economic hardship, and the secularization of society provoked peasant unrest. Antonio Conselheiro, a religious mystic, began to gather followers in the 1890s, especially among the dispossessed peasantry. Eventually, their community, Canudos, contained thousands. The government feared these "fanatics" and sent four military expeditions against Canudos, Conselheiro's "New Jerusalem." The fighting was bloody, and casualties were in the thousands. Conselheiro and his followers put up a determined guerilla defense of their town and their view of the world. The tragedy of Canudos' destruction moved journalist Euclides da Cunha to write *Rebellion in the Backlands* (*Os sertões*, 1902), an account of the events. Like Sarmiento, he saw them as a struggle between civilization and barbarism. However, da Cunha maintained great sympathy for the followers of Antonio Conselheiro (Figure 25.5), and he argued that civilization could not be spread in the flash of a cannon. The book has become a classic of Latin American literature, but the problems of national integration and the disruption of traditional values in the wake of modernization and change remained unresolved.

Figure 25.5 *Refugees of Canudos*

Societies in Search of Themselves

 There was a tension in cultural life between European influences and the desire to express an American reality, or between elite and folk culture. Social change came very slowly for American Indians, blacks, and women, but by the end of the century the desire for progress and economic resurgence was beginning to have social effects.

Cultural Expression After Independence

The end of colonial rule opened up Latin America to direct influences from the rest of Europe. Scientific observers, travelers, and the just plain curious—often accompanied by artists—came to see and record, and while doing so introduced new ideas and fashions.

Artistic and cultural missions sometimes were brought directly from Europe by Latin American governments.

The elites of the new nations adopted the tastes and fashions of Europe. The battles and triumphs of independence were celebrated in paintings, hymns, odes, and theatrical pieces in the neoclassical style in an attempt to use Greece and Rome as a model for the present. Latin Americans followed the lead of Europe, especially France. The same neoclassical tradition also was apparent in the architecture of the early 19th century.

In the 1830s, the generation that came of age after independence turned to romanticism and found the basis of a new nationality in historical images, the American Indian, and local customs. This generation often had a romantic view of liberty. They emphasized the exotic as well as the distinctive aspects of American society. In Brazil, for example, poet António Gonçalves Dias (1823–1864) used the American Indian as a symbol of Brazil and America. In Cuba, novels sympathetic to slaves began to appear by mid-century. In Argentina, writers celebrated the pampas and its open spaces. Sarmiento's critical account of the caudillos in *Facundo* described in depth the life of the gauchos, but it was José Hernández who in 1872 wrote *Martín Fierro*, a romantic epic poem about the end of the way of the gaucho. Historical themes and the writing of history became a political act because studying the past became a way of organizing the present. Many of Latin America's leading politicians were also excellent historians and the theme of their writing was the creation of the nation.

By the 1870s, a new realism emerged in the arts and literature that was more in line with the scientific approach of positivism and the modernization of the new nations. As the economies of Latin America surged forward, novelists appeared who were unafraid to deal with human frailties such as corruption, prejudice, and greed. Chilean Alberto Blest Gana and Brazilian mulatto J. Machado de Assis (1839–1908; Figure 25.6) wrote critically about the social mores of their countries during this era.

Throughout the century, the culture of the mass of the population had been little affected by the trends and tastes of the elite. Popular arts, folk music, and dance flourished in traditional settings, demonstrating a vitality and adaptability to new situations that was often lacking in the more imitative fine arts. Sometimes authors in the romantic tradition or poets such as Hernández turned to traditional themes for

Figure 25.6 *J. Machado de Assis (1839–1908) was a gifted African Brazilian author of humble origins whose psychological short stories and novels won him acclaim as Brazil's greatest novelist of the 19th century.*

their subject and inspiration, and in that way they brought these traditions to the greater attention of their class and the world. For the most part, however, popular artistic expressions were not appreciated or valued by the traditional elites, the modernizing urban bourgeoisie, or the new immigrants.

Old Patterns of Gender, Class, and Race

Although significant political changes make it appealing to deal with the 19th century as an era of great change and transformation in Latin America, it is necessary to recognize the persistence of old patterns and sometimes their reinforcement. Changes took place, to be sure, but their effects were not felt equally by all classes or groups in society, nor were all groups attracted by the promises of the new political regimes and their views of progress.

For example, women gained little ground during most of the century. They had participated actively in the independence movements. Some had taken up arms or aided the insurgent forces, and some—such as Colombian Policarpa (La Pola) Salvatierra, whose final words were "Do not forget my example"—had paid for their activities on the gallows. After independence, there was almost no change in the predominant attitudes toward women's proper role. Expected to be wives and mothers, women could not vote, hold public office, become lawyers, or in some places testify in a court of law. Although there were a few exceptions, unmarried women younger than 25 remained under the power and authority of their fathers. Once married, they could not work, enter into contracts, or control their own estates without permission of their husbands. As in the colonial era, marriage, politics, and the creation of kinship links were essential elements in elite control of land and political power, and thus women remained a crucial resource in family strategies.

Lower-class women had more economic freedom—often controlling local marketing—and also more personal freedom than elite women under the constraints of powerful families. In legal terms, however, their situation was no better—and in material terms, much worse—than that of their elite sisters. Still, by the 1870s women were an important part of the workforce.

The one area in which the situation of women began to change significantly was public education. There had already been a movement in this direction in the colonial era. At first, the idea behind education for girls and women was that because women were responsible for educating their children, they should be educated so that the proper values could be passed to the next generation. By 1842, Mexico City required girls and boys aged 7 to 15 to attend school, and in 1869 the first girls' school was created in Mexico. Liberals in Mexico wanted secular public education to prepare women for an enlightened role within the home, and similar sentiments were expressed by liberal regimes elsewhere. Public schools appeared throughout Latin America, although their impact was limited. For example, Brazil had a population of 10 million in 1873, but only about 1 million men and half that number of women were literate.

The rise of secular public education created new opportunities for women. The demand for teachers at the primary level created the need for schools in which to train teachers. Because most teachers were women, these teacher training schools gave women access to advanced education. Although the curriculum often emphasized traditional female roles, an increasing number of educated women began to emerge who were dissatisfied with the legal and social constraints on their lives. By the end of the 19th century, these women were becoming increasingly active in advocating women's rights and other political issues.

In most cases, the new nations legally ended the old society of castes in which legal status and definition depended on color and ethnicity, but in reality much of that system continued. The stigma of skin color and former slave status created barriers to advancement. Indigenous peoples in Mexico, Bolivia, and Peru often continued to labor under poor conditions and to suffer the effects of government failures. There was conflict. In Yucatan, a great rebellion broke out, pitting the Maya against the central government and the whites, in 1839 and again in 1847. It smoldered for 10 years. Despite the intentions of governments, American Indians resisted changes imposed from outside their communities and were willing to defend their traditional ways. The word *Indian* was still an insult in most places in Latin America. For some mestizos and others of mixed origin, the century presented opportunities for advancement in the army, professions, and commerce, but these cases were exceptions.

In many places, expansion of the export economy perpetuated old patterns. Liberalism itself changed during the century, and once its program of secularization, rationalism, and property rights were made law, it became more restrictive. Positivists of the end of the century still hoped for economic growth, but some were willing to gain it at the expense of individual freedoms. The positivists generally were convinced of the benefits of international trade for Latin America, and large landholdings increased in many areas at the expense of small farms and Indian communal lands as a result. A small, white Creole, landed upper class controlled the economies and politics in most places, and they were sometimes joined in the political and economic functions by a stratum of urban middle-class merchants, bureaucrats, and other bourgeois types. The landed and mercantile elite tended to merge over time to create one group that, in most places, controlled the government. Meanwhile, new social forces were at work. The flood

In Depth

Explaining Underdevelopment

The terms *underdeveloped* and the more benign *developing* describe a large number of nations in the world with a series of economic and social problems. Because Latin America was first among what we now call the *developing nations* to establish its independence and begin to compete in the world economy, it had to confront the reasons for its relative position and problems early and without many models to follow. The Document section of this chapter offers two visions of Latin America's early problems that are similar because both emphasize the Hispanic cultural heritage, as well as its supposed deficiencies or strengths, as a key explanation for the region's history. Such cultural explanations were popular among 19th-century intellectuals and political leaders, and they continue today, although other general theories based on economics and politics have become more popular.

At the time of Latin American independence, the adoption of European models of economy, government, and law seemed to offer great hope. But as "progress," republican forms of government, free trade, and liberalism failed to bring about general prosperity and social harmony, Latin Americans and others began to search for alternative explanations of their continuing problems as a first step in solving them. Some critics condemned the Hispanic cultural legacy; others saw the materialism of the modern world as the major problem and called for a return to religion and idealism. By the 20th century, Marxism provided a powerful analysis of Latin America's history and present reality, although Marxists themselves could not decide whether Latin American societies were essentially feudal and needed first to become capitalist or whether they were already capitalist and were ready for socialist revolution.

Throughout these debates, Latin Americans often implicitly compared their situation with that of the United States and tried to explain the different economic positions of the two regions. At the beginning of the 19th century, both regions were still primarily agricultural, and although a few places in North America were starting small industries, the mining sector in Latin America was far stronger than that of its northern neighbor. In 1850, the population of Latin America was 33 million, the population of the United States was 23 million, and the per capita income in both regions was roughly equal. By 1940, however, Latin America's population was much larger and its economic situation was far worse than in the United States. Observers were preoccupied by why and how this disparity arose. Was there some flaw in the Latin American character, or were the explanations to be found in the economic and political differences between the two areas, and how could these differences be explained? The answers to these questions were not easy to obtain, but increasingly they were sought not in the history of individual countries but in analyses of a world economic and political system.

There had long been a Marxist critique of colonialism and imperialism, but the modern Latin American analysis of underdevelopment grew from different origins. During the 1950s, a number of European and North American scholars developed the concept of *modernization*, or *westernization*. Basing their ideas on the historical experience of western Europe, they believed that development was a matter of increasing per capita production in any society, and that as development took place various kinds of social changes would follow. The more industrialized, urban, and modern a society became, the more social change and improvement were possible as traditional patterns and attitudes were abandoned or transformed. Technology, communication, and the distribution of material goods were the means by which the transformation would take place. Some scholars also believed that as this process occurred there would be a natural movement toward more democratic forms of government and popular participation.

Modernization theory held out the promise that any society could move toward a brighter future by following the path taken earlier by western Europe. Its message was one of improvement through gradual rather than radical or revolutionary change, and thus it tended to be politically conservative. It also tended to disregard cultural differences, internal class conflicts, and struggles for power within nations. Moreover, sometimes it was adopted by military regimes that believed that imposing order was the best way to promote the economic changes necessary for modernization.

The proponents of modernization theory had a difficult time convincing many people in the "underdeveloped" world, where the historical experience had been very different from that of western Europe. In 19th-century Latin America, for example, early

(continued)

attempts to develop industry were faced with competition from the cheaper and better products of already industrialized nations such as England and France, so a similar path to development was impossible. Critics argued that each nation did not operate individually but was part of a world system that kept some areas "developed" at the expense of others.

These ideas were first and most cogently expressed in Latin America. After World War II, the United Nations established an Economic Commission for Latin America (ECLA). Under the leadership of Argentine economist Raul Prebisch, the ECLA began to analyze the Latin American economies. Prebisch argued that "unequal exchange" between the developed nations at the center of the world economy and those like Latin America created structural blocks to economic growth. The ECLA suggested various policies to overcome the problems, especially the development of industries that would overcome the region's dependence on foreign imports.

From the structural analysis of the ECLA and from more traditional Marxist critiques, a new kind of explanation, usually called *dependency theory*, began to emerge in the 1960s. Rather than seeing underdevelopment or the lack of economic growth as the result of failed modernization, some scholars in Latin America began to argue that development and underdevelopment were not stages but part of the same process. They believed that the development and growth of some areas, such as western Europe and the United States, were achieved at the expense of, or because of, the underdevelopment of dependant regions such as Latin America. Agricultural economies at the periphery of the world economic system always were at a disadvantage in dealing with the industrial nations of the center, and thus they would become poorer as the industrial nations got richer. The industrial nations would continually draw products, profits, and cheap labor from the periphery. This basic economic relationship of dependency meant that external forces determined production, capital accumulation, and class relations in a dependant country. Some theorists went further and argued that Latin America and other nations of the Third World were culturally dependant in their consumption of ideas and concepts. Both modernization theory and Mickey Mouse were seen as the agents of a cultural domination that was simply an extension of economic reality. These theorists usually argued that socialism offered the only hope for breaking out of the dependency relationship.

These ideas, which dominated Latin American intellectual life, were appealing to other areas of Asia and Africa that had recently emerged from colonial control. Forms of dependency analysis became popular in many areas of the world in the 1960s and 1970s. By the 1980s, however, dependency theory was losing its appeal. As an explanation of what had happened historically in Latin America, it was useful, but as a theory that could predict what might happen elsewhere, it provided little help. Marxists argued that it overemphasized the circulation of goods (trade) rather than how things were produced and that it ignored the class conflicts they believed were the driving force of history. Moreover, with the rise of multinational corporations and globalization, capitalism itself was changing and was becoming less tied to individual countries. Thus an analysis based on trade relationships between countries became somewhat outdated.

Can development be widespread, as modernization theory argued, or is the underdevelopment of some countries inherent in the capitalist world economy, as the dependency theorists believe? The issue is still in dispute. The search for new explanations and new solutions to the problems of development will continue as peoples throughout the world work to improve their lives.

Questions: In what sense was 19th-century Latin America a dependant economy? Which explanation or prediction about dependancy best fits world economic trends today?

of immigration, beginning in earnest in the 1870s, to Argentina, Brazil, and a few other nations began to change the social composition of those places. Increasingly, rapid urbanization also changed these societies. Still, Latin America, though politically independent, began the 1880s as a group of predominantly agrarian nations with rigid social structures and a continuing dependency on the world market.

The Great Boom, 1880–1920

 Between 1880 and 1920, Latin America, like certain areas of Asia and Africa, experienced a tremendous spurt of economic growth, stimulated by the increasing demand in industrializing Europe and the United States for raw materials, foodstuffs, and specialized tropical crops. Mexico and Argentina are two excellent examples of the effects of these changes, but not all groups shared the benefits of economic growth. By the end of the 19th century, the United States was beginning to intervene directly in Latin American affairs.

Latin America was well prepared for export-led economic expansion. The liberal ideology of individual freedoms, an open market, and limited government intervention in the operation of the economy had triumphed in many places. Whereas this ideology had been the expression of the middle class in Europe, in Latin America it was adopted not only by the small urban middle class but also by the large landowners, miners, and export merchants linked to the rural economy and the traditional patterns of wealth and land owning. In a number of countries, a political alliance was forged between the traditional aristocracy of wealth and the new urban elements. Together they controlled the presidential offices and the congresses and imposed a business-as-usual approach to government at the expense of peasants and a newly emerging working class.

The expansion of Latin American economies was led by exports. Each nation had a specialty: bananas and coffee from the nations of Central America; tobacco and sugar from Cuba; rubber and coffee from Brazil; hennequen (a fiber for making rope), copper, and silver from Mexico; wool, wheat, and beef from Argentina; copper from Chile. In this era of strong demand and good prices, these nations made high profits. This allowed them to import large quantities of foreign goods, and it provided funds for the beautification of cities and other government projects. But export-led expansion was always risky because the world market prices of Latin American commodities ultimately were determined by conditions outside the region. In that sense, these economies were particularly vulnerable and in some ways dependent.

Also, export-led expansion could result in rivalry, hostility, and even war between neighboring countries. Control of the nitrates that lay in areas between Chile, Peru, and Bolivia generated a dispute that led to the War of the Pacific (1879–1883), pitting Chile against Bolivia and Peru. Although all were unprepared for a modern war at first, eventually thousands of troops were mobilized. The Chileans occupied Lima in 1881 and then imposed a treaty on Peru. Bolivia lost Antofagasta and its access to the Pacific Ocean and became a landlocked nation. Chile increased its size by a third and benefited from an economic boom during and after the war. In Peru and Bolivia, governments fell, and a sense of national crisis set in after the defeat in the "fertilizer war."

The expansion of Latin American trade was remarkable. It increased by about 50 percent between 1870 and 1890. Argentina's trade was increasing at about 5 percent a year during this period—one of the highest rates of growth ever recorded for a national economy. "As wealthy as an Argentine" became an expression in Paris, reflecting the fortunes that wool, beef, and grain were earning for some in Argentina. In Mexico, an oligarchic dictatorship, which maintained all the outward attributes of democracy but imposed "law and order" under the dictator Porfirio Díaz, created the conditions for unrestrained profits. Mexican exports doubled between 1877 and 1900. Similar figures could be cited for Chile, Costa Rica, and Bolivia.

This rapidly expanding commerce attracted the interest of foreign investors eager for high returns on their capital. British, French, German, and North American businesses and entrepreneurs invested in mining, railroads, public utilities, and banking. More than half the foreign investments in Latin America were British, which alone were 10 times more in 1913 than they had been in 1870. But British leadership was no longer uncontested; Germany and, increasingly, the United States provided competition. The United States was particularly active in the Caribbean region and Mexico, but not until after World War I did United States capital predominate in the region.

Foreign investments provided Latin America with needed capital and services but tended to place key industries, transportation facilities, and services in foreign hands. Foreign investments also constrained Latin American governments in their social, commercial, and diplomatic policies.

Mexico and Argentina: Examples of Economic Transformation

We can use these two large Latin American nations as examples of different responses within the same general pattern. In Mexico, the liberal triumph of Juárez had set the stage for economic growth and constitutional government. In 1876, Porfirio Díaz, one of

Juárez's generals, was elected president, and for the next 35 years he dominated politics. Díaz suppressed regional rebellions and imposed a strong centralized government. Financed by foreign capital, the railroad system grew rapidly, providing a new way to integrate Mexican regional economies, move goods to the ports for export, and allow the movement of government troops to keep order. Industrialization began to take place. Foreign investment was encouraged in mining, transportation, and other sectors of the economy, and financial policies were changed to promote investments. For example, United States investments expanded from about 30 million pesos in 1883 to more than $1 billion by 1911.

The forms of liberal democracy were maintained but were subverted to keep Díaz in power and to give his development plans an open track. Behind these policies were a number of advisors who were strongly influenced by positivist ideas and who wanted to impose a scientific approach on the national economy. These **cientificos** set the tone for Mexico while the government suppressed any political opposition to these policies. Díaz's Mexico projected an image of modernization led by a Europeanized elite who greatly profited from the economic growth and the imposition of order under Don Porfirio.

Growth often was bought at the expense of Mexico's large rural peasantry and its growing urban and working classes. This population was essentially native, because unlike Argentina and Brazil, Mexico had received few immigrants. They participated very little in the prosperity of export-led growth. Economic expansion at the expense of peasants and American Indian communal lands created a volatile situation.

Strikes and labor unrest increased, particularly among railroad workers, miners, and textile workers. In the countryside, a national police force, the Rurales, maintained order, and the army was mobilized when needed. At the regional level, political bosses linked to the Díaz regime in Mexico City delivered the votes in rigged elections.

For 35 years, Díaz reigned supreme and oversaw the transformation of the Mexican economy. His opponents were arrested or driven into exile, and the small middle class, the landowners, miners, and foreign investors celebrated the progress of Mexico. In 1910, however, a middle-class movement with limited political goals seeking electoral reform began to mushroom into a more general uprising in which the frustrations of the poor, the workers, the peasants, and nationalist intellectuals of various political persuasions erupted in a bloody 10-year civil war, the Mexican Revolution.

At the other end of the hemisphere, Argentina followed an alternative path of economic expansion. By 1880, the American Indians on the southern pampas had been conquered, and vast new tracts of land were opened to ranching. The strange relationship between Buenos Aires and the rest of the nation was resolved when Buenos Aires was made a federal district. With a rapidly expanding economy, it became "the Paris of South America," an expression that reflected the drive by wealthy Argentines to establish themselves as a modern nation. By 1914, Buenos Aires had more than 2 million inhabitants, or about one-fourth of the national population. Its political leaders, the "Generation of 1880," inherited the liberal program of Sarmiento and other liberals, and they were able to enact their programs because of the high levels of income the expanding economy generated.

Technological changes contributed to Argentine prosperity. Refrigerated ships allowed fresh beef to be sent directly to Europe, and this along with wool and wheat provided the basis of expansion. The flood of immigrants provided labor. Some were *golondrinas* (literally, "swallows"), who were able to work one harvest in Italy and then a second in Argentina because of the differences in seasons in the two hemispheres, but many immigrants elected to stay. Almost 3.5 million immigrants stayed in Argentina between 1857 and 1930, and unlike the Mexican population, by 1914 about one-third of the Argentine population was foreign born. Italians, Germans, Russians, and Jews came to "hacer America"—that is, "to make America"—and remained. In a way, they really did Europeanize Argentina, as did not happen in Mexico, introducing the folkways and ideologies of the European rural and working classes. The result was a fusion of cultures that produced not only a radical workers' movement but also the distinctive music of the tango, which combined Spanish, African, and other musical elements in the cafe and red-light districts of Buenos Aires. The tango became the music of the Argentine urban working class.

As the immigrant flood increased, workers began to seek political expression. A Socialist party was formed in the 1890s and tried to elect representatives to office. Anarchists hoped to smash the political system and called for strikes and walkouts. Inspired to some extent by European ideological battles, the struggle spilled into the streets. Violent strikes and government repression characterized the decade after 1910, culminating in a series of strikes in 1918 that led to extreme repression. Development had its social costs.

The Argentine oligarchy was capable of some internal reform, however. A new party representing the emerging middle class began to organize aided by an electoral law in 1912 that called for secret ballots, universal male suffrage, and compulsory voting. With this change, the Radical party, promising political reform and more liberal policies for workers, came to power in 1916, but faced with labor unrest it acted as repressively as its predecessors. The oligarchy made room for middle-class politicians and interests, but the problems of Argentina's expanding labor force remained unresolved, and Argentina's economy remained closely tied to the international market for its exports.

With many variations, similar patterns of economic growth, political domination by oligarchies formed by traditional aristocracies and "progressive" middle classes, and a rising tide of labor unrest or rural rebellion can be noted elsewhere in Latin America. Modernization was not welcomed by all sectors of society. Messianic religious movements in Brazil, American Indian resistance to the loss of lands in Colombia, and banditry in Mexico were all to some extent reactions to the changes being forced on the societies by national governments tied to the ideology of progress and often insensitive to its effects.

Uncle Sam Goes South

After its Civil War, the United States began to take a more direct and active interest in the politics and economies of Latin America. Commerce and investments began to expand rapidly in this period, especially in Mexico and Central America. American industry was seeking new markets and raw materials, while the growing population of the United States created a demand for Latin American products. Attempts were made to create inter-American cooperation. A major turning point came in 1898 with the outbreak of war between Spain and the United States, which began to join the nations of western Europe in the age of imperialism.

The war centered on Cuba and Puerto Rico, Spain's last colonies in the Americas. The Cuban economy had boomed in the 19th century on the basis of its exports of sugar and tobacco grown with slave labor. A 10-year civil war for independence, beginning in 1868, had failed in its main objective but had won the island some autonomy. A number of ardent Cuban nationalists, including journalist and poet José Martí, had gone into exile to continue the struggle. Fighting erupted again in 1895, and the United States joined in 1898, declaring war on Spain and occupying Cuba, Puerto Rico, and the Philippines.

In fact, U.S. investments in Cuba had been increasing rapidly before the war, and the United States had become a major market for Cuban sugar. The **Spanish-American War** opened the door to direct U.S. involvement in the Caribbean. A U.S. government of occupation was imposed on Cuba and Puerto Rico, which had witnessed its own stirrings for independence in the 19th century. When the occupation of Cuba ended in 1902, a series of onerous conditions was imposed on independent Cuba that made it almost an American dependency—a status that was legally imposed in Puerto Rico.

For strategic, commercial, and economic reasons, Latin America, particularly the Caribbean and Mexico, began to attract American interest at the turn of the century. These considerations lay behind the drive to build a canal across Central America that would shorten the route between the Atlantic and Pacific. When Colombia proved reluctant to meet American proposals, the United States backed a Panamanian movement for independence and then signed a treaty with its representative that granted the United States extensive rights over the **Panama Canal.** President Theodore Roosevelt was a major force behind the canal, which was opened to traffic in 1914.

The Panama Canal was a remarkable engineering feat and a fitting symbol of the technological and industrial strength of the United States. North Americans were proud of these achievements and hoped to demonstrate the superiority of the "American way"— a feeling fed to some extent by racist ideas and a sense of cultural superiority. Latin Americans were wary of American power and intentions in the area. Many intellectuals cautioned against the expansionist designs of the United States and against what they saw as the materialism of American culture. Uruguayan José Enrique Rodó, in his essay *Ariel* (1900), contrasted the spirituality of Hispanic culture with the materialism of the United States. Elsewhere in Latin America, others offered similar critiques.

Latin American criticism had a variety of origins: nationalism, a Catholic defense of traditional values, and some socialist attacks on expansive capitalism. In a way, Latin America, which had achieved its political independence in the 19th century and had been part of European developments, was able to articulate the fears and the reactions of the areas that had become the colonies and semicolonies of western Europe and the United States in the age of empire.

 ## GLOBAL CONNECTIONS: New Latin American Nations and the World

During the 19th century, the nations of Latin America moved from the status of colonies to that of independent nation-states. The process was sometimes exhilarating and often painful, but during the course of the century, these nations were able to create governments and begin to address many social and economic problems. These problems were inherited from the colonial era and were intensified by internal political and ideological conflicts and foreign intervention. Moreover, the Latin American nations had to revive their economies after their struggles for independence and to confront their position within the world economic system as suppliers of agricultural products and consumers of manufactured goods.

To some extent Latin America ran against the currents of global history in the 19th century. During the great age of imperialism, Latin America cast off the previous colonial controls. Swept by the same winds of change that had transformed Europe's society and economy and led to the separation of England's North American colonies, Latin American countries struggled with the problems of nation-building while, like China and Russia, holding off colonial incursions. In this sense, and also in some efforts to define a Latin American cultural identity, Latin America became a bit more isolated in the world at large.

The heritage of the past weighed heavily on Latin America. Political and social changes were many, and pressures for these changes came from a variety of sources, such as progressive politicians, modernizing military men, a growing urban population, dissatisfied workers, and disadvantaged peasants. Still, in many ways Latin America remained remarkably unchanged. Revolts were frequent, but revolutions that changed the structure of society or the distribution of land and wealth were few, and the reforms intended to make such changes usually were unsuccessful. The elite con-trolled most of the economic resources, a growing but still small urban sector had emerged politically but either remained weak or had to accommodate the elite, and most of the population continued to labor on the land with little hope of improvement. Latin America had a distinctive civilization, culturally and politically sharing much of the Western tradition yet economically functioning more like areas of Asia and Africa. Latin America was the first non-Western area to face the problems of decolonization, and many aspects of its history that seemed so distinctive in the 19th century proved to be previews of what would follow: decolonization and nation-building elsewhere in the world in the 20th century.

Latin America's global connections included ongoing political and cultural ties with the West. Efforts to imitate the West accelerated in some regions, for example, with the importation of sports like soccer. Growing influence and intervention from the United States was another outside force. New immigration, from southern Europe but also now from Asia, brought additional connections. But Latin America's most significant global link continued to involve its dependant economy, drawing goods, now including machinery, from the West while exporting a growing range of foods and raw materials.

Further Readings

Stanley J. and Barbara Stein's *The Colonial Heritage of Latin America* (1970) is a hard-hitting interpretation of colonial and 19th-century Latin America that emphasizes its continued dependency and its neocolonial status after independence. David Bushnell and Neil Macauley's *The Emergence of Latin America in the Nineteenth Century* (1988) provides an excellent overview that is critical of the dependency thesis. The classic study from the dependency perspective is Fernando Henrique Cardoso and Enzo Faletto's *Dependency and Development in Latin America* (1979). Roberto Cortés Conde's *The First Stages of Modernization in Spanish America* (1974) provides a good economic analysis, as does S. Haber, *Why Latin America Fell Behind* (1997). The movements for independence are described in John Lynch's *The Spanish American Revolutions* (1973). Tulio Halperin Donghi's *The Aftermath of Revolution in Latin America* (1973) analyzes the first half of the 19th century. Claudio Veliz's *The Centralist Tradition in Latin America* (1980) tries to explain the divergent development of Latin America and western Europe, and E. Bradford Burns' *Poverty or Progress: Latin America in the Nineteenth Century* (1973) provides a challenging attack on the liberal programs and a defense of a folk political tradition. Jean Franco's *The Modern Culture of Latin America: Society and the Artist* (1967) is a lively discussion of literature and the arts. Volumes 3 to 5 of *The Cambridge History of Latin America* (1985–1986) contain up-to-date essays on major themes and individual countries. A good essay from the collection is Robert Freeman Smith's "Latin America, the United States, and the European Powers, 1830–1930," vol. 4, 83–120.

There are many single-volume country histories and monographs on particular topics. David Rock's *Argentina* (1985), E. B. Burns' *A History of Brazil* (1980), Michael Meyer and William Sherman's *The Course of Mexican History* (1979), and Herbert Klein's *Bolivia* (1982) are good examples of national histories. There are excellent rural histories, such as Stanley Stein's *Vassouras: A Brazilian Coffee County* (2nd ed., 1989), Charles Berquist's *Coffee and Conflict in Colombia, 1886–1910* (1978), and Arnold Bauer's *Chilean Rural Society* (1975). Silvia Arrom's *The Women of Mexico City* (1985) is a fine example of the growing literature in women's history, some of which is also seen in June Nash and Helen Safa, eds., *Sex and Class in Latin America* (1980). Hobart Spalding Jr.'s *Organized Labor in Latin America* (1977) surveys urban labor, and Charles Berquist's *Labor in Latin America* (1986) is a comparative interpretive essay.

On the Web

Simon Bolívar's views on state formation and his ambivalent attitude toward the United States are examined at http://victorian.fortunecity.com/dadd/453, http://www.emory.edu/COLLEGE/CULPEPER/BAKEWELL/texts/jamaica-letter.html, and http://www.airpower.maxwell.af.mil/airchronicles/aureview/1986/jul-aug/bushnell.html.

The life and career of his co-revolutionist in the South, Jose de San Martín, is beautifully illustrated at http://pachami.com/English/sanmartin1E.htm and described at http://geocities.com/TimesSquare/1848/martin.html.

Bolívar and San Martín lived to see their visions compromised or betrayed, but they avoided the tragic fate of the hero of the Mexican war for independence, Father Miguel de Hidalgo, http://www.mexconnect.com/mex_/travel/ganderson/gadeloresh.html.

The Monroe Doctrine (http://www.yale.edu/lawweb/avalon/monroe.htm) and Thomas Jefferson's comments on its "imperial" implications (http://www.mtholyoke.edu/acad/intrel/thomas.htm) are worthy of close attention. Other sites, including http://usinfo.state.gov/usa/infousa/facts/democrac/50.htm, stress that for all its later foreign policy implications, it was merely a reflection of John Quincy Adams' domestic political concerns. However, discourse over the Monroe Doctrine illuminates the process by which the United States evolved from a revolutionary upstart to a world power. Jefferson himself rejected a seizure of Cuba on moral grounds but noted its value as a possible addition to his country. Other American leaders with fewer scruples would later seize land from their neighbors to the South, a topic addressed at http://www.geocities.com/Athens/Ithaca/9852/usimp.htm and http://www.fordham.edu/halsall/mod/modsbook32.html. The concept of Manifest Destiny as it relates to world history beyond the United States-Mexican conflict is discussed at http://odur.let.rug.nl/~usa/E/manifest/manifxx.htm and http://www.pbs.org/kera/usmexicanwar/dialogues/prelude/manifest/d2aeng.html

For United States and Latin American relations generally, see http://www.uoregon.edu/~caguirre/uslatam.html.

CIVILIZATIONS IN CRISIS: THE OTTOMAN EMPIRE, THE ISLAMIC HEARTLANDS, AND QING CHINA

In the late 19th century, the Chinese were forced to concede port and warehouse areas, such as the one in this painting, to rival imperialist powers. These areas were, in effect, colonial enclaves. They were guarded by foreign troops, flew foreign flags, and were run by Western or Japanese merchant councils.

- From Empire to Nation: Ottoman Retreat and the Birth of Turkey
- IN DEPTH: Western Dominance and the Decline of Civilizations
- Western Intrusions and the Crisis in the Arab Islamic Heartlands
- The Last Dynasty: The Rise and Fall of the Qing Empire in China
- DOCUMENT: Building a New China
- GLOBAL CONNECTIONS: Muslim and Chinese Decline and a Shifting Global Balance

By the early 18th century, it appeared that two of the civilizations—Middle Eastern Islamic and Chinese—still capable of contesting the European drive for global dominance were headed in very different directions. Under the Qing dynasty, which was established by Manchu nomads from north of the Great Wall after the fall of the Ming emperors in the mid-17th century, China was enjoying yet another era of growth and prosperity. The territory controlled by the Manchus was greater than that claimed by any Chinese dynasty since the Tang in the 7th century. China's population was growing steadily, and its trade and agricultural production were keeping pace. Like other "barbarian" peoples, the Europeans were closely controlled by the bureaucrats of the Qing empire. European traders were confined to the ports of Macao and Canton on China's south coast. In the early 18th century, the Qing ruler had severely curtailed missionary activities in China without fear of foreign reprisals. Thus, despite signs of growing poverty and social unrest in some districts, the Manchus appeared to have restored good government and the well-being of the general populace of China.

At the other end of Asia, the fate of the Ottomans appeared to be exactly the reverse. After centuries of able rule and expansion at the expense of their Christian and Muslim neighbors (see Chapter 21), the Ottomans were in full retreat by the early 18th century. The Austrian Habsburgs chipped away at the Ottomans' European possessions from the west while a revived Russia closed in from the north. Muslim kingdoms in north Africa broke away from the empire, and imperial governors and local notables throughout the Arab portions of the Middle East grew more and more independent of the ruling sultan in Istanbul (formerly Constantinople). Political decline was accompanied by rising economic and social disruption. Inflation was rampant throughout much of the empire, and European imports were rapidly destroying what was left of the already battered Ottoman handicraft industries. The empire was racked by social tensions, crime, and rebellion in some areas. The divided Ottoman elite could not agree on a strategy for reinvigorating state and society. Nor could they find a way to halt the advance of the Christian infidels, whose military victories and economic inroads were undoing centuries of hard-won conquests. With the ranks of its Ottoman defenders reduced, the very heartlands of the Islamic world were increasingly at risk.

In little more than a century, the very different paths these two civilizations appeared to be following suddenly converged, and then the

1650 C.E.	**1800 C.E.**	**1850 C.E.**	**1875 C.E.**	**1900 C.E.**
1644 Manchu nomads conquer China; Qing dynasty rules	**1805–1849** Reign of Muhammad Ali in Egypt	**1850–1864** Taiping rebellion in China	**1876** Constitution promulgated for Ottoman Empire	**1905** Fatherland Party established in Egypt
1664–1722 Reign of Kangxi emperor in China	**1807–1839** Reign of Ottoman Sultan Mahmud II	**1854–1856** Crimean War	**1876–1908** Reign of Ottoman Sultan Abdul Hamid	**1908** Young Turks seize power in Istanbul
1727 First printing press set up in Ottoman Empire	**1826** Ottoman Janissary corps destroyed	**1856–1860** Anglo–French war against China	**1877** Treaty of San Stefano; Ottomans driven from most of the Balkans	
1736–1799 Reign of Qianlong emperor in China	**1834** Postal system established in Ottoman Empire	**1866** First railway begun in Ottoman Empire	**1882** British invasion and occupation of Egypt; failed revolt led by Orabi in Egypt	
1768–1774 Disastrous Ottoman war with Russia	**1838** Ottoman treaty with British removing trade restrictions in the empire	**1869** Opening of the Suez Canal	**1883** Mahdist victory over British-led Egyptian expeditionary force at Shakyan	
1772 Safavid dynasty falls in Persia	**1839–1841** Opium War in China	**1870** Ottoman legal code reformed	**1889** Young Turks established in Paris	
1789–1807 Reign of Ottoman Sultan Selim III	**1839–1876** *Tanzimat* reforms in the Ottoman Empire		**1898** British–Egyptian army defeats the Mahdist army at Omdurman	
1798 British embassy to Qianlong emperor in China; French invasion of Egypt; Napoleon defeats Egypt's Mameluk rulers	**1839–1897** Life of Islamic thinker al-Afghani		**1898–1901** Boxer Rebellion in China; 100 Days of Reform in China	
	1849–1905 Life of Muhammad Abduh			

Ottomans gained strength as China fell apart. A combination of internal weaknesses and growing pressure from the industrializing European powers threw China into a prolonged crisis in the early 19th century. If anything, Chinese civilization was revealed as even more vulnerable than the Islamic world, which the Ottomans sought to defend. The Ottomans began to find new sources of leadership and to introduce reforms on the basis of Western precedents. In sharp contrast, the Manchus were paralyzed by the shock of devastating defeats at the hands of the European "barbarians." Overpopulation, administrative paralysis, and massive rebellions sapped China's strength from within, while European gunboats and armies broke down its outer defenses. By the end of the 19th century, internal disruptions and external pressures had demolished the foundations of Chinese civilization—a civilization whose development we have traced over nearly four millennia.

As China imploded, its leaders struggled to find a new and viable system to put in its place. That struggle was carried on throughout a half century (roughly from 1898 to 1949) of foreign invasions, revolution, and social and economic breakdown that produced suffering on a scale unmatched in all human history. In sharp contrast, by the end of the 19th century, new leaders had emerged in the Ottoman Empire who were able to overthrow the sultanate with remarkably little bloodshed and to begin the process of nation-making in the Turkish portions of the empire. Unfortunately, Ottoman weaknesses in earlier decades left the rest of the Middle East exposed to European inroads, and a larger Islamic crisis proved impervious to Turkish solutions.

From Empire to Nation: Ottoman Retreat and the Birth of Turkey

◈ By the early 18th century, the days of the Ottoman Empire appeared numbered. Weakened by internal strife, the Ottomans were unable to prevent their European rivals from whittling away territories on all sides. But beginning in the late 18th century, able Ottoman rulers and committed reformers devised strategies and initiated changes that slowed the decline of the empire and the advance of the European powers. Rather than crash and disappear like so many empires before it, the Ottoman regime was captured from within by leaders committed to remaking it in the image of Western nations.

In part, the Ottoman crisis was brought on by a succession of weak rulers within a political and social order that was centered on the sultan at the top. Inactive or inept sultans opened the way for power struggles between rival ministers, religious experts, and the commanders of the Janissary corps. Competition between elite factions further eroded effective leadership within the empire, weakening its control over the population and resources it claimed to rule. Provincial officials colluded with the local land-owning classes, the ayan, to cheat the sultan of a good portion of the taxes due him, and they skimmed all the revenue they could from the already impoverished peasantry in the countryside.

At the same time, the position of the artisan workers in the towns deteriorated because of competition from imported manufactures from Europe. Particularly in the 18th and early 19th centuries, this led to urban riots in which members of artisan guilds and young men's associations often took a leading role. Merchants within the empire, especially those who belonged to minority religious communities such as the Jews and Christians, grew more and more dependant on commercial dealings with their European counterparts. This pattern accelerated the influx of Western manufactured goods that was steadily undermining handicraft industries within the empire. In this way Ottoman economic dependence on some of its most threatening European political rivals increased alarmingly.

With the Ottoman leaders embroiled in internal squabbles and their armies deprived of the resources needed to match the great advances in weaponry and training made by European rivals, the far-flung Ottoman possessions proved an irresistible temptation for their neighbors (see Map 26.1). In the early 18th century, the Austrian Habsburg dynasty was the

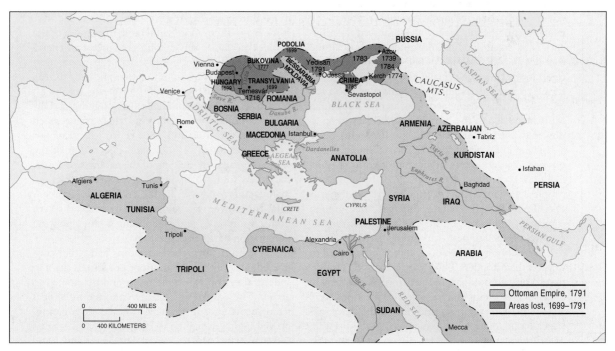

Map 26.1 *The Ottoman Empire in the Late 18th Century*

In Depth

Western Dominance and the Decline of Civilizations

As we have seen in our examination of the forces that led to the breakup of the great civilizations in human history, each civilization has a unique history. But some general patterns have been associated with the decline of civilizations. Internal weaknesses and external pressures have acted over time to erode the institutions and break down the defenses of even the largest and most sophisticated civilizations. In the preindustrial era, slow and vulnerable communication systems were a major barrier to the long-term cohesion of the political systems that held civilizations together. Ethnic, religious, and regional differences, which were overridden by the confidence and energy of the founders of civilizations, reemerged. Self-serving corruption and the pursuit of pleasure gradually eroded the sense of purpose of the elite groups that had played a pivotal role in civilized development. The resulting deterioration in governance and military strength increased social tensions and undermined fragile preindustrial economies.

Growing social unrest from within was paralleled by increasing threats from without. A major factor in the fall of nearly every great civilization, from those of the Indus valley and Mesopotamia to Rome and the civilizations of Mesoamerica, was an influx of nomadic peoples, whom sedentary peoples almost invariably saw as barbarians. Nomadic assaults revealed the weaknesses of the ruling elites and destroyed their military base. Their raids also disrupted the agricultural routines and smashed the public works on which all civilizations rested. Normally, the nomadic invaders stayed to rule the sedentary peoples they had conquered, as has happened repeatedly in China, Mesoamerica, and the Islamic world. Elsewhere, as occurred after the disappearance of the Indus valley civilization in India and after the fall of Rome, the vanquished civilization was largely forgotten or lay dormant for centuries. But over time, the invading peoples living in its ruins managed to restore patterns of civilized life that were quite different from, though sometimes influenced by, the civilization their incursions had helped to destroy centuries earlier.

Neighboring civilizations sometimes clashed in wars on their frontiers, but it was rare for one civilization to play a major part in the demise of another. In areas such as Mesopotamia, where civilizations were crowded together in space and time in the latter millennia B.C.E., older, long-dominant civilizations were overthrown and absorbed by upstart rivals. In most

cases, however, and often in Mesopotamia, external threats to civilizations came from nomadic peoples. This was true even of Islamic civilization, which proved the most expansive before the emergence of Europe and whose rise and spread brought about the collapse of several long-established civilized centers. The initial Arab explosion from Arabia that felled Sasanian Persia and captured Egypt was nomadic. But the incursions of the Arab bedouins differed from earlier and later nomadic assaults on neighboring civilizations. The Arab armies carried a new religion with them from Arabia that provided the basis for a new civilization, which incorporated the older ones they conquered. Thus, like other nomadic conquerors, they borrowed heavily from the civilizations they overran.

The emergence of western Europe as an expansive global force radically changed long-standing patterns of interaction between civilizations as well as between civilizations and nomadic peoples. From the first years of overseas exploration, the aggressive Europeans proved a threat to other civilizations. Within decades of Columbus' arrival in 1492, European military assaults had destroyed two of the great centers of civilization in the Americas: the Aztec and Inca empires. The previous isolation of the Native American societies and their consequent susceptibility to European diseases, weapons, plants, and livestock made them more vulnerable than most of the peoples the Europeans encountered overseas. Therefore, in the first centuries of Western expansion, most of the existing civilizations in Africa and Asia proved capable of standing up to the Europeans, except on the sea. With the scientific discoveries and especially the technological innovations that transformed Europe in the 17th and 18th centuries, all of this gradually changed. The unparalleled extent of the western Europeans' mastery of the natural world gave them new sources of power for resource extraction, manufacture, and war. By the end of the 18th century, this power was being translated into the economic, military, and increasingly the political domination of other civilizations.

A century later, the Europeans had either conquered most of these civilizations or reduced them to spheres they controlled indirectly and threatened to annex. The adverse effects of economic influences from the West, and Western political domination, proved highly damaging to civilizations as diverse as those of west Africa, the Islamic heartlands, and

China. For several decades before World War I, it appeared that the materially advanced and expansive West would level all other civilized centers. In that era, most leading European, and some African and Asian, thinkers and political leaders believed that the rest of humankind had no alternative (except perhaps a reversion to savagery or barbarism) other than to follow the path of development pioneered by the West. All non-Western peoples became preoccupied with coping with the powerful challenges posed by the industrial West to the survival of their civilized past and the course of their future development.

Questions: Can you think of instances in which one preindustrial civilization was a major factor in the collapse of another? Why do you think such an occurrence was so rare? Discuss the advantages that the Native Americans' isolation from civilizations in Europe, Africa, and Asia gave the European intruders in the 16th century. What kinds of advantages did the scientific and industrial revolutions give the Europeans over all other civilized peoples from the 18th century onward? Is the West losing these advantages today?

main beneficiary of Ottoman decadence. The long-standing threat to Vienna was forever vanquished, and the Ottomans were pushed out of Hungary and the northern Balkans.

In the late 1700s, the Russian Empire, strengthened by Peter the Great's forced westernization (see Chapter 18), became the main threat to the Ottomans' survival. As military setbacks mounted and the Russians advanced across the steppes toward warm-water ports in the Black Sea, the Ottomans' weakness was underscored by their attempts to forge alliances with other Christian powers. As the Russians gobbled up poorly defended Ottoman lands in the Caucasus and Crimea, the subject Christian peoples of the Balkans grew more and more restive under Ottoman rule. In 1804, a major uprising broke out in Serbia that was repressed only after years of difficult and costly military campaigns. But military force could not quell the Greek revolt that broke out in the early 1820s, and by 1830 the Greeks had regained their independence after centuries of Ottoman rule. In 1867, Serbia also gained its freedom, and by the late 1870s the Ottomans had been driven from nearly the whole of the Balkans and thus most of the European provinces of their empire. In the decades that followed, Istanbul itself was repeatedly threatened by Russian armies or those of the newly independent Balkan states.

Reform and Survival

Despite almost two centuries of unrelieved defeats on the battlefield and steady losses of territory, the Ottoman Empire somehow managed to survive into the 20th century. Its survival resulted in part from

divisions between the European powers, each of which feared that the others would gain more from the total dismemberment of the empire. In fact, the British concern to prevent the Russians from controlling Istanbul—thus gaining direct access to and threatening British naval dominance in the Mediterranean—led them to prop up the tottering Ottoman regime repeatedly in the last half of the 19th century. Ultimately, the Ottomans' survival depended on reforms from within, initiated by the sultans and their advisors at the top of the imperial system and carried out in stages over most of the 19th century. At each stage, reform initiatives increased tensions within the ruling elite. Some factions advocated far-reaching change along European lines, others argued for reforms based on precedents from the early Ottoman period, and other elite groups had a vested interest in blocking change of any sort.

These deep divisions within the Ottoman elite made reform a dangerous enterprise. Although modest innovations, including the introduction of the first printing press in 1727, had been enacted in the 18th century, Sultan **Selim III** (r. 1789–1807) believed that bolder initiatives were needed if the dynasty and empire were to survive. But his reform efforts, aimed at improving administrative efficiency and building a new army and navy, angered powerful factions within the bureaucracy. They were also seen by the Janissary corps, which had long been the dominant force in the Ottoman military (see Chapter 21), as a direct threat. Selim's modest initiatives cost him his throne—he was toppled by a Janissary revolt in 1807—and his life.

Two decades later, a more skillful sultan, **Mahmud II,** succeeded where Selim III had failed.

After secretly building a small professional army with the help of European advisors, in 1826 Mahmud II ordered his agents to incite a mutiny of the Janissaries. This began when the angry Janissaries overturned the huge soup kettles in their mess area. With little thought given to planning their next move, the Janissaries poured into the streets of Istanbul, more a mob than a military force. Once on the streets, they were shocked to be confronted by the sultan's well-trained new army. The confrontation ended in the slaughter of the Janissaries, their families, and the Janissaries' religious allies.

After cowing the ayan, or provincial notables, into at least formal submission to the throne, Mahmud II launched a program of much more far-reaching reforms than Selim III had attempted. Although the ulama, or religious experts, and some of Mahmud's advisors argued for self-strengthening through a return to the Ottoman and Islamic past, Mahmud II patterned his reform program on Western precedents. After all, the Western powers had made a shambles of his empire. He established a diplomatic corps on Western lines and exchanged ambassadors with the European powers (Figure 26.1). The westernization of the army was expanded from Mahmud's secret force to the whole military establishment. European military advisors, both army and navy, were imported to supervise the overhaul of Ottoman training, armament, and officers' education.

In the decades that followed, Western influences were pervasive at the upper levels of Ottoman society, particularly during the period of the **Tanzimat reforms** between 1839 and 1876. University education was reorganized on Western lines, and training in the European sciences and mathematics was introduced. State-run postal and telegraph systems were established in the 1830s, and railways were built in the 1860s. Newspapers were established in the major towns of the empire. Extensive legal reforms were enacted, and in 1876 a constitution, based heavily on European prototypes, was promulgated. These legal reforms greatly improved the position of minority religious groups, whose role in the Ottoman economy increased steadily.

Some groups were adversely affected by these changes, which opened the empire more and more to Western influences. This was especially true of the artisans, whose position was gravely weakened by an 1838 treaty with the British that removed import taxes and other barriers to foreign trade that had

Figure 26.1   *The European view of the Ottoman Empire as an exotic and bizarrely antique land is captured in this late 18th-century engraving of the Ottoman sultan entertaining the French ambassador and his entourage. Even though the sultan's power was greatly diminished, European diplomats continued to observe long-standing protocols in their visits to the Sublime Porte, where the Ottoman foreign ministry was located. In the 19th century, as a succession of sultans sought to westernize the empire, foreign relations, including a regular exchange of resident ambassadors with each of the European powers, were increasingly brought in line with those of the Ottomans' European rivals.*

protected indigenous producers from competition from the West. Other social groups gained little from the Tanzimat reforms. This was particularly true of women. Proposals for women's education and an end to seclusion, polygamy, and veiling were debated in Ottoman intellectual circles from the 1860s onward. But few improvements in the position of women, even among the elite classes, were won until after the last Ottoman sultan was driven from power in 1908.

Repression and Revolt

The reforms initiated by the sultans and their advisors did improve the Ottomans' ability to fend off, or at least deflect, the assaults of foreign aggressors. But they increasingly threatened the dynasty responsible for them. Western-educated bureaucrats, military officers, and professionals came increasingly to view the sultanate as a major barrier to even more radical reforms and the full transformation of society. The new elites also clashed with conservative but powerful groups, such as the ulama and the ayan, who had a vested interest in preserving as much as possible of the old order.

The Ottoman Sultan **Abdul Hamid** responded to the growing threat from westernized officers and civilians by attempting a return to despotic absolutism during his long reign from 1878 to 1908. He nullified the constitution and restricted civil liberties, particularly the freedom of the press. These measures deprived westernized elite groups of the power they had gained in forming imperial policies. Dissidents or even suspected troublemakers were imprisoned and sometimes tortured and killed. But the deep impact of decades of reform was demonstrated by the fact that even Abdul Hamid continued to push for westernization in certain areas. The military continued to adopt European arms and techniques, increasingly under the instruction of German advisors. In addition, railways, including the famous line that linked Berlin to Baghdad, and telegraph lines were built between the main population centers. Western-style educational institutions grew, and judicial reforms continued.

The despotism of Abdul Hamid came to an abrupt end in the nearly bloodless coup of 1908. Resistance to his authoritarian rule had led exiled Turkish intellectuals and political agitators to found the **Ottoman Society for Union and Progress** in Paris in 1889. Professing their loyalty to the Ottoman regime, the Young Turks (Figure 26.2), as members of the society came to be known, were determined to restore the 1876 constitution and resume far-reaching reforms within the empire. Clandestine printing presses operated by the Young Turks turned out tracts denouncing the regime and outlining further steps to be taken to modernize and thus save the empire. Assassinations were attempted and coups plotted, but until 1908 all were undone by a combination of divisions within the ranks of the westernized dissidents and police countermeasures.

Sympathy within the military for the 1908 coup had much to do with its success. Perhaps even more important was the fact that only a handful of the

Figure 26.2 *Taken after Turkey's defeat in World War I and the successful struggles of the Turks to prevent the partition of their heartlands in Asia Minor by the victorious Greeks, this photo features a group of Young Turks who had survived these challenges and grown a good deal older. The man in the business suit in the center is Mustafa Kemal, or Ataturk, who emerged as a masterful military commander during and after the war, and went on to become the founder of the modern nation of Turkey.*

sultan's supporters were willing to die defending the regime. Although a group of officers came to power, they restored the constitution and press freedoms and promised reforms in education, administration, and even the status of women. The sultan was retained as a political figurehead and the highest religious authority in Islam.

Unfortunately, the officers soon became embroiled in factional fights that took up much of the limited time remaining before the outbreak of World War I. In addition, their hold on power was shaken when they lost a new round of wars in the Balkans and a conflict against Italy over Libya, the Ottomans' last remaining possession in north Africa. Just as the sultans had before them, however, the Young Turk officers managed to stave off the collapse of the empire by achieving last-gasp military victories and by playing the hostile European powers against each other.

Although it is difficult to know how the Young Turks would have fared if it had not been for the outbreak of World War I, their failure to resolve several critical issues did not bode well for the future. They overthrew the sultan, but they could not bring themselves to give up the empire ruled by Turks for over 600 years. The peoples most affected by their decision to salvage what was left of the empire were the Arabs of the Fertile Crescent and coastal Arabia, who still remained under Ottoman control. Arab leaders in Beirut and Damascus had initially favored the 1908 coup because they believed it would bring about the end of their long domination by the Turks. To their dismay, the Arabs discovered that the Young Turks not only meant to continue their subjugation but were determined to enforce state control to a degree unthinkable to the later Ottoman sultans. The quarrels between the leaders of the Young Turk coalition and the growing resistance in the Arab portions of what was left of the Ottoman Empire were suddenly cut short in August 1914.

Western Intrusions and the Crisis in the Arab Islamic Heartlands

The profound crisis of confidence brought on by successive reverses and the ever-increasing strength of the Muslims' old European rivals elicited a wide variety of responses in the Islamic world. Islamic thinkers debated the best way to reverse the decline and drive back the Europeans. Some argued for a return to the Islamic past, others favored a large-scale adoption of Western ways, and others tried to find ways to combine the two approaches. Reformist leaders, such as Muhammad Ali in Egypt, tried to graft on elements of Western culture while preserving the old state and society pretty much intact. Religious leaders, most spectacularly the Mahdi of the Sudan, who was regarded by his followers as a divinely appointed prophet, rose up to lead jihads, or holy wars, against the advancing Europeans.

By the early 1800s, the Arab peoples of the Fertile Crescent, Egypt, coastal Arabia, and north Africa had lived for centuries under Ottoman-Turkish rule. Although most Arabs resented Turkish domination, they could identify with the Ottomans as fellow Muslims, who were both ardent defenders of the faith and patrons of Islamic culture. Still, the steadily diminishing capacity of the Ottomans to defend the Arab Islamic heartlands left them at risk of conquest by the aggressive European powers. The European capture of outlying but highly developed Islamic states, from those in the Indonesian archipelago and India to Algeria in north Africa, engendered a sense of crisis among the Islamic faithful in the Middle Eastern heartlands. From the most powerful adversaries of Christendom, the Muslims had become the besieged. The Islamic world had been displaced by the West as the leading civilization in a wide range of endeavors, from scientific inquiry to monumental architecture.

Muhammad Ali and the Failure of Westernization in Egypt

Although it did not establish a permanent European presence in the Islamic heartlands, Napoleon's invasion of Egypt in 1798 sent shock waves across what remained of the independent Muslim world. Significantly, Napoleon's motives for launching the expedition had little to do with designs for empire in the Middle East itself. Rather, he saw the Egyptian campaign as the prelude to destroying British power in India, where the French had come out on the short end of earlier wars for empire. Whatever his calculations, Napoleon managed to slip his fleet past the

British blockade in the Mediterranean and put ashore his armies in July 1798 (see Map 26.1). There followed one of the most lopsided military clashes in modern history. As they advanced inland, Napoleon's forces were met by tens of thousands of cavalry bent on defending the Mamluk regime that then ruled Egypt as a vassal of the Ottoman sultans. The term *Mamluk* literally meant slave, and it suggested the Turkic origins of the regime in Egypt. Beginning as slaves who served Muslim overlords, the Mamluks had centuries earlier risen in the ranks as military commanders and seized power in their own name. **Murad,** the head of the coalition of Mamluk households that shared power in Egypt at the time of Napoleon's arrival, dismissed the invader as a donkey boy whom he would soon drive from his lands.

Murad's contempt for the talented young French commander was symptomatic of the profound ignorance of events in Europe that was typical of the Islamic world at the time. This ignorance led to a series of crushing defeats, the most famous of which came in a battle fought beneath the pyramids of the ancient Egyptian pharaohs. In that brief but bloody battle, the disciplined firepower of the French legions devastated the ranks of Mamluk cavalry, who were clad in medieval armor and wielded spears against the artillery Napoleon used with such devastating effect.

Because the Mamluks had long been seen as fighters of great prowess in the Islamic world, their rout was traumatic. It revealed just how vulnerable even the Muslim core areas were to European aggression and how far the Muslims had fallen behind the Europeans in the capacity to wage war. Ironically, the successful invasion of Egypt brought little advantage to Napoleon or the French. The British caught up with the French fleet and sank most of it at the Battle of Aboukir in August 1798. With his supply line cut off, Napoleon was forced to abandon his army and sneak back to Paris, where his enemies were trying to use his reverses in Egypt to put an end to his rise to power. Thus, Egypt was spared European conquest for a time. But the reprieve brought little consolation to thoughtful Muslims because the British, not Egypt's Muslim defenders, had been responsible for the French retreat.

In the chaos that followed the French invasion and eventual withdrawal in 1801, a young officer of Albanian origins named **Muhammad Ali** emerged as the effective ruler of Egypt. Deeply impressed by the weapons and discipline of the French armies, the Albanian upstart devoted his energies and the resources of the land that he had brought under his rule to building an up-to-date European-style military force. He introduced Western-style conscription among the Egyptian peasantry, hired French officers to train his troops, imported Western arms, and adopted Western tactics and modes of organization and supply. Within years he had put together the most effective fighting force in the Middle East. With it, he flaunted the authority of his nominal overlord, the Ottoman sultan, by successfully invading Syria and building a modern war fleet that threatened Istanbul on a number of occasions.

Although Muhammad Ali's efforts to introduce reforms patterned after Western precedents were not confined to the military, they fell far short of a fundamental transformation of Egyptian society. To shore up his economic base, he ordered the Egyptian peasantry to increase their production of cotton, hemp, indigo, and other crops that were in growing demand in industrial Europe. Efforts to improve Egyptian harbors and extend irrigation works met with some success and led to modest increases in the revenues that could be devoted to the continuing modernization of the military. Attempts to reform education were ambitious, but little was actually achieved. Numerous schemes to build up an Egyptian industrial sector were frustrated by the opposition of the European powers and the intense competition from imported, Western-manufactured goods.

The limited scope of Muhammad Ali's reforms ultimately checked his plans for territorial expansion and left Egypt open to inroads by the European powers. He died in 1848, embittered by the European opposition that had prevented him from mastering the Ottoman sultans and well aware that his empire beyond Egypt was crumbling. Lacking Muhammad Ali's ambition and ability, his successors were content to confine their claims to Egypt and the Sudanic lands that stretched from the banks of the upper Nile to the south (see Map 26.1). Intermarrying with Turkish families that had originally come to Egypt to govern in the name of the Ottoman sultans, Muhammad Ali's descendants provided a succession of rulers who were known as **khedives** after 1867. The khedives were the formal rulers of Egypt until they were overthrown by the military coup that brought Gamel Abdul Nasser to power in 1952.

Bankruptcy, European Intervention, and Strategies of Resistance

Muhammad Ali's successors made a muddle of his efforts to reform and revitalize Egyptian society. While cotton production increased and the landlord class grew fat, the great majority of the peasants went hungry. The long-term consequences of these developments were equally troubling. The great expansion of cotton production at the expense of food grains and other crops rendered Egypt dependant on a single export. This meant that it was vulnerable to sharp fluctuations in demand (and thus price) on the European markets to which most of it was exported. Some further educational advances were made. But these were mainly at elite schools where French was the language of instruction.

Much of the revenue the khedives managed to collect, despite the resistance of the ayan, was wasted on the extravagant pastimes of the mostly idle elite connected to the palace. Most of what was left was squandered on fruitless military campaigns to assert Egyptian authority over the Sudanic peoples along the upper Nile. The increasing inability of the khedives to balance their books led in the mid-19th century to their growing indebtedness to European financiers. The latter lent money to the khedives and members of the Turkish elite because the financiers wanted continued access to Egypt's cheap cotton. By the 1850s, they had a second motive: a share in the potentially lucrative schemes to build a canal across the Isthmus of Suez that would connect the Mediterranean and Red Seas. The completion of the **Suez Canal** in 1869, depicted while still under construction in Figure 26.3, transformed Egypt into one of the most strategic places on earth. The canal soon became a vital commercial and military link between the European powers and their colonial empires in Asia and east Africa. Controlling it became one of the key objectives of their peaceful rivalries and wartime operations through the first half of the 20th century.

The ineptitude of the khedival regime and the Ottoman sultans, who were their nominal overlords, prompted discussion among Muslim intellectuals and political activists as to how to ward off the growing European menace. In the mid-19th century, Egypt, and particularly Cairo's ancient Muslim University of al-Azhar, became key meeting places of these thinkers from throughout the Islamic world. Some prominent

Islamic scholars called for a jihad to drive the infidels from Muslim lands. They also argued that the Muslim world could be saved only by a return to the patterns of religious observance and social interaction that they believed had existed in the golden age of Muhammad.

Other thinkers, such as **al-Afghani** (1839–1897) and his disciple **Muhammad Abduh** (1849–1905), stressed the need for Muslims to borrow scientific learning and technology from the West and to revive their earlier capacity to innovate. They argued that Islamic civilization had once taught the Europeans much in the sciences and mathematics, including such critical concepts as the Indian numerals. Thus, it was fitting that Muslims learn from the advances the Europeans had made with the help of Islamic borrowings. Those who advocated this approach also stressed the importance of the tradition of rational inquiry in Islamic history. They strongly disputed the views of religious scholars who contended that the Qur'an was the source of all truth and should be interpreted literally.

Although both religious revivalists and those who stressed the need for imports from the West agreed on the need for Muslim unity in the face of the growing European threat, they could not reconcile their very different approaches to Islamic renewal. Their differences, and the uncertainties they have injected into Islamic efforts to cope with the challenges of the West, remain central problems in the Muslim world today.

The mounting debts of the khedival regime and the strategic importance of the canal gave the European powers, particularly Britain and France, a growing stake in the stability and accessibility of Egypt. French and British bankers, who had bought up a good portion of the khedives' shares in the canal, urged their governments to intervene militarily when the khedives proved unable to meet their loan payments. In the early 1880s, a major challenge to the influence of foreign interests was mounted by the supporters of a charismatic young Egyptian officer named **Ahmad Orabi**. The son of a small farmer in lower Egypt, Orabi had attended Qur'anic school and studied under the reform-minded Muhammad Abduh at al-Azhar. Though a native Egyptian, Orabi had risen in the ranks of the khedival army and had become increasingly critical of the fact that the officer corps was dominated by Turks with strong ties to the khedival regime. An attempt by the khedive to save money by disbanding Egyptian regiments and

Figure 26.3 *Building a canal across the desert Isthmus of Suez was a remarkable engineering feat. As this contemporary photo illustrates, a massive investment in up-to-date technology was needed. By creating a water route between the Mediterranean and Red seas, the canal greatly shortened the travel time between Europe and maritime Asia as well as the east coast of Africa. Combined with the growing predominance of steamships, it helped to expand global commerce as well as tourism, which became a major middle-class activity in the late 19th century.*

dismissing Egyptian officers sparked a revolt led by Orabi in the summer of 1882. Riots in the city of Alexandria, associated with mutinies in the Egyptian armies, drove the frightened khedive to seek British assistance. After bombarding the coastal batteries set up by Orabi's troops, the British sent ashore an expeditionary force that crushed Orabi's rebellion and secured the position of the khedive.

Although Egypt was not formally colonized, the British intervention began decades of dominance both by British consuls, who ruled through the puppet khedives, and by British advisors to all high-ranking Egyptian administrators. British officials controlled Egypt's finances and foreign affairs; British troops ensured that their directives were heeded by Egyptian administrators. Direct European control over the Islamic heartlands had begun.

Jihad: The Mahdist Revolt in the Sudan

As Egypt fell under British control, the invaders were drawn into the turmoil and conflict that gripped the Sudanic region to the south. Egyptian efforts to conquer and rule the Sudan, beginning in the 1820s, were resisted fiercely. The opposition forces were led by the camel- and cattle-herding nomads who occupied the vast, arid plains that stretched west and east from the upper Nile (see Map 26.1). The sedentary peoples who worked the narrow strip of fertile land along the river were more easily dominated. Thus, Egyptian authority, insofar as it existed at all, was concentrated in these areas and in river towns such as **Khartoum,** which was the center of Egyptian administration in the Sudan.

Even in the riverine areas, Egyptian rule was greatly resented. The Egyptian regime was notoriously corrupt, and its taxes placed a heavy burden on the peasants compelled to pay them. The Egyptians were clearly outsiders, and the favoritism they showed some of the Sudanic tribes alienated the others. In addition, nearly all groups in the Muslim areas in the north Sudan were angered by Egyptian attempts in the 1870s to eradicate the slave trade. The trade had long been a great source of profit for both the merchants of the Nile towns and the nomads, who attacked non-Muslim peoples, such as the Dinka in the south, to capture slaves.

By the late 1870s, Egyptian oppression and British intervention had aroused deep resentment and hostility. But a leader was needed to unite the diverse and often divided peoples of the region and to provide an ideology that would give focus and meaning to rebellion. **Muhammad Achmad** proved to be that leader. He was the son of a boat builder, and he had been educated by the head of a local Sufi brotherhood. The fact that his family claimed descent from Muhammad and that he had the physical signs—a cleft between his teeth and a mole on his right cheek—that the local people associated with the promised deliverer, or **Mahdi,** advanced his reputation. The visions he began to experience, after he had broken with his Sufi master and established his own sectarian following, also suggested that a remarkable future was in store. What was seen to be a miraculous escape from a bungled Egyptian effort to capture and imprison Muhammad Achmad soon led to his widespread acceptance as a divinely appointed leader of revolt against the foreign intruders.

The jihad that Muhammad Achmad, who came to be known to his followers as the Mahdi, proclaimed against both the Egyptian heretics and British infidels was one of a number of such movements that had swept through sub-Saharan Africa since the 18th century. It represented the most extreme and violent Islamic response to what was perceived as the dilution of Islam in the African environment and the growing threat of Europe. Muhammad Achmad promised to purge Islam of what he saw as superstitious beliefs and degrading practices that had built up over the centuries, thus returning the faith to what he claimed was its original purity. He led his followers in a violent assault on the Egyptians, whom he believed professed a corrupt version of Islam, and on the European infidels. At one point, his successors dreamed of toppling the Ottoman sultans and invading Europe itself.

The Mahdi's skillful use of guerrilla tactics and the confidence his followers placed in his blessings and magical charms earned his forces several stunning victories over the Egyptians. Within a few years the Mahdist forces were in control of an area corresponding roughly to the present-day nation of Sudan. At the peak of his power, the Mahdi fell ill with typhus and died. In contrast to many movements of this type, which collapsed rapidly after the death of their prophetic leaders, the Mahdists found a capable successor for Muhammad Achmad. The **Khalifa Abdallahi** had been one of the Mahdi's most skillful military commanders. Under Abdallahi, the Mahdists built a strong, expansive state. They also sought to build a closely controlled society in which smoking, dancing, and alcoholic drink were forbidden, and theft, prostitution, and adultery were severely punished. Islamic religious and ritual practices were enforced rigorously. In addition, most foreigners were imprisoned or expelled, and the ban on slavery was lifted.

For nearly a decade, Mahdist armies attacked or threatened neighboring states on all sides, including the Egyptians to the north. But in the fall of 1896, the famous British General Kitchener was sent with an expeditionary force to put an end to one of the most serious threats to European domination in Africa. The spears and magical garments of the Mahdist forces proved no match for the machine guns and artillery of Kitchener's columns. At the battle of Omdurman in 1898, thousands of the Mahdist cavalry were slaughtered. Within a year the Mahdist state collapsed, and British power advanced yet again into the interior of Africa.

The 19th century was a time of severe reverses for the peoples of the Islamic world. By the century's end, it was clear that neither the religious revivalists, who called for a return to a purified Islam free of Western influences, nor the reformers, who argued that some borrowing from the West was essential for survival, had come up with a successful formula for dealing with the powerful challenges posed by the industrial West. Failing to find adequate responses and deeply divided, the Islamic community grew increasingly anxious over the dangers that lay ahead. Islamic civilization was by no means defeated. But its continued viability clearly was threatened by its powerful European neighbor, which had become master of the world.

The Last Dynasty: The Rise and Fall of the Qing Empire in China

Although China had been strong enough to get away with its policies of isolation and attitudes of disdain in the early centuries of European expansion, by the late 18th century these policies were outmoded and dangerous. Not only had the Europeans grown much stronger than they had been in the early centuries of expansion, but Chinese society was crumbling from within. More than a century of strong rule by the Manchus and a high degree of social stability, if not prosperity, for the Chinese people gave way to rampant official corruption, severe economic dislocations, and social unrest by the end of the 18th century. With the British in the lead, over the course of the 19th century, the Western powers took advantage of these weaknesses to force open China's markets, humiliate its military defenders, and reduce its Qing rulers to little more than puppets.

Although the Manchu nomads had been building an expansive state of their own north of the Great Wall for decades, their conquest of China was both unexpected and sudden. A local leader named **Nurhaci** (1559–1626) was the architect of unity among the quarrelsome Manchu tribes. He combined the cavalry of each tribe into extremely cohesive fighting units within eight **banner armies,** named after the flags that identified each. In the first decades of the 17th century, Nurhaci brought much of Manchuria, including a number of non-Manchu peoples, under his rule (see Map 26.2). Although he remained the nominal vassal of the Chinese Ming emperor, Nurhaci's forces continually harassed the Chinese who lived north of the Great Wall. During this period, the Manchu elite's adoption of Chinese

Map 26.2   *China During the Qing Era*

ways, which had begun much earlier, was greatly accelerated. The Manchu bureaucracy was organized along Chinese lines, Chinese court ceremonies were adopted, and Chinese scholar-officials found lucrative employment in the growing barbarian state north of the Great Wall.

The weakness of the declining Ming regime, rather than the Manchus' own strength, gave the Manchus an opportunity to seize control in China. Their entry into China resulted from a bit of luck. In 1644, an official of the Ming government in charge of the northern defenses called in the Manchus to help him put down a widespread rebellion in the region near the Great Wall. Having allowed the Manchus to pass beyond the wall, the official found that they were an even greater threat than the rebels. Exploiting the political divisions and social unrest that were destroying what was left of Ming authority, the Manchus boldly advanced on the Ming capital at Beijing, which they captured within the year. It took nearly two decades before centers of Ming and rebel resistance in the south and west were destroyed by the banner armies, but the Manchus soon found themselves the masters of China.

They quickly proved that they were up to the challenge of ruling the largest empire in the world.

Their armies forced submission by nomadic peoples far to the west and compelled tribute from kingdoms such as Vietnam and Burma to the south. Within decades, the Manchu regime, which had taken the dynastic name **Qing** before its conquest of China, ruled an area larger than any previous Chinese dynasty with the exception of the Tang.

To reconcile the ethnic Chinese who made up the vast majority of their subjects, the Manchu rulers shrewdly retained much of the political system of their Ming predecessors. They added to the court calendar whatever Confucian rituals they did not already observe. They made it clear that they wanted the scholar-officials who had served the Ming to continue in office. The Manchus even pardoned many who had been instrumental in prolonging resistance to their conquest. For much of the first century of the dynasty, Chinese and Manchu officials were paired in appointments to most of the highest posts of the imperial bureaucracy, and Chinese officials predominated at the regional and local levels. Manchus, who made up less than two percent of the population of the Qing Empire, occupied a disproportionate number of the highest political positions. But there were few limits as to how high talented ethnic Chinese could rise in the imperial bureaucracy.

Unlike the Mongol conquerors who had abolished it, the Manchus retained the examination system and had their own sons educated in the Chinese classics. The Manchu emperors styled themselves the Sons of Heaven and rooted their claims to be the legitimate rulers of China in their practice of the traditional Confucian virtues. The early Manchu rulers were generous patrons of the Chinese arts, and at least one, **Kangxi** (1661–1722), was a significant Confucian scholar in his own right. Kangxi and other Manchu rulers employed thousands of scholars to compile great encyclopedias of Chinese learning.

Economy and Society in the Early Centuries of Qing Rule

The Manchu determination to preserve much of the Chinese political system was paralleled by an equally conservative approach to Chinese society as a whole. In the early centuries of their reign, the writings of Zhu Xi, which had been so influential in the preceding dynastic eras, continued to dominate official thinking. Thus, long-nurtured values such as respect

for rank and acceptance of hierarchy—that is, old over young, male over female, scholar-bureaucrat over commoner—were emphasized in education and imperial edicts. Among the elite classes, the extended family remained the core unit of the social order, and the state grew increasingly suspicious of any forms of social organization, such as guilds and especially secret societies, that rivaled it.

The lives of women at all social levels remained centered on or wholly confined to the household. There the dominance of elder men was upheld by familial pressures and the state. Male control was enhanced by the practice of choosing brides from families slightly lower in social status than those of the grooms. Because they were a loss to their parents' household at marriage and usually needed a sizeable dowry, daughters continued to be much less desirable than sons. Despite the poor quality of the statistics relating to the practice, there are indications that the incidence of female infanticide rose in this period. In the population as a whole, males considerably outnumbered females, the reverse of the balance between the two in contemporary industrial societies.

Beyond the family compound, the world pretty much belonged to men, although women from lower-class families continued to work in the fields and sell produce in the local markets. The best a married woman could hope for was strong backing from her father and brother after she had gone to her husband's home, as well as the good luck in the first place to be chosen as the wife rather than as a second or third partner in the form of a concubine. If they bore sons and lived long enough, wives took charge of running the household. In elite families they exercised control over other women and even younger men.

Some of the strongest measures the Manchus took after conquering China were aimed at alleviating the rural distress and unrest that had become so pronounced in the last years of Ming rule. Taxes and state labor demands were lowered. Incentives such as tax-free tenure were offered to those willing to resettle lands that had been abandoned in the turmoil of the preceding decades. A sizeable chunk of the imperial budget (up to 10 percent in the early years of the dynasty) was devoted to repairing existing dikes, canals, and roadways and extending irrigation works. Peasants were encouraged to plant new crops, including those for which there was market demand, and to grow two or even three crops per year on their holdings.

Given the growing population pressure on the cultivable acreage and the near disappearance in most areas of open lands that could be settled, the regime had very little success in its efforts to control the landlord classes. After several decades of holding steady, the landlord classes found that they could add to their estates by calling in loans to peasants or simply by buying them out. With a surplus of workers, tenants had less and less bargaining power in their dealings with landlords. If they objected to the share of the crop the landlords offered, they were turned off the land and replaced by those willing to accept even less. As a result, the gap between the rural gentry and ordinary peasants and laborers increased. One could not miss the old and new rich in the rural areas, as they rode or were carried in sedan chairs, decked out in silks and furs, to make social calls on their peers. To further display their superior social standing, many men of the gentry class let their nails grow long to demonstrate that they did not have to engage in physical labor.

The sector of Chinese society over which the Qing exercised the least control was also the most dynamic. The commercial and urban expansion that had begun in the Song era gained new strength in the long peace China enjoyed during the first century and a half of Manchu rule. Regional diversification in crops such as tea was matched by the development of new ways to finance agricultural and artisan production. Until the end of the 18th century, both the state and the mercantile classes profited enormously from the great influx of silver that poured into China in payment for its exports of tea, porcelain, and silk textiles. European and other foreign traders flocked to Canton, and Chinese merchants, freed from the restrictions against overseas travel of the late Ming, found lucrative market outlets overseas. Profits from overseas trade gave rise to a wealthy new group of merchants, the **compradors,** who specialized in the import-export trade on China's south coast. In the 19th century, these merchants proved to be one of the major links between China and the outside world.

Rot from Within: Bureaucratic Breakdown and Social Disintegration

By the late 18th century, it was clear that like so many Chinese dynasties of the past, the Qing was in decline. The signs of decline were pervasive and familiar. The bureaucratic foundations of the Chinese Empire were rotting from within. The exam system, which had done well in selecting able and honest bureaucrats in the early decades of the dynasty, had become riddled with cheating and favoritism. Despite formal restrictions, sons of high officials often were ensured a place in the ever-growing bureaucracy. Even more disturbing was the fact that nearly anyone with enough money could buy a post for sons or brothers. Impoverished scholars could be paid to take the exams for poorly educated or not-so-bright relatives. Examiners could be bribed to approve weak credentials or look the other way when candidates consulted cheat sheets while taking their exams. In one of the most notorious cases of cheating, a merchant's son won high honors despite the fact that he had spent the days of testing in a brothel hundreds of miles from the examination site.

Cheating had become so blatant by the early 18th century that in 1711 students who had failed the exams at Yangzhou held a public demonstration to protest bribes given to the exam officials by wealthy salt merchants. The growing influx of merchants' and poorly educated landlords' sons into the bureaucracy was particularly troubling because few of them had received the classical Confucian education that stressed the responsibilities of the educated ruling classes and their obligation to serve the people. Increasingly, the wealthy saw positions in the bureaucracy as a means of influencing local officials and judges and enhancing family fortunes. Less and less concern was expressed for the effects of bureaucratic decisions on the peasantry and urban laborers.

Over several decades, the diversion of revenue from state projects to enrich individual families devastated Chinese society. For example, funds needed to maintain the armies and fleets that defended the huge empire fell off sharply. Not surprisingly, this resulted in a noticeable drop in the training and armament of the military. Even more critical for the masses were reductions in spending on public works projects. Of these, the most vital were the great dikes that confined the Huanghe or Yellow River in northern China. Over the millennia, because of the silting of the river bottom and the constant repair of and additions to the dikes, the river and dikes were raised high above the densely populated farmlands through which they passed. Thus, when these great public works were neglected for lack of funds and proper official supervision of repairs, leaking dikes and the rampaging waters of the great river meant catastrophe for much of northeastern China.

Nowhere was this disaster more apparent than in the region of the Shandong peninsula (see Map 26.2). Before the mid-19th century, the Huanghe emptied into the sea south of the peninsula. By the 1850s, however, the neglected dikes had broken down over much of the area, and the river had flooded hundreds of square miles of heavily cultivated farmland. By the 1860s, the main channel of the river flowed north of the peninsula. The lands in between had been flooded and the farms wiped out. Millions of peasants were left without livestock or land to cultivate. Tens—perhaps hundreds—of thousands of peasants died of famine and disease.

As the condition of the peasantry deteriorated in many parts of the empire, further signs of dynastic decline appeared. Food shortages and landlord demands prompted mass migrations. Vagabond bands clogged the roads, and beggars crowded the city streets. Banditry, long seen by the Chinese as one of the surest signs of dynastic decline, became a major problem in many districts. As the following verse from a popular ditty of the 1860s illustrates, the government's inability to deal with the bandits was seen as a further sign of Qing weakness:

When the bandits arrive, where are the troops?

When the troops come, the bandits have vanished.

Alas, when will the bandits and troops meet?

The assumption then widely held by Chinese thinkers—that the dynastic cycle would again run its course and the Manchus would be replaced by a new and vigorous dynasty—was belied by the magnitude of the problems confronting the leaders of China. The belief that China's future could be predicted from the patterns of its past ignored the fact that there were no precedents for the critical changes that had occurred in China under Manchu rule. Some of these changes had their roots in the preceding Ming era (see Chapter 22), in which, for example, food crops from the Americas, such as corn and potatoes, had set in motion a population explosion. China desperately needed innovations in technology and organization that would increase its productivity to support its exploding population at a reasonable level. The corrupt and highly conservative late Manchu regime was increasingly an obstacle to, rather than a source of, these desperately needed changes.

Barbarians at the Southern Gates: The Opium War and After

Another major difference between the forces sapping the strength of the Manchus and those that had brought down earlier dynasties was the nature of the "barbarians" who threatened the empire from outside. Out of ignorance, the Manchu rulers and their Chinese administrators treated the Europeans much like the nomads and other peoples whom they saw as barbarians. But the Europeans presented a very different sort of challenge. They came from a civilization that was China's equal in sophistication and complexity. In fact, although European nation-states such as Great Britain were much smaller in population (in the early 19th century, England had 7 million people to China's 400 million), the scientific and industrial revolutions allowed them to compensate for their smaller numbers with better organization and superior technology. These advantages proved critical in the wars between China and Britain and the other European powers that broke out in the mid-19th century.

The issue that was responsible for the initial hostilities between China and the British did little credit to the latter. For centuries, British merchants had eagerly exported silks, fine porcelains, tea, and other products from the Chinese empire. Finding that they had little in the way of manufactured goods or raw materials that the Chinese were willing to take in exchange for these products, the British were forced to trade growing amounts of silver bullion. Unhappy about the unfavorable terms of trade in China, British merchants hit on a possible solution in the form of opium, which was grown in the hills of eastern India. Although opium was also grown in China, the Indian variety was far more potent and was soon in great demand in the Middle Kingdom. By the early 19th century an annual average of 4500 chests of opium, each weighing 133 pounds, were sold, either legally or illegally, to merchants on the south China coast (Figure 26.4). By 1839, on the eve of the **Opium War,** nearly 40,000 chests were imported by the Chinese.

Figure 26.4 *An early 19th-century engraving of a British opium factory gives some sense of the massive scale of the opium trade with China. The opium paste was worked into balls, which were dried on racks like those shown in the illustration. The balls were then packed in chests for shipping to China and other overseas destinations. Although the British forbade the sale of opium in their Indian empire, they went to war with China in 1839–1841 because the Qing rulers tried to put an end to the import of a product that was contributing to the disintegration of Chinese civilization.*

Although the British had found a way to reverse the trade balance in their favor, the Chinese soon realized that the opium traffic was a major threat to their economy and social order. Within years, China's favorable trade balance with the outside world was reversed, and silver began to flow in large quantities out of the country. As sources of capital for public works and trade expansion decreased, agricultural productivity stagnated or declined, and unemployment spread, especially in the hinterlands of the coastal trading areas. Wealthy Chinese, who could best afford it, squandered increasing amounts of China's wealth to support their opium habits. Opium dens spread in the towns and villages of the empire at an alarming rate. It has been estimated that by 1838, one percent of China's more than 400 million people were addicted to the drug. Strung-out officials neglected their administrative responsibilities, the sons of prominent scholar-gentry families lost their ambition, and even laborers and peasants abandoned their work for the debilitating pleasures of the opium dens.

From the early 18th century, Qing emperors had issued edicts forbidding the opium traffic, but little had been done to enforce them. By the beginning of the 19th century, it was clear to the court and high officials that the opium trade had to be stopped. When serious efforts were finally undertaken in the early 1820s, they only drove the opium dealers from Canton to nearby islands and other hidden locations on the coast. Finally, in the late 1830s, the emperor sent one of the most distinguished officials in the empire, **Lin Zexu,** with orders to use every means available to stamp out the trade. Lin, who was famous for his incorruptibility, took his charge seriously. After being rebuffed in his attempts to win the cooperation of European merchants and naval officers in putting an end to the trade, Lin ordered the European trading areas in Canton blockaded, their warehouses searched, and all the opium confiscated and destroyed.

Not surprisingly, these actions enraged the European merchants, and they demanded military action to avenge their losses. Arguing that Lin's measures violated both the property rights of the merchants and principles of free trade, the British ordered the Chinese to stop their anti-opium campaign or risk military intervention. When Lin persisted, war broke out in late 1839. In the conflict that followed, the Chinese were routed first on the sea, where their antiquated war junks were no match for British gunboats. Then they were soundly defeated in their attempts to repel an expeditionary force the British sent ashore. With British warships and armies threatening the cities of the Yangtze River region, the Qing emperor was forced to sue for peace and send Lin into exile in a remote province of the empire.

Their victories in the Opium War and a second conflict, which erupted in the late 1850s, allowed the European powers to force China to open trade and diplomatic exchanges. After the first war, Hong Kong was established as an additional center of British commerce. European trade was also permitted at five other ports, where the Europeans were given land to build more warehouses and living quarters (see the painting that opens the chapter). By the 1890s, 90 ports of call were available to more than 300,000 European and American traders, missionaries, and diplomats. Britain, France, Germany, and Russia had won long-term leases of several ports and the surrounding territory (see Map 26.2).

Although the treaty of 1842 made no reference to the opium trade, after China's defeat the drug poured unchecked into China. By the mid-19th century, China's foreign trade and customs were overseen by British officials. They were careful to ensure that European nationals had favored access to China's markets and that no protective tariffs, such as those the Americans were using at the time to protect their young industries, were established by the Chinese. Most humiliating of all for the Chinese was the fact that they were forced to accept European ambassadors at the Qing court. Not only were ambassadors traditionally (and usually quite rightly) seen as spies, but the exchange of diplomatic missions was a concession that European nations were equal in stature to China. Given the deeply entrenched Chinese conviction that their Middle Kingdom was the civilized center of the earth and that all other peoples were barbarians, this was a very difficult concession to make. European battleships and firepower gave them little choice.

A Civilization at Risk: Rebellion and Failed Reforms

Although it was not immediately apparent, China's defeat in the Opium War greatly contributed to a building crisis that threatened not just the Qing dynasty but Chinese civilization as a whole. Defeat and the dislocations in south China brought on by the growing commercial encroachments of the West spawned a massive rebellion that swept through much of south China in the 1850s and early 1860s and at one point threatened to overthrow the Qing dynasty. Led by a mentally unstable, semi-Christianized prophet named **Hong Xiuquan,** the **Taiping Rebellion** increased the already considerable stresses in Chinese society and further drained the diminishing resources of the ruling dynasty. Widespread peasant uprisings, incited by members of secret societies such as the White Lotus, had erupted as early as the 1770s. But the Taiping movement was the first to pose a serious alternative not only to the Qing dynasty but to Confucian civilization as a whole. The Taipings offered sweeping programs for social reform, land redistribution, and the liberation of women. They also attacked the traditional Confucian elite and the learning on which its claims to authority rested. Taiping rebels smashed ancestral tablets and shrines, and they proposed a simplified script and mass literacy that would have undermined one of the scholar-gentry's chief sources of power.

Their attack on the scholar-gentry was one of the main causes of the Taipings' ultimate defeat. Left no option but to rally to the Manchu regime, the provincial gentry became the focus of resistance to the Taipings. Honest and able Qing officials, such as Zeng Guofan, raised effective, provincially based military forces just in time to fend off the Taiping assault on northern China. Zeng and his allies in the government also carried out much needed reforms to root out corruption in the bureaucracy and revive the stagnating Chinese economy. In the late 19th century, these dynamic provincial leaders were the most responsible for China's **self-strengthening movement,** which was aimed at countering the challenge from the West. They encouraged Western investment in railways and factories in the areas they governed, and they modernized their armies. Combined with the breakdown of Taiping leadership and the declining appeal of a movement that could not deliver on its promises, the gentry's efforts brought about the very bloody suppression of the Taiping Rebellion.

Despite their clearly desperate situation by the late 19th century, including a shocking loss in a war with Japan in 1894 and 1895, the Manchu rulers stubbornly resisted the far-reaching reforms that were the only hope of saving the regime and, as it turned out, Chinese civilization. Manchu rulers occasionally supported officials who pushed for extensive political and social reforms, some of which were inspired by the example of the West. But their efforts were repeatedly frustrated by the backlash of members of the imperial household and their allies among the scholar-gentry, who were determined to preserve the old order with only minor changes and to make no concessions to the West.

The last decades of the dynasty were dominated by the ultraconservative dowager empress **Cixi,** who became the power behind the throne. In 1898, she and her faction crushed the most serious move toward reform. Her nephew, the emperor, was imprisoned in the Forbidden City, and leading advocates for reform were executed or driven from China. On one occasion, Cixi defied the westernizers by rechanneling funds that had been raised to build modern warships into the building of a huge marble boat in one of the lakes in the imperial gardens. With genuine reform blocked by Cixi and her faction, the Manchus relied on divisions among the provincial officials and among the European powers to maintain their position. Members of the Qing household also secretly backed popular outbursts aimed at expelling the foreigners from China, such as the **Boxer Rebellion** (Figure 26.5). The Boxer uprising broke out in 1898 and was put down only through the intervention of the imperialist powers in 1901. Its failure led to even greater control over China's internal affairs by the Europeans and a further devolution of power to provincial officials.

The Fall of the Qing: The End of a Civilization?

By the beginning of the 20th century, the days of the Manchus were numbered. With the defeat of the Taipings, resistance to the Qing came to be centered in rival secret societies such as the Triads and the Society of Elders and Brothers. These underground organizations inspired numerous local uprisings against the dynasty in the late 19th century. All of these efforts

Figure 26.5   *During the Boxer uprisings from 1898 to 1901, allied armies—European, American, and Japanese—entered the Chinese capital at Beijing, where the foreign legations endured nearly two months of siege and assaults by Chinese resistance forces. Once the Boxers had been defeated, the allies imposed large fines on the Chinese, thus forcing them to pay for what was in effect a failed rebellion against the steady takeover of the empire by foreign economic and political interests. For the next half-century, China was a major arena for conflict between the great powers, including the United States and Japan.*

failed because of lack of coordination and sufficient resources. But some of the secret society cells became a valuable training ground that prepared the way for a new sort of resistance to the Manchus.

By the end of the 19th century, the sons of some of the scholar-gentry and especially of the merchants in the port cities were becoming more and more involved in secret society operations and other activities aimed at overthrowing the regime. Because many of these young men had received European-style educations, their resistance was aimed at more than just getting rid of the Manchus. They envisioned

Document

Building a New China

Faced with mounting intrusions by the Western powers into China, which the Manchu dynasty appeared powerless to resist, Chinese political leaders and intellectuals debated the ways by which China could renew itself and thus survive the challenges posed by the industrialized West. As the following passages from his journal *A People Made New* (published from 1902 to 1905) illustrate, Liang Qichao, one of the main advocates of major reforms in Chinese society, recognized the need for significant borrowing from Europe and the United States. At the same time, late 19th- and early 20th-century champions of renewal such as Liang wanted to preserve the basic features of Chinese society as they had developed over two millennia of history.

If we wish to make our nation strong, we must investigate extensively the methods followed by other nations in becoming independent. We should select their superior points and appropriate them to make up our own shortcomings. Now with regard to politics, academic learning, and techniques, our critics know how to take the superior points of others to make up for our own weakness; but they do not know that the people's virtue, the people's wisdom, and the people's vitality are the great basis of politics, academic learning, and techniques.

[Those who are for "renovation"] are worried about the situation and try hard to develop the nation and to promote well-being. But when asked about their methods, they would begin with diplomacy, training of troops, purchase of arms and manufacture of instruments; then they would proceed to commerce, mining, and railways; and finally they would come, as they did recently, to officers' training, police, and education. Are these not the most important and necessary things for modern civilized nations? Yes. But can we attain the level of modern civilization and place our nation in an invincible position by adopting a little of this and that, or taking a small step now and then? I know we cannot.

Let me illustrate this by commerce. Economic competition is one of the big problems of the world today. It is the method whereby the powers attempt to conquer us. It is also the method whereby we should fight for our existence. The importance of improving our foreign trade has been recognized by all. But in order to promote foreign trade, it is necessary to protect the rights of our domestic trade and industry; and in order to protect these rights, it is necessary to issue a set of commercial laws. Commercial laws, however, cannot stand by themselves, and so it is necessary to complement them with other laws. A law which is not carried out is tantamount to no law; it is therefore necessary to define the powers of the judiciary. Bad legislation is worse than no legislation, and so it is necessary to decide where the legislative power should belong. If those who violate the law are not punished, laws will become void as soon as they are proclaimed; therefore, the duties of the judiciary must be defined. When all these are carried to the logical conclusion, it will be seen that foreign trade cannot be promoted without a constitution, a parliament, and a responsible government.

…What, then, is the way to effect our salvation and to achieve progress? The answer is that we must shatter at a blow the despotic and confused governmental system of some thousands of years; we must sweep away the corrupt and sycophantic learning of these thousands of years.

Questions: What does Liang see as the key sources of Western strength? What does he believe China needs most to borrow from Europe and the United States? Do his recommendations strike you as specific enough to rescue China from its many predicaments? If you were the emperor's advisor, what sorts of changes would you recommend, perhaps copying the approaches tried by the leaders of other civilizations in this era?

power passing to Western-educated, reformist leaders who would build a new, strong nation-state in China patterned after those of the West, rather than simply establishing yet another imperial dynasty. For aspiring revolutionaries such as **Sun Yat-sen,** who emerged as one of their most articulate advocates, seizing power was also seen as a way to enact desper-

ately needed social programs to relieve the misery of the peasants and urban workers.

Although they drew heavily on the West for ideas and organizational models, the revolutionaries from the rising middle classes were deeply hostile to the involvement of the imperialist powers in Chinese affairs. They also condemned the Manchus for failing to control the foreigners. The young rebels cut off their *queues* (braided ponytails) in defiance of the Manchu order that all ethnic Chinese wear their hair in this fashion. They joined in uprisings fomented by the secret societies or plotted assassinations and acts of sabotage on their own. Attempts to coordinate an all-China rising failed on several occasions because of personal animosities or incompetence. But in late 1911, opposition to the government's reliance on the Western powers for railway loans led to secret society uprisings, student demonstrations, and mutinies on the part of imperial troops. When key provincial officials refused to put down the spreading rebellion, the Manchus had no choice but to abdicate. In February 1912, the last emperor of China, a small boy named **Puyi,** was deposed, and one of the more powerful provincial lords was asked to establish a republican government in China.

The revolution of 1911 toppled the Qing dynasty, but in many ways a more important turning point for Chinese civilization was reached in 1905. In that year, the civil service exams were given for the last time. Reluctantly, even the ultraconservative advisors of the empress Cixi had concluded that solutions to China's predicament could no longer be found in the Confucian learning the exams tested. In fact, the abandonment of the exams signaled the end of a pattern of civilized life the Chinese had nurtured for nearly 2500 years. The mix of philosophies and values that had come to be known as the Confucian system, the massive civil bureaucracy, rule by an educated and cultivated scholar-gentry elite, and even the artistic accomplishments of the old order came under increasing criticism in the early 20th century. Many of these hallmarks of the most enduring civilization that has ever existed were violently destroyed.

GLOBAL CONNECTIONS: Muslim and Chinese Decline and a Shifting Global Balance

Both Chinese and Islamic civilizations were severely weakened by internal disruptions in the 18th and 19th centuries, and each was thrown into prolonged crisis by the growing challenges posed by the West. Several key differences in the interaction between each civilization and the West do much to explain why Islam, though badly shaken, survived, whereas Chinese civilization collapsed under the burden of domestic upheavals and foreign aggression. For the Muslims, who had been warring and trading with Christian Europe since the Middle Ages, the Western threat had long existed. What was new was the much greater strength of the Europeans in the ongoing contest, which resulted from their global expansion and their scientific and industrial revolutions. For China, the challenges from the West came suddenly and brutally. Within decades, the Chinese had to revise their image of their empire as the center of the world and the source of civilization itself to take into account severe defeats at the hands of peoples they once dismissed as barbarians.

The Muslims could also take comfort from the fact that in the Judeo-Christian and Greek traditions they shared much with the ascendant Europeans. As a result, elements of their own civilization had played critical roles in the rise of the West. This made it easier to justify Muslim borrowing from the West, which in any case could be set in a long tradition of exchanges with other civilizations. Although some Chinese technology had passed to the West, Chinese and Western leaders were largely unaware of early exchanges and deeply impressed by the profound differences between their societies. For the Chinese, borrowing from the barbarians required a painful reassessment of their place in the world—a reassessment many were unwilling to make.

In countering the thrusts from the West, the Muslims gained from the fact that they had many centers to defend; the fall of a single dynasty or regime did not mean the end of Islamic independence. The Muslims also gained from the more gradual nature of the Western advance. They had time to learn from earlier mistakes and try out different responses to the Western challenges. For the Chinese, the defense of their civilization came to be equated with the survival of the Qing dynasty, a line of thinking that the Manchus did all they could to promote. When the dynasty collapsed in the early 20th century, the Chinese lost faith in the formula for civilization they had successfully followed for more than two millennia. Again, timing was critical. The crisis in China seemed to come without warning. Within decades, the Qing went from being the arrogant controller of the barbarians to being a defeated and humbled pawn of the European powers.

When the dynasty failed and it became clear that the "barbarians" had outdone the Chinese in so many fields of civilized endeavor, the Chinese had little to fall back on. Like the Europeans, they had excelled in social and political organization and in mastery of the material world. Unlike the Hindus or the Muslims, they had no great religious tradition with which to counter the European conceit that worldly dominance could be equated with inherent superiority. In the depths of their crisis, Muslim peoples clung to the conviction that theirs was the true faith, the last and fullest of God's revelations to humankind. That faith became the basis of their resistance and their strategies for renewal, the key to the survival of Islamic civilization and its continuing efforts to meet the challenges of the West in the 20th century.

Both China and the Islamic lands of the Middle East and north Africa faced common challenges through the unavoidable intrusion of Western-dominated globalism. While their responses differed, both civilizations were only partially colonized (in contrast to Africa). Their situation also differed from that of Latin America, where connections to the West ran deeper amid an older pattern of economic dependency. They differed, finally, from two other societies, near neighbors, who retained fuller independence amid the same global pressures: Russia and Japan.

Further Readings

The best general introductions to the Ottoman decline and the origins of Turkey are Bernard Lewis' *The Emergence of Modern Turkey* (2nd ed., 1968) and the chapter "The Later Ottoman Empire" by Halil Inalcik in *The Cambridge History of Islam*, vol. 1 (1973). Other recent studies on specific aspects of this process include C. V. Findley's studies of Ottoman bureaucratic reform and the development of a modern civil service in what is today Turkey; Ernest Ramsaur's *The Young Turks* (1957); Stanford Shaw's *Between Old and New* (1971); and David Kusher's essay, *The Rise of Turkish Nationalism* (1977). On Egypt and the Islamic heartlands in this period, see P. M. Holt's *Egypt and the Fertile Crescent, 1516–1922* (1965) or P. J. Vatikiotis' *The History of Egypt* (1985). On the Mahdist movement in the Sudan, see P. M. Holt's *The Mahdist State in the Sudan* (1958) or the fine summary by L. Carl Brown in Robert Rotberg and Ali Mazrui, eds., *Protest and Power in Black Africa* (1970). The latter also includes many informative articles on African resistance to European conquest and rule. On women and changes in the family in the Ottoman realm, see Nermin Abadan-Unat's *Women in Turkish Society* (1981), and in the Arab world, see Nawal el Saadawi's *The Hidden Face of Eve* (1980).

On the Manchu takeover in China, see Frederic Wakeman Jr.'s *The Great Enterprise* (1985) and Jonathan Spence and John E. Willis, eds., *Ming to Ch'ing* (1979). On Qing rule, among the most readable and useful works are Spence's *Emperor of China: Portrait of K'ang-hsi* (1974) and the relevant sections in his recent study, *The Search for Modern China* (1990); Susan Naquin and Evelyn Rawski's *Chinese Society in the 18th Century* (1987); and the essays in John Fairbank, ed., *The Cambridge History of China: Late Ch'ing 1800–1911* (1978). A good survey of the causes and course of the Opium War is provided in Hsin-pao Chang's *Commissioner Lin and the Opium War* (1964). The Taiping Rebellion is covered in Jen Yu-wen's *The Taiping Revolutionary Movement* (1973) and Jonathan D. Spence, *God's Chinese Son: Taiping Heavenly Kingdom of Hong Xiuquan* (1996). The rebellion heralding the last stage of Qing decline is examined in J. W. Esherick's *The Origins of the Boxer Rebellion* (1987).

The first stages of the Chinese nationalist movement are examined in the essays in Mary Wright, ed., *China in Revolution: The First Phase* (1968). The early sections of Elisabeth Croll's *Feminism and Socialism in China* (1980) provide an excellent overview of the status and condition of women in the Qing era.

On the Web

The transitions from the Mongol to Ming to Qing dynasties are reviewed at http://www.bergen.org/AAST/Projects/ChinaHistory/MING.HTM. Links to resources for the study of the art of the Qing Empire can be found at http://www.art-and-archaeology.com/timelines/china/qing.html. The decline of the Qing (http://library.thinkquest.org/26469/history/1900.html and http://www.hoover.archives.gov/exhibits/China/Political%20Evolution/19thc/19thhome.htm) was accelerated by the failure of a reform effort which climaxed in the 103 days from June 11 to September 21, 1898 (http://www-chaos.umd.edu/history/modern3.html). This failure came on top of the Opium War (http://www.wsu.edu/~dee/CHING/OPIUM.HTM and http://www.cyber.law.harvard.edu/ChinaDragon/opiumwar.html). A site at http://web.jjay.cuny.edu/~jobrien/reference/ob29.html encourages discussion of Chinese Opium Commissioner Lin Zexu's letter to Queen Victoria.

The Taiping Rebellion (http://www.chaos.umd.edu/ history/modern2.html) gravely weakened 2,000 years of traditional Chinese government. The Boxer Rebellion (http://geocities.com/CollegePark/Pool/6208/title_ page.htm) provided the coup de grâce.

Major General Charles "Chinese" Gordon (http://www. cis.upenn.edu/~homeier/interests/heros/gordon.html), who took part in the suppression of the anti-foreign, anti-Qing Taiping Rebellion, also had to address another indigenous revolt in Egypt led by Muhammad Ahmad ibn as Sayyid abd Allah (http://sudanhome.com/info/ mahdiyah.htm).

Unlike al-Mahdi, who sought the path of militant revivalism, Mohammad Abduh and Jamal al-din Afghani (http://www.iranchamber.com/personalities/ jasadabadi/jamal_odin_asadabadi.php) sought Western-style modernization within the context of Islam.

Earlier, Muhammad Ali, ruler of Egypt, had sought the same goal through economic transformation, but even the efforts of his successors to build the Suez Canal backfired due to European control over capital flow which ultimately led to increased European control over Egypt (http:// www.emayzine.com/lectures/egypt1798-1924.html).

Much the same fate befell the Tanzimat (http://www. scholars.nus.edu.sg/landow/victorian/history/dora/ dora9.html), the Ottoman effort that paralleled the Qing reformist experiment.

CHAPTER 27

RUSSIA AND JAPAN: INDUSTRIALIZATION OUTSIDE THE WEST

This silk factory, based on imported technology and designed mainly for the burgeoning export trade to the West, is representative of early Japanese industrialization.

- Russia's Reforms and Industrial Advance
- DOCUMENT: Conditions for Factory Workers in Russia's Industrialization
- Protest and Revolution in Russia
- Japan: Transformation Without Revolution
- IN DEPTH: The Separate Paths of Japan and China
- VISUALIZING THE PAST: Two Faces of Western Influence
- GLOBAL CONNECTIONS: Russia and Japan in the World

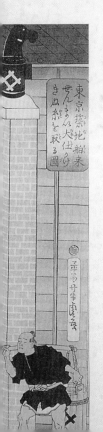

In the 1890s, the Russian government several times proposed a European disarmament conference because weapon costs were soaring. The idea had many justifications in an increasingly dangerous military environment. It also stemmed from the difficulties Russia was facing in keeping up with current expenses amid social unrest and the costs of industrialization.

On a more frivolous front, in 1896 a team of Japanese students defeated a group of American sailors in a baseball game, to their great delight. Growing foreign presence and an effort to imitate aspects of Western education had introduced new pastimes to Japan, including baseball, and within two decades the Japanese were prepared to beat Westerners at their own game.

This chapter deals with two important nations that defied the common pattern of growing Western domination during the 19th century: Russia and Japan. Both did so only after a heightened threat of Western interference, and both had to accept Western advisors and other intrusions. By 1914, however, Russia and Japan had managed to launch significant industrialization and to make other changes designed to strengthen their political and social systems. Neither Russia nor Japan rivaled the industrial might of the West at this point; both were trying to catch up after a late start. Their achievement was economic autonomy—not a share in the West's core position—which enabled both nations to gain sufficient power to participate in the imperialist scramble of the late 19th century.

Russia and Japan differed from the pattern of halting reforms characteristic of China and the Middle East in the 19th century. Theirs were the only societies outside the West to begin a wholesale process of industrialization before the 1960s.

The case of Japan was particularly striking. Japanese industrialization and related reforms seemed less expected in light of previous patterns than did Russia's, where an interest in selective borrowing from the West had developed by 1700. Japan pulled away from the rest of east Asia, at least for a time, whereas Russia continued a pattern of expanding influence in eastern Europe and central Asia.

Russia and Japan did have some common characteristics, which help explain why both could maintain economic and political independence during the West's century of power. They both had prior experience of imitation: Japan from China, Russia from Byzantium and then the West. They knew that learning from outsiders could be profitable and need not destroy their native cultures. They both had improved their political effectiveness during the 17th and 18th centuries, through the Tokugawa shogunate and the tsarist empire, respectively. Both nations could use the state to sponsor changes that in the West had rested in part with private businesses.

1700 C.E.	1800 C.E.	1825 C.E.	1850 C.E.
1720 End ban on Western books	**1800–1850** Growth of "Dutch school"	**1825** Decembrist Revolt	**1853** Perry expedition to Edo Bay
1762–1796 Catherine the Great	**1812** Failure of Napoleon's invasion	**1825–1855** Heightening of repression by Tsar Nicholas I	**1854** Follow-up American and British fleet visit
1773–1775 Pugachev Rebellion	**1815** Russia reacquires Poland through Treaty of Vienna; Alexander I and the Holy Alliance	**1829–1878** Serbia gains increasing autonomy in Ottoman Empire, then independence	**1854–1856** Crimean War
1772–1795 Partitioning of Poland		**1830–1831** Polish nationalist revolt repressed	**1856** Romania gains virtual independence
		1831 Greece wins independence after revolt against Ottomans	**1860–1868** Civil strife
		1833, 1853 Russian–Ottoman wars	**1860s–1870s** Alexander II reforms
		1841–1843 Brief shogun reform effort	**1861** Russian emancipation of serfs
			1865–1879 Russian conquests in central Asia
			1867 Mutsuhito, emperor of Japan
			1867 Russia sells Alaska to U.S.
			1868–1912 Meiji period
			1870 Ministry of Industry established
			1870–1940 Population growth
			1872 Universal military service established
			1872 Education Act (Japan)

Ironically, soon after the reform period began in both countries, Russia and Japan met in new ways, as their expansionist interests brought a clash over influence in Korea. The resultant Russo-Japanese War symbolized the growing importance of both societies in world affairs. The war promoted further change, convincing Japanese leaders that they were on the right course while weakening the Russian establishment.

Reforms in both Russia and Japan raised new questions about each civilization's identity as change cut into distinctive traditions. Individual agents played a great role in initiating and directing the reform process in each country, helping to explain an unusual burst of change.

Russia's Reforms and Industrial Advance

 After half a century of conservatism, Russia moved into an active reform period in 1861. Social and political changes set the basis for initial industrialization by the 1890s. But social strain persisted as Russian leaders tried to defend the tsarist autocracy.

Russia Before Reform

Russian rulers, beginning with Catherine the Great in her later years, sought ways to protect the country from the contagion of the French Revolution. The sense that Western policies might serve as models for Russia faded dramatically. Napoleon's 1812 invasion of Russia also led to a new concern with defense. Conservative intellectuals supported the move toward renewed isolation. In the eyes of these aristocratic writers, Russia knew the true meaning of community and stability. The system of serfdom provided ignorant peasants with the guidance and protection of paternalistic masters—an inaccurate social analysis but a comforting one. To resist Napoleon's pressure early in the 19th century, the government introduced some improvements in bureaucratic training. A new tsar, Alexander I, flirted with liberal rhetoric, but at the Congress of Vienna he sponsored the **Holy Alliance** idea. In this alliance, the conservative monarchies of Russia, Prussia, and Austria would combine in defense of religion and the established

1875 C.E.	**1900 C.E.**
1875–1877 Russian–Ottoman War; Russia wins new territory	**1902** Loose alliance with Britain
1877 Final samurai rising	**1904–1905** Russo–Japanese War
1878 Bulgaria gains independence	**1904–1905** Loss in Russo–Japanese War
1881 Anarchist assassination of Alexander II	**1905–1906** Revolution results in peasant reforms and duma
1881–1905 Growing repression, attacks on minorities	**1910** Annexation of Korea
1884–1887 New gains in central Asia	**1912** Growing party strife in parliament
1884–1914 Beginnings of Russian industrialization; near-completion of trans-Siberian railway (full linkage 1916)	**1912–1918** Balkan Wars
	1914 World War I begins
1890 New constitution and legal code	**1916–1918** Seizure of former German holdings in Pacific and China
1892–1903 Sergey Witte, minister of finance	**1917** Revolution and Bolshevik victory
1894–1895 Sino–Japanese war	
1898 Formation of Marxist Social Democratic Party	

The poet Pushkin, for example, descended from an African slave, used romantic styles to celebrate the beauties of the Russian soul and the tragic dignity of the common people. Because of its compatibility with the use of folklore and a sense of nationalism, the romantic style took deep root in eastern Europe. Russian musical composers would soon make their contributions, again using folk themes and sonorous sentimentality within a Western stylistic context.

While Russia's ruling elite continued to welcome Western artistic styles and took great pride in Russia's growing cultural respectability, they increasingly censored intellectuals who tried to incorporate liberal or radical political values. A revolt of Western-oriented army officers in 1825—the **Decembrist uprising** (see Figure 27.1)—inspired the new tsar, Nicholas I, to still more adamant conservatism. Repression of political opponents stiffened, and the secret police expanded. Newspapers and schools, already confined to a small minority, were tightly supervised. What political criticism there was flourished mainly in exile in places such as Paris and London; it had little impact on Russia.

Partly because of political repression, Russia avoided the wave of revolutions that spread through Europe in 1830 and 1848. Russia seemed to be operating in a different political orbit from that of the West, to the great delight of most Russian officials. In its role as Europe's conservative anchor, Russia even intervened in 1849 to help Austria put down the nationalist revolution in Hungary—a blow in favor of

order. The idea of Russia as a bastion of sanity in a Europe gone mad was appealing, although in fact the alliance itself accomplished little.

Defending the status quo produced some important new tensions, however. Many intellectuals remained fascinated with Western progress. Some praised political freedom and educational and scientific advance. Others focused more purely on Western cultural styles. Early in the 19th century, Russia began to contribute creatively to Europe's cultural output.

Figure 27.1 *In the military Decembrist revolt in St. Petersburg, Loyalist troops put down the insurgent regiments in 1825.*

monarchy but also a reminder of Russia's eagerness to flex its muscles in wider European affairs.

While turning more conservative than it had been in the 18th century, Russia maintained its tradition of territorial expansion. Russia had confirmed its hold over most of Poland at the Congress of Vienna in 1815 after Napoleon briefly sponsored a separate Polish duchy. Nationalist sentiment, inspired by the growth of romantic nationalism in Poland and backed by many Polish landowners with ties to western Europe, roused recurrent Polish opposition to Russian rule. An uprising occurred in 1830 and 1831, triggered by news of the revolutions in the West and led by liberal aristocrats and loyal Catholics who chafed under the rule of an Orthodox power. Tsar Nicholas I put down this revolt with great brutality, driving many leaders into exile.

At the same time, Russia continued its pressure on the Ottoman Empire, whose weakness attracted their eager attention. A war in the 1830s led to some territorial gains. France and Britain repeatedly tried to prop up Ottoman authority in the interest of countering Russian aggression. Russia also supported many nationalist movements in the Balkans, including the Greek independence war in the 1820s; here, a desire to cut back the Turks outweighed Russia's commitment to conservatism. Overall, although no massive acquisitions marked the early 19th century, Russia continued to be a dynamic diplomatic and military force (Map 27.1).

Economic and Social Problems: The Peasant Question

Russia's economic position did not keep pace with its diplomatic aspirations. As the West industrialized and central European powers such as Prussia and Austria introduced at least the beginnings of industrialization, including some rail lines, Russia largely stood pat. This meant that it began to fall increasingly

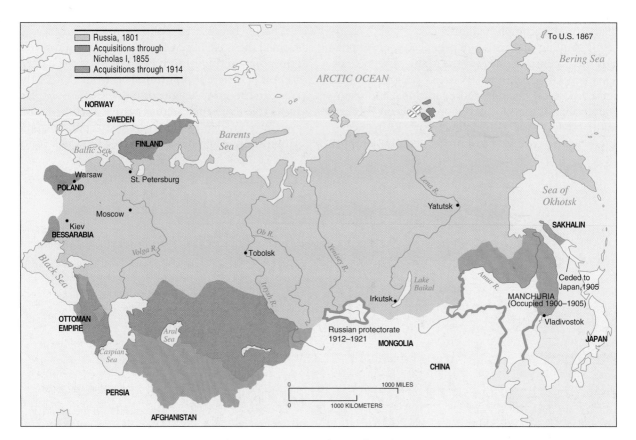

Map 27.1 *Russian Expansion, 1815–1914. Russia continued to push to the west, south, and east. The main conflicts were with the Ottoman Empire. Later, however, conflicts in east Asia loomed larger.*

behind the West in technology and trade. Russian landlords eagerly took advantage of Western markets for grain, but they increased their exports not by improving their techniques but by tightening the labor obligations on their serfs. This was a common pattern in much of eastern Europe in the early 19th century, as Polish and Hungarian nobles also increased labor service to gain ground in the export market. In return for low-cost grain exports, Russia and other east European areas imported some Western machinery and other costly equipment as well as luxury goods for the great aristocrats to display as badges of cultured respectability. A few isolated factories that used foreign equipment were opened up in imitation of western European industrialization, but there was no significant change in overall manufacturing or transportation mechanisms. Russia remained a profoundly agricultural society based mainly on serf labor, but it was now a visibly stagnant society as well.

The widening gap between Russia and the West was driven home dramatically by a minor war in the Crimea between 1854 and 1856. Nicholas I provoked conflict with the Ottoman Empire in 1853, arguing among other things that Russia was responsible for protecting Christian interests in the Holy Land. This time, however, France and Britain were not content with diplomatic maneuverings to limit Russian gains but came directly to the sultan's aid. Britain was increasingly worried about any great power advance in the region that might threaten its hold on India, whereas France sought diplomatic glory and also represented itself as the Western champion of Christian rights. The resultant **Crimean War** was fought directly in Russia's backyard on the Black Sea, yet the Western forces won, driving the Russian armies from their entrenched positions. (Each side lost about 250,000 troops in a truly difficult struggle.) The loss was profoundly disturbing to Russian leadership, for the Western powers won this little war not because of great tactics or inspired principles but because of their industrial advantage. They had the ships to send masses of military supplies long distances, and their artillery and other weapons were vastly superior to Russia's home-produced models. This severe blow to a regime that prided itself on military vigor was a frightening portent for the future.

The Crimean War helped convince Russian leaders, including the new tsar, Alexander II, that it was time for a change. Reform was essential, not to copy the West but to allow sufficient economic adjustments for Russia to keep pace in the military arena. First and foremost, reform meant some resolution of Russia's leading social issue, the issue that most distinguished Russian society from that of the West: serfdom. Only if the status of serfs changed could Russia develop a more vigorous and mobile labor force and so be able to industrialize. Russian concern about this issue paralleled the attacks on slavery in the Americas in the same period, reflecting a desire to meet Western humanitarian standards and a need for cheap, flexible labor.

So for two decades Russia returned to a policy of reform, based on Western standards and examples; serfdom had been abolished in western Europe after 1789 and in east central regions such as Prussia and Hungary in the aftermath of the revolutions of 1848. As before, however, the intention was not to duplicate Western measures fully but to protect distinctive Russian institutions, including the landed aristocracy and tightly knit peasant communities. The result was an important series of changes that, with tragic irony, created more grievances than they resolved while opening the way to further economic change.

The Reform Era and Early Industrialization

The final decision to emancipate the serfs in 1861 came at roughly the same time that the United States and Brazil decided to free slaves. Neither slavery nor rigorous serfdom suited the economic needs of a society seeking an independent position in Western-dominated world trade.

In some ways, the **emancipation of the serfs** was more generous than the liberation of slaves in the Americas. Although aristocrats retained part of the land, including the most fertile holdings, the serfs got most of it, in contrast to slaves, who received their freedom but nothing else. However, Russian emancipation was careful to preserve essential aristocratic power; the tsar was not interested in destroying the nobility, who remained his most reliable political allies and the source of most bureaucrats. Even more, emancipation was designed to retain the tight grip of the tsarist state. The serfs obtained no new political rights at a national level. They were still tied to their villages until they could pay for the land they were given. The redemption money went to the aristocrats to help preserve this class. Redemption payments added greatly to peasants' material hardship (Figure 27.2), and peasants thought that the land belonged to them with no need to pay for its return.

Emancipation did bring change; it helped create a larger urban labor force. But it did not spur a revolution in agricultural productivity because most peasants continued to use traditional methods on their small plots. And it did not bring contentment. Indeed, peasant uprisings became more common as hopes for a brighter future seemed dashed by the limits of change. Explosive rural unrest in Russia was furthered by substantial population growth as some of the factors that had earlier swelled the West's population now spread to Russia, including increased use of the potato. In sum, after 1861 Russia was a classic case of a society in the midst of rapid change where reform did not go far enough to satisfy key protest groups.

Figure 27.2   *This roadside scene in the late 19th century depicts the poverty of a Russian peasant village. What forces produced such poor conditions, even after serfdom had been abolished?*

To be sure, the reform movement did not end with emancipation. Alexander II introduced a host of further measures in the 1860s and early 1870s. New law codes cut back the traditional punishments now that serfs were legally free in the eyes of the law (though subject to important transitional restrictions). The tsar created local political councils, the **zemstvoes,** which had a voice in regulating roads, schools, and other regional policies. Some form of local government was essential now that the nobles no longer directly ruled the peasantry. The zemstvoes gave some Russians, particularly middle-class people such as doctors and lawyers, new political experience, and they undertook important inquiries into local problems. However, the councils had no influence on national policy; the tsar resolutely maintained his own authority and that of his extensive bureaucracy. Another important area of change was the army; the Crimean War had shown the need for reform. The officer corps was improved through promotion by merit and a new organization of essential services. Recruitment was extended, and many peasants learned new skills through their military service. Some strides also were made in providing state-sponsored basic education, although schools spread unevenly.

From the reform era onward, literacy increased rapidly in Russian society. A new market developed for popular reading matter that had some similarities to the mass reading culture developing in the West. Interestingly, Russian potboiler novels, displaying a pronounced taste for excitement and exotic adventure, also attested to distinctive values. For example, Russian "bad guys" never were glorified in the end but always were either returned to social loyalty or condemned—a clear sign of the limits to individualism. Women gained new positions in this climate of change. Some won access to higher education, and, as in the West, a minority of women mainly from the upper classes began to penetrate professions such as medicine. Even sexual habits began to change, as had occurred in the West a century earlier. Fathers' control over their children's behavior loosened a bit, particularly where nonagricultural jobs were available, and sexual activity before marriage increased.

The move toward industrialization was part of the wider process of change. State support was an industrial effort, for Russia lacked a preexisting middle class and capital. State enterprises had to make up

Document

Conditions for Factory Workers in Russia's Industrialization

Russia passed several laws protecting workers, but enforcement was minimal. The Ministry of Finance established a factory inspectorate in the 1880s, which dutifully reported on conditions; these reports usually were ignored. The following passages deal with a number of Moscow factories in the 1880s:

In the majority of factories there are no special quarters for the workers. This applies to workers in paper, wool, and silk finishing. Skilled hand craftsmen like brocade weavers can earn good wages, and yet most of them sleep on or under their looms, for lack of anything else. Only in a few weaving factories are there special sleeping quarters, and these are provided not for the weavers, but for other workers—the winders and dyers, etc. Likewise, the velveteen cutters almost always sleep on the tables where they work. This habit is particularly unhealthy, since the work areas are always musty and the air is saturated with dye fumes—sometimes poisonous ones. Carpenters also generally sleep on their workbenches. In bastmatting factories, workers of both sexes and all ages sleep together on pieces and mats of bast which are often damp. Only the sick workers in these bast factories are allowed to sleep on the single stove....Work at the mill never stops, day or night. There are two twelve-hour shifts a day, which begin at 6:00 A.M. and 6:00 P.M. The men have a half-hour for breakfast (8:30–9:00) and one hour for dinner (1:00–2:00).

The worst violations of hygienic regulations were those I saw in most of the flax-spinning mills where linen is produced.... Although in western Europe all the dust-producing carding and combing machines have long been covered and well ventilated, I saw only one Russian linen mill where such a machine was securely covered. Elsewhere, the spools of these machines were completely open to the air, and the scutching apparatus is inadequately ventilated....

In many industrial establishments the grounds for fines and the sizes of fines are not fixed in advance. The factory rules may contain only one phrase like the following: "Those found violating company rules will be fined *at the discretion of the manager.*"

The degree of arbitrariness in the determination of fines, and thus also in the determination of the worker's wages, was unbelievably extreme in some factories. In Podolsk, for instance, in factories No. 131 and No. 135, there is a ten-ruble forfeit for leaving the factory before the expiration of one's contract. But as applied, this covers much more than voluntary breach of contract on the worker's part. This fine is exacted from every worker who for any reason has to leave the factory. Cases are known of persons who have had to pay this fine three times. Moreover, fines are levied for so many causes that falling under a severe fine is a constant possibility for each worker. For instance, workers who for any reason came into the office in a group, instead of singly, would be fined one ruble. After a second offense, the transgressors would be dismissed—leaving behind, of course, the ten-ruble fine for breach of contract.

In factory No. 135 the workers are still treated as serfs. Wages are paid out only twice a year, even then not in full but only enough to pay the workers' taxes (other necessities are supplied by the factory store). Furthermore this money is not given to the workers directly, but is sent by mail to their village elders and village clerks. Thus the workers are without money the year around. Besides they are also paying severe fines to the factory, and these sums will be subtracted from their wages at the final year-end accounting.

Extreme regulations and regimentation are very common in our factories—regulations entangle the workers at every step and burden them with more or less severe fines which are subtracted from their often already inadequate wages. Some factory administrators have become real virtuosos at thinking up new grounds for fines. A brief description of a few of the fines in factory No. 172 is an excellent example of this variety: on October 24, 1877, an announcement was posted of new fines to be set at the discretion of the office for fourteen different cases of failure to maintain silence and cleanliness. There were also dozens of minor fines prescribed for certain individual offenses: for example, on August 4, 1883, a huge fine of five rubles was set for singing in the factory courtyard after 9:30, or at any time in any unauthorized place. On June 3, 1881, a fine was to be levied from workers who took tea and sugar, bread, or any kind of foodstuffs into the weaving building, "in order to avoid breeding any insects or vermin." On May 14, 1880, a fine was set for anyone who wrote with pencil, chalk, or anything else on the walls in the dyeing or weaving buildings.

Questions: What were the worst features of Russian factories? Were conditions worse than in western Europe during early industrialization, and if so in what ways and why? (Relatedly, what conditions probably were common in the first stages of

(continued)

factory industry everywhere?) How did working conditions and management attitudes help create a revolutionary mood among Russian workers? Think also about the nature of this source. Why would a conservative government sponsor such a critical report? What does the report suggest about tensions at the top of Russian society, between government and business? Would a conservative government be more likely to undertake this kind of inquiry than the more reform-minded regime that had existed a decade earlier? What do you think the results of such a report would be, in the Russian context, or indeed in any early industrial context?

part of the gap, in the tradition of economic activity that went back to Peter the Great.

Russia began to create an extensive railroad network in the 1870s. The establishment of the **trans-Siberian railroad,** which connected European Russia with the Pacific, was the crowning achievement of this drive when it was nearly completed by the end of the 1880s. The railroad boom directly stimulated expansion of Russia's iron and coal sectors. Railroad development also stimulated the export of grain to the West, which now became essential to earn foreign currency needed in payment for advanced Western machinery. The railroads also opened Siberia up to new development, which in turn brought Russia into a more active and contested Asian role.

By the 1880s, when Russia's railroad network had almost quintupled since 1860, modern factories were beginning to spring up in Moscow, St. Peters-burg, and several Polish cities, and an urban working class was growing rapidly (Figure 27.3). Printing factories and metalworking shops expanded the skilled artisanry in the cities, and metallurgy and textile plants recruited a still newer semiskilled industrial labor force from the troubled countryside.

Under Count **Sergei Witte,** Minister of Finance from 1892 to 1903 and an ardent economic modernizer, the government enacted high tariffs to protect new Russian industry, improved its banking system, and encouraged Western investors to build great factories with advanced technology. As Witte put it, "The inflow of foreign capital is…the only way by which our industry will be able to supply our country quickly with abundant and cheap products." By 1900, approximately half of Russian industry was foreign owned and much of it was foreign operated, with British, German, and French industrialists taking the lead. Russia became a debtor nation as huge industrial development loans piled up. By 1900, Russia had surged to fourth rank in the world in steel production and was second to the United States in the newer area of petroleum production and refining. Russian textile output was also impressive. Long-standing Russian economic lags were beginning to yield.

This industrial revolution was still in its early stages. Russia's world rank was a function more of its great size and population, along with its rich natural resources, than of thorough mechanization. Many Russian factories were vast—on average, the largest in the world—but they usually were not up to Western technical standards, nor was the labor force highly trained. Agriculture also remained backward, as peasants, often illiterate, had neither capital nor motives to change their ways.

Other reforms also produced ambiguous results. Russia remained a traditional peasant society in many ways. Beneath the official military reorganization, many peasant-soldiers continued to see their officers

Figure 27.3 *Early Russian industrialization is depicted in this 1888 photo of the commercial department of the Abrikosova and Son factory.*

as landlord-patrons. Discipline and military efficiency were lax. It was not clear that the Russian masses had experienced the kinds of attitudinal changes that had occurred in the West at the time of initial industrialization or even before. Even more obvious was the absence of a large, self-confident middle class of the sort that had arisen earlier in the West. Businesspeople and professionals grew in numbers, but often they were dependant on state initiatives, such as zemstvo employment for doctors and economic guidance for businesspeople. They also lacked the numbers and tradition to become as assertive as their Western counterparts had been (for example, in challenging aristocratic power and values).

Protest and Revolution in Russia

 A rising tide of unrest accompanied Russia's period of transformation by the 1880s, from nationalist agitation to outright revolution. Russia became a profoundly unstable society.

The Road to Revolution

Alexander II's reforms, as well as economic change and the greater population mobility it involved, encouraged minority nationalities to make demands of the great empire. Intellectuals explored the cultural traditions of Ukrainians and other groups. Nationalist beliefs initially were imported from western Europe, but here and elsewhere in eastern Europe, they encouraged divisive minority agitation that multinational states, such as Russia and Austria–Hungary, found very hard to handle. Nationalist pressures were not the main problem in Russia, but given Russia's mainstream nationalist insistence on the distinctive superiorities of a Russian tradition, they did cause concern.

Social protest was more vigorous still, and it was heightened not only by the limitations of reform but by industrialization itself. Recurrent famines provoked peasant uprisings. Peasants deeply resented redemption payments and taxes and often seized and burned the records that indicated what they owed.

Many educated Russians, including some aristocrats, also clamored for revolutionary change. Two strands developed. Many business and professional people, though not very aggressive, began to seek a fuller political voice and new rights such as greater

freedom in the schools and press; they argued for liberal reforms. At the same time, a group of radical **intelligentsia**—a Russian term for articulate intellectuals as a class—became increasingly active. As Russian universities expanded, student groups grew as well, and many were impatient with Russia's slow development and with the visible restrictions on political activity.

Some intellectuals later toned down their goals as they entered the bureaucracy or business life. But many remained inspired by radical doctrines, and more than a few devoted their lives to a revolutionary cause. This kind of intellectual alienation rested on some of the principles that had roused intellectuals in the West, but it went deeper in Russia. It was the first example of a kind of intellectual radicalism, capable of motivating terrorism, which would characterize other societies caught in tense transitions during the 20th century. The Russian intelligentsia wanted political freedom and deep social reform while maintaining a Russian culture different from that of the West, which they saw as hopelessly materialistic. Their radicalism may have stemmed from the demanding task they set themselves: attacking key Russian institutions while building a new society that would not reproduce the injustices and crippling limitations of the Western world.

Many Russian radicals were **anarchists,** who sought to abolish all formal government. Although anarchism was not unknown in the West, it took on particular force in Russia in opposition to tsarist autocracy. Many early anarchists in the 1860s hoped that they could triumph by winning peasant support, and a host of upper-class radicals fanned out to teach the peasantry the beauties of political activism. Failure here led many anarchists to violent methods and thus to the formation of the first large terrorist movement in the modern world. Given the lack of popular support and other political outlets, assassinations and bombings seemed the only way to attack the existing order. As anarchist leader Bakunin put it,

> We have only one plan—general destruction. We want a national revolution of the peasants. We refuse to take any part in the working out of schemes to better the conditions of life; we regard as fruitless solely theoretical work. We consider destruction to be such an enormous and difficult task that we must devote all our powers to it, and we do not wish to deceive ourselves with the

dream that we will have enough strength and knowledge for creation.

Not surprisingly, the recurrent waves of terrorism merely strengthened the tsarist regime's resolve to avoid further political change in what became a vicious circle in 19th-century Russian politics.

By the late 1870s, Alexander II was pulling back from his reform interest, fearing that change was getting out of hand. Censorship of newspapers and political meetings tightened; many dissidents were arrested and sent to Siberia. Alexander II was assassinated by a terrorist bomb in 1881 after a series of botched attempts. His successors, while increasing the effort to industrialize, continued to oppose further political reform. New measures of repression also were directed against minority nationalities, partly to dampen their unrest and partly to gain the support of upper-class conservatives. The Poles and other groups were supervised carefully. Russian language instruction was forced on peoples such as Ukrainians. Persecution of the large Jewish minority was stepped up, resulting in many mass executions—called pogroms—and seizures of property. As a consequence, many Russian Jews emigrated.

By the 1890s, the currents of protest gained new force. Marxist doctrines spread from the Western socialist movement to a segment of the Russian intelligentsia, who became committed to a tightly organized proletarian revolution. One of the most active Marxist leaders was **Vladimir Ilyich Ulyanov,** known as Lenin. Lenin, a man from a bureaucratic family whose brother was hanged after a trial, following his arrest by the political police, introduced important innovations in Marxist theory to make it more appropriate for Russia. He argued that because of the spread of international capitalism, a proletariat was developing worldwide in advance of industrialization. Therefore, Russia could have a proletarian revolution without going through a distinct middle-class phase. Lenin also insisted on the importance of disciplined revolutionary cells that could maintain doctrinal purity and effective action even under severe police repression. Lenin's approach animated the group of Russian Marxists known as **Bolsheviks,** or majority party (though, ironically, they were actually a minority in the Russian Marxist movement as a whole). The approach proved ideal for Russian conditions.

Working-class unrest in the cities grew with the new currents among the intelligentsia. Russian workers became far more radical than their Western counterparts. They formed unions and conducted strikes—all illegal—but many of them also had firm political goals in mind. Their radicalism stemmed partly from the absence of legal political outlets. It arose also from rural unrest—for these new workers pulled in peasant grievances against the existing order—and from the severe conditions of early industrialization, with its large factories and frequent foreign ownership. Although many workers were not linked to any particular doctrine, some became interested in Bolshevism, and they were urged on by passionate organizers.

By 1900, the contradictory currents in Russian society may have made revolution inevitable. The forces demanding change were not united, but the importance of mass protest in both countryside and city, as well as the radical intelligentsia, made it difficult to find a compromise. Furthermore, the regime remained resolutely opposed to compromise. Conservative ministers urged a vigorous policy of resistance and repression.

The Revolution of 1905

Military defeat in 1904 and 1905 finally lit this tinderbox. Russia had maintained its expansionist foreign policy through the late 19th century, in part because of tradition and in part because diplomatic success might draw the venom from internal unrest. It also wanted to match the imperialist strides of the Western great powers. A war with the Ottoman Empire in the 1870s brought substantial gains, which were then pushed back at the insistence of France and Britain. Russia also successfully aided the creation in the Balkans of new Slavic nations, such as Serbia and Bulgaria, the "little Slavic brothers" that filled nationalist hearts with pride. Some conservative writers even talked in terms of a pan-Slavic movement that would unite the Slavic people—under Russian leadership, of course. Russia participated vigorously in other Middle Eastern and central Asian areas. Russia and Britain both increased their influence in Persia and Afghanistan, reaching some uneasy truces that divided spheres of activity early in the 20th century. Russia was also active in China. The development of the trans-Siberian railroad encouraged Russia to incorporate some northern portions of Manchuria, violating the 18th-century Amur River agreement. Russia also joined Western powers in obtaining long-term leases to Chinese territory during the 1890s.

These were important gains, but they did not satisfy growing Russian ambitions, and they also brought trouble. Russia risked an overextension because its diplomatic aspirations were not backed by real increases in military power. The problem first came to a head in 1904. Increasingly powerful Japan became worried about further Russian expansion in northern China and efforts to extend influence into Korea. The **Russo-Japanese War** broke out in 1904. Against all expectations save Japan's, the Japanese won. Russia could not move its fleet quickly to the Pacific, and its military organization proved too cumbersome to oppose the more effective Japanese maneuvers. Japan gained the opportunity to move into Korea as the balance of power in the Far East began to shift.

Unexpected defeat in war unleashed massive protests on the home front in the Russian Revolution of 1905. Urban workers mounted well-organized general strikes that were designed above all for political gains. Peasants led a series of insurrections, and liberal groups also agitated. After trying brutal police repression, which only infuriated the urban crowds, the tsarist regime had to change course. It wooed liberals by creating a national parliament, the **duma.** The interior minister Piotyr Stolypin introduced an important series of reforms for the peasantry. Under the **Stolypin reforms,** peasants gained greater freedom from redemption payments and village controls. They could buy and sell land more freely. The goal was to create a stratified, market-oriented peasantry in which successful farmers would move away from the peasant masses, becoming rural capitalists. Indeed, peasant unrest did die down, and a minority of aggressive entrepreneurs, called **kulaks,** began to increase agricultural production and buy additional land. Yet the reform package quickly came unglued. Not only were a few new workers' rights withdrawn, triggering a new series of strikes and underground activities, but the duma was progressively stripped of power. Nicholas II, a weak man who was badly advised, could not surrender the tradition of autocratic rule, and the duma became a hollow institution, satisfying no one. Police repression also resumed, creating new opponents to the regime.

Pressed in the diplomatic arena by the Japanese advance yet eager to counter internal pressures with some foreign policy success, the Russian government turned once again to the Ottoman Empire and the Balkans. Various strategies to acquire new rights of access to the Mediterranean and to back Slavic allies in the Balkans yielded no concrete results, but they did stir the pot in this vulnerable area and helped lead to World War I. And this war, in which Russia participated to maintain its diplomatic standing and live up to the billing of Slavic protector, led to one of the great revolutions of modern times.

Russia and Eastern Europe

A number of Russian patterns were paralleled in smaller eastern European states such as Hungary (joined to Austria but autonomous after 1866), Romania, Serbia, Bulgaria, and Greece. These were new nations—unlike Russia—and emerging after long Ottoman dominance, they had no access to the diplomatic influence of their giant neighbor. Most of the new nations established parliaments, in imitation of Western forms, but carefully restricted voting rights and parliamentary powers. Kings—some of them new, as the Balkan nations had set up monarchies after gaining independence from the Ottoman Empire—ruled without many limits on their power. Most eastern European nations abolished serfdom either in 1848 or soon after Russia's move, but landlord power remained more extensive than in Russia, and peasant unrest followed. Most of the smaller eastern European nations industrialized much less extensively than Russia, and as agricultural exporters they remained far more dependant on Western markets.

Amid all the problems, eastern Europe enjoyed a period of glittering cultural productivity in the late 19th century, with Russia in the lead. Development of the romantic tradition and other Western styles continued. National dictionaries and histories, along with the collection of folktales and music, helped the smaller Slavic nations gain a sense of their heritage. The Russian novel enjoyed a period of unprecedented brilliance. Westernizers such as Turgenev wrote realistic novels that promoted what they saw as modern values, whereas writers such as Tolstoy and Dostoevsky tried to portray a special Russian spirit. Russian music moved from the romanticism of Tchaikovsky to more innovative, atonal styles of the early 20th century. Polish and Hungarian composers such as Chopin and Liszt also made an important mark. Russian painters began participating in modern art currents, producing important abstract work. Finally, scientific research advanced at levels of fundamental importance. A Czech scientist, Gregor Mendel, furthered the understanding of genetics, and a Russian physiologist, Ivan Pavlov, experimenting on conditioned reflexes, explained unconscious responses in human beings. Eastern Europe thus participated more fully than ever before in a cultural world it shared with the West.

Japan: Transformation Without Revolution

 Like Russia, Japan faced new pressure from the West during the 1850s, although this pressure took the form of a demand for more open trade rather than outright military conflict. Japan's response was more direct than Russia's and more immediately successful. Despite Japan's long history of isolation, its society was better adapted than Russia's to the challenge of industrial change. Market forms were more extensive, reaching into peasant agriculture, and literacy levels were higher. Nevertheless, Japan had to rework many of its institutions during the final decades of the 19th century, and the process produced significant strain.

The Final Decades of the Shogunate

On the surface, Japan experienced little change during the first half of the 19th century, and certainly this was a quiet time compared with the earlier establishment of the Tokugawa shogunate (see Chapter 22) or the transformation introduced after the 1850s.

During the first half of the 19th century, the shogunate continued to combine a central bureaucracy with semifeudal alliances between the regional daimyos and the samurai. The government repeatedly ran into financial problems. Its taxes were based on agriculture, despite the growing commercialization of the Japanese economy; this was a severe constraint. At the same time, maintaining the feudal shell was costly. The government paid stipends to the samurai in return for their loyalty. A long budget reform spurt late in the 18th century built a successful momentum for a time, but a shorter effort between 1841 and 1843 was notably unsuccessful. This weakened the shogunate by the 1850s and hampered its response to the crisis induced by Western pressure.

Japanese intellectual life and culture also developed under the Tokugawa regime. Neo-Confucianism continued to gain among the ruling elite at the expense of Buddhism. Japan gradually became more secular, particularly among the upper classes. This was an important precondition for the nation's response to the Western challenge in that it precluded a strong religious-based resistance to change. Various Confucian schools actively debated into the mid-19th century, keeping Japanese intellectual life fairly creative. Schools and academies expanded, reaching well below the upper class through commoner schools, or **terakoya,** which taught reading, writing, and the rudiments of Confucianism to ordinary people. By 1859, more than 40 percent of all men and over 15 percent of all women were literate—a far higher percentage than anywhere else in the world outside the West, including Russia, and on a par with some of the fringe areas of the West (including the American South).

Although Confucianism remained the dominant ideology, there were important rivals. Tensions between traditionalists and reformist intellectuals were emerging, as in Russia in the same decades. A national studies group praised Japanese traditions, including the office of emperor and the Shinto religion. One national studies writer expressed a typical sentiment late in the 18th century: "The 'special dispensation of our Imperial Land' means that ours is the native land of the Heaven-Shining Goddess who casts her light over all countries in the four seas. Thus our country is the source and fountainhead of all other countries, and in all matters it excels all the others." The influence of the national studies school grew somewhat in the early 19th century, and it would help inspire ultranationalist sentiment at the end of the century and beyond.

A second minority group consisted of what the Japanese called **Dutch Studies.** Although major Western works had been banned when the policy of isolation was adopted, a group of Japanese translators kept alive the knowledge of Dutch to deal with the traders at Nagasaki. The ban on Western books was ended in 1720, and thereafter a group of Japanese scholars interested in "Dutch medicine" created a new interest in Western scientific advances, based on the realization that Western anatomy texts were superior to those of the Chinese. In 1850, there were schools of Dutch Studies in all major cities, and their students urged freer exchange with the West and a rejection of Chinese medicine and culture. "Our general opinion was that we should rid our country of the influences of the Chinese altogether. Whenever we met a young student of Chinese literature, we simply felt sorry for him."

Just as Japanese culture showed an important capacity for lively debate and fruitful internal tension, so the Japanese economy continued to develop into the 19th century. Commerce expanded as big merchant companies established monopoly privileges in many centers. Manufacturing gained ground in the countryside in such consumer goods industries as soy sauce and silks, and much of this was organized by city merchants. Some of these developments were comparable to slightly earlier changes in the West and have given rise to arguments that economically Japan had a running start on industrialization once the Western challenge revealed the necessity of further economic change.

By the 1850s, however, economic growth had slowed—a situation that has prompted some scholars to stress Japan's backwardness compared with the West. Technological limitations constrained agricultural expansion and population increase. At the same time, rural riots increased in many regions from the late 18th century onward. They were not overtly political but rather, like many rural protests, aimed at wealthy peasants, merchants, and landlord controls. Although the authorities put down this unrest with little difficulty, the protests contributed to a willingness to consider change when they were joined by challenge from the outside.

The Challenge to Isolation

Some Japanese had become increasingly worried about potential outside threats. In 1791, a book was issued advocating a strong navy. Fears about the West's growing power and particularly Russia's Asian expansion fed these concerns in later decades.

Fear became reality in 1853 when American Commodore **Matthew Perry** arrived with a squadron in Edo Bay near Tokyo and used threats of bombardment to insist that Americans be allowed to trade. The United States, increasingly an active part of the West's core economy, thus launched for Japan the same kind of pressure the Opium War had created for China: pressure from the heightened military superiority of the West and its insistence on opening markets for its burgeoning economy. In 1854, Perry returned and won the right to station an American consul in Japan;

in 1856, through a formal treaty, two ports were opened to commerce. Britain, Russia, and Holland quickly won similar rights. As in China, this meant that Westerners living in Japan would be governed by their own representatives, not by Japanese law.

The bureaucrats of the shogunate saw no alternative but to open up Japan, given the superiority of Western navies. And of course, there were Japanese who had grown impatient with strict isolation; their numbers swelled as the Dutch schools began to expand. On the other hand, the daimyos, intensely conservative, were opposed to the new concessions, and their opposition forced the shogun to appeal to the emperor for support. Soon, samurai opponents of the bureaucracy were also appealing to the emperor, who began to emerge from his centuries-long confinement as a largely religious and ceremonial figure. Whereas most daimyos defended the status quo, the samurai were more divided. Some saw opportunity in change, including the possibility of unseating the shogunate. The fact was that the complex shogunate system had depended on the isolation policy; it could not survive the stresses of foreign influence and internal reactions. The result was not immediate collapse; indeed, into the late 1850s, Japanese life seemed to go on much as before.

In the 1860s, political crisis came into the open. The crisis was spiced by samurai attacks on foreigners, including one murder of a British official, matched by Western naval bombardments of feudal forts. Civil war broke out in 1866 as the samurai eagerly armed themselves with American Civil War surplus weapons, causing Japan's aristocracy to come to terms with the advantages of Western armaments. When the samurai defeated a shogunate force, many Japanese were finally shocked out of their traditional reliance on their own superiority. One author argued that the nation, compared with the West with its technology, science, and humane laws, was only half civilized.

This multifaceted crisis came to an end in 1868 when the victorious reform group proclaimed a new emperor named Mutsuhito but commonly called "Meiji," or "Enlightened One." In his name, key samurai leaders managed to put down the troops of the shogunate. The crisis period had been shocking enough to allow further changes in Japan's basic political structure—changes that went much deeper at the political level than those introduced by Russia from 1861 onward.

In Depth

The Separate Paths of Japan and China

Japan's ability to change in response to new Western pressure contrasted strikingly with the sluggishness of Chinese reactions into the 20th century. The contrast draws particular attention because China and Japan had been part of the same civilization orbit for so long, which means that some of the assets Japan possessed in dealing with change were present in China as well. Indeed, Japan turned out to benefit, by the mid-19th century, from having become more like China in key respects during the Tokugawa period. The link between Chinese and Japanese traditions should not be exaggerated, of course, and earlier differences help explain the divergence that opened so clearly in the late 19th century. The east Asian world now split apart, with Japan seizing eagerly on Chinese weakness to mount a series of attacks from the 1890s to 1945, which only made China's troubles worse.

Japan and China had both chosen considerable isolation from larger world currents from about 1600 until the West forced new openings between 1830 and 1860. Japan's isolation was the more complete. Both countries lagged behind the West because of their self-containment, which was why Western industrialization caught them unprepared. China's power and wealth roused Western greed and interference first, which gave Japan some leeway.

However, China surpassed Japan in some areas that should have aided it in reacting to the Western challenge. Its leadership, devoted to Confucianism, was more thoroughly secular and bureaucratic in outlook. There was no need to brush aside otherworldly commitments or feudal distractions to deal with the West's material and organizational power. Government centralization, still an issue in Japan, had a long history in China. With a rich tradition of technological innovation and scientific discovery in its past as well, China might have appeared to be a natural to lead the Asian world in responding to the West.

However, that role fell to Japan. Several aspects of Japanese tradition gave it a flexibility that China lacked. It already knew the benefits of imitation, which China, save for its period of attraction to Buddhism, had never acknowledged. Japan's slower government growth had allowed a stronger, more autonomous merchant tradition even as both societies became more commercial in the 17th and early 18th centuries. Feudal traditions, though declining under the Tokugawa shogunate, also limited the heavy hand of government controls while stimulating a sense of military competitiveness, as in the West. In contrast, China's government probably tried to control too much by the 18th century and quashed initiative in the process.

China was also hampered by rapid population growth from the 17th century onward. This population pressure consumed great energy, leaving scant capital for other economic initiatives. Japan's population stability into the 19th century pressed resources less severely. Japan's island status made the nation more sensitive to Western naval pressures.

Finally, China and Japan were on somewhat different paths when the Western challenge intruded in the mid-19th century. China was suffering one of its recurrent dynastic declines. Government became less efficient, intellectual life stagnated, and popular unrest surged. A cycle of renewal might have followed, with a new dynasty seizing more vigorous reins. But Western interference disrupted this process, complicating reform and creating various new discontents that ultimately overturned the imperial office.

In contrast, Japan maintained political and economic vigor into the 19th century. Whereas by the late 19th century China needed Western guidance simply to handle such bureaucratic affairs as tariff collection and repression of peasant rebellion, Japan suffered no such breakdown of authority, using foreign advisors far more selectively.

Once a different pattern of response was established, every decade increased the gap. Western exploitation of Chinese assets and dilution of government power made conditions more chaotic, while Japanese strength grew steadily after a very brief period of uncertainty. By the 20th century, the two nations were enemies—with Japan, for the first time, the stronger—and seemed to be in different orbits. Japan enjoyed increasing industrial success and had a conservative state that would yield after World War II to a more fully parliamentary form. China, after decades of revolution, finally won its 20th-century political solution: communism.

Yet today, at the onset of the 21st century, it is unclear whether east Asia was split as permanently as 19th- and early 20th-century developments had suggested. Japan's industrial lead remains, but China's economy is beginning to soar. Common cultural habits of group cooperation and decision making remind us that beneath different political systems, a fruitful shared heritage continues to operate. The heritage is quite different from that of the West but fully adaptable to the demands of economic change. And so Westerners begin to wonder whether a Pacific century is about to dawn.

Questions: What civilization features had Japan and China shared before the 19th century? In what ways were Japanese political institutions more adaptable than Chinese institutions? Why was Russia also able to change earlier and more fundamentally than 19th-century China?

Industrial and Political Change in the Meiji State

The new Meiji government promptly set about abolishing feudalism, replacing the daimyos in 1871 with a system of nationally appointed prefects (district administrators carefully chosen from different regions; the prefect system was copied from French practice). Political power was effectively centralized, and from this base the Meiji rulers—the emperor and his close advisors, drawn from loyal segments of the aristocracy—began to expand the power of the state to effect economic and social change.

Quickly, the Japanese government sent samurai officials abroad, to western Europe and the United States, to study economic and political institutions and technology. These samurai, deeply impressed by what they saw, pulled back from their earlier antiforeign position and gained increasing voice over other officials in the government. Their basic goal was Japan's domestic development, accompanied by a careful diplomatic policy that would avoid antagonizing the West.

Fundamental improvements in government finance soon followed. Between 1873 and 1876, the Meiji ministers introduced a real social revolution. They abolished the samurai class and the stipends this group had received. The tax on agriculture was converted to a wider tax, payable in money. The samurai were compensated by government-backed bonds, but these decreased in value, and most samurai became poor. This development sparked renewed conflict, and a final samurai uprising occurred in 1877. However, the government had introduced an army based on national conscription, and by 1878 the nation was militarily secure. Individual samurai found new opportunities in political and business areas as they adapted to change. One former samurai, Iwasaki Yataro (1834–1885; Figure 27.4), who started his career buying weapons for a feudal lord, set up the Mitsubishi company after 1868, winning government contracts for railroad and steamship lines designed to compete with British companies in the region. Despite his overbearing personality, Iwasaki built a loyal management group, including other former samurai, and by his death had a stake in shipbuilding, mining, and banking as well as transportation. The continued existence of the samurai, reflecting Japan's lack of outright revolution, would yield diverse results in later Japanese history.

The process of political reconstruction crested in the 1880s. Many former samurai organized political

Figure 27.4 *Iwasaki Yataro*

parties. Meiji leaders traveled abroad to discover modern political forms. In 1884 they created a new conservative nobility, stocked by former nobles and Meiji leaders, that would operate a British-style House of Peers. Next, the bureaucracy was reorganized, insulated from political pressures, and opened to talent on the basis of civil service examinations. The bureaucracy began to expand rapidly; it grew from 29,000 officials in 1890 to 72,000 in 1908. Finally, the constitution, issued in 1889, ensured major prerogatives for the emperor along with limited powers for the lower house of the **Diet,** as the new parliament was called. Here, Germany provided the model, for the emperor commanded the military directly (served by a German-style general staff) and also directly named his ministers. Both the institution and its members' clothing were Western, as the Visualizing the Past segment shows. The Diet could pass laws, upon agreement of both houses, and could approve budgets, but failure to pass a budget would simply reinstate the budget of the previous year. Parliament could thus advise government, but it could not control it. Finally, the conservative tone of this parliamentary experiment was confirmed by high property qualifications set for voting rights. Only about 5 percent of Japanese men had enough wealth to be allowed to vote for representatives to the lower house.

Japan's political structure thus came to involve centralized imperial rule, wielded by a handful of Meiji advisors, combined with limited representative institutions copied from the West. This combination gave great power to a group of wealthy businesspeople and former nobles who influenced the emperor and also pulled strings within the parliament. Political parties arose, but a coherent system overrode their divisions into the 20th century. Japan thus followed its new policy of imitating the West, but it retained its own identity. The Japanese political solution compared interestingly to Russian institutions after Alexander II's reforms: Both states were centralized and authoritarian, but Japan had incorporated business leaders into its governing structure, whereas Russia defended a more traditional social elite.

Japan's Industrial Revolution

Political decisions were essential after the crisis of the 1860s, but they were soon matched by other initiatives. The new army, based on the universal conscription of young men, was further improved by formal officer training and by upgrading armaments according to Western standards. With the aid of Western advisors, a modern navy was established.

Attention also focused on creating the conditions necessary for industrialization. New government banks funded growing trade and provided capital for industry. State-built railroads spread across the country, and the islands were connected by rapid steamers. New methods raised agricultural output to feed the people of the growing cities.

The new economic structure depended on the destruction of many older restrictions. Guilds and internal road tariffs were abolished to create a national market. Land reform created clear individual ownership for many farmers, which helped motivate expansion of production and the introduction of new fertilizers and equipment.

Government initiative dominated manufacturing not only in the creation of transportation networks but also in state operation of mines, shipyards, and metallurgical plants. Scarce capital and the unfamiliarity of new technology seemed to compel state direction, as occurred in Russia at the same time. Government control also helped check the many foreign advisors needed by early Japanese industry; here, Japan maintained closer supervision than its Russian neighbor. Japan established the Ministry of Industry in 1870, and it quickly became one of the key government agencies, setting overall economic policy as well as operating specific sectors. By the 1880s, model shipyards, arsenals, and factories provided experience in new technology and disciplined work systems for many Japanese. Finally, by expanding technical training and education, setting up banks and post offices, and regularizing commercial laws, the government provided a structure within which Japan could develop on many fronts. Measures in this area largely copied established practices in the West, but with adaptation suitable for Japanese conditions; thus, well before any European university, Tokyo Imperial University had a faculty of agriculture.

Private enterprise quickly played a role in Japan's growing economy, particularly in the vital textile sector. Some businesspeople came from older merchant families, although some of the great houses had been ruined with the financial destruction of the samurai class. There were also newcomers, some rising from peasant ranks. Shuibuzawa Eiichi, for example, born a peasant, became a merchant and then an official of the Finance Ministry. He turned to banking in 1873, using other people's money to set up cotton-spinning mills and other textile operations. By the 1890s huge new

Visualizing the Past

Two Faces of Western Influence

These pictures show an 1850s cartoon portraying American Commodore Matthew Perry as a greedy warlord and the first meeting of the Japanese parliament in 1890.

Questions: What was the cartoon meant to convey? What kinds of attitudes toward the West does it represent? What does the picture of parliament convey about attitudes toward the West? What was the model for the design of the meeting room? What do the two pictures suggest about uses of costume in a time of rapid change?

industrial combines, later known as **zaibatsu,** were being formed as a result of accumulations of capital and far-flung merchant and industrial operations.

By 1900, the Japanese economy was fully launched in an industrial revolution. It rested on a political and social structure different from that of Russia—one that had in most respects changed more profoundly. Japan's success in organizing industrialization, including its careful management of foreign advice and models, proved to be one of the great developments of later 19th-century history.

It is important to keep these early phases of Japanese industrialization in perspective. Pre–World War I Japan was far from the West's equal. It depended on imports of Western equipment and raw materials such as coal; for industrial purposes, Japan was a resource-poor nation. Although economic growth and careful government policy allowed

Japan to avoid Western domination, Japan was newly dependent on world economic conditions and was often at a disadvantage. It needed exports to pay for machine and resource imports, and these in turn took hordes of low-paid workers. Silk production grew rapidly, the bulk of it destined for Western markets. Much of this production was based on the labor of poorly paid women who worked at home or in sweatshops, not in mechanized factories. Some of these women were sold into service by farm families. Efforts at labor organization or other means of protest were met by vigorous repression.

Social and Cultural Effects of Industrialization

The Industrial Revolution and the wider extensions of manufacturing and commercial agriculture, along with political change, had significant ramifications within Japanese culture and society. Japanese society was disrupted by massive population growth. Better nutrition and new medical provisions reduced death rates, and the upheaval of the rural masses cut into traditional restraints on births. The result was steady population growth that strained Japanese resources and stability, although it also ensured a constant supply of low-cost labor. This was one of the causes of Japan's class tensions.

The Japanese government introduced a universal education system, providing primary schools for all. This education stressed science and the importance of technical subjects along with political loyalty to the nation and emperor. Elite students at the university level also took courses that emphasized science, and many Japanese students went abroad to study technical subjects in other countries.

Education also revealed Japanese insistence on distinctive values. After a heady reform period in the 1870s, when hundreds of Western teachers were imported and a Rutgers University professor brought in for high-level advice about the whole system, the emperor and conservative advisors stepped back after 1879. Innovation and individualism had gone too far. A traditional moral education was essential, along with new skills, which would stress "loyalty to the Imperial House, love of country, filial piety toward parents, respect for superiors, faith in friends, charity toward inferiors and respect for oneself." The use of foreign books on morality was prohibited, and intense government inspection of textbooks was intended to promote social order.

Many Japanese copied Western fashions as part of the effort to become modern. Western-style haircuts replaced the samurai shaved head with a topknot—another example of the westernization of hair in world history. Western standards of hygiene spread, and the Japanese became enthusiastic toothbrushers and consumers of patent medicines. Japan also adopted the Western calendar and the metric system. Few Japanese converted to Christianity, however, and despite Western popular cultural fads, the Japanese managed to preserve an emphasis on their own values. What the Japanese wanted and got from the West involved practical techniques; they planned to infuse them with a distinctively Japanese spirit. As an early Japanese visitor to the American White House wrote in a self-satisfied poem that captured the national mood,

> We suffered the barbarians to look upon
> The glory of our Eastern Empire of Japan.

Western-oriented enthusiasms were not meant to destroy a distinctive Japanese spirit.

Japanese family life retained many traditional emphases. The birth rate dropped as rapid population growth forced increasing numbers of people off the land. Meanwhile, the rise of factory industry, separating work from home, made children's labor less useful. This trend, developed earlier in the West, seems inseparable from successful industrialization. There were new signs of family instability as well; the divorce rate exploded until legal changes made procedures more difficult. On the more traditional side, the Japanese were eager to maintain the inferiority of women in the home. The position of Western women offended them. Japanese government visitors to the United States were appalled by what they saw as the bossy ways of women: "The way women are treated here is like the way parents are respected in our country." Standards of Japanese courtesy also contrasted with the more open and boisterous behavior of Westerners, particularly Americans. "Obscenity is inherent in the customs of this country," noted another samurai visitor to the United States. Certain Japanese religious values were also preserved. Buddhism lost some ground, although it remained important, but Shintoism, which appealed to the new nationalist concern with Japan's distinctive mission and the religious functions of the emperor, won new interest.

Economic change, and the tensions as well as the power it generated, also produced a shift in Japanese foreign policy. This shift was partly an imitation of Western models. New imperialism also relieved some strains within Japanese society, giving displaced samurai the chance to exercise their military talents elsewhere. Even more than Western countries, which used similar arguments for imperialism, the Japanese economy also needed access to markets and raw materials. Because Japan was poor in many basic materials, including coal and oil for energy, the pressure for expansion was particularly great.

Japan's quick victory over China in the **Sino-Japanese War** for influence in Korea (1894–1895) was a first step toward expansion (Map 27.2). Japan convincingly demonstrated its new superiority over all other Asian powers. Humiliated by Western insistence that it abandon the Liaodong peninsula it had just taken from China, the Japanese planned a war with Russia as a means of striking out against the nearest European state. A 1902 alliance with Britain was an important sign of Japan's arrival as an equal nation in the Western-dominated world diplomatic system. The Japanese were also eager to dent Russia's growing strength in east Asia after the development of the trans-Siberian railroad. Disputes over Russian influence in Manchuria and Japanese influence in Korea led to the Russo-Japanese War in 1904, which Japan won handily because of its superior navy. Japan annexed Korea in 1910, entering the ranks of imperialist powers.

The Strain of Modernization

Japanese achievement had its costs, including poor living standards in the crowded cities. Many Japanese conservatives resented the passion other Japanese displayed for Western fashions. Disputes between generations, with the old clinging to traditional standards and the young more interested in Western styles, were very troubling in a society that stressed the importance of parental authority.

Some tension entered political life. Political parties in Japan's parliament clashed with the emperor's ministers over rights to determine policy. The government often had to dissolve the Diet and call for new elections, seeking a more workable parliamentary majority. Political assassinations and attempted assassinations reflected grievances, including direct action impulses in the samurai tradition.

Another kind of friction emerged in intellectual life. Many Japanese scholars copied Western philosophies and literary styles, and there was enough adaptation to prevent the emergence of a full Russian-style intelligentsia. Other intellectuals expressed a deep pessimism about the loss of identity in a changing world. The underlying theme was confusion about a Japan that was no longer traditional, but not Western either. What *was* it? Thus, some writers spoke of Japan's heading for a "nervous collapse from which

Map 27.2 *Japanese Colonial Expansion to 1914. What were the principal gains? Why did Japan feel frustrated by the ultimate results of its victories?*

we will not be able to recover." Others dealt with more personal conflicts such as those in the following poem:

> Do not be loved by others; do not accept their charity, do not promise anything.... Always wear a mask. Always be ready for a fight—be able to hit the next man on the head at any time. Don't forget that when you make friends with someone you are sooner or later certain to break with him.

As an antidote to social and cultural insecurity, Japanese leaders urged national loyalty and devotion to the emperor, and with some success. The official message promoted Japanese virtues of obedience and harmony that the West lacked. School texts thus stressed,

> Our country takes as its base the family system: the nation is but a single family, the imperial family is our main house. We the people worship the unbroken imperial line with the same feeling of respect and love that a child feels toward his parents....The union of loyalty and filial piety is truly the special character of our national polity.

Japanese nationalism built on traditions of superiority, cohesion, and deference to rulers, as well as on the new tensions generated by rapid change. It became a deep force, probably in Japan more than elsewhere, that played a unique role in justifying sacrifice and struggle in a national mission to preserve independence and dignity in a hostile world. Nationalism, along with firm police repression of dissent and the sweeping changes of the early Meiji years, certainly helps explain why Japan avoided the revolutionary pressure that hit Russia, China, and other countries after 1900.

Yet Japan's very success reminds us of how unusual it was. No other society outside the Western world was yet able to match its achievements. Russia, responding to Western example in its own way, continued its growth as a world power, but amid such social disarray that further upheaval was inevitable. Most of the rest of the world faced the more immediate concern of adjusting to or resisting Western dominance; industrialization was a remote prospect. Even today, when many societies are striving for greater industrialization, the ability to emulate the Japanese pattern of rapid change seems very limited—concentrated, interestingly enough, in other small east Asian nations.

 GLOBAL CONNECTIONS: Russia and Japan in the World

Russia's world role, founded on its huge size and territorial expansion, had already been established in the early modern period. There were, however, new twists during the 19th century. Russian troops and diplomats periodically gained direct roles in western Europe. Russian forces entered France as part of the coalition that defeated Napoleon. A side result was the development of new restaurants in France, called bistros, based on the Russian word for quick. Russian armies helped put down the Hungarian revolution in 1849. Russian involvement in Middle Eastern diplomacy resulted from its steady pressure on the Ottoman Empire. By the later 19th century, Russia extended its influence in eastern Asia, seizing new territories in northern China and claiming a role elsewhere, in China and Korea alike. This set the collision course with Japan.

Japan's world role was much newer, and just emerging by 1914. Long isolated, Japan had experienced only one previous attempt at assertion beyond its borders, the late-16th century invasion of Korea. Now, however, ambitions increased, fueled by economic needs, growing industrial and military strength, and population pressure. Japan sought to be regarded as a great nation along Western imperialist lines. This would bring conflicts with China and Russia before 1914, and wider experiments thereafter. In the long run, it was Japan's striking economic success that would most clearly define its new place in the world. Initially, the unfolding of strength in the eastern Pacific region, along with the complex relationships to the West, marked Japan's dramatic entry as a force to be reckoned with.

The beginnings of serious industrialization in Russia and Japan, and the entry of Japan into world affairs, contributed important new ingredients to the global diplomatic picture by the early 20th century. These developments, along with the rise of the United States, added to the growing sense of competition between the established Western powers. Japan's surge promoted a fear in the West of a new **yellow peril** that should be opposed through greater imperialist efforts. Outright colonial acquisitions by the new powers added directly to the competitive atmosphere, particularly in the Far East.

Further Readings

A. Gerschenkron, *Economic Backwardness in Historical Perspective: A Book of Essays* (1962) helps define the conditions of latecomer industrialization. The best survey of Russia in this transitionary period is Hans Rogger's *Russia in the Age of Modernization and Revolution, 1881-1917* (1983). See also Geoffrey Hosking, *Russia: People and Empire, 1532–1917* (1997). Russian reforms and economic change are discussed in W. Blackwell, *The Industrialization of Russia*, 2nd ed. (1982), and Jerome Blum, *Lord and Peasant in Russia from the Ninth to the Nineteenth Century* (1961). Sidney Harcave, trans., *The Memoirs of Count Witte* (1990), includes a brief biographical sketch and his collected writings of this influential "modernizer." On social and cultural developments, see Victoria Bonnell, ed., *The Russian Worker: Life and Labor Under the Tsarist Regime* (1983); Barbara Engel, *Mothers and Daughters: Women of the Intelligentsia in Nineteenth Century Russia* (1983); and Jeffrey Brooks, *When Russia Learned to Read: Literacy and Popular Culture* (1987). On another vital area of Eastern Europe, see A. Stavrianos, *The Balkans, 1815–1914* (1963).

Japan in the 19th century is viewed from a modernization perspective in R. Dore, ed., *Aspects of Social Change in Modern Japan* (1967). See also W. W. Lockwood, *The Economic Development of Japan: Growth and Structural Change 1868–1938* (1954); J. C. Abegglen, *The Japanese Factory: Aspects of Its Social Organization*, rev. ed. (1985); Andrew Gordon; *The Evolution of Labor Relations in Japan* (1985); and Hugh Patrick, ed., *Japanese Industrialization and Its Social Consequences* (1973). E. O. Reischauer's *Japan, the Story of a Nation* (1981) remains a good general history of the period. For more closely focused works on socio-economic change, see S. Ericson, *The Sound of the Whistle: Railroads and the State in Meiji Japan* (1996); Peter N. Stearns, *Schools and Students in Industrial Society: Japan and the West* (1997); and E. P. Tsurumi, *Factory Girls: Women in the Thread Mills of Meiji Japan* (1990). *The Encyclopedia Britannica* (including its on-line version) has a useful article on the life of Iwasaki Yataro, the founder of Mitsubishi, that puts a face on the modernization of Japan. Several works demonstrate that colonialism was an adjunct to industrialization in Japan as well as in Europe and in the Americas. These studies include R. H. Myers and M. R. Beattie, eds., *The Japanese Colonial Empire 1895–1945* (1984); W. G. Beasley, *Japanese Imperialism, 1894-1945* (1987); and P. Duus, *The Abacus and the Sword, the Japanese Penetration of Korea, 1895-1910* (1995).

On the Web

The glories of Czarist Russia are revealed by a virtual tour of the Alexander Palace at http://www.alexanderpalace.org/palace/. However, the riches of the czars could not conceal the dismal world of the Russian peasantry whose lot was little improved by Russian economic modernization. This world and how it was illuminated by the works of the Russian writer Nikolai Gogol is addressed at http://www.kirjasto.sci.fi/gogol.htm, http://www.spartacus.schoolnet.co.uk/RUSserfs.htm, http://www.geocities.com/Athens/Forum/4123/krimlife.htm, http://cw.mariancollege.edu/cdavis/gogol_information.htm, and http://it.stlawu.edu/~rkreuzer/indv3/peasant.htm.

Russian liberalism reached its high-water mark in the abolition of serfdom, an institution whose rise and demise is described at http://bahai-library.org/resources/tablets-notes/lawh-malik-rus/bio.html and http://www.yale.edu/lawweb/avalon/econ/koval6.htm. A copy of the Emancipation Manifesto ending serfdom can be found at http://www.dur.ac.uk/~dml0www/emancipn.html. However, reaction soon set in.

The failure of the Revolution of 1905 (http://mars.acnet.wnec.edu/~grempel/courses/wc2/lectures/rev1905.html) to achieve any significant degree of political and social reform paved the way for those favoring more radical change, such as the Bolsheviks, led by Vladimir Ilyich Ulyanov, whose life and work is examined at http://www.marxists.org/archive/lenin/ and whose voice can be heard at http://www.soften.ktu.lt/~kaleck/Lenin/lenin2.html. Count Sergei Witte's life and diplomatic and economic policies are glimpsed at http://www.fortunecity.com/victorian/hornton/890/RussiaNew3/Witte.html and http://members.tripod.com/~american_almanac/witte92b.htm.

Marxist intellectual Leon Trotsky's brief evaluation of Witte, found at http://www.marxists.org/archive/trotsky/works/1905/ch10.htm, is dramatically written and full of interest.

The Meiji Restoration's industrial policy is discussed at http://www.japan-guide.com/e/e2130.html and http://kjs.nagaokaut.ac.jp/mikami/IDEAS/home.htm. Iwasaki Yataro's role in this process is illuminated at http://www.mitsubishi.or.jp/e/h/his.html. A key to the process of modernization in Japan is the Constitution of the Empire of Japan (1889), which is reproduced at http://history.hanover.edu/texts/1889con.html. For further insight into this process, this document can be compared with the Constitution of Japan (1947) at http://history.hanover.edu/texts/1947con.html. Life in Meiji Japan can be glimpsed through an exhibition of contemporary woodblock art at http://www.artgallery.sbc.edu/ukiyoe/historyofwoodblockprints.html and http://www.cjn.or.jp/ukiyo-e/.

PART VI

The 20th Century in World History

CHAPTERS

28 Descent into the Abyss: World War I and the Crisis of the European Global Order

29 The World in the 1920s: Challenges to European Dominance

30 The Great Depression and the Authoritarian Response

31 A Second Global Conflict and the End of the European World Order

32 Western Society and Eastern Europe in the Decades of the Cold War

33 Latin America: Revolution and Reaction into the 21st Century

34 Africa, the Middle East, and Asia in the Era of Independence

35 Rebirth and Revolution: Nation-building in East Asia and the Pacific Rim

36 Globalization and Resistance: World History 1990–2003

Introduction

Describing the 20th century is one of the most challenging tasks facing a historian. We are so close to the patterns involved that objectivity is difficult. Previous periods, although they generate continued debate, at least constitute stories whose endings are known. We can easily see that the Industrial Revolution ushered in profound changes for the West and some other parts of the world by 1900. We can even more easily see that during the 19th century, Western nations gained unprecedented power in the world. In other words, it is not difficult to define the 19th century in terms of its contrasts with the early modern period, to see what its new ingredients were and how many of them turned out.

Though now in the 21st century, we are still actively engaged with the 20th century's aftermath, which makes judgment far more tentative. This is not a new problem. In the 19th century, for example, many people were not aware of the Industrial Revolution, even when they were involved in it. They were much more likely to point to some recent political event or cultural current in defining their era. It is hard to get perspective on one's own

time. How significant in world history was the surge of Nazism during the 1930s? Here was a fearsome new political movement that at the time seemed to signify permanent changes in political trends and the whole character of European society. Almost any historian writing in the 1950s, at least in the West, would have seen the rise of Nazism as a major turning point. Yet from the vantage point of the early 21st century, Nazism seems one of many developments that mark a key subperiod rather than a fundamental feature of the whole century. Many Americans by 2003 would rate the rise of Japan to the status of industrial superpower or the revolution in China far more important in creating a novel international context for our century than Nazism was. Nazism's decisive focus has diluted with the passage of time. Even the cold war now seems more an episode than a decisive stage in world history.

The key question is whether the 20th century opened up a new basic period in world history or whether it simply modified the fundamental patterns of the 19th century. The answer seems clear: The 20th century has provided a rare break in world history, comparable in scope to the 15th century or the 5th century. The contemporary period in world history is still taking shape, so it is harder to define than earlier watersheds. Furthermore, there is obvious continuity with some patterns of the 19th century. Nevertheless, several fundamental changes can be defined.

Previous periods in world history have met three criteria: They involved basic geographic rebalancing among major civilization areas, they measurably increased the intensity and extent of contact among civilizations, and partly as a result of new contacts, they demonstrated some new and roughly parallel patterns among many of the major civilizations. The 20th century meets these criteria.

The Repositioning of the West

 The decline of the West is a key feature of the new balance between civilizations that began in the 20th century. This resulted in part from the two highly destructive wars fought between 1914 and 1945. Both wars were global in causes, conduct, and results, but bitter European rivalries played a key role, and the weakening of western Europe's world position was a key consequence.

The West's global position changed in several respects. Western population (including that of the United States) decreased rapidly as a percentage of the world total. Western birth control practices plus rapid population growth rates elsewhere combined to produce this result. The West's population stagnation opened Europe and the United States to rapid immigration from other societies.

More decisive was the decline and then the virtual end of the great Western empires, a process clearly under way by the 1920s and then culminating after 1945. The West, which dominated most of the world directly or indirectly by 1920, ruled little beyond its own borders by 1980. Monopoly over the most advanced weapon systems, a key Western advantage since the 16th century, also declined, although many Western nations, led after 1945 by the United States, retained a major share in leadership. Japan and then the Soviet Union joined the West as world military giants, while other societies, though not quite as advanced, gained ground. Furthermore, alternative forms of warfare, particularly the guerrilla tactics used in colonial struggles, allowed many regions to counter Western military supremacy. From a Western standpoint, the world became more complicated after centuries of a steadily advancing edge in military power.

In 1991, the United States and various allies decisively defeated Iraq in the Persian Gulf War, using a variety of high-technology weapons. Western-dominated military advantages, particularly in air warfare, meant that only a few hundred allied soldiers died in combat, compared with perhaps 100,000 Iraqis. But even this war showed how the 20th century had become more complex than the easy days of Western imperialism. It took months of military buildup, a force of more than half a million men and women, and expenditures of more than $50 billion to defeat a medium-sized Arab state.

The West also lost its unchallenged preeminence as a world trader and manufacturer. Of course, much of the world economic system established in the 16th century persisted. Important regions still sent cheap raw materials, supplied by low-paid labor, into international trade. Only a few societies made the bulk of the profits from international trade because they ran the shipping and banking facilities and produced the most expensive processed products. In this basic sense, there was strong continuity from earlier periods in world history. But the actors changed, which is where the West's decline showed up. Although the West continued to be among the dominant economic agents, by the 1960s it was joined by Japan and an increasing number of other east

Asian centers. Still other societies, such as Brazil and China, gained new ability to compete with the West in selected industrial areas.

On many fronts, the rise of the West, one of the leading processes in world history since the 15th century, leveled off, with the 1920s and 1930s forming a key turning point. No single civilization emerged by the end of the 20th century to claim the kind of growing world leadership the West had long produced. In part, this was because the West itself still remained strong.

Nevertheless, the West's decline opened opportunities for other regional centers. The proliferation of new nations around the world after 1945 brought new opportunities for independence. Successful liberation movements created new opportunities for human agency outside the West. Individual leaders such as Gandhi in India, Mao Zedong in China, and Lenin in Russia put a personal stamp on developments outside the West. The 20th century added to the forces of conformity and mass organization, but there were opportunities for individual initiative in shaping cultural and political change.

International Contacts

 The intensification of international contacts was a basic feature of the 20th century, though there were some complications in the middle decades of the century. Technology was critical: Innovations included faster communication via wireless radio and, later, satellite and computer; faster transport, using the airplane; and larger capacity for communication and the movement of goods. Levels of world trade steadily increased, except during the 1930s, and more and more corporations (particularly from the West and Japan) operated internationally.

World wars and peacetime alliances demonstrated the new levels of international contact on other fronts. Diplomatic contacts were internationalized as never before. International cultural influences also increased in tandem with improved communication and the efforts of multinational corporations. Films, scientific research, and artistic styles all spread widely at both popular and elite levels. By the 1990s, children in nearly every society could identify Mickey Mouse. The result was no single world culture, for regional reactions and the extent of penetration varied widely. But most cultures had to come to some terms with the impact of Hollywood movies, Parisian art, and British–American popular music. International interest in sports was another unprecedented development across civilization

1910 c.e.	1920 c.e.	1930 c.e.	1940 c.e.	1950 c.e.
1910–1920 Mexican Revolution	**1920** Treaty of Sèvres reorganizes Middle East	**1930–1945** Vargas regime in Brazil	**1941** United States enters World War II	**1950–1953** Korean War
1912 African National Congress party formed in South Africa	**1921** Foundation of Chinese Communist party	**1931** Japan invades Manchuria	**1942–1945** Holocaust	**1950** End U.S. occupation in China
1912 Fall of Qing dynasty in China; beginning of Chinese Revolution	**1927–1928** Stalin heads Soviet Union; five-year plans and collectivization	**1931–1947** Gandhi-led resistance in India	**1945** Formation of United Nations	**1955** Warsaw Pact
1914–1918 World War I	**1929–1933** Height of Great Depression	**1933** Nazis rise to power in Germany	**1945** Atomic bomb	**1955** Bandung conference; nonaligned movement
1916 Arab revolts against Ottomans		**1933–1939** New Deal in United States	**1945** Communists proclaim Vietnam independence	**1956** Partial end of Stalinism
1917 United States enters World War I		**1934–1940** Cárdenas reform period in Mexico	**1945–1948** Soviet takeover of eastern Europe	**1957** European Economic Community (Common Market)
1917 Russian Revolution		**1935** German rearmament; Italy conquers Ethiopia	**1946** Philippines proclaim independence	**1957** Ghana becomes first independent African nation
1917 Balfour Declaration promises Jews a homeland in Palestine		**1937** Army officers in power in Japan; invasion of China	**1946–1947** Decolonization begins, especially in Asia and Oceania	**1959** Cuban Revolution
1919 Versailles peace settlement; League of Nations		**1939–1945** World War II	**1947** Peronism in Argentina	
1919 Revolt in Egypt; first Pan-African Nationalist Congress		**1939** Nazi–Soviet Pact	**1947** India and Pakistan gain independence	
			1947–1975 Cold war; Marshall Plan	
			1948 Division of Korea	
			1948 Israel–Palestine partition; first Arab–Israeli war	
			1949 Formation of NATO	
			1949 Communist victory in China	

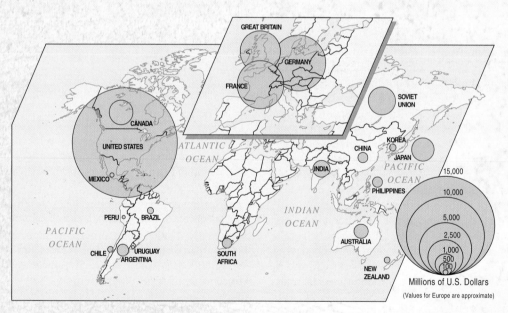

World Distribution of Manufacturing, 1930

lines. Soccer won mass enthusiasm almost everywhere; the Olympic games, which were reestablished in 1896, shifted from initial dominance by the West to genuine global participation.

The growth of international contacts also created unprecedented complexity in international relations. Under the League of Nations and then, after World War II, the United Nations and the World Bank, interna-

664

1960 C.E.	1970 C.E.	1980 C.E.	1990 C.E.
1960s Civil rights movement in United States; revival of feminism	**1972, 1979** Oil crises; height of OPEC power	**1980–1988** Iran–Iraq War	**1990** Reunification of Germany
1962 Algeria declares independence	**1975** Communist victory in Vietnam	**1985 ff.** Gorbachev heads Soviet Union; reforms and unrest through eastern Europe	**1990–1991** Iraq invades Kuwait; Persian Gulf crisis; U.S.–Allied defeat of Iraq
1965–1973 U.S. military intervention in Vietnam	**1975–1998** Democratic regimes spread in Latin America	**1989** Reform movement in South Africa	**1991** Collapse of the Soviet Union
1965–1968 Cultural revolution in China	**1976** Death of Mao; new reform pattern in China	**1989** New regimes throughout eastern Europe	**1992** Full economic integration of Common Market
1968–1973 Student protests in West	**1979** Iranian Revolution; spread of Islamic fundamentalism		**1994** Palestinian autonomy in Israel; full democracy in South Africa, Nelson Mandela president
			1999 Rise of new conflicts, Palestinians, Israelis
			2003 U.S.–British war with Iraq

tional agencies proliferated. Government embassies spread to and from the new nations; never had so many foreign service professionals flourished. More and more businesses divided production and sales facilities between many countries in what came to be called multinational corporations. New streams of immigrants from Africa, Asia, and the Caribbean headed toward the leading industrial centers from the 1920s onward. Some observers wondered whether the balance was shifting away from regional identities toward global homogenization.

International Challenges in Politics and Culture

 Change undermined long-standing traditions in politics, social structures, and culture. Very few societies had the same form of government by 2000 that they had in 1900. Monarchies crumbled and were replaced by democracies, totalitarian governments, or authoritarian regimes. Politically, major civilizations tried to come to terms with Western examples while developing governments vigorous enough to gain or main-

tain independence. Along with new political forms came new functions. Governments generally took on new roles in trying to further economic growth. They also accepted new responsibilities in areas such as education and health care, and their contact with masses of citizens increased greatly as a result.

Changes in previous belief systems formed another current that swept over most national and civilization boundaries. Most of the world's people in 1850 adhered to one of the great religions or philosophical systems created during the classical or postclassical eras, such as Confucianism, Christianity, and Islam. These systems were still lively by 2000, and some were even winning new converts. In most parts of the world, however, they had been modified or challenged by new systems of belief that were more secular in orientation, such as liberalism, nationalism, or communism. They were also challenged by growing interest in science, a staple of the burgeoning mass education systems.

Changes in ideas and politics related to a third general international current: the displacement of long-standing beliefs in rigid social inequalities. All the great agricultural civilizations had developed highly structured systems of inequality. Western ideas, expressed in great

665

movements such as the French Revolution of 1789, had attacked assumptions of structured inequality and legal privilege. Also, the abolition of slavery through most of the world in the 19th century signaled the end of another traditional institution of inequality. The further spread of Western ideas, but also new movements such as Russian and Chinese communism and the nationalisms of Asia and Africa, brought a more widespread attack on rigid inequalities in the 20th century. Caste systems and aristocracies officially crumbled, with rare exceptions. Patriarchal assumptions were challenged, for example by widespread voting rights for women. Inequality did not end, but older ideas yielded to new beliefs.

Innovation did not mean uniformity. Major civilizations developed different political, cultural, and social responses to change. It was the need to innovate that had global force.

The 20th Century as a New Period in World History

◈ The 20th century as a new period in world history unfolded in three phases. Between 1914 and 1945, the world was shaken by a series of catastrophic events—two world wars and an international depression—that led to the new international order, reflecting the West's decline and facilitating the emergence of new centers of activity. Several political upheavals accompanied the West's crises, ushering in new regimes in Russia, Mexico, China, and Turkey.

After 1945, decolonization entered high gear, creating a host of novel governments. New social mobility, changes in gender relations, and redefinitions of government functions moved to center stage. The decades after World War II were also defined by a tense struggle between most communist societies, headed by the Soviet Union, and the United States and its allies. This cold war ushered in unprecedented military buildups and daunting new weaponry, though no catastrophic "hot" wars broke out. These were the decades that saw the emergence of the Pacific Rim as a powerhouse, with Japan becoming the world's second-largest economy.

The late 20th century saw the end of the cold war after the collapse of the Soviet Union. The result was a more uncertain, if in some ways less menacing, international diplomatic and military framework. Regional conflicts took on new importance. At the same time, the continued advance of societies such as China, the impact of worldwide manufacturing growth, and the results of proliferating information technology added to the pressures for change.

The chapters that follow deal first with the decades between 1914 and about 1950. This was the time when the changes in the West's world position began to surface, and also the seeds of decolonization. This was a

The World in 1995

666

time, also, when a first wave of 20th-century revolutions called traditional social and political structures into question in many parts of the world. A second set of chapters (32–35) then deals with key areas of the world during the second half of the 20th century, in the context of decolonization, the cold war, and complex changes in the global economy. A final chapter deals with developments since 1990, in light of the cold war's end and the mounting pace of globalization. All three sections maintain a tension between undeniably rapid change, and the particular responses of individual societies as they reflected traditions built up in earlier stages in the development of major civilizations. In this tension lies a key to the complexity not only of 20th-century world history, but of world historical prospects at the opening of the 21st century.

Globalization

 World history in the 20th and early 21st centuries can be judged from one final general vantage point. As the 20th century began, the pace of globalization was clearly accelerating. The spread of industrialization, new developments in global communication and transportation, and the wave of cultural influences from the West created an unprecedented set of linkages around the world.

But globalization then receded for several decades in many respects. Several large societies pulled out of the global network, at least in part. The United States resisted global politics. The Soviet Union and then China resisted global economics. Nazi Germany and authoritarian Japan tried to create at least regional empires as an alternative to globalization. Many decolonization movements sought to reduce international involvement in favor of national independence and self-expression. The period 1914–1950 saw an unexpected retreat for many of the forces of globalization, despite the ongoing impact of new technologies.

Gradually from 1950 onward, and then with rapid acceleration as the cold war receded and finally ended, a second wave of globalization emerged, extending easily into the early 21st century. Another set of technologies, the formation of multinational companies in the West and the Pacific Rim, plus the emergence of a truly global consumer and media culture easily surpassed the kind of globalization visible in 1900. Decisions by countries like China and Russia to re-enter the global framework both reflected and encouraged the wave of globalization. Here too, however, new resistances arose, often around local nationalisms or larger religious cultures. Globalization and resistance set an underlying context for the histories of individual societies, and they became a dominant theme as the world entered a new century in 2001.

I. To what extent did the Cold War affect the goals of leaders of decolonization movements and new nations in the 1950's and 1960's? What additional types of documents would help in answering this question?

1. Vietnam: Manifesto of the Laodong Party 1951

[Note: By this time China and the Soviet Union had recognized the Party's regime in Vietnam, but it was still struggling for control.]

The main task of the Viet Nam Laodong Party now is:

To unite and lead the working class, the working masses and the entire people of Viet Nam in their struggle to wipe out the French colonialists and defeat the American interventionists; to bring the liberation war of the Viet Nam people to complete victory, thereby making Viet Nam a genuinely independent and united country. . . .

In the field of external affairs, the Viet Nam Laodong Party recommends: The Viet Nam people must actively support the national liberation movements of oppressed peoples; unite closely with the Soviet Union, China and other people's democracies; form close alliances with the peoples of France and the French colonies so as to contribute to the anti-imperialist struggle to defend world peace and democracy!

2. Indonesia: President Sukarno at the opening of the Bandung Conference 1955

No task is more urgent than that of preserving peace. Without peace our independence means little. The rehabilitation and upbuilding of our countries will have little meaning. Our revolutions will not be allowed to run their course. . . .

What can we do? We can do much! We can inject the voice of reason into world affairs. We can mobilise all the spiritual, all the moral, all the political strength of Asia and Africa on the side of peace. Yes, we! We, the peoples of Asia and Africa, 1,400,000,000 strong, far more than half the human population of the world, we can mobilise what I have called the Moral Violence of Nations in favour of peace. We can demonstrate to the minority of the world which lives on the other continents that we, the majority, are for peace, not for war.

3. Speech of Jawaharlal Nehru, first Prime Minister of India 1956

The preservation of peace forms the central aim of India's policy. It is in the pursuit of this policy that we have chosen the path of nonalignment in any military or like pact of alliance [including Cold War alliances]. Nonalignment does not mean passivity of mind or action, lack of faith or conviction. It does not mean submission to what we consider evil. It is a positive and dynamic approach to such problems that confront us. We believe that each country has not only the right to freedom but also to decide its own policy and way of life. Only thus can true freedom flourish and a people grow according to their own genius

We believe, therefore, in nonaggression and non-interference by one country in the affairs of another and the growth of tolerance between them and the capacity for peaceful coexistence. We think that by the free exchange of ideas and trade and other contacts between nations each will learn from the other and truth will prevail. We therefore endeavor to maintain friendly relations with all countries, even though we may disagree with them in their policies or structure of government. We think that by this approach we can serve not only our country but also the larger causes of peace and good fellowship in the world.

4. Egypt: Anwar al-Sadat at the First Afro-Asian People's Solidarity Conference 1957

We cannot live peacefully in a world threatened by the shadow of war. We can no longer enjoy the products of our hands and the fruits of our labour in a world where plunder prevails and flourishes. We can no longer build and reconstruct in a world which manufactures weapons for destruction and devastation. We can no longer raise the standard of living of our peoples and stamp out diseases and epidemics in a world where nations vie with each other for the production of lethal weapons of massacre and annihilation. Gone for ever is the era where the future of war and peace was decided upon in a few European capitals, because today we happen to be strong enough to make the decision ourselves in that respect.

Our weight in the international balance has now become preponderant. Only think of the colossal number of our people, our natural resources, the vastness of the area covered by our respective countries, and our strategic positions. You will surely come to the conclusion that the outbreak of war is impossible so long as we insist on peace, especially if we do not content ourselves with a mere negative attitude, but assume one of positiveness in favour of Peace. This transition from the negative to the positive is a fundamental basis worthy of our adoption.

5. Cuban leader Fidel Castro: Second Declaration of Havana 1962

Since the end of the Second World War, the Latin American nations are becoming pauperized constantly. The value of their per capita income falls. The dreadful percentages of child death rate do not decrease, the number of illiterates grows higher, the peoples lack employment, land, adequate housing, schools, hospitals, communication systems and the means of subsistence. On the other hand, North America investments exceed 10 billion dollars. Latin America, moreover, supplies cheap raw materials and pays high prices for manufactured articles. Like the first Spanish conquerors, who exchanged mirrors and trinkets with the Indians for silver and gold, so the United States trades with Latin America. . . .

The duty of every revolutionary is to make revolution. We know that in America and throughout the world the revolution will be victorious. But revolutionaries cannot sit in the doorways of their homes to watch the corpse of imperialism pass by. The role of Job does not behoove a revolutionary. Each year by which America's liberation may be hastened will mean millions of children rescued from death, millions of minds freed for learning, infinitudes of sorrow spared the peoples.

II. In a context of rapidly growing world population, what was the nature of debate over family planning at the 1994 United Nations Population and Development Conference, and how did the United Nations handle the debate? What additional types of documents would be useful in analyzing this debate?

1. Statement of the Norwegian Prime Minister at the United Nations Population and Development Conference 1994

I am pleased by the emerging consensus that everyone should have access to the whole range of family-planning services at an affordable price. Sometimes religion is a major obstacle. This happens when family planning is made a moral issue. But morality cannot only be a question of controlling sexuality and protecting unborn life. Morality is also a question of giving individuals the opportunity of choice, of suppressing coercion of all kinds and abolishing the criminalization of individual tragedy. Morality becomes hypocrisy if it means accepting mothers' suffering or dying in connection with unwanted pregnancies and illegal abortions, and unwanted children living in misery.

Women's education is the single most important path to higher productivity, lower infant mortality and lower fertility. The economic returns on investment in women's education are generally comparable to those for men, but the social returns in terms of health and fertility by far exceed what we gain from men's education. So let us pledge to watch over the numbers of school-enrollment for girls.

Population growth is one of the most serious obstacles to world prosperity and sustainable development. We may soon be facing new famine, mass migration, and war as peoples compete for ever more scarce land and water resources.

2. Interview with the Iranian Minister Hossain Malekafzali attending the United Nations Population and Development Conference 1994

First of all, is the abortion. We do not accept abortion as it is in the text, as a family planning tool, but also we think that we should have . . . a good quality of services for family planning. Do not take the abortion, so abortion is not permitted, except in a very few cases, when the life of the mother, for example, is in danger . . . and also, the second point is the child education, or adults and education, regarding the sex education. This also is not permitted in Islamic countries like Iran, but when the men and women are in the age of marriage, then it is OK. We can have the sex education for those people who are ready to get married. This is the second point, and the third point is the importance of the family because the thing [is] that the family is the basic unit of the society, and the family role is very clear.

3. Statement of the representative of the United Arab Emirates

The delegation of the United Arab Emirates believes in protecting man and promoting his welfare and enhancing his role in the family and in the State and at the international level. We consider also that man is the central object and the means for attaining sustainable development. We do not consider abortion as a means of family planning, and we adhere to the principles of Islamic law also in matters of inheritance.

We wish to express reservations on everything that contravenes the principles and precepts of our religion Islam, a tolerant religion, and our laws.

4. Statement of the representative of the Holy See [Vatican]

But there are other aspects of the final document which the Holy See cannot support. Together with so many people around the world, the Holy See affirms that human life begins at the moment of conception. That life must be defended and protected. The Holy See can therefore never condone abortion or policies which favor abortion. The final document, recognizes abortion as a dimension of population policy even though it does stress that abortion should not be promoted as a means of family planning and urges nations to find alternatives to abortion.

The chapters also contain references which could be seen as accepting extramarital sexual activity, especially among adolescents. They would seem to assert that abortion services belong within primary health care as a method of choice. . . .

5. Statement by the representative of the Syrian Arab Republic

I should like to put on record that the Syrian Arab Republic will deal with an address the concepts contained in the Programme of Action . . . in full accordance with the ethical, cultural and religious concepts and convictions of our society in order to serve the unit of the family, which is the nucleus of society, and in order to enhance prosperity in our societies.

6. U.N. Report from the United Nations Population and Development Conference 1994

The aim of family-planning programmes must be to enable couples and individuals to decide freely and responsibly the number and spacing of their children and to have the information and means to do so and to ensure informed choices and make available a full range of safe and effective methods. The success of population education and family planning programmes in a variety of settings demonstrates that informed individuals can and will act responsibly in the light of their own needs and those of their families and communities. The principle of informed free choice is essential to the long-term success of family-planning programmes. Any form of coercion has no part to play.

Family-planning programmes have contributed considerably to the decline in average fertility rates for developing countries. However, the full range of modern family-planning methods still remains unavailable to at least 350 million couples world wide. Survey data suggest that approximately 120 million additional women world wide could be currently using a modern family-planning method if more accurate information and affordable services were easily available, and if partners, extended families and the community were more supportive.

As part of the effort to meet unmet needs, all countries should seek to identify and remove all the major remaining barriers to the utilization of family-planning services. Some of those barriers are related to the inadequacy, poor quality and cost of existing family-planning services. It should be the goal of public, private and non-governmental family planning organizations to remove all programme-related barriers to family-planning use by the year 2005. . . .

CHAPTER 28

DESCENT INTO THE ABYSS: WORLD WAR I AND THE CRISIS OF THE EUROPEAN GLOBAL ORDER

With the German invasion into France in 1914, northern France was pockmarked with trenches from which little advance was possible. The Western Front, as it was known, pitted attacking German troops against French and British defenders. Trench warfare, depicted in the painting here, employed the awesome technology of modern war.

- The Coming of the Great War
- A World at War
- **VISUALIZING THE PAST:** Trench Warfare
- Failed Peace
- World War I and the Nationalist Assault on the European Colonial Order
- **DOCUMENT:** Lessons for the Colonized from the Slaughter in the Trenches
- **IN DEPTH:** Women in Asian and African Nationalist Movements
- **GLOBAL CONNECTIONS:** World War and Global Upheavals

The First World War—or the Great War as it was called by those who lived through it and did not know a second conflict of this magnitude lay in their future—was one of several key turning points of world history in the 20th century. Because of the colonial domination and pervasive influence that the industrial powers of Europe had achieved throughout the globe by the late 1800s, a war that in an earlier era might have been confined to Europe spread within weeks to the Middle East and parts of Africa as well as (on a much reduced scale) to east Asia and over the oceans of the world. The epicenters of the conflict in northern France and east-central Europe sucked in manpower and resources from across the globe. Distant Dominions within the British Empire, such as New Zealand, Australia, and Canada, were soon involved directly in combat. The two great industrial nations outside of Europe, Japan and ultimately the United States, also became active participants in a struggle for global supremacy (again, with very different levels of intensity) that raged for four devastating years.

Four years of massive slaughter, with the European imperial powers suffering the bulk of the casualties, severely weakened or utterly shattered existing global systems. The long war also generated new historical forces that dominated the history of the decades that followed and in important ways persist to the present day. In this chapter we will examine the forces that led to the outbreak of the war and the nature of the conflict on the **Western Front,** central and eastern Europe, the Middle East, and a number of key locations in sub-Saharan Africa. In the second half of the chapter, we will explore the ways in which the war undermined the colonial empires of the European powers and led to the decline of a European-dominated global order.

The Coming of the Great War

 By 1914 diplomatic tensions had escalated fairly steadily among the major European powers. Colonial rivalries and arms races had led to the formation, beginning in the 1890s, of two increasingly hostile alliances. Each of the alliances were anchored on secret treaties that committed those who joined to come to each other's assistance in case of attack by an outside rival power. The participants in each alliance also made plans to coordinate both military preparations and operations should war break out in Europe.

Hostile Alliances and Armaments Races

Fear of Germany's growing economic and military power had driven autocratic Russia to ally first with republican France and then with the even more democratic

1870 C.E.	1890 C.E.	1900 C.E.	1910 C.E.	1920 C.E.
1870–1890 Cycle of depressions in Europe and the United States	**1890** End of the Three Emperors' Alliance (Russia, Austria–Hungary, Germany) **1894** Franco-Russian alliance **1899–1901** Anglo-Boer War in South Africa	**1904–1905** Japanese victory over Russia **1906** Dinshawai incident in Egypt **1909** Morley-Minto reforms in India	**1910** Union of South Africa formed **1914–1918** World War I **1916** Beginning of Arab revolt against Ottoman Empire **1917** Russian Revolution **1917** United States enters World War I **1918** Treaty of Brest-Litovsk; Russia withdraws from war **1919** Versailles conference and treaty; League of Nations established **1919** Gandhi leads first nonviolent protest movements in India; revolt in Egypt; Rowlatt Act in India	**1920** French and British mandates set up in Middle East **1920s** Pan-African Congresses in Paris **1923** Treaty of Lausanne recognizes independence of Turkey

Britain (see Map 28.1). Germany's growing power also menaced its neighbor to the west, France. In both cases, from the early 1890s the arrogance and aggressive posturing of Germany's new ruler, Kaiser Wilhelm II, only magnified the threat the emerging colossus seemed to pose for the rest of Europe. The French also hoped that their alliance with Russia would lead to a two-front war that would brake Germany's rising supremacy and allow France to recover the provinces of Alsace and Lorraine, which France had lost to Germany through defeat in the Franco-Prussian War of 1870. Eclipsed by Germany economically and increasingly threatened overseas by a growing German navy, Britain joined with Russia and France to form the Triple Entente alliance in the early 1900s.

In the same years, the Entente powers increasingly confronted a counteralliance consisting of Germany, Austria-Hungary, and (nominally at least) Italy. With the accession of Kaiser Wilhelm II to power, Germany had moved away from a defensive triple alliance with Russia and Austria-Hungary to a growing dependence on the latter alone. Germany had also sought to draw Italy into its coalition with promises of support for its efforts at colonial expansion. But Italian hostility to Austria-Hungary, which still controlled lands the Italians claimed as their own, kept Italy's role as one of the Central Powers tentative and

liable to shift with changing international circumstances. Italian ambivalence became all too clear after the outbreak of war when they not only refused to support Germany and Austria-Hungary, but in 1915 entered the conflict on the side of the Triple Entente.

The alliance system, menacing in itself, was embittered by the atmosphere generated by imperial rivalries that were played out over most of the globe. In the decades leading up to the First World War, most of the European powers had been involved in empire building overseas, and they came to equate the prestige of great power status with the possession of colonies. Rivalries over areas to colonize heightened nationalist sentiments in each country. But by 1900, most of the world's available territories had been colonized by one or another of the states in the two alliance systems. As a result, the scramble in the early 1900s for the few areas as yet unclaimed produced much greater tensions in the European diplomatic system. France maneuvered to annex Morocco to its north African colonies, which already included Algeria and Tunisia (see Map 28.1). Germany twice threatened war if the French advance continued, only to back off when it was clear that none of the other European powers would support it. In the second of the international crises over Morocco in 1911, the Germans had to be bought off by a French concession of territory from their possessions in central Africa.

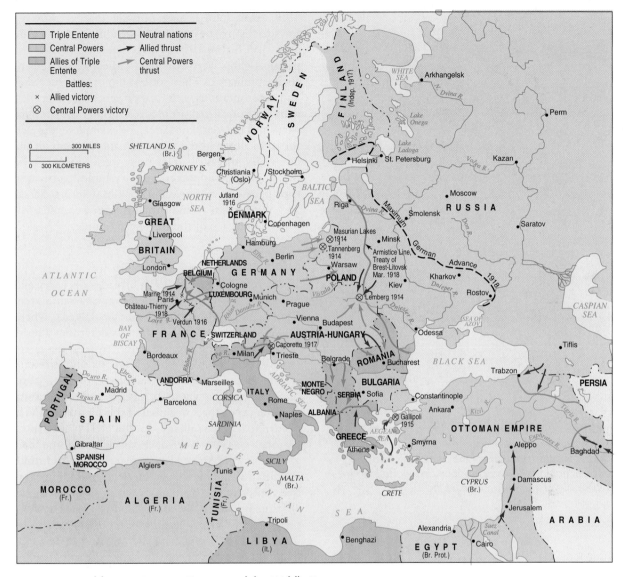

Map 28.1   *World War I Fronts in Europe and the Middle East*

Imperialist rivalries solidified the growing divisions between the two alliances and fed the jingoism (warlike nationalist sentiments that spread widely among the middle and working classes throughout Europe) that had much to do with the coming of the war. Most European leaders of both the great powers and smaller states like those in the Balkans were eager to vie for increased territories and obsessed with keeping their rivals from advancing at their country's expense (see Figure 28.1).

Imperialism and the alliance system were both linked to ever more intense and costly arms races. Naval rivalry was the most apparent and fiercely contested. The Germans' decision to build a navy that could threaten Great Britain's long-standing control of the world's oceans was one of the key reasons for Britain's move for military cooperation with France and (more grudgingly) Russia. It also touched off the greatest arms race in all of history to that time. Huge new warships, such as the *Dreadnought* battleship

BALKAN TROUBLES

THE BOILING POINT.

Figure 28.1 *The obvious fear displayed by an assortment of European leaders in this 1912 Punch cartoon is eerily prescient of the bafflement and concern that later seized European and world leaders in the midst of the Balkan wars of the 1990s.*

launched in 1906 and the German ships built in response, kept the naval rivalry at fever pitch. Serious hopes for arms limitations, much less reductions, faded. Armies grew steadily in size and firepower, and they practiced massive maneuvers that national leaders were prepared to implement in the event of the outbreak of a general war. Not surprisingly, the military buildup helped pave the way to war, as some in the German military in particular pushed for a preemptive strike before army reforms in Russia made it too powerful to overcome.

Diplomatic and military competition tied foreign policy to spiraling domestic tensions. All of the major industrial nations, and those in the process of industrializing like Russia, faced growing labor unrest after

1900. Strikes, the growth of trade unions, and votes for socialist parties mounted steadily in the decade and a half before 1914. The business classes and the political elites were alarmed by these challenges to their dominance. They sought diplomatic successes and confrontations with rival powers to distract their subjects from social problems at home. British ministers and the German kaiser, for examples, appealed for labor peace in the name of national unity in the face of the threat of attack by powerful rivals. Those in power also supported military buildups because they provided employment for the working classes and huge profits to industrialists who were pillars of support for each of the European regimes.

The Outbreak of the War

In the years just before 1914, decades of rivalry and mounting tensions within the European state system were increasingly centered on the Balkans, where Russia sought to back Serbia in its determined resistance to the steady advance of the Austro-Hungarian empire. The complex ethnic divisions and interstate rivalries of the Balkan area mirrored the growing crisis of Europe as a whole. It was not surprising, then, that the event that precipitated the First World War occurred in the Balkans. In July 1914, a Serbian nationalist, Gavriel Princip, assassinated the heir apparent to the Austro-Hungarian throne, **Archduke Ferdinand,** and his wife in **Sarajevo,** the administrative center of the Bosnian province of the Austrian empire. Bolstered by the infamous "blank check" promised by German leaders for reprisals against Serbia, the Austro-Hungarians drew up a list of demands that it was impossible for the Serbs to accede to without surrendering their nation's sovereignty. The ruling circles of Austria-Hungary were determined to put an end to decades of Serbian challenges to their control over portions of the Balkans, and thus they were clearly intent on forcing a war.

When the Russians vowed to support their Slavic brethren in Serbia should war break out with the Austrians, the alliance systems that had been forged in the preceding decades quickly came into play. Within months the confrontation of the two blocs had transformed what might have been a regional war among the Balkan states and their Austrian or Russian backers into the threat of a general European war. Inept diplomacy and a widespread sense of resignation to the eventual outbreak of war, which some believed would sort out the quarrels and tensions that had been building for decades, led to the mobilization of the armies of the great powers in late July 1914.

Although the leaders of most of the powers had long regarded mobilization as a way of applying diplomatic pressure, for the Germans mobilization meant war. Because they had faced the possibility of massive combat on two fronts since the 1890s, the Germans had devised an intricate plan to first attack in the west and defeat France before turning to the more backward, and thus slower to mobilize, Russians in the east. Once Russia mobilized against Germany and the German armies moved to mobilize in retaliation according to a rigid railway timetable that plotted an invasion of neutral Belgium on the way to an all-out assault on France, the alliance systems were locked into a massive war. When the British entered the conflict, officially to defend tiny Belgium, which they had long before pledged to protect, a European conflict was transformed into a global one. Britain's naval ally—Japan—quickly jumped into the fray. British-ruled colonial territories, from the "white" Dominions of Canada, Australia, and New Zealand to Britain's extensive imperial possessions in India and across Africa and southeast Asia, were brought directly into the war. After nearly a century's lapse, Europe was again consumed by a general war that rapidly spread to other parts of the world.

A World at War

 Part of the reason European leaders let their nations blunder into war in 1914 was that most of them expected the conflict to come to be brief and decisive. They saw a war between the European powers as a way to break the logjam of tension and unresolved disputes built up by decades of confrontations between the two alliance systems. Many were also convinced that because the economies of the industrial powers, particularly Britain and Germany, were so interdependent, Europe could simply not remain at war for more than several months or at best a year. Thus, the soldiers of the combatant powers, and most of the leaders who sent them off to war in August 1914, were convinced that the troops would be home by Christmas. But as early as September, with offensives crushed or bogged down on both the Western Front and in the east, it was beginning to be clear that Europe and the world had been plunged into a conflict that was likely to go on for a good deal longer, perhaps many years.

The War in Europe

Perhaps more than any other single factor, the failure of Germany's ambitious plan for a quick victory over France insured that there would be a long war of stalemate and attrition. German political and military leaders counted on their country's superb railway system and huge armies to overwhelm the Belgians and defeat the French before they could even fully mobilize. The French obliged them by launching offensives against deeply entrenched German forces in Alsace-Lorraine that ended in the near destruction of some of France's best armies. But Belgium resisted bravely, slowing the German goliath, and the small but superbly trained British army suddenly appeared to contest the momentum of three German armies, each of which was larger than the total British forces. By the time they reached the frontiers of northern France, the German soldiers were tired and, having left the railways behind in southern Belgium, growing short of boots, food, and ammunition. Reeling from their defeats by the Germans in Alsace-Lorraine, the French forces fled toward Paris, where they regrouped, were reinforced (in part by a famous convoy of Parisian cab drivers), and prepared for the German onslaught. During a five-day battle along the Marne River in early September, the German advance was halted, then thrown back. Paris had been saved and the stage set for over three years of bloody stalemate on the Western Front.

To protect themselves from the withering firepower of the artillery and machine guns of the opposing armies, British and German soldiers began to dig into the ground during and after the clashes along the Marne. Soon northern and western France was crisscrossed by miles and miles of entrenchments that frustrated—with staggering levels of dead and wounded—all attempts to break the stalemate between the opposing forces until well into 1918. The almost unimaginable killing power of the industrial technology wielded by the opposing European armies favored the defensive. Devastating

Visualizing the Past

Trench Warfare

This World War I photograph highlights soldiers in the trenches during one of the many lulls in battle.

Questions: What can be read from the picture? Photographs are an important visual experience in modern history; how can they be interpreted? What were the trenches like? Can the expressions and poses of the soldiers be read to suggest what war meant to them? How did life in the trenches compare with their previous lives in industrial society and with expectations in an age that had vaunted manliness and nationalism? Does the picture raise issues of bias or staging on the part of the photographer, or is it a neutral piece of evidence? Finally, can one move from this picture of war to some speculations about what peacetime life would be like for the veterans who returned home?

artillery, the withering fire of machine guns, barbed-wire barriers, and the use of poison gas turned the Western Front into a killing ground that offered no possibility of decisive victory to either side. The carnage reached unimaginable levels, with the Germans losing 850,000 men, the French 700,000, and the British over 400,000 in the single year of 1916 on just the Western Front.

By the millions, the youth of Europe was killed, maimed, and driven insane, or waited for the next offensive catastrophe in rat- and lice-infested trenches. Like the so-called "primitive" peoples the Europeans had come to dominate overseas, soldiers were exposed to rain and cold and deprived of virtually all of the material comforts that large sections of western European societies had come to regard as their birthright. A German soldier, and later novelist, captured the constant fear, the almost unendurable anxiety the soldiers experienced:

> The front is a cage in which we must await fearfully whatever may happen. We lie under the network of arching shells and live in a suspense of uncertainty. Over us chance hovers.

In so many ways, the war in Europe was centered on the ongoing and senseless slaughter in the trenches. Levels of dead and wounded that would have been unimaginable before the war rose ever higher between 1915 and 1918. They were all the more tragic because neither side could break the stalemate; hundreds of thousands were killed or maimed to gain small patches of ground that were soon lost in counterattacks. Years of carnage made all too evident the lack of imagination and utter incompetence of most of the generals on both sides of the conflict. Few understood that mass assaults on mechanized defenses had become suicidal at this point in the industrial age. The aged officers in the higher commands and overmatched politicians soon demoted or dismissed those who sought to find creative ways out of the trench morass. As the years passed, as a British war poet observed:

> Neither [side] had won or could win the war
> The war had won and would go on winning.

The War in the East and in Italy

In the first weeks of the conflict, the Germans were alarmed by the rapidity with which the Russians were able to mount major offensives against both the Austro-Hungarians and eastern Germany itself. Having committed most of their forces to their own offensives against France, the German high command felt obliged to divert critical resources and manpower to check the advancing Russian armies. In late August the reorganized German forces virtually destroyed an entire Russian army (and sent a second into headlong retreat). In defeat, the Russian forces exhibited many of the weaknesses that resulted in, by far, the highest levels of casualties of any of the combatants and the

ultimate and utter defeat of the tsarist armies. Aristocratic generals dispatched millions of mostly illiterate and poorly trained peasants to certain death in repeated assaults on better-armed and led German forces. Commands in critical battles were sent in uncoded format and readily picked up by their adversaries. Russian artillery, manned by upper-class personnel, usually provided little cover for massed peasant forces, which were reduced to little more than cannon and machine-gun fodder in assaults on the entrenched Germans.

Although the lines shifted over large areas in the east, they inexorably, with horrific human cost, moved east into the provinces of the Russian empire. The poor showing of the Russian commanders, including the hapless tsar **Nicholas II,** who insisted on taking control at the front, did much to spark the mutinies and peasant revolts that were critical forces in the revolutionary waves that destroyed the tsarist regime in 1917.

The Russians fared somewhat better on the Austro-Hungarian front (see Map 28.1), where they faced even more inept generals and multiethnic armies whose soldiers' loyalty to the Austrian emperor was often lukewarm or nonexistent. But the Russians could not prevent the Austrians from crushing Serbia, which held out until the end of 1915. Thanks largely to timely interjections of German soldiers, the Austro-Hungarians managed, again at the cost of millions of casualties, to check repeated Russian offensives. The Austrian forces generally fought much better against the Italians, who entered the war in May 1915. Nine months earlier, Italian leaders had declined to march to war with their Central Power allies, whom the Italians claimed had attacked first and thus nullified what was a defensive treaty. Having wrested British promises of substantial territorial gains, mostly at Austria-Hungary's expense, the Italians launched a series of offensives against the Austrians.

With the Austrians enjoying the high ground in the eastern Alps, the assaults all ended in disaster. Incompetent and corrupt generals, soldiers increasingly disgusted by costly campaigns that went nowhere, and venal politicians double-dealing behind the lines resulted in the near collapse of the Italian front in 1917. Although British and French reinforcements rushed from the Western Front eventually stalled the Austrian advance, Italian soldiers deserted in droves and the war plunged Italy into social and political turmoil. One of the Italian soldiers who was briefly at the front and slightly wounded, Benito Mussolini, would soon exploit this unrest to the fullest in his postwar drive to impose a fascist dictatorship on Italy.

The Homefronts in Europe

As the war dragged on without any sign that decisive victories could be won by either side, soldiers at the fronts across Europe grew resentful of the civilians back home. Their anger was focused on political leaders who cheered them on from the safety of the sidelines far to the rear. But the soldiers were also disturbed, more generally, by the patriotic zeal and insensitivity of the civilian populace, which had little sense of the horrors they were forced to endure at the front. In fact, the commitment of the civilians behind the lines and their hatred for the enemy was usually far more pronounced than that of the soldiers actually in combat. Each of the powers remained able to mobilize ever larger numbers of soldiers and military resources, despite growing food shortages and privations on the homefronts. Governments responded by rationing resources and regulating production to head off potentially crippling labor disputes.

Whole industrial sectors, such as railways, were administered directly by the state. Executive branches of the combatants' governments gradually took over the power of elected parliaments—particularly in Germany, where by late 1916 the General Staff virtually ran the country. Dissent was suppressed, often by force, and newspapers and other media outlets (as well as the letters of the soldiers) were strictly censored. Governments developed propaganda departments that grew more sophisticated and strident as the war dragged on. The British proved the most adept at propaganda. Much of this was aimed at the United States in the hope that the Americans would be drawn into the war. The British and American public were bombarded with stories of German atrocities. As the war went into its second and third years, news of severe setbacks was increasingly denied to the German people. As a consequence, most Germans were stunned by what seemed their sudden defeat in 1918. The extent of the involvement of the civilian population (in some cases as targets of bombardments and aerial assaults) and the power of governments to mobilize men *and* women and control the information they received about the conflict made "The Great War" truly the first total war in human history.

The war in essence sped up many developments already visible in industrial societies. The power of organization increased, particularly through the new interventions of governments. To maintain unified backing of the civilian population, socialists and trade union chiefs were given new recognition and allowed to serve on governing boards in charge of industrial production and negotiate improved working conditions. As their leaders became ever more drawn into the existing governmental system, some labor groups rejected their leadership and became ever more vocal critics of the war. As the war lumbered on, seemingly out of control, these trends became more pronounced, particularly in Russia and Germany. Labor protests in Moscow and St. Petersburg gave powerful momentum to the wave of discontent and mass protest that brought down the tsarist regime in February of 1917 and propelled the Bolsheviks to power in October of the same year (see Chapter 29). In Germany, labor agitation, very often sparked by growing shortages of food and fuel that were intensified by the British naval blockade, also loomed as a threat to the military commanders who ran the country in the last years of the conflict. As the German front in France and Belgium collapsed in the early summer of 1918, leftist leaders and angry laborers pushed the nation to the brink of revolution in late 1918 and 1919.

As a direct consequence of the war, women's participation in the labor force increased greatly, particularly in Germany, Britain, and the United States. Defying prevailing prewar notions about the "natural" gender roles, women proved very able to work even in heavy industry, where many were engaged in the very dangerous production of munitions (Figure 28.2). Better wages and the confidence they gained from their mastery of such demanding and critical roles as factory workers and nurses at the front sparked a broader liberation for women during the war years. From the rising hemlines of their dresses and their license to smoke in public to unchaperoned dating and greatly increased political activism, many women sought to recast gender roles and images.

At war's end, the loss of many of their jobs to men returning from the front as well as government programs consciously designed to force them back into the home reversed many of the gains that women had achieved during the conflict. But in Britain, Germany, and the United States, they gained the vote, which they had struggled for in the decades before 1914. The visibility and influence of the

Figure 28.2 *The drastic shortage of farm and factory workers caused by the insatiable military manpower needs of World War I generals provided abundant (but often dangerous, as the munitions work shown here suggests) job outlets for young women.*

career-oriented and sophisticated "new women" of the 1920s, though a small minority even in Germany and the United States, gave promise of broader advances in the decades to come.

The War Outside Europe

Except for Austria-Hungary, all of the major powers that went to war in 1914 had colonies outside Europe. When it became clear that the war was not to be the quick, decisive clash that most had anticipated, the manpower and resources of these imperial possessions were increasingly sucked into the spreading conflict. By 1915, fighting had spread to the Middle East, west and east Africa, across most of the seas and oceans of the world, and even to China and the islands of the Pacific. Troops from Canada, Australia, New Zealand, and throughout much of Africa had been recruited, mainly to fight for the Triple Entente allies. By 1917 the United States had entered the war, leaving only the nations of South America alone of all of the continents not directly engaged in the struggle.

Britain's participation, more than that of any other power, contributed to the war's globalization. The British navy not only cut off Germany from its colonies in Africa, China, and the Pacific islands, but it hunted down German ships still on the high seas at the outbreak of war. Perhaps most critically, British naval supremacy meant that an effective blockade could be maintained that would deprive the Central

Powers of supplies of food and raw materials from overseas throughout the war. Because the British also controlled trans-Atlantic cable links, they could easily outdo the Germans in propaganda efforts to convince the neutral United States to side with them in the war. The expensive and highly touted German navy fully engaged the British Grand Fleet only once during the war, in 1916 off Jutland in Denmark. Though the Germans sank more ships and killed more British sailors, the high seas fleet was driven back into port and proved of little use to the larger German effort for the rest of the war.

The British entry into the war also meant that its empire and allies were drawn into the fray. Japan, which had joined Britain in a naval pact in 1902, eagerly attacked German colonies in China and the Pacific. These acquisitions, especially the seizure of the Shandong peninsula, would provide great impetus to Japan's imperialist aspirations in China in the 1930s. The islands they captured from the Germans in World War I proved components of the defense perimeter they sought to build in the Pacific during World War II.

The British Dominions—Canada, Australia, and New Zealand—quickly marshalled considerable resources to support the war effort. These areas not only supplied food and critical raw materials; in defiance of the German U-boat fleet in the Atlantic, they swelled the initially meager ranks of Britain's armed forces. Dominion troops were a mainstay of British operations in the Middle East, including the defense of the vital Suez Canal link and the ill-fated assault at **Gallipoli** in 1915. They fought valiantly on the Western Front throughout the war, at times bolstering British lines that were crumbling under massive German assaults. White settler colonials in South Africa also joined those from the Dominions in support of the British, despite bitter opposition from some segments of the Afrikaner population, which had suffered so greatly as a result of draconian British repression in the Anglo-Boer war just over a decade earlier.

The British and the French also received vital support from their nonsettler colonies in Africa, India, and southeast Asia. The massive army, which the British had recruited in India for over a century and a half, did much of the fighting in sub-Saharan Africa and the Middle East. The French deployed tens of thousands of non-European soldiers, recruited mainly in north and west Africa, on the Western Front, where many served with distinction but with scant reward. Unlike the British, who turned mainly to women to replace the millions of farmers and factory workers who went off to war, the French relied heavily on laborers recruited in their colonies from Africa to Vietnam.

Although the Germans quickly lost most of their colonies in Africa and the Far East, superbly led African soldiers recruited and trained in German East Africa (Tanzania today) held off hundreds of thousands of British-led Indian and south African troops until two weeks after the end of hostilities in Europe itself. But Germany's main support outside Europe came from the Ottoman Empire (see Map 28.1), which entered the war in the fall of 1915. The Young Turk leaders, who had consolidated their power in Constantinople in the decade leading up to the war (see Chapter 26), had continued the Ottoman sultans' reliance on German military advisors and financiers. After fending off the British-led campaign to capture the Gallipoli peninsula, the Turks opened up fronts in southern Russia, where they suffered severe defeats, and the Middle East, where their fortunes were more mixed and they remained for years a threat to the British in Egypt and the Suez Canal zone.

The Young Turk leaders sought to transfer blame for the reverses on the Russian front to the Christian Armenian minority, which was concentrated in areas that spanned the two empires in eastern Anatolia and the Caucasus. In fact, remembering earlier pogroms launched by the Turks against them, some of the

Armenians living in Turkish areas had backed the Russians. But most of the minority was loyal or neutral, and poor generalship and bad planning were the main causes of the Turkish military disasters. Struggling to cover their blunders, the Young Turk leaders launched a genocidal assault in 1915 against the Armenians, which claimed as many as a million lives and sent hundreds of thousands of Armenians in flight to Russia and the Middle East.

The last major combatant to enter the global conflagration was the United States, which declared war on Germany in the spring of 1917. The war made the United States into a major global power, culminating developments that had been underway for decades. By 1914, the United States had become an active force in international diplomacy and power politics. It had built a modest Pacific empire, centering on Hawaii and the Philippine islands, and had become increasingly forceful in its interventions in Central America and the Caribbean. The outbreak of the war was greeted with considerable ambivalence on the part of American leaders and the citizenry more generally. Distant from the battlefields, Americans disagreed over which side was in the right and whether or not they should intervene in quarrels that seemed to have little to do with them. But American businesses profited greatly from the war by selling food, raw materials, and eventually weapons, mainly (due to the British blockade) to the Entente allies. American mercantile interests, like their counterparts in Japan, also took advantage of the Europeans' need to concentrate their industrial production on the war effort by taking over new markets in Latin America and Asia. Rapidly rising exports, combined with huge loans to Britain, France, and Russia, which all needed credit to buy American goods, transformed the United States from an international debtor to the world's largest creditor and strongest economy.

Despite all of the gains that the United States had accrued through neutrality, American leadership and a majority of the American public was pro-British. British successes in the propaganda war and ever growing economic ties to the Entente allies did much to explain this sentiment. But clumsy German attempts to influence American opinion and, most critically, the German need to use submarines to counter the British blockade and control of sea access to Europe, did much to drive the United States into the war. Following the resumption of unrestricted submarine warfare in the Atlantic, which President

Woodrow Wilson had earlier warned would force military retaliation by the United States, America entered the conflict in April 1917. American warships were immediately joined with the British to create a convoy system that eventually offset an intensified German submarine campaign designed to starve the British Isles into submission. For much of 1917, the number of American troops sent to Europe was small and largely symbolic. But by early 1918, millions of young Americans were in training and hundreds of thousands arrived in Europe each week. The growing buildup of American reinforcements, and American-produced arms and supplies, convinced the German high command that they must launch a massive strike for a quick victory, before the full manpower and resources of the United States could be brought to bear against their weary soldiers.

Endgame: The Return of Offensive Warfare

For several weeks in March and April of 1918, the massive offensives launched by the Germans on the Western Front looked as if they might bring victory to the Central Powers. An entire British army had been shattered and another was in full retreat; the already demoralized French forces were also falling back toward Paris. Nearly a million German soldiers transferred from the **Eastern Front** after Russia was knocked out of the war, and new assault tactics and the deployment of storm troopers had restored the offensive and broken three long years of bloody stalemate. But just as Paris was again within the range of the great German guns, the advance slowed. Mount-

ing casualties and sheer fatigue on the German side, counteroffensives, new weapons like tanks, and a rapidly increasing influx of fresh and enthusiastic American soldiers stalled the German drive and then began to push the German armies out of northern France. At the same time, the Austrian fronts broke down in both northeast Italy and the Balkans. The Austro-Hungarian empire fragmented along national lines, and the heir to the Habsburg throne abdicated as separate republics in Austria and Hungary sued the Entente allies for peace.

Fearing that their armies were on the verge of collapse and menaced by widespread rebellions at home, the German commanders agreed to an *armistice* (a suspension of fighting) on November 11, 1918. The generals sought to shift the blame for defeat to a civilian government that they had abruptly installed in Berlin. Made up of members of the Center and Socialist parties, Germany's new government was forced to both sue the Entente allies for peace and consent to an armistice agreement delivered by two British admirals and two French generals. Assuming that their armies were on the verge of victory just months before, the German people were stunned by the sudden reversal. Many accepted the myth that Germany had been betrayed by socialist and Jewish politicians, whose alleged "stab in the back" would become a rallying cry for **Adolf Hitler** and the Nazis' drive for power from the early 1920s.

After four years of slaughter, the casualty totals were staggering (see Table 28.1). At least 10 million soldiers were dead and 20 million more wounded. The losses were, by far, the heaviest among the great powers of Europe who had been the main adversaries

TABLE 28.1
World War I Losses

	Dead	Wounded	Prisoner
Great Britain	947,000	2,122,000	192,000
France	1,385,000	3,044,000	446,000
Russia	1,700,000	4,950,000	500,000
Italy	460,000	947,000	530,000
United States	115,000	206,000	4,500
Germany	1,808,000	4,247,000	618,000
Austria–Hungary	1,200,000	3,620,000	200,000
Turkey	325,000	400,000	

Note: The number of known dead (round numbers) was placed at about 10 million and the wounded at about 20 million, distributed among chief combatants.

in the conflict. From France to Russia, virtually every European family had a death to mourn. As the fighting ended, an additional calamity struck. Hundreds of thousands of soldiers and millions of civilians died in an influenza pandemic that began in Asia and spread like wildfire around the globe. Though the direct costs of the long and widespread war and the indirect economic losses it inflicted are almost impossible to calculate with certainty, both totals reached hundreds of billions of dollars. In Belgium and northern France, northern Italy, and across east central Europe, extensive swaths of fertile farmlands and bustling cites were reduced to smoldering ruins. This devastation and a postwar economic downturn that followed the armistice dislocated economies across the globe until well into the mid-1920s and fed into the Great Depression that was to follow a decade later.

Failed Peace

 The widespread bitterness evoked by the unprecedented cost in lives and destruction of the war was redoubled by the utter failure of the peace conference convened by the victorious allies at Versailles. The Germans' willingness to negotiate an armistice owed much to their faith in Woodrow Wilson's frequent promises that he would seek a peace that was not aimed at punishing the defeated powers but focused on establishing a viable new world order in which such a war could never again occur. Whatever Wilson's intentions, his vision of a nonpunitive peace was soon done in by America's Entente allies, who viewed Wilson and his advisors as ill-informed idealists with little grasp of the realities of European power politics.

While the Italians and Japanese scrambled to obtain maximum advantage from their support for the allied cause during the war, the French insisted that they had suffered the most and their losses had to be avenged. **Georges Clemenceau,** the French premier, pushed for the peace conference to brand the Germans the aggressors and thus force them to pay huge reparations to France and the other nations assaulted. He also worked to cut down the size of Germany and funnel its resources to France and the other powers.

Fearing that a reduced Germany would prove fertile ground for the spread of communist revolution, **David Lloyd George,** the British prime minister, attempted with little success both to mediate between Clemenceau and Woodrow Wilson and to win enough reparations to satisfy a disgruntled electorate at home. All of the leaders of the victorious Entente powers, including Wilson, soon closed ranks against the demands welling up from peoples in colonized areas, from the Middle East to Vietnam. Dashing the expectations that he had aroused by his ringing call for the right of peoples to *self-determination*, Wilson soon made it clear that the peoples he had in mind were white folk like the Poles, not Arabs or Vietnamese (Figure 28.3). With Wilson's blessing, the British and French set about shoring up, and in fact expanding, their battered empires, while the Japanese solidified their beachhead in China and island enclaves in the western Pacific. The triumvirate of Wilson, Lloyd George, and Clemenceau, which dominated the proceedings at Versailles, also made certain that a mild antiracist clause never made it into the final draft of the treaty.

The Peace of Paris, which was the most important of a series of treaties that emerged from the gathering at Versailles, was nothing less than the *diktat* (dictated peace, without negotiations) that German politicians across the political spectrum sought to reverse in the postwar era. The German delegation was allowed no part in drafting the treaty, and they were given no opportunity to amend or refuse it. The German representatives were even humiliated by being brought in by the servants' entrance for the signing and being required to stand for hours while the entire draft of the treaty was read aloud before the assembled delegates. The Germans' main allies—the Austrians—were also major targets of the treaties that emerged from the conference. The Austro-Hungarian Empire was dismembered, as nationalist groups carved out the new nations of Czechoslovakia, Hungary, and Yugoslavia. Poland was also reborn, and like Czechoslovakia, it was given substantial chunks of what had been German territory before the war. This left a somewhat fragile Germanic Austria, cut off from its traditional markets, as one of many weak countries between a smaller Germany and a massive Soviet Union to the east.

The fatal flaws of the peace process extended far beyond calculated insults to the Germans. The new

Figure 28.3 *At the Paris peace conference of 1919, the Arabs sought a new voice. The Arab representatives included Prince Feisal, later King of Iraq, and an Iraqi general. A British delegation member, T. E. Lawrence (third from the right), was a long-time friend of the Arabs. The Arabs did not win full national self-determination for their homelands.*

Bolshevik leaders of Russia, who would be treated as pariahs for decades, were not even invited to the conference. Wartime promises to the Arabs in return for their support for the Entente allies in the war were forgotten, as Britain and France divided the Arab heartlands of the Middle East between themselves. China's pleas for protection from Japanese occupation of the Shandong peninsula were dismissed, and a youthful Ho Chi Minh, the future leader of Vietnam, was rudely refused an audience with Woodrow Wilson. Denied their demand that Germany be permanently partitioned, French leaders turned inward on each other and waited despondently for the next German assault they were convinced was inevitable.

Even the United States, whose President Wilson had opened the peace conference with such exuber-

ant expectations, repudiated what had been wrought at Versailles. Despite Wilson's literally near-fatal efforts to win popular support for the treaty, the American Congress voted down the critical clauses establishing a **League of Nations** and later made a separate peace with Germany. Even as the delegates were still at work, it was clear to knowledgeable observers that Versailles was a disaster. One of the most perceptive chroniclers of the war years and their aftermath, Vera Brittain, wrote as the terms of the treaty began to be made public in the press:

> [T]he Big Four were making a desert and calling it peace. When I thought about these negotiations … they did not seem to me to represent at all the kind of "victory" that the young men whom I had loved would have regarded as sufficient justification for their lost lives.

World War I and the Nationalist Assault on the European Colonial Order

Four long years of intra-European slaughter severely disrupted the systems of colonial domination that had been expanded and refined in the century leading up to World War I. The conflict also gave great impetus to the forces of resistance that had begun to well up in the decades before the war. Although the actual process of decolonization would occur in most areas only after a second global conflict two decades later, World War I enhanced the standing of nationalist leaders, such as Gandhi, in major ways. The demands placed on colonized peoples during the war also contributed significantly to popular dissatisfaction with Western domination and widespread protest in a number of colonies during and after the conflict.

Though the European colonizers had frequently quarreled over colonial possessions in the late 19th century, during World War I they actually fought each other in the colonies for the first time. African and Asian soldiers and laborers in the hundreds of thousands served both on the Western Front and in the far-flung theaters of war from Egypt, Palestine, and Mesopotamia to east Africa. The colonies also supplied food for the home populations of the Triple Entente powers, as well as vital raw materials such as oil, jute, and cotton. Contrary to long-standing colonial policy, the hard-pressed British even encouraged a considerable expansion of industrial production in India to supplement the output of their overextended home factories. Thus, the war years contributed to the development in India of the largest industrial sector in the colonized world.

World War I presented the subjugated peoples of Africa and Asia with the spectacle of the self-styled civilizers of humankind sending their young men by the millions to be slaughtered in the horrific and barbaric trench stalemate on the Western Front. For the first time, African and Asian soldiers were ordered by their European officers to kill other Europeans. In the process, the vulnerability of the seemingly invincible Europeans and the deep divisions between them were starkly revealed. During the war years, European troops in the colonies were withdrawn to meet the need for manpower on the many war fronts. The garrisons that remained were dangerously understaffed. The need to recall administrative personnel from British and French colonies meant that colonial officials were compelled to fill their vacated posts with African and Asian administrators, many of whom enjoyed real responsibility for the first time.

To maintain the loyalty of their traditional allies among the colonized and to win the support of the Western-educated elites or new allies such as the Arabs, the British and French made many promises regarding the postwar settlement. Because these concessions often seriously compromised their pre-war dominance or their plans for further colonial expansion, the leaders of the victorious allies repeatedly reneged on them in the years after the war. The betrayal of these pledges understandably contributed a great deal to postwar agitation against the continuance and spread of European colonial domination.

For intellectuals and political leaders throughout Africa and Asia, the appalling devastation of World War I cast doubt on the claims that the Europeans had made for over a century that they were, by virtue of their racial superiority, the fittest of all peoples to rule the globe. The social and economic disruptions caused by the war in key colonies, such as Egypt, India, and the Ivory Coast, made it possible for nationalist agitators to build a mass base for their anticolonial movements for the first time. But in these and other areas of the colonized world, the war gave added impetus to movements and processes already underway rather than initiating new responses to European global domination. Therefore, it is essential to place wartime developments in the colonies and the postwar surge in anticolonial resistance in a longer-term context that takes into account African and Asian responses that extend in some cases back to the last decades of the 19th century. Since it is impossible to relate the history of the independence struggles in all of the European colonies, key movements, such as those that developed in India, Egypt, and British and French west Africa, will be considered in some depth. These specific movements will then be related to broader patterns of African and Asian nationalist agitation and the accelerating phenomenon of decolonization worldwide.

Document

Lessons for the Colonized from the Slaughter in the Trenches

The prolonged and senseless slaughter of the youth of Europe in the trench stalemate on the Western Front did much to erode the image of Europeans as superior, rational, and more civilized beings that they had worked hard to propagate among the colonized peoples in the decades before the Great War. The futility of the seemingly endless slaughter cast doubts on the Europeans' rationality and fitness to rule themselves, much less the rest of the world. The destructive uses to which their science and technology were put brought into question the Europeans' long-standing claims that these material advancements tangibly demonstrated their intellectual and organizational superiority over all other peoples. The excerpts below, taken from the writings of some of the leading thinkers and political leaders of the colonized peoples of Africa and Asia, reflect their disillusionment with the West as a result of the war and the continuing turmoil in Europe in the postwar era.

Rabindranath Tagore

Bengali poet, playwright, and novelist Rabindranath Tagore was one of the earliest non-European recipients of the Nobel Prize for literature.

> Has not this truth already come home to you now when this cruel war has driven its claws into the vitals of Europe? When her hoard of wealth is bursting into smoke and her humanity is shattered on her battlefields? You ask in amazement what she has done to deserve this? The answer is, that the West has been systematically petrifying her moral nature in order to lay a solid foundation for her gigantic abstractions of efficiency. She has been all along starving the life of the personal man into that of the professional.

Mohandas Gandhi

In the years after the First World War, Mohandas Gandhi emerged as India's leading nationalist figure.

> India's destiny lies not along the bloody way of the West, but along the bloodless way of peace that comes from a simple and godly life. India is in danger of losing her soul…. She must not, therefore, lazily and helplessly say, "I cannot escape the onrush from the West." She must be strong enough to resist it for her own sake and that of the world. I make bold to say that the Europeans themselves will have to remodel their outlooks if they are not to perish under the weight of the comforts to which they are becoming slaves.

Léopold Sédar Senghor

Senegalese poet and political leader Léopold Sédar Senghor is widely regarded as one of the 20th century's finest writers in the French language.

> Lord, the snow of your Peace is your proposal
>   to a divided world to a divided Europe
> To Spain torn apart….
> And I forget
> White hands that fired the shots which
>   brought the empires crumbling
> Hands that flogged the slaves, that flogged
>   You [Jesus Christ]
> Chalk-white hands that buffeted You,
>   powdered painted hands that buffeted me
> Confident hands that delivered me to solitude
>   to hatred
> White hands that felled the forest of palm trees
>   once commanding Africa, in the heart of Africa.
>   From *Snow Upon Paris*

Aimé Césaire

West Indian poet Aimé Césaire was a founder of the négritude movement, which asserted black culture in the late 1920s.

> Heia [Praise] for those who have never
>   invented anything
> those who never explored anything
> those who never tamed anything
> those who give themselves up to the essence of
>   all things
> ignorant of surfaces but struck by the
>   movement of all things.
>   From *Return to My Native Land*

Questions: On the basis of this sample, what aspects of the West's claims to superiority would you say were called into question by the suicidal conflict of the leading powers within European civilization? What aspects of their own civilizations do these writers, both implicitly and explicitly, champion as alternatives to the ways of the West? Are these writers in danger of stereotyping both the West and their own civilizations?

India: The Makings of the Nationalist Challenge to the British Raj

Because India and much of southeast Asia had been colonized long before Africa, movements for independence arose in Asian colonies somewhat earlier than in their African counterparts. By the last years of the 19th century, the Western-educated minority of the colonized in India and the Philippines had been organized politically for decades. Their counterparts in Burma and the Netherlands Indies were also beginning to form associations to give voice to their political concerns. Because of India's size and the pivotal role it played in the British Empire (by far the largest of the European imperialist empires), the Indian nationalist movement pioneered patterns of nationalist challenge and European retreat that were later followed in many other colonies. Though it had been under British control for only a matter of decades, Egypt also proved an influential center of nationalist organization and resistance in the pre–World War I era.

Local conditions elsewhere in Asia and in Africa made for important variations on the sequence of decolonization worked out in India and Egypt. But key themes—such as the lead taken by Western-educated elites, the importance of charismatic leaders in the spread of the anticolonial struggle to the peasant and urban masses, and a reliance on nonviolent forms of protest—were repeated again and again in other colonial settings.

The **Indian National Congress party** led the Indians to independence and governed through most of the early decades of the postcolonial era. It grew out of regional associations of Western-educated Indians that were originally more like study clubs than political organizations in any meaningful sense of the term. These associations were centered in the cities of Bombay, Poona, Calcutta, and Madras (see Map 24.3). The Congress party that Indian leaders formed in 1885 had the blessing of a number of high-ranking British officials. These officials viewed it as a forum through which the opinions of educated Indians could be made known to the government, thereby heading off potential discontent and political protest.

For most of its first decades, the Congress party served these purposes quite well. The organization had no mass base and very few ongoing staff members or full-time politicians who could sustain lobbying efforts on issues raised at its annual meetings. Some members of the Congress party voiced concern for the growing poverty of the Indian masses and the drain of wealth from the subcontinent to Great Britain. But the Congress party's debates and petitions to the government were dominated by elite-centric issues, such as the removal of barriers to Indian employment in the colonial bureaucracy and increased Indian representation in all-Indian and local legislative bodies. Most of the members of the early Congress party were firmly loyal to the British rulers and confident that once their grievances were made known to the government, they would be remedied.

Many Western-educated Indians were increasingly troubled, however, by the growing virulence of British racism. This they were convinced had much to do with their poor salaries and limited opportunities for advancement in the colonial administration. In their annual meetings, members of the Congress, who were now able to converse and write in a common English language, discovered that no matter where they came from in India, they were treated in a similar fashion. The Indians' shared grievances, their similar educational and class backgrounds, and their growing contacts through the Congress party gave rise to a sense of common Indian identity that had never before existed in a south Asian environment that was more diverse linguistically, religiously, and ethnically than the continent of Europe.

Social Foundations of a Mass Movement

By the last years of the 19th century, the Western-educated elites had begun to grope for causes that would draw a larger segment of the Indian population into their growing nationalist community. More than a century of British rule had generated in many areas of India the social and economic disruptions and the sort of discontent that produced substantial numbers of recruits for the nationalist campaigns. Indian businessmen, many of whom would become major financial backers of the Congress party, were angered by the favoritism the British rulers showed to British investors in establishing trade policies in India. Indian political leaders increasingly stressed these inequities and the more general loss to the Indian people resulting from what they termed the "drain" of Indian resources under colonial rule. Though the British rebuttal was that a price had to be paid for the peace and good government that had come with colonial rule, nationalist thinkers pointed out that the cost was too high.

A large portion of the government of India's budget went to cover the expenses of the huge army that mainly fought wars elsewhere in the British Empire. The Indian people also paid for the generous salaries and pensions of British administrators, who occupied positions that the Indians themselves were qualified to assume. Whenever possible, as in the purchase of railway equipment or steel for public works projects, the government bought goods manufactured in Great Britain. This practice served to buttress a British economy that was fast losing ground to the United States and Germany. It also ensured that the classic colonial relationship between a manufacturing European colonizer and its raw-material-producing overseas dependencies was maintained.

In the villages of India, the shortcomings of British rule were equally apparent by the last decades of the 19th century. The needs of the British home economy had often dictated policies that pushed the Indian peasantry toward the production of cash crops such as cotton, jute, and indigo. The decline in food production that invariably resulted played a major role in the regional famines that struck repeatedly in the pre–World War I era. Radical Indian nationalists frequently charged that the British were callously indifferent to the suffering caused by food shortages and outbreaks of epidemic disease, and that they did far too little to alleviate the suffering that resulted. In many areas, landlessness and chronic poverty, already a problem before the establishment of British rule, increased markedly. In most places, British measures to control indebtedness and protect small landholders and tenants were too little and came too late.

The Rise of Militant Nationalism

Some of the issues that Indian nationalist leaders stressed in their early attempts to build a mass base had great appeal for devout Hindus. This was particularly true of campaigns for the protection of cows, which have long had a special status for the Hindu population of south Asia. But these religious-oriented causes often strongly alienated the adherents of other faiths, especially the Muslims. Not only did Muslims eat beef, and thus slaughter cattle, but they made up nearly one-fourth of the population of the Indian Empire. Some leaders, such as **B. G. Tilak,** were little concerned by

this split. They believed that since Hindus made up the overwhelming majority of the Indian population, nationalism should be built on appeals to Hindu religiosity. Tilak worked to promote the restoration and revival of what he believed to be the ancient traditions of Hinduism. On this basis, he opposed women's education and the raising of the very low marriage age for women. Tilak also turned festivals for Hindu gods into occasions for mass political demonstrations. He broke with more moderate leaders of the Congress party by demanding the boycott of British-manufactured goods. Tilak also sought to persuade his fellow Indians to refuse to serve in the colonial administration and military. Tilak demanded full independence, with no deals or delays, and threatened violent rebellion if the British failed to comply.

Tilak's oratorical skills and religious appeal made him the first Indian nationalist leader with a genuine mass following. Nonetheless, his popularity was confined mainly to his home base in Bombay and in nearby areas in western India. At the same time, his promotion of a very reactionary sort of Hinduism offended and frightened moderate and progressive Hindus, Muslims, and followers of other religions, such as the Sikhs. When evidence was found connecting Tilak's writings to underground organizations that advocated violent revolt, the British, who had grown increasingly uneasy about his radical demands and mass appeal, arrested and imprisoned him. Six years of exile in Burma for Tilak had a dampening effect on the mass movement he had begun to build among the Hindu population.

The other major threat to the British in India before World War I also came from Hindu communalists who advocated the violent overthrow of the colonial regime. But unlike Tilak and his followers, those who joined the terrorist movement favored clandestine operations over mass demonstrations. Though terrorists were active in several parts of India by the last decade of the 19th century, those in Bengal built perhaps the most extensive underground network. Considerable numbers of young Bengalis, impatient with the gradualist approach advocated by moderates in the Congress party, were attracted to underground secret societies. These were led by quasi-religious, guru-style leaders who exhorted them to build up their physiques with Western-style calisthenics and learn how to use firearms and make bombs. British officials and government buildings were the major targets of terrorist assassination plots and sabotage. On occasion the young revolutionaries also struck at European civilians and collaborators among the Indian population. But the terrorists' small numbers and limited support from the colonized populace as a whole rendered them highly vulnerable to British repressive measures. The very considerable resources the British devoted to crushing these violent threats to their rule had checked the terrorist threat by the outbreak of World War I.

Tilak's removal and the repression campaigns against the terrorists strengthened the hand of the more moderate politicians of the Congress party in the years before the war. Western-educated Indian lawyers came to be the dominant force in nationalist politics, and—as the careers of Gandhi, Jinnah, and Nehru demonstrate—they would provide many of the movement's key leaders throughout the struggle for independence. The approach of those who advocated a peaceful, constitutionalist route to decolonization was given added appeal by timely political concessions on the part of the British. The **Morley-Minto reforms** of 1909 provided educated Indians with considerably expanded opportunities both to vote for and serve on local and all-India legislative councils.

The Emergence of Gandhi and the Spread of the Nationalist Struggle

In the months after the outbreak of World War I, the British could take great comfort from the way in which the peoples of the empire rallied to their defense. Of the many colonies among the tropical dependencies, none played as critical a role in the British war effort as India. The Indian princes offered substantial war loans; Indian soldiers bore the brunt of the war effort in east Africa and the Middle East; and nationalist leaders, including Gandhi and Tilak, toured India selling British war bonds. But as the war dragged on and Indians died on the battlefields or went hungry at home to sustain a conflict that had little to do with them, signs of unrest spread throughout the subcontinent.

Wartime inflation had adversely affected virtually all segments of the Indian population. Indian peasants were angered at the ceilings set on the price of their market produce, despite rising costs. They were also often upset by their inability to sell what they had produced because of shipping shortages linked to the war. Indian laborers saw their already meager wages drop steadily in the face of rising prices. At the same time, their bosses grew rich from profits earned in war production. Many localities suffered from famines, which were exacerbated by wartime transport shortages that impeded relief efforts.

After the end of the war in 1918, moderate Indian politicians were frustrated by the British refusal to honor wartime promises. Hard-pressed British leaders had promised the Indians that if they continued to support the war effort, India would move steadily to self-government within the empire once the conflict was over. Indian hopes for the fulfillment of these promises were raised by the **Montagu-Chelmsford reforms** of 1919. These measures increased the powers of Indian legislators at the all-India level and placed much of the provincial administration of India under their control. But the concessions granted in the reforms were offset by the passage later in the same year of the **Rowlatt Act,** which placed severe restrictions on key Indian civil rights, such as the freedom of the press. These conditions fueled local protest during and immediately after the war. At the same time, **Mohandas Gandhi** emerged as a new leader who soon forged this localized protest into a sustained all-India campaign against the policies of the colonial overlords.

Gandhi's remarkable appeal to both the masses and the Western-educated nationalist politicians was due to a combination of factors. Perhaps the most important was the strategy for protest that he had worked out a decade earlier as the leader of a successful movement of resistance to the restrictive laws imposed on the Indian migrant community in south Africa. Gandhi's stress on nonviolent, but quite aggressive, protest tactics endeared him both to the moderates and to more radical elements within the nationalist movement. His advocacy of peaceful boycotts, strikes, noncooperation, and mass demonstrations—which he labeled collectively **satyagraha,** or truth force—proved an effective way of weakening British control while limiting opportunities for violent reprisals that would allow the British to make full use of their superior military strength.

It is difficult to separate Gandhi's approach to mass protest from Gandhi as an individual and thinker. Though physically unimposing, he possessed an inner confidence and sense of moral purpose that sustained his followers and wore down his adversaries. He combined the career of a Western-educated lawyer with the attributes of a traditional Hindu ascetic and guru. The former had given him considerable exposure to the world beyond India and a rather astute understanding of the strengths and weaknesses of the British colonizers. These qualities and his soon legendary skill in negotiating with the British made it possible for Gandhi to build up a strong following among middle-class, Western-educated Indians, who had long been the dominant force behind the nationalist cause. But the success of Gandhi's protest tactics also hinged on the involvement of ever-increasing numbers of the Indian people in anticolonial resistance. The image of a traditional mystic and guru that Gandhi projected was critical in gaining mass support from peasants and laborers alike. Many of these "ordinary" Indians would walk for miles when Gandhi was on tour. Many did so in order to honor a saint rather than listen to a political speech. Gandhi's widespread popular appeal, in turn, gave him even greater influence among nationalist politicians. The latter were very much aware of the leverage his mass following gave to them in their ongoing contests with the British overlords. Under Gandhi's leadership, nationalist protest surged in India during the 1920s and 1930s.

Egypt and the Rise of Nationalism in the Middle East

Egypt is the one country in the Afro-Asian world in which the emergence of nationalism preceded European conquest and domination (see Map 28.2). Risings touched off by the mutiny of Ahmad Orabi and other Egyptian officers (see Chapter 26), which led to the British occupation in 1882, were aimed at the liberation of the Egyptian people from their alien Turkish overlords as well as the meddling Europeans. British occupation meant, in effect, double colonization for the Egyptian people by the Turkish khedives (who were left in power) and their British advisors.

In the decades following the British conquest, government policy was dominated by the strong-willed and imperious **Lord Cromer.** As High Commissioner of Egypt, he pushed for much-needed economic reforms that reduced but could not eliminate the debts of the puppet khedival regime. Cromer also oversaw sweeping reforms in the bureaucracy and the construction of irrigation systems and other public works projects. But the prosperity the British congratulated themselves for having brought to Egypt by the first decade of the 20th century was enjoyed largely by tiny middle and

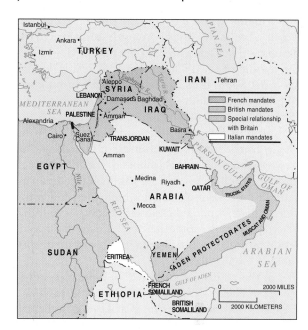

Map 28.2 *The Middle East After World War I*

elite classes, often at the expense of the mass of the population. The leading beneficiaries included foreign merchants, the Turco-Egyptian political elite, a small Egyptian bourgeoisie in Cairo and other towns in the Nile delta, and the ayan, or the great landlords in the rural areas.

The latter were clearly among the biggest gainers. The British had been forced to rely heavily on local, estate-owning notables in extending their control into the rural areas. As a result, the ayan, not the impoverished mass of rural cultivators and laborers, received most of the benefits of the new irrigation works, the building of railways, and the increasing orientation of Egyptian agriculture to the production of raw cotton for the export market. Unfettered by legal restrictions, the ayan greedily amassed ever larger estates by turning smallholder owners into landless tenants and laborers. As their wealth grew, the contrast between the landlords' estate houses and the thatch and mud-walled villages of the great mass of the peasantry became more and more pronounced. Bored by life in the provinces, the well-heeled landed classes spent most of their time in the fashionable districts of Cairo or in resort towns such as Alexandria. Their estates were run by hired managers, who were little more than rent collectors as far as the peasants were concerned.

With the khedival regime and the great landlords closely allied to the British overlords, resistance to the occupation was left mainly to the middle class. Since the middle of the 19th century, this relatively new and small social class had been growing in numbers and influence, mainly in the towns in the Nile delta. With the memory of Orabi's revolt in 1882 still fresh, the cause of Egyptian independence was taken up mainly by the sons of the **effendi,** or the prosperous business and professional families that made up much of this new middle class. Even nationalist leaders who came from rural ayan families built their following among the urban middle classes. In contrast to India, where lawyers predominated in the nationalist leadership, in Egypt, journalists (a number of them educated in France) led the way.

In the 1890s and early 1900s, numerous newspapers in Arabic (and to a lesser extent French and English) vied to expose the mistakes of the British and the corruption of the khedival regime. Egyptian writers also attacked the British for their racist arrogance and their monopolization of well-paying positions in the Egyptian bureaucracy. Like their Indian counterparts, Egyptian critics argued that these could just as well have been filled by university-educated Egyptians. In the 1890s, the first nationalist party was formed. But again in contrast to India, where the Congress party dominated the nationalist movement from the outset, a variety of rival parties proliferated in Egypt. There were three main alternatives by 1907, but none could be said to speak for the great majority of the Egyptians, who were illiterate, poorly paid, and largely ignored urban laborers and rural farmers.

In the years before the outbreak of World War I in 1914, heavy-handed British repression on several occasions put down student riots or retaliated for assassination attempts against high British and Turco-Egyptian officials. Despite the failure of the nationalist parties to unite or build a mass base in the decades before the war, the extent of the hostility felt by the Egyptian masses was demonstrated by the **Dinshawai incident** in 1906. This confrontation between the British and their Egyptian subjects exemplified the racial arrogance displayed by most of the European colonizers. Though the incident at Dinshawai was seemingly a small clash resulting in only limited numbers of fatalities, the excessive British response to it did much to undermine whatever support remained for their continued presence in Egypt.

Most Egyptian villages raised large numbers of pigeons, which served as an important supplement to the meager peasant diet. Over the years, some of the British had turned the hunting of the pigeons of selected villages into a holiday pastime. A party of British officers on leave was hunting the pigeons of the village of Dinshawai in the Nile delta when they accidentally shot the wife of the prayer leader of the local mosque. The angry villagers mobbed the greatly outnumbered shooting party, which in panic fired on the villagers. Both the villagers and the British soldiers suffered casualties in the clashes that followed. In reprisal for the death of one of the officers, the British summarily hung four of the villagers. Though the actual hanging was not photographed, the building of the scaffolding was captured in a photo (see Figure 28.4). The British also ordered that other villagers connected to the incident be publicly flogged or sentenced to varying terms of hard labor.

The harsh British reprisals aroused a storm of protest in the Egyptian press and among the nationalist parties. Some Egyptian leaders later recounted how the incident convinced them that cooperation with the British was totally unacceptable and fixed their resolve to agitate for an end to Egypt's occupation. Popular protests in several areas, and the emergence of ayan support for the nationalist cause, also suggested the possibility of building a mass base for anti-British agitation. More than anything else, the incident at Dinshawai had galvanized support for popular protest across the communal and social boundaries that had so long divided the peoples of Egypt.

By 1913, the British had been sufficiently intimidated by the rising tide of Egyptian nationalism to grant a constitution and representation in a parliament elected indirectly by the men of wealth and influence. World War I and the British declaration of martial law put a temporary end to nationalist agitation. But, as in India, the war unleashed forces in Egypt that could not be stopped and that would soon lead to the revival of the drive for independence with even greater strength than before.

War and Nationalist Movements in the Middle East

In the years after World War I, resistance to European colonial domination, which had been confined largely to Egypt in the prewar years, spread to much of the rest of the Middle East. Having sided with the

Figure 28.4 *This photograph, probably taken without the knowledge of the British authorities, shows the construction of the gallows that were used to hang the four peasants who were executed in reprisal for the attacks on British soldiers at Dinshawai in 1906. The Dinshawai incident exemplified the colonizers' tendency to overreact to any sign of overt resistance on the part of the colonized.*

Central Powers in the war, the Turks now shared in their defeat. The Ottoman Empire disappeared from history, as Britain and France carved up the Arab portions that had revolted against the Young Turk regime during the war. Italy and Greece attacked the Turkish rump of the empire around Constantinople and in Anatolia (Asia Minor) with the intent of sparking a partition of these areas in concert with the other Entente allies. But a skilled military commander, Mustafa Kemal or **Ataturk,** had emerged for the Turkish officer corps during the war years. Ataturk rallied the Turkish forces and gradually drove back the Greek armies intent on colonizing the Turkish homeland.

By 1923, an independent Turkish republic had been established, but at the cost of the expulsion of tens of thousands of ethnic Greeks. As an integral part of the effort to establish a viable Turkish nation, Ataturk launched a sweeping program of reforms. Many of the often radical changes his government introduced in the 1920s and 1930s were modeled on Western precedents, including a new Latin alphabet,

women's suffrage, and introduction, and criticism of, the veil. But in important ways his efforts to secularize and develop Turkey also represented the culmination of transformations made under the Ottomans over the preceding century (see Chapter 26).

With Turkish rule in the Arab heartlands ended by defeat in the war, Arab nationalists in Beirut, Damascus, and Baghdad turned to face the new threat presented by the victorious Entente powers, France and Britain. Betraying promises to preserve Arab independence that the British had made in 1915 and early 1916, French and British forces occupied much of the Middle East in the years after the war. **Hussein,** the sherif of Mecca, had used these promises to convince the Arabs to rise in support of Britain's war against the Turks, despite the fact that the latter were fellow Muslims. Consequently, the allies' postwar violation of these pledges humiliated and deeply angered Arabs throughout the Middle East. The occupying European powers faced stiff resistance from the Arabs in each of the **mandates** they carved out in Syria, Iraq, and Lebanon under the auspices of the League of Nations. Nationalist movements in these countries gained ground during the 1920s and 1930s. The Arabs' sense of humiliation and anger was greatly intensified by the disposition of Palestine, where British occupation was coupled with promises of a Jewish homeland.

The fact that the British had appeared to promise Palestine, for which they received a League of Nations mandate in 1922, to both the Jewish **Zionists** and the Arabs during the war greatly complicated an already confused situation. Despite repeated assurances to Hussein and other Arab leaders that they would be left in control of their own lands after the war, Lord Balfour, the British foreign secretary, promised prominent Zionist leaders in 1917 that his government would promote the establishment of a Jewish homeland in Palestine after the war. This pledge, the **Balfour Declaration,** fed existing Zionist aspirations for the Hebrew people to return to their ancient Middle Eastern lands of origin, which had been nurtured by the Jews of the diaspora for millennia. In the decades before the First World War, these dreams led to the formation of a number of organizations. Some of these were dedicated to promoting Jewish emigration to Palestine; others were committed to the eventual establishment of a Jewish state there.

These early moves were made in direct response to the persecution of the Jews of eastern Europe in the last decades of the 19th century. Particularly vicious *pogroms,* or violent assaults on the Jewish communities of Russia and Romania in the 1860s and 1870s, convinced Jewish intellectuals such as **Leon Pinsker** that assimilation of the Jews into, or even acceptance by, Christian European nations was impossible. Pinsker and other thinkers called for a return to the Holy Land. Like-minded individuals founded Zionist organizations, such as the Society for the Colonization of Israel, to promote Jewish migration to Palestine in the last decades of the 19th century. Until World War I, the numbers of Jews returning to Palestine were small—in the tens of thousands—though Zionist communities were established on lands purchased in the area.

Until the late 1890s, the Zionist effort was generally opposed by Jews in Germany, France, and other parts of western Europe who enjoyed citizenship and extensive civil rights. In addition, many in these communities had grown prosperous and powerful in their adopted lands. But a major defection to the Zionists

occurred in 1894. **Theodor Herzl,** an established Austrian journalist, was stunned by French mobs shouting "Death to the Jews" as they taunted the hapless army officer **Alfred Dreyfus.** Dreyfus was a French Jew who had been falsely accused of passing military secrets to the Germans. His subsequent mistreatment, including exile to the infamous penal colony on Devil's Island, became the flashpoint for years of bitter debate between the left and right in France. Soon after this incident in 1897, Herzl and a number of other prominent, western European Jews joined with Jewish leaders from eastern Europe to form the **World Zionist Organization.** As Herzl made clear in his writings, the central aim of this increasingly well-funded organization was to promote Jewish migration to and settlement in Palestine until a point was reached when a Zionist state could be established in the area. Herzl's nationalist ambitions, as well as his indifference to the Arabs already living in the area, were captured in the often-quoted view of one of his close associates that Palestine was "a land without people for a people [the Jews] without a land."

Lord Balfour's promises to the Zionists and the British takeover of Palestine struck the Arabs as a double betrayal of wartime assurances that Arab support for the Entente powers against the Turks would guarantee them independence after the war. This sense of betrayal was a critical source of the growing hostility the Arabs felt toward Jewish emigration to Palestine and their purchase of land in the area. Rising Arab opposition convinced many British officials, especially those who actually administered Palestine, to severely curtail the rather open-ended pledges that had been made to the Zionists during the war. This shift led in turn to Zionist mistrust of British policies and open resistance to them. It also fed the Zionists' determination to build up their own defenses against the increasingly violent Arab resistance to the Jewish presence in Palestine. But British attempts to limit Jewish emigration and settlement were not matched by efforts to encourage, through education and consultation, the emergence of strong leadership among the Arab population of Palestine. Consequently, in the critical struggles and diplomatic maneuvers of the 1930s and 1940s, the Arabs of Palestine were rarely able to speak for themselves. They were represented by Arab leaders from neighboring lands, who did not always understand Palestinian needs and desires. These non-Palestinian spokespersons also often acted more in the interests of Syrian or Lebanese Arabs than those of the Christian and Muslim Arab communities in Palestine.

Revolt in Egypt, 1919

Because Egypt was already occupied by the British when the war broke out, and it had been formally declared a protectorate in 1914, it was not included in the promises made by the British to the sherif Hussein. As a result, the anticolonial struggle in Egypt was rooted in earlier agitation and the heavy toll the war had taken on the Egyptian people, particularly the peasantry. During the war, the defense of the Suez Canal was one of the top priorities for the British. To guard against possible Muslim uprisings in response to Turkish calls for a holy war, martial law was declared soon after hostilities began. Throughout the war, large contingents of Entente and empire forces were garrisoned in Egypt. These created a heavy drain on the increasingly scarce food supplies of the area. Forced labor and confiscations by the military of the precious draft animals of the peasantry also led to widespread discontent. As the war dragged on, this unrest was further inflamed by spiraling inflation as well as by food shortages and even starvation in some areas.

By the end of the war, Egypt was ripe for revolt. Mass discontent strengthened the resolve of the educated nationalist elite to demand a hearing at Versailles, where the victorious Allies were struggling to reach a postwar settlement. When a delegation (*wafd* in Arabic) of Egyptian leaders was denied permission to travel to France to put the case for Egyptian self-determination to the peacemakers at Versailles, most Egyptian leaders resigned from the government and called for mass demonstrations. What followed shocked even the most confident British officials. Student-led riots touched off outright insurrection over much of Egypt. Especially noteworthy among the demonstrators were large numbers of women, some of whom were from westernized households but joined the majority of women participating by wearing veils and long robes as a sign of their liberation from British cultural domination. At one point, Cairo was cut off from the outside world, and much of the countryside was hostile territory for the occupying power. Though the British army was able, at the cost of scores of deaths, to restore control, it was clear that some hearing had to be given to Egyptian demands.

The emergence of the newly formed **Wafd party** under its hard-driving leader **Sa'd Zaghlul** provided the nationalists with both a focus for unified action and a mass base that far excelled any they had attracted in the prewar decades.

When a special British commission of inquiry into the causes of the upheaval in Egypt met with widespread civil disobedience and continuing violent opposition, it recommended that the British begin negotiations for an eventual withdrawal from Egypt. Years of bargaining followed, which led to a highly qualified independence for the Egyptians. British withdrawal occurred in stages, beginning in 1922 and culminating in the British withdrawal to the Suez Canal zone in 1936. But though they pulled out of Egypt proper, the khedival regime was preserved and the British reserved the right to reoccupy Egypt should it be threatened by a foreign aggressor.

Though they had won a significant degree of political independence, the Egyptian leaders of the Wafd party, as well as its rivals in the Liberal Constitutionalist and Union parties, did little to relieve the increasing misery of the great majority of the Egyptian people. Most Egyptian politicians regarded the winning of office as an opportunity to increase their own and their families' fortunes. Many politicians from ayan households and from the professional and merchant classes used their influence and growing wealth to amass huge estates, which were worked by landless tenants and laborers. Locked in personal and interparty quarrels, as well as the ongoing contest with the khedival regime for control of the government, few political leaders had the time or inclination to push for the land reforms and public works projects that the peasantry so desperately needed.

The utter social bankruptcy of the 40 years of nationalist political dominance that preceded the military coup and social revolution led by Gamal Abdul Nasser in 1952 is suggested by some revealing statistics compiled by the United Nations in the early 1950s. By that time, nearly 70 percent of Egypt's cultivable land was owned by six percent of the population. Some 12,000 families alone controlled 37 percent of the farmland. As for the mass of the people, 98 percent of the peasants were illiterate, malnutrition was chronic among both the urban and rural population, and an estimated 95 percent of rural Egyptians suffered from eye diseases. Such was the legacy of the very unrevolutionary process of decolonization in Egypt.

In Depth

Women in Asian and African Nationalist Movements

One important but often neglected dimension of the liberation struggles that Asian and African peoples waged against their colonial overlords was the emergence of a stratum of educated, articulate, and politically active women in most colonial societies. In this process, the educational opportunities provided by the European colonizers often played as vital a role as they had in the formation of male leadership in nationalist movements. Missionary girls' schools were confined in the early stages of European involvement in Africa and Asia to the daughters of low-class or marginal social groups. But by the end of the 19th century these schools had become quite respectable for women from the growing westernized business and professional classes. In fact, in many cases, some degree of Western education was essential if westernized men were to find wives with whom they could share their career concerns and intellectual pursuits.

The seemingly insurmountable barriers that separated westernized Asian and African men from their traditional—and thus usually without formal education—wives became a stock theme in the novels and short stories of the early nationalist era. This concern was perhaps best exemplified by the works of Rabindranath Tagore. The problem was felt so acutely by the first generation of Indian nationalist leaders that many took up the task of teaching their wives English and Western philosophy and literature at home. Thus, for many upper-class Asian and African women, colonization proved a liberating force. This trend was often offset by the male-centric nature of colonial education and the domestic focus of much of the curriculum in women's schools.

Although women played a small role in the early, elitist stages of Asian and African nationalist movements, they frequently became more and more prominent as the early study clubs and political associations reached out to build a mass base. In India, women who had been exposed to Western education and European ways, such as Tagore's famous heroine in the novel *The Home and the World*, came out of seclusion and took up supporting roles, though they were still usually behind the scenes. Gandhi's campaign to supplant imported, machine-made British cloth with homespun Indian cloth, for example, owed much of whatever success it had to female spinners and weavers. As nationalist leaders moved their anti-colonial campaigns into the streets, women became involved in mass demonstrations. Throughout the 1920s and 1930s, Indian women braved the *lathi*, or billy club, assaults of the Indian police; suffered the indignities of imprisonment; and launched their own newspapers and lecture campaigns to mobilize female support for the nationalist struggle.

In Egypt, the British made special note of the powerful effect that the participation of both veiled women and more westernized upper-class women had on mass demonstrations in 1919 and the early 1920s. These outpourings of popular support did much to give credibility to the Wafd party's demands for British withdrawal. In both India and Egypt, female nationalists addressed special appeals to British and American suffragettes to support their peoples' struggles for political and social liberation. In India in particular, their causes were advanced by feminists such as the English champion of Hinduism, Annie Besant, who became a major figure in the nationalist movement before and after World War I.

When African nationalism became a popularly supported movement in the post–World War II period, women, particularly the outspoken and fearless market women in west Africa, emerged as a major political force. In settler colonies, such as Algeria and Kenya, where violent revolt proved necessary to bring down deeply entrenched colonial regimes, women took on the dangerous tasks of messengers, bomb carriers, and guerrilla fighters. As Frantz Fanon argued decades ago, and as was later beautifully dramatized in the film *The Battle of Algiers*, this transformation was particularly painful for women who had been in seclusion right up to the time of the revolutionary upsurge. The cutting of their hair, as well as the wearing of lipstick and Western clothes, often alienated them from their fathers and brothers, who equated such practices with prostitution.

In many cases, women's participation in struggles for the political liberation of their people was paralleled by campaigns for female rights in societies that, as we have seen, were dominated by males. Upper-class Egyptian women founded newspapers and educational associations that pushed for a higher age of marriage, educational opportunities for women, and an end to seclusion and veiling. Indian women took up many of these causes and also developed programs to improve hygiene and employment opportunities for lower-caste women. These early efforts, as well as the prominent place of women in nationalist struggles, had much to do with the granting of basic civil rights to women. These included suffrage and legal equality, which were key features of the constitutions of many newly independent Asian and African nations. The great majority of women in the new states of Africa and Asia have yet to enjoy most of these rights. Yet their inclusion in constitutions and post-independence laws provides crucial backing for the struggles for women's liberation in the nations of the postcolonial world.

Questions: Why might missionary education for women in the colonies have stressed domestic skills? In what ways do you think measures to "modernize" colonial societies were oriented to males? Can you think of women who have been or are major political figures in contemporary Africa and Asia? Why have there not been more? What sorts of traditional constraints hamper the efforts of women to achieve economic and social equality and major political roles in newly independent nations?

The Beginnings of the Liberation Struggle in Africa

Most of Africa had come under European colonial rule only in the decades before the outbreak of World War I. Nonetheless, precolonial missionary efforts had produced small groups of Western-educated Africans in parts of west and south central Africa by the end of the 19th century. Like their counterparts in India, most Western-educated Africans were staunchly loyal to their British and French overlords during the First World War. With the backing of both Western-educated Africans and the traditional rulers, the British and especially the French were able to draw on their African possessions for manpower and raw materials throughout the war. But this reliance took its toll on their colonial domination in the long run. In addition to local rebellions in response to the forcible recruitment of African soldiers and laborers, the war effort seriously disrupted newly colonized African societies. African merchants and farmers suffered from shipping shortages and the sudden decline in demand for crops, such as cocoa. African villagers were not happy to go hungry so that their crops could feed the armies of the allies. As Lord Lugard, an influential colonial administrator, pointed out, the desperate plight of the British and French also forced them to teach tens of thousands of Africans:

how to kill white men, around whom [they had] been taught to weave a web of sanctity of life. [They] also know how to handle bombs and Lewis guns and Maxims … and [they have] seen the white men budge when [they have] stood fast. Altogether [they have] acquired much knowledge that might be put to uncomfortable use someday.

The fact that the Europeans kept few of the promises of better jobs and public honors, which they had made during the war to induce young Africans to enlist in the armed forces or serve as colonial administrators, contributed a good deal to the unrest of the postwar years. This was particularly true of the French colonies, where opportunities for political organization, much less protest, were severely constricted before, during, and after the war. Major strikes and riots broke out repeatedly after the war. In the British colonies, where there was considerably more tolerance for political organization, there were also strikes and a number of outright rebellions. Throughout colonized Africa, protest intensified in the 1930s in response to the economic slump brought on by the Great Depression.

Though Western-educated politicians did not link up with urban workers or peasants in most African colonies until the 1940s, disenchanted members of the emerging African elite began to organize in the 1920s and 1930s. In the early stages of this process, charismatic African American political figures, such as **Marcus Garvey** and **W. E. B. DuBois**, had a major impact on emerging African nationalist leaders. In the 1920s, much effort was placed into attempts to arouse all-Africa loyalties and build **pan-African** organizations. The fact that the leadership of these organizations was mainly African American and West Indian, and that delegates from colonized areas in Africa itself faced very different challenges under different colonial overlords, had much to do with the fact that pan-Africanism proved unworkable. But its well-attended conferences, especially the early ones in Paris, did much to arouse anticolonial sentiments among Western-educated Africans.

By the mid-1920s, nationalists from French and British colonies were pretty much going separate ways. Because of restrictions in the colonies, and because small but well-educated groups of Africans were represented in the French parliament, French-speaking west Africans concentrated their organizational and ideological efforts in Paris in this period. The **négritude** literary movement nurtured by these exiles did much to combat the racial stereotyping that had so long held the Africans in psychological bondage to the Europeans. Writers such as the Senegalese poet **Léopold Sédar Senghor** (Figure 28.5), Léon Damas from French Guiana, and the West Indian Aimé Césaire celebrated the beauty of black skin and the African physique. They argued that in the precolonial era, African peoples had built societies where women were freer, old people were bet-

Figure 28.5 *In the post–World War I era, African and African American intellectuals such as Léopold Sédar Senghor (pictured here), W. E. B. DuBois, and Aimé Césaire explored in their writings the ravages wrought by the centuries of suffering inflicted on the people of Africa by the slave trade and the forced diaspora that resulted. These intellectuals worked to affirm the genius of African culture and African patterns of social interaction.*

ter cared for, and attitudes toward sex were far healthier than they had ever been in the so-called civilized West.

Except in settler colonies, such as Kenya and Rhodesia, Western-educated Africans in British territories were given greater opportunities to build political associations within Africa itself. In the early stages of this process, African leaders sought to nurture organizations that linked the emerging nationalists of different British colonies, such as the National Congress of British West Africa. By the late 1920s, these pan-colony associations gave way to political groupings concerned primarily with issues within individual colonies such as Sierra Leone, the Gold Coast, or Nigeria. After the British granted some representation in colonial advisory councils to Western-educated Africans in this period, emphasis on colony-specific political mobilization became even more pronounced. Though most of these early political organizations were too loosely structured to be considered true political parties, there was a growing recognition by some leaders of the need to build a mass base. In the 1930s a new generation of leaders made much more vigorous attacks on the policies of the British. Through their newspapers and political associations, they also reached out to ordinary African villagers and the young, who had hitherto played little role in nationalist agitation. Their efforts to win a mass following would come to full fruition only after European divisions plunged humanity into a second global war.

 GLOBAL CONNECTIONS: World War and Global Upheavals

In a multitude of ways the First World War set the global historical agenda for the 20th century. The long war, particularly the horrific and increasingly senseless slaughter in the trenches, did much to undermine Europe's prewar position of global dominance. The war severely disrupted Europe's economy and bolstered already emerging rivals, especially the United States and Japan, for preeminence in world trade and finance. Over much of Europe, the hardships endured by the civilian populations on the home front reignited long-standing class tensions. In Russia, but also elsewhere in east central Europe, growing social divisions sparked full-scale revolutions. In Britain, France, Germany, and other liberal democracies in western Europe, labor parties, some socialist or communist, emerged with much greater power after the conflict. Many shared power, both in coalitions with center parties or in their own right in the 1920s and 1930s. The war saw major changes in gender roles in spheres ranging from employment and marriage to sex and fashion. It also generated growing challenges to the rigid racial hierarchies that had dominated both scientific theorizing and popular attitudes in the decades leading up to the conflict.

The victorious Entente allies, especially the British and French but also the Belgians and Japanese, managed to hold on to, and in fact enlarge, their empires. But the hardships endured by colonized peoples and the empty promises made by their desperate colonial overloads during the war gave great impetus to resistance to their empires that spread from the Middle East and India to Vietnam and China. For African and Asian intellectuals at least, the psychological advantage that racial thinking and scientific and technological superiority had given the Europeans began to dissipate. The essential cooperation of nationalist leaders like Gandhi gave them and their ideologies of liberation access to ever larger numbers of colonized peoples. In the postwar decades, mass civil disobedience campaigns in India and Egypt, and peasant risings in Vietnam and China, established the protest techniques and demands that would ultimately bring down all of the European colonial empires. The revolutionary regime in Russia, which had come to power as a direct consequence of the war, actively abetted efforts to advance the cause of decolonization around the world. Two other industrial nations whose power had been greatly enhanced by the war, the United States and Japan, sought in different ways both to supplant the European colonizers and replace them as the economic and political power centers of the 20th century.

Further Readings

There is a vast literature on the origins of the First World War. A somewhat dated, but still very readable, introduction is available in Laurence Lafore's *The Long Fuse* (1965).

James Joll's *The Origins of the First World War* (1984) includes a much fuller treatment of the many and highly contested interpretations of the causes of the conflict. Fritz Fisher's *Germany's Aims in the First World War* (1967) stirred great controversy by arguing that Germany's leaders purposely provoked the conflict, while Paul Kennedy's *The Rise of the Anglo-German Antagonism, 1860–1914* (1980) covers one of the key rivalries and especially the naval race with a good deal more balance. The impact of colonial disputes on the coming of the war is concisely and convincingly treated in L. F. C. Turner, *Origins of the First World War* (1970).

Of the many general histories of the war on land and sea, the more reliable and readable include *The World in the Crucible, 1914–1919* (1984) by Bernadotte Schmitt and Harold Vedeler, and most recently John Keegan's *The First World War* (1999). Marc Ferro's *The Great War* (1973) remains one of the most stimulating analyses of the conduct of the war. Three of the most successful attempts to understand the war from the participants' perspectives are Paul Fussell's *The Great War and Modern Memory* (1975) and John Cruickshank's *Variations on Catastrophe* (1982), which draw on literary works and memoirs, and Richard Cork's magisterial exploration of artistic images of the conflict in *A Bitter Truth: Avant-Garde Art and the Great War* (1994). Some of the better accounts by the participants include Erich Remarque's classic *All Quiet on the Western Front* (1929); Frederic Manning's *The Middle Parts of Fortune* (1929); Vera Brittain's *Testament of Youth* (1933); and Wilfred Owen's *Poems* (1920; reprinted as *The Collected Poems of Wilfred Owen*, 1964).

The disasters at Versailles and some of their consequences are also chronicled in numerous books and articles. Two of the most readable are Harold Nicholson's *Peace Making, 1919* (1965) and Charles L. Mee Jr.'s *The End of Order: Versailles, 1919* (1980). Samples of varying views on the many controversies surrounding the conference can be found in Ivo J. Lederer, ed., *The Versailles Settlement* (1960). The best book on the wider ramifications of the decisions made at or in connection with the conference is Arno Mayer's *Politics and Diplomacy of Peace-Making, 1918–1919* (1967).

A good general historical narrative of the impact of the war on the struggle for Indian independence can be found in Sumit Sarkar's *Modern India, 1885–1947* (1983). The war also figures importantly in the early sections of Mohandas Gandhi's autobiographical *The Story of My Experiments with Truth* (1927). Louis Fischer's *Gandhi* (1950) still yields valuable insights into the personality of one of the great nationalist leaders and the workings of nationalist politics. Judith Brown's studies of Gandhi as a political leader, including *Gandhi's Rise to Power* (1972), and her recent biography of his life and career provide an approach more in tune with current research. The poems and novels of Rabindranath Tagore yield wonderful insights into the social and cultural life of India through much of this era.

P. J. Vatikiotis' *The History of Egypt* (especially the 1985 edition) has excellent sections on the war and early nationalist era in that country. Interesting, but often less reliable, is Jacques Berque's *Colonialism and Nationalism in Egypt* (1972). Leila Ahmed's *Women and Gender in Islam* (1992) has excellent chapters on the role of women at various stages of the nationalist struggle and in the post-independence era. George Antonius' *The Arab Awakening* (1946) is essential reading on British double dealing in the Middle East during the war, especially as this affected the Palestine question. Alternative perspectives are provided by Aaron Cohen's *The Arabs and Israel* (1970). David Fromkin's *A Peace to End All Peace* (1989) provides a more recent and superb account of wartime and postwar events in the Middle East as a whole.

The early stages of the nationalist struggle, including the war years, in west Africa are well covered by Michael Crowder's *West Africa under Colonial Rule* (1982). A narrative of the history of the First World War as a whole in sub-Saharan Africa can be found in Byron Farwell's *The Great War in Africa* (1986). The continued advance of European colonialism in the Middle East and Africa in the postwar years is analyzed in *France Overseas* (1981) by Christopher Andrew and A. S. Kanya-Forstner.

On the Web

Recent interactive overviews of the Great War and its legacies are provided at http://www.bbc.co.uk/history/war/wwone/index.shtml, http://www.worldwar1.com/index.html and http://www.geocities.com~worldwar1/default.html, and at the Wilfred Owen multimedia archive at http://www.hcu.ox.ac.uk/jtap/. Wilfred Owen joined the British Army to help relieve the suffering of soldiers in the field "directly by leading them as well as an officer can; indirectly, by watching their sufferings that I may speak of them as well as a pleader can." He accomplished both tasks. His life and war poetry are movingly presented at sites such as http://home.tiscali.be/ericlaermans/cultural/owen.html, http://www.rjgeib.com/heroes/owen/owen.html, http://www.pitt.edu/~pugachev/greatwar/owen.html, and http://www.bbc.co.uk/history/3d/trench.shtml, which includes a host of useful links to a wide variety of related subjects, including a virtual tour of a trench. Life in the trenches, including related weapons such as chemical agents, is also explored at http://www.worldwar1.com/. But even this excellent site cannot compare in impact with the personal account of trench warfare found in the diary of Private Donald Fraser of the Canadian Expeditionary Force at http://www.fordham.edu/halsall/mod/1918fraser.html and at http://www.archives.ca/05/0518/05180105/0518010504_e.html, which also provides resources for the study of the battle of Vimy Ridge.

Two of the great battles in the trenches, the Somme and Verdun, are illuminated at http://www.stemnet.nf.ca/beaumont/somme2.htm and http://www.achtungpanzer.com/blitz.htm.

The home fronts of the combatant nations, from food rationing to the impact of the related influenza epidemic, are discussed at http://www.spartacus.schoolnet.co.uk/FWWhome.htm (scroll down to "War and the Home Front").

The text of the Zimmerman Telegram that provided the proximate cause of the U. S. entry into World War I can be found at http://www.firstworldwar.com/source/zimmerman.htm. The role of Canada and Latin American in the war and the war's impact on them are explored at http://www.archives.ca/05/0518_e.html and http://www.worldwar1.com/sfla.htm, respectively. The text of the Treaty of Versailles and many ancillary materials are offered at http://history.acusd.edu/gen/text/versaillestreaty/vercontents.html. A vast collection of other major documents related to the war is offered at http://www.lib.byu.edu/~estu/wwi/ or http://www.ku.edu/~kansite/ww_one.

Colonial and postcolonial discourse that embraces issues such as négritude is the subject of analysis at http://www.postcolonial.org/ (go to Search Tool, enter "négritude" for links on this subject).

Insight into the casual brutality of imperialism that fuelled nationalist revolts can be derived from an account of the Dinshawai incident in Egypt (http://touregypt.net/denshwaymuseum.htm) and the Amritsar massacre in India (http://www.scholars.nus.edu.sg/landow/post/india/history/colonial/massacre.html, http://www.geocities.com/Broadway/Alley/5461/AMRITSAR.htm, and http://lachlan.bluehaze.com.au/churchill/am-man.htm). The African National Congress Party homepage at http://www.anc.org.za/ not only provides current information about the party, but also materials on the freedom struggle in South Africa, such as the life histories, speeches, and writings of African National Congress freedom fighters.

Theodor Herzl's leadership of the early Jewish nationalist movement can be seen from both the Zionist (http://www.israel.org/jspruce/bibliography/hetzl.html) and Palestinian nationalist perspectives (http://www.arab2.com/biography/Arab-Israeli-Conflict.htm).

One of the early leaders of the Indian nationalist movement, Bal Gangadhar Tilak, is briefly examined at http://www.kamat.com/kalranga/itihas/tilak.htm. Mohandas Gandhi's leadership of that movement is explored at http://dwardmac.pitzer.edu/

anarchist_archives/bright/gandhi/Gandhi.html. His famous Salt March (http://www.sscnet.ucla.edu/southasia/History/Gandhi/Dandi.html and http://www.algonet.se/~jviklund/gandhi/ENG.MKG.salt.html) is the subject of a film (http://harappa.com/wall/1930.html). His "Quit India" speech of 1942 is offered at http://www.ibiblio.org/pha/policy/1942/420427a.html. The character of Gandhi's close associate, Jawaharlal Nehru, is offered at http://www.itihaas.com/modern/nehru-profile.html.

The poet laureate of the Indian Independence movement, Rabindranath Tagore, is celebrated at http://www.itihaas.com/modern/tagore-profile.html. A review of the life of Muhammad Ali Jinnah, the Indian Muslim nationalist who led the campaign for the creation of the state of Pakistan and became its first president, is provided at http://www.rediff.com/news/1998/sep/10jinnah.htm, while a short movie made of him delivering one of his key speeches is available at http://www.harappa.com/jinnahmov.html.

CHAPTER 29

THE WORLD IN THE 1920s: CHALLENGES TO EUROPEAN DOMINANCE

The construction of a strong nation built on socialist principles was the message conveyed in public murals after the Mexican Revolution like this one by David Siqueros.

- The Disarray of Western Europe, 1918–1929
- Industrial Societies Outside Europe
- Revolution: The First Waves
- IN DEPTH: A Century of Revolutions
- GLOBAL CONNECTIONS: The 1920s and the World

The 1920s and 1930s are often known as the interwar period. The decades were profoundly shaped by the dislocations of World War I and then the mounting crisis that led to World War II. These were decades of considerable dislocation in the West. Revolutionary regimes in several societies provided another source of change. New, authoritarian political systems were another response to crisis, particularly after the Great Depression, in several parts of the world. All of this occurred even as resistance to European imperialism was mounting.

This chapter focuses on developments in the 1920s but includes three key revolutions that began earlier and fed into this decade. Along with the increasing protests against European colonialism, discussed in Chapter 28, the 1920s were marked by three major patterns. First, western Europe recovered from World War I incompletely, particularly in economics and politics. Cultural creativity was important, and several social developments marked real innovation. But political and economic structures, and European diplomacy as well, rested on shaky foundations.

Outside Europe, growing industrial strength marked the United States and Japan. There were significant changes as well in Canada and Australia. Economic power added to a sense of international competitiveness. Furthermore, though in different ways, political and diplomatic patterns in this wider industrial world raised important new issues. Japan grappled with its political system, the United States with its governmental interactions with the wider world.

Finally, the 1920s saw the ongoing results of a major series of contemporary revolutions in Mexico, Russia, and China. These revolutions had started before the 1920s, but their impact and evolution became clearer in this decade. While the revolutions varied one from the other, they all served to question Western power and key Western assumptions.

Diplomatic Deafness

Relations with the West, including outright protests, took various forms in the 1920s. In India, Gandhi's new nationalist movement built on Hindu traditions while also criticizing the caste system and traditional gender relations—a blend between continuity and change. A new nation in Turkey used a combination of military force and diplomacy. Western powers had planned to divide Turkey among themselves, as they did the rest of the Ottoman Empire. But Turkish nationalists set up an effective army that took over the country, and they then negotiated with the West for recognition. The leading Turkish diplomat, Ismet Inonu, was hard of hearing. To wear out Western officials, he simply turned off his hearing aid during long-winded discussions, reactivating it when his tired colleagues were willing to see things his way. Turkey was recognized, though its relations with Europe continue to be discussed today.

701

1910 C.E.	1920 C.E.
1917 Tsarist regime overthrown in February; Bolshevik revolution in October; Mexican constitution includes revolutionary changes	**1920–1940** Muralist movement in Mexico
1918 Armistice ends World War I in November	**1921** Albert Einstein wins the Nobel Prize; Chinese Communist party founded; Lenin's New Economic Policy in USSR
1919 Versailles conference; Peace of Paris; leftist revolution defeated in Germany; May Fourth movement in China	**1922** Mussolini/fascists seize power in Italy; first commercial radio station in Pittsburgh
	1923–1924 Hyperinflation in Germany
	1923 Defeat of Japanese bill for universal suffrage; Tokyo earthquake
	1927 Charles Lindbergh's solo trans-Atlantic flight; Guomindang (Nationalists) capture north China, purge Communist party
	1927–1928 Stalin pushes the first five-year plan in the Soviet Union, collectivization begins; agricultural slump in United States
	1928–1929 Skyscraper craze in New York

The Disarray of Western Europe, 1918–1929

 The 1920s formed an odd mixture in western Europe and beyond. Wartime dislocations created new, often troubling political and economic patterns. A new political movement, fascism, gained power in Italy. On the other hand, important developments occurred in culture and popular culture. The 1920s also saw significant changes .in east central Europe and also in the United States, Canada, and Australia. Finally, Japan, newly industrial, combined economic advance with political uncertainty; outside the West, its growing economic voice and world power inevitably affected Europe and North America.

World War I quickly shattered the confidence many Europeans had maintained around the turn of the 20th century. The war also caused serious structural damage to the European economy, diplomatic relations among Western states, and political systems in many countries.

Although the ultimate effects of World War I involved Europe's world position, the war also brought tremendous dislocation within Europe. Though some of the damage was quickly repaired, much persisted for the subsequent two decades. The key battlegrounds for four bloody years had been in Europe. The sheer rate of death and maiming, as well

as the frustration of long periods of virtual stalemate, had had a devastating material and psychological impact on the European combatants. More than 10 million Europeans had died. Vast amounts of property had been destroyed. Most governments had failed to tax their populations enough to pay for the war effort—lest they weaken domestic support—so huge debts accumulated, leading to inflationary pressure even before the war was over. Key prewar regimes were toppled when the German emperor abdicated and the Habsburg Empire collapsed.

The Roaring Twenties

Despite all the disruptions, a brief period of stability, even optimism, emerged in the mid-1920s. Diplomatic tensions eased somewhat within Europe, as Germany made some moves to accommodate its reduced position in return for partial relief from war reparations payments. Although Germany refused to accept its new eastern boundaries, it did promise friendship all around. Hopes that the Versailles settlement could be permanent ran so high that an American and a French leader coauthored a treaty outlawing war forever—the **Kellogg-Briand Pact** of 1928, which a number of nations dutifully ratified.

Internal politics also seemed to calm. The war's end and immediate economic dislocations, as well as the impact of the Russian Revolution, had inspired a new political polarization in many western European countries. Many veterans joined groups on the far right that wanted an authoritarian government that would protect national honor; the labor movement on the left split, with a minority wing becoming communist, taking cues from the revolutionary regime in the Soviet Union. Both radical left and radical right scared each other, further complicating parliamentary life. Germany produced an admirable constitution for its new democratic republic, but many groups did not accept it and there were understandable fears for its life. Even Britain, long known for its political stability, saw a major shift as the Labour party replaced the Liberals as the second major political force. Generally, the liberal middle sector of European politics was weakened. Nevertheless, the middle years of the 1920s brought a brief respite, as the extremist groups declined in force.

Economic prosperity buoyed hopes in the middle of the decade. The worst inflationary pressures were resolved at the cost of wiping out the value of savings for many propertied groups. Industrial production boomed, though more markedly in the United States than in western Europe. Mass-consumption standards rose for several years. New products, such as the artificial fiber rayon and radios, spread widely. Household appliances proliferated as technology's impact on daily life reached a new height.

The 1920s also saw a burst of cultural creativity in many parts of the West. Filmmakers experimented for both artistic expression and mass entertainment. Modern artists developed geometrical styles and other innovations, as in Figure 29.1. New forms of architecture and furniture design spread in what was called the "modern" style, as in Figure 29.2. The **cubist movement,** headed by Pablo Picasso, rendered familiar objects as geometrical shapes. Writers and playwrights pioneered new forms, reducing plot lines and often seeking audience involvement in dramas. In retrospect the mood of the 1920s, in terms of high culture and popular culture alike, seemed somewhat frenzied. The defiance of traditional styles—the growing abstraction of modern art and novelists' efforts to capture unconscious impulses over structured plots—attempted to convey some of the menacing tensions beneath the surface of modern life.

Figure 29.1 *Marcel Duchamp, using a modified cubist style, achieved a dramatic visual effect in an approach characteristic of Western art from the 1920s onward.*

Figure 29.2 *The skyscraper, developed first in the United States, became a major expression of artistic innovation and dramatic new structural materials, including novel uses of glass. This Chicago tower was designed by European master Ludwig Mies van der Rohe.*

Important scientific advances continued. In physics, new discoveries about atomic structure would ultimately lead to new weaponry and sources of power. Biologists advanced understanding of genetics. Discoveries complicated older views of an orderly universe, and science became too specialized for ordinary people to grasp. But a sense of progress persisted in this area.

Women, particularly in the middle class, registered important gains. Women's involvement in the labor force during World War I was short-lived, as men pushed them out at war's end. However, postwar legislation granted women suffrage in Britain, Germany, and the United States. Further, prosperity and the declining birth rate gave many women the chance to develop new leisure habits and less restrictive fashions. Women were prominently featured in consumer gains, as in Figure 29.3. Young women in the United States began to date more freely, as a preliminary to courtship. Wives in Britain wrote of new interests in sexual pleasure, while maintaining commitment to marriage. Women began to smoke and drink in public and to enjoy new dance crazes and other leisure activities. Here were developments, like the more general rise of consumerism, that would gain momentum later on. These developments also produced reaction from people who thought women should stay in traditional roles with traditional modesty.

Industrialization continued to advance. The 1920s saw continued gains for assembly-line production and big-business forms. Huge combines developed in key industries, both in Europe and in the United States, and managers learned new ways to coordinate and discipline masses of workers in factories, offices, and sales outlets. Major new product lines developed with artificial fibers like rayon and nylon and other consumer goods.

Fascism in Italy

New signs of political trouble emerged first on the fringes of western Europe. In 1919 a former socialist and (very briefly) a former soldier, **Benito Mussolini,** formed the *fascio di combattimento*, or union for struggle, in Italy. Italian fascists vaguely advocated a corporate state that would replace both capitalism and socialism with a new national unity. They pointed to the need for an aggressive, nationalistic

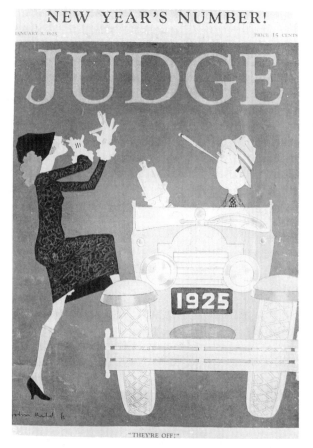

Figure 29.3 *Consumer society, 1920s style: cars, cosmetics, a "new woman," and more open pleasure seeking.*

foreign policy. Above all, fascists worked to seize power by any means and to build a strong state under a strong leader. They violently attacked rival political groups, seeking to promote an atmosphere of chaos.

Fascism had its roots in the late 19th century, with groups disenchanted with liberal, parliamentary systems and with social conflict. Various intellectuals, in many countries, began to urge the need for new, authoritarian leadership and devotion to nationalist values over capitalist profit-seeking and socialist class struggle alike.

Conditions in postwar Italy gave these impulses a huge boost. Nationalists resented the fact that Italy had gained so little new territory in World War I. Veterans often felt abandoned by civilian society, and some thirsted for new action. Labor unrest increased, which convinced some conservatives that new measures were essential against ineffective liberal leadership. The Italian parliament seemed incapable of decisive measures, as political factions jockeyed for personal advantage. In these conditions Mussolini, fascism's leading exponent, could make his mark even with a minority of direct supporters.

Amid growing political divisions and a rising threat from the working-class left, in 1922 the Italian king called on Mussolini to form a new government. Though the fascists themselves had only limited popular support, they seemed the only hope to stem left-wing agitation and parliamentary ineptitude. Once in power, Mussolini eliminated most opposition (Figure 29.4), suspending elections outright in 1926, while seeking greater state direction of the economy and issuing strident propaganda about the glories of military conquest. This first fascist regime moved with some caution, fitting into the briefly hopeful negotiations among European states in the 1920s, but the principles it espoused suggested how far European politics had been unseated from the widespread prewar agreements on parliamentary rule.

The New Nations of East Central Europe

Many of the problems and reactions visible in western Europe after World War I also affected the new nations of east central Europe, though here the challenge of building new political regimes and the predominantly agrarian character of the economy complicated the situation even in the 1920s (see Map 29.1). Most of the new nations looked to western Europe for political inspiration at first, and all were hostile to the new communist regime in the Soviet Union. "Westernization," however, proved difficult, particularly when the West itself was so troubled.

Figure 29.4 *One of the most ominous acts of Mussolini's fascist regime was the burning of books and other literature deemed "subversive."*

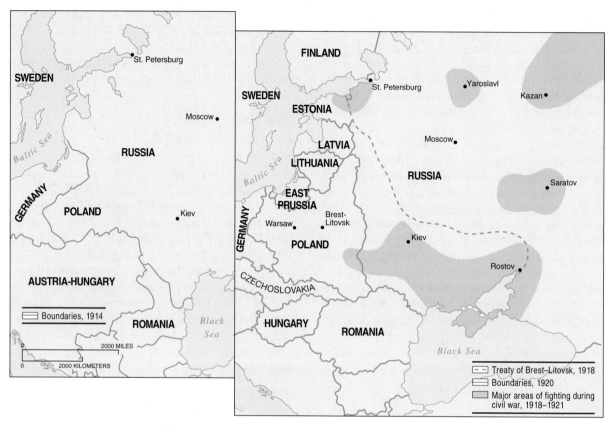

Map 29.1 *Eastern Europe and the Soviet Union, 1919–1939. The Soviet Union regained some territory ceded to Germany in the 1918 peace treaty, but it lost ground to a number of east European states.*

Most of the new nations, from the Baltic states to Yugoslavia, were consumed by nationalist excitement at independence but also harbored intense grievances about territories they had not acquired. Hence there were bitter rivalries among the small eastern European states, which weakened them both diplomatically and economically. Most of the new nations began the interwar period with some form of parliamentary democracy, in imitation of the West, but soon converted to authoritarian rule, either through a dictator (as in Poland) or by a monarch's seizure of new power (as in Yugoslavia, the new nation expanded from Serbia). This political pattern resulted from more underlying social tensions. Most eastern European countries remained primarily agricultural, heavily dependant on sales to western Europe. They were hard hit by the collapse of agricultural prices in the 1920s and then further damaged by the Depression. Furthermore, most countries also refused to undertake serious land reform, despite widely professed intentions. Aristocratic estate owners thus sought desperately to repress peasant movements, which brought them to support authoritarian regimes, which often had vaguely fascist trappings. Peasant land hunger and continued problems of poverty and illiteracy were simply not addressed in most cases.

Industrial Societies Outside Europe

 The 1920s saw important developments in industrial societies outside Europe. Canada and Australia continued political consolidation, while the United States combined economic power with an attempt at political isolation. Japan experienced rapid industrial growth, but domestic politics were unsettled. Industrial expansion outside Europe added to a sense of international competition.

Several former "settler societies" solidified political structures outside Europe (Map 29.2). The participation of Canada, Australia, and New Zealand in World War I, at Britain's side, furthered the idea of a commonwealth, and an imperial conference in 1921 agreed that the self-governing Dominions should be considered coequals with Britain in international affairs. A 1926 resolution defined the Dominions as "autonomous communities" within the British Empire, equal in status, in no way subordinate one to another in any aspect of their domestic or external affairs, though united by a common allegiance to the (British) crown, and freely associated as members of the British Commonwealth of Nations. British representation in the Dominions, aside from the symbolic

monarchy, consisted of a governor-general with no real authority.

Canada was developing not only its national politics but also an increasingly vibrant economy during the early years of the 20th century. Completion of the Canadian Pacific Railway by 1905 spurred rapid development in the western prairie provinces. Exploitation of mineral and forest resources joined with abundant production of wheat, as Canada exported food widely to Europe, as well as minerals and wood pulp to various areas, particularly the United States. Canadian development was marked also by rapid immigration, particularly from eastern Europe. Between 1903 and 1914, 2.7 million immigrants entered Canada, and as late as 1941, 40 percent of the population of the prairie provinces was of central or eastern European origin. French Canadians, centered in the province of Quebec, also increased their representation through one of the highest birth rates in the world, becoming a full quarter of the total Canadian population.

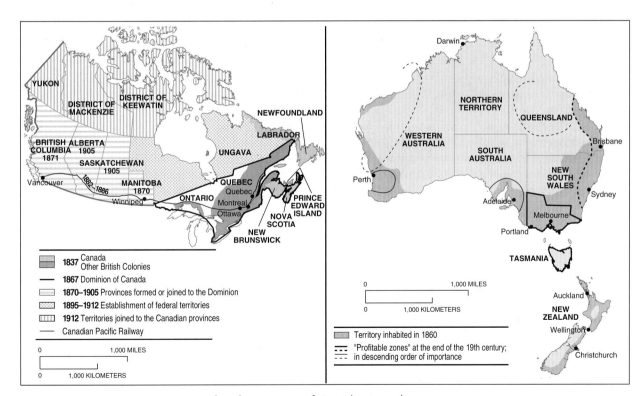

Map 29.2 *From Dominions to Nationhood: Formation of Canada, Australia, and New Zealand*

Australia's independence in 1901 brought important developments in parliamentary institutions early in the 20th century. Like Canada, the new nation consisted of a federation of provinces. More than Canada, Australia strongly emphasized leadership in the field of social legislation. A strong trade union movement prompted increasing attention to government-sponsored arbitration procedures. The government was also active in economic planning, for the country had limited arable land but depended heavily on agricultural exports. Government ownership included railways and shipping lines, banks, and power plants. Participation in World War I gave Australia a new international role and a new sense of national pride. Rapid immigration contributed to a vigorous economy that was, however, severely damaged by the 1930s Depression.

The Rise of the American Colossus

Outside the evolving British Commonwealth, the United States served as a final extension of many aspects of Western society. Because of its size, population, and economic strength, the growing international role of the United States had even greater significance than the emergence of Canada, Australia, and New Zealand.

The United States was late entering World War I, reflecting strong traditions of isolation. The war catapulted the United States into a leadership position, and the nation guided many of the provisions of the Versailles treaty. But the U.S. Senate rejected the treaty, and the United States retreated into an isolationist policy between the world wars, leavened only by participation in international economic and disarmament conferences. Interventionism in Latin America continued, though by the 1930s the United States tried to improve its relations with its southern neighbors and attempted to substitute negotiation for big-stick diplomacy. Vigorous hostility to socialism also marked the United States, with a major "red scare" in reaction to the Russian Revolution. In contrast even to western Europe, labor politics receded.

The U.S. presence in world affairs accelerated during the 1920s, however, in the economic and cultural realms. After a brief postwar readjustment, the U.S. economy boomed during the 1920s. Industrial production doubled between 1921 and 1929. Republican administrations fostered business growth through high tariffs and low taxes on corporations and personal incomes. Many corporations merged into larger and more efficient conglomerates, and technological innovations spawned an increasing array of consumer goods for U.S. and world markets. Within the United States a new level of consumerism developed, as growing numbers of the middle class bought automobiles and electric appliances. Radios and telephones spread even more widely. Humbler products, such as soap and cosmetics, won a growing mass market, and advertising reached new audiences to spur demand. Credit buying expanded, with enhanced reliance on installment buying. A durable new youth culture emerged, as suggested in Figure 29.5.

Besides their sheer growth and their involvement in mass consumerism, U.S. corporations were innovators. Many corporations set up research and development programs, which helped generate new product lines, such as rayon and nylon—artificial fibers that soon rivaled silk in popularity. Organization of work systems combined with new technology to boost productivity. Henry Ford had introduced the assembly line in 1913, using conveyor belts to move automobile assembly through various routine stages, with semi-skilled workers continuously repeating small tasks as the products moved toward completion. Engineers in the United States promoted efficiency studies, which treated workers like additional machinery to be rationalized as fully as possible. During the 1920s industrial psychologists found additional ways to boost output, studying the impact of piped-in music, for example, in unconsciously prompting workers to speed up their pace. Such methods were widely imitated abroad, not only in western Europe but also in the Soviet Union. With growing exports of grain and manufactured products, increasing international investment, and literal world leadership in organizational innovation, the international economic role of the United States gained ground steadily, in marked disparity to its isolationist diplomacy.

The nation also increasingly exported its culture, as it began to give as well as to receive in this vital area. Jazz quickly caught on in Europe; U.S. artists and writers participated in an increasingly internationalized Western culture. But it was in the area of popular culture that the United States made it greatest mark. As the first mass-consumer society, the United States led the way in a number of marketing and advertising developments. The dime store, for

Figure 29.5 *The interwar decades saw the rise of a succession of dance crazes. Adults as well as young people would be caught up in dancing to the new big bands.*

example, spread to England and was copied in France and Germany as a major outlet for low-cost mass merchandise. Hollywood became the world capital of the popular movie industry during the 1920s. Movies quickly began to play a vital role in U.S. culture, with 40 million viewers attending a film at least once a week in 1922; by 1929 that number had risen to 100 million. Hollywood stars—some born in Europe, such as Charlie Chaplin, Greta Garbo, and Rudolph Valentino—became symbols of comedy or sexuality throughout the Western world and beyond. Just as Britain had served as an international source of new sports in the later 19th century, so the United States now led in provision of commercial spectacles. Even its dance crazes, such as the Charleston, quickly spread to European centers, in an increasingly fad-conscious culture.

Japan and Its Empire

Japan was decidedly not a Western nation, either by origin or adoption. However, it had become an industrial power and replaced its traditional, feudal government with a regime in which ministers appointed by the emperor combined, sometimes uneasily, with a parliament. Japan's government in 1900 had resembled that of Germany, except that the vote was much more restricted. Like Germany and other Western nations, Japan would see its new political institutions tested by war and the Depression; like Germany and Italy its commitment to the parliamentary form would decline under this test. In the 1930s Japan turned to a more adventurous foreign policy in response to economic challenge and political change—again, like many nations in the West.

The interwar years were not simply a time of crisis for Japan, however. During the 1920s, particularly, new cultural developments, an expanding economy, and a brief commitment to liberal democracy produced important currents as well—ones that would be called on after World War II.

Agricultural productivity improved steadily, led by progressive landlords who introduced fertilizers and new equipment. Rice production more than doubled between the 1880s and the 1930s. Modern industry advanced more slowly, though it passed well beyond the pilot phase of the late 19th century. Great industrial combines—the *zaibatsu*—sponsored rapid expansion in such fields as shipbuilding, usually relying heavily on tight links with the government bureaucracy, but there were daring individual entrepreneurs as well. Between 1905 and 1918 Japan enjoyed a considerable industrial boom, with rapid advances not only in light industries, such as silk, but also in electrical power, iron, and coal. Japanese life expectancy began to improve, fueled by a higher standard of living. A popular consumer culture emerged, at least in the cities, as workers began to attend movies and read newspapers. Education advanced rapidly, with primary-school attendance universal in the relevant age groups by 1925. Enrollments in secondary schools and technical colleges swelled, improving the nation's capacity to assimilate the newer Western technologies.

Limits on Japanese economic advance included vulnerability to economic conditions abroad. Because Japan exported relatively few items to the West but continued to require considerable imports of raw materials, including fuels and sophisticated equipment, a slump in demand for a product such as silk cloth could be disastrous. In this sense Japan bore some resemblance to dependant economies in the world, despite industrial progress. Population growth was another burden, or at least a mixed blessing. Japan's population soared from 30 million in 1868 to 45 million in 1900 and then to 73 million by 1940. This was a tribute to agricultural advance, as the size of the farm population remained constant, and it facilitated a low-wage industrial economy. It also restricted further improvements in the standard of living and created considerable social dislocation in the crowded, migrant-filled cities. Periodic protests through strikes, demonstration, and some socialist agitation were met with vigorous police response.

Japan experienced ongoing difficulties in assimilating a generally accepted political structure—difficulties that had not been resolved during the first decades of the 20th century. Military leaders began to take a growing role in setting general diplomatic policy from the mid-1920s onward, at the expense of the civilian parties and politicians. Japan's oligarchic political structure, in which elite groups negotiated with one another for appropriate policy rather than fully yielding to any single agency, such as parliament, permitted this kind of realignment. From the Meiji period onward, military leaders, though largely weaned from the samurai tradition, had remained separate from the civilian bureaucracy. They were trained in separate schools and regarded themselves as true guardians of the modern Japanese state as well as older traditions. They reported not to civilian authority but directly to the emperor. Like military leaders in the West during the 1920s but with greater vigor, they resented what they regarded as the selfishness and accommodation to special interests of the political parties, as the latter increasingly resorted to mass political campaigns and vote-getting strategies. Reduction of military budgets during the 1920s hit military leaders hard, and army prestige declined to the point that officers wore civilian clothing when off base. In essence Japan experimented during the 1920s with a liberal political pattern, which seemed to give primacy to party maneuverings and electoral appeals but which also antagonized the military (and other conservative elite groups) while failing to subject them to new controls. Voting rights were extended to all adult males, but this did not produce agreement on political forms.

A Balance Sheet

Changes in Europe, the "settler societies," and Japan during the 1920s were complex. Democratic and parliamentary political forms took further root in Germany and in places like Canada. Significant industrial and social change combined with signs of creativity in culture, in both sciences and the arts. On the other hand, challenges to democracy arose in Italy and in much of east central Europe, while Japanese politics became less stable. The United States tried to isolate itself from world politics. Events would soon prove that the economic foundations of the major industrial powers were shaky as well. Even in the 1920s the economy of western Europe was newly challenged by the greater vigor of the United States and Japan.

Revolution: The First Waves

 An unprecedented surge of political and social revolution seized other key parts of the world. Launched in some cases before World War I, revolution posed a direct challenge to the more established industrial, democratic powers, particularly in the West. Revolutions also set a host of new forces in motion in the societies directly involved. Collectively, revolutions suggested alternatives to economic, political, and social forms emphasized in the West. Along with the surge of anticolonialism in the 1920s, they contributed a new level of complexity to world affairs and suggested the growing vulnerability of Western dominance.

Mexico's Upheaval

Several cataclysmic events launched Latin America into the 20th century and set in motion trends that would determine much of the region's subsequent history. The first of these events was the 10-year civil war and political upheaval of the **Mexican Revolution,** caused primarily by internal forces. Eventually, the Mexican Revolution was also influenced by another major event: the outbreak of World War I. Although most Latin American nations avoided direct participation in the Great War, as World War I was called at the time, the disruption of traditional markets for Latin American exports and the elimination of European sources of goods caused a realignment of the economies of several nations in the region. They were forced to rely on themselves. A spurt of manufacturing continued the process begun after 1870, and some small steps were taken to overcome the traditional dependence on outside supply. Finally, at the end of World War I, the United States emerged as the dominant foreign power in the region, replacing Great Britain in both economic and political terms. That position created a reality that Latin Americans could not ignore and that greatly influenced the economic and political options in the region.

The regime of **Porfirio Díaz** had been in power since 1876 and seemed unshakable. During the Díaz dictatorship, tremendous economic changes had been made, and foreign concessions in mining, railroads, and other sectors of the economy had created a sense of prosperity among the Mexican elite. However, this progress had been bought at considerable expense. Foreigners controlled large sectors of the economy. The hacienda system of extensive landholdings by a small elite dominated certain regions of the country. The political system was corrupt, and any complaint was stifled. The government took repressive measures against workers, peasants, and American Indians who opposed the loss of their lands or the unbearable working conditions. Political opponents often were imprisoned or forced into exile. In short, Díaz ruled with an iron fist through an effective political machine.

By 1910, however, Díaz was 80 years old and seemed willing to allow some political opposition. **Francisco Madero,** a wealthy son of an elite family, proposed to run against Díaz. Madero believed that some moderate democratic political reforms would relieve social tensions and allow the government to continue its economic development with a minimum of popular unrest. This was more than Díaz could stand. Madero was arrested, a rigged election put Díaz back in power, and things returned to normal.

When Madero was released from prison, he called for a revolt.

A general rebellion developed. In the north, small farmers, railroaders, and cowboys coalesced under the colorful former bandit and able commander **Pancho Villa.** In the southern province of Morelos, an area of old conflicts between American Indian communities and large sugar estates, a peasant-based guerrilla movement began under **Emiliano Zapata,** whose goal of land reform was expressed in his motto "Tierra y Libertad" (Land and Liberty). Díaz was driven from power by this coalition of forces, but it soon became apparent that Madero's moderate programs would not resolve Mexico's continuing social problems. Zapata rose in revolt, demanding a sweeping land reform, and Madero steadily lost control of his subordinates. In 1913, with at least the tacit agreement of the U.S. ambassador in Mexico, who wanted to forestall revolutionary changes, a military coup removed Madero from government and he was then assassinated.

General **Victoriano Huerta** sought to impose a Díaz-type dictatorship supported by the large landowners, the army, and the foreign companies, but the tide of revolution could not be stopped so easily. Villa and Zapata rose again against the government and were joined by other middle-class political opponents of Huerta's illegal rule. By 1914 Huerta was forced from power, but the victorious leaders now began to fight over the nature of the new regime and the mantle of leadership. An extended period of warfare followed, and the tides of battle shifted constantly. The railroad lines built under Díaz now moved large numbers of troops, including *soldaderas*, women who sometimes shouldered arms. Matters were also complicated by U.S. intervention, aimed at bringing order to the border regions, and by diplomatic maneuverings after the outbreak of World War I in Europe. Villa and Zapata remained in control in their home territories, but they could not wrest the government from the control of the more moderate political leaders in Mexico City. **Alvaro Obregón,** an able general who had learned the new tactics of machine guns and trenches from the war raging in Europe and had beaten Villa's cavalry in a series of bloody battles in 1915, emerged as leader of the government.

As much as the Mexican Revolution had its own internal dynamic, it is interesting to note that it was roughly contemporaneous with revolutions in other agrarian societies that had also just undergone a period of rapid and disruptive modernization. The Boxer Rebellion in China (1899–1901) and the toppling of the emperor in 1911, the 1905 revolution in Russia, and a revolution in Iran in the same year underlined the rapid changes in these societies, all of which had received large foreign investments from either the United States or western Europe. In each of these countries, governments had tried to establish strong centralized control and had sought rapid modernization, but in doing so they had made their nations increasingly dependant on foreign investments and consequently on world financial markets. Thus, the world banking crisis of 1907 and 1908 cut Mexico and these other countries off from their needed sources of capital and created severe strains on their governments. This kind of dependency, and the fact that in Mexico more than 20 percent of the nation's territory was owned directly by citizens or companies from the United States, fed a growing nationalism that spread through many sectors of society. That nationalist sentiment played a role in each of these revolutions.

By 1920 the civil war had ended and Mexico began to consolidate the changes that had taken place in the previous confused and bloody decade. Obregón was elected president in that year. He was followed by a series of presidents from the new "revolutionary elite" who tried to consolidate the new regime. There was much to be done. The revolution had devastated the country; 1.5 million people had died, major industries were destroyed, and ranching and farming were disrupted. But there was great hope because the revolution also promised (although it did not always deliver) real changes.

What were some of these changes? The new **Mexican Constitution of 1917** promised land reform, limited the foreign ownership of key resources, and guaranteed the rights of workers. It also placed restrictions on clerical education and church ownership of property, and promised educational reforms. The workers who had been mobilized were organized in a national confederation and were given representation in the government. The promised land reforms were slow in coming, though later, under President Lázaro Cárdenas (1934–1940), more than 40 million acres were distributed, most of it in the form of *ejidos*, or communal holdings. The government launched an extensive program of primary and especially rural education.

Culture and Politics in Postrevolutionary Mexico

Nationalism and *indigenism*, or the concern for the indigenous peoples and their contribution to Mexican culture, lay beneath many reforms. Having failed to integrate the American Indians into national life for a century, Mexico now attempted to "Indianize" the nation through secular schools that emphasized nationalism and a vision of the Mexican past that glorified its American Indian heritage and denounced Western capitalism. Artists such as **Diego Rivera** and **José Clemente Orozco** recaptured that past and outlined a social program for the future in stunning murals on public buildings designed to inform, convince, and entertain at the same time. The Mexican muralist movement had a wide impact on artists throughout Latin America even though, as Orozco himself stated, it sometimes created simple solutions and strange utopias by mixing a romantic image of the American Indian past with Christian symbols and communist ideology. Novelists, such as Mariano Azuela, found in the revolution a focus for the examination of Mexican reality. Popular culture celebrated the heroes and events of the revolution in scores of ballads (*corridos*) that were sung to celebrate and inform. In literature, music, and the arts, the revolution and its themes provided a stimulus to a tremendous burst of creativity, as in the following lines of poetry:

> Gabino Barrera rose in the mountains
>
> his cause was noble,
>
> protect the poor and give them the land.
>
> Remember the night he was murdered
>
> three leagues from Tlapehuala;
>
> 22 shots rang out
>
> leaving him time for nothing.
>
> Gabino Barrera and his loyal steed
>
> fell in the hail of rounds,
>
> the face of this man of the Revolution
>
> finally rested, his lips pressed to the ground.

The gains of the revolution were not made without opposition. Although the revolution preceded the Russian Revolution of 1917 and had no single ideological model, many of the ideas of Marxist socialism were held by leading Mexican intellectuals and a few politicians. The secularization of society and especially education met strong opposition from the Catholic church and the clergy, especially in states where socialist rhetoric and anticlericalism were extreme. In the 1920s, a conservative peasant movement backed by the church erupted in central Mexico. These **Cristeros,** backed by conservative politicians, fought to stop the slide toward secularization. The fighting lasted for years until a compromise was reached.

The United States intervened diplomatically and militarily during the revolution, motivated by a desire for order, fear of German influence on the new government, and economic interests. An incident provoked a short-lived U.S. seizure of Veracruz in 1914, and when Pancho Villa's forces had raided across the border, the United States sent an expeditionary force into Mexico to catch him. The mission failed. For the most part, however, the war in Europe dominated U.S. foreign policy efforts until 1918. The United States was suspicious of the new government, and a serious conflict arose when U.S.-owned oil companies ran into problems with workers.

As in any revolution, the question of continuity arose when the fighting ended. The revolutionary leadership hoped to institutionalize the new regime by creating a one-party system. This organization, called the Party of the Institutionalized Revolution (PRI), developed slowly during the 1920s and 1930s into a dominant force in Mexican politics. It incorporated labor, peasant, military, and middle-class sectors and proved flexible enough to incorporate new interest groups as they developed. Although Mexico became a multiparty democracy in theory, in reality the PRI controlled politics and, by accommodation and sometimes repression, maintained its hold on national political life. Some presidents governed much like the strongmen in the 19th century had done, but the party structure and the need to incorporate various interests within the government coalition limited the worst aspects of caudillo, or personalist, rule. The presidents were strong, but the policy of limiting the presidency to one six-year term ensured some change in leadership. The question of whether a revolution could be institutionalized remained in debate. By the end of the 20th century, many Mexicans believed that little remained of the principles and programs of the revolutionaries of 1910.

Revolution in Russia: Liberalism to Communism

In March 1917 strikes and food riots broke out in Russia's capital, St. Petersburg (subsequently renamed Leningrad until 1991, when it was renamed St. Petersburg as a gesture of defiance against the revolutionary legacy). The outbursts were spurred by wartime misery, including painful food shortages. They also and more basically protested the conditions of early industrialization set against incomplete rural reform and an unresponsive political system. And they quickly assumed revolutionary proportions. The rioters called not just for more food and work but for a new political regime as well. A council of workers, called a soviet, took over the city government and arrested the tsar's ministers, after some brutal attempts at military repression. Unable to rely on his own soldiers, the tsar abdicated, thus ending the long period of imperial rule.

For eight months a liberal provisional government struggled to rule the country. Russia seemed thus to launch its revolution on a basis similar to France in 1789, where a liberal period set change in motion. Like Western liberals, Russian revolutionary leaders, such as **Alexander Kerensky,** were eager to see genuine parliamentary rule, religious and other freedoms, and a host of political and legal changes. But liberalism was not deeply rooted in Russia, if only because of the small middle class, so the analogies with the first phase of the French revolution cannot be pressed too far. Furthermore, Russia's revolution took place in much more adverse circumstances, given the pressures of participation in the First World War. The initial liberal leaders were eager to maintain their war effort, which associated their link with democratic France and Britain. Yet the nation was desperately war weary, and prolongation drastically worsened economic conditions while public morale plummeted. Liberal leaders also held back from the massive land reforms expected by the peasantry, for in good middle-class fashion they respected existing property arrangements and did not wish to rush into social change before a legitimate new political structure could be established. Hence serious popular unrest continued, and in November (October, by the Russian calendar) a second revolution took place, which expelled liberal leadership and soon brought to power the radical, Bolshevik wing of the Social Democratic party, soon renamed the Communist party, and Lenin, their dynamic chief (see Figure 29.6).

The revolution was a godsend to Lenin, who had long been writing of Russia's readiness for a communist revolt because of the power of international capitalism and its creation of a massive proletariat, even in a society that had not directly passed through middle-class rule. Lenin quickly gained a strong position among the urban workers' councils in the major cities. This corresponded to his deeply rooted belief that revolution should come not from literal mass action but from tightly organized cells whose leaders espoused a coherent plan of action.

Once the liberals were toppled, Lenin and the Bolsheviks faced several immediate problems. One, the war, they handled by signing a humiliating peace treaty with Germany and giving up huge sections of western Russia in return for an end of hostilities. This treaty was soon nullified by Germany's defeat at the hands of the Western allies, but Russia was ignored at the Versailles peace conference—treated

as a pariah by the fearful Western powers. Much former territory was converted into new nation-states. A revived Poland built heavily on land Russia had controlled for more than a century, and new, small Baltic states cut into even earlier acquisitions. Still, although Russia's deep grievances against the Versailles treaty would later help motivate renewed expansionism, the early end to the war was vital to Lenin's consolidation of power.

Although Lenin and the Bolsheviks had gained a majority role in the leading urban soviets, they were not the most popular revolutionary party, and this situation constituted the second problem faced at the end of 1917. The November seizure of power had led to the creation of the Council of People's Commissars, drawn from soviets across the nation and headed by Lenin, to govern the state. But a parliamentary election had already been called, and this produced a clear majority for the Social Revolutionary party, which emphasized peasant support and rural reform. Lenin, however, shut down the parliament, replacing it with

Figure 29.6   *Moscow workers guard the Bolshevik headquarters during the Russian Revolution of 1917.*

a Bolshevik-dominated Congress of Soviets. He pressed the Social Revolutionaries to disband, arguing that "the people voted for a party which no longer existed." Russia was thus to have no Western-style, multiparty system but rather a Bolshevik monopoly in the name of the true people's will. Indeed, Communist party control of the government apparatus persisted from this point to 1989, a record for continuity much different from the fate of revolutionary groups earlier in the Western past.

Russia's revolution did, however, produce a familiar backlash that revolutionaries in other eras would have recognized quite easily: foreign hostility and, even more important, domestic resistance. The world's leading nations—aside from Germany, now briefly irrelevant—were appalled at the Communist success, which threatened principles of property and freedom they cherished deeply. As settled regimes, they also disliked the unexpected, and some were directly injured by Russia's renunciation of its heavy foreign debts. The result was an attempt at intervention, recalling the attacks on France in 1792. Britain, France, the United States, and Japan all sent troops. But this intervention, although it heightened Russian suspicion of outsiders, did relatively little damage. The Western powers, exhausted by World War I, pulled out quickly, and even Japan, though interested in lingering in Asiatic Russia, stepped back fairly soon.

The internal civil war, which foreign troops slightly abetted, was a more serious matter, as it raged from 1918 to 1921. Tsarist generals, religiously faithful peasants, and many minority nationalities made common cause against the Communist regime. Their efforts were aided by continuing economic distress, the normal result of revolutionary disarray, but also heightened by earlier Communist measures. Lenin had quickly decreed a redistribution of land to the peasantry and also launched a nationalization, or state takeover, of basic industry. Many already landed peasants resented loss of property and incentive and in reaction lowered food production and the goods sent to markets. Industrial nationalization somewhat similarly disrupted manufacturing. Famine and unemployment created more economic hardship than the war had generated, which added fuel to the civil war fires. Even workers revolted in several cities, threatening the new regime's most obvious social base as well as ideological mainstay.

Stabilization of Russia's Communist Regime

Order was restored after the revolution on several key foundations. First, the construction of the powerful new army under the leadership of Leon Trotsky recruited able generals and masses of loyal conscripts. This **Red Army** was an early beneficiary of two ongoing sources of strength for Communist Russia: a willingness to use people of humble background but great ability who could rise to great heights under the new order but who had been doomed to immobility under the old system, and an ability to inspire mass loyalty in the name of an end to previous injustice and a promise of a brighter future. Next, economic disarray was reduced in 1921 when Lenin issued his **New Economic Policy.** Intended as a stopgap measure in recognition of the real-life barriers to immediate construction of communism, the NEP promised considerable freedom of action for small business owners and peasant landowners. The state continued to set basic economic policies, but its efforts were now combined with individual initiative. Under this temporary policy, food production began to recover, and the regime gained time to prepare the more durable structures of the Communist system.

By 1923 the Bolshevik revolution was an accomplished fact. A new constitution set up a federal system of socialist republics. This system recognized the multinational character of the nation, which was called the **Union of Soviet Socialist Republics.** The dominance of ethnic Russians was preserved in the central state apparatus, however, and certain groups, notably Jews, were given no distinct representation. Since the separate republics were firmly controlled by the national Communist party and since basic decisions were as firmly centralized, the impact of the new nationalities' policy was somewhat mixed; yet it was also true that direct nationalities' protests declined notably from the 1920s until the late 1980s.

The apparatus of the central state was another mixture of appearance and reality. The **Supreme Soviet** had many of the trappings of a parliament and was elected by universal suffrage. But competition in elections was normally prohibited, which meant that the Communist party easily controlled the body, which served mainly to ratify decisions taken by the party's central executive. Parallel systems of central bureaucracy and party bureaucracy further confirmed the Communist monopoly on power and the ability to control major decisions from the center. The Soviet political system was elaborated over time. A new constitution in the 1930s spoke glowingly of human rights. In fact, the Communists had quickly reestablished an authoritarian system, making it more efficient than its tsarist predecessor had been, complete with updated versions of political police to ensure loyalty.

Soviet Experimentation

The mid-1920s constituted a lively, experimental period in Soviet history, partly because of the jockeying for power at the top of the power pyramid. Despite the absence of Western-style political competition, a host of new groups found a voice. The Communist party, though not eager to recruit too many members lest it lose its tight organization and elite status, encouraged all sorts of subsidiary organizations. Youth movements, women's groups, and particularly organizations of workers all actively debated problems in their social environment and directions for future planning. Workers were able to influence management practices; women's leaders helped carve legal equality and new educational and work opportunities for their constituents.

One key to the creative mood of these years was the rapid spread of education promoted by the government, as well as educational and propaganda activities sponsored by various adult groups. Literacy gained ground quickly. The new educational system was also bent on reshaping popular culture away from older peasant traditions and, above all, religion, and toward beliefs in Communist political analysis and science. Access to new information, new modes of inquiry, and new values encouraged controversy.

The Soviet regime grappled with other key definitional issues in the 1920s. Rivalries among leaders at the top had to be sorted out. Lenin became ill and then died in 1924, creating an unexpected leadership gap. A number of key lieutenants jostled for power, including the Red Army's flamboyant Trotsky and a Communist party stalwart of worker origins who had taken the name **Stalin,** meaning steel. After a few years of jockeying, Joseph Stalin emerged as undisputed leader of the Soviet state, his victory a triumph also for party control over other branches of government.

Stalin's accession was more than a personal bureaucratic issue, however. Stalin represented a strongly nationalist version of communism, in contrast to the more ideological and international visions of many of his rivals. At the revolution's outset Lenin had believed that the Russian rising would be merely a prelude to a sweeping Communist upheaval throughout the Western industrial world. Many revolutionary leaders actively encouraged communist parties in the West and set up a **Comintern,** or Communist International office, to guide this process. But revolution did not spill over, despite a few brief risings in Hungary and Germany right after World War I. Under Stalin, the revolutionary leadership, although still committed in theory to an international movement, pulled back to concentrate on Russian developments pure and simple—building "socialism in one country," as Stalin put it. Stalin in many ways represented the anti-Western strain in Russian tradition, though in new guise. Rival leaders were killed or expelled, rival visions of the revolution downplayed. Stalin would also accelerate industrial development while attacking peasant land ownership with a new **collectivization** program (see Figure 29.7).

The Russian Revolution was one of the most successful risings in human history, at least for several decades. Building on widespread if diverse popular discontent and a firm belief in centralized leadership, the Bolsheviks beat back powerful odds to create a new, though not totally unprecedented, political regime. They used features of the tsarist system but managed to propel a wholly new leadership group to power not only at the top but also at all levels of the bureaucracy and army. The tsar and his hated ministers were gone, mostly executed, but so was the overweening aristocratic class that had loomed so large in Russian history for centuries.

Toward Revolution in China

The abdication of Puyi, the Manchu boy-emperor in 1912, marked the end of a century-long losing struggle on the part of the Qing dynasty to protect Chinese civilization from foreign invaders and revolutionary threats from within, such as the massive Taiping movement (see Chapter 26). The fall of the Qing opened the way for an extended struggle over which leader or movement would be able to capture the mandate to rule the ancient society that had

Figure 29.7 *Russian children help carry the propaganda for Stalin's campaign for collectivization of agriculture. The banner reads, "Everybody to the collective farms!" These happy faces belie the tragedy resulting from the collectivization program, in which millions fell victim to slaughter or starvation.*

for millennia ordered the lives of at least one-fifth of humankind. The loose alliance of students, middle-class politicians, secret societies, and regional military commanders that overthrew the Manchus quickly splintered into several hostile contenders for the right to rule China. Internal factors and foreign influences paved the way for the ultimate victory of the Chinese Communist party under Mao Zedong.

After the fall of the Qing dynasty, the best-positioned of the contenders for power were regionally based military commanders or warlords, who would dominate Chinese politics for the next three decades. Many of the warlords combined in cliques or alliances to protect their own territories and to crush neighbors and annex their lands. The most powerful of these cliques, centered in north China, was headed by the unscrupulous **Yuan Shikai,** who hoped to seize the vacated Manchu throne and found a new dynasty. By virtue of their wealth, the merchants and bankers of coastal cities like Shanghai and Canton made up a second power center in post-Manchu China. Their involvement in politics resulted from

their willingness to bankroll both favored warlords and Western-educated, middle-class politicians like Sun Yat-sen.

Sometimes supportive of the urban civilian politicians, and sometimes wary of them, university students and their teachers, as well as independent intellectuals, provided yet another factor in the complex post-Qing political equation. Though the intellectuals and students played critical roles in shaping new ideologies to rebuild Chinese civilization, they were virtually defenseless in a situation in which force was essential to those who hoped to exert political influence. Deeply divided, but very strong in some regions, secret societies represented another contender for power. Like many in the military, members of these societies envisioned the restoration of monarchical rule, but under a Chinese, not a foreign, dynasty. As if the situation were not confused enough, it was further complicated by the continuing intervention of the Western powers, eager to profit from China's divisions and weakness. Their inroads, however, were increasingly overshadowed by

In Depth

A Century of Revolutions

Not since the late 18th and early 19th centuries had there been a succession of revolutions like those in the early decades of the 20th century. In contrast to the revolutionary movements of the earlier period, however, the early 20th-century upheavals were just the first waves of a revolutionary tide that struck with renewed fury after 1945. A number of factors account for the successive surges of revolution in the 20th century. Rural discontent was crucial, for peasants provided vital contributions to 20th-century revolutions everywhere they occurred. Peasants were newly spurred by pressures of population growth, combined with resentment against big landowners. Modern state forms tended to increase taxes on the peasantry, while making traditional protests, like banditry, more difficult.

Equally fundamentally, the rise of revolutionary movements was fed by the underlying disruptions caused by the spread of the Industrial Revolution and the Western-centered, global market system. Handicraft producers thrown out of work by an influx of machine-manufactured goods, and peasants, such as those in central Mexico who lost their land to moneylenders, frequently rallied to calls to riot and, at times, ultimately became caught up in revolutionary currents. In the colonies, unemployed Western-educated African and Asian secondary school and college graduates became deeply committed to struggles for independence that promised them dignity and decent jobs. Urban laborers, enraged by the appalling working and living conditions that were characteristic of the early stages of industrialization in countries such as Russia and China, provided key support for revolutionary parties in many countries.

Although global economic slumps did much to fire the revolutionaries' longings, world wars proved even more fertile seed beds of revolutions. Returning soldiers and neglected veterans provided the shock troops for leftist revolutionaries and fascist pretenders alike. Defeated states witnessed the rapid erosion of their power to suppress internal enemies and floundered as their armies refused to defend them or joined movements dedicated to their overthrow. In this regard, the great increase in global interconnectedness in the 20th century was critical. The economic competition and military rivalries of the industrial powers drew them into unwanted wars that they could not sustain without raw materials and manpower drawn from their colonies and other neutral states.

Another key factor that contributed to the sharp rise in the incidence of revolutions in the 20th century was the underlying intellectual climate. Notions of progress and a belief in the perfectibility of human society, which were widely held in the 19th century, deeply influenced such communist theorists as Marx, Lenin, Mao Zedong, and Ho Chi Minh. These and other revolutionary ideologues sought, in part, to overthrow existing regimes that they viewed as exploitative and oppressive. But they were also deeply committed to building radically new societies that would bring justice and a decent livelihood to previously downtrodden social groups, especially the working classes, peasantry, and urban poor. Visions of the good life in peasant communes or workers' utopias were a powerful driving force for revolutionary currents throughout the century from Mexico to China. One measure of their influence is the extent to which highly competitive capitalist societies developed social welfare programs to curb social discontent that could spiral into active protest, and perhaps even revolutionary challenges to the existing social order.

A final common ingredient of 20th-century revolutions was the need to come to terms with Western influence and often to reassert greater national autonomy. Mexico, Russia, and China all sought to reduce Western economic control and cultural influence, seeking alternative models. Many revolutions involved active anti-Western sentiment and attacks on Western investments. In Russia, Stalinism went on the attack against "decadent" Western cultural influence.

Questions: What internal and external forces weakened the governments of Mexico and China in the opening decades of the 20th century and unleashed the forces of revolution? What key social groups were behind the revolutions in Mexico, China, and Russia, and why were they so important in each case? What similarities and differences can you identify among these three early revolutions in the 20th century?

the entry into the contest for the control of China by the newest imperialist power, Japan. From the mid-1890s, when the Japanese had humiliated their much larger neighbor by easily defeating it in war, until 1945, when Japan's surrender ended World War II, the Japanese were a major factor in the long and bloody contest for mastery of China.

China's May Fourth Movement and the Rise of the Marxist Alternative

Sun Yat-sen headed the Revolutionary Alliance, a loose coalition of anti-Qing political groups that had spearheaded the 1911 revolt. After the Qing were toppled, Sun claimed that he and the parties of the alliance were the rightful claimants to the mandate to rule all of China. But he could do little to assert civilian control in the face of warlord opposition. The Revolutionary Alliance had little power and virtually no popular support outside the urban trading centers of the coastal areas in central and south China. Even in these areas, they were at the mercy of the local warlords. The alliance formally elected Sun president at the end of 1911, set up a parliament modeled after those in Europe, and chose cabinets with great fanfare. But their decisions had little effect on warlord-dominated China.

Sun Yat-sen conceded this reality when he resigned the acting presidency in favor of the northern warlord Yuan Shikai in 1912. As the most powerful of the northern clique of generals, Yuan appeared to have the best chance to unify China under a single government. He at first feigned sympathy for the democratic aims of the alliance leaders but soon revealed his true intentions. He took foreign loans to build up his military forces and buy out most of the bureaucrats in the capital at Beijing. When Sun and other leaders of the Revolutionary Alliance called for a second revolution to oust Yuan in the years after 1912, he made full use of his military power and more underhanded methods, such as assassinations, to put down their opposition. By 1915, it appeared that Yuan was well on his way to realizing his ambition of becoming China's next emperor. His schemes were foiled, however, by the continuing rivalry of other warlords, republican nationalists like Sun, and the growing influence of Japan in China. The latter increased dramatically as a result of World War I.

As England's ally according to terms of a 1902 treaty, Japan immediately entered the war on the side of the Entente, or Western allied powers. Moving much too quickly for the comfort of the British and the other Western powers, the Japanese seized German-held islands in the Pacific and occupied the Germans' concessionary areas in China. With all the great powers except the United States embroiled in war, the Japanese sought to establish a dominant hold over their giant neighbor. In early 1915, they presented Yuan's government with Twenty-One Demands, which, if accepted, would have reduced China to the status of a dependant protectorate. Though Sun and the Revolutionary Alliance lost much support by refusing to repudiate the Japanese demands, Yuan was no more decisive. He neither accepted nor rejected the demands, but concentrated his energies on an effort to trump up popular enthusiasm for his accession to the throne. Disgusted by Yuan's weakness and ambition, one of his warlord rivals plotted his overthrow. Hostility to the Japanese won Yuan's rival widespread support, and in 1916, Yuan was forced to resign the presidency. His fall was the signal for a free-for-all power struggle between the remaining warlords for control of China.

As one of the victorious allies, Japan managed to solidify its hold on northern China by winning control of the former German concessions in the peace negotiations at Versailles in 1919. But the Chinese had also allied themselves to the Entente powers during the war. Enraged by what they viewed as a betrayal by the Entente powers, students and nationalist politicians organized mass demonstrations in numerous Chinese cities on May 4, 1919. The demonstrations began a prolonged period of protest against Japanese inroads. This protest soon expanded from marches and petitions to include strikes and mass boycotts of Japanese goods.

The fourth of May, 1919, the day when the resistance began, gave its name to a movement in which intellectuals and students played a leading role. Initially at least, the **May Fourth movement** was aimed at transforming China into a liberal democracy. Its program was enunciated in numerous speeches, pamphlets, novels, and newspaper articles. Confucianism was ridiculed and rejected in favor of a wholehearted acceptance of all that the Western democracies had to offer. Noted Western thinkers, such as Bertrand Russell and John Dewey, toured China, extolling the merits of science, industrial technology, and democratic government and basking in the cheers of enthusiastic Chinese audiences. Chinese thinkers called for the liberation of women, the simplification of the Chinese script in order to promote mass literacy, and the promotion of Western-style individualism. Many of these themes are captured in the literature of the period. In the novel *Family* by Ba Jin, for example, a younger brother audaciously informs his elder sibling that he will not accept the marriage partner the family has arranged for him. He clearly sees his refusal as part of a more general revolt of the youth of China against the ancient Confucian social code.

> Big Brother, I'm doing what no one in our family has ever dared do before—I'm running out on an arranged marriage. No one cares about my fate, so I've decided to walk my own road alone. I'm determined to struggle against the old forces to the end. Unless you cancel the match, I'll never come back. I'll die first.

However enthusiastically the program of the May Fourth movement was adopted by the urban youth of China, it was soon clear that mere emulation of the liberal democracies of the West could not provide effective solutions to China's prodigious problems. Civil liberties and democratic elections were meaningless in a China that was ruled by warlords. Gradualist solutions were folly in a nation where the great mass of the peasantry was destitute, much of it malnourished or dying of starvation. Even if fair elections could be held and a Western-style parliament installed as an effective ruling body, China's crisis had become so severe that there was little time for legislators to squabble and debate. The ministers of an elected government with little military clout would hardly have been able to implement well-meaning programs for land redistribution and subsidies for the poor in the face of deeply entrenched regional opposition from the landlords and the military. It soon became clear to many Chinese intellectuals and students, as well as to some of the nationalist politicians, that more radical solutions were needed. In the 1920s, this conviction gave rise to the Communist left within the Chinese nationalist movement.

The Bolshevik victory and the programs launched to rebuild Russia prompted Chinese intellectuals to give serious attention to the works of Marx and other socialist thinkers and the potential they offered for the regeneration of China. But the careful study of the writings of Marx, Engels, Lenin, and Trotsky in the wake of the Russian Revolution also impressed a number of Chinese intellectuals with the necessity for major alterations in Marxist ideology if it was going to be of any relevance to China or other peasant societies. Marx, after all, had foreseen socialist revolutions occurring in the more advanced industrial societies with well-developed working classes and a strong proletarian consciousness. He had thought that there would be little chance for revolution in Russia. In China, with its overwhelmingly rural, peasant population (and Marx viewed the peasantry as a reactionary or, at best, a conservative, petty bourgeois social element), the prospects for revolution looked even more dismal.

The most influential of the thinkers who called for a reworking of Marxist ideology to fit China's situation was **Li Dazhao.** Li was from peasant origins, but he had excelled in school and eventually become a college teacher. He headed the Marxist study circle that developed after the 1919 upheavals at the University of Beijing. His interpretation of Marxist philosophy placed heavy emphasis on its capacity for promoting renewal and its ability to harness the energy and vitality of a nation's youth. In contrast to Lenin, Li saw the peasants, rather than the urban workers, as the vanguard of revolutionary change. He justified this shift from the orthodox Marxist emphasis on the working classes, which made up only a tiny fraction of China's population at the time, by characterizing the whole of Chinese society as proletarian. All of China, he argued, had been exploited by the bourgeois, industrialized West. Thus, the oppressed Chinese as a whole needed to unite and rise up against their exploiters.

Li's version of Marxism, with alterations or emphasis on elements that made it suitable for China, had great appeal for the students, including the young **Mao Zedong,** who joined Li's study circle. They, too, were angered by what they perceived as China's betrayal by the imperialist powers. They shared Li's hostility (very much a throwback to the attitudes of the Confucian era) to merchants and commerce, which appeared to dominate the West. They, too, longed for a return to a political system, like the Confucian, in which those who governed were deeply committed to social reform and social welfare. They also believed in an authoritarian state, which they felt ought to intervene constructively in all aspects of the peoples' lives. The Marxist study club societies that developed as a result of these discoveries soon spawned a number of more broadly based, politically activist organizations.

In the summer of 1921, in an attempt to unify the growing Marxist wing of the nationalist struggle, a handful of leaders from different parts of China met in secret in the city of Shanghai. At this meeting, closely watched by the agents of the local warlord and rival political organizations, the Communist party of China was born. The party was minuscule in terms of the numbers of their supporters, and at this time it was still dogmatically fixed on a revolutionary program oriented to the small and scattered working class. But the communists at least offered a clear alternative to fill the ideological and institutional void left by the collapse of the Confucian order.

The Seizure of Power by China's Guomindang

In the years when the communist movement in China was being put together by urban students and intellectuals, the **Guomindang,** or Nationalist party, which

was to prove the communists' great rival for the mandate to rule in China, was struggling to survive in the south. Sun Yat-sen, who was the acknowledged head of the nationalist struggle from the 1911 revolution until his death in early 1925, had gone into exile in Japan in 1914, while warlords, such as Yuan Shikai, consolidated their regional power bases. After returning to China in 1919, Sun and his followers attempted to unify the diverse political organizations struggling for political influence in China by reorganizing the revolutionary movement and naming it the Nationalist party of China (the Guomindang).

The Nationalists began the slow process of forging alliances with key social groups and building an army of their own, which they now viewed as the only way to rid China of the warlord menace (Map 29.3). Sun strove to enunciate a nationalist ideology that gave something to everyone. It stressed the need to unify China under a strong central government, to bring the imperialist intruders under control, and to introduce social reforms that would alleviate the poverty of the peasants and the oppressive working conditions of laborers in China's cities. Unfortunately

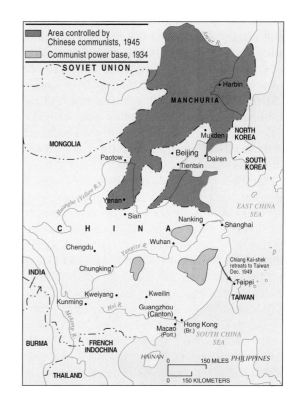

Map 29.3 *China in the Era of Revolution and Civil War*

for the great majority of the Chinese people, for whom social reforms were the main concern, the Nationalist leaders concentrated on political and international issues, such as relations with the Western powers and Japan, and failed to implement most of the domestic programs they proposed, most especially land reform.

In this early stage Sun and the Nationalists built their power primarily on the support provided by urban businessmen and merchants in coastal cities such as Canton. Sun forged an alliance with the communists that was officially proclaimed at the first Nationalist party conference in 1924. For the time being at least, the Nationalist leaders were content to let the communists serve as their major link to the peasants and the urban workers. Nationalist leaders also turned to Soviet Russia, and the Bolsheviks sent advisors and gave material assistance.

In 1924, the **Whampoa Military Academy** was founded with Soviet help and partially staffed by Russian instructors. The academy gave the Nationalists a critical military dimension to their political maneuvering. The first head of the academy was an ambitious young military officer named **Chiang Kai-shek.** The son of a poor salt merchant, Chiang had made his career in the military and by virtue of connections with powerful figures in the Shanghai underworld. He had received some military training in Japan, and managed by the early 1920s to work his way into Sun Yat-sen's inner circle of advisors. Chiang was not happy with the communist alliance. But he was willing to bide his time until he had the military strength to deal with both the communists and the warlords, who remained the major obstacles to the Nationalist seizure of power.

Absorbed by all these political machinations, Sun and other Nationalist leaders had little time left for serious attention to the now severe deterioration of the Chinese economy or providing relief for the huge population whose sufferings mounted as a result. Urban laborers worked for pitiful wages and lived in appalling conditions. But the social condition of the peasantry, which made up nearly 90 percent of China's population, was perhaps the most pressing issue facing China's aspiring national leaders. Over a century of corruption, weak Manchu rule, the Qing collapse in 1911, and the depredations of the warlords had left the peasantry in many regions of China in misery. Big landlords and rich peasants rapaciously amassed great landholdings, which they rented out at exorbitant rates that left the tenants who worked them little to feed and clothe their families. Famine and disease stalked China's heavily populated provinces, while its ancient irrigation systems fell into disrepair. Corrupt warlords and bureaucrats, including those allied to the Nationalist party, colluded with the landlords to extract the maximum taxes and labor services from the peasantry. Many peasants were too poor and starved to perform the most basic of social duties, such as burying their deceased parents, whose bodies were often left to be devoured by vultures and packs of wild dogs.

Though rural China cried out for strong leadership and far-reaching economic and social reform, China's leaders bickered and plotted but did little. Sun gave lip service to the Nationalist party's need to deal with the peasant problem. But his abysmal ignorance of rural conditions was revealed by statements in which he denied that China had exploitative landlords and his refusal to believe that there were "serious difficulties" between the great mass of the peasantry and the landowners.

Mao and the Peasant Option

Though the son of a fairly prosperous peasant, Mao Zedong had rebelled early in his life against his father's exploitation of the tenants and laborers who worked the family fields. Receiving little assistance from his estranged father, Mao was forced to make his own way in the world. Through much of his youth and early adulthood, he struggled to educate himself in the history, philosophy, and economic theory that most other nationalist and revolutionary leaders mastered in private schools. Having moved to Beijing in the post–May Fourth era, Mao came under the influence of thinkers such as Li Dazhao, who placed considerable emphasis on solutions to the peasant problem as one of the keys to China's survival. As the following passage from Mao's early writings reveals, almost from the outset he was committed to revolutionary solutions that depended on peasant support:

> A revolution is an insurrection, an act of violence by which one class overthrows another. A rural revolution is a revolution by which the peasantry overthrows the power of the feudal landlord class. Without using the greatest force, the peasants cannot possibly overthrow the deep-rooted authority of the landlords which has lasted for thousands of years.

The Nationalists' successful drive for national power began only after Sun Yat-sen's death in 1925, which opened the way for Chiang Kai-shek and his warlord allies to seize control of the party. After winning over or eliminating the military chiefs in the Canton area, Chiang marched north with his newly created armies. His first campaign culminated in the Nationalists' seizure of the Yangtze River valley and Shanghai in early 1927. Later his forces also captured the capital at Beijing and the rest of the Huanghe river basin. The refusal of most of the warlords to end their feuding meant that Chiang could defeat them or buy them out, one by one. By the late 1920s, he was the master of China in name and international standing, if not in actual fact. He was, in effect, the head of a warlord hierarchy. But most political leaders within China and in the outside world recognized him as the new president of China.

Chiang quickly turned against the communists, attacking them in various places. A brutal massacre occurred in Shanghai in 1927, with many workers gunned down or beheaded (Figure 29.8). Chiang carefully wooed support from western Europe and the United States, while lining up most police and landlord leaders at home. The offensive propelled Mao Zedong to leadership. An attack on the communist rural stronghold in south-central China, supported by German advisors, caused Mao to spearhead a **Long March** of 90,000 followers in 1934, across thousands of miles to the more remote northwest. Here, in Shanxi, where some peasant communes had already been established, the new communist center took shape (see Map 29.3).

While the Long March solidified Mao's leadership of Chinese communism and gave many followers a sense that they could not be defeated, it was the

Figure 29.8 *The Guomindang's brutal suppression of the workers' organizations in Shanghai in 1927 was a turning point in the history of modern China. The Guomindang–Communist party alliance was shattered, and Mao Zedong's call for a peasant-based revolution became imperative as the vulnerability of the small Chinese working class was exposed.*

Japanese invasions of China in the 1930s that would begin to give communists a new advantage. Chiang had to ally with communists to fight the Japanese threat, while his own power base, along the coast, was eroded by the powerful Japanese advance. The Chinese revolution was far from over.

GLOBAL CONNECTIONS: The 1920s and the World

Globalization retreated after World War I. There were important new connections. The League of Nations sought to provide an opportunity for discussions of diplomatic and military conflicts, but it could not prevent Japanese incursions into China. Various League agencies, like the International Labor Office, did promote better working conditions around the world, collecting significant data in the process. Many large European and American companies continued to expand their international operations. Hollywood solidified its hold as world movie capital, suggesting the acceleration of cultural as well as business contacts.

But these developments paled against the growing political isolation of the United States and the success of the Soviet Union in developing an independent pattern of industrialization, largely outside the world economy. International disarmament discussions produced few results as Japan, for example, defended its rights to expand its navy. Nationalism, gaining not only in the colonies but also in England and the United States, infused international contacts with a sense of bitter rivalry. Globalization retreat would intensify into the 1930s.

Further Readings

Sally Marks' *The Ebbing of European Ascendancy: An International History of the World: 1914–1945* (2002) is the new standard introduction to the diplomacy of the period. The previous standard, her own *The Illusion of Peace* (1976), remains useful due to its brevity and clarity. Good overall studies of the political revolutions of the period include Eric Wolf's *Peasant Wars of the Twentieth Century* (1965); Theda Skocpol's *States and Social Revolutions* (1970); and John Dunn's *Modern Revolutions* (1972). Mark N. Katz's

Reflections on Revolutions (1999) is an accessible survey of historical theories of revolution.

On the Russian Revolution, Sheila Fitzpatrick's *The Russian Revolution* (2nd ed., 1994) is an overview with a rich bibliography. See also E. H. Carr, *The Bolshevik Revolution, 1917–1923* (1978). Rex Wade's *The Russian Revolution, 1917* (2000) is a comprehensive social and political history of the revolution's early years. Edmund Wilson's *To the Finland Station* (1972) offers a dramatic account of the revolution's early phase and the philosophical currents that informed Bolshevik thinking. On specific social groups, see John Keep's *The Russian Revolution: A Study in Mass Mobilization* (1976) and Victoria Bonnell's *Roots of Rebellion: Workers' Politics and Organizations in St. Petersburg and Moscow, 1900–1914* (1983). Leon Trotsky's *History of the Russian Revolution*, a gripping narrative by a participant, surveys social, economic, and political dimensions of the revolution.

On fascism in Italy, R. J. B. Bosworth's *The Italian Dictatorship: Problems and Perspectives in the Interpretation of Mussolini and Fascism* (1998) traces changing historical thinking. Philip Morgan's *Italian Fascism, 1919–1945* (1995) provides a general overview. Emilio Gentile's *The Sacralization of Politics in Fascist Italy* (trans. Keith Botsford) (1996) examines popular political culture. C. F. Delzell's *Mediterranean Fascism, 1919–1945* (1970) provides documents and primary sources.

The economic history of Latin America is summarized in the classic by Brazilian economist Celso Furtado, *Economic Development of Latin America* (2nd ed., 1976), and in John Sheahan's *Patterns of Development in Latin America* (1987). There are many good studies of Latin American politics, but Guillermo O'Donnell's *Modernization and Bureaucratic Authoritarianism* (1973) has influenced much recent scholarship. Also useful are Alan Knight's *The Mexican Revolution*, 2 vols. (1986), and John M. Hart's *Revolutionary Mexico* (1987), which provide excellent analyses of that event. Freidrich Katz's *The Life and Times of Pancho Villa* (1998) is an outstanding biography.

On the cultural aspects of the U.S. influence on Latin America there is Gilbert Joseph et al., eds., *Close Encounters Empire* (1998). The role of the United States is discussed in Abraham Lowenthal's *Partners in Conflict: The United States and Latin America* (1987). Lester D. Langley's *The United States and the Caribbean in the Twentieth Century* (4th ed., 1989) gives a clear account of the recent history in that region, and Walter La Feber's *Inevitable Revolutions* (1984) is a critical assessment of U.S. policy in Central America.

For the United States, William Leuchtenburg's *The Perils of Prosperity, 1914–32* (1958) and David Joseph Goldberg's *Discontented America: The United States in the 1920s* (1999) are both useful introductions. Robert

Cruden, *Body and Soul: The Making of American Modernism* (2000), and Lynn Dumenil and Eric Foner, *The Modern Temper: American Culture and Society in the 1920s* (1995), offer intriguing analyses of the period. Robert Stern, Gregory Gilmartin, and Thomas Mellins, *New York: 1930* (1987), examines American architecture and urbanism between the two world wars. Steve Watson's *The Harlem Renaissance* (1995) is unsurpassed as a general study of African-American culture and society in the "Roaring Twenties." Paula Fass' *The Damned and the Beautiful: American Youth in the 1920's* (1977) remains the best introduction to the "Lost Generation."

Some of the best general studies on China in the early 20th century include Lucian Bianco's *The Communist Revolution in China* (1967); C. P. Fitzgerald's *Birth of Communist China* (1964); Wolfgang Franke's *A Century of Chinese Revolution, 1851–1949* (1970); and Jonathan Spence's *The Search for Modern China* (1990). For firsthand accounts of conditions in the revolutionary era, see especially Graham Peck's *Two Kinds of Time* (1950); Edgar Snow's *Red Star over China* (1938); and Theodore White and Analee Jacoby's *Thunder out of China* (1946).

On the Web

The British Broadcasting System has provided a very user-friendly guide (http://www.bbc.co.uk/education/modern/russia/russihtm.htm) to study the origins of the Russian Revolution, including how global historical forces, such as the First World War, shaped its course. The initial program of the Russian Provisional Government (http://www.dur.ac.uk/~dml0www/provgov1.html), its worst political blunders (http://www.historylearningsite.co.uk/provisional_government.htm), and the revealing lyrics of its national anthem (http://www.national-anthems.net/~davidk/ruf2-txt.htm) are also accessible on the Web. The Lenin Archive (http://www.marxists.org/archive/lenin/) is a good place to find the works, a biography, and images of the Bolshevik leader. Other useful sites for further study of Lenin and other leaders of the early communist movement are http://www2.cddc.vt.edu/marxist/archive/index.html, http://www.campus.northpark.edu/history/WebChron/EastEurope/OctRev.html, and http://www.marxist.com/Russia/rev-betrayed.html.

Benito Mussolini's vision of fascism can be glimpsed at http://www.fordham.edu/halsall/mod/mussolini-fascism.html. Italian fascism and life in fascist Italy is explained at http://www.library.wisc.edu/libraries/dpf/Fascism/Intro.html. An internal link at this site (http://www.library.wisc.edu/libraries/dpf/Fascism/Youth.html) offers a vivid look into the manner in which young fascists were indoctrinated via a magazine, a glimpse of whose front covers are alone worth a visit to the site.

The struggles of Latin Americans in the early 20th century are traced at sites exploring the lives of Pancho Villa, such as http://ojinaga.com/villa/ and http://www.mexconnect.com/mex_/history/panchovilla1.html.

Life in the United States in the 1920s is illuminated at http://www.cvip.fresno.com/~jsh33/roar.html and http://www.webtech.kennesaw.edu/jcheek3/roaring_twenties.htm. Other sites examine in detail the Scopes "Monkey Trial" (http://www.xroads.virginia.edu/~UG97/inherit/1925home.html), Prohibition (http://www.prohibition.history.ohio-state.edu/), and Harlem in the jazz age (http://www.etext.lib.virginia.edu/harlem/index.html). The path that led to the winning of the vote for women is traced at http://www.memory.loc.gov/ammem/naw/nawshome.html, while the role of women peace activists during the Red Scare is examined at http://www.womhist.binghampton.edu/wilpf/intro.htm.

Links to sites illuminating key figures in the fall of the Qing empire can be found at a useful biography of Yuan Shi-Kai at http://www.wikipedia.org/wiki/Yuan_Shikai. The emergence of Republican China, including Sun Yat Sen's early political platform, is treated at http://www.chaos.umd.edu/history/republican.html. The life of Chiang Kai-shek as seen against the background of nationalist politics is provided at http://www.wsu.edu:8001/~dee/MODCHINA/NATIONAL.HTM. An interesting reflection on the legacy of the student-led May the Fourth Movement is offered at http://www.fas.harvard.edu/~asiactr/haq/199903/9903a003.htm. An excellent introduction to the life of Mao Zedong is provided at http://www.asiasource.org/society/mao.cfm.

CHAPTER 30

THE GREAT DEPRESSION AND THE AUTHORITARIAN RESPONSE

Soviet poster: The heroic image of the Russian worker

- The Global Great Depression
- **IN DEPTH:** The Decline of the West?
- Economic and Political Changes in Latin America
- The Militarization of Japan
- Stalinism in the Soviet Union
- **DOCUMENT:** Socialist Realism
- **VISUALIZING THE PAST:** Socialist Realism
- New Political and Economic Realities
- **GLOBAL CONNECTIONS:** Depression and Retreat

The worldwide economic depression that began in 1929—and became known as the **Great Depression**—ushered in a number of important new developments. There were important continuities from the 1920s, which the Depression merely intensified. These included the decline of globalization and the shakiness of Western democracies. But there were outright innovations as well. New regimes arose, such as Nazi Germany and fascist or semifascist governments elsewhere, including Japan. Stalinist Russia solidified a police state, while China turned further away from experiments with democracy. The Depression encouraged new authoritarian regimes in Latin America, along with changes in economic policy. Overall, economic depression and political change led directly to World War II. The global framework that had been established under Western dominance before World War I, already shaken, now seemed to collapse entirely.

The Global Great Depression

 Though centered in the West, the economic collapse that began in 1929 had worldwide causes and effects. Reactions to the Depression varied. The rise of Nazism was a startling change within western Europe.

Coming barely a decade after the turmoil of World War I, the onset of global economic depression constituted a crucial next step in the mounting spiral of international crisis. The crash of the New York stock market hit the headlines in 1929, but in fact the Depression had begun, sullenly, in many parts of the world economy even earlier. The Depression resulted from new problems in the industrial economy of Europe and the United States, combined with the long-term weakness in economies, like those of Latin America, that depended on sales of cheap exports in the international market. The result was a worldwide collapse that spared only a few economies and brought political as well as economic pressures on virtually every society.

Causation

The impact of the First World War on the European economy had led to several rocky years into the early 1920s. War-induced inflation, enhanced by government policies in the years after the war, was a particular problem in Germany, as prices soared daily and ordinary purchases required huge quantities of currency. Forceful government action finally resolved this crisis in 1923 but only by a massive devaluation of the German mark, which did nothing to restore lost savings. More generally, a sharp, brief recession in 1920 and 1921 had reflected other postwar dislocations, though by 1923 production levels had regained or surpassed prewar levels. Great Britain, an industrial pioneer that was already victim of a loss of dynamism before the war, recovered more slowly, in part because of its unusually great dependence on an export market now open to wider competition.

Structural problems affected other areas of Europe besides Britain and lasted well beyond the predictable readjustments to peacetime. Farmers throughout much

1920 C.E.	1930 C.E.
1920–1940 Muralist movement in Mexico	**1930** U.S. Congress passes the Smoot-Hawley tariff; economic downturn in western Europe, especially Germany, and throughout European colonial empires; rapid rise of Nazi party in Germany
1921 Chinese Communist party founded	
1921 Lenin's New Economic Policy in USSR	**1931** Statute of Westminster gives full autonomy to British Dominions of Canada, Australia, New Zealand, South Africa, and the Irish Free State; failed rebellion against Japanese rule in Korea; poor harvests and severe economic dislocations in Japan; Japanese invasion of Manchuria
1922 Fascists seize power in Italy	
1927–1928 Collectivization and first five-year plan under Stalin	
1929 Women given the right to vote in Ecuador; New York stock market crashes	**1932** Franklin Roosevelt begins four-term tenure as United States president and launches the New Deal
	1932–1934 Forced collectivization at height in the USSR; genocidal famine inflicted on the Ukraine and other areas
	1933 Adolf Hitler becomes chancellor of Germany
	1934–1940 Cárdenas president in Mexico, extensive land reform
	1935 Nuremberg laws deprive Jews of German citizenship; Mussolini's armies invade Ethiopia; outbreak of the civil war in Spain
	1936 Popular Front government formed in France; junior army officers revolt in Japan, key political leaders assassinated
	1936–1938 Height of Stalinist purges in USSR
	1937 Full-scale Japanese invasion of China
	1938 *Kristallnacht* begins intensification of attacks on Jews in Germany; Munich agreement allows Hitler to begin destruction of Czechoslovakia
	1938 Japan's military leaders impose state control over economy and social system, Diet approves war budget
	1939 Outbreak of World War II

of the Western world, including the United States, faced almost chronic overproduction of food and resulting low prices. Food production had soared in response to wartime needs; during the postwar inflation many farmers, both in western Europe and in North America, borrowed heavily to buy new equipment, overconfident that their good markets would be sustained. But rising European production combined with large imports from the Americas and New Zealand sent prices down, which lowered earnings and made debts harder to repay. One response was continued population flight from the countryside, as urbanization continued. Remaining farmers were hard pressed and unable to sustain high demand for manufactured goods.

Thus although economies in France and Germany seemed to have recovered by 1925, problems continued: the fears inflation had generated, which in turn limited the capacity of governments to respond to other problems, as well as the weaknesses in the buying power of key groups. In this situation, much of the mid-decade prosperity rested on exceedingly fragile grounds. Loans from U.S. banks to various European enterprises helped sustain demand for goods but on condition that additional loans pour in to help pay off the resultant debts.

Furthermore, most of the dependant areas in the world economy, colonies and noncolonies alike, were suffering badly. Pronounced tendencies toward overproduction developed in the smaller nations of eastern Europe, which sent agricultural goods to western Europe, as well as among tropical producers in Africa and Latin America. Here, continued efforts to win export revenue pressed local estate owners to drive up output in coffee, sugar, and rubber. As European governments and businesses organized their African colonies for more profitable exploitation, they set up large estates devoted to goods of this type. Again, production frequently exceeded demand, which drove prices and earnings down in both Africa and Latin America. This meant, in turn, that many colonies and dependant economies were unable to buy many industrial exports, which weakened demand for Western products precisely when output tended to rise amid growing U.S. and Japanese competition. Several food-exporting regions, including many of the new eastern European nations, fell into a depression, in terms of earnings and employment, by the mid-1920s, well before the full industrial catastrophe.

Governments of the leading industrial nations provided scant leadership during the emerging crisis of the 1920s. Knowledge of economics was often feeble within a Western leadership group not noteworthy for its quality even in more conventional areas. Nationalistic selfishness predominated. Western nations were more concerned about insisting on repayment of any debts owed to them or about constructing tariff barriers to protect their own industries than about facilitating balanced world economic growth. Protectionism, in particular, as practiced even by traditionally free-trade Great Britain and by the many nations in eastern Europe, simply reduced market opportunities and made a bad situation worse. By the later 1920s employment in key Western industrial sectors—coal (also beset by new competition from imported oil), iron, and textiles—began to decline, the foretaste of more general collapse.

The Debacle

The formal advent of the Depression occurred in October 1929, when the New York stock market collapsed. Stock values tumbled as investors quickly lost confidence in prices that had been pushed ridiculously high. Banks, which had depended heavily on their stock investments, rapidly echoed the financial crisis, and many institutions failed, dragging their depositors along with them. Even before this crash, Americans had begun to call back earlier loans to Europe. Yet the European credit structure depended extensively on U.S. loans, which had fueled some industrial expansion but also less productive investments, such as German reparations payments and the construction of fancy town halls and other amenities. In Europe, as in the United States, many commercial enterprises existed on the basis not of real production power but of continued speculation. When one piece of the speculative spiral was withdrawn, the whole edifice quickly collapsed. Key bank failures in Austria and Germany followed the U.S. crisis. Throughout most of the industrial West, investment funds dried up as creditors went bankrupt or tried to pull in their horns.

With investment receding, industrial production quickly began to fall, beginning with the industries that produced capital goods and extending quickly to consumer products fields. Falling production—levels dropped by as much as one-third by 1932—meant falling employment and lower wages, which in turn withdrew still more demand from the economy and led to further hardship. Unemployed and underpaid workers could not buy goods whose production

might give other workers jobs. The existing weakness of some markets, such as the farm sector or the nonindustrial world, was exacerbated as demand for foods and minerals plummeted. New and appalling problems developed among workers, now out of jobs or suffering from reduced hours and reduced pay (see Figure 30.1), as well as among the middle classes. The Depression, in sum, fed on itself, growing steadily worse from 1929 to 1933. Even countries initially less hard hit, such as France and Italy, saw themselves drawn into the vortex by 1931.

In itself the Great Depression was not entirely unprecedented. Previous periods had seen slumps triggered by bank failures and overspeculation, yielding several years of falling production, unemployment, and hardship. But the intensity of the Great Depression had no precedent in the brief history of industrial societies. Its duration was also unprecedented; in many countries, full recovery came only after a decade and only with the forced production schedules provoked by World War II. Unlike earlier depressions, this one

Figure 30.1 *This photo of a woman in the United States exemplifies unemployment and poverty during the Great Depression.*

came on the heels of so much other distress—the economic hardships of war, for example, and the catastrophic inflation of the 1920s—and caught most governments totally unprepared.

The Depression was more, of course, than an economic event. It reached into countless lives, creating hardship and tension that would be recalled even as the crisis itself eased. Loss of earnings, loss of work, or simply fears that loss would come devastated people at all social levels. The suicides of ruined investors in New York were paralleled by the vagrants' camps and begging that spread among displaced workers. The statistics were grim; up to one-third of all blue-collar workers in the West lost their jobs for prolonged periods. White-collar unemployment, though not quite as severe, was also unparalleled. In Germany 600,000 of four million white-collar workers had lost their jobs by 1931. Graduating students could not find work or had to resort to jobs they regarded as insecure or demeaning. Six million overall unemployed in Germany and 22 percent of the labor force unemployed in Britain were statistics of stark misery and despair. Families were disrupted; men felt emasculated at their inability to provide, and women and children were disgusted with authority figures whose authority was now hollow. In some cases wives and mothers found it easier to gain jobs in a low-wage economy than their husbands did, and although this development had some promise in terms of new opportunities for women, it could also be confusing for standard family roles. For many, the agony and personal disruption of the Depression were desperately prolonged, with renewed recession around 1937 and with unemployment still averaging 10 percent or more in many countries as late as 1939.

Inevitably, the Depression affected popular culture, reducing the excitement and experimentation of the 1920s. Women's fashions became more sedate, with skirt lengths dropping. Movies emphasized escapist themes, as consumer culture continued amid growing poverty. In the United States the comic book character Superman was introduced in the late 1930s to provide an alternative to the constraints of normal life.

The Depression, like World War I, was an event that blatantly contradicted the optimistic assumptions of the later 19th century. To many it showed the fragility of any idea of progress, and belief that Western civilization was becoming more humane. To still more it challenged the notion that the parliamentary democracies of the West were able to control their own destinies. Because it was a second catastrophic event within a generation, the Depression led to even more extreme results than the war had done—more bizarre experiments, more paralysis in the face of deepening despair. Just as the Depression had been caused by a combination of specifically Western problems and wider weaknesses in the world economy, so its effects had both Western twists and international repercussions.

A few economies were buffered from the Depression. The Soviet Union, busy building an industrial society under communist control and under the heading **socialism in one country,** had cut off all but the most insignificant economic ties with other nations. The result placed great hardships on many Russian people, called to sustain rapid industrial development without outside capital, but it did prevent anything like a depression during the 1930s. Soviet leaders pointed with pride to the steadily rising production rates and lack of serious unemployment, in a telling contrast with the miseries of Western capitalism at the time.

For most of the world, however, the Depression worsened an already bleak economic picture. Western markets could absorb fewer commodity imports as production fell and incomes dwindled. Hence the nations that produced foods and raw materials saw prices and earnings drop even more than before. Unemployment rose rapidly in the export sectors of the Latin American economy, creating a major political challenge not unlike that faced by the Western nations. Japan, a new industrial country, still heavily depended on export earnings for financing its imports of essential fuel and raw materials. The Japanese silk industry, an export staple, was already suffering from the advent of artificial silklike fibers produced by Western chemical giants. Now Western luxury purchases collapsed, leading to severe unemployment in Japan and a crucial political crisis. Between 1929 and 1931, the value of Japanese exports plummeted by 50 percent. Workers' real income dropped by almost one-third, and more than three million people were unemployed. Depression was compounded by poor harvests in several regions, leading to rural begging and near starvation.

The Great Depression, though most familiar in its Western dimensions, was a truly international collapse, a sign of the tight bonds and serious imbalances that had developed in world trading patterns. The results of the collapse, and particularly the varied responses to it, are best traced in individual cases. For Latin America the Depression stimulated new kinds of effective political action, particularly greater state involvement in economic planning and direction. New government vigor did not cure the economic effects of the Depression, which escaped the control of most individual states, but it did set an important new phase in this civilization's political evolution. For Japan the Depression increased suspicions of the West and helped promote new expansionism designed, among other things, to win more assured markets in Asia. In the West the Depression led to new welfare programs that stimulated demand and helped restore confidence, but it also led to radical social and political experiments, such as German Nazism. What was common in this welter of reactions was the intractable global quality of the Depression, which made it impossible for any purely national policy to restore full prosperity. Even Nazi Germany, which boasted of regaining full employment, continued to suffer from low wages and other dislocations aside from its obvious and growing dependence on military production. The reactions to the Depression, including a sense of weakness and confusion in many quarters inside and outside policy circles, helped to bring the final great crisis of the first half of the 20th century: a second, and more fully international, world war.

Responses to the Depression in Western Europe

In western Europe as in the United States, the Great Depression revealed that neither the economic nor the political achievements of the mid-1920s had been as solidly based as had been hoped. Political consequences were inevitable with so many people out of work or threatened with unemployment. The relatively weak Western governments responded to the onset of the catastrophe counterproductively. National tariffs were raised to keep out the goods of other countries, but this merely worsened the international economy and curbed sales for everyone. Most governments tried to cut spending, reflecting the decline in revenues that accompanied falling production. They were concerned about avoiding renewed inflation, but in fact their measures further reduced economic stimulus and

pushed additional workers—government employees—out of jobs. Confidence in the normal political process deteriorated. In many countries the Depression heightened political polarization. People sought solutions from radical parties or movements, both on the left and on the right. Support for communist parties increased in many countries, and in important cases the authoritarian movement on the right gained increased attention. Even in relatively stable countries, such as Britain, battles between the Conservative party and the labor movement made decisive policy difficult. Class conflict rose to new levels, in and out of politics.

In key cases, the Great Depression led to one of two effects: either a parliamentary system that became increasingly incapacitated, unable to come to grips with the new economic dilemma and too divided to take vigorous action, even in foreign policy, or the outright overturning of the parliamentary system.

France was a prime example of the first pattern. The French government reacted sluggishly to the Depression. Voters responded by moving toward the political extremes. Socialist and then communist parties expanded. Rightist movements calling for a strong leader and fervent nationalism grew, their adherents often disrupting political meetings in order to discredit the parliamentary system by making orderly debate impossible. In response liberal, socialist, and communist parties formed the **Popular Front** in 1936 to win the election. The Popular Front government, however, was unable to take strong measures of social reform because of the ongoing strength of conservative republicans hostile to change and the authoritarian right that looked to forceful leadership to contain the lower classes. The same paralysis crept into foreign policy, as Popular Front leaders, initially eager to support the new liberal regime in Spain that was attacked by conservative army leaders in the Spanish Civil War, found themselves forced to pull back. The Popular Front fell in 1938, but even before this France was close to a standstill.

There were more constructive responses. Scandinavian states, most of them directed by moderate socialist parties, increased government spending, providing new levels of social insurance against illness and unemployment. This foreshadowed the welfare state. British policy was more tentative, but new industrial sectors emerged under the leadership of innovative businessmen. The world's first television industry, for example, took shape in southern

England in the late 1930s, though it was too small to break the hold of the Depression.

The New Deal

After a few years of floundering, the United States generated another set of creative responses. Initial American policies, under President Herbert Hoover, resembled those of western Europe, in seeking higher tariffs and attempting to cut spending in reaction to falling revenues. The United States also sought to accelerate war debt repayments from Europe, which also made matters worse internationally. In 1933 a new administration took over, under Franklin Roosevelt, offering a "new deal" to the American people.

New Deal policies, as they unfolded during the 1930s, offered more direct aid to Americans at risk, through increased unemployment benefits and other measures. Many unemployed people were given jobs on public works projects. A crucial innovation was the Social Security system, based on contributions from workers and employers and designed to provide protection in unemployment and old age. The New Deal also undertook some economic planning and stimulus, for both industry and agriculture, while installing new regulations on banking.

The New Deal ushered in a period of rapid government growth, a watershed in American history particularly as it was followed by the massive expansion of military operations in World War II. The regime did not solve the Depression, which sputtered on until wartime spending ended it in the early 1940s. It also did not install a full welfare state, holding back, for example, from plans to offer a health insurance system. But the New Deal did restore the confidence of most Americans in their political system, preempting more extremist political movements and minimizing the kind of paralysis that afflicted Britain and France in the same years.

Nazism and Fascism

German patterns differed markedly from the wavering responses of Germany's neighbors, and from democratic welfare innovation as well. In Germany the impact of the Depression led directly to a new fascist regime. Germany had suffered the shock of loss in World War I, enhanced by treaty arrangements that cast primary blame for the war on the German nation, which had only recent and shaky parliamentary traditions. A number of factors, in sum, combined to make Germany a fertile breeding ground for fascism, though it took the Depression to bring this current to the fore.

Fascism in Germany, as in Italy, was a product of the war. The movement's advocates, many of them former veterans, attacked the weakness of parliamentary democracy and the corruption and class conflict of Western capitalism. They proposed a strong state ruled by a powerful leader who would revive the nation's forces through vigorous foreign and military policy. While fascists vaguely promised social reforms to alleviate class antagonisms, their attacks on trade unions as well as on socialist and communist parties pleased landlords and business groups. Although fascism won outright control only in Italy in the movement's early years, fascist parties complicated the political process in a number of other nations during the 1920s and beyond. But it was the advent of the National Socialist, or Nazi, regime in Germany under Adolf Hitler that made this new political movement a major force in world history. Here, a Western commitment to liberal, democratic political forms was challenged and reversed.

In his vote-gathering campaigns, in the later 1920s and early 1930s, Hitler repeated standard fascist arguments about the need for unity and the hopeless weakness of parliamentary politics. The state should provide guidance, for it was greater than the sum of individual interests, and the leader should guide the state. Hitler promised many groups a return to more traditional ways; thus many artisans voted for him in the belief that preindustrial economic institutions, such as the guilds, would be revived. Middle-class elements, including big-business leaders, were attracted to Hitler's commitment to a firm stance against socialism and communism. Hitler also focused grievances against various currents in modern life, from big department stores to feminism, by attacking what he claimed were Jewish influences in Germany. He promised a glorious foreign policy to undo the wrongs of the Versailles treaty. Finally, Hitler represented a hope for effective action against the Depression. Although the Nazis never won a majority vote in a free election, his party did win the largest single slice in 1932, and this enabled Hitler to make arrangements with other political leaders for his rise to power legally in 1933.

Once in power, Hitler quickly set about constructing a **totalitarian state**—a new kind of

In Depth

The Decline of the West?

At various points in the 20th century, influential Western thinkers and leaders worried about the decline of Western society. Sometimes their concerns focused on the undeniably relative decline of the West in the world, which set the 20th century off from the periods in world history between the late 18th century and 1920. In the 1980s, for example, various U.S. news magazines began to trumpet the idea of an emerging "Pacific century," dominated by east Asian powers, that would replace the period of Western (and recently, U.S.) preponderance.

The idea of absolute decline has its proponents in the 21st century. The West's relative loss of power over the past 60 years, with decolonization and the rise of Japanese exports, may produce absolute decline compared to earlier Western leadership. Some societies—such as the Roman Empire or the Ottoman Empire—depended on continued expansion to provide labor or booty for the upper class and then began to lose their vitality when further growth became impossible. The West no longer requires colonies to provide slaves, but it may have become so dependant on its ability to dominate other economies that relative decline will spell the beginning of a new period of internal woes.

Furthermore, there have been numerous periods in which developments in the West provoked gloom. Early in the 20th century the German philosopher Oswald Spengler, pondering the growing pleasure-seeking Western culture and its internal divisions, wrote *The Decline of the West*, in which he predicted that Western civilization was going the way of Rome. He argued that the West was doomed to fall before the onslaught of such vigorous but less civilized peoples as the Russians or the Americans. His book was hugely popular after World War I, when it looked as if Western nations had indeed inflicted grievous injury on their own civilization. Other historians, though somewhat less cosmically pessimistic than Spengler, have picked up the theme of what they see as an inevitable decline of societies following periods of vigor. The theme seemed to fit western Europe again immediately after World War II, when both victors and vanquished were suffering through the immense problems of reconstruction. It was revived again in the late 1980s, when the world dominance of the United States seemed in retreat.

Other observers, though less systematic, discerned internal decay. Some focused on cultural trends, bemoaning the lack of standards in art—the tendency to play with novel styles, however frivolous, simply to win attention. Or they criticized popular culture for shallow, manipulable materialism and vulgar sexuality. Some critics saw analogies between modern Western commercialism and the Roman "bread and circuses" approach to the urban masses that, they argued, had weakened the empire's moral fiber and reduced its capacity for work and military valor.

Analogies, however, are inexact, and the role of moral decline in causing Rome's downfall is debatable in any event. One of the problems in comparing current Western trends to past cases of decline—even subtler cases, such as the gradual reduction of Arab vitality in the later postclassical era—is that modern conditions as shaped by industrialization may weaken the applicability of past standards.

Western demography is a case in point. There is no question that the demographic vitality of the West weakened in the late 19th and 20th centuries; the baby boom era, from 1946 to 1963, provided a brief if interesting exception. Birth rates in the West declined fairly steadily in the 1930s and again by the 1980s, reaching a point close to bare reproduction. Indeed, some Western nations, such as Germany, were by the 1980s coming close to falling beneath reproduction levels, with birth rates so low that population decline would soon set in unless compensated by further immigration. Moreover, slow or zero population growth was accompanied by increased percentages of the aged, the result of advancing life expectancy combined with the relatively small number of children being born. In most historic situations, slowing population growth has signaled a general decrease in vitality, causing further decline as competition and the opportunity provided by population increase waned. Unquestionably, the West's demographic trends reduced its percentage of world population, which might relate to its relative decline and certainly opened it to new immigration from various parts of the world. But the total package is difficult to measure, for in the context of an industrial society, which provides a variety of technical aids to human labor and is a heavy consumer of resources, stable populations might prove a source of strength, not weakness,

(continued)

whereas rapid population increase might be a fateful burden that limits effective development.

Judgments about decline, finally, are complicated by the cycles of Western history during the past hundred years and by the nature of modern Western expectations. Periods of great disarray, like the 1930s, have not thus far led to long-term chaos, as Western nations have seemed able to bounce back. Other decades roused anxieties mainly because of the heavy Western commitment to steady progress. Thus during the 1970s, when economic growth slowed, many polls showed that Americans stopped believing that their society would advance in the future (though interestingly they still believed that their own lives would get better). Yet the 1970s brought no huge crisis, simply a slowing in the pace of improvement. The Western habit of expecting steady economic advance could easily lead to temporary exaggerations of what 1970s Americans called "malaise."

Clearly, to paraphrase Mark Twain, reports of the death of the West seem, at the beginning of the 21st century, premature. Yet past examples from world history suggest one other caution: Social decline, if it does set in, typically takes a long time to work through. Rome declined for three centuries before it "fell"; the Ottoman Empire began to turn downward two centuries before it became known as "sick." The first century of decline may be difficult to perceive yet particularly important to monitor in case restorative measures are necessary.

Questions: Did the West shown signs of cultural decline in the 20th century? What is the best case for arguing that 20th-century Western history does not suggest cultural decline? If the West is in decline, what might be done about it? Does world history suggest that decline is reversible?

---

government that would exercise massive, direct control over virtually all the activities of its subjects. Hitler eliminated all opposition parties; he purged the bureaucracy and military, installing loyal Nazis in many posts. His secret police, the **Gestapo,** arrested hundreds of thousands of political opponents. Trade unions were replaced by government-sponsored bodies that tried to appease low-paid workers by offering full employment and various welfare benefits. Government economic planning helped restore production levels, with particular emphasis on armaments construction. Hitler cemented his regime by continual, well-staged propaganda bombardments (see Figure 30.2), strident nationalism, and an incessant attack on Germany's large Jewish minority.

Hitler's hatred of Jews ran deep; he blamed them for various personal misfortunes and also for socialism and excessive capitalism—movements that in his view had weakened the German spirit. Obviously, anti-Semitism served as a catchall for a host of diverse dissatisfactions, and as such it appealed to many Germans. Anti-Semitism also played into Hitler's hands by providing a scapegoat that could rouse national passions and distract the population from other problems. Measures against Jews became more and more severe; they were forced to wear special emblems,

their property was attacked and seized, and increasing numbers were sent to concentration camps. After 1940 Hitler's policy insanely turned to the literal elimination of European Jewry, as the Holocaust raged in the concentration camps of Germany and conquered territories (see Chapter 31).

Hitler's foreign and military policies were based on preparation for war. He wanted to not only recoup Germany's World War I losses, but also create a land empire that would extend across much of Europe, particularly toward the east against what he saw as the inferior Slavic peoples. Progressively Hitler violated the limits on German armaments and annexed neighboring territories, provoking only weak response from the Western democracies.

Hitler suspended German reparation payments, thus renouncing this part of the Versailles settlement; he walked out of a disarmament conference and withdrew from the League of Nations. In 1935 he announced German rearmament and in 1936 brought military forces into the Rhineland—both moves in further violation of the Versailles treaty. When France and Britain loudly protested but did nothing more, and the isolationist United States said even less, Hitler was poised for the further buildup of German strength and further diplomatic adventures that would ultimately lead to World War II.

Figure 30.2 *The adulation that the German masses felt for Adolf Hitler in the mid 1930s is evident in this rally photo. Hitler's popularity rested primarily on his promises to rebuild Germany's deeply depressed economy and restore its world power status by reversing the 1919 Treaty of Paris ending World War I.*

In 1938 Hitler proclaimed a long-sought union, or **Anschluss,** with Austria as a fellow German nation. Western powers complained and denounced but did nothing. War threatened, but at a conference in 1938 in Munich, Hitler persuaded the British prime minister, Neville Chamberlain, that he would be satisfied with the concession of just the heavily German populated Sudetenland portions of Czechoslovakia. In the months following the conference, Nazi armies occupied these regions. Chamberlain, seizing on Hitler's apparent eagerness to compromise, proclaimed that his **appeasement** had won "peace in our time." ("Our time" turned out to be slightly more than a year.) Emboldened by Western weakness, in March 1939 Hitler's forces dismantled the rest of Czechoslovakia and began to press Poland for territorial concessions. He also concluded an agreement with the Soviet Union, which was not ready for war with Germany and had despaired of Western resolve. The Soviets also coveted parts of Poland, the Baltic states, and Finland for their own, and when Hitler invaded Poland, Russia launched its own war to undo the Versailles settlement. Hitler attacked Poland on September 1, 1939, not necessarily expecting general war but clearly prepared to risk it; Britain and France, now convinced that nothing short of war would stop the Nazis, made their own declaration in response. War had been an integral part of Nazism all along; now it moved to center stage.

The Spread of Fascism and the Spanish Civil War

Nazi triumph in Germany inevitably spurred fascism in other parts of Europe. Many east central states, already authoritarian, took on fascist trappings. Explicit fascist movements emerged in Hungary and Romania. Fascism in Austria was vindicated when Hitler proclaimed the union of Austria and Germany in 1938, quickly spreading the apparatus of the Nazi party and state.

Hitler's advent galvanized the authoritarian regime of a nearby power, Italy, where a fascist state had been formed in the 1920s, led by Benito Mussolini. Like Hitler, Mussolini had promised an aggressive foreign policy and new nationalist glories, but in fact his first decade had been rather moderate diplomatically. With Hitler in power, however, Mussolini began to experiment more boldly, if only to avoid being overshadowed completely.

In 1935 Mussolini attacked Ethiopia, planning to avenge Italy's failure to conquer this ancient land during the imperialist surge of the 1890s. The League of Nations condemned the action, but neither it nor the democratic powers in Europe and North America took action. Consequently, after some hard fighting, the Italians won their new colony. Here, then, was another destabilizing element in world politics.

Fascism also spread into Spain, leading to the **Spanish Civil War.** Here, forces supporting a parliamentary republic plus social reform had feuded since 1931 with advocates of a military-backed authoritarian state. In 1936 outright civil war broke out. Spanish military forces, led by General Francisco Franco, were backed by an explicitly fascist party, the Falange, as well as more conventionally conservative landowners and Catholic leaders.

Republican forces included various groups, with support from peasants and workers in various parts of the country. Communists and a large anarchist movement played a crucial role. They won some support also from volunteers from the United States and western Europe, and from the Soviet Union.

Bitter fighting consumed much of Spain for three years. German and Italian forces bombed several Spanish cities, a rehearsal for the bombing of civilians in World War II. France, Britain, and the United States made vague supporting gestures to the republican forces but offered no concrete aid, fearful of provoking a wider conflict and paralyzed by internal disagreements about foreign policy. Franco's forces won in 1939. The resultant regime was not fully fascist, but it maintained authoritarian controls and catered to landlords, church, and army for the next 25 years.

Economic and Political Changes in Latin America

 Latin America, hit hard by the Great Depression, responded with important new political systems and an effort to gain greater economic independence.

In Latin America, the Depression followed more than a decade of social and cultural tension. During and after World War I, Latin American economies had expanded and the population continued to increase, especially in the cities. The growth of middle-class and working-class populations challenged traditional oligarchies and resulted in new political parties, often populist and nationalist. These new parties and the traditional elites attacked liberalism and laissez-faire capitalism, which were clearly in crisis by the time of the world economic crash in 1929. The Mexican Revolution had a limited immediate impact beyond the borders of Mexico, but the outbreak of World War I affected most of Latin America directly.

The economic boom of the late 19th century had continued into the early 20th century. Each nation had its specialized crop or set of exports: coffee from Colombia, Brazil, and Costa Rica; minerals from Bolivia, Chile, and Peru; bananas from Ecuador and Central America; and sugar from Cuba. As long as European demand remained high, groups in control of these exports profited greatly.

World War I had some immediate effects on the Latin American economies. Cut off from supplies of traditional imports, these countries experienced a spurt of industrial growth in what economists call **import substitution industrialization.** Latin Americans had to produce for themselves some of what they had formerly imported. Most of this involved light industry such as textiles (see Figure 30.3). Latin America continued to suffer from a lack of capital, limited markets (because so many people had so little to spend), and low technological levels. Still, changes took place. Moreover, during the war European demand for some products increased. World War I had stimulated the economy, but it was a false start. After the war, a general inflation meant that the real wages of the working classes declined and their worsening condition contributed to increasing political unrest.

That unrest also resulted from population growth, which was rapid in some countries. Immigrants continued to pour into Argentina, Brazil, and some of the other countries with a temperate climate, swelling the ranks of the rural and urban working classes. Cities grew in size and importance. Some, such as Lima, Montevideo, Quito, and Mexico City, so dominated the economic and political resources of their countries that growth outside the capital was difficult. Rapid urban growth created a series of social problems that reflected the transformation of Latin America from agrarian to industrializing societies.

Labor and the Middle Class

The rising importance of urban labor and the growth of an urban middle class led to changes in the political structure of some Latin American nations. The traditional land-owning oligarchy in countries such as Argentina, Chile, and Brazil began to open up the political system to meet the desire of the growing middle class to share political power. In Argentina, for example, a new electoral law in 1912 resulted in the 1916 triumph of the middle-class–based Radical party. After some preliminary attempts to forge an alliance

Figure 30.3 *The growing labor force that resulted from Latin American industrialization began to change the nature of urban life and politics. Here, women in Orizaba, Mexico, are making sacks for coffee.*

with workers, however, that strategy was abandoned in favor of closer ties with the traditional elites. In Brazil, after the establishment of a republic in 1889, a series of conservative presidents from the Republican party in the wealthiest and most powerful states held control of the government. This alliance of traditional landed interests and urban middle classes maintained political stability and a business-as-usual approach to government, but it began to encounter a series of opponents during the 1920s. Reformist military officers, disaffected state politicians, bandits, and millenarian peasant movements seeking a return to a golden age all acted in different ways against the political system and the system of export–import capitalism that seemed to produce increasing inequality while it produced great wealth. Similar criticisms were voiced throughout Latin America.

As in western Europe, in Latin America the growing industrial and urban labor forces began to exert some influence on politics during the first decades of the century. Not surprisingly, many workers were engaged in export production or in related transportation activities. Immigrants from Spain, Italy, and elsewhere in Europe sometimes came with well-developed political goals and ideologies. These ideologies ranged from anarchism, which aimed to smash the state entirely by using the general strike to gain power, to **syndicalism,** which aimed to use the organization of labor to achieve that goal. Railroad, dock, and mining workers often were among the most radical and the first to organize; usually they were met with force. Hundreds of miners in Iquique, Chile, striking against awful conditions in 1907, were shot down by government forces. Between 1914 and 1930, a series of general strikes and labor unrest swept through much of Latin America. Sometimes, as in Argentina in 1919 during the **Tragic Week,** the government reaction to "revolutionary workers," many of whom were foreign born, led to brutal repression under the guise of nationalism. A growing sense of class conflict developed in Latin America as in western Europe during this period, even though most workers were still rural and unorganized.

Ideology and Social Reform

In the 1920s and 1930s, the failures of liberalism were becoming increasingly apparent. A middle class had emerged and had begun to enter politics, but unlike its western European counterpart, it gained power only in conjunction with the traditional oligarchy or the military. In Latin America, the ideology of liberalism was not an expression of the strength of the middle class but rather a series of ideas not particularly suited to the realities of Latin America, where large segments of the population were landless, uneducated, and destitute. Increasing industrialization did not dissolve the old class boundaries, nor did public education and other classic liberal programs produce as much social mobility as had been expected.

Disillusioned by liberalism and World War I, artists and intellectuals who had looked to Europe for inspiration turned to Latin America's own populations and history for values and solutions to Latin American problems. During the 1920s intellectuals complained that Latin America was on a race to nowhere. In literature and the arts, the ideas of rationality, progress, and order associated with liberalism and the outward appearances of democracy were under attack.

Ideas of reform and social change were in the air. University students in Córdoba, Argentina, began a reform of their university system that gave the university more autonomy and students more power within it. This movement soon spread to other countries. There were other responses as well. Socialist and communist parties were formed or grew in strength in several Latin American nations in this period, especially after the Russian Revolution of 1917. The strength of these parties of the left originated in local conditions but sometimes was aided by the international communist movement. Although criticism of existing governments and of liberalism as a political and economic philosophy came from these left-leaning parties, it also came from traditional elements in society such as the Roman Catholic church, which disliked the secularization represented by a capitalist society.

The Great Crash and Latin American Responses

The economic dependency of Latin America and the internal weaknesses of the liberal regimes were made clear by the great world financial crisis. Export sales dropped rapidly. Amid growing poverty, reform movements gained momentum. More important, however, was the rise of a conservative response, hostile to class conflict and supported by church and military leaders. A corporatist movement, aimed at curbing capitalism while avoiding Marxism, won growing attention. **Corporatism** emphasized the organic nature of society, with the state as a mediator adjusting the interests of different social groups; the ideology appealed to conservative groups and the military, in European as well as Latin American societies. Some corporatist leaders sympathized with aspects of Italian and German fascism.

New regimes, as well as a new concern with social problems, characterized much of Latin America in the 1930s. One such reforming administration was that of President **Lázaro Cárdenas** (1934–1940) in Mexico, when land reform and many of the social aspects of the revolution were initiated on a large scale. Cárdenas distributed more than 40 million acres of land and created communal farms and a credit system to support them. He expropriated foreign oil companies that refused to obey Mexican law and created a state oil monopoly. He expanded rural education programs. These measures made him broadly popular in Mexico and seemed to give substance to the promise of the revolution.

Cárdenas in Mexico was perhaps the most successful example of the new political tide that could be seen elsewhere in Latin America. In Cuba, for example, the leaders of a nationalist revolution aimed at social reform and breaking the grip of the United States took power in 1933, and although their rule soon was taken over by moderate elements, important changes and reforms did take place. To some extent, such new departures underlined both the growing force of nationalism and the desire to integrate new forces into the political process. Nowhere was this more apparent than in the populist Vargas regime of Brazil.

The Vargas Regime in Brazil

In Brazil, a contested political election in 1929, in which the state elites could not agree on the next president, resulted in a short civil war and the emergence of **Getúlio Vargas** (1872–1954) as the new president. The Brazilian economy, based on coffee exports, had collapsed in the 1929 crash. Vargas had promised liberal reforms and elimination of the worst abuses of the old system. Once in power, he launched a new kind of centralized political program, imposing federal administrators over the state governments. He held off attempted coups by the communists in 1935 and by the green-shirted fascist "Integralists" in 1937. With the support of the military, Vargas imposed a new constitution in 1937 that established the *Estado Novo* (New State), based on ideas from Mussolini's Italy. It imposed an authoritarian regime within the context of nationalism and economic reforms, limiting immigration and eliminating parties and groups that resisted national integration or opposed the government.

For a while, Vargas played off Germany and the Western powers in the hope of securing armaments and favorable trade arrangements. Despite Vargas' authoritarian sympathies, he eventually joined the Allies during World War II, supplied bases to the United States, and even sent troops to fight against the Axis powers in Italy. In return, Brazil obtained arms, financial support for industrial development, and trade advantages. Meanwhile, Vargas ran a corporatist government, allowing some room for labor negotiations under strict government supervision. Little open opposition to the government was allowed. The state organized many other aspects of the economy. Opposition to Vargas and his repressive policies was building in Brazil by 1945, but by then he was turning increasingly to the left, seeking support from organized labor and coming to terms with the Communist party leaders whom he had imprisoned.

Under criticism from both the right and the left, Vargas committed suicide in 1954. His suicide note emphasized his populist ties and blamed his death on Brazil's enemies:

> Once more the forces and interests which work against the people have organized themselves again and emerge against me.... I was a slave to the people, and today I am freeing myself for eternal life. But this people whose slave I was will no longer be slave to anyone. My sacrifice will remain forever in their souls and my blood will be the price of their ransom....

Much of Brazilian history since Vargas has been a struggle over his mantle of leadership. In death, Vargas became a martyr and a nationalist hero, even to those groups he had repressed and imprisoned in the 1930s.

Argentina: Populism, Perón, and the Military

Argentina was something of an anomaly. There, the middle-class Radical party, which had held power during the 1920s, fell when the economy collapsed in 1929. A military coup backed by a strange coalition of nationalists, fascists, and socialists seized power, hoping to return Argentina to the golden days of the great export boom of the 1890s. The coup failed. Argentina became more dependant as foreign investments increased and markets for Argentine products declined. However, industry was growing, and with it grew the numbers and strength of industrial workers, many of whom had migrated from the countryside. By the 1940s the workers were organized in two major labor federations. Conservative governments backed by the traditional military held power through the 1930s, but in 1943 a military group once again took control of the government.

The new military rulers were nationalists who wanted to industrialize and modernize Argentina and make it the dominant power of South America. Some were admirers of the fascist powers and their programs. Although many of them were distrustful of the workers, the man who became the dominant political force in Argentina recognized the need to create a broader basis of support for the government. Colonel **Juan D. Perón** (1895–1974) emerged as a power in the government. Using his position in the Ministry of Labor, he appealed to workers, raising their salaries, improving their benefits, and generally supporting their demands. Attempts to displace him failed, and he increasingly gained popular support, aided by his wife, Eva Duarte, known as Evita. She became a public spokesperson for Perón among the lower classes. During World War II, Perón's admiration for the Axis powers was well known. In 1946, Perón successfully manipulated an attempt by the United States to discredit him, because of his fascist sympathies, into nationalist support for his presidential campaign.

As president, Perón forged an alliance between the workers, the industrialists, and the military. Like Vargas in Brazil, he learned the effectiveness of the radio, the press, and public speeches in mobilizing public support. He depended on his personal charisma and on repression of opponents to maintain his rule. The Peronist program was couched in nationalistic terms. The government nationalized the foreign-owned railroads and telephone companies, as well as the petroleum resources. The foreign debt was paid off, and for a while the Argentine economy boomed in the immediate postwar years. But by 1949 there were economic problems again. Meanwhile, Perón ruled by a combination of inducements and repression, while Evita Perón became a symbol to the *descamisados*, or the poor and downtrodden, who saw in Peronism a glimmer of hope. Her death in 1952 at age 33 caused an outpouring of national grief.

Perón's regime was a populist government with a broader base than had ever been attempted in Argentina. Nevertheless, holding the interests of the various components of the coalition together became increasingly difficult as the economy worsened. A democratic opposition developed and complained of Perón's control of the press and his violation of civil liberties. Industrialists disliked the strength of labor organizations. The military worried that Perón would arm the workers and cut back on the military's gains. The Peronist party became more radical and began a campaign against the Catholic church. In 1955, anti-Perón military officers drove him into exile.

Argentina spent the next 20 years in the shadow of Perón. The Peronist party was banned, and a succession of military-supported civilian governments tried to resolve the nation's economic problems and its continuing political instability. But Peronism could survive even without Perón, and the mass of urban workers and the strongly Peronist unions continued to agitate for his programs, especially as austerity measures began to affect the living conditions of the working class. Perón and his new wife, Isabel, returned to Argentina in 1973, and they won the presidential election in that year—she as vice president. When Perón died the next year, however, it was clear that Argentina's problems could not be solved by the old formulas. Argentina slid once more into military dictatorship.

The Militarization of Japan

 Although badly damaged by the global economic depression, Japan recovered faster than the West, but amid growing authoritarianism and military expansion.

Authoritarian military rule had taken over in Japan even earlier than in the West. Not fascist outright, it had some clear affinities with the new regimes in Europe, including its aggressive military stance. As early as 1931, as the Depression hit Japan hard, military officials completed a conquest of the Chinese province of Manchuria, without the backing of the civilian government (see Map 30.1)

As political divisions increased in response to the initial impact of the Depression, a variety of nationalist groups emerged, some advocating a return to Shintoist or Confucian principles against the more Western values of urban Japan. This was more than a political response to economic depression. As in Germany, a variety of groups used the occasion for a more sweeping protest against parliamentary forms; nationalism here seemed a counterpoise to alien Western values. Older military officers joined some bureaucrats in urging a more authoritarian state that could ignore party politics; some wanted further military expansion to protect Japan from the uncertainties of the world economy by providing secure markets and sources of raw materials.

In May 1932 a group of younger army officers attacked key government and banking officers and murdered the prime minister. They did not take over the state directly, but for the next four years moderate military leaders headed the executive branch, frustrating both the military firebrands and the political parties. Another attempted military coup in 1936 was put down by forces controlled by the established admirals and generals, but this group, including General Tojo Hideki, increasingly interfered with civilian cabinets, blocking the appointment of most liberal bureaucrats. The result, after 1936, was a series of increasingly militaristic prime ministers.

The military superseded civilian politics, particularly when renewed wars broke out between Japan and China in 1937. Japan, continuing to press the ruling Chinese government lest it gain sufficient strength to threaten Japanese gains, became involved in a skirmish with Chinese forces in the Beijing area in 1937. Fighting spread, initially quite unplanned. Most Japanese military leaders opposed more general war, arguing that the nation's only interest was to defend Manchuria and Korea. However, influential figures on the General Staff held that China's armies should be decisively defeated to prevent trouble in the future. This view prevailed, and Japanese forces quickly occupied the cities and railroads of eastern China. Several devastating bombing raids accompanied this invasion.

Although Japanese voters had continued to prefer more moderate policies, their wishes were swept away by military leaders in a tide of growing nationalism. By the end of 1938 Japan controlled a substantial regional empire, including Manchuria, Korea,

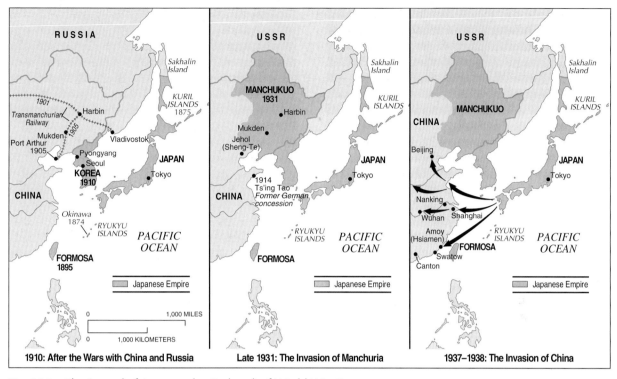

Map 30.1   *The Spread of Japan to the Outbreak of World War II*

and Taiwan (Formosa), within which the nation sold half its exports and from which it bought more than 40 percent of all imports, particularly food and raw materials. Both the military leadership, eager to justify further modernization of Japan's weaponry and to consolidate political control, and economic leaders, interested in rich resources of other parts of Asia—such as the rubber of British Malaya or the oil of the Dutch East Indies—soon pressed for wider conquests as Japan surged into World War II.

As war in Asia expanded, well before the formal outbreak of World War II, Japan also tightened its hold over its earlier empire, particularly in Korea. Efforts to suppress Korean culture were stepped up, and the Japanese military brutally put down any resistance. Japanese language and habits were forced on Korean teachers. Japanese industrialists dominated Korean resources, while peasants were required to produce rice for Japan at the expense of nutrition in Korea itself. Young men were pressed into labor groups, as the population was exhorted to join the Japanese people in "training to endure hardship."

Industrialization and Recovery

Japan's policies in the 1930s quelled the effects of the Depression for Japan even more fully than Hitler's policies were able to do for Germany. While the Depression initially hit Japan hard—half of all factories were closed by 1931, children in some areas were reduced to begging for food from passengers on passing trains, and farmers were eating tree bark—active government policies quickly responded. As a result, Japan suffered far less than many Western nations did during the Depression decade as a whole. Under the 1930s minister of finance, Korekiyo Takahashi, the government increased its spending to provide jobs, which in turn generated new demands for food and manufactured items, yielding not only the export boom but also the virtual elimination of unemployment by 1936. The same policy helped support government military purchasing, but it is not clear that this constituted an essential response.

Indeed, Japan made a full turn toward industrialization after 1931, its economy growing much more rapidly than that of the West and rivaling the surge of the Soviet Union. Production of iron, steel, and chemicals soared. The spread of electric power was the most rapid in the world. The number of workers, mainly men, in the leading industries rose sevenfold during the 1930s. Quality of production increased as assembly-line methods were introduced, and Japanese manufacturing goods began to rival those of the West. As the level of Japanese industrial goods rose, the first Western outcry against Japanese exports was produced—even though in 1936 the Japanese controlled only 3.6 percent of world trade.

Japan also initiated a series of new industrial policies designed to stabilize the labor force and prevent social unrest. These paralleled the growing emphasis on mass patriotism and group loyalty developed by the government. Big companies began to offer lifetime contracts to a minority of skilled workers and to develop company entertainments and other activities designed to promote hard work and devotion. These distinctive Japanese policies, not part of its initial industrialization, proved to be a durable feature of Japanese society.

By 1937 Japan boasted the third largest and the newest merchant marine in the world. The nation became self-sufficient in machine tools and scientific equipment, the fruit of the growth in technical training. The basis had been set for the more significant economic expansion of the later 20th century, delayed by Japan's dash into World War II.

Stalinism in the Soviet Union

 A totalitarian state emerged in the Soviet Union from the late 1920s onward. Here, under communism, the impetus was not the Depression, which the largely independent Soviet economy ignored. Rather, pressures to step up industrialization plus the autocratic hand of a new leader accounted for a new police state. Rhetoric and social policies differed from those of the fascist regimes, but the political structure was uncannily similar.

The experimental mood of the mid-1920s faded quickly in the Soviet Union after 1927, when Joseph Stalin acquired full power over potential rivals. Stalin was eager both to have authoritarian control and to renew the momentum toward socialism, which had

been deflected by the New Economic Policy and the surge of discussion among many mass organizations. By this point the bulk of the land lay in the hands of a minority of wealthy, commercially oriented peasants, the *kulaks*, who were particularly attuned to a profit-based market agriculture. Rural areas seemed inclined to parallel earlier Western experience, in dividing the peasantry among relatively innovative owners and a mass of laborers—and this was not socialism. Even in industry, state-run enterprises and planning had only limited effect, as opposed to small private businesses. Stalin devoted himself to a double task: to make the Soviet Union a fully industrial society and to do so under full control of the state rather than through private initiative and individual ownership of producing property. In essence, Stalin wanted modernization but with a revolutionary, noncapitalist twist. Although he was willing to borrow Western techniques and advice, importing a small number of foreign engineers, for example, he insisted on Soviet control and largely Soviet endeavor.

Economic Policies

A massive program to collectivize agriculture began in 1928. Collectivization meant the creation of large, state-run farms, rather than individual holdings as in the West. Communist party agitators pressed peasants to join in collectives. In addition to being distinctly socialistic, the collectives movement also further offered, at least in theory, the chance to mechanize agriculture most effectively, as collective farms could group scarce equipment, such as tractors and harvesters. Collectivization also allowed more efficient control over peasants, reflecting, though in radical new form, a traditional reluctance to leave peasants to their own devices. Government and party control was desirable not only for political reasons, but also because Stalin's hopes for a speedup of industrialization required that resources be taken from peasants, through taxation, in order to provide capital for industry.

The peasantry responded to collectivization with a decidedly mixed voice. Many laborers, resentful of kulak wealth, initially welcomed the opportunity to have more direct access to land. But most kulaks refused to cooperate voluntarily, often destroying livestock and other property rather than submit to collectivization. Devastating famine resulted from Stalin's insistence on pressing forward. In addition, millions of kulaks were killed or deported to Siberia during the early 1930s, in one of the most brutal oppressions of what turned out to be a brutal century in world history. Gradually, rural resistance collapsed and production began to increase once again; the decimation of the kulaks may indeed have weakened opportunities to oppose Stalin's increasingly authoritarian hold for a generation or two. But collectivization, though increasingly thorough, was not a smash success, for even those peasants who participated often seemed fairly unmotivated. Although the collective farms allowed peasants small plots of their own, as well as job security and considerable propagandizing by the omnipresent Party members, they created an atmosphere of factorylike discipline and rigid planning from above that antagonized many peasants. The centralized planning process allowed few incentives for special efforts and often complicated a smooth flow of supplies and equipment, a problem also exacerbated by the Stalinist regime's priority concentration on the industrial sector. Agricultural production remained a major weakness in the Soviet economy, demanding a higher percentage of the labor force than was common under industrialization.

The collective farms did, however, allow normally adequate if minimal food supplies once the messy transition period had ended, and they did free excess workers to be channeled into the ranks of urban labor. The late 1920s and early 1930s saw a massive flow of unskilled workers into the cities, as the Soviet Union's industrialization, already launched, shifted into high gear.

If Stalin's approach to agriculture had serious flaws, his handling of industry was in most ways a stunning success. A system of **five-year plans** under the state planning commission began to set clear priorities for industrial development, including expected output levels and new facilities. The government constructed massive factories in metallurgy, mining, and electric power to make the Soviet Union an industrial country independent of Western-dominated world banking and trading patterns, with the productive infrastructure also suitable for modern war. There was more than a hint of Peter the Great's policies here, in updating the economy without really westernizing it, save that industrialization constituted a more massive departure than anything Peter had contemplated. The focus, as earlier, was on heavy industry, which built on the nation's great natural resources and also

served to prepare for possible war with Hitler's anti-communist Germany. This distinctive industrialization, which slighted consumer goods production, was to remain characteristic of the Soviet version of industrial society. Further, Stalin sought to create an alternative not simply to private business ownership but also to the profit-oriented market mechanisms of the West. Thus he relied not on price competition but on formal, centralized resource allocation to distribute equipment and supplies. This led to many bottlenecks and considerable waste, as quotas for individual factories were set in Moscow, but there was no question that rapid industrial growth occurred. During the first two five-year plans, to 1937—that is, during the same period that the West was mired in the Depression—Soviet output of machinery and metal products grew 14-fold. The Soviet Union had become the world's third industrial power, behind only Germany and the United States. A long history of backwardness seemed to have ended.

Toward an Industrial Society

For all its distinctive features, the industrialization process in the Soviet Union produced many results similar to those in the West. Increasing numbers of people were crowded into cities, often cramped in inadequate housing stock—for Soviet planners, like earlier Western capitalists, were reluctant to put too many resources into mass housing. Factory discipline was strict, as communist managers sought to instill new habits in a peasant-derived workforce. Incentive procedures were introduced to motivate workers to higher production. Particularly capable workers received bonuses and also elaborate public awards for their service to society. At the same time, communist policy quickly established a network of welfare services, surpassing the West in this area and reversing decades of tsarist neglect. Workers had meeting houses and recreational programs, as well as protection in cases of illness and old age. Soviet industrial society provided only modest standards of living at this point, but a host of collective activities compensated to some degree. Finally, although Soviet industry was directed from the top, with no legal outlet for worker grievances—strikes were outlawed, and the sole trade union movement was controlled by the Party—worker concerns were studied, and identified problems were addressed. The Soviet Union under

Stalin used force and authority, but it also recognized the importance of maintaining worker support—so, informally, laborers were consulted as well.

Totalitarian Rule

Stalinism instituted new controls over intellectual life. In the arts, Stalin insisted on uplifting styles that differed from the modern art themes of the West, which he condemned as capitalist decadence. (Hitler and Stalin, bitter enemies, both viewed contemporary Western culture as dangerous.) Artists and writers who did not toe the line risked exile to Siberian prison camps, and party loyalists in groups like the Writers Union helped ferret out dissidents. **Socialist realism** was the dominant school, emphasizing heroic idealizations of workers, soldiers, and peasants (see Figure 30.4). Science was also controlled. Stalin clamped down hard on free scientific inquiry, insisting for example that evolutionary biology was wrong because it contradicted Marxism. A number of scientists were ruined by government persecution.

Stalin also combined his industrialization program with a new intensification of government police procedures; he used Party and state apparatus to monopolize power, even more thoroughly than Hitler's totalitarian state attempted. Real and imagined opponents of his version of communism were executed. During the great purge of Party leaders that culminated in 1937–1938, hundreds of people were intimidated into confessing imaginary crimes against the state, and most of them were then put to death. Many thousands more were sent to Siberian labor camps. Any possibility of vigorous internal initiative was crushed, as both the state and the Communist party were bent under Stalin's suspicious will. News outlets were monopolized by the state and the Party, and informal meetings also risked a visit from the ubiquitous secret police, renamed the MVD in 1934. Party congresses and meetings of the executive committee, or **Politburo,** became mere rubber stamps. An atmosphere of terror spread.

Stalin's purges, which included top army officials, ironically weakened the nation's ability to respond to growing foreign policy problems, notably the rising threat of Hitler. Soviet diplomatic initiatives after the 1917 revolution had been unwontedly modest, given the nation's traditions, largely because of the intense concentration on internal development. Diplomatic relations with major nations were gradually reestablished, as the fact of communist leadership was accepted, and the Soviet Union was allowed into the League of Nations. A few secret military negotiations, as with Turkey in the early 1920s, showed a flicker of interest in more active diplomacy, and of course the nations continued to encourage and often guide internal Communist party activities in many other countries.

Hitler's rise was a clear signal that more active concern was necessary. A strong Germany was inevitably a threat to Russia from the west, and Hitler was vocal about his scorn for Slavic peoples and communism, about his desire to create a "living room" for Germany to the east. Stalin initially hoped that he could cooperate with the Western democracies in blocking the German threat. The Soviet Union thus tried to participate in a common response to German and Italian intervention during the Spanish Civil War, in 1936–1937. But France and Britain were incapable of forceful action and were in any event almost as suspicious of the Soviets as of the Nazis. So the Soviet Union, unready for war

Figure 30.4 *In his 1949 painting* Creative Fellowship, *Soviet artist Shcherbakov shows the cooperation of scientists and workers in an idealized factory setting. The painting exemplifies the theories and purposes of socialist realism.*

Document

Socialist Realism

One of the most fascinating features of the Soviet system was the attempt to create a distinctive art, different from the art of Western cultures (seen as decadent) and appropriate to the communist mission. This effort involved censorship and forced orthodoxy, but it also was an attempt to resolve earlier Russian problems of relating formal culture to the masses and trying to preserve a national distinctiveness amid the seductions of Western influence. The following effort to define Soviet artistic policy was written by Andrey Zhdanov in 1934, the year Stalin made him the party's spokesperson at the Congress of Soviet Writers.

There is not and never has been a literature making its basic subject-matter the life of the working class and the peasantry and their struggle for socialism. There does not exist in any country in the world a literature to defend and protect the equality of rights of the working people of all nations and the equality of rights of women. There is not, nor can there be in any bourgeois country, a literature to wage consistent war on all obscurantism, mysticism, hierarchic religious attitudes, and threats of hell-fire, as our literature does.

Only Soviet literature could become and has in fact become such an advanced, thought-imbued literature. It is one flesh and blood with our socialist construction....

What can the bourgeois writer write or think of, where can he find passion, if the worker in the capitalist countries is not sure of his tomorrow, does not know whether he will have work, if the peasant does not know whether he will be working on his bit of land or thrown on the scrap heap by a capitalist crisis, if the working intellectual is out of work today and does not know whether he will have work tomorrow?

What can the bourgeois author write about, what source of inspiration can there be for him, when the world, from one day to the next, may be plunged once more into the abyss of a new imperialist war?

The present position of bourgeois literature is such that it is already incapable of producing great works. The decline and decay of bourgeois literature derives from the decline and decay of the capitalist system and are a feature and aspect characteristic of the present condition of bourgeois culture and literature. The days when bourgeois literature, reflecting the victories of the bourgeois system over feudalism, was in the heyday of capitalism capable of creating great works, have gone, never to return. Today a degeneration in subject matter, in talents, in authors and in heroes, is in progress....

A riot of mysticism, religious mania and pornography is characteristic of the decline and decay of bourgeois culture. The "celebrities" of that bourgeois literature which has sold its pen to capital are today thieves, detectives, prostitutes, pimps, and gangsters....

The proletariat of the capitalist countries is already forging its army of writers and artists—revolutionary writers, the representatives of whom we are glad to be able to welcome here today at the first Soviet Writers' Congress. The number of revolutionary writers in the capitalist countries is still small but it is growing and will grow with every day's sharpening of the class struggle, with the growing strength of the world proletarian revolution.

We are firmly convinced that the few dozen foreign comrades we have welcomed here constitute the kernel, the embryo, of a mighty army of proletarian writers to be created by the world proletarian revolution in foreign countries....

Comrade Stalin has called our writers "engineers of the human soul." What does this mean? What obligations does such an appellation put upon you?

It means, in the first place, that you must know life to be able to depict it truthfully in artistic creations, to depict it neither "scholastically" nor lifelessly, nor simply as "objective reality," but rather as reality in its revolutionary development. The truthfulness and historical exactitude of the artistic image must be linked with the task of ideological transformation, of the education of the working people in the spirit of socialism. This method in fiction and literary criticism is what we call the method of socialist realism.

Our Soviet literature is not afraid of being called tendentious, for in the epoch of class struggle there is not and cannot be "apolitical" literature.

And it seems to me that any and every Soviet writer may say to any dull-witted bourgeois, to any philistine or to any bourgeois writers who speak of the tendentiousness of our literature: "Yes, our Soviet literature is tendentious and we are proud of it, for our tendentiousness is to free the working people—and the whole of mankind—from the yoke of capitalist slavery."

To be an engineer of the human soul is to stand foursquare on real life. And this in turn means a break with old-style romanticism, with the romanticism which depicted a nonexistent life and nonexistent heroes, drawing the reader away from the contradictions and shackles of life into an unrealizable and utopian world. Romanticism is not alien to our literature, a literature standing firmly on a materialistic basis, but ours is a romanticism of a new type, revolutionary romanticism. We say that socialist realism is the fundamental method of Soviet fiction and literary criticism, and this implies that revolutionary romanticism will appear as an integral part of any literary creation, since the whole life of our Party, of the working class and its struggle, is a fusion of the hardest, most matter-of-fact practical work, with the greatest

(continued)

heroism and the vastest perspectives. The strength of our Party has always lain in the fact that it has united and unites efficiency and practicality with broad vision, with an incessant forward striving and the struggle to build a communist society.

Soviet literature must be able to portray our heroes and to see our tomorrow. This will not be utopian since our tomorrow is being prepared by planned and conscious work today.

Questions: What were the reasons for culture according to Stalinist intellectuals? How did Soviet cultural leaders analyze Western intellectual life? What were the proper tasks of an artist in Soviet society? How were these tasks expressed in socialist realism? What would the Soviet response be to Western intellectuals who claimed objectivity for their work?

Visualizing the Past

Socialist Realism

How does the picture illustrate the purposes of socialist realism style? How does it compare to the stated purposes of socialist realism in the Document section? Why would it be seen as an inspiration to the Soviet people? How did its themes fit the larger Stalinist system? Is the picture realistic by Western standards? How would official artists defend it against charges of inaccuracy? How did the style and themes compare with the modern, abstract art gaining ground in the West at this point (see Chapter 29)? How did it compare with the popular art shown in commercials for products in the United States and western Europe? Is the picture a good summary of Soviet culture?

This example of socialist realism depicts heroic women workers.

and greatly disappointed in the West, signed a historic agreement with Hitler in 1939. This pact bought some time for greater war preparation and also enabled Soviet troops to attack eastern Poland and Finland, in an effort to regain territories lost in World War I. Here was the first sign of a revival of Russia's long interest in conquest, which would be intensified by the experience of World War II.

New Political and Economic Realities

 The 1930s clearly changed the world balance. Germany rose within Europe. But Europe was challenged by more vigorous regimes elsewhere and by increasing anti-imperial protest.

The Depression further weakened western Europe, which now tended to divide between weak parliamentary regimes and angry fascist states. The Western political tradition, as it had developed since the Enlightenment, was called into question. Japan, also damaged by the Depression, soon rallied, but under authoritarian leadership with growing reliance on military adventurism. The Depression also promoted new initiatives in Latin America, along with severe economic dislocation. Meanwhile, key revolutionary movements continued. The short-term success of Stalinism in Russia was an obvious contrast to the dislocations of the West. Revolutionary forces in China remained active, even as the focus shifted to Japanese invasion.

Movements against Western colonialism continued in many other parts of the world. Particularly decisive developments occurred in the Middle East. In independent Turkey, the leadership of Kemal Ataturk brought many reforms. Traditional Islamic habits were challenged, as the new regime sought to create a secular state. Ataturk even attacked traditional patterns of dress, like the fez, a cap worn by upper-class men: "It was necessary to abolish the fez, which sat on our heads as a sign of ignorance, of fanaticism, of hatred to progress and civilization, and to adopt in its place the hat, the customary head-dress of the whole civilized world." The new regime also spread a secular education system. Women gained the vote.

Turkey and also Persia (whose name changed to Iran in 1935) sought to reduce dependence on the Western economy by promoting industrialization. Particular attention went to the policy of import substitution, as in Latin America. The idea here was to set up factories to produce clothing and other goods, so that fewer imports from the West would be necessary. Persia, like other parts of the Middle East, also began to participate in growing oil exports. Here, however, the hold of Western companies modified the goals of economic independence.

Finally, in the Arab world growing nationalism greeted the efforts by European powers to rule much of the region either as colonies or as League of Nations mandates. Pressures forced European powers to promise independence for countries like Egypt and Syria, and Lebanon won independence under French protection in 1936. The framework of Western imperialism was beginning to unravel.

 GLOBAL CONNECTIONS: **Depression and Retreat**

The Great Depression of the 1930s promoted a growing wave of nationalist reactions and further weakened global ties. Western European countries and the United States increased their tariffs and refused to collaborate in measures the might alleviate economic dislocation. Their narrow policies made economic collapse even worse. Japan, badly hurt by a new United States tariff which cut into silk exports, increased its own nationalism; here was the context for the growing power of younger army officers pushing for overseas expansion. Japan began to think of its own new empire in east Asia that could shield it from worldwide economic trends. Nazi Germany also pulled out of the international community, seeking to make Germany as economically self-sufficient as possible. The Soviet Union still mouthed communist commitment to internationalism, but in fact Stalin concentrated on standing alone, in a nationalist and isolationist version of the great Russian Revolution. The world was falling into pieces, and no society, certainly not the beleaguered West, seemed capable of putting it back together.

Further Readings

On the causes and onset of the Great Depression, C. Kindleberger's *The World in Depression, 1929–1939* (1973) is a solid introduction. See also J. Galbraith, *The Great Crash: 1929* (1980) and, for a useful collection of articles, W. Lacquer and G. L. Mosse, eds., *The Great Depression* (1970). Japan's experience is covered in I. Morris, ed., *Japan, 1931–1945: Militarism, Fascism, Japanism?* (1963).

Ronald Edsforth's *The New Deal: America's Response to the Great Depression* (2000) is a readable introduction to the political history of the New Deal. For a case study of social and political change in the United States during the period, see Lizabeth Cohen's *Making a New Deal: Industrial Workers in Chicago, 1919–1939* (1990). See also William Chafe's *Women and Equality: Changing Patterns in American Culture* (1984).

Alan Bullock's *Hitler: A Study in Tyranny* (1964) remains the best introduction to the Nazi leader. The methods and manner of the rise of German fascism are explored in William S. Allen, *Nazi Seizure of Power in a Single Town, 1930–1935* (1969); Russell G. Lemmons, *Goebbels and Der Angriff: Nazi Propaganda, 1927–1933* (1994); David Schoenbaum, *Hitler's Social Revolution: Class and Status in Nazi Germany* (1997); and Samuel W. Mitchum Jr., *Why Hitler? The Genesis of the Nazi Reich* (1996).

For a standard analysis of the Spanish Civil War, see Hugh Thomas, *The Spanish Civil War* (1977); Paul Preston, *The Spanish Civil War, 1936–1939* (2nd ed., 1994); and Raymond Carr, *The Spanish Tragedy: The Civil War in Perspective* (1993). Peter Carroll's *The Odyssey of the Abraham Lincoln Brigade: Americans in the Spanish Civil War* (1994) deals with one of the civil war's many international aspects.

For the career of Juan Perón and Peronism, there is Frederick C. Turner, *Juan Peron and the Reshaping of Argentina* (1983). Robert M. Levine's *Getulio Vargas: Father of the Poor* (1998) explores Brazil's corporatist state. Luis Aguilar's *Cuba 1933: Prologue to Revolution* (1972) demonstrates that, as in so many other Asian as well as Latin American countries, the post–Second World War revolutionary movement in Cuba led by Fidel Castro was rooted in the events of the 1930s. Irwin Gellman's *The Good Neighbor Diplomacy: United States Policy in Latin America, 1933–1945* (1980) and *Roosevelt and Batista: Good Neighbor Policy in Cuba, 1933–1945* (1973) address the U.S. role in shaping the regimes that were challenged by those later revolutionary movements.

On the Stalinist era and terror state, Robert Conquest's *The Great Terror: A Reassessment* (1990) and Roy Medvedev's *Let History Judge: The Origins and Consequences of Stalinism* (1989) are important studies of the period. Stephen Kotkin's *Magnetic Mountain: Stalinism as Civilization* (1995) assesses the cultural, social, and political impact of Stalin's industrialization program by looking at the experience of a planned industrial city. Sarah Davies'

Popular Opinion in Stalin's Russia: Terror, Propaganda, and Dissent, 1934–1941 (1997) offers a revealing portrayal of everyday cultural life under Stalin. Alan Bullock's *Hitler and Stalin: Parallel Lives* (1993) offers a comparative biography of the two totalitarian leaders.

Mark Selden's *The Yenan Way in Revolutionary China* (1971) provides the fullest account of the development of the Communist movement after the Long March.

On the Web

The causes of the Great Depression are examined at http://www.sos.state.mi.us/history/museum/techstuf/depressn/teacup.html.

Photographic records and personal remembrances of the Great Depression in the United States are recorded at http://memory.loc.gov/ammem/fsowhome.html, http://www.pbs.org/wgbh/amex/dustbowl/peopleevents/pandeAMEXO5.htm, and http://www.sos.state.mi.us/history/museum/techstuf/depressn/teacup.html. The Franklin Delano Roosevelt Library (http://www.fdrlibrary.marist.edu/index.html) offers a gateway to the study of America's longest serving president. His response to the Great Depression, the New Deal, is examined at what is simply one of the finest of all Internet sites, http://www.newdeal.feri.org/.

The origins and future of Stalinism are explored at http://home.mira.net/~andy/bs/index.htm. Stalinism is seen through declassified documents at http://www.utoronto.ca/serap. Stalin offers his view of Soviet industrialization at http://artsci.shu.edu/reesp/documents/Stalin—industrialization.htm. A transcript of one of Stalin's purge trials brings them alive at http://art-bin.com/art/omosc20e.html.

Leon Trotsky's role as an exiled critic of Stalin's regime (http://www.anu.edu.au/polsci/marx/contemp/pamsetc/socfrombel/sfb_7.htm) can be enlivened by a virtual visit to the house in Mexico where he was assassinated by a Stalinist agent (http://www.mexconnect.com/mex_/travel/jmitchell/jmtrotsky.html).

Profiles of Nazi leaders and documents illustrating the rise of German fascism are offered at http://fcit.coedu.usf.edu/holocaust/people/perps.htm. The origins of Hitler's anti-Semitism are revealed at http://www2.h-net.msu.edu/~german/gtext/kaiserreich/hitler1.html.

Leon Trotsky's now classic critique of fascism has been made available at http://eserver.org/history/fighting-fascism/ and http://csf.colorado.edu/psn/marx/Other/Trotsky/Archive/1930-Ger/.

A course lesson plan that offers a very good general introduction to German National Socialism and its totalitarian state and that includes useful definitions of key terms can be found at http://www.remember.org/guide/Facts.root.nazi.html.

The nature of the totalitarian state and the relationship between politics and art can be explored at sites such as http://www.calvin.edu/academic/cas/gpa/politart.htm, http://fcit.coedu.usf.edu/holocaust/arts/artReich.htm, and http://www.humanities.uci.edu/~rmoeller/body/nazi_art.html.

The Spanish Civil War is analyzed at http://www.geocities.com/CapitolHill/9820/ while an excellent related photo file, including Robert Capra's famous "Moment of Death" photograph, can be found at http://history.sandiego.edu/cdr2/WW2Pics/13953.jpg.

The Internet provides some vivid accounts of Latin American in the 1930s at sites examining the lives of Fulgencio Batista (http://www.historyofcuba.com/history/batista.htm), Getulio Vargas (search on http://historicaltextarchive.com/), and Juan Perón, whose followers maintain their own Web page (http://www.falange.org/peron.htm), which is devoid of critical analysis but has excellent contemporary photographs. The Web also offers examinations of larger movements, such as the diplomacy of the period (http://www.mre.gov.br/acs/diplomacia/ingles/h_diplom/ev003i.htm).

CHAPTER 31

A SECOND GLOBAL CONFLICT AND THE END OF THE EUROPEAN WORLD ORDER

Sober-faced and weeping Czechs watch the entry of the Nazi armies into Prague in the spring of 1939, as Hitler completes the takeover of the tiny democracy that was betrayed by the duplicity and cowardice of Allied leaders.

- Old and New Causes of a Second World War
- Unchecked Aggression and the Coming of War in Europe and the Pacific
- IN DEPTH: Total War
- The Conduct of a Second Global War
- DOCUMENT: Japan and the Loss in World War II
- War's End and the Emergence of the Superpower Standoff
- Nationalism and Decolonization
- VISUALIZING THE PAST: On National Leadership
- GLOBAL CONNECTIONS: Persisting Trends in a World Transformed by War

World War II began officially on September 1, 1939, with the German invasion of Poland. But a succession of localized clashes, which were initiated by the Japanese seizure of Manchuria in 1931, can be seen as part of a global conflict that raged for well over a decade between the 1930s and 1945. In contrast to the coming of World War I, which, as we have seen, the leaders of Europe more or less blundered into, the Second World War was provoked by the deliberate aggressions of both Nazi Germany and its Italian ally, and a militarized and imperialist Japan. The failure on the part of the leaders of the Western democracies and the Soviet Union to respond resolutely to these challenges simply fed the militarist expansionism of what came to be called the Axis powers, in reference to the connection between Berlin, Rome, and Tokyo.

National rivalries and especially deep suspicions on the part of the Western democracies of the totalitarian Stalinist regime prevented effective coordination, much less alliances, between Britain and France and the Soviets, and thus limited their ability to counter the moves of the Axis leaders. Strong responses on the part of British and French leaders to repeated Nazi aggressions were made all but impossible by the deep political divisions within each of these democracies, and by lingering guilt about the way the Allies had mishandled the Versailles settlement after World War I. Leaders, such as (most infamously) Neville Chamberlain, long thought that there was some truth to Hitler's strident allegations that the Germans had been unjustly blamed for the war and punished by being stripped of parts of their homeland, colonies, and the means to rebuild a viable economy after the war.

As the 1930s progressed, it was increasingly clear that international security arrangements centered on the League of Nations were impotent. When Japan was censured for its invasion of Manchuria in 1931 and Italy for its brutal takeover of Ethiopia in 1935 and 1936, their leaders contemptuously withdrew from the League and easily fended off the feeble or failed attempts to apply sanctions to punish their aggressions. By the time of Germany's successive annexations in central and eastern Europe in the late 1930s and Japan's full-scale invasion of all of China, the League was little more than a joke shared by the fascist-militarist dictators. And the treaties worked out in good faith by statesmen like Chamberlain were not worth the paper they were written on. Leaders like Hitler and Mussolini scorned the old diplomacy, and viewed treaties as a way to cover their aggressions and delay reprisals while they strengthened their military forces for the general war they believed must eventually come.

751

1930 C.E.	1940 C.E.	1950 C.E.	1960 C.E.
1930s Great Depression	**1941–1945** World War II	**1957** Ghana established as first independent African nation	**1960** Congo granted independence from Belgian rule
1931 Japan invades Manchuria	**1941** Japanese attack Pearl Harbor; United States enters World War II	**1958** Afrikaner Nationalist party declares independence of South Africa	**1962** Algeria wins independence
1933 Nazis to power in Germany	**1941** German invasion of Soviet Union		
1935 Government of India Act	**1942** Fall of Singapore to the Japanese		
1935 Italy invades Ethiopia	**1942** Cripps mission to India; Quit India movement		
1936–1939 Spanish Civil War	**1945** Atomic bomb dropped on Japan; United Nations established		
1936–1939 Arab risings in Palestine	**1947** India and Pakistan gain independence		
1938 Germany's union (Anschluss) with Austria; Munich conference; German armies occupy the Sudetenland	**1947** Cold war begins		
1939 Nazi–Soviet Pact	**1947** Wider decolonization begins with independence of India and Pakistan		
	1948 Israel–Palestine partition, first Arab–Israeli war; beginning of apartheid legislation in South Africa		

Old and New Causes of a Second World War

 The path to World War II was paved by major social and political upheavals in several of the nations that had fought in World War I and had either been defeated, as was the case with Germany, or, like Italy and Japan, had been on the winning side but disappointed by their share of the spoils. Grievances related to World War I were compounded in each case by the economic havoc, and resulting social tensions, brought on by the Depression.

In Japan, social and political dissent had given rise to highly militarist, ultranationalist groups, whose violent outbursts were covered whenever possible by high-ranking officers in the army. The secret societies that were associated with the parties of the far right, such as the Black Dragon Society, opposed westernization and urged the restoration of Shintoism. Their adherents indulged in fanatical emperor-worship. They longed for a Nazi-style authoritarian government free from parliamentary restraints and empowered to quash individualism at home and the diplomatic cooperation with the Western powers abroad that they believed were key sources of Japan's decline. The younger army officers in particular pushed for a military dictatorship that would allegedly fully restore the emperor's

authority. They violently assaulted those who had made in the past or proposed further treaties with the United States or other democracies. And they spearheaded Japanese advances first in Manchuria, and during the late 1930s, in China south of the Great Wall.

The gradual militarization of Japan proceeded despite the solid majorities that moderate political parties continued to win until the very end of the 1930s. And it developed in the context of a succession of regional diplomatic crises. During the later 1920s, nationalistic forces in China began to get the upper hand over the regional warlords who had dominated Chinese politics since the early 1900s. At the head of the Guomindang (or Nationalist) party, General Chiang Kai-shek in particular was able to win the support of intellectuals, students, the business classes, the rural gentry, and even members of the largely discredited Confucian elites and rival military leaders. His military successes against first the southern and later the northern warlords seemed destined to unify China under a strong central government for the first time in decades.

The success of the Guomindang worried Japan's army officers, who feared that a reunited China would move to resist the informal control the Japanese had exerted over Manchuria since their victory in the Russo-Japanese war in 1905. Fearful of curbs on their expansionist aims on the mainland and unimpeded by weak civilian governments at home, the Japanese military seized Manchuria in 1931 and proclaimed it the independent state of Manchukuo. The international crisis that resulted worked to the military's advantage because civilian politicians were reluctant to raise objections that might weaken Japan in negotiations with the United States and the other powers or undermine its armies of occupation in Manchuria and Korea, which the Japanese had declared a colony in 1910.

In contrast to the gradual shift of power to the military in Japan, the change of regimes in Germany was more abrupt and more radical. Parliamentary government in the Weimar era had been under siege from the time its civilian leaders had agreed to the armistice in 1918, and even more so after they signed the punitive treaty at Versailles. Weimar had survived these humiliations, civil war, and the hyperinflation of the mid-1920s, but just as economic recovery appeared to be gaining real momentum, the Great Depression struck. In the social discontent and political turmoil that followed, Adolf Hitler and the **National Socialist** (**Nazi**) party captured a steadily rising portion of the votes and parliamentary seats in a rapid succession of elections. The Nazis promised to put the German people back to work, to restore political stability, and to set in motion a remilitarization program that would allow Germany to throw off the shackles of what Hitler branded the diktat of Versailles. Hitler also promised to turn back the communist bid to capture power in Germany that had grown more and more serious as the Depression deepened. The threat of the communists within was linked to that of the Soviet Union to the east. From the early 1920s, Hitler and his lieutenants had stressed the need to invade and destroy the Soviet empire, and a key part of Hitler's racist vision for the future was to reduce the Russians and other Slavic peoples to virtual slaves in the service of the Aryan master race.

As we have seen in Chapter 30, a major part of the Nazis' political agenda once in power was a systematic dismantling of the political and diplomatic system created by the Versailles settlement. Rearmament from 1935, the militarization of the Rhineland in 1936, a forced union with Austria and the seizure of areas in Czechoslovakia where German-speakers were in the majority in 1938, and the occupation of the rest of the Czechoslovak republic the following year made a shambles of the agreements that had ended World War I. Hitler's successes emboldened Mussolini to embark on military adventures of his own, most infamously in

Ethiopia, where Italian pilots bombed defenseless cities and highly mechanized armies made extensive use of poisonous gases against resistance forces armed with little more than rifles. The fascists stunned much of the rest of the world by routinely unleashing these weapons on a civilian population that had no means of defending itself.

Hitler and Mussolini also intervened militarily in the Spanish Civil War in the mid-1930s in the hope of establishing an allied regime. Once again, Mussolini's mechanized forces proved effective, this time against the overmatched, left-leaning armed forces of the Spanish republic. Both the Italian and German air forces used the Spanish conflict as a training ground for their air forces; in the absence of enemy planes or pilots, however, their main targets were ground forces and, ominously, civilians in Spain's cities and villages. The support of the Axis members was critical to Franco's destruction of the elected republican government and seizure of power, particularly since the Western democracies had refused to counter the Nazi and fascist interventions.

Excepting volunteer forces recruited in England, France, the United States, and other democracies, only the Soviet Union sought to provide military aid to Spain's republicans. Though valiant, these relief attempts proved futile in the face of relentless assaults by Franco's well-supplied legions and the Axis forces. Despite the critical assistance provided by his fellow fascists, Franco refused to join them in the global war that broke out soon after he had crushed the republic and begun a dictatorial rule in Spain that would last for decades.

Unchecked Aggression and the Coming of War in Europe and the Pacific

By the late 1930s a number of patterns were clearly established in the interaction between the new totalitarian states and the democracies. The paramount lesson for the former was that aggression would succeed and at little cost.

Hitler and Mussolini discovered that Britain and France, and even more so the increasingly isolated United States, were quite willing to sacrifice small states, such as Spain and Czechoslovakia, in the false

In Depth

Total War

War had changed long before the 20th century. With state centralization, war lost its ritual characteristics. It became more commonly an all-out battle, using any tactics and weapons that would aid in victory. In other words, war became less restrained than it had been among less bureaucratized peoples who often used bluff and scare more than violence.

The 20th century most clearly saw the introduction of a fundamentally new kind of war, total war, in which vast resources and emotional commitments of the belligerent nations were marshaled to support military effort. The two world wars were thus novel not only in their geographic sweep but in their mobilization of the major combatants. The features of total war also colored other forms of struggle, helping to explain brutal guerrilla and terrorist acts by groups not powerful enough to mount total wars but nonetheless affected by their methods and passions.

Total war resulted from the impact of industrialization on military effort, reflecting both the technological innovation and the organizational capacity that accompanied the industrial economy. Key steps in the development of total war thus emerged in the West from the end of the 18th century. The French Revolution, building new power for the state in contact with ordinary citizens, introduced mass conscription of men, forming larger armies than had ever before been possible. New citizen involvement was reflected in incitements to nationalism and stirring military songs, including aggressive national anthems—a new idea in itself. Industrial technology was first applied to war on a large scale in the U.S. Civil War. Railroads allowed wider movement of mass armies. Mass-produced guns and artillery made a mockery of earlier cavalry charges and redefined the kind of personal bravery needed to fight in war.

However, it was World War I that fully revealed the nature of total war. Steadily more destructive technology included battleships, submarines, tanks, airplanes, poison gas (which had been banned by international agreement before the war), machine guns, and long-range artillery. Organization for war included not only massive, compulsory recruitment—the draft—but also government control of economic activity via obligatory planning and rationing. Another factor was unprecedented control of media, not only through effective censorship and the containment of dissidents but through powerful propaganda designed to incite passionate, all-out commitment to the national cause and deep, unreasoned hatred of the enemy. Vivid posters, flaming speeches, and outright falsehood were combined in the emotional mobilization effort. All of these features returned with a vengeance in World War II, from the new technology of bombing, rocketry, and ultimately the atomic bomb to the enhanced economic mobilization organized by government planners.

The people most affected by the character of total war were the troops, who directly endured—bled from and died from—the new technology. But one measure of total war was a blurring of the distinction between military and civilians, a distinction that had often limited war's impact earlier in world history. Whole civilian populations, not just those unfortunate enough to be near the front lines, were forced into certain types of work and urged to certain types of beliefs. The bombing raids, including the German rockets directed against British cities late in World War II, subjected civilians to some of the most lethal weapons available as many belligerents deliberately focused their attacks on densely populated cities. Correspondingly, psychological suffering, though less common among civilians than among front-line soldiers, could spread throughout the populations involved in war.

Total war, like any major historical development, had mixed results. Greater government economic direction often included new measures to protect workers and give them a voice on management boards. Mobilization of the labor force often produced at least temporary breakthroughs for women. Intense efforts to organize technological research often produced side effects of more general economic benefit, such as the invention of synthetic rubber and other new materials.

Still, total war was notable especially for its devastation. The idea of throwing all possible resources into a military effort made war more economically disruptive than had been the case before. The emotions unleashed in total war produced embittered veterans who might vent their anger by attacking established political values. It certainly made postwar diplomacy more difficult. One result of total war was a tendency for the victor to be inflexible in negotiations at war's end. People who fought so hard found it difficult to treat enemies generously. The results of a quest for vengeance often produced new tensions that led directly, and quickly, to further conflict. War-induced passions and disruptions could also spark new violence at home, as crime rates often soared not only right after the war ended (a traditional result) but for longer periods of time. Children's toys started to reflect the most modern weaponry. Thus, much of the nature of life in the 20th and 21st centuries has been determined by the consequences of total war.

Questions: How did the experience of total war affect social and political patterns after the war's end? Why do many historians believe that total war made rational peacetime settlements more difficult than did earlier types of warfare?

hope that fascist and especially Nazi territorial ambitions would be satisfied and thus war averted. Leaders like Winston Churchill, who warned that a major war was inevitable given Hitler's insatiable ambitions, were kept from power by voters who had no stomach for another world war. Rival politicians, such as Neville Chamberlain and the socialist leaders of France, also feared correctly that rearming as Churchill proposed would put an end to their ambitious schemes to build welfare states as an antidote to further depressions. But in the late 1930s, another round of provocative aggressions pushed the democracies into a war that none had the stomach for or was prepared at that point to fight.

Although Nazi aggressions traditionally have been stressed as the precipitants of World War II, the Japanese military actually moved first. In the second half of 1937, from their puppet state, Manchukuo, which had been carved out of Manchuria, they launched a massive invasion of China proper. Exploiting a trumped-up incident in early July that led to a fire fight between Japanese and Chinese troops, the army launched an ill-advised campaign to conquer the whole of China. Prominent naval leaders and civilian politicians had deep misgivings about this massive escalation of the war in China, and were uneasy about American and British reactions to yet another major round of Japanese aggression. But they were largely cowed into silence by the threat of assassination by fanatical junior army officers and appeals to patriotic solidarity in a situation where Japanese soldiers were at risk.

At first, the advancing Japanese forces met with great success, occupying most of the coastal cities, including Shanghai and, by the end of 1938, Canton as well as the hinterlands behind cities in the north. The Japanese deployed extensive aerial bombing against Guomindang forces and especially the civilian population in the coastal cities. As Chinese resistance stiffened in some areas, Japanese soldiers resorted to draconian reprisals against both the Chinese fighters and civilians. In many instances, most infamously in the capture in December 1937 of the city of Nanjing, the evacuated Guomindang capital, Japanese forces took out their frustrations on retreating Chinese troops and the civilian population (see Figure 31.1). The wanton destruction and pillage, murder of innocent civilians, and rape of tens of thousands of undefended Chinese women that accompanied the Japanese occupation of the ancient city was but a prelude to the unparalleled human suffering of the world war that had now begun.

Deprived of the coastal cities and provinces that were the main centers of their power, Chiang and the Guomindang forces retreated up the Yangtze River, deep into the interior to the city of Chongqing, which became the nationalist capital for the rest of the war. Thus, long before the Japanese attacks on Pearl Harbor and Western colonies throughout southeast Asia in late 1941 that greatly expanded the war in Asia, Japan and China were engaged in a massive and deadly contest for control of all of east Asia.

The Japanese had plunged into war without coordination, or even serious consultation with their likely allies, Germany and Italy. In fact the Tripartite Pact, which joined the three expansive states in a loose alliance, was not signed until September 1940, when the war was well underway in both Europe and east Asia. In fact, Nazi military advisors had contributed greatly to the training of the Guomindang officers and troops that fought to contain the Japanese invasion of China.

With a pause to consolidate his stunning gains in central Europe from 1936 to 1938, Hitler now concentrated his forces on the drive to the Slavic east, which he had long staked out as the region that

Figure 31.1 *Americans and Europeans are generally aware that the Soviet Union lost more than 26 million people in World War II. Fewer are aware, however, that when the Japanese invaded China in 1931, they opened up a series of conflicts that would result in more than 20 million Chinese deaths by 1945. It is hard to comprehend suffering on that scale. Here, in a more limited form, one can see the tragic results of the Japanese invasions.*

would provide living space for the Germanic master race. He bought time to prepare the way for the assault on the main target, the Soviet Union, by signing a nonaggression pact with Stalin in August 1939. Military emissaries of the two dictators negotiated a division of the smaller states that separated their empires, and Stalin swallowed short-term disappoinments, such as the division of Poland, to prepare the Soviet Union for the invasion that most observers were now convinced was inevitable. Within days of signing the agreement, Hitler ordered the Wehrmacht, or Nazi armies, to overrun western Poland; the Soviets then occupied the eastern half of the country, which had been promised to them in the cynical pact just concluded with the Nazis.

The brutal Nazi invasion of Poland on September 1, 1939, put an end to any lingering doubts about Hitler's contempt for treaties and repeated assurances that Germany's territorial ambitions had been satisfied by the absorption of Czechoslovakia into the Nazi Reich. Although they were helpless to assist the overmatched Poles in their futile efforts to oppose the German advance, the British and French had no choice but to declare war on Germany. But the armies of both powers simply dug in along the defensive lines that had been established in eastern France in the late 1920s. There they waited for the Nazis to turn to the west for further conquests, and prepared for another defensive war like the one they had managed to survive, at such horrific cost, between 1914 and 1918. But a second major theater of what rapidly developed into a second world war had been opened, and this conflict would prove radically different in almost all major respects from the one to which the new configuration of powers in Europe and the Pacific believed they were committing themselves.

The Conduct of a Second Global War

 The forces that gave rise to the Second World War meant that there would be more of a balance between a number of theaters spread across Europe, north Africa, and Asia, in contrast to World War I, whose outcome hinged on the battles on the Western Front. Within Europe, the largest and most costly front in lives lost and physical destruction was in the vast expanses of the Soviet Union, where huge, mechanized Nazi and Russian armies and air forces clashed in some of the largest battles in history from 1941 into 1945. The Nazis were also compelled to do battle with the democratic Allies in north Africa (including Egypt), Italy, and—at both the beginning and end of the war—northern France and the Low Countries. After December 1941, the decade-long contest between Japan and China spread across southeast Asia and much of the Pacific, as the United States and Great Britain emerged as the main obstacles to Japan's drive to become the hegemon of east Asia and the western rim of the Pacific.

The reluctance to rearm and react decisively displayed by both the Western democracies and the Soviet Union in the 1930s made possible crushing and almost unremitting victories and rapid territorial advances on the part of the main Axis powers, Germany and Japan, early in the war. But once the Nazis became bogged down in the expanses of the Russian steppes and the United States entered the war, the tide shifted steadily in favor of the Allies. Once the initial momentum of the Axis war machine was slowed, it became increasingly clear that the Anglo-American and Soviet alliance was decidedly more powerful in terms of population size, potential industrial production, technological innovation, and military capacity on land, under and above the seas, and in the air.

Nazi Blitzkrieg, Stalemate, and the Long Retreat

As the Japanese bogged down in China and debated the necessity of tangling with the United States and the European colonial powers, the Nazi war machine captured France and the Low Countries with stunning speed, forced the British armies to beat a fast retreat to their island refuge, and then rolled over eastern Europe and drove deep into the Soviet Union. Germany appeared unstoppable and the fate of a large chunk of humanity seemed destined for a long period of tyrannical Nazi rule. From the outset, German strategy was centered on the concept of **blitzkrieg** or "lightning war," which involved the rapid penetration of enemy territory by a combination of tanks and mechanized troop carriers, backup infantry, and supporting fighter aircraft and bombers. The effective deployment of these forces overwhelmed the Poles in 1939, and more critically routed the French and British within a matter of days in the spring of 1940, thereby accomplishing what the Kaiser's armies failed to do through four long years of warfare between 1914 and 1918. German willingness to punish adversaries or civilian populations in areas that refused to yield greatly magnified the toll of death and destruction left in the wake of Hitler's armies. In early 1940, for example, the Dutch port of Rotterdam was virtually leveled by Nazi bombers, killing over 40,000 civilians.

The rapid collapse of France was, in part, a consequence of the divided and weak leadership the republic had displayed in the successive crises of the 1930s. Governments had come and gone as contemporaries quipped that they were moving in revolving doors. Left and right quarreled and stalemated over rearming, responding to the Nazis and allying with the British and the Soviets. When the war broke out, the citizenry of France was thoroughly demoralized, and the nation's defenses were outdated and extremely susceptible to the Wehrmacht's blitzkrieg offensives. By the summer of 1940, all of north and central France was in German hands, and in the south, a Nazi puppet regime, centered on the city of **Vichy,** was in charge. With the Nazi occupations of Norway and Denmark in the preceding months, Britain alone of the western democracies in Europe survived. But what remained of the British armies had been driven from the continent, while the nation's people and cities were under heavy assault by a markedly superior German air force, which strove to open the way to cross-channel invasion by the much larger and more powerful land forces of the steadily growing Nazi empire.

Remarkably, under the courageous leadership of **Winston Churchill,** the British people weathered what their new prime minister had aptly pronounced the nation's "darkest hour." A smaller British air force proved able to withstand the Nazi air offensive, including saturation bombing of London and other British cities. Victory in what came to be known as the **Battle of Britain** was due to a mix of strong leadership by Churchill and a very able coalition cabinet; innovative air tactics, made possible by the introduction of radar devices for tracking German assault aircraft; and the bravery of Britain's royal family and the high morale of the citizenry as a whole that the bombing raids only seemed to enhance. Unable to destroy Britain's air defenses or break the resolve of its people, Hitler and the Nazi high command had to abandon their plans for conquest of the British Isles. Without air superiority, the Germans could not prevent the Royal Navy from entering the channel and destroying the huge flotilla of landing craft that would be needed to carry the Nazi forces across the narrow but turbulent straits that had for nearly a millennium shielded Britain from outside invasion.

By mid-1941 the Germans controlled most of the continent of Europe and much of the Mediterranean. They had rescued the Italians' floundering campaign to conquer Albania and overrun Yugoslavia and Greece. They had conquered, or in the case of Sweden forced the neutralization of, the Scandinavian countries. They continued on to capture most of the islands of the Mediterranean and launched motorized offensives under the soon-to-be legendary commander Erwin Rommel (Figure 31.2) across north Africa and on to Egypt, with the goal of seizing the Suez Canal and cutting Britain off from its Asian empire (see Map 31.1). Once conquered, the hundreds of millions of peoples subjugated by Nazi aggression were compelled to provide resources, war materials, soldiers, and slave labor to a German war machine then being directed against even more ambitious targets.

Frustrated by resolute British defiance, Hitler and the Nazi high command turned to the south and east to regain the momentum that had propelled them to so many victories in the first years of the war in Europe. As Nazi forces, numbering 3.5 million, drove the poorly prepared and understaffed Soviet forces out of Finland, Poland, the Baltic states, and much of Byelorussia and the Ukraine in the summer

Figure 31.2 *Erwin Rommel and German mechanized forces in north Africa. Rommel was perhaps the most astute and daring Nazi general. But he met his match in the desert war fought against British troops led by Bernard Montgomery.*

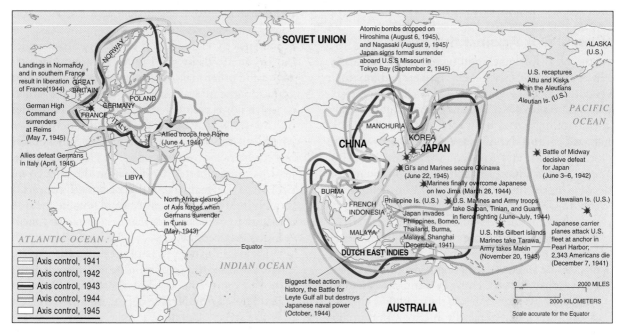

Landings in Normandy
and in southern France
result in liberation
of France(1944)

German High
Command
surrenders
at Reims
(May 7, 1945)

Allied troops free Rome
(June 4, 1944)

Allies defeat Germans
in Italy (April, 1945)

North Africa cleared
of Axis forces when
Germans surrender
in Tunis
(May, 1943)

Atomic bombs dropped on
Hiroshima (August 6, 1945),
and Nagasaki (August 9, 1945)
Japan signs formal surrender
aboard U.S.S Missouri in
Tokyo Bay (September 2, 1945)

U.S. recaptures
Attu and Kiska
in the Aleutians

Battle of Midway
decisive defeat
for Japan
(June 3–6, 1942)

GI's and Marines secure Okinawa
(June 22, 1945)

Marines finally overcome Japanese
on Iwo Jima (March 26, 1944)

U.S. Marines and Army troops
take Saipan, Tinian, and Guam
in fierce fighting (June–July, 1944)

Japan invades
Philippines, Borneo,
Thailand, Burma,
Malaya, Shanghai
(December, 1941)

U.S. hits Gilbert islands
Marines take Tarawa,
Army takes Makin
(November 20, 1943)

Japanese carrier
planes attack U.S.
fleet at anchor in
Pearl Harbor;
2,343 Americans die
(December 7, 1941)

Biggest fleet action in
history, the Battle for
Leyte Gulf all but destroys
Japanese naval power
(October, 1944)

Axis control, 1941
Axis control, 1942
Axis control, 1943
Axis control, 1944
Axis control, 1945

0 _____ 2000 MILES
0 _____ 2000 KILOMETERS
Scale accurate for the Equator

Map 31.1 *The Main Theaters of World War II*

and early fall of 1941, Hitler's grandest victory of all—and unlimited access to cheap labor and such critical resources as oil—seemed within reach. But the Soviet armies, despite appalling losses, did not collapse; they retreated eastward rather than surrender. Stalin ordered Soviet industry relocated across the Ural Mountains to shield them from capture and German aerial attacks.

As with Napoleon's invasion nearly a century and a half earlier, Russian resistance stiffened as winter approached, and the German drive east stalled on the outskirts of Moscow and Leningrad. The harsh winter caught the German forces unprepared while their Russian adversaries used terrain and weather conditions they knew well to counter attack with ferocity on a wide front. The Nazis' mass killings and harsh treatment of the Slavic peoples, including the Ukrainians, many of whom initially were disposed to support the invaders, aroused guerrilla resistance by tens, then hundreds, of thousands of partisans, who fought behind German lines throughout the rest of the war.

Renewed German offensives in the spring of 1942 again drove deep into Russia but failed a second time to capture key cities like Moscow, Leningrad, and Stalingrad, and perhaps as critically, the great Baku oil fields in the southern steppes. The two sides clashed in

some of the greatest battles of the entire war—in fact of all human history—including Kursk, which featured thousands of tanks deployed (and destroyed) by each of the adversaries. As another winter approached, the Germans were further away from knocking the Soviets out of the war than the year before. In fact, the failed Nazi attempt to capture Stalingrad in the bitter winter of 1942 and 1943 ended in the destruction of an entire German army and proved a decisive turning point in the war in the east.

In 1943, the Red armies went on the offensive at numerous points along the overextended, undermanned, and vulnerable German front. With staggering losses in lives and equipment, the Nazi forces, despite Hitler's rantings that they die in place, began the long retreat from the Soviet Union. By late 1944, Red armies had cleared the Soviet Union of Nazi forces and captured Poland and much of east central Europe southward into the Balkans. As the Soviet forces advanced inexorably toward Germany, it was clear that the destruction of Hitler's "thousand-year reich" was only months away. It was also apparent that the almost unimaginable sacrifices and remarkable resilience of Russian soldiers, which included many women, had contributed mightily to the destruction of the vaunted Nazi fighting machine.

From Persecution to Genocide: Hitler's War Against the Jews

As the Nazi war machine bogged down in Russia, Hitler and his Nazi henchmen stepped up their vendetta against Gypsies, leftist politicians, homosexuals, and especially Jews. Jews, Polish intellectuals, and communists had been rounded up and killed in mass executions during the German offensives into eastern Europe and Russia in the early 1940s. But after a "final solution" for the "Jewish problem" was decided upon by prominent Nazi officials at the Wannsee Conference in February 1942, the regime directed its energies explicitly and systematically to genocide. The destruction, rather than the removal, of the Jewish people became the official policy of the Reich. In the three years that remained to Hitler and his henchmen, the concentration camps they had set up in the 1930s to incarcerate their political enemies and groups branded as racially inferior—thus polluting to the Aryan people—were transformed into factories for the mass production of death.

The more the war against the Allies turned against Hitler and the Nazi high command, the more they pressed the genocidal campaign against the largely defenseless Jewish peoples of Europe. In fact, vital resources were regularly diverted from the battle fronts for transportation, imprisonment, and mass murder in the camps, where the destruction of human life reached a frenetic pace in the last years of the regime. Jews and other "undesirables" were identified and arrested throughout the Nazi empire. Shipped to the camps in the east, those deemed physically fit were subjected to harsh forced labor that took a heavy toll in lives. The less fortunate, including the vast majority of the women and children, were systematically murdered, sometimes in experiments carried out by German physicians with the callous disregard for human suffering and humiliation that was a hallmark of the Nazi regime.

As many as 12 million people were murdered in the genocidal orgy that has come to be known as the **Holocaust,** and which will perhaps prove to be what is remembered more than anything else about the Nazi regime. Of these, at least 6 million were Jews, and many millions of others were Slavic peoples mercilessly slaughtered on the Eastern Front. Without question, the Holocaust was by far the most costly genocide of the 20th century, which had begun with the Armenian massacres in 1915, and had the horrors

of Kampuchea, Rwanda, Bosnia, and Kosovo yet to come. With the possible exceptions of the massacres in the Soviet Ukraine in the 1930s and those carried out in the 1970s by the Khmer Rouge, more than any of the other major episodes of the 20th-century genocide, the Holocaust was notable for the degree to which it was premeditated, systematic, and carried out by the Nazi state apparatus and functionaries, who until the very end kept precise and detailed records of their noxious deeds. The Holocaust was at least passively abetted by denial on the part of the people of Germany and the occupied countries, though the Danes and Italians were notable for their resistance to Nazi demands that they turn over "their" Jews for incarceration.

The plight of the Jews of Europe was also greatly exacerbated by the refusal of the Western Allies to accept as emigrants any but the most affluent or skilled Jews fleeing Nazi atrocities, and by the failure of those same Allies to use their military assets to strike at the railway lines and killing chambers they clearly knew were in operation by the last months of the war. These responses to the Nazi horror only steeled the resolve of Zionist leaders in Palestine and elsewhere to facilitate, by negotiations with the hated Nazis if necessary, the flight of the European Jews. It also intensified their determination to establish a Jewish state in Palestine to ensure that there could never be another Holocaust.

Anglo-American Offensives, Encirclement, and the End of the 12-Year Reich

For nearly two years, the British were so absorbed in their own struggle for survival that they could provide little relief for their Soviet allies, hard-pressed by what some have seen as Hitler's foolhardy invasion of Russia. Even before the attack on Pearl Harbor in December 1941, the United States was providing substantial assistance, including military supplies, to beleaguered Britain. Franklin Roosevelt was quite openly sympathetic to the British cause and soon established a good working relationship with Churchill. American forces first entered the war in a major way in the campaigns to counter German U-boat attacks on shipping crossing the Atlantic. Then American tank divisions and infantrymen joined the British in reversing Rommel's gains in North Africa in 1942 and 1943. Having all but cleared Nazi forces from

Africa and the Middle East, Anglo-American armies next struck across the Mediterranean at Sicily and then Italy proper. Their steady, but often costly, advance up the peninsula lasted into early 1945 but eventually toppled the fascist regime and prompted a Nazi takeover of northern Italy. Mussolini and the last of his many mistresses were captured and shot by partisans and enraged civilians and hung upside down on a lamp post near Lake Bellagio.

With significant German forces tied down on the Eastern Front and in Italy, the allied high command, with General Dwight Eisenhower at its head, prepared landings in northern France that would carry the war into the fortress the Nazis had been building in occupied Europe ever since their defeat in the Battle of Britain in 1940. In early June, against fierce resistance, the Allies established beachheads at Normandy, from which they launched liberation campaigns into the Low Countries and the rest of France. Despite Hitler's last-ditch effort to repel the invading Allied armies in what became known as the **Battle of the Bulge** in the winter of 1944–1945, by early in 1945, the Allies had invaded Germany from the west, while the Red armies were pouring in from the east.

In late April, Russian and American troops linked up at the Elbe River, where they became caught up in spontaneous celebrations. The genuine comradery and mutual respect widely displayed by troops on both sides would soon be lost in high-stakes maneuvers by the political leaders in each camp to shape the postwar world order. On April 30, after haranguing his closest advisors for his betrayal by the German people, Adolf Hitler committed suicide in his Berlin bunker. Less than two weeks later, German military leaders surrendered their forces, putting an end to the war in the European and Mediterranean theaters. But the contest between the Anglo-American and Soviet allies for control of Germany had already commenced, and it would soon be extended to Europe as a whole and the rest of the world.

The Rise and Fall of the Japanese Empire in the Pacific War

Long before their sneak attack on **Pearl Harbor** on December 7, 1941, the Japanese had been engaged in a major war on the Chinese mainland. Even after Pearl Harbor, roughly one-third of all Japanese military forces would remain bogged down in China, despite the sudden extension of the Japanese empire

over much of southeast Asia and far out into the Pacific (see Map 31.1). With the American Pacific fleet temporarily neutralized by the attack, Japan's combined air, sea, and army assaults quickly captured the colonial territories of the British in Hong Kong in south China as well as Malaya and Burma. They also overran the Dutch East Indies and the Philippines—despite more determined resistance—and completed the takeover of French Indochina. The Thais managed to stave off the invasion and occupation of Siam by retreating into neutrality and cooperating with the ascendant Japanese. Although Great Britain remained a major combatant, and Australia and New Zealand provided important support, the United States quickly emerged as the major counterforce to Japan's ever-expanding Asian empire.

Though impressive in size and the speed with which it was formed, the Japanese empire soon proved to be highly vulnerable to the Allied forces committed to its destruction. The Japanese had risked alienating virtually all of the European colonial powers by their seizure of much of southeast Asia. They did so because they calculated that since the European metropoles had been overrun or were hard-pressed by the Nazis, the Europeans would not be able to reinforce their colonial enclaves. The Japanese leadership was also aware that the homeland's wartime economy was in desperate need of critical raw materials, including oil and staple foods, that could be imported from southeast Asia. But in their efforts to extract those resources, the Japanese imposed colonial regimes on the peoples of southeast Asia that were a good deal more brutally oppressive than those of any of the displaced Western colonizers. Over time, this produced growing resistance movements from Burma to the Philippines, which drew Japanese soldiers and substantial resources from the war in the Pacific against the advancing Allied forces.

Resistance fighters also cooperated with British and American forces pushing into the area in the latter stages of the war. Southeast Asian guerrilla forces, which often had communist affiliations, played significant roles in sabotaging occupying forces and harassing retreating Japanese armies. The shipping lanes from distant colonial enclaves throughout southeast Asia also proved highly vulnerable to American submarines, which by late 1944 were able to sink a high percentage of the tons of foodstuffs and war materials shipped back to Japan.

The main front of the Pacific theater of the war centered on the widely scattered islands that Japan had begun to occupy before, and especially after, World War I, as well as those seized from the British and Americans after Pearl Harbor. No sooner had the Japanese garrisoned these enclaves than a hastily but well-prepared American advance into the central Pacific put them on the defensive. Having attacked Pearl Harbor when all of the major American aircraft carriers were at sea, the Japanese missed the chance to cripple the most potent weapons in the United States arsenal. Within six months, the United States naval and air forces fought the Japanese to a standoff at the **Battle of the Coral Sea.** In June, less than a month later, off **Midway Island,** they won a decisive victory over a powerful carrier force, commanded by Admiral Yamamoto, the architect of the Pearl Harbor attack. Once the Allied forces had gained the upper hand in the air and on the sea through these engagements, they could begin the assault on the double ring of Pacific island fortresses that protected the Japanese homeland (Figure 31.3).

Keying their amphibious assaults on strategically vital islands, the joint air, sea, and land operations of the Allied forces had come within striking distance of Japan itself by early 1944, despite fierce and unrelenting Japanese resistance. In June of that year, the American Air Force began regular bomber assaults on the Japanese home islands. The high concentration of the Japanese population in urban areas and the wood and paper construction of most Japanese dwellings provided tempting targets for American bomber squadrons. In March 1945, General Curtis Le May, who was in charge of American air operations, ordered mass aerial bombardment of highly vulnerable Japanese cities. In Tokyo alone, these raids killed over 125,000 people, mostly civilians, and destroyed over 40 percent of the city within days. At the same time, Allied naval superiority and submarine attacks had largely cut the home islands off from what remained of the empire in China and southeast Asia.

By the early summer of 1945, Japanese leaders were sending out peace feelers, while the more fanatical elements in the army were promising to fight to the death. The end was sudden and terrifying. On August 6th and three days later on August 9th, atomic bombs were dropped on Hiroshima and Nagasaki, respectively. In moments these cities, which to this point had been spared bombing, were reduced to ashes, with short-term casualties in both well over 100,000, and deaths from radiation sickness increasing this total greatly in the years, and even decades, that followed. Even more than in the European theater, the end of the long and most

Figure 31.3 *The United States advanced on Japan with the invasion and capture of Okinawa in March 1945. Note the huge stores of munitions, food, and other supplies provided for the Allied armies. This awesome material abundance touched off "cargo cult" movements in the Pacific islands after the war.*

Document

Japan and the Loss in World War II

Japan's defeat in World War II brought moral and material confusion. The government was so uncertain of the intentions of the victorious Americans that it evacuated its female employees to the countryside. The following excerpt from the 1945 diary of Yoshizawa Hisako (who became a writer on home economics) reveals more popular attitudes and the mixed ingredients that composed them. The passage also suggests how the American occupation force tried to present itself and the reception it received.

August 15. As I listened to the Emperor's voice announcing the surrender, every word acquired a special meaning and His Majesty's voice penetrated my mind. Tears streamed down my cheeks. I kept on telling myself that we must not fight ourselves and work hard for our common good. Yes, I pledged myself, I must work [for Japan's recovery].

The city was quiet.

I could not detect any special expression in people's faces. Were they too tired? However, somehow they seemed brighter, and I could catch an expression showing a sign of relief. It could have been a reflection of my own feelings. But I knew I could trust what I saw....

The voluntary fighting unit was disbanded, and I was no longer a member of that unit. Each of us burned the insignia and other identifications.

I cannot foresee what kind of difficulty will befall me, but all I know is that I must learn to survive relying on my health and my will to live.

August 16. People do not wear expressions any different from other days. However, in place of a "good morning" or "good afternoon," people are now greeting each other with the phrase "What will become of us?"

During the morning, the city was still placed under air-raid alert.

My company announced that until everything becomes clearer, no female employees were to come to work and urged all of us to go to the countryside, adding that we should leave forwarding addresses. This measure was taken to conform to the step already taken by governmental bureaus. Are they thinking that the occupation army will do something to us girls? There are so many important questions we have to cope with, I cannot understand why governmental officials are so worried about these matters.

We did not have enough power and lost the war.

The Army continued to appeal to the people to resist the enemy to the end. This poses a lot of problems. People can show their true colors better when they are defeated than when they win. I just hope we, as a nation, can show our better side now.

Just because we have been defeated, I do not wish to see us destroying our national characteristics when we are dealing with foreign countries.

August 17. It was rumored that a number of lower echelon military officers were unhappy with the peace, and were making some secret moves. There were other rumors, and with the quiet evacuation of women and children from the cities, our fear seemed to have intensified. After all we have never experienced a defeat before. Our fear may simply be the manifestation of fear of the unknown.

Our airplanes dropped propaganda leaflets.

One of the leaflets was posted at the Kanda Station which said: "Both the Army and Navy are alive and well. We expect the nation to follow our lead." The leaflet was signed. I could understand how those military men felt. However, we already have the imperial rescript to surrender. If we are going to rebuild, we must open a new path. It is much easier to die than to live. In the long history of our nation, this defeat may become one of those insignificant happenings. However, the rebuilding after the defeat is likely to be treated as a far more important chapter in our history.

We did our best and lost, so there is nothing we have to say in our own defense. Only those people who did not do their best may now be feeling guilty, though.

Mr. C. said that everything he saw in the city was so repugnant that he wanted to retreat to the countryside. I was amazed by the narrowness of his thought process. I could say that he had a pure sense of devotion to the country, but that was only his own way of thinking. Beautiful perhaps, but it lacked firm foundation. I wish men like him would learn to broaden their perspectives.

August 18. Rationed bread distribution in the morning. I went to the distribution center with Mrs. A.

August 21. We heard that the Allied advance units will be airlifted and arrive in Japan on the 26th. And the following day, their fleet will also anchor in our harbors. The American Army will be airlifted and land in Atsugi airport.

According to someone who accompanied the Japanese delegation which went to accept surrender conditions, the Americans behaved like gentlemen. They explained to the Americans that certain conditions were unworkable in light of the present situation in Japan. The Americans immediately agreed to alter those conditions. They listened very carefully to what the Japanese delegation had to say.

An American paper, according to someone, reported that meeting as follows: "We cooked thick beefsteak expecting seven or eight Japanese would appear. But seventeen of them came, so we had to kill a turkey to prepare for them. We treated them well before they returned."...When I hear things like this, I immediately feel how exaggerated and inefficient our ways of doing things are. They say that Americans will tackle one item

(continued)

after another at a conference table, and do not waste even 30 seconds....

In contrast, Japanese administration is conducted by many chairs and seals. For example when an auxiliary unit is asked to undertake a task for a governmental bureau, before anything can be done, twenty, or thirty seals of approval must be secured. So there is no concept of not wasting time. Even in war, they are too accustomed to doing things the way they have been doing and their many seals and chairs are nothing but a manifestation of their refusal to take individual responsibilities.

The fact of a defeat is a very serious matter and it is not easy to accept. However, it can bring some positive effects, if it can inculcate in our minds all the shortcomings we have had. I hope this will come true some day, and toward that end we must all endeavor. Even if we have to suffer hunger and other tribulations we must strive toward a positive goal.

Questions: How did Japanese attitudes in defeat help prepare Japan for postwar redevelopment? Did defeat produce new divisions in attitudes among the Japanese? What other kinds of reactions might have been expected? How would you explain the rather calm and constructive outlook the passage suggests? Would American reactions to a Japanese victory have been similar?

destructive war in human history came swiftly. As they had in dealing with Germany, the Allies demanded unconditional surrender by the Japanese. With the exception of retaining the emperor, which was finally allowed, the Japanese agreed to these terms and began to disarm. With the division of Germany that had begun some months earlier, the Allied occupation of the islands set the stage for the third main phase of the 20th century, which would be dominated by the cold war between the Soviet and American superpowers that would be waged amid the collapse of the European colonial order.

War's End and the Emergence of the Superpower Standoff

The final stages of World War II quickly led to a tense confrontation between the United States and the Soviet Untion, each backed by allies. The cold war pitted against each other two different political and economic systems—capitalist versus communist, each of which displayed missionary zeal in attempting to prescribe policies for the rest of the world. The cold war also pitted against each other two military giants—the great victors of World War II, with vast territories, population, and resources—in a bitter rivalry for more territory and influence. After a brief pause immediately after World War II, each side in the cold war embarked on massive military buildups, soon featuring nuclear weaponry and missile delivery systems. Each side sought military alliances and bases almost everywhere.

World War II did not produce the sweeping peace settlements, misguided as most of them turned out to be, which had officially ended World War I. The leaders of the Allies opposed to the Axis powers met on several occasions in an attempt to build the framework for a more lasting peace free of the vindictiveness that was so prominent at the Versailles gathering. A key result of Allied discussions was agreement on establishing the **United Nations.** From the outset, this new international organization was more representative of the world's peoples, in both large and small nations, than the League of Nations. The United States pledged to join, played a major role in the United Nations' planning and finance, and provided the site on the East River in Manhattan where the organization's permanent headquarters was ultimately located. The Soviet Union was also a charter member, along with long-standing great powers, such as Britain and France. China, represented in the first decades after 1945 by the Guomindang, was grouped with these other global powers as a permanent member of the Security Council, the steering committee for United Nations operations. In the decades after the end of the war, the vanquished Axis powers were eventually granted membership, as were the former colonies, soon after each gained their independence.

With the successful establishment of the United Nations, international diplomacy and assistance moved beyond the orbit of the Western powers, who had all but monopolized them for centuries, but through their vetoes in the Security Council they retained considerable control. The United Nations' primary mission was to provide a forum for negotiating international disputes. But it also took over the apparatus of more specialized international agencies, including the World Court of Justice, those concerned with human rights, and those that coordinated programs directed at specific groups and problems, ranging from labor organization and famine relief to agricultural development and women's concerns. Although United Nations interventions to preserve or restore peace to numerous regions have encountered much resistance by both the great powers and regional power brokers, they have repeatedly proved vital to reducing violent conflict and providing refugee relief throughout the globe. The United Nations has also sponsored initiatives, including critical international conferences, that have proved highly influential in shaping policies and programs affecting child labor, women's rights, and environmental protection.

From Hot War to Cold War

The cold war would last until the 1980s, with various points of crisis and confrontation. Direct conflict between the two superpowers did not occur, despite dire forebodings. Much of world history, however, was shaped by cold war maneuverings for over four decades.

The cold war began when the World War II allies turned, in the war's final conferences, to debate the nature of the postwar settlement. It quickly became apparent that the Soviet Union expected massive territorial gains and that Britain and the United States intended to limit these gains through their own areas of influence. Unresolved disputes—for World War II was never ended with a clear set of peace negotiations—then led to the full outbreak of the cold war between 1945 and 1949.

Tensions had clearly surfaced during the 1944 **Tehran Conference,** when the allies agreed on the invasion of Nazi-occupied France. The decision to focus on France rather than moving up from the Mediterranean in effect gave the Soviet forces a free hand to move through the smaller nations of eastern

Europe as they pushed the Nazi armies back. Britain negotiated separately with the Soviets to ensure Western preponderance in postwar Greece as well as equality in Hungary and Yugoslavia, with Soviet control of Rumania and Bulgaria, but the United States resisted this kind of un-Wilsonian scorn for the rights of small nations.

The next settlement meeting was the **Yalta Conference** in the Soviet Crimea early in 1945. President Franklin Roosevelt of the United States was eager to press the Soviet Union for assistance against Japan and to this end promised the Soviets important territorial gains in Manchuria and the northern Japanese islands. The organization of the United Nations was confirmed. As to Europe, however, agreement was more difficult. The three powers easily arranged to divide Germany into four occupation zones (liberated France getting a chunk), which would be disarmed and purged of Nazi influence. Britain, however, resisted Soviet zeal to eliminate German industrial power, seeing a viable Germany as a potential ally in a subsequent Western–Soviet contest. Bitter dispute also raged over the smaller nations of eastern Europe. No one disagreed that they should be friendly to their Soviet neighbor, but the Western leaders also wanted them to be free and democratic. Stalin, the Soviet leader, had to make some concessions by including noncommunist leaders in what was already a Soviet-controlled government in liberated Poland—concessions that he soon violated.

The final postwar conference occurred in the Berlin suburb of **Potsdam** in July 1945. Russian forces now occupied not only most of eastern Europe but eastern Germany as well. This de facto situation prompted agreement that the Soviet Union could take over much of what had been eastern Poland, with the Poles gaining part of eastern Germany in compensation. Germany was divided pending a final peace treaty (which was not to come for more than 40 years). Austria was also divided and occupied, gaining unity and independence only in 1956, on condition of neutrality between the United States and the Soviet Union. Amid great difficulty, treaties were worked out for Germany's other allies, including Italy, but the United States and, later, the Soviet Union signed separate treaties with Japan.

All these maneuvers had several results. Japan was occupied by the United States and its wartime gains stripped away. Even Korea, taken earlier, was freed but was divided between U.S. and Soviet zones of occupation (the basis for the North Korea–South Korea division still in effect today). Former Asian colonies were returned to their old "masters," though often quite briefly, as new independence movements quickly challenged the control of the weakened imperialist powers. China regained most of its former territory, though here, too, stability was promptly challenged by renewed fighting between communist and nationalist forces within the nation, aided by the Soviet Union and the United States, respectively.

The effort to confirm old colonial regimes applied also to the Middle East, India, and Africa. Indian and African troops had fought for Britain during the war, as in World War I, though Britain imprisoned key nationalist leaders and put independence plans on hold. African leaders had participated actively in the French resistance to its authoritarian wartime government. The Middle East and north Africa had been shaken by German invasions and Allied counterattacks. Irritability increased, and so did expectations for change. With Europe's imperial powers further weakened by their war effort, adjustments seemed inevitable, as in those parts of Asia invaded by the Japanese.

In Europe the boundaries of the Soviet Union pushed westward, with virtually all the losses after World War I erased. Independent nations created in 1918 were for the most part restored (though the former Baltic states of Latvia, Lithuania, and Estonia became Soviet provinces because they had been Russian provinces before World War I). Except for Greece and Yugoslavia, the new nations quickly fell under Soviet domination, with communist governments forced on them and Soviet troops in occupation. The nations of western Europe were free to set up or confirm democratic regimes, but most of them lived under the shadow of growing U.S. influence, manifested in continued presence of U.S. troops, substantial economic aid and coordination, and no small amount of outright policy manipulation.

The stage was set, in other words, for two of the great movements that would shape the ensuing decades in world history. The first comprised challenges by subject peoples to the tired vestiges of control by the great European empires—the movement known as "decolonization" that in a few decades would create scores of new nations in Asia, Africa, and the West Indies. The second great theme was the confrontation between the two superpowers that

emerged from the war—the United States and the Soviet Union, each with new international influence and new military might. Many believed that this cold war would soon become a war in a more literal and devastating sense. That these trends constituted a peace settlement was difficult to imagine in 1945 or 1947, yet they seemed the best that could be done.

Nationalism and Decolonization

 The effects of a second global conflict, brought on by the expansionist ambitions of Hitler's Germany and of imperial Japan, proved fatal to the already badly battered European colonial empires. The sobering casualties of yet another war between the industrialized powers sapped the will of the Western colonizers to engage in further conflicts that would clearly be needed to crush resurgent nationalist movements throughout Africa and Asia. From India and Pakistan to west Africa, independence was won in most of the nonsettler colonies with surprisingly little bloodshed and remarkable speed. But in areas such as Algeria, Kenya, and south Africa, where large European settler communities tried to block nationalist agitation, liberation struggles were usually violent and costly and at times far from complete.

The Nazi rout of the French and the stunningly rapid Japanese capture of the French, Dutch, British, and United States colonies in southeast Asia put an end to whatever illusions the colonized peoples of Africa and Asia had left about the strength and innate superiority of their colonial overlords. Because the Japanese were non-Europeans, their early victories over the Europeans and Americans played a particularly critical role in destroying the myth of the white man's invincibility. The fall of the "impregnable" fortress at Singapore on the southern tip of Malaya, and the Americans' reverses at Pearl Harbor and in the Philippines proved to be blows from which the colonizers never quite recovered, even though they went on to eventually defeat the Japanese. The sight of tens of thousands of British, Dutch, and American troops, struggling under the supervision of the victorious Japanese to survive the "death marches" to prison camps in their former colonies, left an indelible impression on the Asian villagers who saw them pass by. The harsh regimes and heavy demands the

Japanese conquerors imposed on the peoples of southeast Asia during the war further strengthened the determination to fight for self-rule and to look to their own defenses after the conflict was over.

The devastation of World War II—a **total war** fought in the cities and countryside over much of Europe—drained the resources of the European powers. This devastating warfare also sapped the will of the European populace to hold increasingly resistant African and Asian peoples in bondage. The war also greatly enhanced the power and influence of the two giants on the European periphery: the United States and the Soviet Union. In Africa and the Middle East, as well as in the Pacific, the United States approached the war as a campaign of liberation. American propagandists made no secret of Franklin Roosevelt's hostility to colonialism in their efforts to win Asian and African support for the Allied war effort. In fact, American intentions in this regard were enshrined in the **Atlantic Charter of 1941.** This pact sealed an alliance between the United States and Great Britain that the latter desperately needed to survive in its war with Nazi Germany. In it Roosevelt persuaded a reluctant Churchill to include a clause that recognized the "right of all people to choose the form of government under which they live." The Soviets were equally vocal in their condemnation of colonialism and were even more forthcoming with material support for nationalist campaigns after the war. In the

cold war world of the superpowers that emerged after 1945, there was little room for the domination that the much-reduced powers of western Europe had once exercised over much of the globe.

The Winning of Independence in South and Southeast Asia

The outbreak of World War II soon put an end to the accommodation between the Indian National Congress and the British in the late 1930s. Congress leaders offered to support the Allies' war effort if the British would give them a significant share of power at the all-India level and commit themselves to Indian independence once the conflict was over. These conditions were staunchly rejected both by the viceroy in India and at home by Winston Churchill, who headed the coalition government that led Britain through the war. Labour members of the coalition government, however, indicated that they were quite willing to negotiate India's eventual independence. As tensions built between nationalist agitators and the British rulers, Sir Stafford Cripps was sent to India in early 1942 to see whether a deal could be struck with the Indian leaders. Indian divisions and British intransigence led to the collapse of Cripps's initiative and the renewal of mass civil disobedience campaigns under the guise of the **Quit India movement,** which began in the summer of 1942 (Figure 31.4).

Figure 31.4 *As this photo of Mahatma Gandhi beside his spinning wheel suggests, he played many roles in the Indian nationalist struggle. The wheel evokes India's traditional status as a textile center and the economic boycotts of British machine-made cloth that were central to Gandhi's civil disobedience campaigns. Gandhi's meditative position projects the image of a religious guru that appealed to large segments of the Indian populace. The simplicity of his surroundings evokes the asceticism and detachment from the material world that had long been revered in Indian culture.*

The British responded with repression and mass arrests, and for much of the remainder of the war, Gandhi, Nehru, and other major Congress politicians were imprisoned. Of the Indian nationalist parties, only the Communists—who were committed to the antifascist alliance—and, more ominously, the **Muslim League** rallied to the British cause. The League, now led by a former Congress party politician, the dour and uncompromising **Muhammad Ali Jinnah,** won much favor from the British for its wartime support. As their demands for a separate Muslim state in the subcontinent hardened, the links between the British and Jinnah and other League leaders became a key factor in the struggle for decolonization in south Asia.

World War II brought disruptions to India similar to those caused by the earlier global conflict. Inflation stirred up urban unrest, while a widespread famine in 1943 and 1944, brought on in part by wartime transport shortages, engendered much bitterness in rural India. Winston Churchill's defeat in the first postwar British election in 1945 brought a Labour government to power that was ready to deal with India's nationalist leaders. With independence in the near future tacitly conceded, the process of decolonization between 1945 and 1947 focused on what sort of state or states would be carved out of the subcontinent after the British withdrawal. Jinnah and the League had begun to build a mass following among the Muslims. In order to rally support they played on widespread anxieties among the Muslim minority that a single Indian nation would be dominated by the Hindu majority, and that the Muslims would become the targets of increasing discrimination. It was therefore essential, they insisted, that a separate Muslim state called Pakistan be created from those areas in northwest and east India where Muslims were the most numerous.

As communal rioting spread throughout India, the British and key Congress party politicians reluctantly concluded that a bloodbath could be averted only by partition—the creation of two nations in the subcontinent: one secular, one Muslim. Thus, in the summer of 1947, the British handed power over to the leaders of the majority Congress party, who headed the new nation of India, and to Jinnah, who became the first president of Pakistan.

In part because of the haste with which the British withdrew their forces from the deeply divided subcontinent, a bloodbath occurred anyway. Vicious Hindu–Muslim and Muslim–Sikh communal rioting, in which neither women nor children were spared, took the lives of hundreds of thousands in the searing summer heat across the plains of northwest India. Whole villages were destroyed; trains were attacked and their passengers hacked to death by armed bands of rival religious adherents. These atrocities fed a massive exchange of refugee populations between Hindu–Sikh and Muslim areas that may have totaled 10 million people. Those who fled were so terrified that they were willing to give up their land, their villages, and most of their worldly possessions. The losses of partition were compounded by the fact that there was soon no longer a Gandhi to preach tolerance and communal coexistence. On January 30, 1948, on the way to one of his regular prayer meetings, he was shot by a Hindu fanatic.

In granting independence to India, the British, in effect, removed the keystone from the arch of an empire that spanned three continents. Burma (known today as Myanmar) and Ceylon (now named Sri Lanka) won their independence peacefully in the following years. India's independence and Gandhi's civil disobedience campaigns, which had done so much to win a mass following for the nationalist cause, also inspired successful struggles for independence in Ghana, Nigeria, and other African colonies in the 1950s and 1960s.

The retreat of the most powerful of the imperial powers could not help but contribute to the weakening of lesser empires such as those of the Dutch, the French, and the Americans. In fact, the process of the transfer of power from United States officials to moderate, middle-class Filipino politicians was well under way before World War II broke out. The loyalty to the Americans that most Filipinos displayed during the war, as well as the stubborn guerrilla resistance they put up against the Japanese occupation, did much to bring about the rapid granting of independence to the Philippines once the war was ended. The Dutch and French were less willing to follow the British example and relinquish their colonial possessions in the postwar era. From 1945 to 1949, the Dutch fought a losing war to destroy the nation of Indonesia, which nationalists in the Netherlands Indies had established when the Japanese hold over the islands broke down in mid-1945. The French struggled to retain Indochina. Communist revolutions in east Asia also emerged victorious in the postwar period. No sooner had the European colonizers suffered these losses than they were forced to deal with new threats to the last bastions of the imperial order in Africa.

The Liberation of Nonsettler Africa

World War II proved even more disruptive to the colonial order imposed on Africa than the first global conflict of the European powers. Forced labor and confiscations of crops and minerals returned, and inflation and controlled markets again cut down on African earnings. African recruits in the hundreds of thousands were drawn once more into the conflict and had even greater opportunities to use the latest European weapons to destroy Europeans. African servicemen had witnessed British and French defeats in the Middle East and southeast Asia, and they fought bravely only to experience renewed racial discrimination once they returned home. Many were soon among the staunchest supporters of postwar nationalist campaigns in the African colonies of the British and French. The swift and humiliating rout of the French and Belgians by Nazi armies in the spring of 1940 shattered whatever was left of the colonizers' reputation for military prowess. It also led to a bitter and, in the circumstances, embarrassing struggle between the forces of the puppet Vichy regime and those of De Gaulle's Free French, who continued fighting the Nazis mainly in France's north and west African colonies.

The wartime needs of both the British and the Free French led to major departures from long-standing colonial policies that had restricted industrial development throughout Africa. Factories were established to process urgently needed vegetable oils, foods, and minerals in western and south central Africa. These, in turn, contributed to a growing migration on the part of African peasants to the towns and a sharp spurt in African urban growth. The inability of many of those who moved to the towns to find employment made for a reservoir of disgruntled, idle workers that would be skillfully tapped by nationalist politicians in the postwar decades.

There were essentially two main paths to decolonization in nonsettler Africa in the postwar era. The first was pioneered by Kwame Nkrumah and his followers in the British Gold Coast colony, which, as the independent nation of Ghana, launched the process of decolonization in Africa. Nkrumah epitomized the more radical sort of African leader that emerged

throughout Africa after the war. (See the Visualizing the Past box.) Educated in African missionary schools and the United States, he had established wide contacts with nationalist leaders in both British and French west Africa and civil rights leaders in America prior to his return to the Gold Coast in the late 1940s. He returned to a land in ferment. The restrictions of government-controlled marketing boards and their favoritism for British merchants had led to widespread, but nonviolent, protest in the coastal cities. But after the police fired on a peaceful demonstration of ex-servicemen in 1948, rioting broke out in many towns.

Though both urban workers and cash crop farmers had supported the unrest, Western-educated African leaders were slow to organize these dissident groups into a sustained mass movement. Their reluctance arose in part from their fear of losing major political concessions, such as seats on colonial legislative councils, which the British had just made. Rejecting the caution urged by more established political leaders, Nkrumah resigned his position as chairman of the dominant political party in the Gold Coast and established his own **Convention Peoples Party (CPP)**. Even before the formal break, he had signaled the arrival of a new style of politics by organizing mass rallies, boycotts, and strikes.

In the mid-1950s, Nkrumah's mass following, and his growing stature as a leader who would not be deterred by imprisonment or British threats, won repeated concessions from the British. Educated Africans were given more and more representation in legislative bodies, and gradually they took over administration of the colony. The British recognition of Nkrumah as the prime minister of an independent Ghana in 1957 simply concluded a transfer of power from the European colonizers to the Western-educated African elite that had been under way for nearly a decade.

The peaceful devolution of power to African nationalists led to the independence of the British nonsettler colonies in black Africa by the mid-1960s. Independence in the comparable areas of the French and Belgian empires in Africa came in a somewhat different way. Hard pressed by costly military struggles to hold on to their colonies in Indochina and Algeria, the French took a much more conciliatory line in dealing with the many peoples they ruled in west Africa. Ongoing negotiations with such highly westernized leaders as Senegal's Léopold Sédar Senghor

Visualizing the Past

On National Leadership

Throughout Africa and Asia, struggles for decolonization and national independence often led to the emergence of leaders with exceptional mass appeal and political skills. But the personal qualities, visions of the future, and leadership styles that made for widespread loyalty to these individuals varied widely depending on the cultures and social settings from which they emerged as well as the nature of the political contests that led to the colonizers' retreat and the establishment of new nations. The following are photos of four of the most charismatic and effective leaders of independence movements in Africa and Asia. Study these photos and the background information on each of these individuals that is provided in earlier sections of this chapter and the relevant section of Chapter 34, and answer the questions about leadership styles and images that follow.

Questions: What do the dress and poses of each of these leaders tell us about the images they projected? Why did the style and approach each adopted win widespread popular support in each of the very different societies in which they emerged as pivotal leaders in the struggles for independence? How well do you think that each of their approaches to leadership served them in dealings with the European colonizers and contests with the rival leaders and political parties they faced in each of the societies in which they arose? What did charisma mean in each of these settings?

Léopold Sédar Senghor, Senegal

Gamal Abdul Nasser, Egypt

Kwame Nkrumah, Ghana

Mahatma Gandhi, India

and the Ivory Coast's Felix Houphouât-Boigny led to reforms and political concessions. The slow French retreat ensured that moderate African leaders, who were eager to retain French economic and cultural ties, would dominate the nationalist movements and the postindependence period in French west Africa. Between 1956 and 1960, the French colonies moved by stages toward nationhood—a process that sped up after de Gaulle's return to power in 1958. By 1960, all of France's west African colonies were free.

In the same year, the Belgians completed a much hastier retreat from their huge colonial possession in the Congo. Their virtual flight was epitomized by the fact that there was little in the way of an organized nationalist movement to pressure them into concessions of any kind. In fact, by design there were scarcely any well-educated Congolese to lead resistance to Belgian rule. At independence in 1960, there were only 16 African college graduates in a Congolese population that exceeded 13 million. Though the Portuguese still clung to their impoverished and scattered colonial territories, by the mid-1960s the European colonial era had come to an end in all but the settler societies of Africa.

Repression and Guerrilla War: The Struggle for the Settler Colonies

The pattern of relatively peaceful withdrawal by stages that characterized the process of decolonization in most of Asia and Africa proved unworkable in most of the settler colonies. These included areas like Algeria, Kenya, and Southern Rhodesia, where substantial numbers of Europeans had gone intending to settle permanently in the 19th and early 20th centuries. South Africa, which had begun to be settled by Europeans centuries earlier, provided few openings for nationalist agitation except that mounted by the politically and economically dominant colonists of European descent. In each case, the presence of European settler communities, varying in size from millions in South Africa and Algeria to tens of thousands in Kenya and Southern Rhodesia, blocked both the rise of indigenous nationalist movements and concessions on the part of the colonial overlords.

Because the settlers regarded the colonies to which they had emigrated as their permanent homes, they fought all attempts to turn political control over to the African majority or even to grant them civil rights. They also doggedly refused all reforms by colonial administrators that required them to give up any of the lands

they had occupied, often at the expense of indigenous African peoples. Unable to make headway through nonviolent protest tactics—which were forbidden—or negotiations with British or French officials, who were fearful of angering the highly vocal settler minority, many African leaders turned to violent, revolutionary struggles to win their independence.

The first of these erupted in Kenya in the early 1950s. Impatient with the failure of the nonviolent approach adopted by **Jomo Kenyatta** and the leading nationalist party, the **Kenya African Union (KAU)**, an underground organization coalesced around a group of more radical leaders. After forming the **Land Freedom Army** in the early 1950s, the radicals mounted a campaign of terror and guerrilla warfare against the British, the settlers, and Africans who were considered collaborators. At the height of the struggle in 1954, some 200,000 rebels were in action in the capital at Nairobi and in the forest reserves of the central Kenyan highlands. The British responded with an all-out military effort to crush the guerrilla movement, which was dismissed as an explosion of African savagery and labeled the "Mau Mau" by the colonizers, not the rebels. In the process, the British, at the settlers' insistence, imprisoned Kenyatta and the KAU organizers, thus eliminating the nonviolent alternative to the guerrillas.

The rebel movement had been militarily defeated by 1956 at the cost of thousands of lives. But the British were now in a mood to negotiate with the nationalists, despite strong objections from the European settlers. Kenyatta was released from prison, and he emerged as the spokesman for the Africans of Kenya. By 1963, a multiracial Kenya had won its independence. Under what was, in effect, Kenyatta's one-party rule, it remained until the mid-1980s one of the most stable and more prosperous of the new African states.

The struggle of the Arab and Berber peoples of Algeria for independence was longer and even more vicious than that in Kenya. Algeria had for decades been regarded by the French as an integral part of France—a department just like Provence or Brittany. The presence of more than a million European settlers in the colony only served to bolster the resolve of French politicians to retain it at all costs. But in the decade after World War II, sporadic rioting grew into sustained guerrilla resistance. By the mid-1950s, the **National Liberation Front (FLN)** had mobilized large segments of the Arab and Berber population of the colony in a full-scale revolt against French rule and settler dominance. High-ranking French army officers came to see the defeat of this movement as a way to restore a reputation that had been badly tarnished by recent defeats in Vietnam (see Chapter 35). As in Kenya, the rebels were defeated in the field. But they gradually negotiated the independence of Algeria after de Gaulle came to power in 1958. The French people had wearied of the seemingly endless war, and de Gaulle became convinced that he could not restore France to great power status as long as its resources continued to be drained by the Algerian conflict.

In contrast to Kenya, the Algerian struggle was prolonged and brutalized by a violent settler backlash. Led after 1960 by the **Secret Army Organization (OAS),** it was directed against Arabs and Berbers as well as French who favored independence for the colony. With strong support from elements in the French military, earlier resistance by the settlers had managed to topple the government in Paris in 1958, thereby putting an end to the Fourth Republic. In the early 1960s, the OAS came close to assassinating de Gaulle and overthrowing the Fifth Republic, which his accession to power had brought into existence. In the end, however, the Algerians won their independence in 1962 (Figure 31.5). After the bitter civil war, the multiracial accommodation worked out in Kenya appeared out of the question as far as the settlers of Algeria were concerned. Over 900,000 left the new nation within months after its birth. In addition, tens of thousands of harkis, or Arabs and Berbers who had sided with the French in the long war for independence, fled to France. They, and later migrants, formed the core of the substantial Algerian population now present in France.

Figure 31.5 *Algerians celebrate in Oran as French barricades are torn down by members of the local Arab militia and Arab civilians just after independence is announced in July 1962. The barricades were erected throughout the colony to keep Europeans' residence areas off limits to the Arabs and Berbers, who made up the overwhelming majority of the population. Although cities such as Oran and Algiers had long been segregated into "native" and European quarters, the protracted and bloody war for independence fought by the Arab and Berber peoples had resulted in full-scale occupation by the French army and the physical separation of settler and Arab–Berber areas.*

The Persistence of White Supremacy in South Africa

In southern Africa, violent revolutions put an end to white settler dominance in the Portuguese colonies of Angola and Mozambique in 1975 and in Southern Rhodesia (now Zimbabwe) by 1980. Only in South Africa did the white minority manage to maintain its position of supremacy. Its ability to do so rested on several factors that distinguished it from other settler societies. To begin with, the white population of South Africa, roughly equally divided between the Dutch-descended Afrikaners and the more recently arrived English speakers, was a good deal larger than that of any of the other settler societies. Though they were only a small minority in a country of 23 million black Africans and 3.5 million East Indians and coloreds (mulattos, in American parlance), by the mid-1980s, South Africa's settler-descended population had reached 4.5 million.

Unlike the settlers in Kenya and Algeria, who had the option of retreating to Europe as full citizens of France or Great Britain, the Afrikaners in particular had no European homeland to fall back upon. They had lived in South Africa as long as other Europeans had in North America, and they considered themselves quite distinct from the Dutch. Over the centuries, the Afrikaners had also built up what was for them a persuasive ideology of white racist supremacy. Though crude by European or American standards, Afrikaner racism was far more explicit and elaborate than that developed by the settlers of any other colony. Afrikaner ideology was grounded in selected biblical quotations and the celebration of their historic struggle to "tame a beautiful but hard land" in the face of opposition from both the African "savages" and the British "imperialists."

Ironically, their defeat by the British in the Anglo-Boer War from 1899 to 1902 also contributed much to the capacity of the white settler minority to maintain its place of dominance in South Africa. A sense of guilt, arising especially from their treatment of Boer women and children during the war—tens of thousands of whom died of disease in what the British called concentration camps—led the victors to make major concessions to the Afrikaners in the postwar decades. The most important of these was internal political control, which included turning over the fate of the black African majority to the openly racist supremist Afrikaners. Not surprisingly, the continued subjugation of the black Africans became a central aim of the Afrikaner political organizations that emerged in the 1930s and 1940s, culminating in the **Afrikaner National Party.** From 1948, when it emerged as the majority party in the all-white South African legislature, the National party devoted itself to winning complete independence from Britain (which came without violence in 1961) and to establishing lasting white domination over the political, social, and economic life of the new nation.

A rigid system of racial segregation (which will be discussed more fully in Chapter 34), called **apartheid** by the Afrikaners, was established after 1948 through the passage of thousands of laws. Among other things, this legislation reserved the best jobs for whites and carefully defined the sorts of contacts permissible between different racial groups. The right to vote and political representation were denied to the black Africans, and ultimately to the coloreds and Indians. It was illegal for members of any of these groups to hold mass meetings or to organize political parties or labor unions. These restrictions, combined with very limited opportunities for higher education for black Africans, hampered the growth of black African political parties and their efforts to mobilize popular support for the struggle for decolonization. The Afrikaners' establishment of a vigilant and brutal police state to uphold apartheid, and their opportunistic cultivation of divisions between the diverse peoples in the black African population, also contributed to their ability to preserve a bastion of white supremacy in an otherwise liberated continent.

Conflicting Nationalisms: Arabs, Israelis, and the Palestinian Question

Along with Egypt, several Middle Eastern states, including Iraq and Syria, had technically gained independence between the world wars, though European influence remained strong. With World War II, independence became more complete, though it was not until the 1970s that governments were strong enough to shake off Western dominance of the oil fields. Egypt's 1952 revolt and independence movements in the rest of north Africa gained ground, though the struggle against France in Algeria was bitter and prolonged. Although virtually all Arab peoples who were not yet free by the end of World War II were liberated by the early 1960s, the fate of Palestine continued to present special problems. Hitler's campaign of genocide against the European Jews had provided powerful support for the Zionists' insistence that the Jews must have their own homeland, which more and more was conceived in terms of a modern national state. The brutal persecution of the Jews also won international sympathy for the Zionist cause. This was in part due to the fact that the leaders of many nations, including the United States and Great Britain, were reluctant to admit Jews fleeing the Nazi terror into their own countries. As Hitler's henchmen stepped up their race war against the Jews, the tide of Jewish immigration to Palestine rose sharply. But growing Arab resistance to Jewish settlement and land purchases in Palestine, which was often expressed in communal rioting and violent assaults on Zionist communities, led to increasing British restrictions on the entry of Jews into the colony.

A major Muslim revolt swept Palestine between 1936 and 1939. The British managed to put down this rising but only with great difficulty. It both decimated the leadership of the Palestinian Arab community and further strengthened the British resolve to stem the flow of Jewish immigrants to Palestine. Government measures to keep out Jewish refugees from Nazi oppression led in turn to violent Zionist resistance to the British presence in Palestine. The Zionist assault was spearheaded by a regular Zionist military force, the **Haganah,** and several underground terrorist organizations.

By the end of World War II, the major parties claiming Palestine were locked into a deadly stalemate. The Zionists were determined to carve out a Jewish state in the region. The Palestinian Arabs and their allies in neighboring Arab lands were equally determined to transform Palestine into a multireligious nation in which the position of the Arab majority would be ensured. Having badly bungled their mandatory responsibilities, and under attack from both sides, the British wanted more than anything else to scuttle and run. The 1937 report of a British commission of inquiry supplied a possible solution: partition. The newly created United Nations provided an international body that could give a semblance of legality to the proceedings. In 1948, with sympathy for the Jews running high because of the postwar revelations of the horrors of Hitler's Final Solution, the member states of the United Nations—with the United States and the Soviet Union in rare agreement—approved the partition of Palestine into Arab and Jewish countries (see Map 31.2).

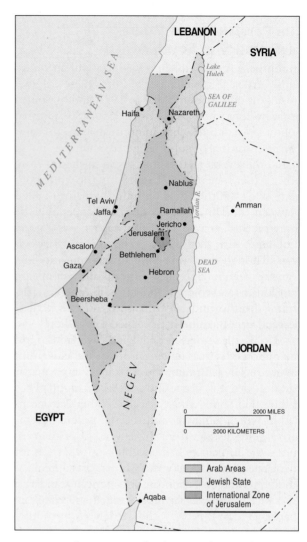

Map 31.2   *The Partition of Palestine After World War II*

The Arab states that bordered the newly created nation of Israel had vehemently opposed the United Nations' action. Soon the two sides were engaged in all-out warfare. Though heavily outnumbered, the Zionists proved to be better armed and much better prepared to defend themselves than almost anyone could have expected. Not only did they hold onto the tiny, patchwork state they had been given by the United Nations, but they expanded it at the Arabs' expense. The brief but bloody war that ensued created hundreds of thousands of Palestinian Arab refugees. It also sealed the persisting hostility between Arabs and Israelis that has been the all-consuming issue in the region and a major international problem to the present day. In Palestine, conflicting strains of nationalism had collided. As a result, the legacy of colonialism proved even more of a liability to social and economic development than in much of the rest of newly independent Africa and Asia.

 ## GLOBAL CONNECTIONS: Persisting Trends in a World Transformed by War

Given the fragile foundations on which it rested, the rather rapid demise of the European colonial order is not really surprising. World War II completed the process that World War I and anticolonial nationalism had begun; the end of Western imperialism came quickly. In this sense, the global framework was transformed. However, the winning of political freedom in Asia and Africa also represented less of a break with the colonial past than the appearance of many new nations on the map of the world might lead one to assume. The decidedly nonrevolutionary, elite-to-elite transfer of power that was central to the liberation process in most colonies, even those where there were violent guerrilla movements, limited the extent of the social and economic transformation that occurred. The Western-educated African and Asian classes moved into the offices and took the jobs—and often the former homes—of the European colonizers. But social gains for the rest of the population in most new nations were minimal or nonexistent. In Algeria, Kenya, and Zimbabwe (formerly Southern Rhodesia), abandoned European lands were distributed to Arab and African peasants and laborers. But in most former colonies, especially in Asia, the big landholders that remained were indigenous, and they have held on tenaciously to their holdings. Educational reforms were carried out to include more sciences in school curricula and the history of Asia or Africa rather than Europe. But Western cultural influences have remained strong in almost all of the former colonies. Indians and many west Africans with higher educations continue to communicate in English.

The liberation of the colonies also did little to disrupt Western dominance of the terms of international trade or the global economic order more generally. In fact, in the negotiations that led to decolonization, Asian and African leaders often

explicitly promised to protect the interests of Western merchants and businessmen in the postindependence era. These and other limits that sustained Western influence and often dominance, even after freedom was won, greatly reduced the options open to nationalist leaders struggling to build viable and prosperous nations. Though new forces have also played important roles, the postindependence history of colonized peoples cannot be understood without a consideration of the lingering effects of the colonial interlude in their history.

Further Readings

Two of the most genuinely global histories of World War II, which also include extensive accounts of the origins of the war in both Europe and the Pacific, are Gerhard L. Weinberg, *A World at Arms: A Global History of World War II* (1994), and Peter Calvocoressi and Guy Wint, *Total War: Causes and Courses of the Second World War* (1972). For a good overview of the coming of the war in Europe from the British perspective, see Christopher Thorne, *The Approach of War 1938–1939* (1967), and from the German viewpoint, Gerhard L. Weinberg, *Germany, Hitler, and World War II* (1995). A fine analysis of the underlying patterns in the European theater can be found in Gordon Wright, *The Ordeal of Total War, 1939–1945* (1968).

From a prodigious literature on the Holocaust, some good works to begin with are Hannah Arendt's brilliant *Eichmann in Jerusalem* (1963) and Raul Hilberg's *Destruction of the European Jews* (1985). Christopher Browning's *Ordinary Men* (1992) provides a chilling account of some of those who actually carried out the killings, while Viktor Frankl's *Man's Search for Meaning* (1959) is one of the most poignant of the numerous autobiographical accounts of the concentration camps. Omer Bartov provides a thoughtful meditation on the wider meanings of the Holocaust for 20th-century history in *Murder in Our Midst* (1996).

On the causes of the Pacific war, see Michael Barnhart, *Japan Prepares for Total War* (1987), and William O'Neill, *A Democracy at War* (1993). On the course of the war in the Pacific from differing perspectives, see Ronald Spector, *Eagle Against the Sun* (1985); Saburò Ienaga, *The Pacific War, 1931–1945* (1978); and John Dower, *War Without Mercy: Race and Power in the Pacific War* (1986). On the end of the war and the forces that led to the cold war, see Martin Sherwin, *A World Destroyed: The Atomic Bomb and the Grand Alliance* (1975); William Craig, *The Fall of Japan* (1967); Herbert Feis, *From Trust to Terror: The Onset of the Cold War, 1945–1950* (1970); and Melvyn Leffler, *A Preponderance of Power: National Security, the Truman Administration, and the Cold War* (1992).

A thoughtful overview of the process of decolonization in the British empire as a whole can be found in the works of John Darwin. In addition to P. J. Vatikiotis' general *History of Egypt*, mentioned in Chapter 5, Jacques Berque's *Egypt: Imperialism and Revolution* (1972) and Peter Mansfield's *The British in Egypt* (1971) provide detailed accounts of the nationalist revolt and early years of quasi-independence. The struggles for decolonization in Africa are surveyed by Ali A. Mazrui and Michael Tidy in *Nationalism and New States in Africa* (1984); J. D. Hargreaves, *Decolonization in Africa* (1988); and W. R. Louis and P. Gifford, eds., *Decolonization in Africa* (1984).

From the very substantial literature on the rise of nationalism in settler societies, some of the best studies include C. Roseberg and J. Nottingham's *The Myth of "Mau Mau"* (1966) on Kenya; the writings of Terrence Ranger on Rhodesia; and Alastair Horne's *A Savage War of Peace* (1977) on Algeria. Of the many works on South Africa, the general histories of S. Throup, B. Bunting, T. D. Moodie, and Leonard Thompson provide a good introduction to the rise of Afrikaner power. The period of the partition and the first Arab-Israeli conflict have been the subject of much revisionist scholarship in recent years. Some of the best of this is included in important books by Benny Morris, Walid Khalidi, Ilan Pappé, and Tom Segev.

On the United States in the cold war decades, see Walter Lafeber's *America, Russia, and the Cold War, 1945–1980* (7th ed., 1993). Ronald Powaski's *The Cold War: The United States and the Soviet Union, 1917–1991* (1998) is a reliable and readable standard political history that synthesizes the historiography of the cold war. Ellen Schrecker's *Many Are the Crimes: McCarthyism in America* (1998) has a broad social history of the political and cultural legacy of the Red Scare. T. H. Etzold and J. L. Gaddis, eds., *Containment: Documents on American Policy and Strategy, 1945–1950* (1978), provides primary source material on the political history of the early cold war.

On the Web

A superb starting point for the on-line study of World War II can be found at http://www.historywiz.com/worldwartwo.htm. The site features links to battle histories, oral histories, and exhibits, and offers an audio file of President's Truman's speech announcing the use of the atomic bomb against Japan. Other useful links can be found at http://history.acusd.edu/gen/ww2_links.html, which leads to sources organized by battles and by countries, including the battle for Stalingrad and the role of Russia in the war. Yale University provides a digital library for Second World War documents at http://www.yale.

edu/lawweb/avalon/wwii/wwii.htm. Rutgers University offers records of personal experiences at http://fas-history.rutgers.edu/oralhistory/orlhom.htm, which can be supplemented by other collections at http://www.ibiscom.com/w2frm.htm, http://clicksmart.co.uk/History/WW2/, http://www.geocities.com/Athens/Oracle/2691/links.htm, and http://www.fsu.edu/~ww2/links.htm, which offer links to sites ranging from combat stories to prisoner of war experiences.

Dramatic recreations or virtual visits to key sites of this conflict abound on the Web. These sites include Hiroshima (http://titan.iwu.edu/~rwilson/hiroshima/), the 1941–1944 siege of Leningrad (http://www.cityvision2000.com/history/900days.htm), and Pearl Harbor (http://execpc.com/~dschaaf/mainmenu.html, http://www.hawaii.navy.mil/cnbdata/cnbdata/7dec98/virtour.htm, and http://plasma.nationalgeographic.com/pearlharbor/). The concept of "lightning war" or blitzkrieg is explained at http://www.achtungpanzer.com/blitz.htm.

The role of the American home front and American women in World War II is explored through photographs and interviews at http://www.pomperaug.com/socstud/stumuseum/web/ARHhome.htm, http://www.u.arizona.edu/~kari/rosie.htm, http://www.wasp-wwii.org/, and http://www.stg.brown.edu/projects/WWII_Women/WomenInWWII.html.

The experience of internment and death camps for civilians and prisoners of war in German, Russian, and Japanese held territories is examined at http://www.vikingphoenix.com/public/rongstad/military/pow/pow.htm and http://www.mansell.com/pow-index.html. The removal of the Japanese American population in America to internment camps during the war is discussed and links on the subject provided at http://www.geocities.com/Athens/8420/main.html. Many Japanese interment camps in America have their own dedicated Web site, such as that at http://www.nps.gov/manz/ and http://www.library.arizona.edu/wracamps/.

Overviews and interactive digital data bases for the Holocaust are provided at http://www.remember.org, http://www.holocaust-history.org, and http://www.ushmm.org. See also the excellent teacher's guide that offers study guides, documents, and essays at and http://fcit.coedu.usf.edu/holocaust/resource/document/DocPropa.htm.

A map of Nazi concentration camps is provided at http://history1900s.about.com/library/holocaust/

blmap.htm. There are several Web pages devoted to those who struggled against the Holocaust, including Oskar Schindler (http://auschwitz.dk/Schindler2.htm) and Raul Wallenberg (http://www.us-israel.org/jsource/biography/wallenberg.html). The struggle against those who seek to deny the genocidal nature of the Nazi regime is addressed in articles offered at http://www.holocaust-history.org/. The search for meaning in the modern European holocaust has been pioneered by one of its victims, Simon Wiesenthal (http://www.wiesenthal.com/). Virtual visits to the Anne Frank homepages (http:// www.annefrank.nl/ and http://www.annefrank.com) and other links (see http://www.nicole-caspari.de/annefrank/e_links.html and http://www.coollessons.org/holocaust.htm) lend a human face to both fascist oppression and the quest for a world without hatred.

That this holocaust is but one of many human genocides is the subject of several sites that offer comparative analyses or links to other examples from Cambodia to Rwanda. These include http://www.ess.uwe.ac.uk/genocide.htm, http://www.yale.edu/cgp/, http://www.webster.edu/~woolflm/holocaust.html, and http://www.sage.edu/RSC/programs/globcomm/division/courses/history/wwwhol.html.

The winning of India's independence, Gandhi's last years, and his assassination did not end the struggle for *satyagraha* (http://www.colorado.edu/conflict/peace/example/wehr7496.htm and http://www.pbs.org/weta/forcemorepowerful/india/satyagraha.html). Many others have followed this path in India and abroad (see examples and resource lists at http://www.pbs.org/weta/forcemorepowerful/classroom/resources.html, http://www.transnational.org/forum/Nonviolence/Nonviolence.html, http://nonviolenceinternational.net/seasia/Learn_%20nonviolence/Index.htm, and http://edition.cnn.com/WORLD/9708/India97/india/gandhi.legacy/). Gandhi can be seen in a short film of a visit to London at http://www.historychannel.com/speeches/index.html. Jawaharlal Nehru's life and role in the freedom movement is explored at http://www.pbs.org/wgbh/commandingheights/shared/minitextlo/prof_jawaharlalnehru.html. His "tryst with destiny speech" that inaugurated a new chapter in the history of the Indian subcontinent can be read at http://www.itihaas.com/independent/speech.html and http://www.fordham.edu/halsall/mod/1947nehru1.html. It can be heard at http://www.harappa.com/sounds/nehru.html.

A newsreel covering the birth of Pakistan can be viewed at http://harappa.com/wall/pakistan.html, while the birth pangs of Bangladesh are traced at http://www.virtualbangladesh.com/.

The generation of leaders that helped secure Africa's freedom is well-represented on the Internet. For Léopold Senghor, poet of négritude and president of Senegal, see http://web.uflib.ufl.edu/cm/africana/senghor.htm. Links to Tanzania's Julius Nyerere's life and speeches can be found at http://www.hartford-hwp.com/archives/30/index-fd.html. Jomo Kenyatta and his role in the Land Freedom Army and Mau Mau movements are listed at http://www.kenyaweb.com/history/struggle/ and http://www.ccs.neu.edu/home/feneric/maumau.html.

The African National Congress Party homepage at http://www.anc.org.za/ traces its anti-colonial role from its earliest beginnings to Nelson Mandela. Apartheid in South Africa is discussed at http://www-cs-students.stanford.edu/~cale/cs201/apartheid.hist.html.

CHAPTER 32

WESTERN SOCIETY AND EASTERN EUROPE IN THE DECADES OF THE COLD WAR

Campus unrest was a Western-style phenomenon in the 1960s. Student uprisings in France in 1968 created a near revolution. Here, students and workers demonstrate in Paris.

- After World War II: International Setting for the West
- The Resurgence of Western Europe
- Political Stability and the Question Marks
- IN DEPTH: The United States and Western Europe: Convergence and Complexity
- Cold War Allies: The United States, Canada, Australia, and New Zealand
- Culture and Society in the West
- VISUALIZING THE PAST: Women at Work in France and the United States
- Eastern Europe After World War II: A Soviet Empire
- Soviet Culture: Promoting New Beliefs and Institutions
- DOCUMENT: 1986: A New Wave of Soviet Reform
- GLOBAL CONNECTIONS: The Cold War and the World

Both western and eastern Europe had been devastated by World War II, and the recovery process was demanding. Yet the Soviet Union emerged within a few years with a new European empire and status as a world superpower, rivaling the United States and its allies. Western Europe bounced back as well, though not to its former world dominance. The United States, defying its earlier traditions, maintained a strong international presence amid massive military expenditures.

The postwar decades were strongly shaped by the emergence and evolution of the cold war rivalries between east and west: capitalist democracies and communist countries on the European continent and beyond. Competing alliance systems formed quickly, and both sides developed large arsenals of nuclear weapons. The cold war did not, however, monopolize developments either in the West or in eastern Europe, particularly after the 1950s.

In the West, the postwar decades saw the emergence of a strong economic surge, with a turn toward a service-based, high-tech economy. Social tensions eased, and dramatic new roles for women took shape. Popular consumer culture reached new heights, as the West experienced significant social transformation. Democratic political forms gained greater solidity, in a striking reversal of the trends that had emerged between the world wars. Western Europe also forged new diplomatic unity, deliberately seeking to overcome the paralyzing nationalisms of the first half of the 20th century.

As the Soviet Union and its new allies shook off the worst effects of World War II, Stalinism was gradually eased. Advancing industrialization brought some social changes not totally unlike those in the West—for example, in a growing emphasis on nuclear families and low birth rates. But the Soviet Union also concentrated strongly on its new world role, seeking unprecedented advances in space exploration and international sports competitions. Finally, in the 1980s, the costs of the cold war began to take a clearer toll in eastern Europe.

After World War II: International Setting for the West

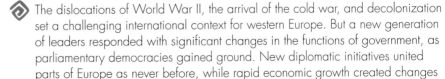

The dislocations of World War II, the arrival of the cold war, and decolonization set a challenging international context for western Europe. But a new generation of leaders responded with significant changes in the functions of government, as parliamentary democracies gained ground. New diplomatic initiatives united parts of Europe as never before, while rapid economic growth created changes in society and culture.

1940 C.E.	1950 C.E.	1960 C.E.	1970 C.E.	1980 C.E.	1990 C.E.	2000 C.E.
1945 End of World War II	**1953** Stalin's death	**1960s** Civil rights movement in U.S.; emergence of new feminist movement	**1970s** Democratic regimes in Spain, Portugal, and Greece	**1981–1988** Reagan president in United States	**1992** End of economic restrictions within Common Market	**2001** Euro currency introduced
1945–1948 Soviet takeover of eastern Europe; new constitutions in Italy, Germany, and France; Labour party victory in Britain; basic measures of welfare states	**1955** Formation of Warsaw Pact		**1973, 1977** Oil crises	**1985–1991** Gorbachev heads Soviet Union	**1993** Division of Czechoslovakia; Clinton inauguration ends three-term Republican tenure in White House	**2001** Growing concern about terrorism
	1956 Stalinism attacked by Khrushchev	**1961** Berlin Wall erected	**1979** Uprisings in Poland and their suppression; Thatcher and new conservatism in Britain; Soviet invasion of Afghanistan; significant recession	**1989** Berlin Wall division ends; new regimes throughout eastern Europe		
	1956 Hungarian revolt and its suppression	**1962** Cuban missile crisis				
1947 Marshall Plan	**1957** Establishment of European Economic Community or Common Market (basis of later European Union)	**1968** Revolt in Czechoslovakia and its repression; Soviet policy (Brezhnev doctrine) proclaims right to intervene in any socialist country				
1947–1960s Emergence and most intense phase of cold war	**1958** De Gaulle's Fifth Republic in France					
1949 East and West German regimes established		**1968–1973** Massive student protests				
1949 Soviet Union develops atomic bomb; North Atlantic Treaty Organization established						

World War II left western Europe in shambles. The sheer physical destruction, caused particularly by bombing raids, disrupted housing and transportation. Downed bridges and rail lines complicated food shipments, leaving many people in France and Germany ill-fed and unable to work at full efficiency. German use of forced foreign labor, as well as the many boundary changes resulting from the war, generated hundreds of thousands of refugees trying to return home or find a new home. For at least two years after 1945 it was unclear that recovery would be possible, as sheer survival proved difficult enough. In the long run Europe's postwar weakness after three decades of strife helped trigger in the former colonial areas a crescendo of nationalist sentiment directed against the West, as well as the fuller emergence of the United States and the Soviet Union, whose size and building industrial strength finally overshadowed Europe's proud nation-states.

Europe and Its Colonies

The two larger changes provoked by the war—decolonization and the cold war—quickly intruded on the West. We have seen that colonies outside Europe, roused by the war, became increasingly restive. When the British returned to Malaya and the Dutch to Indonesia—areas from which they had been dislodged—they found a more hostile climate, with well-organized nationalist resistance. It was soon clear that many colonies could be maintained only at great cost, and in the main the European nations decided that the game was not worth the candle. A few cases proved messy. France tried to defend its holdings in Vietnam against communist guerrillas, yielding only in 1954 after some major defeats. The French clung even more fiercely to Algeria, the oldest African colony and one with a large European minority. The French military joined Algerian settlers in insisting on a war to the death against nationalist forces, and bitter fighting went on for years. The tension even threatened civil war in France, until a new president, Charles de Gaulle, realized the hopelessness of the struggle and negotiated Algeria's independence in 1962.

Overall, decolonization proceeded more smoothly than this between the late 1940s and the mid-1970s, without prolonged fighting that might drain the Western nations. Kenya, Vietnam, and the Algerian morass were bitter exceptions. Western governments typically retained important cultural relations with their former colonies and sometimes provided administrative and military help as well. Both France and Belgium, for example, frequently intervened in Africa after decolonization was officially complete. Finally,

Western economic interests remained strong in most former colonies—particularly in Africa, which exploited mineral and agricultural resources in a pattern of trade not radically different from that of colonial days.

The impact of decolonization on the West should not, however, be minimized. Important minorities of former settlers and officials came home embittered, though, except briefly in France, they were not a significant political force. Europe's overt power in the world was dramatically reduced. Efforts by Britain and France to attack independent Egypt in 1956, to protest Egypt's nationalization of the Suez Canal, symbolized the new state of affairs. The United States and the Soviet Union forced a quick end to hostilities, and what was once a colonial lifeline came into non-Western hands. Yet although decolonization was a powerful change in world affairs, it did not, at least in the short run, overwhelm the West, as neither economic growth nor internal political stability suffered greatly.

The Cold War

The final new ingredient of Europe's diplomatic framework, the cold war between the United States and the Soviet Union, had a more durable ongoing influence on politics and society within the West. The conflict took shape between 1945 and 1947. The last wartime meetings among the leaders of Britain, the United States, and the Soviet Union had rather vaguely staked out the boundaries of postwar Europe, which were certainly open to varied interpretations. By the war's end, Soviet troops firmly occupied most eastern European countries, and within three years the Soviets had installed communist regimes to their liking, while excluding opposition political movements. Thus an **eastern bloc** emerged that included Poland, Czechoslovakia, Bulgaria, Romania, and Hungary. And Soviet boundaries themselves had pushed west, reversing the decisions of the post–World War I Versailles conference. The Baltic states disappeared, and Poland lost territory to Russia, gaining some former German lands as compensation. Finally, Soviet occupation of the eastern zone of Germany gave Russia a base closer toward the heart of Europe than the tsars had ever dreamed possible (see Map 32.1).

Offended by the Soviet Union's heavy-handed manipulation of eastern Europe, including its zone in eastern Germany, U.S. and British policymakers tried to counter. The new American president, **Harry**

Map 32.1 *Soviet and Eastern European Boundaries by 1948. The new communist empire was joined in the Warsaw Pact, formed to respond to the West's North Atlantic Treaty Organization (itself formed in response to a perceived communist threat).*

Truman, was less eager for smooth relations with the Soviets than Franklin Roosevelt had been; Truman was emboldened by the U.S. development of the atomic bomb in 1945. Britain's wartime leader, Winston Churchill, had long feared communist aggression; it was he who in 1946 coined the phrase **iron curtain** to describe the division between free and repressed societies that he saw taking shape in Europe. But Britain frankly lacked the power to resist Soviet pressure, and under the Labour government it explicitly left the initiative to the United States.

The United States responded to Soviet rivalry with vigor. It criticized Soviet policies and denied Soviet applications for reconstruction loans. It bolstered regimes in Iran, Turkey, and Greece that were under Soviet pressure. Then in 1947 the United States proclaimed its **Marshall Plan,** a program of substantial loans that was designed to aid Western nations rebuild from the war's devastation. In Soviet eyes the Marshall Plan was a vehicle for U.S. economic dominance, and indeed there is little question that in addition to humanitarian motives the United States intended to beat back domestic communist movements in countries such as France and Italy by promoting economic growth.

The focal point of the cold war in these early years was Germany, which after the war had been divided into four zones administered by the United States, Britain, France, and the Soviet Union (Map 32.2). Soviet policy in Germany initially concentrated on seizing goods and factories as reparation. The Western Allies soon prevented Soviet intervention in their own zones and turned to some rebuilding efforts in the interests of playing a modest "German card" against growing Soviet strength in the East. That is, although the West, led by the United States, did not intend to resurrect a powerful Germany, it soon began to think in terms of constructing a viable political and economic entity. Allied collaboration started building a unified West Germany in 1946, and local political structures followed by more national ones were established through elections. When in

1947 the West moved to promote German economic recovery by creating a stable currency, the Soviet Union responded by blockading the city of Berlin, the divided former capital that sat in the midst of the Soviet zone. The United States responded with a massive airlift to keep the city supplied, and the crisis finally ended in 1948, with two separate Germanies—East and West—beginning to take clear shape along a tense, heavily fortified frontier.

Cold war divisions spread from Germany to Europe more generally with the formation of two rival military alliances. The **North Atlantic Treaty Organization (NATO)** was formed in 1949, under U.S. leadership, to group most of the western European powers and Canada in a defensive alliance against possible Soviet aggression. The NATO pact soon legitimated some rearmament of West Germany in the context of resistance to communism, as well as the continued maintenance of a substantial U.S. military presence in Germany and in other member nations. In response, the Soviet Union organized the **Warsaw Pact** among its eastern European satellites. When in 1949 the Soviets developed their own nuclear capability, the world—particularly the European world—seemed indeed divided between two rival camps, each in turn dominated by its own superpower. Numerous U.S. and Soviet military units were permanently stationed in Europe on either side of the cold war divide.

The cold war had a number of implications for western Europe. It brought new influences from the United States on internal as well as foreign policy. Through the 1950s and beyond, the United States pressed for acceptance of German rearmament (though under some agreed on limits); it lobbied for higher military expenditures in its old allies France and Britain; and it pressed for acceptance of U.S. forces and weapons systems. The Americans' wishes were not always met, but the United States had vital negotiating leverage in the economic aid it offered (and might withdraw), in the troops it stationed in Europe, and in the nuclear "umbrella" it developed (and might, in theory, also withdraw). Nuclear weapons seemed to offer the only realistic protection should the Soviet Union venture direct attack. The Soviets, for their part, influenced western Europe not only through perceived aggressive intent but also by funding and supporting substantial communist movements in France and Italy, which in turn affected but did not overwhelm the political process.

Map 32.2 *Germany After World War II*

The cold war did not maintain within Europe the intensity it reached in the initial years. Centers of conflict shifted in part outside Europe as Korea, then Vietnam, and recurrently the Middle East became flashpoints. After 1958 France became more and more restive under what it viewed as Anglo-U.S. dominance of NATO, and it finally withdrew its forces from the joint NATO command, requiring also that U.S. troops leave French soil. In the 1970s Germany opened new negotiations with the Soviet Union and eastern bloc countries, wanting increased export opportunities and reduced diplomatic tension. Nevertheless, the cold war and the resultant alliance system continued to describe much of the framework of east–west relations in Europe and elsewhere in the world.

The shifting balance between the United States and Europe produced a crisscrossing of military relationships, whatever the larger implications of the shift. As western Europe abandoned military preeminence, the United States, never before a major peacetime military power, devoted growing resources to its military capacity and gave an increasing voice to its military leaders. Regardless of the political party in power, the percentage of the U.S. government budget going to the military remained stable from the 1950s to the 1980s—when it went up. In contrast, some European leaders boasted that their societies had made a transition toward preeminence of civilian values and goals. Although U.S. and European values and institutions became more similar in key respects after World War II, the difference in military roles signaled ongoing distinctions within Western society.

The Resurgence of Western Europe

 Although the shifts in the West's external environment triggered by World War II were not catastrophic, they constituted major readjustments. Ironically, western Europe's domestic development in this same period was considerably more positive, a strong contrast not only to its reduction in world status but also to the massive troubles that had followed World War I.

A new set of leaders emerged in many European countries, some from wartime resistance movements, eager to avoid the mistakes that had led to economic depression and war. Although their vision was not always realized, from 1945 onward western Europe did move onward on three important fronts: the extension of democratic political systems, a modification of nation-state rivalries within Europe, and a commitment to rapid economic growth that reduced previous social and gender tensions.

The Spread of Liberal Democracy

In politics, defeat in war greatly discredited fascism and other rightist movements that had opposed parliamentary democracy. Vestiges of these movements continued, periodically surfacing in France and Italy but rarely with much muscle. At the same time, key leftist groups, including the strong communist movements that emerged from the war in France and Italy, were committed to democratic politics. Although social protest continued, outright revolutionary sentiment declined. Finally, several new political movements surfaced, notably an important Christian Democratic current, which was wedded to democratic institutions and moderate social reform. Despite national variations, in general western Europe experienced a shift in the political spectrum toward fuller support for democratic constitutions and greater agreement on the need for government planning and welfare activities.

New regimes had to be constructed in Germany and Italy after the defeat of fascist and Nazi leadership. France established a new republic once occupation ended. In Germany, political reconstruction was delayed by the division of the nation by the victorious Allies. As the cold war took shape, however, France, Britain, and the United States progressively merged their zones into what became the Federal Republic of Germany (West Germany), encouraging a new constitution that would avoid the mistakes of Germany's earlier Weimar Republic by outlawing extremist political movements. The new constitutions set up after 1945 in many European countries varied in particulars but uniformly established effective parliaments with universal (now always including female) suffrage. And the regimes endured. Only France, pressed by the Algerian War, changed its constitution in 1958, forming a Fifth Republic, still democratic but with stronger presidential authority.

Western Europe's movement toward more consistent democracy continued in the 1970s, when Spain and Portugal moved from their authoritarian, semifascist constitutions (following the deaths of longtime strongmen) to democratic, parliamentary systems. Greece, increasingly linked to the West, followed the same pattern. By the 1980s western Europe had become more politically uniform than ever before in history. Party dominance shifted, with conservatives, including Christian Democrats, alternating with socialist coalitions, but all major actors agreed on the constitutional system itself.

The Welfare State

The consolidation of democracy also entailed a general movement toward a **welfare state.** Resistance ideas and the shift leftward of the political spectrum helped explain the new activism of the state in economic policy and welfare issues. Wartime planning in the British government had pointed to the need for new programs to reduce the impact of economic inequality and to reward the lower classes for their loyalty (Figure 32.1). Not surprisingly, the governments that emerged at the war's end—Britain's Labour party and the Communist-Socialist–Christian Democrat coalitions in France and Italy—quickly moved to set up a new government apparatus that would play a vigorous role in economic planning and develop new social activities as well. By 1948 the basic nature of the modern welfare state had been established throughout western Europe, as not only the new regimes but also established reformists (as in Scandinavia) extended a variety of government programs. The United States, though somewhat more tentative in welfare measures, added to its New Deal legislation in the 1960s, under President Lyndon Johnson's Great Society programs, creating medical assistance packages for the poor and the elderly. Canada enacted an even more comprehensive medical insurance plan.

The welfare state elaborated a host of social insurance measures. Unemployment insurance was improved. Medical care was supported by state-funded insurance or, as in Britain where it became a centerpiece to the new Labour program, the basic health care system was nationalized. State-run medical facilities provided free care to the bulk of the British population from 1947 onward, although some small fees were later introduced. Family assistance was another category, not entirely new, that was now greatly expanded. All western European governments provided payments to families with several children,

Figure 32.1 *The great sacrifices of the ordinary people in World War II brought great pressure for the establishment of welfare states at war's end. Here, orange juice and vitamins are distributed to children and mothers at a British health clinic in the mid-1950s.*

the amount increasing with family size. In the 1950s a French worker family with low earnings and five children could improve its income by as much as 40 percent through family aid. Governments also became more active in the housing field—a virtual necessity given wartime destruction and postwar population growth. Britain embarked on an ambitious program of "council housing," providing many single-family units that deliberately mixed working-class and middle-class families in new neighborhoods. By the 1950s over one-fourth of the British population was housed in structures built and run by the government.

The welfare state was an important new definition of government functions but hardly a device for social revolution. It cushioned citizens against major expenses and unusual hardships rather than rearranging overall social structure. It protected the purchasing power of the very poor against catastrophe, and it contributed to improved health conditions generally. It also, of course, increased contacts between government and citizen, and it produced a host of new regulations that framed European life.

The welfare state was undeniably expensive. It greatly enlarged government bureaucracies, in addition to channeling tax monies to new purposes. A new breed of bureaucrat, often called a **technocrat** because of intense training in engineering or economics and because of a devotion to the power of national planning, came to the fore in government offices. By the 1950s up to 25 percent of the gross national product of France and Holland was going to welfare purposes, and the figure tended to rise with time. As military expenses began to stabilize, welfare commitments became far and away the largest component of Western government budgets outside the United States. Here was a clear indication of the extent to which the western European state had altered its relationship to the wider society.

An increased governmental role in economic policy paralleled the welfare state. Most postwar governments nationalized some sectors of industry outright. Most European countries also set up new planning offices, responsible for developing multiyear economic projections and for setting goals and the means to meet them. By coordinating tax concessions and directing the flow of capital from state banks, government planners had genuine power to shape, although not directly to run, economic activity. Planning extended to both agriculture and industry. Planning offices regulated crop sizes and encouraged consolidation of land for greater efficiency, and they could require farmers to participate in cooperatives that would improve marketing and purchasing procedures.

Political Stability and the Question Marks

 During most of the postwar decades, political extremes in most Western countries moderated. Conservatives tinkered with the welfare state but did not dismantle it. Socialist parties and, often, even communist groups moderated their tone. Power could and did pass from one side to the other without major disruption.

The Western pattern of political compromise around the mechanisms of parliamentary democracy and the welfare state were severely jolted by a series of student protests that developed in the late 1960s. Even before this, in the United States a vigorous civil rights movement had developed to protest unequal treatment of African Americans (see Figure 32.2). Massive demonstrations, particularly in cities in the American South, attacked segregation and limitations on African American voting rights.

Campus unrest was a Western-wide phenomenon in the 1960s. At major American universities, campus unrest focused on the nation's involvement in the war in Vietnam. Young people in Europe and the United States also targeted the materialism of their societies, including the stodginess of the welfare state, seeking more idealistic goals and greater justice. Student uprisings in France in 1968 created a near revolution. By the early 1970s new rights for students and other reforms, combined with police repression, ended the most intense student protests, whereas passage of civil rights legislation in the United States ultimately reduced urban rioting and demonstrations. The flexibility of postwar Western democracy seemed triumphant. Some additional political concerns, including a new wave of feminism focusing on economic rights and dignity for women, and environmentalist movements entered the arena during the 1970s, partly as an aftermath of the student explosion. The rise of the **Green movement** in several countries in the 1970s signaled a new political tone, hostile to uncontrolled economic growth. Green parliamentary deputies in Germany even refused to wear coats and ties in their efforts to defy established political habits.

As economic growth slowed in the 1970s and the Western world faced its greatest economic recession since the immediate postwar years, other signs of political change appeared. New leadership sprang up within the British Conservative party and the U.S. Republican party, seeking to reduce the costs and coverage of the welfare state. In 1979 British Conservative leader Margaret Thatcher began the longest-running prime-ministership in twentieth-century British history, working to cut welfare and housing expenses and to promote free enterprise. Neither she nor her U.S. counterpart, Ronald Reagan, fully dismantled the welfare state, but they did reduce its impact. Despite important adjustments,

Figure 32.2   *The great civil rights rally in Washington, D.C., August 1963.*

however, the main line of postwar government in the West persisted into the 21st century.

The Diplomatic Context

Along with the extension of democracy and the development of the welfare state, the West showed postwar vigor in addressing some traditional diplomatic problems, notably recurrent nationalistic rivalry, as well as specific manifestations, such as French–German enmity. U.S. guidance combined with innovative thinking in the new European governments.

During the war, many resistance leaders had tempered their hatred of Nazism with a plea for a reconstruction of the European spirit. The Christian Democratic movement, particularly, produced important new advocates of harmony among European nations. By 1947 United States leaders were also eager to spur western Europe's economic recovery, for which they judged coordination across national boundaries an essential precondition. Thus the Marshall Plan required discussion of tariffs and other devel-

opment issues among recipient nations. With simultaneous U.S. insistence on the partial rearmament of Germany and German participation in NATO, the framework for diplomatic reform was complete.

Faced with these pressures and aware of the failure of nationalistic policies between the wars, several French statesmen took a lead in proposing coordination between France and Germany as a means of setting up a new Europe. The nations of the Low Countries and Italy were soon linked in these activities. The idea was to tie German economic activity to an international framework so that the nation's growing strength would not again threaten European peace. Institutions were established to link policies in heavy industry and later to develop atomic power. A measure to establish a united European military force proved too ambitious and collapsed under nationalist objections. But in 1958 the six western European nations (West Germany, France, Italy, Belgium, Luxembourg, and the Netherlands) set up the European Economic Community, or Common Market—later called the **European Union**—to begin to create a

Map 32.3 *The European Union in the Europe of 2003*

single economic entity across national political boundaries (see Map 32.3). Tariffs were progressively reduced among the member nations, and a common tariff policy was set for the outside world. Free movement of labor and investment was encouraged. A Common Market bureaucracy was established, ulti-mately in Brussels, to oversee these operations. The Common Market set up a court system to adjudicate disputes and prevent violations of coordination rules; it also administered a development fund to spur economic growth in such laggard regions as southern Italy and western France.

The Common Market did not move quickly toward a single government. Important national disputes limited the organization's further growth. France and Germany, for example, routinely quarreled over agricultural policy, with France seeking more payments to farmers as a matter of obvious self-interest. But although the European Union did not turn into full integration, it did survive and, on the whole, prosper. It even established an advisory international parliament, ultimately elected by direct vote. Further, in the 1980s firm arrangements were made to dismantle all trade and currency exchange barriers among member states in 1992, creating essentially complete economic unity. A single currency, the euro, was set up in many member countries by 2001. The European Union's success expanded its hold within western Europe. After long hesitations Britain, despite its tradition of proud island independence, decided to join, as did Ireland, Denmark, and later Greece, Spain, Portugal, Austria, Sweden, Denmark, and Finland. By 2002, other nations near to central Europe were ready for membership.

Nationalist tensions within Europe receded to a lower point than ever before in modern European history. After the worst scares of the cold war, focused mainly on the division between communist East and semicapitalist West, Europe became a diplomatically placid continent, enjoying one of the longest periods of substantial internal peace in its history.

Economic Expansion

After a surprisingly short, if agonizing, postwar rebuilding, striking economic growth accompanied political and diplomatic change. The welfare state and the European Union may have encouraged this growth by improving purchasing power for the masses and facilitating market expansion across national boundaries; certainly economic growth encouraged the success of new political and diplomatic systems.

There was no question that by the mid-1950s western Europe had entered a new economic phase. Agricultural production and productivity increased rapidly as peasant farmers, backed by technocrats, adopted new equipment and seeds. European agriculture was still less efficient than that of North America, which necessitated some much-resented tariff barriers by the Common Market. But food pro-

duction easily met European needs, often with some to spare for export. Retooled industries poured out textiles and metallurgical products. Expensive consumer products, such as automobiles and appliances, supported rapidly growing factories. Western Europe also remained a leading center of weapons production, trailing only the United States and the Soviet Union in exports.

Overall growth in gross national product surpassed the rates of any extended period since the Industrial Revolution began; it also surpassed the growth rates of the U.S. economy during the 1950s and 1960s. The German economy, after some basic reconstruction and a currency stabilization in 1948, expanded at 6 percent a year during the 1950s; with a few modest setbacks this pace continued into the early 1970s. France's growth rate reached 8 percent by the late 1950s, maintained almost this level during the 1960s, and returned to rates of over 7 percent annually by the early 1970s. By 1959 the Italian economy, a newcomer to the industrial big leagues, was expanding at an annual rate of 11 percent.

These growth rates depended on rapid technological change. Europe's rising food production was achieved with a steadily shrinking agricultural labor force. France's peasant population—16 percent of the labor force in the early 1950s—fell to 10 percent two decades later, but overall output was much higher than before. During the 1950s the industrial workforce grew as part of factory expansion, but by the 1960s, the relative proportion of factory workers also began to drop, despite rising production. Workers in the service sector, filling functions as teachers, clerks, medical personnel, insurance and bank workers, and performers and other "leisure industry" personnel, rose rapidly in contrast. Europe, like the United States, began to convert technological advance into the provision of larger bureaucracies and service operations without jeopardizing the expanding output of goods. In France half of all paid workers were in the service sector by 1968, and the proportion rose steadily thereafter.

The high rates of economic growth also ensured relatively low unemployment after the immediate postwar dislocations passed. Even Britain, with lagging development, averaged no more than 4 percent unemployment a year during the 1950s and 1960s, whereas France and Germany featured rates of 2 percent to 3 percent a year. Indeed, many parts of the continent were labor-short and had to seek hundreds of thousands of workers from other areas—first from southern Europe, then, as this region industrialized, from Africa, the Middle East, and parts of Asia. The rise of immigrant minorities was a vital development in western Europe and also the United States, where the influx of Asian and Latin American immigrants stepped up markedly.

Unprecedented economic growth and low unemployment meant unprecedented improvements in incomes, even with the taxation necessary to sustain welfare programs. Per capita disposable income rose 117 percent in the United States between 1960 and 1973 and soared 258 percent in France, 312 percent in Germany, and 323 percent in Denmark. Indeed, Scandinavia, Switzerland, and the Federal Republic of Germany surpassed the United States in standards of living by the 1980s, whereas France, long an apparent laggard in modern economic development, pulled even. New spending money rapidly translated into huge increases in the purchase of durable consumer goods, as virtually the whole of Western civilization became an "affluent society." By 1969 two of every ten people in Britain, Sweden, West Germany, and France owned an automobile, and rates continued to climb. Ownership of television sets became virtually universal. France and other countries indulged in a mania for household appliances. Shopping malls and supermarkets, the agents of affluence and extensive but efficient shopping that had first developed in the United States, spread widely, at the expense of more traditional, small specialty shops. A West German company, in fact, took over a key U.S. grocery chain in the late 1970s, on grounds that Europeans now knew mass marketing as well as or better than the U.S. consumer pioneers.

Europe had unquestionably developed a framework of affluent consumerism as fully as had the United States, with at least as much impact on basic social patterns and habits of thought. Advertising was not quite as ubiquitous in Europe as across the Atlantic, particularly because most television channels were state-run and noncommercial. But promptings to buy, to smell good, to look right, to express one's personality in the latest car style began quickly to describe European life (Figure 32.3). The frenzy to find good vacation spots was certainly intense. Millions of Germans poured annually into Italy and Spain, seeking the sun. Britons thronged to Spanish

Figure 32.3 *In the United States, as well as in Japan and western Europe, advertisements increasingly evoked a good life to be achieved by buying the right goods. The newest car was associated with a prosperous home, a loving family, and even happy pets.*

beaches. Europeans were bent on combining efficient work with indulgent leisure.

The West's economic advance was not without some dark spots. Inflation was a recurrent headache when demand outstripped production. Inflation in the 1970s, affecting even the cautious Germans, who were particularly eager to avoid this specter from the past, caused serious dislocation. Pockets of unemployment were troubling. Many immigrant workers from Turkey, north Africa, Pakistan, and the West Indies suffered very low wages and unstable employment. These immigrants, euphemistically labeled "guest workers," were often residentially segregated and victims of discrimination by employers and police, as racism continued to be an important factor in Western society.

In Depth

The United States and Western Europe: Convergence and Complexity

The relationship between the United States and western Europe has been important both historically and analytically for at least two centuries. Many people in the United States have tried to establish a distinctive identity while acknowledging special relationships with Europe; isolationism was one response earlier in this century. Europeans, for their part, have groped for definition of their U.S. "cousins," particularly as U.S. military and cultural influence grew in the 20th century. Were U.S. innovations to be welcomed, as stemming from a kindred society with a special flair for technology and modern mass taste, or should they be resisted as emblems of a superficial, degenerate, and essentially un-European society?

The United States–western Europe relationship has not been constant. Over time, and particularly since 1945, U.S. and European societies have in many important respects converged. Because of heightened imitation and shared advanced industrial economies, some earlier differences have receded.

Western Europe, for example, no longer has a very distinct peasantry. Its farmers, though smaller scale than their U.S. agribusiness counterparts, are commercialized and simply so few in numbers that they no longer set their society apart. European workers, though less likely than those in the United States to call themselves middle class, are now relatively prosperous. They have moved away from some of the political radicalism that differentiated them from their U.S. counterparts earlier in the 20th century. Europe does not, to be sure, have as deep-seated a racial issue as the United States inherited from slavery, but the growing influx of people from the West Indies, north Africa, and Asia has duplicated in Europe some of the same racial tensions and inner-city problems that bedevil the United States. At the other end of the social scale, trained managers and professionals now form a similar upper class in both societies, the fruit of systems of higher education that differ in particulars but resemble each other in producing something of a meritocratic elite.

A shared popular culture has certainly emerged. Although it stemmed mainly from U.S. innovations before World War II, more recently it has involved

By the 1990s, slower economic growth raised new unemployment problems in western Europe. Economic inequality increased throughout the West, though particularly in the United States. Nevertheless, the West's economic vitality, a marked contrast to the interwar decades, underpinned vital social transformations and played a major role in the global economic framework as well.

Cold War Allies: The United States, Canada, Australia, and New Zealand

Important changes in Canada and Australia paralleled developments in western Europe. The growing power of the United States was a vital new factor in global affairs.

Developments in the so-called overseas West in many ways paralleled those in western Europe, but without the sense of grappling with prior collapse. The sheer level of innovation in domestic policy was less great, in part because the crises of the first half of the 20th century had been less severe. Crucial adjustments occurred, however, in foreign policy. The United States led the way in making the changes in its own tradition that were necessary to develop a massive peacetime military force and a global set of alliances. With the decline of European, and particularly British, international power and the emergence of the cold war context, Australia, New Zealand, and Canada tightened their links with the United States and developed new contacts with other areas of the world.

The Former Dominions

Canada forged ahead in welfare policies after World War II, establishing a greater stake in economic plan-

mutual borrowing. The United States, for example, embraced miniskirts and rock groups from Britain in the 1960s, and not only British but also French youth raced to buy the latest style in blue jeans.

Differences remain, of course, some of them going back to earlier historical traditions. The United States has relied more fully on free-market capitalism than did western Europe, with the United States possessing less complete planning, fewer environmental regulations, and a more modest welfare apparatus. The difference was heightened during the 1990s. The United States proved much more religious than did western Europe. Only a minority of people in most western European countries professed religious belief by the 1990s, with less than 10 percent in most cases attending church with any regularity. In contrast the United States remains highly religious, with up to 40 percent regular church attendance, and 70 to 80 percent of its people professing religious belief. The United States made a less complete conversion to a new leisure ethic after World War II than did western Europe; European vacation time advanced toward more than a month a year, whereas the average in the United States remained two weeks or less. Europeans were franker also about teenage sexuality, following the 1960 sexual revolution. They distributed birth control materials to adolescents much more commonly than did their more prudish U.S. counterparts, reducing rates of teenage pregnancy in the process.

In certain important respects, then, the United States constituted a more traditional society, in terms of values, in the later 20th century than did western Europe. Some of the variation between the two societies related to long-established distinctions (as in the degree of suspicion of government power); others emerged for the first time, sometimes surprisingly, after World War II.

The biggest distinctions between the two societies in recent decades, however, followed from their increasingly divergent world roles. Western Europe, though still highly influential in culture and trade on a global scale, concentrated increasingly on its own regional arrangements, including the European Union trading bloc, and decreasingly on military development. The United States moved in the opposite direction. Thus a traditional distinction was reversed; the United States became the more military (and, some would argue, militaristic) society, and many Europeans became committed to more strictly civilian goals.

Questions: Why did the United States and western Europe converge in new ways during the 20th century? Do the two societies remain part of a common civilization? What are the most important issues to resolve in making this judgment?

ning and in state-run medical insurance than did the United States. At the same time, however, Canadian economic integration with the United States continued, with U.S. investments in Canadian resources and mutual exports and imports soaring steadily into the 1970s. By 1980 the Canadian government took some measures to limit further U.S. penetration, and a sense of Canadian nationalism sparked resentment of the giant to the south. In 1988, however, the two nations signed a free-trade agreement, creating a North American trading bloc at a time when European unity was increasing rapidly.

Continued emigration to Canada pointed in new directions also, with growing numbers of people arriving from various parts of Asia. Canada's most distinctive issue, however, involved growing agitation by French Canadians in Quebec for regional autonomy or even national independence. A new separatist party, founded in 1967, took control of the provincial government during the 1970s. Subsequent legis-

lation limited the use of the English language in Quebec's public and commercial life, though referendums for full independence failed during the 1980s. A new Canadian constitution in 1982, however, granted greater voice to the provinces, both to counter French Canadian demand and also to recognize the growing economic strength of the resource-rich western provinces. Separatist tensions continued to simmer, however, into the 21st century.

From 1945 onward Australia and New Zealand moved steadily away from their traditional alignment with Great Britain and toward horizons around the Pacific. The two commonwealths joined a mutual defense pact with the United States in 1951, directed against potential communist aggression in the Pacific. Both nations cooperated with the United States in the Korean War, and Australia backed U.S. intervention in Vietnam. In 1966 the Australian prime minister declared, "Wherever the United States is resisting aggression ... we will go a-waltzing Matilda with you." In the later 1970s and 1980s Australia and especially New Zealand began to distance themselves somewhat from U.S. foreign policy. New Zealand barred U.S. nuclear-armed vessels in 1985.

As Great Britain aligned with the European Union, Australian and New Zealand exports were increasingly directed toward other Pacific nations, notably Japan, whereas investment capital came mainly from the United States and Japan. Indeed, Australia became Japan's chief raw-materials supplier aside from oil. Asian emigration also increasingly altered the population mix, again particularly in Australia. Despite a long-held whites-only immigration policy, the Australian government was powerless to resist growing regional emigration, particularly from Indochina. By 1983 Asians accounted for 60 percent of the total immigrant population in Australia.

The "U.S. Century"?

Amid a host of domestic issues, the big news in U.S. history after 1945 was its assumption—in many ways, its eager assumption—of the superpower mantle, opposing the Soviet Union and serving as the world's leading defender of democratic and capitalistic values. The United States hesitated briefly after 1945, demobilizing its World War II forces rather quickly with some hope that world peace would provide some respite from further international engagement. However, Great Britain's inability to continue to police the world for the West, together with rapid Soviet successes in installing communist governments in eastern Europe, prompted a decisive U.S. stance. In 1947 President Harry Truman promised support for "free peoples who are resisting subjugation by armed minorities or by outside pressures." The doctrine, specifically directed against communist pressures on Greece and Turkey, soon extended into the elaboration of Marshall Plan aid to rebuild the economies of western Europe against the possibility of communist subversion in these war-torn countries. The Republican party was initially tempted to resist these new international engagements, but the 1948 communist takeover of Czechoslovakia checked that impulse. For many decades basic U.S. foreign policy proceeded amid wide bipartisan agreement.

The plunge into the cold war took a toll on the home front, however. The United States entered a period of intense, even frenzied concern about internal communist conspiracies, ferreting out a host of suspected spies and subjecting people in many fields to dismissal from their jobs on grounds of suspected radical sympathies.

Cold war engagement prompted other policy changes in the federal government. The Defense Department was set up in 1947 to coordinate military policy, and the Central Intelligence Agency was established to organize a worldwide information-gathering and espionage network. Military spending increased considerably, with the formation of the Strategic Air Command to stand in constant readiness in case of a Soviet bombing attack. A massive U.S. airlift thwarted Soviet pressure on the western sectors of occupied Berlin. The United States resisted the invasion of South Korea by the communist North, beginning in the 1950s; U.S. troops stationed in Japan were sent in to support the South Koreans. Under General Douglas MacArthur and backed by several allies under a hastily arranged United Nations mandate, the North Korean invasion was repulsed within a few months. The United States then authorized an invasion into North Korea, which brought a retaliatory intervention from communist China. The United States was pushed back, and more than two years of additional fighting ensued before peace was negotiated in 1953—with the new boundary line between the two Koreas relatively close to the previous line. In the meantime annual U.S. spending on the military had increased further, from $13.5 billion to $50 billion.

During the 1950s, under the presidency of Dwight D. Eisenhower, the United States settled into a policy of containment of the Soviet Union, which involved maintenance of large peacetime military forces. The United States also arranged alliances not only with western Europe, in NATO, but also with Australia and New Zealand, with several southeast Asian nations, and with several nations in the Middle East; this alliance system virtually surrounded the Soviet Union. Less novel was recurrent U.S. intervention in Central America against suspected communist movements; thus U.S. aid toppled a new Guatemalan government in 1954. The United States was unable to prevent a takeover in Cuba that eventually propelled Cuba into the communist camp, despite a U.S.-backed invasion attempt by anticommunist Cuban rebels. Nonetheless, the United States maintained its policy of vigilance (under President John Kennedy in 1962) by forcing the Soviet Union to withdraw its missile sites on the island.

The U.S. containment policy yielded a final test that took shape during the 1960s, when intervention against communist revolutionaries in South Vietnam gradually escalated. The U.S. Air Force began bombing communist North Vietnam in 1965. Later that year American troops were sent in, reaching a total of 550,000 by 1968. By this time the United States was spending $2 billion a week on a war that never produced convincing success and gradually bogged down in horrendous bloodshed on both sides. By 1970 more bombs had been dropped on Vietnam than had been dropped by anyone, anywhere previously in the 20th century. By 1968 domestic pressure against the war, centered particularly on U.S. college campuses, began to force changes in strategy. A new U.S. president, Richard Nixon, tried to expand the war to other parts of Indochina, to increase pressure on North Vietnam. Simultaneously, peace negotiations with North Vietnam were launched, resulting finally in an agreement on a cease-fire, in 1973. By 1975, as the United States speedily withdrew, all Vietnam lay in communist hands.

Furor over the Vietnam War led to agonizing policy reassessments in the United States. Some observers judged that new directions might be forged, as the United States had discovered that its massive military might could be stalemated by fervent guerrilla tactics. Both the U.S. military and the public grew more wary of regional wars. Although the national mood sobered, however, decisive policy changes did not ensue. A socialist government in Chile, for example, was ousted with the aid of covert U.S. pressure even as the Vietnam conflict wound down. The socialist government was replaced by a brutal military regime. Then in 1980 the United States overwhelmingly elected a new president, Ronald Reagan, who combined conservative domestic policies with a commitment to bolster military spending and make sure that the United States would "ride tall" again in world affairs. The 1980s saw no major new international involvements, but several punitive raids were conducted against suspected terrorists in the Middle East, and the small West Indian island of Grenada was invaded to topple a leftist regime. President Reagan sponsored a number of expensive new weapons systems, which helped press an afflicted Soviet economy to virtual collapse as its leaders attempted to keep pace. The next president, George Bush, continued an interventionist policy by sending U.S. troops into Panama to evict and arrest an abrasive dictator and then by spearheading a Western and moderate Arab alliance against Iraq's invasion of Kuwait, during 1990–1991. The United States also led participation in military action against forces in the Balkans in the 1990s.

By this point, with the cold war over, the United States emerged as "the world's only superpower." It had taken over and expanded many of the international policing functions once held by Western nations like Britain. Other Western states sometimes resented American leadership, but they generated no clear alternative and usually supported United States initiatives.

Culture and Society in the West

 Classic tensions of industrial society declined in Western societies, but gender relations were profoundly altered by the new work roles for women. Consumerism gained ground, becoming a defining feature of Western civilization. Many observers claimed that a new kind of society was taking shape.

Political and economic changes in Western society progressively altered the contours of earlier industrial development. The West became the first example of an advanced industrial society, especially from the 1950s onward, and both the United States and western Europe shared in leading facets of change.

Social Structure

Economic growth, bringing increasing prosperity to most groups, eased some earlier social conflicts throughout the West. Workers were still propertyless, but they had substantial holdings as consumers, and their sense of social inferiority often declined as a result. Social lines were also blurred by increasing social mobility, as educational opportunities opened further and the size of the white-collar sector expanded. Much unskilled labor was left to immigrants. Economic and political change also altered conditions for western Europe's peasantry and not only by cutting its size. Peasants became increasingly commercial, eager for improvements in standards of living, and participant, through car trips and television, in urban culture. They also became more attuned to bureaucracies, as state regulations pushed them into cooperative organizations.

Social distinctions remained. Middle-class people had more abundant leisure opportunities and a more optimistic outlook than did most workers. Signs of tension continued. Crime rates went up throughout Western society after the 1940s, though the levels were particularly high in the United States. Race riots punctuated U.S. life in the 1950s and 1960s and exploded in immigrant sections of British cities in the 1980s and Germany in the early 1990s.

The Women's Revolution

A key facet of postwar change involved women and the family, and again both western Europe and the United States participated fully in this upheaval. Although family ideals persisted in many ways—with workers, for example, urging that "a loving family is the finest thing, something to work for, to look to and to look after"—the realities of family life changed in many ways. Family leisure activities expanded. Extended family contacts were facilitated by telephones and automobiles. More years of schooling increased the importance of peer groups for children, and the authority of parents undoubtedly declined.

The clearest innovation in family life came through the new working patterns of women. World War II brought increased factory and clerical jobs for women, as the earlier world war had done. After a few years of downward adjustment, the trends continued. From the early 1950s onward, the number of working women, particularly married women, rose steadily in western Europe, the United States, and Canada. (See the Visualizing the Past box.) Women's earlier educational gains had improved their work qualifications; the growing number of service jobs created a need for additional workers—and women, long associated with clerical jobs and paid less than men, were ideal candidates. Many women also sought entry into the labor force as a means of adding to personal or family income, to afford some of the consumer items now becoming feasible but not yet easy to buy, or as a means of personal fulfillment in a society that associated worth with work and earnings.

The growing employment of women, which by the 1970s brought the female segment of the labor force up to 44 percent of the total in most Western countries, represented particularly the employment of adult women, most of them married and many with children. Teenage employment dropped as more

girls stayed in school, but long-term work commitments rose steadily. This was not, to be sure, a full stride to job equality. Women's pay lagged behind men's pay. Most women were concentrated in clerical jobs rather than spread through the occupational spectrum, despite a growing minority of middle-class women who were entering professional and management ranks. Clearly, however, the trends of the 19th-century Industrial Revolution, to keep women and family separate from work outside the home, had yielded to a dramatic new pattern.

Other new rights for women accompanied this shift. Where women had lacked the vote before, as in France, they now got it; of the western European nations, only Switzerland doggedly refused this concession at the national level until 1971. Gains in higher education were considerable, though again full equality remained elusive. Women constituted 23 percent of German university students in 1963, and under socialist governments in the 1970s the figure rose. Preferred subjects, however, remained different from those of men, as most women stayed out of engineering, science (except medicine), and management. Family rights improved, at least in the judgment of most women's advocates. Access to divorce increased, which many observers viewed as particularly important to women. Abortion law eased, though more slowly in countries of Catholic background than in Britain or Scandinavia; it became increasingly easy for women to regulate their birth rate. Development of new birth control methods, such as the contraceptive pill introduced in 1960, as well as growing knowledge and acceptability of birth control, decreased unwanted pregnancies. Sex and procreation became increasingly separate considerations. Although women continued to differ from men in sexual outlook and behavior—more than twice as many French women as men, for example, hoped to link sex, marriage, and romantic love, according to 1960s polls—more women than before tended to define sex in terms of pleasure.

Predictably, of course, changes in the family, including the roles of women, brought new issues and redefined ideals of companionship. The first issue involved children. A brief increase in the Western birth rate ended in the early 1960s and a rapid decline ensued. Women working and the desire to use income for high consumer standards mitigated against children, or very many children, particularly in the middle

Visualizing the Past

Women at Work in France and the United States

A statistical table of the sort presented here is essentially descriptive. What patterns are described? Is there a major change, and how can it be defined? What are the main differences between these two nations? Were they converging, becoming more similar, in 1962? In 1982? Do they end up in a similar situation with regard to women's work roles, or are they more different in 1982 than they were in 1946?

From description, questions of causation arise. Statistical patterns provide a precise framework for a challenging analysis. Why were the United States and France so different in 1946? What might have caused the changes in patterns (for example, in the United States during the 1950s)? What was the role of new feminist demands in 1963? What might have caused the differences in the timing of trends in France and the United States?

Women at Work: The Female Labor Force in France and the United States

	France		United States	
	Women Workers (thousands)	Percentage of Total Force	Women Workers (thousands)	Percentage of Total Force
1946	7,880	37.90	16,840	27.83
1954	6,536	33.93	19,718	29.43
1962	6,478	33.23	24,047	32.74
1968	6,924	34.62	29,242	35.54
1975	7,675	36.48	37,553	39.34
1982	8,473	39.46	47,894	42.81

Sources: B. R. Mitchell, *International Historical Statistics: Europe, 1750–1988*; U.S. Bureau of the Census, *Historical Statistics of the United States, Colonial Times to 1970, Bicentennial Edition, Part 1*; U.S. Bureau of the Census, *Statistical Abstract of the United States: 1984*.

class, where birth rates were lowest. Those children born were increasingly sent, often at an early age, to day-care centers, one of the amenities provided by the European welfare state and particularly essential where new fears about population growth began to surface. European families had few hesitations about replacing maternal care with collective care, and parents often claimed that the result was preferable for children. At the same time, however, some observers worried that Western society, and the Western family, were becoming indifferent to children in an eagerness for adult work and consumer achievements. American adults, for example, between the 1950s and 1980s, shifted their assessment of family satisfaction away from parenthood by concentrating on shared enjoyments between husbands and wives.

Family stability also opened new cracks. Pressures to readjust family roles, women working outside the family context, and growing legal freedoms for women caused men and women alike to turn more readily to divorce. In 1961, 9 percent of all British marriages ended in divorce; by 1965 the figure was 16 percent and rising. By the late 1970s, one-third of all British marriages ended in divorce, and the U.S. rate was higher still.

The development of a new surge of feminist protest, although it reflected much wider concerns than family life alone, showed the strains caused by women's new activities and continued limitations. Growing divorce produced many cases of impoverished women combining work and child care. New work roles revealed the persistent earnings gap between men and women. More generally, many women sought supporting values and organizations as they tried to define new identities less tied to the domestic roles and images of previous decades.

A **new feminism** began to take shape with the publication in 1949 of *The Second Sex* by the French intellectual Simone de Beauvoir. Echoed in the 1950s and 1960s by other works, such as *The Feminine Mystique*, by Betty Friedan of the United States (Figure 32.4), a new wave of women's rights agitation rose after three decades of relative calm. The new feminism tended to emphasize a more literal equality that would play down special domestic roles and qualities; therefore, it promoted not only specific reforms but also more basic redefinitions of what it meant to be male and female.

The new feminism did not win all women, even in the middle class, which was feminism's most avid audience. It also did not cause some of the most

sweeping practical changes that were taking place, as in the new work roles. But it did support the revolution in roles. From the late 1960s onward it pressed Western governments for further change, raising issues that were difficult to fit into established political contexts (Figure 32.5). The movement both articulated and promoted the gap between new expectations and ongoing inequalities in gender. And the new feminism expressed and promoted some unanswered questions about family functions. In a real sense later 20th-century feminism seemed to respond to the same desire for individuality and work identity in women that had earlier been urged on men as part of the new mentality suitable for a commercialized economy. Family remained important in the evolving outlook of women, although some feminist leaders attacked the institution outright as hopelessly repressive. Even for many less ideological women, however, family goals were less important than they had been before.

Western Culture

Amid great innovations in politics, the economy, and social structure—including some pressing new problems—Western cultural life in many respects proceeded along established lines. A host of specific new movements arose, and a wealth of scientific data was assimilated, though basic frameworks had been set earlier, often in the more turbulent but intellectually creative decades of the early 20th century.

One key development was a shift of focus toward the United States. Greater political stability in the United States during the 1930s and 1940s, as well as Hitler's persecutions, had driven many prominent intellectuals to U.S. shores, where they often remained even as western Europe revived. As U.S. universities expanded, their greater wealth fueled more scientific research; what was called a "brain drain," based on dollar power, drew many leading European scientists to the United States even during the 1950s and 1960s. European science remained active, but the costliness of cutting-edge research produced a durable U.S. advantage. Money also mattered in art, as patronage became increasingly important, and thus New York replaced Paris as the center of international styles.

Europeans did participate in some of the leading scientific advances of the postwar years. Francis

Figure 32.4 *Betty Friedan, author of* The Feminine Mystique, *was seen as a leader of the women's rights movement in the 1960s.*

Figure 32.5 *The feminist movement focused particularly on economic gains for women and a rejection of purely domestic roles. The movement first gained momentum in the United States in the late 1960s, in the wake of civil rights agitation, but soon spread to western Europe.*

Crick, of Cambridge University in England, shared with the American James Watson key credit for the discovery of the basic structure of the genetic building block deoxyribonucleic acid (DNA), which in turn opened the way for rapid advances in genetic knowledge and industries based on artificial synthesis of genetic materials. By 2000 work on the human genome project was proceeding rapidly on both sides of the Atlantic. Europeans also participated in nuclear research, often through laboratories funded by the European Union or other inter-European agencies. European space research, slower to develop than Soviet or U.S. initiatives, nevertheless also produced noteworthy achievements by the 1970s, and again there were impor-

tant commercial spin-offs in communications satellites and other activities.

Developments in the arts maintained earlier 20th-century themes quite clearly. Most artists continued to work in the "modern" modes set before World War I, which featured unconventional self-expression and a wide array of nonrepresentational techniques. The clearest change involved growing public acceptance of the modern styles. The shock that had greeted earlier innovations disappeared, and the public, even when preferring older styles displayed in museums or performed by symphony orchestras devoted to the classics, now seemed reconciled to the redefinition of artistic standards. New names were added to the roster of leading modern artists. In Paris Bernard Buffet scored important successes with gaunt, partially abstract figures. The British sculptor Henry Moore produced rounded figures and outright abstractions that conveyed some of the horrors of wartime life and postwar dislocations. A new group of "pop" artists in the 1960s tried to bridge the gap between art and commercial mass culture by incorporating cans and their products, comic strips, and advertisements into paintings, prints, and collages. As also held true in the realm of fully abstract painting, U.S. artists increasingly took the lead.

Europeans retained clearer advantages in artistic films. Italian directors produced a number of gripping, realistic films in the late 1940s, portraying both urban and peasant life without frills. Italy, France, and Sweden became centers of experimental filmmaking again in the 1960s. Jean-Luc Godard and Michelangelo Antonioni portrayed the emptiness of urban life, and Swedish director Ingmar Bergman produced a series of dark psychological dramas. Individual directors in Spain, Britain, and Germany also broke new ground, as Europeans remained more comfortable than their U.S. counterparts in producing films of high artistic merit, relatively free from commercial distractions.

Fragmentation occurred in the social sciences, with no commanding figure rising to the stature of Marx or Weber in previous generations, willing to posit fundamental social dynamics or sweeping theories. Many specific fields in the social sciences turned to massive data collections and pragmatic, detailed observations; in many of these, U.S. practitioners developed a decided advantage. Economics, in particular, became something of an American specialty in the post-Keynesian decades and focused on massive quantitative studies of economic cycles and money supplies. European influence was greater in several new theoretical formulations in the humanities. French intellectuals also contributed to a redefinition of historical study, building on innovations launched between the world wars. Social history, or the focus on changes in the lives of ordinary people, became increasingly the order of the day, giving a great spur to historical research throughout western Europe and the United States.

A Lively Popular Culture

Western society displayed more vitality in its popular culture than in formal intellectual life, which reflected the results of economic and social change. As European economies struggled to recover from the war and as U.S. military forces spread certain enthusiasms

more widely than before, some observers spoke of a U.S. "Coca-cola-nization" of Europe. U.S. soft drinks, blue-jean fashions, chewing gum, and other artifacts became increasingly common. U.S. films continued to wield substantial influence, although the lure of Hollywood declined somewhat. More important was the growing impact of U.S. television series. Blessed with a wide market and revenues generated from advertising, American television was quite simply "slicker" than its European counterparts, and the western drama *Bonanza*, the soap opera *Dallas*, and many other shows appeared regularly on European screens to define, for better or worse, an image of the United States.

In contrast to the interwar decades, however, European popular culture had its own power, and it even began to influence the United States as well. The most celebrated figures of popular culture in the 1960s were unquestionably the Beatles, from the British port city of Liverpool. Although they adopted popular music styles of the United States, including jazz and early rock, the Beatles added an authentic working-class touch in their impulsiveness and their mockery of authority. They also expressed a good-natured desire to enjoy the pleasures of life, which is a characteristic of modern Western popular culture regardless of national context. British popular music groups continued to set standards in the 1970s and had wide impact on western Europe more generally.

Other facets of popular culture displayed a new vigor. Again in Britain, youth fashions, separate from the standards of the upper class, showed an ability to innovate and sometimes to shock. Unconventional uses of color and cut, as in punk hairstyles of the later 1970s, bore some resemblance to the anticonventional tone of modern painting and sculpture.

Sexual culture also changed in the West, building on earlier trends that linked sex to a larger pleasure-seeking mentality characteristic of growing consumerism and to a desire for personal expression. Films and television shows demonstrated increasingly relaxed standards about sexual display. In Britain, Holland, and Denmark sex shops sold a wide array of erotic materials and products.

Like the United States, western Europe experienced important changes in sexual behavior starting around 1960, particularly among young people. Premarital sex became more common. The average age of first sexual intercourse began to go down. Expressive sexuality in western Europe was also evident in the growing number of nude bathing spots, again in interesting contrast to more hesitant initiatives in the

United States. Although the association of modern popular culture with sexuality and body concern was not novel, the openness and diversity of expression unquestionably reached new levels and also demonstrated western Europe's new confidence in defining a vigorous, nontraditional mass culture of its own.

Critics of Western popular culture worried about its superficiality and its role in distracting ordinary people from ongoing problems such as social inequality. But there were no huge reactions, like those of Nazism against the cultural trends of the 1920s. Western popular culture played a major role in setting global cultural standards, enhancing the West's international influence even as its formal political dominance declined.

Eastern Europe After World War II: A Soviet Empire

 Several of the major changes in eastern Europe after 1945 paralleled those in the West. Ongoing industrialization brought some familiar social changes. Cold war competition produced Soviet policies that often mirrored those of the United States. But this was a communist region, and a less developed industrial economy, so key differences surfaced as well. Russia and its new allies continued to seek considerable independence from the world economy. Distinctive traditions maintained a hold as well, including a penchant for territorial expansion and a pronounced ambivalence about whether to accept or reject Western influence.

The Soviet Union as Superpower

By 1945 Soviet foreign policy had several ingredients. Desire to regain tsarist boundaries (though now carried through regarding Finland) joined with traditional interest in expansion and in playing an active role in European diplomacy. Genuine revulsion at Germany's two invasions prompted a feverish desire to set up buffer zones, under Soviet control. As a result of Soviet industrialization and its World War II push westward, the nation also emerged as a world power, like the newcomer United States. Continued concentration on heavy industry and weapons development, combined with strategic alliances and links to communist movements in various parts of the world, helped maintain this status.

Soviet participation in the late phases of the war against Japan provided an opportunity to seize some islands in the northern Pacific. The Soviet Union established a protectorate over the communist regime of North Korea, to match the U.S. protectorate in South Korea. Soviet aid to the victorious Communist party in China brought new influence in that country for a time, and in the 1970s the Soviet Union gained a new ally in communist Vietnam, which provided naval bases for the Soviet fleet. Its growing military and economic strength gave the postwar Soviet Union new leverage in the Middle East, Africa, and even parts of Latin America; alliance with the new communist regime in Cuba was a key step here, during the 1960s. The Soviet Union's superpower status was confirmed by its development of the atomic and then hydrogen bombs, from 1949 onward, and by its deployment of missiles and naval forces to match the rapid expansion of U.S. arsenals. The Soviet Union had become a world power.

The New Soviet Empire in Eastern Europe

As a superpower the Soviet Union developed increasing worldwide influence, with trade and cultural missions on all inhabited continents and military alliances with several Asian, African, and Latin American nations. But the clearest extension of the Soviet sphere developed right after World War II, in eastern Europe (see Map 32.1). Here the Soviets made it plain that they intended to stay, pushing the Soviet effective sphere of influence farther to the west than ever before in history. Soviet insistence on this empire helped launch the cold war, as the Soviet Union displayed its willingness to confront the West rather than relax its grip.

The small nations of eastern Europe, mostly new or revived after World War I, had gone through a troubled period between the world wars. Other than democratic Czechoslovakia, they had failed to establish vigorous, independent economies or solid political systems. Then came the Nazi attack, and ineffective Western response, as Czechoslovakia, Poland, and Yugoslavia were seized by German or Italian forces. Eastern Europe fell under Nazi control for four years. Although anti-Nazi governments formed abroad, only in Yugoslavia was a resistance movement strong enough to seriously affect postwar results.

By 1945 the dominant force in eastern Europe was the Soviet army, as it pushed the Germans back and remade the map. Through the combination of the Soviet military might and collaboration with local communist movements in the nations that remained technically independent, opposition parties were crushed and noncommunist regimes forced out by 1948. The only exceptions to this pattern were Greece, which moved toward the Western camp in diplomatic alignment and political and social systems; Albania, which formed a rigid Stalinist regime that ironically brought it into disagreement with Soviet post-Stalinist leaders; and Yugoslavia, where a communist regime formed under the resistance leader Tito quickly proclaimed its neutrality in the cold war, resisting Soviet direction and trying to form a more open-ended, responsive version of the communist economic and social system.

After what was in effect the Soviet takeover, a standard development dynamic emerged throughout most of eastern Europe by the early 1950s. The new Soviet-sponsored regimes attacked possible rivals for power, including, where relevant, the Roman Catholic church. Mass education and propaganda outlets were quickly developed. Collectivization of agriculture ended the large estate system, without creating a property-owning peasantry. Industrialization was pushed through successive five-year plans, though with some limitation due to Soviet insistence on access to key natural resources (such as Romanian oil) on favorable terms. Finally, a Soviet–eastern European trading zone became largely separate from the larger trends of international commerce.

After the formation of NATO in western Europe, the relevant eastern European nations were also enfolded in a common defense alliance, the Warsaw Pact, and a common economic planning organization. Soviet troops continued to be stationed in most eastern European states, both to confront the Western alliance and to ensure the continuation of the new regimes and their loyalty to the common cause.

Although it responded to many social problems in the smaller nations of eastern Europe, as well as to the desire of the Soviet Union to expand its influence and guard against German or more general Western attack, the new Soviet system created obvious tensions. Particularly tight controls in East Germany brought a workers' rising there in 1953, vigorously repressed by Soviet troops. Faced with a widespread exodus to West Germany, the Soviets built the **Berlin Wall** in 1961 to stem the flow. All along the new borders of eastern Europe, barbed wire fences and armed patrols kept the people in. In 1956 relaxation of Stalinism within the Soviet Union created new hopes that controls might be loosened. More liberal communist leaders arose in Hungary and Poland, with massive popular backing,

seeking to create states that, although communist, would permit greater diversity and certainly more freedom from Soviet domination. In Poland the Soviets accepted a new leader more popular with the Polish people. Among other results, Poland was allowed to halt agricultural collectivization, establishing widespread peasant ownership in its place, and the Catholic church, now the symbol of Polish independence, gained greater tolerance. But a new regime in Hungary was cruelly crushed by the Soviet army and a hard-line Stalinist leadership set up in its place (Figure 32.6).

Yet Soviet control over eastern Europe did loosen slightly overall, for the heavy-handed repression cost considerable prestige. Eastern European governments were given a freer hand in economic policy and were allowed limited room to experiment with greater cultural freedom. Several countries thus began to outstrip the prosperity of the Soviet Union itself. Contacts with the West expanded in several cases, with greater trade and tourism. Eastern Europe remained with the Soviet Union as a somewhat separate economic bloc in world trade, but there was room for limited diversity. Individual nations, such as Hungary, developed new intellectual vigor and experimented with slightly less centralized economic planning. The communist political system remained in full force, however, with its single-party dominance and strong police controls; diplomatic and military alignment with the Soviet Union remained essential.

The limits of experimentation in eastern Europe were brought home again in 1968, when a more liberal regime came to power in Czechoslovakia. Again the Soviet army responded, expelling the reformers and setting up a particularly rigid leader. A challenge came from Poland once more in the late 1970s, in the form of widespread Catholic unrest and an independent labor movement called **Solidarity,** all against the backdrop of a stagnant economy and low morale. Here response was slightly more muted, though key agitators were arrested; the Polish army took over the state, under careful Soviet supervision.

By the 1980s eastern Europe had been vastly transformed by several decades of communist rule. Important national diversity remained, visible both in industrial levels and in political styles. Catholic Poland thus differed from hard-line, neo-Stalinist Bulgaria or Romania. Important discontents remained as well. Yet a communist-imposed social revolution had brought considerable economic change and real social upheaval, through the abolition of the once-dominant aristocracy and the remaking of the peasant masses through collectivization, new systems of

Figure 32.6 *As Soviet troops moved into Hungary to crush the revolt of 1956, freedom fighters in Budapest headed for the front with whatever weapons they could find. This truckload of supporters is being urged on by the crowd.*

mass education, and industrial, urban growth. Earlier cultural ties with the West, though still greater than in the Soviet Union itself, had been lessened; Russian, not French or English, was the first foreign language learned.

The expansion of Soviet influence answered important Soviet foreign policy goals, both traditional and new. The Soviets retained a military presence deep in Europe, which among other things reduced very real anxiety about yet another German threat. Eastern European allies aided Soviet ventures in other parts of the world, providing supplies and advisors for activities in Africa, Latin America, and elsewhere. Yet the recurrent unrest in eastern Europe served as something of a check on Soviet policy as well. The need for continued military presence may have diverted Soviet leaders from emphasizing expansionist ambitions in other directions, particularly where direct commitment of troops might be involved.

Evolution of Domestic Policies

Within the Soviet Union the Stalinist system remained intact during the initial postwar years. The war encouraged growing use of nationalism as well as appeals for communist loyalty, as millions of Russians responded heroically to the new foreign threat. Elements of this mood were sustained as the cold war with the United States developed after 1947, with news media blasting the United States as an evil power and a distorted society. Many Soviets, fearful of a new war that U.S. aggressiveness seemed to them to threaten, agreed that strong government authority remained necessary. This attitude helped sustain the difficult rebuilding efforts after the war, which proceeded rapidly enough for the Soviet Union to regain its prewar industrial capacity and then proceed, during the 1950s, to impressive annual growth rates. The attitude also helped support Stalin's rigorous efforts to shield the Soviet populations from extensive contact with foreigners or foreign ideas. Strict limits on travel, outside media, or any uncensored glimpse of the outside world kept the Soviet Union unusually isolated in the mid-20th-century world—its culture, like its economy, largely removed from world currents.

Stalin's political structure continued to emphasize central controls and the omnipresent Party bureaucracy, leavened by the adulation accorded to Stalin and by the aging leader's endemic suspiciousness. Moscow-based direction of the national economy, along with the steady extension of education, welfare, and police operations, expanded the bureaucracy both of the government and of the parallel Communist party. Recruitment from the ranks of peasant and worker families continued into the 1940s, as educational opportunities, including growing secondary school and university facilities, allowed talented young people to rise from below. Party membership, the ticket to bureaucratic promotion, was deliberately kept low, at about 6 percent of the population, to ensure selection of the most dedicated elements. New candidates for the Party, drawn mostly from the more broadly based communist youth organizations, had to be nominated by at least three Party members. Party members vowed unswerving loyalty and group consciousness.

Soviet Culture: Promoting New Beliefs and Institutions

 Rapid industrialization created new issues in eastern European society and culture. Import literary currents showed impressive vitality, even as Soviet leaders sought alternatives to Western-style consumerism. Beginning in the 1950s, the Stalinist system yielded to greater flexibility, though Communist party control remained tight. New diplomatic and social issues arose by the 1970s.

The Soviet government was an impressive new product, not just a renewal of tsarist autocracy. It carried on a much wider array of functions than the tsars had ventured, not only in fostering industrialization but also in reaching out for the direct loyalties of individual citizens. The government and the Party also maintained an active cultural agenda, and although this had been foreshadowed by the church–state links of tsarist days, it had no full precedent. The regime declared war on the Orthodox church and other religions soon after 1917, seeking to shape a secular population that would maintain a Marxist, scientific orthodoxy; vestigial church activities remained but under tight government regulation. Artistic and literary styles, as well as purely political writings, were carefully monitored to ensure adherence to the Party line. The educational system was used not only to train and recruit technicians and bureaucrats but also to create a loyal, right-thinking citizenry. Mass ceremonies, such as May Day parades, stimulated devotion to the state and to communism.

Although the new regime did not attempt to abolish the Orthodox church outright, it greatly limited the church's outreach. Thus the church was barred from giving religious instruction to anyone under 18, and state schools vigorously preached the doctrine that religion was mere superstition. Although loyalties to the church persisted, they now seemed concentrated in a largely elderly minority. The Soviet regime also limited freedom of religion for the Jewish minority, often holding up Jews as enemies of the state in what was in fact a manipulation of traditional Russian anti-Semitism. The larger Muslim minority was given greater latitude, on condition of careful loyalty to the regime. On the whole, the traditional religious orientation of Soviet society declined in favor of a scientific outlook and Marxist explanations of history in terms of class conflict. Church attendance dwindled under government repression; by the 1950s only the elderly seemed particularly interested.

The Soviet state also continued to attack modern Western styles of art and literature, terming them decadent, but maintained some earlier Western styles, which were appropriated as Russian. Thus Russian orchestras performed a wide variety of classical music, and the Russian ballet, though rigid and conservative by 20th-century Western norms, commanded wide attention and enforced rigid standards of excellence. In the arts, socialist realist principles spread to eastern Europe after World War II, particularly in public displays and monuments. With some political loosening and cold war thaw after 1950, however, Soviet and eastern European artists began to adopt Western styles to some extent. At the popular level, jazz and rock music bands began to emerge by the 1980s, though official suspicion persisted.

Literature in the Soviet Union remained diverse and creative, despite official controls sponsored by the communist-dominated Writers' Union. Leading authors wrote movingly of the travails of World War II, maintaining the earlier tradition of sympathy with the people, great patriotism, and concern for the Russian soul. The most creative Soviet artists, particularly the writers, often skirted a fine line between conveying some of the sufferings of the Russian people in the 20th century and courting official disapproval. Their freedom also depended on leadership mood; thus censorship eased after Stalin and then tightened again somewhat in the late 1960s and 1970s, though not to previous levels. Yet even authors critical of aspects of the Soviet regime maintained distinctive Russian values. **Aleksandr Solzhenitsyn,** for example, exiled to the United States after the publication of his trilogy on Siberian prison camps, *The Gulag Archipelago*, found the West too materialistic and individualistic for his taste. Though barred from his homeland, he continued to seek an alternative both to communist policy and to westernization, with more than a hint of a continuing belief in the durable solidarity and faith of the Russian common people and a mysterious Russian national soul.

Along with interest in the arts and a genuine diversity of expressions despite official party lines, Soviet culture continued to place great emphasis on science and social science. Scientists enjoyed great prestige and wielded considerable power. Social scientific work, heavily colored by Marxist theory, nonetheless produced important analyses of current trends and of history. Scientific research was even more heavily funded, and Soviet scientists generated a number of fundamental discoveries in physics, chemistry, and mathematics. At times scientists felt the heavy hand of official disapproval. Biologists and psychiatrists, particularly, were urged to reject Western theories that called human rationality and social progress into question, though here as in other areas controls were most stringent in the Stalinist years. Thus Freudianism was banned, and under Stalin biologists who overemphasized the uncontrollability of genetic evolution were jailed. But Soviet scientists overall enjoyed considerable freedom and great prestige. As in the West, their work was often linked with advances in technology and weaponry. After the heyday of Stalinism, scientists gained greater freedom from ideological dictates, and exchanges with Western researchers became more common in what was, at base, a common scientific culture.

Shaped by substantial state control, 20th-century Soviet culture overall proved neither traditional nor Western. Considerable ambivalence about the West remained, as Soviets continued to utilize many art forms they developed in common with the West, such as the ballet, while instilling a comparable faith in science. Fear of cultural pollution—particularly, of course, through non-Marxist political tracts but also through modern art forms—remained lively, as Soviet leaders sought a culture that would enhance their goals of building a socialist society separate from the capitalist West.

Economy and Society

The Soviet Union became a fully industrial society between the 1920s and the 1950s. Rapid growth of manufacturing and the rise of urban populations to more than 50 percent of the total were measures of this development. Most of the rest of eastern Europe was also fully industrialized by the 1950s. Eastern European modernization, however, had a number of distinctive features. State control of virtually all economic sectors was one key element; no other industrialized society gave so little leeway to private initiative. The unusual imbalance between heavy industrial goods and consumer items was another distinctive aspect. The Soviet Union lagged in the priorities it placed on consumer goods—not only such Western staples as automobiles but also housing construction and simple items, such as bathtub plugs. Consumer-goods industries were poorly funded and did not achieve the advanced technological level that characterized the heavy-manufacturing sector. The Soviet need to amass capital for development in a traditionally poor society helped explain the inattention to consumer goods; so did the need to create, in a society that remained poorer overall, a massive armaments industry to rival that of the United States. Thus despite an occasional desire to beat the West at its own affluent-society game, eastern Europe did not develop the kind of consumer society that came to characterize the West. Living standards improved and extensive welfare services provided security for some groups not similarly supported in the West, but complaints about poor consumer products and long lines to obtain desired goods remained a feature of Soviet life.

Soviet industrialization also caused an unusual degree of environmental damage. The drive to produce at all costs created bleak zones around factories, where waste was dumped, and in agricultural mining areas up to one quarter of all Soviet territory (and that of the eastern bloc) was environmentally degraded, often with severe health damages as well.

The communist system throughout eastern Europe also failed to resolve problems with agriculture. Capital that might have gone into farming equipment was often diverted to armaments and heavy industry. The arduous climate of northern Europe and Asia was a factor as well, dooming a number of attempts to spread grain production to Siberia, for example. But it seemed clear that the eastern

European peasantry continued to find the constraints and lack of individual incentive in collectivized agriculture deterrents to maximum effort. Thus eastern Europe had to retain a larger percentage of its labor force in agriculture than was true of the industrial West, but it still encountered problems with food supply and quality.

Despite the importance of distinctive political and economic characteristics, eastern European society echoed a number of the themes of contemporary Western social history—simply because of the shared fact of industrial life. Work rhythms, for example, became roughly similar. Industrialization brought massive efforts to speed the pace of work and to introduce regularized supervision. The incentive systems designed to encourage able workers resembled those used in Western factories. Along with similar work habits came similar leisure activities. For decades, sports have provided excitement for the peoples of eastern Europe, as have films and television. Family vacations to the beaches of the Black Sea became cherished respites. Here, too, there were some distinctive twists, as the communist states boosted sports efforts as part of their political program (in contrast to the Western view of sports as a combination of leisure and commercialism). East Germany, along with the Soviet Union, developed particularly extensive athletic programs under state sponsorship, winning international competitions in a host of fields.

Eastern European social structure also grew closer to that of the West, despite the continued importance of the rural population and despite the impact of Marxist theory. Particularly interesting was a tendency to divide urban society along class lines—between workers and a better-educated, managerial middle class. Wealth divisions remained much less great than in the West, to be sure, but the perquisites of managers and professional people—particularly for Communist party members—set them off from the standard of living of the masses.

Finally, the Soviet family reacted to some of the same pressures of industrialization as did the Western family. Massive movements to the cities and crowded housing enhanced the nuclear family unit, as ties to a wider network of relatives loosened. The birth rate dropped. Official Soviet policy on birth rates varied for a time, but the basic pressures became similar to those in the West: Falling infant death rates, with improved diets and medical care, together with increasing periods of schooling and some increase in consumer expectations, made large families less desirable than before. Wartime dislocations contributed to birth rate decline

at points as well. By the 1970s the Soviet growth rate was about the same as that of the West. As in the West, also, some minority groups—particularly Muslims in the southern Soviet Union—maintained higher birth rates than the majority ethnic group—in this case, ethnic Russians—a differential that caused some concern about maintaining Russian cultural dominance.

Patterns of child rearing showed some similarities to those in the West, as parents, especially in the managerial middle class, devoted great attention to promoting their children's education and ensuring good jobs for the future. At the same time children were more strictly disciplined than in the West, both at home and in school, with an emphasis on authority that had political implications as well. Soviet families never afforded the domestic idealization of women that had prevailed in the West during industrialization. Most married women worked, an essential feature of an economy struggling to industrialize and offering relatively low wages to individual workers. As in the peasant past, women performed many heavy physical tasks. They also dominated some professions, such as medicine, though these professionals were much lower in status than were their male dominated counterparts in the West. Soviet propagandists took pride in the constructive role of women and their official equality, but there were signs that many women were suffering burdens from demanding jobs with little help from their husbands at home.

De-Stalinization

The rigid government apparatus created by Stalin and sustained after World War II by frequent arrests and exiles to forced labor camps was put to a major test after Stalin's death in 1953. The results gradually loosened, without totally reversing, Stalinist cultural isolation. Focus on one-man rule might have created immense succession problems, and indeed frequent jockeying for power did develop among aspiring candidates. Yet the system held together. Years of bureaucratic experience had given most Soviet leaders a taste for coordination and compromise, along with a reluctance to strike out in radical new directions that might cause controversy or arouse resistance from one of the key power blocs within the state. Stalin's death was followed by a ruling committee that balanced interest groups, notably the army, the police, and the Party apparatus. This mechanism encouraged conservatism, as each bureaucratic sector defended its existing prerogatives, but it also ensured fundamental stability.

In 1956, however, **Nikita Khrushchev** emerged from the committee pack to gain primary power, though without seeking to match Stalin's eminence. Indeed, Khrushchev attacked Stalinism for its concentration of power and arbitrary dictatorship. In a stirring speech delivered to the Communist party congress, Khrushchev condemned Stalin for his treatment of political opponents, for his narrow interpretations of Marxist doctrine, even for his failure to adequately prepare for World War II. The implications of the de-Stalinization campaign within the Soviet Union suggested a more tolerant political climate and some decentralization of decision making. In fact, however, despite a change in tone, little concrete institutional reform occurred. Political trials became less common, and the most overt police repression eased. A few intellectuals were allowed to raise new issues, dealing, for example, with the purges and other Stalinist excesses. Outright critics of the regime were less likely to be executed and more likely to be sent to psychiatric institutions or, in the case of internationally visible figures, exiled to the West or confined to house arrest. Party control and centralized economic planning remained intact. Indeed, Khrushchev planned a major extension of state-directed initiative by opening new Siberian land to cultivation; his failure in this costly effort, combined with his antagonizing many Stalinist loyalists, led to his quiet downfall.

After the de-Stalinization furor and Khrushchev's fall from power, patterns in the Soviet Union remained stable into the 1980s, verging at times on stagnant. Economic growth continued but with no dramatic breakthroughs and with recurrent worries over sluggish productivity and especially over periodically inadequate harvests, which compelled expensive grain deals with Western nations, including the United States. A number of subsequent leadership changes occurred, but the transitions were handled smoothly.

Cold war policies eased somewhat after Stalin's death. Khrushchev vaunted the Soviet ability to outdo the West at its own industrial game, bragging on a visit to the United States that "we will bury you." The Khrushchev regime also produced one of the most intense moments of the cold war with the United States, as he probed for vulnerabilities. Exploiting the new alliance with Cuba, the Soviets installed missiles in Cuba (see Figure 32.7), yielding only to a firm U.S. response in 1962 by removing the missiles but not

Figure 32.7 *Site of Cuban missile base in San Cristobal in October 1962. Discovery of Soviet installations threatened war, but Soviet prime minister Khrushchev removed the missiles under pressure from the United States.*

their support of the communist regime on the island. Khrushchev had no desire for war, and overall he promoted a new policy of peaceful coexistence. He hoped to beat the West economically and actively expanded the Soviet space program; Sputnik, the first space satellite, was sent up in 1957, well in advance of its U.S. counterpart. Khrushchev maintained a competitive tone, but he shifted away from an exclusive military emphasis. Lowered cold war tensions with the West permitted a small influx of Western tourists by the 1960s as well as greater access to the Western media and a variety of cultural exchanges, which gave some Soviets a renewed sense of contact with a wider world and restored some of the earlier ambiguities about the nation's relationship to Western standards.

At the same time, the Soviet leadership continued a steady military buildup, adding increasingly sophisticated rocketry and bolstered by its unusually successful space program. The Soviets maintained a lead in manned space flights into the late 1980s (see Figure 32.8). Both in space and in the arms race, the Soviet Union demonstrated great technical ability combined with a willingness to settle for somewhat simpler systems than those the United States attempted, which helped explain how it could maintain superpower parity even with a less prosperous overall economy. An active sports program, resulting in a growing array of victories in Olympic games competition, also showed the Soviet Union's new ability to compete on an international scale and its growing pride in international achievements.

The nation faced a number of new foreign policy problems, although maintaining superpower status. From the mid-1950s onward the Soviet Union experienced a growing rift with China, a communist nation with which it shared a long border. Successful courtship of many other nations—such as Egypt, a close diplomatic friend during the 1960s—often turned sour, though these developments were often balanced by new

Figure 32.8 *Soviet advances in science and technology both surprised and threatened the United States and western Europe. Manned space flights were but one area in which the Soviets challenged the material supremacy of the West.*

Figure 32.9 *May Day celebration in Red Square, Moscow.*

alignments elsewhere. The rise of Muslim awareness in the 1970s was deeply troubling to the Soviet Union, with its own large Muslim minority. This prompted a 1979 invasion of Afghanistan, to promote a friendly puppet regime, which bogged down amid guerrilla warfare into the late 1980s. On balance, the Soviet Union played a normally cautious diplomatic game, almost never engaging directly in warfare but maintaining a high level of preparedness (see Figure 32.9).

Problems of work motivation and discipline loomed larger in the Soviet Union than in the West by the 1980s, after the heroic period of building an industrial society under Stalinist exhortation and threat. With highly bureaucratized and centralized work plans and the absence of abundant consumer goods, many workers found little reason for great diligence. High rates of alcoholism, so severe as to cause an increase in death rates, particularly among adult males, also burdened work performance and caused great concern to Soviet leaders. More famil-

iar were problems of youth agitation. Although Soviet statistics tended to conceal outright crime rates, it is clear that many youth became impatient with the disciplined life and eager to have greater access to Western culture, including rock music and blue jeans.

Most observers thought the Soviet Union remained firmly established in the early 1980s, thanks to careful police control, vigorous propaganda, and real, popular pride in Soviet achievements. Even though the U.S. Central Intelligence Agency failed to see major problems, in fact, economic conditions were deteriorating rapidly, and the whole Soviet system would soon come unglued. Yet its collapse was all the more unsettling because of communism's huge success for many decades. At great cost to many people, the Soviet Union had attained world power. Many rejoiced in its fall, but many were also disoriented by it. What could and should replace a system that had dominated huge stretches of Europe and Asia for so long?

Document

1986: A New Wave of Soviet Reform

The following document reflects a wave of reform introduced in 1986 by a new Soviet leader, Mikhail Gorbachev. Gorbachev's policies ultimately ushered in a major new era of Russian history. At the time, however, they represented an attempt to save the key features of the Soviet state while recognizing ominous new problems. The document obviously invites analysis around several issues, including what features of the Soviet state Gorbachev sought to preserve, what new problems he identified, and how he intended to deal with them. You might also speculate about why the reforms eventually spun out of Soviet control.

None of us can continue living in the old way. This is obvious. In this sense, we can say that a definite step toward acceleration has been made.

However, there is a danger that the first step will be taken as success, that we will assume that the whole situation has been taken in hand. I said this in Vladivostok. I want to say it again in Khabarovsk. If we were to draw this conclusion, we would be making a big mistake, an error. What has been achieved cannot yet satisfy us in any way. In general, one should never flatter oneself with what has been accomplished. All of us must learn this well. Such are the lessons of the past decades—the last two, at least. And now this is especially dangerous.

No profound qualitative changes that would reinforce the trend toward accelerated growth have taken place as yet. In general, comrades, important and intensive work lies ahead of us. To put it bluntly, the main thing is still to come. Our country's Party, the entire Party, should understand this well....

We should learn as we go along, accomplishing new tasks. And we must not be afraid of advancing boldly, of doing things on the march, in the course of the active accomplishment of economic and social tasks....

Restructuring is a capacious word. I would equate the word restructuring with the word revolution. Our transformations, the reforms mapped out in the decisions of the April plenary session of the Party Central Committee and the 27th CPSU [Communist Party of the Soviet Union] Congress, are a genuine revolution in the entire system of relations in society, in the minds and hearts of people, in the psychology and understanding of the present period and, above all, in the tasks engendered by rapid scientific and technical progress.

There is a common understanding in the CPSU and in the country as a whole—we should look for answers to the questions raised by life not outside of socialism but within the framework of our system, disclosing the potential of a planned economy, socialist democracy and culture and the human factor, and relying on the people's vital creativity.

Some people in the West do not like this. There everyone lies in wait for something that would mean a deviation from socialism, for us to go hat in hand to capitalism, for us to borrow its methods. We are receiving a great deal of "advice" from abroad as to how and where we should proceed. Various kinds of provocative broadcasts are made, and articles are published, aimed at casting aspersions on the changes taking place in our country and at driving a wedge between the Party leadership and the people. Such improper attempts are doomed to failure. The interests of the Party and the people are inseparable, and our choice and political course are firm and unshakable. On this main point, the people and the Party are united.

But we also cannot allow ingrained dogmas to cloud our eyes, to impede our progress and keep us from creatively elaborating theory and applying it in practice, in the given, concrete historical stage through which our society is passing. We cannot allow this, either.

I am saying this also because among us there are still, of course, people who have difficulty in accepting the word "restructuring" [perestroika] and who even sometimes can pronounce it only with difficulty. In this process of renewal, they often see not what it in fact contains but all but a shaking of foundations, all but a renunciation of our principles. Our political line is aimed at fully disclosing the potential and advantages of the socialist system, removing all barriers and all obstructions to our progress, and creating scope for factors of social progress.

I want to say something else. The farther we advance into restructuring, the more the complexity of this task is revealed, and the more fully the enormous scale and volume of the forthcoming work is brought out. It is becoming clearer to what extent many notions about the economy and management, social questions, statehood and democracy, upbringing and education and moral demands still lag behind today's requirements and tasks, especially the tasks of further development.

We will have to remove, layer by layer, the accumulated problems in all spheres of the life of society, freeing ourselves of what has outlived its time and boldly making creative decisions....

Sometimes people ask: Well, just what is this odd business, restructuring? How do you understand it, "what do you eat it with," this restructuring? Yes, we're all for it, some say, but we don't know what to do. Many say this straight out....

Restructuring proposes the creation of an atmosphere in society that will impel people to overcome accumulated inertia and indifference, to rid themselves, in work and in life, of everything that does not correspond to the principles of socialism, to our world views and way of life. Frankly, there is some work to be done here. But in this instance everyone must look first of all at himself, comrades—in the Politburo, in the primary Party organizations—and everyone must make a specific attempt to take himself in hand. In past years, we got used to some things in an atmosphere of insufficient criticism, openness and responsibility, things that do not all correspond to the principles of socialism. I apply this both to rank-and-file personnel and to officials....

In general, comrades, we must change our style of work. It should be permeated with respect for the people and their opinions, with real, unfeigned closeness to them. We must actually go to people, listen to them, meet with them, inform them. And the more difficult things are, the more often we must meet with them and be with them when some task or other is being accomplished. In our country, people are responsive; they are a wonderful people, you can't find another people like them. Our people have the greatest endurance. Our people have the greatest political activeness. And now it is growing. This must be welcomed and encouraged in every way. Let us consider that we have come to an agreement on this in the Khabarovsk Party organization. [*Applause.*]

In this connection, some words about public openness [glasnost]. It is sometimes said: Well, why has the Central Committee launched criticism, self-criticism and openness on such a broad scale? I can tell you that so far we have lost nothing, we have only gained. The people have felt an influx of energy; they have become bolder and more active, both at work and in public life. Furthermore, you know that all those who had been trying to circumvent our laws immediately began to quiet down. Because there is nothing stronger than the force of public opinion, when it can be put into effect. And it can be put into effect only in conditions of criticism, self-criticism and broad public openness....

Incidentally, it looks as if many local newspapers in cities and provinces are keeping quiet. The central newspapers are speaking out in full voice, supporting everything good and criticizing blunders and shortcomings. But the local papers are silent. When a group of editors assembled in the Central Committee's offices, they said bluntly: "Well, you tell this to our secretaries in the city and district Party committees." And indeed, why shouldn't people know what is going on in the district or the city? Why shouldn't they make a judgment on it and, if need be, express their opinion? This is what socialism is, comrades. Are there any editors present? [*A voice:* Yes, we're here.]

I hope that the secretaries of the city and district Party committees will take our talk into account. They are the managers. These are their newspapers. We must not be afraid of openness, comrades. We are strong, and the people are in favor of socialism, the Party's policy, changes and restructuring. In general, it is impermissible to approach openness with the yardsticks of traditional short-term campaigns. Public openness is not a one-shot measure but a norm of present-day Soviet life, a continuous, uninterrupted process during which some tasks are accomplished and new tasks—as a rule, still more complicated ones—arise. [*Applause.*]

I could say the same thing about criticism and self-criticism. If we do not criticize and analyze ourselves, what will happen? For us, this is a direct requirement, a vital necessity for purposes of the normal functioning of the Party and of society....

Source: From a speech to the Communist Party in Khabarovsk. From Alexander Dallin and Gail Lapidus, eds. *The Soviet System: From Crisis to Collapse* (Boulder: Westview Press, 1994), pp. 284–287.

Questions: What did Gorbachev intend by the policies of glasnost and perestroika? What problems was he focusing on? What aspects of Soviet politics and society did Gorbachev hope to preserve? Why did the reform movement ultimately prove incompatible with the Soviet state?

GLOBAL CONNECTIONS: The Cold War and the World

The massive competition between the West and the Soviet alliance dominated many aspects of world history between 1945 and 1992. It played a key role in other major global themes, such as decolonization and nationalism. But the competition also gave other parts of the world some breathing room, as they could play one side against the other—a contrast to previous decades in which Western imperialism had dominated.

At the same time, Western and Soviet influences were not entirely contradictory. While Western consumerism and Soviet communism were quite different, both were largely secular. Both societies emphasized science. Both societies challenged key social traditions, including purely traditional roles for women. Both eagerly sold weapons on the world market. Both could stimulate hostility to new forms of outside influence and pressures to change. These factors, too, helped shape world history for a crucial half-century.

Further Readings

Important overviews of recent European history are Walter Laqueur's *Europe Since Hitler* (1982); John Darwin's *Britain and Decolonization* (1988); Helen Wallace and others' *Policy-Making in the European Community* (1983); and Alfred Grosser's *The Western Alliance* (1982).

Some excellent national interpretations provide vital coverage of events since 1945 in key areas of Europe, including A. F. Havighurst's *Britain in Transition: The Twentieth Century* (1982) and John Ardagh's highly readable *The New French Revolution: A Social and Economic Survey of France* (1968) and *France in the 1980s* (1982). Volker Berghahn's *Modern Germany: Society, Economy and Politics in the 20th Century* (1983) is also useful.

On post–World War II social and economic trends, see C. Kindleberger, *Europe's Postwar Growth* (1967); V. Bogdanor and R. Skidelsky, eds., *The Age of Affluence, 1951–1964* (1970); R. Dahrendorf, ed., *Europe's Economy in Crisis* (1982); and Peter Stearns and Herrick Chapman, *European Society in Upheaval* (3rd ed., 1991). On the welfare state, see Stephen Cohen's *Modern Capitalist Planning: The French Model* (1977) and E. S. Einhorn and J. Logue's *Welfare States in Hard Times* (1982).

On the relevant Commonwealth nations, see Charles Doran, *Forgotten Partnership: U.S.-Canada Relations Today* (1983); Edward McWhinney, *Canada and the Constitution, 1979–1982* (1982); and Stephen Graubard, ed., *Australia: Terra Incognita?* (1985).

Postwar Soviet history is treated in Richard Barnet, *The Giants: Russia and America* (1977); A. Rubinstein, *Soviet Foreign Policy Since World War II* (1981); Alec Nove, *The Soviet Economic System* (1980); Stephen Cohen et al., eds., *The Soviet Union Since Stalin*; and Ben Eklof's *Gorbachev and the Reform Period* (1988).

On Soviet culture, Jeffrey Brooks, *Thank You, Comrade Stalin! Soviet Public Culture from Revolution to Cold War* (2000), is a cultural history of the Communist press. James von Geldern and Richard Stites, eds., *Mass Culture in Soviet Russia: Tales, Poems, Songs, Movies, Plays, and Folklore, 1917–1953* (1995), is a valuable repository of primary cultural texts and documents.

Postwar eastern Europe is treated in H. Setson Watson's *Eastern Europe Between the Wars* (1962); F. Fetjo's *History of the People's Democracies: Eastern Europe Since Stalin* (1971); J. Tampke's *The People's Republics of Eastern Europe* (1983); Timothy Ash's *The Polish Revolution: Solidarity* (1984); H. G. Skilling's *Czechoslovakia: Interrupted Revolution* (1976) (on the 1968 uprising); and B. Kovrig's *Communism in Hungary from Kun to Kadar* (1979).

A major interpretation of the communist experience is T. Skocpol's *States and Social Revolutions* (1979). On women's experiences, see Barbara Engel and Christine Worobec, eds., *Russia's Women: Accommodation, Resistance, Transformation* (1990).

On the early signs of explosion in eastern Europe, see K. Dawisha's *Eastern Europe, Gorbachev and Reform: The Great Challenge* (1988). Bohdan Nahaylo and Victor Swoboda's *Soviet Disunion: A History of the Nationalities Problem in the USSR* (1990) provides important background. See also Rose Brady's *Kapitalizm: Russia's Struggle to Free Its Economy* (1999). Joseph Rothschild's *Return to Diversity: A Political History of East Central Europe Since World War II* (3rd ed., 2000) stands as the authoritative political history. Sabrina Ramet, ed., *Eastern Europe: Politics, Culture and Society Since 1939* (1998), presents a cultural and social history survey through each country and includes a relevant bibliography.

James T. Patterson, *Grand Expectations: The United States, 1945–1974* (1996), offers a useful overview of the period. Trends in the postwar United States include the civil rights movement, movingly described in David J. Garrow's *Bearing the Cross: Martin Luther King Jr. and the Southern Leadership Conference, 1955-1968* (1986).

Transformation of America's cities is traced by Kenneth T. Jackson, *Crabgrass Frontier: The Suburbanization of the United States* (1985), and the growth of popular culture analyzed in R. Maltby, ed., *The Passing Parade: A History of Popular Culture in the Twentieth Century* (1989), and Lewis MacAdams, *The Birth of Cool: Beat, Bebop, and the American Avant-Garde* (2001). Arthur M. Schlesinger Jr., *A Thousand Days: John F. Kennedy in the White House* (1965); Doris Kearns, *Lyndon Johnson and the American Dream* (1976); and David Stockman, *The Triumph of Politics: Inside Story of the Reagan Revolution* (1987), offer accounts of American political aspirations during three key presidential administrations by authors closely identified with their subjects.

On the Web

Stalin's death heralded much political infighting (http://www.1upinfo.com/country-guide-study/soviet-union/soviet-union65.html), which eventually saw the installation of Nikita Khrushchev (http://www.cnn.com/SPECIALS/cold.war/kbank/profiles/khrushchev/). Khrushchev's famous "We will bury you" remarks are offered at http://www.em.doe.gov/timeline/nov1956.html. Soviet attacks on dissidents are noted at http://www.ibiblio.org/expo/soviet.exhibit/attack.html. The life and work of Russian cold war leader Leonid Brezhnev and the speech which established what became known as the Brezhnev Doctrine can be found at http://www.cnn.com/SPECIALS/cold.war/episodes/14/documents/doctrine/ and http://www.cnn.com/SPECIALS/cold.war/kbank/profiles/brezhnev/. Links for the study of the Soviet space program are offered at http://www.slavweb.com/eng/Russia/space-e0.html. The role of that program in the cold war is examined at http://www.pbs.org/newshour/forum/october97/sputnik_10-13.html and http://socstudy.onysd.wednet.edu/academics/istory/us/coldwar.html.

Excellent overviews of the cold war in text, images, and documents are available at http://cwihp.si.edu/, http://www.coldwar.org/, http://www.fas.harvard.edu/~hpcws/index2.htm, http://www.stmartin.edu/~dprice/cold.war.html, and http://history.acusd.edu/gen/20th/coldwar0.html. American President John F. Kennedy's famous "Ich bin ein Berliner" speech is presented in written and audio format at http://www.coldwar.org/museum/berlin_wall_exhibit.html, a site that also traces the Berlin Wall's rise and demise. The cold war's impact on American domestic politics is illuminated at http://www.spartacus.schoolnet.co.uk/USAmccarthyism.htm.

Czechoslovakia's effort to throw off the Stalinist yoke in 1968 is remembered at http://rferl.org/nca/special/invasion1968/. An overview of the later revolutions in eastern Europe that heralded the end of the Soviet Empire can be found at http://mars.acnet.wnec.edu/~grempel/courses/wc2/lectures/rev89.html.

American intervention in Latin America during the cold war is examined at http://web.mit.edu/cascon/cases/case_els.html, http://www.hartford-hwp.com/archives/47/index-ca.html, http://www.coha.org/WRH_issues/wrh_21_15_nic.htm, and http://www.hartford-hwp.com/archives/47/index-fba.html.

The National Security Archives offers audio tapes of related intelligence briefings, images of Soviet missile bases in Cuba, and minute by minute chronologies of the crisis at http://www.gwu.edu/~nsarchiv/nsa/cuba_mis_cri/.

Feminism and the place of Betty Friedan (http://womenshistory.about.com/library/qu/blqufrie.htm) in the American feminist movement left little doubt that this revolutionary effort ultimately sought the liberation of both men and women. An on-line archival site devoted to the women's liberation movement can be found at http://scriptorium.lib.duke.edu/wlm/.

CHAPTER 33

LATIN AMERICA: REVOLUTION AND REACTION INTO THE 21st CENTURY

The promise of revolutionary change produced figures like Ernesto "Che" Guevara, an Argentine who participated in the Cuban Revolution. His death in Bolivia in 1967 made him an icon of revolution, but it also demonstrated that the forces of reaction and the status quo remained strong.

- Latin America After World War II
- Radical Options in the 1950s
- VISUALIZING THE PAST: Murals and Posters: Art and Revolution
- The Search for Reform and the Military Option
- DOCUMENT: The People Speak
- IN DEPTH: Human Rights in the 20th Century
- Societies in Search of Change
- GLOBAL CONNECTIONS: Struggling Toward the Future in a Global Economy

In 1998, General Augusto Pinochet, the elderly former commander in chief of the Chilean army and virtual dictator of his country from 1974 to 1990, was arrested in London. Accusations against him for crimes against humanity had been filed in Spain that had then led to his arrest in England. In 1973, Pinochet and the army had overthrown the leftist but elected regime of President Salvador Allende, and in the brutal repression that followed, thousands of people had been killed or tortured. Pinochet and his supporters claimed he had no personal role in the abuses and that he had saved the country from anarchy and restored economic prosperity. His opponents looked on his regime as one of brutal oppression. The arrest became an international incident, and even though Pinochet was eventually released and for "reasons of health" was not forced to stand trial, some Chileans believed that at least a message had been sent to such dictators that crimes of oppression would not be tolerated or forgotten. But many Chileans, and Latin Americans in general, remained divided over what to do about the political struggles of the past. In Chile, Argentina, Brazil, Guatemala, and elsewhere, people asked if it was better to seek reconciliation and move ahead, or was it necessary to bring to justice those who had committed abuses and crimes during the political struggles of the late 20th century. The question deeply divided these societies, just as deeply as had the political struggles and alternative visions of society that had generated the conflicts originally. For Latin America, much of the century had been an era of struggle between the forces of revolution and reaction.

The focus of the previous chapter—on the West and eastern Europe—involved societies with very different 20th-century institutions and experiences but with one common bond: the experience of industrialization or its growth. The same holds true for the Pacific Rim, discussed in Chapter 35. This chapter and the next deal with societies grouped in what is sometimes called the **third world,** or developing nations, in contrast to the capitalist industrial nations of the first world and the formerly communist industrial nations of the second world. The developing nations display great diversity, depending on their political traditions—the presence or absence of revolutionary experience, for example—and on cultural emphasis. However, they all faced issues of economic development and the inequality of relating to economically more powerful societies as part of their 20th-century history.

Latin America fit the third world definition closely, despite great regional variety, but it also showed how loose this definition was. During the second half of the 20th century, Latin America continued to take an intermediate position between the nations of the North Atlantic and the developing

1940 C.E.	1960 C.E.	1980 C.E.	1990 C.E.	2000 C.E.
1942 Brazil joins Allies in World War II; sends troops to Europe	**1961** U.S.—backed invasion of Cuba is defeated	**1982** Argentina and Great Britain clash over Falkland Islands (Islas Malvinas)	**1994** Brazil stabilizes economy with new currency: the *Real*	**2000** PRI loses presidency of Mexico; Vicente Fox elected
1944–1954 Arevalo and Arbenz reforms in Guatemala	**1964** Military coup topples Brazilian government	**1983** U.S. invades Grenada	**1994** Zapatista uprising in Chiapas, Mexico	**2001** Economic collapse of Argentina
1947 Juan Péron elected president of Argentina	**1970–1973** Salvador Allende, socialist government in Chile; over-	**1989** Sandinistas lose election in Nicaragua	**1996** Return to civilian government in Guatemala	**2002** "Lula" and Workers party win Brazilian elections
1952–1964 Bolivian Revolution	thrown and assassinated by the military in 1973	**1989** United States invades Panama, deposes General Noriega	**1998** Colombian government initiates negotiations with FARC	**2003** Néstor Kirchner elected president of Argentina and one
1954 Arbenz overthrown with help from United States	**1979** Sandinista Revolution takes control in Nicaragua		guerillas but kidnappings and drug trade continue	wing of the Peronist party returns to power
1959 Castro leads revolution in Cuba			**1998** Colonel Hugo Chavez elected president in Venezuela and new constitution approved in 1999	

countries of Asia and Africa. Although Latin America shared many problems with these other developing areas, its earlier political independence and its often more Western social and political structures placed it in a distinct category. After 1945, and particularly from the 1970s onward, the Latin American elites led their nations into closer ties with the growing international capitalist economy, admittedly over increasing objections from critics within their nations. Investments and initiative often came from Europe and the United States, and Latin American economies continued to concentrate on exports. As a result, Latin America became increasingly vulnerable to changes in the world financial system. For many Latin Americans, this dependency on the markets, the financial situation, and the economic decisions made outside the region was also reflected in a political and even cultural dependency in which foreign influence and foreign models shaped all aspects of national life.

Throughout the 20th century, Latin Americans grappled with the problem of finding a basis for social justice, cultural autonomy, and economic security by adopting ideologies from abroad or by developing a specifically Latin American approach to the problem. Thus, in Latin America the struggle for decolonization has been primarily one of economic disengagement and a search for political and cultural forms appropriate to Latin American realities rather than a process of political separation and independence, as in Asia and Africa.

New groups began to appear on the political stage. Although Latin America continued its 19th-century emphasis on agrarian and mineral production, an industrial sector also grew in some places. As this movement gathered strength, workers' organizations began to emerge as a political force. Industrialization was accompanied by some emigration and by explosive urban growth in many places. A growing urban middle class linked to commerce, industry, and the expanding state bureaucracies also began to play a role in the political process.

With variation from country to country, overall the economy and the political process were subject to a series of broad shifts. There was a pattern to these shifts, with economic expansion (accompanied by conservative regimes that, although sometimes willing to make gradual reforms, hoped to maintain a political status quo) alternating with periods of economic crisis during which attempts were made to provide social justice or to break old patterns. Thus, the political pendulum swung broadly across the region and often affected several countries at roughly the same time, indicating the relationship between international trends and the internal events in these nations.

Latin Americans have long debated the nature of their societies and the need for change. Although much of the rhetoric of Latin America stressed radical reform and revolutionary change in the 20th century, the region has remained remarkably unchanged. Revolutionaries have not been lacking since 1945, but the task of defeating the existing political and social order and creating a new one on which the majority of the population will agree is difficult, especially when this must be done within an international as well as a national context. Thus, the few revolutionary political changes that have had long-term effects stand in contrast to the general trends of the region's political history. At the same time, however, significant changes in education, social services, the position of women, and the role of industry have taken place over the past several decades and have begun to transform many areas of Latin American life.

Latin America After World War II

The end of World War II was not a decisive break for Latin America, as the region had been only modestly involved, but economies had grown. Brazil had made an arrangement with the United States for help with its steel industry in return for allowing military cooperation; this furthered the process of Brazilian industrial growth so that by the 1970s Brazilian steel was competing directly with the industry in the United States. The advent of the cold war helped stimulate a new round of revolutionary agitation in Latin America, partly under Marxist inspiration and with some Soviet backing. The cold war certainly stiffened United States' response to Latin American radicalism. Decolonization, the other great postwar global current, encouraged restiveness about economic dependency, but of course Latin America had already experienced the literal decolonization process.

In 1945, several key Latin American countries were still dominated by authoritarian reformers who had responded to the impact of the Great Depression. Getulio Vargas returned to power in Brazil in 1950, with a program of populist nationalism; the state took over the petroleum industry. Juan Perón (Figure 33.1) ruled in Argentina, again with a populist platform combined with severe political repression.

A military group drove Perón from power in 1955, but the popularity of Peronism, particularly among workers, continued for two decades. This encouraged severe political measures by the military dictators, including torture and execution of opponents in what was called the "dirty war." The military government involved Argentina in a war with Britain in 1982, over the Islas Malvinas (Falkland Islands) which Britain controlled and Argentina claimed. The rulers hoped to gain nationalist support, but they lost the war and the regime was discredited.

Mexico and the PRI

For its part Mexico, in the 1940s and beyond, continued to be controlled by the Party of the Institutionalized

Figure 33.1   *The populist politics of Juan Perón and his wife Evita brought new forces, especially urban workers, into Argentine politics. Their personal charisma attracted support from groups formerly excluded from politics but eventually led to opposition from the Argentine military and Perón's overthrow in 1955.*

in negotiations for the North American Free Trade Agreement (NAFTA), hoping to spur Mexican industry. Results remained unclear by 2003, though trade with the United States did increase, amid Mexican fears of loss of economic control and amid a growing gap between a sizeable middle class and the very poor, including most of Mexico's Indians. Finally in 2000, a national election ended the PRI political monopoly. Vicente Fox, leader of the conservative PAN party, became president, on a platform of cleaning up corruption and improving conditions for Mexican workers in the United States. Again, long-term results remained unclear.

Radical Options in the 1950s

 In the immediate aftermath of World War II, with several key Latin American nations dominated by earlier political patterns, the most important innovation involved a new surge of radical unrest in several smaller countries, which is where the cold war framework quickly came into play. Frustration with the failures of social, political, and economic reforms led to radical solutions that were often influenced by socialist ideas. In Bolivia, Guatemala, and Cuba, revolutionaries tried to change the nature of government and society, but such changes also had to accommodate the reality of the cold war and the interests of the United States.

Revolution, or **PRI** (see Figure 33.2). By the last decades of the 20th century, the stability provided by the PRI's control of politics was undercut by corruption and a lack of social improvement. Many Mexicans believed that little remained of the revolutionary principles of the 1910 revolution. Charges of corruption and repression mounted for several decades. In 1994 an armed guerrilla movement burst forth in the heavily Indian southern state of Chiapas (Figure 33.3). Calling themselves **Zapatistas** in honor of Emiliano Zapata, the peasant leader in the 1910 revolution, the movement showed how key social issues remained unresolved. The Mexican government responded with a combination of repression and negotiation. Also in the 1990s the government joined

The Argentine and Brazilian changes begun by Perón and Vargas were symptomatic of the continuing problems of Latin America, but their personalistic authoritarian solutions were only one possible response. By the 1940s, pressure for change had built up through much of Latin America. Across the political spectrum there was a desire to improve the social and economic conditions throughout the region and a general agreement that development and economic strength were the keys to a better future. How to achieve those goals remained in question, however. In Mexico, as we have seen, one-party rule continued, and the "revolution" became increasingly conservative and interested in economic growth rather than social justice. In a few countries, such as Venezuela and Costa Rica, reform-minded democratic parties were able to win elections in an open political system. In other places, such a solution was less

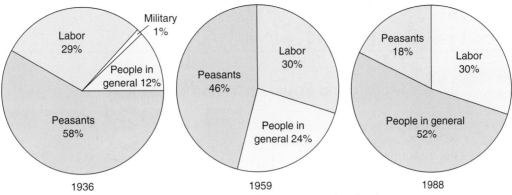

Figure 33.2 *Participation in Mexico's PRI: These graphs reflect party membership by sectors. Note that the population shifted away from rural areas and that labor remained fairly steady.*

likely or less attractive to those who wanted reform. Unlike the Mexican revolutionaries of 1910–1920, those seeking change in the post–World War II period could turn to the well-developed political philosophy of Marxian socialism as a guide. However, such models were fraught with dangers because of the context of the cold war and the ideological struggle between western Europe and the Soviet bloc.

Throughout Latin America, the failures of political democratization, economic development, and social reforms led to consideration of radical and revolution-

ary solutions to national problems. In some cases, the revolutions at first were successful but ultimately were unable to sustain the changes. In predominantly Indian Bolivia, where as late as 1950 90 percent of the land was owned by 6 percent of the population, a revolution erupted in 1952 in which miners, peasants, and urban middle-class groups participated. Although mines were nationalized and some land redistributed, fear of moving too far to the left brought the army back into power in 1964, and subsequent governments remained more interested in order than in reform.

Figure 33.3 *Zapatistas mobilized in Chiapas, one of Mexico's poorest states, and have been able to resist government suppression.*

Visualizing the Past

Murals and Posters: Art and Revolution

Public art for political purposes has been used since ancient Egypt, but with the development of lithography (a color printing process), the poster emerged as a major form of communication. First developed in the late 19th century as a cheap form of advertising using image and text to sell soap, wine, or chocolate or to advertise dance halls and theaters, by the 1880s posters were adapted to political purposes, and in World War I all the major combatants used them. But those opposed to governments could also use posters to convey a revolutionary message to a broad public. In Latin America, the Mexican Revolution made use of public art in great murals, but these were often expensive and took a long time to complete. Both the Cuban Revolution of the 1960s and the Nicaraguan Revolution of the 1980s turned to the poster as a way to convey its policies and goals to a broad public.

Questions: What are the advantages of the poster over the mural, and vice versa? Is poster art really art? Why are images of the past often the subjects of revolutionary art? To whom is political art usually directed?

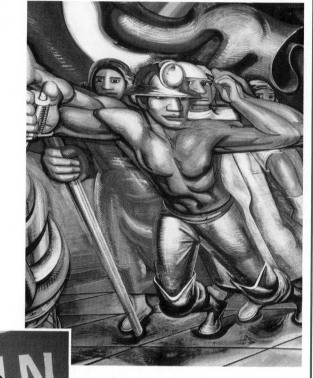

Guatemala: Reform and United States Intervention

The first place where more radical solutions were tried was Guatemala. This predominantly Indian nation had some of the worst of the region's prob-lems. Its population was mostly illiterate and suffered poor health conditions and high mortality rates. Land and wealth were distributed very unequally, and the whole economy depended on the highly volatile prices for its main exports of coffee and bananas. In

1944, a coalition of middle-class and labor elected a reformer, **Juan José Arevalo,** as president. Under a new constitution, he began a series of programs within the context of "spiritual socialism" that included land reform and an improvement in the rights and conditions of rural and industrial workers. An income tax, the first in the nation's history, was projected and educational reforms were planned. These programs and Arevalo's sponsorship of an intense nationalism brought the Arevalo government into direct conflict with foreign interests operating in Guatemala, especially the **United Fruit Company,** the largest and most important foreign concern there, which controlled extensive properties, transportation, and shipping facilities.

In 1951, after a free election, the presidency passed to Colonel Jacobo Arbenz, whose nationalist program was more radical and whose public statements against foreign economic interests and the landholding oligarchy were more extreme than those of Arevalo. Arbenz announced several programs to improve or nationalize the transportation network, the hydroelectric system, and other areas of the economy. A move to expropriate unused lands on large estates in 1953 provoked opposition from the landed oligarchy and from United Fruit, which eventually was threatened with the loss of almost half a million acres of reserve land. The U.S. government, fearing "communist" penetration of the Arbenz government and under considerable pressure from the United Fruit Company, denounced the changes and began to impose economic and diplomatic restrictions on Guatemala. At the same time, the level of nationalist rhetoric intensified, and the government increasingly received the support of the political left in Latin America and in the socialist bloc.

In 1954, with the help of the U.S. Central Intelligence Agency, a dissident military force was organized and invaded Guatemala. The Arbenz government fell, and the pro-American regime that replaced it turned back the land reform and negotiated a settlement favorable to United Fruit. The reform experiment was thus brought to a halt. By the standards of the 1960s and later, the programs of Arevalo and Arbenz seem rather mild, although Arbenz's statements and supposedly his acceptance of arms from eastern Europe undoubtedly contributed to U.S. intervention.

The reforms promised by the United States–supported governments were minimal. Guatemala continued to have a low standard of living, especially for its Indian population. The series of military governments after the coup failed to address the nation's social and economic problems. That failure led to continual violence and political instability. Political life continued to be controlled by a coalition of coffee planters, foreign companies, and the military. A guerrilla movement grew and provoked brutal military repression, which fell particularly hard on the rural Indian population. Guatemala's attempt at radical change, an attempt that began with an eye toward improving the conditions of the people, failed because of external intervention. The failure was a warning that change would not come without internal and foreign opposition.

The Cuban Revolution: Socialism in the Caribbean

The differences between Cuba and Guatemala underline the diversity of Latin America and the dangers of partial revolutions. The island nation had a population of about 6 million, most of whom were the descendants of Spaniards and the African slaves who had been imported to produce the sugar, tobacco, and hides that were the colony's mainstays. Cuba had a large middle class, and its literacy and health care levels were better than in most of the rest of the region. Rural areas lagged behind in these matters, however, and there the working and living conditions were poor, especially for the workers on the large sugar estates. Always in the shadow of the United States, Cuban politics and economy were rarely free of American interests. By the 1950s, about three-fourths of what Cuba imported came from the United States. American investments in the island were heavy during the 1940s and 1950s. Although the island experienced periods of prosperity, fluctuations in the world market for Cuba's main product, sugar, revealed the tenuous basis of the economy. Moreover, the disparity between the countryside and the growing middle class in Havana underlined the nation's continuing problems.

From 1934 to 1944, **Fulgencio Batista,** a strong-willed, authoritarian reformer who had risen through the lower ranks of the army, ruled Cuba. Among his reforms were a democratic constitution of 1940 that promised major changes, nationalization of natural resources, full employment, and land reform. However, Batista's programs of reform were marred by corruption, and when in 1952 he returned to the presidency, there was little left of the reformer but a great deal of the dictator. Opposition developed in various sectors of the society. Among the regime's opponents was **Fidel Castro,** a young lawyer experienced in leftist university politics and an ardent critic of the Batista government and the ills of Cuban society. On July 26, 1953, Castro and a few followers launched an unsuccessful attack on some military barracks. Captured, Castro faced a trial, an occasion he used to expound his revolutionary ideals, aimed mostly at a return to democracy, social justice, and the establishment of a less dependant economy.

Released from prison, Castro fled to exile in Mexico where, with the aid of **Ernesto "Che" Guevara,** a militant Argentine revolutionary, he gathered a small military force. They landed in Cuba in 1956 and slowly began to gather strength in the mountains. By 1958, the "26th of July Movement" had found support from students, some labor organizations, and rural workers and was able to conduct operations against Batista's army. The bearded rebels, or *barbudos,* won a series of victories. The dictator, under siege and isolated by the United States (which because of his excesses refused to support him any longer), was driven from power, and the rebels took Havana amid wild scenes of joy and relief (Figure 33.4).

What happened next is highly debatable, and Castro himself has offered alternative interpretations at different times. Whether Castro was already a Marxist–Leninist and had always intended to introduce a socialist regime (as he now claims) or whether the development of this program was the result of a series of pragmatic decisions is in question. Rather than simply returning to the constitution of 1940 and enacting moderate reforms, Castro launched a program of sweeping change. Foreign properties were expropriated, farms were collectivized, and a centralized socialist economy was put in place. Most of these changes were accompanied by a nationalist and anti-imperialist foreign policy. Relations with the United States were broken off in 1961, and Cuba increasingly depended on the financial support and arms of the Soviet Union to maintain its revolution. With that support in place, Castro was able to survive the increasingly hostile reaction of the United States. That reaction included a disastrous United States–sponsored invasion by Cuban exiles in 1961 and an embargo on trade with Cuba. Dependence on the Soviet Union led to a crisis in 1961, when Soviet nuclear missiles, perhaps placed in Cuba in case of another U.S. invasion, were discovered and a con-

Figure 33.4 *Fidel Castro and his guerrilla army brought down the Batista government in January 1959, to the wild acclaim of many Cubans. Castro initiated sweeping reforms in Cuba that eventually led to the creation of a socialist regime and the hostility of the United States.*

frontation between the superpowers ensued. Despite these problems, to a large extent the Cuban Revolution survived because the politics of the cold war provided Cuba with a protector and a benefactor.

The results of the revolution have been mixed. The social programs were extensive. Education, health, and housing have improved greatly and rank Cuba among the world's leaders—quite unlike most other nations of the region. This is especially true in the long-neglected rural areas. A wide variety of social and educational programs have mobilized all sectors of the population. The achievements have been accompanied by severe restrictions of basic freedoms.

Attempts to diversify and strengthen the economy have been less successful. An effort to industrialize in the 1960s failed, and Cuba turned again to its ability to produce sugar. The world's falling sugar and rising petroleum prices led to disaster. Only by subsidizing Cuban sugar and supplying petroleum below the world price could the Soviet Union maintain the Cuban economy. Since the breakup of the Soviet Union in the 1990s, the Cuban situation has deteriorated; along with China, the island has become one of the last socialist bastions.

Despite these problems, the Cuban Revolution offered an example that has proved attractive to those seeking to transform Latin American societies. Early direct attempts to spread the model of the Cuban Revolution, such as Che Guevara's guerrilla operation in Bolivia, where he lost his life in 1967, were failures, but the Cuban model and the island's ability to resist the pressure of a hostile United States has proved attractive to other nations in the Caribbean and Central America, such as Grenada and Nicaragua, that have also exercised the revolutionary option. U.S. reaction to such movements has been containment or intervention.

The Search for Reform and the Military Option

Programs based in Catholic, Marxist, and capitalist doctrines continued to seek solutions to Latin America's problems. Military governments in the 1960s and 1970s based on nationalism and advocating economic development created new "bureaucratic authoritarian" regimes, which for a while served the cold war interests of the United States. By the 1980s a new wave of democratic regimes was emerging.

The revolutionary attempts of the 1950s, the durability of the Cuban Revolution, and the general appeal of Marxist doctrines in developing nations underlined Latin America's tendency to undertake revolutionary change that left its economic and social structures unchanged. How could the traditional patterns of inequality and international dependency be overcome? What was the best path to the future?

For some, the answer was political stability, imposed if necessary, to promote capitalist economic growth. The one-party system of Mexico demonstrated its capacity for repression when student dissidents were brutally killed during disturbances in 1968. Mexico enjoyed some prosperity from its petroleum resources in the 1970s, but poor financial planning, corruption, and foreign debt again caused problems by the 1980s, and the PRI seemed

to be losing its ability to maintain control of Mexican politics.

For others, the church, long a power in Latin America, provided a guide. Christian Democratic parties formed in Chile and Venezuela in the 1950s, hoping to bring reforms through popularly based mass parties that would preempt the radical left. The church often was divided politically, but the clergy took an increasingly engaged position and argued for social justice and human rights, often in support of government opponents. A few, such as Father Camilo Torres in Colombia, actually joined armed revolutionary groups in the 1960s.

More common was the emergence within the church hierarchy of an increased concern for social justice (see Figure 33.5). By the 1970s, a **liberation theology** combined Catholic theology and socialist principles or used Marxist categories for understanding

Figure 33.5 *The right to a secure life became the goal of many political movements. Here, in a church-sponsored demonstration in São Paulo, Brazil, women and men seek "Land and Peace for All Peoples."*

Document

The People Speak

Scholarly analysis of general trends often cannot convey the way in which historical events and patterns affect the lives of people or the fact that history is made up of the collective experience of individuals. It is often very difficult to know about the lives of common people in the past or to learn about their perceptions of their lives. In recent years in Latin America, however, a growing literature of autobiographies, interpreted autobiographies (in which another writer puts the story down and edits it), and collections of interviews have provided a vision of the lives of common people. These statements, like any historical document, must be used carefully because their authors or editors sometimes have political purposes, because they reflect individual opinions, or because the events they report may be atypical. Nevertheless, these personal statements put flesh and blood on the bones of history and provide an important perspective from those whose voice in history often is lost.

A Bolivian Woman Describes Her Life

Domitilia Barrios de Chungara was a miner's wife who became active in the mine workers' political movement. Her presence at the United Nations–sponsored International Woman's Year Tribunal in 1975 moved a Brazilian journalist to organize her statements into a book about her life. This excerpt provides a picture of her everyday struggle for life.

My day begins at four in the morning, especially when my compañero is on the first shift. I prepare his breakfast. Then I have to prepare salteñas [small meat pastries] because I make about one hundred salteñas every day and I sell them on the street. I do this in order to make up for what my husband's wage doesn't cover in terms of our necessities. The night before, we prepare the dough and at four in the morning I make the salteñas while I feed the kids. The kids help me.

Then the ones that go to school in the morning have to get ready, while I wash the clothes left soaking over night.

At eight I go out to sell. The kids that go to school in the afternoon help me. We have to go to the company store and bring home the staples. And in the store there are immensely long lines and you have to wait there until eleven in order to stock up. You have to line up for meat, for vegetables, for oil. So it's just one line after another. Since everything is in a different place, that's how it has to be.

From what we earn between my husband and me, we can eat and dress. Food is very expensive: 28 pesos for a kilo of meat, 4 pesos for carrots, 6 pesos for onions.... Considering that my compañero earns 28 pesos a day, that's hardly enough is it?

We don't ever buy ready made clothes. We buy wool and knit. At the beginning of each year, I also spend about 2,000 pesos on cloth and a pair of shoes for each of us. And the company discounts some of that each month from my husband's wage. On the pay slips that's referred to as the "bundle." And what happens is that before we finish paying the "bundle" our shoes are worn out. That's how it is.

Well, from eight to eleven in the morning I sell the salteñas. I do the shopping in the grocery store, and I also work at the Housewives Committee talking with the sisters who go there for advice.

At noon, lunch has to be ready because the rest of the kids have to go to school.

In the afternoon I have to wash clothes. There are no laundries. We use troughs and have to get the water from a pump.

I've got to correct the kids' homework and prepare everything I'll need to make the next day's salteñas.

From Peasant to Revolutionary

Rigoberta Menchú, a Quiché Indian from the Guatemalan highlands, came from a peasant family that had been drawn into politics during the repression of Indian communities and human rights in the 1970s. In these excerpts, she reveals her disillusionment with the government and her realization of the ethnic division between Indians and ladinos, or mestizos, that complicates political action in Guatemala.

The CUC [Peasant Union] started growing; it spread like wildfire among the peasants in Guatemala. We began to understand that the root of all our problems was exploitation. That there were rich and poor and that the rich exploited the poor—our sweat, our labor. That's how the rich got richer and richer. The fact that we were always waiting in offices, always bowing to the authorities was part of the discrimination that we Indians suffered.

The situation got worse when the murderous generals came to power although I did not actually know who was the president at the time. I began to know them from 1974 when General Kjell Langerud came to power. He came to our region and said: "We're going to solve the land problem. The land belongs to you. You cultivate the land and I will share it out among you." We trusted him.

I was at the meeting when [he] spoke. And what did he give us? My father tortured and imprisoned.

Later I had the opportunity of meeting other Indians. Achi Indians, the group that lives closest to us. And I got to know some Mam Indians too. They all told me: "The rich are bad. But not all ladinos are bad." And I started wondering: Could it be that not all ladinos are Achi Indians, the group that lives closest to us? And I know some Mam Indians too. They all told me: "The rich are bad."...There were poor ladinos as well as rich ladinos, and they were exploited as well. That's when I began recognizing exploitation. I kept on going to the finca [large farm] but now I really wanted to find out, to prove if that was true and learn the details. There were poor ladinos on the finca. They worked the same, and their children's bellies were swollen like my little brother's.... I was just beginning to speak a little Spanish in those days and I began to talk to them. I said to one poor ladino: "You are a poor ladino, aren't you?" And he nearly hit me. He said: "What do you know about it, Indian!" I wondered: "Why

is that when I say poor ladinos are like us, I'm spurned?" I didn't know then that the same system which tries to isolate us Indians also puts barriers between Indians and ladinos.... Soon afterwards, I was with the nuns and we went to a village in Uspantán where mostly ladinos live. The nun asked a little boy if they were poor and he said: "Yes, we're poor but we're not Indians." That stayed with me. The nun didn't notice, she went on talking. She was foreign, she wasn't Guatemalan. She asked someone else the same question and he said: "Yes, we're poor but we're not Indians." It was very painful for me to accept that an Indian was inferior to a ladino. I kept on worrying about it. It's a big barrier they've sown between us, between Indian and ladino. I didn't understand it.

Questions: What was distinctive about lower-class life and outlook in late 20th-century Latin America? How had lower-class life changed since the 19th century?

society in an effort to improve conditions for the poor. Liberation theologians stressed social equality as a form of personal salvation. When criticized for promoting communism in his native Brazil, Dom Helder da Camara, archbishop of Pernambuco, remarked, "The trouble with Brazil is not an excess of communist doctrine but a lack of Christian justice." The position of the Catholic church in Latin American societies was changing, but there was no single program for this new stance or even agreement among the clergy about its validity. Still, this activist position provoked attacks against clergy such as the courageous Archbishop Oscar Romero of El Salvador, who was assassinated in 1980 for speaking out for social reform, and even against nuns involved in social programs. The church, however, played an important role in the fall of the Paraguayan dictatorship in 1988.

Out of the Barracks: Soldiers Take Power

The success of the Cuban Revolution impressed and worried those who feared revolutionary change within a communist political system. The military forces in Latin America had been involved in politics since the days of the caudillos in the 19th century, and in several nations military interventions had been common. As the Latin American military became more professionalized, however, a new philosophy underlay the military's involvement in politics. The soldiers began

to see themselves as above the selfish interests of political parties and as the true representatives of the nation. With technical training and organizational skills, military officers by the 1920s and 1930s believed that they were best equipped to solve their nations' problems, even if that meant sacrificing the democratic process and imposing martial law.

In the 1960s, the Latin American military establishments, made nervous by the Cuban success and the swing to leftist or populist regimes, began to intervene directly in the political process, not simply to clean out a disliked president or party, as they had done in the past, but to take over government itself. In 1964, the Brazilian military (with the support of the United States and the Brazilian middle class) overthrew the elected president after he threatened to make sweeping social reforms. In Argentina, growing polarization between the Peronists and the middle class led to a military intervention in 1966. In 1973 the Chilean military, which until then had remained for the most part out of politics, overthrew the socialist government of President **Salvador Allende.** He had nationalized industries and banks and had sponsored peasant and worker expropriations of lands and factories. His government was caught in an increasing polarization between groups trying to halt these changes and those pushing for faster and more radical reforms. By 1973, the economy was in serious difficulty, undermined by resistance in Chile and by U.S. policies designed to isolate the country.

Allende was killed during the military coup against him, and throughout Latin America there were demonstrations against the military and U.S. involvement. But Chile was not alone. Similar coups took place in Uruguay in 1973 and in Peru in 1968.

The soldiers in power imposed a new type of bureaucratic authoritarian regime. Their governments were supposed to stand above the competing demands of various sectors and establish economic stability. Now, as arbiters of politics, the soldiers would place the national interest above selfish interests by imposing dictatorships. Government was essentially a presidency, controlled by the military, in which policies were formulated and applied by a bureaucracy organized like a military chain of command. Political repression and torture were used to silence critics, and stringent measures were imposed to control inflation and strengthen the economies. Laws limited political freedoms, and repression often was brutal and illegal. In Argentina, violent opposition to military rule led to a counteroffensive and the "dirty war" in which thousands of people "disappeared."

Government economic policies fell heaviest on the working class. The goal of the military in Brazil and Argentina was development. To some extent, in Brazil at least, economic improvements were achieved, although income distribution became even more unequal than it had been. Inflation was reduced, industrialization increased, and gains were made in literacy and health, but basic structural problems such as land ownership and social conditions for the poorest people remained unchanged.

There were variations within these military regimes, but all were nationalistic. The Peruvian military tried to create a popular base for its programs and to mobilize support among the peasantry. It had a real social program, including extensive land reform, and was not simply a surrogate for the conservatives in Peruvian society. In Chile and Uruguay, the military was fiercely anticommunist. In Argentina, nationalism and a desire to gain popular support in the face of a worsening economy led to a confrontation with Great Britain over the Falkland Islands (Islas Malvinas), which both nations claimed. The war stimulated pride in Argentina and its soldiers and sailors, but defeat caused a loss of the military's credibility.

The New Democratic Trends

In Argentina and elsewhere in South America, by the mid-1980s the military had begun to return government to civilian politicians. Continuing economic problems and the pressures of containing opponents wore heavily on the military leaders, who began to realize that their solutions were no more destined to success than those of civilian governments. Moreover, the populist parties, such as the Peronists and Apristas, seemed less of a threat, and the fear of Cuban-style communism had diminished. Also, the end of the cold war meant that the United States was less interested in sponsoring regimes that, though "safe," were also repressive. In Argentina, elections were held in 1983. Brazil began to restore democratic government after 1985 and in 1989 chose its first popularly elected president since the military takeover. The South American military bureaucrats and modernizers were returning to their barracks.

The process of redemocratization was not easy, nor was it universal. In Peru, Sendero Luminoso (Shining Path), a long-sustained leftist guerrilla movement, controlled areas of the countryside and tried to disrupt national elections in 1990. In Central America, the military cast a long shadow over the government in El Salvador, but return to civilian government took place in 1992. In Nicaragua, the elections of 1990, held under threat of a U.S. embargo, removed the **Sandinista party** from control in Nicaragua. In subsequent elections the party of the Sandinistas could still muster much support, but it could not win back the presidency. The trend toward a return to electoral democracy could be seen in Guatemala as well. By 1996 civilian government had returned to Guatemala as the country struggled to overcome the history of repression and rebellion and the animosities they had created. The United States demonstrated its continuing power in the region in its invasion of Panama and the arrest of its strongman leader, Manuel Noriega.

Latin American governments in the last decades of the 20th century faced tremendous problems. Large foreign loans taken in the 1970s for the purpose of development, sometimes for unnecessary projects, had created a tremendous level of debt that threatened the economic stability of countries such as Brazil, Peru, and Mexico. In 2002, the Argentine government defaulted on its debt and faced economic crisis. High rates of inflation provoked social instability as real wages fell. Pressure from the international banking community to curb inflation by cutting government spending and reducing wages often ignored the social and political consequences of such actions. An international commerce in drugs, which produced tremendous profits, stimulated criminal activity and created powerful international cartels that could even threaten national sovereignty. In Colombia a leftist guerilla movement controlled large areas of the country and funded itself from the drug trade. In countries as diverse as Cuba, Panama, and Bolivia, the narcotics trade penetrated the highest government circles.

But despite the problems, the 1990s seemed to demonstrate that the democratic trends were well established. In Central America there was a return to civilian government. In Venezuela and Brazil, corruption in government led to the fall of presidents and as we have mentioned led to a major political change in Mexico in 2000. In Brazil, a leftist working-class presidential candidate, Lula (Luiz Inacio Lula da Silva), was elected in 2002. More radical options were also still possible. In Colombia the insurgency continued to threaten the nation's stability; in Venezuela, a populist military leader survived a coup in 2002 and threatened to move the country toward a more independent foreign policy. In other countries the military was sometimes troublesome, but a commitment to a more open political system in most of the region seemed firm.

The United States and Latin America: Continuing Presence

As a backdrop to the political and economic story we have traced thus far stands the continuing presence of the United States. After World War I, the United States emerged as the predominant power in the hemisphere, a position it had already begun to assume at the end of the 19th century with the Cuban–Spanish–American War and the building of the Panama Canal. European nations were displaced as the leading investors in Latin America by the United States. In South America, private investments by American companies and entrepreneurs, as well as loans from the American government, were the chief means of U.S. influence. U.S. investments rose to more than $5 billion by 1929, or more than one-third of all U.S. investments abroad.

Cuba and Puerto Rico experienced direct United States involvement and almost a protectorate status. But in the Caribbean and Central America, the face of U.S. power, economic interest, and disregard for the sovereignty of weaker neighbors was most apparent. Military interventions to protect United States–owned properties and investments became so common that there were more than 30 before 1933 (see Map 33.1). Haiti, Nicaragua, the Dominican

Republic, Mexico, and Cuba all experienced direct interventions by U.S. troops. Central America was a peculiar case because the level of private investments by U.S. companies such as United Fruit was very high and the economies of these countries were so closely tied to the United States. Those who resisted the U.S. presence were treated as bandits by expeditionary forces. In Nicaragua, **Augusto Sandino** led a resistance movement against occupying troops until his assassination by the United States–trained Nicaraguan National Guard in 1934. His struggle against U.S. intervention made him a hero and later the figurehead of the Sandinista party, which carried out a socialist revolution in Nicaragua in the 1980s.

The grounds for these interventions were economic, political, strategic, and ideological. The direct interventions usually were followed by the creation or support of conservative governments, often dictatorships that would be friendly to the United States. These became known as **banana republics,** a reference not only to their dependence on the export of tropical products but also to their often subservient and corrupt governments.

Foreign interventions contributed to a growing nationalist reaction. Central America with its continuing political problems became a symbol of Latin America's weakness in the face of foreign influence and interference, especially by the United States. The Nobel Prize–winning Chilean communist poet Pablo Neruda, in his poem "The United Fruit Co." (1950), spoke of the dictators of Central America as "circus flies, wise flies, learned in tyranny" who buzzed over the graves of the people. He wrote the following eight lines with passion:

> When the trumpet sounded, all was prepared in the land,
> and Jehovah divided the world between Coca Cola Inc.,
> Anaconda, Ford Motors, and other companies:
> United Fruit Co. reserved for itself the juiciest part,
> the central coast of my land,
> the sweet waist of America
> and baptized again its lands
> as Banana Republics.

The actions of the United States changed for a time after 1933. In that year, president Franklin D.

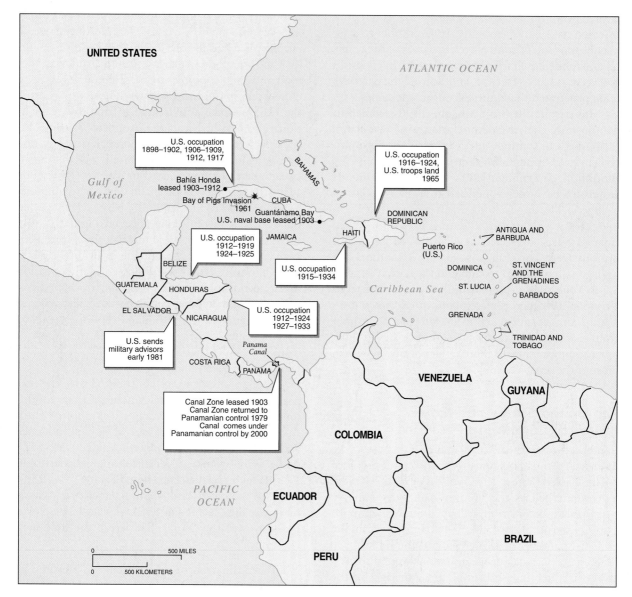

Map 33.1 *U.S. Intervention in Central America and the Caribbean, 1898–1981*

Roosevelt introduced the **Good Neighbor Policy,** which promised to deal more fairly with Latin America and to stop direct interventions. After World War II, however, the U.S. preoccupation with containment of the Soviet Union and communism as an ideology led to new strategies in Latin America. They included participation in regional organizations, the support of governments that at least expressed democratic or anticommunist principles, the covert undermining of governments considered unfriendly to U.S. interests, and, when necessary, direct intervention. Underlying much of this policy was also a firm belief that economic development would eliminate the conditions that contributed to radical political solutions. Thus, U.S. programs such as the **Alliance for Progress,** begun in 1961, aimed to develop the region as an alternative to those solutions. The alliance had limited success despite good intentions and more than $10 billion in aid, but many Latin Americans perceived that it benefited the elites rather

In Depth

Human Rights in the 20th Century

In Latin America, the question of human rights became a burning issue in the 1960s and continued thereafter. The use of torture by repressive governments, the mobilization of death squads and other vigilante groups with government acquiescence, and the use of terrorism against political opponents by the state and by groups opposed to the state became all too common in the region. Latin America's record on the violation of human rights was no worse than that of some other areas of the world. However, the demonstrations by the Argentine "Mothers of the Plaza del Mayo" to focus attention on their disappeared children; the publication of prison memoirs recounting human rights violations in Brazil, Cuba, and Argentina; and films dramatizing events such as the assassination of Archbishop Oscar Romero in El Salvador have all focused attention on the problem in Latin America. Moreover, because Latin America shares in the cultural heritage of Western societies, it is difficult to make an argument that human rights there have a different meaning or importance than in Europe or North America.

The concept of human rights—that is, certain universal rights enjoyed by all people because they are justified by a moral standard that stands above the laws of any individual nation—may go back to ancient Greece. The concept of natural law and the protection of religious or ethnic minorities also moved nations in the 19th century toward a defense of human rights. To some extent, the international movement to abolish the slave trade was an early human rights movement. In modern times, however, the concept of human rights has been strongly attached to the foundation of the United Nations. In 1948, that body, with the experience of World War II in mind, issued a Universal Declaration of Human Rights and created a commission to oversee the human rights situation. The Universal Declaration, which guaranteed basic liberties and freedoms regardless of color, sex, or religion, proclaimed that it should be the "common standard for all peoples and nations." However, one critic has stated that of the 160 nations in the United Nations, only about 30 have a consistently good record on human rights.

A major problem for the international community has been enforcing the Universal Declaration. The United Nations commission did not have any specific powers of enforcement, and much debate has taken place on the power of the United Nations to intervene in the internal affairs of any nation. More recently, various regional organizations have tried to establish the norms that should govern human rights and to create institutions to enforce these norms.

One specialist has claimed that "human rights is the world's first universal ideology." The defense of human rights seems to be a cause that most people and governments can accept without hesitation, but the question is complex. Although the rights to life, liberty, security, and freedom from torture or degrading punishment are generally accepted in principle by all nations, other rights remain open to question. What is a right, and to what extent are definitions of rights determined by culture?

The question of universality versus relativism emerged quickly in the debate over human rights. What seemed to be obvious human rights in Western societies were less obvious in other parts of the world, where other priorities were held. For example, laws prohibiting child labor were enforced by most Western societies, but throughout the world perhaps 150 million children worked, often in unhealthy and exploitive conditions. They worked because of economic necessity in many cases, but in some societies such labor was considered moral and proper. Such cultural differences have led to a position of relativism, which recognizes that there are profound cultural variations in what is considered moral and just. Critics of the original Universal Declaration contend that its advocacy of the right to own property and the right to vote imposed Western political and economic values as universals. Cultural relativism had the advantage of recognizing the variety of cultures and standards in the world, but it has also been used as a shield to deflect criticism and to excuse the continued violation of human rights.

The definition of human rights is also political. The West emphasizes the civil and political rights of the individual. The socialist nations place social and economic justice above individual rights, although by the 1990s movements in eastern Europe and China indicated that there was pressure to modify this approach. In the developing nations, an argument for peoples' rights has emerged in which the "right to development," which calls for a major structural redistribution of the world's resources and economic opportunities, is a central concept. As Léopold Senghor of

(continued)

Senegal put it, "Human rights begin with breakfast"; or as a report on Ghana stated, "'One man, one vote' is meaningless unless accompanied by the principle of 'one man, one bread.'" Whereas developing nations view the right to development as a human right, it is viewed as a political and economic demand in wealthier nations of the West.

Another dimension of human rights is the extent to which it influences national foreign policies. Governments may make statements pledging respect for human rights in their foreign policies, but considerations of national defense, sovereignty, or other goals often move human rights concerns into a secondary position. Disputes over the role of human rights in foreign policy sometimes are posed as a conflict between "moralistic utopians" who see the world as it should be and "pragmatists" who see the world as it is. Neither approach necessarily denies the importance of human rights, but there are differences in priority and strategy. Pragmatists might argue that it is better to maintain relations with a nation violating human rights in order to be able to exercise some influence over it in the future, or that other policy considerations must be weighed along with those of human rights in establishing foreign policy. Moralists would prefer to bring pressure by isolating and condemning a nation that violates international standards.

These different approaches have been reflected in the U.S. policy shifts toward Latin America. In the 1950s, human rights considerations were secondary to opposing the spread of communism in the hemisphere, and the United States was willing to support governments that violated human rights as long as they were anticommunist allies. During the 1960s,

this policy continued, but increasing and systematic abuses by military regimes in Brazil, Uruguay, Chile, Nicaragua, and elsewhere in Latin America began to elicit some changes. In 1977, President Carter initiated a new policy in which human rights considerations would be given high priority in U.S. foreign policy. The U.S. refusal to support or aid governments that violated human rights contributed to the weakening of some regimes and stimulated resistance to human rights violations in Latin America, but by the 1980s a more pragmatic approach had returned to U.S. policy. Criticism of human rights violations sometimes was made selectively, and abuses in "friendly" governments were dismissed. The extent to which human rights concerns must be balanced against issues such as security, the maintenance of peace, and nonintervention continues to preoccupy policymakers.

Attention to human rights will continue to play an important role in international affairs. Problems of definition still remain, and there is no universal agreement on the exact nature of human rights. Controversy on the weight of political and civil rights and social, cultural, and economic rights continues to divide richer and poorer nations. Still, the United Nations Declaration of Human Rights, to which 160 nations are signatories, provides a basic guide and an outline for the future.

Questions: Why might various regimes oppose human rights, and on what basis? Is the human rights movement a Western replacement for imperialism as a way to exert international political influence? Have international human rights movements produced political change?

than the poor. Because of its record, Latin Americans and North Americans both began to question the assumption that development was basically a problem of capital and resources and that appropriate strategies would lead to social and economic improvement, which in turn would forestall revolution.

During the 1970s and 1980s, U.S. policy often was pragmatic, accepting Latin America as it was, which meant dealing on friendly terms with the military dictatorships. President Jimmy Carter (1976–1980) made a new initiative to deal with Latin America and to influence governments there to observe civil liberties. Most significantly, a treaty was

signed with Panama that ceded to that nation eventual control of the Panama Canal.

Increasing violence in Central America in the 1980s and the more conservative presidencies of Ronald Reagan and George Bush led the United States back to policies based on strategic, economic, and defense considerations in which direct intervention or support of counterrevolutionary forces played a part. Thus, in 1989 and 1990, the United States toppled a government in Panama that was authoritarian, defied U.S. policies, and controlled drug smuggling, replacing it with a cooperative regime backed by American troops.

Societies in Search of Change

 Social relations changed slowly in Latin America. Inequalities based on ethnicity continued in some places. Women had entered the labor force in large numbers but began to gain the vote only after 1929. However, their status was in many ways closer to that of women in western Europe than to those of Asia or Africa. Population growth, urbanization, and the migration of workers continued to challenge the region as both politicians and artists tried to identify and confront persistent problems.

Despite frustrated Latin American attempts at profound reform, there were great changes during the 20th century. Social and gender relations changed during the century. We have already seen how countries such as Mexico, Peru, and Bolivia sought to enfranchise their Indian populations during this century in different ways and with differing degrees of success. National ideologies and actual practice often are not the same, and discrimination on the basis of ethnicity continues. To be called Indian is still an insult in many places in Latin America. Although ethnic and cultural mixture characterizes many Latin American populations and makes Indian and African elements important features of national identity, relations with Indian populations often continue to be marked by exploitation and discrimination in nations as diverse as Brazil, Nicaragua, and Guatemala.

Slow Change in Women's Roles

The role of women has changed slowly. After World War I, women in Latin America continued to live under inequalities in the workplace and in politics. Women were denied the right to vote anywhere in Latin America until Ecuador enfranchised women in 1929 and Brazil and Cuba did the same in 1932. Throughout most of the region, those examples were not followed until the 1940s and 1950s. In some nations, the traditional associations of women with religion and the Catholic church in Hispanic life made reformers and revolutionaries fear that women would become a conservative force in national politics. This attitude, combined with traditional male attitudes that women should be concerned only with home and family, led to a continued exclusion of women from political life. In response, women formed various associations and clubs and began to push for the vote and other issues of interest to them.

Feminist organizations, suffrage movements, and international pressures eventually combined to bring about change. In Argentina, 15 bills for female suffrage were introduced in the senate before the vote was won in 1945. Sometimes the victory was a matter of political expediency for those in power: In the Dominican Republic and some other countries, the enfranchisement of women was a strategy used by conservative groups to add more conservative voters to the electorate in an effort to hold off political change. In Argentina, recently enfranchised women became a major pillar of the Peronist regime, although that regime also suppressed female political opponents such as Victoria Ocampo, editor of the important literary magazine *Sur*.

Women eventually discovered that the ability to vote did not in itself guarantee political rights or the ability to have their specific issues heard. After achieving the vote, women tended to join the national political parties, where traditional prejudices against women in public life limited their ability to influence political programs. In Argentina, Brazil, Colombia, and Chile, for example, the integration of women into national political programs has been slow, and women have not participated in proportion to their numbers. In a few cases, however, women played a crucial role in elections.

Some of the earliest examples of mobilization of women and their integration into the national labor force of various Latin American nations came in the period just before World War I and continued thereafter. The classic roles of women as homemakers, mothers, and agricultural workers were expanded as women entered the industrial labor force in growing numbers. By 1911 in Argentina, for example, women made up almost 80 percent of the textile and clothing industry's workers. But women found that their salaries often were below those of comparable male workers and that their jobs, regardless of the skill levels demanded, were considered unskilled and thus less well paid. Under these conditions, women, like other workers, joined the anarchist, socialist, and other labor unions and organizations.

Labor organizations are only a small part of the story of women in the labor force. In countries such as Peru, Bolivia, and Ecuador, women working in the markets control much small-scale commerce and have become increasingly active politically. In the growing service sectors, women have also become an important part of the labor force. Shifts in attitudes about women's roles have come more slowly than political and economic changes. Even in revolutionary Cuba, where a Law of the Family guaranteed equal rights and responsibilities within the home, enforcement has been difficult.

By the mid-1990s, the position of women in Latin America was closer to that in western Europe and North America than to the other areas of the world. Women made up 9 percent of the legislators in Latin America, a percentage higher than in any other region of the world. In terms of demographic patterns, health, education, and place in the workforce, the comparative position of women reinforced Latin America's intermediate position between industrialized and developing nations.

The Movement of People

In 1950 the populations of North America (United States and Canada) and Latin America were both about 165 million, but by 1985 North America's population was 265 million, while Latin America's had grown to more than 400 million. Declining mortality and continuing high fertility were responsible for this situation.

At the beginning of the 20th century, the major trend of population movement was immigration to Latin America, but the region has long experienced internal migration and the movement of people within the hemisphere. By the 1980s, this movement had reached significant levels, fed by the flow of workers seeking jobs, the demands of capital for cheap labor, and the flight of political refugees seeking basic freedoms. In the 1920s, Mexican workers crossed the border to the United States in large numbers at the same time Guatemalans were crossing the border to Mexico to work on coffee estates. During World War II, government programs to supply laborers were set up between the United States and Mexico, but these were always accompanied by extralegal migration, which fluctuated with the economy. Conditions for migrant laborers often were deplorable, although the extension of social welfare to them in the 1960s began to address some of the problems. By the 1970s, more than 750,000 illegal Mexican migrants a year were crossing the border—some

more than once—as the United States continued to attract migrants.

This internationalization of the labor market was comparable in many ways with the movement of workers from poorer countries such as Turkey, Morocco, Portugal, and Spain to the stronger economies of West Germany and France. In Latin America it also reflected the fact that industrialization in the 20th century depended on highly mechanized industry that did not create enough new jobs to meet the needs of the growing population. Much of the migration has been to the United States, but there has also been movement across Latin American frontiers: Haitians migrate to work in the Dominican Republic, and Colombians illegally migrate to Venezuela. By the 1970s, about 5 million people per year were migrating in Latin America and the Caribbean.

Politics has also been a major impulse for migration. Haitians fleeing political repression and abysmal conditions have risked great dangers in small open boats to reach the United States. The Cuban Revolution caused one of the great political migrations of the century. Beginning in 1959, when the Cuban middle class fled socialism, and continuing into the 1980s with the flight of Cuban workers, almost 1 million Cubans left the island. The revolutionary upheaval in Nicaragua, political violence in Central America, and poverty in Haiti have contributed to the flight of refugees. Often, it is difficult to separate political and economic factors in the movement of people from their homelands.

International migration is only part of the story. During the 20th century, there has been a marked movement in Latin America from rural to urban areas (see Table 33.1). Whereas in the 19th century Latin America was an agrarian region, by the 1980s about one-half of the population lived in cities of more than 20,000, and more than 25 of these cities had populations of more than 1 million. Some of these cities had reached enormous size. In 1999, Mexico City had more than 18 million inhabitants, São Paulo had almost 18 million, and Buenos Aires had over 12 million. Latin America was by far the most urbanized area of the developing world and only slightly less urbanized than western Europe.

The problem is not simply size but rate of growth. The urban populations grew at a rate about three times that of the population as a whole, which itself has grown rapidly. Urban economies have not been able to create enough jobs for the rapidly increasing population. Often recent migrants lived in marginal neigh-

TABLE 33.1
Population of Capital Cities as a Percentage of Total Population in 10 Latin American Nations

Nation	Capital	1880	1905	1930	1960	1983	2003
Argentina	Buenos Aires	12	20	20	32	34	33
Brazil	Rio de Janeiro	3	4	4	7	4*	3*
Chile	Santiago	6	10	13	22	37	29
Colombia	Bogotá	1	2	2	8	11	15
Cuba	Havana	13	15	15	18	20	20
Mexico	Mexico City	3	3	5	15	20	9
Panama	Panama City	7	14	16	25	20	15
Peru	Lima	3	3	5	19	27	30
Uruguay	Montevideo	12	30	28	31	40	39
Venezuela	Caracas	3	4	7	20	18	7

*No longer the capital city.

Source: From J. P. Cole, *Latin America: An Economic and Social Geography* (1965), 417; www.world-gazetteer.com.

borhoods or in shantytowns, which have become characteristic of the rapidly growing cities of Latin America. These *favelas*, to use the Brazilian term, have created awful living conditions, but over time some have become poorer neighborhoods within the cities, and community cooperation and action within them have secured basic urban services. More recently, the rate of urban growth has slowed, but the social problems in the cities remain a major challenge.

Although Latin American urbanization increased rapidly after 1940, the percentage of its people living in cities is still less than in western Europe but more than in Asia and Africa. Unlike the 19th-century European experience, the lack of employment in Latin American cities has kept rural migrants from becoming part of a laboring class with a strong identification with fellow workers. Those who do succeed in securing industrial jobs often join paternalistic labor organizations that are linked to the government. Thus, there is a separation between the chronically underemployed urban lower class and the industrial labor force. Whereas industrialization and urbanization promoted a strong class solidarity in 19th-century Europe, which led to the gains of organized labor, in contemporary Latin America nationalist and populist politics have weakened the ability of the working class to operate effectively in politics.

Cultural Reflections of Despair and Hope

Latin America remains an amalgamation of cultures and peoples trying to adjust to changing world realities. Protestant denominations have made some inroads, but the vast majority of Latin Americans are still Catholic. Hispanic traditions of family, gender relations, business, and social interaction influence everyday life and help to determine responses to the modern world.

Latin American popular culture remains vibrant. It draws on African and Indian traditional crafts, images, and techniques but arranges them in new ways. Music is also part of popular culture. The Argentine tango of the turn of the century began in the music halls of lower-class working districts of Buenos Aires and became an international craze. The African-influenced Brazilian samba and the Caribbean salsa have spread widely. They are a Latin American contribution to world civilization.

The struggle for social justice, economic security, and political formulas in keeping with the cultural and social realities of their nations has provided a dynamic tension that has produced tremendous artistic achievements. Latin American poets and novelists have gained worldwide recognition. We have already noted the artistic accomplishments of the Mexican Revolution. In 1922, Brazilian artists, composers, and authors staged a Modern Art Week in São Paulo, which emphasized a search for a national artistic expression that reflected Brazilian realities.

That theme also preoccupied authors elsewhere in Latin America. The social criticism of the 1930s produced powerful realist novels, which revealed the exploitation of the poor, the peasantry, and the Indians. Whether in the heights of the Andes or in the dark streets of the growing urban slums, the plight of the common folk provided a generation of authors with themes worthy of their effort. Social and political criticism has remained a central feature of Latin American literature and art and has played an important role in the development of newer art forms such as film.

The inability to bring about social justice or to influence politics has also sometimes led Latin American artists and intellectuals to follow other paths. In the 1960s a wave of literature took place in which novels that mixed the political, the historical, the erotic, and the fantastic were produced by a generation of authors who used "magical realism" because they found the reality of Latin America too absurd to be described by the traditional forms or logic. Writers such as the Argentine Jorge Luis Borges (1899–1980) and the Colombian Gabriel García Marquez (b. 1928) won acclaim throughout the world. García Marquez's *One Hundred Years of Solitude* (1967) used the history of a family in a mythical town called Macondo as an allegory of Latin America and traced the evils that befell the family and the community as they moved from naive isolation to a maturity that included oppression, exploitation, war, revolution, and natural disaster but never subdued the spirit of its people. In that way, his book outlined the trajectory of Latin America in the 20th century.

GLOBAL CONNECTIONS: Struggling Toward the Future in a Global Economy

As Latin America entered the 21st century, it continued to search for economic growth, social justice, and political stability. No easy solutions were available. In many ways, Latin American societies remained "unrevolutionary," unable to bring about needed changes because of deeply entrenched class interests, international conditions, or power politics. However, the struggle for change had produced some important results. The Mexican and Cuban revolutions brought profound changes in those countries and had a broad impact on the rest of the hemisphere, either as models to copy or as dangers to be avoided. Other nations, such as Bolivia, Peru, and Nicaragua, attempted their own versions of radical change with greater or lesser success. New forms of politics, sometimes populist and sometimes militarist, were tried. New political and social ideas, such as those of liberation theology, grew out of the struggle to find a just and effective

formula for change. Latin American authors and artists served as a conscience for their societies and received worldwide recognition for their depiction of the sometimes bizarre reality they observed. Although tremendous problems continued to face the region, Latin America remained the most advanced part of the developing world. Levels of literacy, for example, easily surpassed those in most of Asia and in Africa.

In the age of globalization, Latin America faces new challenges. The new world economy has created opportunities for expansion, and in the 1990s Latin American economies grew considerably, but this growth has made the problems of the distribution of wealth in Latin America even more acute. Over a third of the population still lives in poverty. Brazil, with one of the strongest economies in the region, had one of the worst records in this regard. Other problems also result from the economic changes. In Mexico, the northern part of the country near the border with the United States has benefited from new trade opportunities while southern Mexico has gotten poorer. Then too, integration into the world economy often threatens traditional cultures. Since the 1980s, various Indian political movements have sought to protect traditional cultures while seeking political and economic opportunities. New technologies could create new opportunities for Latin America, but if it cannot meet the challenges of political openness and social equity, the region will find itself disadvantaged in the new global economy.

Cultural issues remained unresolved as well. Partly reflecting divisions in wealth and urbanism, Latin Americans participated variously in global consumer currents. Middle-class Mexicans, for example, began to copy United States patterns in celebrating Halloween (previously an important traditional holiday focused on the forces of death) and Christmas. To some Mexican intellectuals, this represented a crucial abandonment of identity, and to others the new interests seemed either alien or unobtainable. The spread of new religious movements, including fundamentalist Protestantism, signaled an attempt to provide alternatives to global culture, particularly among urban slum-dwellers. At the same time, Latin American filmmakers, artists, and popular musicians contributed directly to global culture, often incorporating traditional elements in the process. Latin America's global position became increasingly complex.

Further Readings

A considerable literature in many disciplines deals with Latin America as a whole, and there are many country-specific studies. Two good introductory texts, both of which present variations of the "dependency" interpretation, are E. Bradford Burns' *Latin America: A Concise Interpretive History* (4th ed., 1986) and Thomas E. Skidmore and Peter H. Smith's *Modern Latin America* (1989). An excellent overview of Latin American literature and art is provided in Jean Franco's *The Modern Culture of Latin America* (2nd ed., 1970). Aspects of population history are discussed in Nicholas Sánchez-Albornoz's *The Population of Latin America* (1970) and Magnus Morner's *Adventurers and Proletarians: The Story of Migrants in Latin America* (1985). The role of women is presented briefly in June Hahner's *Women in Latin American History* (1976).

The economic history of Latin America is summarized in the classic by Brazilian economist Celso Furtado, *Economic Development of Latin America* (2nd ed., 1976), and in John Sheahan's *Patterns of Development in Latin America* (1987). Two excellent studies of labor that have different emphases are Hobart Spalding Jr.'s *Organized Labor in Latin America* (1977) and Charles Berquist's *Labor in Latin America* (1986). An overview is provided by Richard Salvucci, ed., in *Latin America and the World Economy* (1996).

There are many good studies of Latin American politics, but Guillermo O'Donnell's *Modernization and Bureaucratic Authoritarianism* (1973) has influenced much recent scholarship. The role of the United States is discussed in Abraham Lowenthal's *Partners in Conflict: The United States and Latin America* (1987). Anthony Maingot's *The United States and the Caribbean* (1994) gives a clear account of the recent history in that region, and Walter La Feber's *Inevitable Revolutions* (1984) is a critical assessment of U.S. policy in Central America. Lars Schoultz's *Human Rights and United States Policy Toward Latin America* (1981) details the influence of human rights on foreign policy.

A few good monographs on important topics represent the high level of scholarship on Latin America. Alan Knight's *The Mexican Revolution*, 2 vols. (1986) and John M. Hart's *Revolutionary Mexico* (1987) provide excellent analyses of that event. Freidrich Katz's *The Life and Times of Pancho Villa* (1998) is an outstanding biography. Florencia Mallon's *The Defense of Community in Peru's Central Highlands* (1983) looks at national change from a community perspective. Robert Potash's *The Army and Politics in Argentina 1945–1962* (1980) is one of the best in-depth studies of a Latin American military establishment, and Richard Gott's *Guerrilla Movements in Latin America* (1972) presents analysis and documents on the movements seeking revolutionary change at that time. On the cultural aspects of the U. S. influence on Latin America there is Gilbert Joseph et al., eds., *Close Encounters with Empire* (1998).

On the Web

A great deal on Latin American politics and social conditions can be gathered from the Internet. From a well-researched critical stance, see the North American Congress on Latin America (NACLA) reports at http://www.nacla.org. The revolutions in Chile (http://www.hartford-hwp.com/archives/42a/130. html or http://www.soc.ucsb.edu/projects/casemethod/foran.html), Cuba (http://www.worldsocialist-cwi.org/publications/Cuba/index2.html?/publications/Cuba/cuapp1.html), Guatemala (http://www2.truman.edu/~marc/webpages/revsfall98/guatemala/guatemala.html, http://www.hartford-hwp.com/archives/47/index-ce.html, and http://www.gwu.edu/~nsarchiv/NSAEBB/NSAEBB4/) and Mexico (http://nt2.ec.man.ac.uk/multimedia/Mexican%20Revolution.htm) inspired both joy and deadly reaction.

The leaders of these movements, such as Cuba's Castro (http://www.cnn.com/SPECIALS/cold.war/kbank/profiles/castro/ and http://www.marxists.org/history/cuba/archive/castro/), Mexico's Emiliano Zapata (http://www.cs.utk.edu/~miturria/project/zapata.html and http://www.mexconnect.com/mex_/history/ezapata1.html), and the women of the Mexican revolution (http://www.u.arizona.edu/ic/mcbride/ws200/mex-jand.htm) often seem larger than life; none more so than Che Guevara (http://www.pbs.org/newshour/forum/november97/che.html), whose image remains as current as an icon of revolution today as it did almost a half-century ago (http://www-sul.stanford.edu/depts/hasrg/german/exhibit/GDRposters/che.html/, http://www.pbs.org/newshour/forum/november97/che.html, and http://www.fmch.ucla.edu/Exhibits/guevara.htm.

The hopes of many Latin Americans for a more egalitarian society were celebrated in the works of artists such as Diego Rivera (http://www.diegorivera.com/) and Jose Orozco (http://www.dartmouth.edu/~hood/collections/orozco-murals.html). These hopes were ultimately broken on the anvil of the cold war (http://www.coldwar.org and http://turnerlearning.com/cnn/coldwar/backyard/byrd_ttl.html). They now largely rest with those who see the free market as the solution to poverty and inequality. There are doubts, however, that the free market is the panacea for the region's long-standing economic and social ills. This doubt is particularly strong among the Mayan farmers of Chiapas (http://nativenet.uthscsa.edu/archive/nl/9407/0164.html, http://lanic.utexas.edu/project/Zapatistas/, http://www.american.edu/ted/chiapas.htm, http://www.zapatistas.org, and http://www.providence.edu/polisci/projects/zapatistas/nafta.html).

CHAPTER 34

AFRICA, THE MIDDLE EAST, AND ASIA IN THE ERA OF INDEPENDENCE

Women played a vital role in the mass demonstrations that toppled the shah of Iran and brought Ayatollah Khomeini to power. In many ways women's support for political movements in the postcolonial period was a continuation of their active participation in earlier struggles against European colonial domination. But increasingly in the postcolonial era, women have organized not only to promote political change, but to force social and economic reforms that will improve the quality of their own lives.

- The Challenges of Independence
- **IN DEPTH:** Artificial Nations and the Rising Tide of Communal Strife
- **DOCUMENT:** Cultural Creativity in the Emerging Nations: Some Literary Samples
- Paths to Economic Growth and Social Justice
- **VISUALIZING THE PAST:** Globalization and Postcolonial Societies
- **GLOBAL CONNECTIONS:** Postcolonial Nations in the Cold War World Order

In Gillo Pontecorvo's moving film on the struggle for independence in Algeria, *The Battle of Algiers*, one member of the high command of the National Liberation Front (FLN) reflects on the nature of the revolutionary struggle in a conversation with a young guerrilla fighter, the protagonist of the film. When the young man expresses his anxieties about the outcome of the general strike taking place in the city of Algiers, the thoughtful leader of the FLN seeks to put the immediate crisis in a larger perspective. Revolutions, he observes, are difficult to get going and even harder to sustain. But the real tests, he says, will come when the revolutionary struggle has been successfully concluded. Once independence has been won, the leaders of the liberation struggle must assume power and face the greatest challenges of all: building viable nations and prosperous societies for peoples disoriented and deprived by decades or in many cases centuries of colonial rule.

These reflections on the process of decolonization anticipated the actual experience of the peoples in the new nations carved out of the ruins of the European colonial empires. Once the European colonizers had withdrawn and the initial euphoria of freedom had begun to wear off, Western-educated nationalist leaders were forced to confront the realities of the fragile state structures and underdeveloped economies they had inherited. With the common European enemy gone, the deep divisions between the different ethnic and religious groups that had been thrown together in the postcolonial states became more and more apparent and disruptive. These related challenges, which were faced by all of the newly independent peoples of Africa, the Middle East, and Asia, are explored in the opening sections of this chapter.

The leaders of the new nations found their efforts to spur economic growth limited by concessions made to the departing colonizers and by the nature of the international economy, which heavily favored industrialized nations. They saw their ambitious schemes to improve living standards among formerly colonized peoples frustrated by a shortage of expertise and resources and by population growth rates that quickly ate up whatever advances could be made. Population increase and efforts to spur economic development often had highly detrimental effects on the already ravaged environments of the newly independent nations. Loggers and land-hungry farmers, for example, have cut and burned vast swaths of the rain forests throughout much of Africa and Asia. Unable to afford the expensive antipollution devices that have reduced environmental degradation in wealthier industrialized countries, many developing nations have experienced an alarming fouling of their air, water, and soil in the decades since independence.

1910 C.E.	1920 C.E.	1930 C.E.	1940 C.E.	1950 C.E.	1960 C.E.
1912 African National Congress party formed **1919** First Pan-African Nationalist Congress	**1928** Founding of the Muslim Brotherhood in Egypt	**1930s** Free Officers movement develops in Egypt	**1947** India and Pakistan achieve independence **1948** First Arab–Israeli War; Afrikaner Nationalist party to power in South Africa; beginning of apartheid legislation **1949** Hassan al-Banna assassinated in Egypt	**1951** India's first five-year plan for economic development launched **1952** Farouk and khedival regime overthrown in Egypt; Nasser and Free Officers to power **1955** Bandung Conference; beginning of nonaligned movement **1956** Abortive British–French–Israeli intervention in Suez **1958** South Africa completely independent of Great Britain	**1960** Sharpeville shootings in South Africa **1966** Nkrumah overthrown by military coup in Ghana **1966–1970** Biafran secessionist war in Nigeria **1967** Six-Day War between Israel and the Arabs

The Challenges of Independence

 In the early decades of independence, the very existence of the nation-states that were carved out of the Western colonial empires was often challenged by the internal rivalries, and in some cases civil wars, between different social and ethnic groups. Economic growth was hampered by unprecedented rates of population increase, the structure of the international market, and the underdeveloped state of most colonial economies at the time of independence. Some social groups benefited more than others from the opportunities created by independence, and women continued to find themselves disadvantaged in nearly all areas of their lives.

The nationalist movements that won independence for most of the peoples of Africa, the Middle East, and Asia usually involved some degree of mass mobilization. Peasants and working-class townspeople, who hitherto had little voice in politics beyond their village boundaries or local labor associations, were drawn into political contests that toppled empires and established new nations. To win the support of these groups, nationalist leaders promised them jobs, civil rights, and equality once independence was won. The leaders of many nationalist movements nurtured visions of postindependence utopias in the minds of their followers. The people were told that once the Europeans, who monopolized the best jobs, were driven away and their exploitive hold on the economy was brought to an end, there would be enough to give everyone a good life.

Unfortunately, postindependence realities in almost all of the new nations made it impossible for nationalist leaders to fulfill the expectations they had aroused among their followers and, in varying degrees, among the colonized populace at large. Even with the Europeans gone and the terms of economic exchange with more developed countries somewhat improved, there was simply not enough to go around. Thus, the socialist-inspired ideologies that nationalist leaders had often embraced and promoted were misleading. The problem was not just that goods and services were unequally distributed, leaving some people rich and the great majority poor. The problem was that there were not enough resources to take care of everybody, even if it was possible to distribute them equitably.

When utopia failed to materialize, personal rivalries and long-standing divisions between different classes and ethnic groups (communalism), which had been muted by the common struggle against the alien colonizers, resurfaced or intensified. The European colonizers had established arbitrary boundaries (see Maps 34.1 and 34.2), sometimes combining hostile ethnic or religious groups. In almost all the new states, these rivalries and differences became dominant features of political life. They produced political instability and often threatened the viability of the nations themselves, as with East and West Pakistan (see Figures 34.1 and 34.2), where extreme

1970 C.E.	1980 C.E.	1990 C.E.
1970s Peak period for OPEC cartel	**1980–1988** Iran–Iraq War	**1990** Nelson Mandela released from prison; Iraqi invasion of Kuwait
1971 Bangladesh revolt against West Pakistan; Indo-Pakistani War	**1989** de Klerk charts path of peaceful reform in South Africa	**1991** Persian Gulf War
1972 Bangladesh becomes independent nation		**1994** First democratic elections in South Africa
1973 Third Arab–Israeli War		
1979 Shah of Iran overthrown; Islamic republic declared		

contrasts of topography and culture led to violence and the secession of the area that became **Bangladesh.** The recurring problems of famine and starvation in parts of Africa have stemmed from human conflicts more than natural disasters (Figure 34.3). Rivalries and civil wars in many of the newly decolonized nations consumed resources that might have been devoted to economic development. They also blocked—in the name of the defense of subnational interests—measures designed to build more viable and prosperous states. Absorbed by the task of just holding their new nations together, politicians neglected problems—such as soaring population increases, uncontrolled urban growth, rural landlessness, and environmental deterioration—that soon loomed just as large a threat as political instability to their young nations.

The Population Bomb

The nationalist leaders who led the colonized peoples of Africa and Asia to independence had firmly committed themselves to promoting rapid economic development once colonial restraints were removed. In keeping with their Western-educated backgrounds, most of these leaders saw their nations following the path of industrialization that had brought national prosperity and international power to much of western Europe and the United States. This course of development was also fostered by representatives of the Soviet bloc, who had emphasized heavy industry in their state-directed drives to modernize their economies and societies. Of the many barriers to the

rapid economic breakthroughs postcolonial leaders hoped for, the most formidable and persistent were the spiraling population increases that often overwhelmed whatever economic advances the peoples of the new nations managed to make (Figure 34.4).

Factors making for sustained population increases in already densely populated areas of Asia and Africa had begun to take effect even before the era of high colonialism. Food crops, mostly from the New World, contributed to dramatic population growth in China, India, and Java as early as the 17th century. They also helped sustain high levels of population in areas such as the Niger delta in west Africa, despite heavy losses as a result of the slave trade. The coming of colonial rule reinforced these upward trends in a number of ways. It ended local warfare that had caused population losses and, perhaps more significantly, had indirectly promoted the spread of epidemic diseases and famine. The new railroad and steamship links established by the colonizers to foster the spread of the market economy also cut down on the regional famines that had been a major check against sustained population increase since ancient times. Large amounts of food could be shipped from areas where harvests were good to those where drought or floods threatened the local inhabitants with starvation.

With war and famine—two of the main barriers to population increase—much reduced, growth began to speed up. This was particularly true in areas such as India and Java that had been under European control for decades. Death rates declined, but birth rates remained much the same, leading to increasingly larger net increases. Improved hygiene and medical treatment played little part in this rise until the early 20th century. From that time, efforts to eradicate tropical diseases, as well as global scourges such as smallpox, and to improve sewage systems and purify drinking water have led to further population increases.

Nearly all leaders of the emerging nations headed societies in which population was increasing at unprecedented levels. This increase continued in the early years of independence. In much of Asia, it has begun to level off in recent decades. But in most of Africa, population growth continues at very high rates. In some cases, most notably south Asia, moderate growth rates have produced huge total populations because they were adding to an already large base. As a result, in the 1970s population experts predicted that at the then-current rates, south Asia's population of more than 600 million would more

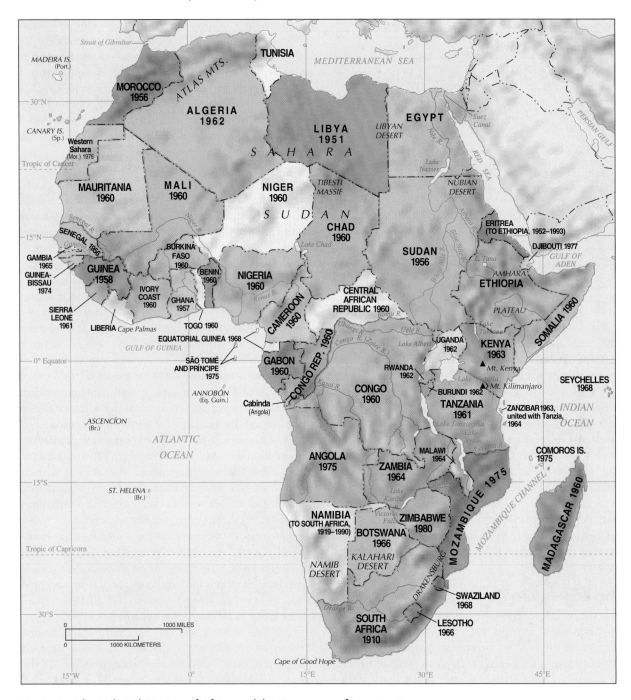

Map 34.1 *The Colonial Division of Africa and the Emergence of New Nations*

than double by the year 2000. With more than one billion people in India alone at present, the prophecy has more than been fulfilled.

In Africa, by contrast, which began with low population levels, relative to its large land area, very high birth rates and diminished mortality rates have resulted in very steep population increases in recent decades. Some population experts predict that if present growth rates continue, by the mid-21st century Nigeria will have a population equal to that of pre-

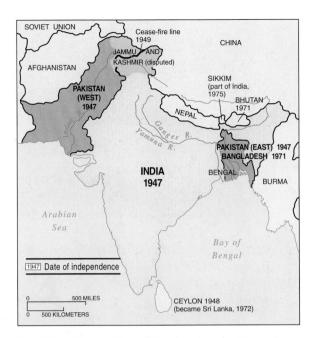

Map 34.2 *The Partition of South Asia: The Formation of India, Pakistan, Bangladesh, and Sri Lanka*

sent-day China. In view of the AIDS epidemic that has spread through much of central and eastern Africa since the 1980s, some of the estimates for population increases in Africa as a whole may have to be revised downward. But recent measures of African produc-

tivity and per capita incomes suggest that even more moderate increases in population may be difficult to support at reasonable living standards. This prospect is underscored by estimates that the 400 million peoples of Africa are supported by a continental economy with a productive capacity equal to just six percent of that of the United States, or roughly equal to that of the state of Illinois.

On the face of it, the conquest of war, disease, and famine was one of the great achievements of European colonial regimes. It was certainly an accomplishment that colonial officials never tired of citing in defense of continued European dominance. But the European policy of limiting industrialization in their colonial dependencies meant that one of the key ways by which Europe had met its own population boom in the 19th and early 20th centuries was not available to the new nations. They lacked the factories to employ the exploding population that moved to the cities from the rural areas, as well as the technology to produce the necessities of life for more and more people. Unlike the Europeans and the Americans, the emerging nations found it difficult to draw food and mineral resources from the rest of the world to feed this growing population. In fact, these were the very things the colonized peoples had been set up to sell to the industrialized nations. Even in countries such as India, where impressive advances in industrialization were made in the postcolonial era,

Figure 34.1 *One of the earliest states to be carved out of the former colonies, Pakistan contained extreme contrasts of lush tropical and arid semidesert environments, as depicted here and in Figure 34.2. The cultures of East and West Pakistan were equally diverse, a diversity that had much to do with the violent secession of what became the nation of Bangladesh in 1971.*

Figure 34.2 *Postcolonial Pakistan's extreme contrasts, from the semiarid area depicted here to the tropical setting shown in Figure 34.1, are also reflected in its diverse cultures. Similar differences have threatened the viability of many emerging nations in the era of independence following colonial domination.*

gains in productivity were swallowed up rapidly by the population explosion.

In most African and Asian countries, there has been resistance to birth control efforts aimed at controlling population growth. Some of this resistance is linked to deeply entrenched social patterns and religious beliefs. In many of these societies, procreation is seen as a sign of male virility. In addition, the capacity to bear children, preferably male children, continues to be critical to the social standing of women. In some cases, resistance to birth control is linked to specific cultural norms. For example, Hindus believe that a deceased man's soul cannot begin the cycle of rebirth until his eldest son has performed special ceremonies over his funeral pyre. This belief increases the already great pressure on Indian women to have children, and it encourages families to have several sons to ensure that at least one survives the father.

In Africa, children are seen as indispensable additions to the *lineage:* the extended network of relatives (and deceased ancestors) that, much more than the nuclear family, makes up the core social group over much of the subcontinent. As in India, sons are essential for continuing the patrilineal family line and performing burial and ancestral rites. The key roles played by women in agricultural production and marketing make girls highly valued in African societies. This is not true in many Asian societies, where high dowries and occupational restrictions limit their contribution to family welfare.

Before the 20th century, the high rates of stillbirths and infant mortality meant that mothers could expect to lose many of the children they conceived. Ten or 12 deaths of 15 or 16 children conceived was not unheard of. Beyond the obvious psychological scars left by these high death rates, they also fostered the conviction that it was necessary to have many children to ensure that some would outlive the parents. In societies where welfare systems and old-age pensions were meager or unknown, surviving children took on special urgency because they were the only ones who would care for their parents once they could no longer work for themselves. The persistence

Figure 34.3 *Since independence, famine has stalked much of the formerly colonized world, particularly in sub-Saharan Africa. Often, as in the case of these young refugees from the Nigerian civil war photographed in the late 1960s, starvation has been caused by human conflicts rather than natural disasters.*

of these attitudes in recent decades, when medical advances have greatly reduced infant mortality, has been a major factor contributing to soaring population growth.

In the early decades after independence, many African and Asian leaders were deeply opposed to state measures to promote family planning and birth control. Some saw these as Western attempts to meddle in their internal affairs; others proudly declared that the socialist societies they were building would be able to take care of the additional population. As it has become increasingly clear that excessive population increase makes significant economic advances impossible, many of these leaders have begun to reassess their attitudes toward birth control. A particular cause for alarm is the fact that in many developing countries a high percentage of the population is under age 15 (as high as 40 percent in some areas) and thus dependant on others for support. But even for those who now want to promote family planning, the obstacles are staggering. In addition to the cultural and social factors just discussed, leaders often find they lack sufficient resources and the educated personnel needed to make these programs effective. High rates of illiteracy, particularly among women, must be overcome, but education is expensive. Perhaps no form of financial and technical assistance from the industrialized to the developing world will be as critical in the coming decades as that devoted to family planning.

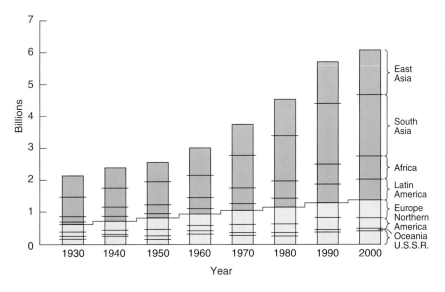

Figure 34.4 *This graph shows the growth of the world population by major global geographic areas between 1930 and 2000. It illustrates the near stabilization of the upswing in populations of the West and the states of the former Soviet Union that began with industrialization in the 18th century. It charts the explosion that occurred in recent decades in the areas of the globe that were colonized, both formally and informally, by the industrial powers in the 19th and early 20th centuries. These increases surpass those of any other epoch in human history.*

In Depth

Artificial Nations and the Rising Tide of Communal Strife

Again and again in the postcolonial era, new states have been torn by internal strife. Often much of what we in the industrialized West know of these areas in Africa, the Middle East, and Asia is connected to the breakdown of their political systems and the human suffering that has resulted. In just the last few years, for example, international news reports have featured descriptions of famines generated by civil wars in Somalia, the Sudan, and Mozambique; by harrowing images of refugees fleeing for their lives from Rwanda, Angola, and Cambodia; by religious riots in India; and mass slaughter in Timor. Western observers are often tempted to take this instability and suffering as proof that the people of these decolonized areas are unfit to rule themselves, that they are incapable of building viable political systems.

Although these responses are understandable given the crisis-focused coverage of the emerging nations by international news agencies, they fail to take into account the daunting obstacles that have confronted African, Middle Eastern, and Asian nation-builders. They ignore the important ways in which Western colonialism contributed to the internal divisions and political weaknesses of newly independent states. They also overlook the deep, often highly disruptive social divisions within Western societies (the long history of racial conflict in the United States, for example, or the vicious civil war in the former European nation of Yugoslavia). Any analysis of the recurring political crises of Africa, the Middle East, and Asia should begin with the realization that nearly all the nations that emerged from decolonization were artificial creations. The division of Africa and Asia by the Western imperialist powers was arbitrary (see, for examples, Maps 34.1 and 34.2). Some colonial boundaries cut peoples apart: the Shans of southeast Asia, the Kurds of the Middle East, the Somalis of the horn of east Africa. Some imposed boundaries tossed together tens, sometimes hundreds, of very different and often hostile ethnic or religious groups. The roads and railways built by the colonizers, the marketing systems they established, and the educational policies they pursued all hardened the unnatural boundaries and divisions established in the late 19th century. It was these artificial units, these motley combinations of peoples that defied the logic of history and cultural affinity, that African, Middle Eastern, and Asian nationalist leaders had to try to meld into nations after World War II.

The point is not that there was perfect harmony or unity among the peoples of these areas before the coming of colonial rule. As we have seen, there was a great diversity of ethnicity, languages, and religions among the peoples who built civilizations in these areas in the precolonial era. Intense competition, communal conflict, and countless wars occurred between different ethnic and religious groups. European colonization worsened these divisions while suppressing violent confrontations between different communities. In fact, European colonial regimes were built and maintained by divide-and-rule tactics. Very often the colonizers selectively recruited minority ethnic or religious groups into their armies, bureaucracies, and police forces. For example, the Tutsi minority in strife-torn Rwanda and Burundi was much favored by first the Belgians and later the French. In the colonial period, the Tutsis had greater access than the Hutu majority to missionary education, military training, and government positions. These advantages gained a disproportionate share of political power and social standing for the Tutsis after independence. But they also made them the obvious target for persecution by disgruntled Hutus. Rivalry and violent conflict between the two groups has often made a shambles of nation-building initiatives in Rwanda and Burundi over the past several decades and reached catastrophic levels in the mid-1990s. It has continued to simmer in the years since, at times spilling over into political struggles in neighboring states such as Congo.

The inequities of the colonial order were compounded by the increasingly frequent use of divide-and-rule policies by European officials in the last years of their rule. In addition, the colonizers' desire to scuttle and run from their colonial responsibilities when it was clear that the days of colonial rule were numbered opened the way for ethnic and religious strife. Communal violence in turn prompted the exodus of refugees that accompanied the winning of independence in many colonies, most notably in south Asia, Nigeria, the Belgian Congo, and Palestine. The Western-educated leaders who came to power in these and other newly independent states soon realized that only a small portion of the population was committed to an overarching nationalist identity. Even among the Westernized elite classes, which had led the decolonization struggle, national loyalties were often shallow and overridden by older, subnational ethnic and religious identities. As a result, many of the new nations of Africa and southeast Asia have been threatened by secessionist movements.

The most spectacular collapse of a new state came in Pakistan, the unwieldy patchwork of a nation the British threw together at the last minute in 1947 to satisfy Jinnah's demands for majority rule in Muslim areas of the Indian subcontinent (see Map 34.2). A glance at the map reveals the vulnerability of Pakistan, split into two parts: West and East Pakistan, separated by India's more than 1000 miles of hostile territory. East and West Pakistan also differed greatly in their natural environments (see Figures 34.1 and 34.2) and in the ethnic makeup of their peoples and the languages they used. They even differed in their approaches to the Islamic faith that had justified including them in the same country in the first place.

Fragile national ties were eroded rapidly by the East Pakistanis' perception that they had been in effect recolonized by West Pakistan. West Pakistanis held highly disproportionate shares of government jobs and military positions, and West Pakistan received the lion's share of state revenues despite the fact that East Pakistan generated most of the new nation's foreign earnings. By the early 1970s, East and West Pakistan were locked in a bloody civil war, which ended with the creation of the nation of Bangladesh from East Pakistan in 1972.

India, which relished the chance to contribute to the breakup of Pakistan, has itself been repeatedly threatened by civil strife between different linguistic, religious, and ethnic groups. In the early 1980s, Sikh guerrillas carried on a violent campaign for separation in the north, and the Indian government was forced to intervene militarily in the violent struggle between different ethnic and religious groups in Sri Lanka (Ceylon), its neighbor to the south. In 1997, an avowedly Hindu communalist party came to power in New Delhi, in defiance of the staunch adherence to the principle of a secular state upheld by leading Indian nationalist figures in the colonial era and all of the earlier postindependence governments. The victory of the Bharatya Janata party (BJP) has intensified the anxieties of the large Muslim minority and other non-Hindu religious groups about the possibility of discrimination and even open persecution.

In Africa, where there was even less of a common historical and cultural basis on which to build nationalism than in south or southeast Asia, separatist movements have been a prominent feature of the political life of new states. Secessionist movements have raged from Morocco in the northwest to Ethiopia in the east and Angola in the south (see Map 34.1). Civil wars, such as the struggle of the non-Muslim peoples of the southern Sudan against the Muslim rulers from the northern parts of that country, have also abounded. Thus far, none of the secessionist movements have succeeded, although that of the Ibo peoples of eastern Nigeria, who proclaimed an independent state of Biafra in 1967, led to three years of bloody warfare in Africa's most populous nation.

In all cases, the artificial nature of the new nations of Africa, the Middle East, and Asia has proved costly. In addition to internal divisions, boundary disputes between newly independent nations have often led to border clashes and open warfare. India and Pakistan have fought three such wars since 1947. Iraq's Saddam Hussein justified his 1990 annexation of Kuwait with the argument that the tiny but oil-rich Arab "sheikhdom" was an artificial creation of the British colonizers, who had carved Kuwait out of land that historically had been part of Iraq.

Democracy has often been one of the main victims of the tensions between rival ethnic groups within many emerging nations and threats from neighbors without. Politicians in nearly all the new states have been quick to play on communal fears as well as on ethnic and religious loyalties to win votes. As a result, freely elected legislatures have often been dominated by parties representing these special interests. Suspicions that those in power were favoring their own or allied groups has led to endless bickering and stalemates in national legislatures, which have become tempting targets for coup attempts by military strongmen. One of the more predictable reasons these usurpers have given for dictatorial rule has been the need to contain the communal tensions aroused by democratic election campaigns.

Questions: How might colonial policies have been changed to reduce the tensions between different ethnic and religious communities? Why were these measures not taken? What can be done now to alleviate these divisions? Should the United Nations or industrialized nations such as the United States or Japan intervene directly to contain communal clashes or civil wars in Africa and Asia? What is to be done with the rapidly growing refugee populations created by these conflicts?

Parasitic Cities and Endangered Ecosystems

As population increase in the rural areas of emerging nations outstripped the land and employment opportunities available to the peasantry, mass migrations to urban areas ensued. The massive movement of population from overcrowded villages to the cities was one of the most dramatic developments in the postcolonial history of most new nations. Ambitious youths and the rural poor crowded into port centers and capital cities in search of jobs and a chance to find the "good life" that the big hotels and restaurants and the neon lights of the city center appeared to offer to all comers. But because most of these cities lacked the rapidly expanding industrial sectors that had made possible the absorption of a similar migrant influx earlier in the West, they were often dead ends for migrants from the rural areas. There were few jobs, and heavy competition for them ensured that wages would remain low for most workers. The growing numbers of underemployed or unemployed migrants turned to street vending, scavenging, huckstering, begging, or petty crime to survive.

In the independence era, the urban poor have become a volatile factor in the political struggles of the elite. They have formed the crowds willing for a price to cheer on one contender or jeer down another, and ready to riot and loot in times of government crisis. In deeply divided societies, the poor, working-class, or idle youths of the urban areas have often formed the shock troops in communal clashes between rival ethnic and religious groups. Fear of outbursts by urban "mobs" has also forced Asian, Middle Eastern, and African regimes to spend scarce resources to subsidize and thus keep low the price of staple foods such as bread, as well as kerosene and other necessities.

The sudden population influx from the rural areas to cities without sufficient jobs or the infrastructure to support them has greatly skewed urban growth in the emerging nations. Within decades, Asian cities have become some of the largest in the world, and Middle Eastern and African urban areas have sprawled far beyond their modest limits in colonial times. As Figure 34.5 dramatically illustrates, the wealth of the upper- and middle-class areas, dominated by glitzy hotels and high-rises, contrasts disturbingly with the poverty of the vast slums that stretch in all directions from the city centers. Little or

Figure 34.5 *In the urban areas of undeveloped nations, the contrast between the wealth of the few and the poverty of the majority is revealed by the juxtaposition of the high-rise apartments of the affluent middle classes and the shantytowns of the urban poor. The city centers in emerging nations are much like those of the industrial West or Japan. But the cities as a whole often are more like collections of large villages than integrated urban units. Many of these villages are vast shantytowns with varying levels of basic services such as running water, sewer systems, and transportation networks to the city center.*

no planning was possible for the slum quarters that expanded as squatters erected makeshift shelters wherever open land or derelict buildings could be found. Originally, most of the slum areas lacked electricity, running water, or even the most basic sewage facilities. As shanties were gradually converted into ramshackle dwellings, many governments scrapped plans to level slum settlements and instead tried to provide them with electrical and sanitary systems. As an increasing number of development specialists have reluctantly concluded, slums often provide the only housing urban dwellers are likely to find for some time to come.

These conditions have burdened many postcolonial societies with parasitic rather than productive cities. This means that they are heavily dependant for survival on food and resources drawn from their own countryside or from abroad. In contrast to the cities of western Europe and North America, even during the decades of rapid urban expansion in the 19th century, few cities of the emerging nations have had the manufacturing base needed to generate growth in their surrounding regions or the nation as a whole. They take from the already impoverished countryside, but they are able to give little in return. Urban dependence on the countryside further stretches the already overextended resources of the rural areas.

Rural overpopulation in the decades after independence has led to soil depletion in many areas that have been worked for centuries or millennia. It has also resulted in an alarming rate of deforestation throughout Africa and Asia. Peasant villagers cut trees for fuel or clear land for farming and livestock grazing. Deforestation and overgrazing not only pose major threats to wild animal life but also upset the balance in fragile tropical ecosystems, producing further soil depletion and erosion and encouraging desertification. This environmental degradation is intensified by industrial pollution from both the developed countries and the emerging nations themselves. Although the industrial sectors in the latter are small, pollution tends to be proportionally greater than in the developed world because developing nations rarely can afford the antipollution technology introduced over the last few decades in western Europe, Japan, and North America.

Women's Subordination and the Nature of Feminist Struggles in the Postcolonial Era

The example of both the Western democracies and the communist republics of eastern Europe, where women had won the right to vote in the early and mid-20th century, encouraged the founders of many emerging nations to write female suffrage into their constitutions. The very active part women played in many nationalist struggles was perhaps even more critical to their earning the right to vote and run for political office. Women's activism also produced some semblance of equality in legal rights, education, and occupational opportunities under the laws of many new nations.

However, the equality that was proclaimed on paper often bore little resemblance to the actual rights that most women could exercise. It also had little bearing on the conditions under which they lived their daily lives. Even the rise to power of individual women such as **Indira Gandhi,** who as India's prime minister proved to be one of the most resolute and powerful of all third-world leaders, or **Corazon Aquino,** president of the Philippines in the post-Marcos era of the late 1980s, is deceptive. In most instances, female heads of state in the emerging nations entered politics and initially won political support because they were connected to powerful men. Indira Gandhi was the daughter of **Jawaharlal Nehru,** India's first prime minister; and Corazon Aquino's husband was the martyred leader of the Filipino opposition to Ferdinand Marcos. **Benazir Bhutto,** a prime minister of Pakistan, was the daughter of a domineering Pakistani prime minister who had been toppled by a military coup and executed in the late 1970s. Lacking these sorts of connections, most African, Middle Eastern, and Asian women have been at best relegated to peripheral political positions and at worst allowed no participation in the political process.

The limited gains made by women in the political sphere are paralleled by the second-class position to which most are consigned in many societies. In some respects, their handicaps are comparable to those that constrict women in the industrialized democracies and communist nations. But the obstacles to female self-fulfillment, and in many cases mere survival, in emerging nations are usually much more blatant and fundamental than the restrictions women have to contend with in developed societies. To begin with, early marriage ages for women and large families are still the norm in most African, Middle Eastern, and Asian societies. This means that women spend their youthful and middle-age years having children. There is little time to think of higher education or a career.

Because of the low level of sanitation in many postcolonial societies and the scarcity of food, all but elite and upper middle-class women experience chronic anxiety about such basic issues as adequate nutrition for their children and their susceptibility to disease. The persistence of male-centric customs directly affects the health and life expectancy of women themselves. For example, the Indian tradition that dictates that women first serve their husbands and sons and then eat what is left has obvious disadvantages. The quantity and nutritional content of the leftovers is likely to be lower than that of the original meals, and in tropical environments flies and other disease-bearing insects are more likely to have fouled the food.

The demographic consequences of these social patterns can be dramatic. In the 1970s, for example, it was estimated that as much as 20 percent of the female population of India was malnourished and that another 30 percent had a diet that was well below acceptable United Nations levels. In sharp contrast to the industrial societies of Japan, the United States, and Europe, where women outnumber (because on the average they outlive) men, in India there are only 930 females for every 1000 males.

Although the highly secular property and divorce laws many new states passed after independence have given women much greater legal protection, many of these measures are ignored in practice. Very often, women have neither the education nor the resources to exercise their legal rights. The spread of **religious revivalism** in many cases has further eroded these rights, even though advocates of a return to tradition often argue that practices such as veiling and stoning for women (but not men) caught in adultery actually enhance their dignity and status. Most Asian, Middle Eastern, and African women continue to be dominated by male family members, are much more limited than men in their career opportunities, and are likely to be less well fed, educated, and healthy than men at comparable social levels.

Neocolonialism, Cold War Rivalries, and Stunted Development

The schemes of nationalist leaders aimed at building an industrial base that would support the rapidly increasing populations of their new nations soon yielded to the economic realities of the postcolonial world. Not only did most of the nations that emerged from colonialism have little in the way of an industrial base, but their means of obtaining one were meager. To buy the machines and hire or train the technical

experts that were essential to get industrialization going, the new nations needed to earn capital they could invest for these ends. Some funds could be accumulated by saving a portion of the state revenues collected from the peasantry. In most cases, however, there was little left once the bureaucrats had been paid, essential public works and education had been funded, and other state expenses had been met. Thus, most emerging nations have relied on the sale of cash crops and minerals to earn the money they need to finance industrialization. As their leaders soon discovered, the structure of the world market worked against them.

The pattern of exchange promoted in the colonial era left most newly independent countries dependant on the export production of two or three food crops or industrial raw materials. The former included cocoa, palm oil, coffee, jute, and hemp. Key among the latter were minerals, such as copper, bauxite, and oil, for which there was a high demand in the industrialized economies of Europe, North America, and increasingly Japan. Since World War II, the prices of these exports—which economists call **primary products**—have not only fluctuated widely but have declined steadily when compared to the prices of most of the manufactured goods emerging nations usually buy from the industrialized world. Price fluctuations have created nightmares for planners in developing nations. Revenue estimates from the sale of coffee or copper in years when the price is high are used to plan government projects for building roads, factories, and dams. Market slumps can wipe out these critical funds, thereby retarding economic growth and throwing countries deeply into debt.

African, Middle Eastern, and Asian leaders have been quick to blame the legacy of colonialism and what they have called the **neocolonial economy**—the global economy dominated by the industrialized nations—for the limited returns yielded thus far by their development schemes. Although there is much truth to these accusations, they do not tell the whole story. These leaders must also share the responsibility for the slow pace of economic growth in much of the developing world. The members of the educated classes that came to dominate the political and business life of newly independent nations often used their positions to enrich themselves and their relatives at the expense of their societies as a whole. Corruption has been notoriously widespread in most of the new nations. Government controls on the import of goods such as automobiles, television sets, and stereos, which

Document

Cultural Creativity in the Emerging Nations: Some Literary Samples

Despite, or perhaps because of, political instability and chronic economic difficulties, postcolonial societies have generated a high level of artistic creativity over the past four or five decades. Nowhere has this creativity been more prominent and brilliant than in literary works, for which African, Middle Eastern, and Asian writers have earned Nobel prizes and won a wide readership far beyond their own nations. The selections that follow are only a small sample of the vast and varied works of these talented writers, from poetry and drama to novels and short stories.

Many of these writers focus on the predicament of the Western-educated elites who dominate the new nations that emerged from the European colonial empires. In the following stanza from the poem "I Run Around with Them," Indonesian poet Chairil Anwar reflects on the lack of purpose and malaise he believed to be widespread among the children of these elite groups.

I run around with them, what else can I
    do, now—
Changing my face at the edge of the street,
    I use their eyes
And tag along to visit the fun house:
These are the facts as I know them
(A new American flic at the Capitol,
The new songs they dance to).
We go home: there's nothing doing
Though this kind of Death is our neighbor,
    our friend, now.
Hanging around at the corner, we wait for the
    city bus
That glows night to day like a gold tooth;
Lame, deformed, negative, we
Lean our bony asses against lamp poles
And jaw away the years.

In the next quotation, from the novel *No Longer at Ease*, widely read Nigerian author Chinua Achebe identifies another dilemma: the pull between Western culture and the ancient civilization of one's own land.

Nothing gave him greater pleasure than to find another Ibo-speaking student in a London bus. But when he had to speak in English with a Nigerian student from another tribe he lowered his voice. It was humiliating to have to speak to one's countryman in a foreign language, especially in the presence of the proud owners of that language. They would naturally assume that one had no language of one's own. He wished they were here today to see. Let them come to Umuofia [the protagonist's home village] now and listen to the talk of men who made a great art of conversation. Let them come and see men and women and children who knew how to live, whose joy of life had not yet been killed by those who claimed to teach other nations how to live.

Like many of the more famous novelists of the emerging nations, V. S. Naipaul is an expatriate, born in the Caribbean and now living in rural England. In his moving and controversial account of his return to his Indian ancestral home, titled *An Area of Darkness*, Naipaul confronts the problem of massive poverty and the responses of foreigners and the Indian elite to it.

To see [India's] poverty is to make an observation of no value; a thousand newcomers to the country before you have seen and said as you. And not only newcomers. Our own sons and daughters, when they return from Europe and America, have spoken in your very words. Do not think that your anger and contempt are marks of your sensitivity. You might have seen more: the smiles on the faces of the begging children, that domestic group among the pavement sleepers waking in the cool Bombay morning, father, mother and baby in a trinity of love, so self-contained that they are as private as if walls had separated them from you; it is your gaze that violates them, your sense of outrage that outrages them.... It is your surprise, your anger that denies [them] humanity.

Questions: Can you think of parallels in U.S. history or contemporary society to the situations and responses conveyed in these passages from recent postcolonial writings? Do they suggest that it is possible to communicate even intimate feelings across cultures, or do you find them alien, different? What other issues would you expect African, Middle Eastern, and Asian postcolonial artists to deal with in their work?

are luxury items beyond the reach of most of the people, have often been lax. As a result, tax revenues and export earnings that could have fueled development have often gone to provide the good life for small minorities within emerging nations. The inability or refusal of many regimes to carry out key social reforms, such as land redistribution, which would spread the limited resources available more equitably over the population, has contributed vitally to the persistence of these patterns.

Badly strapped for investment funds and essential technology, emerging African, Middle Eastern, and Asian nations have often turned to international organizations, such as the World Bank and the International Monetary Fund, or to rival industrial nations for assistance. Although resources for development have been gained in this way, the price for international assistance has often been high. The industrialized nations have demanded major concessions in return for their aid. These have ranged from commitments to buy the products of, and favor investors from, the lending countries to entering into alliances and permitting military bases on the territory of the client state.

Loans from international lending agencies almost invariably have been granted only after the needy nation agreed to conditionalities. These are regulations that determine how the money is to be invested and repaid, and they usually involve promises to make major changes in the economy of the borrowing nation. In recent years, these promises have often included a commitment to remove or reduce state subsidies on food and other essential consumer items. State subsidies were designed to keep prices for staple goods at a level that the urban and rural poor—the great majority of the people in almost all emerging nations—could afford. When carried out, subsidy reductions often have led to widespread social unrest, riots, and the collapse or near collapse of postcolonial regimes.

Paths to Economic Growth and Social Justice

However much the leaders of the new nations of Africa, the Middle East, and Asia might have blamed their societies' woes on the recently departed colonizers, they soon felt the need to deliver on the promises of social reform and economic well-being that had done so much to rally

support to the nationalist cause. Different leaders adopted different approaches, and some tried one strategy after another. Although it is obviously impossible to deal with all of these efforts at nation-building and economic development in depth, the basic elements of several distinctive strategies are considered in this chapter. The discussion of each strategy focuses on a single, prominent case example.

Depending on their own skills, the talents of their advisors and lieutenants, and the resources at their disposal, leaders in the emerging nations have tackled the daunting task of development with varying degrees of success. Ways have been found to raise the living standards of a significant percentage of the population of some of the emerging nations. But these strategies have rarely benefited the majority. It may be too early to judge the outcomes of many development schemes. But so far, none has proved to be the path to the social justice and general economic development that nationalist leaders saw as the ultimate outcome of struggles for decolonization. Although some countries have done much better than others, successful overall strategies to deal with the challenges facing emerging nations have yet to be devised.

Charismatic Populists and One-Party Rule

One of the least successful responses on the part of leaders who found their dreams for national renewal frustrated has been a retreat into authoritarian rule. This approach has often been disguised by calculated, charismatic appeals for support from the disenfranchised masses. Perhaps the career of Kwame Nkrumah, the leader of Ghana's independence movement, illustrates this pattern best. There is little question that Nkrumah was genuinely committed to social reform and economic uplift for the Ghanaian people during the years of his rise to become the first prime minister of the newly independent west African nation of Ghana in 1957 (see Map 34.3). After assuming power, he moved vigorously to initiate programs that would translate his high aspirations for his people into reality. But his ambitious schemes for everything from universal education to industrial development soon ran into trouble.

Rival political parties, some representing regional interests and ethnic groups long hostile to Nkrumah, repeatedly challenged his initiatives and tried to block the efforts to carry out his plans. His leftist leanings

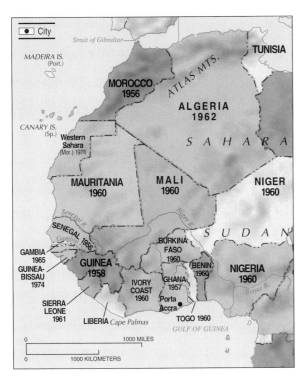

Map 34.3   *The New West African Nations*

won support from the Soviet bloc but frightened away Western investors, who had a good deal more capital to plow into Ghana's economy. They also led to growing hostility on the part of the United States, Great Britain, and other influential noncommunist countries. Most devastatingly, soon after independence, the price of cocoa—by far Ghana's largest export crop—began to fall sharply. Tens of thousands of Ghanaian cocoa farmers were hard hit and the resources for Nkrumah's development plans suddenly dried up.

Nkrumah's response to these growing problems was increasingly dictatorial. He refused to give up or cut back on his development plans. As a result, most failed miserably because of the lack of key supplies and official mismanagement. In the early 1960s, he forcibly crushed all political opposition by banning rival parties and jailing other political leaders. He assumed dictatorial powers and ruled through functionaries in his own Convention People's party.

Nkrumah also sought to hold on to the loyalty of the masses and mobilize their energies by highly staged "events" and the manipulation of largely invented symbols and traditions that were said to be derived from Ghana's past. Thus, he tried to justify his policies and leadership style with references to a uniquely African brand of socialism and the need to revive African traditions and African civilization. Even before independence, he had taken to wearing the traditional garb of the Ghanaian elite. The very name *Ghana*, which Nkrumah himself proposed for the new nation that emerged from the former Gold Coast colony, had been taken from an ancient African kingdom. The original Ghanaian kingdom actually was centered much farther to the north and had little to do with the peoples of the Gold Coast.

Nkrumah went about the country giving fiery speeches, dedicating monuments to the "revolution," which often consisted of giant statues of himself (Figure 34.6). He also assumed a prominent role in the nonaligned movement that was then sweeping the newly independent nations. His followers' adulation knew no bounds. Members of his captive parliament compared him to Confucius, Muhammad, Shakespeare, and Napoleon and predicted that his birthplace would serve as a "Mecca" for all of Africa's leaders. But his suppression of all opposition and his growing ties to the Communist party, coupled with the rapid deterioration of the Ghanaian economy, increased the ranks of his enemies, who waited for a chance to strike. That chance came early in 1966, when Nkrumah went off on one of his many trips, this time a peace mission to Vietnam. In his absence, he was deposed by a military coup. Nkrumah died in exile in 1972, and Ghana moved in a very different direction under its new military rulers.

Military Responses: Dictatorships and Revolutions

Given the difficulties that leaders such as Nkrumah faced after independence and the advantages the military have in crisis situations, the proliferation of coups in the emerging nations is not surprising. Armed forces have at times been divided by the religious and ethnic rivalries that have been so disruptive in new nations. But the regimentation and emphasis on discipline and in-group solidarity in military training often render soldiers more resistant than other social groups to these forces. In conditions of political breakdown and social conflict, the military possesses the monopoly—or near monopoly—of force that is often essential for restoring order. Their occupational conditioning makes soldiers not only more ready than civilian leaders to use the force at their disposal but less concerned with its destructive consequences. Military personnel also tend to have some

Figure 34.6 *Many monumental statues of Kwame Nkrumah, such as this one, rose in the towns and villages of Ghana as he tried to cover the failure of his socialist-inspired development programs with dictatorial rule and self-glorification. Although Nkrumah's efforts to cover his regime's failures through self-glorifying displays and pageantry were extreme, they were not unique. The many photos of the "great leader" of the moment that one finds in many developing nations are a variation on Nkrumah's tactics. These state campaigns to glorify the dictatorial figures are reminiscent of those mounted by the leaders of the communist revolutions in Russia, China, and Cuba.*

degree of technical training, which was usually lacking in the humanities-oriented education of civilian nationalist leaders. Because most military leaders have been staunchly anticommunist, they have often attracted covert technical and financial assistance from Western governments.

Once in control, military leaders have banned civilian political parties and imposed military regimes of varying degrees of repression and authoritarian control. Yet the ends to which these regimes have put their dictatorial powers have differed greatly. At their worst, military regimes—such as those in Uganda (especially under Idi Amin), Myanmar (formerly Burma), and Congo—have quashed civil liberties while making little attempt to reduce social inequities or improve living standards. These regimes have existed mainly to enrich the military leaders and their allies. Military governments of this sort have been notorious for official corruption and for imprisoning, torturing, or eliminating political dissidents. Understandably uneasy about being overthrown, these regimes have diverted a high proportion of their nations' meager resources, which might have gone for economic development, into expenditures on expensive military hardware. Neither the Western democracies nor the countries of the Soviet bloc have hesitated to supply arms to these military despots.

In a few cases, military leaders have been radical in their approaches to economic and social reform. Perhaps none was more so than **Gamal Abdul Nasser** (Figure 34.7), who took power in Egypt after a military coup in 1952. As we have seen in Chapter 28, the Egyptians won their independence in the mid-1930s except for the lingering British presence in the Suez Canal zone (see Map 34.4). But self-centered civilian politicians and the corrupt khedival regime had done little to improve the standard of living of the mass of the Egyptian people. As conditions worsened and Egypt's governing parties did little but rake in wealth for their elitist memberships, revolutionary forces emerged in Egyptian society.

The radical movement that succeeded in gaining power, the **Free Officers movement,** evolved from a secret organization established in the Egyptian army in the 1930s. Founded by idealistic young officers of Egyptian rather than Turco-Egyptian descent, the secret Revolutionary Command Council studied conditions in the country and prepared to seize power in the name of a genuine revolution. For many decades, it was loosely allied to the **Muslim Brotherhood,** another revolutionary alternative to the khedival regime.

The brotherhood was founded by Hasan al-Banna (see Figure 34.8) in 1928. Al-Banna was a schoolteacher who had studied in his youth with the famous Muslim reformer Muhammad Abduh. While at Al-Azhar University in Cairo in the years after World War I, al-Banna had combined a deep interest

Figure 34.7 *After the Free Officers' seizure of power in the 1952 coup, a young general named Nasser emerged as the most charismatic and able of a number of rivals for power. For nearly two decades Nasser dominated Egyptian politics and was a major force in Middle Eastern history.*

in scientific subjects with active involvement in student demonstrations in support of Wafd demands for Egyptian independence. In this period, like many other Egyptian students, al-Banna developed contempt for the wealthy minority of Egyptians and Europeans who flourished in the midst of the appalling poverty of most of his people.

To remedy these injustices and rid Egypt of its foreign oppressors, al-Banna founded the Muslim Brotherhood in 1928. Although members of the organization were committed to a revivalist approach to Islam, the brotherhood's main focus, particularly in the early years, was on a program of social uplift and sweeping reforms. The organization became involved in a wide range of activities, from promoting trade unions and building medical clinics to educating women and pushing for land reform. By the late 1930s, the brotherhood's social service had become highly politicized. Al-Banna's followers fomented strikes and urban riots and established militant youth organizations and paramilitary assassination squads. Despite the murder of al-Banna by the khedive Farouk's assassins in 1949, the members of the brotherhood continued to expand its influence in the early 1950s among both middle-class youths and the impoverished masses.

After Egypt's humiliating defeats in the first Arab-Israeli War of 1948 and in a clash with the British over the latter's continuing occupation of the Suez Canal zone in 1952, mass anger with a discredited khedival and parliamentary regime gave the officers their chance. In July 1952, an almost bloodless military coup toppled the corrupt khedive Farouk from his jewel-encrusted throne (Figure 34.9).

The revolution had begun. The monarchy was ended, and with the installation of Nasser and the Free Officers, Egyptians ruled themselves for the first time since the 6th century B.C.E. By 1954, all political parties had been disbanded, including the Muslim Brotherhood, which had clashed with its former allies in the military and had been suppressed after an attempt on Nasser's life. Nasser was only one of several officers at the head of the Free Officers movement, and by no means was he initially the most charismatic. But after months of internal power struggles in the officer corps, he emerged as the head of a military government that was deeply committed to revolution.

Nasser and his fellow officers used the dictatorial powers they had won in the coup to force through programs that they believed would uplift the long-oppressed Egyptian masses. They were convinced

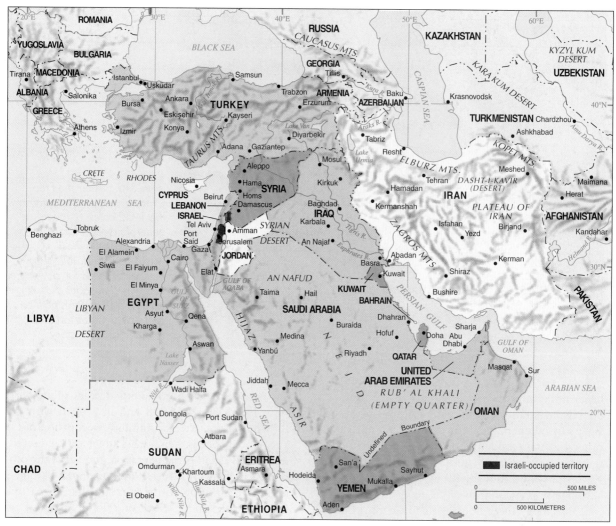

Map 34.4   *The Middle East in the Cold War Era*

that only the state had the power to carry out essential social and economic reforms, and thus they began to intervene in all aspects of Egyptian life. Land reform measures were enacted: Limits were placed on how much land an individual could own, and excess lands were seized and redistributed to landless peasants. State-financed education through the college level was made available to Egyptians. The government became Egypt's main employer; by 1980, more than 30 percent of Egypt's workforce was on the state payroll. State subsidies were used to lower the price of basic food staples, such as wheat and cooking oil. State-controlled development schemes were introduced that emphasized industrial growth, modeled after the five-year plans of the Soviet Union.

To establish Egypt's economic independence, stiff restrictions were placed on foreign investment. In some cases foreign properties were seized and redistributed to Egyptian investors. Nasser also embarked on an interventionist foreign policy that stressed the struggle to destroy the newly established Israeli state, forge Arab unity, and foment socialist revolutions in neighboring lands. His greatest foreign policy coup came in 1956, when he rallied international opinion to finally oust the British and their French allies from the Suez Canal zone. Despite the setbacks suffered by Egyptian military forces, Nasser made good use of the rare combined backing of the United States and the Soviet Union to achieve his aims in the crisis.

Figure 34.8 *Hasan al-Banna, founder of the Muslim Brotherhood, an opposition group in Egypt that established medical clinics and promoted unions, land reform, and women's education.*

Figure 34.9 *Growing Egyptian resistance to the British occupation of the Suez Canal zone was expressed in this effigy of a British soldier that was strung up on a Cairo street corner in January 1952. The Arabic banner that accompanies the mock hanging reminds Egyptians of the Dinshawai incident, discussed in Chapter 28, and the need to sustain resistance to British domination. Within months of this protest, mass demonstrations and a military coup freed the Egyptian people from both the British occupation and the repressive khedival regime.*

However well intentioned, many of Nasser's initiatives misfired. Land reform efforts were frustrated by bureaucratic corruption and the clever strategies devised by the landlord class to hold on to their estates. State development schemes often lacked proper funding and failed because of mismanagement and miscalculations. Even the Aswan Dam project, which was the cornerstone of Nasser's development drive, was a fiasco. Egypt's continuing population boom quickly canceled out the additional cultivable lands the dam produced. The dam's interference with the flow of the Nile resulted in increasing numbers of parasites that cause blindness. It also led to a decline in the fertility of farmlands in the lower Nile delta, which were deprived of the rich silt that normally was washed down by the river. Foreign investment funds from the West, which Egypt desperately needed, soon dried up. Aid from the much poorer Soviet bloc could not begin to match what was lost, and much of this assistance was military. In the absence of sufficient foreign investment and with Egypt's uncontrolled population rising at an alarming rate, the state simply could not afford all the ambitious schemes to which Nasser and the revolutionary officers had committed it. The gap between aspirations and means was increased in the later years of Nasser's reign (in the 1960s) by the heavy costs of his mostly failed foreign adventures, including the disastrous Six-Day War with Israel in 1967.

Although he had to move slowly at first, Nasser's successor, **Anwar Sadat,** had little choice but to dismantle the massive state apparatus that had been created. He favored private rather than state initiatives. During Sadat's tenure in office the middle class, which had been greatly restricted by Nasser, emerged again as a powerful force. After fighting the Israelis to a stalemate in 1973, Sadat also moved to end the costly confrontation with Israel as well as Egypt's support for revolutionary movements in the Arab world. He expelled the Russians and opened Egypt to aid and investment from the United States and western Europe.

Sadat's shift in direction has been continued by his successor, **Hosni Mubarak.** But neither the attempt at genuine revolution led by Nasser nor the move to capitalism and more pro-West positions under his successors has done much to check Egypt's alarming population increases and the corruption of its bloated bureaucracy. Neither path to development has had much effect on the glaring gap between the living conditions of Egypt's rich minority and its impoverished masses. No better gauge of the discontent that is bred by these inequities can be found than the proliferation of Muslim fundamentalist movements. One of these succeeded in assassinating Sadat; others have sustained terrorist campaigns aimed at overthrowing the Mubarak regime.

The Indian Alternative: Development for Some of the People

Although the approach to nation-building and economic development followed by the leaders of independent India has shared the Nasserite emphasis on socialism and state intervention, India's experience has differed from Egypt's in several significant ways. To begin with, the Indians have managed to preserve civilian rule throughout the nearly five decades since they won their independence from Great Britain. In fact, in India the military has consistently defended secular democracy against religious extremism and other would-be authoritarian trends. In addition, although India, like Egypt, has been saddled with a crushing burden of overpopulation, it came to independence with a larger industrial and scientific sector, a better communication system and bureaucratic grid, and a larger and more skilled middle class in proportion to its total population than most other emerging nations.

During the first decades of its freedom, India had the good fortune to be governed by leaders such as Jawaharlal Nehru and his allies in the Congress party, who were deeply committed to social reform and economic development as well as the preservation of civil rights and democracy. India's success at the latter has been remarkable. Despite continuous threats of secession by religious and linguistic minorities, as well as poverty, unemployment, and recurring natural disasters, India remains the world's largest functioning democracy. Except for brief periods of rule by coalitions of opposition parties, the Congress party has ruled at the center for most of the independence era. But opposition parties have controlled many state and local governments, and they remain vocal and active in the national parliament. Civil liberties, exemplified by a very outspoken press and free elections, have been upheld to an extent that sets India off from much of the rest of the emerging nations.

Nehru's approach to government and development also differed from Nasser's in his more moderate mix of state and private initiatives. Nehru and his successors pushed state intervention in some sectors but also encouraged foreign investment from countries in both of the rival blocs in the cold war. As a consequence, India has been able to build on its initial advantages in industrial infrastructure and its skilled managerial and labor endowment. Its significant capitalist sector has encouraged ambitious farmers, such as those in the Punjab in the northwest, to invest heavily in the **Green Revolution**—the introduction of improved seed strains, fertilizers, and irrigation as a means of producing higher crop yields. Industrial and agrarian growth has generated the revenue necessary for the Indian government to promote literacy and village development schemes, as well as family planning, village electrification, and other improvement projects in recent decades. Indians have also developed one of the largest and most sophisticated high-tech sectors in the postcolonial world, including its own "silicon valleys" in cities like Bangalore in southern India. From the late 1980s India also provided tens of thousands of computer and Internet experts for advanced industrial societies such as those found in the United States and Europe.

Despite its successes, India has suffered from the same gap between needs and resources that all developing nations have had to face. Whatever the government's intentions—and India has been hit by corruption and self-serving politicians, like most nations—there have simply not been the resources to raise the living standards of even a majority of its huge population. The middle class has grown, perhaps as rapidly as that of any postcolonial nation. Its presence is striking in the affluent neighborhoods of cities such as Bombay and Delhi and is proclaimed by the Indian film industry, the world's largest, and in many sitcoms and dramas about the lives of Indian-style yuppies. But as many as 50 percent of India's people have gained little from the development plans and economic growth that have occurred since independence.

In part, this is because population growth has offset economic gains. But social reform has been slow in most areas, both rural and urban. Groups such as the wealthy landlords, who supported the nationalist drive for independence, have continued to dominate the great mass of tenants and landless laborers, just as they did in the precolonial and colonial eras. Some development measures, most notably those associated with the Green Revolution, have greatly favored cultivators with the resources to invest in new seeds and fertilizer. They have increased the gap between rich and poor people over much of rural India. Thus, the poor have paid and will continue to pay the price for Indian gradualism.

Iran: Religious Revivalism and the Rejection of the West

No path of development adopted by a postcolonial society has provided more fundamental challenges to the existing world order than revolutionary Iran under the direction of the **Ayatollah Ruhollah Khomeini.** In many respects, the Khomeini revolution of 1979 was a throwback to the religious fervor of such anticolonial resistance movements as that led by the Mahdi of the Sudan in the 1880s. Core motivations for the followers of both movements were provided by the emphasis on religious purification and the rejoining of religion and politics, which leaders such as the Mahdi and Khomeini have seen as central to the Islamic tradition. The call for a return to the kind of society believed to have existed in the past "golden age" of the prophet Muhammad was central to the policies pursued by both the Mahdist and Iranian regimes once they had gained power. Both movements were aimed at toppling Western-backed governments: the Mahdists' the Anglo-Egyptian presence in the Sudan, Khomeini's the autocratic Iranian shah and the Pahlavi dynasty.

Although they came from the Sunni and Shi'a religious traditions, respectively, both the Mahdi and Khomeini claimed to be divinely inspired deliverers. Each promised to rescue the Islamic faithful from imperialist Westerners and from corrupt and heretical leaders within the Muslim world. Both leaders promised their followers magical protection and instant paradise should they fall while waging the holy war against the heretics and infidels. Each leader sought to build a lasting state and social order on the basis of what were believed to be Islamic precedents. Thus, each revivalist movement aimed at defending and restoring what its leaders believed to be the true beliefs, traditions, and institutions of Islamic civilization. The leaders of both movements sought to spread their revolutions to surrounding areas, both Muslim and infidel, and each believed he was setting in motion forces that would eventually sweep the entire globe.

Though proclaimed as an alternative path for development that could be followed by the rest of the emerging nations, Khomeini's revolution owed its initial success in seizing power to a combination of circumstances that was unique to Iran (see Map 34.4). Like China, Iran had not been formally colonized by the European powers but rather had been reduced to a sphere of informal influence, divided between Great Britain and Russia. As a result, neither the bureaucratic nor the communication infrastructures that accompanied colonial takeovers were highly developed there. Nor did a substantial Western-educated middle class emerge. Thus, the impetus for "modernization" came suddenly and was imposed from above by the Pahlavi shahs. The initiatives taken by the second shah in particular, which were supported by Iran's considerable oil wealth, wrenched Iran out of the isolation and backwardness in which most of the nation lived until the mid-20th century. The shah tried to impose economic development and social change by government directives. Although advances occurred, the regime managed to alienate the great mass of the Iranian people in the process.

The shah's dictatorial and repressive regime deeply offended the emerging middle classes, whom he considered his strongest potential supporters. His flaunting of Islamic conventions and his neglect of Islamic worship and religious institutions enraged the *ayatollahs*, or religious experts. They also alienated the *mullahs*, or local prayer leaders and mosque attendants, who guided the religious and personal lives of the great majority of the Iranian population. The favoritism the shahs showed foreign investors and a handful of big Iranian entrepreneurs with personal connections to highly placed officials angered the smaller bazaar merchants, who had long maintained close links with the mullahs and other religious leaders. The shah's half-hearted land reform schemes alienated the land-owning classes without doing much to improve the condition of the rural poor. Even the urban workers, who benefited most from the boom in construction and light industrialization the shah's development efforts had stimulated, were dissatisfied. In the years before the 1979 revolution, a fall in oil prices had resulted in an economic slump and widespread unemployment in urban areas such as the capital, Tehran.

Although he had treated his officers well, the shah had badly neglected the military rank-and-file, especially in the army. So when the crisis came in 1978, the shah found that few soldiers were prepared to defend his regime. His armies refused to fire on the growing crowds that demonstrated for his removal and the return of Khomeini, then in exile in Paris. Dying of cancer and disheartened by what he saw as betrayal by his people and by allies such as the United States, the shah fled without much of a fight. Khomeini's revolution triumphed over a regime that looked powerful but proved to be exceptionally vulnerable.

After coming to power, Khomeini, defying the predictions of most Western "experts" on Iranian affairs, followed through on his promises of radical change. Constitutional and leftist parties allied to the revolutionary movement were brutally repressed. Moderate leaders were replaced quickly by radical religious figures who were eager to obey Khomeini's every command. The "satanic" influences of the United States and western Europe were purged; at the same time, Iran also distanced itself from the atheistic communist world. Secular influences in law and government were supplanted by strict Islamic legal codes, which included such punishments as the amputation of limbs for theft and stoning for women caught in adultery. Veiling became obligatory for all women, and the career prospects for women of the educated middle classes, who had been among the most favored by the shah's reforms, suddenly were limited drastically.

Khomeini's planners also drew up grand schemes for land reform, religious education, and economic development that accorded with the dictates of Islam. Most of these measures came to little because soon after the revolution, Saddam Hussein, the military leader of neighboring Iraq, sought to take advantage of the turmoil in Iran by annexing its western, oil-rich provinces. The First Gulf War that resulted swallowed up Iranian energies and resources for almost the entire decade after Khomeini came to power. The struggle became a highly personal vendetta for Khomeini, who was determined to destroy Saddam Hussein and punish the Iraqis. His refusal to negotiate peace caused heavy losses and untold suffering to the Iranian people. This suffering continued long after it was clear that the Iranians' aging military equipment and hand-ful of allies were no match for Hussein's more advanced military hardware and an Iraqi war machine bankrolled by its oil-rich Arab neighbors, who were fearful that Khomeini's revolution might spread to their own countries.

As the support of the Western powers, including the United States (despite protestations of neutrality), for the Iraqis increased, the position of the isolated Iranians became increasingly intolerable. Hundreds of thousands of poorly armed and half-trained Iranian conscripts, including tens of thousands of untrained and nearly weaponless boys, died before Khomeini finally agreed to a humiliating armistice in 1988. Peace found revolutionary Iran in shambles. Few of its development initiatives had been pursued, and shortages in food, fuel, and the other necessities of life were widespread.

Iran's decade-long absorption in the war and its continuing isolation makes it impossible to assess the potential of the religious revivalist, anti-Western option for other postcolonial nations. What had seemed at first to be a viable path to independent development had become mired in brutal internal repression and misguided and failed development schemes. By the 1990s, however, although control by Islamic leaders continued, more open elections began to occur in Iran, presenting new alternatives for the future.

South Africa: The Apartheid State and Its Demise

South Africa was by no means the only area still under some form of colonial dominance decades after India gained its independence in 1947. Portugal, the oldest and long considered the weakest of the European colonizers, held onto Angola, Mozambique, and its other African possessions until the mid-1970s. Until 1980, Zimbabwe (formerly Southern Rhodesia) was run by white settlers, who had unilaterally declared their independence from Great Britain. Southwest Africa became fully free of South African control only in 1989, and some of the smaller islands in the West Indies and the Pacific remain under European or American rule to the present day.

By the 1970s, however, South Africa was by far the largest, most populous, richest, and most strategic area where most of the population had yet to be liberated from colonial domination. Since the 1940s, the white settlers, particularly the Dutch-descended Afrikaners, had solidified their internal control of the country under the leadership of the Nationalist party.

Visualizing the Past

Globalization and Postcolonial Societies

Although many of the areas colonized by the industrialized nations of the West had participated in long-distance trade from early times, colonial rule greatly intensified their integration into the capitalist-dominated world system. Colonization also brought more remote areas that had been only marginally affected by cross-cultural trade into the world system for the first time. As we have seen in Chapter 24 and the present chapter, new market linkages not only affected the elites and trading classes of African, Middle Eastern, and Asian societies, but they also increasingly involved the peasants, who made up the great majority of the population of colonial societies, as well as smaller numbers of workers in the towns and cities.

In the postcolonial era, this process of global market integration has accelerated steadily. One key feature of advancing globalization has been the specialized production of mineral and agricultural exports for foreign consumption. Another has been the growing proportion of uprooted farmers and urban laborers in postcolonial societies employed in factories manufacturing clothing, household furnishings, audiovisual equipment, and other consumer goods for sale overseas, particularly in wealthy societies such as those in North America, western Europe, and Japan. These shifts have greatly increased trading links and economic independence between postcolonial societies and those that had formerly colonized them.

The pervasiveness of these connections in the daily lives of peoples around the globe can be readily seen in the shoes, clothing, and watches worn by the teacher and students in your class, and by the equipment and furnishings of your classrooms. Poll the class to determine where these items and other school supplies were produced. Discuss household and other personal items that were likely to have been manufactured, or at least assembled, in similar locales. Then consider the conditions under which the laborers who made these products were likely to have worked, and the international corporations that oversee and market these products.

Questions: Who benefits the most from the profits made in the international marketing of goods from postcolonial societies? How does the fact they are imported in massive quantities affect the wages and working conditions of American factory laborers? What measures can be taken to improve the situation of both workers in emerging nations and those in the United States, or are the interests of the two irreconcilable?

In stages and through a series of elections in which the blacks, who made up the majority of South Africans, were not allowed to vote, the Nationalists won complete independence from Great Britain in 1960. From 1948, when the Nationalist party first came to power, the Afrikaners moved to institutionalize white supremacy and white minority rule by passing thousands of laws that, taken together, made up the system of apartheid (see Chapter 31) that dominated all aspects of South African life until the 1990s.

Apartheid was designed not only to ensure a monopoly of political power and economic dominance for the white minority, both British- and Dutch-descended, but also to impose a system of extreme segregation on all races of South Africa in all aspects of their lives. Separate and patently unequal facilities were established for different racial groups for recreation, education, housing, work, and medical care. Dating and sexual intercourse across racial lines were strictly prohibited, skilled and high-paying jobs were reserved for white workers, and nonwhites were required to carry passes that listed the parts of South Africa where they were allowed to work and live. If caught by the police without their passes or in areas where they were not permitted to travel, nonwhite South Africans were routinely given stiff jail sentences.

Spatial separation was also organized on a grander scale by the creation of numerous **homelands** within South Africa, each designated for the main ethnolinguistic or "tribal" groups within the black African population. Though touted by the Afrikaners as the ultimate solution to the racial "problem," the homelands scheme would have left the black African majority with a small portion of some of the poorest land in South Africa. Because the homelands were overpopulated and poverty-stricken, the white minority was guaranteed a ready supply of cheap black labor to work in their factories and mines and on their farms. Denied citizenship in South Africa proper, these laborers would have been forced eventually to return to the homelands, where they had left their wives and children while emigrating in search of work.

To maintain the blatantly racist and inequitable system of apartheid, the white minority had to build a police state and expend a large portion of the federal budget on a sophisticated and well-trained military establishment. Because of the land's great mineral wealth, the Afrikaner nationalists were able to find the resources to fund their garrison state for decades. Until the late 1980s, the government prohibited all forms of black protest and brutally repressed even nonviolent resistance. Black organizations such as the **African National Congress** were declared illegal, and African leaders such as **Walter Sisulu** and **Nelson Mandela** were shipped off to maximum-security prisons. Other leaders, such as **Steve Biko,** one of the young organizers of the Black Consciousness movement, were murdered while in police custody.

Through spies and police informers, the regime tried to capitalize on personal and ethnic divisions within the black majority community. Favoritism was shown to some leaders and groups to keep them from uniting with others in all-out opposition to apartheid. With all avenues of constitutional negotiation and peaceful protest closed, many advocates of black majority rule in a multiracial society turned to guerrilla resistance from the 1960s onward. The South African government responded in the 1980s by declaring a state of emergency, which simply intensified the restrictions already in place in the garrison state. The government repeatedly justified its repression by labeling virtually all black protest as communist-inspired and playing on the racial fears of the white minority.

Through most of the 1970s and early 1980s, it appeared that the hardening hostility between the unyielding white minority and the frustrated black majority was building to a very violent upheaval. But from the late 1980s, countervailing forces were taking hold in South African society. An international boycott greatly weakened the South African economy. In addition, the South African army's costly and futile involvement in wars in neighboring Namibia and Angola seemed to presage never-ending struggles against black liberation movements within the country. Led by the courageous **F. W. de Klerk,** moderate Afrikaner leaders pushed for reforms that

began to dismantle the system of apartheid. The release of key black political prisoners, such as the dramatic freeing of Nelson Mandela in 1990, signaled that at long last the leaders of the white majority were ready to negotiate the future of South African politics and society. Permission for peaceful mass demonstrations and ultimately the enfranchisement of all adult South Africans for the 1994 elections provided a way out of the dead end in which the nation was trapped under apartheid.

The well-run and remarkably participatory 1994 elections brought to power the African National Congress party, led by Nelson Mandela, who became the first black president of South Africa. He has proved to be one of the most skillful and respected political leaders on the world scene as well as a moderating force in the potentially volatile South African arena. The peaceful surrender of power by F. W. de Klerk's losing party, which was supported by most of the white minority, suggested that a pluralist democracy might well succeed in South Africa (Figure 34.10). But major obstacles remain. Bitter interethnic rivalries within the black majority community, which periodically flared into bloody battles between Zulus and Xhosas in 1990s, have yet to be fully resolved. Hard-line white supremacist organizations among the Afrikaners continue to defy the new regime. And the tasks of reforming the institutions and redistributing the wealth of South Africa in ways that will make for a just and equitable social order are formidable. Well into the 21st century, South Africa is likely to remain one of the most interesting and promising social experiments of an age in which communalism and ethnic hostility threatened to engulf much of the globe.

Comparisons of Emerging Nations

This chapter has focused on many of the common problems faced by newly independent nations in Asia, the Middle East, and Africa in the final decades of the 20th century. Some of these problems, obviously, resemble issues in Latin America discussed in Chapter 33, where new nations' problems were less salient than for the regions discussed here but where population pressure, environmental change, and considerable economic dependence also loomed large.

Despite common issues, it is also important to distinguish particular patterns in the late 20th century, some of which reflected older traditions in key civilizations. India's success in maintaining democ-

Figure 34.10 *This photograph of a long line of newly enfranchised citizens waiting to vote in South Africa provides a striking contrast with the decreasing participation in elections in the United States and other older democracies in the West. For the first time, the Bantu-speaking peoples, coloreds, and Indians who made up the vast majority of South Africa's population were allowed to vote in free elections. Their determination to exercise their hard-won right to vote was demonstrated by the peoples' willingness to wait, often in stifling heat, for many hours in the long lines that stretched from polling stations throughout the country.*

racy, for example, contrasts with the experience of most of the Middle East and, until recently, much of Africa. India was less completely a new nation than its counterparts elsewhere. It reflected enlightened leadership and its complex relationship with Great Britain. Earlier Indian traditions of considerable decentralization showed in the federal system of the huge democracy. The abolition of the caste system, a massive change, did not remove considerable social inequality based in part on the caste heritage. While it too changed in some ways, the persistence of Hinduism as the majority religion marked India as well.

Developments in the Middle East reflected massive changes, ranging from the tensions over Israel to the region's growing control over its oil revenues. Despite distinguished traditions, most nations in this region were new, and political patterns also reflected the absence of a dominant regional state since the fall of the Ottoman Empire. Important tensions continued between secular and religious leaders. The significance of Islam, as in the Iranian revolution, also linked this region to earlier traditions, raising issues about the relationship between religion and politics and the role of women that had distinctive regional elements as well.

Africa had particular features of its own. The new nations of sub-Saharan Africa came late to independence, and they had been subjected to increasing Western economic dominance well into the postcolonial decades. This was one reason that Africa was poorer than most of Asia by the century's end. Massive cultural changes included growing conversions to Islam or Christianity: by 2000, about 40 percent of all sub-Saharan Africans were Muslim, about 40 percent Christian, while the number of traditional polytheists had shrunk to 20 percent (from 80 percent) during the course of the century. Nationalism, consumer culture, and some Marxism constituted other new cultural components. Yet here too, some observers found important elements of tradition. Many Africans combined older beliefs and artistic styles with their new religions. In some nations, emphasis on powerful authoritarian rulers reflected not only the tensions of new nationhood, but an earlier tradition of "Big Man" rule.

GLOBAL CONNECTIONS: Postcolonial Nations in the Cold War World Order

The years of independence for the nations that have emerged from the colonial empires in Asia, the Middle East, and Africa have been filled with political and economic crises and social turmoil, and tensions between tradition and change. At the same time, it is important to put the recent history of these areas in a larger perspective. Most of the new nations that emerged from colonialism have been in existence for only a few decades. They came to independence with severe handicaps, many of which were a direct legacy of their colonial experiences. It is also important to remember that developed countries, such as the United States, took decades filled with numerous boundary disputes and outright wars to reach their current size and structure. Nearly a century after the original 13 colonies broke from Great Britain and formed the United States, a civil war, the most costly war in the nation's history, was needed to preserve the union. If one takes into account the artificial nature of the emerging nations, most have held together rather well.

What is true in politics is true of all other aspects of the postcolonial experience of the African, Middle Eastern, and Asian peoples. With much lower populations and far fewer industrial competitors, as well as the capacity to draw on the resources of much of the rest of the world, European and North American nations had to struggle to industrialize and thereby achieve a reasonable standard of living for most of their people. Even with these advantages, the human cost in terms of horrific working conditions and urban squalor was enormous, and we are still paying the high ecological price. African, Middle Eastern, and Asian countries

(and, as we saw in Chapter 27, this includes Japan) have had few or none of the West's advantages. Most of the emerging nations have begun the "great ascent" to development burdened by excessive and rapidly increasing populations that overwhelm the limited resources that developing nations often must export to earn the capital to buy food and machines. The emerging nations struggle to establish a place in the world market system that is structured in favor of the established industrial powers.

Despite the cultural dominance of the West, which was one of the great legacies or burdens of the colonial era, Asian, Middle Eastern, and African thinkers and artists have achieved a great deal. If much of this achievement has depended on Western models, one should not be surprised, given the educational backgrounds and personal experiences of the emerging nations' first generations of leaders. The challenge for the coming generations will be to find genuinely African, Middle Eastern, and Asian solutions to the problems that have stunted political and economic development in the postcolonial nations. The solutions arrived at are likely to vary a great deal, given the diversity of the nations and societies involved. They are also likely to be forged from a combination of Western influences and the ancient and distinguished traditions of civilized life that have been nurtured by African, Middle Eastern, and Asian peoples for millennia.

Further Readings

Much of the prolific literature on political and economic development in the emerging nations is focused on individual countries, and it is more helpful to know several cases in some depth than to try to master them all. Robert Heilbroner's writings, starting with *The Great Ascent* (1961), still provide the most sensible introduction to challenges to the new states in the early decades of independence. Peter Worsley's *The Third World* (1964) provides a provocative, if somewhat disjointed, supplement to Heilbroner's many works. Though focused mainly on south and southeast Asia, Gunnar Myrdal's *Asian Drama* (3 vols., 1968), is the best exploration in a single cultural area of the complexities of the challenges to development. A good overview of the history of postindependence south Asia can be found in W. N. Brown's *The United States and India, Pakistan, and Bangladesh* (1984 ed.), despite its misleadingly Western-centric title. Perhaps the best account of Indian politics is contained in Paul Brass' *The Politics of India Since Independence* (1990) in the *New Cambridge History of India* series.

On development policy in India, see Francine R. Frankel's *India's Political Economy, 1947–1977* (1978).

Ali Mazrui and Michael Tidy's *Nationalism and New States in Africa* (1984) provides a good survey of developments throughout Africa. Also useful are S. A. Akintoye's *Emergent African States* (1976) and H. Bretton's *Power and Politics in Africa* (1973). For the Middle East, John Waterbury's *The Egypt of Nasser and Sadat* (1983) provides a detailed account of the politics of development, and Peter Mansfield's *The Arabs* (1978) supplies a decent (if now a bit dated) overview.

On military coups, see Ruth First's *The Barrel of a Gun* (1971) and S. Decalo's *Coups and Army Rule in Africa* (1976). Shaul Bakhash's *The Reign of the Ayatollahs* (1984) is perhaps the most insightful of several books that have appeared about Iran since the revolution. Brian Bunting's *The Rise of the South African Reich* (1964) traces the rise of the apartheid regime in great (and polemical) detail, while Gail Gerhart's *Black Power in South Africa* (1978) is one of the better studies devoted to efforts to tear that system down. Among the many fine African, Middle Eastern, and Asian authors whose works are available in English, some of the best include (for Africa) Chinua Achebe, Wole Soyinka, and Ousmene Sembene; (for India) R. K. Narayan and V. S. Naipaul; (for Egypt) Nawal el Saadawi and Naguib Mahfouz; and (for Indonesia) Mochtar Lubis and P. A. Toer. For white perspectives on the South African situation, the fictional works of Nadine Gordimer and J. M. Coetzee are superb.

On the Web

A timeline for decolonization is provided at http://smccd.net/accounts/helton/decoloni.htm and http://campus.northpark.edu/history/WebChron/World/Decolonization.html. An overview of famed African novelist Chinua Achebe's writing on imperialism and decolonization can be found at http://www.postcolonialweb.org/achebe/achebeov.html and http://www.webster.edu/~barrettb/achebe.htm.

Kwame Nkrumah's classic indictment of neocolonialism can be found at http://www.fhsu.edu/history/virtual/nkrumah.htm, while a classically neoconservative view condemning neocolonialism, but not modernization, is offered at http://www.afbis.com/analysis/neo-colonialism.html. The postcolonial burdens of

African leaders are addressed at sites devoted to Léopold Senghor (http://web.uflib.ufl.edu/cm/africana/senghor.htm) and the life and speeches of Tanzania's Julius Nyerere (http://www.hartford-hwp.com/archives/30/index-fd.html).

Gamal Abdul Nasser's cold war era experiments with Arab socialism as the best means of negotiating modernization are discussed at http://www.arab.net/egypt/et_nasser.htm and http://www.1upinfo.com/country-guide-study/egypt/egypt44.html.

The debate over the role of religion as a solution to the moral malaise as well as the disparity of wealth that has come to characterize the postmodern era is illuminated by the works of Hasan al-Banna of the Muslim Brotherhood (http://www.glue.umd.edu/~kareem/rasayil/, http://www.nmhschool.org/tthornton/hasan_al.htm, and http://www.ummah.org.uk/ikhwan/) and the life of Iran's Ayatollah Ruhollah Khomeini (http://www.iranchamber.com/history/rkhomeini/ayatollah_khomeini.php and http://www.asiasource.org/society/khomeini.cfm). For further information regarding Khomeini's role as the supreme leader of the Islamic revolution in Iran, see http://www.bbc.co.uk/persian/revolution/rev_01.shtml and http://www.fordham.edu/halsall/mod/1979khom1.html. Current moderating trends in this seedbed of the Islamic movement are analyzed at http://www.brown.edu/Departments/Anthropology/publications/IranisChanging.htm and http://www.brown.edu/Departments/Anthropology/Beeman.html.

A useful review of India's first 50 years of independence may be found at http://www.itihaas.com/independent/contrib7.html. Jawaharlal Nehru's views on Marxism, capitalism, and nonalignment are available at http://www.fordham.edu/halsall/mod/1941/nehru.html. His commitment to world disarmament (http://www.indianembassy.org/policy/Disarmament/India_Disarmament.htm) failed to move the world, and as a result, India later went down the path to nuclear confrontation with Pakistan. The growing place of religion in Indian political life, which Nehru would have also opposed, is embodied in the platform of the Bharatiya Janata Party (http://www.bjp.com). Indira Gandhi's role in postcolonial India is explored at http://www.sscnet.ucla.edu/southasia/History/Independent/Indira.html

CHAPTER 35

REBIRTH AND REVOLUTION: NATION-BUILDING IN EAST ASIA AND THE PACIFIC RIM

Mao Zedong as the friend and father of the people is the theme emphasized in this colorful poster from the Maoist era. Soldiers, peasants, women, children, and peoples from many regions of China are pictured here rallying to Mao's vision of a strong, just, and prosperous China.

- East Asia
  in the Postwar
  Settlements
- Japan, Incorporated
- The Pacific Rim:
  New Japans?
- VISUALIZING THE PAST:
  Pacific Rim
  Growth
- IN DEPTH: The Pacific
  Rim as a U.S.
  Policy Issue
- Mao's China
  and Beyond
- DOCUMENT: Women in
  the Revolutionary
  Struggle
- Colonialism
  and Revolution
  in Vietnam
- GLOBAL CONNECTIONS:
  East Asia and the
  Pacific Rim in the
  Contemporary
  World

In many respects, the recent histories of China and the peoples of Japan, Korea, and Vietnam, whose cultures were so profoundly affected by Chinese civilization, have been fundamentally different from those of much of the rest of Asia and Africa. Particularly in the past century, the experience of the Japanese has diverged the most from those of other Asian and African peoples. The ethnically homogenous, politically unified, and militarily adept Japanese not only were able to beat off Western imperialist advances against their island home but they have been one of the few non-Western peoples to achieve a high level of industrialization. Within decades of the forced "opening" of Japan by the United States in the 1850s, Japan also became the only African or Asian nation to join the ranks of the great powers. In imitation of its Western rivals, it embarked on its own campaign of imperialist expansion overseas. Although Korea was colonized early in the 20th century by its powerful Japanese neighbor, in the decades since World War II it has emerged as one of the leading industrial centers of the **Pacific Rim.** Since World War II as well, Korea, Taiwan, and several other centers experienced rapid industrial advances, propelling the Pacific Rim to new importance in world affairs.

In contrast to industrialized Japan and to Korea in the past three decades or so, with their high standards of living and global economic power, China and Vietnam have had a good deal in common with the rest of the emerging nations. China and Vietnam suffered heavily from the assaults and exploitive terms of exchange imposed by imperialist powers, both Western and Japanese. Each has had to contend with underdevelopment, overpopulation, poverty, and environmental degradation. But unlike most of the rest of the formerly colonized peoples, the Chinese and the Vietnamese have had to deal with these awesome challenges in the midst of the collapse of the patterns of civilized life each had followed for thousands of years.

As disruptive as imperialist conquest and its effects were in the rest of the Asian and African worlds, most colonized peoples managed to preserve much of their precolonial cultures and modes of social organization. The defense and revival of traditional customs, religious beliefs, and social arrangements played a key role in their struggles for decolonization. This was not the case in China and Vietnam, where a combination of external aggression and internal upheavals discredited and destroyed the Confucian system that had long been synonymous with civilized life. With their traditional order in shambles, the peoples of China and Vietnam had no choice but to embark on full-scale revolutions that would clear away the rubble of the failed Confucian system. They needed to remove the obstacles posed by imperialist dominance and build new, viable states and societies. In contrast to much of the rest of the colonized world, the countries of China and

863

1750 C.E.	1910 C.E.	1925 C.E.	1940 C.E.
1770s Tayson Rebellion in Vietnam	**1911** Revolution in China	**1925** VNQDD founded in Vietnam; first communist organization also established	**1942** Japanese occupation of French Indochina
1802 Establishment of the Nguyen dynasty; Vietnam unified	**1912** Fall of the Qing dynasty in China	**1927** Nationalists capture Shanghai; purge of communists and workers	**1945** Ho Chi Minh proclaims the Republic of Vietnam
1858–1862 Beginning of the French conquest of Vietnam	**1919** May Fourth Movement begins; founding of Guomindang or Nationalist party	**1929** Failed VNQDD-inspired uprising in Vietnam	**1948** U.S.-sponsored Republic of (South) Korea established
1883 French conquest of Vietnam is completed	**1921** Communist party of China founded	**1930** Failed communist uprising in Vietnam	**1949** Victory of the communists in China; People's Republic of China established
c.1900 Korean Communist party founded (in exile)		**1931** Japanese invasion of Manchuria	**1950–1951** Purge of the landlord class in China
		1937 Japanese invasion of China proper	**1950–1953** Korean War
			1952 End of U.S. occupation of Japan
			1953 Beginning of China's first five-year plan
			1954 French defeated at Dien Bien Phu; Geneva accords, French withdrawal from Vietnam; beginning of the Sino-Soviet split

Vietnam derived few benefits from European domination, either informal or formal. Imperialist pressures eroded and smashed their political institutions rather than building up a bureaucratic grid and imparting political ideologies that could form the basis for nation-building. Both China and Vietnam already had the strong sense of identity, common language, and unifying polity that were among the major legacies of colonialism in other areas.

Because of economic development (in the Pacific Rim, and more recently in China) and the forces of revolution, east Asia has been fundamentally recast in the decades since World War II and has gained new importance in world affairs. Patterns vary, between the combination of industrialization and reform of the Pacific Rim, in close connection to the West, and the fluctuations of major revolution. The legacy of earlier patterns in east Asia, including Confucianism, has similarly been redefined and utilized in different ways. But the themes of growing independence and self-assertion provide some commonalities to east Asia in contemporary world history, and many observers have also found some shared uses of the Confucian cultural and organizational heritage.

East Asia in the Postwar Settlements

 Adjustments at the end of World War II defined the Pacific Rim into the 1950s as a zone of reasonably stable noncommunist states developed. Linked to the West, these states maintained a neo-Confucian emphasis on the importance of conservative politics and a strong state.

The victors in World War II had some reasonably clear ideas about how east Asia was to be restructured. Korea was divided between a Russian zone of occupation in the north and an American zone in the south. The island of **Taiwan** was restored to China, which in principle was ruled by a Guomindang government headed by Chiang Kai-shek. The United States regained the Philippines and pledged to grant independence quickly, retaining some key military bases. European powers restored controls over their

1955 c.e.	1970 c.e.
mid-1950s Buildup of U.S. advisors in South Vietnam	**1975** Communist victory in Vietnam; collapse of the Republic of South Vietnam
1957 "Let a Hundred Flowers Bloom" campaign in China	**1976** Death of Zhou Enlai and Mao Zedong; purge of Gang of Four
1958–1960 "Great Leap Forward" in China	**1994** Death of North Korean leader Kim Il-Sung
1960 Syngman Rhee forced from office by student demonstrations	
1963 Beginning of state family planning in China	
1965–1968 Era of the Cultural Revolution in China	
1965–1973 Direct U.S. military intervention in Vietnam	
1968 Tet offensive in Vietnam	

holdings in Vietnam, Malaya, and Indonesia. Japan was occupied by American forces bent on introducing major changes that would prevent a recurrence of military aggression.

New Divisions and the End of Empires

Not surprisingly, the Pacific regions of Asia did not quickly settle into agreed-upon patterns. A decade after the war's end, not only the Philippines but also Indonesia and Malaya were independent, as part of the postwar tide of decolonization (see Map 35.1). Taiwan was still ruled by Chiang Kai-shek, but the Chinese mainland was in the hands of a new and powerful communist regime. Chiang's nationalist regime claimed a mission to recover China, but in fact Taiwan was a separate republic. Korea remained divided but had undergone a brutal north-south conflict in which only U.S. intervention preserved South Korea's independence. Japan was one of the few Pacific regions where matters had proceeded somewhat according to plan, as the nation began to recover while accepting a very different political structure.

Japanese Recovery

Japan in 1945 was in shambles. Its cities were burned, its factories destroyed or idle, its people impoverished and shocked by the fact of surrender and the trauma of bombing, including the atomic devastation of Hiroshima and Nagasaki. However, like the industrial nations of the West, Japan was

capable of reestablishing a vigorous economy with surprising speed. Its occupation by U.S. forces, eager to reform Japan but also eager to avoid punitive measures, provided an opportunity for a new period of selective westernization.

The American occupation government, headed by General Douglas MacArthur, worked quickly to tear down Japan's wartime political structure. (Occupation lasted until 1952, a year after Japan signed a peace treaty with most of its wartime opponents.) Japan's military forces were disbanded, the police decentralized, many officials removed, and political prisoners released. For the long run, American authorities pressed for a democratization of Japanese society by giving women the vote, encouraging labor unions, and abolishing Shintoism as a state religion. Several economic reforms were also introduced, breaking up landed estates for the benefit of small farmers—who quickly became politically conservative—and dissolving the holdings of the zaibatsu combines, a measure that had little lasting effect as Japanese big business regrouped quickly.

A new constitution tried to cut through older limitations by making the parliament the supreme

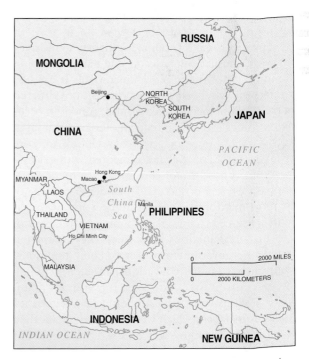

Map 35.1 *The Pacific Rim Area by 1960. Geographic locations and political systems created new contacts and alignments.*

overnment body. Several civil liberties were guaranteed, along with gender equality in marriage and collective bargaining rights. Military forces with "war potential" were abolished forever, making Japan a unique major nation in its limited military strength. The emperor became merely a symbolic figurehead, without political power and with no claims to Shinto divinity. Even as Japan accepted many political and legal concepts, it inserted its own values into the new constitution. Thus, a 1963 law called for special social obligations to the elderly, in obvious contrast to Western approaches: "The elders shall be loved and respected as those who have for many years contributed toward the development of society, and a wholesome and peaceful life shall be guaranteed to them."

These new constitutional measures were embraced by the Japanese people, many of whom became avid opponents of any hint of military revival. Military power and responsibility in the region were retained by the United States, which long after the occupation period kept important bases in Japan. Many of the political features of the new constitution worked smoothly—in large part because the Japanese had experienced parliamentary and political party activity for extended periods in previous decades. Two moderate parties merged in 1955 into the new **Liberal Democratic party**, which monopolized Japan's government into the 1990s.

Japan became a genuine multiparty democracy but with unusual emphasis on one-party control in the interests of order and elite control. It granted women the vote, but women's conditions differed markedly from men's. In education, American occupation forces insisted on reducing the nationalism in textbooks and opening secondary schools to more social groups. These changes merged with existing Japanese enthusiasm for education, heightening the emphasis on school success. Japan developed one of the most meritocratic systems in the world, with students advanced to university training on the basis of rigorous examinations. But once the occupation ended, the government reasserted some traditional components in this education package, including careful controls over textbooks. In 1966, for example, the Ministry of Education attacked "egotistic" attitudes in Japan, which were producing "a feeling of spiritual hollowness and unrest." Schools in this situation should generate ethical discipline and group consciousness, touching base with more customary goals while preparing students for their role in Japan's

expanding economy. As one conservative put it in the 1980s, "You have to teach tradition [to the children] whether they like it or not."

Korea: Intervention and War

Korea's postwar adjustment period was far more troubled than Japan's. The leaders of the great Allied powers during World War II had agreed in principle that Korea should be restored as an independent state. But the United States' eagerness to obtain Soviet help against Japan resulted in Soviet occupation of the northern part of the peninsula. As the cold war intensified, American and Soviet authorities could not agree on unification of the zones, and in 1948 the United States sponsored a **Republic of Korea** in the south, matched by a Soviet-dominated **People's Democratic Republic of Korea** in the north. North Korea's regime drew on an earlier Korean Communist party founded in exile in the 1900s. North Korea quickly became a communist state with a Stalinist-type emphasis on the power of the leader, Kim Il-Sung, until his death in 1994. The South Korean regime, bolstered by an ongoing American military presence, was headed by nationalist Syngman Rhee. Rhee's South Korea developed parliamentary institutions in form but maintained a strongly authoritarian tone.

In June 1950, North Korean forces attacked South Korea, hoping to impose unification on their own terms (see Figure 35.1). The United States reacted quickly (after some confusing signals about whether South Korea was inside the U.S. "defense perimeter"). President Truman insisted on drawing another line against communist aggression, and he orchestrated United Nations sponsorship of a largely American "police action" in support of South Korean troops. In the ensuing **Korean War,** under General MacArthur's leadership, Allied forces pushed North Korea back, driving on toward the Chinese border; this action roused concern on the part of China's communist regime, which sent "volunteers" to force American troops back toward the south. The front stabilized in 1952 near the original north-south border. The stalemate dragged on until 1953, when a new American administration was able to agree to an armistice.

Korea then continued its dual pattern of development. North Korea produced an unusually isolated version of one-man rule as Kim concentrated his

Figure 35.1 *A tank unit of the North Korean People's Army assembled in September 1950. Military buildup was part of the preparation for invading South Korea.*

powers over the only legal political party, the military, and the government. Even Soviet liberalization in the late 1980s brought little change. South Korea and the United States concluded a mutual defense treaty in 1954; American troop levels were reduced, but the South Korean army gained more sophisticated military equipment and the United States poured economic aid into the country, initially to prevent starvation in a war-ravaged land. The political tenor of South Korea continued to be authoritarian. In 1961, army officers took over effective rule of the country, although sometimes a civilian government served as a front.

However, economic change began to gain ground in South Korea, ushering in a new phase of activity and international impact. Tensions between the two Koreas continued to run high, with many border clashes and sabotage, but outright warfare was avoided.

Emerging Stability in Taiwan, Hong Kong, and Singapore

Postwar adjustments in Taiwan involved yet another set of issues. As the communist revolutionary armies gained the upper hand in mainland China, between 1946 and 1948 the Guomindang (Nationalist) regime prepared to fall back on its newly reacquired island, which the communists could not threaten because they had no navy. The result was imposition over the Taiwanese majority of a new leadership plus a massive military force drawn from the mainland.

The authoritarian political patterns the nationalists had developed in China, centered on Chiang Kai-shek's personal control of the government, were amplified by the need to keep disaffected Taiwanese in check. Hostility with the communist regime across the Taiwan Strait ran high. In 1955 and 1958, the communists bombarded two small islands controlled by the nationalists, Quemoy and Matsu, and wider conflict threatened as the United States backed up its ally. Tensions were defused when communist China agreed to fire on the islands only on alternate days, while United States ships supplied them on the off-days, thus salvaging national honor. Finally, the United States induced Chiang to renounce any intentions of attacking the mainland, and conflict eased into mutual bombardments of propaganda leaflets. During this period, as in South Korea, the United States gave economic aid to Taiwan, ending assistance only in the 1960s when growing prosperity seemed assured.

Two other participants in the economic advances of the Pacific Rim were distinguished by special ties to Britain. **Hong Kong** remained a British colony after World War II; only in the 1980s was an agreement reached between Britain and China for its 1997 return to the Chinese fold. Hong Kong gained increasing autonomy from direct British rule. Its Chinese population swelled at various points after 1946 as a result of flights from communist rule.

Singapore retained a large British naval base until 1971, when Britain abandoned all pretense of power in east Asia. Singapore grew into a vigorous free port, and became an independent nation in 1965.

Overall, by the end of the 1950s a certain stability had emerged in the political situation of many smaller east Asian nations. From the 1960s onward these same areas, combining Western contacts with important traditions of group loyalty, moved from impressive economic recovery to new international influence on the basis of manufacturing and trade.

Japan, Incorporated

 The keynotes of Japanese history from the 1950s onward were a fierce concentration on economic growth and distinctive political and cultural forms as the nation proved that industrial success did not depend on a strict Western pattern.

Japan's Distinctive Political and Cultural Style

The chief emphasis of Japanese politics lay in conservative stability. The Liberal Democratic party held the reins of government from 1955 onward. This meant that Japan, uniquely among the democratic nations of the postwar world, had no experience with shifts in party administration until 1993. Changes in leadership, which at times were frequent, were handled through negotiations among the Liberal Democratic elite, not directly as a result of shifts in voter preference.

Clearly, this system revived many of the oligarchic features of Meiji Japan and the Japan of the 1920s. During the prosperous 1970s and 1980s, economic progress and the Liberal Democrats' willingness to consult opposition leaders about major legislation reinforced Japan's effective political unity. Only at the end of the 1980s, when several Liberal Democratic leaders were branded by corruption of various sorts, were new potential questions raised.

Japan's distinctive political atmosphere showed clearly in strong cooperation with business. The state set production and investment goals while actively lending public resources to encourage investment and limit imports. The government-business coordination to promote economic growth and export expansion prompted the half-admiring, half-derisory Western label "Japan, Incorporated."

The government actively campaigned to promote birth control and abortion, and population growth slowed. This was another product of the strong national tradition of state-sponsored discipline.

As in politics and education, Japanese culture preserved important traditional elements, which provided aesthetic and spiritual satisfactions amid rapid economic change (see Figure 35.2). Customary styles in poetry, painting, tea ceremonies, and flower arrangements continued. Each New Year's Day, for example, the emperor presided at a poetry contest, and masters of traditional arts were honored by being designated as Living National Treasures. Kabuki and No theater also flourished. Japanese films and novels

Figure 35.2 *Traditional settings are found in modern Japan. The yomei-mon gateway, at the Mausoleum of Leyasu in Nikko, is a traditional place for contemplation.*

often recalled the country's earlier history. Japanese painters and architects participated actively in the "international style" pioneered in the West, but they often infused it with earlier Japanese motifs such as stylized nature painting. City orchestras played the works of Western composers and native compositions that incorporated passages played on the Japanese flute and zither. At the same time, aside from interior decoration and film, Japanese contributions to world culture were negligible; this was not where national creativity showed an international face.

Cultural combinations were not always smooth. Both before and after World War II, key intellectuals used art and literature to protest change, not merely to blend Western and traditional styles. The flamboyant postwar writer Hiraoka Kimitoke (pen name Yukio Mishima, 1925–1970) was a case in point. His novels and dramas, which began to appear in 1949, dealt with controversial themes such as homosexuality while also updating versions of the No plays. A passionate nationalist, he was too sickly for military service in World War II, though he later built up his body. At first he enjoyed many Western contacts and interests, but he came to hate Western ways. In 1968 he formed a private army centered on restoring Japanese ideals. After finishing a final major novel, Mishima performed his own ritual suicide in 1970. He wrote to an American friend shortly before his death, "I came to wish to sacrifice myself for this old beautiful tradition of Japan, which is disappearing very quickly day by day."

The Economic Surge

Particularly after the mid-1950s, rapid economic growth made Japan's clearest mark internationally and commanded the most intense energies at home. By 1983, the total national product was equal to the combined totals of China, both Koreas, Taiwan, India, Pakistan, Australia, and Brazil. Per capita income, though still slightly behind that of the leading Western nations such as West Germany, had passed that of many countries, including Britain. Annual economic growth reached at least 10 percent regularly from the mid-1950s onward, surpassing the regular levels of every other nation during the 1960s and 1970s, as Japan became one of the top two or three economic powers in the world (see Figure 35.3). Leading Japanese corporations, such as the great automobile manufacturers and electronic equipment producers, became known not simply for the volume of their international exports but for the high quality of their goods.

A host of factors fed this astounding economic performance. Active government encouragement was a major ingredient. Educational expansion played a major role as Japan began to turn out far more engineers than did more populous competitors such as the United States. Foreign policy also played a role. Japan was able to devote almost its whole capital to investment in productive technology, for its military expenses were negligible given its reliance on United States protection.

Japan's distinctive labor policies functioned well. Workers were organized mainly in company unions that were careful not to impair their companies' productivity. Leading corporations solidified this cooperation, which spurred zealous work from most employees. Social activities, including group exercise sessions before the start of the working day, promoted and expressed group loyalty, and managers took active interest in suggestions by employees. The Japanese system also ensured lifetime employment to an important part of the labor force, a policy aided by economic growth, low average unemployment rates, and an early retirement age. This network of policies and attitudes made Japanese labor seem both less class-conscious and less individualistic than labor forces in the advanced industrial nations of the West; it reflected older traditions of group solidarity in Japan, going back to feudal patterns.

Japanese management displayed a distinctive spirit, again as a result of adapting older traditions of leadership. There was more group consciousness, including a willingness to abide by collective decisions and less concern for quick personal profits than was characteristic of the West, particularly the United States. Few corporate bureaucrats changed firms, which meant that their efforts were concentrated on their company's success. Leisure life remained meager by Western standards, and many Japanese were reluctant to take regular vacations.

Japan's distinctiveness extended to family life, despite some features similar to the West's industrial experience. Japanese women, though increasingly well educated and experiencing an important decline in birth rates, did not follow Western patterns precisely. A feminist movement was confined to a small

Figure 35.3   *Tokyo at night at the beginning of the 21st century epitomizes the resurgence of Asian economies following World War II.*

number of intellectuals. Within the family, women shared fewer leisure activities with their husbands, concentrating more heavily on domestic duties and intensive child-rearing than was true in the West by the 1970s. In child-rearing, conformity to group standards was emphasized far more than in the West or in communist China. A comparative study of nursery schools showed that Japanese teachers were bent on effacing their own authority in the interests of developing strong bonds between the children. Shame was directed toward nonconformist behaviors, a disciplinary approach the West had largely abandoned in the early 19th century. Japanese television game shows, superficially copied from those of the West, imposed elaborate, dishonoring punishment on losing contestants.

The nation had few lawyers, for it was assumed that people could make and abide by firm arrangements through mutual agreement. Psychiatrists reported far fewer problems of loneliness and individual alienation than in the West. Conversely, situations that promoted competition between individuals, such

as university entrance tests, produced far higher stress levels than did analogous Western experiences. The Japanese had particular ways to relieve tension. Bouts of heavy drinking were more readily tolerated than in the West, seen as a time when normal codes of conduct could be suspended under the helpful eyes of friends. Businessmen and some politicians had recourse to traditional geisha houses for female-supplied cosseting, a normal and publicly accepted activity.

Japanese popular culture was not static, both because of ongoing attraction to Western standards and because of rapid urbanization and economic growth. The U.S. presence after World War II brought a growing fascination with baseball, and professional teams flourished. Japanese athletes began also to excel in such sports as tennis and golf. In the mid-1980s, the government, appalled to discover that a majority of Japanese children did not use chopsticks but preferred knives and forks in order to eat more rapidly, invested money to promote chopsticks training in the schools. This was a minor development, but it indicates the ongoing tension between change, with its Western connotations, and a commitment to Japanese identity (see Figure 35.4). The veneration of old age was challenged by some youthful assertiveness and by the sheer cost of supporting the rapidly growing percentage of older people, for Japan relied heavily on family support for elders.

Other issues were associated with change. By the 1960s, pollution became a serious problem as cities and industry expanded rapidly; traffic police, for example, sometimes wore masks to protect their lungs. The government (eager to preempt a potential opposition issue) paid increasing attention to environmental issues after 1970.

The 1990s brought some new questions to Japan. Mired in political corruption, the Liberal Democrats were replaced by shaky coalition governments. A severe economic recession caused widespread unemployment. Even as Japanese methods were being touted in the West as a basis for economic and social revitalization, some of the critical patterns of postwar development were at least temporarily disrupted.

The Pacific Rim: New Japans?

 Economic and to some extent political developments in several other middle-sized nations and city-states on Asia's Pacific coast mirrored important elements of Japan's 20th-century history, though at a slightly later date. Political authoritarianism was characteristic, though usually with periodic bows to parliamentary forms and with recurrent protests from dissidents who wanted greater freedom. Government functions extended to careful economic planning and rapid expansion of the educational system, which emphasized technical training. Group loyalties promoted diligent labor and a willingness to work hard for low wages. Economic growth burgeoned, although new clouds appeared on the horizon at the end of the 1990s.

The Korean Miracle

South Korea was the most obvious example of the spread of new economic dynamism to other parts of the Pacific Rim. The Korean government rested normally in the hands of a political strongman, usually from army ranks. Syngman Rhee was forced out of office by student demonstrations in 1960; a year later, a military general, Park Chung-hee, seized power. He retained his authority until his assassination in 1979 by his director of intelligence. Then another general seized power. Intense student protest, backed by wider popular support, pressed the military from power at the end of the 1980s, but a conservative politician won the ensuing general election, and it was not clear how much the political situation had changed. Opposition activity was possible in South Korea, though usually heavily circumscribed, and many leaders were jailed. There was some freedom of the press although it did not extend to publications from communist countries.

Figure 35.4 *As this photo of an ultra-modern skyscraper in Hong Kong amply illustrates, some of the most innovative architecture of the age of globalization can be found in the great commercial centers along the Pacific Rim. The region also boasts the world's tallest building, a twin-tower office complex in the Malaysian capital of Kuala Lumpur.*

As in postwar Japan, the South Korean government from the mid-1950s onward placed its primary emphasis on economic growth, which in this case started from a much lower base after the Korean War and previous Japanese exploitation. Huge industrial firms were created by a combination of government aid and active entrepreneurship. By the 1970s, when growth rates in Korea began to match those of Japan, Korea was competing successfully in the area of cheap consumer goods, as well as in steel and automobiles, in a variety of international markets. In steel, Korea's surge—based on the most up-to-date technology, a skilled engineering sector, and low wages—pushed past Japan's. The same held true in textiles, where Korean growth (along with that of Taiwan) erased almost one-third of the jobs held in the industry in Japan.

Huge industrial groups such as Daewoo and **Hyundai** resembled the great Japanese holding companies before and after World War II and wielded great political influence. For example, Hyundai was the creation of entrepreneur Chung Ju Yung, a modern folk hero who walked 150 miles to Seoul, South Korea's capital, from his native village to take his first job as a day laborer at age 16. By the 1980s, when Chung was in his sixties, his firm had 135,000 employees and 42 overseas offices throughout the world. Hyundai virtually governed Korea's southeastern coast. It built ships, including petroleum supertankers; it built thousands of housing units sold to low-paid workers at below-market rates; it built schools, a technical college, and an arena for the practice of the traditional Korean martial art Tae Kwon Do. With their lives carefully provided for, Hyundai workers responded in kind, putting in six-day weeks with three vacation days per year and participating in almost worshipful ceremonies when a fleet of cars was shipped abroad or a new tanker launched (see Figure 35.5).

South Korea's rapid entry into the ranks of newly industrialized countries produced a host of more general changes. The population soared: By the 1980s more than 40 million people lived in a nation about the size of the state of Indiana, producing one of the highest population densities on earth: about 1000 people per square mile. This was one reason, even amid growing prosperity, why many Koreans emigrated. The government gradually began to encourage couples to limit their birth rates. Seoul expanded to embrace 9 million people; it developed intense air pollution and a hothouse atmosphere of deals and business maneuvers. Per capita income grew despite the population increase, rising almost 10 times from the early 1950s to the early 1980s, but to a level still only one-ninth of that of Japan. Huge fortunes coexisted with widespread poverty in this setting, although the poor were better off than those of less developed nations.

Figure 35.5 *Hyundai loading dock for export to the United States.*

Visualizing the Past

Pacific Rim Growth

How can the figures in the table be used to illustrate the industrial emergence of the Pacific Rim (Japan, South Korea, Singapore, Hong Kong)? Which countries most clearly have been undergoing an industrial revolution since the 1960s, and how can this be measured? How do the key Pacific Rim areas compare in growth to the neighboring "little tigers," Indonesia, Malaysia, and Thailand? Do the Philippines constitute another "little tiger?" Finally, how do Japanese patterns compare with the newer areas of the Pacific Rim, and how can this relationship be explained?

Note: Growth at 2.3 percent per year doubles the category in 30 years; 7 percent per year doubles in 10 years.

Indices of Growth and Change in the Pacific Rim

Gross National Product (GNP) 1965–1996

	Per Capita GNP East and Southeast Asia, annual growth rates (%)	
	1965	1996
China	8.5	6.7
Hong Kong	7.5	5.6
Indonesia	6.7	4.6
Japan	4.5	3.6
Korea (South)	8.9	7.3
Malaysia	6.8	4.1
Philippines	3.5	0.9
Singapore	8.3	6.3
Thailand	7.3	5.0
For comparison		
All preexisting industrial countries	3.0	2.2
United States	2.4	1.4
India	4.5	2.3

	Social and Economic Data			
	% labor force in agriculture		% population urban	
	1965	1996	1965	1996
China	78	72	17	31
Indonesia	66	55	41	82
Japan	20	7	71	78
Korea (South)	49	18	41	82
Malaysia	54	27	34	54
Thailand	80	64	13	20

Adapted from World Bank, World Development Indicators (Washington, D.C., 1998).

Advances in Taiwan and the City-States

The Republic of China, as the government of Taiwan came to call itself, experienced a high rate of economic development. Productivity in both agriculture and industry increased rapidly, the former spurred by land reform that benefited small commercial farmers. The government concentrated increasingly on economic gains as its involvement in plans for military action against the mainland communist regime declined. As in Japan and Korea, formal economic planning reached high levels, though allowing latitude for private business. Money was poured into education, and literacy rates and levels of technical training rose rapidly. The result was important cultural and economic change for the Taiwanese people. Traditional medical practices and ritualistic popular religion remained lively but were expanded to allow simultaneous use of modern, Western-derived medicine and some of the urban entertainment forms popular elsewhere.

The assimilation of rapid change gave the Taiwanese government great stability despite a host of new concerns. The U.S. recognition of the People's Republic of China brought with it a steadily decreasing official commitment to Taiwan. In 1978, the United States severed diplomatic ties with the Taiwanese regime, although unofficial contacts—through the American Institute in Taiwan and the Coordination Council for North American Affairs, established by the republic in Washington—remained strong. The Taiwanese also built important regional contacts with other governments in eastern and southeastern Asia that facilitated trade. For example, Japan served as the nation's most important single trading partner, purchasing foodstuffs, manufactured textiles, chemicals, and other industrial goods.

Taiwan also developed some informal links with the communist regime in Beijing, although the latter continued to claim the island as part of its territory. The republic survived the death of Chiang Kai-shek and the accession of his son, **Chiang Ching-kuo,** in 1978. The young Chiang emphasized personal authority less than his father had, and he reduced somewhat the gap between mainland-born military personnel and native Taiwanese in government ranks. However, a strong authoritarian strain continued, and political diversity was not encouraged.

Conditions in the city-state of Singapore, though less tied to great power politics, resembled those in Taiwan in many ways. The prime minister, **Lee Kuan Yew,** took office in 1965, when the area first gained independence, and held power for the next three decades. The government established tight controls over its citizens, going beyond anything attempted elsewhere in the Pacific Rim. Sexual behavior and potential economic corruption, as well as more standard aspects of municipal regulation and economic planning, were scrutinized carefully. The government proclaimed the necessity of unusual discipline and restraint because such a large population crowded into a limited space. One result was unusually low reported crime rates, and another was the near impossibility of serious political protest. The dominant People's Action party suppressed opposition movements. The authoritarian political style was rendered somewhat more palatable by extraordinarily successful economic development, based on a combination of government controls and initiatives and free enterprise. Already the world's fourth largest port, Singapore saw manufacturing and banking surpass shipping as sources of revenue. Electronics, textiles, and oil refining joined shipbuilding as major sectors. By the 1980s Singapore's population enjoyed the second highest per capita income in Asia. Educational levels and health conditions improved accordingly.

Finally, Hong Kong retained its status as a major world port and branched out as a center of international banking, serving as a bridge between the communist regime in China and the wider world. Export production combined high-speed technology with low wages and long hours for the labor force, yielding highly competitive results. Textiles and clothing formed 39 percent of total exports by the 1980s, but other sectors, including heavy industry, developed impressively as well. As in other Pacific Rim nations, a prosperous middle class emerged, with links to many other parts of the world, Western and Asian alike. In 1997, after careful negotiation with the British, Hong Kong was returned to China. The communist government promised to respect the territory's free market economic system and maintain democratic political rights, although the changeover raised questions for the future.

Common Themes and New Problems

The Pacific Rim states had more in common than their rapid growth rates and expanding exports. They all stressed group loyalties against excessive individualism or protest and in support of hard work. Confucian morality often was used, implicitly or explicitly, as part of this effort. The Pacific Rim states also shared reliance on government planning and direction amid limitations on dissent and instability. Of course, they benefited greatly from the expansion of the Japanese market for factory goods, such as textiles, as well as raw materials.

The dynamism of the Pacific Rim spilled over to neighboring parts of southeast Asia by the 1980s. "Little tigers" such as Indonesia, Malaysia, and Thailand began to experience rapid economic growth,

In Depth

The Pacific Rim as a U.S. Policy Issue

Whenever power balances change between nations or larger civilizations, a host of policy issues arises for all parties involved. The rise of the Pacific Rim economies posed some important questions for the West, particularly for the United States because of its military role in the Pacific as well as its world economic position. The United States had actively promoted economic growth in Japan, Korea, and Taiwan as part of its desire to discourage the spread of communism. Although American aid was not solely responsible for Pacific Rim advance, and although it tapered off by the 1960s, the United States took some satisfaction in demonstrating the vitality of noncommunist economies. The United States also was not eager to relinquish its military superiority in the region, which gave it a stake in Asian opinion.

Yet the threats posed by increasing Pacific Rim economic competition were real and growing. Japan seemed to wield a permanent balance-of-payments superiority; its exports to the United States regularly exceeded imports by the 1970s and 1980s, which contributed greatly to the United States' unfavorable overall trade balance. Japanese investment in American companies and real estate increased the United States' growing indebtedness to foreign nations. The symbolic problems were real as well. Japanese observers pointed out with some justice that Americans seemed more worried about Japanese investments than about larger British holdings in the United States, an imbalance that smacked of racism. Certainly, Americans found it harder to accept Asian competition than they did European, if only because it was less familiar. Japanese ability to gain near monopolies in key industries such as electronic recording systems as well as the growing Korean challenge in steel and automobiles meant or seemed to mean loss of jobs and perhaps a threat of more fundamental economic decline in years to come.

In the 1980s, several observers urged American imitation of the bases of Pacific Rim success: The United States should open more partnerships between government and private industry and do more economic planning, it should teach managers to commit themselves to group harmony rather than individual profit seeking, and it should build a new concord between management and labor, based on greater job security and cooperative social programs. Some firms in the United States did introduce certain Japanese management methods, including more consultation with workers, with some success.

Other observers, also concerned about long-term erosion of American power on the Pacific Rim, urged a more antagonistic stance. A few wanted the United States to pull out of costly Japanese and Korean military bases so that the Pacific Rim would be forced to shoulder more of its own defense costs. Others wanted to impose tariffs on Asian goods, at least until the Pacific Rim nations made it easier for American firms to compete in Asian markets. Aggrieved American workers sometimes smashed imported cars and threatened Asian immigrants, although many American consumers continued to prefer Pacific Rim products. The options were complex, and no clear change in American policy emerged.

Pacific Rim nations also faced choices about their orientation toward the West, particularly the United States. Questions that arose earlier about what Western patterns to copy and what to avoid continued to be important, as the Japanese concern about forks and chopsticks suggests. Added were issues about how to express pride and confidence in modern achievements against what were seen as Western tendencies to belittle and patronize. In 1988, the summer Olympic games were held in South Korea, a sign of Korea's international advance and a source of great national pride. During the games, Korean nationalism flared against the U.S. athletes and television commentators, based on their real or imagined tendencies to seek out faults in Korean society. South Korea, like Japan, continued to rely on Western markets and U.S. military assistance, but there was a clear desire to put the relationship on a more fully equal footing. This desire reflected widespread public opinion, and it could have policy implications.

The Pacific Rim crisis in 1998 raised a new set of questions. American leaders urged assistance to beleaguered economies such as those of South Korea and Indonesia, but they also, with some self-satisfaction, tried to insist on introducing a more Western-style market economy. Asian leaders recognized the need for some change, but they did not welcome advice that seemed to ignore successful components from the past and threatened some of the privileges of established political and business elites.

Questions: How great were the challenges posed by the Pacific Rim to the U.S. world position and well-being? What are the most likely changes in American–Pacific Rim relations over the next two decades?

along with the pollution problems that accompanied new manufacturing and larger cities.

However, the final years of the 20th century revealed unexpected weaknesses in this dynamic region. Growth faltered, unemployment rose, and currencies from South Korea to Indonesia took a drastic hit. Many Western observers argued that this crisis could be resolved only by reducing the links between governments and major firms and introducing more free-market competition. In essence, they contended that only a Western industrial model could be successful, and agencies such as the World Bank tried to insist on reforms in this direction as a condition for economic assistance. In the meantime, political pressures increased amid economic distress, and in 1998 the long-time authoritarian ruler of Indonesia was overturned in favor of pledges for future democracy. By 1999, however, economic growth rates in the region began to pick up. It was not clear that basic patterns had to be rethought.

Mao's China and Beyond

In assuming power in 1949, China's communists faced the formidable task of governing a vast nation in ruins. But in contrast to the Bolsheviks, who in 1917 seized power in Russia quite easily only to face years of civil war and foreign aggression, the communists in China claimed a unified nation from which foreign aggressors had been expelled. Unlike the Bolsheviks, the communist leadership in China could move directly to the tasks of social reform and economic development that China so desperately needed. In so doing, they could build on the base they had established in the "liberated" zones during their long struggle for power.

Just as he was convinced that he was on the verge of victory, Chiang Kai-shek's anticommunist crusade had been rudely interrupted by the Japanese invasion of the Chinese mainland (see Chapter 31). Obsessed with the communists, Chiang had done little to block the steady advance of Japanese forces in the early 1930s into Manchuria and the islands along China's coast. Even after the Japanese launched their assaults, aimed at conquering China, Chiang wanted to continue the struggle against the communists (see Map 35.2).

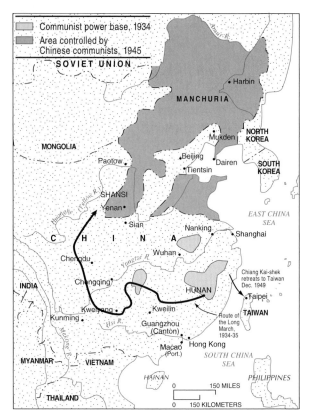

Map 35.2 *China in the Years at the End of World War II, the Final Phase of the Civil War*

Forced by his military commanders to concentrate on the Japanese threat, Chiang grudgingly formed a military alliance with the communists. Although he did all he could to undermine the alliance and continue the anticommunist struggle by underhanded means, for the next seven years the war against Japan took priority over the civil war in the contest for control of China.

Although it brought more suffering to the Chinese people, the Japanese invasion was enormously advantageous for the Communist party. The Japanese invaders captured much of the Chinese coast, where the cities were the centers of the business and mercantile backers of the Nationalists. Chiang's conventional military forces were pummeled by the superior air, land, and sea forces of the Japanese. The Nationalists' attempts to meet the Japanese in conventional battles led to disaster; their inability to defend the coastal provinces lowered their standing in the eyes of the Chinese people. Chiang's hasty and humiliating retreat to Chongqing (see Map 35.2), in the interior of China, further eroded his reputation as the savior of the nation and rendered him more dependant than ever on his military allies, the rural landlords, and—perhaps most humiliating—foreign powers such as the United States.

The guerrilla warfare the communists waged against the Japanese armies proved far more effective than Chiang's conventional approach. With the Nationalist extermination campaigns suspended, the communists used their anti-Japanese campaigns to extend their control over large areas of north China. By the end of World War II, the Nationalists controlled mainly the cities in the north; they had become (as Mao prescribed in his political writings) islands surrounded by a sea of revolutionary peasants. The communists' successes and their determination to fight the Japanese won them the support of most of China's intellectuals and many of the students who had earlier supported the Nationalists. By 1945, the balance of power within China was clearly shifting in the communists' favor. In the four-year civil war that followed, communist soldiers, who were well treated and fought for a cause, consistently routed the much-abused soldiers of the Nationalists, many of whom switched to the communist side. By 1949, it was over. Chiang and what was left of his armies fled to the island of Formosa, renamed Taiwan, and Mao proclaimed the establishment of the **People's Republic of China** in Beijing.

The Japanese invasion proved critical in the communist drive to victory. But equally important were the communists' social and economic reform programs, which eventually won the great majority of the peasantry, the students and intellectuals, and even many of the bureaucrats to their side. Whereas Chiang, whatever his intentions, was able to do little to improve the condition of the great mass of the people, Mao made uplifting the peasants the central element in his drive for power. Land reforms, access to education, and improved health care gave the peasantry a real stake in Mao's revolutionary movement and good reason to defend their soviets against both the Nationalists and the Japanese. In contrast to Chiang's armies, whose arrival meant theft, rape, and murder to China's villagers, Mao's soldiers were indoctrinated with the need to protect the peasantry and win their support. Lest they forget, harsh penalties were levied, such as execution for stealing an egg.

As guerrilla fighters, Mao's soldiers had a much better chance to survive and advance in the ranks than did the forcibly conscripted, brutally treated foot soldiers of the Nationalists. Mao and the commanders around him, such as **Lin Biao,** who had been trained at Chiang's Whampoa Academy in the 1920s, proved far more gifted—even in conventional warfare—than the often corrupt and inept Nationalist generals. Thus, although the importance of the Japanese invasion cannot be discounted, the communists won the mandate to govern China because they offered solutions to China's fundamental social and economic problems. Even more critically, they actually put their programs into action in the areas that came under their control. In a situation in which revolutionary changes appeared to be essential, the communists alone convinced the Chinese people that they had the leaders and the program that could improve their lives.

The Communists Come to Power

The communists' long struggle for control had left the party with a strong political and military organization that was rooted in the **party cadres** and the **People's Liberation Army.** The continuing importance of the army was indicated by the fact that most of China was administered by military officials for five years after the communists came to power. But the army remained clearly subordinate to the Party. Cadre advisors were attached to military contingents at all levels, and the central committees of the party were dominated by nonmilitary personnel.

With this strong political framework in place, the communists moved quickly to assert China's traditional preeminence in east and much of southeast Asia. Potential secessionist movements were forcibly repressed in Inner Mongolia and Tibet, although resistance in the latter has erupted periodically and continues to the present day. In the early 1950s, the Chinese intervened militarily in the conflict between North and South Korea, an intervention that was critical in forcing the United States to settle for a stalemate and a lasting division of the peninsula. Refusing to accept a similar but far more lopsided two-nation outcome of the struggle in China itself, the communist leadership has periodically threatened to invade the Nationalists' refuge on Taiwan, often touching off international incidents. China also played an increasingly important role in the liberation struggle of the Vietnamese to the south, although that did not peak until the height of American involvement in the conflict in the 1960s.

By the late 1950s, the close collaboration between the Soviet Union and China that marked the early years of Mao's rule had broken down. Border disputes, focusing on territories the Russians had seized during the period of Qing decline, and the Chinese refusal to play second fiddle to Russia, especially after Stalin was succeeded by the less imposing Khrushchev, were key causes of the split. These causes of the breakdown in collaboration worsened the differences resulting from the meager economic assistance provided by the Soviet "comrades." They also fed Mao's sense that with the passing of Stalin, he was the chief theoretician and leader of the communist world. In the early 1960s, the Chinese flexed their military and technological muscle by defeating India in a brief war that resulted from a border dispute. More startling, however, was the Chinese success in exploding the first nuclear device developed by a non-industrial nation.

Planning for Economic Growth and Social Justice

On the domestic front, the new leaders of China moved with equal vigor, though with a good deal less success. Their first priority was to complete the social revolution in the rural areas that had been carried through to some extent in communist-controlled areas during the wars against the Japanese and Guomindang. Between 1950 and 1952, the landlord class and the large landholders, most of whom had been spared in the earlier stages of the revolution, were dispossessed and purged. Village tribunals, overseen by party cadre members, gave tenants and laborers a chance to get even for decades of oppression. Perhaps as many as 3 million people who were denounced as members of the exploitive landlord class were executed. At the same time, the land taken from the land-owning classes was distributed to peasants who had none or little. For a brief time at least, one of the central pledges of the communist revolutionaries was fulfilled: China became a land of peasant smallholders.

However, communist planners saw rapid industrialization, not peasant farmers, as the key to successful development. With the introduction of the first Stalinist-style five-year plan in 1953, the communist leaders turned away from the peasantry, which

had brought them to power, to the urban workers as the hope for a new China. With little foreign assistance from either the West or the Soviet bloc, the state resorted to stringent measures to draw resources from the countryside to finance industrial growth. Some advances were made in industrialization, particularly in heavy industries such as steel. But the shift in direction had consequences that were increasingly unacceptable to Mao and his more radical supporters in the Party. State planning and centralization were stressed, Party bureaucrats greatly increased their power and influence, and an urban-based privileged class of technocrats began to develop. These changes, and the external threat to China posed by the U.S. intervention in Korea and continuing U.S.-China friction, led Mao and his followers to force a change of strategies in the mid-1950s.

Mao had long nurtured a deep hostility toward elitism, which he associated with the discredited Confucian system. He had little use for Lenin's vision of revolution from above, led by a disciplined cadre of professional political activists. He distrusted intellectuals, disliked specialization, and clung to his faith in the peasants rather than the workers as the repository of basic virtue and the driving force of the revolution. Acting to stem the trend toward an elitist, urban-industrial focus, Mao and his supporters pushed the **Mass Line** approach, beginning with the formation of agricultural cooperatives in 1955. In the following year, cooperatives became farming collectives that soon accounted for more than 90 percent of China's peasant population. The peasants had enjoyed their own holdings for less than three years. As had occurred earlier in the Soviet Union, the leaders of the revolution, who had originally given the land over to the mass of the peasants, later took it away from them through collectivization.

In 1957 Mao struck at the intellectuals through what may have been a miscalculation or perhaps a clever ruse. Announcing that he wanted to "let a hundred flowers bloom," Mao encouraged professors, artists, and other intellectuals to speak out on the course of development under communist rule. His request stirred up a storm of angry protest and criticism of communist schemes. Having flushed the critics into the open (if the campaign was indeed a ruse) or having been shocked by the vehemence of the response, the party struck with demotions, prison sentences, and banishment to hard labor on the collectives. The flowers rapidly wilted in the face of this betrayal.

The Great Leap Backward

With political opposition within the party and army apparently in check (or in prison), Mao and his supporters launched the **Great Leap Forward** in 1958. The programs of the Great Leap were a further effort to revitalize the flagging revolution by restoring its mass, rural base. Rather than huge plants located in the cities, industrialization would be pushed through small-scale projects integrated into the peasant communes. Instead of the communes' surplus being siphoned off to build steel mills, industrial development would be aimed at producing tractors, cement for irrigation projects, and other manufactures needed by the peasantry. Enormous publicity was given to efforts to produce steel in "backyard" furnaces (Figure 35.6) that relied on labor rather than machine-intensive techniques. Mao preached the benefits of backwardness and the joys of mass involvement, and he looked forward to the withering away of the meddling bureaucracy. Emphasis was placed on self-reliance within the peasant communes. All aspects of the lives of their members were regulated and regimented by the commune leaders and the heads of the local labor brigades.

Within months after it was launched, all indicators suggested that the Great Leap Forward and rapid collectivization were leading to economic disaster. Peasant resistance to collectivization, the abuses of commune leaders, and the dismal output of the backyard factories combined with drought to turn the Great Leap into a giant step backward. The worst famine of the communist era spread across China. For the first time since 1949, China had to import large amounts of grain to feed its people, and the numbers of Chinese to feed continued to grow at an alarming rate. Defiantly rejecting Western and United Nations proposals for family planning, Mao and like-thinking radicals charged that socialist China could care for its people, no matter how many they were. Birth control was seen as a symptom of capitalist selfishness and inability to provide a decent living for all of the people.

Like those of India, China's birth rates were actually a good deal lower than those of many emerging nations. Also like India, however, the Chinese were adding people to a massive population base. At the time of the communist rise to power, China had approximately 550 million people. By 1965, this had risen to approximately 750 million. By the year 2000, China's population was approximately 1.3 billion.

In the face of the environmental degradation and overcrowding that this leap in population produced,

Figure 35.6 *The famous backyard steel furnaces became a central symbol of China's failed drive for self-sufficiency during the Great Leap Forward in the late 1950s.*

even the Party ideologues came around to the view that something must be done to curb the birth rate. Beginning in the mid-1960s, the government launched a nationwide family planning campaign designed to limit urban couples to two children and those in rural areas to one. By the early 1970s, these targets had been revised to two children for either urban or rural couples. By the 1980s, however, just one child per family was allowed. Although there is evidence of official excesses—undue pressure for women to have abortions, for example—these programs have greatly reduced the birth rate and have begun to slow China's overall population increase. But again, the base to which new births are added is already so large that China's population will not stabilize until well into the 21st century. By that time there will be far more people than now to educate, feed, house, and provide with productive work.

Advances made in the first decade of the new regime were lost through amateurish blunders, excesses of overzealous cadre leaders, and students' meddling. China's national productivity fell by as much as 25 percent. Population increase soon overwhelmed the stagnating productivity of the agricultural and industrial sectors. By 1960, it was clear that the Great Leap must be ended and a new course of development adopted. Mao lost his position as State Chairman (although he remained the head of the Party's Central Committee). The **pragmatists**, including Mao's old ally **Zhou Enlai,** along with **Liu Shaoqui** and **Deng Xiaoping,** came to power determined to restore state direction and market incentives at the local level.

"Women Hold Up Half of the Heavens"

In Mao's struggles to renew the revolutionary fervor of the Chinese people, his wife, **Jiang Qing,** played an increasingly prominent role. Mao's reliance on her was consistent with the commitment to the liberation of Chinese women he had acted upon throughout his political career. As a young man he had been deeply moved by a newspaper story about a young girl who had committed suicide rather than be forced by her family to submit to the marriage they had arranged for her with a rich but very old man. From that point onward, women's issues and women's support for the communist movement became important parts of Mao's revolutionary strategy. Here he was drawing on a well-established revolutionary tradition, for women had been very active in the Taiping Rebellion of the mid-19th century, the Boxer Revolt in 1900, and the 1911 revolution that had toppled the Manchu regime. One of the key causes taken up by the May Fourth intellectuals, who had a great impact on the youthful Mao Zedong, was women's rights. Their efforts put an end to footbinding. They also did much to advance campaigns to end female seclusion, win legal rights for women, and open educational and career opportunities to them.

The attempts by the Nationalists in the late 1920s and 1930s to reverse many of the gains made by women in the early revolution brought many women into the communist camp. Led by Chiang's wife, Madam Chiang Kai-shek, the Nationalist counteroffensive (like comparable movements in the fascist countries of Europe at the time) tried to return Chinese women to the home and hearth. Madam Chiang proclaimed a special Good Mother's Day and declared that for women, "virtue was more important than learning." She taught that it was immoral for a wife to criticize her husband (an ethical precept she herself ignored regularly).

The Nationalist campaign to restore Chinese women to their traditional domestic roles and dependence on men contrasted sharply with the communists' extensive employment of women to advance the revolutionary cause. Women served as teachers, nurses, spies, truck drivers, and laborers on projects ranging from growing food to building machine-gun bunkers. Although the Party preferred to use them in these support roles, in moments of crisis women became soldiers on the front lines. Many won distinction for their bravery under fire. Some rose to become cadre leaders, and many were prominent in the antilandlord campaigns and agrarian reform. Their contribution to the victory of the revolutionary cause bore out Mao's early dictum that the energies and talents of women had to be harnessed to the national cause because "women hold up half of the heavens."

As was the case in many other Asian and African countries, the victory of the revolution brought women legal equality with men—in itself a revolutionary development in a society such as China's. For example, women were given the right to choose their marriage partners without familial interference. But arranged marriages persist today, especially in rural

Document

Women in the Revolutionary Struggle

Even more than in the nationalist movements in colonized areas such as India and Egypt, women were drawn in large numbers into revolutionary struggles in areas such as China and Vietnam. The breakdown of the political and social systems weakened the legal and family restrictions that had subordinated women and limited their career choices. The collapse of the Confucian order also ushered in decades of severe crisis and brutal conflict in which women's survival depended on their assumption of radically new roles and their active involvement in revolutionary activities. The following quotations are taken from Vietnamese and Chinese revolutionary writings and interviews with women involved in revolutionary movements in each country. They express the women's goals, their struggle to be taken seriously in the uncharacteristic political roles they had assumed, and some of the many ways women found self-respect and redress for their grievances as a result of the changes wrought by the spread of the new social order.

> Women must first of all be masters of themselves. They must strive to become skilled workers … and, at the same time, they must strictly observe family planning. Another major question is the responsibility of husbands to help their wives look after children and other housework.

> We intellectuals had had little contact with the peasants and when we first walked through the village in our Chinese gowns or skirts the people would just stare at us and talk behind our backs. When the village head beat gongs to call out the women to the meeting we were holding for them, only men and old women came, but no young ones. Later we found out that the landlords and rich peasants had spread slanders among the masses saying "They are a pack of wild women. Their words are not for young brides to hear."

> Brave wives and daughters-in-law, untrammelled by the presence of their menfolk, could voice their own bitterness … encourage their poor sisters to do likewise, and thus eventually bring to the village-wide gatherings the strength of "half of China" as the more enlightened women, very much in earnest, like to call themselves. By "speaking pains to recall pains," the women found that they had as many if not more grievances than the men, and that given a chance to speak in public, they were as good at it as their fathers and husbands.

> In Chingtsun the work team found a woman whose husband thought her ugly and wanted to divorce her. She was very depressed until she learned that under the Draft Law [of the Communist party] she could have her own share of land. Then she cheered up immediately. "If he divorces me, never mind," she said. "I'll get my share and the children will get theirs. We can live a good life without him."

Questions: On the basis of these quotations, identify the traditional roles and attitudes toward women (explored in earlier chapters on China and Vietnam) that women engaged in revolutionary movements in China and Vietnam have rejected. What do they believe is essential if women are to gain equality with men? How do the demands of the women supporting these revolutionary movements compare with those of women's rights advocates in the United States?

areas, and the need to have Party approval for all marriages is a new form of control. Since 1949, women have also been expected to work outside the home. Their opportunities for education and professional careers have improved greatly. As in other socialist states, however, openings for employment outside the home have proved to be a burden for Chinese women. Until the late 1970s, traditional attitudes toward child-rearing and home care prevailed. As a result, women were required not only to hold down a regular job but also to raise a family, cook meals, clean, and shop, all without the benefit of the modern appliances available in Western societies.

Although many women held cadre posts at the middle and lower levels of the Party and bureaucracy, the upper echelons of both were overwhelmingly controlled by men. The short-lived but impressive power amassed by Mao's wife, Jiang Qing, in the early 1970s ran counter to these overall trends, but Jiang Qing got to the top because she was married to Mao. She exercised power mainly in his name and was toppled soon after his death when she tried to rule in her own right.

Mao's Last Campaign and the Fall of the Gang of Four

Having lost his position as head of state but still the most powerful and popular leader in the Communist party, Mao worked throughout the early 1960s to establish grassroots support for yet another renewal of the revolutionary struggle. He fiercely opposed the efforts of Deng Xiaoping and his pragmatist allies to scale back the communes, promote peasant production on what were in effect private plots, and push economic growth over political orthodoxy. By late 1965, Mao was convinced that his support among the students, peasants, and military was strong enough to launch what would turn out to be his last campaign, the **Cultural Revolution.** With mass student demonstrations paving the way, he launched an all-out assault on the "capitalist-roaders" in the Party.

Waving "little red books" of Mao's pronouncements on all manner of issues, the infamous **Red Guard** student brigades (Figure 35.7) publicly ridiculed and abused Mao's political rivals. Liu Shaoqui was killed, Deng Xiaoping was imprisoned, and Zhou Enlai was driven into seclusion. The aroused students and the rank and file of the People's Liberation Army were used to pull down the bureaucrats from their posi-tions of power and privilege. College professors, plant managers, and the children of the bureaucratic elite were berated and forced to confess publicly their many crimes against "the people." Those who were not imprisoned or, more rarely, killed were forced to do manual labor on rural communes to enable them to understand the hardships endured by China's peas-antry. In cities such as Shanghai, workers seized con-trol of the factories and local bureaucracy. As Mao had hoped, the centralized state and technocratic elites that had grown steadily since the first revolu-tion won power in 1949 were being torn apart by the rage of the people.

However satisfying for advocates of continuing revolution such as Mao, it was soon clear that the Cultural Revolution threatened to return China to the chaos and vulnerability of the prerevolutionary era. The rank-and-file threat to the leaders of the People's Liberation Army eventually proved decisive in prompting countermeasures that forced Mao to call off the campaign by late 1968. The heads of the armed forces moved to bring the rank and file back into line; the student and worker movements were disbanded and in some cases forcibly repressed. By the early 1970s, Mao's old rivals had begun to sur-face again. For the next half decade, a hard-fought

Figure 35.7 *In launching the Cultural Revolution in the mid-1960s, Mao Zedong and his allies tried to restore the revolutionary fervor of the 1930s and 1940s that they felt had been eroded by the growing bureaucratization of China. In this photo a crowd of Mao's zealous young supporters rally in Beijing. The vicious assaults on anyone branded as elitist or pro-Western by those in support of the Cultural Revolution led to killings, torture, and imprisonment on a scale that is not yet fully understood. As the movement degenerated into mindless radicalism for its own sake, many of the gains a more moderate approach had made in the preceding decade were lost.*

struggle was waged at the upper levels of the Party and the army for control of the government. The reconciliation between China and the United States that was negotiated in the early 1970s suggested that, at least in foreign policy, the pragmatists were gaining the upper hand over the ideologues. Deng's growing role in policy formation from 1973 onward also represented a major setback for Jiang Qing, who led the notorious **Gang of Four** that increasingly contested power on behalf of the aging Mao.

The death in early 1976 of Zhou Enlai, who was second only to Mao in stature as a revolutionary hero and who had consistently backed the pragmatists, appeared to be a major blow to those whom the Gang of Four had marked out as "capitalist-roaders" and betrayers of the revolution. But Mao's death later in the same year cleared the way for an open clash between the rival factions. While the Gang of Four plotted to seize control of the government, the pragmatists acted in alliance with some of the more influential military leaders. The Gang of Four were arrested, and their supporters' attempts to foment popular insurrections were foiled easily. Later tried for their crimes against the people, Jiang Qing and the members of her clique were purged from the Party and imprisoned for life after their death sentences were commuted.

Since the death of Mao, the pragmatists have been ascendant, and leaders such as Deng Xiaoping have opened China to Western influences and capitalist development, if not yet democratic reform. Under Deng and his allies, the farming communes were discontinued and private peasant production for the market was encouraged. Private enterprise has also been promoted in the industrial sector, and experiments have been made with such capitalist institutions as a stock exchange and foreign hotel chains.

Although it has become fashionable to dismiss the development schemes of the communist states as misguided failures, the achievements of the communist regime in China in the late 20th and early 21st centuries have been impressive. Despite severe economic setbacks, political turmoil, and a low level of foreign assistance, the communists have managed a truly revolutionary redistribution of the wealth of the country. China's very large population remains poor, but in education, health care, housing, working conditions, and the availability of food, most of it is far better off than it was in the prerevolutionary era. The Chinese have managed to provide a decent standard of living for a higher proportion of their people than perhaps any other large developing country. They have also achieved higher rates of industrial and agricultural growth than neighboring India, with its mixed state–capitalist economy and democratic polity. The Chinese have done all of this with much less foreign assistance than most developing nations have had. If the pragmatists remain in power and the champions of the market economy are right, China's growth in the 21st century should be even more impressive. But the central challenge for China's leaders will be to nurture that growth and the improved living standards without a recurrence of the economic inequities and social injustice that brought about the revolution in the first place.

Colonialism and Revolution in Vietnam

 Like most of the peoples of the former colonies in Africa and Asia, the Vietnamese, as well as their neighbors in Laos and Cambodia, were brought under European colonial rule in the second half of the 19th century. But because the Vietnamese had long modeled their polity on the Confucian system of their giant neighbor to the north and had borrowed heavily from China in the social and cultural spheres, their encounter with the expansive West had much in common with that of the Chinese. The Vietnamese were also shocked by the sudden and forcible intrusion of Western influences into their formerly sheltered world. As was the case in China, the failure of Vietnam's Confucian emperor and bureaucracy to repel the foreign French invaders discredited and eventually led to the complete collapse of the system around which the Vietnamese had organized civilized life for nearly two millennia. Just as in China, this collapse led to violent revolution against colonial rule and a search for a viable social and political order.

French interest in Vietnam reached back as far as the 17th century. Driven from Japan by the founders of the Tokugawa shogunate, French missionaries fell back on coastal Vietnam. Vietnam attracted them both because its Confucian elite seemed similar to that of the Japanese and because the continuing wars between rival dynastic houses in the Red River valley and central

Vietnam gave the missionaries ample openings for their conversion efforts (see Map 35.3). From this time onward, French rulers, who considered themselves the protectors of the Catholic missions overseas, took an interest in Vietnamese affairs. As the numbers of converts grew into the tens of thousands and French merchants began to trade at Vietnamese ports, the French stake in the region increased.

By the late 18th century, French involvement had become distinctly political as a result of the power struggles that convulsed the whole region. In the south, a genuine peasant rebellion, the **Tayson Rebellion,** toppled the Nguyen dynasty in the late 1770s. In the years that followed, the **Trinh** dynasty, the northern rival of the Nguyen, was also dethroned. The Tayson controlled most of the country, eliminated the Trinh, and all but wiped out the Nguyen. Seeing a chance to win influence in the ruling house, the French head of the Vietnam mission, the Bishop of Adran, threw his support behind the one surviving prince of the southern house, **Nguyen Anh.**

Anh had fled into the Mekong wilderness with a handful of supporters, thus escaping death at the hands of the Tayson. With the arms and advice of the French, he rallied local support for the dynasty and soon fielded a large army. After driving the Tayson from the south, Nguyen Anh launched an invasion of Tayson strongholds in the north. His task of con-

quest was made easier by bitter quarrels between the Tayson leaders. By 1802, the Nguyen armies had prevailed, and Nguyen Anh had proclaimed himself the Gia Long emperor of Vietnam.

Gia Long made the old Nguyen capital at Hue in central Vietnam the imperial capital of a unified Vietnam. His French missionary allies were rewarded with a special place at court, and French traders were given greater access to the port of Saigon, which was rapidly emerging as the leading city of the Mekong River valley region in the south. The Nguyen dynasty was the first in centuries to rule all of Vietnam and the first to rule a Vietnamese kingdom that included both the Red River and Mekong deltas. In fact, the Mekong region had only begun to be settled extensively by Vietnamese in the century or so before Gia Long rose to power.

Gia Long and his successors proved to be arch-traditionalists deeply committed to strengthening Confucianism in Vietnam. Their capital at Hue was intended to be a perfect miniature of the imperial palace at Beijing. The dynasty patronized Confucian schools and built its administration around scholar-bureaucrats who were well versed in Confucian learning. The second emperor, **Minh Mang** (1820–1841), prided himself on his knowledge of the Confucian classics and his mastery of the Chinese script. He even had the audacity to criticize the brushwork of the reigning Chinese emperor, who was not any more Chinese than Minh Mang but was descended from Manchu nomads. All of this proved deeply disappointing to the French missionaries, who hoped to baptize Gia Long and then carry out through the Vietnamese the sort of top-down conversion that the Jesuits had hoped for ever since their arrival in Asia.

Things actually got much worse. Gia Long's ultra-Confucian successor, Minh Mang, came to see the Catholics as a danger to the dynasty. His persecution of the Vietnamese Catholic community not only enraged the missionaries but also contributed to the growing political and military intervention of the French government in the region. Pushed both by political pressures at home and military defeats in Europe, French adventurers and soldiers exploited quarrels with the Nguyen rulers to justify the piecemeal conquest of Vietnam and neighboring Cambodia and Laos, beginning in the late 1840s (see Map 35.3). By the 1890s, the whole of the country was under French control, and the Nguyen dynasty had been reduced to the status of puppet princes. In the decades that followed, the French concentrated on

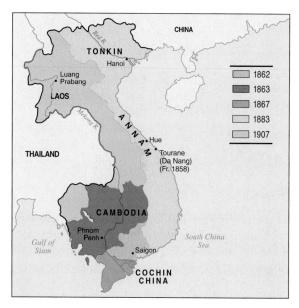

Map 35.3 *Vietnam: Divisions in the Nguyen and French Periods*

drawing revenue and resources from Vietnam while providing very little in return.

The French determination to make Vietnam a colony that was profitable for the homeland worsened social and economic problems that were already severe under the Nguyen rulers. Most of the densely packed peasant population of the north lacked enough land for a subsistence livelihood. French taxes and the burden of obligatory purchases by each village of set amounts of government-sold opium and alcohol drove many peasants into labor in the mines. Even larger numbers left their ancestral villages and migrated to the Mekong region to work on the plantations established there by French and Chinese entrepreneurs. Other migrants chose to become tenants on the great estates that had been carved out of sparsely settled frontier regions by Vietnamese and Chinese landlords.

Migration brought little relief. Plantation workers were paid little and were treated much like slave laborers. The unchecked demands of the Mekong landlords left their tenants with scarcely enough of the crops they grew to feed, clothe, and house their families. The exploitive nature of French colonialism in Vietnam was graphically revealed by the statistics the French themselves collected. These showed a sharp drop in the food consumed by the peasantry in all parts of the colony between the early 1900s and the 1930s, a drop that occurred despite the fact that Vietnam became one of the world's major rice-exporting areas.

Vietnamese Nationalism: Bourgeois Dead Ends and Communist Survival

The failure of the Nguyen rulers after Minh Mang to rally the forces of resistance against the French did much to discredit the dynasty. But from the 1880s into the first decades of the 20th century, guerrilla warfare was waged in various parts of the country in support of the "Save the King" movement. Because this resistance was localized and small, the French were able to crush it on a piecemeal basis. In any case, French control over the puppet emperors who remained on the throne at Hue left the rebels with little cause worth fighting for. The failure of the Nguyen and the Confucian bureaucratic classes to defend Vietnam against the French did much to discredit the old order in the eyes of the new generations that came of age in the early decades of French rule.

Perhaps because it was imported rather than home-grown, the Vietnamese were quicker than the Chinese to reject Confucianism once its failings were clear, and they did so with a good deal less trauma. But its demise left an ideological and institutional vacuum that the Vietnamese, again like the Chinese, would struggle for decades to fill.

In the early 20th century, a new Western-educated middle class, similar to that found in other colonial settings (see Chapters 24 and 34), was formed. It was made up mainly of the children of the traditional Confucian elite and the emerging landlord class in the Mekong region. Some, taking advantage of their parents' wealth, went to French schools and emerged speaking fluent French and with a taste for French fashions and frequent holiday jaunts to Paris and the French Riviera. Many of them went to work for the French as colonial administrators, bank managers, and even labor recruiters. Others pursued independent careers as lawyers, doctors, and journalists. Many who opted for French educations and French lifestyles were soon drawn into nationalist organizations. Like their counterparts elsewhere in the colonies, the members of these organizations initially concentrated on protesting French racism and discrimination, improving their wages, and gaining access to positions in the colonial government held by French people.

As in other colonies, nationalist newspapers and magazines proliferated. These became the focal point of an extended debate over the approach that should be taken toward winning freedom from French rule and, increasingly, what needed to be done to rebuild Vietnam as a whole. Because the French forcibly repressed all attempts to mount peaceful mass demonstrations or organize constitutional agitation, those who argued for violent resistance eventually gained the upper hand. In the early 1920s, the nationalist struggle was centered in the clandestine **Vietnamese Nationalist party** (Vietnamese Quoc Dan Dong, or VNQDD), which was committed to violent revolution against the French colonizers. Although the VNQDD made some attempt to organize urban laborers and peasant villagers, the party members were drawn overwhelmingly from the children of the landlord elite and urban professional classes. Their secret codes and elaborate rituals proved little protection against the dreaded Sûreté, or French secret police. A series of failed uprisings, culminating in a 1929 attempt to spark a general revolution with the assassination of a much-hated French official in charge of labor recruitment, decimated the party. It was particularly hard hit by the ensuing French campaign of repression, execution, and imprisonment. From that point onward, the bourgeois nationalists were never again the dominant force in the struggle for independence.

The demise of the VNQDD left its major rival, the **Communist party of Vietnam,** as the main focus of nationalist resistance in Vietnam. As in China and Korea, the communist wing of the nationalist movement had developed in Vietnam during the 1920s, often at the initiative of leaders in exile. By the late 1920s, the party was dominated by the charismatic young Nguyen Ai Quoc, who would later be known as **Ho Chi Minh.** Ho had discovered Marxism while studying in France and Russia during and after World War I. Disillusioned by his failure to gain a hearing for his plea for the Vietnamese right to self-determination at the post–World War I Paris Peace Conference, Ho dedicated himself to a revolutionary struggle to drive the French from Indochina.

In the early 1930s, the Communist party still held to the rigid but unrealistic orthodox vision of a revolution based on the urban working classes. Because the workers in Vietnam made up as small a percentage of the population as they had in China, the orthodox strategy made little headway. A sudden shift in the early 1930s to a peasant emphasis, in part to take advantage of widespread but not communist-inspired peasant uprisings in central Vietnam, led to a disaster almost as great as that which had overtaken the VNQDD a year before. French repression smashed the communist party hierarchy and drove most of the major communist leaders into exile. But the superior underground organization of the communists and the support they received from the comintern helped them survive the French onslaught. When the French were weakened by the Japanese invasion of Indochina in 1941, the Vietnamese communists were ready to use the colonizers' setbacks to advance the struggle for national liberation.

The War of Liberation Against the French

During World War II, operating out of bases in south China, the communist-dominated nationalist movement, known as the **Viet Minh,** established liberated areas throughout the northern Red River delta (see Map 35.3). The abrupt end of Japanese rule left a vacuum in Vietnam, which only the Viet Minh was prepared to fill. Its programs for land reform and

mass education had wide appeal among the hard-pressed peasants of the north, where they had been propagated during the 1930s and especially during the war. The fact that the Viet Minh actually put their reform and community-building programs into effect in the areas they controlled won them very solid support among the rural population. The Viet Minh's efforts to provide assistance to the peasants during the terrible famine of 1944 and 1945 also convinced the much-abused Vietnamese people that here at last was a political organization genuinely committed to improving their lot.

Under the leadership of general **Vo Nguyen Giap,** the Viet Minh skillfully used guerrilla tactics similar to those devised by Mao in China. These offset the advantages that first the French and then the Japanese enjoyed in conventional firepower. With a strong base of support in much of the rural north and the hill regions, where they had won the support of key non-Vietnamese "tribal" peoples, the Viet Minh forces advanced triumphantly into the Red River delta as the Japanese withdrew. By August 1945, the Viet Minh were in control of Hanoi, where Ho Chi Minh proclaimed the establishment of the independent nation of Vietnam.

Although the Viet Minh had liberated much of the north, they had very little control in the south. In that part of Vietnam a variety of communist and bourgeois nationalist parties jostled for power. The French, eager to reclaim their colonial empire and put behind them their humiliations at the hands of the Nazis, were quick to exploit this turmoil. With British assistance, the French reoccupied Saigon and much of south and central Vietnam. In March 1946, they denounced the August declaration of Vietnamese independence and moved to reassert their colonial control over the whole of Vietnam and the rest of Indochina. An unsteady truce between the French and the Viet Minh quickly broke down. Soon Vietnam was consumed by a renewal of the Viet Minh's guerrilla war for liberation, as well as bloody infighting between the different factions of the Vietnamese.

After nearly a decade of indecisive struggle, the Viet Minh had gained control of much of the Vietnamese countryside, and the French, with increasing American financial and military aid, clung to the fortified towns. In 1954, the Viet Minh decisively defeated the French by capturing the giant fortress they had built at **Dien Bien Phu** in the mountain highlands hear the Laotian border. The victory gained international recognition at a 1954 conference in Geneva for an independent state, the Democratic Republic of Vietnam, in the north. At Geneva, elections throughout Vietnam were also promised in the treaty within two years to decide who should govern a reunited north and the still politically fragmented south.

The War of Liberation Against the United States

The promise at Geneva that free elections would be held to determine who should govern a united Vietnam was never kept. Like the rest of east Asia, Vietnam had become entangled in the cold war maneuvers of the United States and the Soviet Union. Despite very amicable cooperation between the Viet Minh and United States armed forces during the war against Japan, U.S. support for the French in the First Indochina War and the growing fame of Ho Chi Minh as a communist leader drove the two further and further into opposition. The anticommunist hysteria in the United States in the early 1950s fed the perception of influential American leaders that South Vietnam, like South Korea, must be protected from communist takeover.

The search for a leader to build a government in the south that the United States could prop up with economic and military assistance led to **Ngo Dinh Diem.** Diem appeared to have impeccable nationalist credentials. In fact, he had gone into exile rather than give up the struggle against the French. His sojourn in the United States in the 1940s and the fact that he was Catholic also recommended him to American politicians and clergy. Unfortunately, these same attributes would alienate him from the great majority of the Vietnamese people.

With U.S. backing, Diem was installed as the president of Vietnam. He tried to legitimatize his status in the late 1950s by holding rigged elections in the south, in which the communists were not permitted to run. Diem also mounted a series of campaigns to eliminate by force all possible political rivals. Because the communists posed the biggest threat (and were of the greatest concern to Diem's American backers), the suppression campaign increasingly focused on the communist cadres that remained in the south after Vietnam had been divided at Geneva. By the mid-1950s, the **Viet Cong** (as the Diem regime dubbed the communist resistance) were threatened with extermination. In response to this threat, the communist regime in the north began to send weapons, advisors, and other resources to the southern cadres, which were reorganized as the National Liberation Front in 1960.

As guerrilla warfare spread and Diem's military responses expanded, both the United States and the North Vietnamese escalated their support for the warring parties. When Diem proved unable to stem the communist tide in the countryside, the United States authorized his generals to overthrow him and take direct charge of the war. When the Vietnamese military could make little headway, the United States stepped up its military intervention.

From thousands of special advisors in the early 1950s, the United States commitment rose to nearly 500,000 men and women, who made up a massive force of occupation by 1968. But despite the loss of nearly 60,000 American lives and millions of Vietnamese casualties, the Americans could not defeat the communist movement. In part, their failure resulted from their very presence, which made it possible for the communists to convince the great majority of the Vietnamese people that they were fighting for their independence from yet another imperialist aggressor.

Although more explosives were dropped on tiny Vietnam, North and South, than in all of the theaters of World War II, and the United States resorted to chemical warfare against the very environment of the South Vietnamese they claimed to be trying to save, the communists would not yield. The Vietnamese emerged as the victors of the Second Indochina War. In the early 1970s, U.S. diplomats negotiated an end to direct American involvement in the conflict. Without that support, the unpopular military regime in the south fell apart by 1975 (Figure 35.8). The communists united Vietnam under a single government for the first time since the late 1850s. But the nation they governed was shattered and impoverished by decades of civil war, revolution, and armed conflict with two major colonial powers and the most powerful nation of the second half of the 20th century.

After Victory: The Struggle to Rebuild Vietnam

In the years since 1975 and the end of what was, for the Vietnamese, decades of wars for liberation, communist efforts to complete the revolution by rebuilding Vietnamese society have failed. In part, this failure can be linked to Vietnam's isolation from much of the rest of the international community. This isolation resulted in part from pressures applied by a vengeful United States against relief from international agencies. It was increased by border clashes with China that were linked to ancient rivalries between the two countries. Deprived of assistance from abroad and faced with a shattered economy and a devastated environment at home, Vietnam's aging revolutionary leaders pushed hard-line Marxist-Leninist (and even Stalinist) political and economic agendas. Like their Chinese counterparts, they devoted their energies to persecuting old enemies (thus setting off mass migrations from what had been South Vietnam) and imposed a dictatorial regime that left little room for popular responses to government initiatives. In contrast to the Chinese in the past decade, however, the Vietnamese leadership also tried to maintain a highly centralized command economy. The rigid system that resulted stifled growth and, if anything, left the Vietnamese people almost as impoverished as they had been after a century of colonialism and decades of civil war.

By the late 1980s, the obvious failure of these approaches and the collapse of communist regimes throughout eastern Europe prompted measures aimed at liberalizing and expanding the market sector within the Vietnamese economy. The encouraging responses of Japanese and European corporations, eager to open up Vietnamese markets, have done much to stimulate growth in the Vietnamese economy. Growing investments by their industrial rivals have placed increasing pressure on American firms to move into the Vietnamese market (see Figure 35.9).

Figure 35.8 *After decades of struggle against foreign invaders, Vietnamese guerrillas march with the regular forces of the North Vietnamese army into Saigon in May 1975. The capture of the city marked the end of the long wars to free a unified Vietnam. It followed a return to conventional warfare by North Vietnamese and Viet Cong forces, which led to the rapid collapse of the South Vietnamese military and regime.*

Figure 35.9 *By the mid-1990s, the failed efforts of the United States to isolate Vietnam gave way to increasing economic and diplomatic contacts. One example of American corporate penetration is depicted in this street scene from Hanoi in 1993. The opening of Vietnam to foreign investment, assistance, and tourism accelerated through the 1990s. In this atmosphere it has been possible to begin to heal the deep wounds and animosities generated by decades of warfare waged by the Vietnamese people against advanced industrial nations such as Japan, France, and the United States.*

These trends have been strengthened by the genuine willingness shown by Vietnamese leaders in the past decade to work with U.S. officials to resolve questions about prisoners of war and soldiers missing in action from the Vietnam War. But, like many other postcolonial nations, Vietnam has paid a high price for its efforts at integraton into the globalizing economy. Many of its workers have had to endure the sweatshop conditions widely found in foreign factories, social inequality has increased markedly, and the free education system and other public services once provided by the communist state have declined or have entirely disappeared.

 ## GLOBAL CONNECTIONS: East Asia and the Pacific Rim in the Contemporary World

There can be little doubt that the ancient civilizations of both China and Vietnam went through revolutionary transformations in the 20th century. Monarchies or autocratic colonial regimes have been replaced with Communist party cadres who seized power in the name of the peasants and workers. Whole social classes, such as the scholar-gentry and the landlords, have been eliminated. Education and writing systems developed by and centered on the elite have been replaced by mass-oriented schooling and simplified scripts designed to promote literacy. Women have greatly improved their legal status and position within the family, and a wide range of career opportunities, most of which would have been unthinkable under the prerevolutionary Confucian order, have opened to them. Marxist-Leninist theories have blended in recent years with experiments in Western-style capitalism, replacing Confucianism as the state ideology and providing the philosophical basis for the new social order.

The breadth and depth of these changes might lead one to conclude that the patterns of civilized life nurtured by China and Vietnam for over two millennia disappeared. But upon closer examination, it becomes clear that much more has been preserved than these gauges of radical change and the rhetoric of the ruling parties of China and Vietnam might lead one to believe. For example, both societies have retained deeply ingrained suspicions of the commercial and entrepreneurial classes. Both continue to stress that those who wield political power are obligated to rule in ways that promote the welfare of the mass of the people. Both China and Vietnam still adhere to ideological systems that stress secularism, social harmony, and life in this world rather than religious concerns and life hereafter. These continuities caution us against overstating the extent to which the history of the 20th century marked a decisive break with the past. Just as the Bolsheviks in Russia drew on the political traditions of the tsarist era and nationalists in India and Africa invoked the ancient symbols and beliefs of their societies, Chinese and Vietnamese revolutionaries struggled to build new societies that owed much to their Confucian past. These continuities also remind us of the resilience of ideas and patterns of civilized life that have been nurtured over centuries and, in the cases of China and Vietnam, over millennia. Civilizations weave dense and complex webs of human interaction. These patterns may be changed profoundly by the sort of revolutionary upheavals that occurred in the 20th century. But more often than not, the changes are less sweeping, and much more is preserved than revolutionary leaders would like to admit.

Japan and the Pacific Rim have not undergone the kinds of revolutionary change that China and Vietnam experienced, and in some respects—for example, conditions for women—they remain more traditional societies. But change has affected all aspects of life, blending with distinctive emphases on group loyalty and a strong state role inherited from Confucian principles. Not only industrial advance, but also democratization have provided key spurs to change. As China and, to a less extent, Vietnam move toward more market economies, modifying earlier revolutionary patterns, many observers wonder if a broadly common set of east Asian institutions will emerge.

Revolution and economic change have combined to make east Asia a growing force in world affairs by the early 21st century—and of course, largely independent of Western control in contrast to the previous period of imperialism. China's size and revolutionary recovery, plus the surge of the Pacific Rim, prompted some observers by the 1980s to wonder if the next century would be the "century of east Asia." Japan and South Korea became centers of multinational corporations, along with the West. Japanese exports, including toys like Pokemon and also animated films, became part of global consumer culture. Japanese scientific capacity, in areas like supercomputing, often led the world, while China and Japan alike played growing roles in space technology. China became a dominant nation in global athletics competitions. In various ways, including standard diplomatic and economic channels but more besides, east Asia, despite its divisions, became more active in world affairs than ever before. The result reflected the huge changes in the region, but promised changes in global patterns as well.

Further Readings

The best account of contemporary Japanese society and politics is E. O. Reischauer's *The Japanese* (1988). For a recent history, see M. Hane's *Modern Japan: A Historical Survey* (2nd ed., 1992); William G. Beasley's *The Rise of Modern Japan* (1995); and Edward R. Beauchamp, ed., *Women and Women's Issues in Post World War II Japan* (1998).

Several novels and literary collections are accessible and useful. J. Tanizaki's *The Makioka Sisters* (1957) deals with a merchant family in the 1930s; see also H. Hibbett, ed., *Contemporary Japanese Literature: An Anthology of Fiction, Film, and Other Writing Since 1945* (1992). An important study of change, focusing on postwar rural society, is G. Bernstein, *Haruko's World: A Japanese Farm Woman and Her Community* (1983). Another complex 20th-century topic is assessed in R. Storry's *The Double Patriots: A Story of Japanese Nationalism* (1973).

On the Pacific Rim concept and its implications in terms of the world economy, see David Aikman, *Pacific Rim: Area of Change, Area of Opportunity* (1986); Philip West et al., eds., *The Pacific Rim and the Western World: Strategic, Economic, and Cultural Perspectives* (1987); Stephen Haggard and Chung-In Moon, *Pacific Dynamics: The International Politics of Industrial Change* (1988); and Roland A. Morse et al., *Pacific Basin: Concept and Challenge* (1986). Vera Simone's *The Asian Pacific: Political and Economic Development in a Global Context* (1995) is a comparative survey of postcolonial state building and international cultural connections. Also see S. Ichimura, *The Political Economy of Japanese and Asian Development* (1998).

Excellent introductions to recent Korean history are Bruce Cumings' *The Two Koreas* (1984) and his *Korea's Place in the Sun: A Modern History* (1997), and David Rees' *A Short History of Modern Korea* (1988). A variety of special topics are addressed in Marshal R. Pihl, ed., *Listening to Korea: Economic Transformation and Social Change* (1989). See also Paul Kuznet's *Economic Growth and Structure in the Republic of Korea* (1977) and Dennis McNamara's *The Colonial Origins of Korean Enterprise, 1910–1945* (1990).

For a fascinating exploration of cultural change and continuity in Taiwan regarding issues in health and medicine, see Arthur Kleinman's *Patients and Healers in the Context of Culture* (1979). On Singapore, Janet W. Salaff's *State and Family in Singapore* (1988) is an excellent study; see also R. N. Kearney, ed., *Politics and Modernization in South and Southeast Asia* (1975).

A good summary of the final stages of the civil war in China is provided in Lucien Bianco's *Origins of the Chinese Revolution, 1915–1949* (1971). Perhaps the best overview of modern Chinese history from the Qing dynasty era through the Tiananmen Square massacres can be found in Jonathan D. Spence, *The Search for Modern China* (1990). Other useful accounts of the post-1949 era include Maurice Meisner's *Mao's China and After 1984* (1984); Michael Gasster's *China's Struggle to Modernize* (1987 ed.), and Immanuel C. Y. Hsu, *China Without Mao* (1983). On the pivotal period of the Cultural Revolution, see Roderick MacFarquhar's two-volume study on *The Origins of the Cultural Revolution* (1974, 1983), and Lowell Dittmer's *Liu Shao-ch'i and the Chinese Cultural Revolution* (1974). For a highly critical assessment of the Maoist era, it is difficult to surpass Simon Leys' *Chinese Shadows* (1977). On cultural life in the postrevolutionary era, see the essays in R. MacFarquhar, ed., *The Hundred Flowers Campaign and the Chinese Intellectuals*, and Lois Wheeler Snow, *China on Stage* (1972). Elisabeth Croll's *Feminism and Socialism in China* (1978) remains by far the best single work on the position of women in revolutionary and Maoist China.

The first war of liberation in Vietnam is covered in Ellen J. Hammer's *The Struggle for Indochina, 1940–1955* (1966 ed). The best of many surveys of the second war, often called the American War in Vietnam, is Marilyn Young's *The Vietnam Wars, 1945–1990* (1989). Of a number of fine studies on the origins of American intervention in the area, two of the best are Archimedes Patti's *Why Vietnam?* (1980) and Lloyd Gardner's *Approaching Vietnam* (1988). On the conduct of the war, Jeffrey Races' *The War Comes to Long An* (1972); Eric Bergerud's *The Dynamics of Defeat: The Vietnam War in Hau Nghia Province* (1991); and Marc Jason Gilbert, ed., *Why the North Won the Vietnam War* (2002), are useful for the stress they place on the role of the Vietnamese in determining this conflict's course and ultimate outcome. Powerful firsthand accounts of the guerrilla war and U.S. combat include Mark Baker's *Nam* (1981); Philip Caputo's *A Rumor of War* (1977); and Troung Nhu Tang's *A Viet Cong Memoir* (1985).

On the Web

The career arc of leading personalities in the rise of modern Korea, such as Syngman Rhee (http://www.kimsoft.com/2000/rhee.htm and http://us.cnn.com/SPECIALS/cold.war/kbank/profiles/rhee/), and much of the history of postwar Japan, was shaped by the

Korean War (http://mcel.pacificu.edu/as/students/ stanley/home.html). The nature of the Korean economy and the dominant role of large corporate entities, *chaebol*, in postwar Korea are explored at http://www. megastories.com/seasia/skorea/chaebol/chaebol.htm, and http:// 1upinfo.com/country-guide-study/ south-korea/south-korea92.html, where they are compared with Japanes *zaibatsu* and *keiretsu*.

The life of General Douglas MacArthur and the art and society of the occupation or "Confusion" era in Japan is discussed at http://educate.si.edu/spotlight/korean. html. Japan's difficulty in accepting responsibility for its wartime atrocities, particularly the abuse of Korean and other Asian women by Japanese occupation troops, is discussed at http://online.sfsu.edu/~soh/comfortwomen. html, http://online.sfsu.edu/~soh/cw-links.htm, and http://csf.colorado.edu/bcas/sample/comfdoc.htm.

Korekiyo Takahashi's role in the building of the modern Japanese economy and his conflict with the war party led by Tojo Hideki is examined at http://netec.mcc.ac.uk/ WoPEc/data/Papers/hithitueca395.html and http:// www.historynet.com/ (search name for many links). The place of Takahashi's policies in today's Japan is examined at http://www.atimes.com/Japan-econ/ AB12Dh01.html.

Much of the postwar recovery of east Asian economies was due to close cooperation between business and government (http://www.kimsoft.com/1997/sk-econ.htm and http://www.let.leidenuniv.nl/history/econgs/ japan.html), which recently has been criticized even in Japan, where politicians were caught with trunks full of cash provided by leading Japanese companies. This pattern was followed by the eastern Pacific Rim's economic tigers as part of an authoritarian development strategy, most clearly expressed by Singapore's Lee Kwan Yew, who has made comparisons between himself and Machiavelli (http://www.sfdonline.org/Link%20Pages/ Link%20Folders/Political%20Freedom/Machiavelli.html). However, a recent economic recession in the region, discussed at http://www.rice.edu/rtv/speeches/ 19981023lee.html, has forced some to question whether the east Asian model of economic growth is worthy of emulation elsewhere. A close look at the roots of the continuing Asian economic crisis of the 1990s is explored at http://www.stern.nyu/globalmacro/. (click on "Asia Crisis" at left-hand margin).

The story of the Red Guards as viewed through their songs can be explored at http://www.indiana.edu/ ~easc/resources/working_papers/10b_song.htm.

The limits of the recent movement toward liberalization in China, and by extension in the remaining communist nations, were tested during the student occupation of Tiananmen Square in 1989. A Web site exploring this event (http://www.tsquare.tv/) offers film and music clips, a photo gallery, and a transcript of Deng Xiaoping's June 9, 1989, speech declaring martial law.

The transcript of the Public Broadcasting Company's superb documentary on the protests in China in 1989 can be found at http://www.pbs.org/wgbh/pages/ frontline/gate/. The National Security Archives' briefing book on the Tiananmen Square protests (http://www. gwu.edu/~nsarchiv/NSAEBB/NSAEBB16/) contains a wealth of documents, while still photography of the protests, their repression, and ongoing efforts at democratization in China is offered at http://www.christusrex. org/www1/sdc/tiananmen.html. A moving 360 degree view of the Square can be accessed at http://www. roundtiananmensquare.com/.

A balanced survey of Vietnamese history encompassing the Vietnamese revolution and its aftermath can be found at http://www.viettouch.com/history/.

The Web is particularly rich in sites documenting Vietnam's wars for national liberation, including the Emperor Bao Dai's letter of abdication of August 25, 1945, and Vietnam's Declaration of Independence of September 2, 1945 (http://www.vwip.org/doc-top.html or http:// www.vwip.org/vwiphome.html), the Viet Cong's Program of 1962 (http://www.fordham.edu/halsall/ mod/1962vietcong1.html), and excerpts from a host of American documents on the war (http://depts.vassar. edu/~vietnam/).

Audio feed and visual images of Robert McNamara's speech on the instability of the Republic of Vietnam, President Johnson's announcement of his decision not to run for reelection and focus on a negotiated settlement of the war, the screams of students reacting to a National Guard unit's shooting of passers-by as well as antiwar demonstrators at Kent State University, and President Nixon's announcement that he had achieved peace with honor in Vietnam can all be found at http://www. historychannel.com/speeches/index.html.

CHAPTER 36

GLOBALIZATION AND RESISTANCE: WORLD HISTORY 1990–2003

Breaching the Berlin Wall in 1989: West and East Germany meet.

- The End of the Cold War
- The Great Powers and New Disputes
- **IN DEPTH:** How Much Historical Change?
- Globalization
- **DOCUMENT:** Protests Against Globalization
- A World of Religious and Ethnic Conflict
- Global Warming and Other Perils
- Toward the Future
- **GLOBAL CONNECTIONS:** Civilizations and Global Forces

In the 1990s, the last chronological decade of the 20th century, global history took an abrupt turn. With the remarkably sudden collapse of the Soviet Union and the communist regimes of eastern Europe, the long and tense cold war came to an end. By this time, the parallel process of decolonization had been completed. This was symbolized by the admission of well over a hundred new states into the United Nations between the 1960s and 1980s. The end of colonialism opened up new possibilities for global historical development. Some of these gave promise of human improvement, especially the spread of new technologies and medicines. Others, which were often revivals of earlier patterns, threatened to become new sources of social conflict and international confrontations.

By the 1990s, the early 20th-century map of the world set in place by a final burst of colonial expansion had been utterly redrawn. Not only had the European, American, and Japanese empires been replaced by a patchwork of emerging nation-states, but the Soviet empire had also disintegrated. It too was replaced by numerous successor states, from the reborn Baltic republics to the new states of the Muslim steppe regions that now flanked the Russian core of the old empire across the south. The new political alignment of the globe remained volatile and the source of ongoing civil wars and interstate clashes. But in stark contrast to the political division of the world at the onset of the 20th century, there was far greater local and regional sovereignty, however much different ethnic and religious groups might contest who had the right to exercise it.

The collapse of the communist bloc of eastern Europe and the end of the cold war standoff of the superpowers also opened up the possibility of a truly globalized economy. The smaller nations of the former Warsaw Pact allies, such as Poland and Hungary, quickly moved to throw off the state regulations that had stifled economic growth and to integrate their economies into the market-oriented network dominated by their European neighbors, the United States, and Japan. With greater difficulty, Russia also struggled to make the transition from communism to capitalism. With surprisingly little time lag and greater ease, the People's Republic of China, Vietnam, and to a lesser extent Cuba soon followed suit. Communist regimes that resisted these trends, such as North Korea and Albania, were soon isolated, impoverished, and under siege, if not toppled. The demise of the communist option also gave added impetus to international trade agreements, such as NAFTA and GATT, which were designed to break down barriers to the exchange of goods, and especially the movement of capital investment. It also brought even greater power to international lending agencies, such as the World Bank and the International Monetary Fund,

893

1980 c.e.	1990 c.e.	2000 c.e.
1988 Soviet withdrawal from Afghanistan	**1990** Iraqi invasion of Kuwait	**2000** International Human Rights Conference, South Africa; Milosevic forced out as Serbian president; seeming end of Yugoslav civil wars
1988–1991 Independence movements in eastern Europe and in minority states in Soviet Union	**1991** End of Soviet Union, Yeltsin to power in Russia; civil wars begin in Yugoslavia, and Slovenia and Croatia secede; Persian Gulf War, Iraq defeated	**2000–2002** Second Intifada in Palestine and Israel
1989–1990 Collapse of Soviet Union and Warsaw Pact regimes	**1992** North American Free Trade Association (NAFTA) inaugurated; Bosnia withdraws from Yugoslavia; first World Environmental Conference in Brazil	**2001** Mass demonstrations against World Trade Organization in Genoa; terrorist attacks on World Trade Center and Pentagon; U.S.-Northern Alliance coalition topples Taliban regime in Afghanistan
	1992–1993 UN-U.S. interventions in Somalia	**2002** India and Pakistan mobilize armies over Kashmir dispute; euro becomes common currency in much of European Union
	1994 Mass genocide in Rwanda	**2003** U.S. and allies conquer Iraq
	1994 U.S. intervention in Haiti	
	1995 U.S.-NATO interventions in Bosnia	
	1997 Second World Environmental Conference, Kyoto, Japan	
	1998 Serbian assault on Albanians in Kosovo	
	1999 U.S.-NATO war against Yugoslavia; Putin becomes president of Russia	

which had played such a major role in shoring up the economies and stabilizing the polities of the capitalist block in the cold war era.

Although many, especially in the West, greeted these globalizing trends as forces that would liberate humanity and make possible decent standards of living globally, their impact thus far has been much more varied, and in important respects a cause for concern. New wealth was generated on an unprecedented scale in the 1990s, but this increase tended to favor the social groups, both in developing and industrialized areas, that were already well-to-do. These groups controlled the capital, educational advantages, and contacts that made it possible for them to take best advantage of the potential for innovation and profit that globalization opened up. New—and in the case of countries like India, Japan, and Korea, very sizeable—middle classes emerged worldwide. But in most cases the absolute numbers of the poor and malnourished grew even more rapidly, especially in postcolonial societies, which in most cases actually fell further behind Japan and the West in scientific and technological advancement.

The poor and unskilled working classes participated to some extent in the vastly expanded consumer culture that was spreading globally. In many areas, jobs in assembly or processing plants provided sources of income that would not have been available without global linkages. But for the most part workers were drawn into the globalizing economy at the very lowest levels. Working-class and rural men and women alike were integrated into the global network mainly as poorly paid sweatshop workers, who labored in regimented, unhealthy, and often dangerous assembly-line environments. The designer clothes and electronic devices they produce are shipped mainly to markets in more affluent countries or sold to the wealthy elites in their own societies. The profits of their labors are overwhelmingly reaped by international corporations and the mercantile networks associated with them. The new global economy also accelerated environmental damage in many parts of the world.

The end of the cold war and new globalization raised cultural and political issues as well. Conflicts among ethnic groups intensified as the cold war framework receded, particularly in former communist countries but also in parts of Africa and the Middle East. Religious movements resisted key aspects of global consumerism and the political and diplomatic power of the United States, contributing to renewed tensions in the Middle East and elsewhere and a new, global surge of terrorism.

The End of the Cold War

 After 1985, reforms unintentionally ushered in the collapse of communism in eastern Europe and an end to much of the Soviet empire. Democracy gained ground amid considerable uncertainty about the future.

The cold war had lasted for 30 years when its context began to shift. The Russian Empire had been expanding, off and on, for 500 years, interrupted only briefly by World War I and the initial phases of the Russian Revolution before it resumed its growth, to unprecedented levels. What could cause these two firmly established patterns, the cold war and the Russian Empire, to change course dramatically?

Leadership was surely one component. After Stalin and then Khrushchev, Soviet leadership had turned conservative. Party bureaucrats, eager to protect the status quo, often advanced only mediocre people to top posts, men whose major leadership characteristic was their unwillingness to rock the boat. Many of these leaders then continued to hold power when their own aptitude declined with illness and age.

Of more general significance was the reassertion of initiative from some parts of the world surrounding the Soviet Union, despite continued pressures from the superpowers. The rise of Islamic fervor, evident in the Iranian Revolution of 1979, inevitably created anxiety in the Soviet Union with its large Muslim minority. To reduce this new threat, late in 1979 the Soviets invaded neighboring Afghanistan, hoping to set up a puppet regime that would protect Russian interests; the move drew widespread international disapproval. The war proved difficult, as Afghan guerrillas, with some backing from the United States, held their ground fiercely. Costs and casualties mounted, and the war—the first formal action the Soviets had indulged in since World War II—quickly proved unpopular at home.

At the same time, the success of western Europe's economy pushed communism into a defensive and retreating posture throughout eastern Europe. The attraction of Western institutions and consumer standards gained ground. Within the Soviet empire itself, a new free trade union movement resumed in Poland, linked to the Catholic church, and while it was repressed through Soviet-mandated martial law in 1981, the stress of keeping the lid on was likely to increase.

Changes in Chinese policy entered in. China of course had separated itself from Soviet direction in the 1960s. But in 1978 the regime made a choice to participate in the world economy and to admit more market forces and competitive free enterprise in the internal economy as well. There was no relaxation of political controls, and a democratic movement was vigorously quashed in 1989. But the Chinese economy now differed dramatically from that of the Soviet Union, and change was quickly rewarded, both with international investment and with rapid growth. The Soviets now had to contend not only with China's massive population, but with its superior economic performance.

Finally, United States diplomatic policy tightened. While President Jimmy Carter hoped to reduce tensions in the late 1970s, he was a vigorous human rights advocate, particularly eager to point out Soviet deficiencies. American conservatives heightened their own opposition to the Soviet Union. A new strategic arms limitation agreement (SALT II) was negotiated in 1979, but quickly encountered resistance in the U. S.

Senate. Then came the Soviet move into Afghanistan. President Carter reacted vigorously, claiming that the move was a "stepping stone to their possible control over much of the world's oil supplies" and, even more dramatically, the "gravest threat to world peace since World War II." American participation in the 1980 Moscow Olympics was cancelled.

Then, in 1980, the new, conservative president, Ronald Reagan, who had denounced the Soviet Union as an "evil empire," announced a massive increase in U.S. defense spending. The size of domestic programs declined relative to the federal budget as a whole, and some programs were cut outright (promoting, among other things, a surge in homelessness), but conservatives accepted a growing budget deficit in favor of the new military outlays. The president also announced a "Reagan doctrine" of assisting anticommunism anywhere, and followed up with an invasion of a small, Marxist-controlled Caribbean island, Grenada, and support for anti-Marxist military action in Central America.

These moves put new pressure on the Soviets, already stretched to the limit to maintain military and global competition with the United States, and beset with an unpopular war and new regional pressures as well. The stage was set for the events that, initially promoted for quite different reasons, undid the cold war.

The Explosion of the 1980s and 1990s

From 1985 onward the Soviet Union entered a period of intensive reform, soon matched by new political movements in eastern Europe that effectively dismantled the Soviet empire. The initial trigger for this extraordinary and unanticipated upheaval lay in the deteriorating Soviet economic performance, intensified by the costs of military rivalry with the United States. There were reasons for pride in the Soviet system as well, and many observers believed that public attitudes by the 1980s were shaped much less by terror than by satisfaction with the Soviet Union's world prestige and the improvements the communist regime had fostered in education and welfare. But, to a degree unperceived outside the Soviet Union, the economy was grinding to a standstill. Forced industrialization had produced extensive environmental deterioration throughout eastern Europe. According to Soviet estimates, half of all agricultural land was endangered by the late 1980s; more than 20 percent of Soviet citizens lived in regions of ecological disaster. Rates and

severity of respiratory and other diseases rose, impairing both morale and economic performance. Infant mortality rates also rose in several regions, sometimes nearing the highest levels in the world.

More directly, industrial production began to stagnate and even drop as a result of rigid central planning, health problems, and poor worker morale. Growing inadequacy of housing and consumer goods resulted, further lowering motivation. As economic growth stopped, the percentage of resources allocated to military production escalated, toward a third of all national income. This reduced funds available for other investments or for consumer needs. At first only privately, younger leaders began to recognize that the system was near collapse.

The Age of Reform

Yet the Soviet system was not changeless, despite its heavy bureaucratization. Problems and dissatisfactions, though controlled, could provoke response beyond renewed repression. After a succession of leaders whose age or health precluded major initiatives, the Soviet Union in 1985 brought a new, younger official to the fore. **Mikhail Gorbachev** quickly renewed some of the earlier attacks on Stalinist rigidity and replaced some of the old-line Party bureaucrats. He conveyed a new, more Western style, dressing in fashionable clothes (and accompanied by his stylish wife), holding relatively open press conferences, and even allowing the Soviet media to engage in active debate and report on problems as well as successes. Gorbachev also further altered the Soviet Union's modified cold war stance. He urged a reduction in nuclear armament, and in 1987 he negotiated a new agreement with the United States that limited medium-range missiles in Europe. He ended the war in Afghanistan, bringing Soviet troops home.

Internally, Gorbachev proclaimed a policy of **glasnost,** or openness, which implied new freedom to comment and criticize. He pressed particularly for a reduction in bureaucratic inefficiency and unproductive labor in the Soviet economy, encouraging more decentralized decision making and the use of some market incentives to stimulate greater output. The sweep of Gorbachev's reforms, as opposed to an undeniable new tone in Soviet public relations, remained difficult to assess. Strong limits on political freedom persisted, and it was unclear whether Gorbachev could cut through the centralized planning apparatus that controlled the main lines of the Soviet economy. There was also uncertainty about how well the new leader could balance reform and stability.

Indeed, questions about Gorbachev's prospects recalled many basic issues in Soviet history. In many ways Gorbachev's policies constituted a return to a characteristic ambivalence about the West as he reduced Soviet isolation while continuing to criticize aspects of Western political and social structure. Gorbachev clearly hoped to use some Western management techniques and was open to certain Western cultural styles without, however, intending to abandon basic control of the communist state. Western analysts wondered if the Soviet economy could improve worker motivation without embracing a Western-style consumerism or whether computers could be more widely introduced without allowing freedom for information exchange.

Gorbachev also sought to open the Soviet Union to fuller participation in the world economy, recognizing that isolation in a separate empire had restricted access to new technology and limited motivation to change. Although the new leadership did not rush to make foreign trade or investment too easy—considerable suspicion persisted—the economic initiatives brought symbolic changes, such as the opening of a McDonald's restaurant in Moscow and a whole array of new contacts between Soviet citizens and foreigners (see Figure 36.1).

Gorbachev's initial policies did not quickly stir the Soviet economy, but they had immediate political effects, some of which the reform leader had almost certainly not anticipated. The keynote of the reform program was **perestroika,** or economic restructuring, which Gorbachev translated into more leeway for private ownership and decentralized control in industry and agriculture. Farmers, for example, could now lease land for 50 years, with rights of inheritance, and industrial concerns were authorized to buy from either private or state operations. Foreign investment was encouraged. Gorbachev pressed for reductions in Soviet military commitments, particularly through agreements with the United States on troop reductions and limitations on nuclear weaponry, in order to free resources for consumer goods industries. He urged more self-help among the Soviets, including a reduction in drinking, arguing that he wanted to "rid public opinion of ... faith in a 'good Tsar,' the all powerful center, the notion that someone can bring about order and organize pere-

Figure 36.1 *Young capitalist selling Pepsi on a Moscow street, 1993.*

stroika from on high." Politically, he encouraged a new constitution in 1988, giving considerable power to a new parliament, the Congress of People's Deputies, and abolishing the Communist monopoly on elections. Important opposition groups developed both inside and outside the Party, pressing Gorbachev between radicals who wanted a faster pace of reform and conservative hard-liners. Gorbachev himself was elected to a new, powerful presidency of the Soviet Union in 1990.

Reform amid continued economic stagnation provoked agitation among minority nationalities in the Soviet Union, from 1988 onward. Muslims and Armenian Christians rioted in the south, both against each other and against the central state. Baltic nationalist and other European minorities also stirred, some insisting on independence (notably in Lithuania), some pressing for greater autonomy. Again, results of this diverse unrest were difficult to forecast, but some observers predicted the end of Soviet control of central Asia and the European borderlands.

Even social issues were given uncertain new twists. Gorbachev noted that Soviet efforts to establish equality between the sexes had burdened women with a combination of work and household duties. His solution—to allow women to "return to their purely womanly missions" of housework, childrearing, and "the creation of a good family atmosphere"—had a somewhat old-fashioned ring to it.

Dismantling the Soviet Empire

Gorbachev's new approach, including his desire for better relations with Western powers, prompted more definitive results outside the Soviet Union than within, as the smaller states of eastern Europe uniformly pushed for greater independence and internal reforms. Bulgaria moved for economic liberalization in 1987 but was held back by the Soviets; pressure resumed in 1989 as the Party leader was ousted and free elections were arranged. Hungary changed leadership in 1988 and installed a non-Communist president. A new constitution and free elections were planned; the Communist party renamed itself Socialist. Hungary also reviewed its great 1956 rising, formally declaring it "a popular uprising … against an oligarchic system … which had humiliated the nation." Hungary moved rapidly toward a free-market economy. Poland installed a non-communist government in 1988 and again moved quickly to dismantle the state-run economy; prices rose rapidly as government subsidies were withdrawn. The Solidarity movement, born a decade before through a merger of non-communist labor leaders and Catholic intellectuals, became the dominant political force. East Germany displaced its communist government in 1989, expelling key leaders and moving rapidly toward unification with West Germany. The Berlin Wall was dismantled (see the chapter opener photograph), and in 1990 non-communists won a free election. German unification occurred in 1991, a dramatic sign of the collapse of postwar Soviet foreign policy. Czechoslovakia installed a new government in 1989, headed by a playwright, and sought to introduce free elections and a more market-driven economy.

Although mass demonstrations played a key role in several of these political upheavals, only in Romania was there outright violence, as an exceptionally authoritarian communist leader was swept out by force. As in Bulgaria, the Communist party retained considerable power, though under new leadership, and reforms moved less rapidly than in Hungary and Czechoslovakia. The same held true for Albania, where the unreconstructed Stalinist regime was dislodged and a more flexible communist leadership installed.

New divergences in the nature and extent of reform in eastern Europe were exacerbated by clashes among nationalities, as in the Soviet Union. Change and uncertainty brought older attachments to the fore. Romanians and ethnic Hungarians clashed; Bulgarians attacked a Turkish minority left over from the Ottoman period. In 1991 the Yugoslavian communist regime, though not Soviet-dominated, also came under attack, and a civil war boiled up from disputes among nationalities. Minority nationality areas, notably Slovenia, Croatia, and Bosnia-Herzegovina, proclaimed independence, but the national, Serbian-dominated army applied massive force to preserve the Yugoslav nation.

Amid this rapid and unexpected change, prospects for the future became unpredictable. Few of the new governments fully defined their constitutional structure, and amid innovation the range of new political parties almost compelled later consolidations. Like the Soviet Union itself, all the eastern European states suffered from sluggish production, massive pollution, and economic problems that might well lead to new political discontent.

With state controls and protection abruptly withdrawn by 1991, tensions over the first results of the introduction of the market economy in Poland brought rising unemployment and further price increases. These in turn produced growing disaffection from the Solidarity leadership. Diplomatic linkages among small states—a critical problem area between the two world wars—also had yet to be resolved.

The massive change in Soviet policy was clear. Gorbachev reversed postwar imperialism completely, stating that "any nation has the right to decide its fate by itself." In several cases, notably Hungary, Soviet troops were rapidly withdrawn, and generally it seemed unlikely that a repressive attempt to reestablish an empire would be possible (see Map 36.1). New contacts with Western nations, particularly in the European Economic Community, seemed to promise further realignment in the future.

Renewed Turmoil in 1991 and 1992

The uncertainties of the situation within the Soviet Union were confirmed in the summer of 1991, when

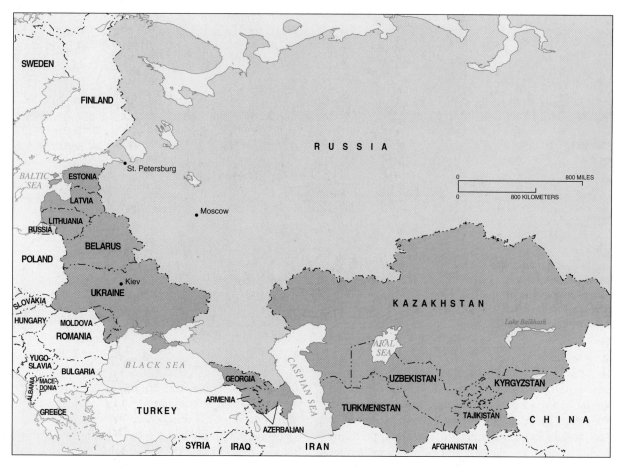

Map 36.1 *Post–Soviet Union Russia, Eastern Europe, and Central Asia. The boundaries of east central Europe and central Asia were substantially redrawn.*

an attempted coup was mounted by military and police elements. Gorbachev's presidency and democratic decentralization were both threatened. Massive popular demonstrations, however, asserted the strong democratic current that had developed in the Soviet Union since 1986. The contrast with earlier Soviet history and the suppression of democracy in China two years before was striking.

In the aftermath of the attempted coup, Gorbachev's authority weakened. Leadership of the key republics, including the massive Russian Republic, became relatively stronger. The three Baltic states used the occasion to gain full independence (see Figure 36.2), though economic links with the Soviet Union remained. Other minority republics proclaimed independence as well, but Gorbachev struggled to win agreement on continued economic union

and some other coordination. By the end of 1991 leaders of the major republics, including Russia's **Boris Yeltsin,** proclaimed the end of the Soviet Union, projecting a commonwealth of the leading republics, including the economically crucial Ukraine, in its stead. Amid the disputes Gorbachev fell from power, doomed by his attempts to salvage a presidency that depended on some survival of a greater Soviet Union. His leadership role was taken over by Boris Yeltsin, who as president of Russia and an early renouncer of communism now emerged as the leading, though quickly beleaguered, political figure. Yeltsin soon used force to bring Russia's parliament under some control (see Figure 36.3).

The former Soviet Union gave way to the loose Commonwealth of Independent States, which won tentative agreement from most of the now indepen-

Figure 36.2   *As part of the independence of the Baltic nation of Latvia, crowds toppled Soviet symbols—in this case, a giant statue of Lenin, in 1991.*

dent republics. But tensions immediately surfaced about economic coordination amid rapid dismantling of state controls; about control of the military, where Russia—still by far the largest unit—sought predominance, including nuclear control amid challenges from the Ukraine and from Kazakhstan (two of the other republics with nuclear weaponry on their soil); and about relationships between the European-dominated republics, including Russia, and the cluster of central Asian states. How much unity might survive in the former Soviet Union was unclear.

The fate of economic reform was also uncertain. Russian leaders hesitated to convert to a full market system lest transitional disruption further antagonize the population.

By the late 1990s, the leadership of Boris Yeltsin deteriorated as the economy performed badly, individual profiteers pulled in huge fortunes, and Yeltsin's health worsened. A new president, Vladimir Putin, was named in 1999, vowing to clean up corruption and install more effective government controls over separate provinces. Putin declared his commitment to democracy and a free press but also sponsored new attacks on dissident television stations and newspapers. Many Russians seemed to agree that stronger measures were needed—why should a leader tolerate public criticism? Others longed for a return to the Soviet days of greater economic security and national

glory. Still others, eager to embrace a more liberal society and often enjoying new prosperity and consumer choice, worried about the future. At the same time, the Russian legislature filled with more reform-minded parties, as Communist election success declined somewhat.

The Spread of Democracy

The end of the cold war was associated with another large trend in the world at the end of the 20th century: the spread of multiparty democracy with (reasonably) freely contested elections (see Figure 36.4). We have seen that, through much of the century, several different government forms competed for success amid a general climate of change: communism, fascism, and other authoritarianism, and democracy itself. But from the late 1970s onward, the tide seemed to turn toward democracy in many regions that had long been inhospitable.

Economic and political success in western Europe, including the drawing power of the Common Market, helped propel Spain, Portugal, and Greece to democratic systems in the mid-1970s, after long periods of authoritarian control. Then the democratic wave hit Latin America, backed by U.S. and western European support. Beginning with new regimes in Argentina and Brazil, authoritarian controls were replaced by free elec-

Figure 36.3 *Using the army to attack the parliament building in Moscow, Boris Yeltsin consolidated his position against dissident delegates, many of them former communists, though he lost the ensuing parliamentary elections.*

tions (see Chapter 33). The process continued through the 1990s, when literally all Latin American countries except Cuba were in the democratic camp. Revolutionaries in Central America accepted the system in the late 1980s; Paraguay was the final authoritarian regime to yield a decade later. In 2000, Mexico elected its first president from a party other than the PRI, the party that had monopolized control since the revolution.

Democratic systems gained ground in South Korea and Taiwan in the 1980s. In the Philippines, an authoritarian ruler was cast aside, amid considerable popular pressure, in favor of an elected government. By this point, of course, the democratic current captured the Soviet bloc, with democratic systems winning out in most of east central Europe, Russia itself, and to a degree in the former Soviet republics in central Asia.

While most of Africa remained authoritarian, democratic change spread to this region by the 1990s, headed of course with the triumph of democracy over apartheid in South Africa. After new assertions of military control, Nigeria, the continent's most populous country, turned to democracy in 1999. At this point also, a near-revolution toppled another authoritarian system, in Indonesia, and replaced it with competitive elections.

Never before had democracy spread so widely, among so many otherwise different societies. Only China and parts of the Middle East seemed to hold apart completely. In China, the major democratic demonstration in Beijing in 1989 echoed the global democratic current but was brutally put down. Elsewhere, the political stability, cultural prestige, and economic success of Western democracy, supplemented by the strength of democratic systems in Japan and India, seemed to win the day. The fall of European communism both reflected and encouraged the trend. One of democracy's main competitors was now discredited. The end of the cold war worked to the same effect, reducing the need for great powers to support authoritarian systems in return for military alliance. The United States, in particular, became more consistent in its encouragement to democratic reforms, under Jimmy Carter and again in the 1990s.

Figure 36.4   *Russian elections, 1993*

Huge questions remained about democracy's future. The link to economic expectations—the sense that democracy was a precondition for freer markets and economic growth that supported many Latin American conversions and also Gorbachev's reforms in Russia—was an obvious vulnerability: What if the economy did not improve? New uncertainties emerged by 2000. Still, the global trend was undeniable at least for a time, and it conjoined with the hopes born of the reduction of cold war tensions.

The Great Powers and New Disputes

 The most obvious result of the end of the cold war was the further ascendancy of the United States. Economic developments encouraged steps toward regional collaborations. But a new set of conflicts, including bitter ethnic strife, followed from the end of the Soviet system as well.

The end of the cold war and the spread of democracy raised important issues for the world's great powers. Most obviously, the United States became the lone superpower, the only country with the capability of military intervention around the globe. Russian power declined dramatically. The nation faced severe economic problems, as economic growth was limited. Military forces were cut back, a portion of the fleet simply left to rust in harbors. By 2001 military spending, at $4 billion a year, was only $1/30$ of that of the United States (where levels remained high). The splitting off of Ukraine and Kazakhstan, where some former Soviet missiles had been mounted, further reduced Russian capacity. The United States contributed a bit of funding to help pay for the retirement of some missiles and nuclear weapons. Russian weaponry remained considerable, though its state of readiness was questionable. Russian leaders alternated between playing up to the United States and Western powers and attempting to assert a more independent role. They enjoyed some success in influencing some of the former Soviet republics, notably Belarus and Moldova, through political alliances, economic influence, and even continued troop placement. But there was no question that the Russian counterweight to the United States was a thing of the past.

Other countries worried visibly about unchallenged American strength. China, particularly, alternated between seeking favorable economic arrangements with the U.S. government (China enjoyed a great balance of trade advantage with the United States) and seeking to increase military rivalry. China's claims to control Taiwan, combined with U.S. involvement in defense of the island, were a particularly fruitful source of tension. China's military buildup, however, did not threaten the United States directly. Efforts to forge alliances against U.S. power, by greater cooperation with Russia or with other countries like Iran, roused United States concern but they did not emerge as full-fledged partnerships.

By 2001, even western European countries expressed some misgivings about U.S. strength, particularly when the United States seemed to ignore international collaboration in areas such as the environment. In 2001, in an interesting gesture of anti-Americanism, the United Nations excluded the United States from membership on its Human Rights Commission, the first time this had happened since the commission was formed.

Still, no systematic counterpoise to U.S. power emerged in the decade plus after the cold war's end. U.S. power was indeed enhanced, through most of the 1990s, by unusually rapid economic growth and by U.S. leadership in burgeoning new fields of information technology and bioengineering. Even Japan did not keep pace with U.S. innovations in technology and business organization, as the Pacific Rim encountered new economic difficulties at the very end of the 20th century.

What was the United States to do with its world power? U.S. leaders clearly felt emboldened to tell other parts of the world how to organize their societies. Both business and political experts argued that the U.S. model of a free market economy should be adopted everywhere—for example, as a cure-all against the economic doldrums of the more state-directed Pacific Rim. U.S. leaders also worried about new kinds of threats that would replace the old great-power confrontations. Thus they identified small nations that sponsored terrorism or that might manage to send isolated but deadly nuclear weapons against the United States, such as Iran, Iraq, and North Korea. These threats justified considerable military expenditure in the United States and focused new efforts to assemble allies willing to pressure or isolate what the United States sometimes termed "rogue states."

The United States also took a role in a number of regional conflicts. Its leadership in a large coalition of European and Arab states against the Iraqi invasion of the small nation of Kuwait was in part designed to protect vital oil supplies. A short **Persian Gulf War** in 1991 pushed the Iraqis out of Kuwait and led to a decade of control over parts of Iraqi territory. The United States also intervened, more reluctantly, in conflicts in the Balkans because instability in Europe still seemed threatening. U.S. allies pressed for help, and atrocities against civilian populations were dramatic. The exact principles of U.S. operations in the post–cold war world remained unclear, however, and many Americans were wary of serving as the world's police force.

The terrorist attacks on the United States on September 11, 2001, raised another set of issues. Clearly, U.S. power was drawing fire from groups concerned both about specific policies in the Middle East and about wider U.S. power or, as they termed it, arrogance. To the Middle Eastern terrorists, the United States interfered with Middle Eastern countries, defiling "sacred ground" by stationing troops in Saudi Arabia and offending further by strongly supporting Israel. The terrorist response, hijacking airliners to crash into buildings symbolic of U.S. financial and military might, killed approximately 3000 people—but the terrorists regarded this as justifiable retaliation against a nation they could not hope to fight by conventional means. Backed by most of the world's nations, the United States vowed to end terrorism, and successfully toppled the Islamic fundamentalist regime in Afghanistan that had harbored the terrorists behind the September 11th attacks.

Regional Disputes and Alliances

The end of the cold war framework highlighted certain regional rivalries. Many of them were not new, but they became more acute as the controlling influence of U.S.–Soviet rivalry disappeared. At the same time, efforts to form regional cooperative arrangements also gained ground. Europe took the lead here, in building further on its Common Market structure, but there were developments also in Asia and the Americas.

The collapse of the Soviet empire raised obvious questions for the principal alliance systems in western Europe. The North Atlantic Treaty Organization (NATO) had been formed specifically to block Soviet expansionism. What was its purpose now that the Soviet threat had receded? NATO officials continued to see the alliance as a desirable stabilizing force in Europe and perhaps beyond. We will see that NATO did play a direct role in the greatest pocket of instability, the Balkans. Coordination of military planning continued. Several former eastern bloc countries requested admission to NATO, to herald their new orientation toward the West and to insure against Russian intervention, and NATO has granted admission to a number of east central European countries since the end of the 1990s.

The economic alliance of western Europe—the European Union—was another matter, since its purposes of economic integration and stimulus to growth were unaffected by the cold war's end. Most eastern European countries, along with Turkey, sought entry into the European Union. Their economies were in throes of conversion from communist systems to market arrangements, and their standards of living were noticeably below those of western Europe. In some cases, questions persisted also about commitments to democracy and human rights. Full integration with the European Union would clearly be a drawn-out process. But by 2002 candidacies of several countries

In Depth

How Much Historical Change?

As the cold war drew to a close, a number of analysts, primarily in the United States, looked forward to dramatic shifts in human affairs. There were two related lines of argument. The first, summed up in the "end of history" concept, emphasized the new dominance of the democratic form of government. The contest among political and economic systems, particularly between democracy and communism, was over; democracy would now sweep over the world. With this, the need for basic questioning about political institutions would also end: Democracy worked best, and it was here to stay. Further, the change in political structure also had implications for power rivalries. Some analysts contended that democracies never war on each other. Once the people control affairs of state through their votes, the selfishness and power trips that lead to war would end. Ordinary people understand the horror of war. They appreciate the common humanity they share with other democratic peoples. Just as democracy resolves internal conflicts through votes, democracies resolve external conflicts through bargaining and compromise. People do not vote for wars of aggression, at most sanctioning defense against attack.

Another argument, which might be combined with the democracy approach, focused on the spread of consumer capitalism around the world. As put forward by a U.S. journalist in a popular book called *The Lexus and the Olive Tree*, the consumer capitalism approach emphasized the benefits of a global economy. In this, everyone would gain access to greater material abundance and the wonders of consumerism, and they would not wish to jeopardize this prosperity

through war. Shared interests, rather than traditional disputes over limited resources, would carry the day.

These kinds of arguments assumed that the world was poised to depart substantially from prior history, based on new political systems or new economic systems or both. This is a challenging kind of forecasting because it cannot be easily disproved, until the future does not correspond to the dramatic projections. The consumerism argument, particularly, had no precedent in the past. At the same time, the predictions also could not be proved, for example by pointing to some prior historical analogy. How, then, should they be assessed?

Questions: Following the end of the cold war, did the world change as rapidly and fundamentally as these predictions implied? Did new systems spread as uniformly and consistently as the democracy and global consumerism arguments implied? Were past rivalries and cultural and institutional commitments to war and dispute so easily wiped away? These predictions were issued in the wake of the excitement surrounding the cold war's end. Developments later in the 1990s and in 2001 did not necessarily live up to the idea of fundamental transformation. How wrong were the predictions, and why did very intelligent people find them plausible in the first place? Or was the world in the early stages of the kinds of transition the forecasters suggested? How significant, in other words, was the cold war's end in reshaping global relationships?

where market reforms had been most successful, such as Poland and Hungary, were well advanced, and full membership for at least some of the applicants was assured. Poland voted approval for entry in 2003. In the meantime the European Union continued to strengthen internal integration. Amid dispute, many existing members agreed on a common currency, the "euro," which went into effect in early 2002. The experiment in European unity continued.

Other areas sought benefits from economic alliances, though without moving to the level of integration Europe had achieved. During the 1990s a free trade agreement—the **North American Free Trade Agreement (NAFTA)**—joined the United States, Mexico, and Canada. Opponents worried

about loss of jobs to cheaper Mexican labor, and about environmental damage as firms moved to more loosely regulated regions. But a considerable trade increase did result, seeming to benefit all participants but particularly Mexico.

East and southeast Asia and the Pacific Rim formed the final center for new discussions about new levels of international economic arrangements. Several discussions explored opportunities for tariff reduction and policy coordination. Clearly, economic issues had replaced cold war rivalries as the motor for regional diplomatic experiments.

But the continued potential for regional diplomatic and military conflict was striking as well. Most of the conflicts were not new. But the end of the cold war and the decline of Russian influence at the very least highlighted regional clashes and the maturing military power of many regional players, including nuclear capacity in several cases. The United States and the United Nations sought to keep the peace in most instances, but their efforts were not always successful.

The Middle East remained a trouble spot during the 1990s. Even before the end of the cold war, Iraq and Iran had conducted a long, casualty-filled war, with the ambitions of Iraq's dictatorial leader, Saddam Hussein, pitted against the Islamic revolutionary regime in Iran. Iraq prevailed, and then later, in 1990, invaded the small oil-rich state of Kuwait. This galvanized the international coalition, of Western and moderate Arab states, which defeated Iraq in the 1991 Persian Gulf War while leaving Saddam Hussein in power. The United States maintained a large military presence in the Persian Gulf region, which drew criticism from many Arabs and Muslims.

Amid growing concern about terrorism directed against the United States, another war in the Persian Gulf region broke out in 2003, when the United States and Britain conquered Iraq with the avowed intention of destroying Saddam Hussein's regime and introducing democracy. The war reflected the newness of nations like Iraq, whose boundaries had been created by Western colonial powers after the fall of the Ottoman Empire, and also the prevalence of harsh authoritarian—and in this case, ambitious—regimes in the region. Whether a new assertion of Western power could resolve these issues, further complicated by tensions between some Muslim groups and Western authorities, remains to be seen.

Israeli–Palestinian tensions serve as another Middle Eastern flashpoint. Israeli relations with the huge Palestinian minority deteriorated after the cold war ended, despite some promising peace moves in the mid-1990s. Though an autonomous Palestinian government was set up over two territories within Israel, tensions continued. Bitter violence between Israelis and Palestinians revived between 2001 and 2003. A wave of suicide bombings by Palestinians targeted Israeli civilians, while the Israeli government attacked Palestinian cities and refugee camps in turn. Clearly, key issues in this complex region remain to be resolved.

Tensions between India and Pakistan also escalated, with various border clashes particularly around the disputed territory of Kashmir. By 2000 both countries had conducted tests of nuclear weapons. This was the most open case of nuclear dissemination, as the limited nuclear group of the cold war began to expand. Increased Hindu nationalism within India was matched by fiercer Muslim rhetoric in Pakistan.

There was no clear global pattern of activity resulting from the end of the cold war. The tensions between impulses toward integration, based primarily on economic goals, and the indulgence of rivalries, sometimes spiced by military expansion, were obvious.

Ethnic Conflict

The upsurge of ethnic conflict in several areas constituted a strikingly novel feature of the post–cold war scene. Ethnic rivalries were not of course new, but several components helped explain the new and troubling outbreak.

New levels of global interaction increased the potential for group identities to generate hostilities. Some groups clearly increased their investment in ethnic identity as a means of countering outside influences and global pressures. At the same time, the collapse of several key multinational states, notably the Soviet Union and Yugoslavia (see Map 36.2), opened the door to a reassertion of ethnic identity as a means of replacing discredited ideologies such as communism and as part of the conflict for control within new political units.

Within Europe, a number of ethnic groups developed new opportunities for expression, as the hold of the classic nation-state declined. The British government, for example, gave limited autonomy to Scottish

Map 36.2 *The Implosion of Yugoslavia, 1991–1999*

and Welsh governments. France and Spain became more tolerant toward linguistic minorities such as the Bretons and the Catalans. During the 1990s, a number of European countries saw the rise of new political movements bent on reducing immigration in favor of protecting jobs and cultural identity for the majority national group. A National Front group in France won up to 10 percent of all votes during the mid-1990s, though it then fell back a bit. Austria generated a controversial right-wing national government rhetorically hostile to immigrants, and in 2001 a new government leader in Italy emphasized an antiforeign plank. Violence against immigrant groups, such as Turks in Germany, flared recurrently as well.

More systematic violence broke out in several of the territories of the former Soviet Union. Czechoslovakia split peacefully into two ethnic segments, the Czech Republic and Slovakia, but this was not the common pattern. New or newly freed states witnessed frequent ethnic conflicts. Hungarian minorities in Romania and Turkish minorities in Bulgaria faced new pressures during the 1990s. A bloody revolt broke out in a Muslim region of Russia, Chechnya, where a regional leader proclaimed independence in 1990. On two occasions during the ensuing decade, heavy fighting broke out between the Russian military and rebels seeking an independent Muslim nation. Acts of terrorism, including bombs placed in several Moscow apartment buildings and theaters, helped push Russian public opinion to greater acceptance of military action. Neither side achieved full victory, though Russian resistance to this kind of regional and ethnic claim seemed firm.

Ethnic tension also surfaced in southeastern Europe and central Asia. Recurrent fighting occurred among ethnic groups in the newly independent nation of Georgia. More serious warfare erupted periodically between Armenian Christians and their Muslim neighbors in Azerbaijan.

Yugoslavia was the most important case where elimination of a multiethnic state, successfully united under communism, brought bloodshed and turmoil. Ethnic patterns were unusually complex in this region. Slavs differed linguistically from Albanians (many of whom, also, were Muslim). Slavs themselves were divided among groups like Serbs and Croats, with different alphabets, religions, and historical experiences. There were also Muslim Slavs in the territory of Bosnia. Groups had been pitted against each other from the Turkish conquest and the differential reactions to German occupation in World War II.

After the death of the strong communist leader in Yugoslavia, Marshall Tito, ethnic divisions became more open, with rising tensions between Albanians in the region of Kosovo and the dominant Serbian group. Individual Serbian nationalist leaders, like Slobodan Milosevic, began to gain increasing attention.

Then came the Soviet collapse, which emboldened several regions to seek independence. Slovenia and Croatia pulled away in 1991, and fierce fighting erupted between Croats and Serbs before the latter reluctantly agreed to a dismemberment of a country they believed they should dominate. The government of Bosnia and Herzegovina declared independence in 1992, but this led to bitter fighting among internal groups—Catholic Croats, Orthodox Serbs, and Muslims—aided by outside intervention particularly from Serbia (see Figure 36.5). Massive

Figure 36.5 *Civil war in Yugoslavia as the separate Slavic groups splinter. The Yugoslav army here attacks the historic Croatian city of Dubrovnik in 1991. The Croats later achieved independence.*

killing resulted, with many atrocities against civilians under the heading of "ethnic cleansing"—which often meant killing or removing non-Serb populations to facilitate Serb control. Tremendous diplomatic pressure from western Europe and the United States, supplemented by Russia, led to some tenuous cease-fires, but finally, in 1995, an international military force had to step in to impose an uneasy peace. At the end of the 1990s, warfare broke out between Serbs and Muslims in the province of Kosovo, with atrocities on both sides. Purely diplomatic efforts to stop the killing failed, and NATO forces, headed by the United States, began a bombing campaign against Yugoslavia that finally forced an end to hostilities and the installation of another international occupying force. By 2000, Milosevic was forced out of the Yugoslav presidency.

Ethnic attacks were not confined to the lands once ruled by communism. In the 1990s another set of bloody conflicts broke out in central Africa, pitting tribal groups, the Hutus and the Tutsis, against each other particularly in the nation of Rwanda (see Figure 36.6). Here, too, old rivalries blended with disputes over current power; the Tutsis had long ruled, but they were outnumbered by resentful Hutus. Intervention from neighboring states like Uganda contributed to the confusion. Tremendous slaughter resulted, with hundreds of thousands killed and many more—over two million—driven from their homes. While outside powers, the Organization of African States, and the United Nations urged peace, there was no decisive outside intervention. Bloodshed finally ran its course, but ethnic disputes continued in central Africa, contributing to civil war in countries like Congo. Ethnic and religious disputes were also involved in a number of other African trouble spots, including Muslim attacks on Christians in Sudan, and warfare among military gangs in countries like Sierra Leone and Liberia.

Clearly, ethnic tensions were leading not just to warfare, but to renewed acts of genocide that targeted civilians, including women and children, and the creation of massive refugee populations. Reactions from the world at large varied. In some instances, violence seemed sufficiently menacing to major powers that intervention occurred, though never without great hesitation. No policies emerged that offered great promise of pushing back the potential for ethnic conflict.

Figure 36.6 *In the last decade of the 20th century, the specter of genocide returned to a century that had seen more examples of this extreme form of violence against whole peoples than any other period in world history. Genocide infected the Balkans and, as this picture shows, the nation of Rwanda in east central Africa.*

Globalization

 Several factors complicated the unfolding of globalization by the early 21st century. They included lingering nationalism, new subnational loyalties, a significant religious surge, and novel forms of terrorism.

The collapse of the Soviet Union and the Warsaw Pact alliance, which effectively ended the long cold war stalemate, abruptly opened up possibilities for new transglobal connections that had been limited after 1914 by successive wars and international crises. In many instances the new linkages between states and regions that were created or greatly expanded after 1989 represented revivals of processes that had begun to flourish in the decades before World War I. But major, late 20th-century innovations in communications, banking, and computing—all of which came together in quite remarkable ways on the Internet—made possible transmissions of information, economic exchanges, and cultural collaborations at a speed and intensity beyond anything imaginable in earlier epochs. Particularly noteworthy was the rapidity with which the republics that emerged from the former Soviet Union, including Russia, and the former communist states of eastern Europe, were incorporated into expanding global networks. Mainland China, which remained communist politically, also moved to adopt market capitalism and increase its trade with the United States, Japan, and the other industrial nations of the European Union.

Many experts saw what they called globalization as the dominant theme of present and future world history. **Globalization** meant the increasing interconnectedness of all parts of the world, particularly in communication and commerce but in culture and politics as well. It meant accelerating speed for global connections of various sorts. It meant openness to exchanges around the world.

The new focus on globalization in the 1990s legitimately reflected two or three new developments beyond the networks established from the later 19th century onward. First, the end of the cold war and the absence of systematic patterns of international conflict meant new opportunities for, and new attention to, global connections. China, as well as the former Soviet Union, became much more fully open to international trade and many if not all the other facets of globalization. More broadly, the growing commitment around the world to more free market arrangements, and less state intervention, opened up opportunities for foreign investment and the extension of manufacturing operations to additional areas. Latin America, India, and other places participated in this movement, along with the communist and former communist world. By the 1990s only a handful of spots—Myanmar, North Korea, the former Yugoslavia—were largely outside the network of globalization.

Second, the late 20th century saw a new round of technical developments, associated particularly with the computer, that greatly accelerated the speed and amount of global communication. The new technology particularly facilitated international commerce, but there were global cultural and political implications as well.

Finally, though more tentatively, more people around the world became accustomed to global connections (see Figure 36.7). At least in some areas, intensive nationalism declined in favor of a more cosmopolitan interest in wider influences and contacts. The spread of English as a world language, though incomplete and often resented, was part of this connection. English served airline travel, many sports, and the early Internet as a common language. This encouraged and reflected other facets of global change.

The New Technology

A globalization guru tells the following story. In 1988 a U.S. government official was traveling to Chicago and was assigned a limousine with a cellular phone. He was so delighted to have this novelty that he called his wife just to brag. Nine years later, in 1997, the same official was visiting Ivory Coast in west Africa and went to a remote village, reachable only by dugout canoe, to inaugurate a new health facility. As he prepared to leave, climbing in the canoe, a government official handed him a cellular phone and said he had a call from Washington. Cellular phones became increasingly common, one of the key new communication devices that, by the 1990s, made almost constant contact with other parts of the world feasible, and for some people unavoidable. Western Europe and east Asia led in the cellular phone revolution, but leading groups in all parts of the world participated.

Figure 36.7 *Midnight, December 31, 1999: Celebration of the new millennium in Sydney, Australia. Thanks to telecommunications, festivities in most time zones were broadcast worldwide, making for a great global party.*

During the 1980s steady improvements in miniaturization made computers increasingly efficient. By the 1990s, the amount of information that could be stored on microchips increased by over 60 percent annually. Linkages among computers improved as well, starting with halting efforts in the 1960s mainly for defense purposes. E-mail was introduced in 1972. In 1990 a British software engineer working in Switzerland, Tim Berners, developed the World Wide Web, and the true age of the Internet was born. Almost instantaneous contact by computer became possible around the world, with it the capacity to send vast amounts of text, imagery, and even music (both legally and illegally). While the Internet was not available to everyone—by 2001 only 25 percent of the world's population had any access to it—it did provide global contacts for some regions otherwise fairly remote. In eastern Russia, for example, international mail service was agonizingly slow, telephone access often interrupted—but a student could sit at an Internet café in Vladivostok and communicate easily with counterparts in the United States or Brazil.

Satellite linkages for television formed a final communications revolution, making simultaneous broadcasts possible around the world. A full quarter of the world's population now could, and sometimes did, watch the same sporting event, usually World Cup soccer or the Olympics, a phenomenon never before possible or even approachable in world history. Global technology gained new meaning.

Business Organization and Investment

Thanks in part to new technology, in part to more open political boundaries, international investment accelerated rapidly at the end of the 20th century. Stock exchanges featured holdings in Chinese utilities or Brazilian steel companies as well as the great corporations of the West and Japan. U.S. investments abroad multiplied rapidly, almost doubling in the first half of the 1970s. By the 1980s foreign operations were generating between 25 and 40 percent of all corporate profits in the United States. Japan's foreign investment rose fifteenfold during the 1970s. During the 1980s Japanese car manufacturers set up factories in the United States, Europe, and other areas. German cars, French tires, German chemicals and pharmaceuticals, and Dutch petroleum all had substantial U.S. operations. At the end of the 1990s the German Volkswagen firm introduced an imaginative new car design, the bug, with production facilities entirely based in Mexico, but marketing in the United States and around the world.

Globalization in business involved rapid increases in exports and imports, the extension of business organization across political boundaries—the so-called **multinational corporations**—and division of labor on a worldwide basis. Cars in the United States were manufactured by assembling parts made in Japan, Korea, Mexico, and elsewhere. Japanese cars often had more American-made parts in them than Detroit products had. Such was the new structure of global production. Firms set up operations not simply to produce closer to markets in order to save transportation costs; they also looked for centers of cheap labor and relaxed environmental regulations. Computer boards were made by women in the West Indies and Africa. India developed a huge software industry, subcontracting for firms in the United States and western Europe. The linkages were dazzling.

International firms continued a long-standing interest in finding cheap raw materials. Companies in the West and Japan thus competed for access to oil and minerals in the newly independent nations of central Asia, after the collapse of the Soviet Union. International investments also followed interest rates. During the 1990s relatively attractive U.S. interest rates drew extensive investment from Europe, Japan, and the oil-rich regions in the Middle East.

While multinational companies sometimes faced government regulation, many of them had more power, and far more resources, than the governments of most of the countries within which they operated. They could thus determine most aspects of labor and environmental policy. They could and did pull up stakes in one region if more attractive opportunities opened elsewhere, regardless of the impact in terms of unemployment and empty facilities. Yet the spread of multinationals also promoted industrial skills in many previously agricultural regions, and they depended on improvements in communications and transportation that could bring wider changes (see Figure 36.8).

American factories located in northern Mexico, designed to produce goods largely for sale back in the United States, showed the complexity of the new international economy. The factories unquestionably sought low-paying labor and lax regulations. Factories often leaked chemical waste. Wages were barely 10 percent of U.S. levels. But the foreign factories

Figure 36.8   *Change and continuity in rural India. New irrigation and electrification combine with traditional methods of tilling the soil as agricultural production rises.*

often paid better, nevertheless, than their Mexican counterparts. Many workers, including large numbers of women, found the labor policies more enlightened and the foremen better behaved in the foreign firms as well. Evaluation was tricky. A key question, not yet answerable, involved what would happen next: Would wages improve, and would the industrial skills of the new factory workers allow a widening range of opportunities? Or would the dependence on poverty-level wages persist?

Migration

Broad international patterns of migration had developed by the 1950s and 1960s, with the use of "guest workers" from Turkey and north Africa in Europe for example. Here, patterns in the 1990s built clearly on previous trends. But the fact was that easier travel back and forth plus the continued gap between slowly growing populations in the industrial countries, and rapidly growing populations in Latin America, Africa, and parts of Asia, maintained high levels of exchange. A few areas, like Italy, Greece, and Japan, had almost ceased internal population growth by the 1990s, which meant that new labor needs, particularly at the lower skill levels, had to be supplied by immigration. Japan hoped to avoid too much influx by relying on high-technology solutions, but even here worker groups were brought in from the Philippines and southeast Asia. Migration into Europe and the United States was far more extensive, producing truly multinational populations in key urban and commercial centers. By 2000 at least 25 percent of all Americans, mostly people of color, came from households where English was not the first language. Ten percent of the French population in 2003 was Muslim (see Figure 36.9). Here was an important source of tension, with local populations often fearing foreigners and worried about job competition. Here also was a new opportunity, not just for new laborers but for new cultural inspiration as well.

Cultural Globalization

Thanks in part to global technologies and business organization, plus reduced political barriers, the pace

Figure 36.9 *The mixtures of peoples and cultures that had become a prominent feature of world history by the end of the 20th century is wonderfully illustrated by this group of Muslim schoolchildren in a French school. By 2003, 10 percent of the French population was Islamic.*

of cultural exchange and contact around the world accelerated at the end of the 1990s. Much of this involved mass consumer goods, spread from the United States, western Europe, and Japan. But art shows, symphony exchanges, scientific conferences, and Internet contact increased as well. Music conductors and artists held posts literally around the world, sometimes juggling commitments among cities like Tokyo, Berlin, and Chicago within a single season. Science laboratories filled with researchers from around the world, collaborating (usually in English) with little regard for national origin.

The spread of fast-food restaurants from the United States, headed by McDonald's, formed one of the most striking international cultural influences from the 1970s onward. The company began in Illinois in 1955 and started its international career in 1967 with outlets in Canada and Puerto Rico. From then on, the company entered an average of two new nations per year and accelerated the pace in the 1990s. By 1998 it was operating in 109 countries overall. The company won quick success in Japan, where it gained its largest foreign audience; "makadonaldo" first opened in Tokyo's world famous Ginza, already known for cosmopolitan department stores, in 1971. McDonald's entry into the Soviet Union in 1990 was a major sign of the ending of cold war rivalries and the growing Russian passion for international consumer goods. The restaurants won massive patronage despite (by Russian standards) very high prices. Even in gourmet-conscious France, McDonald's and other fast-food outlets were winning 26 percent of all restaurant dining by the 1990s. Not everyone who patronized McDonald's really liked the food. Many patrons in Hong Kong, for example, said they went mainly to see and be seen, and to feel part of the global world.

Cultural globalization obviously involved increasing exposure to American movies and television shows. Series like *Baywatch* won massive foreign audiences. Movie and amusement park icons like Mickey Mouse, and products and dolls derived from them, had international currency. Western beauty standards, based on the models and film stars, won wide exposure, expressed among other things in widely sought international beauty pageants. MTV spread Western images and sounds to youth audiences almost everywhere.

Holidays took on an international air. American-style Christmas trappings, including gift giving, lights, and Santa Claus, spread not only to countries of Chris-

tian background, like France, but also places like Muslim Istanbul. Northern Mexico picked up American Halloween trick-or-treating, as it displaced the more traditional Catholic observance of All Saints' Day.

Consumer internationalization was not just American. Japanese rock groups gained wide audience. The Pokemon toy series, derived from Japanese cultural traditions, won a frenzied audience among American children in the 1990s, who for several years could not get enough. A Japanese soap opera heroine became the most admired woman in Muslim Iran. South Korea, historically hostile to Japan, proved open to popular Japanese music groups and cartoon animation. European popular culture, including fashion and music groups, gained large followings around the world as well.

Dress was internationalized to an unprecedented extent. American-style blue jeans showed up almost everywhere. A major export item for Chinese manufacturing involved Western clothing pirated from famous brand names. A "Chinese market" in the cities of eastern Russia contained entirely Western-style items, mainly clothing and shoes.

Cultural internationalization obviously involved styles from industrial countries, wherever the products were actually made, spreading to other areas, as well as within the industrial world itself. Degrees of penetration varied—in part by wealth and urbanization, in part according to degrees of cultural tolerance. Foreign models were often adapted to local customs. Thus foods in McDonald's in India (where the chain was not very popular in any event) included vegetarian items not found elsewhere. Comic books in Mexico, originally derived from U.S. models, took on Mexican cultural images, including frequent triumphs over "gringo" supermen. Cultural internationalization was a real development, but it was complex and incomplete.

Institutions of Globalization

On the whole, political institutions globalized less rapidly than technology or business, or even consumer culture. Many people worried about the gap between political supervision and control and the larger globalization process. UN activity accelerated a bit in the 1990s. With the end of the cold war, more diplomatic hotspots invited intervention by multinational military forces. UN forces tried to calm or prevent disputes in a number of parts of Africa, the Balkans, and the Middle East. Growing refugee populations called for UN humanitarian intervention, often aided by other international groups. UN conferences broadened their scope, dealing for example with gender and population control issues. While the results of the conferences were not always clear, a number of countries did incorporate international standards into domestic law. Women in many African countries, for example, were able to appeal to UN proclamations on gender equality as a basis for seeking new property rights in the courts. By 2001, the United Nations became increasingly active as well in encouraging assistance to stem the AIDS epidemic.

As more nations participated actively in international trade, the importance of organizations in this arena grew. The International Monetary Fund (IMF) and the World Bank had been founded after World War II to promote trade. Guided by the major industrial powers, these organizations offered loans and guidance to developing areas and also to regions that encountered temporary economic setbacks. Loans to Mexico and to southeast Asia during the 1990s were intended to promote recovery from recessions that threatened to affect other areas. Loans were usually accompanied by requirements for economic reform, usually through reduced government spending and the promotion of more open competition. These guidelines were not always welcomed by the regions involved. The IMF and the World Bank were widely viewed as primary promoters of the capitalist global economy.

Annual meetings of the heads of the seven leading industrial powers (four from Europe, two from North America, plus Japan) also promoted global trade and policies toward developing regions. Finally, the regional economic arrangements that had blossomed from the 1950s onward gained growing importance as globalization accelerated. The European Union headed the list, but the North American Free Trade Agreement and other regional consortiums in Latin America and east Asia also pushed for lower tariffs and greater economic coordination.

Protest and Economic Uncertainties

Accelerating globalization attracted a vigorous new protest movement by the end of the 1990s. Meetings of the World Bank or the industrial leaders were increasingly marked by huge demonstrations and some violence. The current movement began with massive protests in Seattle in 1999, and they continued at key gatherings thereafter (see Figure 36.10). Protesters came from various parts of the world and

Figure 36.10 *In recent years, the periodic meetings of the World Trade Organization have prompted protests against the inequities of globalization. In 1999, protesters confronted police in Seattle; demonstrations periodically turned violent, though most of the participating groups sought nonviolent tactics.*

Document

Protests Against Globalization

In December 1999, a series of protests rocked Seattle on the occasion of a World Trade Organization (WTO) meeting designed to discuss further international tariff cuts in the interests of promoting global trade. The following passage was written by Jeffrey St. Clair, a radical journalist who is co-editor of the political newsletter *CounterPunch*. St. Clair describes the atmosphere of the Seattle protests and some of the groups involved. The Seattle protests foreshadowed a regular sequence of popular demonstrations at the meetings of such groups as the World Bank, which continue into the 21st century, involving many of the same groups and issues.

Monday

And the revolution will be started by: sea turtles. At noon about 2,000 people massed at the United Methodist Church, the HQ of the grassroots [organizations], for a march to the convention center. It was Environment Day and the Earth Island Institute had prepared more than 500 sea turtle costumes for marchers to wear. The sea turtle became the prime symbol of the WTO's threats to environmental laws when a WTO tribunal ruled that the U.S. Endangered Species Act, which requires shrimp to be caught with turtle excluder devices, was an unfair trade barrier.

But the environmentalists weren't the only ones on the street Monday morning. In the first showing of a new solidarity, labor union members from the Steelworkers and the Longshoremen showed up to join the march. In fact, Steelworker Don Kegley led the march, alongside environmentalist Ben White. (White was later clubbed in the back of the head by a young man who was apparently angry that he couldn't do his Christmas shopping. The police pulled the youth away from White, but the man wasn't arrested. White played down the incident.) The throng of sea turtles and blue-jacketed union folk took off to the rhythm of a familiar chant that would echo down the streets of Seattle for days: "The people will never be divided!"

I walked next to Brad Spann, a Longshoreman from Tacoma, who hoisted up one of my favorite signs of the entire week: "Teamsters and Turtles Together at Last!" Brad winked at me and said, "What the hell do you think old Hoffa [former Teamster leader] thinks of that?"

The march, which was too fast and courteous for my taste, was escorted by motorcycle police and ended essentially in a cage, a protest pen next to a construction site near the convention center. A large stage had been erected hours earlier and Carl Pope, the director of the Sierra Club, was called forth to give the opening speech. The Club is the nation's most venerable environmental group....

Standing near the stage I saw Brent Blackwelder, the head of Friends of the Earth. Behind his glasses and somewhat shambling manner, Blackwelder looks ever so professional. And he is by far the smartest of the environmental CEOs. But he is also the most radical politically, the most willing to challenge the tired complacency of his fellow green executives....

Blackwelder's speech was a good one, strong and defiant. He excoriated the WTO as a kind of global security force for transnational corporations whose mission is "to stuff unwanted products, like genetically engineered foods, down our throats."...

After the speechifying most of the marchers headed back to the church. But a contingent of about 200 ended up in front of McDonald's where a group of French farmers had mustered to denounce U.S. policy on biotech foods. Their leader was José Bove, a sheep farmer from Millau in southwest France and a leader of Confederation Paysanne, a French environmental group. In August, Bove had been jailed in France for leading a raid on a McDonald's restaurant under construction in Larzac. At the time, he was already awaiting charges that he destroyed a cache of Novartis' genetically engineered corn. Bove said his raid on the Larzac McDonald's was promoted by the U.S. decision to impose a heavy tariff on Roquefort cheese in retaliation for the European Union's refusal to import American hormone-treated beef. Bove's act of defiance earned him the praise of Jacques Chirac and Friends of the Earth. Bove said he was prepared to start a militant worldwide campaign against "Frankenstein" foods. "These actions will only stop when this mad logic comes to a halt," Bove said. "I don't demand clemency but justice."

Bove showed up at the Seattle McDonald's with rounds of Roquefort cheese, which he handed out to the crowd. After listening to a rousing speech against the evils of Monsanto, and its bovine growth hormone and Roundup Ready soybeans, the crowd stormed the McDonald's breaking its windows and urging customers and workers to join the marchers on the streets. This was the first shot in the battle for Seattle.

Who were these direct action warriors on the front lines? Earth First, the Alliance for Sustainable Jobs and the Environment (the new enviro-steelworker alliance), the Ruckus Society (a direct action training center), Jobs with Justice, Rainforest Action Network, Food Not Bombs, Global Exchange, and a small contingent of Anarchists, the dreaded Black Bloc.

There was also a robust international contingent on the streets Tuesday morning: French farmers, Korean greens [environmentalists], Canadian wheat growers, Mexican environmentalists, Chinese dissidents, Ecuadorian anti-dam organizers, U'wa tribespeople from the Columbian rainforest, and British campaigners against genetically modified foods. Indeed earlier, a group of Brits had cornered two Monsanto lobbyists behind an abandoned truck carrying an ad for the *Financial Times*. They detained the corporate flacks long enough to deliver a stern warning about the threat of frankencrops to wildlife, such as the Monarch butterfly. Then a wave of tear gas wafted over them and the Monsanto men fled, covering their eyes with their neckties....

As the march turned up toward the Sheraton and was beaten back by cops on horses, I teamed up with Etienne Vernet and Ronnie Cumming. Cumming is the head of one of the feistiest groups in the U.S., the PureFood Campaign, Monsanto's chief pain in the ass. Cumming hails from the oil town of Port Arthur, Texas. He went to Cambridge with another great foe of industrial agriculture, Prince Charles. Cumming was a civil rights organizer in Houston during the mid-sixties. "The energy here is incredible," Cumming said. "Black and white, labor and green, Americans, Europeans, Africans, and Asians arm in arm. It's the most hopeful I've felt since the height of the civil rights movement."

Vernet lives in Paris, where he is the leader of the radical green group EcoRopa. At that very moment the European delegates inside the convention were capitulating on a key issue: The EU, which had banned import of genetically engineered crops and hormone-treated beef, had agreed to a U.S. proposal to establish a scientific committee to evaluate the health and environmental risks of biotech foods, a sure first step toward undermining the moratorium. Still Vernet was in a jolly mood, lively and invigorated, if a little bemused by the decorous nature of the crowd. "Americans seem to have been out of practice in these things," he told me. "Everyone's so polite. The only things on fire are dumpsters filled with refuse." He pointed to a shiny black Lexus parked on Pine Street, which throngs of protesters had scrupulously avoided. In the windshield was a placard identifying it as belonging to a WTO delegate. "In Paris that car would be burning."

[David] Brower [environmental leader] was joined by David Foster, Director for District 11 of the United Steelworkers of America, one of the most articulate and unflinching labor leaders in America. Earlier this year, Brower and Foster formed an unlikely union, a coalition of radical envi-

ronmentalists and Steelworkers called the Alliance for Sustainable Jobs and the Environment, which had just run an amusing ad in the *New York Times* asking, "Have You Heard the One about the Environmentalist and the Steelworker?" The groups had found they had a common enemy: Charles Hurwitz, the corporate raider. Hurwitz owned the Pacific Lumber company, the northern California timber firm that is slaughtering some of the last stands of ancient redwoods on the planet. At the same time, Hurwitz, who also controlled Kaiser Aluminum, had locked out 3,000 Steelworkers at Kaiser's factories in Washington, Ohio, and Louisiana. "The companies that attack the environment most mercilessly are often also the ones that are the most anti-union," Foster told me. "More unites than divides us."

I came away thinking that for all its promise this tenuous marriage might end badly. Brower, the master of ceremonies, isn't going to be around forever to heal the wounds and cover up the divisions. There are deep, inescapable issues that will, inevitably, pit Steelworkers, fighting for their jobs in an ever-tightening economy, against greens, defending dwindling species like sockeye salmon that are being killed off by hydrodams that power the aluminum plants that offer employment to steel workers. When asked about this potential both Brower and Foster danced around it skillfully. But it was a dance of denial. The tensions won't go away simply because the parties agree not to mention them in public. Indeed, they might even build, like a pressure cooker left unwatched. I shook the thought from my head. For this moment, the new, powerful solidarity was too seductive to let such broodings intrude for long.

Questions: What were the principal groups involved in the globalization protests? Why did they feel such passion? Was this a global protest, or did different parts of the world have different issues? Is the movement likely to hold together? Can you think of other reasons to oppose globalization? What were the key arguments of defenders of globalization who disapproved of this kind of protest and of its goals?

From Alexander Cockburn, Jeffrey St. Clair, Allan Sekula, *5 Days That Shook the World* (London: Verso, 2000), 16–21, 28, 29, 36–37.

---

raised a number of issues. Many people believed that rapid global economic development was threatening the environment. Others blasted the use of cheap labor by international corporations, which was seen as damaging labor conditions even in industrial nations. Rampant consumerism was another target.

Most generally, many critics claimed that globalization was working to the benefit of rich nations and the wealthy generally, rather than the bulk of the world's population. They pointed to figures that suggested growing inequalities of wealth, with the top quarter of the world's population growing richer during the 1990s while the rest of the people increasingly suffered. This division operated between regions, widening the gap between affluent nations and the more populous developing areas. It also operated within regions, including the United States and parts of western Europe, where income gaps were on the rise. Bitter disagreements increasingly divided the supporters and opponents of globalization.

Quite apart from formal protest, different regions interpreted globalization variously, depending on economic results. From the mid-1990s onward, new economic problems affected areas such as southeast Asia, Russia, and Turkey, where unfavorable balances of trade drove down the values of national currency, while production declined and unemployment increased. International economic organizations like the World Bank tried to help, but on condition of reforms that might, for example, force the closing of less effective enterprises that would temporarily drive up unemployment. By 2002, major economic crises hit Argentina and to a lesser extent Brazil. These led to widespread beliefs that globalization was hurting rather than helping local prosperity. Whether global ties could survive these continuing regional problems was unclear.

A World of Religious and Ethnic Conflict

 A resurgence of many particularistic loyalties greatly complicated the globalization process and could threaten to reverse it. Not only regional conflicts but also new assertions of nationalism and religion arose. Some observers predicted a "clash of civilizations" on the basis of divisions of this sort, offering a dire and different model of the future from globalization. A new surge of international terrorism emerged from the most extreme tensions, using some of the connections that globalization had spawned.

Nationalism and Religious Currents

Several trends ran counter to globalization as the 21st century began. Nationalism was one. While many nations were partially bypassed by globalization—many countries were much less powerful than the multinational corporations—nationalist resistance to globalization surfaced in many ways. Many countries opposed the erosion of traditions by global cultural patterns. Thus the Japanese government subsidized training in the use of chopsticks, because so many Japanese children seemed to be relying on forks and fast foods instead of customary manners. The French

government periodically resisted the incorporation of English words into the French language. Many European countries tried to regulate the number of immigrants from Africa, Asia, and the West Indies, in the interests of preserving dominance for families and workers of European background. The United States rejected a wide variety of international treaties, including a provision for regulation against war crimes, because they might interfere with national sovereignty. China and other states periodically bristled against international criticism of internal policies concerning political prisoners.

What might be called subnational loyalties also surged around 2000, in part in the wake of the breakup of the Soviet empire. In China, the ongoing struggles of the Tibetans and a number of the Muslim minority peoples of western China quite often prompted forcible, at times brutal, responses on the part of the Maoist regime and its allegedly less repressive communist successors. In important ways these confrontations represented the continuation of the historic Chinese domination of neighboring non-Chinese peoples and minority ethnic groups after the establishment of the Communist People's Republic. Similar neocolonial policies were pursued by the communist regime in unified Vietnam. There the lives of the so-called tribal or hill peoples and ethnic minorities, such as the Khmers (Cambodians) and Chams, were subjected to ever more stringent state regulation and campaigns by the majority Vietnamese to undermine the cultures and weaken the separate identities of minority peoples. The Vietnamese also asserted their dominance over neighboring peoples, such as the Laotians and especially the Cambodians, whose genocidal, Khmer Rouge leadership was driven from power by a Vietnamese invasion.

In other areas, particularly parts of Africa, ethnic competition for political and economic dominance led to the complete breakdown of several newly independent states in the 1980s and 1990s. In countries like Sierra Leone and Liberia, political power devolved to local warlords and their often vicious gangs who warred with each other, with remnants of postcolonial governments and with UN forces sent in to restore order. Mercenary bands, including many armed children, killed and mutilated many civilians.

Religious differences contributed to many subnational conflicts. Catholic–Eastern Orthodox–Muslim clashes complicated ethnic rivalry in the former

Yugoslavia. Muslim–Christian clashes occurred in Indonesia and the Sudan. Hindus and Muslims disputed in India, Protestants and Catholics in Northern Ireland, and Jews with Muslim and Christian Arabs in Israel and Palestine. Fervent religious belief, combined with growing intolerance, often proved the basis for extremist politics and growing violence.

Religious Revivals

In addition to religious tensions within particular regions, a global religious revival developed in the final decades of the 20th century. Religious movements were not necessarily opposed to globalization, but they tended to insist on their distinctiveness, against any uniform global culture, and they also bred suspicions of the consumerism and sexuality highlighted in many manifestations of globalization, including films and tourism.

As communism collapsed in eastern Europe, many people returned to previous religious beliefs, including Orthodox Christianity. Protestant fundamentalists, often from the United States, were also busy in the region. Protestant fundamentalism also spread rapidly in parts of Latin America, such as Guatemala and Brazil. In India, Hindu fundamentalism surged by the 1990s, with Hindu nationalist politicians capturing the nation's presidency. Fundamentalism also gained ground in Islam, particularly in the Middle East and nearby parts of Africa and south central Asia. Whether Christian, Hindu, or Islamic, fundamentalists tended to urge a return to the primacy of religion and religious laws and often opposed greater freedoms for women. Frequently, fundamentalists urged government support for religious values.

Religious fundamentalism ran counter to globalization in several ways, even though many religious leaders became adept at using new global technologies such as the Internet. It tended to appeal particularly to impoverished urban groups who seemed to be left behind in the global economy. Fundamentalism also tended to increase intolerance, even in religious traditions that had historically been reasonably open. Hindu fundamentalists thus frequently clashed with Muslims in India. While some advocates of globalization assumed that religious traditionalism would decline,

the balance was in fact unclear as the 21st century opened.

Global Terrorism

Around 2000, a new wave of international terrorism built on some of the nationalist, subnationalist, and religious currents in various parts of the world. The new terrorism used some of the apparatus of globalization, particularly to reach across regional boundaries; it also attacked key institutions and principles of globalization in some instances.

Terrorists used secret military operations to counter the power of regular military forces, often targeting civilians. Terrorism was not new: bombing and assassination attempts had dotted the later 19th century, for example in Russia, directed against political regimes the terrorists viewed as oppressive. It was a terrorist assassination of an Austrian prince that had launched World War I. By the later 20th century, terrorism usually involved a minority nationalist movement, like the Basque terrorists in northern Spain or an Indian separatist group in Sri Lanka, or a religious cause. Technological advances, including the miniaturization of bombs, expanded the destructive power of terrorist acts and their capacity to sow fear. As governments improved security protections for political leaders, terrorists increasingly turned to more random civilian targets, in hopes of destabilizing a society and undermining a hated political regime.

The attack on the United States on September 11, 2001, which killed about 3000 people, was an unusually brazen act by a group of Islamic terrorists. It obviously protested American power and policies in the Middle East, but the terrorists also chose a symbol of economic globalization, the World Trade Center in New York.

Terrorism normally provoked extensive retaliation by the police and military in societies under attack. This retaliation sometimes caused far more casualties, even among civilians, than the terrorist acts themselves. Terrorists seldom seemed to achieve many of their stated goals, but eliminating their threat proved very difficult. As terrorism went global, particularly with the attacks on the United States, it threatened to complicate some of the institutions of globalization—for example, by provoking new limitations on international travel. Here was a key theme for at least the early 21st century.

Global Warming and Other Perils

 New environmental issues were a fundamental feature of globalization. International conferences recognized the issues but struggled to come up with solutions. Rapid international travel increased the chances of rapid spread of disease.

Perhaps the most sobering revelations that soon muted the initial triumphalism of the Western democracies over communism were those associated with the environment. Here, in turn, was another set of issues confronting humanity in the 21st century. Increased access for travelers and reporters to once restricted areas of the Soviet Union and eastern Europe made it clear that the drive for industrial development in the communist nations had been even more environmentally devastating than the capitalist variant of that process, even in its colonial manifestations. Perhaps most daunting was the realization that if communism had not failed economically, it would have eventually rendered utterly unsustainable the environmental underpinnings of the societies it had captured, and those to which it would have continued to spread.

The impact of these revelations was intensified by the prospect of communist China's new "market-Leninist" path to industrialization, which stressed grafting free market capitalism onto dictatorial, highly bureaucratized political systems like those long associated with communism. With China's population of over a billion people building on a resource base that is already severely depleted and degraded—including widespread water shortages—long-term prognoses for the dire outcomes of unrestrained global development may prove to be understatements. Equally alarming have been reports on the ecological fallout of rapid development in southeast Asia, where multinationals based in Japan and in the newly industrialized countries of east Asia are extracting resources with abandon and where the rain forest is disappearing even more rapidly than in Brazil. Similar trends have been documented in sub-Saharan Africa, where imminent economic collapse and environmental demise are now routinely predicted.

An additional repercussion of the environmental and economic breakdown of societies in eastern Europe and the former Soviet Union has been the virtual elimination of these major sources of financial assistance, technology, and technical expertise for postcolonial societies in Asia and Africa. It has also occasioned a significant and growing shift of Western investment aid and technology transfer to formerly communist areas at the expense of other developing regions, particularly sub-Saharan Africa. In view of growing disillusionment with the alternative development or modernization strategies of the Western democracies, the available options for ecologically sound, sustained growth in the postcolonial world and Latin America are questionable at best.

By the early 1990s, even the ever-optimistic experts at the World Bank and the IMF conceded that 40 years of development strategy have been largely a failure both in terms of raising living standards and in terms of the devastation they have wrought in the fragile African environment. Throughout the cold war, both capitalist planners and their communist rivals have promoted large-scale, high-tech development schemes that have rarely taken into account local needs or the environmental costs of development. These projects have favored industry over agriculture and ignored grassroots resistance and counterproposals. They have also very often been forced on postcolonial regimes that have lacked the organizational and managerial skills, and that have been too riddled with cronyism and corruption to implement them effectively. The bottom line is that "development" in both its communist and free market guises has failed to close the gap between rich and poor nations. In fact, that divide increased dramatically in the last decades of the 20th century.

By century's end, the wealthy one-fifth of humanity living in the industrialized nations consumed four-fifths of all marketed goods and resources. They also produced over 70 percent of the earth's pollution. In 1998, tiny Belgium, with 9 million people, had a Gross Domestic Product equal to that of the 40 countries of sub-Saharan Africa, whose combined population was 450 million. It has been estimated that, at present rates of economic growth, it would take most developing nations 150 years to reach the average levels of productivity achieved in 1980 by wealthy nations like the United States, Japan, and those of western Europe. Many of these societies may not have even a fraction of this time to find sustainable solutions to dilemmas of mass poverty, overpopulation, and environmental degradation. In apocalyptic idioms the journalist Marc Cooper recently chronicled the outcome of political inertia and failed development strategies for the citizenry of the world's largest conurbation, Mexico City, where oxygen is now widely sold by peddlers in the streets:

> the city's poised on the abyss of a world-class bio/technic disaster … its infrastructure is crumbling, …the drinking water mixes with sewer effluent, … many of the scars of the 1985 killer quake won't be healed before the next tremblor strikes. [And even then] Mexico City still beats the eternally depressed, sun-baked countryside.

Environmental Issues as Global Concerns

At the turn of the 21st century, environmental issues have emerged as focal points of public debate and government policy in most human societies. After a century of unprecedented levels of mechanized warfare, scientific experimentation, and the spread of industrialization, a wide variety of complex and often interrelated environmental disruptions threaten not only humanity but all other life forms on the planet Earth (see Figure 36.11).

Most scientists now agree that the greenhouse effect caused by the buildup in the atmosphere of excessive amounts of carbon dioxide and other heat-trapping gases has led to a substantial warming of the planet in recent decades. Some of the chief sources of the pollutants responsible for the atmospheric buildup are industrial wastes—including those resulting from energy production through the burning of fossil fuels like coal—and exhaust from millions of cars, trucks, and other machines run by internal combustion engines that burn petroleum. But other major sources of the greenhouse effect are both surprising and at present essential to the survival of large portions of humanity. Methane, another greenhouse gas, is introduced into the atmosphere in massive quantities as a by-product of the stew of fertilized soil and water in irrigated rice paddies, which feed a majority of the peoples of Asia, the world's most populous continent.

Figure 36.11 *Oil and the environment. A massive spill in the Persian Gulf, off the coast of Saudi Arabia, in 1991.*

Methane is also released by flatulent cattle, which produce milk and meat for human populations over much of the globe. Other gases have had equally alarming effects. Chlorofluorocarbons (CFCs), for example, which were once widely used in refrigeration, air conditioning, and spray cans, deplete the ozone layer, thereby removing atmospheric protection from the ultraviolet rays emanating from the sun.

If scientific predictions are correct, global warming will increasingly cause major shifts in temperatures and rainfall throughout much of the globe. Fertile and well-watered areas now highly productive in foods for humans and animals may well be overwhelmed by droughts and famine. If widely accepted computer simulations are correct, coastal areas at sea level—which from Bangladesh to the Netherlands to New Jersey are among the most densely populated in the world—are likely to be inundated. These coastal areas are threatened not just by rising water levels in the world's oceans but by hurricanes and tropical storms that may in the coming decades generate winds up to 200 miles an hour. As climates are drastically altered, vegetation and wildlife in many areas will be radically altered. Temperate forests, for example, may die off in many regions and be replaced by scrub, tropical vegetation, or desert flora. Some animal species may migrate or adapt and survive, but many, unable to adjust to such rapid climatic changes, will become extinct.

Not all of the sources of global warming are the product of the Industrial Revolution and its rapid spread and intensification, which has been a major theme in 20th-century world history. Most human societies have raised cattle and sheep for millennia, and methane has been flowing from rice paddies into the atmosphere since the Neolithic revolution, which began in some areas as early as the middle of the 9th millennium B.C.E. But the intensification of industrial processes and resource demands has accelerated the greenhouse effect and global warming. The cutting and burning of the world's forests is one of the more notable examples. Not only does the smoke produced contribute massively to carbon dioxide buildup in the atmosphere, but the destruction of the rain forests, in particular, deprives the earth of the natural "sinks" of plant life that suck up carbon dioxide and turn it into oxygen.

The destruction of the rain forests is especially troublesome since, unlike the temperate woodlands, they cannot regenerate themselves. And in terms of evolution, the rain forests have been the source of most of the species of plant and animal life that now inhabit the earth. In this and other ways, human interventions now affect global climate and weather in the short term and will determine the fate of the planetary environment in the centuries, perhaps millennia, to come.

International discussions of environmental regulation increased from 1997 onward. A major conference in Kyoto, Japan, set limits on greenhouse gas emissions, in order to curtail global warming. It was not clear, however, whether these limits would have any effect. Many individual nations, including the United States by 2001, opposed the limits proposed because of potential damage to national economies. Here was another area where global politics did not seem to be keeping pace with globalization.

Disease

Changes in global contacts have usually involved disease, and globalization is no exception. Rapid international travel helped spread the AIDS epidemic from 1980 onward. Southern and eastern Africa were hit most severely, but AIDS also spread to the United States and western Europe. The epidemic took on even larger proportions in places like Brazil. By the early 21st century, rates of increase in parts of Asia and in Russia began to accelerate. These were regions that had initially felt relatively safe but where global contact ultimately brought new levels of contagion. In 2003 a small but persistent outbreak of a new illness, Severe Acute Respiratory Syndrome (SARS), raised fears of another global contagion.

The result, to be sure, was less severe than some of the earlier epidemics associated with global contacts, though some experts warned of even greater disease problems in the future. Environmental issues, newer on the global scale, may have replaced disease as the clearest downside of international connections.

Toward the Future

 As the 21st century opened, many people tried to look to the future. Forecasts always use history, but in quite different ways. The huge innovations of the 20th century, and the further changes that emerged in the 1990s, made forecasting particularly difficult. The tensions between globalization and cultural and economic divisions clouded forecasts as well.

Human beings have always wanted to know what the future will hold. Various societies looked to the configurations of the stars for predictions, and astrology still has partisans in the contemporary world. Some societies generated beliefs in cycles, predicting that the future would repeat patterns already seen in the past; many Chinese scholars developed a cyclical approach. Still other societies assume that the future will differ from the past; from the Enlightenment onward, Western culture developed an additional belief in progress.

History suggests the futility of many efforts at forecasting. It has been estimated that well over half of the "expert" forecasts generated in the United States since World War II have been wrong. This includes predictions that by 2000 most Americans would be riding to and from work in some kind of airship, or that families would be replaced by promiscuous communes. Yet if history debunks forecasts, it also provides the basis for thinking about the future.

Projecting from Trends

The most obvious connection between history and the future involves the assessment of trends that are likely to continue at least for several decades. Thus we "know" that global population growth will slow up, because it is already slowing up. Many forecasts see stabilization by 2050, based on rapidly falling birth rates around the world. We also "know" that populations will become older; that is, the percentage of older citizens will increase. This is already happening in western Europe, the United States, and Japan and will occur elsewhere as birth rates drop. What we don't "know" of course is how societies will react to the demands of the increasing numbers of older people, or how much the environment will have deteriorated by the time global population stabilizes. Even trend-based forecasts can be thrown off by unexpected events, like wars. Thus in the 1930s experts "knew" that the American birth rate would fall, because it was already falling; but then war and prosperity created a totally unexpected baby boom, and the experts were wrong for at least two decades.

Trend-based forecasting is even chancier when the trends are already fragile. The late 20th century saw a genuine global spread of democracy, though admittedly not to every region. It was possible to venture predictions about the triumph of this form of government. But by 2002 it was hard to be confident that democracies were entirely secure in parts of Latin America or even in Russia. The hold of earlier, less democratic political traditions or the sheer pressure of economic stagnation might unseat the trend.

Forecasting is at least as complex when two different trends are in play. The 20th century saw a fairly steady rise in consumerism, which spread to all parts of the world. The appeal of mass media, commercialized sports, and global fashions reaches across traditional boundaries. But the last 30 years have also seen a pronounced increase in religious interest, in many if not all parts of the world. Some people participate in both trends, but overall, the priorities are different. Is one of the two trends likely to predominate? Or should we think of the future in terms of division and tension among cultural interests?

Big Changes

Some analysts have looked at the world's future in terms of stark departures from its past. They argue that trend analysis is inadequate because we are on the verge of a major shift in framework. In the 1960s, a "population bomb" analysis won considerable attention. The argument was that rapid population growth was about to overwhelm all other developments, leading to resource depletion, new wars over resources, and a world far different from what we had previously known. In fact, this particular scenario has fallen from favor, despite continued rapid population growth. The slowing rate of growth, combined with the fact that food production has on the whole kept pace, has displaced this disturbing scenario. But other forecasts, of dramatic climate change and of resource exhaustion, provide some environmentalists with another dire picture of the world's future, in which other issues, like the fate of particular political systems, fade in importance.

Another scenario that has enjoyed recurrent popularity is the vision of a postindustrial world. Some pundits argue that computer technology, genetic engineering, and other technological advances are undermining the conditions of industrial society. Information, not production, becomes the key to economic growth and to social structures. The functions of cities shift from production to entertainment. Work will become more individualized and less time consuming, creating a new premium for expressive leisure. Again, the emphasis is on a dramatically different future. Here too, however, critics express doubts. Many parts of the world are not yet industrial, much less postindustrial. Work does not seem to be heading toward less routine; for example, computers promote repetitious activities as much as new creativity. As is always true with intriguing predictions of massive change, the jury is still out.

The Problem of the Contemporary Period

One of the reasons prediction is particularly difficult—though also compelling—is that world history has undergone so many fundamental changes during the past century. We know, for example, that the dominance of western Europe, for centuries a staple of world history, is a thing of the past, despite the continued vitality of the region. But what will replace it? Continued United States ascendancy, with military outposts in many parts of the world? Or the rise of China or east Asia? Or perhaps no single dominant region at all? We know there's a question about the world balance that will replace Western control, but the answer is unclear.

The same applies to conditions for women. Improvements in women's education plus the decline of the birth rate add up to significant changes for women around the world. The pace of change varies with the region, to be sure. Many regions also have given new legal and political rights to women. But is there a new model for women's roles that might be applicable around the world? Continued disputes about women's work roles, significant male backlash against change, and even disputes by women themselves about the relevance of a Western model for women's lives make forecasting difficult. We can assume continued change, but it's hard to pinpoint the results.

 GLOBAL CONNECTIONS: Civilizations and Global Forces

A key question for the future involves the fate of individual civilizations. World history has been shaped by the characteristics of key civilizations for over 5000 years, granting that not everyone has been part of a major civilization and that in some cases civilizations are not easy to define. Some observes argue that, by the 21st century, the separate characteristics of civi-

lizations are beginning to yield to homogenizing forces. Many scientists, athletes, and businesspeople feel more commitment to their professional interests than to their region of origin—which means that global professional identities can override civilizational loyalties. The downtowns of most cities around the world look very much alike. The same products, stores, and restaurants can be found in most urban areas. Globalization may be outpacing regional labels.

Yet we have also seen that globalization can falter, as it did in the middle decades of the 20th century. Even when it accelerates, as in the 1990s, it brings efforts to reassert separate identities. Even as it participates in the global economy, China remains different, reflecting for example some of the political characteristics that were launched 3000 years ago. The Japanese easily move in global economics and culture, but with an emphasis on group identity measurably different from the personal goals emphasized in the United States. Major religions like Hinduism and Islam continue to mark their regions, and in some ways their influence seems to be on the rise.

World history has long been defined by a tension between regional features and larger connections. The specifics change, for example with shifts in technology and organizational capacity. But it may be premature to assume that some kind of global homogeneity is going to change the equation altogether.

Further Readings

On the future of NATO, see Martin A. Smith, *NATO in the First Decade After the Cold War* (2000). On the struggle to build the European community, see G. W. White, *Nationalism and Territory: Constructing Group Identity in Southeastern Europe* (2000), and Andrew Valls, ed., *Ethics in International Affairs: Themes and Cases* (2000).

For the explosion of the 1980s and 1990s, David Kotz and Fred Weir's *Revolution from Above: The Demise of the Soviet System* (1997) explores the internal dissolution of the Soviet leadership. Mikhail Gorbachev's *Memoirs* (1995) is the central participant's reflections on the end of the Soviet Union. Raymond L. Garthoff's *The Great Transition: American-Soviet Relations at the End of the Cold War* (1994) provides the foreign policy context. Karen Dawisha and Bruce Parrott, eds., *The Consolidation of Democracy in East-Central Europe* (1997), discusses recent experience toward democratization and includes a country-by-country survey. Nanette Funk and Magda Mueller's *Gender Politics and Post-Communism: Reflections from Eastern Europe and the Former Soviet*

Union (1993) deals with the role of women in this transition. Tina Rosenberg's *The Haunted Land: Facing Europe's Ghosts After Communism* (1995) is an engaging narrative that explores the legacies of repression in Germany, Poland, and the Czech Republic.

Walter Laqueur's *Fascism: Past, Present, Future* (1997) is the authoritative analysis of present-day fascism, with an excellent bibliographical essay and several solid regional studies of far-right political movements. Paul Hockenos, *Free to Hate: The Rise of the Right in Post-Communist Eastern Europe* (rev. ed., 1994), provides accessible reportage that explores neofascist movements on a country-by-country basis. J. Luccassen and L. Luccassen, eds., *Migration, Migration, History, History: Old Paradigms and New Perspectives* (1997), is a recent comparative social history—in addition to an extensive bibliography it includes chapters on conceptual issues (periodization, definitions, etc.) and several regional historical case studies. Alistair Ager's *Refugees: Perspectives on the Experience of Forced Migration* (1998) is a useful survey.

For very different takes on the resurgence of globalization since 1989, see Thomas Friedman's cautious celebration in *The Lexus and the Olive Tree: Understanding Globalization* (2000); John Gray's more sober appraisal in *False Dawn* (1998); and Thomas Frank's lively critique in *One Market Under God* (2000). Differing perspectives on the cultural ramifications of the new global economic order are provided by Peter Stearns, *Consumerism in World History* (2001); Walter LaFeber, *Michael Jordan and the New Global Capitalism* (2000); and the contributions to James Watson, ed., *Golden Arches East: McDonald's in East Asia* (1998). See also Lewis Solomon, *Multinational Corporations and the Emerging World Order* (1978); Stephen Rees, *American Films Abroad* (1997); Theodore von Laue, *The World Revolution of Westernization* (1997); Peter N. Stearns, *The Industrial Revolution in World History* (2nd ed., 1998); and Bruce Mazlish and Ralph Buultjens, eds., *Conceptualizing Global History* (1993).

For a detailed, long-term historical perspective on the successive conflicts in the Balkans, see Misha Glenny, *The Balkans: Nationalism, War and the Great Powers, 1804–1999* (2000). On the religious dimensions of the Yugoslavia wars, see the essays in Paul Mojzes, ed., *Religion and War in Yugoslavia* (1998). On the successive conflicts of the mid-1990s more specifically, see Laura Silber and Allan Little, *Yugoslavia: Death of a Nation* (1995) and Tim Judah, *Kosovo: War and Revenge* (2000). Gérard Prunier's *The Rwanda Crisis: History of a Genocide* is one of the most detailed accounts, and Mahmood Mamdani's *When Victims Become Killers* (2001) is an interesting analysis of the conflict's larger political and philosophical implications. Levon Chorbajian and George Shirinian's *Studies in Comparative Genocide* (1999) is a good place to begin an exploration of the darker side of 20th-century history.

Of the numerous and highly contentious writings on Islamic revivalism, Dilip Hiro's *Holy Wars: The Rise of Islamic Fundamentalism* (1989) is insightful and more balanced than most. A counterpart on Judaism is Arthur Hertzberg's *Jewish Fundamentalism* (1991). For Hinduism, see Gurdas Ahuja, *BJP and Indian Politics* (1994). For a comparative view covering Christian movements, see Richard Antoun's *Understanding Fundamentalism* (2001).

The September 11, 2001, terrorist attacks and persisting communal struggles, such as those in Northern Ireland and between Israelis and Palestinians, have produced a great proliferation of journalistic books and articles on terrorism in recent decades. A manageable place to begin an investigation of this highly contested and fluid category of social movement is Alexander Yonan et al., eds., *Terrorism: Theory and Practice* (1979). A historical overview with a global range for the modern period can be found in Albert Parry's *Terrorism* (1976). A very substantial literature has developed on the 1991 Persian Gulf War. The essays in Ibrahim Ibrahim, ed., *The Gulf Crisis* (1992) provide a good historical introduction to the conflict. Two of the better general accounts of the war are Lawrence Freedman and Efraim Karsh's *The Gulf Conflict, 1990–1991* (1993) and Michael Gordon and Bernard Trainor's *The General's War* (1995). An Arab viewpoint of the conflict is provided in Mohamed Heikal, *Illusions of Triumph* (1992); a strong critique of the media coverage and technowar aspects of the conflict is *The Persian Gulf TV War* (1992) by Douglas Kellner.

For a provocative and detailed account of U.S. interventionism since the end of the cold war, a good place to begin is David Halberstam's *War in a Time of Peace* (2001). Less compellingly written, but useful for differing perspectives, is Lester Brune's *The United States and Post-Cold War Interventions* (1998). On specific flashpoints that provoked extensive international involvement and policy debate in the United States and elsewhere, some of the best work is on Somalia, including Mark Bowden's superb recounting of the mission in crisis in *Black Hawk Down* (1990) and Jonathan Stevenson's more policy-oriented *Losing Mogadishu* (1995).

For genuinely global perspectives on environmental issues, see Bill McKibben, *The End of Nature* (1999 edition); Mark Hertsgaard, *Earth Odyssey* (1998); and Ramachandra Guha, *Environmentalism: A Global History* (2000). The best accounts of environmental degradation in key regions of the world include: (1) Brazil—Susanna Hecht and Alexander Cockburn, *The Fate of the Forest* (1990); (2) China—Judith Shapiro, *Mao's War against Nature* (2001); and Vaclav Smil, *The Bad Earth* (1984) and *China's Environmental Crisis* (1993); (3) the Soviet Union—Murray Feshback and Alfred Friendly Jr., *Ecocide in the USSR* (1992); (4) the United States—Marc Reisner,

Cadillac Desert (1993); and (5) India—Madhav Gadgil and Ramachandra Guha, *Ecology and Equity* (1995).

Several serious books (as well as many more simplistic, popularized efforts) attempt to sketch the future of the world or the West. On the concept of the postindustrial society, see Daniel Bell's *The Coming of Post-Industrial Society* (1974). For other projections, consult R. L. Heilbroner's *An Inquiry into the Human Prospect* (1974) and L. Stavrianos' *The Promise of the Coming Dark Age* (1976).

On environment and resource issues, D. H. Meadows and D. L. Meadows' *The Limits to Growth* (1974); Al Gore's *Earth in the Balance* (1992); and L. Herbert's *Our Synthetic Environment* (1962) are worthwhile. M. ul Haq's *The Poverty Curtain: Choices for the Third World* (1976) and L. Solomon's *Multinational Corporations and the Emerging World Order* (1978) cover economic issues, in part from a non-Western perspective. On a leading social issue, see P. Huston's *Third World Women Speak Out* (1979).

On the Web

As NATO and the Warsaw Pact seem to be merging, it is appropriate to examine their parallel histories and the impact of their past antagonisms on world history, an effort attempted at http://www.isn.ethz.ch/php/. An examination of the nature and future of NATO, and analyses of recent events and significant speeches in Europe, as well as analyses of NATO actions, can be found at http://www.nato.int/. The European quest for union is explored at http://www.eurunion.org and http://europa.eu.int/index_en.htm.

Resources for the study of the collapse of communism, the changes within the former Soviet Union since 1991 (including the attempted breakaway of Chechnya from the Russian Federation), and the establishment of a post–cold war "New World Order" are provided at http://www.historyteacher.net/APEuroCourse/WebLinks/WebLinks-NewWorldOrder.htm.

A survey of the lives of Alexander Dubcek (http://rferl.org/nca/special/invasion1968), Vaclav Havel and his Velvet Revolution (http://www.radio.cz/history/history15.html), and Lech Walesa (http://www.achievement.org/autodoc/page/wal1int-1) illuminate the process that led to the fall of the Berlin Wall. Both the rise and demise of that wall is traced in text, video, and photographs at http://www.coldwar.org/museum/berlin_wall_exhibit.html and http://members.aol.com/johball/berlinw2.htm. The history of Lenin's mausoleum, perhaps the greatest relic of the Communist era in Russia, is traced at http://www.aha.ru/~mausoleu/m-hist_e.htm.

For the breakup of Yugoslavia and the continuing crisis in the Balkans, see http://www.truthinmedia.org and http://www.historyguy.com/balkan_war_third.htm

For links to documents on conflicts in this region, go to http://www.mtholyoke.edu/acad/intrel/bosnia.htm

Analyses and links to both sides of the globalization debate are offered at http://globalization.about.com/library/weekly/aa080701a.htm and http://www.emory.edu/SOC/globalization/. Of the many other sites on globalization, some of the more interesting and historically grounded include http://www.stephweb.com/capstone/index.htm and http://www.epinet.org/subjectpages/trade.html, which reports on international trade. One site highly critical of economic globalization (http://www.ifg.org/analysis.htm) offers a dark analysis of the role of the World Trade Organization, the World Bank, and the United Nations in this process. The World Bank (http://www1.worldbank.org/economicpolicy/globalization/) and the International Monetary Fund offer their own more roseate view of globalization at http://www.imf.org/external/np/exr/ib/2000/041200.htm. Another site (http://www.pbs.org/globalization/) examines the impact of globalization on human rights.

For general coverage of the 1991 Persian Gulf War, see http://www.pbs.org/wgbh/pages/frontline/gulf/index.html, and on the debate over the inconclusive end of the war and continuing conflict in the region, see http://www.pbs.org/wgbh/pages/frontline/shows/syndrome/.

The UN-U.S. intervention in Somalia and its troubling outcomes are considered from different vantage points at http://www.netnomad.com/ and http://www.unsomalia.org/.

A militant view of the alleged ills of the affluent society and the growing dominance of multinational and non-state organizations in the postmodern era is presented at http://www.socialconscience.com/. A less radical view that nonetheless suggests that the twin pillars of Western civilization (the market economy and democracy) are more likely to undermine than support each other can be found at http://www.mtholyoke.edu/acad/intrel/attali.html.

An indispensable discussion of recent trends in Islamic nationalism/fundamentalism is provided at http://wrc.lingnet.org/islamf.htm.

Links to virtually every aspect of recent conflicts within Islamist states and with non-Islamist nations, including the origins of the Taliban and counter-Taliban attacks on

Afghanistan by much of the world community, can be found at http://www.library.vanderbilt.edu/romans/terrorism/afghanistan.html. The roots and results of the Taliban movement can currently be studied via an on-line version of David B. Edwards' *Before Taliban: Genealogies of the Afghan Jihad* (2002) at http://ark.cdlib.org/ark:/13030/ft3p30056w/. For the place of Hamas in Islamist efforts, see http://www.prisonplanet.com/news_lert_hamas2.html and http://www.meta-religion.com/Hate_Groups/extremism_islamic.htm.

The terrorist attacks on September 11, 2001, on New York City and Washington, D.C., are recounted from many perspectives at http://www.freepint.com/gary/91101.html. On this subject, see also http://www.lib.umich.edu/govdocs/usterror.html.

The text of, and debate over the accuracy of, Samuel Huntington's argument that the world is heading toward a "clash of civilizations" can be found at http://www.alamut.com/subj/economics/misc/clash.html, http://www.lander.edu/atannenbaum/Tannenbaum%20courses%20folder/POLS%20103%20World%20Politics/103_huntington_clash_of_civilizations_full_text.htm, http://www.shunya.net/Text/Articles/EdwardSaid.htm, http://csf.colorado.edu/wsystems/jwsr/archive/vol4/v4n2r2.htm, and http://www.ndsu.nodak.edu/ndsu/ambrosio/civ.html.

A Web site that seeks to debunk concerns over global warming (http://www.globalwarming.org/about.htm) may be usefully compared with other public interest Web sites expressing those concerns (http://www.sierraclub.org/globalwarming/dangerousexperiment/ and http://www.climatehotmap.org/). Pace University's Web site, http://www.law.pace.edu/env/energy/globalwarming.html, offers useful links to all sides of this controversy. The text of the Kyoto Protocol on global warming that the United States has refused to sign is offered at http://www.cnn.com/SPECIALS/1997/global.warming/stories/treaty/. Another interesting site (http://www.americans-world.org/digest/global_issues/global_warming/gw2.cfm) is devoted to analyzing shifts in public opinion on the Kyoto Protocols.

GLOSSARY

Pronunciation guidance is supplied in square brackets, [ ], after difficult words. The symbols used for pronunciation are found in the table below. Syllables for primary stress are *italicized*.

a	act, bat, marry	I	bite, ice	u	sum, up	
AY	age, rate	j	just, tragic	U	sue, blew, through	
âr	air, dare	k	keep, cop	ûr	turn, urge, cur	
ä	ah, part, calm	ng	sing	zh	vision, pleasure	
ch	chief, beach	o	ox, hot	uh	*a*lone, syst*e*m, eas*i*ly, gall*o*p, circ*u*s	
e	edge, set	O	hope, over	A	as in French *a*mi	
EE	equal, seat, bee	ô	order, ball	KH	as in German a*ch*, i*ch*	
EER	here, ear	oi	oil, joint	N	as in French bo*n*	
g	give, trigger	oo	book, tour	OE	as in French d*eux*	
h	here	ou	plow, out	R	as in French *r*ouge	
hw	which, when	sh	she, fashion	Y	as in German f*ü*hlen	
i	if, big	th	thin, ether			

Abbasid [uh bas *id*, ab *uh* sid] Dynasty that succeeded the Umayyads as caliphs within Islam; came to power in 750 C.E. (p. 135)

Abbas the Great Safavid ruler from 1587 to 1629; extended Safavid domain to greatest extent; created slave regiments based on captured Russians, who monopolized firearms within Safavid armies; incorporated Western military technology. (p. 486)

Abdallahi, Khalifa [uh dool *ä hEE*] Successor of Muhammad Achmad as leader of Mahdists in Sudan; established state in Sudan; defeated by British General Kitchener in 1898. (p. 628)

Abduh, Muhammad Disciple of al-Afghani; Muslim thinker at end of 19th century; stressed need for adoption of Western scientific learning and technology, recognized importance of rational inquiry. (p. 626)

Abdul Hamid Ottoman sultan who attempted to return to despotic absolutism during reign from 1878 to 1908; nullified constitution and restricted civil liberties; deposed in coup in 1908. (p. 623)

Abelard, Peter Author of *Yes and No*; university scholar who applied logic to problems of theology; demonstrated logical contradictions within established doctrine. (p. 224)

absolute monarchy Concept of government developed during rise of nation-states in western Europe during the 17th century; featured monarchs who passed laws without parliaments, appointed professionalized armies and bureaucracies, established state churches, imposed state economic policies. (p. 391)

Achmad, Muhammad Head of a Sudanic Sufi brotherhood; claimed descent from prophet Muhammad; proclaimed both Egyptians and British as infidels; launched revolt to purge Islam of impurities; took Khartoum in 1883; also known as the Mahdi. (p. 628)

African National Congress Black political organization within South Africa; pressed for end to policies of apartheid; sought open democracy leading to black majority rule; until the 1990s declared illegal in South Africa. (p. 858)

Afrikaner National party Emerged as the majority party in the all-white South African legislature after 1948; advocated complete independence from Britain; favored a rigid system of racial segregation called apartheid. (p. 773)

age of revolution Period of political upheaval beginning roughly with the American Revolution in 1775 and continuing through the French Revolution of 1789 and other movements for change up to 1848. (p. 536)

Akbar Son and successor of Humayan; oversaw building of military and administrative systems that became typical of Mughal rule in India; pursued policy of cooperation with Hindu princes; attempted to create new religion to bind Muslim and Hindu populations of India. (p. 490)

al-Afghani Muslim thinker at the end of the 19th century; stressed need for adoption of Western scientific learning and technology; recognized importance of tradition of rational inquiry. (p. 626)

al-Ghazali Brilliant Islamic theologian; struggled to fuse Greek and Qur'anic traditions; not entirely accepted by ulama. (p. 156)

al-Mahdi [al-*mä* dEE] Third of the Abbasid caliphs; attempted but failed to reconcile moderates among Shi'a to Abbasid dynasty; failed to resolve problem of succession. (p. 147)

al-Rashid, Harun [al-rä *shEEd*] Most famous of Abbasid caliphs; renowned for sumptuous and costly living; dependant on Persian advisors early in reign; death led to civil wars over succession. (p. 148)

Alexander the Great Successor of Philip II; successfully conquered Persian Empire prior to his death in 323 B.C.E.; attempted to combine Greek and Persian cultures. (p. 51)

Alexandria, Egypt   One of many cities of that name founded by Alexander the Great; site of ancient Mediterranean's greatest library; center of literary studies. (p. 72)

Ali   Cousin and son-in-law of Muhammad; one of orthodox caliphs; focus for Shi'a. (p. 128)

Ali, Muhammad   Won power struggle in Egypt following fall of Mamluks; established mastery of all Egypt by 1811; introduced effective army based on Western tactics and supply and a variety of other reforms; by 1830s was able to challenge Ottoman government in Constantinople; died in 1848. (p. 625)

Allah   Supreme God in strictly monotheistic Islam. (pp. 99, 121)

Allende, Salvador   [ä *yAHn* dAY, ä *yen* dEE] President of Chile; nationalized industries and banks; sponsored peasant and worker expropriations of lands and foreign-owned factories; overthrown in 1973 by revolt of Chilean military with the support of the United States. (p. 823)

Alliance for Progress   Begun in 1961 by the United States to develop Latin America as an alternative to radical political solutions; enjoyed only limited success; failure of development programs led to renewal of direct intervention. (p. 826)

Almohadis   [*äl* mO häd EEz] A reformist movement among the Islamic Berbers of northern Africa; later than the Almoravids; penetrated into sub-Sahara Africa. (p. 174)

Almoravids   [al muh *räv* udz] A puritanical reformist movement among the Islamic Berber tribes of northern Africa; controlled gold trade across Sahara; conquered Ghana in 1076; moved southward against African kingdoms of the savanna and westward into Spain. (p. 174)

Amaru, Tupac   Mestizo leader of Indian revolt in Peru; supported by many among lower social classes; revolt eventually failed because of Creole fears of real social revolution. (p. 443)

American Civil War   Fought from 1861 to 1865; first application of Industrial Revolution to warfare; resulted in abolition of slavery in the United States and reunification of North and South. (p. 547)

American Revolution   Rebellion of English American colonies along Atlantic seaboard between 1775 and 1783; resulted in independence for former British colonies and eventual formation of United States of America. (p. 537)

amigos del país   [uh *mEE* gOs, ä *mEE-*, del päEEs] Clubs and associations dedicated to improvements and reform in Spanish colonies; flourished during the 18th century; called for material improvements rather than political reform. (p. 440)

anarchists   Political groups that sought the abolition of all formal government; particularly prevalent in Russia; opposed tsarist autocracy; eventually became a terrorist movement responsible for assassination of Alexander II in 1881. (p. 649)

Anglican church   Form of Protestantism set up in England after 1534; established by Henry VIII with himself as head, at least in part to obtain a divorce from his first wife; became increasingly Protestant following Henry's death. (p. 384)

animism   A religious outlook that sees gods in many aspects of nature and propitiates them to help control and explain nature; typical of Mesopotamian religions. (p. 110)

Anschluss   Hitler's union of Germany with the German-speaking population of Austria; took place in 1938, despite complaints of other European nations. (p. 735)

apartheid   Policy of strict racial segregation imposed in South Africa to permit the continued dominance of whites politically and economically. (p. 773)

appeasement   Policy of Neville Chamberlain, British prime minister who hoped to preserve peace in the face of German aggression; particularly applied to Munich Conference agreements; failed when Hitler invaded Poland in 1939. (p. 735)

Aquinas, Thomas   Creator of one of the great syntheses of medieval learning; taught at University of Paris; author of several *Summas;* believed that through reason it was possible to know much about natural order, moral law, and nature of God. (p. 225)

Aquino, Corazon   First president of the Philippines in the post-Marcos era of the late 1980s; Aquino, whose husband was assassinated by thugs in the pay of the Marcos regime, was one of the key leaders in the popular movement that toppled the dictator. (p. 845)

Aragon   Along with Castile, a regional kingdom of the Iberian peninsula; pressed reconquest of peninsula from Muslims; developed a vigorous military and religious agenda. (p. 343)

Arevalo, Juan José   Elected president of Guatemala in 1944; began series of socialist reforms including land reform; nationalist program directed against foreign-owned companies such as United Fruit Company. (p. 819)

Argentine Republic   Replaced state of Buenos Aires in 1862; result of compromise between centralists and federalists. (p. 603)

Aristotle   Greek philosopher; teacher of Alexander the Great; knowledge based on observation of phenomena in material world. (p. 79)

Armenian genocide   Assault carried out by mainly Turkish military forces against Armenian population in Anatolia in 1915; over a million Armenians perished and thousands fled to Russia and the Middle East. (p. 680)

Aryans   Indo-European nomadic pastoralists who replaced Harappan civilization; militarized society. (p. 52)

Asante Empire   [uh *san* tEE, uh *sän*] Established in Gold Coast among Akan people settled around Kumasi; dominated by Oyoko clan; many clans linked under Osei Tutu after 1650. (p. 456)

asantehene   [un san tAY hAY nAY] Title taken by ruler of Asante Empire; supreme civil and religious leader; authority symbolized by golden stool. (p. 457)

Ashikaga Shogunate   Replaced the Kamakura regime in Japan; ruled from 1336 to 1573; destroyed rival Yoshino center of imperial authority. (p. 294)

Ashikaga Takuaji   [ä shEE kä gä tä kwä ji] Member of the Minamoto family; overthrew the Kamakura regime and established the Ashikaga Shogunate from 1336–1573; drove emperor from Kyoto to Yoshino. (p. 294)

Ashoka   [uh *sO* kuh] Grandson of Chandragupta Maurya; completed conquests of Indian subcontinent; converted to Buddhism and sponsored spread of new religion throughout his empire. (p. 54)

Asian sea trading network   Prior to intervention of Europeans, consisted of three zones: Arab zone based on glass, carpets, and tapestries; India based on cotton textiles; and China based on paper, porcelain, and silks. (p. 501)

Ataturk   Also known as Mustafa Kemal; leader of Turkish republic formed in 1923; reformed Turkish nation using Western models. (p. 691)

Atlantic Charter of 1941   World War II alliance agreement between the United States and Britain; included a clause that recognized the right of all people to choose the form of government under which they live; indicated sympathy for decolonization. (p. 767)

audiencia   Royal court of appeals established in Spanish colonies of New World; there were 10 in each viceroyalty; part of colonial administrative system; staffed by professional magistrates. (p. 434)

Augustine (Saint)   Influential church father and theologian (354–430 C.E.); born in Africa and ultimately Bishop of Hippo in Africa; champion of Christian doctrine against various heresies and very important in the long-term development of Christian thought on such issues as predestination. (p. 103)

Augustus Caesar   Name given to Octavian following his defeat of Mark

Anthony and Cleopatra; first emperor of Rome. (p. 73)

Aurangzeb [*ôr* uhng zeb] Son and successor of Shah Jahan in Mughal India; determined to extend Mughal control over whole of subcontinent; wished to purify Islam of Hindu influences; incessant warfare exhausted empire despite military successes; died in 1707. (p. 493)

Axum Kingdom located in Ethiopian highlands; replaced Meroë in first century C.E.; received strong influence from Arabian peninsula; eventually converted to Christianity. (p. 93)

ayan [ä yän] The wealthy landed elite that emerged in the early decades of Abbasid rule. (p. 140)

Babur Founder of Mughal dynasty in India; descended from Turkic warriors; first led invasion of India in 1526; died in 1530. (p. 489)

Babylonian empire Unified all of Mesopotamia c. 1800 B.C.E.; collapsed due to foreign invasion c. 1600 B.C.E. (p. 19)

Baghdad Capital of Abbasid dynasty located in Iraq near ancient Persian capital of Ctesiphon. (p. 138)

Baibars [bI *bars*] Commander of Mamluk forces at Ain Jalut; originally enslaved by Mongols and sold to Egyptians. (p. 325)

Bakr, Abu [*bak* uhr, uh bU] One of Muhammad's earliest converts; succeeded Muhammad as first caliph of Islamic community. (p. 131)

bakufu Military government established by the Minamoto following the Gempei Wars; centered at Kamakura; retained emperor, but real power resided in military government and samurai. (p. 294)

Balboa, Vasco de First Spanish captain to begin settlement on the mainland of Mesoamerica in 1509; initial settlement eventually led to conquest of Aztec and Inca empires by other captains. (p. 370)

Balfour Declaration British minister Lord Balfour's promise of support for the establishment of Jewish settlement in Palestine issued in 1917. (p. 692)

Balkan nationalism Movements to create independent nations within the Balkan possessions of the Ottoman Empire; provoked a series of crises within the European alliance system; eventually led to World War I. (p. 558)

banana republics Term given to governments supported or created by the United States in Central America; believed to be either corrupt or subservient to U.S. interests. (p. 825)

band A level of social organization normally consisting of 20 to 30 people; nomadic hunters and gatherers; labor divided on a gender basis. (p. 14)

Bangladesh Founded as an independent nation in 1972; formerly East Pakistan. (p. 837)

banner armies Eight armies of the Manchu tribes identified by separate flags; created by Nurhaci in early 17th century; utilized to defeat Ming emperor and establish Qing dynasty. (p. 629)

Batavia Dutch fortress located after 1620 on the island of Java. (p. 504)

Batista, Fulgencio Dictator of Cuba from 1934 to 1944; returned to presidency in 1952; ousted from government by revolution led by Fidel Castro. (p. 819)

Battle of Britain The 1940 Nazi air offensive including saturation bombing of London and other British cities, countered by British innovative air tactics and radar tracking of German assault aircraft. (p. 758)

Battle of the Bulge Hitler's last-ditch effort to repel the invading Allied armies in the winter of 1944–1945. (p. 761)

Battle of the Coral Sea World War II Pacific battle; United States and Japanese forces fought to a standoff. (p. 762)

Battle of Kulikova Russian army victory over the forces of the Golden Horde; helped break Mongol hold over Russia. (p. 323)

Battle on the River Zab Victory of Abbasids over Umayyads; resulted in conquest of Syria and capture of Umayyad capital. (p. 137)

Battle of Siffin Fought in 657 between forces of Ali and Umayyads; settled by negotiation that led to fragmentation of Ali's party. (p. 133)

Batu Ruler of Golden Horde; one of Chinggis Khan's grandsons; responsible for invasion of Russia beginning in 1236. (p. 320)

bedouin Nomadic pastoralists of the Arabian peninsula; culture based on camel and goat nomadism; early converts to Islam. (p. 122)

Belisarius One of Justinian's most important military commanders during period of reconquest of western Europe; commanded in north Africa and Italy. (p. 196)

Benedict of Nursia Founder of monasticism in what had been the western half of the Roman Empire; established Benedictine Rule in the 6th century; paralleled development of Basil's rules in Byzantine Empire. (p. 108)

Benin Powerful city-state (in present-day Nigeria) which came into contact with the Portuguese in 1485 but remained relatively free of European influence; important commercial and political entity until the 19th century. (p. 187)

Berke [*ber* kuh] A ruler of the Golden Horde; converted to Islam; his threat to Hulegu combined with the growing power of Mamluks in Egypt forestalled further Mongol conquests in the Middle East. (p. 325)

Berlin Wall Built in 1961 to halt the flow of immigration from East Berlin to West Berlin; immigration was in response to lack of consumer goods and close Soviet control of economy and politics; torn down at end of cold war in 1991. (p. 800)

Bernard of Clairvaux [*bûr* närd uhv klär *vO*] Emphasized role of faith in preference to logic; stressed importance of mystical union with God; successfully challenged Abelard and had him driven from the universities. (p. 224)

bhaktic cults [*buk* tEEk] Hindu groups dedicated to gods and goddesses; stressed the importance of strong emotional bonds between devotees and the god or goddess who was the object of their veneration; most widely worshipped gods were Shiva and Vishnu. (p. 163)

Bhutto, Benazir Twice prime minister of Pakistan in the 1980s and 1990s; first ran for office to avenge her father's execution by the military clique then in power. (p. 845)

Biko, Steve An organizer of Black Consciousness movement in South Africa, in opposition to apartheid; murdered while in police custody. (p. 858)

Bismarck, Otto von Conservative prime minister of Prussia; architect of German unification under Prussian king in 1870; utilized liberal reforms to attract support for conservative causes. (p. 546)

Black Death Plague that struck Europe in 14th century; significantly reduced Europe's population; affected social structure. (p. 232)

blitzkrieg German term for lightning warfare; involved rapid movement of troops, tanks, and mechanized carriers; resulted in early German victories over Belgium, Holland, and France in World War II. (p. 757)

bodhisattvas [bO duh *sut* vuhs] Buddhist holy men; built up spiritual merits during their lifetimes; prayers even after death could aid people to achieve reflected holiness. (p. 105)

Boers Dutch settlers in Cape Colony, in southern Africa. (p. 376)

Boer Republics Transvaal and Orange Free State in southern Africa; established to assert independence of Boers from British colonial government in Cape Colony in 1850s; discovery of diamonds and precious metals caused British migration into the Boer areas in 1860s. (p. 583)

Boer War Fought between 1899 and 1902 over the continued independence of Boer republics; resulted in British victory, but began the process of decolonization in southern Africa. (p. 583)

Bolívar, Simon Creole military officer in northern South America; won series of victories in Venezuela, Colombia, and Ecuador between 1817 and 1822; military success led to creation of independent state of Gran Colombia. (p. 592)

Bolsheviks Literally, the majority party; the most radical branch of the Russian Marxist movement; led by V.I. Lenin and dedicated to his concept of social revolution; actually a minority in the Russian Marxist political scheme until its triumph in the 1917 revolution. (p. 650)

Bonaparte, Napoleon Rose within the French army during the wars of the French Revolution; eventually became general; led a coup that ended the French Revolution; established French Empire under his rule; defeated and deposed in 1815. (p. 540)

Boxer Rebellion Popular outburst in 1898 aimed at expelling foreigners from China; failed because of intervention of armies of Western powers in China; defeat of Chinese enhanced control by Europeans and the power of provincial officials. (p. 635)

boyars Russian aristocrats; possessed less political power than did their counterparts in western Europe. (pp. 207, 404)

British East India Company Joint stock company that obtained government monopoly over trade in India; acted as virtually independent government in regions it claimed. (p. 364)

British Raj British political establishment in India; developed as a result of the rivalry between France and Britain in India. (p. 565)

Bronze Age From about 4000 B.C.E., when bronze tools were first introduced in the Middle East, to about 1500 B.C.E., when iron began to replace it. (p. 13)

Buddha Creator of major Indian and Asian religion; born in 6th century B.C.E. as son of local ruler among Aryan tribes located near Himalayas; became an ascetic; found enlightenment under bo tree; taught that enlightenment could be achieved only by abandoning desires for all earthly things. (p. 59)

Bulgaria Slavic kingdom established in northern portions of Balkan peninsula; constant source of pressure on Byzantine Empire; defeated by Emperor Basil II in 1014. (p. 197)

bushi Regional warrior leaders in Japan; ruled small kingdoms from fortresses; administered the law, supervised public works projects, and collected revenues; built up private armies. (p. 292)

Buyids Regional splinter dynasty of the mid-10th century; invaded and captured Baghdad; ruled Abbasid Empire under name of sultan; retained Abbasids as figureheads. (p. 151)

Byzantine Empire Eastern half of Roman Empire following collapse of western half of old empire; retained Mediterranean culture, particularly Greek; later lost Palestine, Syria, and Egypt to Islam; capital at Constantinople. (p. 102)

Cabral, Pedro Alvares Portuguese leader of an expedition to India; blown off course in 1500 and landed in Brazil. (p. 435)

Caesar, Julius Roman general responsible for conquest of Gaul; brought army back to Rome and overthrew republic; assassinated in 44 B.C.E. by conservative senators. (p. 73)

Calcutta Headquarters of British East India Company in Bengal in Indian subcontinent; located on Ganges; captured in 1756 during early part of Seven Years' War; later became administrative center for all of Bengal. (p. 376)

caliph The political and religious successor to Muhammad. (p. 131)

calpulli Clans in Aztec society, later expanded to include residential groups that distributed land and provided labor and warriors. (p. 244)

Calvin, Jean French Protestant (16th century) who stressed doctrine of predestination; established center of his group at Swiss canton of Geneva; encouraged ideas of wider access to government, wider public education; Calvinism spread from Switzerland to northern Europe and North America. (p. 384)

candomble [kan dom *blä*] African religious ideas and practices in Brazil, particularly among the Yoruba people. (p. 468)

Canton One of two port cities in which Europeans were permitted to trade in China during the Ming dynasty. (p. 514)

Cape Colony Dutch colony established at Cape of Good Hope in 1652 initially to provide a coastal station for the Dutch seaborne empire; by 1770 settlements had expanded sufficiently to come into conflict with Bantus. (p. 376)

Cape of Good Hope Southern tip of Africa; first circumnavigated in 1488 by Portuguese in search of direct route to India. (p. 361)

capitaincies Strips of land along Brazilian coast granted to minor Portuguese nobles for development; enjoyed limited success in developing the colony. (p. 435)

caravels Slender, long-hulled vessels utilized by Portuguese; highly maneuverable and able to sail against the wind; key to development of Portuguese trade empire in Asia. (p. 501)

Cárdenas, Lázaro President of Mexico from 1934 to 1940; responsible for redistribution of land, primarily to create ejidos, or communal farms; also began program of primary and rural education. (p. 738)

Caribbean First area of Spanish exploration and settlement; served as experimental region for nature of Spanish colonial experience; encomienda system of colonial management initiated here. (p. 422)

Carolingians Royal house of Franks after 8th century until their replacement in 10th century. (p. 216)

Carthage Originally a Phoenician colony in northern Africa; became a major port and commercial power in the western Mediterranean; fought the Punic Wars with Rome for dominance of the western Mediterranean. (p. 73)

Castile Along with Aragon, a regional kingdom of the Iberian peninsula; pressed reconquest of peninsula from Muslims; developed a vigorous military and religious agenda. (p. 343)

Castro, Fidel Cuban revolutionary; overthrew dictator Fulgencio Batista in 1958; initiated series of socialist reforms; came to depend almost exclusively on Soviet Union. (p. 820)

Çatal Hüyük [*chät* l hU *yook*] Early urban culture based on sedentary agriculture; located in modern southern Turkey; was larger in population than Jericho, had greater degree of social stratification. (p. 14)

Catherine the Great German-born Russian tsarina in the 18th century; ruled after assassination of her husband; gave appearance of enlightened rule; accepted Western cultural influence; maintained nobility as service aristocracy by granting them new power over peasantry. (p. 409)

Catholic Reformation Restatement of traditional Catholic beliefs in response to Protestant Reformation (16th century); established councils that revived Catholic doctrine and refuted Protestant beliefs. (p. 384)

caudillos [kou *thEE* lyos, -*thEE* yos] Independent leaders who dominated local areas by force in defiance of national policies; sometimes seized national governments to impose their concept of rule; typical throughout newly independent countries of Latin America. (p. 595)

Cavour, Count Camillo di [kä *voor*] Architect of Italian unification in 1858; formed an alliance with France to attack Austrian control of northern Italy; resulted in creation of constitutional monarchy under Piedmontese king. (p. 546)

centralists   Latin American politicians who wished to create strong, centralized national governments with broad powers; often supported by politicians who described themselves as conservatives. (p. 595)

Chabi   Influential wife of Kubilai Khan; promoted interests of Buddhists in China; indicative of refusal of Mongol women to adopt restrictive social conventions of Chinese. (p. 326)

Chaldiran   [*chäl duh rán*] Site of battle between Safavids and Ottomans in 1514; Safavids severely defeated by Ottomans; checked western advance of Safavid Empire. (p. 483)

Chams   Indianized rivals of the Vietnamese; driven into the highlands by the successful Vietnamese drive to the south. (p. 308)

Chan Buddhism   Known as Zen in Japan; stressed meditation and appreciation of natural and artistic beauty; popular with members of elite Chinese society. (p. 268)

Chandragupta Maurya   [*chun druh gUp tuh mour EE uh*] Founder of Maurya dynasty; established first empire in Indian subcontinent; first centralized government since Harappan civilization. (p. 54)

Changan   Capital of Tang dynasty; population of 2 million, larger than any other city in the world at that time. (p. 266)

Charlemagne   [*shär luh mAYn*] Charles the Great; Carolingian monarch who established substantial empire in France and Germany c. 800. (p. 217)

Charles III   Spanish enlightened monarch; ruled from 1759 to 1788; instituted fiscal, administrative, and military reforms in Spain and its empire. (p. 441)

Chartist movement   Attempt by artisans and workers in Britain to gain the vote during the 1840s; demands for reform beyond the Reform Bill of 1832 were incorporated into a series of petitions; movement failed. (p. 542)

Chiang Ching-kuo   [*jEE äng ching gwO*] Son and successor of Chiang Kai-shek as ruler of Taiwanese government in 1978; continued authoritarian government; attempted to lessen gap between followers of his father and indigenous islanders. (p. 874)

Chiang Kai-shek   [*chang kiy shek*] A military officer who succeeded Sun Yat-sen as the leader of the Guomindang or Nationalist party in China in the mid-1920s; became the most powerful leader in China in the early 1930s, but his Nationalist forces were defeated and driven from China by the Communists after World War II. (p. 722)

Chichimecs   American hunting-and-gathering groups; largely responsible for the disruption of early civilizations in Mesoamerica. (p. 23)

chinampas   Beds of aquatic weeds, mud, and earth placed in frames made of cane and rooted in lakes to create "floating islands"; system of irrigated agriculture utilized by Aztecs. (p. 245)

Chinggis Khan   [*jeng guhs kän*] Born in 1170s in decades following death of Kabul Khan; elected khagan of all Mongol tribes in 1206; responsible for conquest of northern kingdoms of China, territories as far west as the Abbasid regions; died in 1227, prior to conquest of most of Islamic world. (p. 158)

Chongzhen   [*choong juhn*] Last of the Ming emperors; committed suicide in 1644 in the face of a Jurchen invasion of the Forbidden City at Beijing. (p. 517)

Choson   Earliest Korean kingdom; conquered by Han emperor in 109 B.C.E. (p. 299)

Churchill, Winston   British prime minister during World War II; responsible for British resistance to German air assaults. (p. 758)

Cicero   Conservative Roman senator; Stoic philosopher; one of great orators of his day; killed in reaction to assassination of Julius Caesar. (p. 76)

cientificos   Advisors of government of Porfirio Díaz who were strongly influenced by positivist ideas; permitted government to project image of modernization. (p. 612)

city-state   A form of political organization typical of Mesopotamian civilizations; consisted of agricultural hinterlands ruled by an urban-based king. (p. 19)

civilization   Societies distinguished by reliance on sedentary agriculture, ability to produce food surpluses, and existence of nonfarming elites, as well as merchant and manufacturing groups. (p. 15)

Clemenceau, Georges   French prime minister in last years of World War I and during Versailles Conference of 1919; pushed for heavy reparations from Germans. (p. 682)

Clive, Robert   Architect of British victory at Plassey; established foundations of British Raj in northern India (18th century). (p. 567)

Clovis   Early Frankish king; converted Franks to Christianity c. 496; allowed establishment of Frankish kingdom. (p. 215)

collectivization   Creation of large, state-run farms rather than individual holdings; allowed more efficient control over peasants, though often lowered food production; part of Stalin's economic and

political planning; often adopted in other communist regimes. (p. 716)

Columbian exchange   Biological and ecological exchange that took place following Spanish establishment of colonies in New World; peoples of Europe and Africa came to New World; animals, plants, and diseases of two hemispheres were transferred. (p. 430)

Columbus, Christopher   Genoese captain in service of king and queen of Castile and Aragon; successfully sailed to New World and returned in 1492; initiated European discoveries in Americas. (p. 362)

Comintern   International office of communism under USSR dominance established to encourage the formation of Communist parties in Europe and elsewhere. (p. 716)

Communist Party of Vietnam   Originally a wing of nationalist movement; became primary nationalist party after decline of VNQDD in 1929; led in late 1920s by Nguyen Ai Quoc, alias Ho Chi Minh. (p. 886)

compradors   Wealthy new group of Chinese merchants under the Qing dynasty; specialized in the import-export trade on China's south coast; one of the major links between China and the outside world. (p. 631)

Comte, Auguste   [*koNt*] French philosopher (19th century); founder of positivism, a philosophy that stressed observation and scientific approaches to the problems of society. (p. 600)

Comunero Revolt   One of popular revolts against Spanish colonial rule in New Granada (Colombia) in 1781; suppressed as a result of divisions among rebels. (p. 443)

Confucius   Also known as Kung Fuzi; major Chinese philosopher; born in 6th century B.C.E.; author of *Analects;* philosophy based on need for restoration of order through advice of superior men to be found among the shi. (p. 37)

Congress of Vienna   Meeting in the aftermath of Napoleonic Wars (1815) to restore political stability in Europe and settle diplomatic disputes. (p. 541)

conservatives   Political viewpoint with origins in western Europe during the 19th century; opposed revolutionary goals; advocated restoration of monarchy and defense of church. (p. 541)

Constantine   Roman emperor from 312 to 337 C.E.; established second capital at Constantinople; attempted to use religious force of Christianity to unify empire spiritually. (p. 73)

consulado   Merchant guild of Seville; enjoyed virtual monopoly rights over goods shipped to America and handled much of the silver received in return. (p. 433)

consuls Two chief executives or magistrates of the Roman republic; elected by an annual assembly dominated by aristocracy. (p. 76)

Convention Peoples party (CPP) Political party established by Kwame Nkrumah in opposition to British control of colonial legislature in Gold Coast. (p. 769)

Cook, Captain James Made voyages to Hawaii from 1777 to 1779 resulting in opening of islands to the West; convinced Kamehameha to establish unified kingdom in the islands. (p. 584)

Copernicus Polish monk and astronomer (16th century); disproved Hellenistic belief that the earth was at the center of the universe. (p. 388)

Copts Christian sect of Egypt; tended to support Islamic invasions of this area in preference to Byzantine rule. (pp. 103, 132)

core nations Nations, usually European, that enjoyed profit from world economy; controlled international banking and commercial services such as shipping; exported manufactured goods for raw materials. (p. 367)

Corinthian Along with Doric and Ionian, distinct style of Hellenistic architecture; the most ornate of the three styles. (p. 82)

Cornwallis, Lord Charles Reformer of the East India Company administration of India in the 1790s; reduced power of local British administrators; checked widespread corruption. (p. 570)

Coronado, Francisco Vázquez de Leader of Spanish expedition into northern frontier region of New Spain; entered what is now United States in search of mythical cities of gold. (p. 427)

corporatism Political ideology that emphasized the organic nature of society and made the state a mediator, adjusting the interests of different social groups; appealed to conservative groups in European and Latin American societies and to the military. (p. 738)

Cortés, Hernán Led expedition of 600 to coast of Mexico in 1519; conquistador responsible for defeat of Aztec Empire; captured Tenochtitlan. (p. 426)

cossacks Peasants recruited to migrate to newly seized lands in Russia, particularly in south; combined agriculture with military conquests; spurred additional frontier conquests and settlements. (p. 404)

Council of the Indies Body within the Castilian government that issued all laws and advised king on all matters dealing with the Spanish colonies of the New World. (p. 434)

Creole slaves American-born descendants of saltwater slaves; result of sexual exploitation of slave women or process of miscegenation. (p. 467)

Creoles Whites born in the New World; dominated local Latin American economies; ranked just beneath peninsulares. (p. 438)

Crimean War Fought between 1854 and 1856; began as Russian attempt to attack Ottoman Empire; Russia opposed by France and Britain as well; resulted in Russian defeat in the face of Western industrial technology; led to Russian reforms under Tsar Alexander II. (p. 645)

Cristeros Conservative peasant movement in Mexico during the 1920s; most active in central Mexico; attempted to halt slide toward secularism; movement resulted in armed violence. (p. 713)

Cromer, Lord British adviser in khedival Egypt; pushed for economic reforms that reduced but failed to eliminate the debts of the khedival regime. (p. 689)

Crusades Series of military adventures initially launched by western Christians to free Holy Land from Muslims; temporarily succeeded in capturing Jerusalem and establishing Christian kingdoms; later used for other purposes such as commercial wars and extermination of heresy. (p. 151)

cubist movement 20th-century art style; best represented by Spanish artist Pablo Picasso; rendered familiar objects as geometrical shapes. (p. 703)

Cultural Revolution Movement initiated in 1965 by Mao Zedong to restore his dominance over pragmatists; used mobs to ridicule Mao's political rivals; campaign was called off in 1968. (p. 882)

cuneiform [kyU *nEE* uh fôrm, *kyU* nEE uh-] A form of writing developed by the Sumerians using a wedge-shaped stylus and clay tablets. (p. 15)

curacas Ayllu chiefs with privileges of dress and access to resources; community leaders among Andean societies. (p. 254)

Cyril Along with Methodius, missionary sent by Byzantine government to eastern Europe and the Balkans; converted southern Russia and Balkans to Orthodox Christianity; responsible for creation of written script for Slavic known as Cyrillic. (p. 203)

Cyrus the Great Established massive Persian Empire by 550 B.C.E.; successor state to Mesopotamian empires. (p. 70)

da Gama, Vasco Portuguese captain who sailed for India in 1497; established early Portuguese dominance in Indian Ocean. (p. 343)

Dahomey Kingdom developed among Fon or Aja peoples in 17th century; center at Abomey 70 miles from coast; under King Agaja expanded to control coastline and port of Whydah by 1727; accepted Western firearms and goods in return for African slaves. (p. 458)

daimyos Warlord rulers of 300 small states following Onin War and disruption of Ashikaga Shogunate; holdings consolidated into unified and bounded ministates. (p. 294)

Damascus Syrian city that was capital of Umayyad caliphate. (p. 133)

Daoism Philosophy associated with Laozi; stressed need for alignment with Dao or cosmic force. (p. 35)

Darwin, Charles Biologist who developed theory of evolution of species (1859); argued that all living species evolved into their present form through the ability to adapt in a struggle for survival. (p. 551)

Decembrist uprising Political revolt in Russia in 1825; led by middle-level army officers who advocated reforms; put down by Tsar Nicholas I. (p. 643)

Declaration of the Rights of Man and the Citizen Adopted during the liberal phase of the French Revolution (1789); stated the fundamental equality of all French citizens; later became a political source for other liberal movements. (p. 538)

Deism Concept of God current during the Scientific Revolution; role of divinity was to set natural laws in motion, not to regulate once process was begun. (p. 390)

de Klerk, F. W. White South African prime minister in the late 1980s and early 1990s. Working with Nelson Mandela and the African National Congress, de Klerk successfully dismantled the apartheid system and opened the way for a democratically elected government that represented all South Africans for the first time. (p. 858)

de la Cruz, Sor Juana Inés Author, poet, and musician of New Spain; eventually gave up secular concerns to concentrate on spiritual matters. (p. 434)

Demak Most powerful of the trading states on north coast of Java; converted to Islam and served as point of dissemination to other ports. (p. 165)

demographic transition Shift to low birth rate, low infant death rate, stable population; first emerged in western Europe and United States in late 19th century. (p. 184)

demography The study of population. (p. 184)

Deng Xiaoping [dung shee ow ping] One of the more pragmatic, least ideological of the major Communist leaders of China; joined the party as a young man in the 1920s, survived the legendary Long March and persecution during the Cultural Revolution of the 1970s, and emerged as China's most influential leader in the early 1980s. (p. 880)

Descartes, René [dAY *kärt*] Established importance of skeptical review of all received wisdom (17th century); argued that human reason could then develop laws that would explain the fundamental workings of nature. (p. 389)

Deshima Island port in Nagasaki Bay; only port open to non-Japanese after closure of the islands in the 1640s; only Chinese and Dutch ships were permitted to enter. (p. 521)

Devi Mother goddess within Hinduism; widely spread following collapse of Guptas; encouraged new emotionalism in religious ritual. (p. 99)

dharma [*där* muh, *dur-*] The caste position and career determined by a person's birth; Hindu culture required that one accept one's social position and perform occupation to the best of one's ability in order to have a better situation in the next life. (p. 54)

dhimmi Literally "people of the book"; applied as inclusive term to Jews and Christians in Islamic territories; later extended to Zoroastrians and even Hindus. (p. 134)

dhows Arab sailing vessels with triangular or lateen sails; strongly influenced European ship design. (p. 139)

Díaz, Porfirio One of Juárez's generals; elected president of Mexico in 1876; dominated Mexican politics for 35 years; imposed strong central government. (p. 711)

Diem, Ngo Dinh Political leader of South Vietnam; established as president with United States support in the 1950s; opposed Communist government of North Vietnam; overthrown by military coup supported by United States. (p. 887)

Dien Bien Phu Most significant victory of the Viet Minh over French colonial forces in 1954; gave the Viet Minh control of northern Vietnam. (p. 886)

Diet Japanese parliament established as part of the new constitution of 1889; part of Meiji reforms; could pass laws and approve budgets; able to advise government, but not to control it. (p. 656)

Din-i-Ilahi [din i ilähee, dEEn] Religion initiated by Akbar in Mughal India; blended elements of the many faiths of the subcontinent; key to efforts to reconcile Hindus and Muslims in India, but failed. (p. 492)

Dinshawai incident [din shä wAY] Clash between British soldiers and Egyptian villagers in 1906; arose over hunting accident along Nile River where wife of prayer leader of mosque was accidentally shot by army officers hunting pigeons; led to Egyptian protest movement. (p. 690)

Diocletian Roman emperor from 284 to 305 C.E.; restored later empire by improved administration and tax collection. (p. 73)

direct democracy Literally rule of the people; as interpreted in Athens, all decisions emanated from popular assembly without intermediation of elected representatives. (p. 75)

Disraeli, Benjamin Leading conservative political figure in Britain in the second half of the 19th century; took initiative of granting vote to working-class males in 1867; typical of conservative politician making use of popular politics. (p. 546)

Doric Along with Ionian and Corinthian, distinct style of Hellenistic architecture; the least ornate of the three styles. (p. 82)

Dreyfus, Alfred French Jew falsely accused of passing military secrets to the Germans; his mistreatment and exile to Devil's Island provided flashpoint for years of bitter debate between the left and right in France. (p. 692)

DuBois, W.E.B. African American political leader; had a major impact on emerging African nationalist leaders in the 1920s and 1930s. (p. 695)

duma National parliament created in Russia in the aftermath of the Revolution of 1905; progressively stripped of power during the reign of Tsar Nicholas II; failed to forestall further revolution. (p. 651)

Dutch East India Company Joint stock company that obtained government monopoly over trade in Asia; acted as virtually independent government in regions it claimed. (p. 364)

Dutch Studies Group of Japanese scholars interested in implications of Western science and technology beginning in the 18th century; urged freer exchange with West; based studies on few Dutch texts available in Japan. (p. 652)

Dutch trading empire Based on control of fortified towns and factories, warships on patrol, and monopolized control of products—particularly spices. (p. 505)

eastern bloc Nations favorable to the Soviet Union in eastern Europe during the cold war—particularly Poland, Czechoslovakia, Bulgaria, Romania, Hungary, and East Germany. (p. 781)

Eastern Front Most mobile of the fronts established during World War I; lacked trench warfare because of length of front extending from the Baltic to southern Russia; after early successes, military defeats led to downfall of the tsarist government in Russia. (p. 681)

edict of Nantes Grant of tolerance to Protestants in France in 1598; granted only after lengthy civil war between Catholic and Protestant factions. (p. 385)

Edo Tokugawa capital city; modern-day Tokyo; center of the Tokugawa Shogunate. (p. 519)

effendi Class of prosperous business and professional urban families in khedival Egypt; as a class generally favored Egyptian independence. (p. 690)

Einstein, Albert Developed mathematical theories to explain the behavior of planetary motion and the movement of electrical particles; after 1900 issued theory of relativity. (p. 552)

El Mina Most important of early Portuguese trading factories in forest zone of Africa. (p. 449)

emancipation of the serfs Tsar Alexander II ended rigorous serfdom in Russia in 1861; serfs obtained no political rights; required to stay in villages until they could repay aristocracy for land. (p. 645)

Empress Wu Tang ruler 690–705 C.E. in China; supported Buddhist establishment; tried to elevate Buddhism to state religion; had multistory statues of Buddha created. (p. 269)

encomendero [AYn kO mAYn *dAU* rO] The holder of a grant of Indians who were required to pay a tribute or provide labor. The encomendero was responsible for their integration into the church. (p. 422)

encomienda Grants of Indian laborers made to Spanish conquerors and settlers in Mesoamerica and South America; basis for earliest forms of coerced labor in Spanish colonies. (p. 421)

English Civil War Conflict from 1640 to 1660; featured religious disputes mixed with constitutional issues concerning the powers of the monarchy; ended with restoration of the monarchy in 1660 following execution of previous king. (p. 385)

Enlightenment Intellectual movement centered in France during the 18th century; featured scientific advance, application of scientific methods to study of human society; belief that rational laws could describe social behavior. (p. 395)

Ethiopia A Christian kingdom that developed in the highlands of eastern Africa under the dynasty of King Lalaibela; retained Christianity in the face of Muslim expansion elsewhere in Africa. (p. 93)

European-style family Originated in 15th century among peasants and artisans of western Europe, featuring late marriage age, emphasis on the nuclear family, and a large minority who never married. (p. 383)

European Union Began as European Economic Community (or Common Market), an alliance of Germany, France, Italy, Belgium, Luxembourg, and the Netherlands, to create a single economic entity across national boundaries in 1958; later joined by Britain, Ireland, Denmark, Greece, Spain, Portugal, Sweden, Austria, Finland, and other nations for further European economic integration. (p. 786)

factories Portuguese trading fortresses and compounds with resident merchants; utilized throughout Portuguese trading empire to assure secure landing places and commerce. (p. 449)

fascism Political philosophy that became predominant in Italy and then Germany during the 1920s and 1930s; attacked weakness of democracy, corruption of capitalism; promised vigorous foreign and military programs; undertook state control of economy to reduce social friction. (p. 704)

fazendas Coffee estates that spread within interior of Brazil between 1840 and 1860; created major export commodity for Brazilian trade; led to intensification of slavery in Brazil. (p. 605)

federalists Latin American politicians who wanted policies, especially fiscal and commercial regulation, to be set by regional governments rather than centralized national administrations; often supported by politicians who described themselves as liberals. (p. 595)

feminist movements Sought various legal and economic gains for women, including equal access to professions and higher education; came to concentrate on right to vote; won support particularly from middle-class women; active in western Europe at the end of the 19th century; revived in light of other issues in the 1960s. (p. 549)

Ferdinand, Archduke Heir apparent to the Austro-Hungarian throne whose assassination in Sarajevo started World War I. (p. 674)

Ferdinand of Aragon Along with Isabella of Castile, monarch of largest Christian kingdoms in Iberia; marriage to Isabella created united Spain; responsible for reconquest of Granada, initiation of exploration of New World. (p. 421)

feudalism The social organization created by exchanging grants of land or fiefs in return for formal oaths of allegiance and promises of loyal service; typical of Zhou dynasty and European Middle Ages; greater lords provided protection and aid to lesser lords in return for military service. (p. 219)

five pillars The obligatory religious duties of all Muslims; confession of faith, prayer, fasting during Ramadan, zakat, and hajj. (p. 130)

five-year plans Stalin's plans to hasten industrialization of USSR; constructed massive factories in metallurgy, mining, and electric power; led to massive state-planned industrialization at cost of availability of consumer products. (p. 743)

flying money Chinese credit instrument that provided credit vouchers to merchants to be redeemed at the end of the voyage; reduced danger of robbery; early form of currency. (p. 276)

footbinding Practice in Chinese society to mutilate women's feet in order to make them smaller; produced pain and restricted women's movement; made it easier to confine women to the household. (p. 279)

Francis I King of France in the 16th century; regarded as Renaissance monarch; patron of arts; imposed new controls on Catholic church; ally of Ottoman sultan against Holy Roman emperor. (p. 383)

Frederick the Great Prussian king of the 18th century; attempted to introduce Enlightenment reforms into Germany; built on military and bureaucratic foundations of his predecessors; introduced freedom of religion; increased state control of economy. (p. 394)

Free Officers movement Military nationalist movement in Egypt founded in the 1930s; often allied with the Muslim Brotherhood; led coup to seize Egyptian government from khedive in July 1952. (p. 850)

French Revolution Revolution in France between 1789 and 1800; resulted in overthrow of Bourbon monarchy and old regimes; ended with establishment of French Empire under Napoleon Bonaparte; source of many liberal movements and constitutions in Europe. (p. 538)

Freud, Sigmund Viennese physician (19th–20th centuries); developed theories of the workings of the human subconscious; argued that behavior is determined by impulses. (p. 552)

Fujiwara Japanese aristocratic family in mid-9th century; exercised exceptional influence over imperial affairs; aided in decline of imperial power. (p. 291)

Fulani [ʃU lä nEE, foo lä-] Pastoral people of western Sudan; adopted purifying Sufi variant of Islam; under Usuman Dan Fodio in 1804, launched revolt against Hausa kingdoms; established state centered on Sokoto. (p. 460)

Galileo Published Copernicus' findings (17th century); added own discoveries concerning laws of gravity and planetary motion; condemned by the Catholic church for his work. (p. 389)

galleons Large, heavily armed ships used to carry silver from New World colonies to Spain; basis for convoy system utilized by Spain for transportation of bullion. (p. 433)

Gallipoli Peninsula south of Istanbul; site of decisive 1915 Turkish victory over Australian and New Zealand forces under British command during World War I. (p. 680)

Gálvez, José de Spanish minister of the West Indies and chief architect of colonial reform; moved to eliminate Creoles from upper bureaucracy of the colonies; created intendants for local government. (p. 442)

Gandhi, Indira Daughter of Jawaharlal Nehru (no relation to Mahatma Gandhi); installed as a figurehead prime minister by the Congress party bosses in 1966; a strong-willed and astute politician, she soon became the central figure in India politics, a position she maintained through the 1970s and passed on to her sons. (p. 845)

Gandhi, Mohandas Led sustained all-India campaign for independence from British Empire after World War I; stressed nonviolent but aggressive mass protest. (p. 688)

Gang of Four Jiang Qing and four political allies who attempted to seize control of Communist government in China from the pragmatists; arrested and sentenced to life imprisonment in 1976 following Mao Zedong's death. (p. 883)

Garvey, Marcus African American political leader; had a major impact on emerging African nationalist leaders in the 1920s and 1930s. (p. 695)

Gempei Wars [gem pe] Waged for five years from 1180, on Honshu between Taira and Minamoto families; resulted in destruction of Taira. (p. 294)

Gestapo Secret police in Nazi Germany, known for brutal tactics. (p. 734)

Giap, Vo Nguyen Chief military commander of the Viet Minh; architect of the Vietnamese victory over the French at Dien Bien Phu in 1954. (p. 886)

glasnost Policy of openness or political liberation in Soviet Union put forward by Mikhail Gorbachev in the late 1980s. (p. 896)

globalization The increasing interconnectedness of all parts of the world, particularly in communication and commerce but also in culture and politics. (p. 908)

Glorious Revolution English overthrow of James II in 1688; resulted in affirmation of parliament as having basic sovereignty over the king. (p. 394)

Goa Portuguese factory or fortified trade town located on western India coast; site for forcible entry into Asian sea trade network. (p. 503)

Golden Horde   One of the four subdivisions of the Mongol Empire after Chinggis Khan's death, originally ruled by his grandson Batu; territory covered much of what is today south central Russia. (p. 320)

Good Neighbor Policy   Established by Franklin D. Roosevelt for dealing with Latin America in 1933; intended to halt direct intervention in Latin American politics. (p. 826)

Gorbachev, Mikhail   USSR ruler after 1985; renewed attacks on Stalinism; urged reduction in nuclear armament; proclaimed policies of glasnost and perestroika. (p. 896)

Gothic   An architectural style developed during the Middle Ages in western Europe; featured pointed arches and flying buttresses as external supports on main walls. (p. 226)

Gran Colombia   Independent state created in South America as a result of military successes of Simon Bolívar; existed only until 1830, at which time Colombia, Venezuela, and Ecuador became separate nations. (p. 592)

Grand Canal   Built in 7th century during reign of Yangdi during Sui dynasty; designed to link the original centers of Chinese civilization on the north China plain with the Yangtze river basin to the south; nearly 1200 miles long. (p. 275)

Great Depression   International economic crisis following the First World War; began with collapse of American stock market in 1929; actual causes included collapse of agricultural prices in 1920s; included collapse of banking houses in the United States and western Europe, massive unemployment; contradicted optimistic assumptions of 19th century. (p. 727)

Great Leap Forward   Economic policy of Mao Zedong introduced in 1958; proposed industrialization of small-scale projects integrated into peasant communes; led to economic disaster; ended in 1960. (p. 879)

great trek   Movement of Boer settlers in Cape Colony of southern Africa to escape influence of British colonial government in 1834; led to settlement of regions north of Orange River and Natal. (p. 462)

Great Wall   Chinese defensive fortification intended to keep out the nomadic invaders from the north; initiated during Qin dynasty and reign of Shi Huangdi. (p. 38)

Great Zimbabwe   Bantu confederation of Shona-speaking peoples located between Zambezi and Limpopo rivers; developed after 9th century; featured royal courts built of stone; created centralized state by 15th century; king took title of Mwene Mutapa. (p. 188)

Greek fire   Byzantine weapon consisting of mixture of chemicals that ignited when exposed to water; utilized to drive back the Arab fleets that attacked Constantinople. (p. 197)

Greek Revolution   Rebellion in Greece against the Ottoman Empire in 1820; key step in gradually dismantling the Ottoman Empire in the Balkans. (p. 541)

Green movement   Political parties, especially in Europe, focusing on environmental issues and control over economic growth. (p. 785)

Green Revolution   Introduction of improved seed strains, fertilizers, and irrigation as a means of producing higher yields in crops such as rice, wheat, and corn; particularly important in the densely populated countries of Asia. (p. 854)

Gregory VII   Pope during the 11th century who attempted to free church from interference of feudal lords; quarreled with Holy Roman Emperor Henry IV over practice of lay investiture. (p. 223)

griots   [grEE *O*, *gr*EE *O*, *gr*EE ot] Professional oral historians who served as keepers of traditions and advisors to kings within the Mali Empire. (p. 177)

guano   Bird droppings utilized as fertilizer; exported from Peru as a major item of trade between 1850 and 1880; income from trade permitted end to American Indian tribute and abolition of slavery. (p. 599)

Guevara, Ernesto "Che"   Argentine revolutionary; aided Fidel Castro in overthrow of Fulgencio Batista regime in Cuba; died while directing guerrilla movement in Bolivia in 1967. (p. 820)

guilds   Sworn associations of people in the same business or trade in a single city; stressed security and mutual control; limited membership, regulated apprenticeship, guaranteed good workmanship; often established franchise within cities. (p. 230)

guillotine   [*gil* uh tEEn, *gEE* uh-, gil uh *tEEn*, gEE uh-] Introduced as a method of humane execution; utilized to execute thousands during the most radical phase of the French Revolution known as the Reign of Terror. (p. 538)

Guomindang   [*gwo min däng*] Chinese Nationalist party founded by Sun Yat-sen in 1919; drew support from local warlords and Chinese criminal underworld; initially forged alliance with Communists in 1924; dominated by Chiang Kai-shek after 1925. (p. 721)

Guptas   Dynasty that succeeded the Kushans in the 3rd century C.E.; built empire that extended to all but the southern regions of Indian subcontinent; less centralized than Mauryan Empire. (p. 55)

gurus   Brahmans who served as teachers for the princes of the imperial court of the Guptas. (p. 58)

Gutenberg, Johannes   Introduced movable type to western Europe in 15th century; credited with greatly expanded availability of printed books and pamphlets. (p. 383)

Habsburg, Maximilian von   Proclaimed Emperor Maximilian of Mexico following intervention of France in 1862; ruled until overthrow and execution by liberal revolutionaries under Benito Juárez in 1867. (p. 602)

haciendas   Rural estates in Spanish colonies in New World; produced agricultural products for consumers in America; basis of wealth and power for local aristocracy. (p. 433)

hadiths   Traditions of the prophet Muhammad. (p. 135)

Haganah   Zionist military force engaged in violent resistance to British presence in Palestine in the 1940s. (p. 774)

Hagia Sophia   [hä juh sä *fEE* uh] New church constructed in Constantinople during reign of Justinian. (p. 195)

hajj   Pilgrimage to the holy city of Mecca to worship at the Ka'ba. (p. 130)

Hammurabi   The most important ruler of the Babylonian empire; responsible for codification of law. (p. 19)

Han dynasty   Chinese dynasty that succeeded the Qin in 202 B.C.E.; ruled for next 400 years. (p. 38)

Hangzhou   [*häng jO*] Capital of later Song dynasty; located near East China Sea; permitted overseas trading; population exceeded 1 million. (p. 276)

Hannibal   Great Carthaginian general during Second Punic War; successfully invaded Italy but failed to conquer Rome; finally defeated at Battle of Zama. (p. 73)

Hanseatic League   An organization of cities in northern Germany and southern Scandinavia for the purpose of establishing a commercial alliance. (p. 229)

Harappa   Along with Mohenjo-daro, major urban complex of the Harappan civilization; laid out on planned grid pattern. (p. 21)

Harappan civilization   First civilization of Indian subcontinent; emerged in Indus River valley c. 2500 B.C.E. (p. 26)

Harvey, William   English physician (17th century) who demonstrated circular movement of blood in animals, function of heart as pump. (p. 389)

Hausa   Peoples of northern Nigeria; formed states following the demise of Songhay Empire that combined Muslim and pagan traditions. (p. 180)

Hellenistic period   That culture associated with the spread of Greek influence as a result of Macedonian conquests; often seen as the combination of Greek culture with eastern political forms. (p. 72)

Henry the Navigator   Portuguese prince responsible for direction of series of expeditions along the African coast in the 15th century; marked beginning of western European expansion. (p. 343)

Herzl, Theodor   [*hûrt* suhl, *hârt-*] Austrian journalist and Zionist; formed World Zionist Organization in 1897; promoted Jewish migration to Palestine and formation of a Jewish state. (p. 692)

Hidalgo, Father Miguel de   Mexican priest who established independence movement among American Indians and mestizos in 1810; despite early victories, was captured and executed. (p. 591)

Hideyoshi, Toyotomi   [tO yO tO mAY] General under Nobunaga; succeeded as leading military power in central Japan; continued efforts to break power of daimyos; constructed a series of alliances that made him military master of Japan in 1590; died in 1598. (p. 518)

Himalayas   Mountain region marking the northern border of the Indian subcontinent; site of the Aryan settlements that formed small kingdoms or warrior republics. (p. 52)

Hispaniola   First island in Caribbean settled by Spaniards; settlement founded by Columbus on second voyage to New World; Spanish base of operations for further discoveries in New World. (p. 422)

Hitler, Adolf   Nazi leader of fascist Germany from 1933 to his suicide in 1945; created a strongly centralized state in Germany; eliminated all rivals; launched Germany on aggressive foreign policy leading to World War II; responsible for attempted genocide of European Jews. (p. 681)

Ho Chi Minh   Also known as Nguyen Ai Quoc; led Vietnamese Communist party in struggle for liberation from French and U.S. dominance and to unify north and south Vietnam. (p. 886)

Hojo   Warrior family closely allied with Minamoto; dominated Kamakura regime and manipulated Minamoto rulers; claimed to rule in name of Japanese emperor at Kyoto. (p. 294)

Holocaust   Term for Hitler's attempted genocide of European Jews during World War II; resulted in deaths of 6 million Jews. (p. 760)

Holy Alliance   Alliance among Russia, Prussia, and Austria in defense of religion and the established order; formed at Congress of Vienna by most conservative monarchies of Europe. (p. 642)

Holy Roman emperors   Emperors in northern Italy and Germany following split of Charlemagne's empire; claimed

title of emperor c. 10th century; failed to develop centralized monarchy in Germany. (p. 218)

homelands   Under apartheid, areas in South Africa designated for ethnolinguistic groups within the black African population; such areas tend to be overpopulated and poverty-stricken. (p. 857)

Homo sapiens   The human species that emerged as most successful at the end of the Paleolithic period. (p. 8)

Hong Kong   British colony on Chinese mainland; major commercial center; agreement reached between Britain and People's Republic of China returned colony to China in 1997. (p. 867)

Hong Xiuquan   [*hoong* shEE *U* chY *än*] Leader of the Taiping rebellion; converted to specifically Chinese form of Christianity; attacked traditional Confucian teachings of Chinese elite. (p. 634)

Hongwu   First Ming emperor in 1368; originally of peasant lineage; original name Zhu Yuanzhang; drove out Mongol influence; restored position of scholar-gentry. (p. 508)

huacas   Sacred spirits and powers that resided or appeared in caves, mountains, rocks, rivers, and other natural phenomena; typical of Andean societies. (p. 253)

Huancavelica   [wäng kuh vuh *IEE* kuh] Location of greatest deposit of mercury in South America; aided in American silver production; linked with Potosí. (p. 432)

Huanghe   Also known as Yellow River; site of the development of sedentary agriculture in China. (p. 21)

Huerta, Victoriano   Attempted to reestablish centralized dictatorship in Mexico following the removal of Madero in 1913; forced from power in 1914 by Villa and Zapata. (p. 711)

Huitzilopochtli   [wEE tsEE lO *pOch* tlEE] Aztec tribal patron god; central figure of cult of human sacrifice and warfare; identified with old sun god. (p. 243)

Hulegu   Ruler of the Ilkhan khanate; grandson of Chinggis Khan; responsible for capture and destruction of Baghdad. (p. 158)

humanism   Focus on humankind as center of intellectual and artistic endeavor; method of study that emphasized the superiority of classical forms over medieval styles, in particular the study of ancient languages. (p. 382)

Humayan   Son and successor of Babur; expelled from India in 1540, but restored Mughal rule by 1556; died shortly thereafter. (p. 490)

Hundred Years' War   Conflict between England and France from 1337 to 1453; fought over lands England possessed in

France and feudal rights versus the emerging claims of national states. (p. 221)

hunting and gathering   Means of obtaining subsistence by human species prior to the adaptation of sedentary agriculture; normally typical of band social organization. (p. 11)

Hussein   Sherif of Mecca; used British promise of independence to convince Arabs to support Britain against the Turks in World War I; angered by Britain's failure to keep promise. (p. 691)

Hyundai   Example of huge industrial groups that wield great power in modern South Korea; virtually governed Korea's southeastern coast; vertical economic organization with ships, supertankers, factories, schools, and housing units. (p. 872)

Ibn Batuta   Arabic traveler who described African societies and cultures in his travel records. (p. 177)

Ibn Khaldun   [i buhn kal *dUn*, KHUn] A Muslim historian; developed concept that dynasties of nomadic conquerors had a cycle of three generations—strong, weak, dissolute. (p. 152)

iconoclasm   Religious controversy within the Byzantine Empire in the 8th century; emperor attempted to suppress veneration of icons; literally "breaking of images"; after long struggle, icon veneration was restored. (p. 200)

icons   Images of religious figures that became objects of veneration within Christianity of the Byzantine Empire; particularly prevalent in Eastern monasticism. (p. 200)

ideographic writing   Pictographic characters grouped together to create new concepts; typical of Chinese writing. (p. 22)

Ieyasu, Tokugawa   [tO koog ä wä] Vassal of Toyotomi Hideyoshi; succeeded him as most powerful military figure in Japan; granted title of shogun in 1603 and established Tokugawa Shogunate; established political unity in Japan. (p. 519)

Ifriqiya   [if ree *ki* uh] The Arabic term for eastern north Africa. (p. 174)

Iliad   Greek epic poem attributed to Homer but possibly the work of many authors; defined gods and human nature that shaped Greek mythos. (p. 81)

imams   According to Shi'ism, rulers who could trace descent from Ali. (p. 486)

import substitution industrialization Typical of Latin American economies; domestic production of goods during the 20th century that had previously been imported; led to light industrialization. (p. 736)

Inca   Group of clans centered at Cuzco that were able to create empire incorporating various Andean cultures; term also used for leader of empire. (p. 96)

Inca socialism A view created by Spanish authors to describe Inca society as a type of utopia; image of the Inca Empire as a carefully organized system in which every community collectively contributed to the whole. (p. 250)

Indian Misnomer created by Columbus referring to indigenous peoples of New World; implies social and ethnic commonality among Native Americans that did not exist; still used to apply to Native Americans. (p. 239)

Indian National Congress party Grew out of regional associations of Western-educated Indians; originally centered in cities of Bombay, Poona, Calcutta, and Madras; became political party in 1885; focus of nationalist movement in India; governed through most of postcolonial period. (p. 686)

Indies piece Term utilized within the complex exchange system established by the Spanish for African trade; referred to the value of an adult male slave. (p. 453)

Indra Chief deity of the Aryans; depicted as a colossal, hard-drinking warrior. (p. 53)

Indus River valley River sources in Himalayas to mouth in Arabian Sea; location of Harappan civilization. (p. 21)

Industrial Revolution Series of changes in economy of Western nations between 1740 and 20th century; stimulated by rapid population growth, increase in agricultural productivity, commercial revolution of 17th century, and development of new means of transportation; in essence involved technological change and the application of machines to the process of production. (p. 535)

intelligentsia [in teli *jent* sEE uh, *-gent-*] Russian term denoting articulate intellectuals as a class; 19th-century group bent on radical change in Russian political and social system; often wished to maintain a Russian culture distinct from that of the West. (p. 649)

investiture Practice of state appointment of bishops; Pope Gregory VII attempted to ban the practice of lay investiture, leading to war with Holy Roman Emperor Henry IV. (p. 223)

Ionic Along with Doric and Corinthian, distinct style of Hellenistic architecture; more ornate than Doric but less than Corinthian. (p. 82)

iron curtain Phrase coined by Winston Churchill to describe the division between free and communist societies taking shape in Europe after 1946. (p. 781)

Isabella of Castile Along with Ferdinand of Aragon, monarch of largest Christian kingdoms in Iberia; marriage to Ferdinand created united Spain; responsible for reconquest of Granada, initiation of exploration of New World. (p. 421)

Isandhlwana [EE sän dl *wä* nuh] Location of battle fought in 1879 between the British and Zulu armies in southern Africa; resulted in defeat of British; one of few victories of African forces over western Europeans. (p. 575)

Isfahan [is fuh *hän*] Safavid capital under Abbas the Great; planned city laid out according to shah's plan; example of Safavid architecture. (p. 487)

Islam Major world religion having its origins in 610 C.E. in the Arabian peninsula; meaning literally submission; based on prophecy of Muhammad. (pp. 99, 121)

Ismâ'il Sufi commander who conquered city of Tabriz in 1501; first Safavid to be proclaimed shah or emperor. (p. 483)

Iturbide, Augustín de Conservative Creole officer in Mexican army who signed agreement with insurgent forces of independence; combined forces entered Mexico City in 1821; later proclaimed emperor of Mexico until its collapse in 1824. (p. 591)

Ivan III Also known as Ivan the Great; prince of Duchy of Moscow; claimed descent from Rurik; responsible for freeing Russia from Mongols after 1462; took title of tsar or Caesar—equivalent of emperor. (p. 403)

Ivan IV Also known as Ivan the Terrible; confirmed power of tsarist autocracy by attacking authority of boyars (aristocrats); continued policy of Russian expansion; established contacts with western European commerce and culture. (p. 404)

Janissaries Ottoman infantry divisions that dominated Ottoman armies; forcibly conscripted as boys in conquered areas of Balkans, legally slaves; translated military service into political influence, particularly after 15th century. (p. 475)

Jesuits A new religious order founded during the Catholic Reformation; active in politics, education, and missionary work; sponsored missions to South America, North American, and Asia. (p. 384)

Jesus of Nazareth Prophet and teacher among the Jews; believed by Christians to be the Messiah; executed c. 30 C.E. (p. 106)

Jiang Qing [*jyäng* ching] Wife of Mao Zedong; one of Gang of Four; opposed pragmatists and supported Cultural Revolution of 1965; arrested and imprisoned for life in 1976. (p. 880)

jihad Islamic holy war. (p. 132)

Jin Also known as Qin; kingdom north of the Song Empire; established by Jurchens in 1115 after overthrowing Liao dynasty. (p. 274)

Jinnah, Muhammad Ali Muslim nationalist in India; originally a member of the National Congress party; became leader of Muslim League; traded Muslim support for British during World War II for promises of a separate Muslim state after the war; first president of Pakistan. (p. 768)

jinshi [chin shEE] Title granted to students who passed the most difficult Chinese examination on all of Chinese literature; became immediate dignitaries and eligible for high office. (p. 267)

jizya [*jiz* yuh] Head tax paid by all non-believers in Islamic territories. (p. 134)

João VI Portuguese monarch who established seat of government in Brazil from 1808 to 1820 as a result of Napoleonic invasion of Iberian peninsula; made Brazil seat of empire with capital at Rio de Janeiro. (p. 593)

Juárez, Benito Indian governor of state of Oaxaca in Mexico; leader of liberal rebellion against Santa Anna; liberal government defeated by French intervention under Emperor Napoleon III of France and establishment of Mexican Empire under Maximilian; restored to power in 1867 until his death in 1872. (p. 601)

junks Chinese ships equipped with watertight bulkheads, sternpost rudders, compasses, and bamboo fenders; dominant force in Asian seas east of the Malayan peninsula. (p. 275)

Jurchens Founders of the Qin kingdom that succeeded the Liao in northern China; annexed most of Yellow River basin and forced Song to flee to south. (p. 274)

Justinian Eastern Roman emperor between 527 and 565 C.E.; tried to restore unity of old Roman Empire; issued most famous compilation of Roman law. (p. 102)

juula [jUlä] Malinke merchants; formed small partnerships to carry out trade throughout Mali Empire; eventually spread throughout much of west Africa. (p. 177)

Ju Yuanzhang [jU yU *än jäng*, y*Yän*] Chinese peasant who led successful revolt against Yuan in 14th century; founded Ming dynasty. (p. 331)

Ka'ba Most revered religious shrine in pre-Islamic Arabia; located in Mecca; focus of obligatory annual truce among bedouin tribes; later incorporated as important shrine in Islam. (p. 126)

Kabir Muslim mystic during 15th century; played down the importance of ritual differences between Hinduism and Islam. (p. 163)

Kamasutra Written by Vatsayana during Gupta era; offered instructions on all aspects of life for higher caste males, including grooming, hygiene, etiquette, selection of wives, and instruction on lovemaking. (p. 60)

Kamehameha I [kä *mAY* hä *mAY* hä, kuh *mAY* uh *mAY* uh] Fought series of wars backed by British weapons and advisors resulting in unified Hawaiian kingdom by 1810; as king he promoted economic change encouraging Western merchants to establish export trade in Hawaiian goods. (p. 585)

Kangxi [*käng shEE*] Confucian scholar and Manchu emperor of Qing dynasty from 1661 to 1722; established high degree of Sinification among the Manchus. (p. 630)

Karakorum Capital of the Mongol Empire under Chinggis Khan. (p. 320)

Karbala Site of defeat and death of Husayn, son of Ali; marked beginning of Shi'a resistance to Umayyad caliphate. (p. 133)

Kautilya Political advisor to Chandragupta Maurya; one of the authors of *Arthashastra;* believed in scientific application of warfare. (p. 56)

Kellogg-Briand Pact A treaty coauthored by American and French leaders in 1928; in principle outlawed war forever; ratified subsequently by other nations. (p. 702)

Kenya African Union (KAU) Leading nationalist party in Kenya; adopted nonviolent approach to ending British control in the 1950s. (p. 771)

Kenyatta, Jomo Leader of the nonviolent nationalist party in Kenya; organized the Kenya Africa Union (KAU); failed to win concessions because of resistance of white settlers; came to power only after suppression of the Land Freedom Army, or Mau Mau. (p. 771)

Kerensky, Alexander Liberal revolutionary leader during the early stages of the Russian Revolution of 1917; sought development of parliamentary rule, religious freedom. (p. 713)

Khadijah First wife of the prophet Muhammad, who had worked for her as a trader. (p. 127)

khagan Title of the supreme ruler of the Mongol tribes. (p. 318)

khanates Four regional Mongol kingdoms that arose following the death of Chinggis Khan. (p. 313)

Khartoum River town that was administrative center of Egyptian authority in Sudan. (p. 628)

khedives [kuh *dEEv*] Descendants of Muhammad Ali in Egypt after 1867; for-

mal rulers of Egypt despite French and English intervention until overthrown by military coup in 1952. (p. 625)

Khitans Nomadic peoples of Manchuria; militarily superior to Song dynasty China but influenced by Chinese culture; forced humiliating treaties on Song China in 11th century. (p. 272)

Khmers Indianized rivals of the Vietnamese; moved into Mekong River delta region at time of Vietnamese drive to the south. (p. 303)

Khomeini, Ayatollah Ruhollah [KHO *mAY* nEE, kO-, äyuh *tO* luh] Religious ruler of Iran following revolution of 1979 to expel the Pahlavi shah of Iran; emphasized religious purification; tried to eliminate Western influences and establish purely Islamic government. (p. 855)

Khrushchev, Nikita [*kroosh* chef, -chof, *krUsh*-] Stalin's successor as head of USSR; attacked Stalinism in 1956 for concentration of power and arbitrary dictatorship; failure of Siberian development program and antagonism of Stalinists led to downfall. (p. 805)

Kiev Trade city in southern Russia established by Scandinavian traders in 9th century; became focal point for kingdom of Russia that flourished to 12th century. (p. 205)

Koguryo Tribal people of northern Korea; established an independent kingdom in the northern half of the peninsula; adopted cultural Sinification. (p. 299)

Kongo Kingdom, based on agriculture, formed on lower Congo River by late 15th century; capital at Mbanza Kongo; ruled by hereditary monarchy. (p. 188)

Korean War Fought from 1950 to 1953; North supported by USSR and later People's Republic of China; South supported by United States and small international United Nations force; ended in stalemate and continued division of Korea. (p. 866)

Kubilai Khan Grandson of Chinggis Khan; commander of Mongol forces responsible for conquest of China; became khagan in 1260; established Sinicized Mongol Yuan dynasty in China in 1271. (p. 325)

kulaks Agricultural entrepreneurs who utilized the Stolypin and later NEP reforms to increase agricultural production and buy additional land. (p. 651)

kuriltai Meeting of all Mongol chieftains at which the supreme ruler of all tribes was selected. (p. 318)

Kush An African state that developed along the upper reaches of the Nile c. 1000 B.C.E.; conquered Egypt and ruled it for several centuries. (p. 21)

Kushans Dynasty that succeeded the Mauryas in northwestern India; sponsors of Buddhism; empire did not extend to Ganges River valley. (p. 55)

La Reforma The liberal rebellion of Benito Juárez against the forces of Santa Anna. (p. 602)

Land Freedom Army Radical organization for independence in Kenya; frustrated by failure of nonviolent means, initiated campaign of terror in 1952; referred to by British as the Mau Mau. (p. 771)

Las Casas, Bartolomé de Dominican friar who supported peaceful conversion of the Native American population of the Spanish colonies; opposed forced labor and advocated Indian rights. (p. 424)

League of Nations International diplomatic and peace organization created in the Treaty of Versailles that ended World War I; one of the chief goals of President Woodrow Wilson of the United States in the peace negotiations; the United States was never a member. (p. 683)

Lee Kuan Yew Ruler of Singapore from independence in 1959 through three decades; established tightly controlled authoritarian government; ruled through People's Action party to suppress political diversity. (p. 874)

Lepanto Naval battle between the Spanish and the Ottoman Empire resulting in a Spanish victory in 1571; demonstrated European naval superiority over Muslims. (p. 367)

Lesotho Southern African state that survived mfecane; not based on Zulu model; less emphasis on military organization, less authoritarian government. (p. 464)

letrados University-trained lawyers from Spain in the New World; juridical core of Spanish colonial bureaucracy; exercised both legislative and administrative functions. (p. 434)

Liao dynasty Founded in 907 by nomadic Khitan peoples from Manchuria; maintained independence from Song dynasty in China. (p. 272)

Li Bo Most famous poet of the Tang era; blended images of the mundane world with philosophical musings. (p. 283)

liberal Political viewpoint with origins in western Europe during the 19th century; stressed limited state interference in individual life, representation of propertied people in government; urged importance of constitutional rule and parliaments. (p. 541)

Liberal Democratic party Monopolized Japanese government from its formation in 1955 into the 1990s;

largely responsible for the economic reconstruction of Japan. (p. 866)

liberation theology Combined Catholic theology and socialist principles in effort to bring about improved conditions for the poor in Latin America in 20th century. (p. 821)

Li Dazhao [*lEE dä jaU*] Chinese intellectual who gave serious attention to Marxist philosophy; headed study circle at the University of Beijing; saw peasants as vanguard of revolutionary communism in China. (p. 720)

Lin Biao Chinese commander under Mao; trained at Chiang Kai-shek's Whampoa Academy in the 1920s. (p. 877)

Lin Zexu Distinguished Chinese official during the early 19th century; charged with stamping out the opium trade in southern China; ordered blockade of European trading areas in Canton and confiscation of opium; sent into exile following the Opium War. (p. 633)

Liu Shaoqui Chinese Communist pragmatist; with Deng Xiaoping, came to power after Mao; determined to restore state direction and market incentives at local level. (p. 880)

Li Yuan Also known as Duke of Tang; minister for Yangdi; took over empire following assassination of Yangdi; first emperor of Tang dynasty; took imperial title of Gaozu. (p. 266)

Lloyd George, David Prime minister of Great Britain who headed a coalition government through much of World War I and the turbulent years that followed. (p. 682)

Locke, John English philosopher during 17th century; argued that people could learn everything through senses and reason; argued that power of government came from the people, not divine right of kings; offered possibility of revolution to overthrow tyrants. (p. 390)

loess [*lO* es, les, lus] Fine grained soil deposited in Ordos bend by winds from central Asia; created fertile soil for sedentary agricultural communities. (p. 26)

Long March Communist escape from Hunan province during civil war with Guomindang in 1934; center of Communist power moved to Shaanxi province; firmly established Mao Zedong as head of the Communist party in China. (p. 723)

Louis XIV French monarch of the late 17th century who personified absolute monarchy. (p. 391)

Louis XVI Bourbon monarch of France who was executed during the radical phase of the French Revolution (1792). (p. 538)

L'Overture, Toussaint [*lU* veR *tYR*] Leader of slave rebellion on the French sugar island of St. Domingue in 1791; led to creation of independent republic of Haiti in 1804. (p. 591)

Luanda Portuguese factory established in 1520s south of Kongo; became basis for Portuguese colony of Angola. (p. 450)

Luo Nilotic people who migrated from Upper Nile valley; established dynasty among existing Bantu population in lake region of central eastern Africa; center at Bunyoro. (p. 460)

Luther, Martin German monk; initiated Protestant Reformation in 1517 by nailing 95 theses to door of Wittenberg church; emphasized primacy of faith over works stressed in Catholic church; accepted state control of church. (p. 384)

Luzon Northern island of Philippines; conquered by Spain during the 1560s; site of major Catholic missionary effort. (p. 505)

Macao One of two ports in which Europeans were permitted to trade in China during the Ming dynasty. (p. 513)

Macedon Kingdom located in northern Greece; originally loosely organized under kings; became centralized under Philip II; served as basis for unification of Greece and later Macedonian Empire. (p. 71)

Machiavelli, Niccolo [mak EE uh *vel* EE] Author of *The Prince* (16th century); emphasized realistic discussions of how to seize and maintain power; one of most influential authors of Italian Renaissance. (p. 382)

Madero, Francisco Moderate democratic reformer in Mexico; proposed moderate reforms in 1910; arrested by Porfirio Díaz; initiated revolution against Díaz when released from prison; temporarily gained power, but removed and assassinated in 1913. (p. 711)

Magellan, Ferdinand Spanish captain who in 1519 initiated first circumnavigation of the globe; died during the voyage; allowed Spain to claim Philippines. (p. 363)

Maghrib [*mug* ruhb] The Arabic word for western north Africa. (p. 174)

Magna Carta Great Charter issued by King John of England in 1215; confirmed feudal rights against monarchical claims; represented principle of mutual limits and obligations between rulers and feudal aristocracy. (p. 220)

Mahabharata [muh *hä bär* uh tuh] Indian epic of war, princely honor, love, and social duty; written down in the last centuries B.C.E.; previously handed down in oral form. (p. 52)

Mahdi In Sufi belief system, a promised deliverer; also name given to Muhammad Achmad, leader of late 19th-century revolt against Egyptians and British in the Sudan. (p. 628)

Mahayana Chinese version of Buddhism; placed considerable emphasis on Buddha as god or savior. (p. 105)

Mahmud II Ottoman sultan; built a private, professional army; fomented revolution of Janissaries and crushed them with private army; destroyed power of Janissaries and their religious allies; initiated reform of Ottoman Empire on Western precedents. (p. 621)

Mahmud of Ghazni Third ruler of Turkish slave dynasty in Afghanistan; led invasions of northern India; credited with sacking one of wealthiest of Hindu temples in northern India; gave Muslims reputation for intolerance and aggression. (p. 161)

Malacca Portuguese factory or fortified trade town located on the tip of the Malayan peninsula; traditionally a center for trade among the southeastern Asian islands. (pp. 165, 503)

Mamluks Muslim slave warriors; established a dynasty in Egypt; defeated the Mongols at Ain Jalut in 1260 and halted Mongol advance. (p. 158)

mandates Governments entrusted to European nations in the Middle East in the aftermath of World War I; Britain occupied Iraq and Palestine, while France occupied Syria and Lebanon after 1922. (p. 691)

Mandate of Heaven The divine source for political legitimacy of Chinese rulers; established by Zhou to justify overthrow of Shang. (p. 26)

Mandela, Nelson Long-imprisoned leader of the African National Congress party; worked with the ANC leadership and F. W. de Klerk's supporters to dismantle the apartheid system from the mid-1980s onward; in 1994, became the first black prime minister of South Africa after the ANC won the first genuinely democratic elections in the country's history. (p. 858)

manifest destiny Belief of the government of the United States that it was destined to rule the continent from coast to coast; led to annexation of Texas and Mexican-American War. (p. 601)

manorialism System that described economic and political relations between landlords and their peasant laborers during the Middle Ages; involved a hierarchy of reciprocal obligations that exchanged labor or rents for access to land. (p. 215)

Mao Zedong Communist leader in revolutionary China; advocated rural reform and role of peasantry in Nationalist revolution; influenced by Li Dazhao; led

Communist reaction against Guomindang purges in 1920s, culminating in Long March of 1934; seized control of all of mainland China by 1949; initiated Great Leap Forward in 1958. (p. 720)

Marattas Western India peoples who rebelled against Mughal control early in 18th century. (p. 496)

Marquis of Pombal Prime minister of Portugal from 1755 to 1776; acted to strengthen royal authority in Brazil; expelled Jesuits; enacted fiscal reforms and established monopoly companies to stimulate the colonial economy. (p. 442)

Marshall Plan Program of substantial loans initiated by the United States in 1947; designed to aid Western nations in rebuilding from the war's devastation; vehicle for American economic dominance. (p. 781)

Martel, Charles Carolingian monarch of Franks; responsible for defeating Muslims in battle of Tours in 732; ended Muslim threat to western Europe. (p. 216)

Marx, Karl German socialist of the mid-19th century; blasted earlier socialist movements as utopian; saw history as defined by class struggle between groups out of power and those controlling the means of production; preached necessity of social revolution to create proletarian dictatorship. (p. 548)

mass leisure culture An aspect of the later Industrial Revolution; based on newspapers, music halls, popular theater, vacation trips, and team sports. (p. 550)

Mass Line Economic policy of Mao Zedong; led to formation of agricultural cooperatives in 1955; cooperatives became farming collectives in 1956. (p. 878)

Mataram Kingdom that controlled interior regions of Java in 17th century; Dutch East India Company paid tribute to the kingdom for rights of trade at Batavia; weakness of kingdom after 1670s allowed Dutch to exert control over all of Java. (p. 565)

Mauryas Dynasty established in Indian subcontinent in 4th century B.C.E. following invasion by Alexander the Great. (p. 54)

mawali Non-Arab converts to Islam. (p. 134)

May Fourth movement Resistance to Japanese encroachments in China began on this date in 1919; spawned movement of intellectuals aimed at transforming China into a liberal democracy; rejected Confucianism. (p. 719)

Maya Classic culture emerging in southern Mexico and Central America contemporary with Teotihuacan; extended over broad region; featured monumental architecture, written language, calendrical and mathematical systems, highly developed religion. (p. 96)

Mecca City located in mountainous region along Red Sea in Arabian peninsula; founded by Umayyad clan of Quraysh; site of Ka'ba; original home of Muhammad; location of chief religious pilgrimage point in Islam. (p. 125)

Medina Also known as Yathrib; town located northeast of Mecca; grew date palms whose fruit was sold to bedouins; became refuge for Muhammad following flight from Mecca (hijra). (p. 126)

Mehmed II [me *met*] Ottoman sultan called the "Conqueror"; responsible for conquest of Constantinople in 1453; destroyed what remained of Byzantine Empire. (p. 474)

mercantilism Economic theory that stressed governments' promotion of limitation of imports from other nations and internal economies in order to improve tax revenues; popular during 17th and 18th centuries in Europe. (p. 367)

Mesopotamia Literally "between the rivers"; the civilizations that arose in the alluvial plain of the Tigris–Euphrates river valleys. (p. 16)

mestizos People of mixed European and Indian ancestry in Mesoamerica and South America; particularly prevalent in areas colonized by Spain; often part of forced labor system. (p. 368)

Methodius Along with Cyril, missionary sent by Byzantine government to eastern Europe and the Balkans; converted southern Russia and Balkans to Orthodox Christianity; responsible for creation of written script for Slavic known as Cyrillic. (p. 203)

Mexican-American War Fought between Mexico and the United States from 1846 to 1848; led to devastating defeat of Mexican forces, loss of about one-half of Mexico's national territory to the United States. (p. 601)

Mexican Constitution of 1917 Promised land reform, limited foreign ownership of key resources, guaranteed the rights of workers, and placed restrictions on clerical education; marked formal end of Mexican Revolution. (p. 712)

Mexican Revolution Fought over a period of almost ten years from 1910; resulted in ouster of Porfirio Díaz from power; opposition forces led by Pancho Villa and Emiliano Zapata. (p. 711)

Mexico City Capital of New Spain; built on ruins of Aztec capital of Tenochtitlan. (p. 426)

mfecane [um fuh *ka* nAY] Wars of 19th century in southern Africa; created by Zulu expansion under Shaka; revolution-ized political organization of southern Africa. (p. 462)

Middle Ages The period in western European history from the decline and fall of the Roman Empire until the 15th century. (p. 213)

Middle Passage Slave voyage from Africa to the Americas (16th–18th centuries); generally a traumatic experience for black slaves, although it failed to strip Africans of their culture. (p. 466)

Midway Island World War II Pacific battle; decisive U.S. victory over powerful Japanese carrier force. (p. 762)

Minamoto Defeated the rival Taira family in Gempei Wars and established military government (bakufu) in 12th-century Japan. (p. 293)

Minas Gerais [*mEE* nuhs zhi *RIs*] Region of Brazil located in mountainous interior where gold strikes were discovered in 1695; became location for gold rush. (p. 437)

Mindanao Southern island of Philippines; a Muslim kingdom that was able to successfully resist Spanish conquest. (p. 505)

Ming dynasty Succeeded Mongol Yuan dynasty in China in 1368; lasted until 1644; initially mounted huge trade expeditions to southern Asia and elsewhere, but later concentrated efforts on internal development within China. (p. 331)

Minh Mang [*min mäng*] Second emperor of a united Vietnam; successor of Nguyen Anh; ruled from 1820 to 1841; sponsored emphasis of Confucianism; persecuted Catholics. (p. 884)

Ministry of Rites Administered examinations to students from Chinese government schools or those recommended by distinguished scholars. (p. 267)

Mira Bai Celebrated Hindu writer of religious poetry; reflected openness of bhaktic cults to women. (p. 163)

mita Labor extracted for lands assigned to the state and the religion; all communities were expected to contribute; an essential aspect of Inca imperial control. (p. 254)

Moctezuma II [mok te *sU* mä] Last independent Aztec emperor; killed during Hernán Cortés's conquest of Tenochtitlan. (p. 426)

Mohenjo Daro Along with Harappa, major urban complex of the Harappan civilization; laid out on planned grid pattern. (p. 21)

moldboard Heavy plow introduced in northern Europe during the Middle Ages; permitted deeper cultivation of heavier soils; a technological innovation of the medieval agricultural system. (p. 215)

Mongols Central Asian nomadic peoples; smashed Turko-Persian kingdoms; captured Baghdad in 1258 and killed last Abbasid caliph. (p. 158)

monotheism The exclusive worship of a single god; introduced by the Jews into Western civilization. (p. 27)

Monroe Doctrine American declaration stated in 1823; established that any attempt of a European country to colonize in the Americas would be considered an unfriendly act by the United States; supported by Great Britain as a means of opening Latin American trade. (p. 598)

monsoons Seasonal winds crossing Indian subcontinent and southeast Asia; during summer bring rains. (p. 52)

Montagu-Chelmsford reforms Increased the powers of Indian legislators at the all-India level and placed much of the provincial administration of India under local ministries controlled by legislative bodies with substantial numbers of elected Indians; passed in 1919. (p. 688)

Morley-Minto reforms Provided educated Indians with considerably expanded opportunities to elect and serve on local and all-India legislative councils. (p. 688)

Mu'awiya [mU *ä* wEE ä] Leader of Umayyad clan; first Umayyad caliph following civil war with Ali. (p. 133)

Mubarak, Hosni President of Egypt since 1981, succeeding Anwar Sadat and continuing his policies of cooperation with the West. (p. 854)

Mughal Empire Established by Babur in India in 1526; the name is taken from the supposed Mongol descent of Babur, but there is little indication of any Mongol influence in the dynasty; became weak after rule of Aurangzeb in first decades of 18th century. (p. 473)

Muhammad Prophet of Islam; born c. 570 to Banu Hashim clan of Quraysh tribe in Mecca; raised by father's family; received revelations from Allah in 610 C.E. and thereafter; died in 632. (p. 121)

Muhammad ibn Qasim Arab general; conquered Sind in India; declared the region and the Indus valley to be part of Umayyad Empire. (p. 160)

Muhammad of Ghur Military commander of Persian extraction who ruled small mountain kingdom in Afghanistan; began process of conquest to establish Muslim political control of northern India; brought much of Indus valley, Sind, and northwestern India under his control. (p. 162)

Muhammad Shah II Turkic ruler of Muslim Khwarazm kingdom; attempted to resist Mongol conquest; conquered in 1220. (p. 319)

Muhammad the Great Extended the boundaries of the Songhay Empire; Islamic ruler of the mid-16th century. (p. 180)

mullahs Local mosque officials and prayer leaders within the Safavid Empire; agents of Safavid religious campaign to convert all of population to Shi'ism. (p. 486)

multinational corporations Powerful companies, mainly from the West or Pacific Rim, with production as well as distribution operations in many different countries. Multinationals surged in the decades after World War II. (p. 910)

Mumtaz Mahal Wife of Shah Jahan; took an active political role in Mughal court; entombed in Taj Mahal. (p. 495)

Murad Head of the coalition of Mamluk rulers in Egypt; opposed Napoleonic invasion of Egypt and suffered devastating defeat; failure destroyed Mamluk government in Egypt and revealed vulnerability of Muslim core. (p. 625)

Muslim Follower of Islam. (p. 121)

Muslim Brotherhood Egyptian nationalist movement founded by Hasan al-Banna in 1928; committed to fundamentalist movement in Islam; fostered strikes and urban riots against the khedival government. (p. 850)

Muslim League Founded in 1906 to better support demands of Muslims for separate electorates and legislative seats in Hindu-dominated India; represented division within Indian nationalist movement. (p. 768)

Mussolini, Benito Italian fascist leader after World War I; created first fascist government based on aggressive foreign policy and new nationalist glories. (p. 704)

Mvemba, Nzinga King of Kongo south of Zaire River from 1507 to 1543; converted to Christianity and took title Alfonso I; under Portuguese influence attempted to Christianize all of kingdom. (p. 450)

nabobs Name given to British representatives of the East India Company who went briefly to India to make fortunes through graft and exploitation. (p. 570)

Nadir Khan Afshar Soldier-adventurer following fall of Safavid dynasty in 1722; proclaimed himself shah in 1736; established short-lived dynasty in reduced kingdom. (p. 489)

Nasser, Gamal Abdul Took power in Egypt following a military coup in 1952; enacted land reforms and used state resources to reduce unemployment; ousted Britain from the Suez Canal zone in 1956. (p. 850)

Natal British colony in south Africa; developed after Boer trek north from Cape Colony; major commercial outpost at Durban. (p. 583)

National Liberation Front (FLN) Radical nationalist movement in Algeria; launched sustained guerilla war against France in the 1950s; success of attacks led to independence of Algeria in 1958. (p. 771)

National Socialist party Also known as the Nazi party; led by Adolf Hitler in Germany; picked up political support during the economic chaos of the Great Depression; advocated authoritarian state under a single leader, aggressive foreign policy to reverse humiliation of the Versailles treaty; took power in Germany in 1933. (p. 753)

négritude Literary movement in Africa; attempted to combat racial stereotypes of African culture; celebrated the beauty of black skin and African physique; associated with origins of African nationalist movements. (p. 696)

Nehru, Jawaharlal [n*AΥ*rU, *nâr* U] One of Gandhi's disciples; governed India after independence (1947); committed to program of social reform and economic development; preserved civil rights and democracy. (p. 845)

neocolonial economy Industrialized nations' continued dominance of the world economy; ability of the industrialized nations to maintain economic colonialism without political colonialism. (p. 846)

neo-Confucians Revived ancient Confucian teachings in Song era China; great impact on the dynasties that followed; their emphasis on tradition and hostility to foreign systems made Chinese rulers and bureaucrats less receptive to outside ideas and influences. (p. 273)

Neolithic Age The New Stone Age between 8000 and 5000 B.C.E.; period in which adaptation of sedentary agriculture occurred; domestication of plants and animals accomplished. (p. 10)

Neolithic revolution The succession of technological innovations and changes in human organization that led to the development of agriculture, 8500–3500 B.C.E. (p. 11)

Nestorians A Christian sect found in Asia; tended to support Islamic invasions of this area in preference to Byzantine rule; cut off from Europe by Muslim invasions. (p. 132)

New Deal President Franklin Roosevelt's precursor of the modern welfare state (1933–1939); programs to combat economic depression enacted a number of social insurance measures and used government spending to stimulate the economy; increased power of the state and the state's intervention in United States social and economic life. (p. 732)

New Economic Policy Initiated by Lenin in 1921; state continued to set basic economic policies, but efforts were now combined with individual initiative; policy allowed food production to recover. (p. 715)

new feminism New wave of women's rights agitation dating from 1949; emphasized more literal equality that would play down domestic roles and qualities for women; promoted specific reforms and redefinition of what it meant to be female. (p. 796)

New France French colonies in North America; extended from St. Lawrence River along Great Lakes and down Mississippi River valley system. (p. 371)

New Spain Spanish colonial possessions in Mesoamerica; included most of central Mexico; based on imperial system of Aztecs. (p. 427)

Newton, Isaac English scientist during the 17th century; author of *Principia;* drew the various astronomical and physical observations and wider theories together in a neat framework of natural laws; established principles of motion; defined forces of gravity. (p. 389)

Nezhualcoyotl [nez wät l coiOt l] Leading Aztec king of the 15th century. (p. 243)

Nguyen [ngI en, ngu yen] Rival Vietnamese dynasty that arose in southern Vietnam to challenge traditional dynasty of Trinh in north at Hanoi; kingdom centered on Red and Mekong rivers; capital at Hue. (p. 309)

Nguyen Anh [ngI en, ngu yen än] Last surviving member of Nguyen dynasty following Tayson Rebellion in Vietnam; with French support retook southern Vietnam; drove Tayson from northern Vietnam by 1802; proclaimed himself emperor with capital at Hue; also known as Gia Long. (p. 884)

Nicholas II Tsar of Russia 1894–1917; forcefully suppressed political opposition and resisted constitutional government; deposed by revolution in 1917. (p. 677)

nirvana The Buddhist state of enlightenment, a state of tranquility. (p. 59)

Nobili, Robert di Italian Jesuit missionary; worked in India during the early 1600s; introduced strategy to convert elites first; strategy later widely adopted by Jesuits in various parts of Asia; mission eventually failed. (p. 507)

Nobunaga Japanese daimyo; first to make extensive use of firearms; in 1573 deposed last of Ashikaga shoguns; unified much of central Honshu under his command; killed in 1582. (p. 518)

Nok Culture featuring highly developed art style flourishing between 500 B.C.E. and 200 C.E.; located in forests of central Nigeria. (p. 186)

nomads Cattle- and sheep-herding societies normally found on the fringes of civilized societies; commonly referred to as "barbarian" by civilized societies. (p. 15)

North American Free Trade Agreement (NAFTA) Agreement that created an essentially free trade zone among Mexico, Canada, and the United States, in hopes of encouraging economic growth in all three nations; after difficult negotiations, went into effect January 1, 1994. (p. 904)

North Atlantic Treaty Organization (NATO) Created in 1949 under United States leadership to group most of the western European powers plus Canada in a defensive alliance against possible Soviet aggression. (p. 782)

Northern Renaissance Cultural and intellectual movement of northern Europe; began later than Italian Renaissance c. 1450; centered in France, Low Countries, England, and Germany; featured greater emphasis on religion than Italian Renaissance. (p. 383)

Nur Jahan Wife of Jahangir; amassed power in court and created faction of male relatives who dominated Mughal empire during later years of Jahangir's reign. (p. 495)

Nurhaci Architect of Manchu unity; created distinctive Manchu banner armies; controlled most of Manchuria; adopted Chinese bureaucracy and court ceremonies in Manchuria; entered China and successfully captured Ming capital at Beijing. (p. 629)

obeah African religious ideas and practices in the English and French Caribbean islands. (p. 468)

Obregón, Alvaro Emerged as leader of the Mexican government in 1915; elected president in 1920. (p. 711)

Odyssey Greek epic poem attributed to Homer but possibly the work of many authors; defined gods and human nature that shaped Greek mythos. (p. 81)

Ogedei Third son of Chinggis Khan; succeeded Chinggis Khan as khagan of the Mongols following his father's death. (p. 320)

Old Believers Russians who refused to accept the ecclesiastical reforms of Alexis Romanov (17th century); many exiled to Siberia or southern Russia, where they became part of Russian colonization. (p. 406)

Olmec culture Cultural tradition that arose at San Lorenzo and La Venta in Mexico c. 1200 B.C.E.; featured irrigated agriculture, urbanism, elaborate religion, beginnings of calendrical and writing systems. (p. 96)

Olympic games One of the pan-Hellenic rituals observed by all Greek city-states; involved athletic competitions and ritual celebrations. (p. 71)

Opium War Fought between the British and Qing China beginning in 1839; fought to protect British trade in opium; resulted in resounding British victory, opening of Hong Kong as British port of trade. (p. 632)

Orabi, Ahmad Student of Muhammad Abduh; led revolt in 1882 against Turkish influence in Egyptian army; forced khedive to call on British army for support. (p. 626)

Ormuz Portuguese factory or fortified trade town located at southern end of Persian Gulf; site for forcible entry into Asian sea trade network. (p. 503)

Orozco, José Clemente Mexican muralist of the period after the Mexican Revolution; like Rivera's, his work featured romantic images of the Indian past with Christian symbols and Marxist ideology. (p. 712)

Ottoman Empire Turkic empire established in Asia Minor and eventually extending throughout Middle East; responsible for conquest of Constantinople and end of Byzantine Empire in 1453; succeeded Seljuk Turks following retreat of Mongols. (pp. 151, 473)

Ottoman Society for Union and Progress Organization of political agitators in opposition to rule of Abdul Hamid; also called "Young Turks"; desired to restore 1876 constitution. (p. 623)

Ottomans Turkic people who advanced from strongholds in Asia Minor during 1350s; conquered large part of Balkans; unified under Mehmed I; captured Constantinople in 1453; established empire from Balkans that included most of Arab world. (p. 473)

Pachacuti Ruler of Inca society from 1438 to 1471; launched a series of military campaigns that gave Incas control of the region from Cuzco to the shores of Lake Titicaca. (p. 252)

Pacific Rim Region including Japan, South Korea, Singapore, Hong Kong, Taiwan; typified by rapid growth rates, expanding exports, and industrialization; either Chinese or strongly influenced by Confucian values; considerable reliance on government planning and direction, limitations on dissent and instability. (p. 863)

Paekche Independent Korean kingdom in southeastern part of peninsula; defeated by rival Silla kingdom and its Chinese Tang allies in 7th century. (p. 299)

Palmares Kingdom of runaway slaves with a population of 8,000 to 10,000 people; located in Brazil during the 17th century; leadership was Angolan. (p. 469)

Paleolithic Age The Old Stone Age ending in 12,000 B.C.E.; typified by use of crude stone tools and hunting and gathering for subsistence. (p. 7)

pan-African Organization that brought together intellectuals and political leaders from areas of Africa and African diaspora before and after World War I. (p. 695)

Panama Canal An aspect of American intervention in Latin America; resulted from United States support for a Panamanian independence movement in return for a grant to exclusive rights to a canal across the Panama isthmus; provided short route between Atlantic and Pacific oceans; completed 1914. (p. 613)

parliamentary monarchy Originated in England and Holland, 17th century, with kings partially checked by significant legislative powers in parliaments. (p. 394)

parliaments Bodies representing privileged groups; institutionalized feudal principle that rulers should consult with their vassals; found in England, Spain, Germany, and France. (p. 220)

partition of Poland Division of Polish territory among Russia, Prussia, and Austria in 1772, 1793, and 1795; eliminated Poland as independent state; part of expansion of Russian influence in eastern Europe. (p. 410)

party cadres Basis of China's communist government organization; cadre advisors were attached to military contingents at all levels. (p. 877)

Pasteur, Louis Discoverer of germs; discovery led to more conscientious sanitary regulation by the 1880s. (p. 544)

Paul One of the first Christian missionaries; moved away from insistence that adherents of the new religion follow Jewish law; use of Greek as language of Church. (p. 107)

Paulistas Backwoodsmen from São Paulo in Brazil; penetrated Brazilian interior in search of precious metals during 17th century. (p. 437)

Pearl Harbor American naval base in Hawaii; attack by Japanese on this facility in December 1941 crippled American fleet in the Pacific and caused entry of United States into World War II. (p. 761)

Pedro I Son and successor of João VI in Brazil; aided in the declaration of Brazilian independence from Portugal in 1822; became constitutional emperor of Brazil. (p. 593)

Peloponnesian Wars Wars from 431 to 404 B.C.E. between Athens and Sparta for dominance in southern Greece; resulted in Spartan victory but failure to achieve political unification of Greece. (p. 71)

peninsulares People living in the New World Spanish colonies but born in Spain. (p. 438)

People's Democratic Republic of Korea Northern half of Korea dominated by USSR; long headed by Kim Il-Sung; attacked south in 1950 and initiated Korean War; retained independence as a communist state after the war. (p. 866)

People's Liberation Army Chinese Communist army; administered much of country under People's Republic of China. (p. 877)

People's Republic of China Communist government of mainland China; proclaimed in 1949 following military success of Mao Zedong over forces of Chiang Kai-shek and the Guomindang. (p. 877)

perestroika [per uh *stroi* kuh] Policy of Mikhail Gorbachev calling for economic restructuring in the USSR in the late 1980s; more leeway for private ownership and decentralized control in industry and agriculture. (p. 897)

Pericles Athenian political leader during 5th century B.C.E.; guided development of Athenian Empire; died during early stages of Peloponnesian War. (p. 71)

Perón, Juan D. Military leader in Argentina who became dominant political figure after military coup in 1943; used position as Minister of Labor to appeal to working groups and the poor; became president in 1946; forced into exile in 1955; returned and won presidency in 1973. (p. 739)

Perry, Matthew American commodore who visited Edo Bay with American fleet in 1853; insisted on opening ports to American trade on threat of naval bombardment; won rights for American trade with Japan in 1854. (p. 653)

Persian Gulf War 1991 war led by United States and various European and Middle Eastern allies, against Iraqi occupation of Kuwait. The war led to Iraqi withdrawal and a long confrontation with Iraq about armaments and political regime. (p. 903)

Peter I Also known as Peter the Great; son of Alexis Romanov; ruled from 1689 to 1725; continued growth of absolutism and conquest; included more definite interest in changing selected aspects of economy and culture through imitation of western European models. (p. 406)

Petrarch, Francesco One of the major literary figures of the Western Renaissance; an Italian author and humanist. (p. 340)

pharaoh Title of kings of ancient Egypt. (p. 20)

Philip II Ruled Macedon from 359 to 336 B.C.E.; founder of centralized kingdom; later conquered rest of Greece, which was subjected to Macedonian authority. (p. 71)

Phoenicians Seafaring civilization located on the shores of the eastern Mediterranean; established colonies throughout the Mediterranean. (p. 25)

Pinsker, Leon European Zionist who believed that Jewish assimilation into Christian European nations was impossible; argued for return to Middle Eastern Holy Land. (p. 692)

Pizarro, Francisco Led conquest of Inca Empire of Peru beginning in 1535; by 1540, most of Inca possessions fell to the Spanish. (p. 370)

Plassey Battle in 1757 between troops of the British East India Company and an Indian army under Sirāj ud-daula, ruler of Bengal; British victory resulted in control of northern India. (p. 566)

Plato Greek philosopher; knowledge based on consideration of ideal forms outside the material world; proposed ideal form of government based on abstract principles in which philosophers ruled. (p. 80)

pochteca [poKH tAY cä] Special merchant class in Aztec society; specialized in long-distance trade in luxury items. (p. 246)

polis City-state form of government; typical of Greek political organization from 800 to 400 B.C.E. (pl. poleis). (p. 75)

Politburo Executive committee of the Soviet Communist party; 20 members. (p. 744)

Polynesia Islands contained in a rough triangle whose points lie in Hawaii, New Zealand, and Easter Island. (p. 97)

pope Bishop of Rome; head of the Christian Church in western Europe. (p. 107)

Popular Front Combination of socialist and communist political parties in France; won election in 1936; unable to take strong measures of social reform because of continuing strength of conservatives; fell from power in 1938. (p. 731)

population revolution Huge growth in population in western Europe beginning about 1730; prelude to Industrial Revolution; population of France increased 50 percent, England and Prussia 100 percent. (p. 536)

positivism French philosophy based on observation and scientific approach to problems of society; adopted by many Latin American liberals in the aftermath of independence. (p. 600)

Potosí Mine located in upper Peru (modern Bolivia); largest of New World silver mines; produced 80 percent of all Peruvian silver. (p. 432)

Potsdam Conference Meeting among leaders of the United States, Britain, and the Soviet Union just before the end of World War II in 1945; Allies agreed upon Soviet domination in eastern Europe; Germany and Austria to be divided among victorious Allies. (p. 765)

pragmatists Chinese Communist politicians such as Zhou Enlai, Deng Xiaoping, and Liu Shaoqi; determined to restore state direction and market incentives at the local level; opposed Great Leap Forward. (p. 880)

presidencies Three districts that made up the bulk of the directly ruled British territories in India; capitals at Madras, Calcutta, and Bombay. (p. 568)

Prester John Name given to a mythical Christian monarch whose kingdom had supposedly been cut off from Europe by the Muslim conquests; Chinggis Khan was originally believed to be this mythical ruler. (p. 323)

PRI Party of the Institutionalized Revolution; dominant political party in Mexico; developed during the 1920s and 1930s; incorporated labor, peasant, military, and middle-class sectors; controlled other political organizations in Mexico. (p. 816)

primary products Food or industrial crops for which there is a high demand in industrialized economies; prices of such products tend to fluctuate widely; typically the primary exports of Third World economies. (p. 846)

princely states Domains of Indian princes allied with the British Raj; agents of East India Company were stationed at the rulers' courts to ensure compliance; made up over one-third of the British Indian Empire. (p. 568)

proletariat Class of working people without access to producing property; typically manufacturing workers, paid laborers in agricultural economy, or urban poor; in Europe, product of economic changes of 16th and 17th centuries. (p. 387)

Protestantism General wave of religious dissent against Catholic church; generally held to have begun with Martin Luther's attack on Catholic beliefs in 1517; included many varieties of religious belief. (p. 384)

proto-industrialization Preliminary shift away from agricultural economy in Europe; workers become full- or part-time producers of textile and metal products, working at home but in a capitalist system in which materials, work orders, and ultimate sales depended on urban merchants; prelude to Industrial Revolution. (p. 537)

Pugachev rebellion During 1770s in reign of Catherine the Great; led by cossack Emelian Pugachev, who claimed to be legitimate tsar; eventually crushed; typical of peasant unrest during the 18th century and thereafter. (p. 409)

Punic Wars Fought between Rome and Carthage to establish dominance in the western Mediterranean; won by Rome after three separate conflicts. (p. 72)

pure land Buddhism Emphasized salvationist aspects of Chinese Buddhism; popular among masses of Chinese society. (p. 268)

Puyi Last emperor of China; deposed as emperor while still a small boy in 1912. (p. 637)

pyramids Monumental architecture typical of Old Kingdom Egypt; used as burial sites for pharaohs. (p. 20)

Qin dynasty [chin] Established in 221 B.C.E. at the end of the Warring States period following the decline of the Zhou dynasty; fell in 207 B.C.E. (p. 37)

Qing Manchu dynasty that seized control of China in mid-17th century after decline of Ming; forced submission of nomadic peoples far to the west and compelled tribute from Vietnam and Burma to the south. (p. 630)

Quetzalcoatl [ket säl kO ät l] Toltec deity; Feathered Serpent; adopted by Aztecs as a major god. (p. 240)

quipu System of knotted strings utilized by the Incas in place of a writing system; could contain numerical and other types of information for censuses and financial records. (p. 256)

Quit India movement Mass civil disobedience campaign that began in the summer of 1942 to end British control of India. (p. 767)

Qur'an [koo *rän*, *-ran*] Recitations of revelations received by Muhammad; holy book of Islam. (p. 121)

Quraysh [koor *Ish*] Tribe of bedouins that controlled Mecca. (p. 125)

Qutb-ud-din Aibak [kUt bUd *dEEn* I *bäk*] Lieutenant of Muhammad of Ghur; established kingdom in India with capital at Delhi; proclaimed himself Sultan of India. (p. 162)

radical Political viewpoint with origins in western Europe during the 19th century; advocated broader voting rights than liberals; in some cases advocated outright democracy; urged reforms in favor of the lower classes. (p. 541)

Rajput [*räj* pUt] Regional princes in India following collapse of empire; emphasized military control of their regions. (p. 99)

Ramadan Islamic month of religious observance requiring fasting from dawn to sunset. (p. 130)

Ramayana One of the great epic tales from classical India; traces adventures of King Rama and his wife, Sita. (p. 52)

Recopilación [rAY kO pEEl ä sEE *On*] Body of laws collected in 1681 for Spanish possessions in New World; basis of law in the Indies. (p. 434)

Red Army Military organization constructed under leadership of Leon Trotsky, Bolshevik follower of Lenin; made use of people of humble background. (p. 715)

Red Guard Student brigades utilized by Mao Zedong and his political allies during the Cultural Revolution to discredit Mao's political enemies. (p. 882)

Red Heads Name given to Safavid followers because of their distinctive red headgear. (p. 483)

Reform Bill of 1832 Legislation passed in Great Britain that extended the vote to most members of the middle class; failed to produce democracy in Britain. (p. 541)

reincarnation The successive attachment of the soul to some animate form according to merits earned in previous lives. (p. 58)

religious revivalism An approach to religious belief and practice that stresses the literal interpretation of texts sacred to the religion in question and the application of their precepts to all aspects of social life; increasingly associated with revivalist movements in a number of world religions, including Christianity, Islam, Judaism, and Hinduism. (p. 846)

Renaissance Cultural and political movement in western Europe; began in Italy c. 1400; rested on urban vitality and expanding commerce; featured a literature and art with distinctly more secular priorities than those of the Middle Ages. (p. 340)

Republic of Korea Southern half of Korea sponsored by United States following World War II; headed by nationalist Syngman Rhee; developed parliamentary institutions but maintained authoritarian government; defended by UN forces during Korean War; underwent industrialization and economic emergence after 1950s. (p. 866)

revisionism Socialist movements that at least tacitly disavowed Marxist revolutionary doctrine; believed social success could be achieved gradually through political institutions. (p. 549)

Rhodes, Cecil British entrepreneur in south Africa around 1900; manipulated political situation in south Africa to gain entry to resources of Boer republics; encouraged Boer War as means of destroying Boer independence. (p. 583)

Ricci, Matteo [*rEEt* chEE] Along with Adam Schall, Jesuit scholar in court of Ming emperors; skilled scientist; won few converts to Christianity. (p. 516)

Ridda Wars Wars that followed Muhammad's death in 632; resulted in defeat of rival prophets and some of larger clans; restored unity of Islam. (p. 131)

Rio de Janeiro Brazilian port; close to mines of Minas Gerais; importance grew with gold strikes; became colonial capital in 1763. (p. 437)

Rivera, Diego [ri *vär* uh] Mexican artist of the period after the Mexican Revolution; famous for murals painted on walls of public buildings; mixed romantic images of the Indian past with Christian symbols and Marxist ideology. (p. 712)

Roman republic The balanced constitution of Rome from c. 510 to 47 B.C.E.; featured an aristocratic Senate, a panel of magistrates, and several popular assemblies. (p. 72)

Romance of the West Chamber Chinese dramatic work written during the Yuan period; indicative of the continued literary vitality of China during Mongol rule. (p. 329)

Romanov, Alexis Second Romanov tsar; abolished assemblies of nobles; gained new powers over Russian Orthodox church. (p. 406)

Romanov dynasty Dynasty elected in 1613 at end of Time of Troubles; ruled Russia until 1917. (p. 405)

romanticism Artistic and literary movement of the 19th century in Europe; held that emotion and impression, not reason, were the keys to the mysteries of human experience and nature; sought to portray passions, not calm reflection. (p. 552)

Rosas, Juan Manuel de Strongman leader in Buenos Aires; took power in 1831; commanded loyalty of gauchos; restored local autonomy. (p. 598)

Rowlatt Act Placed severe restrictions on key Indian civil rights such as freedom of the press; acted to offset the concessions granted under Montagu-Chelmsford reforms of 1919. (p. 688)

Roy, Ram Mohun Western-educated Indian leader, early 19th century; cooperated with British to outlaw sati. (p. 572)

Royal African Company Chartered in 1660s to establish a monopoly over the slave trade among British merchants; supplied African slaves to colonies in Barbados, Jamaica, and Virginia. (p. 453)

Rurik Legendary Scandinavian, regarded as founder of the first kingdom of Russia based in Kiev in 855 C.E. (p. 205)

Russian Orthodoxy Russian form of Christianity imported from Byzantine Empire and combined with local religion; king characteristically controlled major appointments. (p. 206)

Russo-Japanese War War between Japan and Russia (1904–1905) over territory in Manchuria; Japan defeated the Russians, largely because of its naval power; Japan annexed Korea in 1910 as a result of military dominance. (p. 651)

Sadat, Anwar Successor to Gamal Abdul Nasser as ruler of Egypt; acted to dismantle costly state programs; accepted peace treaty with Israel in 1973; opened Egypt to investment by Western nations. (p. 853)

Safavid dynasty Originally a Turkic nomadic group; family originated in Sufi mystic group; espoused Shi'ism; conquered territory and established kingdom in region equivalent to modern Iran; lasted until 1722. (p. 473)

Sahara Desert running across northern Africa; separates the Mediterranean coast from southern Africa. (p. 95)

sahel The extensive grassland belt at the southern edge of the Sahara; a point of exchange between the forests to the south and northern Africa. (p. 176)

Sail al-Din [sä EEl al din, dEEn] Early 14th-century Sufi mystic; began campaign to purify Islam; first member of Safavid dynasty. (p. 482)

Saladin Muslim leader in the last decades of the 12th century; reconquered most of the crusader outposts for Islam. (p. 151)

saltwater slaves Slaves transported from Africa; almost invariably black. (p. 467)

samurai Mounted troops of Japanese warrior leaders (bushi); loyal to local lords, not the emperor. (p. 292)

San Martin, José de Leader of independence movement in Rio de la Plata; led to independence of the United Provinces of the Rio de la Plata by 1816; later led independence movement in Chile and Peru as well. (p. 592)

Sandinista party Nicaraguan socialist movement named after Augusto Sandino; successfully carried out a socialist revolution in Nicaragua during the 1980s. (p. 824)

Sandino, Augusto Led a guerrilla resistance movement against U.S. occupation forces in Nicaragua; assassinated by Nicaraguan National Guard in 1934; became national hero and symbol of resistance to U.S. influence in Central America. (p. 825)

Sanskrit The sacred and classical Indian language. (p. 52)

Santa Anna, General Antonio López de Seized power in Mexico after collapse of empire of Mexico in 1824; after brief reign of liberals, seized power in 1835 as caudillo; defeated by Texans in war for independence in 1836; defeated by United States in Mexican-American War in 1848; unseated by liberal rebellion in 1854. (p. 598)

Santa Cruz, Andrés Mestizo general who established union of independent Peru and Bolivia between 1829 and 1839. (p. 595)

Sarajevo Administrative center of the Bosnian province of Austrian Empire; assassination here of Archduke Ferdinand in 1914 started World War I. (p. 674)

Sarmiento, Domingo F. Liberal politician and president of Argentine Republic; author of *Facundo*, a critique of caudillo politics; increased international trade, launched internal reforms in education and transportation. (p. 604)

satyagraha [*sut* yuh gruhuh, suht *yä* gruh-] Literally, "truth-force"; strategy of nonviolent protest developed by Mohandas Gandhi and his followers in India; later deployed throughout the colonized world and in the United States. (p. 688)

Schall, Adam Along with Matteo Ricci, Jesuit scholar in court of Ming emperors; skilled scientist; won few converts to Christianity. (p. 516)

scholar-gentry Chinese class created by the marital linkage of the local land-holding aristocracy with the office-holding shi; superseded shi as governors of China. (p. 62)

scholasticism Dominant medieval philosophical approach; so-called because of its base in the schools or universities; based on use of logic to resolve theological problems. (p. 225)

school of National Learning New ideology that laid emphasis on Japan's unique historical experience and the revival of indigenous culture at the expense of Chinese imports such as Confucianism; typical of Japan in 18th century. (p. 521)

Scientific Revolution Culminated in 17th century; period of empirical advances associated with the development of wider theoretical generalizations; resulted in change in traditional beliefs of Middle Ages. (p. 388)

Secret Army Organization (OAS) Organization of French settlers in Algeria; led guerrilla war following independence during the 1960s; assaults directed against Arabs, Berbers, and French who advocated independence. (p. 772)

self-determination Right of people in a region to determine whether to be independent or not. (p. 682)

Seljuk Turks Nomadic invaders from central Asia via Persia; staunch Sunnis;

ruled in name of Abbasid caliphs from mid-11th century. (p. 151)

Selim III Sultan who ruled Ottoman Empire from 1789 to 1807; aimed at improving administrative efficiency and building a new army and navy; toppled by Janissaries in 1807. (p. 621)

Senate Assembly of Roman aristocrats; advised on policy within the republic; one of the early elements of the Roman constitution. (p. 76)

Senghor, Léopold Sédar One of the post–World War I writers of the négritude literary movement that urged pride in African values. (p. 696)

sepoys Troops that served the British East India Company; recruited from various warlike peoples of India. (p. 565)

seppuku Ritual suicide or disembowelment in Japan; commonly known in West as hara-kiri; demonstrated courage and a means to restore family honor. (p. 293)

serfs Peasant agricultural laborers within the manorial system of the Middle Ages. (p. 215)

settlement colonies Areas, such as North America and Australia, that were both conquered by European invaders and settled by large numbers of European migrants who made the colonized areas their permanent home and dispersed and decimated the indigenous inhabitants. (p. 576)

Seven Years' War Fought both in continental Europe and also in overseas colonies between 1756 and 1763; resulted in Prussian seizures of land from Austria, English seizures of colonies in India and North America. (p. 372)

Shah-Nama Written by Firdawsi in late 10th and early 11th centuries; relates history of Persia from creation to the Islamic conquests. (p. 154)

Shang First Chinese dynasty for which archeological evidence exists; capital located in Ordos bend. (p. 24)

Sharia [shä *rEE* ä] Islamic law; defined among other things the patrilineal nature of Islamic inheritance. (p. 181)

shaykhs [shAYks] Leaders of tribes and clans within bedouin society; usually men with large herds, several wives, and many children. (p. 123)

Shi Huangdi [*shOE hwäng dEE*] Founder of the brief Qin dynasty in 221 B.C.E. (p. 37)

Shi'a Also known as Shi'ites; political and theological division within Islam; followers of Ali. (p. 133)

Shinto Religion of early Japanese culture; devotees worshipped numerous gods and spirits associated with the natural world; offers of food and prayers made to gods and nature spirits. (p. 96)

Shiva The Brahman, later Hindu, god of destruction and reproduction; worshipped as the personification of cosmic forces of change. (p. 58)

shoguns Military leaders of the bakufu (military government in 12th-century Japan). (p. 294)

Shrivijaya [srEE wi *jō* yuh] Trading empire centered on Malacca Straits between Malaya and Sumatra; controlled trade of empire; Buddhist government resistant to Muslim missionaries; fall opened up southeastern Asia to Muslim conversion. (p. 165)

Sikhs Sect in northwest India; early leaders tried to bridge differences between Hindu and Muslim, but Mughal persecution led to anti-Muslim feeling. (p. 496)

Silk Roads The most famous of the trading routes established by pastoral nomads connecting the European, Indian, and Chinese civilizations; transmitted goods and ideas among civilizations. (pp. 49, 94)

Silla Independent Korean kingdom in southeastern part of peninsula; defeated Koguryo along with their Chinese Tang allies; submitted as a vassal of the Tang emperor and agreed to tribute payment; ruled united Korea by 668. (p. 299)

Sinification Extensive adaptation of Chinese culture in other regions; typical of Korea and Japan, less typical of Vietnam. (p. 299)

Sino-Japanese War War fought between Japan and Qing China between 1894 and 1895; resulted in Japanese victory; frustrated Japanese imperial aims because of Western insistence that Japan withdraw from Liaodong peninsula. (p. 659)

Sisulu, Walter Black African leader who, along with Nelson Mandela, opposed apartheid system in South Africa. (p. 858)

slash and burn agriculture A system of cultivation typical of shifting cultivators; forest floors cleared by fire are then planted. (p. 13)

Smith, Adam Established liberal economics (*Wealth of Nations*, 1776); argued that government should avoid regulation of economy in favor of the operation of market forces. (p. 395)

social question Issues relating to repressed classes in western Europe during the Industrial Revolution, particularly workers and women; became more critical than constitutional issues after 1870. (p. 548)

socialism Political movement with origins in western Europe during the 19th century; urged an attack on private property in the name of equality; wanted state control of means of production, end to capitalist exploitation of the working man. (p. 548)

socialism in one country Joseph Stalin's concept of Russian communism based solely on the Soviet Union rather than the Leninist concept of international revolution; by cutting off the Soviet Union from other economies, the USSR avoided worst consequences of the Great Depression. (p. 730)

socialist realism Attempt within the USSR to relate formal culture to the masses in order to avoid the adoption of western European cultural forms; begun under Joseph Stalin; fundamental method of Soviet fiction, art, and literary criticism. (p. 744)

sociedad de castas American social system based on racial origins; Europeans or whites at top, black slaves or Native Americans at bottom, mixed races in middle. (p. 438)

Socrates Athenian philosopher of later 5th century B.C.E.; tutor of Plato; urged rational reflection of moral decisions; condemned to death for corrupting minds of Athenian young. (p. 80)

Solidarity Polish labor movement formed in 1970s under Lech Walesa; challenged USSR-dominated government of Poland. (p. 800)

Solzhenitsyn, Aleksandr [sOl zhuh *nEEt* sin, sol-] Russian author critical of the Soviet regime but also of Western materialism; published trilogy on the Siberian prison camps, *The Gulag Archipelago*. (p. 803)

Songhay Successor state to Mali; dominated middle reaches of Niger valley; formed as independent kingdom under a Berber dynasty; capital at Gao; reached imperial status under Sunni Ali (1464–1492). (p. 180)

Sophocles Greek writer of tragedies; author of *Oedipus Rex*. (p. 81)

Southern Song Rump state of Song dynasty from 1127 to 1279; carved out of much larger domains ruled by the Tang and northern Song; culturally one of the most glorious reigns in Chinese history. (p. 275)

Spanish-American War War fought between Spain and the United States beginning in 1898; centered on Cuba and Puerto Rico; permitted American intervention in Caribbean, annexation of Puerto Rico and the Philippines. (p. 613)

Spanish Civil War War pitting authoritarian and military leaders in Spain against republicans and leftists between 1936 and 1939; Germany and Italy supported the royalists; the Soviet Union supported the republicans; led to victory of the royalist forces. (p. 736)

split inheritance Inca practice of descent; all titles and political power went to successor, but wealth and land remained in hands of male descendants for support of cult of dead Inca's mummy. (p. 252)

Stalin, Joseph   Successor to Lenin as head of the USSR; strongly nationalist view of communism; represented anti-Western strain of Russian tradition; crushed opposition to his rule; established series of five-year plans to replace New Economic Policy; fostered agricultural collectivization; led USSR through World War II; furthered cold war with western Europe and the United States; died in 1953. (p. 716)

stateless societies   African societies organized around kinship or other forms of obligation and lacking the concentration of political power and authority associated with states. (p. 173)

Stoics   Hellenistic group of philosophers; emphasized inner moral independence cultivated by strict discipline of the body and personal bravery. (p. 79)

Stolypin reforms   Reforms introduced by the Russian interior minister Piotyr Stolypin intended to placate the peasantry in the aftermath of the Revolution of 1905; included reduction in redemption payments, attempt to create market-oriented peasantry. (p. 651)

stupas   Stone shrines built to house pieces of bone or hair and personal possessions said to be relics of the Buddha; preserved Buddhist architectural forms. (p. 61)

Sudanic states   Kingdoms that developed during the height of Ghana's power in the region; based at Takrur on the Senegal River to the west and Gao on the Niger River to the east; included Mali and Songhay. (p. 176)

Suez Canal   Built across Isthmus of Suez to connect Mediterranean Sea with Red Sea in 1869; financed by European investors; with increasing indebtedness of khedives, permitted intervention of British into Egyptian politics to protect their investment. (p. 626)

Sufis   Mystics within Islam; responsible for expansion of Islam to southeastern Asia. (p. 156)

Sui   Dynasty that succeeded the Han in China; emerged from strong rulers in northern China; united all of northern China and reconquered southern China. (p. 98)

Sumerians   People who migrated into Mesopotamia c. 4000 B.C.E.; created first civilization within region; organized area into city-states. (p. 17)

Sun Yat-sen   Head of Revolutionary Alliance, organization that led 1911 revolt against Qing dynasty in China; briefly elected president in 1911, but yielded in favor of Yuan Shikai in 1912; created Nationalist party of China (Guomindang) in 1919; died in 1925. (p. 636)

Sundiata   The "Lion Prince"; a member of the Keita clan; created a unified state that became the Mali Empire; died about 1260. (p. 177)

Sunnis   Political and theological division within Islam; followers of the Umayyads. (p. 133)

Supreme Soviet   Parliament of Union of Soviet Socialist Republics; elected by universal suffrage; actually controlled by Communist party; served to ratify party decisions. (p. 715)

Suriname   Formerly a Dutch plantation colony on the coast of South America; location of runaway slave kingdom in 18th century; able to retain independence despite attempts to crush guerrilla resistance. (p. 469)

Swazi   New African state formed on model of Zulu chiefdom; survived mfecane. (p. 464)

syndicalism   Economic and political system based on the organization of labor; imported in Latin America from European political movements; militant force in Latin American politics. (p. 737)

Taika reforms   [*tI* kä] Attempt to remake Japanese monarch into an absolute Chinese-style emperor; included attempts to create professional bureaucracy and peasant conscript army. (p. 288)

Taiping rebellion   Broke out in south China in the 1850s and early 1860s; led by Hong Xiuquan, a semi-Christianized prophet; sought to overthrow Qing dynasty and Confucian basis of scholar-gentry. (p. 634)

Taira   Powerful Japanese family in 11th and 12th centuries; competed with Minamoto family; defeated after Gempei Wars. (p. 293)

Taiwan   Island off Chinese mainland; became refuge for Nationalist Chinese regime under Chiang Kai-shek as Republic of China in 1948; successfully retained independence with aid of United States; rapidly industrialized after 1950s. (p. 864)

Taj Mahal   Most famous architectural achievement of Mughal India; originally built as a mausoleum for the wife of Shah Jahan, Mumtaz Mahal. (p. 494)

tambos   Way stations used by Incas as inns and storehouses; supply centers for Inca armies on move; relay points for system of runners used to carry messages. (p. 254)

Tang   Dynasty that succeeded the Sui in 618 C.E.; more stable than previous dynasty. (p. 98)

Tangut   Rulers of Xi Xia kingdom of northwest China; one of regional kingdoms during period of southern Song; conquered by Mongols in 1226. (p. 274)

Tanzimat reforms   Series of reforms in Ottoman Empire between 1839 and 1876; established Western-style university, state postal system, railways, extensive legal reforms; resulted in creation of new constitution in 1876. (p. 622)

Tatars   Mongols; captured Russian cities and largely destroyed Kievan state in 1236; left Russian Orthodoxy and aristocracy intact. (p. 208)

Tayson Rebellion   Peasant revolution in southern Vietnam during the late 1770s; succeeded in toppling the Nguyen dynasty; subsequently unseated the Trinh dynasty of northern Vietnam. (p. 884)

technocrat   New type of bureaucrat; intensely trained in engineering or economics and devoted to the power of national planning; came to fore in offices of governments following World War II. (p. 785)

Tehran Conference   Meeting among leaders of the United States, Britain, and the Soviet Union in 1943; agreed to the opening of a new front in France. (p. 765)

Temple of the Sun   Inca religious center located at Cuzco; center of state religion; held mummies of past Incas. (p. 253)

Tenochtitlan   [tAY nôch tEE *tlän*] Founded c. 1325 on marshy island in Lake Texcoco; became center of Aztec power; joined with Tlacopan and Texcoco in 1434 to form a triple alliance that controlled most of central plateau of Mesoamerica. (p. 242)

Teotihuacan   [tAY O tEE wä *kän*] Site of classic culture in central Mexico; urban center with important religious functions; supported by intensive agriculture in surrounding regions; population of as much as 200,000. (p. 96)

terakoya   Commoner schools founded during the Tokugawa Shogunate in Japan to teach reading, writing, and the rudiments of Confucianism; resulted in high literacy rate, approaching 40 percent, of Japanese males. (p. 652)

The Tale of Genji   Written by Lady Murasaki; first novel in any language; relates life history of prominent and amorous son of the Japanese emperor; evidence for mannered style of Japanese society. (p. 290)

third Rome   Russian claim to be successor state to Roman and Byzantine empires; based in part on continuity of Orthodox church in Russia following fall of Constantinople in 1453. (p. 404)

third world   Also known as developing nations; nations outside the capitalist industrial nations of the first world and the industrialized communist nations of the second world; generally less economically powerful, but with varied economies. (p. 813)

Thirty Years' War   War within the Holy Roman Empire between German Protestants and their allies (Sweden, Denmark, France) and the emperor and his ally,

Spain; ended in 1648 after great destruction with Treaty of Westphalia. (p. 385)

three-field system System of agricultural cultivation by 9th century in western Europe; included one-third in spring grains, one-third fallow. (p. 215)

Tilak, B. G. Believed that nationalism in India should be based on appeals to Hindu religiosity; worked to promote the restoration and revival of ancient Hindu traditions; offended Muslims and other religious groups; first populist leader in India. (p. 687)

Timbuktu Port city of Mali; located just off the flood plain on the great bend in the Niger River; population of 50,000; contained a library and university. (p. 179)

Time of Troubles Followed death of Ivan IV without heir early in 17th century; boyars attempted to use vacuum of power to reestablish their authority; ended with selection of Michael Romanov as tsar in 1613. (p. 405)

Timur-i Lang Also known as Tamerlane; leader of Turkic nomads; beginning in 1360s from base at Samarkand, launched series of attacks in Persia, the Fertile Crescent, India, and southern Russia; empire disintegrated after his death in 1405. (p. 331)

Tlaloc [tlä *lOk*] Major god of Aztecs; associated with fertility and the agricultural cycle; god of rain. (p. 242)

Tokugawa Shogunate Founded 1603 when Tokugawa Ieyasu made shogun by Japanese emperor; ended the civil wars and brought political unity to Japan. (p. 519)

Toltec culture Succeeded Teotihuacan culture in central Mexico; strongly militaristic ethic including human sacrifice; influenced large territory after 1000 C.E.; declined after 1200 C.E. (p. 240)

Topiltzin Religious leader and reformer of the Toltecs; dedicated to god Quetzalcoatl; after losing struggle for power, went into exile in the Yucatan peninsula. (p. 240)

totalitarian state A new kind of government in the 20th century that exercised massive, direct control over virtually all the activities of its subjects; existed in Germany, Italy, and the Soviet Union. (p. 732)

Tragic Week Occurred in Argentina in 1919; government response to general strike of labor forces led to brutal repression under guise of nationalism. (p. 737)

trans-Siberian railroad Constructed in 1870s to connect European Russia with the Pacific; completed by the end of the 1880s; brought Russia into a more active Asian role. (p. 648)

trasformismo Political system in late 19th-century Italy that promoted alliance of conservatives and liberals; parliamentary deputies of all parties supported the status quo. (p. 547)

Treaty of Guadalupe-Hidalgo Agreement that ended the Mexican-American War; provided for loss of Texas and California to the United States; left legacy of distrust of the United States in Latin America. (p. 601)

Treaty of Paris Arranged in 1763 following Seven Years' War; granted New France to England in exchange for return of French sugar island in Caribbean. (p. 372)

Treaty of Tordesillas [tor duh *sEEl* yäs, -*sEE-*] Signed in 1494 between Castile and Portugal; clarified spheres of influence and rights of possession in New World; reserved Brazil and all newly discovered lands east of Brazil to Portugal; granted all lands west of Brazil to Spain. (p. 434)

Treaty of Westphalia Ended Thirty Years' War in 1648; granted right to individual rulers within the Holy Roman Empire to choose their own religion—either Protestant or Catholic. (p. 385)

triangular trade Commerce linking Africa, the New World colonies, and Europe; slaves carried to America for sugar and tobacco transported to Europe. (p. 454)

Trinh Dynasty that ruled in north Vietnam at Hanoi; rivals of Nguyen family in south. (pp. 309, 884)

Triple Alliance Alliance among Germany, Austria–Hungary, and Italy at the end of the 19th century; part of European alliance system and balance of power prior to World War I. (p. 558)

Triple Entente Alliance among Britain, Russia, and France at the outset of the 20th century; part of European alliance system and balance of power prior to World War I. (p. 558)

Truman, Harry American president from 1945 to 1952; less eager for smooth relations with the Soviet Union than Franklin Roosevelt; authorized use of atomic bomb during World War II; architect of American diplomacy that initiated the cold war. (p. 781)

Trung sisters Leaders of one of the frequent peasant rebellions in Vietnam against Chinese rule; revolt broke out in 39 C.E.; demonstrates importance of Vietnamese women in indigenous society. (p. 306)

tumens Basic fighting units of the Mongol forces; consisted of 10,000 cavalrymen; each unit was further divided into units of 1000, 100, and 10. (p. 318)

Tutu, Osei [*tU* tU] Member of Oyoko clan of Akan peoples in Gold Coast region of Africa; responsible for creating unified Asante Empire; utilized Western firearms. (p. 457)

Twantinsuyu [twän tin sU yU] Word for Inca Empire; region from present-day Colombia to Chile and eastward to northern Argentina. (p. 251)

ulama Orthodox religious scholars within Islam; pressed for a more conservative and restrictive theology; increasingly opposed to non-Islamic ideas and scientific thinking. (p. 156)

Ulyanov, Vladimir Ilyich [Ul *yä* nuhf] Better known as Lenin; most active Russian Marxist leader; insisted on importance of disciplined revolutionary cells; leader of Bolshevik Revolution of 1917. (p. 650)

Umayyad [U *mI* yad] Clan of Quraysh that dominated politics and commercial economy of Mecca; clan later able to establish dynasty as rulers of Islam. (p. 125)

umma Community of the faithful within Islam; transcended old tribal boundaries to create degree of political unity. (p. 129)

Union of Soviet Socialist Republics Federal system of socialist republics established in 1923 in various ethnic regions of Russia; firmly controlled by Communist party; diminished nationalities protest under Bolsheviks; dissolved 1991. (p. 715)

United Fruit Company Most important foreign economic concern in Guatemala during the 20th century; attempted land reform aimed at United Fruit caused U.S. intervention in Guatemalan politics leading to ouster of reform government in 1954. (p. 819)

United Nations International organization formed in the aftermath of World War II; included all of the victorious Allies; its primary mission was to provide a forum for negotiating disputes. (p. 764)

untouchables Lowest caste in Indian society; performed tasks that were considered polluting—street sweeping, removal of human waste, and tanning. (p. 53)

Upanishads [U *pan* i shad, U *pä* ni shäd] Later books of the Vedas; contained sophisticated and sublime philosophical ideas; utilized by Brahmans to restore religious authority. (p. 52)

Urban II Called First Crusade in 1095; appealed to Christians to mount military assault to free the Holy Land from the Muslims. (p. 221)

Uthman Third caliph and member of Umayyad clan; murdered by mutinous warriors returning from Egypt; death set off civil war in Islam between followers of Ali and the Umayyad clan. (p. 132)

Valdivia, Pedro de Spanish conquistador; conquered Araucanian Indians of Chile and established city of Santiago in 1541. (p. 427)

Vargas, Getúlio [*vär* guhs] Elected president of Brazil in 1929; launched centralized political program by imposing federal administrators over state governments; held off coups by communists in 1935 and fascists in 1937; imposed a new constitution based on Mussolini's Italy; leaned to communists after 1949; committed suicide in 1954. (p. 738)

varnas Clusters of caste groups in Aryan society; four social castes—Brahmans (priests), warriors, merchants, and peasants; beneath four Aryan castes was group of socially untouchable Dasas. (p. 53)

vassals Members of the military elite who received land or a benefice from a lord in return for military service and loyalty. (p. 219)

Vedas Aryan hymns originally transmitted orally but written down in sacred books from the 6th century B.C.E. (p. 52)

viceroyalties Two major divisions of Spanish colonies in New World; one based in Lima; the other in Mexico City; direct representatives of the king. (p. 434)

Vichy French collaborationist government established in 1940 in southern France following defeat of French armies by the Germans. (p. 757)

Viet Cong Name given by Diem regime to communist guerrilla movement in southern Vietnam; reorganized with northern Vietnamese assistance as the National Liberation Front in 1958. (p. 887)

Viet Minh Communist-dominated Vietnamese nationalist movement; operated out of base in southern China during World War II; employed guerrilla tactics similar to the Maoists in China. (p. 886)

Vietnamese Nationalist party Also known as the Vietnamese Quoc Dan Dong or VNQDD; active in 1920s as revolutionary force committed to violent overthrow of French colonialism. (p. 885)

Vikings Seagoing Scandinavian raiders from Sweden, Denmark, and Norway who disrupted coastal areas of western Europe from the 8th to the 11th centuries. (p. 214)

Villa, Pancho [*vEE* uh] Mexican revolutionary and military commander in northern Mexico during the Mexican Revolution; succeeded along with Emiliano Zapata in removing Díaz from power; also participated in campaigns that removed Madero and Huerta. (p. 711)

Vishnu The Brahman, later Hindu, god of sacrifice; widely worshipped. (p. 58)

Vivaldis Two Genoese brothers who attempted to find a Western route to the "Indies"; disappeared in 1291; precursors of thrust into southern Atlantic. (p. 343)

vizier [vi *zEEr*, *viz* yuhr] Ottoman equivalent of the Abbasid wazir; head of the Ottoman bureaucracy; after 15th century often more powerful than sultan. (p. 477)

Vladimir I Ruler of Russian kingdom of Kiev from 980 to 1015; converted kingdom to Christianity. (p. 205)

vodun African religious ideas and practices among descendants of African slaves in Haiti. (p. 468)

Wafd party [wäft] Egyptian nationalist party that emerged after an Egyptian delegation was refused a hearing at the Versailles treaty negotiations following World War I; led by Sa'd Zaghlul; negotiations eventually led to limited Egyptian independence beginning in 1922. (p. 693)

Wang Anshi Confucian scholar and chief minister of a Song emperor in 1070s; introduced sweeping reforms based on Legalists; advocated greater state intervention in society. (p. 274)

War of the Spanish Succession Resulted from Bourbon family's succession to Spanish throne in 1701; ended by Treaty of Utrecht in 1713; resulted in recognition of Bourbons, loss of some lands, grants of commercial rights to English and French. (p. 441)

Warsaw Pact Alliance organized by Soviet Union with its eastern European satellites to balance formation of NATO by Western powers in 1949. (p. 782)

wazir Chief administrative official under the Abbasid caliphate; initially recruited from Persian provinces of empire. (p. 138)

Wendi Member of prominent northern Chinese family during period of Six Dynasties; proclaimed himself emperor; supported by nomadic peoples of northern China; established Sui dynasty. (p. 264)

welfare state New activism of the western European state in economic policy and welfare issues after World War II; introduced programs to reduce the impact of economic inequality; typically included medical programs and economic planning. (p. 784)

Western Front Front established in World War I; generally along line from Belgium to Switzerland; featured trench warfare and horrendous casualties for all sides in the conflict. (p. 671)

Whampoa Military Academy Founded in 1924; military wing of the Guomindang; first head of the academy was Chiang Kai-shek. (p. 722)

White Dominions Colonies in which European settlers made up the overwhelming majority of the population; small numbers of native inhabitants were typically reduced by disease and wars of conquest; typical of British holdings in North America and Australia with growing independence in the 19th century. (p. 576)

White Lotus Society Secret religious society dedicated to overthrow of Yuan

dynasty in China; typical of peasant resistance to Mongol rule. (p. 329)

white racial supremacy Belief in the inherent mental, moral, and cultural superiority of whites; peaked in acceptance in decades before World War I; supported by social science doctrines of social Darwinists such as Herbert Spencer. (p. 580)

Wilberforce, William British statesman and reformer; leader of abolitionist movement in English parliament that led to end of English slave trade in 1807. (p. 470)

William the Conqueror Invaded England from Normandy in 1066; extended tight feudal system to England; established administrative system based on sheriffs; established centralized monarchy. (p. 220)

witchcraft persecution Reflected resentment against the poor, uncertainties about religious truth; resulted in death of over 100,000 Europeans between 1590 and 1650; particularly common in Protestant areas. (p. 388)

Witte, Sergei [*vit* uh] Russian minister of finance from 1892 to 1903; economic modernizer responsible for high tariffs, improved banking system; encouraged Western investors to build factories in Russia. (p. 648)

Wollstonecraft, Mary Enlightenment feminist thinker in England; argued that new political rights should extend to women. (p. 397)

World Zionist Organization Founded by Theodor Herzl to promote Jewish migration to and settlement in Palestine to form a Zionist state. (p. 692)

Wuzong Chinese emperor of Tang dynasty who openly persecuted Buddhism by destroying monasteries in 840s; reduced influence of Chinese Buddhism in favor of Confucian ideology. (p. 270)

Xavier, Francis [*zAY* vEE uhr, *zav* EE-, *zAY* vyuhr] Spanish Jesuit missionary; worked in India in 1540s among the outcaste and lower caste groups; made little headway among elites. (p. 507)

Xi Xia Kingdom of Tangut people, north of Song kingdom, in mid-11th century; collected tribute that drained Song resources and burdened Chinese peasantry. (p. 274)

Xuanzong [*shU* än jonh, shwantsong] Leading Chinese emperor of the Tang dynasty who reigned from 713 to 755 though he encouraged overexpansion. (p. 271)

Yalta Conference Meeting among leaders of the United States, Britain, and the Soviet Union in 1945; agreed to Soviet entry into the Pacific war in return for possessions in Manchuria, organization of the

United Nations; disputed the division of political organization in the eastern European states to be reestablished after the war. (p. 765)

yanas A class of people within Inca society removed from their ayllus to serve permanently as servants, artisans, or workers for the inca or the Inca nobility. (p. 255)

Yang Guifei [*yäng gwä fä*] Royal concubine during reign of Xuanzong; introduction of relatives into royal administration led to revolt. (p. 271)

Yangdi Second member of Sui dynasty; murdered his father to gain throne; restored Confucian examination system; responsible for construction of Chinese canal system; assassinated in 618. (p. 265)

Yaroslav Last of great Kievan monarchs; issued legal codification based on formal codes developed in Byzantium. (p. 206)

Yellow River Also known as the Huanghe; site of development of sedentary agriculture in China. (p. 21)

Yellow Turbans Chinese Daoists who launched a revolt in 184 C.E. in China promising a golden age to be brought about by divine magic. (p. 98)

Yeltsin, Boris Began to move up the ladder of the Communist party in Soviet Union in 1968, becoming First Secretary of the Moscow City Party Committee in 1985; initially a loyal backer of Gorbachev but increasingly criticized him for slow pace of reform; stood up to a coup attempt in 1991 but then managed to displace Gorbachev; in his position as president of the Russian republic, sponsored several subsequent constitutional provisions and weathered battles with opponents in parliament. (p. 899)

Yi Korean dynasty that succeeded Koryo dynasty following period of Mongol invasions; established in 1392; ruled Korea to 1910; restored aristocratic dominance and Chinese influence. (p. 302)

Yoruba City-states developed in northern Nigeria c. 1200 C.E.; Ile-Ife featured artistic style possibly related to earlier Nok culture; agricultural societies supported by peasantry and dominated by ruling family and aristocracy. (p. 186)

Yuan Shikai [yU *än shEE kI, yŸän*] Warlord in northern China after fall of Qing dynasty; hoped to seize imperial throne; president of China after 1912; resigned in the face of Japanese invasion in 1916. (p. 717)

Zaghlul, Sa'd Leader of Egypt's nationalist Wafd party; their negotiations with British led to limited Egyptian independence in 1922. (p. 693)

zaibatsu [zI *bät* sU] Huge industrial combines created in Japan in the 1890s as part of the process of industrialization. (p. 657)

zakat Tax for charity; obligatory for all Muslims. (p. 129)

Zapata, Emiliano Mexican revolutionary and military commander of peasant guerrilla movement after 1910 centered in Morelos; succeeded along with Pancho Villa in removing Díaz from power; also participated in campaigns that removed Madero and Huerta; demanded sweeping land reform. (p. 711)

Zapatistas Guerrilla movement named in honor of Emiliano Zapata; originated in 1994 in Mexico's southern state of Chiapas; government responded with a combination of repression and negotiation. (p. 816)

zemstvoes [*zemst* vO, pl. -stvos] Local political councils created as part of reforms of Tsar Alexander II (1860s); gave some Russians, particularly middle-class professionals, some experience in government; councils had no impact on national policy. (p. 646)

Zen Buddhism Known as Chan Buddhism in China; stressed meditation and the appreciation of natural and artistic beauty. (p. 268)

Zenj Arabic term for the east African coast. (p. 183)

Zhao Kuangyin [jaoo *kwän yin*] Founder of Song dynasty; originally a general following fall of Tang; took title of Taizu; failed to overcome northern Liao dynasty that remained independent. (p. 272)

Zhenghe Chinese Muslim admiral who commanded series of Indian Ocean, Persian Gulf, and Red Sea trade expeditions under third Ming emperor, Yunglo, between 1405 and 1433; only Chinese attempt to create worldwide trade empire. (p. 337)

Zhou Originally a vassal family of Shang China; possibly Turkic in origin; overthrew Shang and established second historical Chinese dynasty. (p. 36)

Zhou Enlai [*jO* en *lI*] After Mao Zedong, the most important leader of the Communist party in China from the 1930s until his death in 1976; premier of China from 1954; notable as perhaps the most cosmopolitan and moderate of the inner circle of Communist leaders. (p. 880)

Zhu Xi [tsU shEE, ju shEE] Most prominent of neo-Confucian scholars during the Song dynasty in China; stressed importance of applying philosophical principles to everyday life and action. (p. 273)

ziggurats Massive towers usually associated with Mesopotamian temple complexes. (p. 18)

Zionism Movement originating in eastern Europe during the 1860s and 1870s that argued that the Jews must return to a Middle Eastern holy land; eventually identified with the settlement of Palestine. (p. 692)

Zoroastriansim [zôr O *as* trEE uh niz uhm, zOr-] Animist religion that saw material existence as battle between forces of good and evil; stressed the importance of moral choice; righteous lived on after death in "House of Song"; chief religion of Persian Empire. (p. 70)

CREDITS

Literary Credits

PART II

Document Based Questions

1-1. Francis MacDonald Cornford, trans., *The Republic of Plato* (1945; Repr., London: Oxford University Press, 1982), 171–174. Used by permission of Oxford University Press.

1-2. Aristotle, *The Politics of Aristotle,* trans. Benjamin Jowett (New York: Colonial Press, 1900), 4–9; Ancient History Sourcebook (http://www.fordham.edu/halsall/ancient/greek-slaves.html#Aristotle).

1-3. Tacitus, *The Annals,* Book XIV, 42–45, trans. Alfred John Church and William Jackson Brodribb, in *Great Books of the Western World* 14 (Chicago: Britannica, 1991), 151–152.

1-4. Excerpt from second century C.E. textbook by Gauis. Peter Stearns, ed., *World History in Documents: A Comparative Reader* (New York: New York University Press, 1998), 60–63.

1-5. *The Laws of Manu,* trans. G. Buhler; Indian History Sourcebook (http://www.fordham.edu/halsall/india/manu-full.html).

2-1. Confucius, *Analects,* quoted in Kevin Reilly, *Readings in World Civilizations,* Vol. 1, *The Great Traditions,* 3rd ed. (New York: St. Martin's Press, 1995), 153–155.

2-2. Hans Feizi, *The Complete Works,* 2 vols., trans. W. K. Liao (London: Arthur Probsthain, 1959), Vol. 2, 323–333; quoted in Peter N. Stearns, Stephen S. Gosch, and Erwin P. Grieshaber, *Documents in World History,* Vol. 1, *The Great Traditions: From Ancient Times to 1500,* 3rd ed. (New York: Longman, 2003), 44–45, 47.

2-3. Thucydides, *History of the Peloponnesian War,* trans. Charles Smith (Cambridge, MA: Harvard University Press, 1919–1923); quoted in Peter Stearns, ed., *World History in Documents: A Comparative Reader* (New York: New York University Press, 1998), 50–51.

2-4. Herodotus, *The History,* trans. George Rawlinson, (New York: Dutton, 1862); Ancient History Sourcebook (http://www.fordham.edu/halsall/ancient/herodotus-persdemo.html).

2-5. Herodotus, *The History,* trans. George Rawlinson, (New York: Dutton, 1862); Ancient History Sourcebook (http://www.fordham.edu/halsall/ancient/polybius6.html).

PART III

Document Based Questions

1-1. Ahmed Ali, *Al-Qur'ān: A Contemporary Translation* (Princeton: Princeton University Press, 1993). Selections are from the following sura and verses: 4:1, 4:32, 4:34, 5:32.

1-2. Elka Klein, trans.; Internet Medieval Sourcebook (http://www.fordham.edu/halsall/source/jewishwomen-grace.html).Excerpt from *Tosafist commentary on Mishnah 1 and Babylonian Talmud Berakhot 45b,* by Elka Klein, 1998.

1-3. S. P. Scott, ed., *The Civil Law,* vol. 17, *The Novels of Emperor Leo VI* (Cincinnati: Central Trust, 1932); 240; quoted in Peter Stearns, ed., *World History in Documents: A Comparative Reader* (New York: New York University Press, 1998), 134–135.

1-4. Patricia Buckley Ebrey, ed. and trans., *Chinese Civilization: A Sourcebook,* 2nd ed. (New York: Free Press, 1993), 168. Reprinted with permission of The Free Press, a Division of Simon & Schuster Adult Publishing Group. Copyright © 1993 by Patricia Buckley Ebrey. All rights reserved.

1-5. Said Hamdun and Noël King, trans. and eds., *Ibn Battuta in Black Africa,* with an introduction by Ross Dunn (Noel King, 1975); quoted in Peter N. Stearns, Stephen S. Gosch, and Erwin P. Grieshaber, *Documents in World History,* Vol. 1, *The Great Traditions: From Ancient Times to 1500,* 3rd ed. (New York: Longman, 2003), 267, 269–270. Copyright © 1975 Noël King. Used by permission of Marcus Wiener Publishers.

2-1. The Hadith were collections of Islamic law, compiled mainly from the 8th century onward.

2-2. Peter N. Stearns, Stephen S. Gosch, and Erwin P. Grieshaber, *Documents in World History,* Vol. 1, *The Great Traditions: From Ancient Times to 1500,* 3rd ed. (New York: Longman, 2003), 287, 288.

2-3. Peter N. Stearns, Stephen S. Gosch, and Erwin P. Grieshaber, *Documents in World History,* Vol. 1, *The Great Traditions: From Ancient Times to 1500,* 3rd ed. (New York: Longman, 2003), 288–289.

2-4. J. P. Migne, ed., *Patrologiae Cursus Completus* (Paris, 1855), Vol. 214, 493; reprinted in Roy C. Cave and Herbert H. Coulson, *A Source Book for Medieval Economic History* (Milwaukee: Bruce Publishing, 1936; reprinted New York: Biblo & Tannen, 1965), 104–105; Internet Sourcebook: (http://www.fordham.edu/hasall/source/1198popevenz.html).

2-5. Roy C. Cave and Herbert H. Coulson, *A Source Book for Medieval Economic History* (Milwaukee: Bruce Publishing, 1936; reprinted New York: Biblo & Tannen, 1965), 113; Internet Sourcebook: (http://www.fordham.edu/halsall/source/1250medfairs.html) .

2-6. Patricia Buckley Ebrey, ed. and trans., *Chinese Civilization: A Sourcebook,* 2nd ed. (New York: Free Press, 1993), 216. Reprinted with permission of The Free Press, a Division of Simon & Schuster Adult Publishing Group. Copyright © 1993 by Patricia Buckley Ebrey. All rights reserved.

Chapter 7

From Rosenthal, Franz; *The Mudquaddimah: An Introduction to History, Vol. 1.* Copyright © 1958 by Princeton University Press. Reprinted by permission of Princeton University Press.

Chapter 10

From *The Goodman of Paris,* translated by Eileen Power. London: George Routledge and Sons, 1929.

Chapter 11

Map of Inca Empire from *Atlas of Ancient America* by Coe, Snow and Benson, copyright ©1986, p. 196. Reprinted by permission of Andromeda Oxford Ltd., Abington, UK.

Chapter 13

Poem by Ki no Tsurayuki from *Japanese Culture,* © 1977 by H. Paul Varley. Reprinted by permission of Henry Holt and Company, LLC.

From *Cultural Atlas of Japan* by M. Collcutt, copyright © 1988. Reprinted by permission of Andromeda Oxford Ltd., Abington, UK.

Chapter 14

Abridgment of "The Mongols in the Eyes of the Europeans" from *History of the Mongols* by Bertold Spuler, translated by Helga and Stuart Drummond, copyright 1988. Copyright © 1972 by Routledge Kegan Paul. Reprinted with permission of the The Regents of the University of California.

PART IV

Document Based Questions

1-1. From Vespucci (Florence, 1505–1506), trans. "M. K." for Quaritch's edition, London, 1885; Internet History Sourcebook: (http://www.fordham.edu/halsall/mod/1497vespucci-america.html).

1-2. Peter Hulme and Noel Whitehead, eds., *Wild Majesty: Encounters with Caribes from Columbia to the Present Day* (Oxford: Clarendon Press, 1953), 13–14; quoted in Peter Stearns, ed., *World History in Documents: A Comparative Reader* (New York: New York University Press, 1998), 203–204. Used by permission of Oxford University Press.

1-3. Hernando Cortés, *Five Letters of Cortes to the Emperor,* trans. J. Bayard Morris (New York: Norton, 1991), 50–52; quoted in Peter Stearns, ed., *World History in Documents: A Comparative Reader* (New York: New York University Press, 1998), 205–206.

1-4. *Voyages of Samuel de Champlain, 1604–1618,* ed. W. L. Grant (New York: Scribner, 1907), 71–74; quoted in Peter Stearns, ed., *World History in Documents: A Comparative Reader* (New York: New York University Press, 1998), 211–212.

1-5. Miguel Leon-Portilla, *The Broken Spears,* quoted in Peter Stearns, ed., *World History in Documents: A Comparative Reader* (New York: New York University Press, 1998), 216. © 1962, 1990 by Miguel Leon-Portilla. Expanded and Updated Edition © 1992 by Miguel Leon-Portilla. Reprinted by permission of Beacon Press, Boston.

2-1. Basil Dmytryshn, *Imperial Russia: A Sourcebook, 1700–1917* (New York: Holt, Rinehart and Winston, 1967); quoted in Peter Stearns, ed., *World History in Documents: A Comparative Reader* (New York: New York University Press, 1998), 260.

2-2. *Chinese Repository* 9 (March 1850), quoted in Peter Stearns, ed., *World History in Documents: A Comparative Reader* (New York: New York University Press, 1998), 263–264.

2-3. Charles Stewart, ed., *Travels of Mirza Abu Taleb Khan in Asia, Africa, and Europe* (New Delhi: Sona Publications, 1814; reprint 1917); quoted in Peter Stearns, ed., *World History in Documents: A Comparative Reader* (New York: New York University Press, 1998), 270–271.

2-4. *An Arabic History of Kilwa Kisiwani (1520)*, from G. S. P. Freeman-Grenville, *The East African Coast* (Oxford: Clarendon Press, 1962), pp. 47–48; quoted in Peter N. Stearns, Stephen S. Gosch, and Erwin P. Grieshaber, *Documents in World History*, Vol. 2, *The Modern Centuries: From 1500 to the Present*, 2nd ed. (New York: Longman, 2000), 58.

2-5. Wake Forest University Electronic Resource (http://www.wfu.edu/~watts/w03_Japancl.html).

Chapter 18

Excerpt from *Imperial Russia: A Source Book, 1700–1917*, edited by Basil Dymtryshyn. Copyright © 1967 by Academic International Press, Gulf Breeze, FL. Reprinted with the permission of the publisher.

Chapter 20

Excerpts from *Africa Remembered: Narratives by West Africans from the Era of the Slave Trade* by Philip Curtin. (Long Grove, IL; Waveland Press, Inc., 1967 [reissued 1997]). Reprinted by permission of Waveland Press, Inc. All rights reserved.

Chapter 22

From *Cultural Atlas of Japan* by M. Collcutt, copyright © 1988. Reprinted by permission of Andromeda Oxford Ltd., Abington, UK.

PART V

Document Based Questions

1-1. John Hall Stewart, ed., *A Documentary Survey of the French Revolution* (New York: Macmillan, 1951), 381–84; quoted in Peter Stearns, ed., *World History in Documents: A Comparative Reader* (New York: New York University Press, 1998), 282.

1-2. James Harvey Robinson, ed., *Readings in European* History, vol. 2 (New York: Ginn, 1966), 522–23, quoted in Peter Stearns, ed., *World History in Documents: A Comparative Reader* (New York: New York University Press, 1998), 283.

1-3. Vicente Lecuna, ed., *Selected Writings of Bolivar* (New York: Colonial Press, 1951), I: 191–192; quoted in Peter Stearns, ed., *World History in Documents: A Comparative Reader* (New York: New York University Press, 1998), 288.

1-4. Carlos B. Gil, ed., *The Age of Porfirio Diaz: Selected Readings* (Albuquerque: University of New Mexico Press, 1977), 35–36; quoted in Peter N. Stearns, Stephen S. Gosch, and Erwin P. Grieshaber, *Documents in World History*, Vol. 2, *The Modern Centuries: From 1500 to the Present*, 2nd ed. (New York: Longman, 2000), 114. Copyright © 1977. Used by permission of University of New Mexico Press.

1-5. Nikolai Danilevsky, *Russia and Europe*, in *The Mind of Modern Russia*, ed. Hans Kohn (New Brunswick, NJ: Rutgers University Press, 1955), 200–211; quoted in Peter Stearns, ed., *World History in Documents: A Comparative*

Reader (New York: New York University Press, 1998), 336.

2-1. Albertine-Adrienne Necker de Saussure, *The Study of the Life of Woman* (Philadelphia, 1844), 27–29; quoted in Peter Stearns, ed., *World History in Documents: A Comparative Reader* (New York: New York University Press, 1998), 318–319.

2-2. Horace Mann, *On the Education of Free Men* (New York: Columbia University Press, 1987), 49–59; quoted in Peter N. Stearns, Stephen S. Gosch, and Erwin P. Grieshaber, *Documents in World History*, Vol. 2, *The Modern Centuries: From 1500 to the Present*, 2nd ed. (New York: Longman, 2000), 134.

2-3. Eliza Duffey, *No Sex in Education; or an Equal Change for Both Girls and Boys* (Philadelphia, 1874), 100–101; quoted in Peter Stearns, ed., *World History in Documents: A Comparative Reader* (New York: New York University Press, 1998), 323.

2-4. Ryusaku Tsunoda, W. T. de Bary, and Donald Keene, eds., *Sources of Japanese Tradition II* (New York: Columbia University Press, 1958), 139–140, 189–191; quoted in Peter N. Stearns, Stephen S. Gosch, and Erwin P. Grieshaber, *Documents in World History*, Vol. 2, *The Modern Centuries: From 1500 to the Present*, 2nd ed. (New York: Longman, 2000), 137.

2-5. *The Autobiography of Yukichi Fukuzawa*, trans. Eüchi Kiyooka (New York: Columbia University Press, 1966), 214–217; quoted in Peter N. Stearns, Stephen S. Gosch, and Erwin P. Grieshaber, *Documents in World History*, Vol. 2, *The Modern Centuries: From 1500 to the Present*, 2nd ed. (New York: Longman, 2000), 136–137.

Chapter 24

Map from *A Short History of Indonesia* by Ailsa Zainu'ddin. Copyright © 1970 by Praeger Publishers. Reproduced with permission of Greenwood Publishing Group, Inc., Westport, CT.

Chapter 26

From an abridgement of "A People Made New (1902–1905)" by Liang Qichao, from *Sources of Chinese Tradition* by William T. deBary, Tait Chan, and Burton Watson. Copyright © 1960 by Columbia University Press. Reprinted with permission of the publisher.

PART VI

Document Based Questions

1-1. New China News Agency, April 6, 1951; Internet Sourcebook (http://www.fordham.edu/halsall/mod/1945-burma-ukpolicy.html).

1-2. *Africa-Asia Speaks from Bandong* (Djakarta Indonesian Ministry of Foreign Affairs, 1955), 19–29; Internet Sourcebook (http://www.fordham.edu/halsall/mod/1955sukarno-bandong.html).

1-3. From a speech in Washington, D.C., December 18, 1956, printed in the U.S. *Department of State Bulletin*, January 14, 1957, 49–50; Internet Sourcebook (http://www.fordham.edu/halsall/mod/1941nehru.html).

1-4. *The First Afro-Asian People's Solidarity Conference, 26 December 1957 to January 1, 1958*, ed. (Cairo: Permanent Secretariat of the Organization for Afro-Asian People's Solidarity, 1958), 7–12; Internet Sourcebook (http://www.fordham.edu/halsall/mod/1957sadat-afroasian1.html).

1-5. James Nelson Goodsell, *Fidel Castro's Personal Revolution in Cuba: 1959–1973*; (New

York: Knopf, 1975), pp. 264–268; Internet Sourcebook (http://www.fordham.edu/halsall/mod/1962castro.html).

2-1. United Nations, *Report of the International Conference on Population and Development*, Cairo, September 5–13, 1994, Addendum, 18–22; quoted in Peter Stearns, ed., *World History in Documents: A Comparative Reader* (New York: New York University Press, 1998), 451, 452.

2-2. Interview of September 6, 1994, *CNN Specials*, transcript 380; quoted in Peter Stearns, ed., *World History in Documents: A Comparative Reader* (New York: New York University Press, 1998), 453.

2-3. United Nations, *Report of the International Conference on Population and Development*, Cairo, September 5–13, 1994, Addendum, 141, 146–49; quoted in Peter Stearns, ed., *World History in Documents: A Comparative Reader* (New York: New York University Press, 1998), 457.

2-4. United Nations, *Report of the International Conference on Population and Development*, Cairo, September 5–13, 1994, Addendum, 141, 146–149; quoted in Peter Stearns, ed., *World History in Documents: A Comparative Reader* (New York: New York University Press, 1998), 457–458.

2-5. United Nations, *Report of the International Conference on Population and Development*, Cairo, September 5–13, 1994, 46–49; quoted in Peter Stearns, ed., *World History in Documents: A Comparative Reader* (New York: New York University Press, 1998), 454, 456.

Chapter 28

Excerpts from *One Hundred Poems of Kabir*, translated by Rabindranath Tagore, copyright © 1961, p. 1.

Excerpt from the poem "Snow Upon Paris" from *Selected Poems* by L.S. Senghor, translated by J. Reed and Clive Wake. Copyright © 1964 by Oxford University Press. Reprinted by permission of Oxford University Press.

Chapter 30

Excerpt from *Readings in Russian Civilization, Volume III,* edited by Thomas Riha. Copyright © 1969 by The University of Chicago Press. Reprinted by permission of The University of Chicago Press.

Adaptation of map, "The Civil War," from *The World Atlas of Revolutions* by Andrew Wheatcroft, pp. 86–87 (Hamish Hamilton, 1983). Text copyright © 1983 Andrew Wheatcroft, cartography copyright © 1983 Hamish Hamilton Ltd. Reproduced by permission of Hamish Hamilton Ltd.

Chapter 35

Adaptation of two maps, "The Northern Expedition" and "Warlord Groups," from *The Times Atlas of World History*, edited by G. Barraclough. Copyright © 1984 by Times Books, a division of Harper Collins. Reprinted by permission.

Adaptation of a map, "The Development of the World Economy," from *The Times Atlas of World History*, edited by G. Barraclough. Copyright © 1984 by Times Books, a division of Harper Collins. Reprinted by permission.

Adaptation of a map, "Industrialization Outside of Europe and North America," from *The Times Atlas of World History*, edited by G. Barraclough. Copyright © 1984 by Times Books, a division of Harper Collins. Reprinted by permission.

Photo Credits

PART 1
CHAPTER 1
Chapter Opener 01 Douglas Mazonowicz/Art Resource, NY; **Visualizing the Past** Woodfin Camp & Associates; **Figure 01.02** University of Pennsylvania Museum (neg. #S4-13970); **01.04** MacQuitty International Photographic Collection; **01.05** Musée Cerneuschi, Paris

PART II
CHAPTER 2
Chapter Opener 02 Robert Harding Picture Library; **Figure 02.01** From *Five Tracts of Hasan al-Banna: A Section from the Majmu 'At Rasa" Il Al-' Imam Al-Shahid Hasan Al Banna'*, translated and edited by Charles Wendell, University of California Press/Berkeley, 1978. Copyright © 1978 The Regents of the University of California

CHAPTER 3
Chapter Opener 03 *Adoration of the Bodhi Tree*, India, Amaravati Satavhana period, 2nd–3rd century. Limestone, 80 x 57.1cm. The Cleveland Museum of Art, 2001, Purchase from the J. H. Wade Fund. 1970.43; **Figure 03.01** Cleveland Museum of Art, Purchase from the J. H. Wade Fund, 30.331; **03.02** Courtesy of the Trustees of the British Museum, London

CHAPTER 4
Chapter Opener 04 Courtesy of the Trustees of the British Museum, London (PS112376); **Figure 04.01** Alinari/Art Resource, NY; **04.02 Image 1** Alison Frantz Collection, American School of Classical Studies at Athens; **Image 2** Hirmer Verlag; **04.03** Musée de l'Arles et de la Provence Antiques (Cl. M. Lacanaud); **Visualizing the Past** Bibliothèque Nationale de France, Paris

CHAPTER 5
Chapter Opener 05 The Granger Collection, New York; **Figure 05.01** Lepsius, Denkmaler

PART III
CHAPTER 6
Chapter Opener 06 Courtesy of the author; **Figure 06.01** Exclusive News Agency/Popperfoto; **06.02** Spencer Collection, New York Public Library, Astor, Lenox and Tilden Foundations; **06.03** Bettmann/Corbis; **06.04** By permission of the British Library (Folio 17V/MS.2884); **06.05** Noel Quidu/Getty Images/Liaison Agency; **06.06** Bridgeman Art Library; **Visualizing the Past Image 1** Shostal/© SuperStock, Inc.; **Image 2** © SuperStock, Inc.; **Image 3** Robert Frerck/Odyssey Productions, Chicago; **Image 4** © SuperStock, Inc.

CHAPTER 7
Chapter Opener 07 From *The Art of India*, English translation copyright © 1985 by Holle Verlag GmbH, Germany. Used by permission of Crown Publishers, a division of Random House, Inc.; **Figure 07.01** Courtesy of the Arthur M. Sackler Museum, Harvard University Art Museums, Gift of John Goelet, formerly in the collection of Louis J. Cartier (1958.76); **07.02** YAN; **07.03** Erich Lessing/Art Resource, NY; **07.04** Topkapi Museum, Istanbul; **07.06** British Library, London/Bridgeman Art Library

CHAPTER 8
Chapter Opener 08 Bibliothèque Nationale de France, Paris; **Figure 08.01** Floyd Norgaard/Ric Ergenbright Photography; **08.02** © SuperStock, Inc.; **08.03** Brooklyn Museum of Art; **08.04** National Museum of African Art, Smithsonian Institution, Washington, D.C./Aldo Tutino/Art Resource, NY; **08.05** Authenticated News International

CHAPTER 9
Chapter Opener 09 Erich Lessing/Art Resource, NY; **Figure 09.01** Alinari/Art Resource, NY; **Visualizing the Past** Dumbarton Oaks Research Library and Collections; **09.02** Biblioteca Nacional, Madrid; **09.03** Erich Lessing/Art Resource, NY; **09.04** From Miniatures Armeniennes, © 1960 Editions Cercle d'Art, Paris; **09.05** Staatsbibliothek Preussischer Kulturbesitz, Berlin/Bildarchiv Preussischer Kulturbesitz; **09.06** Biblioteca Nacional, Madrid; **09.07** Sovfoto

CHAPTER 10
Chapter Opener 10 Giraudon/Art Resource, NY; **Figure 10.01** Sächsische Landesbibliothek Staats- und Universitätsbibliothek Dresden, Germany; **10.02** Giraudon/Art Resource, NY; **10.03** By permission of the British Library (ADD.42130 f82); **10.04** Scala/Art Resource, NY; **Visualizing the Past** Giraudon/Art Resource, NY; **10.06** By permission of the British Library (ADD.27695 f8); **10.07** Historical Pictures/Stock Montage, Inc.; **10.08** Courtesy of the Newberry Library, Chicago; **10.09** Bibliothèque Royale Albert Ier, Brussels

CHAPTER 11
Chapter Opener 11 Peter Menzel; **Figure 11.02** Scala/Art Resource, NY; Instituto Nacional de Antropologia e Historia; **11.03** Bibliotecca Medicea Laurenziana, Florence, Italy (Med. Palat 218, c. 315); **11.04** Courtesy of the Newberry Library, Chicago; **Visualizing the Past Image 1** Ric Ergenbright Photography; **11.05** American History Division, The New York Public Library, Astor, Lenox and Tilden Foundations; **11.06** Elizabeth Hamlin/Stock, Boston

CHAPTER 12
Chapter Opener 12 *Court Ladies Preparing Newly Woven Silk*, China, early 12th century; Emperor Huizong, Chinese (1082–1125) Handscroll; ink, color and gold on silk; H x W: 14 5/8 x 57 3/16 in. (37 x 145.3 cm) The Museum of Fine Arts, Boston. Special Chinese and Japanese Fund, 12.886; **Figure 12.01** Metropolitan Museum of Art , Rogers Fund, 1918 (18.124.5) Photograph © 2003 The Metropolitan Museum of Art; **12.02** SEF/Art Resource, NY; **12.03** The Granger Collection, New York; **12.04** Courtesy of the Freer Gallery of Art, Smithsonian Institution, Washington, D.C. F1957.14; **12.05** Werner Forman Archive, Peking Place Museum/Art Resource, NY; **12.06** Courtesy of the Trustees of the British Museum, London; **12.07** From *East Asia: Tradition and Transformation*, rev. ed., by John Fairbank, Edwin O. Reischaller, and Albert M. Craig, 1989 by Houghton Mifflin Company, used with permission; **12.08** Ma Yuan, Chinese, active 1190–1235; Southern Song dynasty, *Bare Willows and Distant Mountains*. Round fan mounted as album leaf; ink and light color silk,

23.8 x 24.2 cm. Museum of Fine Arts, Boston. Special Chinese and Japanese Fund

CHAPTER 13
Chapter Opener 13 © Kyodo News Service; **Figure 13.01** Art Resource, NY; **13.02** Art Resource, NY; **13.03** Metropolitan Museum of Art, The Brashford Dean Memorial Collection (147.1) Photograph © 2003 The Metropolitan Museum of Art; **13.04** Robert Harding Picture Library; **13.05** The Nelson-Atkins Museum of Art, Kansas City, Missouri (Purchase, Nelson Trust) 45-51/2; **13.06** Cameramann International, Ltd.; **13.07** Bridgeman Art Library; **Visualizing the Past Image 1** Metropolitan Museum of Art, The Brashford Dean Memorial Collection (147.1) Photograph © 2003 The Metropolitan Museum of Art; **Image 2** Courtesy of the Newberry Library, Chicago; Image 3 By permission of the British Library (ADD.27695 f8); **Image 4** Metropolitan Museum of Art, Rogers Fund, 1918 (18.124.5) Photograph © 2003 The Metropolitan Museum of Art; **13.08** John Elk III/Stock, Boston

CHAPTER 14
Chapter Opener 14 Bibliothèque Nationale de France, Paris; **Figure 14.01** Corbis; **14.02** The Granger Collection, New York; **14.03** Bildarchiv Preussischer Kulturbesitz; **14.04** National Palace Museum, Taipei, Taiwan, Republic of China; **14.05** The Granger Collection, New York; **14.06** Bibliothèque Nationale de France, Paris; **14.07** John Massey Stewart

CHAPTER 15
Chapter Opener 15 Giraudon/Art Resource, NY; **Figure 15.01** Duomo, Florence, Italy/Alinari/Art Resource, NY.; **15.02** The Granger Collection, New York; **15.03** The Granger Collection, New York

PART IV
CHAPTER 16
Chapter Opener 16 The Asian Art Museum of San Francisco, The Avery Brundage Collection, B60 D78+ (detail); **Figure 16.01** North Wind Picture Archives; **16.03** Bibliotecca Medicea Laurenziana, Florence, Italy; **16.04** Corbis; **16.05** Library of Congress; **16.06** The Granger Collection, New York; **16.07** V&A Picture Library

CHAPTER 17
Chapter Opener 17 Alinari/Art Resource, NY; **Figure 17.02** On loan to the Scottish National Portrait Gallery, by permission of the Earl of Rosbery; **17.03** Prints Division, New York Public Library, Astor, Lenox and Tilden Foundations; **17.04** Art Resource, NY

CHAPTER 18
Chapter Opener 18 © Fotocommissie/Rijksmuseum Foundation, Amsterdam; **Figure 18.01** Sovfoto; **18.03** Hillwood Museum, Washington, D.C.; **Visualizing the Past** Sovfoto; **18.04** Sovfoto

CHAPTER 19
Chapter Opener 19 Bibliothèque Nationale de France, Paris (RCB 19094); **Figure 19.01** Bridgeman Art Library; **19.02** Library of Congress; **19.03** Courtesy of the Hispanic Society of America, New York; **19.07** Arxiu, MAS; **19.08** DeBry. *America*, 1585; **19.09** Laurie Platt Winfrey/Carousel, Inc.

INDEX

Note: Page numbers followed by f, m, and t indicate figures, maps, and tables, respectively.

A

Abbas I (Safavid shah), 486, 487, 489
Abbas II (Safavid shah), 489
Abbasid Empire
  Christian crusades and, 151–153
  commerce and, 139–140, 142
  cultural advances during, 142, 153–155
  decline of, 147–148, 158
  elite society and, 140
  fall of Umayyads and, 135, 137
  family structure and role of women in,
    150–151
  imperial extravagance and succession disputes
    in, 149–150
  middle and late periods of, 147–153, 159m
  Mongols and, 324, 324f
  nomadic incursions during, 151
  religious trends in, 156
  science in, 155–156
  spread of Islam under, 138–139
Abduh, Muhammad, 626, 850
Abdul Hamid (Ottoman sultan), 623
Abdullahi, Khalifa, 628
Abelard, Peter, 224
Abolitionist movement, 470
Abortion, 794
Absolute monarchy, 390–392
Abu Bakr, 131, 135
Abu Taleb, 127, 481, 482, 357
Achebe, Chinua, 847
Achmad, Muhammad (Mahdi), 628
Afghanistan
  demise of fundamentalist regime in, 903
  Mughal conquests in, 495
  Russian influence in, 650
  Soviet invasion of, 807, 895
Africa. See also Slave trade; specific countries
  agriculture in, 11–12, 14, 95
  artificial nations in, 842, 843
  art in, 186–187f
  artisans in, 459, 459f
  Belgians in, 769
  Benin and, 187
  British in, 582–583
  characteristics of east coast of, 459–460
  Christianity in, 174
  city dwellers and villagers in, 179–180
  coastal trading stations in, 376–377
  colonial division of, 838m
  democratic change in, 901
  demographic transitions in, 184, 185
  early human species in, 9
  economic growth in postcolonial, 846, 848
  education in colonial, 571–572
  ethnic conflict in, 907, 907f, 916
  European explorations in, 344
  European partition of, 564
  fertility rate in, 185
  in 1400, 347
  kingdoms in central, 188
  Kongo and, 188–189

liberation of nonsettler, 769–771
Mali and, 177–180
nationalist movements in, 694–696, 769–772
oral tradition in, 178
population growth in, 837, 840
Portuguese interests in, 183, 187, 190, 361,
  363, 459, 482, 771, 773
post–World War I, 728
religions in, 468, 860
slavery in, 181
Songhay kingdom and, 180–181
spread of Islam to, 132, 147, 171–177,
  179–190, 447, 460
Sudanic states in, 176–177, 179–182
Swahili coast in, 182–183
symbols of kingship in, 458, 458f
trade in, 182–183, 367, 376, 449, 451, 459
tropical dependencies in, 576
white settlers and Africans in southern,
  461–462
World War I and, 679, 680, 684
World War II and, 757, 758, 758f, 769–771
Yorbas and, 186–187
African Americans, 554
African National Congress, 858
African societies
  Christian, 175–176
  common elements in, 173–174
  diversity in, 172
  north of Sahara, 174
  slave trade and, 454–461, 464, 466
  stateless, 173
Afrikaner National Party (South Africa), 773,
  856
Agaja (king of Dahomey), 458
Agriculture
  in Africa, 11–12, 14, 95
  in Americas, 12, 258
  in ancient Greece, 84–85
  in ancient Rome, 84–85
  in China, 14, 46, 48, 277–279, 278f, 513
  collectivization of, 742–743, 800
  in eastern Europe, 800
  estate, 368–369, 413
  in India, 61
  in Japan, 96
  in Latin America, 433
  manorial system and, 215
  in Mesoamerica, 245–246
  in Middle Ages, 215, 218–219,
    227–228
  in Middle East, 11, 13, 14, 16–17, 19
  in Neolithic Age, 11–13, 12m
  patriarchalism and, 45–46
  population growth and, 184, 845
  in postclassical period, 118
  in 17th- and 18th-century Europe, 398
  slash and burn, 13–14
  in Soviet Union, 742–743, 896
  in 20th- century Europe, 788

in Vietnam, 303–304
women and, 45, 46, 61, 137
Aibak, Qutb-ud-din, 162
AIDS, 839, 920
Aisha, 135
Akan people, 456–457
Akbar (Mughal emperor), 490–492, 496
Akkadians, 19
al-Abbas, Abu, 135, 137
al-Afghani, 626
Alamán, Lucas, 597
Alaska, 9, 410
Albania, 758, 800, 898
al-Banna, Hasan, 850–851, 853f
Alberdi, Juan Bautista, 603
Al-Biruni, 163
al-Din, Rashid, 312f
al-Din, Sail, 483
Alexander I, tsar of Russia, 642
Alexander II, tsar of Russia, 649, 650
Alexander the Great
  epic of Sundiata and, 178
  influence of, 71, 72, 88
  invasion of India by, 51, 54
  Persian Empire and, 71
Alexandria, Egypt, 72
Algeria
  French in, 672, 771–772, 772f, 780
  independence of, 780, 835
Algerian War, 783
al-Ghazali, 156
Ali (clansman of Muhammad), 128, 131, 133
Allah, 99, 121
Allende, Salvador, 813, 823–824
Alliance for Progress, 826
al-Mahdi (Abbasid caliph), 147–148
al-Ma'mun (Abbasid caliph), 150
Almohadis, 174
Almoravids, 174, 176
al-Rashid, Haroun, 140f
al-Razi, 155
al-Sahili, Ishak, 179
al-Tusi, 388–389
al-Urdi, 388–389
American Civil War, 547, 554
American Indians
  civilization among, 23
  in classical period, 97
  displacement of, 374–375
  diversity among, 259–260
  European sensibilities and, 250
  exploitation of, 429–431
  morality and conquest of, 428
  outside contacts with, 184
  population decline of, 184
  view of European settlers by, 16
American Philosophical Society, 374
American Revolution
  background of, 536, 537
  effects of, 538, 554, 566, 591

Americas. *See also* Mesoamerica
  agriculture in, 12, 258
  in classical period, 96–97, 97*m*
  explorations to, 345–347
  migration from Asia to, 9–10
Amigos del país, 440
Amin, Idi, 850
Anarchists, 649
Anatolia, 474, 680
Ancient Egypt. *See also* Egypt
  art in, 21, 93*f*
  civilization in, 20–21, 21m, 29
  contact between Mesopotamia and, 28
  contributions of, 25
  trade in, 28, 29
  women in, 45
Ancient Greece. *See also* Greece
  architecture in, 25
  art in, 68f, 72, 81–83
  characteristics of, 71–72, 77, 78
  concept of civilization in, 23
  culture in, 80–83, 86
  economy in, 84–85, 87
  literature in, 81
  overview of, 69–70
  political institutions in, 74–76
  religion in, 79–80
  slavery in, 85
  social structure in, 62, 87
  trade in, 71, 85
Ancient Rome. *See also* Roman Empire
  architecture in, 82–83
  art in, 81–83, 81*f*, 83*f*
  characteristics of, 77, 78
  concept of civilization in, 23
  culture in, 80–83
  economy in, 84–85, 87
  fall of, 73–74
  family structure in, 87
  literature in, 81
  military orientation of, 72–74
  overview of, 69–70
  political institutions in, 74–76, 78–79
  religion in, 78–80
  slavery in, 85
  trade in, 85
Andean societies, Mesoamerican vs., 256–257
Anglican church, 384
Anglo-Boer War, 773
Angola, 376, 773
Animal husbandry, 366–367
Animals
  domestication of, 11, 16
  introduction of new species of, 430–431
Animism
  in Africa, 173
  explanation of, 165
  in Russia, 206, 207
An Lashan, 272
Anschluss, 735
Antigua, 368
Antonioni, Michelangelo, 798
Anwar al-Sadat, 668
Anwar, Chairil, 847
Apartheid, 773, 857–858, 901
Aquinas, Thomas, 214, 225, 234
Aquino, Corazon, 845
Arabia. *See also* Arabs
  bedouins in, 122–123
  marriage and family in, 126
  physical aspects of, 122, 123*m*, 124*f*, 125*m*
  poetry in, 126
  religion in pre-Islamic, 126–127
  social organization in, 123–125
  towns and trade in, 125–126

Arab-Israeli War of 1948, 851
Arabs. *See also* Islam; Islamic civilizations
  conquests by, 131–137
  family and gender roles among, 134–137
  Islam and, 129
  nationalism among, 689–693
  Sasanian Empire and, 132
  Umayyad, 125, 128–137
  World War I and, 683, 683*f*, 684
Aragon, 343
Araucanians, 427
Arbenz, Jacobo, 819
Architecture. *See also* Art
  in ancient Egypt, 21, 25
  in ancient Greece, 25, 81–82, 82*f*
  in China, 27, 269*f*
  in France, 391, 391*f*
  in India, 26, 494, 494*f*
  Islamic, 120f, 142–144, 143*f*, 144*f*, 153, 154*f*, 161*f*
  in Japan, 297*f*, 298*f*
  in Mesoamerica, 244*f*
  in Middle Ages, 226, 226*f*, 235
  in Ottoman Empire, 478, 478*f*, 479
  in Persia, 487–488, 487*f*
  in Russia, 206–207, 208*f*
  20th-century, 703, 703*f*
  in Vietnam, 307*f*
Arevalo, Juan José, 819
Argentina
  economy in, 612–613, 739, 824
  Falkland Islands and, 815, 824
  government and politics in, 824, 900
  immigrants in, 601, 610, 612, 736
  independence of, 591, 592
  labor unrest in, 737
  middle class in, 736
  in 19th-century, 602–605, 604*f*
  Perón regime in, 739–740, 815, 816*f*, 823
  popular culture in, 831
  trade in, 599, 604
  universities in, 738
  voting rights in, 829
Argentine Republic, 603–604
Ariel (Rodó), 613
Aristocracy
  in ancient Greece, 76
  in China, 44, 46
  in Middle Ages, 232–233
Aristotle, 32, 79, 85, 336, 428
Armenians, slaughter of, 680, 760
Art. *See also* Architecture
  in Africa, 186–187*f*
  in ancient Egypt, 21, 93*f*
  in ancient Greece, 68f, 72, 81–83
  in ancient Rome, 81–83, 81*f*, 83*f*
  in Byzantine Empire, 196*f*, 198–200, 199*f*, 201*f*, 202*f*
  in China, 22, 22*f*, 34*f*, 43, 44*f*, 262*f*, 267*f*, 270*f*, 271*f*, 277*f*, 281–284, 283*f*, 512*f*–513*f*, 514
  in Europe, 534*f*, 552, 553*f*
  in India, 50*f*, 58*f*, 60*f*, 61, 164, 164*f*, 377*f*
  in Islamic civilizations, 128*f*, 140*f*, 146*f*, 149*f*, 153–154, 155*f*, 156*f*
  in Japan, 290*f*, 291*f*, 297–298, 298*f*, 498*f*, 640*f*, 868, 869
  in Korea, 301, 301*f*
  in Latin America, 712, 831
  in Mesoamerica, 243, 243*f*, 244
  in Mesopotamia, 25
  in Mexico, 712
  in Middle Ages, 216*f*–217*f*, 221*f*, 226–227, 228f–230*f*, 234*f*, 235*f*
  in Paleolithic Age, 6

  in Persia, 472*f*
  religious themes in, 226–227, 281
  in Renaissance, 340, 341*f*, 380*f*, 382
  revolution and, 818, 818*f*
  in Russia, 206–207, 206*f*, 406*f*, 651
  social values and, 281
  in Soviet Union, 744, 746, 803
  of Sumerians, 17–18
  20th-century, 703, 703*f*, 797–798
  in Ukraine, 206–207
  in United States, 554
Artisans
  in Africa, 459, 459*f*
  in China, 328–329
  in India, 493
  in Islamic civilizations, 153–154
  in Mesoamerica, 256
  in Middle Ages, 230–231
  in Ottoman Empire, 479, 622
  in Persia, 487
  political protest by European, 542, 542*f*
Aryans, in India, 52–53
Asante, 456–457, 456*f*
Ashikaga Shogunate, 294, 298
Ashikaga Takuaji, 294
Ashoka, 54–55, 59, 61
Asia. *See also specific countries or regions*
  artificial nations in, 842, 843
  coastal trading stations in, 376–377
  demographic transition in, 185
  early civilizations in, 21–22, 24–27
  economic growth in postcolonial, 846, 848
  education in colonial, 570–572
  European expansion into, 499–508, 506*m*
  migration to Americas from, 9
  missionaries in, 507–508
  nomadic groups in, 16
  population growth in, 837, 840
  shift to land empires in, 564–573
  spread of Buddhism in, 59, 67
  spread of Islam to, 158–168
  tropical dependencies in, 576
  World War I and, 684
Asian trading network
  characteristics of, 501–502
  military advantages of Europeans and, 505
  Portuguese and, 502–503
  zones in, 501, 502*m*
Assis, J. Machado de, 607, 607*f*
Assyrians, 20, 31, 330
Astronomy
  in India, 60
  Islamic advances in, 155
  in 16th- and 17th-century Europe, 388–390
  Sumerian advances in, 18, 25
Aswan Dam, 853
Atahuallpa, 373–374
Ataturk (Mustafa Kemal), 623*f*, 691
Athens, 71, 75, 76, 82. *See also* Ancient Greece
Atlantic Charter of 1941, 767
Atomic weapons
  cold war and, 782
  development of, 781
  World War II and, 762
Audiencias, 434
Augustine, 103, 224
Augustus Caesar, 73
Aurangzeb (Mughal emperor), 376, 493, 495–496
Australia
  emigration to, 553–554, 792
  European settlements in, 554–556
  independence of, 708
  post–World War I, 707*m*, 708
  relationship with United States, 791–792

trade with Japan, 792
World War I and, 675, 679
World War II and, 761
Austria
  anti-immigrant sentiments in, 906
  European Union and, 788
  fascist movement in, 735
  Great Depression and, 729
  Nazi Germany and, 735, 753
  political protest in, 542
  post–World War I, 682
  Russian policies toward, 410, 643–644
  socialist movement in, 549
Austria-Hungary
  pre–World War I, 558, 672, 674
  World War I and, 677, 682
Averroës (Ibn Rushd), 336
Axis powers, 751. *See also* World War II
Axum, 21*m*, 93, 175
Ayan, 140, 142
Azerbaijan, 906
Azores, 343, 361
Aztecs
  accomplishments of, 23, 249
  description of, 239
  economy of, 245–246
  gender roles of, 247–249
  human sacrifice by, 242, 250–251
  Incas vs., 256–257
  reactions to European encounter, 356-357
  religion of, 242–244
  rise to power of, 241–242
  social contract of, 242
  social structure of, 246–247
  Spanish conquest of, 345, 370, 419, 426
  technological constraints of, 247, 249
  Tenochtitlan and, 244–245
Azuela, Mariano, 712

B

Baba, Ahmad, 455
Babur (Mughal warrior prince), 489, 490
Babylonians, 19, 25, 31
Bacon, Roger, 225
Bactria, 54
Baghdad, Iraq
  Abbasids and, 138, 160
  Mongols and, 158, 324, 325
Bahia, 468
Bai, Mira, 163, 164
Baibars (Egyptian commander), 325
Ba Jin, 720
Bakufu, 294
Bakunin, Mikhail, 649
Balboa, Vasco de, 370
Balfour, Lord, 692
Balfour Declaration, 692
Balkans
  Byzantine Empire and, 196, 197, 201, 203
  Eastern Orthodox Church and, 203
  independence of, 651
  nationalist movements in, 644
  Ottoman Empire in, 474, 541, 558, 621, 624
  pre–World War I, 673, 674
  Russia and, 650, 651
  trade in, 415
  U.S. intervention in, 2, 793, 903
Balkan Wars, 558, 559*m*, 674*f*
Bambara kingdom, 460
Banana republics, 825
Bands, 14
Bangladesh, 837, 839*f*
Banking
  in Middle Ages, 228–231

in Renaissance, 382
twentieth-century crises in, 712, 729
Banner armies, 629
Bantu peoples
  Boers and, 583
  characteristics of, 460
  languages of, 183, 461
  migration of, 173, 182, 188
  in southern Africa, 461
Banu Hashim, 127
Baquaqua, Mahommah Gardo, 447
Barbados, 452, 466
Barbarians, 15, 23
Barreda, Gabino, 532
Basil II (Byzantine emperor), 197–198
Batavia, 503–505, 565, 569
Batista, Fulgencio, 819–820
Batouala (Maran), 581
Battle of Aboukir, 625
Battle of Britain, 758, 761
Battle of the Bulge, 761
Battle of the Camel, 133
Battle of the Coral Sea, 762
Battle of Kulikova, 323
Battle of Lepanto, 367
Battle of Omdurman, 628
Battle on the River Zab, 137
Battle of Siffin, 133
Battle of Tours, 216
Batu (Mongol commander), 320–324
The Beatles, 798
Beaumere, Madame de, 397
Beauvoir, Simone de, 796
Bedouins
  clan rivalries among, 124–125, 131
  conversion to Islam, 134
  explanation of, 122–123
  gender roles among, 126, 136, 137
  religion of, 126–127
  social organization of, 123–124
  trade with, 126
Bela, King of Hungary, 324
Belarus, 902
Belgian Congo, 580, 580*f*
Belgium
  European Union and, 786
  industrialization in, 541–542
  parliament in, 541
  World War I and, 675, 682
  World War II and, 769
Belisarius (Byzantine general), 196
Benedict, 108
Bengal, 566–567, 570
Benin
  description of, 187, 458
  Portuguese interest in, 449–450
Bentham, Jeremy, 570
Beowulf, 227
Berbers, 174, 175
Bergman, Ingmar, 798
Berke (khan of Golden Horde), 325
Berlin Wall, 800, 892*f*, 898
Bernard of Clairvaux, 224
Berners, Tim, 909
Bernier, François, 493
Bhagavad Gita, 59
Bhaktic cults, 163–164
Bhutto, Benazir, 845
Biko, Steve, 858
Birth control, 794, 840
Birth rate, 794–795, 840, 879
Bismarck, Otto von, 546, 548, 558
Black Death (Bubonic plague), 232, 338
Black Dragon Society, 752
Blitzkrieg, 757

Boccaccio, Giovanni, 342
Bodhisattvas, 105
Boer Republics, 583
Boers
  profile of, 583
  settlement of, 376, 461–462, 582
  tensions between British and, 583
Boer War, 583
Bohemia, 415
Bolívar, Simon, 532, 592, 594–597
Bolivia
  drug trade in, 825
  government in, 601
  independence of, 595
  labor force in, 830
  in 20th-century, 817, 821
Bolsheviks, 650, 713–716, 720, 722
Borges, Jorge Luis, 832
Borneo, 165
Bosnia, 760, 906
Bosnia-Herzegovina, 898, 905
Bourbon dynasty, 441–442
Boxer Rebellion, 575, 635, 712
Brahmanism, 57. *See also* Hinduism
Brahmans, 53, 57, 61
Brazil
  Dutch holdings in, 364, 437
  economy in, 605–606, 824
  18th-century population in, 443
  gold rush in, 437
  immigrants in, 601, 605, 610, 736
  independence of, 593
  middle class in, 736, 737
  politics in, 598, 823–825, 900
  Portuguese control of, 362, 363, 435, 444, 593
  Protestantism in, 917
  slavery in, 435, 438, 443, 452, 468, 594, 605–606
  sugar production in, 435–437
  trade in, 599, 605
  in 20th-century, 815, 816, 824, 828
  Vargas regime in, 738–739
  voting rights in, 829
British colonies. *See also* British Raj; England; Great Britain
  in Africa, 582–583, 769
  in India, 565–573, 578 (*See also* India)
  in New Zealand, 584
  in 19th-century, 568, 686
  in North America, 371–372, 374–376
  in 17th-century, 371
British East India Company, 364, 366, 370, 376, 377, 564, 565, 568, 570
British Raj. *See also* India
  consolidation of, 568–569, 568*m*
  education in, 570, 571, 578
  events leading to, 565–568
  Indian independence movement and, 686–689, 767–768
  social hierarchies in, 578
  social reform in, 570–573
British Royal Society, 374
Brittain, Vera, 683
Bronze Age, 13
Bubonic plague (Black Death), 232, 338
Buchan, John, 581
Buddha, 53, 59
Buddhism
  art and, 50*f*, 60*f*, 281
  beliefs and practices of, 59, 104
  in China, 43, 104, 268–270
Buddhism cont.
  in India, 54
  in Japan, 59, 106, 288–289, 293–294, 658

in Korea, 106, 299, 301
Mahayana, 268
rise and spread of, 59, 65, 67, 95, 104–106, 110, 167
in Vietnam, 106, 307
women and, 106
Zen, 268, 270
Buffet, Bernard, 797–798
Bulgaria
Byzantine Empire and, 197–198
independence of, 650, 651
post–World War II, 765, 781
reforms in, 898
Soviet influence in, 801, 898
Turkish minorities in, 906
Burma, 761, 768, 850
Bush, George H. W., 793
Bushi, 292
Buyids, 151
Byelorussia, 758–759
Byzantine Empire
Arab invasions and, 132, 197–198
art in, 196f, 198–200, 199f, 201f, 202f
contact between Kievan Rus' and, 205–206
decline of, 201–202, 203m, 208, 210, 335
description of, 193, 197m
Eastern and Western versions of Christianity and, 200–201
Justinian's achievements in, 195–196
nomadic tribes of, 127
origins of, 102–103, 195
Russia and, 193–194
society and politics in, 198–200
trade in, 199–200
women in, 198

C

Cabral, Pedro Alvares, 435
Caesar, Julius, 73
Cahokia (Illinois), 241
Calcutta, 376–377
Calicut, 500–502
California, 601
Caliph, 131
Caliphate of Córdoba, 137
Calligraphy, 43
Calpulli, 244, 246, 247
Calvin, John, 384
Calvinism, 371, 374, 384
Camara, Dom Helder da, 823
Cambodia, 309
Cambodians, 916
Cambrai, Raoul de, 225
Canada
11th century expeditions to, 221
European settlements in, 364, 371–372, 374, 554–556
French Canadian separatist movement in, 791
NAFTA and, 904
post–World War I, 707, 707m
in second half of 20th century, 790–791
trade in, 707
World War I and, 675, 679
Canary Islands, 343, 344, 451
Candomble, 468
Canning, Lord, 598–599
Canterbury Tales (Chaucer), 227
Canton, 514
Canudos, 606, 606f
Cape Colony, 376, 461, 583
Cape of Good Hope, 361, 376, 449, 450, 461, 500
Capetian kings (France), 220
Capitaincies, 435

Capitalism
in China, 883, 889, 918
colonialism and, 577
in Eastern Europe, 893
rise of, 398, 463
rise of consumer, 904
in Russia, 893
Caravel ships, 501
Cárdenas, Lázaro, 712, 738
Caribbean. See also specific countries
indigenous populations in, 428
introduction of new animal species to, 430
slavery in, 436f, 438, 452, 453, 467f, 468
Spanish conquests in, 422–424
trade in, 433, 442
U.S. interest in, 613, 680, 825, 826m
Carolingians, 216–217
Carrera, Rafael, 595
Carter, Jimmy, 828, 895, 901
Carthage, 73, 174
Castas, 438–440
Caste system
in India, 52–53, 56, 59–63, 163
inequality and, 62–63
Castile, 343
Castro, Fidel, 668, 820
Çatal Hüyük, 14–15
Catalonia, 220
Catherine the Great (queen of Russia), 397, 409–410, 409f, 415
Catholic church. See Christianity; Orthodox Christianity; Roman Catholic church
Catholic Reformation, 384, 385
Caudillos, 595, 601
Causation, 365
Cave painting, 6, 6f
Cavour, Count Camillo di, 546
Cellular phones, 908
Centralists, 602
Césaire, Aimé, 685, 696f
Ceylon, 377, 505, 768
Chabi (wife of Kubilai Khan), 326–327, 327f, 329
Chaitanya, 164
Chaldiran battle, 483–486
Chamberlain, Neville, 735, 751, 755
de Champlain, Samuel, 356
Chams, 308, 309, 916
Chanca, Dr. Diego Alverez, 356
Chandragupta Maurya, 54
Changan, 276
Chaplin, Charles, 709
Charity, 129
Charlemagne (Charles the Great), 200, 216–219, 217f, 218m
Charles I, king of England, 385, 386f
Charles II, king of Spain, 441
Charles III, king of Spain, 441
Charles Martel (Charles the Hammer), 216
Chartist movement, 542
Chechnya, 906
Chiang Ching-kuo, 874
Chiang Jiang, 31
Chiang Kai-shek, 722, 723, 752, 755, 864, 865, 867, 874, 876, 877
Chichimec peoples, 23, 241
Children
effects of industrialization on, 544
of slave mothers, 181–182
Chile
government and politics in, 598, 601, 821, 823, 828
independence of, 592, 595
labor strikes in, 737

middle class in, 736
overthrow of Allende in, 823–824
Pinochet and, 813
Spanish conquest of, 427
trade in, 599
U.S. intervention in, 793
Chimor, 251
China. See also specific dynasties
agriculture in, 14, 37, 46, 48, 277–279, 278f, 513
architecture in, 27, 269f
art in, 22, 22f, 27, 34f, 43, 44f, 262f, 267f, 270f, 271f, 277f, 281–284, 283f, 512f–513f, 514
artisans in, 328–329
Boxer Rebellion in, 575, 712
Buddhism in, 59, 268–270
capitalist development in, 883, 889, 893, 918
civil service examination in, 509–510, 510f, 637
classical period in, 30–49, 51, 66, 77, 78, 91, 92, 94, 98–99
communism in, 720–722, 867, 876–878, 889
culture in, 43, 47–48, 66
democratic demonstration of 1989 in, 901
early civilization in, 21–22, 24–27
economy in, 44, 878, 895
ethnic issues in, 916
expansion and, 514–516
family structure in, 39, 47, 278, 279, 630
feudalism in, 295
Han dynasty and, 36m, 38, 41, 46, 98, 99, 263, 275, 303
influence on Korea, 299–302
influence on Vietnam, 303–306, 878
Japanese invasion of, 724, 740, 752, 755, 757, 761, 876, 877
link between Japan and, 287–294, 309, 310, 654–655, 679
literature in, 43, 282–283, 514, 720
Long March in, 723–724
Mao and, 722–724
Marxist ideology and, 720–721
May Fourth movement in, 719–720
Middle Kingdom of, 37, 52
Ming dynasty in, 331, 337, 508–517
missionaries in, 516
Mongols in, 320, 325–329, 331, 337, 508, 509
Nationalist party in, 721–723, 723f
in 19th century, 617–618
Opium War and, 632–634, 653
peasants in, 42–44, 49, 511, 517, 720, 722
plagues in, 338, 508
political institutions and thought in, 38–41
population growth in, 32, 837, 879–880, 883, 918
post–World War II, 766, 876m
Qin dynasty and, 36m, 37–38, 302–303, 325
Qing dynasty in, 509, 617, 629–638, 716
relationship between U.S. and, 902
religion in, 40–43, 48, 268–270
revolution in, 637, 716–718, 721m, 867
scholar-gentry in, 62, 304–305, 328, 509–512, 635–636
science in, 43, 47–48, 390
Shang era, 22f, 24, 26, 27
slavery in, 44, 46
social structure in, 39, 44–46, 62, 63
Song dynasty in, 272–283
Soviet Union and, 722, 807, 878
Sui dynasty in, 98, 263–269, 278
Tang dynasty in, 99, 266–282

technological advances in, 27, 46, 95, 280, 282
trade in, 33, 38, 46, 49, 63–65, 165–167, 183, 275–276, 337–338, 369, 374, 501, 632–634, 908
women in, 45, 106, 279–280, 512, 630, 880–881
Zhou dynasty in, 25–27, 35, 40, 46, 264, 295
Chinampas, 245
Chinese language, Mandarin, 37
Chinggis Khan, 158, 284, 314
  death of, 320
  early career of, 316–318
  leadership skills of, 318
  Mongol Empire under, 319–320, 321*m*
Chopin, Frederic, 651
Choson, 299
Christian crusades
  explanation of, 151
  impact on Islam of, 152–153, 156
Christian Democratic movement, 783, 786, 821
Christianity. *See also* Orthodox Christianity; Protestantism; Roman Catholic church; *specific denominations*
  in Africa, 175–176
  beliefs and practices of, 104, 107–108
  in eastern Europe, 203–207
  in Ethiopia, 93
  in Middle Ages, 215–216, 224–226
  origins of, 27
  in postclassical period, 193–194
  Protestant Reformation and, 384
  Roman Empire and, 78, 79, 101, 103, 107
  in Spain, 343
  spread of, 96, 103–104, 106–108, 115
  women and, 108
Christians
  conflicts in Balkans between Muslims and, 2
  in Ottoman Empire, 476–477, 619
  slaves as, 468
Chungara, Domitilia Barnos, 822
Chung-hee, 871
Chung Ju Yung, 872
Churchill, Winston
  election of 1945 and, 768
  World War II and, 755, 758, 760, 767
Cicero, 76, 79, 86
Cimabue, 340
Circuses, 398
City-states
  in ancient Greece, 71, 74, 76
  in ancient Middle East, 19, 25, 85
  medieval Italian, 218
Civil disobedience, 767*f*, 768
Civilization
  artistic creativity and values of, 281
  causation approach to, 365
  characteristics of, 15–16
  decline of, 620–621
  definition of, 15, 23
  emergence of early, 13–16
  gender and, 136–137
  heritage of early civilizations, 24–28
  postclassical period expansion of, 114
  in world historical perspective, 23–24
Civil rights movement, 785, 786*f*
Civil service examinations
  in China, 509–510, 510*f*, 637
  in Western nations, 548
Civil War. *See* American Civil War
Cixi (Manchu empress), 635, 637
Classical Greece. *See* Ancient Greece
Classical period. *See also specific civilizations*

characteristics of, 30–33, 91
in China, 30–49, 98–99
comparison of civilizations during, 77–78
expansion and integration during, 31–33, 91–95
in Greece and Rome, 69–88, 99–103
in India, 30–33, 50–67, 98–99
religion in, 40–43, 48, 53, 54, 57–60, 77, 78–80, 103–110
timeline of, 32
trade in, 33, 46, 55, 63, 64, 71, 85, 93, 94, 94*m*
Clemenceau, Georges, 682
Clive, Robert, 567–568
Clovis (king of Franks), 90*f*, 215
Coale, Ansley, 185
Coeur, Jacques, 229–230
Cold war
  containment policy during, 792–793
  end of, 895–896
  Latin America and, 815
  overview of, 764–766
  realignment following, 898–900
  Soviet Union and, 764–766, 781–783, 805, 896–898
  spread of democracy following, 900–902, 904
  U.S. allies and, 790–792
  western Europe and, 781–783
Collectivization
  in eastern Europe, 800, 801
  in Soviet Union, 742–743
Colombia
  drug trade in, 825
  economy in, 595
  independence of, 592
  Spanish control in, 370
Colonialism. *See* Imperialism; *specific countries*
Columbian exchange, 430
Columbus, Christopher, 342, 344*f*, 362
  expedition to Americas, 362–363, 421
  1492 expedition of, 373
  introduction of crops by, 431
Comintern, 716
Common Market, 786–788, 900, 903. *See also* European Union
Communism
  in Africa, 849
  in China, 720–722, 867, 876–879
  in eastern Europe, 800–801, 888, 895, 898
  post–World War II, 792
  in Soviet Union, 714–716, 742, 744, 802, 805, 895
  Spanish Civil War and, 736
  in Vietnam, 886, 887
Communist Party of Vietnam, 886
Computers, 908, 909
Comte, Auguste, 600
Comunero Revolt, 443
Concubines, 181
Condorcet, Marquis de, 535
Confucianism
  in China, 38, 41–42, 47, 48, 98, 99, 106, 267–269, 273–274, 889
  in Japan, 288, 521, 652, 740
  in Korea, 301
  rejection of, 719–721, 889
  social ideals and thought of, 41–42, 47, 75, 328, 329
  in Vietnam, 306, 883, 885
  women and, 45
Confucian system, 637
Confucius, 33, 37, 40–41, 91

Congo, 850, 907
Congress of Vienna, 541, 642, 644
Conselheiro, Antonio, 606
Conservatism, 541, 785
Constable, John, 534*f*, 552
Constantine (Roman emperor), 73–74, 101, 195
Constantinople
  during Byzantine Empire, 195, 197, 199, 200, 202, 210
  Crusades in, 222
  fall to Turks, 208, 335, 355
  during Ottoman Empire, 477*f*, 478–479
  during Roman Empire, 101, 102
Consulado, 433
Consuls, 76
Consumer capitalism, 904
Containment policy, 793
Convention Peoples party (CPP), 769
Cook, James, 585
Cooper, Marc, 919
Copernicus, 388–389, 415
Copts, 103, 132, 175
Corinthian style, 82
Corn, 366
Cornwallis, Charles, 570
Coronado, Francesco Vázquez de, 427
Corporations
  multinational, 910
  in United States, 708
  in western Europe, 544, 544*f*
Corporatism, 738, 739
Cortés, Hernán, 419, 426
Cortés, Hernando, 356
Cossacks, 404, 415
Costa Rica, 601, 816
Council of People's Commissars, 714
Council of the Indies, 434
Creoles, 438–439
Creole slaves, 467
Cresques, Abraham, 179
Crete
  Egyptian influence on, 25, 71
  Ottomans in, 475
Crick, Francis, 796–797
Crimean War, 645, 646
Cripps, Sir Stafford, 767
Cristeros, 713
Croatia, 898, 906
Cromer, Lord, 689
Crops, 360, 366, 431. *See also* Agriculture
Crosby, Alfred, 430
Crusades
  explanation of, 151
  function of, 221–222
  impact of, 152–153, 156, 361
Cruz, Juana Inéz de la, 434, 435*f*
Cuba
  drug trade in, 825
  economy in, 599, 613, 820–821, 893
  gender roles in, 830
  independence of, 591
  revolution in, 819–821, 823, 830
  slavery in, 594
  social reform in, 738
  Soviet relationship with, 806, 806*f*, 820–821
  Spanish control of, 370, 422, 442
  U.S. involvement in, 613, 792, 825
  voting rights in, 829
Cubist movement, 703
Cultural Revolution (China), 882, 883
Culture. *See also* Art; Literature; Music; Poetry; Popular culture
  in China, 43, 47–48

in Europe, 550–552, 703–704, 790–791, 796–799
globalization and, 911–912
Muslim influences on, 153
in Soviet Union, 802–803
in United States, 554, 708–709, 790–791, 796, 798
Cuneiform writing, 15, 17, 18
Cushitic, 460
Cuzco, 252, 254, 427
Cyprus, 475
Cyrebe, 174
Cyril (missionary), 203
Cyrus the Great, 70
Czechoslovakia
collapse of communism in, 898
German annexation of, 735, 753, 756, 800
post–World War I, 682
post–World War II, 781, 792
Soviet intervention in, 801
spread of civilization to, 204
Czech Republic, 906

D
da Cunha, Euclides, 606
Daewoo, 872
da Gama, Vasco, 343, 362, 499–501, 503, 507
Dahomey, 453, 455
Damas, Léon, 696
Damascus, Syria, 133
Dance, 80, 709, 709*f*, 803, 831
Dan Fodio, Usuman, 460
Danilevsky, Nikolai, 532
Daoism
description of, 35, 42–43
effects of, 48, 98, 390
impact of Buddhism on, 106, 269
Darwin, Charles, 23, 551
da Silva, Luiz Inacio Lula, 825
da Vinci, Leonardo. *See* Leonardo da Vinci
Decembrist uprising, 643, 643*f*
Declaration of Independence, 537
Declaration of the Rights of Man and the Citizen, 538
Decolonization, 668
artificial nations created by, 842–843
economic development and, 846, 848
impact of, 781, 835
Latin America and, 815
nonsettler Africa and, 769–771
post–World War II, 668, 766–767, 779–781
settler colonies and, 771–772
South Africa and, 771–773
south and southeast Asia and, 767–770
Deforestation, 16, 845
De Gaulle, Charles, 771, 772, 780
Deism, 390
de Klerk, F. W., 858
Demak, 165–166
Democracy
European liberal, 783–784
in India, 854, 858–859
in Japan, 866
late 20th-century spread of, 900–902, 904
in Latin America, 824–825, 900–901
Demographic transition, 184–185
Demography
explanation of, 184
Western, 733–734
Deng Xiaoping, 880, 882, 883
Denmark
Bismarck and, 546
economic growth in, 789

European Union and, 788
industrialization in, 544
World War II and, 757, 760
Dependency theory, 610
Depression. *See* Great Depression
Descartes, René, 389
Deshima, 521
The Destruction of Philosophy, 336
Developing nations. *See also* Postcolonial era
appeal of Marxism in, 821
economic growth in, 846, 848
endangered ecosystems in, 844–845, 844*f*
explanation of, 813
human rights in, 827–828
in Latin America, 813–814
literature in, 847
Devi, 99
Dewey, John, 719
Dharma, 54, 57, 59
Dhimmis, 134, 476–477
Dhows, 139
Dias, António Gonçalves, 607
Díaz, Porfirio, 602, 611–612, 711
Dickens, Charles, 552
Diderot, Denis, 395, 395*f*, 397
Diem, Ngo Dinh, 887
Dien Bien Phu, 886
Din-i-Ilahi, 492–493
di Nobili, Robert, 507
Dinshawai incident, 690
Diocletian (Roman emperor), 73, 100–101, 193
Disease. *See also* Plagues
in African and Pacific colonies, 582, 585, 586
American Indian exposure to European, 374–375, 428, 430
HIV/AIDS, 839, 920
international contacts and, 366–367
population and, 839
in Roman Empire, 100
in Soviet Union, 896
in Spanish colonies, 423–424, 428
Disraeli, Benjamin, 546
Divine Comedy (Dante), 341
Dominican Republic
independence of, 595
U.S. involvement in, 825
voting rights in, 829
Doric style, 82
Dostoevsky, Fyodor, 651
Douglass, Frederick, 465
Dreyfus, Alfred, 692
Drug trade, 824–825
Du Bois, W.E.B., 695, 696*f*
Duffy, Eliza, 533
Duma, 651
Dutch colonies. *See also* Netherlands
in Asia, 372
in Brazil, 364
in 17th century, 364, 371
Dutch East India Company
in Africa, 376, 461
explanation of, 364
interests of, 564
Dutch East Indies, 761
Dutch Studies, 652–653

E
Early modern period
change in, 356
description of, 350–351
gunpowder empires in, 354–355
rise of western Europe in, 351–352
timeline for, 352–353

trends in, 356–357
world boundaries in, 353–354, 354*m*
world economy and global contacts in, 352–353
Eastern bloc, 781
Eastern Europe. *See also specific countries*
boundaries between western and, 209
economy in, 804, 898
at end of postclassical era, 209–210
estate agriculture in, 413
ethnic conflict in, 898, 905–907
industrialization in, 800, 804, 896
Jews in, 204
map of, 706*m*
post–World War I, 728
post–World War II, 781–782, 781*m*, 792
religious revivals in, 917
Russia and, 415, 651–652
social structure in, 804
Soviet dominance in, 799–802, 893
spread of civilization in, 203–210, 205*m*
trade in, 204–205, 370, 415
East Germany. *See also* Germany
creation of, 782, 782*m*
Soviet control of, 800
unification of, 858
Economic Commission for Latin America (ECLA), 610
Economic thought, 395
Economy
in ancient Greece, 84–85, 87
in ancient Rome, 84–85, 87
of Aztecs, 245–246
in China, 44, 878, 895
Common Market and, 786–788
in Cuba, 820–821
democracy and, 902, 904
in early modern period, 352–353
of 18th-century Russia, 408–409
expansionist trends and, 370–378
governmental role in, 785
imperialism and, 580–582
in India, 61, 63, 65
industrialization and world, 530
international contacts and, 366–367, 369–370
international trade and, 367
in Japan, 869
in Kongo, 188–189
in Latin America, 599–601, 610–613, 736, 824
in Mali, 177, 179
in Middle Ages, 218–219
in Pacific Rim, 873, 889, 903
in postcolonial era, 846, 848
post–World War I, 727–729
in Renaissance, 383
in Russia, 413–414, 902
in 1970s, 785
in 17th- and 18th-century Europe, 397–398
in 16th-century Europe, 386–387
slavery and, 368, 369, 454
in Soviet Union, 742–743, 803–804, 808, 896, 897
in 20th-century Europe, 788–790, 793
in United States, 708, 788, 789, 903
in Vietnam, 888
Ecuador
independence of, 592
labor force in, 830
voting rights in, 829
Edict of Nantes, 385
Edo, 519
Edo peoples, 187
Education. *See also* Universities

in British India, 570, 571, 578
in China, 631
in European colonies, 570–572
in India, 60
in Japan, 652–653, 658, 709–710, 866
Jewish emphasis on, 204
in Mexico, 608, 712
in Middle Ages, 219, 235
in 19th-century 533
in 19th-century Europe, 548
in Ottoman Empire, 622
in Soviet Union, 716, 896
in Vietnam, 885
of women, 794, 922
Effendi, 690
Egypt. *See also* Ancient Egypt
  British control of, 627, 686, 689, 690, 693, 781
  conflicts between Israel and, 851, 852
  Coptic church in, 103, 132, 175
  French invasion of, 624–625
  independence of, 773, 850, 851
  khedival regime in, 626
  Mubarak and, 854
  Muhammad Ali's reforms in, 625
  Muslims in, 157
  Nasser and, 850–853
  nationalist movement in, 689–690, 694
  Ottomans in, 474
  revolt in, 693–694
  Sadat and, 853–854
  Soviet Union and, 807, 852–854
  Suez Canal and, 781
  World War I and, 684
Ehrmann, Marianne, 397
Einstein, Albert, 552
Eisenhower, Dwight D., 761, 792
Elizabeth I, queen of England, 384
El Mina, 449
El Salvador, 824
Encomiendas, 422, 429
Encyclopaedia Britannica, 397
England. *See also* British colonies; Great Britain
  art in, 534*f*
  end of slave trade and, 470
  establishment of parliament in, 220
  expeditions by, 363–364
  feudalism in, 220
  Industrial Revolution in, 527
  interest in Africa, 450
  parliamentary monarchy in, 394
  religious conflict in, 385
  Renaissance in, 383
  trade in, 364, 366, 370, 505
English Civil War, 385, 386*f*
Enlightenment
  changes during, 397, 536
  colonial interest in, 374
  explanation of, 381, 395
  in France, 395, 397, 538
Entertainment, 550
Environmental issues
  global warming and, 918–920
  impact of civilization and, 16
  industrialization and, 845, 896
  in late 20th century, 918–919
  in postcolonial societies, 844–845, 844*f*
  United States and, 902
Epic Age (India), 52, 53, 56–58, 61
Equality
  in classical period, 77, 78, 92
  concept of, 62–63
Equiano, Olaudah, 465
Era of the Warring States, 37

Ernensky, Alexander, 713
Estonia, 766
Ethiopia
  ancient Egyptian interactions with, 29
  Italian attack on, 735, 753
  spread of Christianity to, 175–176, 175*f*
  trade in, 93
Ethnic conflict
  in Africa, 907, 907*f*
  in eastern Europe, 898, 905–907
  nationalism and, 916
  religious fundamentalism and, 917
  terrorism and, 917
  in western Europe, 906
Ethnocentrism, 24, 346
Euclid, 80
Eunuchs, 136, 181
Euro, 788
Europe. *See also* Eastern Europe; Western Europe; *specific countries or regions*
  age of revolution in, 536–543
  boundaries between eastern and western, 209
  in classical period, 96
  colonial territories in, 566*m*
  demographic transition in, 184–185
  diplomatic tensions in pre–World War I, 558–559
  economic growth in, 788–790
  expeditions to Asia by, 499–508, 515–516, 519–520
  impact of decolonization on, 781
  interwar period in, 701–706
  maritime dominance of, 366–369
  Middle Ages in western, 213–236 (*See also* Middle Ages)
  migration in, 911
  political movements in, 541
  post–World War II, 766
  religious conflict in 16th and 17th century, 384–386
  Scientific Revolution in, 389–390
  threat of Mongols to, 320, 323–324
  World War I in, 670*f*, 671–679, 673*m*, 681–682, 684
European Economic Community (Common Market), 786–788. *See also* European Union
European Union
  economic integration through, 903–904
  establishment of, 786–788, 787*m*
Evangelicals, 570
Eware the Great, 187
Exploration
  in Africa, 357
  in the Americas, 356-357
  in Asia, 357
  of Greenland, 221
  in Latin America, 419–420
  western European, 221, 343–345, 360–366

F

Facundo (Sarmiento), 604
Falange, 736
Falkland Islands, 815, 824
Family (Ba Jin), 720
Family structure
  among slaves, 468
  in ancient Greece, 87
  in ancient Rome, 87
  of bedouins, 126
  in China, 39, 47, 278, 279, 630
  in India, 61, 63
  industrialization and, 529
  in Islamic societies, 134–137, 150–151
  in Japan, 658, 869–870

in Renaissance, 383–384
in 17th-century Europe, 396
in Soviet Union, 804–805
in 20th-century West, 794
Famine, 837, 841*f*
Fanon, Frantz, 695
Farming. *See* Agriculture
Fascism
  in Italy, 704–705, 705*f*, 732
  origins of, 732, 734
  post–World War II decline in, 783
  in Spain, 736
  spread of, 735–736
Federal Republic of Germany. *See* West Germany
Feisal (Jordanian prince), 683*f*
Female suffrage. *See* Voting rights
The Feminine Mystique (Friedan), 796
Feminism. *See also* Gender roles; Women
  in 18th century, 397
  in 19th century, 545, 548–550
  in postcolonial era, 845–846
  in 20th century, 785, 795–796, 797*f*, 829, 845–846, 869–870
Ferdinand (Austro-Hungarian archduke), 674
Ferdinand of Aragon, 221, 343, 421
Feudalism
  in China, 295
  explanation of, 219–220
  in Japan, 221, 295–296
  limited government under, 220–221
Feudal monarchies, 219–221, 390
Fez, Morocco, 174
Fiji islands, 97
Film industry. *See* Motion picture industry
Finland, 758, 788, 799
First Indochina War, 887
Five pillars, 130
Flying money, 276
Fon peoples, 453, 458
Foods
  colonization and exchange of, 431
  from New World crops, 360, 366
Footbinding, 279–280, 326
Forbidden city (China), 635
Ford, Henry, 708
Foreign policy, 828
Formosa, 741
Fox, Vicente, 816
France. *See also* French colonies
  absolute monarchy in, 390–392
  architecture in, 391, 391*f*
  campus unrest in, 778*f*, 785
  demographic transition in, 184
  economic growth in, 788–789
  Enlightenment in, 395, 397
  ethnic minorities in, 906
  European Union and, 786, 788
  exploration by, 364
  feudalism in, 220
  Fifth Republic in, 783
  Great Depression in, 731
  industrialization in, 541–542
  interest in Africa, 450
  interest in India, 376–377
  invasion of Egypt, 624–625
  involvement in Vietnam, 571, 772, 883–886
  in Middle Ages, 214, 219, 220, 229, 233–234
  Morocco and, 558, 672
  Muslims in, 911, 911*f*
  Napoleon and, 540–541
  NATO and, 783
  Ottoman Empire and, 644, 645
  parliamentary tradition in, 220, 541, 547

post–World War I, 728
post–World War II, 783
pre–World War I, 563, 671–673
religious conflict in, 384, 385
Renaissance in, 383
socialist movement in, 549
trading companies and, 364, 370
welfare state in, 784, 785
women in labor force in, 795
World War I and, 675–677, 680–684
World War II and, 751, 753, 755–757, 761, 765
Francis I, king of France, 383
Francis of Assisi, 222
Franco, Francisco, 736, 753
Franco-Prussian War of 1870, 672
Franks, 133, 216
Frederick the Great (king of Prussia), 394–395
Free Officers movement (Egypt), 850, 851f
French colonies. See also France
in Africa, 558, 672, 769, 771–772, 780
in Canada, 371, 372, 374
in Caribbean, 591
education in, 571
in North America, 371–372, 374–376
in 17th century, 371
French East India Company, 370
French Guiana, 469
French Indochina, 761
French Revolution of 1789
background of, 538
Latin American and, 591
radical and authoritarian phases of, 538–540
Russia and, 410, 411
French Revolution of 1830, 541
Freud, Sigmund, 552
Friedan, Betty, 796, 796f
Fujiwara, 291
Fulani, 460

G

Galen, 80, 225
Galileo, 389
Gallipoli, 680
Gálvez, José de, 442
Gana, Alberto Blest, 607, 607f
Gandhi, Indira, 845
Gandhi, Mohandas, 685, 688–689, 697, 767f, 768, 770
Ganges River, 31
Gang of Four, 883
Gao, 176, 180
Garbo, Greta, 709
Garvey, Marcus, 695
Gatekeeper elites, 304–305
Gautama Buddha. See Buddha
Gempei Wars, 294
Gender roles. See also Women
among Incas, 255, 255f
of Aztecs, 247–249
of bedouins, 126, 136, 137
in China, 279–280
civilization and, 136–137
convergence of Mongol and Chinese culture and, 326–327
in Islamic societies, 134–137, 150–151
in Latin America, 829
in Ottoman and Safavid Empires, 488–489
in postcolonial era, 845–846
in Russia, 646
in Spanish colonies, 439–440
General Agreement of Tariffs and Trade (GATT), 893
The General History of the Things of New Spain (Sahagún), 248–249

Georgia, 906
Germanic kingdoms, 101, 101m, 103
Germany
annexation of Czechoslovakia, 735, 753, 756
cold war and, 782, 783
concentration camps of, 734
division of, 765, 782, 782m, 783
economic growth in, 788–789
European Union and, 786, 788
fascism in, 732, 734
Great Depression in, 729–732
Hitler and, 732, 734–735
industrialization in, 541–542
invasion of Poland, 735, 751, 756, 757
in Middle Ages, 214, 218–219, 221, 229
nationalism in, 546
in 19th century, 546–547, 547m, 558
parliamentary tradition in, 220
political protest in, 542
post–World War I, 702, 727, 728
post–World War II, 781, 782m
pre–World War I, 558, 559, 671–675
religious conflict in, 384, 385
Renaissance in, 383
socialist movement in, 548–549
Spanish Civil War and, 736
trade in, 229
Turks in, 906
unification of, 898
voting rights for women in, 678
World War I and, 675–678, 680–683
World War II and, 751, 753–761, 764, 767
Gestapo, 734
Ghana
colonizers in, 578, 579f
independence of, 768, 769, 848
Nkrumah and, 848–849
Ghana (Sudanic kingdom)
characteristics of life in, 179–180, 454
Islam in, 176
rise of, 95, 176
Ghost Dance religion, 575
Gia Long, 884
Giotto, 340
Glasnost, 896
Globalization
business organization and investment and, 910–911
cultural, 911–912
disease and, 920
future outlook for, 921–922
industrialization and, 533
institutions of, 912–913
Latin America and, 832
migration and, 911
overview of, 893–895, 908
in postcolonial societies, 857, 889
post–World War I, 724, 727
protest against, 913–916, 913f
technological advances and, 908–909
Global warming, 919–920. See also Environmental issues
Glorious Revolution, 394
Goa, 363
The Goals of Education, 533
Godard, Jean-Luc, 798
Gold Coast, 696, 769, 849
Golden Horde, 320–321, 323–325
Gold rush, 437
Good Neighbor Policy, 826
The Good Wife, 231
Gorbachev, Mikhail, 809, 896–898
Gothic architecture, 226, 226f, 235
Government, 33-34
Granada, 421

Granada War, 421
Gran Colombia, 592, 595
Grand Canal (China), 275, 280
Great Britain. See also British colonies; British Raj; England
in Africa, 628, 695, 696, 769, 771
American Revolution and, 537
control of India by, 376–377, 565–572, 578
economic growth in, 788–789
in Egypt, 627, 686, 689, 690, 693
European Union and, 788, 792
Falklands controversy and, 815
Great Depression and, 730–732
in India, 376–377, 565–573, 568m, 578, 686–689, 767–768
invasion of Iraq by U.S. and, 905
naval power of, 673, 679
Ottoman Empire and, 644, 645
Palestine and, 774
political change in, 541
political protest in, 542
post–World War I, 702, 727, 729
post–World War II, 765
pre–World War I, 558, 559, 577, 672, 673
recognition of Latin American sovereignty by, 598
South Africa and, 582–583
Suez Canal and, 850–852, 853f
trade in, 229, 632
voting rights for women in, 678
welfare state in, 784, 785
World War I and, 675–684
World War II and, 751, 753–758, 760–762, 764, 767–769
Great Depression
causes of, 727–729
description of, 727, 729–731
effects of, 747
in Japan, 730, 731, 740, 741
Latin American and, 730, 736, 738, 815
western European responses to, 731–732
World War I and, 682
Great Leap Forward, 879, 879f, 880
Great trek, 462
Great Wall of China, 38, 43, 263
Great Zimbabwe, 188–189, 189f
Greece. See also Ancient Greece
democracy in, 900
establishment of parliamentary system in, 784
European Union and, 788
independence of, 644, 651
Ottoman rule in, 541
post-World War II, 781, 792, 800
World War II and, 758, 765
Greek fire, 197
Greek Revolution, 541
Greenland, 221
Green movement, 785
Green Revolution, 854, 855
Gregory VII, Pope, 223
Grenada, 793, 821
Griots, 177, 178
Guaman Poma de Ayala, 425
Guatemala
government in, 822–824
in 19th century, 594–595
Protestantism in, 917
U.S. intervention in, 792, 818–819
Guevara, Ernesto "Che," 812f, 820, 821
Guilds, 230
Guillotine, 538
The Gulag Archipelago (Solzhenitsyn), 803
Gunboat diplomacy, 574f
Gunpowder empires
decline of, 496

explanation of, 354–365, 355f, 455
global power shifts and, 484–485
Guns, 355, 369. See also Weaponry
Guomindang (Nationalist Party of China), 721–722, 752, 755, 764, 867, 878
Gupta dynasty, 55–56, 55m, 59–61, 66, 98, 99
Gurus, 58
Gypsies, 760

H

Habsburg Empire
  collapse of, 702
  Ottomans and, 475, 619, 621
  Portugal and, 437
  power of, 392–393
  reach of, 415
Haciendas, 433
Hadiths, 119, 135
Hagia Sophia, 195
Haiti
  independence of, 591
  in 19th century, 594, 595
  political repression in, 830
  slave trade and, 452
  U.S. involvement in, 825
Hajj, 130, 171
Hammurabi, 19
Hammurabi's Code, 19–20, 45
Han dynasty
  characteristics of, 38, 43, 48
  Confucianism and, 41
  decline of, 98, 99, 263
  map of, 36m
  political institutions and thought in, 39–41, 48
  population increase in, 275
  technological advances in, 46
  trade in, 49
  Vietnam and, 303
Han Feizi, 33
Hangzhou, 276
Hannibal, 73
Hanseatic League, 229
Harappan civilization
  characteristics of, 21, 22f, 26
  demise of, 27, 330
  legacy of, 26, 27
Harem, 136, 150
Harris, Marvin, 251
Harun al-Rashid (Abbasid caliph), 149, 150
Harvey, William, 389
Hausa, 180
Hawaii
  American control of, 586
  settlement of, 345–346, 584–586
  U.S. interests in, 680
Health
  industrialization and, 544
  population increase and, 837
  of women, 846
Health care, 784
Heian period
  court life in, 289–291
  explanation of, 288
Hellenistic period. See also Ancient Greece
  Alexander the Great and, 51, 54
  description of, 72, 73m
  ethical beliefs during, 79–80
  science in, 80
Henry IV, Holy Roman Emperor, 223
Henry the Navigator, 343, 361, 361f
Henry VIII, king of England, 384
Hernández, José, 607
Herodotus, 33–34
Herzl, Theodor, 692

Hidalgo, Miguel de, 591
Hideki, Tojo, 740
Hideyoshi, Toyotomi, 518–519, 521
Himalayas, 52
Hinduism
  beliefs of, 57–59, 840
  challenges of Buddhism to, 59–60
  challenges of Islam to, 99, 163–165
  rise and spread of, 54, 57, 59, 65, 110, 115
  ritual suicide and, 250, 492, 493f, 570, 572
Hindus
  attempts to Christianize, 507
  Indian nationalist movement and, 687–688
  in Mughal Empire, 492, 496
Hiroshima, Japan, 762
Hisako, Yoshizawa, 761
Hispaniola, 370, 422, 441, 469
Hitler, Adolf
  persecution of Jews, 760, 773–774
  rise of, 681, 732, 744
  Spanish Civil War and, 753
  suicide of, 761
  totalitarian state under, 732, 734
  World War II and, 751, 753
HIV/AIDS, 839, 920
Ho Chi Minh (Nguyen Ai Quoc), 683, 718, 886, 887
Hojo, 294
Holbein, Hans, 385f
Holland. See Dutch colonies; Netherlands
Holocaust, 734, 760
Holy Alliance, 642–643
Holy Roman emperors, 218, 220
Homo erectus, 8
Homo sapiens sapiens, 8, 28
Hong Kong
  Japanese capture of, 761
  post–World War II, 867–868
Hongwu emperor, 508–512
Hong Xiuquan, 634
Hoover, Herbert, 732
Hopewell culture, 241–242
Houphouët-Boigny, Felix, 771
House of Lords (England), 220
Ho Zuan Huong, 306
Hsu Kuang-Chi, 357
Huancavelica, 432
Huanghe valley civilization, 21–22, 24, 28, 35, 37
Huari, 251
Huayna Capac, 252
Huerta, Victoriano, 711
Huitzilopochtli, 243, 249
Hulegu (Mongol ruler), 158, 324, 325
Humanism, 382, 383
Human rights, 827–828
Human Rights Commission (United Nations), 902
Human sacrifice
  among Aztecs, 242
  interpretations of, 250–251
Human species, distinctive features of, 7
Humayan (Mughal warrior), 490
Humbert de Romans, 119
Hundred Years' War, 221, 232, 234f, 338–339
Hungary
  communism in, 800
  fascist movement in, 735
  in Habsburg Empire, 415
  independence of, 651
  Mongols and, 324
  Ottomans and, 474
  political protest in, 542
  post–World War I, 682
  post–World War II, 765, 781, 800

Renaissance in, 383
Soviet intervention in, 800, 801
transition from communism to capitalism in, 893, 898
Huns
  in China, 38
  in India, 55
  invasions by, 98, 99
Hunting and gathering
  in Americas, 16, 258–259
  in Neolithic Age, 11, 12
  in Paleolithic Age, 8–9
Husayn, 133, 135
Hussein, Saddam, 856, 905
Hutus, 907
Hymn to Wisdom, 268–269
Hyundai, 872

I

Ibn al-Athir, 325
Ibn Batuta, 118, 177, 183
Ibn Khaldun, 119, 152, 331
ibn Qasim, Muhammad, 160, 161
Iceland, 221
Ideographic symbols, 22
Ieyasu, Tokugawa, 519, 521
Ifriqiya, 174
Iliad (Homer), 81
Imams, Shi'a, 486
Imperialism. See also specific countries and regions
  capitalism and, 577
  economic extraction methods and, 580–582
  education and, 570–572
  industrialization and, 559–560
  Marxist critique and, 609
  in Pacific, 582–586
  patterns of dominance and, 576, 578–586
  resistance to, 578
  social hierarchies and, 578
  social reform and, 570, 572–573
  social relations between colonizers and colonized and, 578–580
  in South Africa, 582–583
  technological advances in weaponry and, 573–575
  World War I and, 673–674, 679, 684, 685
  World War II and, 766–775
Import substitution industrialization, 736
Incas
  Aztecs vs., 256–257
  conquests by, 252
  cultural achievements of, 256
  description of, 96, 251, 252m
  gender roles for, 255, 255f
  imperial rule of, 254–256
  political practices of, 252–253
  religion of, 252–253
  rise to power of, 251–252
  Spanish conquest of, 370, 427
India
  agriculture in, 61
  architecture in, 494, 494f
  art in, 50f, 58f, 61, 164, 164f, 281, 377f
  artisans in, 493
  British control of, 376–377, 565–573, 568m, 578, 686–689
  caste system in, 52–53, 56, 59–63, 163
  classical period in, 30–33, 50–67, 54m, 77, 78, 91, 92, 98–99
  communal strife in, 843
  conversion to Islam in, 162–163
  cultural influence of, 65–67
  democracy in, 854, 858–859
  early civilizations in, 21, 22f, 25–27, 330

economy in, 61, 63, 65
family structure in, 61, 63
Gupta dynasty in, 55–56, 55*m*, 59–61, 66, 98, 99
independence movement in, 686–689, 694–695, 701, 767–768
industrialization in, 839–840
Islamic influences in, 160–161, 163, 164
literature in, 52, 53, 57–58, 60, 847
mathematics in, 60, 61
Mauryan dynasty in, 54–55, 64, 65, 67
missionaries in, 376, 570
Mughal Empire in, 489–496
Muslim invasions in, 157, 160–162
political institutions in, 55–57
population growth in, 837
Portuguese in, 500–503
postcolonial, 854–855
religion in, 53, 54, 57–60, 77, 115, 163–165, 250, 492, 493*f*, 570, 572, 840
religious conflicts in, 917
science in, 60, 61
technological advances in, 63, 854
tensions between Pakistan and, 905
topography of, 51–52
trade in, 55, 63, 64, 376, 493, 501
Vedic and Epic Ages in, 52–53, 56–58, 61
women in, 61, 63, 492, 495, 687
World War I and, 675, 684
World War II and, 767–768
Indian, 239
Indies piece, 453
Indochina, 761, 793
Indo-Europeans
in ancient Greece, 71
in ancient Middle East, 20, 21, 26
in India, 52
migration of, 330
Indonesia
economic growth in, 874, 876
independence of, 865
Muslims in, 158
poetry in, 847
trade in, 165
Indra, 53
Indulgences, 384
Indus River civilization, 21, 25–27, 52. *See also* Aryans; Harappan civilization
Industrialization
consumption and leisure activities and, 550
cultural advances and, 552
diverse reactions for, 531
in eastern Europe, 800, 804, 896
economic issues and, 573
environmental deterioration and, 845, 896
expansion of West and, 552–557
globalization and, 533
imperialism and, 563, 839
import substitution, 736
in Japan, 641, 656–660, 741–742, 863
key features of, 528, 543*m*
in Latin America, 814, 815
origins of, 525–526, 525*m*, 528
political trends and, 544, 546–550
population movements and, 530–531
proto-, 537
revolutions and, 541–543, 718
in Russia, 641, 645–649, 713
scientific advances and, 551–552
social and economic inequality and, 533
social impact of, 528–529, 544
in Soviet Union, 743–744, 799, 804, 896
in 20th century, 704
in United States, 541–542, 703

as Western phenomenon, 530–531
women and, 545–546
Industrial Revolution, 527, 535, 920
Inflation, 789
Inner Mongolia, 877
Inonu, Ismet, 701
An Interesting Narrative: Biography of Mahommah G. Baquaqua (Baquaqua), 447
International Monetary Fund (IMF), 848, 893–894, 913, 918
Internet, 909, 912
Investiture, of Roman Catholic bishops, 223
Ionic style, 82
Iran. *See also* Persia
industrialization in, 747
Muslims in, 157
post–World War II, 781
religious fundamentalism in, 855–856
revolution in 1905 in, 712
revolution in 1979 in, 855–856, 895
as "rogue state," 903
war with Iraq, 856, 905
Iraq
Arab invasion and, 132
independence of, 773
invasion of Kuwait, 793, 903, 905
League of Nations mandates and, 691–692
Muslims in, 157
as "rogue state," 903
U.S.-British invasion of, 905
war with Iran, 856, 905
Ireland, 788
Ironmaking, 22, 46, 95, 96, 204, 230
Isabella of Castile, 221, 343, 421
Isandhlwana battle, 562*f*, 575
Islam
Arabs and, 129
bedouins and, 134
beliefs and practices of, 104, 129–130, 174, 224
as challenge to Hinduism, 163–165
Crusades as attack against, 221–222
Mongols and, 324–325
origins of, 27, 123, 127–129
rise and spread of, 95, 99, 104, 108, 110, 113–115, 121–122, 147, 148*m*, 166–167
slavery and, 137, 140, 150–151, 181–182, 455, 463
statistics for distribution of, 157–158
Sufism and, 167–168, 336
Sunni-Shi'a split, 132–133
universal elements in, 129–130
women and, 134–137, 150–151
Islamic civilizations. *See also* Arabs; *specific groups*
Abbasid Empire and (*See* Abbasid Empire)
accomplishments of, 142, 145, 153, 155–156, 160, 168
in Africa, 132, 147, 171–177, 179–190, 447, 460
art and architecture in, 120*f*, 128*f*, 140*f*, 142–144, 143*f*–144*f*, 146*f*, 149*f*, 153–154, 154*f*–156*f*, 161, 161*f*
artisans in, 153–154
commerce in, 139–140, 142
contradictory trends in, 156
family and gender roles in, 134–137
influence of, 153
literature in, 141, 154–155, 336
rise of, 121, 142, 145
scholarship in, 142
in south Asia, 159–165
in southeast Asia, 165–168
timeline of, 148

trade in, 153, 155
Umayyads, 130–137
weakening of, 637
Islamic fundamentalism
causes of, 854
in Iran, 855–856, 895
rise of, 917
terrorism and, 903
terrorist attack of September 11, 2001 and, 917
Ismā'il (Safavid commander), 483–485
Israel
creation of state of, 774–775
tensions between Palestinians and, 905, 917
terrorism against, 905
U.S. support of, 903
wars with Egypt, 851, 853
Italy. *See also* Ancient Rome
anti-immigrant sentiments in, 906
attack on Ethiopia, 735, 753
economic growth in, 788
European Union and, 786
exploration by, 221, 343
fascism in, 704–705, 705*f*, 732, 735
in Middle Ages, 214, 218–219, 229
nationalism in, 546
pre–World War I, 558, 672
Renaissance in, 340–342, 382–384
Spanish Civil War and, 736
trade in, 341–342
transformism in, 547
unification of, 546, 547*m*
welfare state in, 784
World War I and, 677–678, 682
World War II and, 751, 753, 758, 760, 761
Iturbide, Augustín de, 591
Ivan III (Ivan the Great), 403–405
Ivan IV (Ivan the Terrible), 404, 405
Ivory Coast, 684, 771

J

Jackson, Andrew, 541
Jahangir (Mughal emperor), 493–495
Jamaica
slaves in, 452, 468
Spanish control in, 370
James, Henry, 554
Janissaries, 475–476, 486, 622
Japan
age of warlords in, 294
agriculture in, 96
architecture in, 297*f*, 298*f*
art in, 290*f*, 291*f*, 297–298, 298*f*, 498*f*, 640*f*
background of, 289*m*
Buddhism in, 59, 106, 288–289, 293–294, 658
colonial expansion by, 659, 659*m*
control of Manchuria by, 740–741, 752–753
culture and society of, 652–653, 658–660, 868–869, 916
decline of imperial power in, 291–292
democracy in, 866
economy in, 869
education in, 652–653, 658, 709–710, 866
feudalism in, 221, 295–296
Great Depression in, 730, 731, 740, 741
Heian era in, 289–291
industrialization in, 641, 656–660, 741–742, 863
interest in Korea, 519, 651, 659, 740–741, 753
invasion of China by, 724, 740, 755, 757, 761
isolationist nature of, 520–521, 653

link between China and, 287–294, 654–655, 679
literature in, 290–291, 869
Meiji government in, 655–656
militarization in, 296–297, 740–742, 752, 753
missionaries in, 519–521
modernization in, 659–660
neo-Confucianism in, 521, 652
in 19th century, 652
Pearl Harbor attack by, 755
political and social change in, 656, 657, 659
population growth in, 710
post–World War I, 709–710, 740–742, 741*m*
post–World War II, 765–766, 865–866
pre–World War I, 657–658, 660
religion in, 96, 288–289, 293–294, 297–298
Sino–Japanese War and, 659
in 16th century, 517–519
Taika reforms in, 288–289
trade in, 501, 519, 742, 792, 889
U.S. policy and, 875
war between China and, 635
warrior elite in, 292–293
war with Russia, 651
women in, 658
World War I and, 675, 679, 682, 719
World War II and, 751, 755–757, 761–764, 766–767
Java
  Dutch in, 505, 564, 565, 569–570, 578
  education in, 571, 578
  population growth in, 837
  Portuguese in, 504
  puppet shadow plays in, 168
Jawaharlal Nehru, 668
Jerusalem, 222
Jesuits, 384, 441, 443, 507, 517*f*
Jesus of Nazareth, 106–107, 192*f*
Jews
  in Abbasid era, 139, 153
  beliefs of, 27
  in eastern Europe, 650, 692
  educational emphasis of, 204
  Hitler's persecution of, 760, 773–774
  migration to eastern Europe by, 204
  origins of, 25, 27–28
  in Ottoman Empire, 476–477, 619
  role of women and, 45
  in Russia, 650
  in Soviet Union, 803
  in Spain, 134–134*f*, 421
  in Spanish colonies, 435
  Zionist movement and, 692, 774
Jiang Qing, 880, 881, 883
Jingoism, 673
Jin kingdom, 274
Jinnah, Muhammad Ali, 768
Jizya, 134
Joan of Arc, 232
João VI, king of Portugal, 593
John, king of England, 220
Journal des Dames, 397
Juárez, Benito, 588*f*, 589, 601, 602, 603*f*
Judaism. *See also* Jews
  beliefs of, 27–28
  emergence of, 24, 27
  in Ethiopia, 93
Junks, 275
Jurchens, 274
Justinian (Byzantine emperor), 102, 195–196
Juula, 177
Ju Xi, 281
Ju Yuanzhang, 331

K

Ka'ba, 126, 128, 128*f*, 130, 130*f*
Kabir, 163–164
Kamakura regime, 294
Kamasutra, 60
Kamehameha (Hawaiian prince), 585
Kampuchea, 760
Kangxi (Manchu ruler), 630
Kano, 180
Karakorum, 320, 324
Karbala, 133
Kashmir, 905
Katsina, 180
Kautilya, 56
Kay, James, 398
Kazakhstan, 902
Kellogg–Briand Pact, 702
Kemal, Mustafa (Ataturk), 623*f*, 691
Kennedy, John F., 792
Kenya, 696, 771
Kenya African Union (KAU), 771
Kenyatta, Jomo, 771
Kepler, Johannes, 389, 389*f*, 390
Kerensky, Alexander, 713
Khadijah, 127, 135, 136
Khanates, 313, 322*m*
Khartoum, 628
Khayyam, Omar, 154
Khedives, 625–627, 690
Khitan peoples, 272, 274
Khmer Rouge, 760
Khmers, 916
  Vietnam and, 303, 308–309
Khoikhoi, 461, 582
Khomeini, Ayatollah Ruhollah, 834*f*, 855, 856
Khrushchev, Nikita, 805, 806
Khwarazm Empire, 323, 324
Kiev, 205, 322
Kievan Rus'
  decline of, 208–209
  explanation of, 204–206
  institutions and culture in, 206–207
Kilwa, 183
Kim Il-Sung, 866–867
Kimitoke, Hiraoka, 869
Kitchner, General, 628
Koguryo, 299, 300
Koguryo kingdom, 299, 300
Koken, Empress, 288
Kongo
  economic and social characteristics of, 188–189, 454, 455
  Portuguese interest in, 450
Korea
  background of, 299, 299*m*
  Buddhism in, 59, 106, 299
  Chinese influence on, 299–302, 309, 310
  conquest of, 300
  division of, 766
  elite culture in, 301–302
  Japanese control of, 519, 651, 659, 740–741, 753
  post–World War II, 866–867
  Shi dynasty and, 265
  tributary system and, 301
  U.S. policy and, 875
  Yi dynasty in, 302
Korean War, 791, 866
Koryo dynasty, 300, 302
Kosovo, 760, 906, 907
Krishna, 164, 164*f*
Kshatriyas, 53
Kubilai Khan, 284, 313, 325–329, 326*f*

Kush
  Coptic influence in, 175
  kingdom of, 21, 21*m*, 29, 93, 95
Kushans, 55, 59
Kuwait, 793, 903, 905

L

Labor force
  in Japan, 869
  in Latin America, 829–830
  in 20th-century Europe, 788
  women in, 754, 794, 795, 829–830
Labor movements
  late 19th-century, 544
  in Latin America, 737
  in Poland, 801
  post–World War I, 708, 731
  pre–World War I, 674
Labor strikes
  in late 19th century, 544
  in Mexico, 612
  pre–World War I, 674
Labor unions
  in Canada, 708
  in Europe, 544, 674
Lalibela (Ethiopian king), 175
Landa, Diego de, 434
Land Freedom Army (Kenya), 771
Languages. *See also* specific languages
  of Bantu peoples, 183, 461
  in China, 37
  in Middle Ages, 217–218
  in Paleolithic Age, 9
Laodong Party, Manifesto of, 668
Laozi, 42, 91
La Reforma, 602
Las Casas, Bartolomé de, 424, 424*f*, 428
Lascaux, France, 6
Latin America. *See also specific countries*
  agriculture in, 433
  art in, 712, 831
  Catholic church in, 594, 598, 602, 713, 821, 823, 829, 831
  caudillos in, 595, 601
  chronology of conquest of, 421–426
  colonial economics and governments in, 432–435
  conquerors of, 427–428
  cultural expression in, 606–607, 612, 831–832
  democracy in, 824–825, 900–901
  demographic transition in, 185
  destruction and transformation of indigenous societies in, 428–431
  development in, 609–610
  drug trade in, 824–825
  economy in, 599–601, 610–613, 736, 738
  in 18th century, 440–444, 590
  European diseases in, 430
  European exploration in, 419–420
  gender, class, and race in, 607–608, 610, 829–830
  government in, 595–598, 815
  Great Depression and, 730, 736, 738, 815
  human rights in, 827–828
  ideology and social reform in, 737–738
  independence of, 591–594, 594*m*, 613–614
  industrialization in, 814, 815
  introduction of animals and crops to, 430–431
  labor unrest in, 737
  literature in, 607, 713, 738, 822–823, 831–832
  middle class in, 736–737
  morality of conquest of, 428

multiracial societies in, 437–440
in 19th century, 589–594
paths of conquest of, 426–427
plantation colonies in, 435–437
politics in, 594–595, 599–601, 821, 823–825
population movement in, 736, 830–831
post–World War I, 728, 736–738
post–World War II, 815–816
Protestantism in, 831, 917
reform in, 738, 821, 823
slavery in, 368, 422, 435, 438, 443, 452, 466–467, 594, 605
trade in, 433, 599, 604–605, 611, 736, 814
in 20th century, 710–711, 728–736–872, 792, 793, 813–832
Latin America cont.
   U.S. involvement in, 613–614, 680, 708, 792, 825–826, 826m, 828
   women in, 594, 608, 829–830
   World War I and, 711, 736
Latvia, 766, 900f
Lawrence, T. E., 683f
The Laws of Manu, 33
League of Nations
   establishment of, 683
   function of, 724
   German withdrawal from, 734
   Middle East mandates and, 691–692
   Soviet Union and, 744
   World War II and, 751
Lebanon, League of Nations mandates and, 691–692
Le dynasty, 306–307
Lee Kuan Yew, 874
Legalism, 41
Legizamon, Mancio Sierra de, 428
Leisure activities
   industrialization and, 529
   in 19th-century Europe, 550, 551f
   in 17th-century Europe, 398
   in 20th-century Europe and United States, 791
Le May, Curtis, 762
Lenin (Vladimir Ilyich Ulyanov), 650, 714–716, 718, 720, 900f
Leon, Pedro Cieza de, 426
Leonardo da Vinci, 380f, 382
Lesotho, 464
Letrados, 434
"Letter of Jamaica" (Bolívar), 596
The Lexus and the Olive Tree (Friedman), 904
Liang Qichao, 636
Liao dynasty, 272
Liberalism
   in Latin America, 738
   in 19th-century Europe, 541
   in Russia, 713–714
Liberation theology, 821–822
Liberia, 907, 916
Li Bo, 283
Libya, 558
Li Dazhao, 720, 722
Lin Biao, 877
Lin Zexu, 633–634
Liszt, Franz, 651
Literacy
   in Brazil, 608
   in India, 854
   in Japan, 652
   in Russia, 646
   in 16th-century Europe, 386
Literature
   in Africa, 696

in ancient Greece, 81
in China, 43, 282–283, 514, 720
in Europe, 552
in India, 52, 53, 57–58, 60, 847
in Islamic societies, 141, 154–155, 336
in Japan, 290–291, 869
in Latin America, 607, 713, 738, 822–823, 831–832
in Middle Ages, 227, 232
in postcolonial nations, 847
in Russia, 206, 208, 643, 646, 651
in Soviet Union, 745–746, 803
in United States, 554
Lithuania, 415
   post–World War II, 766, 897
   spread of civilization to, 204
Liu Shaoqui, 880
Livestock, introduced to Latin America, 430–431
Lloyd George, David, 682
Locke, John, 374, 390, 394
Lodi dynasty, 490
Loess zone, 26, 27
Louisiana Purchase, 554
Louis XIV, king of France
   accomplishments of, 391–392
   wars during reign of, 393–394
Louis XVI, king of France, 538
L'Overture, Toussaint, 591
Low Countries. See also Belgium; Netherlands
   government in, 220
   in Middle Ages, 214, 219
   Renaissance in, 383
   trade in, 227, 229
   World War II and, 757, 761
Luba peoples, 188
Lugard, Lord, 695
Luther, Martin, 384
Luxembourg, 786
Luzon, 507
Lydians, 25

M
Macao, 363, 513
MacArthur, Douglas, 792, 865, 866
Macaulay, Thomas Babington, 570, 571
Macedonia, 74
Machiavelli, Niccolo, 382
Madagascar, 182
Madeira, 344, 451
Madero, Francesco, 711
Magellan, Ferdinand, 363
Maghrib, 174
Magna Carta, 220
Mahabharata, 52, 63
Mahayana Buddhism, 105, 268. See also Buddhism
Mahdist Revolt, 628, 855
Mahmud II (Ottoman sultan), 621–622
Mahmud of Ghazni, 161, 162
Maize, 431
Maji Maji uprisings, 575
Malacca, 503, 504
Malaya, 165, 761, 766, 865
Malaysia, 63, 874, 876
Mali
   characteristics of life in, 179–180, 179f
   economy in, 177, 179
   government in, 176
   spread of Islam to, 170f, 171, 176–177
Malinke, 177
Malvina islands, 815, 824
Mamluks
   background of, 625

defeat of Mongols by, 325
explanation of, 158
Manchukuo, 753, 755. See also Manchuria
Manchuria
   Japanese control of, 740–741, 752–753, 755
   post–World War II, 765
   Russia and, 650
   in 17th century, 629
Manchus
   conquest of China by, 629–630
   contact with British, 632
   fall of, 635–637, 717
   political and social efforts of, 630–631
   war with Japan, 635
Mandarin Chinese language, 37
Mandarins, 44
Mandela, Nelson, 858
Manet, Eduard, 602
Mangkubumi, 565
Mann, Horace, 533
Manorialism, 215, 542
Mansa Musa, 170f, 171, 177, 179
Manufacturing
   in China, 27, 46, 369
   in India, 63, 67
   in Japan, 653, 658, 742
   in Middle Ages, 231
   in 19th-century Europe, 563
   in postclassical period, 118–119
   in Russia, 413–414
   in 17th- and 18th-century Europe, 398, 399f, 537
   in 16th-century Europe, 387
   in 20th-century Europe, 788
Maoris
   communities of, 584
   culture and society of, 347, 556
Mao Zedong
   China under, 878–880
   influence of, 718, 862f, 882f
   rise of, 717, 722–723
Maran, René, 581
Marattas, 496
Marco Polo, 317, 327, 328f
Maroons, 469
Marquez, Gabriel García, 832
Marriage
   in China, 279
   in India, 61, 63
   in patriarchal societies, 45
   in pre-Islamic Arabia, 126
   in Spanish colonies, 438, 439
Marshall Plan, 781–782, 786, 792
Martel, Charles, 133, 174
Martí, José, 613
Marx, Karl, 548, 549, 720, 798
Marxism
   in China, 720–721, 889
   influence of, 718
   in Latin America, 609, 620, 712–713, 820–822
   in Russia, 650, 802, 803
   in Vietnam, 886
Mataram, 565
Mathematics
   in ancient Egypt, 21, 25
   in ancient Greece, 80
   in China, 43
   in India, 60, 61
   in Islamic civilization, 153, 155, 160, 388–389
   in postclassical period, 117
Matrilineal societies
   explanation of, 126
   Sudanic, 181

Mauritius, 459
Maurya, Chandragupta, 54
Mauryan dynasty, 54–55, 64, 65, 67
Mawali, 134, 138, 139
Maximilian von Habsburg, emperor of Mexico, 589, 602, 603f
Maya, 96
May Fourth Movement, 719–720
Mazdak, 132
Mbundu peoples, 450
McDonalds, 912
Mecca
  background of, 123, 125, 126
  gender roles in pre-Islamic, 136
  Muhammad in, 127–128
  pilgrimages to, 130, 130f
  trade in, 127
  under Umayyads, 133
Medicine
  in India, 60, 61
  in Middle Ages, 219
Medieval Europe. See Middle Ages
Medina
  background of, 123, 126
  Muhammad in, 128
Mehmed II (Ottoman sultan), 474, 478
Meiji government (Japan), 655–656, 868
Menchu, Rigoberre, 822
Mencius, 47
Mendel, Gregor, 651
Mercantilists, 502
Mesoamerica. See also Latin America; specific civilizations
  architecture in, 244f
  art in, 243, 243f, 244
  artisans in, 256
  Aztecs in, 239, 241–249
  cultural patterns in, 258–259
  diversity in, 259–260
  Maya in, 239, 241–249
  population estimates for, 257–258
  postclassical era of, 239–246
  Toltecs in, 238f, 240–241
Mesolithic Age, 10, 13
Mesopotamia
  Arab migration to, 127
  art in, 25
  early civilization in, 16–17, 17m, 18f, 29
  as influence on ancient Egypt, 20, 25
  legacy of, 25–28
  Mongols in, 324
  women in, 45
Mestizos, 368, 438, 594
Methodism, 570
Methodius (missionary), 203
Mexican-American War, 601
Mexican Revolution, 711–712, 736
Mexico
  art in, 712
  Aztecs in, 239, 241, 241f, 242
  Constitution of 1917, 712
  culture and politics in, 712–713, 901
  early civilizations in, 257
  economy in, 611–612, 821, 824
  education in, 608, 712
  in 18th century, 443
  foreign intervention in, 588f, 589, 601, 602
  independence of, 591
  indigenous populations in, 428–429, 429f, 431
  NAFTA and, 904
  in 19th century, 594, 595, 601–602
  revolution in, 711–712, 816, 817, 817f, 818, 818f, 831

Roman Catholic church and, 598
silver in, 432
Spanish conquests in, 363, 426–427
in 20th century, 711–713, 738, 815–817, 816f, 821–822, 825
U.S. interest in, 613
Mexico City, Mexico, 426, 919
Mfecane, 462
Michael II (Byzantine emperor), 199
Michelangelo, 382
Middle Ages
  agriculture in, 215, 218–219, 227–228
  architecture in, 226, 226f, 235
  art and literature in, 216f, 217f, 221f, 226–227, 228f–230f, 232, 234f, 235f
  artisans in, 230–231
  assimilating faith and reason in, 224–225
  Catholic church in, 215–216, 222–224
  Charlemagne and his successors in, 216–218
  decline of, 232–235
  description of, 213–215
  developments during, 235–236
  economic and urban vigor in, 218–219
  education in, 219, 235
  expansionist activity in, 221–222
  explanation of, 213–215, 218m
  feudal monarchies in, 219–220
  High, 224
  limited governments in, 220–221
  manorial system in, 215
  maps of, 218m, 233m
  popular religion in, 225–226
  religious reform and evolution in, 222–224
  rural life in, 227–228
  timeline of, 214
  trade and banking in, 219, 227–231
  women in, 231–232
Middle East. See also specific areas
  agriculture in, 11, 13, 14, 16–17, 19
  artificial nations in, 842, 843
  in cold war era, 852m
  early civilizations in, 16–20, 25, 27–29
  economic growth in postcolonial, 846, 848
  late 20th-century conflicts in, 905
  Mongols in, 324–325, 337
  nationalist movements in, 690–693, 773–775
  in postclassical period, 119
  post–World War I, 689m
  social and cultural change in, 336–337
  trade in, 63, 127, 336
  World War I and, 679, 680, 683
Middle Kingdom (China), 37, 52
Middle Passage, 465–466, 468
Midway Island, 762
Military
  in China, 27
  in classical period, 32
  in former Soviet Union, 902
  industrialization and, 553
  in Japan, 296–297, 369, 740–742
  in Latin America, 823–824, 828
  in postcolonial era, 849–854
  technological advances for, 361, 484–485
Mill, James, 570
Milosevic, Slobodan, 907
Minamoto, 293, 294
Minas Gerais, 437, 593
Ming dynasty
  agriculture in, 513
  art and literature in, 514
  court politics and, 510–511
  decline of, 516–517
  economic growth in, 513–514
  establishment of, 331, 508

exposure to Europeans in, 516
scholar-gentry in, 509–512
social structure in, 337, 511–512
women in, 512
Zhenghe expeditions and, 514, 514m
Minh Mang, 884
Mining
  in colonized areas, 581
  in Latin America, 432, 737
Minoan civilization, 31
Mishima, Yukio, 869
Missionaries
  in Africa, 450
  in Asia, 507–508, 517, 519–521
  Christianity and, 106
  in India, 376, 570
  Jesuit-sponsored, 384, 435
  in Middle East, 54
  19th-century, 551, 563, 570, 579
  Orthodox, 203–204, 215
  in Philippines, 377
  Roman Catholic, 203, 204, 215, 507–508
Mitsubishi company, 655
Moctezuma, 419
Moctezuma II, 242
Modernization theory, 609–610
Modern period. See Early modern period
Mohenjo Daro, 21, 22f
Moldboard, 215, 218
Moldova, 902
Monarchies
  absolute, 390–394
  feudal, 219–221, 390
  parliamentary, 394
Monasteries
  Christian, 108
  in Middle Ages, 216, 218–219, 222
  women in, 222
Mongols
  background of, 158, 314–315
  in China, 325–329, 331, 337, 508, 509
  under Chinggis Khan, 313–320, 314m
  defeat of, 325
  in Europe, 323–324
  gender roles and, 326–327
  impact of, 320, 330–333, 337, 339, 340, 360, 473
  invasions by, 113
  life under, 319–320
  in Muslim empires, 324–325
  in Russia, 208, 210, 320–323, 403, 404
  tolerant views of, 327–328
  weaponry used by, 484
Monk's Mound, 241
Monotheism
  influence of, 127
  origins of, 27, 28
Monroe Doctrine, 554, 598
Monsoons, 52
Montagu-Chelmsford reforms, 688
Moore, Henry, 798
Moral issues, 428
Morley-Minto reforms, 688
Morocco
  French interests in, 558, 672
  Muslims in, 158
Moscow, 323
Motion picture industry
  in Europe, 798
  in India, 854
  in 1920s, 703, 709
  in United States, 703, 709
Mozambique, 773
Mu'awiya, 133

Mughal Empire
  Akbar and, 490–492
  artistic achievements of, 494
  decline of, 376, 377, 495–496, 568
  description of, 473, 489–490, 490*m*
  politics in, 494–495
  Sikhs in, 496
  social reform in, 492
  statistics regarding, 491
  textile trade in, 493
  women in, 495
Muhammad Ali (Egyptian ruler), 624, 625
Muhammad (prophet)
  death of, 130, 131
  family and gender issues and, 134–136
  life of, 121, 127–128, 136
  Umayyads and, 128–130
Muhammad the Great (Songhay leader), 180
Mulattos, 467
Mullahs, 486
Multinational corporations, 910
Mumtaz Mahal, 495
The Muqaddimah (Ibn Khaldun), 152
Murad, 625
Murasaki, Lady, 290, 308
Music
  ancient Chinese, 22
  in Latin America, 831
  in Middle Ages, 227
  in Russia, 643, 651
  in Soviet Union, 803
  in United States, 708
Muslim Brotherhood, 850, 851, 853*f*
Muslim fundamentalism. *See* Islamic
  fundamentalism
Muslim League (India), 768
Muslims. *See* Islam; Islamic civilizations
Mussolini, Benito
  rise of, 704, 705, 735
  Spanish Civil War and, 753
  World War II and, 751, 753, 761
Mutsuihito (Japanese emperor), 653
Mwene Mutapa, 189
Myanmar, 768, 850, 908
Mycenae, 71
Mystery religions, 79

N

Nabobs, 570
Nadir Khan Afshar, 489
NAFTA. *See* North American Free Trade
  Agreement (NAFTA)
Nagasaki, Japan, 762
Nahuatl language, 242, 434
Naipaul, V. S., 847
Nam Viet, 302
Napier, Charles, 572
Napoleon Bonaparte
  expansionist interests of, 540, 540*m*
  invasion of Egypt, 624–625
  invasion of Russia, 642
  nationalist movements, 532
  Poland and, 644
Napoleon III, emperor of France, 602
Nara period, 287–288
Nasser, Gamal Abdul, 625, 693, 770*f*, 850–853
Natal, 583
National Congress of British West Africa, 696
National Congress party (India), 686, 687,
  767–768, 854
National Convention in France, Decree of, 532
Nationalist movements
  in Africa, 695–696
  during and after French Revolution, 532,
    540–541

  in Egypt, 689–690
  ethnic issues and, 916
  in India, 686–689, 701
  in Latin America, 738–739, 820, 821, 824
  in Middle East, 689–693, 773–775
  militant, 687–688
  in 19th-century Europe, 546, 560
  post–World War I, 684, 697
  realities facing, 836–837
  religious issues and, 916–917
  role of women in, 694–695
National Liberation Front (FLN) (Algeria),
  771–772, 835
National Socialist party (Germany). *See* Nazis
Nation-states, 394
Native Americans. *See* American Indians
NATO. *See* North American Treaty
  Organization (NATO)
Navigation
  in northern Europe, 363–364
  technological advances in, 361, 372*f*, 553
Nazis
  Holocaust and, 760
  political agenda of, 753, 755
  racial purification and, 23
  rise of, 681, 731, 732, 734, 753
  World War II and, 755–761, 765, 786 (*See
    also* World War II)
Necker de Saussure, Albertine-Adrienne, 533
Négritude literary movement, 685, 696
Nehru, Jawaharlal, 768, 845, 854
Neocolonial economy, 846
Neo-Confucians
  explanation of, 273–274
  in Japan, 521, 652
  male dominance and, 279–280
  in Ming dynasty, 511
Neolithic Age
  civilization in, 14–16, 14*f*
  development of agriculture in, 11–13, 12*m*
  profile of, 10, 10*m*
Neolithic revolution
  agriculture and, 11–13
  population growth and, 184
Neruda, Pablo, 825
Nestorians, 132
Netherlands. *See also* Dutch colonies
  in Brazil, 364, 437
  expeditions by, 363, 364
  industrialization in, 544
  interest in Africa, 450
  in Java, 505, 565, 567*m*, 569–571
  parliamentary structure in, 394
  trade in, 376, 504–506
  trading companies and, 276, 364
  welfare state in, 785
Nevskii, Alexander, 323
New Deal, 732
New England, 388
New France, 371
New Granada, 443, 595
New Spain, 427, 434
New Stone Age. *See* Neolithic Age
Newton, Isaac, 389–390, 551
New Zealand
  emigration to, 553–554
  European settlements in, 347, 554, 555*m*,
    556, 584
  Maori culture and society in, 347, 556, 584
  relationship with United States, 791–792
  World War I and, 675, 679, 707
Nezhualcoyotl, 243–244
Nguni peoples, 461, 462, 464
Nguyen Anh, 309, 885
Niane, D. T., 178

Nicaragua
  politics in, 824, 828
  revolution in, 818, 821
  U.S. involvement in, 825
Nicholas I, tsar of Russia, 643–645
Nicholas II, tsar of Russia, 651, 677
Nigeria
  democracy in, 901
  independence of, 768
  literature in, 847
  Muslims in, 157
  political mobilization in, 696
  population growth in, 838–839
  Yoruba people of, 186–187
Nirvana, 59
Niu Su, 268
Nixon, Richard, 793
Nkrumah, Kwame, 769, 770, 848, 850*f*
Nobunaga, 518, 520
Nok, 186
Nomads
  bedouin, 122–126
  in China, 26, 27
  in classical period, 94–95, 98
  impact of, 16, 330
  in Neolithic Age, 13
  view of, 15
Noriega, Manuel, 824
North Africa
  characteristics of societies in, 173–174
  Mongols in, 324
  Ottomans in, 474
  spread of Islam to, 174, 176
  World War II and, 757, 760–761, 766
North America. *See also* Canada; United States
  English and French colonies in, 371–372,
    374–376
  slavery in, 375–376, 466–470
  western civilization and, 376
North American Free Trade Agreement
  (NAFTA), 816, 893, 904
North American Treaty Organization (NATO)
  establishment of, 782
  France and, 783
  in late 20th century, 903, 907
Northern Renaissance, 383
North Korea. *See also* Korea
  attempted invasion of South Korea by, 792,
    866, 867*f*
  creation of, 866–867
  in late 20th century, 908
  as "rogue state," 903
  Soviet Union and, 799
Norway, 757
Novgorod, 322, 323
Nubia, 175
Nurhaci, 629
Nur Jahan, 495
Nzinga Mvemba, 450

O

Oba, 187
Obeah, 468
Obregón, Alvaro, 711, 712
Ocampo, Victoria, 829
Odyssey (Homer), 81
Oedipus complex, 81
Ogedei (Mongol grand khan), 320, 324
Old Believers, 406
Old Stone Age. *See* Paleolithic Age
Olmec culture, 28, 96
Olympic games, 71
One Hundred Years of Solitude (Marquez), 832
Opium War, 632–634, 653
Orabi, Ahmad, 626–627, 689, 690

Oral tradition, 178, 346
Orange Free State, 583
Order of St. Clare, 222
Orkney Islands, 14f
Ormuz, 503
Orozco, José Clemente, 712
Orthodox Christianity
    establishment of, 200
    missionaries of, 203–204, 215
    in Russia, 206, 208, 323, 403, 802–803
Osman, 474
Ottoman Empire
    architecture in, 478, 478f, 479
    artisans in, 479, 622
    background of, 473–475
    Battle of Lepanto and, 367
    culture in, 478–479
    decline of, 479–480, 480f, 541, 558, 617,
        619–624, 733
    expansion of, 404–405, 473, 475m, 476m,
        619m
    reform and survival of, 621–623
    repression and revolt in, 623–624
    rise of, 336, 337, 340, 361
    Russian clashes with, 407, 409, 410, 644,
        645, 650
    society and gender roles in, 488–489
    statistics regarding, 491
    sultans in, 476–477
    warfare and, 475–476, 477f, 481–482
    women in, 622
Ottoman Society for Union and Progress, 623
Oyo, 459
Ozbeg tribes, 486, 489

P

Pachacuti, 252
Pacific Islands. See Polynesia; specific islands
Pacific Rim. See also specific countries
    common themes and problems facing,
        874, 876
    economic growth in, 873, 889, 903
    Japan and, 868–871
    Korea and, 871–872
    post–World War II settlements and,
        864–868
    rise of, 863, 864, 865m, 889–890
    Taiwan and, 873–874
    U.S. policy and, 875
Paekche, 299, 300
Pahlavi shahs, 855
Painting. See Art
Pakistan
    climate in, 839f, 840f
    creation of, 843
    culture in, 839f
    Muslims in, 157, 843
    tensions between India and, 905
Paleo-Indians, 171
Paleolithic Age
    cave paintings in, 6
    development and spread of human species
        during, 8–10
    overview of, 7–8
Palestine
    Arab invasion and, 132
    Arab resistance to Jews in, 692–693, 774
    British control of, 692, 774
    Jewish homeland in, 692, 760, 774
    partition of, 774, 774m
Palestinian-Israeli conflict, 905, 917
Palmares, 469
Pamela (Richardson), 397
Panama
    drug trade in, 825

independent of, 613
    Spanish conquest of, 370, 427
    U.S. involvement in, 793, 824, 828
Panama Canal, 613, 825, 828
Panchatantra, 60
Pankhurst, Christabel, 550
Pankhurst, Emmeline, 549–550, 549f
Pankhurst, Richard, 550
Papermaking, 95
Paraguay, 592
    Catholic church in, 823
    democracy in, 901
    independence of, 595
    war of triple alliance against, 606
Parliaments
    establishment of, 541, 547
    origin of, 220
Parthian Empire, 38, 102, 103
Party of the Institutionalized Revolution (PRI)
    (Mexico), 713, 815–816, 817f, 821
Pasteur, Louis, 544
Patriarchal structure
    in agricultural civilizations, 45–46
    in India, 63
Paul, 107
Paulistas, 437
Paul I (tsar of Russia), 409
Pavlov, Ivan, 651–652
Peace of Paris, 682–683, 683f
Pearl Harbor attack, 755, 761, 762
Peasants
    in China, 42–44, 49, 511, 517, 720, 722
    revolutionary movements and, 718, 720
    in Russia, 412–413, 414f, 645–646,
        648–649, 651
Pedro I, emperor of Brazil, 593, 605
Pedro II, emperor of Brazil, 605
Peloponnesian Wars, 71, 75
Peninsulares, 438
Penn, William, 371
A People Made New (Liang Qichao), 636
People's Democratic Republic of Korea. See
    North Korea
People's Republic of China, 877. See also China
Pericles, 33, 71, 75
The Periplus of the Erythraean Sea, 182
Perón, Evita, 739, 740
Perón, Isabel, 740, 816f
Perón, Juan D., 739–740, 815, 816f
Perry, Matthew, 653
Persia. See also Iran
    accomplishments of, 31, 70–71
    architecture in, 487–488, 487f
    art in, 472f
    artisans in, 487
    Byzantine Empire and, 196
    conversion to Islam, 139
    industrialization in, 747
    literature in, 154–155, 155f
    poetry in, 336
    Safavids in, 482–489
    Sasanian Empire in, 132
    Shi'ism in, 486, 487
    trade in, 183, 487–488
Persian Gulf War, 903, 905
Peru
    Christianity in, 434
    coup in 1968 in, 824
    early civilizations in, 254f
    economy in, 824
    Inca heritage of, 250, 254f, 257
    independence of, 591–593, 595
    Indian revolt in, 443–444
    labor force in, 830
    political and social reform in, 824

silver in, 432
slavery in, 468
Spanish conquest of, 427, 429
trade in, 599
Peter III, tsar of Russia, 409, 410
Peter I of Russia (Peter the Great), 357, 402f,
    406–409, 413, 743
Petrarch, Francesco, 342, 381, 382
Pharoahs, 20
Phidias, 82
Philip of Anjou, 441
Philip II of Macedon, 71
Philippines
    independence of, 865
    missionaries in, 507–508
    Muslims in, 158
    post–World War II, 864
    Spanish control of, 363, 376, 505,
        507–508
    trade in, 433
    U.S. interests in, 680
    World War II and, 761, 766
Philosophy
    in ancient Greece, 79–80
    division between Mesopotamian and
        Chinese, 25
    in Middle Ages, 224–225
Phoenicians, 25, 28
Picasso, Pablo, 703
Pinochet, Augusto, 813
Pinsker, Leon, 692
Pius XII, Pope, 223
Pizarro, Francisco, 370–371, 371f
Plagues. See also Disease
    in Asia, 100, 338, 508
    in Middle Ages, 232
    in Roman Empire, 100
Plassey battle, 566–567
Plato, 80
Poetry
    in ancient Rome, 80
    of Aztecs, 243–244
    in China, 43, 282–283
    in Japan, 290, 291
    in Latin America, 825, 831
    in Mexico, 712
    in Middle Ages, 227
    in 19th-century Europe, 552
    in Persia, 336
    in pre-Islamic Arabia, 126
    in Vietnam, 305, 306
Pogroms, 650, 692
Pointillism, 552
Poland
    communism in, 800
    free trade union movement in, 895
    German invasion of, 735, 751, 756, 757, 800
    Jews in, 204
    in Middle Ages, 221
    partition of, 410
    post–World War I, 682
    post–World War II, 781
    Renaissance in, 383
    Russian policies toward, 410, 415, 644
    spread of civilization to, 204
    transition to capitalism in, 893, 895, 898
Polis, 75
Politburo, 744
Political organization
    in ancient Egypt, 20–21, 25
    in ancient Greece, 74–76
    in ancient Rome, 74–76, 78–79
    in Byzantine Empire, 198–200
    in China, 38–40
    of Incas, 252–253

in India, 55–57
in Song dynasty, 272–273
in Songhay, 180–181
in Spain and Portugal, 421
in Sudanic states, 181–182
of Sumerians, 19
Politics
in 18th-century Europe, 394–395
in Latin America, 594–595, 599–601, 821, 823–825
in 19th-century Europe, 541, 542, 544, 546–547
post–World War II trends in, 783–785
religion and, 859
in Renaissance, 383
Pollution, 845, 918. *See also* Environmental issues
Polynesia. *See also* specific islands
conquests in, 345–346
partition of, 576*m*
settlement of, 97, 345–346, 347*m*
Pombal, Marquis of, 442–443
Pontecorvo, Gillo, 835
Pope, 107, 215
Pope Innocent III, 119
Popular culture. *See also* Culture
in Japan, 870–871, 912
in Latin America, 831
in West, 798–799, 912
Popular Front, 731
Population
in China, 32, 837, 879–880, 883, 918
in classical period, 32
economic growth and, 837
growth in the twentieth century, 669-670
in 18th century, 431, 536–537
in India, 837
industrialization and, 530–531, 839–840
in Japan, 710
in Latin America, 736, 830–831
in Mesolithic Age, 10
in Middle Ages, 219
in postcolonial era, 844–845, 844*f*, 854, 855
in Roman Empire, 100
transitions in, 184–185
trends in, 339, 841*f*
Portugal
African interests of, 183, 187, 190, 363, 459, 482, 771, 773
commercial outreach of, 367
democracy in, 900
effect of Napoleonic invasions on, 593
18th-century reforms in, 440, 441
European Union and, 788
expeditions to India, 361, 362, 500–503
exploration by, 343–344, 361–362, 362*m*, 364, 420, 422*m*, 499
international commerce and, 502–503, 503*f*
Japanese exclusion of, 357
missionaries in, 507
political structure in, 421, 783–784
Pombal reforms in, 442–443
reactions to the first arrivals in East Africa, 357
slave trade and, 376, 449–451
social structure in, 421
Portuguese colonies
in Africa, 363, 436, 771, 773
in Asia, 436
in Brazil, 362, 363, 424, 435, 436, 444, 593
chronology of, 421–422
Positivism, 600
Postclassical period
in China, 263–264
Christian civilizations in, 193–194
chronology of, 112–113
exchange and imitation in, 118–119

expansion of civilization in, 114, 116*m*, 117*m*
rise of Islam in, 113–114
timeline of, 114–115
in western Europe, 213–236
world history themes in, 118
world network in, 113, 116–117
world religions in, 115–116
Postcolonial era
artificial nations in, 842–843
charismatic populists and one-party rule in, 848–849
comparisons of emerging nations in, 858–860
dictatorships and revolutions in, 849–854
economic issues in, 846, 848
globalization in, 857
in India, 854–855
in Iran, 855–856
literature in, 847
overview of, 835–837
population growth in, 837–841
in South Africa, 856–858
urbanization and endangered ecosystems in, 844–845
women and feminist struggles in, 845–846
Potato
impact of, 398, 537
introduction in Europe of, 366, 431
Potosí, 432
Potsdam Conference, 765
Potter's wheel, 13
Prester John (Buchan), 323, 324, 581
Primary products, 846
Princip, Gavriel, 674
Principia Mathematica (Newton), 390
Printing press, 434
Procopius, 195
Proletariats, 387–388
Protectionism, 729
Protestantism
in Latin America, 831, 917
missionary interests of, 376
origins of, 384
role of women and, 396
in 16th- and 17th-century Europe, 384–386
in Spanish colonies, 435
Protestant Reformation
effects of, 385
explanation of, 384
western Europe during, 384–388, 387*m*
Protoindustrialization, 537
Prussia
Bismark and, 546–547
Frederick the Great in, 394–395
political change in, 546
Russian policies and, 410, 415
Ptolemy, 80
Puerto Rico
independence of, 591
slavery in, 594
Spanish control of, 370, 422
U.S. involvement in, 613, 825
Pugachev, Emelian, 409, 415, 415*f*
Pugachev rebellion, 409, 415
Punic Wars, 72–73
Puritans, 384
Pushkin, Alexander, 643
Putin, Vladimir, 900
Puyi (Chinese emperor), 637, 716
Pyramids, 20
Pythagoras, 80

Q

Qin dynasty
characteristics of, 37–38
map of, 36*m*
Mongols and, 325

political institutions and though in, 39–41
rise of, 37
Vietnam and, 302–303
Qing dynasty
breakdown and disintegration in, 631–632
description of, 509, 617, 629*m*
economy in, 630
fall of, 635–638, 716
Opium War and, 632–634
rebellion and failed reforms in, 634–635
social structure in, 630, 631
Qin-Han era, 263, 264
Qin Shi Huangdi, 37
Quakers, 374
Quebec, Canada, 371, 707, 791
Quechua language, 254
Quetzalcoatl, 240
Quipu, 256
Quit India movement, 767–768
Qur'an, 118, 121, 128, 129, 134–137, 139, 156, 163
Quraysh, 125, 127, 129

R

Racism
colonizer-colonized relations and, 580, 686
concept of civilization and, 23–24
in South Africa, 773, 857–858
Radicalism, 541
Railroads
in Canada, 707
in Latin America, 599
in Russia, 648, 650
Rajput princes, 99
Ramadan, 130
Ramayana, 52
Reagan, Ronald, 785, 793, 896
Rebellion in the Backlands (da Cunha), 606
Recopilación, 434
Red Army, 715, 716
Red Guard, 882
Red Heads, 483
Reform Bill of 1832 (Great Britain), 541
Reginald of Durham, 119
Reign of Terror, 538
Reincarnation, 58
Religion. *See also* Islamic fundamentalism; Theology; *specific religions*
among slaves, 468
animistic, 165, 173, 206, 207
art and, 226–227, 281
Aztec, 242–244
of bedouins, 126–127
in China, 40–43, 48, 268–270
conversion and accommodation in spread of, 166–167
Din-i-Ilahi, 492
ethnic conflict and, 916–917
fundamentalist trends in, 917
Inca, 252–253
in India, 53, 57–60, 77, 115, 163–165, 250, 492, 493*f*, 570, 572, 840
in Latin America, 594, 598, 602
in Middle Ages, 215–216, 224–226
mystery, 79
in 19th-century Europe, 550, 551
origin of monotheistic, 27–28
politics and, 859
reasons for changing, 115–116
in Renaissance, 382, 383
Scientific Revolution and, 390
in 16th and 17th century Europe, 384–386
in Soviet Union, 802–803
in Spanish colonies, 434
spread of world, 103–108, 109*m*, 110, 115–116

of Sumerians, 18
in 20th-century Europe, 791
in 20th-century United States, 791
women's rights and, 846
Renaissance
art in, 340, 341*f*, 380*f*, 382
explanation of, 340, 381, 387*m*
family structure in, 383–384
human values and culture of,
340–342
impact of, 383
in Italy, 340–342, 382–383
Northern, 383
technological advances in, 383
Republic of Korea. *See* Korea
Revisionism, 549
Revolutionary Alliance (China), 719
Revolutions. *See also specific countries*
in America, 536–538, 554, 566, 591
art and, 818, 818*f*
in China, 637, 716–718, 721*m*
in Europe, 410, 411, 536–543
factors contributing to, 718
industrialization and, 541–543, 718
in Latin America, 816–821
in Mexico, 711–712, 816, 817, 817*f*
in Russia, 651, 702, 712–715, 718
Rhodes, 475
Rhodes, Cecil, 583
Rhodesia, 696
Ricci, Matteo, 516
Richard, king of England, 221*f*
Ridda Wars, 131
Rig-Veda, 52, 53, 57
Rivera, Diego, 588*f*, 712
River valley civilizations
Chinese, 21–22, 22*f*, 26, 27
Egyptian, 20–21, 21*m*
Harappan, 21, 22*f*, 26, 27, 330
legacy of, 24–25, 28, 31, 71
Mesopotamian, 16–19, 26, 27
Roaring Twenties, 702–704
Robespierre, Maximilien, 538–539
Rodó, José Enrique, 613
Roman Catholic church
establishment of, 200
in Latin America, 594, 598, 602, 713, 821,
823, 829, 831
in Middle Ages, 214–216, 222–224
missionaries of, 203, 204, 215, 507–508
in Poland, 800, 801
political and spiritual power of, 215–216
in 16th century, 384
in Spanish colonies, 434
The Romance of the Rose (Villon), 227
The Romance of the West Chamber, 329
Roman Empire. *See also* Ancient Rome
accomplishments of, 78–79, 88
Christianity and, 78, 79, 101, 103, 107
decline of, 73–74, 99–103, 833
manorial system in, 215
map of, 74*m*
political institutions in, 25, 75, 76, 78–79
population in, 32, 100
trade in, 38, 63
Romania
collapse of communism in, 898
fascist movement in, 735
Hungarian minorities in, 906
independence of, 651
post–World War II, 765, 781
Soviet influence in, 801
Romanov, Alexis, 406
Romanov dynasty, 405–406
Romanticism, 552
Rome. *See* Ancient Rome

Romero, Oscar, 823
Rommel, Erwin, 758, 758*f*, 760
Roosevelt, Franklin
Latin America and, 825–826
New Deal and, 732
World War II and, 760, 767
Yalta Conference and, 765
Rosas, Manuel de, 602–603
Rousseau, Jean-Jacques, 470, 536, 538
Rowlatt Act, 688
Roy, Ram Mohun, 572
Royal African Company, 453
Rubaiyat (Khayyam), 154
Rurik dynasty, 205, 403, 404
Russell, Bertrand, 719
Russia. *See also* Soviet Union
architecture in, 206–207, 208*f*
art in, 206–207, 206*f*, 406*f*, 651
attempted French invasion of, 540
Byzantine Empire and, 193–194, 210
Chechnya conflict in, 906
Crimean War and, 645, 646
eastern Europe and, 651–652
economy in, 413–414, 902
expansionist policies in, 403–406, 405*m*, 410,
412*m*, 644, 650–651
factories in, 647, 648, 648*f*
industrialization in, 641, 645–649, 713
institutions and culture in, 206–207, 643
literature in, 206, 208, 643, 646, 651
Mongols in, 208, 210, 320–323, 403, 404
multinational character of, 416, 649, 650
Napoleon's invasion of, 642
in 19th century, 642–644
Orthodox Christianity in, 206
Ottoman Empire and, 407, 409, 410, 644,
645, 650
peasants in, 412–413, 414*f*, 645–646,
648–649, 651
pogroms in, 650
post–Soviet Union, 898*m*
prerevolutionary, 649–650
pre–World War I, 558, 644*m*, 651, 660,
671–675
revolution of 1905 in, 651, 702, 712
revolution of 1917 in, 712–715, 718, 895
serfs in, 412–413, 642, 645–646
social unrest in, 414–415, 644, 713
spread of civilization to, 204–206
support for nationalist movements in Balkans,
644
as third Rome, 404
trade and economic dependence in, 413–414
transition from communism to capitalism in,
893
Ukrainians in, 649, 650
war with Japan, 651
westernization of, 406–412, 407*m*, 621
World War I and, 677, 678, 680, 682, 683
Russian Orthodox church, 206
Russian Revolution of 1917, 712–716, 718
Russo-Japanese War, 651, 752
Rwanda, 760, 907

S

Sadat, Anwar, 853–854
Safavid Empire
decline of, 482, 489
description of, 473, 482–483, 483*m*
Ottomans and, 483–485
politics and war in, 485–486
religion in, 486–487
society and gender roles in, 488–489
statistics regarding, 491
trade and culture in, 487–488
Sahagún, Bernardino de, 248, 434

Sahara, 95, 176
Sahel, 176
Saint Godric, 119
Saint Sophia, 478
Saladin (Salah-ud-Din), 151, 221*f*, 222
Salt II, 895–896
Saltwater slaves, 467
Salvatierra, Policarpa, 608
Samoa, 97
Samurai, 292–293, 292*f*, 655–656, 659
Sandinista party (Nicaragua), 824, 825
Sandino, Augusto, 825
San Martín, José de, 592
San people, 461
Sanskrit, 52, 99, 227
Santa Anna, Antonio López de, 601
Santa Cruz, Andrés, 595
Santo Domingo, 422, 423*f*
Sao Tomé, 451
Sappho, 80
Sarajevo, 674
Sarmiento, Domingo F., 596–597, 604
Sasanian Empire, 71, 103, 127, 132
Sati, 250, 492, 493*f*, 570, 572
Saudi Arabia, 903
Scandinavia. *See also specific countries*
economic growth in, 789
Great Depression in, 731
parliamentary tradition in, 220
trade in, 204–205, 229
Viking raids and, 214–215
welfare state in, 784
Schall, Adam, 516
Scholar-gentry
in China, 62, 304–305, 328, 509–512,
635–636
in Vietnam, 307
Scholasticism, 225
Science
in China, 43, 47–48, 390
in early river valley civilizations, 25
in Hellenistic period, 80
in India, 60, 61
in Islamic civilization, 155–156, 160
in Middle Ages, 219, 225
in 19th-century Europe, 551–552
in Renaissance, 380*f*, 381
in 17th-century Europe, 388–390, 393
in Soviet Union, 744, 806, 807*f*
in 20th century, 704, 796–797
Scotland, 905–906
Sculpture. *See* Art
Second Indochina War, 887
The Second Sex (Beauvoir), 796
Secret Army Organization (OAS) (Algeria), 772
Sego, 460
Sekou, Ahmadou, 575
Sekou, Samory, 575
Self-determination, 682
Selim (Ottoman sultan), 483
Selim III (Ottoman sultan), 621
Seljuk Turks
Byzantine Empire and, 201, 202
collapse of, 474
explanation of, 151
Semitic people, 20, 25. *See also* Arabs; Jews
Senate, 76
Sendero Luminoso, 824
Senegal, 571, 578
Senghor, Léopold Sédar, 685, 696, 696*f*, 769,
770*f*, 771, 827–828
Sepoys, 565, 566
Seppuku, 293
Sépulveda, Juan Gines de, 428
Serbia
Byzantine Empire and, 201

ethnic conflict and, 906–907
independence of, 621, 650, 651, 706
World War I and, 558, 674, 677
Serfdom
end of, 543, 651
explanation of, 215, 219
in Russia, 412–413, 642, 645–646
Settlement colonies. *See also specific areas*
in Africa, 582–583, 696, 771–772
explanation of, 576, 578
in Pacific, 583–586
social structure in, 582
Seurat, Georges, 552
Seven Years' War, 371–372, 376, 377, 442
Severe Acute Respiratory Syndrome, 920
Sexual behavior, 798–799
Shah Jahan (Mughal emperor), 493–495
Shah-Nama (Firdawsi), 154
Shaka, 462
Shang dynasty
accomplishments of, 24, 26, 27
art of, 22*f*
decline of, 35
Sharia, 181
Shaykhs, 123
Shi'a
Abbasids and, 138, 147, 150
explanation of, 133, 135
Safavid Empire and, 482, 485–487
Shi Huangdi, 37–39
Shintoism
influence of, 298
rise of, 96
in 20th-century Japan, 740, 752
Shiva, 58, 58*f*, 163, 164
Shoguns, 294
Shrivijaya, 165
Siam, 761
Siberia, 9, 410
Siddhartha Gautama. *See* Buddha
Sierra Leone, 696, 907, 916
Sijilimas, 174
Sikhs, 496
Silk manufacturing, 27, 49
Silk Roads, 49, 67, 94
Silla, 299–301
Silver, 432, 432*f*
Singapore, 766, 868
Sinification
in Korea, 299–301
in Vietnam, 303–306
Sino-Japanese War, 659
Siraj ud-daula, 567
Sisulu, Walter, 858
Six Dynasties, 275
Skara Brae, 14*f*
Slash and burn agriculture, 13–14
Slavery
in Africa, 181
American Civil War and, 554
in ancient Greece, 32–33, 85
in ancient Rome, 32–33, 85
in Brazil, 435, 438, 443, 452, 468, 594, 605
in China, 44, 46
in early modern period, 367–369
in French colonies, 539
human society and, 463–464
in Islamic societies, 137, 140, 150–151, 181–182, 455, 463
in Latin America, 368, 422, 435, 438, 443, 452, 466–467, 594, 605
in North American colonies, 375–376, 466–470
opponents of, 470

serfdom vs., 645
in Sumerian society, 19
Slaves
African-American culture among, 468
in Americas, 466–467
in ancient Greece, 71
communities for runaway, 469
Creole, 467
female, 455, 468
Middle Passage for, 465–466, 468
personal descriptions of, 465–466
religious practices of, 468
resistance and rebellion among, 469
saltwater, 467
social structure of American, 467–468
Slave trade
African politics and, 455–456
African societies and, 454–455
in Asante, 456–458
in Dahomey, 458–459
demographic patterns in, 453
in east Africa and Sudan, 459–461
end of, 469–470
European interests in, 376
organization of, 453–454
Portuguese, 449–451, 459
profitability of, 454
statistics regarding, 451–453, 452t
Slavs
Byzantine Empire and, 199
in Russia and eastern Europe, 204, 205, 906
Slovakia, 906
Slovenia, 906
Smallpox, 61
Smith, Adam, 395, 470
Socialism
in Africa, 849, 850*f*
in Cuba, 820–821
in Europe, 548–549
in United States, 708
Socialism in one country (Soviet Union), 730
Socialist Fabian Society, 550
Social protest
in 17th- and 18th-century Russia, 414–415
in 16th- and 17th-century Europe, 387–388
Social question, 548
Social reform
in India, 492, 570
in Latin America, 738, 821, 823
Social Revolutionary party (Russia), 714–715
Social sciences
in 19th-century Europe, 552
in Soviet Union, 803
Social structure
in Ancient Greece, 62
in Arabia, 123–125
of Aztecs, 246–247
caste system and, 62–63 (*See also* Caste system)
in China, 39, 44–46, 62, 63
between colonizers and colonized, 578–580
in eastern Europe, 804
in Mesoamerica, 247
in Ming dynasty, 337
in Ottoman Empire, 479
in Portugal, 421
in Songhay, 181
in Soviet Union, 804
in Spain, 421
in Spanish colonies, 438–440
in 20th-century West, 793–794
Sociedad de castas, 438
Society for the Colonization of Israel, 692

Society Islands, 345, 347
Socrates, 32, 80, 91
Sokoto state, 460
Solidarity movement (Poland), 801, 898
Solzhenitsyn, Aleksandr, 803
Somalia, 175
Song dynasty
agriculture in, 277–279
art in, 281–284
commercial expansion in, 275–276
decline of, 274, 284
family and society in, 279
founding of, 272, 273*m*
gender roles in, 279–280
Mongols and, 325, 329
politics in, 272–273
prosperity in, 275–282
revival of Confucian thought in, 273–274
southern, 275
technological advances in, 280, 281
urban growth in, 276
Songhay
characteristics of, 176–177, 455
political and cultural structure in, 180–181
social structure in, 181
The Song of Roland, 227
Soninke, 176
Sophocles, 81, 83
Sotho, 461, 464
South Africa
apartheid in, 773, 857–858, 901
Boers in, 376, 461–462, 582, 583
British involvement in, 582, 583, 856, 857
coloreds in, 582
European settlers in, 553, 578, 582, 856
homelands in, 857–858
independence of, 857
postcolonial, 856–858
South America. *See* Latin America
South Asia
population increase in, 837–838
spread of Islam to, 158–165
World War II and, 767–768
Southeast Asia
colonial regimes in, 578
partition of, 576*m*
spread of Islam to, 165–168
trade in, 63, 338, 501
World War II and, 766–769
Southern Song dynasty, 275
South Korea. *See also* Korea
attempted North Korea invasion of, 792
economic development in, 871–872, 889
post–World War II, 866–867
United States and, 799
South Pacific, 583–586
Soviet Union. *See also* Russia; *specific countries*
agriculture in, 742–743, 896
art in, 744, 746, 803
artistic policy in, 745–746
attempted coup in, 898–899
China and, 722, 807, 878
cold war and, 764–766, 781–783, 805, 896–897
collapse of, 808, 893, 899–900, 905, 908
containment policy toward, 792–793
Cuba and, 820, 821
de-Stalinization in, 805–808
domestic policies in, 802
dominance of eastern Europe by, 799–802
eastern Europe and, 799–802
economy in, 742–743, 803–804, 808, 896, 897
education in, 716, 896

Egypt and, 807, 852–854
environmental deterioration in, 896
establishment of, 715–716
experimental period in, 716
during Great Depression, 730
Hitler and, 735, 744, 753, 756, 760
industrialization in, 743–744, 799, 804, 896
invasion of Afghanistan, 807, 895
literature in, 745–746, 803
Muslims in, 803, 807, 895, 897
post–World War II, 765, 766, 781*m*
reforms in, 809–810, 896–898, 897*f*
social issues in, 804, 807–808, 898
as superpower, 799
totalitarian rule in, 744, 747
women in, 898
World War II and, 756–761, 764, 765
Space program, 806
Spain
amigos del país in, 440
Bourbon dynasty in, 441–442
characteristics of conquerors from, 427
commercial outreach of, 367
democracy in, 900
18th-century reforms in, 440–442
establishment of parliamentary system in, 783–784
ethnic minorities in, 906
European Union and, 788
exploration by, 221, 343–344, 362–363, 362*m*, 422*m*
fascism in, 736, 753
inquisition in, 343
Jews in, 134–134*f*, 343, 421
in Middle Ages, 214, 216, 221
missionaries from, 507
Muslims in, 133, 174, 221, 236, 343, 421
parliamentary tradition in, 220
political structure in, 421
Popular Front and, 731
social structure in, 421
trade in, 433
Spanish-American War, 613, 825
Spanish Civil War, 736, 744, 753
Spanish colonies
bureaucratic control of, 433–434
in Caribbean, 370–371, 422–424, 591, 599
chronology of, 421–422
in Florida, 363
in Mexico, 426–427, 589
in Philippines, 363, 376, 505, 507–508
shifting balance in, 441
Sparta, 71, 75, 76, 79, 88. *See also* Ancient Greece
Spengler, Oswald, 733
Spice trade, 503–505, 504*f*
Split inheritance, 252, 253
Sports
in ancient Greece, 71
in Japan, 871
in 19th-century Europe, 550
Sputnik, 806
Sri Lanka
British control of, 377
independence of, 768
mortality rate in, 185
spread of Buddhism to, 59
St. Clair, Jeffrey, 914
St. Clare of Assisi, 222–223
St. Domingue, 452, 468, 591
Stalin, Joseph, 716, 742, 744, 802, 805
Stamp Act of 1765, 537
Stateless societies, 173
Stock market crash of 1929, 727, 729

Stoicism, 67
Stoics, 79
Stolypin, Piotyr, 651
Stone Age. *See* Neolithic Age; Paleolithic Age
Stupas, 61
Suárez, Ines, 427
Sub-Saharan Africa
in 1400, 347
classical period in, 93, 95
colonial regimes in, 578, 859
economy in, 918
Islam in, 172, 173, 447, 449
slave trade in, 451
World War I and, 680
Sudan
Egyptian interests in, 627–628
Muslim attack on Christians in, 907
Muslim reform movements in, 460, 461, 855
Sudanic states. *See also* Ghana (Sudanic kingdom); Mali; Songhay
cities and villages in, 179–180
explanation of, 176–177
political and social life in, 181–182
slavery in, 181, 455
Sudras, 53
Suez Canal, 626, 627*f*, 680, 693, 781, 850–852, 853*f*
Sufism
in Africa, 460
explanation of, 156
impact of, 336
in India, 162
Safavid dynasty and, 482–483
southeast Asian Islam and, 167–168
Sugar plantations, 377–378, 431, 435–436, 451, 452, 466
Sui dynasty
excesses and collapse of, 265–266
explanation of, 263, 265*m*
land distribution in, 278
rise of, 98, 264
state and religion in, 267–269
Sukarno, 668
Suleyman the Magnificent, 478
Suleyman, Shag, 472*f*
Suleymaniye mosque, 478
Sumatra, trade and, 165
Sumerians, 17–19, 25, 31
Sundiata (Malinke leader), 177, 181, 178
Sunni Ali (Songhay leader), 180, 181
Sunnis
Abbasids and, 138
explanation of, 133
Ottoman Empire and, 483
Seljuk, 151
Sun Yat-sen, 636, 717, 719, 721–723
Suriname, 469, 469*f*
Swahili language, 183
Swahili states
mixture of cultures in, 183
overview of, 182, 182*m*
trading ports in, 182–183
Swazi, 464
Sweden
European Union and, 788
Russian hostilities with, 407
Swetham, Joseph, 396
Switzerland
economic growth in, 789
voting rights for women in, 794
Syndicalism, 737
Syphilis, 430
Syria

Arab invasion of, 132, 137
independence of, 773
League of Nations mandates and, 691–692
Ottomans in, 474

T
Tae Kwon Do, 872
Tagore, Rabindranath, 685
Taika period
explanation of, 287–288
reforms in, 288–289
Taiping Rebellion, 634, 635, 880
Taira, 293
Tais, 303
Taiwan
economic growth in, 873–874
Japanese control of, 741
post–World War II, 864, 867
U.S. policy and, 875
Taizong (Chinese emperor), 269
Tacitus, 32
Taj Mahal, 494, 494*f*, 495
Takahashi, Korekiyo, 741
Takrur, 176
The Tale of Genji (Murasaki), 290–291, 308
Talmasp I (Safavid shah), 486
Tamils, 63, 99
Tang dynasty
agriculture in, 277–279
art in, 281–284
bureaucracy in, 266
commercial expansion in, 275–276
decline of, 271–272
emergence of, 98–99, 266
examination system in, 266–267
explanation of, 263–264, 265*m*
family and society in, 279
gender roles in, 279–280
Korea and, 300
poetry in, 282–283
prosperity in, 275–282
state and religion in, 267–270
technological advances in, 280, 281
urban growth in, 276
Tangut tribes, 274, 320
Tanzimat reforms, 622
Tatars, 208, 210, 322, 323
Tatu, 326
Tayson Rebellion, 884
Tchaikovsky, Pyotr, 651
Technocrats, 785
Technological advances
in China, 27, 46, 280, 282
in early modern period, 361
in east Asia and Pacific Rim, 889
globalization and, 908–909
in India, 63, 854
in Islamic societies, 155
in Middle Ages, 215, 218
in navigation, 361
in Neolithic Age, 13
in 19th century, 573
nomadic mobility and, 95
in postclassical period, 116–118
in Renaissance, 383
in 17th and 18th century, 398
terrorism and, 917
in toolmaking, 9, 10
in 20th century, 788
in United States, 903
in weaponry, 95, 361, 484–485
Teheran Conference, 765
Television, 798, 912

Tenochtitlan, 242–246, 419, 426
Teotihuacan, 96
Terakoya, 652
Terrorism
  Chechyna conflict and, 906
  globalization and, 917
  Islamic fundamentalism and, 903
  against Israel, 905
  against United States, 2, 905
Terrorist attack of September 11, 2001, 2, 903, 917
Texas, 601
Thailand, 874, 876
Thatcher, Margaret, 785
Theodora (Byzantine empress), 195, 198
Theology. See also Religion
  liberation, 821, 823
  in postclassical era, 224–225
Third world, 813. See also Developing nations
Thirty Years' War, 385
The Thousand and One Nights, 141, 149
Three-field system, 215, 218
Tiano people, 422
Tibet, 877
Tigris-Euphrates civilization, 16–20
Tihuanaco, 251, 252
Tilak, B. G., 687, 688
Time of Troubles, 405
Timur-i Lang (Timur the Lame), 313, 323, 330, 331–332, 332f, 473, 489
Tito, Marshall, 906
Tlaloc, 242
Tokugawa Shogunate, 518m, 519, 521, 652, 883
Tolstoy, Leo, 651
Toltecs
  explanation of, 240
  influence of, 240–242
  temples in, 238f
Tools, in Paleolithic Age, 9, 10
Topac Yupanqui, 252
Topiltzin, 240
Toritomo, 294
Torres, Camilo, 821
Totalitarian states
  Germany as, 732, 734
  Soviet Union as, 744, 747
Total war, 754–755, 767. See also Warfare
Trade. See also Slave trade
  in Abbasid age, 139
  in Africa, 182–183, 367, 376, 449, 451, 459
  in ancient Greece, 71, 85
  in ancient Rome, 85
  in Arabia, 125–126
  Asian network zones for, 501–502
  with bedouins, 126
  in Borneo, 165
  in Byzantine Empire, 199–200
  in Canada, 707
  in Caribbean, 433, 442
  in China, 28, 46, 49, 63–65, 165–167, 183, 275–276, 337–338, 374, 501, 632–634
  in classical period, 33, 46, 55, 63, 64, 71, 85, 93, 94
  in early civilizations, 28, 29
  in early modern period, 352, 367
  in eastern Europe, 204–205, 370, 415
  effects of, 369–370
  in England, 364, 366, 370, 505
  European maritime power and, 360–361, 500–507
  in India, 55, 63, 64, 376, 493, 501
  in Indonesia, 165

international agreements for, 893
  in Islamic civilizations, 153, 155
  in Italy, 341–342
  in Japan, 501, 519, 742, 889
  in Korea, 302
  in Latin America, 433, 599, 604, 605, 611, 736, 814
  in Malaya, 165
  in Middle Ages, 219, 227–229
  in Middle East, 63, 127, 336
  NAFTA and, 904
  in Netherlands, 504
  in Persia, 183, 487
  in Philippines, 433
  in postclassical period, 116–117, 118–120
  in postcolonial era, 846, 848
  post–World War I, 728
  in primary products, 846
  in Roman Empire, 38, 63
  in Russia, 413
  in Spain, 433
  spread of religions and, 95, 110
  in Sumatra, 165
  in Vietnam, 884
  in western Europe, 340
Trade routes
  in classical period, 64–65, 64m, 94m
  under Mongols, 320
  spread of religions along, 95, 110
Trade unions. See Labor unions
Tragic Week, 737
Trans-Siberian railroad, 648, 650
Transvaal, 583
Treaty of Guadalupe-Hidalgo, 601
Treaty of Paris (1763), 372
Treaty of Tordesillas, 434
Treaty of Utrecht, 441
Treaty of Westphalia, 385
Trench warfare, 676, 676f, 677, 685
Trinh, 309
Trinity, 107
Tripartite Pact, 755
Triple Entente Alliance, 558, 606, 672, 679, 684, 719. See also World War I
Tropical dependencies, 576, 578
Trotsky, Leon, 715, 720
Truman, Harry, 781, 792, 866
Trung sisters, 306
Tswana, 461
Tunisia
  French in, 571, 672
  Muslim rule in, 174
Tupac Amaru (Jose Gabriel Condorcanqui), 443–444
Turgenev, Ivan, 651
Turkey
  European Union and, 903
  independence of, 691
  industrialization in, 747
  nationalist movement in, 701
  post–World War II, 781, 792
Turks
  Armenians and, 680
  Byzantine Empire and, 201, 202
  explanation of, 176
  fall of Constantinople to, 208
Tutsis, 907
Tutu, Osei, 457
Twantinsuyu. See Incas
Twelve Tablets, 76
Tyranny, 75

U

Uganda, 850

Ukraine
  art in, 206–207
  independence of, 902
  massacres in, 760
  spread of civilization to, 204
  World War II and, 758–759
Ulama, 156
Umayyads
  conquests of, 133–134
  decline of, 135, 137
  explanation of, 125
  Muhammad and, 128–130
  social organization and, 134–135
  Sunnis and, 133
Umma, 129, 174
Underdevelopment, 609–610
Unemployment, 729, 730
Union of Soviet Socialist Republics. See Soviet Union
Unitarians, 602–603
United Fruit Company, 819
United Nations
  Africa and, 916
  establishment of, 764
  function of, 765
  globalization and, 912, 913
  Human Rights Commission, 902
  Israel and, 774
  Universal Declaration of Human Rights, 827
United Provinces of the Rio de la Plata, 592, 602
United States
  campus unrest in, 785
  civil rights movement in, 785, 786f
  cold war and, 764–766, 781–783, 792–793
  containment policy of, 792–793
  culture in, 554, 708–709, 790–791, 796, 798, 799
  economic growth in, 708, 788, 789, 903
  explanation of, 764–766
  immigrant minorities in, 789
  industrialization in, 541–542, 703
  influence of ancient Greece and Rome on, 69
  Latin American interests of, 613–614, 680, 708, 713, 792, 818–821, 825–826, 828
  Mexican migrants in, 830
  NAFTA and, 904
  New Deal in, 732
  Pacific Rim and, 875
  political change in, 541
  popular culture in, 798
  post–World War I, 708–709, 825
  relationship between western Europe and, 790–791
  relationship with Australia, 791–792
  relationship with Canada, 791
  relationship with New Zealand, 791–792
  relationship with Soviet Union, 895–896
  as superpower, 902–903
  terrorist attacks against, 903, 917
  Vietnam War and, 887, 888f
  voting rights for women in, 678
  women in, 794–796
  in world history, 556–557
  World War I and, 678–683, 708
  World War II and, 760–762, 767
Universal Declaration of Human Rights (United Nations), 827
Universities. See also Education
  in India, 60
  in Latin America, 738
  in Middle Ages, 219
  in 19th-century Europe, 551
  in Spanish colonies, 434

unrest in, 778*f*, 785
women attending, 794
Untouchables, 53, 56. *See also* Caste system
Upanishads, 52, 53, 57–58
Urban II, Pope, 221
Urbanization
 endangered ecosystems and, 844–845, 844*f*
 industrialization and, 528–529, 543–544
 in Latin America, 830–831
Uruguay
 coup in 1973 in, 824
 independence of, 595
 military regime in, 828
Uthman, 132–133
Utilitarians, 570

V

Vaisyas, 53
Valdivia, Pedro de, 427
Valentino, Rudolph, 709
van der Rohe, Ludwig Mies, 703*f*
Vargas, Getúlio, 738–739, 815
Vassals, 219
Vedas, 52
Vedic Age (India), 52, 53, 61
Vega, Garcilaso de la, 250
Venezuela
 economy in, 595
 independence of, 591, 592
 politics in, 821, 825
 in 20th century, 816
Vergil, 81
Versailles (France), 391, 391*f*
Vesalius, 389
Vespucci, Amerigo, 356
Viceroyalties, 434
Viet Cong, 887
Viet Minh, 886, 887
Vietnam
 agriculture in, 303–304
 architecture in, 307*f*
 background of, 303, 303*m*, 863–864
 Buddhism in, 106, 307
 Chinese influence on, 303–306, 309, 310, 878
 contact with Chams and Khmers, 308–309
 education in, 885
 French involvement in, 571, 772, 883–887
 independence from China, 306–307
 nationalism in, 885–886, 889, 916
 rebuilding of, 887–889
 Soviet Union and, 799
 trade in, 884
 women in, 303
Vietnamese Nationalist party (VNQDD), 885, 886
Vietnam War
 Australia and, 791–792
 campus unrest and, 785
 events during, 793
 United States and, 887, 888*f*
Viets, 302
Vikings
 explanation of, 214–215, 219
 in Greenland, 361
 in Iceland, 221, 361
Villa, Pancho, 711
Vishnu, 58, 164
Vivaldis brothers, 343
Vizier, 477
Vladimir I (Kievan prince), 205–207
Vodun, 468
Volland, Sophie, 397
Vo Nguyen Giap, 886
Voting rights

in Europe, 546, 548, 550
in Latin America, 829
for women, 550, 678, 704, 794, 829, 845

W

Wales, 906
Wang Anshi, 274
Wannsee Conference, 760
Warfare. *See also* Weaponry; *specific wars*
 in India, 53–54
 in Mesoamerica, 242
 in Ottoman Empire, 475–476, 481–482
 population and, 837
 in Safavid Empire, 486
 in Sumerian society, 19
 technological advances in, 95, 361, 573–575
 total, 754–755
 trench, 676, 676*f*, 677, 685
War of the Pacific, 611
War of the Spanish Succession, 441
Warsaw Pact, 782, 800, 893, 908
Watson, James, 797
Wazir, 138
Wealth of Nations (Smith), 395
Weaponry. *See also* Warfare
 in classical civilizations, 31
 colonial rule and, 574–575
 invention of, 355
 in Japan, 369
 technological advances in, 16, 95, 361, 573–574
 toys to resemble, 755
Weber, Max, 798
Wei, Empress, 271
Weimar Republic, 783
Welfare state
 conservatism and, 785
 economic expansion and, 788
 in western Europe, 784–785, 795
Wendi (Chinese nobleman), 264
Wesley, John, 470
Western civilization
 between 1450 and 1750, 381, 382
 decline of, 733–734
 definition of, 223
 evaluation of nonwestern civilizations by, 250–251
 North America and, 376
 postclassical version of, 224
Western Europe. *See also* Europe; *specific countries and time periods*
 age of revolution in, 536–543
 culture in, 796–799
 in early modern period, 351–352, 357
 economic growth in, 788–790
 elites and masses in, 393
 exploration by, 221, 343–345, 360–366
 in 14th and 15th centuries, 338–340
 as global force, 620
 Great Depression in, 729–732
 immigrant minorities in, 789
 impact of colonial successes on, 377–378
 interwar period in, 701–706
 Middle Ages in, 213–236
 post–World War II, 779–780
 relationship between United States and, 790–791
 Renaissance in, 340–343, 387m
 revolutions of 1848 in, 541–543
 spread of liberal democracy in, 783–784
 welfare state in, 784–785, 795
 women in 20th century, 794–796
Westernization

in eastern Europe, 705–706
of Russia, 406–412, 407*m*, 621
West Germany. *See also* Germany
 creation of, 782, 782*m*
 economic growth in, 789
 European Union and, 786
 regime in, 783
 unification of, 898
West Indies
 Bourbon reforms in, 441–442
 slavery in, 368
 Spanish colonies in, 370, 434, 441
 trade in, 433
Whampoa Military Academy, 722
Wheel, 256
Whistler, James McNeill, 554
White, John, 375*f*
White Dominions, 576, 584, 675
White Lotus Society, 329
Wilberforce, William, 470
Wilhelm II, kaiser of Germany, 672
William the Conqueror, 153, 176, 220
Wilson, Woodrow, 556, 682, 683
Witchcraft, 388, 393, 396
Witte, Sergei, 648
Wollstonecraft, Mary, 397
Women. *See also* Feminism; Gender roles
 in African and Asian nationalist movements, 694–695
 in agricultural societies, 45, 46, 61, 137
 in ancient Rome, 87
 Buddhism and, 106
 in China, 45, 106, 279–280, 512, 630, 880–881
 Christianity and, 108
 colonizer-colonized relations and, 579
 education of, 794, 922
 in India, 61, 63, 492, 495, 687
 industrialization and, 544–546
 in Islamic societies, 134–137, 150–151, 488–489
 in Japan, 658
 in Latin America, 594, 608, 829–830
 in Mesoamerica, 247–249, 255, 255*f*
 in Middle Ages, 231–232
 in Mughal Empire, 492
 in Ottoman Empire, 622
 in Paleolithic Age, 9
 in patriarchal societies, 45–46
 political change and, 542, 829, 834f, 881
 in postclassical civilizationsm 118
 in Russia, 408, 646
 in 17th century Europe, 396
 in Soviet Union, 898
 in Spanish colonies, 439–440
 in Sudanic societies, 181
 in 20th century, 704, 794–796
 in United States, 794–796
 in Vietnam, 303
 voting rights for, 550, 678, 704, 794, 829
 during World War I, 678–679, 679*f*, 704
 during World War II, 754
Women's movements. *See* Feminism
World Bank, 848, 893–894, 913, 916, 918
World Court of Justice, 764–765
World Trade Center, 917
World Trade Organization (WTO), 913*f*, 914
World War I. *See also specific countries and regions*
 casualties in, 681–682, 681*t*, 702
 effects on Europe of, 702
 in Europe, 670*f*, 671, 673*m*, 675–679, 681–682
 European colonial order and, 684

hostilities and diplomatic tensions leading to, 558–559, 671–674
Latin America and, 711, 736
outbreak of, 674–675
outside Europe, 673m, 679–681
overview of, 671, 759m
peace treaty following, 682–683, 714, 719, 732, 734, 753, 781, 886
propaganda during, 678, 754
as total war, 754–755
women during, 678–679, 679f, 704
World War II
British and American offensives in, 760–761
causes of, 752–753
collapse of Reich and, 761
events during, 757–764
events leading to, 734–735, 753, 755–756
genocidal campaign against Jews and, 760
India and, 767–768
Japan and, 752–753, 761–764
Latin America and, 739
overview of, 751
peace settlement following, 764–766
postwar conferences and, 764–766
as total war, 767
women during, 754
World Wide Web, 909
World Zionist Organization, 692
Writing
ancient Chinese, 22, 27
ancient Egyptian, 21, 93
calligraphy and, 43
cuneiform, 15, 17, 18, 18f
in early river valley civilizations, 24–25
Harappan, 26
Phoenician, 25
Wu, Empress, 269, 271
Wu Bao, 268
Wu Ti, 38, 39

Wuzong, Emperor, 270

X
Xavier, Francis, 507, 519–520, 520f
Xhosa, 461
Xi Xia, 274, 320, 325
Xuanzong, Emperor, 271–272

Y
Yalta Conference, 765
Yamamoto, Isoroku, 762
Yanas, 255
Yuan Cai, 118
Yangdi, 265, 275
Yang Guifei, 271, 272
Yangtze River, 31, 37
Yaroslav (Kievan prince), 206, 207
Yataro, Iwasoki, 655, 655f
Yathrib, 126. See also Medina
Yellow peril, 660
Yellow River (China), 21, 26, 31
Yellow Turbans, 98
Yeltsin, Boris, 899, 900
Yes and No (Abelard), 224
Yin/yang, 35
Yoga, 58
Yoruba, 186–187
Young Turks, 623, 623f, 624, 680, 691
Yuan era
decline of, 329, 330
Mongols and, 326, 327, 329
Yuan Shikai, 717, 719, 721
Yucatan, 601, 608
Yugoslavia
ethnic conflict in, 898, 905–907, 905m, 917
post–World War I, 682, 706
post–World War II, 765, 800
World War II and, 758, 800
Yunglo emperor, 511, 514

Yukichi Fukuzawa, 533

Z
Zainab, 135
Zakat, 129, 130
Zanzibar, 460
Zapata, Emiliano, 711, 816
Zapatistas, 816, 817f
Zemstvoes, 646
Zen Buddhism
explanation of, 268, 270
in Japan, 297–298
Zeng Guofan, 634
Zenj, 183
Zhao Kuangyin, 272
Zhang Han, 119–120
Zhdanov, Andrey, 745–746
Zhenghe expeditions, 337, 514–516, 514m
Zhou dynasty
accomplishments of, 26, 37, 43
characteristics of, 36–37
decline of, 37
feudal society during, 295
migration and settlement of, 25, 264
religion and culture in, 40, 43
trade in, 46
Zhou Enlai, 880, 882, 883
Zhu Xi, 273
Zhu Yuanzhang, 508
Ziggurats, 18
Zionists
explanation of, 692
World War II and, 760, 774
Zoë (Byzantine empress), 198
Zoroastrianism
Islamic conquests and, 132, 134, 165
rise of, 70–71, 103
Zulus, 461, 462, 462f, 464, 575
Zulu Wars of 1870s, 464
Zuni Indians, 16

ARCTIC OCEAN

GREENLAND

ICELAND

BERING
SEA

GULF OF
ALASKA

ALEUTIAN ISLANDS

Arctic Circle

Yukon R.

ROCKY MOUNTAINS

NORTH
AMERICA

HUDSON
BAY

60°N

40°N

PACIFIC
OCEAN

Mississippi R.

APPALACHIAN MTS.

ATLANTIC
OCEAN

ATL.
MT

Tropic of Cancer

20°N

HAWAIIAN
ISLANDS

GULF OF
MEXICO

WEST INDIES

CARIBBEAN SEA

0° — Equator

Amazon R.

GUIANA
HIGHLANDS

SOUTH
AMERICA

ANDES MOUNTAINS

20°S

BRAZILIAN
HIGHLANDS

Tropic of Capricorn

ATACAMA
DESERT

Paraná R.

PACIFIC
OCEAN

40°S

60°S

Arctic Circle

Antarctic Circle

80°S

160°W   140°W   120°W   100°W   80°W   60°W   40°W   20°W

80°N